Handbook of Latin American Studies: No. 19

A SELECTIVE AND ANNOTATED GUIDE TO RECENT PUBLISHED
MATERIAL ON
ANTHROPOLOGY, ART, ECONOMICS, EDUCATION, GEOGRAPHY,
GOVERNMENT, HISTORY, INTERNATIONAL RELATIONS,
LABOR AND SOCIAL WELFARE, LANGUAGE AND
LITERATURE, LAW, MUSIC, PHILOSOPHY,
AND SOCIOLOGY

Advisory Board

HANDBOOK OF
LATIN AMERICAN STUDIES

No. 19

PREPARED IN
THE HISPANIC FOUNDATION
IN
THE LIBRARY OF CONGRESS
BY
A NUMBER OF SCHOLARS

●

FRANCISCO AGUILERA, *Editor*
PHYLLIS G. CARTER, *Assistant Editor*

1957
UNIVERSITY OF FLORIDA PRESS
GAINESVILLE

TO THE MEMORY

OF

ARCHER MILTON HUNTINGTON

10 MARCH 1870—11 DECEMBER 1955

THE PRESENT VOLUME

OF THE

HANDBOOK OF LATIN AMERICAN STUDIES

IS

DEDICATED

IN RECOGNITION OF

HIS GREAT CONTRIBUTION

TO LATIN AMERICAN STUDIES

Contributing Editors

Francisco Aguilera, *The Library of Congress*, LITERATURE

George Boehrer, *Georgetown University*, HISTORY

David Bushnell, *Holloman Air Force Base, N. Mex.*, HISTORY

Manoel Cardozo, *The Catholic University of America*, HISTORY

Phyllis G. Carter, *The Library of Congress*, STATISTICS

Robert S. Chamberlain, *Washington, D. C.*, HISTORY

Asher N. Christensen, *University of Minnesota*, GOVERNMENT

Helen L. Clagett, *The Library of Congress*, LAW

Mercer Cook, *Howard University*, LANGUAGE AND LITERATURE

Raymond E. Crist, *University of Florida*, GEOGRAPHY

Frank Dauster, *Rutgers University*, LITERATURE

Ralph Edward Dimmick, *Pan American Union*, LANGUAGE AND LITERATURE

Dirección de Investigaciones Económicas, Nacional Financiera, S. A., *Mexico City*, ECONOMICS

Irene de Menezes Doria, *Instituto Nacional de Estudos Pedagógicos, Rio de Janeiro*, EDUCATION

Robert C. Eidt, *Los Angeles State College*, GEOGRAPHY

Clifford Evans, *Smithsonian Institution*, ANTHROPOLOGY

Carl H. Farman, *Department of Health, Education, and Welfare*, SOCIAL WELFARE

Ángel Flores, *Queens College*, LITERATURE

Siegfried Garbuny, *Washington, D. C.*, ECONOMICS

Arch C. Gerlach, *The Library of Congress*, CARTOGRAPHY

Charles Gibson, *State University of Iowa*, HISTORY

Charles C. Griffin, *Vassar College*, GENERAL

Roscoe R. Hill, *The National Archives* (retired), HISTORY

Roland D. Hussey, *University of California, Los Angeles*, HISTORY

Preston E. James, *Syracuse University*, GEOGRAPHY

Contents

Editor's Note

INTRODUCTION

T HE present issue of the *Handbook of Latin American Studies* marks the departure of the *Handbook* from the policy of including only publications issued during one year, and the beginning of the policy of including all the important publications seen for the first time by the Handbook office staff and the Contributing Editors during the year since the preparation of the last volume, regardless of their imprint date.

In practice the new chronological policy has resulted in a larger book this year, since essentially all of the publications of 1953 were reviewed for it as well as those of 1954 and 1955 and (in a few cases) 1956 which had come to the attention of the Editors by the time the book went to press. *Handbook No. 18* included only publications issued during 1952. It is expected that subsequent numbers will return to the former size.

As always, the *Handbook* is a highly selective bibliography. The staff of the Handbook office goes through all the Hispanic material coming into the Library of Congress, selecting those books and pamphlets which appear to be of interest and calling them to the attention of the Contributing Editors in their respective fields. The Contributing Editors make a further selection and, at the same time, add other items of interest which they have encountered in the course of their work and review the periodical literature in their fields for articles of especial importance. The judgment involved in this final selection is one of the most important responsibilities of our hard-working collaborators.

This volume includes 4225 entries. For convenience in the preparation of the manuscript, a block of numbers was assigned to each section at the beginning of the work, each such block to be a safe margin larger than the expected number of items for the section. Thus, large gaps in the item numbering appear between most sections; and also, the number of the last entry (6726) is appreciably larger than the total number of entries.

CHANGES OF CONTRIBUTING EDITORS

Several new names appear in this volume among the Contributing Editors. Clifford Evans and Betty J. Meggers are now in charge of the section on ethnology pertaining to Western and Southern America which John Howland Rowe edited in Nos. 14-18.

Siegfried Garbuny has succeeded Wendell C. Gordon, who served in Nos. 15-18 as editor of the section on economics for all countries but Argentina, Brazil, and Mexico. Dr. Garbuny has the added responsibility for Argentina, which is no longer given as a separate section.

Marjorie C. Johnston has taken over the section on education (Spanish America and Haiti) which Frank A. Knapp, Jr., consented to prepare as a one-year assignment in No. 18.

Frank Dauster has assumed responsibility for Spanish American drama of the nineteenth and twentieth centuries, which hitherto had been in the charge of José Juan Arrom (Nos. 11-18).

George Boehrer has joined Manoel Cardozo (active as editor from No. 13 on) in the preparation of the Brazilian history section.

Thomas F. Mosimann has assumed responsibility for Labor, thus relieving Carl H. Farman, who prepared the Labor and Socal Welfare section in Nos. 10, 11, and 13-18, of part of his work. Dr. Farman continues in charge of Social Welfare.

Robert S. Chamberlain consented to review a number of historical items of a general character for the present volume.

Asher N. Christensen resumes his work on Government, after a one-year absence during which he was substituted by Philip B. Taylor, Jr.

Phyllis G. Carter resumes her work on Statistics after a one-year absence.

Hilgard O'Reilly Sternberg did not contribute to Brazilian geography in the present number, but will return next year. Dr. James assumed responsibility for the whole section in this volume.

The section on Spanish American and Haitian art, normally contributed by Harold E. Wethey, was omitted from this volume, for reasons beyond control of either the editorial office or Dr. Wethey. The latter will resume his work in the next issue with due attention to items published during 1953.

The contributions of Arch C. Gerlach, on cartography, Roscoe R. Hill, on archival materials, Charles C. Griffin, on various topics listed under "General," and Robert S. Chamberlain and J. H. Parry, on history, are scattered through the volume under various headings according to their subjects.

THE NEW ADVISORY BOARD

The modified composition of the Advisory Board presented on one of the front pages of this volume is the result of a new policy approved by the Librarian of Congress. By virtue of this decision, the Board will consist of as many as eight members, appointed to definite, staggered terms. Four of the members who had served on the Board for the last few years were reappointed by the Librarian of Congress with terminal dates as follows: C. H. Haring, July 1958; M. Burgin, July 1958; H. G. Doyle, July 1957; and C. Krusé, July 1957. The new members so far appointed are J. Malagón (term ending July 1959), G. R. Willey (July 1959), and A. H. Mayor (July 1960). The Librarian of Congress has appointed Dr. Haring Chairman of the Board for the duration of his term.

EXPLANATORY NOTES

AUTHOR INDEX. Includes names of individual authors ("Bandeira, Manuel") and names of corporate authors ("Instituto Panamericano de Geografía e Historia"). Under "Anonymous" are listed, alphabetically, authorless titles.

SUBJECT INDEX. Includes names of individuals ("Bolívar, Simón"), corporate bodies ("Organization of American States"), countries ("Haiti"), areas (Central America"), and topics ("Population"), when they are dealt with as subjects of study.

SPANISH ACCENTS. In the annotations in English, Spanish accents are used only for names of persons and organizations. Accents are no longer used in such annotations for names of places or geographical features, or for names of Indian tribes, because so many of these names have been incorporated in English without the accents.

PERIODICAL CITATIONS. The following abbreviated citation is a typical one: 20:2, Oct. 1954, p. 175-186 (meaning, vol. 20, no. 2, October 1954, pages 175-186). Variations often occur, such as the following: 2. época, año 47, 19:55-57 (segunda época, año 47, vol. 19, no. 55-57); n. s., 42, 1953 (nouvelle série, no. 42, 1953); 122, Aug. 1955 (no. 122, August 1955); fasc. 4; out.-dez. 1953 (fascículo 4, outubro-dezembro 1953).

ABBREVIATIONS: Attention is called to the "Key to Periodicals and Other Title Abbreviations," which is self-explanatory. Throughout the bibliography various standard abbreviations are used ("v." for volume, "t." for *tomo,* "set." for *setembro,* etc.). "B. A.," "N. Y.," and "Rio" are used as abbreviations for Buenos Aires, New York, and Rio de Janeiro, respectively.

FRANCISCO AGUILERA

The Hispanic Foundation
The Library of Congress
Washington, D. C.

Anthropology

GENERAL

1. Aguirre Beltrán, Gonzalo. Formas de gobierno indígena. México, Imp. Universitaria (Cultura mexicana, 5), 1953. 221 p.

Una breve introducción sobre el sistema político azteca a la llegada de los españoles, seguida de tres estudios de grupos indígenas contemporáneos: tarahumaras, tzeltal-tzotiles y tarascos. Las formas de gobierno se analizan en función de los procesos de transculturación y de integración nacional. [A. Palerm]

2. Arze, José Antonio. Sociografía del inkario. ¿ Fué socialista o comunista el imperio inkaiko? La Paz, Fénix, 1952. xvii, 160 p.

Brief analysis and description of the population, social organization, and social institutions of the ancient Incan empire. Most of the volume is devoted to a Spanish translation of *L'empire des incas et leur communisme autocratique* by the Belgian economist, Georges Rouma. [T. L. Smith]

3. B.B.A.A. Boletín bibliográfico de antropología americana. México, Instituto Panamericano de Geografía e Historia. T. 15-16, partes 1-2, 1952-1953, i.e. 1954.

The publication of this standard yearly review of research on American anthropology had been suspended for two years because of administrative difficulties. The 1952 and 1953 volumes are now published jointly in an effort to catch up. As before, they include summaries of activities in Europe as well as the Americas, lists of the articles appearing in anthropological journals, reviews of the literature, and an incomplete list of recent publications. There are obituaries of Enrique Juan Palacios, Wendell C. Bennett, Ralph Linton, and P. Wilhelm Schmidt; and bibliographies of Bennett, Barbro Dalhgren, Johanna Faulhaber, and Eduardo Seler. An index of the personal bibliographies published in previous volumes will be useful. [I. Rouse]

4. Baudin, Louis. El imperio socialista de los Incas. 3. ed., corr. y aumentada. Santiago, Zig-Zag (Historia y documentos), 1953. 339 [i.e. 439] p.

A new edition of the well-known work of Louis Baudin, first published in French in 1928. [C. Gibson]

5. ————. La vie quotidienne au temps des derniers Incas. Paris, Hachette (La vie quotidienne), 1955. 301 p.

The equivalent for Incaic society of Soustelle's examination of Aztec daily life (see item 35) and a work in the same series. A comprehensive view, not exhaustive, but intelligent and useful. Chapters deal with space and time, political and military structure, and intellectual, social, and economic life. Well documented. [C. Gibson]

6. Bidney, David. Theoretical anthropology. N. Y., Columbia University Press, 1953. 506 p.

An important and strikingly eclectic consideration of anthropological theories, which reflects Bidney's background as humanist and philosopher but demands of anthropologists a review of their own theoretical positions, whether they agree with him or not. The volume is an expansion of Bidney's numerous papers printed in various journals over the past decade. [D. B. Stout]

7. Borhegyi, Stephen de. Cultura folk y cultura compleja en el área maya meridional (Cien Soc, 5:26, abril 1954, p. 50-63).

Análisis de los períodos de desarrollo, desde el año 1000 antes de Cristo a la actualidad, con un ensayo de caracterización de la cultura folk y de la cultura compleja. [A. Palerm]

8. Canals Frau, Salvador. Las civilizaciones prehispánicas de América. B. A., Editorial Sudamericana, 1955. 648 p.

The most successful and up-to-date general textbook on American archaeology. It is well illustrated, methodically organized, and clearly presented. [R. Wauchope]

9. Comas, Juan. Bibliografía selectiva de las culturas indígenas de América. México, Instituto Panamericano de Geografía e Historia (Publ. no. 166; Comisión de

Historia, 64; Bibliografías, 1), 1953. 284 p., 5 maps.
A generally successful selection, with emphasis on ethnography and ethnology; entries are grouped under the major headings of "Historical" and "Contemporary," with subdivisions for nations and culture areas. [D. B. Stout]

9A. ————. Los Congresos Internacionales de Americanistas: Síntesis histórica e índice bibliográfico general (1875-1952). México, Instituto Indigenista Interamericano, 1954. lxxxiii, 224 p., illus.
A comprehensive history of the first 30 International Congresses of Americanists, with a valuable general index to all the volumes of the Congress proceedings. [D. B. Stout]

9B. ————. Indigénisme; raison d'être du mouvement indigéniste (B Soc Suisse Am, 6, 1953, p. 1-10).
An excellent analysis of the social and psychological sources and functions of the *indianismo* movement. [D. B. Stout]

9C. ————. Influencia indígena en la medicina hipocrática, en la Nueva España del siglo XVI (Am Indíg, 14:4, oct. 1954, p. 327-361).
Importante examen de un aspecto del proceso de transculturación hispano-indígena. [A. Palerm]

10. Devereux, George. A study of abortion in primitive societies. Julian Press, N. Y., 1955. 394 p.
A comparative study, based on some 400 different societies, of which a number are of Latin American provenience. Psychoanalytic theory is heavily emphasized in the interpretation, but it is in a separate section from those in which the primary data are reviewed. [D. B. Stout]

11. Dittmer, Kunz. Allgemeine Völkerkunde: Formen und Entwicklung der Kultur. Braunschweig, F. Vieweg, 1954. 314 p., illus.
A general text for ethnology and culture history in which the basic orientation is that of the Kulturkreise school, despite the employment of functionalist concepts in some instances; thus, New World agriculture is ascribed to an Asiatic Megalithic Kulturkreise. [D. B. Stout]

12. Erasmus, Charles. Las dimensiones de la cultura: historia de la etnología en los Estados Unidos entre 1900 y 1950. Bogotá, Iqueima, 1953. 198 p.
A comprehensive, but compactly presented, review of the development of ethnological theories and methods in the U. S. during the past half-century. Designed as a manual for Latin American students of anthropology, it successfully fulfills this aim. Extensive bibliography. [D. B. Stout]

13. Foster, George M. Cofradía and compadrazgo in Spain and South America (SW J Anthr, 9:1, spring 1953, p. 1-28).
Comparative study of the history and function performed by the institutions of religious brotherhoods and the godparent complex in the folk cultures of Spanish America. [D. B. Stout]

14. Gillin, John. Ethos components in modern Latin American culture (Am Anthr, 57:3, pt. 1, June 1955, p. 488-500).
Yet another, and generally convincing, attempt by the author to identify and describe the major values and implicit premises that give contemporary Latin American culture its special flavor and set it apart from all other major variants of Western Civilization. [D. B. Stout]

15. Heizer, Robert F. Aboriginal fish poisons. Washington, Smithsonian Institution, Bureau of American Ethnology (Bull., 151; Anthropological papers, 38), 1953, p. 225-383.
Survey of the use of fish poisoning throughout the world. The Guianas are thought to be the New World center of the practice, and lines of diffusion are postulated to Brazil, the Antilles and southeastern United States, and northwestern South America, Middle America, and the western United States. [I. Rouse]

16. Hibben, Frank C. Treasure in the dust. Archaeology in the New World. London, Cleaver-Hulme Press, 1953. 280 p. [R. Wauchope]

17. Instituto Panamericano de Geografía e Historia. Comisión de Historia. Boletín bibliográfico de antropología americana. México. V. 15-16, parte 1, 1952-1953, i.e. 1954—v. 17, parte 2, 1954, i.e. 1955.
The welcome resumption of the single most important bibliographic aid for American anthropology, after a suspension of a year or so. Contains reports of activities in various countries, the tables of contents of a great many anthropological journals, reviews of works in all branches of anthropology, and obituaries of prominent workers in the discipline. [D. B. Stout]

18. Inter-American Indian Congress, III, La Paz, Aug. 1954. Acta final (B Indig, 14:4, sept. 1954, suppl., 30 p.).
Official report of resolutions, policies, etc. [D. B. Stout]

19. International Labour Office. Indigenous peoples. Living and working conditions of aboriginal populations in independent countries. Geneva, 1953. 628 p., maps, plates, tables. (Studies and reports, n. s., 35).
Demographic data, descriptions of diet, housing, health conditions, occupations and crafts, and the various policies concerning all of these in each of the Latin American nations as well as elsewhere in the world. About 300

pages are devoted specifically to Latin America. [D. B. Stout]

20. Jenness, Diamond. Did the Yahgan Indians of Tierra del Fuego speak an Eskimo tongue? (Intl J Am Ling, 19:2, Apr. 1953, p. 128-131).
Brief roster of a number of correspondences in grammar and vocabulary between the Yahgan and Eskimo languages, with the tentative conclusion that they might be genetically related. If further, more rigorous and intensive analysis confirms this relationship, a whole new series of questions will arise concerning New World language affiliations. [D. B. Stout]

21. Keesing, Felix M. Culture change; an analysis and bibliography of anthropological sources to 1952. Stanford, Calif., Stanford University Press (Stanford anthropological series, 1), 1953. 242 p.
Contains a list of the principal works on culture change in all fields of anthropology and a summary of their contributions. The approach is historical, but a theoretical framework for study of the subject is also included. [I. Rouse]

22. Kroeber, A. L. (ed.). Anthropology today. An encyclopedic inventory. Chicago, Ill., University of Chicago Press, 1953. 966 p.
50 papers prepared for the International Symposium on Anthropology, held in 1952 and sponsored by the Wenner-Gren Foundation for Anthropological Research. Each paper is a review of the present status of knowledge, methodological and theoretical development of some aspect of anthropology ranging from archaeology and prehistory through physical anthropology, linguistics, ethnology, and applied anthropology. Most of the contributions are of extremely high quality; the whole volume indeed offers a most searching and complete inventory of the discipline and should serve as an indispensable source and guide for the next academic generation, both in the U. S. and in Latin America. Two of the chapters (see items 752 and 552) deal specifically with Latin American culture history. [D. B. Stout]

23. Lehmann, Henri. Les civilisations précolombiennes. Paris, Presses Universitaires de France (Coll. Que sais-je? 567), 1953. 128 p.
One of the few general books on American archaeology by a recognized authority, this serves a definite purpose, although for Mesoamerica it is disappointing in its stress on Mexican civilizations and for both continents it contains some weak and often out-of-date sections. [R. Wauchope]

24. Litter, Víctor A. Clasificación decimal de la bibliografía antropológica: proyecto de extensión. B. A., I.D.E.A., 1953. 44 p.
Admittedly, anthropological writings of all kinds are not now well accommodated by either the Library of Congress or Dewey Decimal systems of classification, but Litter's proposed scheme to adopt an expanded system based on the Universal Decimal (or Brussels) system is surely doomed to failure, for it involves, for a given book, numbers comprised of 20 to 30 digits and half a dozen or more decimal points, parentheses, and other symbols. [D. B. Stout]

25. Lussagnet, Suzanne. Bibliographie américaniste (J Soc Am, n. s., 43, 1954, p. 249-349).
Continuation of comprehensive yearly bibliography. Covers physical anthropology, archaeology, ethnology and folklore, linguistics, history, geography, and biography. [I. Rouse]

26. McQuown, Norman A. The indigenous languages of Latin America (Am Anthr, 57:3, pt. 1, June 1955, p. 502-570, 5 maps).
An extremely valuable and useful complete list and classification of all the indigenous languages and language families in Middle and South America and the Antilles. The principles and methods on which the classification rests are fully described, and the languages and families are listed in alphabetical order with appended code number according to an expansion of the Trager coding system, geographic coordinates, a number which is also shown on one of the maps and symbols for those that have become extinct or are questionable as to affiliation. The maps are enhanced in their usefulness with additional lists arranged by number. [D. B. Stout]

27. Mead, Margaret, and Nicolas Calas (eds.). Primitive heritage, an anthropological anthology. N. Y., Random House, 1953. 592 p. [R. Wauchope]

28. Meillet, A., and Marcel Cohen (eds.). Les langues du monde. 2. ed. Paris, Société de Linguistique de Paris, Centre National de la Recherche Scientifique, 1952. xlii, 1296 p., maps.
An improvement over the 1924 edition in that the range of contributors is greater and the bibliographies are more extensive. Many of the language groups are illustrated with analyzed texts. There is less attention given to the languages of Middle and South America than they merit. (Middle America, p. 1067-1097; South America and Antilles, p. 1099-1160). [D. B. Stout]

29. Nicholson, H. B. On a supposed Mesoamerican "thin orange" vessel from Ecuador (Am Antiq, 19:2, Oct. 1953, p. 164-166).
Evidence against Jijón's identification (*HLAS, no. 15, 1949,* item 274) of a South American specimen as of Mesoamerican origin. [R. Wauchope]

30. Oberg, Kalervo. Types of social structure among the lowland tribes of South and Central America (Am Anthr, 57:3, pt. 1, June 1955, p. 472-487).

A stimulating and provocative analysis of indigenous social structures, in which a typology embracing six major classes (homogenous tribes, segmented tribes, politically organized chiefdoms, feudal type states, city states, and theocratic empires) is offered. [D. B. Stout]

31. Permanent International Committee of Linguists. Linguistic bibliography for the year 1950 and supplement for previous years. Utrecht-Anvers, 1952. 275 p.

American languages, p. 250-353. Bibliographies for 1948 and 1949 listed in *HLAS, no. 18, 1952,* items 14 and 15. [D. B. Stout]

32. Rendón, Silvia. ¿Fué el maíz originario de América? (Am Indíg, 13:3, julio 1953, p. 223-230).

Review of selected linguistic and historic data with the conclusion that maize is not American in origin, but that it probably originated in the Danube basin or in Transcaucasia. [D. B. Stout]

33. Rojas, Ricardo. Silabario de la decoración americana. B. A., Losada (Obras completas de Ricardo Rojas, 29), 1953. 314 p., illus.

A superficial and incomplete attempt at providing a handbook for Indian designs in the New World. [D. B. Stout]

34. Service, Elman R. Indian-European relations in colonial Latin America (Am Anthr, 57:3, pt. 1, June 1955, p. 411-425, map).

Penetrating analysis of the relation between the degree of complexity of Indian societies and cultures and the various policies employed by the Spanish and Portuguese colonial settlers, missionaries, and officials. [D. B. Stout]

35. Soustelle, Jacques. La vie quotidienne des Aztèques à la veille de la conquête espagnole. Paris, Hachette (La vie quotidienne), 1955. 318 p.

Comprehensive and informed survey of Aztec life at the outset of the 16th century. Political structure, social classes, cosmology, and daily life are handled with an awareness of sources and modern interpretations. Emphasis is on written sources rather than archaeology. The best modern treatment of the subject in French. [C. Gibson]

36. Tax, Sol; Loren C. Eiseley; Irving Rouse; and Carl F. Voegelin (eds.). An appraisal of anthropology today. Chicago, Ill., University of Chicago Press, 1953. 395 p.

A remarkable report in which there has been skillfully preserved even the shortest of the discussions by the 82 participants of the 50 papers prepared for the International Symposium on Anthropology, held at the Wenner-Gren Foundation for Anthropological Research. The quality of these discussions is indeed remarkable, and the interchange of ideas, the sustained, constructively critical spirit that they

portray, will surely be the source of significant future developments in all branches of anthropology. See also item 22. [D. B. Stout]

37. Termer, Franz. Mittelamerikanische Museen (Zeit Ethn, 80:1, 1955, p. 38-58).

Account of leading anthropological museums in Central America, with photos of selected exhibits. [R. Wauchope]

38. Thomas, William L., Jr. (ed.). Yearbook of anthropology, 1955. N. Y., Wenner-Gren Foundation for Anthropological Research, 1955. 836 p.

The first of a new series of annual roundups for all aspects of anthropology. This first Yearbook contains 23 articles, by as many contributors, on recent developments in physical anthropology, prehistory, archaeology, theories, and the applications of anthropology, and 13 articles concerning current and recent developments in the various nations of Europe and southwest Asia. A subsequent volume will contain articles on Latin America; the whole cycle of coverage is planned to be topical in alternate years and regional every four years. A section on reference data includes titles of Ph.D. dissertations, lists of awards and memorial lectures and lists of anthropological societies and associations. This Yearbook is an enormously valuable contribution to the discipline, as will be the ones to follow. [D. B. Stout]

39. ————, and Anna M. Pikelis (eds.). International directory of anthropological institutions. N. Y., Wenner-Gren Foundation for Anthropological Research, 1953. 468 p.

The most complete directory for anthropology ever compiled, and as definitive as such compilations ever can be. The section for each country or region is prepared with a statement concerning the present general status of anthropology; the listings cover museums, universities, research institutes and societies, and include addresses, names of principal officers, data on research facilities and interests, collections, names of faculty members, and a wealth of other helpful information. The entries for Latin America cover pages 277 to 329. [D. B. Stout]

40. Thompson, J. Eric S. The rise and fall of Maya civilization. Norman, Okla., University of Oklahoma Press, 1954. 287 p., illus., maps.

Seguramente, la obra de síntesis más importante sobre los mayas desde el libro clásico de Morley, *The ancient Maya.* El autor no se limita a presentar los resultados generalmente aceptados de las investigaciones realizadas, sino que usa sus excepcionales conocimientos para exponer sus propias ideas e interpretaciones. [A. Palerm]

41. ————. Tabla astrológica de los buenos y malos días (Tlatoani, 1:1, enero 1952, p. 20). [A. Palerm]

42. ————. Tabla de los números en varias lenguas mayas (Tlatoani, 1:1, enero 1952, p. 8). [A. Palerm]

43. Valcárcel, Daniel. La historia como ciencia antropológica. Trujillo, Perú, Universidad Nacional de Trujillo (Biblioteca José Faustino Sánchez Carrión, Monografías y ensayos, 1), 1952. 38 p.
Examines the position of history within anthropology (broadly conceived) in a philosophical context derivative from Dilthey and Cassirer. Divides history into historiography (descriptive) and historiology (interpretive), identifying two subgroups (heuristic and narrative) for the former and four (hermeneutic, theoretic, genetic, and "meta-historic") for the latter. Favors theoretic historiology. [C. Gibson]

44. Verrill, A. Hyatt, and **Ruth Verrill.** America's ancient civilizations. N. Y., Putnam, 1953. 334 p.
An entertaining but irritatingly immodest book. There is probably a place in our literature for the spectacular adventure-type books on archaeology, but it is unfortunate that commercial publishers will not also insist that they be authentic and accurate. [R. Wauchope]

45. Wagley, Charles, and **Marvin Harris.** A typology of Latin American subcultures (Am Anthr, 57:3, pt. 1, June 1955, p. 428-451).

Brief characterization of nine major subcultural types which are identifiable variants of the major cultural traditions in Latin America, and as a typology is a big step in the direction of providing a systematic framework which will accommodate the cultural differences which recur throughout Latin America. [D. B. Stout]

46. Willey, Gordon R. A pattern of diffusion-acculturation (SW J Anthr, 9:4, winter 1953, p. 369-384).
Patterns and function in three prehistoric cultural colonization case studies. A unique analysis of archaeological data. [R. Wauchope]

47. Wilson, Robert B. Beekeeping in Mexico (Gleanings Bee Cult, 81:2, Feb. 1953, p. 79-82; 81:3, Mar. 1953, p. 143-146).
Native Mexican customs connected with beekeeping, from prehistoric times. [R. Wauchope]

48. Wolf, Eric R. Types of Latin American peasantry; a preliminary discussion (Am Anthr, 57:3, pt. 1, June 1955, p. 452-471).
Yet another (compare to item 45 above) endeavor to provide a typology and guide for future research on the culture of rural groups in a Latin American context. [D. B. Stout]

ARCHAEOLOGY: MIDDLE AMERICA

ROBERT WAUCHOPE

NORTHERN MEXICO, often neglected archaeologically between the active programs carried on in the southwest United States and Central Mexico, saw some interesting investigations. The American Philosophical Society conducted a survey of southern Sonora and northern Sinaloa, directed by George E. Fay. Walter W. Taylor, Smithsonian Institution, excavated in Coahuila caves, as did Pablo Martínez del Río. The University of Southern Illinois and the Instituto Nacional de Antropología e Historia, Mexico, excavated the Shroeder site in Durango, with J. Charles Kelley and Ramón Piña Chan in charge. Robert H. Lister and Agnes M. Howard wrote a general review of Chalchihuites culture. Richard MacNeish continued important excavations in early agricultural remains in Tamaulipas caves.

As usual, the Instituto Nacional de Antropología e Historia of Mexico carried on the broadest program of archaeological studies in Middle America. Excavation, repair, and restoration went on at Tula (Jorge Acosta, Rafael Orellana, Ponciano Salazar), Chalco (Richard MacNeish), Tlatilco (Ramón Piña Chan), Tlalpan (José Gorbea), Loma de Extepete (José Corona Núñez), Teotihuacan (Agustín Villagra), Tamuin and Xochicalco (Rafael Orellana), Teopanzolco, Morelos (Piña Chan), Oaxaca (Carlos Margain, C. Lorenzo Gamio), Ixtapantongo (Villagra), El Tajin (José García Payon) and elsewhere in Veracruz (Eduardo Noguera, Juan Valenzuela), Palenque, Chichen Itza, and Uxmal (Alberto Ruz Lhuillier, César Sáenz), Kabah (Ponciano Salazar), Sayil and Labna (César Sáenz).

Other institutions carried on smaller projects in Mexico, sometimes in the same regions listed above. The Carnegie Museum, Pittsburgh, excavated a cordmarked pottery site at El Risco on Lake Texcoco (William J. Mayer-Oakes). Mexico City

College (Ignacio Bernal and students) dug in Oaxaca near Mitla and Yagul. Alfonso Medellín, Department of Anthropology, state of Veracruz, made a Chicontepec survey and excavated at Los Cerros and Dicha Puerta. Waldtraat Hangert of Germany excavated at Santa Cruz Juarez. The Bureau of American Ethnology (Philip Drucker) and the Instituto Nacional (Eduardo Contreras) continued investigations at La Venta. The New World Archaeological Foundation (Thomas Ferguson and Edwin M. Shook) did reconnaissance and excavated in the Grijalva Basin, finding strong Formative period occupations at Chiapa de Corzo and Acala. El Centro de Investigaciones Antropológicas of Mexico sent an expedition to Lake Miramar, eastern Chiapas (Juan Leonard and Frederick Peterson). Others active in El Centro work, not hitherto listed, were Carmen Cook de Leonard, Florence Müller, César Lizardi Ramos, and H. K. and U. Erben. Also working in Campeche was Heinrich Berlin, for the Carnegie Institution of Washington, at Managua, Chinikiha, and Miraflores. Frans Blom, for the Mayan Order of San Antonio, Texas, continued work at Moxviquil near San Cristobal Las Casas, assisted by C. W. Weiant of the Explorers' Club. Agustín Delgado did reconnaissance in the Valle Nacional area, Vera Snyder made pottery collections in the Tepinapa region, and Robert Weitlaner and Howard Brunson excavated sites around San Felipe de Leon and the Cerro Bobo.

The Carnegie Institution of Washington completed its last three field seasons at Mayapan, Yucatan, under the direction of H. E. D. Pollock. Investigations were carried on in house mounds (Karl Ruppert and A. Ledyard Smith), cenotes (Robert E. Smith), and various temples and other structures (Edwin M. Shook, Tatiana Proskouriakoff, J. E. S. Thompson, Gustav Strömsvik, and graduate student assistants). Shook and R. E. Smith made ceramic tests at Chichen Itza; Ruppert and A. L. Smith worked at Chacchob. William T. Sanders made a survey of Cozumel Island and the East Coast, and Heinrich Berlin did reconnaissance in the lower Usumacinta. A program was initiated by the Escuela Nacional de Antropología e Historia, Pablo Martínez del Río, director, and Fernando Cámara Barbachano, secretary.

In British Honduras, the Peabody Museum of Harvard University (Gordon R. Willey and graduate student assistants) carried on three seasons of excavation in the Belize Valley. Michael Steward of the British Museum dug at Benque Viejo. Stephen F. de Borhegyi reported new sites from Santa Rosa and Jalapa, Guatemala. Jesús Núñez Ch. carried on investigations at Copan. In El Salvador, Stanley Boggs directed archaeological and museum activities at San Salvador, Tazumal, and Cihuatan, and Franz Termer and W. Haberland explored the Pipil region. New exhibit halls opened in the Museo Nacional of Costa Rica.

European institutions were active. The University of Paris, the Museum of Man, and the Institute of Ethnology sent missions to Guatemala (Henri Lehmann) and the Huasteca (Guy Stresser-Péan). The Société des Américanistes de Paris continued its fine work of research and publishing. The Institute des Hautes Études de l'Amérique Latine began work in 1954, led by Paul Rivet, Jacques Soustelle, and officials of the University of Paris.

At the Institut für Völkerkunde at Vienna University, a course on the high civilizations of America was offered by K. A. Nowotny. The Museum für Völkerkunde carried on research and writing (F. Katz, R. Heine-Geldern). Franz Termer visited Central America for the Museum of Ethnology and Prehistory in Hamburg. Two important series of publications were continued: *Quellenwerke zur alten Geschichte Amerikas*, and *Corpus codicum Americanorum mediaevi*. The Société Suisse des Américanistes carried on a program of research and publishing (Hans Dietschy, René Navelle, Guy Stresser-Péan, Eugene Pittard, Raoul d'Harcourt, Georges Barbey, M. Paranhos da Silva, and Arnold Ith).

The VI Mesa Redonda of the Sociedad Mexicana de Antropología was held at Chapultepec Castle, Mexico, in 1954. The XXXI International Congress of Americanists met in São Paulo, Brazil, in 1954 also; five papers on Middle American archaeology were presented there. As usual, the meetings of the Society for American Archaeology listed many papers on the same subject.

A volume in honor of Manuel Gamio was being assembled in Mexico by Eusebio Dávalos Hurtado and Juan Comas.

Archaeologists were saddened by the death of three of their greatest scholars: Enrique Juan Palacios, in 1953 (for a tribute and bibliography, see *Yan,* no. 2, 1953, p. 125-134); Alfred Marsten Tozzer, in 1954 (see *American antiquity,* vol. 21, no. 1, July 1955, p. 72-80); and George W. Brainerd, in 1955.

GENERAL

50. Baseball in the year 1000? (Mex This Month, 1:4, July 1955, p. 14-15).
Good pictures of Tarascan figurines.

51. Borhegyi, Stephen F. de. A brief essay on the development of Maya art (Palacio, 61:1, Jan. 1954, p. 3-8).
Short outline of Mayan prehistory and accompanying art development.

52. ─────. Chinese figurines in Mesoamerica (Am Antiq, 20:3, Jan. 1955, p. 286-288).
Further discussion of the date and manner of arrival of Chinese figurines in Middle America.

53. ─────. Cultura folk y cultura compleja en el área maya meridional (Cien Soc, 5:26, abril 1954, p. 50-63).
A bold and stimulating attempt to test a sociocultural hypothesis on the prehistoric (as well as historic) horizons, involving cultural interpretation of artifacts. Borhegyi addresses himself to the matter of the coexistence of "folk" and complex societies.

54. ─────. Installation of archaeological and ethnological material in the Guatemalan National Museum (Museum, 7:1, Jan.-Mar. 1954, p. 52-63).
Well-illustrated description (followed by French translation) of the magnificent new Guatemalan museum.

55. ─────. Jointed figurines in Mesoamerica and their cultural implication (SW J Anthr, 10:3, autumn 1954, p. 268-277).
Also published in Spanish (Antr Hist, 6:2, junio 1954, p. 1-9). Distribution of two types of jointed figurines, with interesting deductions and speculations as to their origin and use.

56. ─────. Pottery mask tradition in Mesoamerica (SW J Anthr, 11:3, autumn 1955, p. 205-213).
Geographical and chronological distribution of clay masks and their probable uses.

57. Brainerd, George W. Archeological findings (*in* Faunal and archeological researches in Yucatan caves, by Robert Torrens Hatt and others. Bloomfield Hills, Michigan, Cranbrook Institute of Science (Bull., 33), 1953, p. 108-119).
Assigns the pottery and artifacts to the prehistoric Yucatecan ceramic sequence.

58. ─────. The Maya civilization. Los Angeles, Calif., Southwest Museum, 1954. 93 p.
A fine series of articles that have been running in *Masterkey,* here published under one cover.

59. Brew, J. O. Eighty-seventh report on the Peabody Museum of Archaeology and Ethnology, Harvard University, 1952-53. (Reprinted from the Report of the President). Cambridge, Mass., 1954. 31 p.
Includes an account of the Museum's activities in British Honduras and Panama, remodeling of exhibits, and publications of the staff.

60. Christensen, Ross T. Ancient diffusion from Mesoamerica to the "Mound Area" of eastern United States: an annotated bibliography (B U Archaeol Soc, 1, May 1950, p. 13-19).
Inclines toward the view that there was an actual ethnic movement from the region of Tamaulipas and San Luis Potosi, through the Gilmore Corridor of Texas, to the eastern U. S. at the close of the Formative period and thereafter.

61. Coe, William R., II. Early man in the Maya area (Am Antiq, 20:3, Jan. 1955, p. 271-273).
Warns that certain supposedly ancient artifacts in the Peten and at Concepcion, Campeche, are not yet demonstrated to be so.

62. Covarrubias, Miguel El águila, el jaguar y la serpiente (Tlatoani, 8-9, nov. 1954, p. 65-70).
Hypotheses regarding the origins of various American cultures, with data supporting theories of Chinese contact. There is a chart correlating chronologies of American cultures.

63. Dahlgren de Jordan, Barbro. La Mixteca, su cultura e historia prehispánicas. México, Imprenta Universitaria (Cultura mexicana, 11), 1953. 400 p.
Assembles information from archaeological and native documentary sources to reconstruct the history and culture of what is now Oaxaca and surrounding area.

64. Ekholm, Gordon F. A possible focus of Asiatic influence in the Late Classic culture of Mesoamerica (Am Antiq, 18:3, pt. 2, Jan. 1953, p. 72-89).
Examines a specific series of analogous traits in the cultures of southeast Asia and America, concluding that this "Complex A" was intrusive in Mesoamerica in late Classic times, and was absorbed and modified by existing vigorous cultures there.

65. Enciso, Jorge. Design motifs of ancient Mexico. N. Y., Dover Publications, 1953. 153 p., illus.
Catalog of designs, particularly from stamps, categorized and with provenience, but lacking any interpretation.

66. Escalona Ramos, Alberto. Una interpretación de la cultura maya mexica. Madrid, Instituto Gonzalo Fernández de Oviedo, Consejo Superior de Investigaciones Científicas, 1952. 127 p.
Great miscellany of odd information is brought under one cover. The interpretation is superficial.

67. Ferdon, Edwin N., Jr. A trial survey of Mexican-Southwestern architectural parallels. Santa Fe, N. Mex., School of American Research, Museum of New Mexico (Monographs, 21), 1955. 35 p.
Suggestions regarding Mexican-Southwest relationships, including the proposal that Quetzalcoatl worship entered the Southwest with round structures there. The period of contact is estimated at 1050-1300 A. D., and it is suggested that trading *pochteca* groups invaded the Hohokam, or possibly groups from Tula seeking a new home after 1168.

68. García Ruiz, Alfonso. El derecho premial entre los mayas y los chibchas (Estud Hist Am, p. 477-516).
Examines native American political structure and processes and their ramifications, calling attention to the formal legal status of some Indian judicial systems.

69. Grace, F. J. S. "Pok-Ta-Pok," the lost rubber ball game. N. Y., 1954. 46 p.
Assembles various accounts of the rubber ball game.

70. Groth-Kimball, Irmgard. The art of ancient Mexico. Text and notes by Franz Feuchtwanger. London and N. Y., Thames and Hudson, 1954. 30 p., illus.
Also published in German (Zürich, Atlantis Verlag, 1953). The introduction is a brief art appraisal, not a true anthropological background, but the 105 illustrations are truly thrilling.

71. ————. Kunst im alten Mexiko. Mit Einleitung und Anmerkungen von Franz Feuchtwanger. Zürich, Atlantis Verlag, 1953. 127 p., illus.
31 pages of introduction and 105 superb illustrations.

72. Hatt, Robert Torrens; Harvey I. Fisher; Dave A. Langebartel; and George W. Brainerd. Faunal and archeological researches in Yucatan caves. Bloomfield Hills, Michigan, Cranbrook Institute of Science (Bull. 33), 1953. 119 p., illus., maps.
See also item 57.

73. Howard, Agnes McClain. Cruciform artifacts of the Sierra Occidental (Am Antiq, 20:2, Oct. 1954, p. 174-175).
An unusual type of artifact found in northern Mexico, especially Durango, and the southwest U. S.

74. Lehmann, Henri. On Noel Morss' "Cradled infant figurines" (Am Antiq, 19:1, July 1953, p. 78-80).
Further discussion of recumbent figures.

75. Martí, Samuel. Música prehispánica. Guía de la Sala de Música Prehispánica. México, Museo Nacional de Antropología, 1954. 15 p.
Prehistoric musical instruments, scales, harmony, etc., with illustrations from the museum. The same data are in an article, "Música precortesiana," (Cuad Am, año 13, 78:6, nov.-dic. 1954, p. 149-155).

76. Orozco y Berra, Manuel. Historia antigua y de las culturas aborígenes de México. México, Ediciones Fuente Cultural, 1954. 2 v. 544, 510 p.
Profusely illustrated with often inferior engravings, but with fairly up-to-date introductory sections by Mexican scholars such as Wigberto Jiménez Moreno, Pablo Martínez del Río, and E. Núñez Mata.

77. Ortega y Medina, Juan A. Monroísmo arqueológico: un intento de compensación de americanidad insuficiente (Cuad Am, año 12, 71:5, sept.-oct. 1953, p. 168-189; año 12, 72:6, nov.-dic. 1953, p. 158-187).
The first part is devoted largely to a comparative study of the ideas, writings, and sources of John Lloyd Stephens and Benjamin N. Norman. The second part interprets Stephens' attitudes as a reflection of general North American Monroism.

78. Palerm, Ángel. The agricultural bases of urban civilization in Mesoamerica (*in* Irrigation civilizations: a comparative study. Washington, Pan American Union (Social science monographs), 1955, p. 28-42).

Classification of Middle American agricultural systems relative to population density and settlement pattern, the characteristics of prehistoric irrigation there, and its importance. A useful assemblage of data on canals and aqueducts, with interesting speculations regarding their extent and significance.

79. ————. La secuencia de la evolución cultural de Mesoamérica (BBAA, 17:1, 1954, i.e. 1955, p. 205-233).

Comparative study of three recent summaries of Middle American prehistory by Pedro Armillas, Alfonso Caso, and Ignacio Bernal, with the author's own suggestions. Broad trends of culture in each major period are reviewed.

80. **Pollock, H. E. D.** Annual report of the director of the Department of Archaeology (*in* Carnegie Institution of Washington. Year book, no. 52, for the year 1952-1953, p. 249-296; and no. 53, for the year 1953-1954, p. 263-300).

These reports contain excellent general statements on the Institution's program in Middle America, with fairly detailed preliminary reports on the individual projects.

81. **Rands, Robert L.** Some manifestations of water in Mesoamerican art. Washington, Smithsonian Institution, Bureau of American Ethnology (Bull., 157; Anthropological papers, 48), 1954, p. 265-293.

Valuable analysis of a series of interlocking complexes relating to falling water in Mesoamerican art, such as tears, the hand, the mouth, containers, urination and other physiological associations, the configurations of death, destruction, and misfortune, and associated deities. Contains detailed appendices, tables, and photographic illustrations.

82. ————. The water lily in Maya art: a complex of alleged Asiatic origin. Washington, Smithsonian Institution, Bureau of American Ethnology (Bull., 151, no. 34), 1953, p. 75-153.

Detailed analysis of this important motif, its symbolic associations, and distribution. The water lily forms part of a complex with the Long-Nosed God and beings perhaps related to the Serpent Bird. Notes close correspondences between the motif in Yucatan and the Usumacinta. "To explain the elaborated water lily as of Asiatic derivation, it would appear necessary to postulate a complex series of waves of fundamental influence which accounted for new traits on various time levels." Suggests that the possible basic relationship between Old and New World theocracies, and the cursive tendencies in Maya and Indian art, may explain the parallels in Maya and Hindu-Buddhist depictions.

83. **Rivet, Paul.** Cités maya. 2nd ed. Paris, Albert Guillot (Les hauts lieux de l'histoire, 4), 1954. 195 p., illus.

Superbly illustrated selection of Mayan objects of art. The new pictures of Palenque and the color reproductions of Bonampak are especially good. Text is for the art student, not the anthropologist.

84. **Rubín de la Borbolla, Daniel F.,** and **Pedro Rivas.** Honduras: monumentos históricos y arqueológicos. México, Instituto Panamericano de Geografía e Historia (Publ. 146; Comisión de Historia, 44; Monumentos históricos y arqueológicos, 8), 1953. 98 p., map, 61 pl.

85. **Sears, Paul B.** The interdependence of archeology and ecology, with examples from Middle America (Trans NY Ac Sci, ser. 2, 15:4, Feb. 1953, p. 113-117).

Pollen counts provide possible environmental explanations of cultural trends in Mexican prehistory.

86. **Séjourné, Laurette.** El mensaje de Quetzalcóatl (Cuad Am, año 13, 77:5, sept.-oct. 1954, p. 159-172).

Nature and significance of the Quetzalcoatl myth, and its tremendous influence on later Mexican prehistoric culture.

87. **Sorenson, John L.** Indications of early metal in Mesoamerica (B U Archaeol Soc, 5, Oct. 1954, p. 1-15).

Assembles information on Classic period metallurgy and possibly earlier metal specimens from Middle America.

88. **Stirling, M. W.** Seventeenth annual report of the Bureau of American Ethnology, 1952-1953. Washington, Smithsonian Institution, 1954. 33 p.

Includes an account of archaeological investigations in Panama and the Olmec area of Mexico.

89. **Stresser-Péan, Guy.** Les nahuas du sud de la Huasteca et l'ancienne extension meridionale des huastèques (R Mex Estud Antr, 13:2-3, 1952-1953, p. 287-290).

Advances the hypothesis that Nahuatl and Huastec cultures merged in the southern Huasteca.

90. **Termer, Franz.** Die Hochkultur der Maya und ihre Erforschung durch die moderne Amerikanistik (Universitas, Stuttgart, 8:1, 1953, p. 149-159).

Reviews highlights of Mayan civilization, the various hypotheses that are still being examined, and the correlation problem.

91. **Thompson, J. Eric S.** The rise and fall of Maya civilization. Norman, Okla., University of Oklahoma Press, 1954. 287 p.

Thoughtful and entertaining study of the Mayas, one of the few general works on this subject written by an authority on Middle American archaeology. Well illustrated and certainly the best and most authentic introduction that we have.

92. Wauchope, Robert. Implications of radiocarbon dates from Middle and South America (Mid Am Research Rec, 2:2, Feb. 1954, p. 17-40).
Implications of the C¹⁴ dates relative to the calendar correlation question and the apparently parallel rise of high civilizations in Mesoamerica and the Andes.

93. Willcox, Horace. Removal and restoration of the monuments of Caracol (B U Mus, 18:1-2, June-Aug. 1954, p. 46-72).
Interesting and instructive account of the problems and techniques involved in the removal and repair of heavy stone monuments and sculptures. Well illustrated.

94. Woodford, Irene Briggs. The "tree of life" in ancient America: its representations and significance (B U Archaeol Soc, 4, Mar. 1953, p. 1-18).
Describes and interprets the elements of this motif and concludes that it was an emblem especially of Itzamna or Quetzalcoatl, and that it was also a symbol of life of good in opposition to evil, and a tree of knowledge. The Old World occurrences of this motif are also mentioned.

RECONNAISSANCE, EXCAVATIONS, REGIONAL STUDIES

95. Acosta, Jorge R. Exploraciones arqueológicas efectuadas en Chichén Itzá, Yucatán, 1951 (A Inst Nac Antr Hist, 6, pt. 1 (no. 34), 1952, i.e. 1955, p. 27-40).
Well-illustrated account of excavations at the Temple of the Eagles, the Tzompantli, and other structures.

96. Adams, Robert M., Jr. Some small ceremonial structures of Mayapan (Cur Rept, 9, Dec. 1953, p. 144-179).
Shrines, platforms, and associated features described and well illustrated.

97. Aguilar P., Carlos H. Retes, un depósito arqueológico en las faldas del Irazú. San José, Universidad de Costa Rica (Sección Tesis de grado y ensayos, 5), 1953. 52 p., illus.
Cache of aboriginal artifacts dating to about 1564, after Spanish contact. There are stone, wooden, and cotton remains; detailed description of carved drum types.

98. Arguedas R. de la Borbolla, Sol, and Luis Aveleyra Arroyo de Anda. A Plainview point from northern Tamaulipas (Am Antiq, 18:4, Apr. 1953, p. 392-393).
The first Plainview point so far recorded from Mexico, and the southernmost reported specimen.

99. Aveleyra Arroyo de Anda, Luis. El segundo mamut fósil de Santa Isabel Iztapan, México, y artefactos asociados. Apéndice por Manuel Maldonado-Koerdell. México, Instituto Nacional de Antropología e Historia, Dirección de Prehistoria (Publ., 1), 1955. 30 p.
Report on the important discovery of human artifacts associated with mammoth in Mexico.

100. Aveleyra Arroyo de Anda, Luis, and Manuel Maldonado-Koerdell. Association of artifacts with mammoth in the Valley of Mexico (Am Antiq, 18:4, Apr. 1953, p. 332-340).
Hunting and butchering tools associated with mammoth remains at Santa Isabel Iztapan. English version of 1952 article (listed in *HLAS*, no. 18, 1952, item 26).

101. Belser, Carlos. El jade precolombino de Costa Rica. San José, Museo Nacional, 1953. 25 p.
Brief study of techniques of manufacture, styles, and significance of jade objects from prehistoric Costa Rica.

102. Berlin, Heinrich. Archaeological reconnaissance in Tabasco (Cur Rept, 7, Dec. 1953, p. 102-135).
Notes on this little-known archaeological region. Contains a useful map of sites.

103. ————. A new temple at Tikal (Archaeology, 6:2, summer 1953, p. 82-86).
Account of the discovery and a description of the sixth major pyramid recently discovered at this greatest of ancient Maya cities.

104. Blom, Frans. Ossuaries, cremation and secondary burials among the Maya of Chiapas, Mexico (J Soc Am, n.s., 43, 1954, p. 123-135).
Various examples of disposal of the dead in prehistoric Chiapas.

105. Borhegyi, Stephen F. de. Comments on incense burners from Copán, Honduras (Am Antiq, 20:3, Jan. 1955, p. 284-286).
A supposed tripod incense burner is shown to be a three-pronged type instead.

106. Bullard, William R., Jr. Boundary walls and house lots at Mayapan (Cur Rept, 13, Feb. 1954, p. 234-253).
Data bearing on house groups and settlement pattern, house lots, lanes and routes of passage, and boundary interpretations in archaeological excavation. Map.

107. Burland, C. A. The Atelco frescoes (New W Antiq, 10, 1954, p. 6-9).
Further interpretation of the Atelco frescoes at San Juan Teotihuacan, Mexico.

108. Caso, Alfonso. El pueblo del sol.

México, Fondo de Cultura Económica, 1953. 125 p.
With fine illustrations, many in color, by Miguel Covarrubias, this expansion of Caso's earlier work, *La religión de los aztecas*, is a popularly written though no less authentic study of Mexican prehistoric religion.

109. **Coe, William R.** Excavations in El Salvador (B U Mus, 19:2, June 1955, p. 14-21).
Preliminary account of investigations in pre-Classic or Formative period mounds at El Trapiche.

110. **Drucker, Philip.** The Cerro de las Mesas offering of jade and other materials. Washington, Smithsonian Institution, Bureau of American Ethnology (Bull., 157; Anthropological papers, 44), 1954, p. 25-68.
Figurines, plaques, earspools, celts, beads, and other objects, and their possible Middle American relationships in time and space. 28 pages of photographs.

111. **Drucker, Philip, and Eduardo Contreras.** Sitios arqueológicos en la parte oriental del territorio olmeca (Tlatoani, 8-9, nov. 1954, p. 36-41).
Archaeological reconnaissance of Tabasco and Veracruz, resulting in tentative boundaries for the Olmec culture at various stages of its development.

112. **Dutton, Bertha P.** Tula of the Toltecs (Palacio, 62:7-8, July-Aug. 1955, p. 195-251).
Detailed account of the architecture and artifacts of Tula and their relationships elsewhere, with a brief introductory account of the Toltecs and a history of investigations. Generously illustrated.

113. **Ekholm, Gordon F.** Exploración arqueológica en Sonora y la parte norte de Sinaloa (Yan, 1, 1953, p. 34-36).
General account of archaeological discoveries in this little-known zone.

114. Excavations in the Mixteca Alta (Mesoam Notes, 3, 1953, 50 p.).
Report prepared by faculty and students of Mexico City College, Department of Anthropology. Correlations with the Monte Alban sequence are suggested.

115. **Fay, George E.** The archaeological cultures of the southern half of Sonora, Mexico (Y Am Philos Soc, 1953, p. 266-269).
Preliminary report on an archaeological survey in the region west and south of Hermosillo, southward to Los Mochis in northern Sinaloa.

116. **Ferdon, Edwin N., Jr.** Tonalá, Mexico. An archaeological survey. Santa Fe, N. Mex., School of American Research

(Monograph, 16), 1953. xvi, 126 p., illus., maps.
Tonala became a ceremonial site in the Formative period, probably contemporaneously with the Danzantes at Monte Alban. Mexican influence from Veracruz was felt during Late Classic and the site was abandoned soon thereafter. Many photographs, maps, plans, and elevations.

117. **Foshag, William F., and Robert Leslie.** Jadeite from Manzanal, Guatemala (Am Antiq, 21:1, July 1955, p. 81-83).
Analysis of jade from the vicinity of one of the few known jade outcrops in Middle America. A useful background statement on New World jades is included.

118. **Haberland, Wolfgang.** The golden battle discs of Chichen Itza (Ethnos, 19:1-4, 1954, p. 94-104).
A re-analysis of the discs from Chichen Itza described by Lothrop. Sees less Toltec influence, and prefers a dating between 10.8.0.0.0 and 10.10.0.0.0.

119. **Howard, Agnes McClain.** Ancestor of pottery? (Am Antiq, 20:2, Oct. 1954, p. 175-176).
Grass container, covered with clay in coiled style, from a cave in Durango.

120. **Instituto Panamericano de Geografía e Historia. Comisión de Historia.** Monumentos históricos y arqueológicos de América. V. 1- . México, 1950- .
This series prints the legislation of the various countries designed to protect their antiquities, gives sample bibliographies, and photographic illustrations of famous sites and artifacts. The countries represented are: 1, Panama (by Ángel Rubio, 1950); 2, United States (by Ronald F. Lee, 1951); 3, Brazil (by Rodrigo Melo Franco de Andrade, 1952); 4, Chile (by Roberto Montandón, 1952); 5, Haiti (by Catts Pressoir, 1952); 6, Guatemala (by Daniel F. Rubín de la Borbolla and Hugo Cerezo, 1953) [see item 160]; 7, Mexico (by Rubín de la Borbolla, 1953) [see item 159]; 8, Honduras (by Rubín de la Borbolla and Pedro Rivas) [see item 84]; and 9, Ecuador (by Fr. José María Vargas, 1953). There is considerable variation in the thoroughness with which the various countries are treated; thus Guatemala and Honduras are only small booklets, while Mexico is a 487-page volume with 475 magnificent illustrations.

121. **Jakeman, M. Wells.** An archaeological reconnaissance of the Xicalango area of western Campeche, Mexico (B U Archaeol Soc, 3, Aug. 1952, p. 16-44).
Report of explorations in the southern Gulf coast area, with a brief description of structures and pottery collected.

122. **Kelley, J. Charles, and William J. Shackelford.** Preliminary notes on the Weicker site, Durango, Mexico (Palacio, 61:5, May 1954, p. 145-150).

Architecture, pottery, and other artifacts of a small agricultural community, and its possible relations to the Chalchihuites prehistoric culture.

123. León, Antonio de. Antigüedades zapotecas. Descubrimientos hechos recientemente en las ruinas de Guiengola, departamento de Oajaca. México, Vargas Rea (Biblioteca de historiadores mexicanos), 1953. 45 p.

A 3800-word article stretched into a 45-page bound book. This should have been a brief news item in some journal.

124. Lister, Robert H. Excavations in Cave Valley, Chihuahua, Mexico (Am Antiq, 19:2, Oct. 1953, p. 166-169).

Preliminary account of cave excavations indicating Mogollon culture 300 miles south of its previously known distribution.

125. Lister, Robert H., and Agnes M. Howard. The Chalchihuites culture of northwestern Mexico (Am Antiq, 21:2, Oct. 1955, p. 122-129).

Descriptive summary of material culture and its possible affiliations elsewhere.

126. López González, Valentín. Breve historia antigua del estado de Morelos. Cuernavaca, México, Departamento de Turismo y Publicidad de Morelos (Cuadernos de cultura morelense, 1), 1953. 38 p.

Brief review of the prehistory of the state of Morelos; an introductory guide but not for the specialist.

127. Loreau, Leonard. Caltonac (Palacio, 61:1, Jan. 1954, p. 13-19).

A visit to ruins in Puebla, Mexico.

128. Lorenzo, José L. A fluted point from Durango, Mexico (Am Antiq, 18:4, Apr. 1953, p. 394-395).

Clovis-type fluted point from a hilltop surface in the Sierra Madre Occidental.

129. Lothrop, S. K. Jade and string sawing in northeastern Costa Rica (Am Antiq, 21:1, July 1955, p. 43-51).

Ingenious use of jade styles and techniques to analyze the relationships of Costa Rican jade ornament.

130. MacNeish, Richard Stockton. Ancient maize and Mexico (Archaeology, 8:2, summer 1955, p. 108-115).

Excellent and well-illustrated preliminary report on important Basic Agricultural and Formative period cave discoveries in northeastern Mexico.

131. ————. An early archaeological site near Panuco, Vera Cruz (Trans Am Philos Soc, n.s., 44:5, Oct. 1954, p. 539-641).

Report on excavations, with an important discussion of their bearing on the Middle American pre-Classic (Formative) cultures. Numerous illustrations and tables.

132. Margain, Carlos R. La zona arqueológica de Tulancingo (A Inst Nac Antr Hist, 6, pt. 1 (no. 34), 1952, i.e. 1955, p. 41-48).

Brief account of discoveries in Hidalgo. Inferior illustrations.

133. Martí, Samuel. Flautilla de la penitencia: fiesta grande de Tezcatlipoca (Cuad Am, año 12, 72:6, nov.-dic. 1953, p. 148-157).

Identification of prehistoric artifacts and their use, from native sources and early accounts.

134. Martínez del Río, Pablo. La cueva mortuoria de la Candelaria, Coahuila (Cuad Am, año 12, 70:4, julio-agosto 1953, p. 177-204).

Results of important discoveries in a Coahuila cave yielding, among much other material, woven and wooden artifacts.

135. Mayer-Oakes, Nita. Archeología [sic] mexicana (Carnegie Mag, 28:5, May 1954, p. 149-152, 156).

In English. Popular account of excavations at El Risco in search of cordmarked pottery.

136. Medellín Zenil, Alfonso, and Frederick A. Peterson. Smiling head complex from central Vera Cruz, Mexico (Am Antiq, 20:2, Oct. 1954, p. 162-169).

Discovery of about 1200 new examples of "smiling heads" enables the authors to make a thorough descriptive analysis of this strange prehistoric complex.

137. Millon, René F. Irrigation at Teotihuacán (Am Antiq, 20:2, Oct. 1954, p. 176-180).

Results of an investigation having an important bearing on basic matters of ancient Middle American culture. Concludes that irrigation is necessary for maize cultivation in the valley of Teotihuacan today, and that it was probably necessary in ancient times there and elsewhere in Middle America.

138. Noguera, Eduardo. La cerámica de Cholula. México, Guarania (Biblioteca de historia y arqueología americanas), 1954. 315 p.

Pottery of Cholula, from Formative to protohistoric times, as established through stratigraphic studies and comparative research. Profusely illustrated, with many figures in color.

139. Orellana T., Rafael. La cabecita del mangal, Veracruz (Yan, 2, 1953, p. 140-141).

Splendid example of late Formative period art, a modeled clay head from Veracruz.

140. ————. Petroglifos y pinturas rupestres de Sonora (Yan, 1, 1953, p. 29-33).
Human, animal, geometric, and abstract symbols. Illustrated.

141. **Paddock, John** (ed.). Excavations in the Mixteca Alta: source materials published by the faculty and students of the Anthropology Department, Mexico City College (Mesoam Notes, 3, 1953, 50 p.).
Report on a field trip to the sites of Yatachio and Pueblo Viejo in northern Oaxaca. Includes map, chronological chart, and illustrations.

142. **Peso, Charles C. di.** The clay figurines of Acambaro, Guanajuato, Mexico (Am Antiq, 18:4, Apr. 1953, p. 388-389).
Exposure of an archaeological hoax in Mexico.

143. **Peterson, Frederick Alvin.** "Doughnut-shaped" vessels and bird bowls of Chupícuaro, Mexico (Ethnos, 20:2-3, 1955, p. 137-145).
Provenience of two striking ceramic forms, one rare, the other interesting because of its conventionalized variations.

144. ————. Faces that are really false (Nat Hist, 62:4, Apr. 1953, p. 176-180).
Well-illustrated exposé of the most recent faked archaeological relics manufactured in Mexico.

145. ————. Falsificaciones de Chupícuaro (Yan, 2, 1953, p. 150-156).
Another of this author's useful articles on fakes. Well illustrated.

146. ————. Preliminary report — archaeology (CIAM expedition — 1955). México, Centro de Investigaciones Antropológicas de México, 1955.
Preliminary report on expedition to the Lacandone Forest.

147. ————. Smiling heads from Vera Cruz (Ethnos, 19:1-4, 1954, p. 80-93).
Description and interpretation of the smiling heads, and a complex of associated objects and traits. Well illustrated, this is an imaginative and informative study.

148. ————. Women warriors and laughing faces (Nat Hist, 63:5, May 1954, p. 210-215, 239).
Famous smiling heads, their provenience and chronological position in prehistoric Mexico, with superb photographs of some of the finest specimens.

149. **Piña Chan, Román.** Una figurilla de Tlatilco (Yan, 2, 1953, p. 148-149).
Sees in this unusual seated figure a reflection of the changing Formative period society.

150. ————. Hallazgos arqueológicos en tierras de Oaxaca (Tlatoani, 8-9, nov. 1954, 31-33).

Large photographs and a brief description of sculptures at Tututepec and Rio Grande.

151. ————. Tlatilco y la cultura preclásica del Valle de México (A Inst Nac Antr Hist, 4 (32), 1949-1950, i.e. 1952, p. 33-43).
The strata "Atoto Reciente" and "Atoto de Transición" correspond to Late Tlatilco and Transition, respectively, and are closely related to Middle Upper Zacatenco and Arbolillo II.

152. **Pollock, H. E. D.** The northern terminus of the principal sacbe at Mayapan (Cur Rept, 15, July 1954, p. 1-14).
The ancient Maya road was one of the latest constructions at Mayapan.

153. **Pollock, H. E. D.,** and **Gustav Strömsvik.** Chacchob, Yucatan (Cur Rept, 6, Jan. 1953, p. 82-101).
An interesting walled city, first reported in 1845 but only now investigated by competent archaeologists. Evidences of a Puuc period occupation.

154. **Porter, Muriel Noé.** Tlatilco and the pre-Classic cultures of the New World. N. Y., Wenner-Gren Foundation for Anthropological Research (Viking Fund publications in anthropology, 19), 1953. 104 p., plus 14 pl.
Comparative study of the significant traits from Tlatilco, the famous Formative period Mexican site. Some interesting relationships are suggested, but the study lacks broad integration of Mesoamerican Formative cultures.

155. **Proskouriakoff, Tatiana.** Varieties of Classic Central Veracruz sculpture. Washington, Carnegie Institution of Washington (Publ., 606; Contributions to American anthropology and history, 58), 1954, p. 61-121.
Another excellent study by the leading analyst of Middle American art, it is of importance to the archaeologist and the art theorist. Details of subject matter and of style are arranged in categories applicable to problems of ethnic relationships, chronology, and art history.

156. **Richards, Annette H.** The dancers of Monte Alban (Pac Discov, 8:4, July-Aug. 1955, p. 12-17).
Assembles the many interpretations of Los Danzantes.

157. ————. The mystery of the first Mexican (Nat Hist, 62:4, Apr. 1953, p. 168-174).
Well-illustrated account of the discovery of human artifacts associated with mammoth at Santa Isabel Iztapan.

158. **Roys, Ralph L.** Conquest sites and the subsequent destruction of Maya architecture in the interior of northern Yucatan (Contrib Am Anthr Hist, 54, 1952, p. 131-182).

A most thorough and interesting study showing that many towns are located at their pre-Spanish sites, their churches and plazas often at the old ceremonial centers, with sequences of earlier buildings underneath. Illustrated.

159. **Rubín de la Bordolla, Daniel F.** México: monumentos históricos y arqueológicos. México, Instituto Panamericano de Geografía e Historia (Publ. 145; Comisión de Historia, 43; Monumentos históricos y arqueológicos, 7), 1953. 487 p., map, and 475 pl.

The first 232 illustrations and pages 101-280 treat of archaeological materials. Fine pictures.

160. **Rubín de la Borbolla, Daniel F., and Hugo Cerezo.** Guatemala: monumentos históricos y arqueológicos. México, Instituto Panamericano de Geografía e Historia (Publ. 144; Comisión de Historia, 42; Monumentos históricos y arqueológicos, 6), 1953. 115 p., map, 34 pl.

161. **Ruppert, Karl, and A. Ledyard Smith.** Excavations in house mounds at Mayapan: III (Cur Rept, 17, Sept. 1954, p. 27-52).

More data on domestic architecture, with special attention to tombs.

162. ————, and ————. Two new gallery-patio type structures at Chichen Itza (Notes Mid Am Archaeol Ethn, 122, Aug. 1955, p. 59-62).

These two new discoveries bring to 13 the number of structures of this type found at, and, so far as is known, limited to Chichen Itza.

163. **Ruppert, Karl; J. Eric S. Thompson; and Tatiana Proskouriakoff.** Bonampak, Chiapas, Mexico. Copies of the mural paintings by Antonio Tejeda F. Identification of pigments by Rutherford J. Gettens. Washington, Carnegie Institution of Washington (Publ., 602), 1955. 71 p.

Although there have been numerous popular and semi-official descriptions of this famous site, this is the definitive professional publication on it. Attacking the subject in all its aspects—geographical, historical, architectural, epigraphic, and artistic—a team of experts has produced a meaningful interpretation and reconstruction of ancient Mayan life. Magnificent color reproductions.

164. **Ruz Lhuillier, Alberto.** Exploraciones arqueológicas en Palenque, 1949 (A Inst Nac Antr Hist, 4 (32), 1949-1950, i.e. 1952, p. 49-60).

Account of the 1949 season's explorations and restorations in the Palace, the Temple of the Tablets, and the zone of burials.

165. ————. Exploraciones en Palenque: 1952 (A Inst Nac Antr Hist, 6, pt. 1 (no. 34), 1952, i.e. 1955, p. 79-110).

Excavations at the Palace and the Temple of the Inscriptions, with a detailed account and many illustrations of the spectacular tomb underneath the latter.

166. ————. The mystery of the Temple of the Inscriptions (Archaeology, 6:1, spring 1953, p. 2-11).

Another general and preliminary but well-illustrated account of the spectacular discoveries at Palenque.

167. ————. La pirámide-tumba de Palenque (Cuad Am, año 13, 74:2, marzo-abril 1954, p. 141-159).

One of a series by this author in this same journal, describing the famous discoveries at Palenque.

168. ————. The pyramid tomb of a prince of Palenque (Illus London News, 223:5967, Aug. 29, 1953, p. 321-323).

Stirring account of the discovery at Palenque, well illustrated, including two full-page color photos of the pyramid and the jade mask.

169. ————. Uxmal: temporada de trabajos 1951-1952 (A Inst Nac Antr Hist, 6, pt. 1 (no. 34), 1952, i.e. 1955, p. 49-67).

Illustrated account of excavations at the Monjas and the Governor's Palace, with additional photographs of work at the Magician Pyramid.

170. **Sanders, William T.** An archaeological reconnaissance of northern Quintana Roo (Cur Rept, 24, Feb. 1955, p. 179-224).

Further description of ruins previously noted by Escalona Ramos and Miguel Ángel Fernández, plus some new discoveries in the little-known area.

171. **Satterthwaite, Linton, Jr.** Piedras Negras archaeology: architecture. Part 6. Unclassified buildings and substructures. Philadelphia, Pa., University of Pennsylvania, University Museum, 1954. 23-92 p.

Continuation of the excellent and detailed reporting of excavations at Piedras Negras. Profusely illustrated with drawings and photographs.

172. **Séjourné, Laurette.** Teotihuacán, la ciudad sagrada de Quetzalcóatl (Cuad Am, año 13, 75:3, mayo-junio 1954, p. 177-205).

Presents his reasons for believing Teotihuacan, not Tula, was the capital of the Toltecs.

173. ————. Tula, la supuesta capital de los toltecas (Cuad Am, año 13, 73:1, enero-feb. 1954, p. 153-169).

First of three articles presenting the hypothesis that Teotihuacan, not Tula, was capital of the Toltecs and that it was the home of Quetzalcoatl.

174. **Shook, Edwin M.** A round temple at Mayapan, Yucatan (Cur Rept, 16, July 1954, p. 15-26).
A shrine was set in its stairway, containing a carved stone idol, as yet unidentified.

175. ————. The Temple of Kukulcan at Mayapan (Cur Rept, 20, Dec. 1954, p. 89-108).
The succession of building events at the main structure is deduced from stratigraphic excavation.

176. ————. Three temples and their associated structures at Mayapan (Cur Rept, 14, June 1954, p. 254-291).
One contained a deep shaft which held 40 human skeletons and other remains. Many photographs and some excellent plans and sections.

177. ————. The X-Coton temples at Mayapan (Cur Rept, 11, Dec. 1953, p. 207-221).
Two structures associated with the two major entrances through the Great Wall and with the cenote. One contained an interesting crematory shaft; the other supported twin temples.

178. **Shook, Edwin M.,** and **William N. Irving.** Colonnaded buildings at Mayapan (Cur Rept, 22, Jan. 1955, p. 127-168).
Detailed study of the architecture and artifacts, with suggestions regarding the function of these specialized colonnaded halls.

179. **Smith, A. Ledyard.** Archaeological reconnaissance in central Guatemala. Washington, Carnegie Institution of Washington (Publ., 608), 1955. 85 p., 140 pl.
Profusely illustrated with excellent maps, plans, sections, and restorations, this reports on the first thorough archaeological survey of Huehuetenango, Quiche, and the Verapaz. The architectural and assemblage data will be particularly important in interpreting prehistoric trends in this little-known archaeological area.

180. **Smith, A. Ledyard,** and **Karl Ruppert.** Excavations in house mounds at Mayapan: II (Cur Rept, 10, Dec. 1953, p. 180-206).
Description, drawings, and photographs of small structures and associated artifacts.

181. **Smith, Philip E.** Excavations in three ceremonial structures at Mayapan (Cur Rept, 21, Jan. 1955, p. 109-126).
A sequence of three building phases is established for the ritual center of the city.

182. **Smith, Robert E.** Cenote exploration at Mayapan and Telchaquillo (Cur Rept, 12, Jan. 1954, p. 222-233).
Evidence that red earth for pottery slips and for house walls was mined in cenotes.

183. ————. Cenote X-Coton at Mayapan (Cur Rept, 5, Jan. 1953, p. 67-81).
Evidence that this cenote was used ceremonially as well as for water, with possible division into ceremonial precincts.

184. ————. Exploration on the outskirts of Mayapan (Cur Rept, 18, Sept. 1954, p. 53-70).
Discoveries at Santa Cruz and Telchaquillo, which were occupied from Formative times into the Mayapan period.

185. **Sokoloff, V. P.,** and **J. Luis Lorenzo.** Modern and ancient soils at some archaeological sites in the Valley of Mexico (Am Antiq, 19:1, July 1953, p. 50-55).
Pedologic-geochemical study of soils indicates a relatively gradual climatic change from the Wisconsin glaciation to the present, from a cold pluvial, through moderately pluvial continental, to the present seasonally arid.

186. **Stirling, Matthew W.** Stone monuments of the Rio Chiquito, Veracruz, Mexico.. Washington, Smithsonian Institution, Bureau of American Ethnology (Bull., 157; Anthropological papers, 43), 1955. 24 p.
Collosal stone heads and other important sculptures in an area of "Olmec-type" remains. Includes 26 pages of photographs.

187. **Strömsvik, Gustav.** A portal vault and temple at Mayapan (Cur Rept, 8, Dec. 1953, p. 136-143).
Details of construction, and a summary of the pottery types found.

188. **Strömsvik, Gustav; H. E. D. Pollock;** and **Heinrich Berlin.** Exploration in Quintana Roo (Cur Rept, 23, Feb. 1955, p. 169-178).
Notes, maps, sketches, and photos.

189. **Szécsy, Janos de.** Investigaciones en Iximché (Humanidades, 1:6, sept. 1953, p. 1-15).
Report on preliminary archaeological study of the capital of the ancient Cakchiquel kingdom.

190. **Thompson, Donald E.,** and **J. Eric S. Thompson.** A noble's residence and its dependencies at Mayapan (Cur Rept, 25, Aug. 1955, p. 225-251).
Interesting deductions and speculations regarding an assemblage of structures. The function of the family oratory in Maya life is discussed.

191. **Thompson, J. Eric S.** A presumed residence of the nobility at Mayapan (Cur Rept, 19, Dec. 1954, p. 71-88).
Architectural data, caches, burials, and artifacts described, plus speculations regarding the structure's use and history. Evidence for the Xipe Totec cult in Yucatan.

192. **Villagra, Agustín.** Trabajos realizados en Teotihuacán: 1952 (A Inst Nac Antr Hist, 6, pt. 1 (no. 34), 1952, i.e. 1955, p. 69-78).
Explorations in Tetitla and Atetelco. Illustrated, including a color plate of murals.

193. **Willey, Gordon R., and Charles R. McGimsey.** The Monagrillo culture of Panama. With an appendix on archaeological marine shells by Robert E. Greengo. Cambridge, Mass., Harvard University, Peabody Museum of American Archaeology and Ethnology (Papers, v. 49, no. 2), 1954. 160 p.
Important report on presumably early shell mound remains and the related ceramic complex of Parita Bay, Panama. This is one of the first projects to fill in some of the missing archaeological chronology of this region.

194. **Willey, Gordon R., and Theodore L. Stoddard.** Cultural stratigraphy in Panama: a preliminary report on the Girón site (Am Antiq, 19:4, Apr. 1954, 332-343).
Time-depth complexity within the Cocle area, demonstrating that the "culture areas" of Central America are now ready to be modified and further defined in terms of chronology. This report marks an important stride in our progress toward understanding Central American prehistory.

195. **Willey, Gordon R.; William R. Bullard, Jr.; and John B. Glass.** The Maya community of prehistoric times (Archaeology, 8:1, spring 1955, p. 18-25).
Well-illustrated preliminary account of the interesting excavations in the Belize Valley, British Honduras.

196. **Woodbury, Richard B., and Aubrey S. Trik.** The ruins of Zaculeu, Guatemala. With an introduction by John M. Dimick. Special contributions by Charles Weer Goff, William C. Root, T. Dale Stewart, Nathalie F. S. Woodbury. N. Y., United Fruit Co., 1953. 2 v. 466 p., illus., maps, plans.
Final report on the architecture and artifacts of this highland site excavated and restored by the United Fruit Company. Somewhat short on broad interpretations, this work nevertheless contains numerous stimulating ideas and is an important contribution to the factual data on Mesoamerican archaeology. The second volume is devoted to illustrations.

NATIVE SOURCES, EARLY HISTORY, AND EPIGRAPHY

197. The annals of the Cakchiquels; translated from the Cakchiquel Maya by Adrián Recinos and Delia Goetz. Title of the lords of Totonicapán; translated from the Quiché text into Spanish by Dionisio José Chonay; English version by Delia Goetz. Norman, Okla., University of Oklahoma Press, 1953. 217 p.
A fine English version of the Spanish edition of 1950.

198. **Apenes, Ola.** Las páginas 21 y 22 de Códice Borbónico (Yan, 2, 1953, p. 102-104).
Analysis of the Borbonicus pages containing the 52 years of the Xiuhmolpilli cycle bearing their respective day names and the appropriate Lord of the Night. Also presents a method of determining the name of the year from its position in the Mexican calendar.

199. **Barra y Valenzuela, Pedro.** Los nahoas; historia, vida y lengua. México, Bartolomé Trucco, 1953. 246 p., illus.
Introduction suitable for the beginning student. Almost half of this book is devoted to language (grammar and vocabulary).

200. **Barthel, Thomas S.** Maya-Palaeographik: die Hieroglyphe Strafe (Ethnos, 20:2-3, 1955, p. 146-151).
Connects symbols of "wood" and "stone" with the concept of punishment in Maya hieroglyphic writing.

201. ————. Regionen des Regengottes (Ethnos, 18:1-2, 1953, p. 86-105).
This paper interprets pages 65-69 of the Dresden Codex.

202. **Burland, Cottie Arthur.** Magic books from Mexico. Harmondsworth, England, Penguin Books, 1953. 30 p., 16 pl.
Color reproductions of selected pages from prehistoric and early historic Mexican codices, with an introduction and notes on each page reproduced.

203. **Caso, Alfonso.** Interpretación del códice Gómez de Orozco. México, Talleres de Impresión de Estampillas y Valores, 1954. 20 p.
A post-European but early fragment of a codex probably from the Mixtec region of Oaxaca, although said to come from Cuicatlan. Includes a fine reproduction in natural color.

204. ————. Un problema de interpretación (Yan, 2, 1953, p. 105-107).
Tests the hypothesis of Lizardi and Apenes (see items 214, 198) by three of its implications and finds it does not correspond to historically known dates. Suggests that while the year may not have begun with the day whose name it bore, the day may have determined the Lord of the Night accompanying that year.

205. Catálogo de obras escritas en lenguas indígenas de México o que tratan de ellas. De la biblioteca particular de Salvador Ugarte. Prólogo de Daniel Kuri Breña.

2. ed. México, Offset Vilar, 1954, i.e. 1955. 307 p., facsms.
Useful listing of a private library's holdings on native Mexican languages. Some new titles have been added to the 1949 listing.

206. Díaz Vasconcelos, Luis Antonio. Norma e institución jurídicas mayas. Guatemala, Universidad de San Carlos de Guatemala, Instituto de Investigaciones Científicas (Publ., 9), 1953. 120 p.
Attempts to reconstruct prehistoric Maya legal systems and political institutions, relying heavily on Torquemada and others.

207. Escalona Ramos, Alberto. Otra interpretación cronológica (Tlatoani, 8-9, nov. 1954, p. 74-75).
Further data bearing on the synchronizing of Mexican, Mayan, and European calendars, and on the question of whether years were named for the first or last day.

208. Garibay K., Ángel María. Historia de la literatura nahuatl. 1. parte. México, Porrúa, 1953. 501 p.
Résumé of works, with many quotations, from what was perhaps the most important native American Indian language so far as "literature" is concerned.

209. Henning, Paul. Comments on the religion of the Toltecs (B U Archaeol Soc, 5, Oct. 1954, p. 16-21).
Extracts from the chronicle of Ixtlilxochitl.

210. Jakeman, M. Wells. An unusual tree-of-life sculpture from ancient Central America (B U Archaeol Soc, 4, Mar. 1953, p. 26-49).
The scene depicted on Stela 5, Iztapa, is compared in 13 elements to details of Lehi's vision of the tree of life in the Book of Mormon.

211. ———— (trans.). The Relación de Motul (B U Archaeol Soc, 5, Oct. 1954, p. 22-29).
Extracts, which treat of religious beliefs and practices, some social organizations, wars, and some material culture.

212. Jäschke, Paul P. Zum Correlationsproblem der Maya-Zeitrechnung (Zeit Ethn, 78:2, 1953, p. 231-238).
Subjects various correlation formulae to astronomical tests and, as one would expect from this method, concludes that the Kreichgauer correlation is best.

213. Kelley, Dave. Further comment to an article on ancient Mexican stellar beliefs by C. A. Burland (New W Antiq, 10, 1954, p. 3-6).
The bearing of Luiseño, Huichol, and other native beliefs on ancient Mexican astrology.

214. Lizardi Ramos, César. Los acompañados del Xiuhmolpilli en el Códice Borbónico (Yan, 2, 1953, p. 95-101).
Examination of the hypothesis that the day which gives its name to the year is the same as the Year Bearer. Illustrations from the Codex Borbonicus.

215. Maler, Teobert, and Sylvanus G. Morley. El dintel 42 de Yaxchilán (Yan, 2, 1953, p. 135-139).
Joins the Maler description with the Morley analysis and adds a fine photograph by D. Juan Leonard.

216. Nicholson, H. B. The birth of the Smoking Mirror (Archaeology, 7:3, autumn 1954, p. 164-170).
Description and analysis of scenes and symbols on an ancient Mexican carved monument, and the religious mythology they depict.

217. ————. Montezuma's zoo (Pac Discov, 8:4, July-Aug. 1955, p. 3-11).
Assembles from eye-witness and other early accounts all data on the zoo and aviary of Tenochtitlan. Nuremberg map of the city and pictures of animals and birds from the codices.

218. ————. Native historical traditions of nuclear American and the problem of their archeological correlation (Am Anthr, 57:3, June 1955, p. 594-613).
Excellent appraisal of methodology involved in attempts to link archaeology to native sources of myth and history.

219. Roys, Ralph L. The Maya katun prophecies of the books of Chilam Balam, Series I. Washington, Carnegie Institution of Washington (Publ., 606; Contributions to American anthropology and history, 57), 1954, p. 1-60.
Valuable translation and commentary on the native Maya prophetic literature of colonial times.

220. Sahagún, Bernardino de. Florentine codex. General history of the things of New Spain. Book 7. The sun, moon, and stars, and the binding of the years. Translated from the Aztec into English with notes and illustrations by Arthur J. O. Anderson and Charles E. Dibble. Santa Fe, N. Mex., School of American Research and University of Utah (Monographs of the School of American Research, 14, part 8), 1953. 81 p.
Another fine translation in this series, with notes and illustrations.

221. Satterthwaite, Linton, Jr. Sculptured monuments from Caracol, British Honduras (B U Mus, 18:1-2, June-Aug. 1954, p. 2-45).
Beautifully illustrated description, analysis, and translation of inscriptions on sculptures from this spectacular new Mayan site.

222. Schultze Jena, Leonhard (ed.). Gliederung des alt-Aztekischen Volks in

Familie, Stand und Beruf. Aus dem Aztekischen Urtext Bernardino de Sahagun's. Quellenwerke zur alten Geschichte Amerikas Aufgezeichnet in den Sprachen der Eingeborenen V. Stuttgart, Kohlhammer Verlag, 1954. 337 p.
Facing Nahuatl and German text of Sahagún. No illustrations. Full Nahuatl glossary at end.

223. Seler, Eduard. La lápida de Huitzuco, estado de Guerrero (Yan, 2, 1953, p. 142-147).
Seler's 1904 paper, translated into Spanish, with new photographs by Carmen Cook Leonard.

224. Soustelle, Jacques. La vie quotidienne des Aztèques, à la veille de la conquête espagnole. Paris, Hachette, 1955. 318 p.
Ethnology of the Aztecs at the time of the conquest, largely as described in native codices and early histories.

225. Thompson, J. Eric S. La inscripción jeroglífica de tablero de El Palacio, Palenque (A Inst Nac Antr Hist, 4, (32), 1949-1950, i.e. 1952, p. 61-68).
Two examples of number "eleven." Palenque utilized the lunar system of measuring time.

226. Ulving, Tor. A new decipherment of the Maya glyphs (Ethnos, 20:2-3, 1955, p. 152-158).
Useful summary of the recent papers by Jurij Valentinovie Knorozov, whose works on the decipherment of Mayan hieroglyphs have been publicized but not often read by modern scholars. This article explains the principle on which Knorozov based his studies of Maya glyphs, and condenses the findings of his 1955 paper. Ulving finds Knorozov's approach and method to be sound and feels that he must be on the right track.

227. Weitlaner, Roberto, and Carlo Antonio Castro. El lienzo de Tlacoatzintepec (Yan, 2, 1953, p. 108-113).
Description of the original of the post-Conquest cotton woven map of San Juan Tlacoatzintepec and surrounding area, pointing out differences between it and a copy made in 1892.

ARCHAEOLOGY: WEST INDIES, VENEZUELA, AND BRAZIL

IRVING ROUSE

The years 1953-1955 have been marked by a number of publications which refute the so-called Circum-Caribbean theory, propounded by Julian H. Steward (see *HLAS, no. 13, 1937,* item 97, and *no. 15, 1949,* item 238). This does not detract from the value of the theory; it was developed by Steward as a hypothesis to stimulate work on the culture history of the area and it has served its purpose well, even though it now appears to be incorrect.

The theory assumed (1) original settlement of the Caribbean region by "Marginal," or hunting-gathering people; (2) spread of Indians northward from the Central Andes, introducing "Circum-Caribbean" culture, which is characterized by intensive agriculture, social stratification, and a priest-temple-idol cult; and (3) degeneration of some of the Circum-Caribbean tribes to a "Tropical Forest" level, with simpler, slash-and-burn agriculture and a lack of both social stratification and the priest-temple-idol cult. Since certain Marginal tribes appear to have survived in out-of-the-way places until the coming of Europeans, Steward's theory explains nicely the coexistence of all three types of culture in the Caribbean region at the time of Columbus.

First intimation that the Circum-Caribbean theory is incorrect was provided by Evans and Meggers (see *HLAS, no. 16, 1950,* item 245) when they discovered that the Circum-Caribbean Marajoara culture at the mouth of the Amazon, far from being a center of development, as Steward had assumed, was intrusive into an area previously occupied by Tropical Forest peoples. The writer then pointed out (in item 254) that only Marginal and Tropical Forest cultures are represented at the mouth of the Orinoco River, there being no trace of the degeneration from the Circum-Caribbean level of development which is called for by the theory, while in the Greater Antilles, Tropical Forest culture actually appears to have evolved into Circum-Caribbean culture. Finally, Evans and Meggers have shown that Circum-Caribbean culture is also absent from the Guianas, one of the places where Steward thought that degeneration to Tropical Forest culture had taken place (see items 251 and 289).

These facts lead to the conclusion, contrary to Steward's theory, that Marginal culture developed immediately into Tropical Forest culture, and that the latter then evolved further into Circum-Caribbean culture in certain restricted parts of the area. Meggers suggests (in item 252) that limitations of the environment inhibited development from the Tropical Forest to the Circum-Caribbean stage in the rest of the area under consideration here.

The outstanding field work of 1953-1955 was Meggers and Evans' survey of the Guianas in 1952-1953, already cited (item 289). John M. Goggin and the writer excavated nonceramic and mission sites on Trinidad in 1953, and J. M. Cruxent and the writer dug in the eastern part of Venezuela in 1955, in both cases obtaining charcoal samples for radiocarbon analysis (see item 253). Hale G. Smith, of Florida State University, dug a ceramic site in central Cuba in 1953 (item 273); and a party from Harvard, including H. B. Nicholson and Gordon R. Willey, worked with Ricardo E. Alegría, of the University of Puerto Rico, in a nonceramic and a ceramic site on that island in 1954 (item 280). Otherwise, local archaeological activity has fallen off in the past three years, particularly in Cuba.

GENERAL

250. Acosta Saignes, Miguel. Zona circumcaribe. Período indígena. México, Instituto Panamericano de Geografía e Historia (Publ. 162; Comisión de Historia, 60), 1953. 101 p.
Outline of the contact-period ethnology of the Circum-Caribbean region, including the Antilles, northern South America, and Central America. Archaeology is covered only incidentally except in an appendix by Gerardo Reichel-Dolmatoff on the Caribbean sections of Colombia.

251. Evans, Clifford. New archeological interpretations in northeastern South America (*in* New interpretations of aboriginal American culture history: 75th anniversary volume. Washington, Anthropological Society of Washington, 1955, p. 82-94).
Refutation of the Circum-Caribbean theory, as it applies to Brazil and the Guianas. Archaeology shows that the mouth of the Amazon was not a center whence Circum-Caribbean influence radiated but a peripheral region where Circum-Caribbean culture penetrated late and was short lived. Similarly, the Guianas were a refuge area rather than a place of cultural development.

252. Meggers, Betty J. Environmental limitation on the development of culture (Am Anthr, 56:5, part 1, 1954, p. 801-824).
Uses the archaeology of lowland South America as an example of environmental limitation. She theorizes that the latter is the reason Tropical Forest culture did not evolve into Circum-Caribbean culture in most of the area.

253. Preston, Richard S.; Elaine Person;

and **E. S. Deevey.** Yale natural radiocarbon measurements, II (Science, 122: 3177, Nov. 18, 1955, p. 954-960).
Includes dates obtained by the Carbon-14 method for a nonceramic site on Trinidad and for two ceramic sites in Venezuela. Evaluation of their significance must await completion of further radiocarbon analyses, now underway.

254. Rouse, Irving. The Circum-Caribbean theory, an archeological test (Am Anthr, 55:2, part 1, Apr.-June 1953, p. 188-200).
Refutation of the Circum-Caribbean theory, as it applies to Venezuela and the Antilles (see introductory comments). Archaeology shows that Tropical Forest culture preceded Circum-Caribbean culture in the area, contrary to the theory. Also published in Spanish translation: "La teoría del circumcaribe sometida a prueba arqueológica" (Cien Soc, 5:25, feb. 1954, p. 24-35).

255. Stern, Theodore. A note on Rouse's "The Circum-Caribbean theory, an archeological test," with a reply by Rouse (Am Anthr, 56:1, Feb. 1954, p. 106-108).
Stern takes issue with Loven's hypothesis that the Antillean ball game originated in Middle America, as elaborated by Rouse (in item 254). Stern favors an origin among the Otomac of the upper Orinoco, whereas Rouse would derive the Otomac ball game independently from Middle America.

WEST INDIES

GENERAL

256. Brown, William L. Maize of the West Indies (Trop Agr, 30:7-9, July-Sept. 1953, p. 141-170).

Classification of the current varieties of maize in the West Indies into eight races. One is a dent variety which the author suggests may have spread from Mexico to Cuba in prehistoric time.

257. Bullen, Ripley P., and D. D. Laxon. Some incised pottery from Cuba and Florida (Fla Anthr, 7:1, Mar. 1954, p. 23-25).

Newly excavated pottery from the Glades culture of southern Florida is compared with sub-Taino pottery from Cayo Ocampo, Cuba, to strengthen the case for connection between the two, originally pointed out by Rouse (see *HLAS, no. 15, 1949*, item 326). Illustrated.

258. Morales Patiño, Oswaldo; Fernando Royo García; Luis Cabrera Torrens; Leandro de Oña; and Justo S. Cabrera. La expedición científica cubana (R Arqueol Etn, 2. época, 7:15-16, enero-dic. 1952, p. 93-202).

Reprinted as *Contribución del Grupo Guamá, Antropología,* no. 23, Habana, Editorial Lex, 1952, 112 p. Leading Cuban archaeologists visit Jamaica, Haiti, Puerto Rico, and the Virgin Islands, examining sites and specimens. Well illustrated.

259. Pérez de la Riva, Francisco. La agricultura indoantillana: su aporte a los cultivos y alimentación del hombre (R Arqueol Etn, 2. época, 7:15-16, enero-dic. 1951, p. 228-266).

Includes illustrations of numerous archaeological specimens, such as cassava graters, metates, and *zemis.*

260. Sears, William H. The sociopolitical organization of pre-Columbian cultures on the Gulf Coastal Plain (Am Anthr, 56:3, June 1954, p. 339-346).

Reviews the evidence for the existence on the Gulf Coastal Plain in the southeastern U. S. of a "class-stratified social system" during the Weeden Island-Kolomoki period (1100-1300 A.D.). He suggests that this was a local development as the result of stimulus from the Antilles prior to the time of "late Arawak expansion" in the latter area. This theory fails to take into consideration the fact that the predecessors of the late Arawak show no traces of class stratification.

CUBA

261. Álvarez Conde, José. Huesos marcados en la isla de Cuba (Mem Soc Cub Hist Nat "Felipe Poey," 22:4, julio 1954, p. 383-388).

Discussion of the significance of haphazardly incised human bones found in the cave of La Jutia, near Fomento in Las Villas Province, Cuba. It is suggested that they may indicate the practice of cannibalism among the Ciboney (Guanajatabey) Indians.

262. Cancela Femenías, Pedro. Algo más sobre la encomienda del Padre Las Casas (R Arqueol Etn, 2. época, 7:15-16, enero-dic. 1952, p. 247-249).

Discovery of two shell deposits of unknown cultural affiliation during the search for Las Casas' encomienda (see also items 265 and 270).

263. García y Grave de Peralta, Fernando. Excursiones arqueológicas: IX-XI (R Arqueol Etn, 2, época, 7:13-14, enero-dic. 1951, p. 36-98).

Fifth installment in the account of the author's archaeological research in eastern Cuba. (See also item below.)

264. ————. Excursiones arqueológicas: XII-XIV (R Arqueol Etn, 2. época, 7:15-16, enero-dic. 1952, p. 31-92).

Sixth installment in the account of the author's archaeological research in eastern Cuba. (See also *HLAS, no. 4, 1938,* item 146c; *no. 15, 1949,* item 334; *no. 16, 1950,* item 224; this volume, item 263.)

265. González Muñoz, Antonio. El mound de la Vega del Palmar (R Arqueol Etn, 2. época, 7:15-16, enero-dic. 1952, p. 243-244).

Ciboney refuse and burial site, discovered during the search for Las Casas' encomienda (see also items 262 and 270).

266. Herrera Fritot, René, and Manuel Rivero de la Calle. La cueva funeraria de Carbonera, Matanzas. Contribución de la Sociedad Espeleológica de Cuba al Décimo Congreso Nacional de Historia. Habana, 1954. 45 p., illus.

Excavation of a Ciboney cave on the north coast of Cuba in 1950. List of stone and shell artifacts. Detailed description of human remains.

267. Morales Patiño, Oswaldo. Arqueología colonial cubana. Resumen de actividades durante el año 1951 (R Arqueol Etn, 2. época, 7:15-16, enero-dic. 1952, p. 5-30).

Summary of field work in Cuba and publications pertinent to the local archaeology during 1951.

268. ————. Arqueología cubana. Relación de actividades durante el año 1950 (R Arqueol Etn, 2. época, 7:13-14, enero-dic. 1951, p. 8-35).

Summary of archaeological research and publications in Cuba during 1950. The discovery of a series of Ciboney and sub-Taino sites in Moron, Camaguey Province, is notable.

269. ————. Los complejos o grupos culturales indocubanos (R Arqueol Etn, 2. época, 7:15-16, enero-dic. 1952, p. 259-267).

Reprinted as *Contribución del Grupo Guamá, Antropología,* no. 25, Habana, Editorial Lex, 1952, 11 p. Trait lists, with illustrations, of the three principal cultures of Cuba: Complejo I (i.e., Guayabo Blanco), Complejo II (Cayo Redondo), and Complejo III (Baní and Pueblo Viejo).

270. ————. ¿Dónde estuvo la encomienda del Padre Las Casas? (R Arqueol Etn, 2. época, 7:15-16, enero-dic. 1952, p. 239-242).

Unsuccessful attempt to locate the site of the encomienda of Father Las Casas around the mouth of the Arimao River near Cienfuegos, Cuba (see also items 262 and 265).

271. ————. Estudio comparativo del pendiente efigie de oro encontrado en Banes (R Arqueol Etn, 2. época, 7:13-14, enero-dic. 1951, p. 166-227).

Reprinted as *Contribución del Grupo Guamá, Antropología,* no. 19-20, Habana, Editorial Lex, 1951, p. 11-72. Thorough comparative study of the gold pendant found in eastern Cuba. He finds the closest resemblances to be with Costa Rica, Panama, and Colombia.

272. **Rodríguez, Alexis; Aurelio Sánchez Agramonte; Gilberto Silva; Justo Salvador Cabrera; and Rafael Cepero.** Exploración arqueológica a ventas de Casanova, Contramaestre, Oriente (R Arqueol Etn, 2. época, 7:15-16, enero-dic. 1952, p. 227-238).

Reprinted as *Contribución del Grupo Guamá, Antropología,* no. 24, Habana, Editorial Lex, 1952, 14 p. Brief report of excavations in a sub-Taino village site.

273. **Smith, Hale G.** Excavations at La Finca de Dos Marías, Camagüey, Cuba (Fla Anthr, 7:1, Mar. 1954, p. 19-21).

Preliminary report of excavations in 1953 at a newly discovered site near Jatibonico, Camaguey Province, Cuba. Its single occupation is referred to the sub-Taino Indians of the 14th and 15th centuries A. D.

274. **Tabio, Ernesto E.** Culturas más primitivas de Cuba precolombina (R Arqueol Etn, 2. época, 7:13-14, enerodic. 1951, p. 117-157).

Reprinted as *Contribución del Grupo Guamá, Antropología,* no. 18, Habana, Editorial Lex, 1951, 43 p. Comprehensive summary, with illustrations and comparative tables, of the two Ciboney cultures of Cuba, Complejo I (i.e., Guayabo Blanco) and Complejo II (i.e., Cayo Redondo).

275. **Utset, Bernardo.** Exploraciones arqueológicas en la región sur de Oriente (R Arqueol Etn, 2. época, 7:13-14, enerodic. 1951, p. 99-109).

Describes his explorations in Ciboney ("Complejo II" in the local terminology) sites on the south shore of eastern Cuba, in which he obtained the first archaeological evidence that

the Ciboney survived until historic time. Several new types of artifacts, such as stone dippers and perforated stone weights, are illustrated.

HAITI, DOMINICAN REPUBLIC

276. **Fischer, Kurt.** L'archéologie en Haïti (Conjonction, 37, fevr. 1952, p. 45-49).

277. **Pressoir, Catts.** Haïti: monuments historiques et archéologiques. México, Instituto Panamericano de Geografía e Historia (Publ. 143; Comisión de Historia, 41; Monumentos históricos y arqueológicos, 5), 1952. 32 p., illus.

History of archaeological research in Haiti, with brief bibliography and a detailed map of sites.

278. **Schweeger-Hefel, Annemarie.** Ein rätselhaftes Stück aus der alten Ambraser Sammlung (Archiv für Völkerkunde, 6-7, 1951-1952, p. 209-228).

Description of a girdle, made of cotton cordage and shell beads, in the Vienna Museum für Völkerkunde. In the absence of a record of provenience, this was originally identified as Indonesian, then African, but the author shows by comparison with archaeological specimens that it probably comes from Santo Domingo.

279. **Suro, Darío.** Arte taíno (Cuad Hispanoam, 35, nov. 1952, p. 21-26).

OTHER ISLANDS

280. **Alegría, Ricardo; H. B. Nicholson; and Gordon R. Willey.** The Archaic tradition in Puerto Rico (Am Antiq, 21:2, Oct. 1955, p. 113-121).

Reports excavation of a stratified cave near Loiza, Puerto Rico. The lower level, which was preceramic, contained a type of hammerstone otherwise known only from the Monagrillo culture of Panama. Includes a good summary of the nonceramic remains in the Caribbean.

281. **Boyrie Moya, Emile de.** L'archéologie indigène et coloniale dans la République Dominicaine (R Fr, 6:56, mai 1954, p. 52-56).

Organization of archaeological research in the Dominican Republic, the principal colonial and Indian sites, and a concise summary of the Indian archaeology. Well illustrated.

282. ————. Monumento megalítico y petroglifos de Chacuey, República Dominicana. Ciudad Trujillo, Universidad de Santo Domingo (Publ., serie 7, v. 97, no. 1), 1955. 223 p., 63 pl., 8 figs.

Detailed report on the excavation of a Taino ball court, a dance plaza, in 1948, 1951, and 1952. Well done.

283. Bullbrook, J. A. On the excavation of a shell mound at Palo Seco, Trinidad, B. W. I. New Haven, Conn., Yale University Press (Yale University publ. in anthropology, 50), 1953. 114 p., illus.
Report, originally written in 1919, of excavations under the auspices of the Trinidad government. The site was stratified, but with the two layers differing only in minor details of ceramic style. It is the type site for the Palo Seco style, which is well described and illustrated here. An appendix by Irving Rouse relates the site to more recent work on the island.

284. Cotter, C. S. A comment on the Windsor site, Jamaica (Am Antiq, 20:2, Oct. 1954, p. 173-174).
Follows up the article by De Wolf on Indian sites in northern Jamaica (item 285). De Wolf had referred incidentally to earthworks, probably of European origin, near one of her sites. Cotter describes his excavations in the earthworks in 1951, which indicate that they are of 16th-century Spanish origin, not 19th-century English as De Wolf had thought.

285. De Wolf, Marian. Excavations in Jamaica (Am Antiq, 18:3, Jan. 1953, p. 230-238).
Report of 1933 excavations at three sites in northern Jamaica. The Little River site yielded a new, painted type of pottery, related to the Ostiones style in Puerto Rico and hence dated in Period IIIa. The other two sites contained the usual incised pottery of Periods IIIb and IV in this area. See also item 284.

286. Jesse, C. Rock-cut basins on Saint Lucia (Am Antiq, 18:2, Oct. 1952, p. 166-168).
Illustrated description of a petroglyph and basins at Dauphin, St. Lucia. A map of sites on the island is included.

287. Wagenaar Hummelinck, P. Rotstekeningen van Curaçao, Aruba en Bonaire (West Indische Gids, 34:2-3, oct. 1953, p. 173-209).
Detailed, well-illustrated description of rock paintings and carvings on the Dutch Leeward Islands, prefaced by a history of archaeological research on the islands, with full bibliography. English summary.

GUIANAS

288. Henderson, Gilroy. Stone circles and tiger's lairs (Timehri, 31, 1952, p. 62-66).
Description of rock paintings and stone heaps made by the Macusi Indians to commemorate success in hunting tigers.

289. Meggers, Betty J., and **Clifford Evans.** Preliminary results of archeological investigations in British Guiana (Timehri, 34, 1955, p. 5-26).
The authors define and place in chronological sequence seven archaeological phases. They conclude that the Guianas were not a zone for transmission of Circum-Caribbean culture, nor a culture center in themselves, as previously assumed; instead, they were a refuge area, settled relatively late in the history of the American Indians.

290. Rouse, Irving. Guianas. Indigenous period. México, Instituto Panamericano de Geografía e Historia (Publ., 157; Comisión de Historia, 55), 1953. 100 p.
Outline of the archaeology and ethnology of the Guianas in terms of the principal cultures and tribes. The former are grouped into four prehistoric periods and the latter into two historic periods. There are brief commentaries and bibliographies for each, with a synthesis at the end.

VENEZUELA

292. Acosta Saignes, Miguel. Arqueología de la Guajira Venezolana (B Soc Suisse Am, 7, 1953, p. 6-8).
Preliminary report of investigation of a shell heap north of Maracaibo being destroyed in road construction. Its elaborate polychrome pottery is related to that of Reichel-Dolmatoff's first painted horizon in the Rancheria district of the Colombian Guajira. See also HLAS, no. 17, 1951, item 195.

293. Cruxent, J. M. Archéologie de Barrancas (R Fr, 6:52, janv. 1954, p. 77-80).
Evaluation and interpretation of the Barrancas style of pottery, from the lower Orinoco River. The author considers it an outstanding form of art. He thinks it shared a common origin with the Santarem ceramic style, on the middle Amazon, and suggests that the two have passed independently through three stages of development: archaic, classic, and decadent.

294. ————. Artes e industrias rurales de Venezuela; la influencia indígena (B Indig Ven, año 1, 1:3, julio-sept. 1953, p. 423-431).
Notes that the modern Indians of Venezuela have regressed in arts and crafts from the accomplishments of their prehistoric ancestors and pleads for a revival. Illustrated.

295. ————. Expediciones en tierra venezolana (Mundo Hisp, número dedicado a Venezuela, 83, supl., 1955, p. 59, 95-96).
Spanish version of an article originally published in 1951. See HLAS, no. 17, 1951, item 164.

296. ————. Trincheras en la arqueología venezolana (Acta Cien Ven, 2:2, 1951, p. 160).
Announcement of the discovery of trenches dug by the Indians in Territorio Amazonas, southern Venezuela. Wooden paddles and potsherds, of unknown style, have been found there.

297. Riley, Carroll L. Two sites in western Bolívar, Venezuela (Am Antiq, 18:3, Jan. 1953, p. 265-268).

Description of surface collections made at Cedeno and Punta Brava near Caicara on the middle Orinoco River. The pottery is of the Late Ronquin style, previously found by Howard further down the river (see *HLAS, no. 9, 1943,* item 446).

BRAZIL

298. Andrade, Rodrigo Melo Franco de. Brasil: monumentos históricos e arqueológicos. México, Instituto Panamericano de Geografía e Historia (Publ. 122; Comisión de historia, 35; Monumentos historicos y arqueológicos, 3), 1952. 223 p., illus.
Includes an annotated bibliography of "arte indígena" (p. 137-139), six plates illustrating sites and specimens, and two maps of sites. All are relatively superficial.

299. Barata, Frederico. A arte oleira dos Tapajó. 3. Alguns elementos novos para a tipologia de Santarém. Belém, Brazil, Instituto de Antropologia e Etnologia do Pará (Publ., 6), 1953.
Continuation of a series describing Santarem pottery in Brazilian collections. See also *HLAS, no. 16, 1950,* item 242 and *no. 17, 1951,* item 170.

300. Faria, Luiz de Castro. Le problème des sambaquis du Brésil: récentes excavations du gisement de Cabeçuda (Laguna Santa Catarina) (*in* Proceedings of the 30th International Congress of Americanists at Cambridge in 1952, 1955, p. 86-91).
Account of excavations in which were found human skeletons; stone axes, bolas, mortars, etc.; and bone projectile points.

301. Godói, Manuel Pereira de. Cachimbos tupis-guaranis de Pirassununga (*in* Indian tribes of aboriginal America. Selected papers of the XXIX International Congress of Americanists. Sol Tax, ed. Chicago, Ill., University of Chicago Press, 1952, p. 314-322).
Description, with illustrations, of three clay pipes found in the vicinity of Pirassununga, São Paulo, Brazil.

302. Godoy, Pereira de. Tupi-Guarani pottery at Pirassunga (*in* Proceedings of the 30th International Congress of Americanists at Cambridge in 1952, 1955, p. 243-246).
Excavation of urn-burial sites on the Mogi-Guassu river in the state of São Paulo, Brazil. Map of sites and illustrations of specimens, including a corrugated urn and painted potsherds.

303. Hilbert, Peter Paul. A cerâmica arqueológica da região de Oriximiná.

Belém, Brazil, Instituto de Antropologia e Etnologia do Pará (Publ., 9), 1955. 76 p., 10 pl., 34 figs., 1 map.
Description of pottery from 41 sites between the rivers Trombetas and Jamunda in the north central part of the Amazon Basin. There are some resemblances to the Santarem style on the Amazon but also differences; e.g., tripod legs recall instead the pottery of the Venezuelan llanos.

304. Meggers, Betty J., and Clifford Evans. Uma interpretação das culturas da Ilha de Marajó. Belém, Brazil, Instituto de Antropologia e Etnologia do Pará (Publ., 6), 1953. 12 p., illus.
Outline of the archaeological sequence on Marajo Island, again stressing that the classic Marajoara culture is intrusive. See also *HLAS, no. 6, 1950,* item 245, and *no 18, 1952,* item 140.

305. Silva, Mauricio Paranhos da. Archéologie de la Guyane Brésilienne (B Soc Suisse Am, 9, 1955, p. 1-16).
Summary of results of Evans and Meggers' 1949 excavations in Brazilian Guiana. See also *HLAS, no. 16, 1950,* item 245.

305a. ————. Archéologie du delta de l'Amazone (Mu Genève, 12:8, sept. 1955).
Brief summary of the archaeological sequence established by Evans and Meggers as the result of their 1949 excavations on Marajo Island. See *HLAS, no. 16, 1950,* item 245.

306. ————. Les phases culturelles de la Guyane Brésilienne (Mus Genève, 12:7, juillet-août 1955).
Brief summary of cultures of the area. Largely duplicates item 291.

FLORIDA

307. Goggin, John M. Space and time perspective in northern St. Johns archeology, Florida. New Haven, Conn., Yale University Press (Yale University publ. in anthropology, 47), 1952.
On p. 71-74, summarizes what is known of the "Spanish-Indian tradition," i.e., of the archaeology during the Spanish colonial period in Florida. Both mission and secular influences are considered.

308. Goggin, John M., and Frank H. Sommer, III. Excavations on Upper Matecumbe Key, Florida. New Haven, Conn., Yale University Press (Yale University publ. in anthropology, 41), 1949. 104 p.
Includes (p. 23-28) an account of the Spanish contacts with the Indians of the Florida Keys.

ARCHAEOLOGY: WESTERN AND SOUTHERN SOUTH AMERICA

CLIFFORD EVANS AND BETTY J. MEGGERS

PERHAPS the most noticeable increase of outstanding archaeological monographs in western South America has occurred in Colombia, with the publications of Gerardo and Alicia Reichel-Dolmatoff dealing with the department of Magdalena, the Sierra Nevada de Santa Marta, and a shell midden at Barlovento near Cartagena. The artifacts are described as types and the reports are well written, in the modern up-to-date archaeological format with good illustrations. This work is filling important gaps in an area that should show aboriginal linkage with Venezuela, Ecuador, and Middle America. Two months of field work in 1955 by the Reichel-Dolmatoffs at the site of Momil on the Lower Sinu River has produced a complex of stone and pottery artifacts that is related to materials from western Venezuela and is also felt by them to be related to the Formative period of Middle America. Haury and Cubillo's report of their 1949-1950 excavations in Chibcha sites in the region around Bogota was released. It reports the absence of archaeological evidence to verify the "greatness" claimed for the Chibcha culture in the Spanish chronicles.

During 1954 the U. S. public viewed select pieces of aboriginal gold work in the traveling temporary exhibit of objects from the Museo del Oro, Banco de la República, Bogota. This superb collection was also featured in the two-volume work by José Pérez de Barradas, *Orfebrería prehispánica de Colombia, estilo calima* (Madrid, 1954, 2 v., [v. 1], Texto; [v. 2], Láminas). Not only is the work a masterpiece of reproduction of the gold specimens in both color and black and white, but the detailed descriptions, analysis, and data on each object are of immense value for the scholar.

Ecuador was an area of general archaeological inactivity between the death of Jijón y Caamaño and 1953 when Emilio Estrada of Guayaquil became interested in salvaging archaeological material being uncovered in the Guayas Basin as a result of intensified agricultural and roadbuilding activity. Estrada has preserved material from coastal sites and published some of his preliminary viewpoints in *Ensayo preliminar sobre arqueología del Milagro*. On his invitation, Clifford Evans and Betty J. Meggers made stratigraphic excavations in the Guayas Basin in September and October of 1954. This work was carried out on the Rio Daule and Rio Babahoyo as well as in the Milagro area. An important result was the identification in the lowest levels of materials definitely related to the Formative period cultures in both Peru and Middle America.

The most publicized archaeological find in Chile was the discovery in early 1954 in the Chilean Andes of a child mummy with associated objects of the Inca period. Popularly written reports appeared in various newspapers and picture magazines, and a scientific paper delivered by Greta Mostny at the XXXI International Congress of Americanists meeting in São Paulo during August 1954 will appear in the proceedings of the Congress.

The Peruvian-Bolivian area, as in the past, produces the greatest number of field projects and publications, many of which, based on field work done decades ago, have finally appeared. A few major contributions may be mentioned. The Textile Museum of Washington, D. C., produced a classic work combining technical data, magnificence of photographic detail, and faithful color reproduction of textiles in the book, *Paracas fabrics and Nazca needlework, 3rd century B.C.-3rd century A.D.* written by Junius Bird and Louisa Bellinger. The last works to come from the pen of Wendell C. Bennett before his death were *Excavations of Wari, Ayacucho, Peru,* which definitely assigns this culture to the Tiahuanaco Horizon, and the art volume, *Ancient arts of the Andes*, based on the aboriginal objects borrowed from various museums of the world by the Museum of Modern Art for a traveling exhibit in the U. S. during 1954. A. L. Kroeber published *Proto Lima: a Middle period culture of Peru*, based on his 1925 field work in the Rimac and Chillon Valleys, and a series of articles by Louis M. Stumer on the same area begin to fill out the literature on this part of the central coast, so that its archaeological history is becoming as well known as that of other culture areas of aboriginal Peru. The Paracas Cavernas and Chavin problem was further discussed by Kroeber (1953); it is most useful when read with Willey's "The Chavin problem: a review and critique" (SW J Anthr, 7:2, summer 1951, p. 103-144). The Columbia University Expedition in the Ica and Nazca Valleys in 1952-1953, led by William Duncan Strong, has not published a preliminary report of their stratigraphic finds except for a very brief and generalized framework based on a talk given by Strong to the New York Academy of Sciences. Two more publications resulting from the famous Viru Valley Project of 1946 on the north coast of Peru are the outstanding study by Willey, entitled *Prehistoric settlement patterns in the Virú Valley, Peru*, and Collier's *Cultural chronology and change as reflected in the ceramics of the Virú Valley, Peru*. The Chavin horizon specimens from the central coast based on the excavations of the Institute of Andean Research program of 1941-1942 in Peru have been described and discussed by Willey and Corbett in *Early Ancon and early Supe culture: Chavin Horizon sites of the central Peruvian coast* (1954).

Of a general nature one must call attention to the appearance in 1953 of Heyerdahl's massive volume presenting his evidence for trans-Pacific contacts. All scholars of aboriginal America must be familiar with his detailed arguments even if they do not agree with his thesis or proof; it is entitled *American Indians in the Pacific: the theory behind the Kon-Tiki expedition*.

In contrast to the above countries, where Americans have played a major part in the archaeological activity, work in Argentina and Uruguay has been by local archaeologists. Among the important contributions are the identification of several distinct preceramic complexes, among them the Ongamira culture described by Menghin and González, and the delineation by González of the cultural sequence in the Valle del Hualtin, northwestern Argentina, revealing striking parallels with the sequence in the southwestern U. S., not only in the evolution of house forms (from pit house to surface masonry room to large pueblo), but in the pottery, stone tools, and other artifacts. The explanation for this parallel development is one of the fascinating problems for archaeologists to solve. In Uruguay, the members of the Sociedad Amigos de la Arqueología continue to salvage and report on their country's aboriginal remains.

GENERAL

350. **Bennett, Wendell C.** Ancient arts of the Andes. Introduction by René d'Harnoncourt. N. Y., Museum of Modern Art, 1954. 186 p., 208 illus., maps.
Based on art exhibition starting in 1954 at the Museum of Modern Art, N. Y., of objects of western South American aboriginal manufacture borrowed from collections all over the world. Many shown and illustrated for first time. Of value to the layman and art historian. Text and captions unfortunately are filled with errors owing to Bennett's death while book still in manuscript form. Superb plates. See also item 371.

351. ————. Area archeology (Am Anthr, 55:1, Jan-Mar. 1953, p. 5-16).
Excellent theoretical discussion on value of the area approach, illustrated especially by work in Central Andes of Peru. Permits establishment of framework for findings.

352. **Bird, Junius.** Fechas del radiocarbono para Sud-América (R Mus Nac, 21, 1952, p. 8-34).
Translation of the English article, "Radiocarbon dating," by Junius Bird, *Memoirs of the Society for American Archaeology*, 8, 1951 (item 175 in *HLAS, no. 17, 1951*).

353. **Bushnell, G. H. S., and Adrian Dig-**

by. Ancient American pottery. N. Y., Pitman, 1955. 51 p., and 80 pl.
Superb photographs of typical ancient American pottery of Mexico, Peru, and southwestern U. S., with brief but good descriptions of the various cultures. The majority of the specimens are in the British Museum or Cambridge University Museum.

354. **Galimberti Miranda, Carlos A.** Las armas de guerra incaicas i su evolución (R Mus Inst Arqueol, 7:13-14, dic. 1951, p. 87-137, illus.).
Good discussion of the weapons of war used by the Incas as described by the chroniclers and verified by the actual specimens in the Cuzco Museum.

354a. **González, Alberto Rex.** La boleadora: sus áreas de dispersión y tipos (R Mus U Eva Perón, n. s., Sección Antropología, 4, 1953, p. 133-292).
Comprehensive study of the typology and world distribution of the bola, both archaeologically and ethnographically.

354b. ————. Mazas líticas del Uruguay y Patagonia (R Mus Paulista, n. s., 8, 1954, p. 261-280, illus.).
Description of six stone club heads with multiple protuberances, found at various places in Uruguay and Patagonia.

355. **Heredia, Florencio Daniel.** El Paititi (R Mus Inst Arqueol, 7:13-14, dic. 1951, p. 19-53).
Discussion of the possible existence and location of the site of Paititi or Musu culture on the Madre de Dios River near the mouth of the Beni River. Supposedly reached by the Inca. Reviews literature and suggests need for scientific exploration for the site.

356. **Heyerdahl, Thor.** American Indians in the Pacific: the theory behind the Kon-Tiki expedition. Chicago, Rand McNally, 1953. 821 p., 90 pl., maps.
Much interesting data, with a new approach to the peopling of the New World; but indiscriminate use of references, including the omission of all recent stratigraphic work in Peru, highly prejudices the arguments in favor of his theories.

357. **Hoffstetter, Robert.** La antigüedad del hombre americano. Progresos recientes en cronología prehistórica (B Inf Cient Nac, 4:47, mayo 1952, p. 794-816).
Review of methods of absolute dating, and major early man finds, in the Americas, indicating that man first reached this hemisphere about 12,000 years ago.

358. ————. Sobre los perros americanos prehispánicos (B Inf Cient Nac, 5:48, junio-julio 1953, p. 102-136, illus.).
Discussion of the origin and antiquity of the dog in America, leading to the conclusion that the dog was brought to this continent by man, rather than domesticated from American wild species.

359. **Homs, Joseph A.** Los orígenes indianos (B Inf Cient Nac, 4:44, enero-feb. 1951, p. 514-527).
Accepts theories of Australian and Melanesian migrations to South America, arriving at a reconstruction of the origin of the American Indians that is unacceptable to modern anthropology.

360. **Imbelloni, José.** El "superstratum" y los "substrata" en una cartografía antropológica correcta (Arch Ethnos, 1:2, sept. 1952, p. 29-34, illus., maps).
The author feels that broad-scale maps of racial, linguistic, or cultural areas obscure important evidence of earlier horizons. This difficulty may be removed by detailed examination of small regions. The California Peninsula and Patagonia are cited as examples.

361. **Márquez Miranda, Fernando.** Región meridional de América del Sur: período indígena. México, Instituto Panamericano de Geografía e Historia (Publ., 178; Comisión de Historia, 71), 1954. 240 p.
Succinct review of status of knowledge and interpretation in Argentina, Chile, and Uruguay, with representative bibliography.

362. **Mendoza, Angélica.** Arte antiga dos Andes (Américas, PAU, Portuguese ed., 6:8, agôsto 1954, p. 16-19, 27, illus.).
Good popular account of the "Art of the Andes" exhibit in N. Y. Some of the most artistic objects illustrated.

363. **Nordenskiöld, Erland.** Investigaciones arqueológicas en la región fronteriza de Perú y Bolivia. Traducción de Carlos Ponce Sanginés y Stig Rydén. La Paz, Alcaldía Municipal (Biblioteca paceña), 1953. 163 p., illus.
Description of artifacts and sites found on survey and excavation along Peru-Bolivian border. Mostly of background interest to more recent archaeological work in the area.

364. **Nordmann, Jo.** Determinación de la edad de los materiales arqueológicos con la ayuda del carbono radioactivo (C^{14}) (R Mus Nac, 21, 1952, p. 35-36).
Translation of article appearing in *Journal de la Société des Américanistes*, n. s., t. 39, 1952.

367. **Rowe, John H.** Forged Tiahuanaco-style keros (Am Antiq, 20:4, pt. 1, Apr. 1955, p. 392-393).
Evidence and description of four carved keros of Tiahuanaco designs proved now to be forgeries; all keros are Inca or post-Conquest.

368. **Schaedel, Richard.** El radiocarbono

14 y la arqueología del Perú y Chile (R Mus Nac, 21, 1952, p. 7).
Introductory statement to the article, by Bird on radio-carbon dating, which follows on p. 8-34 of same issue (see item 352).

369. **Schuster, Carl.** Human figures in South American petroglyphs and pictographs as excerpts from repeating patterns (A Mus Hist Nat, 2. serie, 6:6, 1955, p. 1-13).
After extensive investigation of repetitive patterns interpreted as having genealogical significance, the author suggests that human figures of certain kinds depicted singly on pictographs have been "borrowed" from repetitive patterns.

370. **Serrano, Antonio.** Normas para la descripción de la cerámica arqueológica. Córdoba, Argentina, Universidad Nacional de Córdoba, Instituto de Arqueología, Lingüística y Folklore Dr. Pablo Cabrera ([Publ.], 24), 1952. 25 p., illus.
Presentation of standard terminology, for naming and describing pottery types, which has been widely adopted in archaeological reporting by Americans.

371. **32 masterworks of Andean art.** A supplement to *Ancient arts of the Andes.* N. Y., Museum of Modern Art, 1955. 32 pl.
Illustration of gold, metal, inlay, wood, and pottery objects either not illustrated in Bennett's *Ancient arts of the Andes* or reproduced again to obtain a more artistic and clear picture. Invaluable, for several objects have never been illustrated before. See also item 350.

372. **Valcárcel, Luis E.** Altiplano andino: período indígena. México, Instituto Panamericano de Geografía e Historia (Publ., 156; Comisión de Historia, 54), 1953. 141 p.
Summary in Spanish of geography, ecology, and political and social life of ancient Peru, as well as the recent archaeological findings. Presents themes to follow in the study of pre-Spanish Peru, with good bibliographic references for each.

373. **Willey, Gordon R.** The prehistoric civilizations of nuclear America (Am Anthr, 57:3, pt. 1, June 1955, p. 571-593).
Good summary article, dealing with development of civilizations in America. Compares specific traits in Middle America and Peru in detail as well as from a time sequence standpoint. Excellent "references cited" section.

ARGENTINA

374. **Ardissone, Romualdo, and Mario F. Grondona.** La instalación aborigen en Valle Fértil. B. A., Universidad Nacional de B. A., Instituto de Geografía (Serie A, 18), 1953. 160 p., illus.
Analysis of the historical documentation and the number and distribution of stone mortars in an effort to determine the approximate size of the aboriginal population in the vicinity of San Agustín de Valle Fertil, province of San Juan, Argentina.

375. **Canals Frau, Salvador.** Las poblaciones indígenas de la Argentina: su origen, su pasado, su presente. B. A., Editorial Sudamericana, 1953. 575 p., illus., maps.
General description of the indigenous cultures of Argentina, beginning with a summary of the prehistoric sequence. The Indians are discussed in two major sections, one on the tribes of the pampas and the other on the tribes of the Andean region. Numerous illustrations of arts and crafts, habitat, and Indians. Good for general reference.

376. **Emperaire, J., and A. Laming.** La Grotte du Mylodon, Patagonie occidentale (J Soc Am, n. s., 43, 1954, p. 173-205).
Review of explorations from 1895 to date in a large cave containing Pleistocene fauna and human remains. The author does not feel that human occupation can be demonstrated until after the extinction of the sloth and other Pleistocene fauna. A good presentation of the evidence and its interpretation by various investigators.

376a. **González, Alberto Rex.** Concerning the existence of the pit house in South America (Am Antiq, 18:3, Jan. 1953, p. 271-272).
Discovery of pit houses in northwest Argentina. Highly significant item until full monograph is published.

376b. ————. Las ruinas de Loma Rica y alrededores (Natura, 1:1, 1954, p. 75-94, illus.).
Discussion of Loma Rica and abundant other archaeological sites in the Santa Maria Valley in support of a proposal to make this area a national park, to preserve and restore the ruins.

377. **Márquez Miranda, Fernando.** En la quebrada de Humahuaca, Argentina (*in* Proceedings of the XXX International Congress of Americanists, Cambridge, England, in 1952, 1955, p. 101-109).
Description and photographs of stone house structures.

378. **Menghin, Osvaldo F. A.** Derrotero de los indios canoeros (Arch Ethnos, 1:2, sept. 1952, p. 9-19, illus.).
Attempt to reconstruct the derivation of the "Canoe Indians" of Patagonia using archaeological evidence.

379. ————, **and Alberto Rex González.** Excavaciones arqueológicas en el yacimiento de Ongamira, Córdoba (Rep.

Arg.). Nota preliminar (Notas Mus Eva Perón, Antropología, 17:67, nov. 1954, p. 213-274).
Description of an important early site in Argentina, with detailed analysis of the stratigraphy and artifacts. Thorough and well presented.

380. Montes, Aníbal. El holoceno en relación con nuestra prehistoria. Córdoba, Argentina, Universidad Nacional de Córdoba, Museo de Mineralogía y Geología (Comunicaciones, 25), 1955. 33 p., illus.
Correlation of geological, paleontological, and archaeological evidence for the reconstruction of Holocene events in Argentina.

381. Pedersen, Asbjorn. El infrarrojo y su aplicación en la investigación de pinturas rupestres (Runa, 6, 1953-1954, p. 216-218, pl.).
Demonstration of the value of infra-red photography to reveal faded portions of rock paintings. Paired illustrations show the design visible to the eye and its original form as detected with infra-red. Five examples from the Sierras de Cordoba are used for demonstration.

382. ————. Objetos de bronce de la zona del Río Salado, región chaco-santiagueña (in Proceedings of the XXX International Congress of Americanists, Cambridge, England, in 1952, 1955, p. 92-100, illus.).
Brief text accompanied by tables giving chemical analysis of 28 objects, most of them illustrated on plates.

383. Pericot, L. South American prehistory: a review (Antiquity, 39:114, June 1955, p. 89-94).
Summary of results reported by Menghin in two articles on the prehistory of Patagonia. Chart shows chronological sequence.

386. Serrano, Antonio. Contenido e interpretación de la arqueología argentina. El área litoral (R U Nac Litoral, 29, 1954, 38 p., illus.).
Map of 17 archaeological areas in Argentina and detailed description of the "área litoral," encompassing the Parana and Uruguay Rivers.

387. Vignati, Milcíades Alejo. Aportes al conocimiento antropológico de la provincia de Mendoza (Notas Mus Eva Perón, Antropología, 16:55, abril 1953, p. 27-50, 10 pl.).
Description of sites, stone artifacts, and ceramics from the Guanacache lake region, and of a rock containing petroglyphs at Viluco.

BOLIVIA

388. Ibarro Grasso, Dick Edgar. New archaeological cultures from the departments of Chuquisaca, Potosi, and Tarija,

Bolivia (Am Antiq, 19:2, Oct. 1953, p. 126-129).
Of extreme importance to knowledge of aboriginal cultures of central and southern Bolivia, an area usually ignored in favor of Tiahuanaco area. Descriptive.

389. ————. Un nuevo panorama de la arqueología boliviana (Cuad Am, año 12, 71:5, sept.-oct. 1953, p. 143-167, 10 pl.).
Generalized discussion of the archaeology of Bolivia, emphasizing that the early cultures are related to northwest Argentina, and the spread of Tiahuanaco, and the "Nazcoid" influence. Illustrations of types of ceramics.

390. Menghin, Osvaldo F. A. Culturas precerámicas en Bolivia (Runa, 6, 1953-1954, p. 125-132, illus.).
Summary of the nonceramic, lithic cultures of Bolivia, especially as defined by the field work of Dick Ibarra Grasso in Viscachani, south of La Paz. Compares Bolivian types and proposed ages with central and northwest Argentina. Although many will not agree with his comparisons with Sandia, the general sequence is of extreme importance to the study of the Paleo Indian in the New World.

391. Mitre, Bartolomé. Las ruinas de Tiahuanaco. Estudio preliminar de Fernando Márquez Miranda. B. A., Hachette (Col. El pasado argentino), 1954. 203 p.
Comments on Mitre's 1838 visit to Tiahuanaco as well as the original account. Useful only as a literary, historical document.

392. O'Hara, Hazel. El coronel de los huacos (Américas, PAU, 7:8, agosto 1955, p. 14-18, illus.).
Description of collection of Diez de Medina of Bolivia; Tiahuanaco objects. Misleading, for all the worst theories are expounded here.

393. Portugal, Max. Acotaciones sobre antropología boliviana (G Campesina, 1:1, agosto 1952, p. 30-33).
Statement of what should be done in research. Of limited value to archaeologists.

394. Vellard, Jehan. Las ruinas de Khonkho Wancane (R Mus Nac Antr Arqueol, 2:2, 1. semestre 1955, p. 151-154, illus.).
Photos and description of carved monoliths in Tiahuanaco style near city of Jesus de Machaca in the Desaguadero area at site known as Khonkho-Wankane.

CHILE

395. Becher, Hans. Ein archäologischer Beleg für das vorkolumbische Auftreten der Robbenhaut-Balso an der Nordkuste Chiles (Zeit Ethn, 78:2, 1953, p. 257-261, illus.).
Carved stone vessel in form of reed balsa of type used along Chilean coast in pre-Columbian times.

396. Clues in killing of a noble Inca child (Life, 36:14, Apr. 5, 1954, p. 25-27). News and picture account of finding of child mummy in Chilean Andes. Some of best photographs of the find and its associated objects published so far in nontechnical journal. A few of statements slightly exaggerated. See also item 401.

397. **Cornely, Francisco L.** Cultura de El Molle. Santiago, Museo Arqueológico de la Serena, 1953. 32 p., illus. A revision of the author's earlier published ideas on the archaeology of the Valle de Elqui near El Molle, with better illustrations, additional data, and good diagrams.

398. ————. Las sepulturas de los indios diaguitas chilenos, provincias de Coquimbo y Atacama (Publ Mus Soc Arqueol La Serena B, 7, 1953, p. 5-12, illus.). Stone-lined graves; mostly Inca-influenced pottery in association.

399. **Gajardo Tobar, R.** Algunas consideraciones sobre la interpretación de decorados en la alfarería diaguita (Publ Mus Soc Arqueol La Serena B, 7, 1953, p. 19-21, illus.). Discussion of division of Diaguita designs into archaic, transition, classic, and Inca-influenced.

400. **Iribarren Charlin, Jorge.** Petroglifos en las estancias de La Laguna y Piedras Blancas, Río Hurtado (Publ Mus Soc Arqueol La Serena B, 7, 1953, p. 1-4, illus.). Descriptive article on petroglyphs in various localities in Rio Hurtado Valley near La Serena, central Chile.

401. **Naville, René.** L'enfant momifié du Cerro El Plomo (B Soc Suisse Am, 9, 1955, p. 26-28, illus.). Description of a child mummy found entombed at 5400 meters in the Chilean Andes, with illustration of the child and associated objects.

COLOMBIA

402. **Burke, Malcolm K.** Parque de monolitos (Américas, PAU, 7:6, junio 1955, p. 20-23, illus.). Good popular discussion of the establishment of an archaeological park at the site of San Agustin with the massive stone carvings. Good illustrations of some of the figures.

403. **Crane, Jane Watson.** Patrimonio de oro (Américas, PAU, 6:5, mayo 1954, p. 24-28, illus.). A good layman's account of the exhibit of aboriginal gold brought to the U. S. from the famous Museo del Oro collection of Banco de la República, Colombia. Excellent pictures.

404. **Cubillos Ch., Julio César,** and **Víc-**

tor **A. Bedoya.** Arqueología de las riberas del Río Magdalena, Espinal-Tolima (R Colomb Antr, 2:2, 1954, p. 116-144, illus., map). Excellent description and illustration, in modern archaeological format and terminology, of the pottery and other objects found at La Jabonera on the left bank of the upper Magdalena River, department of Tolima. Fits into the cultural materials found by the Reichel-Dolmatoffs in their Magdalena River excavations.

405. **Dussán de Reichel, Alicia.** Crespo: un nuevo complejo arqueológico del norte de Colombia (R Colomb Antr, 3, 1954, p. 171-188, illus.). Discussion of archaeological site at airport of Crespo, Cartagena, excavated by Reichel-Dolmatoffs in 1954. Excellent descriptions and illustrations, in modern archaeological terminology. Culture probably contemporaneous with Tairona period II. Shell axes of a type common to the Antilles found for first time in Colombia.

406. 80 masterpieces from the Gold Museum. Bogotá, Banco de la República, 1954. Unpaged, 80 pl. with text. Colored and black-and-white illustrations with good descriptive text of the seven styles of aboriginal gold objects, from the Banco de la República collection, which were loaned for temporary exhibition in 1954 in major museums of the U. S.

407. **Giraldo Jaramillo, Gabriel.** Temas de antropología e indigenismo. Bogotá, Los Andes (Sociedad Colombiana de Etnología, 2), 1954. 94 p. Of no value to archaeologists.

408. **Haury, Emil W.** Some thoughts on Chibcha culture in the high plains of Colombia (Am Antiq, 19:1, July 1953, p. 76-78). Good summary statement of larger study of Haury and Cubillos (see following item) demonstrating that Chibcha culture did not reach the peak once thought from Spanish descriptions.

409. ————, and **Julio César Cubillos.** Investigaciones arqueológicas en la sabana de Bogotá, Colombia (cultura chibcha). Tucson, Ariz., University of Arizona (Bulletin, 24:2; Social science bulletin, 22), 1953. 104 p., illus. Detailed account of archaeological survey and stratigraphic excavations in the southern part of the old Chibcha area in the Colombian Andes, 1949-1950. The conclusions are highly significant, for archaeology does not produce evidence to verify the greatness of Chibcha culture as it was previously inferred from the Spanish accounts. There is no evidence that Chibcha had a long history in the area.

410. **Lehmann, Henri.** Archéologie du

sud-ouest colombien (J Soc Am, n. s., 42, 1953, p. 199-270, 10 pl.).
Detailed description of excavations of prehistoric burial chambers in the Popayan region. Good diagrams of the shaft graves and illustrations of the artifacts recovered.

411. Medem, Federico. El cocodrilo. Estudio inicial sobre las representaciones zoomorfas precolombinas en el arte indígena de Colombia. Bogotá, Imp. del Banco de la República, 1953. Unpaged, 26 figs.
Discussion of the art motif of the caiman in aboriginal gold, stone, and pottery. Good data and illustrations, as far as they go; not exhaustive.

412. Nachtigall, Horst. Eine versunkene Hochkultur in Südkolumbien (Umschau in Wissenschaft und Technik, 54:5, März 1954, p. 144-146, illus.).

Good generalized discussion of the subterranean tombs at Tierradentro, Colombia, showing the wall decorations are identical to pottery decorations. Excellent photographs and diagrams of tombs.

413. Pérez de Barradas, José. Orfebrería prehispánica de Colombia. Estilo calima. Obra basada en el estudio de las colecciones del Museo del Oro del Banco de la República, Bogotá. Madrid, Copyright by Banco de la República (Bogotá, Colombia), 1954. 2 v. [V. 1], Texto, 367 p., 201 figs., 20 color pl.; [v. 2], Láminas, 300 illus.
Complete data on Calima style objects in Museo del Oro collection of Banco de la República, Colombia, with good, detailed description, metallurgical analysis, measurements, etc. The entire archaeological problem of the Calima region is briefly handled. Some scholars will disagree with the last chapters on interpretation of relationships of the Calima style with San Agustin stone carvings, and certain Pacific cultures. Illustrations excellent. The second volume contains black-and-white photos of Calima style aboriginal gold work, the finest reproduction yet of these specimens; many are illustrated for first time.

414. Reichel-Dolmatoff, Gerardo. Colombia: período indígena. México, Instituto Panamericano de Geografía e Historia (Publ., 151; Comisión de Historia, 49), 1953. 54 p.
Brief but good summary of ethnology and archaeology of Colombia, with bibliographic references.

415. ————. Contactos y cambios culturales en la Sierra Nevada de Santa Marta (R Colomb Antr, 2. época, 1:1, junio 1953, p. 15-122).
One chapter deals with the relationships between the archaeology of the Tairona culture and the various modern tribes of the Sierra Nevada, especially the Kogi. Extremely interesting and significant conclusions.

416. ————. Excavaciones en los conchales de la costa de Barlovento (R Colomb Antr, 4, 1955, p. 249-272, illus., maps).
Excavation and description of the first shell midden to be scientifically studied in Colombia. The site is on the coast near Cartagena in an area known as Coast of Barlovento. Stratigraphic excavations revealed a profusion of shell, stone artifacts, and over 20,000 sherds mostly with incised designs. Author believes it representative of first prehistoric settlements of fishers and gatherers and nonagriculturists in Colombia. Highly significant work.

417 ————. Investigaciones arqueológicas en la Sierra Nevada de Santa Marta. Partes 1 y 2 (R Colomb Antr, 2:2, 1954, p. 147-206, illus., map).
Detailed, excellent description of the site, Pueblito, which was first excavated by Mason in 1922 but extensively worked by the Reichel-Dolmatoffs at various times from 1946-1949. Uses the best modern archaeological technique, classification, and description of artifacts; and establishment of pottery types. Aboriginal material is of Tairona period II. See also items below.

418. ————. Investigaciones arqueológicas en la Sierra Nevada de Santa Marta. Parte 3 (R Colomb Antr, 3, 1954, p. 141-170, illus.).
Description of four sites in the Pueblito area which along with the aboriginal cultural materials had objects of European origin and manufacture in direct association. Now divides the Tairona period II into Tairona IIa (prehistoric classical) and Tairona IIb (historic). Excellent, very important study. See also items above and below.

419. ————. A preliminary study of space and time perspective in northern Colombia (Am Antiq, 19:4, Apr. 1954, p. 352-366, illus.).
First good English summary of the Reichel-Dolmatoffs' important archaeological survey and excavation work for past 10 years in the department of Magdalena. Cultures and periods discussed by five archaeological areas, with pottery types described and illustrated.

420. ————, and **Alicia Reichel-Dolmatoff.** Investigaciones arqueológicas en el departamento del Magdalena, Colombia, 1946-1950. Parte 3. Barranquilla, Colombia, Universidad del Atlántico, Instituto de Investigación Etnológica (Divulgaciones etnológicas, 3:4), 1953. 96 p., 23 laminas, map.
Divides the department of Magdalena into five archaeological areas. Detailed description of sites and artifacts from entire area. A very important study. Parts 1 and 2 were published in 1951 (see *HLAS, no. 17, 1951,* item 195).

421. ————, and ————. Investigaciones arqueológicas en la Sierra Nevada de Santa Marta. Parte 4 (R Colomb Antr, 4, 1955, p. 191-245, illus.).
Detailed description of architecture, artifacts, and stratigraphic cuts in habitation sites of Tairona period II in Pueblito. See also items above.

422. Wassén, S. Henry. Algunos datos del comercio precolombino en Colombia (R Colomb Antr, 4, 1955, p. 89-109).
Of interest to archaeologists is the section discussing the pre-Columbian trade of gold and copper objects and emeralds in Colombia. Based on study of early Spanish records.

ECUADOR

423. Andrade Marín, Jorge. La excavación arqueológica de Huaraquí, 1953 (B Inf Cient Nac, 5:54, mayo 1953, p. 746-758, illus.).
Description of rectangular receptacles found in the excavation of a mound near Tabacundo, in the Ecuadorian highlands, and speculations about their use.

424. Brainerd, George W. A cylindrical stamp from Ecuador (Masterkey, 27:1, Jan.-Feb. 1953, p. 14-17).
Fragment of cylindrical stamp, from south of Esmeraldas, with stylized speech scrolls, which suggests Mesoamerican contact.

425. Christensen, Ross T. A recent excavation in southern coastal Ecuador (B U Archaeol Soc, 5, Oct. 1954, p. 30-54, illus.).
Discussion of excavations and artifacts found at mound sites on Hacienda La Esperanza, Machala, province of El Oro, Ecuador, during June 1950. Well-presented data. The author recognizes he is in non-Peruvian materials, and relates the spindle whorls to Puna Island, and some of the other pottery and metal work to Manteno cultures of Manabi province. Considering the confused literature on this area, his conclusions are quite valid. It is interesting to note that La Esperanza mounds and their contents are part of the late Milagro period found by Evans and Meggers in the Guayas Basin around Guayaquil, Ecuador, in 1954. Of extreme importance, for Christensen's work is the first scientific excavation in El Oro province, Ecuador.

426. Corbett, John M. Some unusual ceramics from Esmeraldas, Ecuador (Am Antiq, 19:2, Oct. 1953, p. 145-152, illus.).
Description of artifacts, plus some theoretical implications with reference to Ecuador and Middle America.

427. Estrada, Emilio. Ensayo preliminar sobre arqueología del Milagro. Guayaquil, Ecuador, Cervantes, 1954. 113 p., illus.
Description of seven major sites in the Milagro area on the Ecuadorian coast east of Guayaquil, with numerous illustrations of pottery and metal objects, as well as site plans and profiles. The archaeological remains are linked with the Cayapa Indians, historic occupants of the region. The first detailed account of the archaeology of the Milagro area.

428. Evans, Clifford, and Betty J. Meggers. Preliminary report on archaeological investigations in the Guayas Basin, Ecuador (Cuad Hist Arqueol, año 4, 4:12, dic. 1954, p. 308-336, 4 pl.).
English version on one page, Spanish on opposite page, of stratigraphic excavations along Babahoyo and Daule Rivers and Milagro area of Guayas Basin in September-October 1954. Formative period cultures found. Very generalized statement for non-professional audience.

429. González C., Celiano E. Estudios arqueológicos en el cantón Zaruma (B Inf Cient Nac, 6:56, agosto-sept. 1953, p. 187-198, illus.).
Investigation of stone ruins at Cerro de Tocto, near Guanazan, canton of Zaruma, province of El Oro, believed to be built during Inca times by Túpac Yupanque. See also item below.

430. ————. Estudios arqueológicos en el cantón Zaruma (B Inf Cient Nac, 6:57, oct.-nov. 1953, p. 303-313, illus.).
Investigation of stone ruins at Cerro de Tocto, zan, canton of Zaruma, province of El Oro. Materials in cave suggest occupation by many groups. Lacks good description of finds or conditions of discovery, therefore cannot be used for comparative purposes. Author agrees with Rivet's earlier comments about the site. See also item above.

431. Guignabaudet, Philippe. Nuevos descubrimientos arqueológicos en las tolas de Huaraquí (B Inf Cient Nac, 6:56, agosto-sept. 1953, p. 168-186, illus.).
Further excavations at the subterranean "bottle-shaped" tombs of Huaraqui (see item 423) in the canton Pedro Moncayo of the province of Pichincha. Presence of pottery fragments of same vessel with different bodies in same tomb causes the author to speculate on possibility of the same funeral rites for all the dead giving each body a fragment so they could all benefit in the next world—a sort of symbolic ritualism.

432. Haro Alvear, Silvio Luis. Puruha: estudios arqueológicos (Cuad Hist Arqueol, año 1, 1:2-3, dic. 1951, p. 79-124; año 2, 2:6, dic. 1952, p. 131-166; año 3, 3:9, dic. 1953, p. 137-166; illus., maps).
Historical data, archival information, linguistics, chronicler's accounts, and archaeological evidence to demonstrate the importance of the Puruha "kingdom" of the provinces of Chimborazo, Bolivar, and Cañar. Many of Jijón y Caamaño's ideas restated.

433. Holm, Olaf. El tatuaje entre los aborígenes prepizarrianos de la costa ecuatoriana (Cuad Hist Arqueol, año 3, 3:7-8, agosto 1953, p. 56-92, illus.).

Discussion of how archaeological evidence indicates that the pre-Spanish coastal peoples tattooed the face and parts of the body. Quotes Spanish sources as supporting evidence.

434. ————. Verruga peruana en un cerámico patográfico ecuatoriano (Cuad Hist Arqueol, año 4, 4:12, dic. 1954, p. 207-223, illus.).

Description of a ceramic vessel from province of Manabi which shows modeling on the face suggesting that the person had the warty skin disease known as *verruga peruana* (Carrion's disease).

435. Huerta Rendón, Francisco. Una urna funeraria de La Libertad y su "muerte" ritual (R Hitos, 1, 1954, p. 1-6).

Burial vessel from La Libertad with a hole in the side which according to author is like the ceremonial killing of vessels found in southwestern U. S.

436. Larrea, Carlos M. Informe (B Inf Cient Nac, 5:54, mayo 1953, p. 759-773, illus.).

Discussion of the possible purpose of the rectangular receptacles found in certain Ecuadorian highland sites.

437. Nicholson, H. B. On a supposed Mesoamerican "thin orange" vessel from Ecuador (Am Antiq, 19:2, Oct. 1953, p. 164-166).

Further comment on the Cusín vessel proposed by Uhle and Jijón y Caamaño to demonstrate evidence of trade with Mesoamerica. Interesting comments, but lacking in absolute proof.

438. Robinson Pérez, Lillian. Middle American mosaic crossroads of culture on Ecuador's coast (Pac Discov, 8:5, Sept.-Oct. 1955, p. 16-25, illus.).

Demonstrates with text and superb illustrations several heretofore unpublished specimens to show the relationships of certain pottery figurines from northern Manabi, La Tolita, and Esmeraldas, on the north coast of Ecuador, with Middle America.

PERU

439. Actas de la mesa redonda sobre "Terminología arqueológica" (B Soc Antr Per, 1, 1953, p. 3-18).

Important to the serious scholar of Peruvian archaeology, for it shows the old terminology of cultures, periods, and epochs, and the current ones proposed. Some changes are good; others will merely add confusion to an already complex situation.

440. Alicina Franch, José. Nuevas interpretaciones de la figura del shaman en la cerámica chimú (Miscel Am, 1, 1951, p. 45-66, illus.).

Theory that in the Mochica ceramics (the author uses the old terminology of Chimu) the various representations of central figures of birds, snakes, crabs, humans with different masks, etc. are shamans. Detailed arguments to support his viewpoint.

441. Ballesteros-Gaibrois, Manuel. La crónica de Murúa y la crítica del inkario (Runa, 6, 1953-1954, p. 97-117, illus.).

Comparison of two manuscripts on Inca rulers (especially Pachakuti or Yupanqui, the ninth Inca), known as the MS. Wellington, based upon the original by Fray Martín de Murúa entitled "Historia del origen y genealogía de los reyes incas del Perú," and the MS. Loyola (Urteaga). Of especial interest to students of Peruvian history as recorded by various chroniclers. See also item 461.

442. Bennett, Wendell C. Excavations at Wari, Ayacucho, Peru. New Haven, Conn., Yale University Press (Yale University publ. in anthropology, 49), 1953. 121 p., 12 pl.

Last major work of Bennett written before his death. Detailed account of field work undertaken in summer of 1950 at Wari (Huari). Well illustrated, with descriptions of pottery series. Wari culture assigned definitely to the widespread Tiahuanaco horizon of Peru and Bolivia.

443. Bird, Junius, and Louisa Bellinger. Paracas fabrics and Nazca needlework, 3rd century B. C.—3rd century A. D. Catalogue raisonné. Washington, Textile Museum, 1954. 126 p., 127 pl.

Detailed description and analysis of 90 odd textiles from the Paracas Peninsula with a few related ones from Nazca, Peru. Magnificent color and black-and white photos. By far the most superbly illustrated and best technical study to date on Paracas textiles.

444. Carrión Cachot, Rebeca. El culto al agua en el antiguo Perú (R Mus Nac Antr Arqueol, 2:2, 1. semestre 1955, p. 50-140, illus.).

The religious and ceremonial practice of running water in channels or out of spouts of pottery, stone, or wooden vessels has been termed "paccha" in Andean literature. The author makes a complete survey of mythology, archive records, Spanish chroniclers, museum specimens, carved stones at ruins, etc., describing in detail the practice and its related beliefs and ceremonialism. Excellent and important illustrations. A most significant, thorough study; first of its kind on this subject.

445. Chase, Kathleen Barantzen. El desierto entrega sus tesoros (Américas, PAU, 6:5, mayo 1954, p.. 17-19, illus.).

Account of burials found at Ancon, central coast Peru; a nonscientific article.

446. Christensen, Ross T. Preliminary report of excavations in the Piura Valley, Peru (B U Archaeol Soc, Sept. 1951, p. 36-53, illus.).
Description of excavations in the Piura Valley. Good map of sites in this archaeologically unknown area; data too generalized and brief to be of much value for comparative purposes but results from strata-cut investigations should eventually prove to be of unusual significance due to location between well-defined stratigraphy in Ecuador and north Peru.

447. Collier, Donald. Cultural chronology and change as reflected in the ceramics of the Virú Valley, Peru. Chicago, Ill., Chicago Natural History Museum (Fieldiana: Anthropology, 43), 1955. 226 p. illus.
Another of the reports to come out of the famous 1946 Viru Valley project based on intense survey and excavation. Collier's problem was to work on the late prehistoric period but he also found materials dealing with the late Guañape period. Well illustrated with good clear reproduction. Most useful if used with the other Viru Valley project reports (see his preface, p. 8, for complete listings).

448. Cosío, José Gabriel. Vitcos, la última capital de los incas (R Mus Inst Arqueol, 7:13-14, dic. 1951, p. 7-18).
Discussion of the argument that Vitcos, the last capital of the Incas, was not Machu Picchu but instead the ruin of Rosaspata, San Miguel Valley.

449. Espejo Núñez, Julio. Bibliografía básica de arqueología andina. 3. Cultura Paracas (B Bibl, Lima, año 27, 24:1-4, dic. 1954, p. 16-22).
Very complete bibliography of basic references on archaeology and physical anthropology of Paracas culture; contains 107 items by title, indexed by author.

450. Faublée, Jacques. Sculptures Mochica des îles Macabi (J Soc Am, n. s., 43, 1954, p. 149-150, illus.).
Description of three carved wooden staff heads in the collection of the Musées de Bordeaux, excavated in 1868 from beneath 10 meters of guano. Two are illustrated.

451. Fawcett, Raymond (ed.). How did they live? —Peru. London, Gawthorn, 1953? 47 p., illus.
Popular account of Inca culture. Overstated at times.

452. Fester, G. A. Algunos colorantes de una antigua civilización sudamericana (R Mus Nac Antr Arqueol, 2:2, 1. semestre 1955, p. 155-160).
Translation of the English version of this article, but without plates.

453.————. Einige Farbstoffe Sud Amerikanischer Kulturvolker (Isis, 44:1-2, June 1953, p. 13-16, illus.).

Devoted mainly to the study of dyes of Paracas material; the only available chemical study of dyes of this period in Peru. See also item below.

454.————. Some dyes of the ancient South American civilizations (Dyestuffs, 40:9, July 1954, p. 238-244, illus.).
Translation of the original German article (see item above).

455. Ford, James A. The history of a Peruvian valley (Sci Am, 191:2, Aug. 1954, p. 28-34, illus.).
Good popular account of the famous Viru Valley expedition in 1946 and some of its basic archaeological finds. Clear charts and good illustrations.

456. Gayton, A. H. A new type of ancient Peruvian shirt (Am Antiq, 20:3, Jan. 1955, p. 263-270, illus.).
Unique example of a new construction principle of a shirt from Rimac Valley, associated with ceramics of 1400-1500 A. D.

457. Harcourt, Raoul d'. Une broderie sur filet de Nazca, Pérou (B Soc Suisse Am, 8, 1954, p. 1-2).
Description of an embroidered belt from a grave containing objects showing Inca influence excavated at Copara in the Nazca Valley.

458.————. Les formes du tambour à membranes dans l'ancien Pérou (J Soc Am, n. s., 43, 1954, p. 155-159, illus.).
Description of double-ended drums of pottery from archaeological sites at Ica, Huacho, Huaura, Chancay Valley, and Nazca Valley. One example with the heads in place and two lacking them are illustrated.

459. Heyerdahl, T. Aboriginal navigation in Peru; objects and results of the Kon-Tiki expedition (*in* Proceedings of the XXX International Congress of Americanists, Cambridge, England, in 1952, 1955, p. 72-81).
Discussion of balsa raft navigation of aboriginal Peruvians and how the Kon-Tiki expedition demonstrated the seaworthiness of this type of raft. A good concise statement.

460. Houtzager, M. Elisabeth. De schatten van Peru. Utrecht, Centrall Museum, 1954. 24, 99 p., illus.
A sort of catalogue-handbook with illustrations from European museums of aboriginal Peruvian specimens. No new data.

461. Imbelloni, J. Sobre comparación de los textos del Padre Murúa (Runa, 6, 1953-1954, p. 118-124).
Comment on the validity of the comparison by Ballesteros-Gaibrois (see item 441) of the MS. Wellington and MS. Loyola about the Inca Pachakuti (Yupanqui).

462. Kidder, Alfred, II. Algunos problemas de la primitiva arqueología de la hoya del Titicaca (R Mus Nac Antr Arqueol, 2:2, 1. semestre 1955, p. 46-49). Brief, generalized statement of research needs for the perfection and extension of time sequences for the Lake Titicaca Basin as well as for a better interpretation of the existing archaeological data.

463. Kroeber, A. L. Paracas Cavernas and Chavín (U Calif Publ Am Archaeol Ethn, 40:8, 1953, p. 313-348, illus.).
Written to express in detail Kroeber's viewpoint that he, like Tello, sees a "Chavín minority ingredient as indubitable and significant" in Paracas Cavernas-Ocucaje, Peru pottery. Most useful when used in conjunction with Willey's 1951 review and critique of "The Chavín problem" (SW J Anthr, 7:2, summer 1951, p. 103-144).

464. ————. Proto-Lima, a Middle period culture of Peru. With appendix: Cloths, by Dwight T. Wallace. Chicago, Ill., Chicago Natural History Museum (Fieldiana: Anthropology, 44:1), 1954. 157 p., illus.
Detailed descriptive account of Kroeber's 1925 field work relating to the earlier (Proto-Lima) cultures found in the Rimac and Chillon Valleys of central coast Peru. Useful data on architecture, burial patterns, and pottery and other artifacts. Section by Wallace on textiles is competently handled in the current format and terminology of textile experts. Valuable section on differences in viewpoints of Uhle, Jijón y Caamaño, Willey, Bennett, and Kroeber on the Maranga site.

465. ————. Proto-Lima: un período cultural intermedio del Perú. Síntesis e interpretación (R Mus Nac Antr Arqueol, 2:2, 1. semestre 1955, p. 141-145).
Description of Huaca 15, Rimac Valley finds, and relation of this Proto-Lima site to coastal Peruvian archaeology. See also item above.

466. ————. Quantitative analyses of ancient Peruvian metal (Am Antiq, 20:2, Oct. 1954, p. 160-162).
Chemical analysis of metal objects from Uhle collection at University of California Museum, representing Mochica, Tiahuanacoid, Middle Ica, and Inca periods.

467. Kutscher, Gerdt. Nordperuanische Keramik. Figürlich Verzierte Gefässe der Früh-Chimu. Berlin, Gebr. Mann (Monumenta Americana, 1), 1954. 79 p., and 80 p. of illus.
The scenes, designs, figures, ceremonies, etc., on Proto or Early Chimu (Mochica) pottery from the north coast of Peru. Excellent discussion of Mochica life as depicted on these archaeological specimens, as well as detailed data on provenience, size, paint, etc., of each pottery vessel.

468. Lothrop, Samuel K. A Peruvian goldsmith's grave (Archaeology, 7:1, spring 1954, p. 31-36, illus.).
Unique collection of gold objects from Chimu period grave near Huarmey, Peru, now in Robert Woods Bliss Collection, National Gallery of Art, Washington. Detailed discussion and good illustrations of objects.

469. ————. Tumba de un orfebre peruano (R Mus Nac Antr Arqueol, 2:2, 1. semestre 1955, p. 146-150, illus.).
An exact translation, with all the same plates except one, of the item above.

470. Petersen, George. Adorno labial de oro usado por los tallanes (R Mus Nac Antr Arqueol, 2:2, 1. semestre 1955, p. 161-168, illus.).
Illustration and description of lip plugs from graves of Campamento Los Organos, near Mancora and Cabo Blanco in the province of Paita, department of Piura, Peru. Compares them favorably with Ecuadorian material.

471. Porras Barrenechea, Raúl. Quipu i quilca (R Mus Inst Arqueol, 7:13-14, dic. 1951, p. 19-53).
Review of the history and study of writing in ancient Peru—pictographs, beans, quipu, etc. No new data.

472. Puga, Mario. Los incas: sociedad y estado. México, Centauro, 1955. 203 p.
Well-documented discussion of society and state of Inca empire with especial emphasis on ayllu, administration, distribution, etc. Some of the archaeological data lack the most up-to-date reference data.

473. Reiche, Maria. Prehistoric ground drawings in Peru (Photographie und Forschung, 6:4, Jan. 1955, p. 97-108, illus.).
Superb color and black-and-white reproductions of extensive ground drawings near Nazca, with good descriptive text.

474. Rostworowski Tovar de Diez Canseco, María. Pachacutec Inca Yupanqui. Lima, Imp. Torres Aguirre, 1953. 280 p.
Well-documented study of Inca empire, especially the expansion under the ninth ruler, Pachacuti (Pachacutec).

475. Rydén, Stig. Drinking tubes on archaeological vessels from western South America (Am Antiq, 20:2, Oct. 1954, p. 149-153).
New approach to problem of spouts on pottery and metal vessels. Good illustrations, well documented, with cross references.

476. Sawyer, Alan R. The Nathan Cummings Collection of Ancient Peruvian art. Chicago, Ill., Art Institute of Chicago (Handbook), 1954. 48 p., illus.

Select specimens from the former Wassermann-San Blas Collection of Peruvian pottery (mostly Mochica, Chimu and Nazca), acquired by Cummings and now at the Chicago Art Institute, are illustrated with explanatory text. Good photographs; nothing new to Peruvianists except better photographs of some of the metal objects.

477. Strong, William Duncan. Recent archeological discoveries in south coastal Peru (Trans NY Ac Sci, series 2, 16:4, Feb. 1954, p. 215-218).
Brief preliminary report of generalized framework of culture epochs from Columbia University archaeological expedition in Ica and Nazca Valleys in 1952-1953.

478. Stumer, Louis Michael. The Chillón Valley of Peru: excavation and reconnaissance, 1952-53 (Archaeology 7:3, autumn 1954, p. 171-178, illus.; 7:4, winter 1954, p. 220-228, illus.).
Well-presented layman's discussion of archaeological finds from Chillon Valley, just north of Lima, made by Stumer, 1952-1953. Culture and pottery only briefly mentioned for each site. Most important information to the archaeologist in his culture sequence for Chillon Valley with typical sites for each period.

479. ————. History of a dig (Sci Am, 192:3, Mar. 1955, p. 98-104, illus.).
Popularized account of one type of archaeological investigation at Cerra Culebra site, central coast, Peru.

480. ————. Investigaciones de superficie en Caldera, Valle de Huaura (R Mus Nac, 21, 1952, p. 37-67, illus.).
Description of site and artifacts on hacienda Caldera in Huaura Valley, with detailed comparison with Central Coast periods of Coastal Tiahuanaco through Chancay.

481. ————. Playa Grande: primitive elegance in pre-Tiahuanaco Peru (Archaeology, 6:1, spring 1953, p. 42-48, illus.).
Description of excavations and artifacts, Playa Grande site, a few miles north of Lima.

482. ————. Population centers of the Rimac Valley of Peru (Am Antiq, 20:2, Oct. 1954, p. 130-148, illus., maps).
Discussion of sites by cultural periods, thus showing development and change of settlement patterns through time. Useful in light of settlement-pattern approach of Willey (see item 488).

483. ————. Report on the south Peruvian coast: Chala to Arica (Am Antiq, 19:4, Apr. 1954, p. 384-386).
Brief description of sites found in survey. Cultures mostly Tiahuanacoid, with lack of post-Tiahuanacoid and pre-Inca cultures.

484. Tello, Julio C. El país de los Inkas (R Mus Nac Antr Arqueol, 2:2, 1. semestre 1955, p. 24-45).
Reprint of Tello's article originally appearing in the book, *Perú en cifras*, Lima, 1945. One

of Tello's best-generalized theoretical articles on general background, history, and development of Inca empire, with limited discussion of his pre-Inca culture sequence.

485. Van Stan, Ina. Peruvian domestic fabrics from Supe. A study of the Uhle Collection of painted cloths. Tallahassee, Fla., Florida State University, Department of Anthropology and Archaeology (Notes in anthropology, 1:3), 1955. 56 p., illus.
Excellent discussion of aboriginal painted Peruvian textiles, in modern terminology; useful in comparative work.

486. ————. Weaver education in ancient Peru. Tallahassee, Fla., Florida State University (Series, 16, Anthropology), 1954, p. 87-118, illus.
Demonstration from four textile specimens in Florida State University Carter Collection that weavers were taught with samples and samplers. Method of instruction identical to teaching manual arts today. Detailed description of the specimens.

487. Von Hagen, Victor W. Highway of the sun. N. Y., Duell, Sloan, and Pearce, 1955. 320 p., illus., maps.
Highly popularized account of 1952-1954 Inca Highway Expedition tracing roads both in the highlands and on the coast. Of limited value scientifically because of the absence of full description of new finds; primarily written for the layman as an adventure story.

488. Willey, Gordon R. Prehistoric settlement patterns in the Virú Valley, Peru. Washington, Smithsonian Institution, Bureau of American Ethnology (Bulletin, 155), 1953. 453 p., 88 figs., maps, 60 pl.
One of the reports developing out of the famous Viru Valley project of 1946. Utilizing the sequence set up by Ford from survey and stratigraphic data of ceramic sequences, Willey places the settlement patterns of the valley in proper sequence. A unique study never before attempted through such a long time scale in the New World. His stress of settlement patterns (living arrangements, temples, roads, irrigation works, public buildings, etc.) offers new clues to the understanding of the development of aboriginal coastal Peruvian cultures through time with reference to man's use of his natural resources.

489. ————, and **John M. Corbett.** Early Ancón and early Supe culture: Chavín horizon sites of the central Peruvian coast. With special sections: Textiles, by Lila M. O'Neale; Plant remains, by Margaret Ashley Towle; A mummified dog from the lighthouse site, Supe, by W. G. Haag; The human physical type and cranial deformation, by Marshall T. Newman. N. Y., Columbia University Press (Columbia studies in archeology and ethnology, 3), 1954. 169 p., 31 pl.

Detailed description of stratigraphic excavations, artifacts, pottery types, architecture, etc., of early sites at Ancon and Supe excavated in 1941-1942 as Project 3 of the Institute of Andean Research. Line drawings of pottery are excellent, but photographs are poor except for those of textiles. Invaluable to all Peruvianists, for it defines in detail the distinctive features of the Chavin Horizon of the central coast. Many of these types are identical to those found in 1946 in early sites on the north coast.

URUGUAY

490. Freitas, Carlos A. de. Alfarería del delta del Río Negro, paradero La Blanqueada (R Soc Ami Arqueol, 12, 1953, p. 65-121, 31 figs.).
Reprint of a paper originally published in *Revista histórica*, año 36, Montevideo, 1942, giving a detailed discussion of archaeological ceramic finds from a site at the mouth of the Rio Negro in western Uruguay.

491. ————. Alfarería indígena. Hallazgos de trozos de vasijas construídas por los primitivos habitantes del litoral uru-

guayo (R Soc Ami Arqueol, 12, 1953, p. 41-49, illus.).
Description of potsherds from a site at the mouth of the Rio Negro, western Uruguay.

492. ————. Algunos aspectos de la arqueología del Río Uruguay (R Soc Ami Arqueol, 12, 1953, p. 147-183).
Summary of archaeological and documentary evidence concerning the aboriginal occupation of the Uruguay River, at present the boundary between Uruguay and Argentina.

493. ————, and **Silvio S. Geranio.** Informe sobre una vasija ornitomorfa del Río Negro (R Soc Ami Arqueol, 12, 1953, p. 51-64, 12 figs.).
Reprint of an article originally published in v. 9 of the same journal, describing a pottery vessel found in the Rio Negro and said to represent a stylized bird form.

494. Sanz, Víctor. La propiedad en el Charrúa. Montevideo, Hispania, 1955. 48 p.
Discussion of type of ownership of land and goods characteristic of the Charrua, as indicated by documentary sources.

ETHNOLOGY: MIDDLE AMERICA AND THE WEST INDIES

ÁNGEL PALERM AND SIDNEY W. MINTZ

GENERAL

550. Bernal, Ignacio, and **Eusebio Dávalos Hurtado** (eds.). Huastecos, totonacos y sus vecinos (R Mex Estud Antr, 13:2-3, 1952-1953, 567 p.).
Los trabajos de carácter etnológico contenidos en el volumen, tienen entradas separadas en esta sección. Otros trabajos, de carácter histórico, figuran en las secciones respectivas. [A. Palerm]

551. Caso, Alfonso. Calendarios de los totonacos y huastecos (R Mex Estud Antr, 13:2-3, 1952-1953, p. 337-350, illus.). [A. Palerm]

552. ————. New World culture history: Middle America (*in* Kroeber, A. L. (ed.). Anthropology today. An encyclopedic inventory. Chicago, Ill., University of Chicago Press, 1953, p. 226-237).
Concise summary of the principal periods of cultural history in Middle America. See also item 22. [D. B. Stout]

553. Crowley, Daniel J. American credit institutions of Yoruba type (Man, 53:5, May 1953, p. 80).
A credit institution similar to that found today among the Yoruba, as well as in British

Guiana and Trinidad, is reported to occur in the Bahamas as well. [S. W. Mintz]

554. Dahlgren, Barbro. Etnografía prehispánica de la costa del Golfo (R Mex Estud Antr, 13:2-3, 1952-1953, p. 145-156).
Lista de elementos culturales característicos de la costa, y comparación y discusión de los elementos de otras áreas. [A. Palerm]

555. Germán Parra, Manuel, and **Wigberto Jiménez Moreno.** Bibliografía indigenista de México y Centroamérica (1850-1950). México, Instituto Nacional Indigenista (Memorias, 4), 1954. ci, 342 p. [A. Palerm]

556. Kruijer, G. J. Kerk en religie op de Bovenwindse Eilanden der Nederlandse Antillen (West-Indische Gids, 34:4, Dec. 1953, p. 238-251).
Improved economic conditions in St. Martin, St. Eustatius, and Saba have led to a declining importance of magic. Afro-European religious life among lower-class Caribbean populations comes from both the African tradition (e.g., the individual identifying with the supernatural) and from the lower-class social and economic situation. [S. W. Mintz]

557 ————. Saint Martin and Saint Eustatius Negroes as compared with those of St. Thomas (West-Indische Gids, 34:4, Dec. 1953, p. 225-237).
A culture-and-personality study of the people of St. Martin and St. Eustatius which draws heavily on A. Campbell's study of St. Thomas. [S. W. Mintz]

558. Landes, Ruth. Negro slavery and female status (Afr Aff, 52:206, Jan. 1953, p. 54-57).
". . . the sexually-weighted favouritism of New World masters combined with cultural precedents of Africa to elevate the status of slave women in the western hemisphere." Brief reference is made to the position of female slaves in the Caribbean. [S. W. Mintz]

559. Leroi-Gourhan, André, and Jean Poirier. Ethnologie de l'Union Française. Paris, Presses Universitaires de France (Pays d'outre-mer, 6 série; Peuples et civilizations d'outre-mer, 1-2), 1953. 2 v. 1083 p., maps, pl.
V. 2 contains demographic and ethnologic descriptions for the Antilles and French Guiana. Each area is accorded an extensive bibliography, and the tribal lists and maps are very useful. [D. B. Stout]

560. Lichtveld, Lou. Enerlei Creools? (West-Indische Gids, 35:1-2, Apr. 1954, p. 59-71).
The author argues for a comparative study of Caribbean Creole languages, claiming that it is impossible to apply the linguistic categories of European languages to Creole without distortion. The sociohistorical circumstances under which Creole languages formed, and the inner character of such languages, cannot be handled by reference to the European background. [S. W. Mintz]

561. Martí, Samuel. Música precortesiana (Cuad Am, 78:6, nov.-dic. 1954, p. 149-155).
El autor es uno de los escasos especialistas en este campo. [A. Palerm]

562. Moreno, Manuel M. La organización gremial entre los aztecas (R Mex Trab, 5. época, 1:7-8, julio-agosto 1954, p. 29-49).
Reedición de un trabajo importante, aunque superado en muchos aspectos. [A. Palerm]

563. Palerm, Ángel. La distribución del regadío en el área central de Mesoamérica (Cien Soc, 5:25, feb. 1954, p. 2-15; 5:26, abril 1954, p. 64-74, map).
Utilizando fuentes documentales, el autor establece la distribución geográfica del regadío en el área central de Mesoamérica y en el momento del contacto con los españoles. Se localizan en el mapa y en las tablas correspondientes 382 lugares con riego. [A. Palerm]

564. ————. La secuencia de la evolución cultural de Mesoamérica (BBAA, 17:1, 1954, i.e. 1955, p. 205-233).
Primera parte de un artículo de crítica de las ideas e interpretaciones propuestas por Caso, Armillas y Bernal. Comprende desde el Arcaico (Formativo) al fin del mundo Clásico. [A. Palerm]

565. Price-Mars, Jean. Puissance de la foi religieuse chez les nègres de Saint-Domingue dans l'insurrection générale des esclaves de 1791 à 1803 (R Hist Colonies, 42:1, 1954, p. 5-13). [S. W. Mintz]

566. Rodríguez Demorizi, Silveria R. de. Arcaísmos en Santo Domingo (B Ac Dom Lengua, 14:45, agosto 1954, p. 18-28).
Retentions of archaic words in contemporary speech in Santo Domingo, with references to early published usages. [S. W. Mintz]

567. Sauer, Carl O. Economic prospects of the Caribbean (in Wilgus, A. Curtis (ed.). The Caribbean: its economy [see item 1376], p. 15-27).
Contains a brief discussion of conuco subsistence farming and of the plantation economy. [S. W. Mintz]

568. Sherlock, Philip M. West Indian folklore (Libr J, 78:4, Feb. 15, 1953, p. 283-287).
A popular comment on the heterogeneity of Caribbean culture and its expression in folklore. [S. W. Mintz]

569. Smith, Michael G. Some aspects of social structure in the British Caribbean about 1820 (Soc Ec Stud, 1:4, Aug. 1953, p. 55-80).
A cultural-historical study of social differentiation on the islands of St. Vincent and Jamaica during the early decades of the 19th century. [S. W. Mintz]

570. Tejera, Emiliano. Palabras indígenas de la isla de Santo Domingo (B Ac Dom Lengua, 13:43, abril 1953, p. 24-34; 13:44, nov. 1953, p. 22-34).
A list of presumed indigenous terms presented alphabetically. The two entries listed here cover Maguacochios to Managua, and Managuayabo to Mato. This series of articles by Dr. Tejera was begun in 1946. [S. W. Mintz]

571. Thompson, Donald E. Maya paganism and Christianity. A history of the fusion of two religions. New Orleans, La., Middle American Research Institute, 1954. 36 p. [A. Palerm]

COSTA RICA

572. Clemens, René. Informe general

sobre la mesa redonda acerca de la enseñanza de las ciencias sociales, celebrada en San José de Costa Rica (Cien Soc, 6:33, junio 1955, p. 130-155).
La mesa redonda reunió a representantes y especialistas de México, Centroamérica y otros países ribereños del Caribe. El informe incluye las recomendaciones aprobadas por los participantes. [A. Palerm]

573. **James, Preston; Ernest Moore; Robert Shafer; David Stout; and Martin Travis.** Proyecto de estudio integral del área costarricense (Cien Soc, 4:24, dic. 1953, p. 242-259).
Ensayo de enfoque interdisciplinario para el estudio de un área. Para preparar el proyecto se reunieron representantes de las siguientes disciplinas: geografía, humanidades, historia, antropología y ciencias políticas. [A. Palerm]

574. **Norris, Thomas L.** Decision-making activity sequences in a hacienda community (Hum Org, 12:3, fall 1953, p. 26-30).
El caso analizado es el de una hacienda en el cantón de Turrialba, Costa Rica. [A. Palerm]

CUBA

575. **Bascom, William R.** Yoruba acculturation in Cuba (Mém IFAN, 27, 1953, p. 163-167).
Field work in Cuba has definitely established the survival of African linguistic and religious materials in relatively pure form, though "there is no record of contact with Africa since the end of the slave trade in the 1880's." [S. W. Mintz]

576. **Cabrera, Lydia.** El dueño de Ewe (Oluwa-Ewe) (Mém IFAN, 27, 1953, p. 169-180).
Information regarding the conceptions of Osain, the leading divinity of the Lucumí (Yoruba) cult groups in Cuba, as held by cult adherents. [S. W. Mintz]

577. **Lachatañere, Rómulo.** Rasgos bantú en la santería (Mém IFAN, 27, 1953, p. 181-184).
An effort to indicate Bantu elements in Afro-Cuban cult practices, as believed by the author to be distinguishable from Ewe, Ibo, and Yoruba elements. [S. W. Mintz]

578. **Montero de Bascom, Berta.** Influencias africanas en la cultura cubana (Cien Soc, 5:27, junio 1954, p. 98-102).
An enumeration of certain derivative elements of Cuban culture, compared with parallel items as they occur among the Yoruba of Nigeria. [S. W. Mintz]

579. **Olmsted, David L.** Comparative notes on Yoruba and Lucumí (Language, 29:2, Apr.-June 1953, p. 157-164).
An attempt to test by linguistic comparison Bascom's assertion that Lucumi, a Cuban cult language, is derived from Yoruba. The conclusions support this hypothesis, but raise problems concerning the degree of diference between the two languages. [S. W. Mintz]

580. **Ortiz, Fernando.** Los instrumentos de la música afrocubana. V. 4. Los membranófonos abiertos (N a Z); Los bimembranófonos y otros tambores especiales. Habana, Ediciones Cárdenas, 1954. 452 p.
The fourth volume in Ortiz' five-volume study of Afro-Cuban music and instruments. This encyclopedic study is unquestionably the most ambitious project of its kind ever attempted. [S. W. Mintz]

581. **Törnberg, Gerda.** Musical instruments of the Afro-Cubans (Ethnos, 19: 1-4, 1954, p. 105-126).
A description of form and use of a number of Afro-Cuban instruments; the author bases herself largely on the work of Ortíz and others. [S. W. Mintz]

GUATEMALA

582. **Arrot, Charles R.** La cerámica moderna, hecha a mano, de Santa Apolonia (Antr Hist Guat, 5:1, enero 1953, p. 3-10, illus.).
Descripción de las técnicas utilizadas en la actualidad en este poblado de Guatemala. [A. Palerm]

583. **Hoyt, Elizabeth E.** El trabajador indígena en las fincas cafetaleras de Guatemala (Cien Soc, 6:35, oct. 1955, p. 258-268).
Datos reunidos durante una temporada de campo. Se refieren principalmente a las condiciones materiales de existencia. [A. Palerm]

584. **Kelley, David H.** Historia prehispánica del Totonacapán (R Mex Estud Antr, 13:2-3, 1952-1953, p. 303-210). [A. Palerm]

585. **Raynaud, Georges.** Rabinal-achí. El varón de Rabinal. Traducido al castellano por Luis Cardoza y Aragón. Guatemala, Ministerio de Educación Pública (Biblioteca de cultura popular, 43), 1953. 108 p.
Traducción al español de los textos quichés vertidos al francés por el profesor Raynaud. [A. Palerm]

586. **Schultze Jena, Leonhard.** La vida y las creencias de los indígenas quichés de Guatemala. Traducción de Antonio Goubaud Carrera y Herbert D. Sapper. Guatemala, Ministerio de Educación Pública (Biblioteca de cultura popular, 49), 1954. 133 p. [A. Palerm]

587. Skinner Klee, Jorge. Legislación indigenista de Guatemala. México, Instituto Indigenista Interamericano, 1954. 135 p. [A. Palerm]

588. Tax, Sol. Penny capitalism. A Guatemalan Indian economy. Washington, Smithsonian Institution, Institute of Social Anthropology (Publ., 16), 1953. 230 p., charts, maps, tables.
Descripción de la economía de un pueblo guatemalteco (Panajachel) dentro del marco local y usando técnicas antropológicas. [A. Palerm]

HAITI

589. Bourguignon, Erika E. Class structure and acculturation in Haiti (Ohio J Sci, 52:6, Nov. 1952, p. 317-320).
An application of Herskovits' concepts of retention, re-interpretation, and syncretism to differential transculturation along class lines in Haiti. Spanish translation published by Pan American Union with title: "Clases y transculturación en Haití" (Cien Soc, 6:32, abril 1955, p. 122-126). [S. W. Mintz]

590. ─────. Dreams and dream interpretation in Haiti (Am Anthr, 56:2, pt. 1, Apr. 1954, p. 262-268).
Several dreams of Haitian peasants are analyzed to demonstrate that the materials may be used not only as personal documents, but also in the study of "the validation of the culturally patterned world view." [S. W. Mintz]

591. Comhaire, Jean L. Religious trends in African and Afro-American urban societies (Anthr Q, n.s., 1:4, Oct. 1953, p. 95-108).
Information on social structure and religious affiliation in Port-au-Prince, in comparison with relevant data from African societies. [S. W. Mintz]

592. Denis, Lorimer. Origine des loas (Mém IFAN, 27, 1953, p. 195-199).
A myth, told to the author by a Haitian *vodun* cult leader, concerning the migration of the *loas, vodun* divinities, to Haiti from Africa. [S. W. Mintz]

593. Deren, Maya. Divine horsemen. The living gods of Haiti. London, N. Y., Thames and Hudson, 1953. 350 p., illus.
An extremely personal artistic interpretation of Haitian *vodun* by an observer having, in her own words, "no anthropological background (and anticipations) from other ethnic cultures, no systematized approach to an established methodology for collecting data, no plan of questions to ask, which might have created a self-consciousness and distorted the normal distribution of emphasis. . . . What emerges from this research is the fact that the African culture in Haiti was saved by the Indian culture which . . . . provided the Negroes with divinities sufficiently aggressive . . . . to be the moral force behind the revolution." Enchanting but not convincing. 23 pl., line drawings, appendices, notes, glossary, references. [S. W. Mintz]

594. Efron, Edith. French and Creole patois in Haiti (Carib Q, 3:4, Aug. 1954, p. 199-213).
A discussion of the sociological and cultural implications of French versus Creole in Haitian life. [S. W. Mintz]

595. Leiris, Michel. Note sur l'usage de chromolithographies catholiques par les vodouisants d'Haïti (Mém IFAN, 27, 1953, p. 201-207).
A brief study of religious syncretism as revealed in the use of saints' pictures in *vodun* ceremonial houses. The saints are identified with African gods according to specific similarities in dress, role, etc.; the variety of names and attributes of both saints and gods has aided the syncretic process by increasing the possibilities of identification and interpretation. [S. W. Mintz]

596. Loughlin, Elmer H. The truth about voodoo (Nat Hist, 63:4, Apr. 1954, p. 168-179).
A popularly written but sound description of Haitian *vodun*. Excellent photographs. [S. W. Mintz]

597. Mabille, Pierre. Pierres-tonnerre. Pierres à feux (Mém IFAN, 27, 1953, p. 209-211).
On the use of polished stones of indigenous origin by the Haitian rural people as cult objects associated with fire and thunder [S. W. Mintz]

598. Mars, Louis. Nouvelle contribution à l'étude de la crise de possession (Mém IFAN, 27, 1953, p. 213-233).
A psychological analysis of the phenomenon of possession associated with *vodun* ceremonies. [S. W. Mintz]

599. Mennesson-Rigaud, Odette. Vodou haïtien. Quelques notes sur ses réminiscences africaines (Mém IFAN, 27, 1953, p. 235-238).
A brief attempt to relate particular elements of modern *vodun* practice to the traditions of specific African peoples, representatives of whom were carried to Haiti as slaves. [S. W. Mintz]

600. Métraux, Alfred. Les croyances animistes dans le vodou haïtien (Mém IFAN, 27, 1953, p. 239-244).
Animistic elements in *vodun* beliefs and practices. [S. W. Mintz]

601. ─────. Croyances et pratiques magiques dans la Vallée de Marbial, Haïti (J Soc Am, n. s., 42, 1953, p. 135-198).
A very detailed and useful study. [S. W. Mintz]

602. ————. Médecine et voudou en Haïti (Acta Trop, 10:1, 1953, p. 28-68).
Haitian folk medicine assumes most illnesses are caused by malevolent spirits, or by ghosts sent by witch doctors. Therapy is based on *vodun* practices, and on practices derived from European medical theory of the 17th and 18th centuries. Acceptance of scientific medical knowledge increases as contact with the city increases, and is especially characteristic in the case of widespread diseases such as yaws and malaria. [S. W. Mintz]

603. ————. Vodou et protestantisme (R Hist Relig, 144:2, oct.-déc. 1953, p. 198-216).
The sociological relationship of Catholicism, Protestantism and *vodun* in Marbial Valley, Haiti. [S. W. Mintz]

604. **Oddon, Yvonne.** Une cérémonie funéraire haïtienne (Mém IFAN, 27, 1953, p. 245-248).
A brief description of a Haitian funerary ceremony (*retirer les morts de l'eau*). [S. W. Mintz]

605. **Price-Mars, Jean.** Les survivances africaines dans la communauté haïtienne (Mém IFAN, 27, 1953, p. 249-253).
A comment on the historical background of African survivals, religious and linguistic, in Haiti. [S. W. Mintz]

606. **Rigaud, Milo.** La tradition voudoo et le voudoo haïtien (son temple, ses mystères, sa magie). Paris, 1953. 432 p., 50 photos, figs.
A valuable but uneven study of *vodun* ritual. Some of the materials on origins and on sociological functions are sketchy; those on rituals and procedures are very detailed. There is hardly a single citation of other works on *vodun*, and there is no bibliography. The photographs and the data for several chapters were supplied by Odette Mennesson-Rigaud. There is a glossary. [S. W. Mintz]

607. **Simpson, George E.** Magical practices in northern Haiti (J Am Folk, 67: 266, Oct.-Dec. 1954, p. 395-403).
Magical beliefs and practices associated with *vodun* are described. [S. W. Mintz]

608. ————. Peasant children's games in northern Haiti (Folk-Lore, 65, Sept. 1954, p. 65-73).
A description of children's games from the Bassin section of the commune of Plaisance. The author believes these games, some of them sung in French rather than in Creole, have changed little since Colonial times. [S. W. Mintz]

609. **Sterlin, Philippe.** Vèvès vodou, série 1. Port-au-Prince, Dessins, 1953. 63 p.
A set of characteristic ritual symbol representations of African godheads (*vèvès*) portrayed in color drawings, with comments by the author on the characteristics of each god represented. [S. W. Mintz]

610. Tomorrow, quarterly review of psychical research. N. Y. V. 3, no. 1, autumn 1954, special Haiti issue. 161 p.
This periodical's special issue contains previously published materials from the works of M. J. Herskovits and Louis Mars. Other relevant articles on Haiti include "Religion and magic," by Maya Deren (p. 21-34); "Gods of Haiti," by Harold Courlander (p. 53-60); "Africa in the Americas," by Jean Price-Mars (p. 75-84); "Voodoo, Gnosis, Catholicism," by Louis Maximilien (p. 85-90); and "Instruments of rhythm," by Emerante de Pradines (p. 123-126). [S. W. Mintz]

JAMAICA

611. **Asprey, G. F., and Phyllis Thornton.** Medicinal plants of Jamaica (West In Med J, 2:4, Dec. 1953, p. 233-252; 3:1, Mar. 1954, p. 17-41; 4:2, June 1955, p. 69-82; 4:3, Sept. 1955, p. 145-168).
An invaluable listing of plants used for folk medicine in Jamaica. Upwards of 160 species are dealt with in detail. Common names are given, and the most-used common name indicated; common and botanical names are cross-referenced in appendices. A list of plants formerly and presently used for specific ailments is provided. No compound medicines are described, and informants are not named or located, however. This is the best article of its kind on Caribbean folk medicine known to the writer. [S. W. Mintz]

612. **Broom, Leonard.** The social differentiation of Jamaica (Am Sociol R, 19:2, Apr. 1954, p. 115-125).
This article outlines "the development and present character of the system of social differentiation in Jamaica with special reference to ethnicity and color." A presentation of the historical background is followed by a description of the present-day class and ethnic character of the island population. [S. W. Mintz]

613. **Cassidy, Frederic G.** Language and folklore (Carib Q, 3:1, [1953], p. 4-12).
The folk-etymology of modern Jamaican rural speech. [S. W. Mintz]

614. **Clarke, Edith.** Land tenure and the family in four communities in Jamaica (Soc Ec Stud, 1:4, Aug. 1953, p. 81-118).
An important article analyzing the relationship of land tenure to social organization, based on data collected in four rural Jamaican communities. [S. W. Mintz]

615. **Cohen, Yehudi A.** The social organization of a selected community in Jamaica (Soc Ec Stud, 2:4, Mar. 1954, p. 104-133).
A study of the economic and social organization of a Jamaican rural village, which asserts

that the inability of local villagers to cooperate economically "has kept them from strengthening the family and from forming true social groups outside the individual family group." [S. W. Mintz]

616. Cumper, George E. A modern Jamaican sugar estate (Soc Ec Stud, 3:2, Sept. 1954, p. 119-160).
Historical, sociological, and cultural data concerning one of Jamaica's largest sugar plantations. [S. W. Mintz]

617. Edwards, David T. An economic study of agriculture in the Yallahs Valley of Jamaica (Soc Ec Stud, 3:3-4, Dec. 1954, p. 316-341).
A painstaking study of the economics of peasant agriculture in a Jamaican rural area. Useful cultural data are to be found in the descriptions of local conditions of farming, marketing, etc. [S. W. Mintz]

618. Hall, Douglas G. The apprenticeship period in Jamaica, 1834-1838 (Carib Q, 3:3, Dec. 1953, p. 142-166).
A valuable historical paper giving background on the rise of the Jamaican peasantry after the Emancipation. [S. W. Mintz]

619. Kerr, Madeline. Some areas in transition (Phylon, 14:4, 4th quarter 1953, p. 410-412).
Brief comments on changing race relations in Jamaica. [S. W. Mintz]

620. Parry, J. H. Salt fish and ackee (Carib Q, 2:4, [1953], p. 29-35).
Historical data on the introduction of food crops into Jamaica. [S. W. Mintz]

621. Simpson, George E. Begging in Kingston and Montego Bay (Soc Ec Stud, 3:2, Sept. 1954, p. 197-211).
A sociological analysis of begging in Jamaica's two leading urban communities. [S. W. Mintz]

622. ————. Jamaican cult music. Introduction and notes. N. Y., Ethnic Folkways Library (Album, P461), 1954. 10 p.
A description of various types of cult music recorded in West Kingston, Jamaica, with some information on the historical and cultural background of the cults, musical forms, instruments, etc. [S. W. Mintz]

623. Smith, Michael G. Slavery and emancipation in two societies (Soc Ec Stud, 3:3-4, Dec. 1954, p. 239-290).
An attempt at controlled cultural-historical comparison of the slavery institution and the effects of emancipation in two societies: Zaria (northern Nigeria) and Jamaica. The writer concludes that a comparison of slavery in these societies without reference to other institutions is not fruitful, and is led to a comparison of societal types rather than of single institutions. [S. W. Mintz]

MEXICO

624. Aguirre Beltrán, Gonzalo. Teoría de los Centros Coordinadores (Cien Soc, 6:32, abril 1955, p. 66-77).
Se expone la teoría implícita en la creación y desarrollo de los Centros Coordinadores organizados en México por el Instituto Nacional Indigenista. [A. Palerm]

625. ————. Teoría y práctica de la educación indígena. México, Instituto Nacional Indigenista, 1954. 93 p.
El autor, Subdirector del Instituto Nacional Indigenista de México, revisa las experiencias obtenidas en el proceso de educación de los grupos indígenas. [A. Palerm]

626. Barlow, Robert H. Los tepaneca después de la caída de Azcapotzalco (Tlalocan, 3:3, 1952, p. 285-287).
Sobre la suerte de los tepaneca, después de la destrucción de su imperio por tenochcas y acolhuas. [A. Palerm]

627. Barrios, Miguel. Tepanecos y mexicanos: su desaparición en San Juan Tlilhuacan (Tlalocan, 3:3, 1952, p. 287-288). [A. Palerm]

628. Bernal, Ignacio (ed.). Relación de Tancítaro (Arimao y Tepalcapetec) (Tlalocan, 3:3, 1952, p. 205-235).
Relación geográfica del lugar, con notas por el editor. [A. Palerm]

629. Bonilla Domínguez, Celia. El proceso de cambio cultural en medicina. México, Instituto Nacional Indigenista, 1953. 62 p.
Resumen de experiencias de la autora en el estudio de una comunidad indígena de Chiapas, México. [A. Palerm]

630. Brambila, David, and José Vergara Bianchi. Gramática rarámuri. México, Buena Prensa, 1953. 644 p. [A. Palerm]

631. Cámara Barbachano, Fernando. El jarocho (Soc Méx, 1:13, abril 1953, p. 97-99).
Notas sobre la subcultura mexicana de la zona central de la costa del Golfo de México. [A. Palerm]

632. Carrasco, Pedro. Paganismo mixe (Tlatoani, 1:3-4, mayo-agosto 1952, p. 6).
Sobre las creencias religiosas actuales de los mixes de México. [A. Palerm]

633. ————, and Roberto Weitlaner. El sol y la luna (Tlalocan, 3:2, 1952, p. 168-174).
Versiones mixe y chinanteca de una leyenda. [A. Palerm]

634. Caso, Alfonso (and others). Métodos y resultados de la política indigenista en México. México, Instituto Nacional Indigenista (Memorias, 6), 1954. 303 p.

Contiene cuatro estudios: "Instituciones indígenas precortesianas," por Alfonso Caso; "Instituciones indígenas en la Colonia," por José Miranda y Silvio Zavala; "Instituciones indígenas en México independiente," por Moisés Gonzalo Navarro; "Instituciones indígenas en el México actual," por Gonzalo Aguirre Beltrán y Ricardo Pozas. Un examen completo de la política indigenista en México. [A. Palerm]

635. Castro, Carlo Antonio. Testimonio pame-meridional para la etimología de México (Tlatoani, 1:2, marzo-abril 1952, p. 33). [A. Palerm]

636. Christensen, Bodil. Los otomíes del estado de Puebla (R Mex Estud Antr, 13:2-3, 1952-1953, p. 259-268, illus.).

Notas etnográficas sobre un grupo otomí del noroeste de la sierra de Puebla. [A. Palerm]

637. Cline, Howard F. Una subdivisión tentativa de los chinantecos históricos (R Mex Estud Antr, 13:2-3, 1952-1953, p. 281-286).

Cuadro esquemático de las subdivisiones de los chinantecos. [A. Palerm]

638. Cook de Leonard, Carmen. Distribución de los pueblos sonorenses en el siglo XVIII, según Pfefferkorn (Tlatoani, 1:1, enero 1952, p. 19-20). [A. Palerm]

639. ————. Los popolocas de Puebla (R Mex Estud Antr, 13:2-3, 1952-1953, p. 423-445).

Un ensayo de identificación arqueológica de un grupo cultural. [A. Palerm]

640. Cowan, George M. El idioma silbado entre los mazatecos de Oaxaca y los tepehuas de Hidalgo, México (Tlatoani, 1:3-4, mayo-agosto 1952, p. 31-33). [A. Palerm]

641 ————. La importancia social y política de la faena mazateca (Am Indíg, 14:1, enero 1954, p. 67-92).

Estudio de campo sobre el trabajo comunal obligatorio en una comunidad indígena de la cuenca del Papaloapan, México. [A. Palerm]

642. Farias Galindo, José. Folklore mexicano. Miccailhuitl en Tianquistenco. México, Vargas Rea (Biblioteca de historiadores mexicanos), 1953. 38 p.

Only 75 copies were printed. A record in the form of a daily journal of observations at the traditional *fiesta del muerto*, October 31 and early November, in the state of Hidalgo. [R. D. Hussey]

643. Field, Henry. Notes on medicinal plants used in Tepoztlán, Morelos, México (Am Indíg, 13:4, oct. 1953, p. 291-300). [A. Palerm]

644. Fuente, Julio de la. El Centro Coordinador Tzeltal-Tzotzil (Am Indíg, 13:1, enero 1953, p. 55-64).

Breve informe sobre la organización y funcionamiento del primero de los nuevos Centros Coordinadores creados por el Instituto Nacional Indigenista de México. [A. Palerm]

645. Garibay, Ángel María. Versiones discutibles del texto nahuatl de Sahagún (Tlalocan, 3:2, 1952, p. 187-190). [A. Palerm]

646. Gessain, Robert. Les indiens tepehuas de Huehuetla (R Mex Estud Antr, 13:2-3, 1952-1953, p. 187-211).

Descripción etnográfica, basada en estudios de campo modernos. [A. Palerm]

647. Gibson, Charles. Rotation of alcaldes in the Indian cabildo of Mexico City (HAHR, 33:2, May 1953, p. 212-223).

Estudio de la trasmisión del sistema municipal castellano a México, y de su adaptación y combinación con la organización indígena. [A. Palerm]

648. Hayner, Norman S. Mexicans at play: a revolution (Sociol Soc Re, 38:2, Nov.-Dec. 1953, p. 80-83).

Breve análisis de los cambios producidos en México en el campo del recreo personal y diversiones. [A. Palerm]

649. Heizer, Robert F., and William C. Massey. Aboriginal navigation off the coasts of Upper and Baja California. Washington, Smithsonian Institution, Bureau of American Ethnology (Bulletin, 151; Anthropological papers, 39), 1953. p. 285-312. [A. Palerm]

650. Hewes, G. W. Mexicans in search of the "Mexican" (Am J Ec Sociol, 13:2, (Am J Ec Sociol, 13:2, Jan. 1954, p. 209-223).

Una revisión de la bibliografía de los estudios sobre lo "mexicano," con especial acento en los análisis antropológicos. [A. Palerm]

651. Humphrey, Norman D. The Mexican image of Americans (A Am Ac Pol Soc Sci, 295, Sept. 1954, p. 116-125).

Examen de las ideas de los mexicanos sobre los Estados Unidos; especial atención a la situación de clase o grupo social. [A. Palerm]

652. Infield, Henrik F., and Koka Freier. People in ejidos. A visit to cooperative farms of Mexico. N. Y., Frederick Praeger, 1954. 151 p.

Trabajo de carácter bastante superficial. Contiene, sin embargo, datos de interés. [A. Palerm]

653. Jiménez Moreno, Wigberto. Cronología de la historia de Veracruz (R Mex Estud Antr, 13:2-3, 1952-1953, p. 311-313).
Cuadro con correlaciones cronológicas entre diversas fuentes y calendarios. [A. Palerm]

654. Johnson, Irmgard Weitlaner. El quechquemitl y el huipil (R Mex Estud Antr, 13:2-3, 1952-1953, p. 241-257, illus.).
Estudio del estilo y distribución de estas dos prendas femeninas de vestir. [A. Palerm]

655. Kelly, Isabel. The modern Totonac (R Mex Estud Antr, 13:2-3, 1952-1953, p. 175-186).
Descripción etnográfica, basada principalmente en trabajos de campo en la región de Papantla y en la de Ahuacatlán. [A. Palerm]

656. Key, Harold, and Mary Ritchie de Key (comps.). Vocabulario mejicano de la Sierra de Zacapoaxtla, Puebla. México, Instituto Lingüístico de Verano, 1953. 232 p., illus. [A. Palerm]

657. Lewis, Oscar. La cultura campesina en la India y en México (Cien Soc, 6:34, agosto 1955, p. 194-218).
Análisis comparativo de dos pueblos rurales: Rani Khera, India, y Tepoztlán, México. El autor plantea el problema de cómo estos dos lugares pueden ser tan semejantes en términos de su economía, y tan diferentes en términos de su organización social. [A. Palerm]

658. ————. Tepoztlán restudied. A critique of the folk-urban conceptualization of social change (Rural Soc, 18:2, June 1953, p. 121-134).
El artículo va acompañado de una breve discusión por Ralph L. Beals. [A. Palerm]

659. Madsen, William. Hot and cold in the universe of San Francisco Tecospa, Valley of Mexico (J Am Folk, 68:268, Apr.-June 1955, p. 123-139).
Sobre las ideas de alimentos "fríos" y "calientes." [A. Palerm]

660. ————. Shamanism in Mexico (SW J Anthr, 11:1, spring 1955, p. 48-57).
Especialmente en relación con la curación de enfermedades. [A. Palerm]

661. Marroquín, Alejandro. Tlaxiaco, una ciudad mercado. México, Instituto Nacional Indigenista, 1954. 87 p.
Un importante estudio de Tlaxiaco, en la Mixteca de México. El autor se ocupa del ambiente físico, demografía, economía, propiedad, etc., pero centra su estudio en el mercado y en su papel como centro regional. [A. Palerm]

662. Maza, Antonio de la. La pamería a través de los tiempos (R Mex Estud Antr, 13:2-3, 1952-1953, p. 269-280).
Resumen muy sintética de una obra del autor sobre los pames. [A. Palerm]

663. McAfee, Byron (trans.). Danza de la Gran Conquista (Tlalocan, 3:3, 1952, p. 246-273).
Versión preparada por McAfee. [A. Palerm]

664. McIntosh, Juan B., and José Grimes. Vocabulario huichol-castellano y castellano-huichol. México, Instituto Lingüístico de Verano, 1954. 113 p. [A. Palerm]

665. Meade, Joaquín. Historia prehispánica de la Huasteca (R Mex Estud Antr, 13:2-3, 1952-1953, p. 291-302). [A. Palerm]

666. Melgarejo Vivanco, José Luis. Códices veracruzanos (R Mex Estud Antr, 13:2-3, 1952-1953, p. 333-335).
Relación de los códices veracruzanos conocidos, con indicación de su localización. [A. Palerm]

667. Mendieta y Núñez, Lucio (ed.). Estudios sociológicos. Memoria del III Congreso Nacional de Sociología. México, Universidad Nacional Autónoma de México, 1954. 426 p.
Los artículos siguientes son de interés desde el punto de vista de esta sección: "La delincuencia en los grupos indígenas de México," por R. de la Cerda, p. 221-230; "La delincuencia en el pueblo indígena de San Antonio de la Cal (Oaxaca)," por Pedro Yescas Peralta, p. 231-246; "Contribución al estudio de la realidad y factores operantes en la delincuencia indígena," por J. del Valle, p. 407-419. [A. Palerm]

668. Miller, Walter S. Algunos manuscritos y libros mixes del Museo Nacional (Tlalocan, 3:2, 1952, p. 179-183). [A. Palerm]

669. Monzón, Arturo. La estructura social de los seris (Soc Méx, 1:12, feb. 1953, p. 89-92).
Breve nota sobre la estructura y la organización social de este grupo indígena de la costa del Golfo de California, México. [A. Palerm]

670. Paddock, John. Inferencias psicológicas en el estudio de los mixes (Am Indíg, 14:4, oct. 1954, p. 303-314). [A. Palerm]

671. Palerm, Ángel. Etnografía antigua totonaca (R Mex Estud Antr, 13:2-3, 1952-1953, p. 163-173).
Resumen preparado a base de fuentes documentales. [A. Palerm]

672. Plancarte, Francisco M. El problema indígena tarahumara. México, Instituto Nacional Indigenista (Memorias, 5), 1954. 110 p. & illus.

El autor ha sido, desde su fundación, Director del Centro Coordinador de la Tarahumara. En este obra examina la etnografía y la historia de la región, los problemas más urgentes de su población y las soluciones que se han pensado. [A. Palerm]

673. Rey, Harold, and Mary Ritchie. Vocabulario mexicano (Sierra de Zacapoaxtla, Puebla). México, Instituto Lingüístico de Verano, 1953. 232 p. [A. Palerm]

674. Robe, Stanley L. *Coloquios de pastores* from Jalisco, Mexico. Berkeley, Calif., University of California Press, 1954. 158 p. [A. Palerm]

675. Sanders, William T. The anthropogeography of central Veracruz (R Mex Estud Antr, 13:2-3, 1952-1953, p. 27-78). Relaciones del hombre y la cultura con el medio ambiente. Interpretación ecológica de algunas características del desarrollo de las civilizaciones mesoamericanas. [A. Palerm]

676.———. Estudios sobre el patrón de asentamiento del poblado de Xochimilco (Tlatoani, 1:2, marzo-abril 1952, p. 32). [A. Palerm]

677.———. El mercado de Tlatelolco. Un estudio en economía urbana (Tlatoani, 1:1, enero 1952, p. 14-16). Notas sobre el gran mercado de Tlatelolco, México, en el momento del contacto con los españoles. [A. Palerm]

678. Seaford, Enrique. Un breve resumen de la economía chocha (R Mex Estud Antr, 13:2-3, 1952-1953, p. 235-240). [A. Palerm]

679. Shore, Aarón. Autoritarismo y agresión en una aldea mexicana. México, 1954. 63 p. Estudio psicosociológico basado, principalmente, en la aplicación de la prueba TAT a un grupo de niños de Zihuatanejo, México. [A. Palerm]

680. Sociedad Folklórica de México. Aportaciones a la investigación folklórica de México. México, Imp. Universitaria, 1953. 115 p. El volumen contiene una serie de trabajos interesantes: "Fray Bernardino de Sahagún: relación de los textos que no aprovechó en su obra; su método de investigación," por Ángel María Garibay; "La investigación folklórica en el campo: mis experiencias," por Virginia de Mendoza; "La sección de Investigaciones Musicales del Instituto Nacional de Bellas Artes y su labor folklórica," por Baltasar Samper; "La investigación folklórica-musical," por Virginia de Mendoza; "La investigación folklórica en bibliotecas y archivos," por Ernesto Mejía Sánchez; "Cincuenta años de investigaciones folklóricas en México," por Vicente Mendoza. [A. Palerm]

681. Spicer, Edward. Potam, a Yaqui village in Sonora (Am Anthr, 56:4, pt. 2), Aug. 1954. 220 p. Descripción de la estructura social, de los cambios culturales y de las relaciones de Potam con la cultura mayor y con otras comunidades yaquis. Un importante trabajo. [A. Palerm]

682. Starr, Betty W. Levels of communal relations (Am J Sociol, 60:2, Sept. 1954, p. 125-135). Análisis basado en el estudio de tres comunidades rurales de Veracruz, México. [A. Palerm]

683. Stavenhagen, Rolf. En la cuenca del Papaloapan: aspectos de antropología social aplicada (Tlatoani, 2. época, 7, oct.-dic. 1953, p. 30-35). Notas sobre uno de los experimentos sociales más importantes del México actual. [A. Palerm]

684. Stresser-Péan, Guy. Les indiens huasteques (R Mex Estud Antr, 13:2-3, 1952-1953, p. 213-234). Descripción etnográfica, incluyendo datos, bien discriminados, de las fuentes históricas y de los trabajos de campo del autor. [A. Palerm]

685. ———. Les nahuas du sud de la Huasteca et l'ancienne extension meridionale des huastèques (R Mex Estud Antr, 13:2-3, 1952-1953, p. 287-290). [A. Palerm]

686. Tudela de la Orden, José. Las clases sociales entre los tarascos (R Intl Soc, 10:38, abril-junio 1952, p. 439-457). [A. Palerm]

687. Velásquez Gallardo, Pablo (ed.). Título de tierras de Cherán Hatzicurin (Tlalocan, 3:3, 1952, p. 238-245). Original en tarasco y versión española preparada por el editor. [A. Palerm]

688. Viqueira, Carmen, and Ángel Palerm. Alcoholismo, brujería y homicidio en dos comunidades rurales de México (Am Indíg, 14:1, enero 1954, p. 7-36). Estudio de estos tres problemas, con métodos combinados psicológicos y etnológicos. [A. Palerm]

689. Wallis, Ethel Emilia. Problemas de aculturación implícitos en la educación indígena del otomí del Mezquital (Am Indíg, 13:4, oct. 1953, p. 243-258). [A. Palerm]

690. Williams García, Roberto. Etnografía prehispánica de la zona central de Veracruz (R Mex Estud Antr, 13:2-3, 1952-1953, p. 157-161). Esbozo muy sumario de elementos culturales, parcialmente construído a base de "supervivencias." [A. Palerm]

691. Weitlaner, Roberto J., and Carlo Antonio Castro. Papeles de la Chinantla. 1. Mayultianguis y Tlacoatzintepec. México, Museo Nacional de Antropología, 1954. 272 p. [A. Palerm]

692. Wolf, Eric. La formación de la nación. Un ensayo de formulación (Cien Soc, 4:20, abril 1953, p. 50-62; 4:21, junio 1953, p. 98-111; 4:22, agosto 1953, p. 146-171).
Análisis, desde un punto de vista antropológico, del proceso de formación de una nación; México, en este caso. Se mantiene que este proceso es de naturaleza semejante a aquellos llamados de transculturación por los antropólogos. El desarrollo teórico del problema va acompañado de un importante examen histórico de la formación de México como nación independiente. [A. Palerm]

693. Wonderly, William L. Sobre la propuesta filiación lingüística de la familia totonaca con las familias zoqueana y mayense (R Mex Estud Antr, 13:2-3, 1952-1953, p. 105-113).
El autor rebate la hipótesis de McQuown, que había relacionado provisionalmente al totonaco con las lenguas mayenses y zoques. [A. Palerm]

694. Yescas Peralta, Pedro. Teotitlán del Valle: muestra en el proceso de transculturación (R Mex Soc, año 16, 16:3, sept.-dic. 1954, p. 397-408).
Observaciones sobre el cambio cultural en un pueblo zapoteco de México. [A. Palerm]

PUERTO RICO

695. Alegría, Ricardo E. La fiesta de Santiago Apóstol en Loíza Aldea. Madrid, Artes Gráficas (Colección de estudios puertorriqueños), 1954. xxv, 76 p.
A study of the fiesta in honor of Santiago Apóstol in the Puerto Rican town of Loíza Aldea. It is suggested that Santiago may represent a syncretic assimilation of the Yoruba god Shangó to Catholic belief; hence the perpetuation of the ceremonies, in which "Santiago finds his most faithful devotees among the Negro population." [S. W. Mintz]

696. Malaret, Augusto. Puerto Rico indígena (Perú Indíg, 5:12, dic. 1953, p. 128-142).
Mainly a list of terms attributed to the indigenous population of Puerto Rico. [S. W. Mintz]

697. Manners, Robert A., and Julian H. Steward. The cultural study of contemporary societies: Puerto Rico (Am J Sociol, 59:2, Sept. 1953, p. 123-130).
A summary report on an anthropological study of four rural Puerto Rican communities representing different subcultural manifestations within Puerto Rican society. [S. W. Mintz]

698. Mintz, Sidney W. The culture history of a Puerto Rican sugar cane plantation, 1876-1949 (HAHR, 33:2, May 1953, p. 225-251).
El autor ha combinado el método antropológico de entrevistas con informantes con el análisis de documentos escritos, a fin de reconstruir la historia de una plantación. Analiza el cambio de las formas de vida, y muestra la relación entre las formas sociales y los sistemas agrícolas. [A. Palerm]

699. Steward, Julian H. Culture patterns of Puerto Rico (A Am Ac Pol Soc Sci, 285, Jan. 1953, p. 95-103).
This article deals "with the culture patterns or life-ways of certain classes or segments of the Puerto Rican people." [S. W. Mintz]

TRINIDAD

700. Braithwaite, Lloyd. The problem of cultural integration in Trinidad (Soc Ec Stud, 3:1, June 1954, p. 82-96).
An interesting discussion of the quest for foci of cultural integration in an economically and ethnically differentiated society. Carnival and the steel band "movement" are among the cultural phenomena described. [S. W. Mintz]

701. ————. Social stratification in Trinidad. A preliminary analysis (Soc Ec Stud, 2:2-3, Oct. 1953, p. 5-175).
A lengthy sociological analysis of contemporary Trinidadian social structure. [S. W. Mintz]

702. Carr, Andrew. A Rada community in Trinidad (Carib Q, 3:1, [1953], p. 35-54).
An important article describing the perpetuation of a Dahomean cult-group in Trinidad from about 1870 to the present day by members of the last group of African immigrants to reach Trinidad and by their descendants. Detailed lists of deities and ceremonies, and excellent photographs, are provided. [S. W. Mintz]

703. Matthews, Dom Basil. Crisis of the West Indian family. A sample study. Kingston, Jamaica, B.W.I., University College of the West Indies, Extra-Mural Department (Caribbean affairs publ.), 1954? 117 p.
A cultural-historical and sociological study by a Catholic priest of "non-legal" marriage in Trinidad. Father Matthews concludes: "On the basis of the available evidence, the African heritage has little to do with the origin, and still less with the continuance of the non-legal union, directly or indirectly, even in the case of the Negro." [S. W. Mintz]

704. Mayhew, Frank. My life (Carib Q, 3:1, [1953], p. 13-23).
A brief but valuable autobiographical document written by the pastor of a revivalistic cult group in Trinidad. [S. W. Mintz]

OTHER AREAS

705. Chamberlain, Robert S. The conquest and colonization of Honduras, 1502-1550. Washington, Carnegie Institution of Washington (Publ. 598), 1953. 264 p., map.
Importante y excelente trabajo, no limitado a los aspectos puramente históricos; abundante información antropológica. [A. Palerm]

706. Crowley, Daniel J. Form and style in a Bahamian folktale (Carib Q, 3:4, Aug. 1954, p. 218-234).
An analysis of two versions of a folktale of European provenience, now modified by African influence, with some data on the background and character of storytelling in the Bahamas. [S. W. Mintz]

707. Hartog, Johannes. Aruba. Zoals het was, zoals het werd. Van de tijd der indianen tot op heden. Aruba, Netherlands West Indies, De Wit, 1953. 480 p., illus.
A history of Aruba; contains data on aborigines and prehistory, p. 1-25. [S. W. Mintz]

708. Heath, C. R., and **W. G. Marx.** Diccionario mískito-español, español-mískito. Tegucigalpa, Imp. Calderón, 1953. 236 p. [A. Palerm]

709. Jesse, C. A note on Bequia, cradle of the Black Carib (Carib Q, 3:1, [1953], p. 55-56).
A report on presumptive evidence of rock working in Bequia in the Grenadines, which the author attributes to the original Carib inhabitants. [S. W. Mintz]

710. Jourdain, Elodie. Creole, a folk language (Carib Q, 3:1, [1953], p. 24-30).

Notes on Creole, particularly as spoken in Martinique, and its origins. [S. W. Mintz]

711. ————. Le verbe en créole martiniquais (West-Indische Gids, 35:1-2, Apr. 1954, p. 39-58).
The author seeks to establish that the verbs of Martinique Creole have their origins in four or five different French forms. [S. W. Mintz]

712. Lardé, Jorge. La población de El Salvador: su origen y distribución geográfica (A Mus Nac, 4:12, marzo 1953, p. 73-92).
Los datos se refieren, principalmente, a la población indígena y al período de contacto con los españoles; se usan fuentes históricas. [A. Palerm]

713. Lasserre, Guy. Les indiens de Guadeloupe (Cahiers d'Outre-Mer, 6:22, avril-juin 1953, p. 128-158).
A short cultural-historical and anthropological description of the East Indian population of Guadeloupe. [S. W. Mintz]

714. Pearse, Andrew C. While Carriacou makes music and dances, we study . . . (Carib Q, 3:1, [1953], p. 31-34).
Photographs and comments based on a brief visit to Carriacou in the Grenadines to collect data on the African-derived music and dances of that island. [S. W. Mintz]

715. Thomas, Léon. La Dominique et les derniers Caraïbes insulaires (Cahiers d'Outre Mer, 6:21, jan.-mars 1953, p. 37-60).
An introductory sketch of the human geography of the Caribs of Dominica. The article provides little new information. [S. W. Mintz]

716. Ycaza Tigerino, Julio. Las clases sociales en Nicaragua (Cién Soc, 6:31, feb. 1955, p. 2-11). [A. Palerm]

ETHNOLOGY: SOUTH AMERICA

D. B. STOUT

THE new policy of including items in *Handbook no. 19* for more than one year, which for this section meant entries mainly for 1953-1955, has provided a new perspective concerning the development of ethnology in South America. In reviewing the output for a three-year period it became clearer than ever before that Brazil, Colombia, and Venezuela are the leading South American nations in the development of an eclectic, scientifically based ethnology. This is evident not only in the number of significant works published each year, but in their consistent high quality and in the fact that many are based on field researches in which modern methods were employed.

The celebration in 1954 of the Fourth Centennial of São Paulo, Brazil, was the occasion of the 31st International Congress of Americanists, Aug. 23-28, 1954. At the same time there was created an International Congress of Folklore, and the first meeting held. The anthropologists of Brazil have now become numerous enough to warrant and support annual meetings, two of which have been held in 1953 and 1954, respectively. The III Congreso Indigenista Interamericano was held in La Paz, Bolivia, Aug. 2-13, 1954.

For further information on congresses, meetings, research activities, and the like, in the various South American nations, see the BBAA, 15-16:1, 1952-1953, i.e. 1954, and 17:1, 1954, i.e. 1955. The reader's attention is also invited to the *International directory of anthropological institutions,* Wenner-Gren Foundation for Anthropological Research, N. Y., 1953, for an accurate listing of South American anthropological institutes, research centers, universities with anthropological curricula, etc.

Several new journals made their appearance during the period 1953-1955: in Brazil, the *Revista de antropologia,* v. 1, no. 1, junho 1953, Faculdade de Filosofia, Ciências e Letras, Universidade de São Paulo; in Venezuela, the *Boletín indigenista venezolano,* año 1, t. 1, no. 1, enero-marzo 1953, Comisión Indigenista, Ministerio de Justicia, Caracas; in Peru, *Folklore americano,* v. 1, no. 1, nov. 1953, Lima, Comité Interamericano de Folklore, Comisión de Historia, Instituto Panamericano de Geografía e Historia; and in Colombia the *Revista colombiana de antropología,* época 2, v. 1, no. 1, junio 1953, Instituto Colombiano de Antropología, Ministerio de Educación Nacional, Bogotá, which replaces the *Revista del Instituto Etnológico Nacional* and the *Boletín de arqueología.* It should also be noted that the *Revista de folklore* (reported in *HLAS, no. 18, 1952,* p. 26) has been changed in title to *Revista colombiana de folklore,* beginning with no. 2, junio 1953. In addition, *Primitive man,* published at The Catholic University of America, Washington, has been retitled *Anthropological quarterly,* v. 1, no. 1, Jan. 1953, and the *Revue anthropologique,* Institut International d'Anthropologie, Paris, has been revived with a new series, commencing with no. 1, juin 1955. Both of these journals may be expected to contain articles on South America from time to time.

GENERAL

750. Ayrosa, Plínio. Apontamentos para a bibliografia da língua Tupi-Guarani. 2. ed. São Paulo, Universidade de São Paulo, Faculdade de Filosofia, Ciências e Letras (Boletim, 169; Etnografia e Tupi-Guarani, 28), 1954. 261 p.
Amplification, with inclusion of the sources overlooked in the first edition of 1943 (see *HLAS, no. 9, 1943,* item 477).

751. Baldus, Herbert. Bibliografia crítica da etnologia brasileira. São Paulo, Comissão do IV Centenário da Cidade de São Paulo, Serviço de Comemorações Culturais, 1954. 859 p., 11 pl.
A monumental and most valuable volume, containing 1785 entries covering the period 1500 to 1953, with geographic, tribal, subject, and author indexes. The annotations and comments on each entry range from brief notes to critical reviews and are most helpful. A number of entries are included for tribes that live in other nations bordering on Brazil.

752. Bennett, Wendell C. New World culture history: South America (*in* Kroeber, A. L. (and others). Anthropology today: an encyclopedic inventory. Chicago, Ill., University of Chicago Press, 1953, p. 211-225).
"A summary and analysis of the anthropological approaches to the broad subject of culture history as exemplified by studies done on South American materials," and as such a very authoritative and stimulating statement.

753. Carluci, María Angélica. La *couvade* en Sudamérica (Runa, 6, 1953-1954, p. 142-174, maps).
Thorough compilation of sources describing this custom and its distribution. There are 124 societies in South America possessing this custom—the heaviest concentration in the world.

754. Friede, Juan. Los Andakí, 1538-1947. Historia de la aculturación de una tribu selvática. México, Fondo de Cultura Económica, 1953. 304 p., maps.
An ethnohistorical study of the Andaki, once residents of the eastern slope of the Andes, who have since moved into the upper Magdalena River valley. An excellent study based on a full use of the chronicles and other written sources.

755. Ibarra Grasso, Dick Edgar. La escritura indígena andina. La Paz, Biblioteca Paceña, 1953. 318 p., illus.

A complete reappraisal of ideographic writing used by Andean Indians. Suggests possible pre-Columbian origin. [C. Evans and B. J. Meggers]

756. Núñez del Prado, Óscar. Aspects of Andean native life (Kroeber Anthr Soc Pap, 12, spring 1955, p. 1-21).
Translated and abridged from the original "Problemas antropológicos del área andina, Perú—Bolivia—Ecuador" (R U, Cuzco, 42:104, 1. semestre 1953, p. 272-320). Excellent, concise observations on various aspects of contemporary Andean Indian culture and its relation to the nation.

757. Rowe, John H. Map of the Indian tribes of South America, 1:8,000,000. Berkeley, Calif., Berkeley Blue Print Co., 1951. Map.
Revised as of January 1951. Printed in blueprint form and as a black outline; the latter is designed to serve as an overlay on the National Geographic Society map of South America, 1950.

758. Rubio Orbe, Gonzalo. Aculturaciones de indígenas de los Andes (Am Indíg, 13:3, julio 1953, p. 187-222).
Results of a survey done in 1952-1953 of the degree and mode of acculturation among Indians of Bolivia, Peru, and Ecuador.

759. Rübbo Müller, Antonio. Um estudo da organização social de tribos indígenas da América do Sul (Sociologia, 15:1, março 1953, p. 44-83; 2, maio, p. 166-177; 3, agôsto, p. 277-285; 4, out. 1953, p. 394-453).
See *HLAS, no. 18, 1952,* item 327, for previous three sections of this monograph.

760. Schaden, Egon. Aspectos fundamentais da cultura Guarani. São Paulo, Universidade de São Paulo, Faculdade de Filosofia, Ciências e Letras (Boletim, 188; Antropologia, 4), 1954. 216 p.
Excellent analysis of Guarani culture with respect to its major themes, focal aspects, and distinctive patterns, and their relation to the processes of acculturation as undergone by the various Guarani tribes in Brazil and Paraguay. Based on the author's extensive field work with Guarani groups during the past decade.

761. Simmons, Ozzie G. Popular and modern medicine in mestizo communities of coastal Peru and Chile (J Am Folk, 68:267, Jan.-Mar. 1955, p. 57-71).

762. Zerries, Otto. The bull-roarer among South American Indians (R Mus Paulista, n. s., 7, 1953, p. 275-309, map).
A most welcome compilation of the occurrences and uses of the bull-roarer among some 40 tribes and areas of South America. (The bull-roarer is a thin piece of wood with string attached at one end which is whirled about over the head of the user.) The present article

is an amplification of part of the author's previous monograph *Das Schwirrholz* (Strecker und Schröder, Stuttgart, 1942) wherein he discussed the bull-roarer throughout the world.

763. ————. Wild- und Buschgeister in Südamerika: eine Untersuchung jägerzeitlichen Phänomene im Kulturbild südamerikanischer Indianer. Weisbaden, Germany, Franz Steiner Verlag, 1954. 401 p., illus., 4 pl., map.
An exhaustive compendium of materials bearing on South American Indian beliefs in animal souls, animal and bush spirits, etc. The author interprets the data according to the *Kulturkreise* doctrine of culture history.

BRAZIL

764. Baldus, Herbert. Karajá-Mythen (*in* Jahrbuch des Linden-Museums, Stuttgart, 1952 und 1953. Stuttgart, Germany. Museum für Länder- und Völkerkunde, 1953, p. 210-218).

765. ————. Os Oti (R Mus Paulista, n. s., 8, 1954, p. 79-92).
A gathering of the slender information on the Oti tribe, sometimes also called the Shavante of São Paulo.

766. Becher, Hans. Cintos e cordões de cintura dos índios sul-americanos, nâoandinos (R Mus Paulista, n. s., 9, 1955, p. 7-179, 12 pl.).
An exhaustive study of the various forms and functions of belts of all kinds made and worn by the Indians of non-Andean South America. Based on an intensive use of primary and secondary sources. English and German summaries are provided.

767. Biocca, E. Pesquisas sôbre o método de preparação do curare pelos índios (R Mus Paulista, n. s., 8, 1954, p. 165-226, 16 pl.).
Comprehensive and authoritative study of the preparation and use of curare, with detailed observation of preparation among the Makú Indians.

768. Cadogan, León. Ayvu Sapyta (R Antr, 1:1, junho 1953, p. 35-41; 1:2, dez. 1953, p. 123-132; 2:1, junho 1954, p. 37-46).
Texts, translations, and commentary of Mbaya myths.

769. Caspar, Frank. Some sex beliefs and practices of the Tupari Indians, western Brazil (R Mus Paulista, n. s., 7, 1953, p. 203-248, 4 pl.).

770. Christiano de Sousa, Cicero. O método de Rorschach aplicado a um grupo de índios Kaingang (R Mus Paulista, n. s., 7, 1953, p. 311-341, tables).

Additional discussion and analysis of Rorschach tests of 32 Kaingang Indians originally done by Herbert Baldus (see item 778, and *HLAS, no. 13, 1947,* item 314).

771. Fernandes, Eurico. Algumas notas sôbre os Waiano e os Apalaí do Rio Jarí. Belém, Brazil, Instituto de Antropologia e Etnologia do Pará, 1952. xiii, 12 p., illus.

772. Frikel, G. P. Kamáni (R Mus Paulista, n. s., 7, 1953, p. 257-274).
Full description of preparing an arrow poison (kamani) used by the Kachuyana Indians.

773. Galvão, Eduardo. Cultura e sistema de parentesco das tribos do Alto Rio Xingu. 1 (B Mus Nac, Rio, n. s., Antropologia, 14, 1953, 56 p., 25 pl.).
First of a series of bulletins concerning the Indian tribes of the Upper Xingu River area. This one reports extensive data on the social organization and kinship systems of six Carib-speaking, four Arawakan-speaking, and two Tupi-speaking tribes, and the linguistically isolated Trumai. The appendix gives the kinship terms in both Portuguese and English. Galvão regards these tribes as possessing enough cultural similarities, despite their linguistic diversity, to warrant their classification in a single culture area which he has named the Uluri area.

774. Hohenthal, W. Notes on the Shucurú Indians of Serra Ararobá, Pernambuco, Brazil (R Mus Paulista, n. s., 8, 1954, p. 93-166).
Comprehensive and valuable account, based on field work done in 1951-1952, of a tribe that has undergone considerable acculturation.

775. Koch-Grünberg, Theodor. Mitos e lendas dos índios Taulipáng e Arekuná (R Mus Paulista, n. s., 7, 1953, p. 9-202). Translated from the German original edition, *Vom Roraima zum Orinoco,* v. 2, Stuttgart, 1924.

776. Lessa, Luís Carlos. Chimarrão (R Arq Mun, 19:155, jan.-março 1953, p. 361-460).
The story of *yerba mate:* its history, the equipment employed in and the etiquette of its use, and superstitions and folklore pertaining to it in south Brazil.

777. Lima, Pedro E. de. Deformações tegumentares e mutilação dentária entre os índios Tenetehára. 1 (B Mus Nac, Rio, n. s., Antropologia, 16, out. 1954, 22 p., illus.).
Description of body painting, tattooing, and dental mutilation. The last is practiced on the incisors and is ascribed to Negro influences in slavery times.

778. Miranda de Menezes, Cinira. O psico-diagnóstico miocinético aplicado a índios Kaingang (R Mus Paulista, n. s., 7, 1953, p. 343-356).
Further analysis of 32 Rorschach protocols taken from as many Kaingang Indians (see item 770, and *HLAS, no. 13, 1947,* item 314).

779. Murphy, Robert F., and Buell Quain. The Trumaí Indians of central Brazil. N. Y., American Ethnological Society (Monographs, 24). xii, 108 p., pl., map.
A valuable and comprehensive study, based on careful editing by Murphy of Buell Quain's field notes from his 1938 expedition to the Upper Xingu River. The Trumai are now nearly extinct as a society.

780. Nimuendajú, Curt. Apontamentos sôbre os Guarani (R Mus Paulista, n. s., 8, 1954, p. 9-57, map, fig., chart).
Annotated translation by Egon Schaden of a manuscript by the late Nimuendajú which contains additional information on the Apacocuva Guarani not included in Nimuendajú's original article, based on the same manuscript, which appeared as "Die Sagen von der Eschaffung und Vernichtung der Welt als Grundlagen der Religion der Apapocuva-Guarani" (Zeit Ethn, 46, 1914, p. 284-403).

781. ————. Os Tapajó (R Antr, 1:1, junho 1953, p. 53-61).
Brief historical study of the Tapajo, published posthumously.

782. Oberg, Kalervo. Indian tribes of northern Mato Grosso, Brazil. With appendix: Anthropometry of the Umotina, Nambicuara, and Iranxe, with comparative data from other northern Mato Grosso tribes, by Marshall T. Newman. Washington, Smithsonian Institution, Institute of Social Anthropology (Publ., 15), 1953. 144 p., illus., maps.
Excellent ethnographic account, based on field work in 1947-1949, with emphasis on the Camayura, and lesser attention given to the Bacairi, Nambicuara, and Umotina. See also item 890.

783. Röder, Josef, and Hermann Trimborn. Maximilian Prinz zu Wied: Unveröffentlichte Bilder und Handschriften zur Völkerkunde Brasiliens. Bonn, Germany, F. Dümmlers Verlag, 1954. 150 p., 16 figs., 42 pl.
Valuable manuscript and pictorial materials, recently discovered in the Wied family archives, which were written and drawn by Prince Maximilian during and after his travels in Brazil in 1815-1817. The most important new data in this work are those pertaining to the Botocudo tribe.

784. Rondon, Cândido Mariano da Silva. Índios do Brasil das cabeceiras do Rio Xingu, dos Rios Araguáia e Oiapóque. V. 2. Rio, Conselho Nacional de Proteção

aos Índios (Publ., 98), 1953. 363 p., illus.
Second of a projected 15-volume album. Like the first, this volume contains a great many (974) excellent photographs. See *HLAS, no. 13, 1947,* item 367, for review of first volume.

785. Sampaio, Mário Arnaud. Dicionário guaraní-português (R Mus Castilhos, 1:2, junho 1952, p. 39-50; 2-3, jan. 1953, p. 365-390; 3:4, 1954, p. 369-385).
First three parts, "A" through "M." To be continued.

786. Schaden, Egon. O estudo do índio brasileiro—ontem e hoje (Panorama, 2:6, 1953, p. 48-65).
Compressed, but useful, history of ethnology in Brazil.

787. Schultz, Harald. Vinte e três índios resistem à civilização. Prefácio de Herbert Baldus. São Paulo, Edições Melhoramentos, 1953. 79 p., illus.
Brief, popular account of Umutina Indians on the upper Paraguay River, based on field work done in 1943-1945. Excellent photographic illustrations.

788. Shell, Olive. Grammatical outline of Kraho, Ge family (Intl J Am Ling, 18:3, July 1952, p. 115-129).
Based on original field notes by the late Buell Quain.

789. Souza, Lincoln de. Os Xavantes e a civilização. Ensaio histórico. Rio, Serviço Gráfico do Instituto Brasileiro de Geografia e Estatística, 1953. 58 p.
An outline of the history of the Shavante tribe's contact with European-derived culture since 1774.

790. Spalding, Walter. Tradições e superstições do Brazil sul. Rio, Organização Simões (Col. Rex, 3), 1955. 223 p.
An interesting study wherein especial attention is given to folklore elements from Madeira and the Azores.

791. Wagley, Charles. Amazon town. A study of man in the tropics. N. Y., Macmillan, 1953. 305 p., illus.
Fully rounded description of a small community on the lower Amazon river system, based on intermittent visits between 1942 and 1948; of great value in understanding the relationship of humans and their institutions to the tropical habitat.

792. Watson, James B. Way station of Westernization: the Brazilian caboclo (*in* Watson, James B.; Theresa Sherrer Davidson; and Carl W. Thomas. Brazil. Papers presented in the Institute for Brazilian Studies, Vanderbilt University. Nashville, Tenn., Vanderbilt University Press, 1953, p. 9-58).

An excellent and perceptive description and analysis of *caboclo* culture and its relation to the other cultural manifestations of Brazil.

793. Watson, Virginia. An ethnographic account of contemporary Cayuá Indian architecture (R Mus Paulista, n. s., 9, 1955, p. 235-245, 8 pl.).
Thorough analysis of house forms and techniques of construction, and the influence of metal tools on them.

794. Weyer, Edward, Jr. Jungle quest. N. Y., Harper, 1955. 198 p., 24 pl., maps.
A popular account of travels in the Upper Xingu River area and on the Rio das Mortes, with generally accurate and sympathetic comments on the Camayura and Shavante Indians.

795. Willems, Emílio. Brasil: período indígena. México, Instituto Panamericano de Geografía e Historia (Publ., 169; Comisión de Historia, 67), 1953. 110 p.
Authoritative and comprehensive, though compressed, account of the Indian cultures of Brazil. Excellent bibliography (58 pages).

COLOMBIA

796. José Agustín de Barranquilla, Padre. Así es la Guajira. Itinerario de un misionero capuchino. 2. ed. Bogotá, Imp. Nacional, 1953. 237 p., illus.
Incomplete ethnographic account based on missionary experiences. The first edition appeared in 1946 (Empresa Litográfica, Barranquilla).

797. Ortiz, Sergio Elías. Estudios sobre lingüística aborigen de Colombia. Bogotá, Ministerio de Educación Nacional (Biblioteca de autores colombianos, 75), 1954. 503 p.
Systematic review of Indian language classifications in Colombia, with tables of *toponimias,* etc.

798. ————. Los indios yurumangui (B Ac Hist Valle Cauca, 4. época, 20:94, feb. 1953, p. 3-16).
Introduction to a study of the ethnography and language of the Yurumangui Indians, now disappearing as a distinct entity.

799. Otero, Jesús M. Etnología caucana. Popayán, Colombia, Editorial Universidad del Cauca, 1952. 322 p., maps, pl., tables.
Synthesis of the major sources on the Paez, Cholo, Guanaca, Kokonuko, and Guambiano.

800. Reichel-Dolmatoff, Gerardo. Algunos aspectos de la medicina popular en una población mestiza de Colombia (Folk Am, 3:3, nov. 1955, p. 3-17).
Excellent account of folk-medicine beliefs and practices, pertaining to Santa Marta, Colombia. The author concludes that most of them have their source in European culture.

801. ————. Colombia: período indígena. México, Instituto Panamericano de Geografía e Historia (Publ., 151; Comisión de Historia, 49), 1953. 62 p.

Authoritative but highly compressed account of the Indian cultures of Colombia. Extensive bibliography.

802. ————. Contactos y cambios culturales en la Sierra Nevada de Santa Marta (R Colomb Antr, 2. época, junio 1953, p. 15-122, maps, illus.).

An excellent synthesis and interpretation of this author's previous very substantial results of his historical, archaeological, and ethnological researches.

THE GUIANAS

803. Darbois, Dominique. Indiens d'Amazonie. Préface de Bertrand Flornoy. Texte de Francis Mazière. Paris, Duca (Coll. Mondes et visages), 1953. Unpaged, illus.

90 excellent photographs, six in color, of Indian life in the border country between French Guiana and Brazil.

804. Dark, Philip J. C. Bush Negro art; an African art in the Americas. London, Tiranti, 1954. 66 p., 52 pl.

A pioneer, and generally successful, endeavor to describe the characteristics and cultural setting of the arts of the Bush Negroes of Dutch Guiana.

805. Hawkins, W. Neill, and Robert E. Hawkins. Verb inflections in Waiwai (Carib) (Intl J Am Ling, 19:3, July 1953, p. 201-211).

806. Hickerson, Nancy P. Ethnolinguistic notes from lexicons of Lokono (Arawak) (Intl J Am Ling, 19:3, July 1953, p. 181-190).

PARAGUAY

807. Dabbs, Jack Autrey. A Messiah among the Chiriguanos (SW J Anthr, 9:1, spring 1953, p. 45-58).

An unusually detailed, original account, taken from recently examined archives, of a Messiah or self-appointed culture hero among the Chiriguano of Paraguay in 1778 which sheds additional light on the Tupi-Guarani Messiah pattern.

808. Lowes, R. H. G. Alphabetical list of Lengua Indian words with English equivalents (J Soc Am, n.s., 43, 1954, p. 85-109).

809. Service, Elman R. Spanish-Guarani relations in early colonial Paraguay. Ann Arbor, Mich., University of Michigan, Museum of Anthropology (Anthropological papers, 9), 1954. 106 p.

An ethnohistorical study covering the period 1537 to 1620 which establishes much of the background for understanding the present-day character of Paraguayan society and culture.

810. Service, Elman R., and Helen S. Service. Tobatí, Paraguayan town. Chicago, Ill., University of Chicago Press, 1954. 337 p., illus.

An excellent community study of a town some 35 miles from Asuncion, carefully selected for its representativeness of rural Paraguayan culture. The authors make a convincing case for the general interpretation that there is less of a Guarani Indian cultural component in present-day Paraguayan life than has been assumed and alleged hitherto. Based on nearly a year of field work.

PERU

811. Alencastre G., Andrés, and Georges Dumézil. Fêtes et usages des indiens de Langui (J Soc Am, n. s., 42, 1953, p. 1-118).

Notes on the language, eight texts, and extensive commentary on them, from the province of Canas, department of Cuzco.

812. Bird, Junius. Paracas fabrics and Nazca needlework, 3rd century B. C.—3rd century A. D. Washington, Textile Museum (Catalog raisonné), 1954. 126 p., 127 pl., end maps.

A tour-de-force of analysis and description. The author provides excellent ethnological commentary and interpretation for these archaeological materials. The photographs and drawings illustrating technical details are extraordinarily clear.

813. Dirks, Sylvester. Campa (Arawak) phonemes (Intl J Am Ling, 19:4, Oct. 1953, p. 302-304).

814. Fast, Peter W. Amuesha (Arawak) phonemes (Intl J Am Ling, 19:3, July 1953, p. 191-194).

815. Matteson, Esther. The Piro of the Urubamba (Kroeber Anth Soc Pap, 10, spring 1954, p. 25-99, map, pl.).

816. Raspail, Jean. Terres et peuples incas. Paris, René Julliard (Coll. La Croix-du-Sud), 1954. 262 p.

Good popular account of the Inca state and its fall, with descriptions of present-day natives.

817. Reichlen, Henry. Fêtes, danses et rites des indiens de Cajamarca, Pérou (J Soc Am, n. s., 42, 1953, p. 391-413, 5 pl.).

818. **Reyburn, William D.** Quechua I: phonemics (Intl J Am Ling, 20:3, July 1954, p. 210-214).

819. **Rivet, Paul,** and **Georges de Cré-qui-Montfort.** Bibliographie des langues aymará et kičua. V. 3. 1916-1940. Paris, Université de Paris, Institut d'Ethnologie (Travaux et mémoires, 51), 1953. 782 p.
Continuation of this monumental and definitive bibliography. For v. 1 see *HLAS, no 17, 1951,* item 332; for v. 2 see *HLAS, no. 18, 1952,* item 360.

820. **Rivet, Paul,** and **Robert de Wavrin.** Les Nonuya et les Okáina (J Soc Am, n. s., 42, 1953, p. 333-390, map).
Extensive linguistic evidence that these two small tribes speak a dialect of Witoto.

VENEZUELA

821. **Acosta Saignes, Miguel.** El área cultural prehispánica de los Andes venezolanos (Arch Ven Folk, 1:1, enero-junio 1952, p. 45-72, map).
Refinement of the author's previous delineations of indigenous culture areas in Venezuela, with particular attention to the Andean, or Timoto-Cuica, area. Based on thorough use of historical, archaeological, and ethnological sources.

822. ————. Estudios de etnología antigua de Venezuela. Prólogo de Fernando Ortiz. Caracas, Universidad Central de Venezuela, Facultad de Humanidades y Educación, 1954. 302 p.
Thorough review of the major indigenous cultures at the time of the Conquest and analysis of acculturation since then. Based on original chronicles and sources and on extensive use of recent interpretive writings, all of which are carefully assessed. Two maps and an excellent index.

823. **Dupouy, Walter.** El indio en el mapa de Venezuela (Tierra Firme, 2:15, mayo 1953, p. 18-20, maps).
Contains useful distribution map of present tribal locations.

824. ————. Noticias preliminares sobre la comunidad indígena de San Joaquín de Parire, estado Anzoátegui (B Indig Ven, 1:1, enero-marzo 1953, p. 91-125, map, illus.).
Demographic data and brief information on the society and culture of acculturated Carib Indians.

825. **Le Besnerais, Henry.** Contribution à l'étude des indiens yaruro (J Soc Am, n. s., 43, 1954, p. 110-123).
Mainly demographic data, including the different distributions in the rainy and dry seasons.

826. **Riley, Carroll L.** Notes on the Panare Indians of Venezuela (Kroeber Anthr Soc Pap, 10, spring 1954, p. 10-24, map).

827. **Sociedad de Ciencias Naturales La Salle.** La región de Perijá y sus habitantes. Caracas, Universidad del Zulia, 1953. 556 p., illus.
Chapters 3-6 are devoted to ethnographic notes on the Chake Indians of western Venezuela.

OTHER AREAS

828. **Buitron, Aníbal** (and others). La Paz: un pueblo mestizo de la provincia del Carchi. Quito, Instituto Ecuatoriano de Antropología y Geografía, 1952. 125 p., illus.
Excellent and comprehensive description of a mestizo community.

829. **Canals Frau, Salvador.** División y unidad en las poblaciones prehispánicas del Noroeste argentino (A Inst Étn Nac, 4:2, 1951, p. 67-88).
The author, on the basis of archaeological, historical, and linguistic evidence, distinguishes six major groups (or tribes), whose locations are shown on a map.

830. **Firestone, Homer L.** Chama phonology (Intl J Am Ling, 21:1, Jan. 1955, p. 52-55).

831. **Flornoy, Bertrand.** Jivaro. Among the headshrinkers of the Amazon. Foreword by Brian Fawcett. N. Y., Elek, 1953, 224 p., illus.
A sympathetic travel account wherein genuine insight is revealed concerning the life of the Jivaro. Excellent plates.

832. **Koissler Ilg, Bertha.** Cuentan los araucanos. B. A., Espasa-Calpe (Col. Austral, 1208), 1954. 153 p.
35 freely rendered folk tales.

833. **Mostny, Grete; Fidel Jeldes; Raúl González;** and **F. Oberhauser.** Peine, un pueblo atacameño. Santiago, Universidad de Chile, Instituto de Geografía (Publ., 4), 1954. 170 p., illus.
A comprehensive ethnographic account, based on field work done in 1948 and 1949, which provides valuable ethnographic data on a little-known area.

834. **Needham, Rodney.** Siriono and Penan: a test of some hypotheses (SW J Anthr, 10:2, summer 1954, p. 228-232).
An intriguing comparison of the Siriono, and

Holmberg's analysis of that society, with the Penan of Borneo, to the end that Holmberg's hypotheses, concerning the food quest and its influence on social and psychological factors when done under difficulties, are not all borne out.

835. **Rosemberg, Tobías.** El alma de la montaña. Folklore del Aconquija. Edición anotada. B. A., Raigal, 1953. 129 p.
Comprehensive compilation, fully annotated and presented in an eminently readable style.

PHYSICAL ANTHROPOLOGY

T. D. STEWART

The bibliographical items assembled below show an unusually heavy concentration in the Circum-Caribbean area, particularly Mexico and Venezuela. A high percentage of these items for the area at large are by U. S. writers, which is not surprising in view of geographical proximity. On the other hand, a large proportion of the items for Venezuela are the work of the late Eduardo Fleury Cuello (1904-1954). Dr. Fleury was educated in Europe, obtaining his doctorate in medicine and anthropology at the University of Berlin. He was returning from another trip to Germany when he died on shipboard on Oct. 29, 1954. Although Dr. Fleury spent most of his time in medical practice in Caracas, the writer recalls his active and wise participation in the scientific sessions of the II Inter-American Indian Conference in Cuzco in 1949. A man of such accomplishments and influence will be greatly missed. In this connection it should be mentioned that Dr. Fleury was instrumental in persuading Martin Gusinde to study the "pygmies" of the Sierra de Perija, Venezuela, in 1954 (item 923).

From Mexico come reports of further discoveries bearing on the antiquity of man in the New World. On Dec. 31, 1952, George C. O'Neill of Columbia University found fossilized human remains and crude stone implements at the pueblo of Santa Maria Aztahuacan some 26 kilometers southeast of Mexico City. Thereafter A. Romano and others from the Dirección de Prehistoria excavated two skulls and a few associated bones (A Inst Nac Antr Hist, 7:36, 1955, p. 65-74). Although an antiquity approaching that of "Tepexpan Man" is suggested, the problem of geological dating at this new site is very difficult.

More recently (1955) the first publication of the Dirección de Prehistoria (Mexico) describes the uncovering of a second fossil mammoth at Santa Isabel Iztapan (item 856). This time, besides an array of stone artifacts, there is good evidence that the trapped animal was butchered by man.

A different but very important contribution is being made in Central America by a group of workers headed by Nevin S. Scrimshaw. Although much of the work is clinical in nature, evidence is emerging of the close relationship of food and physique. From the time children are weaned until they reach school age their nutritional status is precarious and as a result their physical development often suffers. These findings may help explain the low statures in Middle America.

South America was the scene of two international gatherings during 1954. From August 2 to 12 the III Inter-American Indian Conference met in La Paz, Bolivia. Although little attention was given to physical anthropology, the writer, a member of the American delegation, contributed a paper on "Studies on the physical differentiation of immigrants and especially Mexican Indians migrating to the U. S. A.," and M. T. Newman of the U. S. National Museum sent a paper on "The significance of racial and environmental factors in public health studies of South American Indians."

From August 22 to 28 the XXXI International Congress of Americanists met in São Paulo, Brazil. The program included the following papers in physical anthropology: Castro Faria, Luiz de, "O estado atual da antropologia-física no Brasil";

HANDBOOK OF LATIN AMERICAN STUDIES

Imbelloni, J., "Los constructores de Sambaquí (sector Paraná y Santa Catarina Norte)"; Loureiro Fernandes, J., "Contribuição à antropometria e à hematologia dos Kaingang do Paraná"; Pourchet, Maria Julia, "Contribuição ao estudo antropofísico de descendentes de imigrantes portugueses"; Stewart, T. D., and H. V. Walter, "Fluorine analysis of putatively ancient human and animal bones from the Confins Cave, Minas Gerais, Brazil."

Of more local significance was the VI Mesa Redonda of the Sociedad Mexicana de Antropología which met in Mexico City, Sept. 4-11, 1954. Although eight papers were originally scheduled for the section on physical anthropology under the chairmanship of Eusebio Dávalos Hurtado, only four seem to have been given (cf. BBAA, 15-16:1, 1952-1953, i.e. 1954, p. 199, and 17:1, 1954, i.e. 1955, p. 147). Judging from the titles of the papers, the subject matter covered was largely medical anthropology.

During the early months of 1952 and 1953 the Institute of Demogenetic Research of the University of Cordoba, Argentina, worked in the vicinity of Lake Titicaca under the direction of Alfredo Sacchetti (B Indig, 12:4, dic. 1952, p. 288-295; 13:4, dic. 1953, p. 326-335). Some of the serological results already have been reported (item 892).

In April 1953, Walter F. Harper, Professor of Anatomy, University College of the West Indies, Jamaica, studied deformed Indian skulls from the Antilles in the collections of the U. S. National Museum.

Finally, attention is called to the fact that Juan Comas, a frequent contributor to the literature of this section, resigned as Secretary of the Inter-American Indian Institute on Aug. 1, 1955, and was named to the post of career researcher in the National University of Mexico.

GENERAL

850. Comas, Juan. Las fantasías prehistóricas y antropológicas de Leo Pucher. México, 1955. 21 p.
Author cites modern authors to disprove statements contained in article entitled "El homo ivoensis" (U San Fran Xavier, 14:33-34, enero-dic. 1946, p. 351-387).

851. Cook, Robert C. Latin America: area of population explosion (Popul B, 9:6, Oct. 1953, p. 65-75).
Broad summary of demographic trends and their significance for human biology.

852. Genovés, Santiago. The problem of the sex of certain fossil hominids, with special reference to the Neandertal skeletons from Spy (J Royal Anthr Inst, 84: 1-2, Jan.-Dec. 1954, p. 131-144).
Represents research accomplished on a British Council scholarship in the United Kingdom and during a visit to Brussels. Reviews the diversity of opinions regarding the sex of seven Neandertal specimens. Shows clearly that the interpretations of fossil man are influenced by the subjective identification of sex.

853. Stewart, T. D. Amériques (in Vallois, Henri V., and Hallam L. Movius, Jr., eds. Catalogue des hommes fossiles. XIXᵉ Congrès Géologique International, Alger,

1952, Comptes rendus, fasc. 5, p. 293-299).
Includes data on nine finds of reasonably certain antiquity from South and Central America. Data consist of discoverer, location of site, list of remains and indication of age, repository, and bibliography.

854. Von Verschuer, Otmar Frhr. Resultados da genética para a antropologia (R Antr, 1:1, junho 1953, p. 5-17).
Commemorating the 50th anniversary of the rediscovery of Mendel's theory, reviews recent developments in the field. 78 references.

855. Wormington, Hannah M. Origins, indigenous period. México, Instituto Panamericano de Geografía e Historia (Publ. 153; Comisión de Historia, 51; Program of the history of America, I, 1), 1953. 118 p.
Theme 5 deals with "Some human remains of presumed antiquity." Theme 6D deals with "Theories based on physical anthropological and serological evidence." Pertinent references.

MIDDLE AMERICA AND THE ANTILLES

856. Aveleyra Arroyo de Anda, Luis. El segunda mamut fósil de Santa Isabel Iztapán, México, y artefactos asociados.

México, Instituto Nacional de Antropología e Historia, Dirección de Prehistoria, 1955. 59 p., illus.
Describes, largely by means of photographs, the uncovering of a mammoth skeleton. Shows that the animal became mired and then was butchered by prehistoric man. Important evidence of the contemporaneity of man and elephant in the New World. Appendix on stratigraphy by Manuel Maldonado-Koerdell.

857. Blom, Frans. Ossuaries, Cremation and secondary burials among the Maya of Chiapas, Mexico (J Soc Am, n. s., 43, 1954, i.e. 1955, p. 123-135).
Figures 10-12 give a fair idea of the types of deformity present. There is no indication whether any cranial material was saved.

859. Faulhaber de Sáenz, J. Los huastecos y mexicanos en relación con otras poblaciones de la faja costeña del Golfo de México (R Mex Estud Antr, 13:2-3, 1952-1953, p. 79-93).
Reports measurements on 103 male and 60 female Huastecos from the *ranchería* of Silosuchitl near Tantoyuca, and 93 male and 100 female Mexicanos from Chiconamel. Comparisons are with Starr's earlier measurements.

860. Field, Henry. Los indios de Tepoztlán (México). Coral Gables, Fla., University of Miami Press, 1954. 87 p.
Analysis of observations and measurements obtained in 1947 on 3 series of males: 164 adults from Tepoztlan, 11 juveniles (11-17 years) from Tepoztlan, and 36 adults from Gabriel Mariaca, a nearby town. Comparative data for all Mexico, assembled with the aid of Johanna Faulhaber, are presented on p. 52-83.

861. Gates, R. Ruggles. Studies in race crossing. VI. The Indian remnants in eastern Cuba (Genetica, 27:1-2, 1954, p. 65-96).
Reviews racial history of island. Records observations on hair, skin, eye, ear, and nose for 47 "Indians" from Caridad de los Indios and Vara. Portraits but no pedigrees.

862. Hurtarte E., Augusto, and Nevin S. Scrimshaw. Dental findings in a nutritional study of school children in five Guatemalan highland villages (J Dent Re, 34:3, June 1955, p. 390-396).
442 school children from 6 to 14 years of age were examined in five villages near Antigua, Guatemala, in the department of Sacatepequez. Dental findings are correlated with blood serum analyses. Compared with U. S. standards, these children showed retardation of over one year in eruption of permanent teeth, over one year in bone age, and over two years in height and weight.

863. Keeler, Clyde E. The Caribe Cuna moon-child and its heredity (J Her, 44:5, Sept.-Oct. 1953, p. 163-171).
Summary of observations made in 1950-1953.

Covers morphology, physiology, psychosomatic behavior, and heredity. Good photographs, a map of the Caribe-Cuna towns, and pedigrees of the moon-child condition are included.

864. Lasker, Gabriel Ward. The age factor in bodily measurements of adult male and female Mexicans (Hum Biol, 25:1, Feb. 1953, p. 50-63).
Purpose "is to indicate to what extent comparisons of measurements on groups of unrelated adults are affected by differences in the ages of the individuals." Uses 268 "sedentes" measured by the author in Paracho in 1948, and 608 adults measured in various parts of Mexico by Goldstein prior to 1943.

865. ————. Ethnic identification in an Indian mestizo community. II. Racial characteristics (Phylon, 14:2, 2nd quarter 1953, p. 187-190).
In the Tarascan town of Paracho "practically the whole range of physical types occurs both in individuals whose parents are described as Indians and in those whose parents are considered to be Mestizos or Spanish." This evidence confirms Kaplan's finding (part 1) that ethnic identification is considered a cultural and linguistic rather than biological matter.

866. ————. Human evolution in contemporary communities (SW J Anthr, 10:4, winter 1954, p. 353-365).
Computes the effective breeding population and random genetic drift for six Middle American communities. Comparisons include Panajachel, Guatemala, and Camayura, Brazil.

867. ————. Photoelectric measurement of skin color in a Mexican mestizo population (Am J Phys Anthr, n.s., 12:1, Mar. 1954, p. 115-122).
Reflectance values were recorded for the forehead and inner arm of 243 Tarascan Indian children. The instrument used is the "Photoelectric Reflection Meter, model 610," manufactured by the Photovolt Corp., N. Y.

868. ————. The question of physical selection of Mexican migrants to the U. S. A. (Hum Biol, 26:1, Feb. 1954, p. 52-58).
Of 297 adult males measured by author in 1948, 61 were later selected for contract labor in the U. S. Comparisons of the measurements of the two series show that selection was not based on physique.

869. Lothrop, S. K. Suicide, sacrifice and mutilations in burials at Venado Beach, Panama (Am Antiq, 19:3, Jan. 1954, p. 226-234).
In the light of historic documents analyzes a total of 369 burials, of which 19% are listed as different types of mutilations. 14 illustrations.

870. Martínez del Río, Pablo. A preliminary report on the mortuary cave of Candelaria, Coahuila, Mexico (B Tex Archaeol Soc, 24, 1953, p. 208-256).

The findings of Dr. Faulhaber on the skeletal material are briefly reported on p. 215-221. Plate 23 shows three skulls with syphilitic lesions.

871. Murrill, Rupert Ivan. Racial blood pressure studies. A critique of methodology, with special reference to the effect of age, nutrition, climate and race on blood pressure in Puerto Rico (Pro Am Phil Soc, 99:4, Aug. 1955, p. 277-324).
Part 1 gives data on 2500 individuals of each sex, selected in 1948 on a census basis, and analyzed by sex, age, weight, nutrition, and environment. Part 2 reviews racial blood pressure studies on a world basis, with special emphasis on methods used. There are 21 references for the Latin American area.

872. Romero, Javier. Ensayo sobre geometría craneana. México, Instituto Nacional de Antropología e Historia, 1955. 44 p.
The author, in collaboration with five students, applies the scheme of Klaatsch, as expanded by Imbelloni, to a series of 100 male skulls. Three of the students contribute sections and all participated in various ways. This constituted a practical system of teaching. The results are given in detail.

873. Schreider, Eugène. Recherches anthropologiques sur les Otomis de la région d'Ixmiquilpan (Mexique) (Anthropologie, 57:5-6, mars 1954, p. 453-489; 59:3-4, nov. 1955, p. 251-296).
First part deals with general characteristics of population. Two male series were studied in 1936, one raised in the native environment and the other in a boarding school ("collégiens"). The largest number of measurements reported is 112. Few comparisons. Second part deals with problems and biological hypotheses. Included are environmental, nutritional, and physiological data.

874. Scrimshaw, Nevin S.; Moisés Behar; Carlos Pérez; and Fernando Viteri. Nutritional problems of children in Central America and Panama (Pediatrics, 16:3, Sept. 1955, p. 378-397).
Important review article because of emphasis on relationship between nutrition and physique. 52 references.

875. Terra, Helmut de. A strange Pleistocene fossil locality in Mexico (Science, 118:3077, Dec. 18, 1953, p. 748-749).
The nature of this site (five miles west of Tlalnepantla) suggests that early man may have catapulted boulders from a higher slope on top of animals bogged on a lake shore. No man-made artifacts were found.

875a. Veracruz (state). Antropología física de Veracruz, por Johanna Faulhaber. México, Editorial Cultura, 1950-1956. 2 v. liv, 239 p., and 31 tables comprising second volume.

The racial elements of the state are represented by 15 groups of 200 individuals (100 of each sex). Measurements and observations thereon were obtained in 1951-1953, as follows: Juan José Araiza, 6 groups; Johanna Faulhaber, 5 groups; Santiago Genovés, 3 groups; Felipe Montemayor, 1 group. The data are presented with the usual statistical constants. In addition Pearson's CRL (coeficiente de divergencia tipológica) has been computed for all possible combinations. Maps show the distribution of traits, and photographs show the racial types (a male and a female from each group). In a separate section the descendants of French and Italian immigrants are studied in the same way. Introduction is by Jorge A. Vivó, prologue by Eusebio Dávalos Hurtado, and ethnographic map by José Luis Melgarejo Vivanco.

ARGENTINA

876. Bórmida, Marcelo. Los antiguos patagones. Estudio de craneología (Runa, 6, 1953-1954, p. 5-96 and 8 pl.).
Reviews earlier studies relating to subject, describes sources of material studied, analyzes deformity types present in series, and then presents a metrical analysis. In a short conclusion reconstructs the peopling of Patagonia from the cranial evidence. The sample (350 skulls) is the largest yet studied, but still is unidentified archaeologically.

877. Emperaire, J., and A. Laming. La grotte du Mylodon, Patagonie occidentale (J Soc Am, n.s., 43, 1954, i.e. 1955, p. 173-205).
Reviews the history of this remarkable site which first became known in 1895 with the discovery of a fresh-looking skin attributed to a Mylodon. The C-14 dating from dung is 10,832 ± 400 years. The authors report a visit to the site in 1953. 54 references.

878. Imbelloni, José. Otra vez sobre Pascua (Runa, 5, 1952, p. 204-210).
Additional notes relating to item 375, *HLAS, no. 18, 1952.*

879. Males, Branimiro. Algunas observaciones sobre la representación espacial del maxilar superior (R Inst Antr, 5-6, 1949-1951, i.e. 1954, p. 21-43).
Using a method attributed to Sergio Sergi, the author has measured the distances between four landmarks (metanasion, prosthion, catazigion, and alvion) and calculated the angles associated therewith. Over 125 skulls were studied, mostly modern Romans, Melanesians, Fuegian Indians, and Indians from northwest Argentina. Results are reported in detail.

880. ———. La biodinámica y la biogénesis racial en el estudio de la población (R Inst Antr, 5-6, 1949-1951, i.e. 1954, p. 7-20).
Defines biogenesis as the study of the morphological and functional formation of a particular racial type, and biodynamics as the science which gives an understanding of the

biogenetic facts. From this point of view the author examines race mixture in general terms and states a number of "laws" relating to the populations resulting from mixture of racial types.

881. **Males, Branimiro, and Elva S. Molina.** Ubicación espacial de la nariz y la boca (R Inst Antr, 5-6, 1949-1951, i.e. 1954, p. 77-81).
Further elaboration, without actual application, of a method presented earlier. See *HLAS, no. 14, 1948,* items 591 and 592.

882. **Paulotti, O., and A. S. Giménez.** Coloración de la piel y del iris en los indígenas chaquenses (Runa, 5, 1952, p. 44-71).
Interesting experiment in which the second author, an artist, matched the color tones of the skin (five areas) and iris in water colors. In this way a color scale was made for each human group studied (altogether 721, from the following tribes: Toba, Pilaga, Mataco, Chulupi, Chorote, Tapiete and Maka). An attempt is made to equate the results with earlier observations.

883. **Paulotti, O., and T. Martínez de Paulotti.** Tipos craneanos del noroeste argentino (R Inst Antr, 5-6, 1950-1951, i.e. 1954, p. 45-76 and 14 fold. charts).
Gives 42 measurements, 25 indices, and numerous observations for each of 122 skulls of Argentine Indians from three collections (two in Santiago del Estero and a third in Tucuman). Without further explanation the skulls are classified and the observations thus resummarized according to the authors' scheme of stocks, racial types, morphological types and varieties, which uses mainly South Pacific names ("Tasmánida," "Melanésida," "Píguida," "Austrálido," and "Indonésido").

884. **Tofini, Paolo.** La scapola dei Fuegini (R Antr, Roma, 41, 1954, p. 3-78 and 16 p. of tables, 10 pl.).
On the basis of a new orientation, presents 128 measurements and indices on six male and seven female paired scapulae from the Museum of Anthropology, University of Rome. Comparisons are made with seven male and four female pairs from modern Romans.

885. **Vignati, Milcíades Alejo.** Nuevos trofeos en cráneos humanos del territorio argentino. I. Taza-trofeo de la región cuyana. II. Trofeos con ablasión del hueso malar. III. Cráneos-trofeo del Noroeste (Notas Mus Eva Perón, Antr, 16:64-66, dic. 29, 1953, i.e. 1955, p. 321-355 and 25 pl.).
The first specimen is the vault of a skull shaped like a bowl. It was found in a pottery vessel. The second group (10 skulls) simply have part of the malar bone broken away. The illustrations give no support to the idea that such damage was intentional. The third group (20 skulls) is consistent in showing a small hole at the vertex and a large hole in the base. Outline drawings of four of these skulls, in several planes, are included.

BOLIVIA AND BRAZIL

886. **Landogna Cassone, Francesco.** Contributo alla conoscenza antropologica delle popolazioni indigene del Brasile (Arch Antr Etn, 82, 1952, i.e. 1953, p. 5-32 and 7 pl.).
Describes in detail four hitherto unrecorded "Botocudo" skulls in the Anthropological Museum of the University of Florence (no. 3925, 3982, 4399, 4400). Two are from Parana and two from Santa Catarina. One of the latter (no. 4400) shows deformity resulting probably from healed osteoporosis. Considers these skulls in relation to the paleo-Indians. 34 references.

887. ————. Radio-stratigrafia; prime applicazioni in craniologia antropologica (Arch Antr Etn, 82, 1952, i.e. 1953, p. 83-90 and 12 pl.).
Uses the same four Brazilian skulls as in item above. Gives particular attention to the form and dimensions of the sella turcica. Ignores the interesting pathology in no. 4400.

888. **Lestrange, Monique de.** Dermatoglyphes digitaux et palmaires de 33 Indiens Caingangues, Parana, Brésil (B Mém Soc Anthr, 10. série, 5:3-6, 1954, i.e. 1955, p. 310-311).
Brief analysis without comparisons except for statement relative to findings in series reported in item below.

889. ————. Dermatoglyphes digitaux et palmaires de 47 Indiens du Brésil (B Mém Soc Anthr, 10. série, 5:1-2, 1954, p. 85-86).
Few details of the digital and palmar ridges and flexion creases in a series of 27 male and 20 female Indians from Ivai, municipality of Pitanga, state of Parana.

890. **Newman, Marshall T.** Anthropometry of the Umotina, Nambicuara, and Iranxe, with comparative data from other northern Mato Grosso tribes (*in* Indian tribes of Northern Mato Grosso, Brazil, by Kalervo Oberg. Washington, Smithsonian Institution, Institute of Social Anthropology (Publ., 15), 1953, p. 128-135).
In 1949 Kaoro Onaga, under the supervision of K. Oberg, measured 22 Umotina (14 males, 8 females), 13 Eastern Nambicuara (7 males, 6 females) of the Waklitisu band, and 5 Iranxe males. The mean measurements are here compared with data reported by Ranke, Ehenreich, and Roquette-Pinto.

891. **Otero, Gustavo Adolfo.** Figura y carácter del indio (los ando-bolivianos). 2. ed. La Paz, Juventud, 1954. 205 p. & illus.

Part 2 deals with "La morfología del indio." Although such things as stature and weight are discussed, the sources of the data are not indicated. No changes have been made in this part of the text since the first edition of 1935.

892. Sacchetti, Alfredo. Studi ematologici nella zona del Lago Titicaca, Bolivia (R Antr, Roma, 40, 1953, p. 189-231).

Based on 100 subjects studied in 1953 during the second expedition of the Institute of Demogenetical Research of the University of Cordoba. Reports ABO results (82% group O, 13% A, 4% B, and 1% AB) and Rh results (98% positive). Develops the thesis that there are three racial systems of Rh distributions: Oceanic-Mongolic-American, White, and Negro-Negroid.

CHILE, COLOMBIA, ECUADOR

893. Arcila Vélez, Graciliano. Aporte a la antropometría de los indios katío (Juntas de Nutibara) y los caramanta de Jardín (departamento de Antioquia, Colombia) (B Inst Antr, 1:2, sept. 1954, p. 119-169).

Took 22 measurements and a few observations on 35 Catio (26 males, 9 females) and 15 Caramanta (11 males, 4 females). Measurements and indices are reported individually. Derives body types in outline drawings.

894. ————. Grupos sanguíneos de los indios katíos de Antioquia (B Inst Antr, 1:1, nov. 1953, p. 65-79).

Gives A-B-O frequencies for 129 Catio Indians from the *municipios* of Dabeiba, Frontino, Cañasgordas, and Alto Sinu in the department of Antioquia. Combined with the "Caramanta" (*HLAS, no. 12, 1946,* item 516) they yield 92% group O, 4% A, and 4% B.

895. Esquerra Gómez, Alfonso. La adolescencia como una etapa de la vida humana (R Ac Colomb Cien Exact Fis Nat, 9:33-34, mayo 1953, p. 44-75).

A study of body build said to be based on 500 adolescents: 300 students from the Escuela Militar de Ramírez in Bogota, and 200 children between the ages of 11 and 21 years from an orphanage at Cajica, near Bogota. Although the two groups represent contrasting social levels, the author does not give the sources of any of the 67 individuals shown nude in photographs. Also, some of the graphs deal with a series of 183 adolescents between the ages of 12 and 18 years from the Reformatory of Fagua (1950). Much of the text is concerned with statistical concepts and definitions of stages of human life. The main technique used is that of Viola. This is related somewhat to the ideas of Pende, Sheldon, and Wetzel.

896. Holm, Olaf. Verruga peruana en un ceramio patográfico ecuatoriano (Cuad Hist Arqueol, año 4, 4:12, dic. 1954, p. 207-223).

Discusses the possibility that a ceramic human figure from the province of Manabi portrays an endemic skin disease known as Carrion's disease. Good illustrations.

897. Sandoval, Luis, and Carlos Henckel. The ABO, MNS, and Rh-Hr blood groups of the Mapuche Indians of Cautin Province, Chile (Hum Biol, 26:4, Dec. 1954, p. 324-329).

Based on 258 specimens which yield estimate of 25% white admixture (79.45% group O, 13.56% A, 6.97% B; 47.22% M, 8.33% N, 44.44% MN; all Rh positive).

898. Santiana, Antonio. La abrasión dentaria en los aborígenes sudamericanos (G Méd, Guayaquil, 9:3, mayo-junio 1954, 28 p.).

Reports 3 grades of dental wear (slight, moderate, marked) in percentages for 1182 living Indians from Ecuador, for a few Fuegian Indians, and for 9 skulls and 6 mandibles from Ecuador.

899. ————. Antropología morfológica de los órganos internos en las razas del Ecuador (G Méd, Guayaquil, 8:4, julio-agosto 1953, p. 366-396).

Extensive data on the weight of the liver, spleen, and thymus; lobation of the thymus and lungs; and division of the sciatic nerve and the relationship of the parts to the piriformis muscle. In addition to sex and age, race is considered (mestizos vs. Indians). Comparisons are made with European data.

900. ————. Los indios del Ecuador y sus características serológicas. Resultados del examen en la totalidad de los mismos (B Inf Cient Nac, 6:55, junio-julio 1953, p. 52-74).

Author summarizes his studies of the A-B-O blood groups in 9326 Indians, divided as follows: Andean sector, 7707; Amazonian sector, 1036; western sector, 159. As would be expected, the Amazonian Indians have the highest percentage of blood group O (98.2%). English version on p. 64-74. Spanish version reprinted with illustrations of racial types in *Zeitschrift für Ethnologie,* 78:2, 1953, p. 262-271.

PERU

901. Espejo Núñez, Julio. Bibliografía básica de arqueología andina. II. Trepanación en el antiguo Perú (B Bibl, Lima, año 26, 23:1-4, dic. 1953, p. 87-95).

List of 154 items supplemented by an index of authors.

902. Espejo Núñez, Teófilo. *La antigüedad de la sífilis en el Perú,* de Julio C. Tello (Am Indíg, 14:1, enero 1954, p. 37-51).

Tello presented this thesis in 1908 to the Facultad de Medicina, Universidad Mayor de

San Marcos. The present review gives some background, quotes extensively, and generally comments in an approving fashion. The subject is not brought up to date.

903. Gómez Calderón, María. Investigación sobre el tipo morfológico del mestizo limeño (R Cien, año 55:485-486, 3.-4. trimestre 1953, p. 203-218).
Applies the method of Viola and the classification of Barbara to 250 males and 250 females between the ages of 18 and 21 years. The subjects were examined at 4 *colegios nacionales.*

904. Graña, Francisco; Esteban D. Rocca; and Luis Graña R. Las trepanaciones craneanas en el Perú en la época pre-hispánica. Lima, 1954. 340 p.
Based on 250 trephined skulls assembled in the museums of Lima and Cuzco. Analysis is largely from medical viewpoint, with details conveyed mainly by means of 251 illustrations. Describes an operation on a living subject using prehistoric instruments.

905. Hamperl, H., and P. Weiss. Über die spongiöse Hyperostose an Schädeln aus Alt-Peru (Virchows Archiv, 327:6, Dec. 1955, p. 629-642).
Describes the pathological changes in three skulls which anthropologists have been calling symmetrical osteoporosis. Prefers the term "hyperostosis spongiosa cranii (Müller)." Was unable to tell from the skulls whether the condition was due to a hemolytic anemia or to rickets. Good illustrations.

906. Hartweg, Raoul, and Bertrand Flornoy. Notes anthropologiques sur les Indiens Iawa, Amazonie péruvienne (J Soc Am, n. s., 43, 1954, i.e. 1955, p. 151-154).
Brief general description based on about 10 males. Photographs of one individual in front and side views. The tribe is located in the Peruvian province of Loreto in the region where Peru, Brazil, and Colombia come together.

907. Monge M., Carlos. Biological basis of human behavior (*in* Anthropology today. Prepared under the chairmanship of A. L. Kroeber. Chicago, Ill., University of Chicago Press, 1953, p. 127-144).
Another summary of the Peruvian studies on man in high altitudes considered from the standpoint of broad anthropological theory. 121 references. Further comment is supplied by author (p. 169-170) in the sequel to this book, *An appraisal of anthropology today* (Sol Tax and others, eds., Chicago, Ill., University of Chicago Press, 1953, 395 p.).

908. ————. Características de los seres aclimatados en el altiplano; revista de conjunto sobre la función respiratoria del andino (Perú Indíg, 4:3, abril 1953, p. 4-21).

Summary of physiological data as presented in 1948 in lectures at the University of San Agustín in Arequipa and at the University of San Francisco Javier in La Paz, Bolivia.

909. ————. Man, climate and changes of altitude (Meteor Mono, 2:8, Oct. 1954, p. 50-60).
Another summary of man's physiological adaptation to high altitude.

910. Monge M., Carlos; Jean Vellard; Carlos Monge Cassinelli; and Alberto Cagorla. Aclimatación en los Andes. Antropología fisiológica comparada del hombre del Altiplano. Forma y función del tórax (Perú Indíg, 5:13, dic. 1954, p. 9-21).
Restates the findings from several recent papers

911. Perú. Departamento de Nutrición. La familia peruana; suma y resta de su nutrición. Lima, 1954. 151 p. & illus. (Biblioteca de la revista *Salud y bienestar social,* 1).
Reports results of nutritional studies made in five localities between 1951 and 1953: Hacienda San Nicolas and Caleta de Carquin (department of Lima), Chancan (department of Cuzco), Vicos (department of Ancash) and Yurimaguas (department of Loreto). The relation to physique is mentioned only occasionally (as for instance, the comparison of size of adolescents in Vicos and Huancayo, p. 95).

912. Valle, M. M. Observaciones sobre geografía; geografía ecológica del hombre. 3. ed. Lima, Lumen, 1953. 371 p. and 26 pl.
First part, p. 37-91, gives an up-to-date account of "La influencia del clima sobre los rasgos físicos del hombre."

913. Weiss H., Pedro. Casos peruanos prehistóricos de cauterizaciones craneanas. T sincipital de Manouvrier (R Mus Nac Antr Arqueol, 2:2, 1. semestre 1955, p. 3-23 and 8 pl.).
Presents 24 skulls with scarring at the vertex or around trephine openings and argues that these cases are like the ones reported earlier from France by Manouvrier. The majority are females and subadults.

914. ————. Las trepanaciones peruanas estudiadas como técnica y en sus relaciones con la cultura (R Mus Nac, 22, 1953, p. 17-34).
Contrasts the methods of trephining and associated culture traits in the central and southern regions of Peru. Shows that the Incas in the South had developed a more refined technique.

URUGUAY, VENEZUELA

915. Díaz Ungría, Adelaida G. de. El

tetraedo facial y su aplicación al grupo étnico motilón (Mem Soc Cien Nat La Salle, 13:34, enero-abril 1953, p. 57-77).
Applies a geometrical method of analyzing the face, developed by Hoyos Sáinz, to the 14 skulls from the region of Perija described separately by Fleury Cuello (item 917).

916. Emmer, F. Guajiros. Aplicación del tetraedro facial a los guajiros (B Indig Ven, año 1, 1:2, abril-junio 1953, p. 205-252, and 1 fold. table).
Applies the geometrical scheme of Hoyos Sáinz to 12 skulls of Guajiros described separately by Fleury Cuello (item 918). Comparisons are made with skulls from Spain and with those of Motilones studied by A. G. de Díaz Ungría.

917. Fleury Cuello, Eduardo. Estudio antropométrico de la colección de cráneos motilones (Mem Soc Cien Nat La Salle, 13:34, enero-abril 1953, p. 9-56).
Detailed description of 19 skulls (8 males, 7 females, 4 subadults) collected in 1947 in the region of Perija, west of Lake Maracaibo. Comparison with specimens reported by Marcano in the 1890's shows majority of the Perija Motilones to be higher headed. Individual measurements are listed, along with photographs of 8 and stereographic drawings of all 19.

918. ————. Guajiro. Estudio craneométrico (A U Cent Ven, 34, junio 1953, p. 137-206).
Reports 55 measurements individually for 14 male, 7 female, and 5 subadult skulls. Includes also 5 well-drawn views of each of 8 skulls and 5 stereographic diagrams of each of 13 skulls. The angles of Wacker and Klaatsch are carefully worked out.

919. ————. Guajiro. Notas preliminares para el estudio antropológico de los actuales habitantes de la Guajira, pertenecientes al grupo Guajiro I (A U Cent Ven, 34, junio 1953, p. 207-227).
Reports stature and nine head measurements individually for 34 males and 18 females.

920. ————. Indios caribe: Cachama. Notas para el estudio antropométrico de los indios de la Mesa de Guanipa en el estado Anzoátegui (Venezuela), I (B Indig Ven, año 1, 1:1, enero- marzo 1953, p, 127-136).
Reports stature and 9 head measurements individually for 15 males and 10 females.

921.————. Indios caribe: San Joaquín. Notas preliminares para el estudio antropométrico de los indios de la Mesa de Guanipa en el estado Anzoátegui (Venezuela), II (B Indig Ven, año 1, 1:1, enero-marzo 1953, p. 137-148).
Reports stature and 10 head measurements individually for 22 adult males, 7 adult females, 12 juvenile males, and 3 juvenile females.

922. ————. Über Zwergindianer in Venezuela (Zeit Morph Anthr, 45:2, 1953, p. 259-268, with 2 tables).
Reports the stature and head form of 37 male and 37 female "pygmies" from four localities in the Sierra de Perija. The data were collected by J. M. Cruxent during the 1948-1949 expedition of the Sociedad de Ciencias Naturales La Salle. Comparisons are made with African and Asiatic pygmies. Further data and conclusions will appear elsewhere.

923. Gusinde, Martin. Meine Forshungsreise zu den Yupa-Indianern im westlichen Venezuela (Anthropos, 50:1-3, 1955, p. 418-427).
General account of reasons for, and circumstances surrounding, trip to Sierra de Perija in 1954 to study the so-called "pygmies" (people with mean stature below 150 centimeters).

924. Layrisse, Miguel; Tulio Arends; and R. Domínguez Sisco. Nuevo grupo sanguíneo encontrado en descendientes de indios. Su capacidad productora de incompatibilidad materno-fetal e importancia antropológica. Comunicación previa (Acta Méd Ven, 3:4, julio-agosto 1955, p. 132-138).
The so-called "Diego" blood factor was discovered in 1954 in a pregnant woman from Venezuela, the only example among 200 people studied in North America. Present study extends the testing to 826 individuals in Venezuela. Following are the positive results: general population of Caracas, 2.26%; population of Barcelona, 3.28%; Carib Indians, 35.54%; Arawak Indians, 5.26%; mixed Negro population, 7.33%. Suggests that "Indian factor" would be a better designation.

925. Muñoa, Juan I. Contribuciones a la antropología física del Uruguay. 1. Los primitivos pobladores del este (A Mus Hist Nat, 2. serie, 6:4, abril 1954, p. 1-19, map, and 7 pl.).
Briefly describes (with measurements) 11 more or less complete skulls (some with long bones) from five sites. Gives some general comparative data and computes stature by Manouvrier's tables. Good illustrations.

926. Sociedad de Ciencias Naturales La Salle. La región de Perijá y sus habitantes. Caracas, Universidad del Zulia, 1953. 556 p. illus.
Part 2 of chapter 3 (p. 27-29) outlines the anthropometric work of J. M. Cruxent and briefly characterizes the physique of the groups studied. Plates at end of book include physical types. Chapters 7 and 8 (p. 101-171) report detailed studies of the human skulls.

Art

BRAZIL

ROBERT C. SMITH

During the period of 1952-1955 Brazilian art has attracted a great deal of favorable comment in Europe and the U. S. This is particularly true of the contemporary architecture of Rio de Janeiro and São Paulo. In the latter city an international exposition held in 1954 to commemorate the 400th anniversary of the founding of the city brought thousands of distinguished visitors to see the buildings of Oscar Niemeyer. Equally impressive were the large Brazilian participations in the Second and Third Biennial Art Exhibitions which took place in São Paulo in 1953 and 1955 and in the Biennale of Venice in 1954. An exhibition of photographs of the gardens of Roberto Burle Marx toured the U. S. with great success in 1955, inspiring a number of articles in professional journals. So numerous were these writings and others devoted to contemporary buildings in Brazil that space could not be found to note them all in this bibliography. For the complete list of articles in the Brazilian *Habitat,* the English *Architectural review,* the American *Architectural record,* the Italian *Domus,* the Swiss *Werk,* and the French *Architecture d'aujourd'hui,* the reader is referred to the *Art index.*

Nor was the older art of Brazil neglected in this period. In 1954 two cultural congresses devoted special sessions to the subject. In July a conference on the art of the Northeast was held at Recife as a part of a meeting of historians honoring the 300th anniversary of the expulsion of the Dutch from Pernambuco (item 1249). In September the Second International Colloquium on Luso-Brazilian Studies, sponsored by the University of São Paulo, included a fine arts section which discussed Portuguese art in India and Brazil (item 1247). In 1953 Vanderbilt University's volume on the first Colloquium appeared with abstracts of papers on the colonial art of Brazil presented in Washington in 1950 (item 6713). In 1953 and 1954 the long-delayed 10th and 11th volumes of the *Revista do patrimônio histórico e artístico nacional,* corresponding to the years 1946 and 1947 respectively, contributed several excellent articles to the rapidly expanding bibliography of colonial art. An English collection of essays on Luso-Brazilian culture published in 1953 offers two studies of different aspects of the colonial art of Brazil, which are pioneer undertakings (items 1212 and 1245). In the field of 19th-century Brazilian art, special attention is called to an Italian study of the architecture of São Paulo in that period (item 1256) and to Gilberto Ferrez's fine catalogs of the exhibitions of views of Petrópolis (item 1206) and Recife (item 1266). Interest in the iconography of Brazilian cities, which is rapidly growing in Brazil, is reflected in several articles in *Habitat* and will be further stimulated by the appointment, late in 1954, as director of the Museu Imperial of Petrópolis, of Francisco Marques dos Santos, the distinguished antiquarian, who has done so much to locate and preserve old views of the cities of Brazil.

The scholarly bibliography of Brazilian art from 1943 to 1954 prepared by José Valladares (item 1214), which follows closely the format of the *Handbook of Latin American Studies,* maintains a high standard of selection and criticism.

GENERAL

1200. Arroyo, Leonardo. Igrejas de São Paulo. Rio, Olympio, 1954. 407 p., 49 illus.
The first history of the churches of São Paulo. The information provided is disappointing.

1201. Azevedo, Carlos de. Lopes Mendes no Brasil. Un diário inédito do autor de *A India Portuguesa.* Lisboa, Ministério do Ultramar, 1955. 10 p., illus.
This delightful essay offers the text of a brief diary written by the Portuguese traveler Antônio Lopes Mendes on a journey in Brazil in 1883 together with a biography in both Portuguese and English. The drawings of Lopes Mendes, reproduced in actual size, two in color, include panoramas of parts of Rio de Janeiro, Manáus, Recife, Vitória, and Fortaleza, and a view of the old Carmelite establishment in Olinda.

1202. Barata, Mário. A arquitetura brasileira dos séculos XIX e XX (*in* Aspectos da formação e evolução do Brasil. Estudos publicados em 1952, no *Jornal do Commercio,* no seu 125. aniversário. Rio, 1953, p. 251-264).
This is the fullest statement now available on the introduction and development of neoclassical architecture in Brazil and the movements that have followed it down to the present day. Illustrated with 26 views of the earlier buildings.

1203. Bento, Antônio. Manet no Brasil. Estudo comemorativo da passagem do centenário da visita do pintor ao Rio de Janeiro, 1849-1949. Rio, Ministério da Educação e Saúde, Serviço de Documentação, 1953. 113 p., illus.
"J'ai visité plusieurs églises, elles ne valent pas les nôtres, c'est tout doré, tout illuminé, mais manquant de goût." "J'oubliais de te parler du palais de l'empereur: c'est une vraie bicoque, c'est mesquin . . ." These lines, written in 1849 to his mother, leave no doubt as to the low opinion of Brazilian art formed by the great French Impressionist when he came to Rio at the beginning of his career.

1204. Comissão do IV Centenário da Cidade de São Paulo. Serviço de Comemorações Culturais. São Paulo antigo; plantas da cidade. São Paulo, 1954. 3 p., illus.
Facsimile reproductions of 11 plans of the city, ranging in date from 1810 to 1897. There is a brief introduction by Sérgio Milliet.

1205. Deinhard, Hanna. Two research needs for the future development of Luso-Brazilian studies in the field of the fine arts (Intl Colloq, p. 122-123).
The author recommends that more attention be given to the study of monuments and less to documents and that a photographic service be established for art historians working outside Portugal and Brazil.

1207. Galvão, Alfredo. Subsídios para a história da Academia Imperial e da Escola Nacional de Belas Artes. Rio, Universidade do Brasil, 1954. 142 p.
Contains brief biographies of the directors and professors of the national school of art since its inception with the French Mission of 1816.

1208. Jorge, Fernando. Vidas de grandes pintores do Brasil (incluindo os principais caricaturistas). Introdução de Carlos Burlamaqui Kopke. Ilustrações de Mick Carnicelli. São Paulo, Martins, 1954. 308 p., illus.
Short biographical essays, in popular vein, on outstanding painters of all periods. Includes a useful bibliography.

1209. Machado, Lourival Gomes. Mário de Andrade, crítico de arte (Habitat, 21, 1955, p. 36-39).
A fine analysis of the contribution of this noted writer of São Paulo to the evaluation of Brazilian art with special reference to his interpretation of Aleijadinho.

1210. Outras peças do Museu Pigorini de Roma (Habitat, 9, 1952, p. 36-41, illus.).
Combs, fetiches, pipes, and decorated gourds of Brazilian Indians.

1211. Santos, Noronha. Fontes e chafarizes do Rio de Janeiro (R Pat Hist Art Nac, 10, 1946, i.e. 1953, p. 7-134, illus.).
An excellent, fully documented study of nine fountains of the 18th and early 19th centuries, which at least in part supplants previous accounts by Magalhães Corrêa (1939) and Vieira Fazenda (1921-1927). Much of the information is taken from unpublished documents at the Arquivo Nacional. There is a full bibliography of all materials consulted.

1212. Sousa-Leão Filho, Joaquim de. Decorative art: the azulejo (*in* Livermore, H. V. (ed.). Portugal and Brazil; an introduction. Oxford, Clarendon Press, 1953, p. 385-394).
A carefully prepared and useful general statement on the subject of painted tiles in Brazilian architecture of all periods.

1213. Torres, Heloisa Alberto. Museums of Brazil. Translated by John Knox. Rio,

Ministry of Foreign Affairs, Cultural Division, Publication Office, 1955? 82 p.
Among the federal, state, municipal, ecclesiastical, and private museum here listed appear those with collections of Brazilian art. This valuable publication gives addresses and brief statements of the history and holdings of each institution but no names of staff members are listed.

1214. **Valladares, José.** Arte brasileira, publicações de 1943-1954. Salvador, Brazil, 1955. 78 p.
An annotated bibliography of 506 items in eight separate categories. This extremely useful and admirably prepared work was undertaken in continuation of the *Manual bibliográfico de estudos brasileiros* (*HLAS, no. 15, 1949,* item no. 27). The format used is that of the *HLAS.*

COLONIAL

1215. **Albuquerque, A. P. de.** Arquiteto Antônio José Landi (Habitat, 11, 1953, p. 38-41, illus.).
Brief mention of the principal colonial architect of the far north of Brazil, the Bolognese Landi (1708-1790), including a photograph, among others, of his ruined chapel on the estate of Murutucu near Belem, Para.

1216. **Alves, Marieta.** Igreja de N. S. da Conceição da Praia. Salvador, Brazil, Prefeitura Municipal (Pequeno guia das igrejas da Bahia, 15), 1954. 31 p., illus.
Continuing her notable series of booklets on the churches of Salvador based on original research, the distinguished archivist here presents the largest of the 18th-century parish churches of the city. Her account is based in large measure upon a fortunate find in the Biblioteca Nacional in the form of a history made in 1847 from parish records which now seem to be lost. From this source it is possible to attribute the building (1739-1765) to the engineer Manuel Cardoso de Saldanha, the high altar of 1765 to João Moreira do Espírito Santo, and the painting of the wooden ceiling of the nave to José Joaquim da Rocha (1773).

1217. **Barreto, Paulo Thedim.** Características do quadro arquitetônico brasileiro colonial (Intl Colloq, p. 118-119).
General facts about colonial building.

1218. ————. Casas de câmara e cadeia (R Pat Hist Art Nac, 11, 1947, i.e. 1954, p. 9-196, illus.).
A detailed and comprehensive study of municipal buildings originally prepared as a thesis in competition for the chair of Brazilian architecture at the Universidade do Brasil. It is an outstanding contribution to the study of civil building in the Americas during the colonial period. The author, who is an architect employed by DPHAN (Diretoria do Patrimônio Histórico e Artístico Nacional) has made excellent use of the information in the archive of this government organization in listing and analyzing all known town halls in various parts of the country. Particularly valuable for details of construction and decoration.

1219. **Bazin, Germain.** Originalidade da arquitetura barroca em Pernambuco (Arquivos, Recife, 1-2, 1945-1951, i.e. 1953, p. 171-177, illus.).
A brief but enthusiastic and well-informed account of the characteristics of some of the outstanding old buildings of Recife and Olinda.

1220. **Brancante, E. F.** Nossa antiga São Paulo (Habitat, 13, 1953, p. 35-42, illus.).
A selection of late 19th-century photographs of old lost buildings in São Paulo, including the churches of Bom Jesus de Matozinhos (1860), Companhia de Jesus, São Gonçalo (1862), São Francisco (1890), and the cathedral.

1221. **Bruno, Ernani Silva.** História e tradições da cidade de São Paulo. Rio, Olympio (Col. Documento brasileiros, 80, 80-A, 80-B), 1953-1954. 3 v. 1541 p., illus., maps, plans.
In this history of the city of São Paulo prepared for the 400th anniversary of its foundation, considerable attention is paid to early buildings, which are listed if not described in detail, and to old travelers' reports of São Paulo's appearance as well as to the growth of streets and squares. The book is therefore valuable from the standpoint of both architecture and city planning.

1222. **Bury, John B.** The "Borrominesque" churches of colonial Brazil (Art B, 37:1, Mar. 1955, p. 27-54, illus.).
This important stylistic study is directed primarily to a minute analysis of a group of late 18th-century buildings of Minas Gerais, thought to be the work of Antônio Francisco Lisboa (Aleijadinho), which the author rightly considers the most baroque structures of colonial architecture because of the complicated use of space they display, after the fashion of the Italian architect Francesco Borromini. Special attention is given to the rounded form of towers and the serpentine design of façades. In relation to both these matters there are enigmas which cannot now and possibly never will be explained. The article, outstanding for its scholarship, also surveys the general development of religious architecture in Minas Gerais during the 18th century.

1223. ————. Portuguese and Brazilian architecture of the 17th and 18th centuries: relation of exceptional monuments to their European architectural background (Intl Colloq, p. 119-120).
Recommends a study of the "seaweed"-like façade decoration of the chapel of the Franciscan Third Order in Salvador as a forerunner of similar all-over decoration in Spain and Mexico and a study of certain churches of Minas Gerais, which the author himself has subsequently done with great distinction (item 1222).

1224. **Cruz, Ernesto.** Igrejas e sobrados do Maranhão (São Luís e Alcântara).

Rio, Livros de Portugal, 1953. 118 p., illus.
An introductory study of the early buildings of the principal centers of the northern state of Maranhão, modest structures most of which have been extensively rebuilt.

1225. Cunha, Armando. Salvar e conservar as imagens (Habitat, 10, 1953, p. 56-60).
Interesting for its many photographic details of primitive woodcarved and terracotta images.

1226. Dias, João Pereira. Os azulejos do claustro da ordem terceira de S. Francisco da Baía (Belas Artes, 2. série, 7, 1954, p. 31-34, illus.).
A famous series of blue and white Lisbon tiles is here identified convincingly as representing the marriage procession of Joseph I through Lisbon. The tiles are undated and there are no documents to supply this information. Since, however, the royal wedding took place in 1729, they must be somewhat later than this year.

1227. Documentário iconográfico de cidades e monumentos do Brasil (A Mus Hist Nac, 7, 1953, p. 7-34, illus.).
Descriptive catalog of a collection of watercolors and drawings by A. Norfini representing colonial buildings in various parts of Brazil, made for the most part in 1921. There are many excellent illustrations, some of which are in color.

1228. Falcão, Edgard de Cerqueira. Nas paragens do Aleijadinho. Guia das Minas Gerais. Carta-prefácio do Prof. Basílio de Magalhães. Ilustrações de J. Wasth Rodrigues. São Paulo, Emprêsa Gráfica da Revista dos Tribunais, 1955. 199 p., illus.
A résumé of information, originally published in the author's *Relíquias da terra do ouro,* about the chief colonial buildings of Minas Gerais. Includes a check list, organized by D. Clemente Maria da Silva Nigra, of 57 craftsmen. The text contains English, French, and German translations.

1229. Figueiredo, Napoleão. A fortaleza de Macapá (Habitat, 13, 1953, p. 43-48, illus., plans.).
An account, extremely important for the history of military architecture in Brazil, of the great fortress of São José de Macapá in the territory of Amapá at the northern end of the Brazilian coast. Begun about 1765 on the plans of a group of military engineers, the huge construction was completed in 1782 under the direction of Gaspar Geraldo Gronfelts. It is worth noting that the design was the same as that of the old fort in Maranhão (item 1249), being based on the same model by Manuel de Azevedo Fortes. In this article is published a design for Macapá made in 1739, by the student of military engineering, Manuel Luiz Alves, once again on the lines of the model in Fortes' book.

1230. Géo-Charles. Art baroque en Amé-

rique latine. Paris, Plon, 1954. 32 p., illus.
A picture book which contributes nothing new to the total knowledge of the subject, although a surprising amount of space is devoted to Brazil, receiving as it does 10 pages of the text and 36 of the 66 illustrations.

1231. Kelly, Celso. Três gênios rebeldes. Rio, Ministério da Educação e Cultura, Serviço de Documentação (Os cadernos de cultura, 62), 1953. 49 p.
Contains an essay on Aleijadinho (p. 18-33) in which the author stresses the independence of this enigmatic master in relation to outside influences.

1232. Kochnitzky, Leon. Barroco português e brasileiro na África central (Habitat, 10, 1953, p. 53-55, illus.).
Remarks on the similarity of style between provincial Portuguese buildings in Brazil and Angola. The principal monument illustrated is the Carmelite church of Luanda, the doorway of which is known to have been brought from Madeira about 1691 (M. N. Teague, Portugal's permanence in Africa, Geog Mag, 28:7, Nov. 1955, p. 328).

1233. Leite, Serafim. Artes e ofícios dos jesuítas no Brasil (1549-1760). Rio, Livros de Portugal, 1953. 324 p.
In the course of preparing his monumental 10-volume history of the Jesuits in Brazil, Father Leite collected considerable information on the architects, sculptors, painters, and other craftsmen of the order. This is here published in the form of a biographical dictionary which will be of great service to scholars. Surprisingly few works by these men are known and even fewer have survived.

1234. Lopes, Francisco Antônio. Câmara e cadeia de Vila Rica (An Mus Incon, 1952, p. 106-251).
New information on various aspects of the history and structure of the colonial town hall of Ouro Preto.

1235. Maurits de braziliaan; tentoonstelling. 's-Gravenhage, Koninklijk Kabinet van Schilderijen, 1953. 72 p., illus.
Catalog of an important exhibition held April 7-May 17 in The Hague of a loan collection of paintings, engravings, drawings, and tapestries related to the regime of Count John Maurice of Nassau-Siegen in Pernambuco (1637-1644). There is an essay on the work of the painters Frans Post and Albert Eckhout by J. de Sousa-Leão Filho.

1236. Nossa Senhora nas artes. Exposição organizada pela Sociedade Brasileira de Arte Cristã em colaboração com entidades culturais e religiosas e catalogada pelo Arquivo Nacional, Museu Nacional de Belas Artes, 8 a 31 de dezembro de 1954. Catálogo. Rio, Companhia Brasileira de Artes Gráficas, 1954. 63 p., illus.

1237. Ott, Carlos. Noções sôbre a procedência da arte de pintura na província da Bahia, manuscrito da Biblioteca Nacional (R Pat Hist Art Nac, 11, 1947, i.e. 1954, p. 197-224).
The subject of this study is an anonymous undated 16-page manuscript on late 18th- and early 19th-century painting and sculpture in the state of Bahia. Dr. Ott believes that it was written between 1866 and 1876, possibly by the Bahian painter José Rodrigues Nunes, and that it served as a source for the later book of Manuel Querino, *Artistas bahianos*. The manuscript, printed here in its entirety, contributes some new light on the subject.

1238. Prado, J. F. de Almeida. Tomas Ender, pintor austríaco na côrte de D. João VI no Rio de Janeiro. Um episódio da formação da classe dirigente brasileira, 1817-1818. São Paulo, Companhia Editora Nacional (Biblioteca pedagógica brasileira, Brasiliana, série 5, Grande formato, 7), 1955. 383 p., illus.
Thomas Ender, a young Austrian artist, visited Brazil in 1817 as a member of a scientific expedition which accompanied the Archduchess Leopoldina in her journey to marry the future Emperor Peter I. Ender's fine watercolors of local scenes remained virtually forgotten in the library of the Viennese Akademie der Bildenden Künste until they were shown last year in Brazil on the occasion of the 400th anniversary of the founding of São Paulo. This is in no sense a biography of the painter but rather an evocation of Rio de Janeiro in his time, written by a distinguished art collector and historian who has included an informative chapter of the architecture and physiognomy of the capital city in the second decade of the 19th century.

1239. Reis, Artur César Ferreira. O palácio velho de Belém (R Pat Hist Art Nac, 10, 1946, i.e. 1953, p. 305-312).
After an exhaustive study of source materials concerning a colonial residence in Belém, Pará, known as the Old Palace, the author reaches the conclusion that it is not possible to determine whether this building, recently restored by the government, served as the residence of the governors of Pará before the construction of the new palace in 1767.

1240. Reitoria da Universidade da Bahia. Catálogo dos azulejos. Salvador, 1953. 254 p., illus.
A luxuriously printed catalog compiled by José Valladares, with 84 illustrations of the collection of 18th-century Portuguese painted tiles from the Solar Aguiar now installed in the administration building of the Universidade da Bahia at Salvador. In his introduction the author deals with the history of this characteristic decorative device of Portugal and Brazil.

1241. Relíquias de Nicolau Taunay (Ilus Br, 44:220, agôsto 1953, unpaged).
Five landscapes of the 15 by Nicolas-Antoine Taunay recently acquired in France by the collector Djalma da Fonseca Hermes. All were painted before the artist's arrival in Brazil in 1816. With them is reproduced a portrait of Taunay by Julien Boilly.

1242. Santos, Noronha. Vestígios de fortim colonial no Engenho novo (R Pat Hist Art Nac, 11, 1947, i.e. 1954, p. 225-232, illus.).
An interesting and cleverly documented reference to the remains of a redoubt (*fortim de fachina*) erected by order of the viceroy Count of Resende between 1793 and 1795, which is known to have been commanded by one Caetano Madeira as one of the minor defences of the Bay of Guanabara.

1243. Schenone, Héctor. Tallistas portugueses en el Río de la Plata (A Inst Arte Am, 8, 1955, p. 40-56, illus.).
The influence of Luso-Brazilian craftsmanship in the Buenos Aires area during the late colonial period, already acknowledged in the field of cabinet making, is here documented in relation to woodcarved altarpieces as well. The author has assembled the names of 16 Portuguese woodcarvers of the 17th and 18th centuries, some of whom are known to have come to the Río de la Plata by way of the Portuguese Colônia de Sacramento, the modern Uruguay.
One of these men, José de Sousa Cavadas, can be identified as the author of two high altars in Luján (1759) and B. A. (1761) respectively, while another at Yaguarón in Paraguay can be attributed to him. All belong to the Italianate or Joanine type of retable, used in Portugal in the first half of the 18th century. The altar by Pedro Carmona at San Francisco in B. A., which may date from as late as 1817, is an example of the late rococo style of the time in Brazil.

1244. Smith, Robert C. As artes na Bahia. 1. parte. Arquitetura colonial. Salvador, Brazil, Prefeitura Municipal (Evolução histórica da cidade do Salvador, 4), 1954, 94 p., illus.
Using the scheme advanced in item 1245, the author examines the colonial architecture of Salvador in the first of a series of volumes to be devoted to the art of that city, the old capital of Brazil. Among the points discussed are the authorship of the Solar Saldanha and the origin of the façade of Santa Teresa. This is the most comprehensive book on the subject.

1245. ————. Brazilian baroque architecture (*in* Livermore, H. V. (ed.). Portugal and Brazil; an introduction. Oxford, Clarendon Press, 1953, p. 349-384, illus.).
The first attempt to discuss as a whole, in the light of accepted standards of art history, the development of Brazilian colonial architecture, this essay offers a scheme for its classification and that of the woodcarved altarpieces and ceiling paintings.

1246. ————. The Caetano prospect, an eighteenth century view of Recife in Brazil (Americas, Franciscan Hist, 10:4, Apr. 1954, p. 391-408, illus).
A study of a watercolor copy of a view

of Recife made in 1759 by José Caetano, S. J., which illustrates the manuscript of Luiz dos Santos Vilhena's *Recopilacão de notícias sotero-politanas* in the Biblioteca Nacional at Rio de Janeiro. This panorama, one of the earliest and most detailed known views of the city, is studied in connection with a map of Recife of 1773 from the same manuscript. The analysis is principally from the standpoint of the buildings represented and the plan of the town.

1247. ————. Colonial towns of Spanish and Portuguese America (J Soc Archit Hist, 14:4, Dec. 1955, p. 1-12, illus.).
After pointing out the dichotomy between the regularity of terrain and grid plan of the former and the irregularity of site and *arruamento* of the latter, which has long been recognized, the author presents a precise analysis, based on the Laws of the Indies in the first case and the descriptions of travelers and old views of specific towns in the second. Finally, a number of parallels between Brazilian towns and those of Portugal and the Portuguese empire in the East are cited.

1248. ————. Décadas do Rosário dos Pretos, documentos da irmandade (Arquivos, Recife, 1-2, 1945-1951, i.e. 1953, p. 143-170, illus.).
From a study of old expense books, the author has assembled the names of some 30 carpenters, sculptors, masons, ironworkers, silversmiths, and painters employed in the early 18th century at the church of the Negro brotherhood in Recife. Using information from this source, an attempt is here made to date the church's fine façade.

1249. ————. Una fortaleza de Portugal en el Marañón (A Inst Arte Am, 8, 1955, p. 27-39, illus.).
This paper, submitted to a congress of Brazilian history held at Recife in 1954, is concerned with a description and drawing of the fort of Ponta da Areia in the harbor of São Luiz do Maranhão. The documents, in the Arquivo Histórico Ultramarino of Lisbon, were signed by the military engineer Pedro de Azevedo Carneiro in 1692. The description reveals many interesting details of the practice of military architecture by the Portuguese of the time and in particular the use of specific instructions published by Luiz Serrão Pimentel (1613-1679) in his *Método lusitânico* of 1680.

1250. ————. Os mausoléus de D. João V nas quatro partes do mundo (R Fac Let, 2. série, 21:1, 1955, p. 5-38, illus.).
An effort to record the impact of an event in Portugal upon the art and social history of Portuguese America, Africa, and India, this study concerns the funeral monuments erected to King John V in those places, following his death at Lisbon on July 31, 1750. Among the Brazilian examples only the one designed by the soldier Antônio de Moraes Sarmento for the parish church of São João del Rei seems to have been engraved. This is reproduced along with quotations from the official description. Other references to the catafalques of the king at Bahia, Belém, and Recife are given.

1251. ————. Recommendations for research and research aids in the history of the 17th and 18th century architecture of Portugal and Brazil (Intl Colloq, p. 126-130).
Recommends the publication of: (1) illustrated regional guides to Brazilian monuments; (2) archival findings of DPHAN; (3) a new edition of the *Santuário Mariano* of Frei Agostinho da Cruz.

1252. ————. The seventeenth- and eighteenth-century architecture of Brazil (Intl Colloq, p. 109-116).
Now superseded by item no .

1253. Sousa-Leão Filho, Joaquim de. Palácio das Torres (R Pat Hist Art Nac, 10, 1946, i.e. 1953, p. 135-168, illus.).
This article brings together all available information on the palace of Vrijburg, built for the Dutch governor of Pernambuco, Count John Maurice of Nassau-Siegen, at Recife in 1639, which remained in large part intact until about 1789. It contains a good deal of new information concerning the construction plan, and later history of the building.

1254. Tricentenário da Restauração Pernambucana. Comissão Organizadora e Executiva. Exposição comemorativa de escultura religiosa. (Coleção Abelardo Rodrigues). Recife, 1954. 10 p., illus.
A catalog of 200 statuettes of wood or terracotta from one of the major private collections of colonial religious sculpture in Brazil. An introduction by Robert C. Smith summarizes the little that is known about wood sculpture in Pernambuco, where most of the objects exhibited were made, during the 17th and 18th centuries.

NINETEENTH CENTURY

1255. Calçadas (Habitat, 13, 1953, p. 54-55, illus.).
Photographs made in Salvador by Alice Brill of nine characteristic black and white stone mosaic sidewalks.

1256. Debenedetti, Emma, and Anita Salmoni. Architettura italiana a San Paolo. São Paulo, Instituto Cultural Italo-Brasileiro (Col. Pasquale Petraccone, 1), 1953. 106 p., illus.
An essay on the stylistic development of São Paulo's architecture in the last 70 years. The authors emphasize the contribution of Italians to the neo-classic phase, to the work of Ramos de Azevedo, to the *estilo floreal* or *art nouveau* movement, and finally to contemporary building.

1257. Ferrez, Gilberto. A fotografia no Brasil e um de seus mais dedicados servidores: Marc Ferrez, 1843-1923 (R Pat Hist Art Nac, 10, 1946, i.e. 1953, p. 169-304, illus.).

In assembling this first extensive account of the work of his relative, the photographer Marc Ferrez, the author has assembled a world of information about the use of the camera in Brazil, which goes back to 1840. The monograph is illustrated with a number of photographs of colonial buildings made in the late 19th century. Bibliography.

1258. ————. A iconografia do Recife no século XIX (Diário de Pernambuco, abril 26, 1953).
Indentifies F. Kaus as the author and D. Braunsdorff of Dresden as the lithographer of two views of Recife in 1848, representing the Rua do Crespo and the Cais de Ponte Uchoa.

1258a. ————. Iconografia petropolitana (1800-1890). Petrópolis, Brazil, Museu Imperial, 1955. 33 p., illus.
A handsome catalog in the form of an album, designed to commemorate an exhibition of 135 views of the imperial town of Petrópolis and its buildings, all of which are illustrated. The legends are admirably composed by Gilberto Ferrez, who organized this impressive exhibition.

1259. ————. Três gravuras do Recife de 1847-48 (Diário de Pernambuco, out. 18, 1953).
Presents two large lithographs of Recife, offered for sale in 1848, now in the Biblioteca Nacional of Rio de Janeiro, and identifies another set of six views by W. Bassler of Dresden.

1260. Floreal (Habitat, 12, 1953, p. 58-61, illus.).
Examples of *art nouveau* architecture and decoration in São Paulo, featuring a house attributed to the architect Victor Dubugras (Rua Marques de Itú), the Galeria Wainberg (1905) and the villa of D. Marguerita Marchesini.

1261. Inéditos do Rio (Habitat, 11, 1953, p. 36-37, illus.).
Two water views of the city by the French painter Étienne-François-Auguste Mayer (1805-1890) in the collection of Ambassador Cavalcanti de Lacerda and one of the church of Nossa Senhora da Glória do Outeiro seen from the rear, painted in 1844 by the Austro-Hungarian Ludwig Czerni (1821-1880).

1262. Paliteiros numa coleção (Habitat, 11, 1953, p. 33-35, illus.).
Dr. Osvaldo Riso's fine collection of 19th-century silver toothpick holders. Well illustrated.

1263. Rodrigo Júnior [i.e., João Baptista Carvalho de Oliveira]. Curitiba em 1853 (Ilus Br, 44:224, dez. 1953, p. 42).
From a drawing of the capital city of Paraná made by J. H. Elliot in 1855, the author identifies and discusses the principal buildings.

1264. São Paulo e o "art nouveau" (Habitat, 10, 1953, p. 3-30, illus.).
Repercussions of Victor Horta's decorative movement in the Villa Penteado, designed by

Carlos Ekman, a Swedish architect, in 1902. There are many illustrations, some in color.

1265. Taunay, Affonso de E. Outras aventuras de um artista malogrado: Adriano Taunay (Habitat, 11, 1953, p. 38-43, illus.).
Excerpts from letters of the artist and a friend during a journey to Mato Grosso in 1827-1828, with illustrations of an album of watercolors made by Taunay, 1820-1825, of subjects in Rio de Janeiro.

1266. Tricentenário da Restauração Pernambucana. Comissão Organizadora e Executiva. Iconografia do Recife; século XIX. (Col. Gilberto Ferrez e outros). Recife, 1954. 59 p., illus.
An outstanding catalog, prepared by Gilberto Ferrez, of 232 watercolors, drawings, and prints representing maps or views of Recife from 1809 to 1898. Among these, and here illustrated, are a number of little-known but fascinatingly fresh and revealing work by the English artists Charles Landseer (1799-1879) and H. Lewis, active in 1825-1826 and 1848 respectively. In his introduction, which deals with source material for the subject of the exhibition, Ferrez announces a plan to publish several volumes on views of Recife in the 19th century, including collections of the prints of E. Bauch, L. Schlappriz, and F. H. Carls.

CONTEMPORARY

1267. Os afrescos da igreja de Batatais (Habitat, 11, 1953, p. 18-21, illus.).
Recent religious paintings in the church of a town near the painter Portinari's home. The remarkable eclecticism of the artist is here seen to have centered upon the style of Florentine painting of the 15th century.

1268. Aquino, Flávio de. Max Bill critica a nossa moderna arquitetura (Manchete, 60, junio 13, 1953, p. 38-39).
Report of a now famous interview with a prominent European architect who severely attacked modern Brazilian building. The interview provoked a storm of criticism (item 1275).

1269. B., R.F. Um pintor pernambucano (Habitat, 12, 1953, p. 74-81, illus.).
A large number of illustrations of the folklore paintings of Lula Cardoso Ayres of the period 1940-1944, in combination with photographs of some of his subjects.

1270. La biennale di Venezia. Venezia, 1954. 431 p.
In the Brazilian section (p. 198-202) the work of 12 prominent artists is included.

1271. Borba, Rosy Frontini de. Roupa de couro do vaqueiro nordestino (Habitat, 12, 1953, p. 50-55, illus.).
Descriptions of the unique leather boots, suits, hats, and gloves worn by herdsmen of northern Brazil, with quotations from Euclides da Cunha and other writers.

1272. Braga, Rubem. Três primitivos. Rio, Ministério da Educação e Cultura,

Serviço de Documentação (Os cadernos de cultura, 63), 1953. 19 p., illus.
Brief appreciative essays by a leading critic on the genre painting of the folk artists, José Bernardo Cardoso, Jr. (1861-1947), and Heitor dos Prazeres (b. 1898) of Rio de Janeiro, and the Paulista Antônio da Silva (b. 1909).

1273. Burle Marx e dei giardini brasiliani (Domus, 279, feb. 1953, p. 14-18).
On the "Brazilian garden" as represented in the gardens, tiles, murals, and fabrics designed by Roberto Burle Marx.

1274. Conjunto residencial Prefeito Mendes de Morais-Pedregulho (Br Arquit Cont, 1, agôsto-set., 1953, p. 4-16, illus.).
Extensive description with 33 illustrations of A. E. Reidy's housing development in the São Cristovão district of Rio de Janeiro, including decorations by R. Burle Marx and Portinari.

1275. Costa, Lúcio. A nossa arquitetura moderna, oportunidade perdida (Manchete, 63, julio 4, 1953, p. 49).
Brief reply by an outstanding Brazilian architect and critic to the criticism of Max Bill (item 1268).

1276. A época do "Spam" (Habitat, 10, 1953, p. 49-60, illus.).
Notice of a group of modern artists in São Paulo in 1932-1934, with Lasar Segall's decorations for one of their balls, including four color reproductions of fantastic birds and animals.

1277. Exposição de história de S. Paulo no quadro da história do Brasil (Habitat, 20, 1955, p. 58-59).
Gives the list of Brazilian artists who worked on the decoration of the pavilion containing the exhibition of the history of São Paulo at the 1954 exposition in that city. Mural paintings by Clovis Graciano and Fernando Lemos are illustrated.

1278. Exposição Portinari; catálogo. Edição patrocinada pelas Companhias de Seguro e Capitalização do grupo Sul América e Banco Lar Brasileiro. Rio, Museu de Arte Moderna, 1953. Unpaged.
Catalog of a retrospective exhibition of paintings by Cândido Portinari from 1937 to 1952 with selections from the writings of a number of Brazilian and foreign critics.

1279. Guimarães, Mário. São Paulo; 4 séculos de luta. Rio, Gráfica Vitória, 1954. 184 p., illus.
In this brief history of São Paulo, 14 early paintings and drawings by Portinari are included as illustrations.

1280. Lima, Herman. Alvarus e os seus bonecos. Rio, Ministério da Educação e Cultura, Serviço de Documentação (Col. Artistas brasileiros), 1954. Unpaged, illus.

An album of two-tone reproductions of caricatures of public figures by Álvaro Cotrim, one of the outstanding caricaturists of Brazil, active since 1925. English and French translation.

1281. Machado, Anibal M. Goeldi. Rio, Ministério da Educação, Servico de Documentação (Col. Artistas brasileiros), 1955. Unpaged, illus.
Woodcuts and drawings of a contemporary artist, born in Pará and trained in Europe, whose landscapes have something of the sad and lonely feeling of Utrillo's. The reproductions are very good. English and French translations of the text are provided.

1282. Martins, Luís. Emiliano di Cavalcanti. São Paulo, Museu de Arte Moderna, 1953, 24 p. illus.
A biographical and critical statement coinciding with the Cavalcanti exhibition in Rio de Janeiro.

1283. II Bienal do Museu de Arte Moderna de São Paulo. Catálogo geral. São Paulo, Edições Americanas de Arte e Arquitetura, 1953. xxxix, 346 p., illus.
The Brazilian section (p. 2-51) of the catalogue, in addition to the listing of the competitors in the international exhibition, includes introductions to the special showings of the work of the Impressionist Elyseu Visconti (1867-1944) and of Brazilian landscape painting before 1900.

1284. Terceiro Bienal de Arte de São Paulo (Habitat, 22, 1955, p. 33-63, illus.).
An extensive critical report on the Brazilian participation in the international exposition of contemporary art at São Paulo, containing no less than 122 illustrations and individual statements by the following artists and critics: José G. Vieira, Lívio Abramo, Sérgio Milliet, P. M. Bardi, Maria E. Franco, Antônio Bento, Elena Goerg, L. G. Machado, Wolfgang Pfeifer, Francisco C. P. Cuoco, José Gómez Sicre, E. F. Brancante, Paulo Duarte, Bruno Giorgi. There are six photographs of the new murals by Portinari destined for the United Nations headquarters in N. Y. They show the influence of José Clemente Orozco and other Mexican artists.

1285. III Bienal do Museu de Arte Moderna de São Paulo. Catálogo geral. São Paulo, Edições Americanas de Arte e Arquitetura, 1955. 290 p., illus.
The regular Brazilian section (p. 13-37) is preceded by an account of special exhibitions (p. 1-13), including 12 paintings entitled A guerra by Portinari and 18 paintings and 13 sculptures by Lasar Segall.

1286. Thiollier, René. Depoimento inédito sôbre a "Semana de Arte Moderna" (Habitat, 12, 1953, p. 44-49, illus.).
Letters of Graça Aranha, Paulo Prado and Ronald de Carvalho proving that the author took a prominent part in the organization of the Week of Modern Art, held in São Paulo in 1922.

Economics

GENERAL

1350. Bande, Jorge. La política del seguro privado. Inquietudes y anhelos de la institución del seguro en las Américas. Santiago, Editorial Universitaria, 1953. 328 p.
A learned and thorough discussion of private insurance. Its history is traced from ancient times to the present, its cultural and sociological importance is stressed. The fields covered by private insurance are presented, and the types of insurance companies, their agents and customers reviewed. Insurance techniques are discussed, and the role of the State indicated. All this the author unravels not only from the Chilean point of view, but from a general position, drawing heavily on German and U. S. experiences. [S. Garbuny]

1351. Carrillo Flores, Antonio. El desarrollo económico en Iberoamérica (R Fisc Fin, 15:90, dic. 1954, p. 15-22).
Discurso pronunciado el 23 de noviembre de 1954, por Antonio Carrillo Flores, jefe de la delegación de México y vicepresidente de la Conferencia Económica Interamericana, que tuvo lugar en Quitandinha, Petrópolis, Brasil. [Nacional Financiera]

1352. Ducassi y Mendieta, Francisco. Desempleo y falta de ventas. Habana, Emp. Editora de Publicaciones, 1953. 153 p.
The book consists of one major essay, which gave the title, and a collection of other articles of the author published previously in the daily press. The major essay is a restatement of the underconsumption theory of unemployment and economic crisis, and advocates increased civilian consumption over military as a means to fight depressions and their concomitants. The other articles deal with similar problems in brief journalistic fashion. [S. Garbuny]

1353. Fernández-Arias da Cunha, Carlos. Los movimientos internacionales de capital en Hispanoamérica y España. Madrid, Ediciones Cultura Hispánica, 1953. 108 p.
A very brief discussion with good statistical background on the importance of international capital movements for Spain and the individual Latin American countries is followed by a review of the regulations of capital transfers and a review of the accounting for capital items in the balances of payments of the various Hispanic countries. [S. Garbuny]

1354. Financial and business review of the Americas (N Y Times, 103:35,046, Jan. 6, 1954, p. 47-81, illus.).
An annual financial and business review of the American nations north and south of the U. S. border. The Latin American republics are well featured, with numerous articles on their specific problems at the beginning of 1954. Large advertisements by some of them, such as Brazil, Mexico, and the Dominican Republic, present what is noteworthy for the U. S. in the judgment of these countries. [S. Garbuny]

1355. Fuentes Irurozqui, Manuel. El bloque económico iberoamericano. Punto de vista de un español. Madrid, Ediciones Cultura Hispánica (Col. Hombres e ideas), 1953. 171 p.
A subjective discussion of Latin American economic problems by a Spaniard. The author reviews the generally known data on South America and some recommendations of inter-American conferences of recent years. His ultimate goal is a one-bloc Spanish America centered around Spain economically, culturally, and politically. [S. Garbuny]

1356. Gaines, Thomas A. Profits with progress. Latin America's bright investment future. Stamford, Conn., Latin American Investment Council, 1954. 99 p.
After reducing the existing prejudices against investments in Latin America, the author proceeds to establish the general advantages of investments in the area. He follows up with a country-by-country description of investment opportunities in Latin America and presents a comprehensive rating of investment situations in the individual South American economies. [S. Garbuny]

1357. Grace, Joseph Peter. W. R. Grace, 1832-1904, and the enterprises he created. N. Y., Newcomen Society in North America, 1953. 28 p., illus.
A tribute to W. R. Grace, founder of the W. R. Grace Enterprises and grandfather of the author, who is now at the helm of the family corporation. A personal account describing the founder and the history of his enterprise in the U. S. and Latin America. [S. Garbuny]

1358. Hermida Herrero-Beaumont, Ramón. Relaciones comerciales entre Hispanoamérica y América sajona. Madrid,

Ediciones Cultura Hispánica (Col. Hombres e ideas), 1953. 277 p., illus.

A country-by-country review of commodity movements and resulting import or export surpluses between the Latin American countries on the one hand and the U. S. and Canada on the other. Trade statistics for selected years of the middle and late 1940's serve as a model. The author uses mostly official sources of the countries under study. [S. Garbuny]

1359. Inter American Statistical Institute. Manual de codificación para la aplicación de la Clasificación Uniforme para el Comercio Internacional (CUCI). 1. ed. (preliminar). Washington, Unión Panamericana, 1953. 284 p.

A preliminary manual of commodity indexes for the Standard International Trade Classification of the United Nations. It shall ultimately serve the uniform classification of merchandise in international trade statistics. This Spanish edition lists essentially goods of Latin American international trade. [S. Garbuny]

1360. Malenbaum, Wilfred. The world wheat economy, 1885-1939. Cambridge, Mass., Harvard University Press, 1953. 262 p.

A study, grown out of a doctoral dissertation, of wheat as an international problem. It does not deal especially with wheat as a Latin American, especially Argentine, problem, but brings in all facts that concern Latin America as a wheat producer or consumer. The study is thorough and scholarly and offers reliable statistical material. [S. Garbuny]

1361. McGraw-Hill International Corporation. Overseas Business Service. Listing of United States firms with investments overseas. 2d ed. N. Y., 1954. 63 p.

A list of 1000 U. S. firms (and their presidents) which have investments overseas. The investments are manifested in branches, subsidiaries, and offices only. It is not a list of export transactions, though many firms are exporters. No regions of investments are indicated, so that no special reference to Latin America is made. [S. Garbuny]

1362. Mikesell, Raymond F. Foreign exchange in the postwar world. N. Y., Twentieth Century Fund, 1954. 658 p., tables.

An extremely competent study of foreign exchange developments after World War II. The book deals with exchange problems wherever they occur in the world, and discusses techniques and organizations pertinent to it on a global level. Chapter 8, dealing with multiple exchange rates, and chapter 13, on exchange controls in Latin America, are especially useful to the student of Latin American economic affairs. [S. Garbuny]

1363. Peña Suárez, José Luis de la. El petróleo en Hispanoamérica. Madrid, Ediciones Cultura Hispánica, 1953. 155 p.

A brief review of the petroleum facts of the oil-producing countries in South America, and also Trinidad and the Philippines. To the extent permitted by the available data, it covers in brief oil production, refining, exports, by-products, legislation, and the names of the oil companies. [S. Garbuny]

1364. Pennsylvania State College. School of Mineral Industries. Division of Mineral Economics. Materials survey on tin. Prepared for the National Security Resources Board under contract to the National Production Authority. Washington, U. S. Government Printing Office, 1953. Various pagings, illus., maps, tables.

A comprehensive study of tin, its chemical properties, its geological data, its production and treatment, shipment and consumption. Governmental and international controls of the tin market are also discussed. It is a worldwide study and gives full information on Bolivian tin and its connection with the world market. Excellent statistics, bibliography, and maps. [S. Garbuny]

1365. Shere, Louis. Sugar taxation in the Caribbean and Central American countries. Washington, Pan American Union, 1952. Variously paged.

A study carried out by the author in Washington, D. C., without field trips. A description of the sugar industry in the Caribbean and Central American countries is followed by an analysis of the various sugar markets. Sugar taxes and general taxes affecting the sugar industry are thoroughly discussed. Valuable statistical tables. [S. Garbuny]

1366. Torrente, Vicente, and Gabriel Mañueco. Las relaciones económicas de España con Hispanoamérica. Madrid, Ediciones Cultura Hispánica, 1953. 544 p., tables.

A comprehensive study of the balance of payments of Spain in relation to Latin America. An analysis of the components of the balance is followed by a thorough, but brief chapter on the historical development of Spain's commercial relations with Latin America. More than half of the book consists of statistical trade tables for selected years between 1931 and 1948. The texts of Spain's trade agreements with Bolivia, Chile, Uruguay, and Brazil, respectively, form the end of the book. [S. Garbuny]

1367. Torres Martínez, Manuel de; Carlos Muñoz Linares; Hernán Cortés Rodríguez; and Carlos Fernández-Arias da Cunha. Las relaciones comerciales entre España e Hispanoamérica. Madrid, Ediciones Cultura Hispánica, 1952. 141 p.

The author and his research staff give a summary review of Spain's trade relations and their development with the individual Latin American countries in the time between 1930 and 1950. The discussion is brief and the statistical material all too scanty. [S. Garbuny]

1368. **United Nations. Department of Economic Affairs.** Instability in export markets of under-developed countries in relation to their ability to obtain foreign exchange from exports of primary commodities, 1901-1950. N. Y., 1952. 94 p. (Doc. E/2047/Rev. 1; ST/ECA/15).
Published also in Spanish: *La inestabilidad de los mercados de exportación de los países insuficientemente desarrollados . . . ,* 1952, i.e. 1953, 91 p. A theoretical study of the fluctuations of the export and import markets of underdeveloped countries. All underdeveloped countries in the world are examined, including those of Latin America. The study is concerned with yearly, cyclical, and long-range fluctuations and their interrelationships. The study covers fluctuations in prices, volume, and income of the commodity trade, and their interconnections, and, finally, compares the foreign exchange income of underdeveloped countries from the commodity trade with the exchange income from other sources. Statistical material for selected years of the last half century supports the discussion. [S. Garbuny]

1369. ————. ————. The international flow of private capital, 1946-1952. N. Y., 1954. 61 p., tables. (Doc. E/2531, ST/ECA/22).
Published also in Spanish: *La corriente internacional de capitales privados, 1946-1952.* Capital movements from the U. S., United Kingdom, Switzerland, France, Belgium, and Canada are analyzed. The purpose of the investments is scrutinized as to direct and portfolio investment and to the type of industry favored. The factors which limit these capital movements are equally described. [S. Garbuny]

1370. ————. ————. United States income taxation of private United States investments in Latin America. A description of the United States system and some of its implications. N. Y., 1953. 80 p., graphs, tables. (ST/ECA/18).
This volume deals with the special tax problems of the U. S. investor in Latin America. It discusses U. S. treatment of foreign income under the American income tax system with special reference to Latin America. It analyzes the effect of the American income tax on investments in Latin America. Problems of tax relief, tax credits, are laid bare. The implications of American taxation for the Latin American countries are scrutinized. The volume also contains criticism of the factual material discussed and recommendations for future regulation. Issued also in Spanish: *Régimen tributario aplicado por los Estados Unidos de América a las inversiones privadas estadounidenses en la América Latina.* [S. Garbuny]

1371. ————. **Economic Commission for Latin America.** Possibilities for the development of the pulp and paper industry in Latin America. A joint study by the Economic Commission for Latin America and the Food and Agriculture Organization of the United Nations. N. Y., 1954. 142 p., tables. (Doc. E/CN.12/294/rev. 2).

Issued also in Spanish: *Posibilidades de desarrollo de la industria de papel y celulosa en la América Latina.* After a general introduction on the need to promote the development of the paper industry in Latin America and on the technical possibilities for the purpose, the individual situation in 14 republics and in Surinam, British Guiana, and French Guiana is taken up in detail. The thorough investigation is accompanied by a large amount of statistical material. [S. Garbuny]

1372. ————. ————. Study on iron and steel industry and report on meeting of experts held in Bogotá and sponsored by the Economic Commission for Latin America and Technical Assistance Administration. Santiago, 1953. 2 v. (v. 1, 163 p.; v. 2, variously paged), maps, diagrs., tables. (Doc. E/CN.12/293).
A study on the technical and economic details of the iron and steel industry as they become pertinent for Latin America, including a survey on the raw materials that are basic in this industry. The alternative processes for steel making and the technical equipment they require as well as their suitability and applicability in Latin America are ventilated. Existing steel plants are listed and their performance indicated. The report reflects a conference discussion rather than final findings. [S. Garbuny]

1373. ————. ————. A study of trade between Latin America and Europe. Prepared by the Secretariats of the Economic Commission for Latin America, the Economic Commission for Europe and the Food and Agriculture Organization of the United Nations. Geneva, 1953. 117 p., tables. (Doc. E/CN.12/225).
The problems of Latin America-European trade are discussed essentially from the Latin American point of view. The competitive position of Latin American exports in European markets is analyzed; European commercial policies in their effects on Latin America are described; the changes through industrialization in Latin America and their consequences for European trade are observed. The relative position of the U. S. and the European countries in Latin American markets is adequately discussed. Appendices deal with special commodities in Latin American-European trade. Statistical tables accompany the text. Also published in Spanish: *Estudio del comercio entre América Latina y Europa,* 1953, 117 p. [S. Garbuny]

1374. ————. ————. Technical assistance activities under the expanded programme in the countries in the ECLA region. Rio, 1953. 161 p. (Doc. E/CN. 12/302).
A mimeographed summary of the technical assistance programs of the various international organizations in the countries concerning the Economic Commission for Latin America. A useful guide. [S. Garbuny]

1375. **United States. Senate.** Study of Latin American countries; interim report.

A study of the operations in Latin American countries of the Export-Import Bank and the International Bank and their relationship to the expansion of international trade, pursuant to S. Res. 25, 83d Congress, 1st session. Washington, U. S. Government Printing Office, 1954. 648 p., illus.

Senator Homer E. Capehart's report on the Capehart Mission, a committee authorized by the U. S. Senate Committee on Banking and Currency to study, in 14 Latin American countries, the operations of the Export-Import Bank of Washington and the International Bank for Reconstruction and Development, and their relationship to the expansion of international trade. The visit to each nation is described. The schedule for the mission in each country is reproduced, and the findings of the members submitted. Though already dated by later events in some countries, the volume contains valuable factual material. [S. Garbuny]

1376. Wilgus, A. Curtis (ed.). The Caribbean: its economy. Gainesville, University of Florida Press, School of Inter-American Studies (Publ., series 1, 4), 1954. 286 p.

A collection of papers presented at the Fourth Annual Caribbean Conference at the University of Florida. The topics deal with resources and production in the Caribbean area, with manufacturing and investments, transportation and marketing, labor and general cultural problems. All presentations are brief and general. [S. Garbuny]

LATIN AMERICA (EXCEPT BRAZIL AND MEXICO)

SIEGFRIED GARBUNY

ARGENTINA

1400. Argentina. Dirección Nacional del Servicio Estadístico. IV censo general de la nación. T. 2. Censo agropecuario. B. A., 1955? 491 p., tables.

A comprehensive census of agricultural units and cattle based on direct inquiries by statistical interviewers in 1947. The tabulations show the size of the farms, their legal status as to ownership, as well as the types of cattle and their incidence in the various regions.

1401. ————. Ministerio de Industria de la Nación. Informativo mensual. Publicación oficial. Año 1, no. 1-5, agosto-diciembre 1954.

The first issue contains the names of the directors of various state enterprises which were under the supervision of the Ministry of Industry during the Perón regime in 1954. Next to the names of the various directors are given a number of resolutions of the Ministry of Industry or of the directorates of the respective state enterprises.

1402. Engelbeen, Carlos H. La pesca marítima en la Argentina. Pasado—presente—porvenir. B. A., Ediciones Librería del Colegio, 1955. 216 p.

A thorough study of Argentine fishery: its geological and biological conditions; fishing instruments used; past and present economic significance of fishing for Argentina; economic comparisons with the fishing industries of other countries; questions of domestic consumption, of processing fish at home, of exportation and commercialization of the fish catch; discussion of the role of the State in Argentine fishing. The book is an interesting contribution in view of Argentina's attempt at present to plan the development of a fishing industry.

1403. Tucumán (prov.). Estación Experimental Agrícola. Revista industrial y agrícola de Tucumán. T. 39, enero 1953-sept. 1955.

This issue contains an article on the production of garden seeds in the U. S., other articles dealing exclusively with technical agricultural problems of the Experiment Station, and bibliographical material concerning publications received in the Experiment Station library. Concludes with meteorological tables for the period from January 1953 to September 1955.

1404. Universidad Nacional de Buenos Aires. Facultad de Ciencias Económicas. Revista de la Facultad . . . . B. A. Año 6, no. 51-52, marzo-abril 1953— no. 59-60, nov.-dic. 1953.

The March-April issue is specially dedicated to the Second Argentine Five-Year Plan; it contains articles on the Plan which are preceded by a graphic presentation of the Plan objectives. The September-October issue deals with special Argentine economic problems, ranging from the Argentine-Bolivian treaty to pipelines for gas and oil, and from railroad transportation problems to selected topics on agriculture and forestry. The others contain articles on fiscal, corporation, and banking problems.

1405. Universidad Nacional de Córdoba. Facultad de Ciencias Económicas. Revista de la Facultad . . . . Córdoba, Argentina. Año 7, no. 1-2, 1.-2. trimestres 1954—año 7, no. 3-4, 3.-4. trimestres 1954.

The two 1954 issues of the Review of the Faculty of Economics at the University of Córdoba. Articles on the Second Argentine Five-Year Plan, bank credit, the Guatemalan economy, econometrics, economic development, and special accounting problems of corporations. The articles are followed by notes on contemporary national and international economic events and book reviews.

1406. Universidad Nacional de Eva Perón. Facultad de Ciencias Económicas. Económica. Revista de la Facultad . . . . Publicación trimestral. Ciudad Eva Perón (La Plata). Año 1, no. 1, julio-septiembre 1954.
The first issue of an economic review issued by the Faculty of Economics of the National University at La Plata, then Eva Perón University. The issue contains an article on the Second Argentine Five-Year Plan by Luis Cardoso of La Plata University, as well as articles on public finance and economic theory. The issue ends with book reviews and publication lists.

1407. Universidad Nacional del Litoral. Facultad de Ciencias Económicas, Comerciales y Políticas. Revista de la Facultad . . . . Rosario, Argentina. No. 64-69, enero 1951-dic. 1952, i. e. 1954.
The biennial issue for 1951-1952 contains homages to the late Eva Perón, articles on regional planning, on statistical quality control and mathematical problems, and a disquisition on the state which is accompanied by a comprehensive bibliography. Other articles deal with national Argentine economic problems. The volume ends with an extensive bibliography on topics of interest to the Review.

BOLIVIA

1408. Bolivia. Dirección General de Economía Rural. Departamento de Muestreos y Padrones. Estadística de índices de precios de productos agropecuarios de la república de Bolivia, años 1945-1950. La Paz, 1954. 135 p., graphs, tables.
A collection of price indices for the years 1945-1950. 1945 is the base year. The indices are for agricultural products by location. The indices are also shown in graphic form, the price rises being represented by curves.

1409. ————. Subsecretaría de Prensa, Informaciones y Cultura. El libro blanco de la reforma agraria. La Paz, 1954? 180 p.
A so-called white book on the agrarian reform in Bolivia, sponsored by the MNR. The book presents the agrarian reform as the present government and its party see it, and gives a phase-by-phase history of the reform. It enumerates the laws, decrees, and measures which the reform made necessary, and reprints public utterances on the merits of the reform, especially the words of President Paz Estenssoro.

1410. Guevara Arze, Wálter. Plan de política económica de la revolución nacional. La Paz, Ministerio de Relaciones Exteriores y Culto, 1955. 200 p., maps.
In conjunction with other key administrators in Bolivia, the author, a past foreign minister, reviews the economic problems of his country sector by sector and the plans to solve them through the development of Bolivia's native re-

sources and the acceptance of foreign, especially U. S. assistance. Valuable maps and statistics.

1411. Núñez Rosales, José. La estrategia capitalista para combatir las instituciones estatales. La Paz, Universo, 1954. 147 p.
A collection of articles written at the turn of 1949 to 1950 and published in the Bolivian newspaper Última hora. The author was at that time general manager of the Bolivian Mining Bank. He defends the activities of the state bank and compares them with the actions of the large mining corporations and their leaders. The comparison turns out all well for the bank and rather badly for the large companies.

CHILE

1412. Laherrere, Raymond. Reflexiones sobre la economía chilena. Santiago, Zig-Zag, 1953. 162 p.
A speculative treatise on the ills and cures of the Chilean economy. A lengthy discussion of Chilean inflation, and a theoretical exposition of monetary and credit measures that can cure it. A plea for full use of Chile's resources and for an intensified campaign for foreign investments in Chile. The author's philosophical approach to the problems of Chile make the book somewhat unrealistic.

1413. Margaño Mena, Carlos. Hacia el reino del consumidor. Santiago, 1953. 118 p.
A short treatise on low-cost housing for the working classes. A plea is made for home-ownership on a cooperative basis in the light of existing social conditions in Chile. The theoretical and partisan approach of the author narrows the scope of the study.

1414. Pinto, Aníbal. Hacia nuestra independencia económica. Santiago, Editorial del Pacífico (Col. Estudios económico-sociales, 7), 1953. 219 p.
Based to a large extent on the findings of the Economic Commission for Latin America of the United Nations and the views of its director, Dr. Raúl Prebisch, the author undertakes a painstaking study of the concepts of economic planning for the development of a country like Chile. Using economic freedom and economic democracy as the goal towards which Chile should strive, the book is not without polemic. The argument and the material used are, however, of scientific strictness.

1415. Vila, Tomás. Recursos minerales no-metálicos de Chile. 3. ed. actualizada. Santiago, Editorial Universitaria, 1953. 449 p.
A thorough presentation of the nonmetallic minerals in Chile. The data include physical locations, geological characteristics, status of exploitation, market qualities, prices and export data for the products. The work is extensive and very scholarly and covers 26 nonmetallic major mineral groups.

COLOMBIA

1416. Angarita Niño, Marco J. Eco-

nomía e industria del petróleo en Colombia. Bogotá, Comando General de las Fuerzas Militares (Biblioteca del oficial, 32), 1953. 298 p., graphs, tables.
A thesis in economics, it considers the whole of the petroleum industry in the world in general and in Colombia in particular. Geophysical data are followed by economic and statistical information, useful especially where it deals with Colombia. Special reference is made in the fourth part of the book to the significance of oil in a war economy, taking Colombia as a hypothetical example.

1417. Cañón, José J. Aspectos económicos de la ganadería en Colombia. 2. ed. Bogotá, Ministerio de Agricultura, 1952, i.e. 1953. 118 p., illus.
A descriptive exposition of cattle raising in Colombia for recent years. Geographic and veterinary data are followed by information on investments in land and animals. The volume of animal products and its value are treated equally with market and price problems. Domestic consumption and exports of animals are also part of the discussion, which is accompanied by graphs and tables.

1418. Cavelier, Germán. A statement of the laws of Colombia in matters affecting business. 2d ed., revised and enlarged. Washington, Pan American Union, Division of Law and Treaties, 1953. 186 p.
A synopsis of the laws of Colombia as they affect individual persons and businesses, national or foreign. All major subjects of constitutional, civil, and commercial law are touched upon, and adequate sources for further reference are given.

1419. Colombia. Contraloría General de la República. Economía colombiana. Revista. Año 1, v. 1, no. 1, mayo 1954.
A new periodical. It deals with economic subjects exclusively. The presentation of the topics, which cover the Colombian economic panorama, is semi-scientific. The easily read text is accompanied by graphs, statistics, and cartoon-like pictures. A bibliography of economic books, however, reveals the serious intent.

1420. —————. Departamento Administrativo Nacional de Estadística. Directorio industrial nacional (industria manufacturera colombiana), 1952-1953. Bogotá, 1953. 248 p.
A directory of firms employing more than three employees. Classified by industrial activity and geographical location.

1421. —————. Dirección Nacional de Planeación Económica y Fiscal. Plan de Santander, 1954-1958. Bogotá, 1955. 87 p.
A detailed plan for the development of the department of Santander. Graphs and statistics of the economic, climatic, and geographic facts of the area underpin the development scheme which lists in detail the investments that must be made between 1954 and 1958 to meet the requirements of the project.

1422. —————. Superintendencia Bancaria. Los seguros: aspectos técnicos, comerciales, económicos, jurídicos y sociales. Bogotá, 1954. 236 p.
A symposium on various aspects of insurance in Colombia. Some chapters deal with different types of insurance such as life, fire, maritime, and social insurance. Other chapters attend to the technical details of the insurance contract, again others with the duties of the insurance agent and the social and economic significance of the insurance system.

1423. Cruz Santos, Abel. Temas de economía. Bogotá, Minerva, 1953. 263 p.
A well-organized textbook on economics. It considers past and present theories and institutions. Contains useful references to special economic facts and organizations in Colombia. It is best described as a college text.

1424. Villaveces R., Carlos. Economía y fomento. Bogotá, Imp. Nacional, 1953. 168 p.
A collection of speeches and public utterances of the Colombian Minister of Economic Development in 1952 and 1953, followed by the text of decrees to which the minister referred in his statements. The book is interesting as a personal document for a brief period of Colombia's economic history.

1425. —————. Política fiscal y reforma tributaria. Bogotá, Imp. Nacional, 1953. 115 p.
Essentially a collection of speeches by Finance Minister Villaveces on fiscal and economic problems and on the tax reform of 1953. A speech of President Rojas Pinilla on the reform, and the text of the legislation, are also reproduced.

CUBA

1426. Banco Nacional de Cuba. Revista del . . . . Habana. Año 1, no. 1, enero de 1955.
The first issue of the Revista of Cuba's National Bank. It contains an essay on Cuba's national economy, another on national and international aspects of Cuba's economy. An article on national income follows. The slender issue ends with excellent statistical tables of essential financial and commodity data. It also contains a bibliography of books and periodicals which the National Bank's library received in January 1955.

1427. Casas Fernández, Baldomero. Un análisis de la política azucarera cubana. Conferencia dictada por . . . ante el Instituto de Investigaciones Económicas, Universidad de Oriente. Santiago, Cuba, El Siglo XX, 1955. 29 p.
A lecture on Cuba's sugar policies. The author outlines the facts of the policies on the basis of Cuba's special economic problems. He then

collates them with the International Sugar Convention and with the island's particular economic relations with the U. S. To all this he adds his personal criticisms.

1428. Cuba. Comisión Nacional de Propaganda y Defensa del Tabaco Habano. Memoria de la labor realizada durante los años de 1946-1950. Habana, Lex, 1953. 552 p., illus.
A report on the work of the National Committee for the Promotion and Defense of Habana Tobacco. The volume consists of brief reports for each calendar year of the period. The individual annual reports deal with tobacco experiments, exports, advertising, tobacco legislation, and miscellaneous questions of the period, and contain statistics.

1429. ————. ————. Memoria de la labor realizada durante los años de 1951-1952. Habana, 1953. 238 p., illus.
A report on the work of the National Committee for the Promotion and Defense of Habana Tobacco. See also item above.

1430. López Fresquet, Rufo. El año económico de 1952-1953. Habana, Lex, 1953. 403 p.
A collection of articles written by the author as columnist for the Cuban newspaper *El mundo*. They deal with every aspect of current economic life in Cuba as well as with some international problems. Economic journalism, not scholarly.

1431. Masnata de Quesada, David. Tributación de la industria azucarera. Habana, Lex, 1953. 137 p.
An enlarged reproduction of a brief submitted in November 1953 to the first National Forum in Defense of Sugar at Santiago, Cuba. A detailed enumeration of all direct taxes and imports on sugar through all stages of the sugar economy. The history, the scale, and the manner of collection of each tax are laid out minutely. Criticisms and suggestions for tax reforms are another vital part of the essay.

DOMINICAN REPUBLIC

1432. Pan American Union. Division of Law and Treaties. Selected bibliography on legal and related matters affecting business in the Dominican Republic. Washington, 1953. 5 p.
A selected bibliography of books essentially published in Ciudad Trujillo on various phases of the law: administrative and constitutional law, bankruptcy and commercial law, corporations and money and banking, social security, and international law. The bibliography includes works from 1930 on.

1434. Tellado (hijo), Antonio. A statement of the laws of the Dominican Republic in matters affecting business. 2d ed., revised and enlarged. Washington, Pan American Union, Division of Law and Treaties, 1953. 209 p.

A synopsis of the laws of the Dominican Republic as they affect individual persons and businesses. All major subjects of constitutional, civil, and commercial law are touched upon, and adequate sources for further reference are given.

EL SALVADOR

1435. Ehrhardt, Lucien Andre. La hacienda pública en El Salvador. Preparado para el gobierno de El Salvador. N. Y., Naciones Unidas, Programa de Asistencia Técnica, 1954. 125 p. (Doc. ST/TAA/K/ El Salvador/6).
A short study on El Salvador's public finance system. The bulk of the book deals with the budget and examines the items of income and expenditure. The appendices include brief reviews of the budget for the autonomous institutions, of the extraordinary budget, and of El Salvador's public debt.

1436. El Salvador. Dirección General de Estadística y Censos. Primer censo industrial y comercial, 1951. V. 1. San Salvador, 1955. 334 p., tables.
Though actually an agricultural economy, commerce and industry have made their mark in El Salvador. To establish their magnitude, this first census presents data on the essential features of the different industries, their products and personnel. The appendices give the legal bases of the census and the forms used.

1437. ————. Ministerio de Economía. Proyecto de aprovechamiento hidroeléctrico del Río Lempa. Antecedentes y documentos, 1949-1951. San Salvador, 1953. 2 v. 350; 357-763 p.
A report on the use of the river Lempa in El Salvador for the generation of electric power. The individual parts of the report deal with the background legislation, the engineering aspects of the project, the mission of the World Bank to El Salvador to appraise the financial feasibility of the undertaking, the negotiations and the contracts with the World Bank, the issue of bonds for the financing of the project in the local market, and the start of the project.

1438. Hoselitz, Bert F. Desarrollo industrial de El Salvador. Preparado para el gobierno de El Salvador. N. Y., Naciones Unidas, Programa de Asistencia Técnica, 1954. 107 p. (Doc. ST/TAA/K/El Salvador/10).
A report on the industrial development of El Salvador. The report studies the raw material situation in El Salvador, the industrial structure of the country, the expansion and diversification possibilities for the native industries, as well as the problems of foreign trade and development finance. The text is accompanied by statistical data.

1439. Lundell, John E. Telecommunications in El Salvador. Prepared for the government of El Salvador. N. Y., United Nations, Technical Assistance Pro-

gramme (Doc. ST/TAA/K/El Salvador/4), 1954. 78 p.
A detailed description of all types of telecommunications that exist in El Salvador. The technical and the administrative sides of the subject are equally well laid out. The geographic distribution of the system and the statistical magnitudes are minutely enumerated.

1440. **Moureau, Karl.** Producción y distribución de energía eléctrica en El Salvador. Preparado para el gobierno de El Salvador. N. Y., United Nations, Technical Assistance Program, 1954. 97 p., ilus., fold. map in pocket. (UN [doc] ST/TAA/K/El Salvador/7).
A detailed description of the electrical industry in El Salvador. The production of hydroelectric and thermoelectric power plants, their location and problems, are thoroughly described, and a full account is given of the electric companies, the rates, the legislation, and the financing of the industry. The volume contains valuable graphs and statistics.

1441. **Ortiz, Ricardo M.** The harbor system of El Salvador. Prepared for the government of El Salvador. N. Y., United Nations, Technical Assistance Program (Doc. ST/TAA/K/El Salvador/3), 1954. 140 p. and fold. maps.
A study of the economic activities of the people of El Salvador and the population data of the country precedes a detailed study of all the ports of the republic as to their technical, geographic, and administrative aspects. Special recommendations by the author for the future of the harbors conclude the work, which also contains valuable maps and statistics.

GUATEMALA

1442. Censo cafetalero, 1950 (B Direc Gen Est, Guatemala, 44-45, agosto-oct. 1953, p. 1-187, tables).
A part of the general agricultural census of 1950, this volume presents comprehensive coffee statistics. Nearly 185 pages give information about all details of Guatemalan coffee as to production, quality, location, grades, plantations, workers and supervisors, areas under cultivation, warehousing and transportation; but no price or export statistics are given. The method and the purpose of the census are explained.

1443. **Goicolea Villacorta, Domingo.** Proteccionismo industrial en Guatemala. Guatemala, Universidad de San Carlos de Guatemala, Facultad de Ciencias Económicas, 1955. 318 p., graphs, tables.
A review of Guatemala's economic development opens the discussion. A description of the authorities entrusted with one aspect or another of industrial development precedes the presentation of measures taken for the development of selected industries. Statistical tables and graphs and excerpts from pertinent legal texts amplify the thorough study. Thesis.

1444. **Guatemala. Ministerio de Eco-**

nomía y Trabajo. Decreto número 445. Reglamento del código de petróleo. Guatemala, 1955. 140 p.
The text of the regulations accompanying the Petroleum Code of Guatemala and as such an important appendix to the Code itself.

1445. **Rodas Cruz, Manuel.** El cooperativismo. El movimiento cooperativo en Guatemala y su legislación. Guatemala, Tip. Nacional, 1954. 98 p.
In the first part of the book the cooperative movement is followed in its theory and realization with main reference to France, Germany, and Great Britain. The second part describes the development of cooperatives in Guatemala, discusses the legal provisions for cooperatives, and gives a survey of existing cooperatives in Guatemala. Thesis, University of San Carlos, Guatemala.

1446. **Toledo Morán, Salvador.** Bases para una política petrolera en Guatemala. Guatemala, Universidad de San Carlos de Guatemala, Facultad de Ciencias Económicas, 1955. 74 p.
The author discusses the possible regulation of the petroleum industry in Guatemala, should enough oil be found to make the industry profitable. While he would prefer a State-owned and State-operated industry, he realizes that private capital, and indeed foreign corporations, will have to be invited for the exploitation of the possible mineral wealth. A short but point-by-point review of the problems thus presenting themselves to Guatemala form the core of the small volume. Thesis.

HONDURAS

1447. **Honduras. Dirección General de Censos y Estadísticas.** Primer censo agropecuario, 1952. Tegucigalpa (printed in San Salvador), 1954. 592 p., maps, tables.
The first census of agriculture. The tables are preceded by explanatory notes on how the census was taken. The statistics show the number and the size of the farms in different areas of the country, and data on land tenure. They also show figures on products and plants and cattle.

1448. **Osorio Pavón, Jorge.** Mercado de dinero y posibilidades de un mercado de valores en la República de Honduras. México, Universidad Nacional Autónoma de México, Escuela Nacional de Economía, 1955. 129 p. & tables.
Discusses the money market and the possibilities for an organized securities market in Honduras. The parts dealing with Honduras' central bank and fiscal organization contain valuable information. A review of business in Honduras is equally interesting. Thesis.

1449. **Tosco, M., and M. Napky.** Ingresos del gobierno local, 1924-25—1951-52. Tegucigalpa, Banco Central de Honduras, 1953. 70 p.

A comprehensive review of local income of municipal and provincial units in Honduras. All sources of taxes, customs duties, imports, and fees and fines are listed and explained. Statistical tables for the period 1924-1952 show the actual proceeds from the different sources. Values are given in the local currency.

PERU

1450. Ferrero, Rómulo A. La historia monetaria del Perú en el presente siglo. Lima, Tip. Peruana, 1953. 23 p.

A very short monetary history of Peru for the span 1900-1953, dividing the periods encompassed according to the existence of the free gold standard, the gold exchange standard, the paper standard, and the various types of exchange controls. The succinct presentation contains valuable statistics which increase the lucidity of the study.

1451. International Petroleum Company, Ltd. Petróleo. Aspectos de su industrialización en el Perú y en el mundo. Lima, 1954. 256 p., illus.

A book on petroleum, its geology and technology. Discusses the organization of the industry internationally and in Peru particularly. Great detail is devoted to the Peruvian oil industry, its structure, production, exports, and consumption.

1452. Perú. Instituto Nacional de Investigación y Fomento Mineros. División de Estadística y Economía Mineras. Anuario de la industria minera del Perú en 1953. Breve reseña de la minería peruana en los últimos cincuenta años (1903-1953). Lima, 1954. 361 p., tables. (Boletín, 11).

The yearbook giving the pertinent data for all metals and nonmetallic minerals produced in Peru in 1953. Total and regional tables are presented, and comparisons with statistics of previous years are offered. The tabulations are accompanied by brief and lucid textual interpretations.

1453. Sociedad Nacional de Industrias. Panorama económico del Perú en 1952-1953. Lima, Tip. Peruana, 1955. 183 p.

A succinct survey of all business activities in Peru, from agriculture through mining and forestry to manufacturing and banking. Important business units are briefly described, statistical reviews of whole economic branches presented, lists of all national products offered, development plans and service industries discussed.

1454. Torre, Benjamín de la. Perú: statistical and economic review. London, Tinling, 1953. 112 p., illus.

A brief guide through the economic activities and geographic points of interest in Peru. The statistical data are for first glance information, but are not a source for research. Pictures and maps enliven the narrative.

PANAMA

1455. Panamá. Dirección de Estadística y Censo. Censos nacionales de 1950. Primer censo agropecuario. V. 1. Producción. Panamá, 1954. 310 p., tables.

National census of agricultural production and livestock by product and region. A few historical data precede the tables as do pages of definitions and explanations.

1456. ———. ———. Estudio de los ingresos, gastos y costo de la vida, Ciudad de Panamá, 1952-1953. Preparado . . . por Pauline B. Paro. . . . Panamá, 1954. 99 p., tables & map.

A detailed study of the cost of living of the individual family in Panama City in 1952-1953. The analysis of the "typical" family precedes the analysis of their typical costs. The methods of establishing the index are discussed. The data, presented with ample statistical material, are based on interviews with housewives, social workers, and suppliers of the goods and services which make up the cost-of-living index.

1457. Rijken van Olst, H. El ingreso nacional y las cuentas nacionales de la República de Panamá: años 1944-1952. Panamá, Dirección de Estadística y Censo, 1953. 88 p., tables.

A useful presentation of the national income of Panama for the years 1944-1952. The text gives a ready explanation of the items composing the national accounts. The statistical tables are comprehensive in their detail. Values are indicated in balboas and U. S. dollars.

VENEZUELA

1458. Baptista, Federico G. Breve reseña histórica de la industria petrolera en Venezuela. Caracas, Excélsior, 1955. 40 p., illus. & tables.

A brief narrative of oil development in Venezuela and an account of the participation of the international petroleum companies in Venezuelan oil production. A tabular presentation of the existing oil fields and their yield make the booklet a valuable introduction to Venezuelan oil.

1459. Corporación Venezolana de Fomento. Objetivos y doctrina económica de la C. V. F. Caracas, Ragon, 1955? 31 p.

An analysis of the tasks of the Venezuelan Development Corporation. The Corporation is charged with seeing to completion a plan for the electrification of the country, a plan for providing the nation with enough sugar and rice, a plan to promote large investments which existing financial institutions cannot underwrite. The Corporation shall establish a regional system of development banks to bring about the necessary local financing of economic development. Another major task of the Corporation is to organize systematic economic research to help it in its tasks.

1460. **Mehren, George L.** El mercadeo de los productos agrícolas en Venezuela. Caracas, Consejo de Bienestar Rural, 1954. 206 p. & illus.
A thorough study of the conditions of the marketing of Venezuelan agricultural products and livestock. Every item of the agricultural sector of the Venezuelan economy is described in its physical and economic aspects. The deficiencies of marketing methods for each agricultural product are presented, as are comparisons with American and European types of farming and recommendations for Venezuela. Export and import problems are reviewed, and the role of the government in agricultural marketing thoroughly scrutinized.

1461. **United States. Department of State.** Venezuela: oil transforms a nation. Washington, 1953. 11 p., illus. (Publ. 4946; Inter-American series 45).
A brief pictorial, graphic, and textual description of the impact of the oil industry in Venezuela on the country and its people. The very succinct description contains a multitude of historical data from the early beginnings of Venezuela to the present time.

1462. **Venezuela. Consejo de Bienestar Rural.** Problemas económicos y sociales de los Andes venezolanos. Parte 1. Caracas? 1955? 331 p., illus., tables.
A detailed survey of historical and anthroposociological facts in the Venezuelan Andes. All problems of the economy of the region, including the human factor, agriculture and cattle, water problems, and transportation facilities are considered. Maps of particular areas, pictorial devices, statistics, and photographs.

1463. ————. **Instituto Agrario Nacional.** Aspectos de la reforma agraria en Venezuela. Caracas, 1954. 52 p., illus.
The pamphlet gives a brief survey on the colonization projects of the government's agrarian reform. Colonists, native and immigrant, are depicted and described in their daily activities. Figures on the actual production and the planned output of the settlements are given. The general statistics and good photographs put the problem of the agrarian reform in good perspective.

1464. ————. **Servicio Informativo Venezolano.** Venezuela bajo el nuevo ideal nacional. Realizaciones durante el gobierno del Coronel Marcos Pérez Jiménez, 2 de diciembre de 1952—19 de abril de 1954. Caracas, 1954. 134 p., graphs & illus.
The book deals with the achievements of the regime of Col. Marcos Pérez Jiménez. A short biographical sketch of the president is followed by the reproduction of seven of his speeches between 1952 and 1954. A review of the economic data of Venezuela is followed by a tabular list of government activities and successes in various sectors of the economy. A reproduction of press comments on the regime, a selection of the president's personal maxims,

and a series of photographs of Venezuelan highlights form the last part of the book.

OTHER AREAS

1465. **American Academy of Political and Social Science.** Puerto Rico, a study in demographic development (A Am Ac Pol Soc Sci, 285, Jan. 1953, 246 p.).
A special issue of the *Annals* devoted to Puerto Rico of today. 21 brief sketches cover in bold strokes major aspects of political and economic development, the fusion of cultures, population problems, and prospects for the future. An array of brilliant authors of different backgrounds assures a diversified discussion of the problems of the Commonwealth.

1466. **Banco Central de Costa Rica.** Ley orgánica del. . . . San José, 1953? 24 p.
The text of the organic law of Costa Rica's central bank, followed by general legal provisions and transitory regulations.

1467. **Benoit, Pierre V.** Évolution budgétaire et développement économique d'Haïti. Port-au-Prince, Deschamps, 1954. 134 p., tables.
A study of the Haitian budget, its legal sources, its components and its development over the last 120 years. The study tries to present the influence of the budget on the economic development of the Haitian Republic. The statistical tables should prove helpful to any researcher in the field.

1468. **Carey Jones, N. S.** The pattern of a dependent economy. The national income of British Honduras. Cambridge, England, Cambridge University Press, 1953. 162 p., illus.
A short, learned discussion of national income in a British colony. Official data of the colony's government are supplemented by data the author collected in various ways over several years in British Honduras. His findings are presented in national income tables which are discussed as to sources and methods used.

1469. **Couture, Eduardo J., and H. Barbagelata.** A statement of the laws of Uruguay in matters affecting business. 2d. ed. Washington, Pan American Union, Division of Laws and Treaties, 1952, i. e. 1953. 122 p.
A summary of the principal provisions of the laws and regulations which may in one way or another affect business activities in Uruguay. Problems of immigration, nationality, taxation, banking, insurance, and currency are discussed, along with a review of commercial, patent, trademark, and copyright legislation. Legal sources are indicated, and may serve for further research.

1470. **Eastman, Samuel Ewer, and Daniel Marx, Jr.** Ships and sugar. An evaluation of Puerto Rican offshore shipping.

Río Piedras, University of Puerto Rico Press, 1953. 239 p., illus., maps.
This study is the final report of the External Transportation Project, maintained by the University of Puerto Rico and four shipping companies partaking in Puerto Rican water transport. It assembles as much information on the island's external transportation as public and private records would yield at this time, and also analyzes the various aspects of ocean freight moving between the island and the U. S. Its statistics and source references up to the very present are very useful.

1471. International Bank for Reconstruction and Development. The economic development of Nicaragua. Report of a mission organized by the . . . at the request of the government of Nicaragua. Baltimore, Md., Johns Hopkins Press, 1953. 424 p.
This report consists of five parts. Part 1 is the main report, recommending a five-year development program. Parts 2 and 3 include a review of industries, power, mining, and transportation and communications in their present stages. Part 4 does the same for agriculture and part 5 for the fiscal system. The report is condensed and matter-of-fact.

1472. Moore, O. Ernest. Monetary-fiscal policy and economic development in Haiti (Pub Fin, 9me année, 9:3, oct. 1954, p. 230-256).
The author, a UN financial expert with the Haitian government, gives a historical and institutional review of the fiscal and monetary problems of Haiti in relation to the Republic's development. The presentation is brief but thorough.

1473. Sancho Castro, Álvaro. Comercio internacional de Costa Rica (R Banco Cent, C R, 17, marzo 1954, p. 62-88).
A brief description of the items and problems of Costa Rica's balance of payments during the years 1948-1953. Special reference is made to the foreign exchange income of the country and to the direction of trade according to countries. The statistics are based on data of the General Bureau of Statistics and the census and of the Central Bank of Costa Rica.

1474. Sapena Pastor, Raúl. A statement of the laws of Paraguay in matters affecting business. Washington, Pan American Union, Division of Law and Treaties, 1953. 138 p.
A summary of the principal provisions of the laws and regulation which may in one way or another affect business activities in Paraguay. Problems of immigration, nationality, taxation, banking, insurance, and currency are discussed, along with a review of commercial, patent, trademark, and copyright legislation. Legal sources are included, and may serve for further research.

1475. Williams, Gertrude. The economics of everyday life in the West Indies. Kingston, Jamaica, Extra-Mural Department, University College of the West Indies, 1953. 52 p.
At head of title: Caribbean Affairs. A brief scholarly essay on the economics of the West Indies. Three topics are treated: the economic activities of the area, the currency problem of a region caught between the dollar and the sterling power, and the standard of living of the native population.

BRAZIL

HENRY WILLIAM SPIEGEL

1700. As soluções indicadas pela Comissão Mista Brasil-EE.UU. (Obs Ec Fin, 20: 230, abril 1955, p. 27-55; 231, maio, p. 26-53; 232, junho, p. 36-63; 233, julho, p. 51-63; 236, out., p. 22-41; 237, nov., p. 39-48; 238, dez. 1955, p. 42-55).
Selections from a new report of the U. S.-Brazil Development Commission.

1701. Banco do Brasil. Relatório apresentado à assembléia geral ordinária dos acionistas realizada em 25 de abril de 1955. Rio, 1955. 462 p., tables.
A continuation of this indispensable reference work along customary lines of completeness and reliability.

1702. Barros, Henrique de. A estrutura agrária como obstáculo à ação agronômica. A reforma agrária como problema econômico. São Paulo, Escola de Socio-

logia e Política de São Paulo (Estudos de economia teórica e aplicada, 7), 1954. 40 p.
General thoughts about land reform and agricultural structure. The author is an employee of FOA.

1703. Bastos, Humberto. A crise comercial. Aspectos da conjuntura do comércio exterior. São Paulo, Martins, 1953. 114 p.
The foreign-trade position of Brazil and other Latin American regions is discussed here with the view of finding means for improvement. The proposals of the author include relaxation of export duties and other benefits to exporters, domestic reforms, etc.

1704. ————. País de bolsos vazios. São Paulo, Martins, 1955. 188 p.
Thoughts on miscellaneous economic and financial subjects of current significance, with especial emphasis on government policies, which

are subjected to a critical though unsystematic review.

1705. Brazil. Comissão de Abastecimento do Nordeste. O que foi a CAN: suas atividades, seus planos, suas contas. Rio, 1953. 207 p.
Documents and statistics relating to government efforts aiming at the relief of northern Brazilian regions from the effects of periodic droughts.

1706. ————. Conselho Nacional do Petróleo. Relatório de 1952. Rio, 1954. 276 p. & illus., maps, tables.
Continuation of the report of the government agency in charge of petroleum development.

1707. ————. Diretoria de Aeronáutica Civil. Divisão do Tráfego. Secção de Estatística. Estatística do tráfego aéreo comercial, 1953. Unpaged, tables.
Statistics of civil aviation, indicating an impressive rate of growth during the past 10 years.

1708. ————. Instituto de Pesquisas Tecnológicas. Relatório das atividades desenvolvidas em 1952. . . . São Paulo, 1953. 52 p., illus.
Annual report of this technological research agency which now employs 69 professional people and 287 others.

1709. ————. Instituto de Resseguros do Brasil. Relatório. Décimo quarto exercício, janeiro a dezembro de 1953. (Publ., 53). Rio, 1954. 289 p., tables.
Continuation of the report of the government reinsurance organization.

1710. ————. Instituto Nacional do Mate. Boletim estatístico, 1952. Rio, 1953. 43 p.
Production, trade, and consumption of mate.

1711. ————. Ministério do Trabalho, Indústria e Comércio. Índice do Boletim do Ministério do Trabalho, Indústria e Comércio. Nos 101 a 147. Rio, Serviço de Documentação, 1953. 196 p., tables.
Index volume, indispensable for users of this important periodical.

1712. Camargo, Rogério de, and Adalberto de Queiroz Telles Jr. O café no Brasil: sua aclimação e industrialização. Rio, Ministério da Agricultura, Serviço de Informação Agrícola (Série Estudos brasileiros, 4), 1953. 2 v. 535, 720 p. & illus.
This comprehensive study bids fair to become the standard source of reference with respect to the farm management aspects of coffee production. The book treats primarily of natural-science and technological matters. There are 50 pages on shade trees and more on fertilizer. The educational value of a work like this is potentially enormous.

1713. Carbano de Kretschmer, Elba. Análisis del comercio triguero. El mercado del Brasil. B. A., Universidad de Buenos Aires, Facultad de Agronomía y Veterinaria, Escuela de Agronomía (Publ., 2), 1953. 88 p., graphs, tables.
Brazil's wheat import position, as seen by a resident of Argentina. Argentina buys timber, coffee, and fruit from Brazil, while Brazil in turn has to rely on imports for the greater part of her wheat requirements. This trade, the author declares, is instrumental in creating close ties among Latin American countries.

1714. Carvalho, Joaquim Bertino de Moraes. Ensinar, pesquisar, documentar, cooperar. Dificuldades e facilidades do I. O. em 1952. Relatório de. . . . Rio, Ministério da Agricultura, Instituto de Óleos, 1953. 413 p.
Documentation and statistics relating to vegetable oil production and marketing.

1715. Figueiredo, Nuno Fidelino de. Dimensão e produtividade na indústria de São Paulo. São Paulo, Escola de Sociologia e Política de São Paulo (Estudos de economia teórica e aplicada, 6), 1953. 91 p., tables.
An investigation of the relationship between productivity and size of firm, wages, and related factors.

1716. ————. As gratificações ao pessoal e os lucros na indústria e no comércio. São Paulo, Escola de Sociologia e Política de São Paulo (Estudos de economia teórica e aplicada, 3), 1953. 32 p.
A statistical investigation of the relationship between wages and profits.

1717. ————. As reservas técnicas de seguros e de capitalização e o desenvolvimento econômico. São Paulo, Escola de Sociologia e Política de São Paulo (Estudos de economia teórica e aplicada, 4), 1953. 88 p.
The reserves of life insurance companies, their regulation, and how they can be utilized for development projects.

1718. Furtado, Celso. A economia brasileira. Contribuição à análise do seu desenvolvimento. Rio, A Noite, 1954. 246 p.
This new book by the well-known associate of Raúl Prebisch applies modern theories of economic development to the specific problems of Brazil. Mr. Furtado is abreast of current economic thought and makes original contributions of high value. One of the more important books in the field of economic theory.

1719. Hermes Filho, Gabriel. A Amazô-

nia e o problema da borracha (Obs Ec Fin, 20:238, dez. 1955, p. 20-26).
This and the article immediately following (see item 1723) contain information on current rubber requirements and domestic production.

1720. Instituto Rio Grandense do Arroz. 9.° anuário estatístico do arroz. Safra 1952-1953. Pôrto Alegre, Brazil, 1954. 120 p., tables.
Statistics on all aspects of the highly developed Rio Grande rice economy.

1721. Macedo, Jozé Norberto. Fazendas de gado no vale do São Francisco. Rio, Ministério da Agricultura, Serviço de Informação Agrícola (Documentário da vida rural, 3), 1952. 70 p., tables & illus.
A "rural life" study of the livestock economy of the São Francisco Valley.

1722. Marçal, Joseph N., Jr. Problemas de transporte no Brasil. Rio, Departamento Administrativo do Serviço Público, Serviço de Documentação, 1955, 9 p. "Separata da *Revista do Serviço Público* de abril de 1955."
An expert discussion of the Brazilian transportation problem with especial emphasis on maritime transportation. The author recommends government subsidization of private merchant shipping companies.

1723. Möller, Floriano. A borracha e os transportes no país (Obs Ec Fin, 20:238, dez. 1955, p. 28-33).
See also item 1719.

1724. Morse, Richard M. São Paulo in the twentieth century: social and economic aspects (Interam Ec Aff, 8:1, summer 1954, p. 3-60).
A lively and informative case study of rapid urbanization and its social consequences.

1725. Murray, Carl, and Jamil Munhoz Bailão. Panorama das finanças públicas do estado de São Paulo. São Paulo, Escola de Sociologia e Política de São Paulo (Estudos de economia teórica e aplicada, 8), 1954. 39 p., tables.
Statistics of interest to the student of regional economies.

1726. The Paraíba-Piraí diversion (Water Power, 5:8, Aug. 1953, p. 286-293).
A report on a hydroelectric power project designed to provide more energy for the Rio de Janeiro region.

1727. Pereira, Evaldo Simas. Trigo nacional: deficiências e escândalo (Obs Ec Fin, 20:229, março 1955, p. 66-71).
Current problems of the wheat economy.

1728. Pinto, Ariosto. A Caixa Econômica Federal do Rio de Janeiro em 1953.

Relatório. Rio, Gráfica Olímpica Editôra, 1954. 427 p., graphs, tables.
Continuation of this annual report of the Rio de Janeiro savings bank.

1729. Pôrto, Adolpho Faustino. Posição de Pernambuco na economia nacional. Recife, Brazil, Diretoria de Documentação e Cultura, Prefeitura Municipal do Recife, 1953? 79 p., illus.
Although economic activities continue to be concentrated in southern Brazil, expansion is noted also in the state of Pernambuco. The author traces recent regional developments and explores the obstacles facing the regional economy.

1730. Recuperação do solo e do homem brasileiros (Obs Ec Fin, 20:234, agôsto 1955, p. 50-86).
New ways in commercial fertilizer production.

1731. Revista de história da economia brasileira. São Paulo. Ano 1, no. 1, junho 1953.
A new scholarly periodical cultivating a field not formerly in the possession of such an outlet. The first issue carries a portrait and memorial to Roberto Simonsen and recalls his contribution to the economic history of Brazil. The issue contains articles, documents, and book reviews. The articles—by Hélio Schlittler Silva, Stanley J. Stein, and others—are of high quality. They treat mainly of 19th-century developments, except for one, which deals with the 18th-century sugar economy of Minas Gerais.

1732. Richers, Raimar. O café no comércio exterior do Brasil. São Paulo, 1954. 91 p., tables.
A careful investigation of the structure of foreign trade since the late 1930's with especial reference to the role of coffee exports.

1733. Rio Grande do Sul (state). Secretaria de Estado dos Negócios da Fazenda. Gabinete de Orçamento e Finanças. Organização do sistema orçamentário estadual. Pôrto Alegre, Brazil, 1953. 37 p.
Of interest to students of federal finance.

1734. Stein, Stanley J. The Brazilian cotton textile industry, 1850-1950 (Interam Ec Aff, 8:1, summer 1954, p. 69-91).
A scholarly study of this highly fluctuating industry, which, after temporary wartime prosperity, finds itself again confronted with the difficulties which faced it during the 1930's. The author thinks that the present situation contains an additional element of instability arising from the critical temper of the Brazilian consumer.

1735. Távora, Juarez. Petróleo para o Brasil. Rio, Olympio, 1955. 319 p.
This is a collection of studies undertaken since

1947 and all relating to various aspects of the Brazilian petroleum position. The author discusses a number of legislative proposals made during the last few years.

1736. Tourinho, Borba. Custo de um agrônomo na Universidade Rural: quase um milhão e meio (Obs Ec Fin, 20:231, maio 1955, p. 22-25).
The cost of technical training is high in per capita terms because of the low number of trainees. Proposals for reform.

1737. Viana, Arízio de. Organization of central offices and coordinating procedures required for the conduct of economic development and technical assistance programs. Rio, International Institute of Administrative Sciences, Serviço de Documentação do DASP (Publ., 487), 1955. 23 p.
Administrative problems related to development programs and technical assistance.

MEXICO

DIRECCIÓN DE INVESTIGACIONES ECONÓMICAS, NACIONAL FINANCIERA, S. A.

GENERAL

1850. Ahumada, Jorge. Preparación y evaluación de proyectos de desarrollo económico (Trim Ec, 22:3, julio-sept. 1955, p. 265-296, tables).
Ensayo sobre proyectos de desarrollo económico normados por la distribución de recursos, la técnica de producción y la selección adecuada de proyectos que deben elaborarse.

1851. Alanís Patiño, Emilio. La riqueza nacional (Inv Ec, 15:1, 1. trimestre 1955, p. 53-81, tables).
Datos anteriores a 1945, pero aún con valor actual para estimaciones y análisis. Estudio realizado a través de la dinámica de la economía mexicana y la composición de la riqueza nacional y su monto estimado en términos monetarios.

1852. Almacenes Nacionales de Depósito. Campeche, esquema social y económico. México, 1955. 31 p., map.

1853. ————. Coahuila, esquema social y económico. México, 1955. 40 p., map.

1854. ————. Estado de Baja California, esquema social y económico. México, 1955. 23 p., map.

1855. ————. Territorio de Baja California, esquema social y económico. México, 1955. 27 p., map.

1856. Arce Ibarra, Roxana. La navegación fluvial en el sistema del Río Papaloapan (Tráfico). México, Comisión del Papaloapan, 1955. 87 p., graphs, tables.
Este trabajo reúne antecedentes y datos de gran valor informativo que cubren la navegación fluvial en la Cuenca, en relación a su economía actual y sus perspectivas.

1857. Attolini, José. Geografía del mexicano (Inv Ec, 15:4, 4. trimestre 1955, p. 433-448).

Ensayo sobre la caracterización del medio geográfico del territorio nacional y su habitante, como base de las posibilidades actuales y futuras del mexicano y su economía.

1858. Ayensa, Alfonso. La escuela nacional de economía y los problemas del desarrollo económico de México (Inv Ec, 14:3, 3. trimestre 1954, p. 453-481).

1859. Banco de México, S. A. Bibliografía económica de México (B Trim, 1, 1955).

1860. Bravo, Manuel. Observaciones del Señor Manuel Bravo, Representante de México, relativas al Programa de Cooperación Técnica, en la Sesión de la Subcomisión 3 de la Comisión II, Asuntos Económicos, celebrada el 18 de marzo de 1954 (R Ec, México, 17:4, abril 1954, p. 108-113).
Décima Conferencia Interamericana.

1861. Bullejos, José. Diez años de literatura económica, 1943-1953. México, Escuela Nacional de Economía, Instituto de Investigaciones Económicas, 1954. 162 p.

1862. Campos Salas, Octaviano. El informe Randall (Com Ext, México, 4:2, febrero 1954, p. 51).
Expone los principales capítulos del informe y comenta los aspectos en que se beneficiaría México con la adopción de las medidas propuestas.

1863. Cardoso, Alfonso (and others). Experiencias en economía. Estudios sobre México, la India, Bolivia y la República Dominicana. México, EDIAPSA, 1953. 208 p.

1864. Carrillo Flores, Antonio. Condiciones actuales del desarrollo económico

de México. Discurso del Secretario de Hacienda y Crédito Público en la XXI Convención Bancaria (Prob Agr Ind Méx, 7:1, enero-marzo 1955, p. 325-332, illus.).
Publicado también en: *Revista bancaria*, 3:1, enero-feb. 1955, p. 82-88; *Bancos*, 5:5, mayo 1955, p. 8-11 ff.; *Revista fiscal y financiera*, 15:94, abril 1955, p. 11-25, illus.; *El mercado de valores*, 15:18, p. 208 ff. Junto con el informe presidencial (ver *El mercado de valores*, 15:36, sept. 5, 1955, p. 421 ff.), este documento constituye una de las fuentes más autorizadas sobre la situación económica de México.

1865. ————. La moderna función del gasto público (R Fisc Fin, 13:75, sept. 1953, p. 15-19).

1866. ————. Prosecución del esfuerzo constructivo para el bienestar del país (R Fisc Fin, 12:71, mayo 1953, p. 11-21).

1867. Cervantes Mejía, Rodolfo. La zona libre de Baja California: su desarrollo económico (R Ec, México, 18:3, marzo 1955, p. 74-82, tables).

1868. Confederación de Cámaras Industriales, Asamblea General Ordinaria, 1953. Posición y metas de la economía nacional. México, 1953. 46 p., illus.

1869. Consejo Interamericano de Comercio y Producción. Carta de México. México, 1954. 76 p.
Recomendaciones del VII Plenario del CICYP, celebrado en la ciudad de México, oct. 1954, y acuerdos aprobados en N. Y., oct. 1954.

1870. Cosío Villegas, Daniel. Lección de la barbarie. Comentario sobre *México bárbaro* (Prob Agr Ind Méx, 7:2, abril-junio 1955, p. 187-193).
Crítica y evalúa como historiador las fallas y aciertos de la obra *México bárbaro* de Turner. (Ver párrafo no. 1916).

1871. ———— (ed.). Historia moderna de México. La República restaurada. [T. 2]. La vida económica, por Francisco R. Calderón. México, Hermes, 1955. 812 p., illus., tables.
Esta obra constará de 6 v. Abarcará de 1887 a 1911, en dos períodos: 1867-1876, la República restaurada; 1877-1911, el Porfiriato. Cada período será relatado en 3 v.: 1, la vida política; 2, la económica, y 3, la social. (También está publicado *Vida política del país*, 1. período).

1872. Dekoster Fuentes, Pedro. Estudio económico de la costa de Hermosillo; desarrollo económico basado en el progreso de la agricultura. México, 1953. 200 p., illus., maps, tables.
Estudio económico regional de una zona

desértica transformada en productiva por medio del riego y la mecanización. Incluye un análisis demográfico. (Mención, Premio de Economía, Banco Nacional de México, 1953). Tesis.

1873. Diez Barroso, Fernando. El balance económico (Bancos, 5:3, marzo 1955, p. 6-9 ff., tables).

1874. Durán Ochoa, Julio. El crecimiento de la población mexicana (Trim Ec, 22:3, julio-sept. 1955, p. 331-349, tables).
El artículo corresponde al estudio *Población*, de la serie *Estructura económica y social de México*, realizado bajo el patrocinio de Nacional Financiera, S. A.

1875. ————. Población. México, Fondo de Cultura Económica (Estructura económica y social de México), 1955. 277 p., graphs, maps, tables.
Quinto volumen publicado de la obra que, bajo el rubro general de *Estructura económica y social de México*, realiza la Nacional Financiera a través de su Dirección de Investigaciones Económicas. (Ver párrafo 988 del *HLAS, no. 18, 1952*.) Estudio dividido en tres grandes partes: "Estado de la población," "Movimiento de la población" y "Política demográfica." En la primera parte se examina el aspecto estático de la población en comparación con otros países, subrayándose las tendencias que acusan los últimos censos nacionales. En la segunda, se analiza el aspecto dinámico, también sobre bases de comparación internacional, señalándose los elementos que determinan el movimiento y el crecimiento demográficos. La tercera parte es un ensayo tendiente a analizar los problemas de población, las medidas practicadas, los resultados obtenidos y la política que reclama la evolución demográfica de México.

1876. Escuela Nacional de Economía. La intervención del Estado en la economía. Cursos de invierno de 1955. México, Universidad Nacional Autónoma de México, Instituto de Investigaciones Económicas, 1955. 302 p., graphs, tables.
Recopilación de las conferencias y mesas redondas de los cursos de invierno de 1955 de la Escuela Nacional de Economía, que tuvieron como base de los temas desarrollados la intervención del Estado en la economía.

1877. ————. Niveles de vida y desarrollo económico. México, Universidad Nacional Autónoma de México, 1953. 306 p., tables.
Recopilación de las conferencias y mesas redondas de los cursos de invierno de 1953.

1878. ————. Problemas actuales de México. México, Universidad Nacional Autónoma de México, Instituto de Investigaciones Económicas, 1954. 164 p., tables.
Recopilación de las conferencias y mesas redondas de los cursos de invierno de 1954 de la Escuela Nacional de Economía.

1879. **Flores de la Peña, Horacio.** Crecimiento demográfico, desarrollo agrícola y desarrollo económico (Inv Ec, 14:4, 4. trimestre 1954, p. 519-535, map, tables).

1880. ————. Los obstáculos al desarrollo económico; el desequilibrio fundamental. México, Universidad Nacional Autónoma de México, Escuela Nacional de Economía, 1955. 168 p., graphs, tables.
Análisis de los problemas económicos funcionales que obstaculizan el desarrollo económico, a través de la elasticidad de la oferta, la mecánica de la inflación y la concentración del ingreso hasta el examen de la demanda efectiva. Tesis profesional.

1881. **García Treviño, Rodrigo.** Precios, salarios y mordidas. México, Editorial América, 1953. 302 p.

1882. **Ginstra-Bleeker, R. J. P. van.** Algunos aspectos de la emigración y la inmigración (Inv Ec, 18:1, 1. trimestre 1953, p. 27-53).

1883. **González Ramírez, Manuel.** Los planes políticos y la revolución (Prob Agr Ind Méx, 7:2, abril-junio 1955, p. 195-213).
Ensayo sobre la caracterización de la Revolución Mexicana, con un análisis de los problemas obreros y agrarios del país.

1884. **González Rojo, Enrique** ¿Insuficiencia del mexicano o insuficiencia económica del mexicano? (Cuad Am, año 12, 69:3, mayo-junio 1953, p. 98-109).

1885. **Goodspeed, Stephen Spencer.** El papel del jefe del ejecutivo en México (Prob Agr Ind Méx, 7:1, enero-marzo 1955, p. 13-208, illus.).
Biografía de cada uno de los regímenes revolucionarios a través de los hombres que ocuparon la presidencia del país. Finaliza con un estudio legal, político y económico del Ejecutivo como poder dominante en México. Acompaña a este trabajo una valiosa colección de caricaturas políticas, tomadas de la Hemeroteca Nacional de México.

1886. **Instituto Panamericano de Geografía e Historia.** Los estudios sobre los recursos naturales en las Américas. T. 4. Estudio preliminar en México. México, 1953-1954. 2 v. 1. parte, Investigación, 505 p., illus., maps, tables; 2. parte, Enseñanza, 431 p.

1887. **Lombardo Toledano, Vicente.** La perspectiva de México: una democracia del pueblo (Prob Agr Ind Méx, 7:2, abril-junio 1955, p. 247-280).
Analiza y critica desde el punto de vista histórico, político y económico la situación actual de México y sus perspectivas.

1888. **López Rosado, Diego G.** La política de elevación de los niveles de vida (Inv Ec, 13:3, 3. trimestre 1953, p. 295-322).

1889. **Lurie, Samuel.** Estabilidad y desarrollo económico. México, Centro de Estudios Monetarios Latinoamericanos, 1955. 157 p., tables.
Análisis teórico a través del ingreso nacional y su composición de los problemas de desarrollo económico, con referencia a América Latina y México.

1890. **McWilliams, [Carey].** Los cuervos vuelan hacia el norte (Prob Agr Ind Méx, 6:2, abril-junio 1954, p. 171-182).
Traducción del capítulo 13 de la obra *Ill fares the land*, por McWilliams, en que se describen las condiciones del trabajo agrícola migratorio en los Estados Unidos, en la década 1940-1950.

1891. **Maldonado, Adolfo.** La economía cooperativa en México. México, Banco Nacional de Fomento Cooperativo, S. A., 1955. 204 p.
Estudio del cooperativismo dentro de la teoría económica. El movimiento cooperativista en México desde el punto de vista económico y jurídico.

1892. **Mancera Ortiz, Rafael.** Actitud de México ante los programas de desarrollo (R Fisc Fin, 14:82, abril 1954, p. 29-41).
Ponencia presentada en el IX Congreso Internacional de Ciencias Administrativas, 1953.

1893. **Margain, Hugo B.** El derecho, la economía y la contabilidad en el derecho fiscal (R Fisc Fin, 15:99, sept. 1955, p. 9-34).

1894. ————. La política hacendaria y la industrialización de México (R Fisc Fin, 15:89, nov. 1954, p. 9-18, illus.).

1895. **Martín Echeverría, Leonardo.** La leyenda dorada sobre la riqueza de México (Inv Ec, 14:2, 2. trimestre 1954, p. 231-287).
El presente artículo constituye la introducción histórica a un estudio en preparación sobre los recursos naturales de México.

1896. **Martínez Domínguez, Guillermo.** Propuestas prácticas para elevar los niveles de vida (Inv Ec, 13:3, 3. trimestre 1953, p. 393-417).

1897. **Molina Enríquez, Andrés.** Los grandes problemas nacionales (Prob Agr Ind Méx, 5:1, enero-marzo 1953, suple., p. 9-197, illus).
Contenido: Los antecedentes indeclinables; Los problemas de orden primordial.

1898. Moore, Wilbert E. El impacto del industrialismo en la población (Prob Agr Ind Méx, 6:2, abril-junio 1954, p. 1-166, graphs, illus., tables; comentarios, p. 183-222).

Estudia la importancia que el abastecimiento adecuado de mano de obra tiene para la economía mexicana en desarrollo. Se basa en la población de una región seleccionada por sus características como representativa del problema. Al final se presentan comentarios a la obra: "Moore y la trasculturación en México," por Pedro Armillas; "La obra de Moore: síntesis y consideraciones," por Wigberto Jiménez Moreno; "Consideraciones sobre el *Impacto del industrialismo en la población,*" por Alejandro D. Marroquín; "Las limitaciones del industrialismo moderno," por Arturo Monzón; "Moore: *idéologo* del Punto IV," por Antonio Pérez Elías; "Síntesis crítica del estudio de Wilbert E. Moore," por Roberto J. Weitlaner.

1899. Moreno Sánchez, Manuel. Mas allá de la revolución mexicana (Prob Agr Ind Méx, 7:2, abril-junio 1955, p. 215-245).

Pretende revisar el movimiento revolucionario en función de los problemas actuales del país, para darles una solución distinta al espíritu económico y social de la Revolución Mexicana.

1900. Nathan, Paul. México en la época de Cárdenas (Prob Agr Ind Méx, 7:3, julio-sept. 1955, p. 17-176, illus.; comentarios, p. 177-262).

Trabajo muy criticado por sus deficiencias. Acompañan al trabajo los siguientes comentarios: "Un México de Tepalcate," por José Alvarado; "Cárdenas y el Cardenismo," por Victoriano Anguiano; "Hechos y no palabras," por Silvano Barba González; "El Cardenismo en la Revolución Mexicana," por Valentin Campa; "Significación del Cardenismo," por R. García Treviño; "Un estudio norteamericano sobre Cárdenas; ejemplo de un buen gobierno," por J. Rojo Gómez; "Un estudio más sobre México," por J. Silva Herzog; "Cárdenas, símbolo mexicano," por Leopoldo Zea.

1901. Navarrete, Alfredo, Jr. Algunos efectos de la situación económica internacional en la economía mexicana (Inv Ec, 13:2, 2. trimestre 1953, p. 247-257).

Conferencia sustentada por el autor en los cursos de invierno de 1953 de la Escuela Nacional de Economía. Destaca algunas relaciones entre los cambios de la economía internacional y sus efectos sobre la economía nacional, con el propósito de definir los problemas derivados que merecen estudio especial.

1902. ————. Los problemas del desarrollo económico y su financiamiento en la Décima Conferencia Interamericana de Caracas (Inv Ec, 14:3, 3. trimestre 1954, p. 365-371).

Conferencia sustentada en la Escuela Nacional de Economía, abril 1954. Análisis de los problemas de desarrollo económico que se presentaron en la X Conferencia Interamericana, con referencias a México. Posición de la delegación de México y comentarios sobre los resultados.

1903. Ortiz Mena, Raúl; Víctor L. Urquidi; Albert Waterston; and Jonas H. Haralz. El desarrollo económico de México y su capacidad para absorber capital del exterior. México, Nacional Financiera, S. A. (distribuído por el Fondo de Cultura Económica), 1953. 505 p., maps, tables.

Ver *HLAS, no. 18, 1955,* prólogo a la bibliografía económica de México (p. 67), y párrafo 979.

1904. Pelissier, Raymond F. American business managers and technicians in Mexican business (Interam Ec Aff, 7:3, winter 1953, p. 73-80).

1905. ————. Intensification of competition in Mexico through the entry of American private enterprise (Interam Ec Aff, 7:2, autumn 1953, p. 80-91).

1906. Portes Gil, Emilio. Rectificación a un libro de W. C. Townsend que contiene la biografía del señor General Cárdenas. México, 1955. 14 p.

1907. Ramirez Gómez, Ramón. El problema de la habitación y los niveles de vida (Inv Ec, 13:3, 3. trimestre 1953, p. 323-377).

1908. Rivera Marín, Guadalupe. Los conflictos de trabajo en México (Trim Ec, 22:2, abril-junio 1955, p. 181-208, tables). Tomado de la obra más abajo citada.

1909. ————. El mercado de trabajo; relaciones obrero-patronales. México, Fondo de Cultura Económica (Estructura económica y social de México), 1955. 314 p., graphs, maps, tables.

Cuarto volumen publicado de la obra que bajo el rubro general de *Estructura económica y social de México,* realiza la Nacional Financiera a través de su Dirección de Investigaciones Económicas. (Ver párrafo 988 del *HLAS, no. 18, 1955).* Este libro es el primero de dos que abarcarán el tema mercado de trabajo en México. Dividido en seis partes y un apéndice que comprende la reproducción de documentos internacionales y nacionales de gran significación histórica para el tema, el estudio tiene la finalidad de examinar las instituciones del trabajo, su origen, estructura y función, así como sus interrelaciones y conflictos. Cada uno de los capítulos contiene importante información y cifras recopiladas en fuentes oficiales y privadas que dan singular objetividad a la obra. (Primer lugar, Premio Anual de Economía, Banco Nacional de México, 1954).

1910. **Rodríguez Mata, Emilio.** Evolución de la población de México y de algunas entidades típicas (Inv Ec, 14:3, 3. trimestre 1954, p. 385-396, graphs, tables).

1911. **Schaeffer, Wendell Karl Gordon.** La administración pública mexicana (Prob Agr Ind Méx, 7:1, enero-marzo 1955, p. 209-314, illus.).
Estudio histórico-crítico de administración comparado sobre el caso de México, con capítulos sobre la administración financiera y sobre planeación. Ilustrado con caricaturas políticas de gran valor histórico, proporcionadas por la Hemeroteca Nacional de México.

1912. **Silva Herzog, Jesús.** El desarrollo de la enseñanza de las ciencias económicas en México, 1925-1953 (Trim Ec, 21:1, enero-marzo 1954, p. 1-5).
Ponencia al Congreso de la Unión de Universidades Latinoamericanas, Santiago de Chile, diciembre 1953.

1913. **Tamayo, Jorge L.** Influencia de las condiciones fisiográficas de México en su desarrollo económico (Inv Ec, 15:3, 3. trimestre 1955, p. 363-379, tables).
Describe el territorio nacional como escenario de la economía mexicana y determina en algunos casos de la localización y encauce de actividades económicas primarias, secundarias y terciarias.

1914. **Torres Gaitán, Ricardo.** El desarrollo de la economía nacional y de sus principales sectores (Inv Ec, 18:2, 2. trimestre 1953, p. 135-167).

1915. **Townsend, William Cameron.** Lázaro Cárdenas, demócrata mexicano. Intr. de Frank Tannenbaum, versión castellana y notas de Avelino Ramírez A., rev. de Luis García Carrillo. México, Grijalbo, 1954. 280 p.
Estudia los problemas actuales de México enmarcados en sus raíces históricas más profundas. Destaca el papel decisivo desempeñado por el Presidente Cárdenas en la edificación de un régimen democrático, y su firmeza para consolidar la integridad económica de México.

1916. **Turner, John Kenneth.** México bárbaro (Prob Agr Ind Méx, 7:2, abril-junio 1955, p. 15-158, illus.).
Obra sensacional sobre la explotación de los trabajadores y el movimiento obrero durante la dictadura de Porfirio Díaz, así como sobre el papel de las inversiones, la prensa y el gobierno estadunidense durante esa época de la historia mexicana.

1917. **United Nations. Population Division.** Población de América Central y México en el período de 1950 a 1980. N. Y., 1954. 84 p. (Estudios sobre población, 16; Cálculos de la población futura por sexo y edad, informe 1).

1918. **Universidad Nacional Autónoma de México.** IV Centenario de la Universidad de México, 1551-1951. México, 1954. (Memoria del Congreso Científico Mexicano; Ciencias sociales; v. 13, Economía).

1919. **Velasco, Gustavo R.** La ley sobre atribuciones al ejecutivo en materia económica (Bancos, 3:12, dic. 1953, p. 18-22).

1920. **Vidal, Rodrigo V.** La teoría del desarrollo económico (Inv Ec, 15:1, 1. trimestre 1955, p. 19-30, graphs, tables).
Expone la diferencia entre análisis y teoría para enmarcar los elementos de la teoría keynesiana en una economía avanzada y una en desarrollo. Compara las estructuras económicas y los desequilibrios estructurales de México y Estados Unidos.

1921. **Whetten, Nathan L.** México rural (Prob Agr Ind Méx, 5:2, abril-junio 1953, p. 11-413, graphs, illus., tables).

1922. **Zamora, Francisco.** Tratado de teoría económica. México, Fondo de Cultura Económica, 1953. 764 p., graphs.

FOREIGN TRADE

1923. **Carrillo Flores, Antonio.** El necesario incremento de nuestro comercio exterior (R Fisc Fin, 14:80, feb. 1954, p. 8-10).

1924. **Iturbide, Aníbal de.** Algunas consideraciones sobre comercio exterior e ingreso nacional (Bancos, 5:5, mayo 1955, p. 24-28 ff.).

1925. **Mora, Gonzalo.** Las reuniones sobre comercio exterior (Inv Ec, 14:2, 2. trimestre 1954, p. 311-333).

1926. **Potash, Robert.** El comercio exterior de México de Miguel Lerdo de Tejada: un error estadístico (Trim Ec, 20:3, julio-sept. 1953, p. 474-479).

1927. **Ramón Llige, Herminia.** Importancia del comercio exterior para el desarrollo económico (Inv Ec, 15:2, 2. trimestre 1955, p. 263-277, table).
Estudia la importancia del comercio exterior para las economías insuficientemente desarrolladas a través de las distintas teorías del comercio internacional, estableciendo las diferencias y caracterizando a las economías avanzadas y a las subdesarrolladas.

1928. Sweeney, Timothy D. La balanza de pagos de México, 1947-1950 (Trim Ec, 20:4, oct.-dic. 1953, p. 642-675, tables).

Este estudio se publicó en inglés en *Staff papers* (publicación del Fondo Monetario Internacional), 3:1, abril 1953, bajo el título "The Mexican balance of payments, 1947-50."

1929. Torres Gaytán, Ricardo. Aspectos de la política de comercio exterior mexicana en la Décima Conferencia Interamericana (R Ec, México, 17:6, junio 1954, p. 165-173).

INDUSTRY (AGRICULTURE, MANUFACTURING, MINING)

1930. Alanís Patiño, Emilio. La energía en México. México, Escuela Nacional de Economía, Instituto de Investigaciones Económicas, 1954. 122 p., tables.

Estudia los problemas más importantes de la energía en México y su impacto en nuestro proceso de desarrollo económico. Señala los beneficios que se obtienen al canalizar las inversiones hacia las fuentes de energía.

1931. Alanís Patiño, Emilio; José López Bermúdez; and Manuel Mesa Andraca. Problemas de la tenencia y aprovechamiento de la tierra en México (Prob Agr Ind Méx, 5:4, oct.-dic. 1953, p. 83-167, tables, illus.).

Contenido: (1) Los recursos naturales, agrícolas y forestales de México; (2) El régimen territorial en México. (2do. lugar, Premio Anual de Economía, Banco Nacional de México, 1953).

1932. Anaya Cárdenas, Raúl Enrique. El azúcar y su industria en México (R Ec, México, 18:4, abril 1955, p. 107-110).

1933. Anzaldúa R., Roberto. El problema cafetalero mexicano (R Ec, México, 18:4, abril 1955, p. 104-107).

1934. Ateneo Nacional Agronómico. Nueva agronomía. México, Atenagro, 1954. 318 p., figs.

Estudios del campo mexicano. Conferencias y opiniones expresadas en las Asambleas del Ateneo Nacional Agronómico.

1935. Banco de México. Oficina de Investigaciones Industriales. La industria azucarera de México. T. 1. México, 1953. 432 p., graphs, maps. (Monografías industriales)

Este tomo comprende consideraciones generales, legislación azucarera extranjera y estadísticas mexicanas y de otros países.

1936. Banco Nacional de Comercio Exterior. La industria eléctrica mexicana (Com Ext, México, 4:2, feb. 1954, anexo, xv p.).

Analiza el desarrollo de esta industria en sus aspectos principales durante el período 1933-1952.

1937. ————. La industria siderúrgica (Com Ext, México, 4:4, abril 1954, anexo, 16 p.).

Expone los antecedentes históricos de las plantas siderúrgicas, desde la primera fundición de hierro establecida en 1835 hasta los hornos eléctricos instalados en 1950-1953.

1938. Beltrán, Enrique. Los recursos naturales de México; estado actual de las investigaciones forestales. México, Instituto Mexicano de Recursos Naturales Renovables, 1955. 125 p.

Publicado en inglés (versión de T. Gill) como parte del trabajo planeado por la Society of American Foresters, que abarca América del Norte. Esta parte sobre México en español es más completa que la publicada en inglés. Tiene un capítulo sobre economía forestal de México y una excelente bibliografía sobre la materia, p. 69-125.

1939. Bermúdez, Antonio J. La industria petrolera mexicana en pleno desarrollo (Prob Agr Ind Méx, 6:4, oct.-dic. 1954, p. 231-236, illus.).

1940. ————. El petróleo en el progreso de México (Prob Agr Ind Méx, 7:1, enero-marzo 1955, p. 333-339).

Informe del Director General de Petróleos Mexicanos, marzo 1955.

1941. ————. El petróleo mexicano a 16 años de la expropiación (Prob Agr Ind Méx, 6:2, abril-junio 1954, p. 233-242, tables).

1942. Bravo J., Manuel. Revisión de ideas sobre la planeación industrial (Inv Ec, 13:2, 2. trimestre 1953, p. 271-289).

Contribución al esclarecimiento de principios que influyen sobre la política de industrialización. (Mereció mención especial, Premio Anual de Economía, Banco Nacional de México, 1953).

1943. Cámara Minera de México. Informe (R Fisc Fin, 14:95, mayo 1955, p. 27-57, tables).

1944. Cámara Nacional de la Industria de Transformación, 2. Congreso, México, 1953. Memoria y documentos. Carta de los industriales mexicanos de transformación y antecedentes. 2a. ed. México, EDIAPSA, 1953. 401 p.

1945. Carrillo Flores, Antonio. Estímulo y apoyo al proceso industrial de México (R Fisc Fin, 13:74; agosto 1953, p. 9-11).

1946. Cassaigne, Héctor; José Domingo Lavín; León Ávalos Vez; Gustavo Maryssael; Rolfo Ortega Mata; and Roberto Atwood. Energética. Notas y estudios para su planeación en México. México, EDIAPSA, 1953. 258 p.

1947. Confederación de Cámaras Industriales. Promoción industrial en México. México, 1953. 83 p., maps. (Publicación conmemorativa del XXXV aniversario, Serie Política económica, 4).

1948. Covarrubias, José F. La trascendencia política de la reforma agraria (Prob Agr Ind Méx, 5:3, julio-sept. 1953, p. 121-180, illus.).

1948a. Crowley, José. Azufre. Notas sobre su importancia en el desarrollo económico de México. México, EDIAPSA, 1953. 173 p.

1949. Esteve Torres, Adrián. La crisis minera y sus repercusiones en México (Inv Ec, 14:2, 2. trimestre 1954, p. 289-309).
Estudia las causas del descenso de la producción minera y propone algunas medidas para aumentarla.

1949a. ————. Recursos ferríferos de México (Inv Ec, 14:4, 4. trimestre 1954, p. 537-551, illus., map).

1950. Fabila Montes de Oca, Gilberto. Economía de la agricultura. México, Año del Centenario de la Escuela Nacional de Agricultura, 1954. 584 p., graphs, tables.

1950a. Fernández y Fernández, Ramón. La consolidación y perfeccionamiento de los resultados de la reforma agraria (Bancos, 4:2-3, feb.-marzo 1954, p. 14-15 ff.; 4:4, abril 1954, p. 30-32).
El autor se basa en los lineamientos de la reforma agraria para hacer una revisión completa del régimen de tenencia de la tierra, con el propósito de mejorar y consolidar la política agraria de México.

1951. ————. Esbozo de una política agrícola para México (R Ec, México, 16:7, julio 1953, p. 210-215).

1951a. ————. El informe presidencial y la agricultura (R Ec, México, 18:3, marzo 1955, p. 91-96).

1952. ————. La regulación de precios de los productos agrícolas (Trim Ec, 22:3, julio-sept. 1955, p. 297-330).
Analiza la experiencia de Estados Unidos y otros países para caracterizar las formas en que se han regulado los precios agrícolas en Méxi-co, exponiendo finalmente un esquema doctrinario para el caso de México.

1952a. Flores, Edmundo. Significación, naturaleza y ámbito de la economía agrícola (Inv Ec, 15:3, 3. trimestre 1955, p. 303-326).
Capítulo 1 y prólogo de un *Tratado de economía agrícola* por salir. Definida, enuncia un nuevo enfoque de la economía agrícola aplicada a países en desarrollo; se basará en los casos de México, Bolivia y Perú.

1953. García Sáinz, Ricardo. Problemas algodoneros (R Fisc Fin, 15:98, agosto 1955, p. 7-16).

1953a. Girault, Manuel. El ejido. Callejón sin salida (Prob Agr Ind Méx, 5:4, oct.-dic. 1953, p. 1-26, illus., tables).

1954. González Roa, Fernando. El aspecto agrario de la Revolución Mexicana (Prob Agr Ind Méx, 5:3, julio-sept. 1953, p. 7-120, illus., tables).

1954a. Guillén Díaz, Pedro. Regulación de los precios del mercado y del ingreso agrícolas (B Estud Espec, 1955, p. 210-219).
Análisis teórico y crítico del método seguido en México en la materia y las posibilidades de aplicar otros métodos.

1955. Herrera Gómez, Hugo. Redituabilidad de las obras de riego por bombeo en la región central del Bajío. México, Banco Nacional de Crédito Ejidal, 1954. 154 p., graphs.

1955a. Huerta Robles, Miguel. La insuficiente producción agrícola (B Azuc Mex, 4:55, enero 1954, p. 11).
La Organización de la Industria Azucarera como ejemplo para aumentar la producción agrícola en general.

1956. Lara Beautell, Cristóbal. La industria de energía eléctrica. México, Fondo de Cultura Económica (Estructura económica y social de México), 1953. 561 p., maps, tables.
Preparado bajo la dirección del Departamento de Estudios Financieros de la Nacional Financiera. Tercer volumen publicado de la obra *Estructura económica y social de México* que realiza la Nacional Financiera, S. A., a través de su Dirección de Investigaciones Económicas (ver párrafo 988 del *HLAS, no. 18, 1952*). Investigación sobre el estado actual de la industria eléctrica de México, con un análisis de los principales factores que influyen en su desarrollo, con el propósito de cuantificar las necesidades futuras de energía y la magnitud de la obra por realizarse en el país en materia de electrificación. (Primer lugar, Premio Anual de Economía, Banco Nacional de México, 1953).

1956a. Lavín, José Domingo. Revisión de la industria petrolera mexicana. México, Sindicato Mexicano de Electricistas, 1955. 48 p.
Evaluación de la importancia que para la libertad económica de México y su progreso tiene la nacionalización de la industria petrolera. Contesta con cifras y hechos la crítica y propaganda centraria a la empresa estatal Petróleos Mexicanos.

1957. Leyva A., Alberto, and José Espinosa R. Principales problemas del algodón mexicano (R Ec, México, 16:1, enero 1953, p. 13-18, tables).

1957a. Margain, Hugo B. La industrialización frente al derecho fiscal mexicano (R Fisc Fin, 15:94, abril 1955, p. 47-68).

1958. Martín Echeverría, Leonardo. Progresos recientes de la agricultura mexicana (Prob Agr Ind Méx, 6:4, oct.-dic. 1954, p. 9-114, illus., tables).

1958a. Mesa Andraca, Manuel. La situación henequenera en Yucatá (Prob Agr Ind Méx, 7:2, abril-junio 1955, p. 281-306).
Estudia los antecedentes de la economía henequenera de Yucatán para enmarcar los problemas económico-sociales a que hace frente en la actualidad la península.

1959. Molina Enríquez, Andrés. Filosofía de mis ideas sobre reformas agrarias. Contestación al folleto del Sr. Lic. Don Wistano Luis Orozco (Prob Agr Ind Méx, 5:1, enero-marzo 1953, suple., p. 221-228).

1959a. Moyo Porras, Edmundo (and others). Transportes (R Ec, México, 18:8, agosto 1955, p. 185-199, tables).
Estudio y discusión sobre los transportes dentro del marco de la economía mexicana y su situación actual.

1960. Organización de Estados Americanos. Estudio de economía de producción agrícola en el Bajío; diseño y selección de la muestra estadística (B Estud Espec, 1955, p. 325-339, illus., tables).
Detalla el proceso por el cual se obtuvieron los datos básicos y elabora el diseño y selección de la muestra estadística para el estudio enunciado.

1960a. Orozco, Wistano Luis. La cuestión agraria (Prob Agr Ind Méx, 5:1, enero-marzo 1953, suple., p. 199-219).

1961. Ortega Mata, Rolfo. Necesidad de la nacionalización progresiva de la industria de servicios eléctricos públicos (Inv Ec, 15:3, 3. trimestre 1955, p. 335-352).

Analiza en todos sus niveles el estado actual y las perspectivas de la industria eléctrica de México, para mostrar la necesidad de su nacionalización en el sentido de que quede en manos de la iniciativa privada mexicana y del Estado.

1961a. Parra, Germán. La industrialización de México. México, Imp. Universitaria, 1954. 203 p.

1962. El petróleo y la economía mexicana. Informe del Comité Wolverton a la Cámara de Diputados de los Estados Unidos (Prob Agr Ind Méx, 6:4, oct.-dic. 1954, p. 135-229, illus., tables).

1962a. Petróleos Mexicanos. Breve enumeración de las plantas productoras de lubricantes y parafinas de la refinería "A. M. Amor" de Salamanca, Gto. México, Pemex, 1955. 22 p., illus.

1963. ————. Reynosa. México, Pemex, 1955. 40 p., illus., map.
Proporciona valiosa información sobre las nuevas plantas de Reynosa, Tamps., México, los campos petroleros del noroeste, etc.

1963a. Portes Gil, Emilio. La reforma agraria a través de los regímenes de 1910 a 1930 (B Soc Mex Geog Est, 78:1, julio-agosto 1954, p. 73-96, tables).

1964. Rippy, Merrill. El petróleo y la Revolución Mexicana (Prob Agr Ind Méx, 6:3, julio-sept. 1954, p. 9-180, illus., tables; comentarios, p. 181-196).
Comentarios: "El petróleo y la Revolución Mexicana," por Antonio J. Bermúdez; "Pasado, presente y futuro de nuestro petróleo," por Alejandro Carrillo; "Notas al libro de Merrill Rippy," por José Domingo Lavín.

1964a. Rodríguez Adame, Julián. Antecedentes y realizaciones de la reforma agraria mexicana (Prob Agr Ind Méx, 5:4, oct.-dic. 1953, p. 67-82, illus., tables).

1965. Silva Herzog, Jesús. La epopeya del petróleo en México (Cuad Am, año 12, 67:1, enero-feb. 1953, p. 7-63).
Recopilación de una serie de conferencias dadas por el autor en el Colegio Nacional, con fines de divulgación de la historia del petróleo en México, la expropiación, sus consecuencias inmediatas y la consolidación de la industria nacionalizada.

MONEY AND BANKING

1965a. Alcocer, Mariano. Apuntes para la historia de la banca en México y sus operaciones (R Banc, 2. época, 1, enero-feb. 1953, p. 25-30; 3, mayo-junio 1953, p. 320-327; 4, julio-agosto 1953, p. 412-

417; 5, sept.-oct. 1953; 6, nov.-dic. 1953, p. 607-613; 2:3, mayo-junio 1954, p. 193-199; 2:5, sept.-oct. 1954, p. 325-328).

1966. Asociación de Banqueros de México. Comentarios de la Asociación de Banqueros de México sobre las nuevas disposiciones relacionadas con las instituciones de crédito y organizaciones auxiliares, o que interesan a las mismas (R Banc, 3:1, enero-feb. 1955, p. 31-40).

1966a. ————. Informe del Consejo, XIX Convención Bancaria, abril 1953. México, Cultura, 1953. 39 p., tables.
Aparece también en *Revista bancaria* (2. época, 2, marzo-abril 1953, p. 133-145).

1967. Banco de México, S. A. Departamento de Fideicomiso. Fondo de garantía y fomento para la agricultura, la ganadería y la silvicultura. México, 1955. 36 p.

1967a. Banco Nacional de Crédito Ejidal, S. A. Lineamiento de una política de crédito ejidal (B Estud Espec, 1:5, enero 4, 1954, p. 73).

1968. Banco Nacional de México, S. A. La experiencia monetaria y de crédito en México, 1925-1951 (R Banc, 2. época, 6, nov.-dic. 1953, p. 583-591).
Ponencia presentada por el Banco Nacional de México, S. A., a la Convención Internacional de Crédito, Roma, Italia, octubre de 1951.

1968a. Batiza, Rodolfo. Una nueva estructuración del fideicomiso en México (R Banc, 2. época, 4, julio-agosto 1953, p. 391-399).

1969. Carrillo Flores, Antonio. Causas y efectos de la devaluación monetaria de abril de 1954 (Prob Agr Ind Méx, 6:3, julio-sept. 1954, p. 197-204).

1969a. ————. Discurso del Secretario de Hacienda y Crédito Público en la XX Convención Bancaria, Acapulco, Gro., abril 1954 (R Banc, 2:2, marzo-abril 1954, p. 98-106).
Publicado también por *Comercio exterior*, 4:4, abril 1954, p. 137. Expone el panorama general de la economía mexicana y explica los motivos que hubo para modificar el tipo de cambio, su influencia en la balanza de pagos y los consiguientes procesos de ajuste.

1970. Cervantes Ahumada, Raúl. Títulos y operaciones de crédito. México, Porrúa, 1954. 499 p., illus.

1970a. Comisión Nacional de Valores.

Ley de sociedades de inversión. México, 1955. 46 p.

1971. Cuspinera, Juan L. Estadística de los resultados del crédito (B Estud Espec, 1:5, enero 4, 1954, p. 84).
Estudia los resultados obtenidos a través de los créditos del Banco Nacional de Crédito Ejidal.

1971a. Dávila Gómez Palacios, Roberto. Concentración financiera privada de México (Inv Ec, 15:2, 2. trimestre 1955, p. 249-262, tables).
Analiza elementos que pueden revelar un proceso de concentración financiera a través de las relaciones del crédito, la inversión y la producción.

1972. deBeers, John S. El peso mexicano, 1941-1949 (Prob Agr Ind Méx, 5:1, enero-marzo 1953, p. 7-134, graphs, illus., tables; comentarios, p. 135-152).
Comentarios: *"El peso mexicano"* de John deBeers," por Octavio G. de Bulhoes; "A propósito de *El peso mexicano,*" por Ernesto Fernández Hurtado; "¿Exceso de inversiones o deficiencia de ahorro?" por Juan F. Noyola Vázquez; "Una política financiera dirigida a estimular el desarrollo económico," por Felipe Pazos; "Comentarios sobre *El peso mexicano* de John S. deBeers," por Rafael Urrutia Millán.

1972a. Durán, Marco Antonio. Política de crédito cooperativo (Trim Ec, 20:2, abril-junio 1953, p. 231-241).

1973. Fernández y Fernández, Ramón. Compilación y notas de documentos para la historia del crédito agrícola en México, 1900-1910 (B Estud Espec, 2:15, julio 12, 1954, p. 45; 16, sept. 5, 1954, p. 61; 17, sept. 10, 1954, p. 89; 18, sept. 25, 1954, p. 134; 19, sept. 27, 1954, p. 156; 20, oct. 10, 1954, p. 175).

1973a. Gómez, Rodrigo. Firmeza de la banca mexicana (R Fisc Fin, 15:94, abril 1955, p. 25-29).

1974. Grove, David L. Política monetaria en países sub-desarrollados. México, Centro de Estudios Monetarios Latinoamericanos, 1955. 112 p.
Estudio teórico e histórico de los objetivos de la política monetaria y el papel de la banca central, hasta sus aportaciones al desarrollo económico. Con referencia a América Latina y México.

1974a. Kemerer, Edwin Walter. Inflación y revolución. La experiencia mexicana de 1912 a 1917 (Prob Agr Ind Méx, 5:1, enero-marzo 1953, p. 169-210, graphs, tables).

1975. Kuri Breña, Daniel. Bases para un

sistema de crédito agrícola (Prob Agr Ind Méx, 6:2, abril-junio 1954, p. 223-231).
Estudia el problema del crédito a la agricultura analizando la insuficiencia de la acción estatal y particular en ese aspecto.

1975a. Luna Olmedo, Agustín. Las cuestiones monetarias (R Fisc Fin, 12:68, feb. 1953, p. 24-27).

1976. Margain, Hugo B. Las relaciones entre el fisco y los contribuyentes (R Fisc Fin, 15:92, feb. 1955, p. 7-16).

1976a. Márquez, Javier. Bonos de poder adquisitivo constante (Trim Ec, 21:1, enero-marzo 1954, p. 6-43).
Examina parte de la literatura relativa al tema y la posibilidad de la aplicación del sistema a la América Latina, especialmente a México. (Segundo lugar, Premio Anual de Economía, Banco Nacional de México, 1954).

1977. México. Comisión Nacional Bancaria. Directorio de instituciones de crédito y organizaciones auxiliares. México, 1954. 222 p.

1977a. ————. Comisión Nacional de Valores. Comisión Nacional de Valores. Órgano de la CNV. México. V. 1, no. 1, enero 1954.
Proporciona datos sobre el mercado de valores en México, con indicadores económicos y financieros y una reproducción de leyes, decretos y circulares sobre valores.

1978. Montes de Oca, Luis. Cinco artículos sobre la devaluación monetaria. México, 1954. 35 p.
Refuta los argumentos más importantes expuestos para explicar la devaluación del peso.

1978a. Morales Treviño, Jorge. Comentario y estadísticas sobre la actividad de las Financieras en 10 años (R Banc, 3:5, sept.-oct. 1955, p. 310-317, graphs).

1979. Nacional Financiera, S. A. Índice de la actividad financiera en México (Merc Val, 14:6, 1954, p. 41 ff.).
Explica el procedimiento seguido para calcular el índice de actividad financiera que, a partir de este número, publica la revista.

1979a. ————. Nueva paridad del peso mexicano (Merc Val, 14:17, 1954, p. 137 ff.).
Reproduce los documentos que explican las causas que aconsejaron la modificación del tipo de cambio respecto al dólar.

1980. ————. Dirección de Investigaciones Económicas. El mercado de valores. México, año 15, no. 1-52, 1955.
Nuevo formato (21.5 x 28.5 cms.) a partir del primer número de 1955. Contiene materiales de información y divulgación económica

y financiera nacionales e internacionales, especialmente sobre mercado de capitales, desarrollo económico y estudios específicos indicadores del progreso de la industrialización de México. Secciones permanentes: análisis del mercado de valores, índice de actividad financiera, indicadores económicos y financieros y cotizaciones de valores.

1980a. Navarrete, Ifigenia M. de. El proceso de desarrollo económico y la política fiscal (Inv Ec, 15:2, 2. trimestre 1955, p. 229-247).
Estudia los elementos relevantes del proceso de desarrollo económico en que puede apoyarse o determinar una política fiscal conducente al fomento económico en economías primarias.

1981. Navarro Sánchez, Joaquín. El problema del crédito agrícola (Bancos, 3:10, oct. 1953, p. 20).

1981a. Ortíz Mena, Raúl. La moneda mexicana; análisis histórico de sus fluctuaciones; las depreciaciones y sus causas. México, Banco de México, S. A., Departamento de Estudios Económicos, 1955. 188 p.
Reimpresión en multilith de tesis profesional publicada en 1942 por Editorial América, edición agotada. Sus dos primeras partes, la teórica y la de antecedentes monetarios en México, dan base al análisis histórico que el autor hace de la moneda mexicana a partir de la depreciación de la plata y la reforma monetaria de 1905 hasta la devaluación del peso en 1938 y sus fluctuaciones en los tres años siguientes.

1982. Pani, Alberto J. El problema supremo de México. Ensayo de crítica constructiva a la política financiera. México, Inversiones ARPA, S. A., 1955. 202 p.
El autor, ex-secretario de hacienda (1923-1926 y 1932-1933), hace un examen de su gestión y un análisis crítico de la política financiera que ha conducido a las devaluaciones del peso mexicano.

1982a. Potash, Robert. Alamán y el Banco de Avío (Inv Ec, 13:4, 4. trimestre 1953, p. 499-511).

1983. Rodríguez, Antonio L. Crédito y técnica al campo (Bancos, 4:2-3, feb.-marzo 1954, p. 26-32; 4:4, abril 1954, p. 37-38).

1983a. Sandoval, Fernando B. Antecedentes del crédito agrario en México (Inv Ec, 14:1, 1. trimestre 1954, p. 131-149).

1984. Solana, Mateo. La devaluación. La dinámica del crédito. México, Fondo de Cultura Económico-Jurídica, 1954. 360 p.

1984a. Villaseñor, Eduardo. La estructura

bancaria y el desarrollo económico de México (Trim Ec, 20:2, abril-junio 1953, p. 199-230).

PUBLIC FINANCE AND FOREIGN INVESTMENT

1985. Aguilar M., Alonso. La inversión extranjera. México, Círculo de Estudios Mexicanos, 1955. 32 p.
Examen de las inversiones extranjeras en la economía mexicana para enunciar una política económica frente a ellas.

1895a. Albareda, José Daniel. Origen del impuesto sobre la renta (R Fisc Fin, 13:73, julio 1953, p. 20-24; 75, sept. 1953, p. 63-67; 76, oct. 1953, p. 41-46).

1986. Ávila C., Fernando. El seguro agrícola integral en México y lo que el país puede esperar de su funcionamiento (R Banc, 3:6, nov.-dic. 1955, p. 356-361).

1986a. Bullejos, José. Bibliografía sobre inversiones extranjeras en América Latina (Inv Ec, 15:1, 1. trimestre 1955, p. 5-17).

1987. Bustamante, Eduardo. La política fiscal y los niveles de vida (Inv Ec, 13:3, 3. trimestre 1953, p. 379-391).

1987a. ————. La política fiscal y los niveles de vida (R Fisc Fin, 14:82, abril 1954, p. 41-54).

1988. Ceceña, José Luis. Inversiones internacionales privadas en el siglo XX (Inv Ec, 18:2, 2. trimestre 1953, p. 169-211).

1988a. Comité México - Americano de Hombres de Negocios. Investing in Mexico. A report by the Mexico-United States Committee. Washington, Chamber of Commerce of the U. S., Foreign Commerce Department, 1953. 12 p.

1989. Ebenstein, William. Premisas históricas y tendencias del gobierno mexicano (Prob Agr Ind Méx, 7:1, enero-marzo 1955, p. 315-324).
Publicado originalmente en inglés en *Public administration review*, 10:2, Apr. 1950. Describe y analiza la administración pública en México y sus tendencias, señalando sus progresos y la situación de la organización financiera gubernamental. Hace comparaciones con Estados Unidos y Gran Bretaña.

1989a. Fayerweather, John. Las inversiones en México desde el punto de vista de los hombres de negocios de los Estados

Unidos (R Banc, 3:6, nov.-dic. 1955, p. 348-355).

1990. ————. Papel que representan las inversiones de los Estados Unidos en el desarrollo económico de México (R Banc, 3:5, sept.-oct. 1955, p. 302-309).

1990a. Gleason Galicia, Rubén. Créditos internacionales a largo plazo; su importancia dentro del desarrollo económico de México. México, Nacional Financiera, S. A., 1955. 134 p., tables.
Analiza los créditos a largo plazo que México ha contratado en el exterior a través de la Nacional Financiera, así como la importancia que han tenido en la realización de programas de industrialización del país. Tesis profesional.

1991. ————. Papel de los créditos del exterior en el financiamiento del desarrollo económico (Inv Ec, 15:4, 4. trimestre 1955, p. 497-558, tables).

1991a. González Casanova, Pablo. La ideología norteamericana sobre inversiones extranjeras. México, Universidad Nacional Autónoma de México, Instituto de Investigaciones Económicas, Escuela Nacional de Economía, 1955. 189 p.
Ensayo de análisis sociológico del concepto estadunidense de inversiones extranjeras, correspondiente a la sociología del conocimiento (económico), a través de los enfoques teóricos del problema y los enfoques prácticos y políticos, utilizando el pensamiento o la exposición de representantes de dichos enfoques.

1992. Lavín, José Domingo. Inversiones extranjeras. Análisis, experiencias y orientaciones para la conducta mexicana. México, EDIAPSA, 1954. 137 p., graphs.

1992a. Legorreta, Luis G. Punto de vista de México acerca de las inversiones extranjeras (R Banc, 3:1, enero-feb. 1955, p. 9-10).

1993. Mancera Ortiz, Rafael. La administración pública en los planes de desarrollo económico (R Fisc Fin, 12:70, abril 1953, p. 9-24, illus.).

1993a. ————. El presupuesto como estabilizador del desarrollo económico (R Fisc Fin, 14:81, marzo 1954, p. 11-29, illus., tables).
IX Congreso Internacional de Ciencias Administrativas, 1953.

1994. Margain, Hugo B. Organización fiscal en México (R Fisc Fin, 12:67, enero 1953, p. 24-31).

1994a. Navarrete, Alfredo, Jr. La programación de la inversión pública en México: un comentario (R Ec, México, 17:7, julio 1954, p. 200-201).

1995. ————. Las relaciones financieras internacionales de México (Inv Ec, 15:2, 2. trimestre 1955, p. 179-189).

Resumen de una conferencia del autor en el ciclo Relaciones Financieras México-Norte-americanas organizado por Occidental College y auspiciadas por Southern California Economic Association y University of California at Los Angeles, abril 1955. Para enmarcar y evaluar las relaciones financieras entre México y Estados Unidos, con un análisis de su intercambio comercial y la posición de las inversiones estadunidenses dentro de la economía mexicana, describe y analiza con cifras elocuentes el desarrollo económico de México, sus problemas y sus perspectivas, y explica la mecánica de su proceso y la participación del gobierno.

1995a. ————. Las técnicas de captación del ahorro utilizadas por la Nacional Financiera de México (R Ec, México, 16:10, oct. 1953, p. 299-303).

Resumen de una conferencia dada por el autor en el Centro de Estudios Monetarios Latinoamericanos. Análisis de las técnicas de captación de ahorro empleadas por la Nacional Financiera, S. A., con antecedentes sobre la institución y un examen de los resultados obtenidos a través de las emisiones de certificados de participación y títulos financieros, con abundancia de datos pertinentes.

1996. Navarrete, Ifigenia M. de. Gastos de capital del gobierno federal (R Ec, México, 17:3, marzo 1954, p. 81-86, tables).

Trabajo presentado a la Reunión Técnica sobre Administración Presupuestaria, celebrada por las Naciones Unidas, México, 1953.

1996a. ————. El presupuesto y el gasto

público (R Ec, 17:3, marzo 1954, p. 76-80).

Analiza la estructura y funciones del presupuesto de egresos de México para 1954. Hace referencia a los organismos descentralizados y empresas estatales y explica los objetivos del Comité de Inversiones.

1997. Palacios Macedo, Miguel. Dos documentos sobre política hacendaria mexicana (Prob Agr Ind Méx, 5:1, enero-marzo 1953, p. 153-161).

Contenido: origen, consecuencias y remedios del alza de los precios interiores (memorándum presentado al H. Consejo de Administración del Banco de México, S. A., en septiembre de 1937, y formulado por el Lic. Miguel Palacios Macedo); orígenes y consecuencias de la inflación monetaria.

1997a. Paredes Arévalo, Óscar. Los almacenes generales de depósito en México. México, ANDSA, 1955. 40 p.

1998. Scott, Robert E. Budget making in Mexico (Interam Ec Aff, 9:2, autumn 1955, p. 3-20).

Describe y enjuicia la elaboración y ejercicio del presupuesto en México desde el punto de vista legal y político, señalando la preponderancia del Ejecutivo sobre los demás poderes.

1998a. Urquidi, Víctor. Le financement des investissements au Mexique et en Amérique Latine (R Sci Leg Fin, 46:3, juillet-sept. 1954, p. 752-760).

Trata de la tendencia deficitaria de la balanza de pagos y de las consecuencias que de ello se derivan.

1999. Urrutia, Rafael. La política económica y el presupuesto nacional (R Ec, México, 16:9, sept. 1953, p. 269-272).

1999a. Velasco, Gustavo R. Reflexiones sobre las inversiones extranjeras (R Banc, 3:1, enero-feb. 1955, p. 16-20).

Education

GENERAL

2000. **Alarco, Luis Felipe.** Lecciones de filosofía de la educación. 2. ed. Lima, Juan Mejía Baca & P. L. Villanueva, 1954. 257 p.

After an exposition of the theory and reality of education the author analyzes the structure of education and the interdependence of educator, student, content, aim, and method. Educational anthropology raises questions concerning civic, moral, and religious education. Each chapter is followed by a discussion questionnaire and brief bibliography. [M. C. Johnston]

2001. **Andrade Filho, Bento de.** História da educação. 2. ed. São Paulo, Saraiva, 1953. 258 p.

Pequena história da educação desde a antiguidade aos nossos dias. [I. Doria]

2002. Breves ensayos sobre universidades. Santiago, Universidad de Chile, Departamento de Extensión Cultural, 1953. 233 p.

From lecture series arranged by Department of Cultural Extension, University of Chile, in collaboration with Organizing Commission, Second University Congress and First General Assembly of the Union of Latin American Universities. Contains two essays on medieval and 18th-century universities, seven on contemporary universities of France, Italy, Germany, England, U. S., Mexico, Chile, and five on present problems of the university world. [M. C. Johnston]

2003. **Committee on Instructional Materials.** Instructional materials in Latin American schools. A requirements evaluation. Washington, 1953. 30 p.

Survey of instructional materials in vocational education in Latin America made by a committee created by Institute of Inter-American Affairs in cooperation with Pan American Union and U. S. Office of Education; conclusions, recommendations, bibliography, and list of instructional materials in Spanish and Portuguese; reports on countries visited: Nicaragua, Panama, Peru, Paraguay, Brazil, Puerto Rico. [M. C. Johnston]

2004. **Corrêa, Roberto Alvim.** Hebe ou da educação. Rio, Ministério de Educação e Cultura, Serviço de Documentação (Os

cadernos de cultura), 1953. 40 p.

Considerações filosóficas, pensamentos, etc. sôbre educação. [I. Doria]

2005. **Guevara, Tristán E.** Las maestras norteamericanas que trajo Sarmiento. Washington, Servicio Cultural e Informativo de los Estados Unidos de América (Col. Grandes figuras de América), 1954? 31 p.

Address in celebration of Teachers' Day, Sept. 10, 1954, in B. A. Sympathetic appraisal of the contributions of North American teachers who established the first normal schools authorized by the Argentine Congress in 1869. [M. C. Johnston]

2006. **Inter-American Cultural Council.** Carta cultural de América. I. Recopilación de normas culturales. 1. Educación. Washington, Unión Panamericana, Departamento de Asuntos Culturales, 1953. 4 v. [Parte] A, Conferencias internacionales americanas (1889-1948)—Conferencias sanitarias panamericanas (1902-1950), 121 p.; [parte] B, Congresos, conferencias y seminarios de educación (1908-1950)—Conferencias femeninas interamericanas (1915-1951), 123-455 p.; [parte] C, Congreso Americano de Ciencias Sociales (5-10 de julio de 1916)—Conferencias interamericanas de agricultura (1930-1950), 457-666 p.; [parte] D, Conferencias del trabajo de estados americanos miembros de la Organización Internacional del Trabajo (1936-1949)—Reunión Técnica sobre Extensión Agrícola (23 de agosto-3 de septiembre de 1949), 668-862 p.

Section A contains (1) an index of 120 pages for the four volumes covering all the conferences and congresses from 1889 to 1951 in which resolutions were passed pertaining to education, (2) text of the conventions and resolutions for the International American Conferences, 1889-1948, and (3) text of the educational provisions of the inter-American scientific congresses, 1898-1940. Section B includes (1) the congresses, conferences, and inter-American seminars on education, 1908-1950, and (2) resolutions on education adopted by Inter-American Women's Conferences, 1915-1951. Section C covers (1) the American Congress of Social Sciences, July 5-10, 1916, and (2) the inter-American conferences on agriculture, 1930-1950. Section D contains (1) the text pertaining to education of the conferences on labor, held by the American members of the International Labour Organization, 1936-1949, and (2) the Technical Meeting on Agricultural Extension, August 23-September 3, 1949. [M. C. Johnston]

2007. ―――――. Carta cultural de América. II. Índice analítico de la recopilación de normas culturales. 1. Educación. Washington, Unión Panamericana, Departamento de Asuntos Culturales, 1954. 62 p.

Alphabetical subject index, with cross references, to the four volumes on education of the "Recopilación de normas culturales," Series I of Carta cultural de América. [M. C. Johnston]

2008. Inter-American Seminar on Vocational Education, College Park, Md., Aug. 3-Sept. 6, 1952. Lista de documentos técnicos en castellano y portugués. Washington, Unión Panamericana (Seminario Interamericano de Educatión, 4; Serie A de educación vocacional, 2), 1953. 34 p.

Agenda for the seminar dealing with vocational education, its nature and purposes, agriculture, industry, commerce, and homemaking; list of work papers, giving title, author, and corresponding agenda item; list of basic library materials used by conference participants. [M. C. Johnston]

2009. ―――――. Vocational education textbooks; exhibit catalog. Washington, Pan American Union (Inter-American seminar on education, 4), 1953. 57 p.

Published also in Spanish: Catálogo de la exposición de textos de educación vocacional. Textbooks exhibited from 21 countries of Europe and America are listed by country under the following topics: vocational education—general, agricultural, industrial, business, and education for home and family life. A directory of publishers is also included. [M. C. Johnston]

2010. Palacín Iglesias, Gregorio B. La educación en Latinoamérica. Coral Gables, Fla., University of Miami, 1952. 135 p., illus.

Lessons in Spanish for course on Education in Hispanic America at University of Miami. Explanation of educational systems in Latin American countries, their problems, and the principal differences between those systems and U. S. education; separate descriptions of education in Central America and the 14 other republics. [M. C. Johnston]

2011. Pan American Union. Division of Education. La enseñanza de las ciencias naturales en la escuela primaria. Wash-

ington, 1953. 91 p. (Biblioteca panamericana del maestro, 3).

Prepared by Pedro Ángel Cebollero. Account of purposes, program, methodology, and resources for elementary school science teaching. Material adapted from report prepared for the Inter-American Seminar on Elementary Education (Montevideo, 1950) and from Methods and activities in elementary school science by Glenn O. Blough and Albert J. Hugget (Dryden Press. N. Y.) [M. C. Johnston]

2012. ―――――. ―――――. Opportunities for summer study in Latin America. Compiled by Estellita Hart and Janet Lippincott. Washington, 1953. 36 p.

Condensed information about (1) summer courses offered by Latin American institutions, (2) summer courses offered in Latin America by U. S. institutions, and (3) other educational tours and summer projects. [M. C. Johnston]

2013. Parker, William Riley. The national interest and foreign languages. A discussion guide and work paper . . . for citizen consultations initiated by the U. S. National Commission for UNESCO, Department of State. Prelim. ed. Washington, 1954. 131 p.

Highly useful information on the current academic situation with respect to foreign languages in elementary and secondary schools, colleges, graduate and professional schools; historical summary of modern language instruction in the U. S.; survey of present and future foreign language needs; discussion of questions awaiting answers. Includes study outline and suggested readings. [M. C. Johnston]

2014. Ravera, Alfredo. Apreciación de los resultados de la acción educativa. B. A., Kapelusz, 1953. 181 p., illus.

Discussion of what evaluation is, the need for it, and the method in preschool and primary age groups. Author believes that evaluating learning experiences requires both subjective and objective techniques. Chapter 5 includes 55 sample tests in language, mathematics, and sciences—social and natural. [M. C. Johnston]

2015. Río, Ángel del (ed.). Responsible freedom in the Americas. Garden City, N. Y., Doubleday (Columbia University Bicentennial conference series), 1955. 554 p.

Three of the six parts of this volume deal with education: part 1, nine essays on elementary, primary, and secondary education; part 2, nine essays on university education; part 5, six essays on the role of government in education. Each series is followed by discussion and commentary reflecting opinions of conference participants. The authors, from the U. S., Brazil, Haiti, and 12 Spanish American countries, were dissociated from official government circles. A very useful compendium of current thought on the school in society. [M. C. Johnston]

2016. Seminario Interamericano de Educación Secundaria, Santiago, dic. 29,

1954-enero 22, 1955. Recomendaciones aprobadas por el . . . . Washington, Unión Panamericana, División de Educación, 1955. 37 p.

Recommendations of six groups: 1, nature and purposes of secondary education; 2, organization and administration; 3, plans and programs; 4, methods and techniques; 5, teaching staff; 6, relations of secondary education to professional or specialized preparation. Special recommendations concerning school regulations, school buildings, and definition of pedagogical terms. [M. C. Johnston]

2017. Ugarteche, Pedro. Formación del diplomático peruano. Lima, Villanueva, 1955. 111 p.

Description of diplomatic training in Peru, the U. S., Spain, Brazil, Belgium, and Chile. Advocates plan for an academy of diplomacy for preparation in politics and jurisprudence, economics, commerce, tourism, national defense, journalism, modern languages, and technical subjects. [M. C. Johnston]

2018. Unión de Universidades Latinoamericanas. Planes de estudios de las universidades latinoamericanas. Guatemala (Biblioteca universitaria latinoamericana, 2), 1953. 1xv, 1004 p.

Invaluable reference work containing: (1) list of Latin American universities; (2) list of faculties in each university, by country; (3) index to plans of study, classified according to field of study—law, economics, humanities, medicine, dentistry, pharmacy, obstetrics, agronomy and veterinary medicine, surveying, engineering, architecture, fine arts; and (4) complete programs of study, listing subjects by year (and hours per week for some programs). [M. C. Johnston]

2019. United Nations Educational, Scientific and Cultural Organization. Progress of literacy in various countries. A preliminary statistical study of available census data since 1900. Paris, 1953. 224 p., illus. (Monographs on fundamental education, 6)

Contains chapter on criteria for measuring progress in literacy and reports from 26 countries. The Latin American countries included are Argentina, Brazil, Chile, Colombia, Cuba, Honduras, and Mexico. The year of the most recent data ranges from 1938 for Colombia to 1947 for Argentina. [M. C. Johnston]

SPANISH AMERICA AND HAITI

MARJORIE C. JOHNSTON

ARGENTINA

2050. Bregazzi, Violeta E. Didáctica especial. B. A., Librería del Colegio, 1955. 213 p.

Textbook for normal school students preparing to teach the subjects of the elementary school curriculum: language, reading, composition, arithmetic, geometry, natural sciences, physical and chemical sciences, geography, history, moral and religious education, civics, art, music, manual training, domestic and physical education.

2051. González, Hilario. Fundamentos de pedagogía. Córdoba, Argentina, Assandri, 1954. 281 p.

Philosophical discussion of education—its characteristics, anthropological foundations, relations to religion, family, and patriotism, teaching methods. Last chapter describes educational reforms in Argentina and the second five-year plan.

2052. Grandoli, Mariano J. Iniciativas escolares. Proyectos, discursos . . . (1948-1949). B. A., Tall. Gráf. Guadalupe, 1954. 147 p., illus.

Copies of letters, memoranda, and speeches by the author during his term of office as School Adviser in the Almirante Brown district of the province of Buenos Aires. Sample subjects: school movies, school clubs, ex-students' association, sports, excursions, music, lunchrooms, names of schools.

2053. Luchetti de Monjardín, María Adela. Observación, práctica y crítica en la escuela normal argentina. Planes de clases. 2. ed. B. A., Raigal, 1953. 331 p.

Textbook for students in fourth and fifth years of normal school. Discussion of things to observe in classroom, methods for the various subjects of the elementary school program, ways of planning lessons, evaluation of practice in teaching.

2054. Manganiello, Ethel M., and Violeta E. Bregazzi. Historia de la educación, general y argentina. 5. ed., corregida y aumentada. B. A., Librería del Colegio, 1955. 334 p.

Brief history of education for normal school students, beginning with primitive society and general characteristics of education in Egyptian, Indian, Chinese, Hebrew, Greek, and Roman cultures. Chapters 5-11 treat education from the Middle Ages to the 20th century; the last four chapters describe education in Argentina from the pre-Hispanic period to contemporary reforms.

BOLIVIA

2055. Donoso Torres, Vicente. Bases para una reforma integral de la educación.

Ponencia presentada al Primer Congreso Boliviano de Sociología. La Paz, Don Bosco, 1953. 55 p.
Summary of the state of education in Bolivia; statement of need for an organic law of national education to include (a) organization and administration, (b) objectives, (c) financing, (d) preschool, (e) primary and vocational education, (f) secondary and professional preparation, (g) teacher training, (h) university and technological education; proposed statute of national education and school organization.

2056. Suárez Arnez, Faustino; F. Yolanda Suárez C.; and Nelly Suárez C. Hacia la nueva educación nacional. La Paz, Universo, 1953. 198 p.
The problem of secondary education and its reforms; an organic plan for education in Bolivia; essay on rural education; proposed statute of national education; talks on educational psychology, methods, and language teaching. A family of teachers appraises the system of education, with special attention to the needs of the Indian population.

2057. Torrico Prado, Benjamín. La pedagogía en Bolivia. La Paz, Don Bosco, 1947. 308 p.
History of education in Bolivia from pre-Conquest days to 1946. Chapter highlights: importation of pedagogical ideas and methods by the Jesuits and other orders, Bell and Lancaster, San Juan Bosco, Alfred Fouiller, Andrés Ferreira; summaries of national plans of education by Bolivian leaders; organization of the Sucre normal school; reforms in primary education after 1915; educational statistics.

CHILE

2058. United Nations Educational, Scientific and Cultural Organization. Women and education. Paris, 1953. 264 p. (Problems in education, 5).
Includes bibliographies. Chapters on education for women in Chile, India, and Yugoslavia, followed by recommendation no. 34 adopted by Fifteenth International Conference on Education, Geneva, 1952, "Access of women to education." Part 1, "Women and education in Chile," written by Amanda Labarca H., discusses the status of women in Chile, the cultural evolution of the nation, primary education, secondary education, and higher education.

2059. Universidad de Chile. Leyes, decretos y reglamentos. Recopilación y notas por Enrique L. Marshall. T. 2. Reglamentación de los servicios dependientes de las facultades. Santiago, Editorial Universitaria, 1954. 366 p.
Regulations and plans of study for the faculties of philosophy and letters, juridical and social sciences, medicine, dentistry, chemistry and pharmacy, physical and mathematical sciences, architecture, economics, agronomy, animal husbandry and veterinary medicine, music, plastic arts, and sciences. Appendices contain laws governing the liberal professions and supple-

mentary legislation pertaining to university education.

2060. Universidad Técnica del Estado. Prospecto general. Santiago, 1955. 17 p.
Catalog of the new university for training industrial engineers, technicians, and teachers of industrial subjects.

2061. Vega, Julio. La racionalización de nuestra enseñanza. Santiago, Universidad de Chile (Col. de estudios histórico-sociales), 1954. 277 p.
Author discusses sociological foundations for educational policy, strongly advocating a consideration of the whole problem in relation to (1) the characteristics of the population to be educated, and (2) the type of citizen desired; patchwork reforms are inadequate. A projected organic law for educational services is included.

COLOMBIA

2062. Colombia. Departamento de Educación Campesina. Colombia campesina. Revista mensual. Bogotá. Época 1, no. 1, 1953.
Miscellany of practical, cultural, and recreational reading for rural homes.

2063. Universidad Nacional de Colombia. Estatutos de la Universidad Nacional. Bogotá, 1953. 127 p.
Complete legislation governing the National University of Colombia: organic law 68, 1935, with subsequent decrees; statutes of the university, 34 chapters.

2064. Universidad Pedagógica de Colombia. Aulas. Publicación colombiana al servicio de la educación. Bogotá. V. 1, no. 9-10, nov.-dic. 1953.
Special edition of the journal, devoted to the origin, development, and future plans of the Universidad Pedagógica de Colombia, established in Tunja in 1953.

CUBA

2065. Chacón y Calvo, José María. El Padre Varela y su apostolado. Habana, Comisión Nacional Cubana de la UNESCO (Cuadernos de divulgación cultural), 1953. 40 p.
Essay and bibliography on the life and works of Varela published under the auspices of the Cuban National Commission for UNESCO.

2066. Fernández Mascaró, Guillermo. La obra de un libertador en educación popular. Pref. por Ramiro Guerra y Sánchez. Habana, Lex, 1953. 902 p., illus.
Achievements of Guillermo Fernández Mascaró during his term as secretary of public education in Cuba, 1925 and 1926. A compendium of documents from official sources, with one section containing his speeches and

educational activities while director of the Instituto de Segunda Enseñanza de Santiago de Cuba. Biographical information given in preface.

2067. Lancís Sánchez, Antonio. Cuestiones universitarias. Habana, Lex, 1954. 36 p.
Observations and proposals pertaining to university reforms and modifications in program, offered by a professor of social sciences and public law, University of Habana.

HAITI

2068. Auguste, Charles A. Pour une éducation haïtienne. Port-au-Prince, Les Presses Libres, 1954. 132 p. & illus.
Exposition of underlying principles of Haitian education. For use of parents, teachers, student teachers, and supervisors. General topics, such as education and culture, education and liberty, education as a factor in progress, and specific treatment of preschool and primary education —its experimental basis, civic education, social activities, scientific training, Christian teaching.

2069. Fernández Ballesteros, Alberto. Toulon. Una experiencia en Haití. México, Beatriz de Silva, 1954. 485 p.
Documented account of UNESCO's pilot project in fundamental education located in the Marbial Valley in Haiti. Very interesting and revealing diary of its first director, covering the period 1947-1949.

2070. Haïti. Département de l'Éducation Nationale. Bulletin du Département de l'Éducation Nationale. Port-au-Prince. Oct.-nov. 1953.
First issue of bulletin which continues the *Bulletin officiel du Département de l'Instruction Publique,* published 1894-1942, according to note in preface. Contains list of administrative personnel; copies of circulars sent to school directors; statistics on enrollments in the various types of schools; report of progress in literacy campaign, production of instructional materials, and reform of primary education.

HONDURAS

2071. Bardales B., Rafael. La educación en Honduras. Madrid, Oficina de Educación Iberoamericana, Instituto de Cultura Hispánica, 1953? 54 p.
Statement of objectives, programs of study, and statistical information for each level of the school system: preschool, primary (urban and rural), secondary, normal, vocational, university, and literacy or adult education. Brief introduction containing essential facts about the country.

2072. Guardiola Cubas, Esteban. Historia de la Universidad de Honduras en la primera centuria de su fundación. Tegucigalpa, Tall. Tipog. Nacionales, 1952. 207 p.

Chronicle of the development of the University of Honduras from 1845 to 1947, preceded by a summary of colonial education in Honduras. Last 88 pages are devoted to a critique of the *Pastorelas* of José Trinidad Reyes, poet, priest, and teacher.

2073. Sánchez, Roberto M. Significado de la Escuela Nacional de Bellas Artes de Honduras, 1940-1953. Tegucigalpa, Tall. Tipog. Nacionales, 1953. 22 p.
Record of the accomplishments of the National School of Fine Arts during its first 13 years: expositions, lecture series, contests, library, and archaeological museum. Last chapter gives opinions expressed by national and foreign artists.

2074. Thompson, M. Weldon. Education in Honduras. Edited by Marjorie C. Johnston. Washington, Office of Education (Bulletin, 1955, 7), 1955. 33 p.
Background information on the country; description of the school system; programs of study for secondary, commercial, and normal schools, for university faculties, and for schools of arts and trades and agriculture; bibliography.

MEXICO

2075. Ceniceros, José Ángel. Nuestra constitución política y la educación mexicana. México, Impresora Popular, 1955. 44 p.
Significant interpretation and historical review of the educational provisions of the Constitution of 1917, articles 3, 27, and 123; principles upon which the national policies of education rest, and the responsibility of the teaching profession to carry them out. Prepared by the secretary of public education for the Junta Nacional de Educación Normal.

2076. ————. El problema de la alfabetización. México, Secretaría de Educación Pública, 1953. 16 p.
Analysis of results of the literacy campaign, 1944-1952, in which a 15% reduction in illiteracy in the nation was effected; measures under consideration for intensifying the effort. Address by the secretary of public education to commemorate the literacy law of 1944 in Mexico.

2077. Garrido, Luis. Palabras universitarias, 1951-1953. México, Ediciones Botas, 1954. 222 p.
Collection of speeches, not included in the volume *Discursos y mensajes,* given by Luis Garrido during his term as rector of the National Autonomous University of Mexico.

2078. Salazar Páez, Antonio. El San Francisco de la educación mexicana. Semblanza de Carlos A. Carrillo. México, El Dictamen, 1955. 79 p.
Account of the life, educational theories, and achievements of Carlos A. Carrillo (1855-1893), a schoolmaster from Cordoba, Veracruz, who ranks with Gabino Barreda, Justo Sierra, and

Manuel Gutiérrez as a distinguished precursor of modern education in Mexico.

2079. **Siegrist Clamont, Jorge.** El sistema jurídico de la universidad mexicana. T. 1. México, Universidad Nacional Autónoma de México, Facultad de Derecho, 1954. 569 p.

Discussion, starting with the medieval antecedents of the Royal and Pontifical University of New Spain, of the University of Mexico in the following periods: 1551-1910, 1910-1929, and 1929-1954. Author examines critically the present university system, including higher education outside the capital, and recommends an administrative reorganization of the entire system.

2080. **Tirado Benedí, Domingo.** Educadores de México. Bosquejos biográficos. México, Secretaría de Educación Pública (Biblioteca enciclopédica popular, nueva época, 225), 1955. 102 p.

Short biographies of 39 Mexican educators who made significant contributions to the nation's educational progress. Interesting and informational sketches in chronological order beginning with Pedro de Gante and ending with Moisés Sáenz.

2081. —————. Problemas de la educación mexicana. México, Secretaría de Educación Pública (Biblioteca enciclopédica popular, nueva época, 224), 1955. 110 p.

Two chapters deal with the system of education —its objectives, organization, materials, and methods. Two chapters treat the educational responsibilities of the family and the important relationships between the home and the school. A final chapter presents the important role of the press in the diffusion of education.

2082. **United Nations Educational, Scientific and Cultural Organization.** New horizons at Tzentzenhuaro. One year of work at a fundamental education centre for Latin America. Paris, 1953. 33 p., illus.

Description of the way trainees from Latin American countries work in villages near UNESCO's Fundamental Education Centre, Patzcuaro, Mexico, to improve standards of living. Integration of new skills into the life of the villagers, community changes, improvements in health, recreation, crop production, home industries, literacy.

2083. **Universidad Nacional Autónoma de México.** Anuario general 1954. México, 1954. 278 p.

Catalog of all schools, faculties, and research institutes of the National Autonomous University of Mexico, including historical sketch, organic law and statutes, degree requirements, programs of study, and list of "incorporated" schools.

2084. —————. **Instituto de Investigaciones Sociales.** Primer censo nacional universitario, 1949. México, Stylo, 1953. civ, 518 p., illus., tables.

Introduction giving historical and social antecedents of higher education in Mexico; part 1, organization and financial resources of the National Autonomous University of Mexico, general census of students and teaching staff (number, sex, age, place of birth, father's occupation, school placement and attendance, chief interests); part 2, analysis of students and staff by faculties and schools; part 3, institutions in the states (school, family, home, economic, and social characteristics).

PUERTO RICO

2085. **Puerto Rico. Department of Education.** Catálogo de publicaciones de la Editorial del Departamento de Instrucción. San Juan, 1953. 31 p.

List of 162 publications, largely in Spanish, classified as follows: (1) addresses, lectures, messages, essays; (2) translations, reproductions, adaptations, revisions, summaries; (3) books, manuals; (4) bulletins, courses of study, plans, reports; (5) research; (6) statistics; (7) annual reports; (8) veterans' education.

2086. **Universidad de Puerto Rico.** Catálogo general, descriptivo de facultades, colegios y dependencias, así como de los cursos y programas. 1903-1953 cincuentenario. México, 1953. 306 p., illus.

50th anniversary catalog of the University of Puerto Rico. Contains sections descriptive of organization, degrees, services, student activities; complete programs of study for faculties of general studies, humanities, social sciences, natural sciences, business administration, education, pharmacy, law, college of agricultural and mechanical arts, school of medicine, and other schools, laboratories, and institutes; 46 photographs.

2087. —————. **Colegio de Pedagogía.** Pedagogía. Río Piedras, Puerto Rico. V. 1, no. 1, junio 1953.

Semiannual journal inaugurated in the 50th anniversary year of the University. Seven articles (five in Spanish, two in English) of historical and general interest: University of Puerto Rico, School of Education, foundations of the Puerto Rican school system, in-service training for beginning teachers, intelligence in the modern world, education and the humanities, psychology of friendship.

OTHER COUNTRIES

2088. **Bartolomé Herrera, 1808-1864.** Tramos de una vida de lucha. Ideas. Documenta. Lima, Gran Unidad Escolar Bartolomé Herrera, 1953. 67 p.

Homage to a Peruvian cleric and educator who, as rector of the Colegio de San Carlos, influenced educational thought and action a century ago. Contains biographical sketch, historical setting, and quotations from Herrera's writings.

2089. Olaizola, Sabas. El plan de maestros asociados. Una nueva estructura de la escuela común aplicado al proyecto de formación de maestros. Quito, Casa de la Cultura Ecuatoriana, 1955. 212 p.

This book for teachers discusses the "centers of interest" method and its application to improvements in education, both national and universal. The new common school structure developed in UNESCO projects in teacher education organizes the curriculum about large areas of experience.

2090. Sánchez Urteaga de Peña, Isabel. Guía para jardines de la infancia. Educación pre-escolar a base de música. Desarrollada de acuerdo con el plan vigente de educación. Lima, CIP, 1953. 95 p., illus.

Course for kindergartens containing two units on the child and his individual needs (the school and home, cleanliness) and six units on the child in relation to others: mother, Mother of Heaven, grandmother, the Sierra Indian and his customs, father and his occupations, the Peruvian coat of arms, and San Martín. 64 songs included.

2091. Tosta, Virgilio. Ideas educativas de venezolanos eminentes. Caracas, Ministerio de Educación, Dirección de Cultura y Bellas Artes (Biblioteca venezolana de cultura, Col. Andrés Bello), 1953. 166 p.

Historical origins of Venezuelan education and discussion of ideas advocated by Miguel José Sanz, Simón Rodríguez, Andrés Bello, Simón Bolívar, José María Vargas, Fermín Toro, and Cecilio Acosta. An appendix of 72 pages contains these leaders' writings on education.

2092. Universidad de Costa Rica. Planes de estudio y reglamentos internos de las escuelas universitarias. San José, Trejos, 1953. 206 p.

Introductory view and statement of future plans; regulations and programs of study in schools of agronomy, fine arts, music, sciences, law, economics and social sciences, pharmacy, philosophy and letters, engineering, dentistry, education. Material for each school is paged separately; no index.

2093. Universidad de San Carlos de Guatemala. Labores realizadas durante el período 1950-1954. Guatemala, Imprenta Universitaria, 1954. Unpaged, illus.

Photograph album showing progress in higher education during school years 1950-1954. Tables give summary of activities and numbers of graduates from the various faculties and schools of the university: juridical and social sciences, medicine, engineering, chemical sciences and pharmacy, economic sciences, dentistry, midwifery, humanities, agronomy, journalism, library science.

2094. ———. Facultad de Humanidades. Planes de estudio. Guatemala, 1955. 47 p.

Programs of study for 1955 in the Faculty of Humanities of the University of San Carlos de Guatemala. Departments included are philosophy, letters, history, education, psychology, library science, and journalism.

2095. Universidad Nacional del Zulia. Facultad de Ciencias Médicas. Maracaibo, Venezuela, Publicaciones de la Dirección de Cultura, 1953? 199 p., illus.

Historical summary, officers and teaching staff, regulations, program of study, course content, and enrollments for the six-year course in medicine.

2096. Yglesias R., Eduardo. La escuela de ciencias económicas y sociales. Estudio sobre su desarrollo y organización académica. San José, Universidad de Costa Rica (Sección Tesis de grado y ensayos, 7), 1953. 128 p.

Notes on cultural development of Costa Rica and the organization of the University of Costa Rica; plans of study for School of Economic and Social Sciences (sections: economics, statistics and mathematics, administration and accounting, social service); basic minimum programs in economic sciences for Central American universities; statistical tables for 1943-1953.

BRAZIL

IRENE DE MENEZES DORIA

2200. Abreu, Jaime. Considerações sôbre o Seminário Inter-Americano de Educação Secundária (R Br Estud Ped, 23-58, abril-junho 1955, p. 105-178).

2201. ———. A educação secundária no Brasil. Rio, Campanha de Inquéritos e Levantamentos do Ensino Médio e Elementar, 1954. 104 p.

Contribuição ao Seminário Inter-Americano de Educação Secundária a ser realizado em Santiago do Chile de 29 de dezembro de 1954 a 29 de janeiro de 1955. Abrange 5 temas: natureza e fins da educação secundária; organização e administração; currículo e programas; métodos e técnicas; e o professorado.

2202. Abu-Merhy, Nair Fortes. Importância do estudo dirigido no curso secun-

dário (R Br Estud Ped, 20-51, julho-set. 1953, p. 73-89).
Indicações para metodização do estudo, visando especialmente aos alunos do curso secundário que não alcançam geralmente bom apreveitamento por deficiências no modo de estudar. Finalidades do estudo. Os métodos de estudo: as notas, na leitura e na preleção; a bôa leitura; o trabalho no laboratório e no seminário. [A. Coutinho]

2203. Almeida, João Carlos de. Campanha Nacional de Educação de Adultos (B Dept Est, 16:1, jan. 1954, p. 159-183).
Resultados, em 1953, da campanha de educação de adultos em São Paulo, fornecidos pelo Departamento de Estatística do estado. Dados sôbre cursos instalados e extintos, matriculados e aproveitamento, com discriminação municipal. [A. Coutinho]

2204. ———. O ensino primário em São Paulo em 1953 (B Dept Est, 15:3, 1953? p. 51-65).
Focaliza, através de quadros demonstrativos, a situação do ensino primário nos 369 municípios paulistas, com os resultados preliminares do ano letivo de 1953, obtidos por inquérito realizado junto às Delegacias de Ensino do Estado. Inclui um quadro comparativo dos anos de 1940, 1950, 1953. [Salvio Oliveira]

2205. Almeida Júnior, A. O drama do ensino superior brasileiro (Anhembi, ano 4, 15:43, junho 1954, p. 30-49).
Largo panorama do ensino superior brasileiro, estudando a situação atual depois de haver analisado a do Império e dos princípios da República. Acredita que temos melhorado em diversos aspectos, mas que temos ainda muito que fazer. Denuncia os vícios que atualmente mais ressaltam à visão do observador e que prejudicam uma das funções primordiais da educação: a transmissão da cultura. Em seguida, analisa a comercialização do ensino, que da escola secundária, passou para a superior. Apela para as associações de classe no sentido de a agirem para a solução dos problemas que afligem o ensino superior. [A. Coutinho]

2206. ———. Enquanto se espera pelas diretrizes e bases (R Fac Dir, Paraná, 1:1, dez. 1953, p. 73-90).
Critica severamente o vício brasileiro de confiar demasiado nas reformas do ensino, no sentido de considera-las capazes de corrigir todas as insuficiências das instituições educacionais. Depois de historiar as reformas do ensino, desde tempo do Império, conclui que estas só por sí não bastam. É mister aperfeiçoar os homens que executam as leis e os professores que as aplicam, de forma a torna-los bons cumpridores dos deveres funcionais, cultores do bom ensino, da seriedade nos exames e da assiduidade.

2207. ———. Palestra no curso de aperfeiçoamento de professôres, organizado em São Paulo pela Campanha de Aperfeiçoamento e Difusão do Ensino Secundário. Rio, Diretoria do Ensino Secundário, 1954. 16 p. (Documentário, 2).
Retrata a situação do ensino secundário no Brasil em sua evolução nos últimos cem anos, a transformação do ensino da elite em aspiração das classes menos favorecidas, as consequências que resultaram de suas conquistas por estudantes provenientes dos mais diversos níveis sociais e a diversidade da situação atual e aquela para que foi planejada a Lei Orgânica do Ensino Secundário.

2208. Amado, Gilberto. História da minha infância. Rio, Olympio, 1954. 287 p.
Estudando a sua infância em Sergipe (Estáncia Itaporanga, Aracajú), o autor traça um quadro da vida infantil na zona dos engenhos de açúcar do Nordeste. Problemas de socialização, de educação e de instrução são ventilados. Oferece-nos também retratos vivos da instrução primária e secundária nos fins do século dezenove e início do século vinte. [A. Coutinho]

2209. Andrada, Carlos dos Anjos Duarte de. O curso de didática nas faculdades de filosofia e suas vantagens (Kriterion, 7:29-30, julho-dez. 1954, p. 249-261).
Partindo dos textos legais que regulam o funcionamento das faculdades de filosofia, descreve e comenta a atual estrutura do curso de didática. [Elza N. Alves]

2210. Angelini, Arrigo Leonardo. Quais os cursos preferidos pelos alunos dos nossos ginásios? (Arq Br Psico, 6:3, 1954, p. 11-25).
Pesquisa realizada entre alunos do 4. ano de um ginásio público de São Paulo, com o intuito de verificar seus interesses profissionais. Os resultados indicam que a maioria das moças escolhem a carreira do magistério e que os rapazes preferem os cursos de engenharia. A concentração das escolhas em quasi uma só carreira representa ao que parece uma situação anômala decorrente de falta de orientação vocacional. Os resultados dessa pesquisa concordam com outras realizadas no país. [R. Tavares]

2211. Antipoff, Helena. Os retardados mentais e seus tipos (R SENAC, 1:4, 1953, p. 40-49).
Após descrever as características bio-psicológicas dos retardados mentais, a autora focaliza o problema dos retardados na escola primária e secundária, concluindo por sugerir um programa educativo, a ser desenvolvido de preferência pelo Ministério da Educação, em benefício da infância excepcional. [E. N. Alves]

2212. Avila, José Bastos de. Desenvolvimento físico do escolar (B Inst Pesq Educacionais, 1:1, 1953, 93 p.; 1:3, 1954, 106 p.).
Num amplo trabalho de revisão das tabelas divulgadas em 1940, concernentes ao desenvolvimento físico de criança em idade escolar, apresenta, na primeira parte, o estudo relativo ao tronco e às extremidades, na segunda o estudo da extremidade cefálica dividido em duas partes, a primeira interessando ao crâneo e a segunda à

face. Baseiam-se as pesquisas em cêrca de 5.400 fichas de escolares de um e outro sexo, de 7 a 15 anos de idade, distribuidos pelos três grupos, branco, pardo e preto. As tabelas apresentadas, além dos valores médios e respectivas variações, registram também o desvio-padrão, a fim de que os resultados coligidos possam ser comparados com trabalhos congêneres de outros centros do país ou do estrangeiro. [E. N. Alves]

2213. Azevedo, Fernando de. Educação de educadores; conferência (Anhembi, ano 3, 12:34, set. 1953, p. 25-38).
Depois de historiar rápidamente a formação dos institutos de ensino em Campinas, S. Paulo, mostra que os progressos das instituições do ensino normal e a influência que exerceram derivaram da missão que eram chamadas as escolas normais a cumprir: a formação de professores para o ensino primário. Além disso constituiram elas centros de estudo básicos de nível médio e focos de vida intelectual nas cidades onde existiam. [A. Coutinho]

2214. Barros, N. C. Brito, and Orlando José da Silva. Programas educativos nas unidades sanitárias do serviço especial de saúde pública (R Serv Espec Saú Púb, 6:1, 1953, p. 219-284).

2215. Benjamin, Abraão. Molduras da filosofia e história da educação. São Paulo, Martins, 1954. 241 p.
Após abordar em capítulos introdutórios os temas genéricos e fundamentadores da educação, suas raizes e seus processos e sua problemática, passa o autor ao exame da história da educação, em tôdas as suas fases e teorias, inclusive em capítulo especial, da história da educação no Brasil. [A. Coutinho]

2216. Bittencourt, Raul. A educação brasileira no Império e na República (R Br Estud Ped, 19:49, jan.-março 1953, p. 41-76).
Ensaio sôbre a evolução do sistema educacional brasileiro, caracterizando a educação dentro de cada um dos períodos de nossa formação histórica. [S. Oliveira]

2217. Brandão Filho, A. Sugestões e críticas ao projeto das diretrizes e bases da educação nacional (R Br Estud Ped, 20-52, out.-dez. 1953, p. 3-26).
Considerações em tôrno do problema da carreira de magistério, mostrando como o sistema não funciona com a atual organização do magistério superior, e fazendo sugestões para que êle seja uma realidade. Debate o problema da promoção no ensino superior e por último o da vocação, propondo a exigência de testes de personalidade e exames de sanidade mental para o ingresso no curso superior. [A. Coutinho]

2218. Brazil. Campanha de Aperfeiçoamento e Difusão do Ensino Secundário. Manual do secretário para uso nos estabelecimentos de ensino secundário.

Rio, Ministério da Educação e Cultura, 1955. 127 p.
Trabalho de equipe no qual se inclui um programa de lições para secretários, organizado pela Diretoria do Ensino Secundário.

2219. ————. Campanha Nacional de Aperfeiçoamento de Pessoal de Nível Superior. Atividades da CAPES em 1953 —programação atual (B Inf CAPES; 23, 1954, p. 3-15).

2220. ————. Campanha Nacional de Educação Rural. Uma experiência de educação de base no Brasil. São Paulo, Congresso Interamericano de Educação de Base, 1954. 14 p.
Exposição sôbre a estrutura, objetivos e realizações da CNER que, criada em 1951 pelo Ministério de Educação e Cultura, vem obtendo, nos anos de 1952, 1953 e 1954 os melhores resultados no que chama de "experiência" em benefício das populações rurais.

2221. ————. Departamento Nacional de Educação. O Departamento Nacional de Educação no exercício de 1954. Rio, 1955. 125 p.
Relatório apresentado ao Ministro da Educação. Dá notícia dos planos de trabalho para 1954 e 1955, da estrutura e atividades de vários órgãos e de sua situação orçamentária e administrativa. [Otávio Martins]

2222. ————. Diretoria do Ensino Secundário. Adaptação de cursos. Rio, 1954. 129 p.
Legislação e pareceres do Conselho Nacional e da Consultoria Jurídica do Ministério de Educação e Cultura sôbre adaptação ao curso secundário, de alunos provindos de outros cursos de nível médio.

2223. ————. ————. Assuntos diversos: ates e pareceres do Conselho Nacional de Educação e do Consultor Jurídico sôbre assuntos diversos referentes ao ensino secundário. Rio, 1954. 20 p.

2224. ————. ————. Documentário no. 1. Rio, 1954. 46 p.
Discursos pronunciados por ocasião da transmissão do cargo de diretor do ensino secundário ao prof. Armando Hildebrand, acompanhados do plano de trabalho do novo diretor.

2225. ————. ————. Exames de suficiência. Rio, 1955. 60 p. (Documentário, 7).
Reúne todos os dispositivos legais e regulamentares vigentes sôbre a realização dos exames de suficiência para professores do ensino secundário. [Regina Tavares]

2226. ————. ————. Fundo nacional do ensino médio. Rio, 1955. 62 p. (Documentário, 5).

Reúne um documentário acêrca da instituição do Fundo nacional de ensino médio, pela lei 2.342 de novembro de 1954. A publicação contem um histórico do projeto, desde sua apresentação em 1953 até a sua regulamentação em 1955, o texto da lei, justificativas e exposições de motivos e o decreto de junho de 1955, que regulamentou a aplicação dos recursos do Fundo. [A. Coutinho]

2227. ————. ————. Provas parciais e exames. Rio, 1954. 106 p.

Pareceres da Diretoria do Ensino Secundário sôbre provas e exames, acompanhados de breve orientação em que são condensados os pontos essenciais da matéria. [R. Tavares]

2228. ————. ————. Relação dos estabelecimentos de ensino secundário. Rio, 1955? 365 p.

Lista atualizada (1955)—nome e endereço—de estabelecimentos de ensino secundário dos Estados e territórios brasileiros, num total de 2004 unidades. [G. Vieira]

2229. ————. ————. Fundação do Ensino Secundário. Fundação para manter estabelecimentos de ensino secundário. Rio, 1955. 24 p.

Refere-se aos seguintes aspectos: apresentação, meios para constituir uma fundação, minuta de escrituração de constituição, sugestões para projeto de lei que autoriza a criação da fundação, modêlo de estatutos e de petição para aprovação pelo ministério público, extrato dos estatutos para publicação e legislação aplicavel às fundações. [G. Vieira]

2230. ————. Distrito Federal. Prefeitura. Departamento de Geografia e Estatística. Aspectos gerais do ensino público (Mens Est, DF, 152, 1953, p. 142-151).

2231. ————. ————. ————. Secretaria Geral de Educação e Cultura. Ementário de legislação 1935-1953. Rio, 1955. 220 p.

Reúne as principais leis federais e municipais, relativas à educação no Distrito Federal, desde a criação da Secretaria. [A. Coutinho]

2232. ————. Instituto Brasileiro de Geografia e Estatística. Conselho Nacional de Estatística. Ensino primário geral. Ensino médio (B Est, Rio, 13:49, jan.-março 1955, p. 64-74).

Quadros demonstrativos relativos ao ensino primário geral e ao ensino médio, com as seguintes espicificações: Ensino pre-primário infantil; Ensino fundamental comum; Ensino fundamental supletivo, ensino complementar e ensino em geral. Ensino Médio: (1) distribuição municipal dos estabelecimentos de ensino por unidades da federação, 1954; (2) unidades escolares e alunos matriculados, no início do ano letivo de 1954 e conclusões de curso em 1953, segundo os ramos de ensino e as entidades mantenedoras; (3) unidades escolares, segundo os ramos de ensino e ciclos didáticos

por unidades da federação e capitais, 1954; (4) alunos matriculados, segundo os ramos de ensino e ciclos didáticos, 1954; (5) conclusões de curso, segundo os ramos de ensino e os ciclos didáticos, 1953. [R. Tavares]

2233. ————. ————. ————. Estudos sôbre a alfabetização da população do Brasil. Rio, 1955. 159 p. (Estudos de estatística teórica e aplicada; Estatística cultural, 8).

Compreendendo estudos sôbre Minas Gerais e São Paulo, completa a série de estudos baseados no censo de 1950 sobre alfabetização, segundo o sexo e a idade, por estados, zonas fisiográficas, municípios e cuadros administrativos (cidades, vila e zonas rurais). Os quadros dão números e percentagens dos que sabem ler e escrever na população de 5 anos e mais, relacionados em geral com os valores correspondentes ao censo de 1940. Nos quadros por idade, esta só é dada para grupos de 10 anos (salvo o primeiro de 5 a 9). [O. Martins]

2234. ————. ————. ————. Sinópse estatística do ensino médio, 1954. Rio, 1954. 15 p.

2235. ————. ————. ————. Sinópse estatística do ensino primário geral, 1954. Rio, 1954. 13 p.

2236. ————. ————. ————. Sinópse estatística do ensino superior. Rio, 1954. 24 p.

2237. ————. Ministério da Educação e Cultura. A Campanha de Educação Rural em 1953. 14 p., illus.

Origem, estrutura e atividades da campanha de Educação Rural, incluindo documentação fotográfica de alguns resultados dos trabalhos realizados. [Salvio Oliveira]

2238. ————. ————. Exames de suficiência; programas . . . Rio, Campanha de Aperfeiçoamento e Difusão do Ensino Secundário, 1955.

Série de oito publicações. Cada uma compreende duas partes: a primeira se refere a inscrições, cursos e exames de suficiência dos candidatos ao magistério secundário; a segunda aborda problemas metodológicos da matéria em questão, bem como apresentação do programa de ciências naturais, filosofia, francês, geografia, história, história natural-física-química, latim e matemática. Cita bibliografia. [G. Vieira]

2239. ————. ————. Principais aspectos do ensino no Brasil. Rio, 1953. 194 p.

A publicação traz como sub-título: "Sinopse comemorativa do 20. aniversário do Convênio Interadministrativo de Estatísticas Educacionais e Conexas, firmado na capital da república, em 20 de dezembro de 1931, sob os auspícios da Associação Brasileira de Educação" e apresentada até 1949. Na introducação é traçado um histórico dos progressos verificados neste setor e expõe a classificação estatística do ensino adotada pelo Convênio de 1931 e suas alterações posteriores. O trabalho se divide em duas partes: a primeira trata dos principais aspectos do ensino de todos os graus e ramos, a segunda apresenta dados mais detalhados sôbre êsses mesmos aspectos, relativos apenas ao ensino primário geral. [Otávio Martins]

2240. ————. ————. Serviço de Documentação. Lei orgânica do ensino secundário e legislação complementar. Organizado por Francisco de Assis Vieira. . . . 2. ed. Rio, 1955. 420 p. (Col. Documentos).
Edição ampliada contendo atos legislativos a partir de 1942 até 1955. 1. edição, 1953.

2241. ————. ————. Serviço de Estatística da Educação. Sinopse estatística do ensino médio, 1955. Rio, 1955. 47 p.
Mostra em quadros sinópticos, a situação do ensino médio no início de 1955.

2242. ————. Ministério das Relações Exteriores. Situação cultural; educação (*in* Brasil. Rio, 1955, p. 83-128, illus.).
De referência ao aspecto cultural, expõe a situação da educação nos varios tipos e graus,— primário, secundário, superior, industrial, agrícola, veterinário, militar, informando alem disso, sôbre vários centros de produção cultural do país. Gráficos e ilustrações documentam o trabalho, que é, assim, um repositório de informes e dados sobre o Brasil, destinado sobretudo a divulgação no estrangeiro. [A. Coutinho]

2243. **Brejon, Moisés.** Cursos e bôlsas de estudo. São Paulo, Universidade de São Paulo, Seção de Publicações, 1953. 15 p.
Inquérito realizado entre alunos do curso noturno da Faculdade de Filosofia, Ciências e Letras da Universidade de São Paulo, afim de verificar o gráu de viabilidade da substituição dos cursos universitários noturnos pela prática das bolsas de estudo, ideia esta suscitada pelas restrições que se fazem ao funcionamento daqueles cursos. [A. Coutinho]

2244. **Burkinski, Francisco.** A crise brasileira e a operação município. Prefácio de Araujo Cavalcanti. Rio, Inst. Int. Cienc. Adm., Seção Brasil, 1955. 69 p.
Exposição de projetos de recuperação e desenvolvimento municipais, denominado "operação município," o qual inclui um programa ligado à educação, com ampliação da rêde escolar, sobretudo de finalidade rural, com formação de profissionais. [A. Coutinho]

2245. **Café Filho, João.** Educação e cultura. Mensagem ao Congresso Nacional (Diário do Congresso Nacional, março 16, 1955, p. 198-207).
Exposição sôbre as diretrizes gerais do ensino, nos diversos graus e tipos, bem como as atividades e medidas do govêrno para resolver e

enfrentar as dificuldades verificadas na educação nacional.

2246. **Camarinha, José.** Programas e métodos na alfabetização e educação de adultos (Ed Ad, junho 1954, p. 18-27).

2247. **Campos, Ernesto de Sousa.** História da Universidade de São Paulo. São Paulo, Saraiva, 1954. 502 p., illus.
Trabalho fartamente documentado que relata a história da Universidade de S. Paulo, desde a sua fundação em 1934.

2248. **Cândido, António.** A estrutura da escola. Contribuição sociológica aos cursos especializados de administração escolar. São Paulo, Universidade de São Paulo, Faculdade de Filosofia, Ciências e Letras (Caderno, 5), 1953. 33 p.
Estuda a estrutura total da escola como resultante não só da estrutura administrativa como tambem da própria dinâmica do grupo social escolar, envolvendo relações que escapam à previsão dos administradores. Focaliza esquemáticamente as formas de agrupamento que se apresentam na escola como entidade social— grupos de idade, de sexo associativos, de ensino, "status"—e analisalhes os mecanismos de sustentação—a liderança, normas de conduta escolar, as sanções e os símbolos. Conclui considerando não bastar ao educador o conhecimento de estrutura interna da escola, sendo necessário que paralelamente compreenda a integração desta na estrutura geral da sociedade, em que funciona como fator preponderante de contrôle social. [D. F. Monteiro]

2249. **Carvalho, Irene Mello.** O ensino por unidades didáticas; seu ensáio no Colégio Nova Friburgo. Rio, Fundação Getúlio Vargas, 1954. 219 p.
O trabalho se refere a um ensáio de aplicação do plano de ensino por unidades segundo o sistema Morrison, no Colégio Nova Friburgo.

2250. **Chaves, Nelson.** Universidade, pesquisa e humanismo (R Br Estud Ped, 24-60, out.-dez. 1955, p. 104-120).
Focaliza o papel da universidade moderna que deve reunir o espírito filosófico e científico, o adestramento técnico, a capacidade de pesquisa. Sômente associando universidade, pesquisa e humanismo se dará fundamento à civilização e solução aos graves problemas da sociedade moderna. [A. Coutinho]

2251. **Coelho, Elói do Egito.** Análise dos resultados da escola industrial de Teresina (B CBAI, 9:6. junho 1955, p. 142-1332).
Série de quadros indicando, em números, a situação geral dos alunos, desde a admissão à sua colocação no mercado de trabalho, no campo do ensino técnico e industrial, com detalhes sôbre o recrutamento dos candidatos, matrícula, frequência e aproveitamento. O número de alunos diplomados é elevado, sendo a escola que maior número de alunos diplomou até hoje, na rêde federal.

2252. **Collins, Dwane R.,** and **Theodor M. Simon.** Uma técnica realista para o treinamento de professôres (R Ped, ano 1, 1:1, 1955, p. 11-20).
Descreve e analisa uma técnica prática experimentada com êxito no Instituto Tecnológico de Aeronáutica de São José dos Campos para "ensinar aos professôres a ensinar melhor." [G. Vieira]

2253. **Dória, Ana Rimoli de Faria.** Compêndio de educação da criança surda-muda. Rio, 1954. 179 p.
Destina-se aos professores e aos pais de uma criança surda-muda ou melhor a todos os que convivem com eia e desejam auxiliá-la no seu esfôrço de adaptação à sociedade em que vive.

2254. **Faria Góis Sobrinho.** A dinámica nervosa da aprendizagem (B Inst Psicol, 5:3-4, 1955, p. 1-10).
Exposição da teoria que o autor vem desenvolvendo, em seus cursos de fundamentos biológicos da educação, sôbre o substrato físico, orgânico, dos comportamentos. Sustenta que a aprendizagem, o ato típico da educação, implica progresso orgânico do sistema nervoso, e que esse mecanismo da aprendizagem é concorde com Dewey de que educação é crescimento.

2255. **Fontoura, Amaral.** Metodologia do ensino primário; contendo matéria dos 2. e 3. anos do curso normal. Rio, Gráf. Ed. Aurora, 1955. 470 p.

2256. **Franca, Leonel.** Obras completas. 5. Alocuções e artigos. Rio, 1954. 2 v.
Nestes dois volumes de alocuções e artigos de diversas épocas, o ilustre pensador, jesuita e primeiro Reitor da Pontifícia Universidade Católica do Rio de Janeiro, trata de diversos assuntos relacionados com a história da educação no Brasil, especialmente com a vida da Universidade. São particularmente dignos de menção os estudos sôbre a Companhia de Jesus (v. 1) em que oferece uma síntese da pedagogia dos jesuítas. [A. Coutinho]

2257. **Freitas, Zoraide Rocha de.** História do ensino profissional no Brasil. São Paulo, 1954. 384 p., illus.
Mostra os pródromos do ensino profissional desde o Brasil Império, quando a indústria nascente se tornou mais exigente quanto a operários especializados e eficientes. Houve a preocupação, nas províncias, da criação de estabelecimentos de ensino industrial: ora casas de educandos artífices, ora casas de artes e ofícios. Daí se foi desenvolvendo o ensino profissional, até à época atual, de profundo sentido técnico. [A. Coutinho]

2258. **Freyre, Gilberto.** Em tôrno da situação dos professôres no Brasil (R Ed Cult, 1:1, 1955, p. 5-37).
Ensaio sôbre o papel exercido pelo professor na civilização brasileira, na Colônia e no Império, em contraste com a sua situação no Brasil atual sob o impacto da industrialização.

2259. **Giordana, Ernestina.** Conhecimentos que os adolescentes possuem a respeito dos cursos necessários à sua formação profissional. São Paulo, Universidade de São Paulo, Faculdade de Ciências Econômicas e Administrativas, Instituto de Administração (Contribuição ao estudo da orientação educacional e profissional na escola secundária, 1), 1954. 19 p.

2260. ————. Previsões dos adolescentes sôbre a realização do seu ideal profissional. São Paulo, Universidade de São Paulo, Faculdade de Ciências Econômicas e Administrativas, Instituto de Administração (Contribuição ao estudo da orientação educacional e profissional na escola secundária, 2), 1954. 13 p.
Inquérito realizado pelo Instituto de Administração da Universidade de São Paulo para conhecer as aspirações profissionais dos alunos de ginásios. Foram ouvidos 1435 adolescentes da 4. série ginasial sôbre quais os cursos que deveriam fazer para seguir sua profissão preferida. O inquérito revela que a escolha da profissão se faz com grande dose de ignorância a respeito dos estudos necessários para a respectiva formação. Isso patenteia a tarefa que se impõe aos serviços de orientação profissional das escolas secundárias quanto a orientação do adolescente na escolha da profissão. [A. Coutinho]

2261. **Grisi, Rafael.** Didática mínima. 2. ed. São Paulo, Ed. Brasil, 1954. 102 p.
Analisa os erros mais comuns à prática didática no curso secundário, comentando-os partir de fatos e flagrantes das salas de aulas. No último capítulo, trata do que classifica como "diálogo fecundo," o qual importa no encorajamento dos alunos em suas curiosidades e tentativas de manifestação do seu pensamento, não somente no que diz respeito às matérias escolares, mas tambem a si próprios em suas dúvidas, inaptações e perplexidades em face da vida. [D. F. Monteiro]

2262. **Instituto Nacional de Estudos Pedagógicos.** Projeto de uma escola primaria pilôto do Centro Brasileiro de Pesquisas Educacionais. Rio, 1955. 24 p.
O projeto no. 21 de 1955, elaborado pela Coordenação dos Cursos de Instituto Nacional de Estudos Pedagógicos, estabelece a criação, mediante acôrdo firmado com a Secretaria Geral de Educação e Cultura da Prefeitura do Distrito Federal e funcionamento da primeira escola experimental do I. N. E. P., localizada no Rio. Em 13 documentos, apresenta o plano geral de trabalho para o ano de 1955. [G. Vieira]

2263. ————. Campanha de Inquéritos e Levantamentos do Ensino Médio e Elementar. A educação no Paraná: síntese sôbre o ensino público elementar e médio. [Por Erasmo Piloto]. Rio, 1954. 128 p. (Publ., 3).

Trabalho realizado por solicitação e planejamento da Campanha de Inquéritos e Levantamentos do Ensino Médio e Elementar (CILEME) como contribuição do estado à série de estudos regionais que estão sendo promovidos no país, visando a efetivar preliminarmente uma sondagem objetiva da realidade educacional brasileira. [G. Vieira]

2264. ————. ————. A escola elementar e a formação do professor primário no Rio Grande do Sul. [Por Roberto Moreira]. Rio, 1954. 317 p. (Publ., 5).

O autor apresenta, após fixar os aspectos culturais do Rio Grande do Sul, uma análise apreciativa do sistema educacional focalizando: a organização administrativa da educação; as despesas com educação e cultura; a escola primária, nos seus aspectos administrativos numéricos e materiais, funcionais e qualitativos; o professor primário e sua formação.

2265. ————. ————. Estudos sôbre o Ceará. [Por Joaquim Moreira de Sousa]. Rio, 1955. 240 p. (Publ., 8).

O autor observa que o sistema educacional predominante no Ceará sempre foi puramente alfabetizante e intelectual, não concorrendo para minorar a miseria do povo e os desequilíbrios econômicos em fatôres climáticos hostís. Conclui pela necessidade de organização de um sistema de ensino orientado para a restauração do solo e reabilitação do homem, para vitalizar a economia coletiva. Propõe o preparo adequado do professor primário, através de uma Escola Normal, cujos programas sejam moldados pelas necessidades e características físicas, morais e econômicas do meio. Observa apenas como digno de realce o trabalho realizado pelo prof. Lourênço Filho, quando diretor geral da instrução de 1922 a 1923.

2266. ————. ————. Introdução ao estudo de currículos da escola primária. [Por J. Roberto Moreira]. Rio, 1955. 218 p. (Publ., 7).

Estudo histórico-crítico de currículo da escola primária brasileira, em face de seu condicionamento filosófico, social, econômico e cultural. Inclui ainda uma exposição sôbre os princípios fundamentais e a técnica de elaboração do currículo, além de sugerir medidas imediatas que poderiam ser adotadas com o fim de melhorar o currículo da escola elementar brasileira. [E. N. Alves]

2267. ————. ————. O sistema educacional fluminense; uma tentativa de interpretação e crítica. [Por Jaime Abreu]. Rio, 1955. 371 p. (Publ., 6).

Dentro do programa de estudos dos aspectos gerais e administrativos dos sistemas estaduais de educação, o INEP, através da CILEME apresenta o resultado das pesquisas levantadas no sistema de educação do estado do Rio de Janeiro. O estudo baseado em ampla documentação, empreende o exame do sistema fluminense de educação em relação ao meio social e econômico; analisa o resultado da escola elementar e da escola média, oferecendo sugestões para o desenvolvimento da educação naquele estado.

2268. Instituto Nacional de Estudos Pedagógicos—Centro Brasileiro de Pesquisas Educacionais (R Br Estud Ped, 23:59, julho-set. 1955, p. 118-136).

Apresenta os objetivos que o Centro Brasileiro de Pesquisas Educacionais do INEP, funcionando com a colaboração da UNESCO, se propõe realizar e, em face deles, traça um planejamento de suas atividades, através de estudos e pesquisas cuja execução ficará a cargo de especialistas. [D. F. Monteiro]

2269. Kelly, Celso. A educação na assistência técnica. Rio, Comissão Nacional de Assistência Técnica (O desenvolvimento econômico do Brasil e a assistência técnica; Ciclo de estudos, 3), 1953. 28 p.

Descrevendo o programa ampliado de assistência técnica promovido pela Nações Unidas e suas agências destinado a diminuir a desigualdade entre as nações e concorrer para o progresso econômico e bem estar social, focaliza o papel da ciência e do conhecimento, bem como a obra da UNESCO, especialmente quanto à educação de base. Entre as modalidades de assistência técnica, salienta especialmente as missões e as bolsas. [O. Martins]

2270. ————. Educação popular e obrigatoriedade do ensino (R Br Estud Ped, 23:59, julho-set. 1955, p. 103-113).

Estuda o problema, de modo geral, em face dos Direitos do Homem e passa, em seguida, a particularizá-lo à luz da Constituição Brasileira e das soluções práticas para o mesmo adotadas no âmbito federal e estadual. [D. F. Monteiro]

2271. Kessel, Moisés I. A evasão escolar no ensino primário (R Br Estud Ped, 22:56, out.-dez. 1954, p. 53-72).

Estudos procedidos pelo Instituto Nacional de Estudos Pedagógicos mostrando o gráu de evasão escolar no ensino primário. Em todo o país, de cada dez mil alunos matriculados na primeira série primária apenas 15% são aprovados na quarta série. No Rio Grande do Sul, a percentagem é de 34% nas escolas urbanas e 11.5% nas rurais; em São Paulo de 52 e 27%. Os índices apresentados neste estudo indicam a necessidade de mudança radical na conceituação da escola primária.

2272. Leme, Pascoal. Estudos de educação. Rio, Tupã, 1953. 262 p.

O autor aborda vários problemas educacionais como: fundamentos sociais e psicológicos; a evolução da educação de adultos com uma experiencia de cursos de continuação, aperfeiçoamento e oportunidade, realizada no Distrito Federal; a situação do ensino no Brasil, apresentada à base de estatísticas oficiais de 1945; a situação da educação no Brasil atual. [R. Almeida]

2273. Lima Filho, Francisco da Gama. O estado atual do ensino comercial e o SENAC (R SENAC, 2, 1953, p. 28-38).

Passa em revista a evolução do ensino comercial no Brasil, ressaltando o maior sentido de formação humanística atribuido atualmente a êsse ensino, em contraposição ao caráter essencialmente profissional que tivera no passado. Expõe as realizações dô Serviço Nacional de Aprendizagem Comercial, quer no domínio do ensino para trabalhadores menores e adultos, quer no da assistência ao ensino comercial de formação. [E. N. Alves]

2274. Lopes, José Stênio. Escola rural no município. Rio, Departamento Administrativo do Serviço Público, Serviço de Documentação (Estudos municipais, 1), 1954, p. 17-30.
Descreve e analisa os tipos de escolas primárias dos municípios cearences, contando suas deficiências e apresentando um plano de escola típica rural (localização, prédio, organização, horários, programas, etc.). Conclui dizendo que a tarefa de alfabetização dos habitantes das zonas rurais está a exigir um tipo de escola mais flexível, "escolas móveis" de um a outro sítio, e de ação mais rápida, ao lado das unidades fixas nos povoamentos e vilas. Acha que a tarefa educativa do município não pode ser limitada a alfabetização e sim preparar também o homem do campo para os encargos da mecanização da lavoura e da agricultura, sendo aconselhaveis convênios intermunicipais ou com o estado para realização de um programa de escolas rurais no interior. [R. Tavares]

2275. Lourenço Filho, M. B. A formação do professorado primário (R Br Estud Ped, 23-57, jan.-março 1955, p. 42-51).
Depois de notícia histórica da formação do professor primário no mundo, estuda o ensino normal no Brasil desde os seus primórdios, mostrando as diversas etapas, as reformas que sofreu, a organização geral da educação, programas e cursos de formação. [A. Coutinho]

2276. ――――. A pedagogia de Rui Barbosa. São Paulo, Melhoramentos, 1954. 128 p.
Estudo sôbre os escritos pedagógicos de Rui Barbosa, focalizando as diretrizes filosóficas e as orientações metodológicas. Observa que o pensamento de Rui em matéria de educação resultou da convergência de princípios políticos (o liberalismo), de idéias sociais (a organização das classes médias), dos fundamentos filosóficos que o caracterizaram (o idealismo de Kant e Fichte). Examinando os famosos pareceres sôbre o ensino, a tradução de Lição de Coisas e outros trabalhos de Rui, acentua o autor a influência que tiveram as suas idéias em matéria pedagógica sôbre o conjunto de sua filosofia política, tendo sido Rui o primeiro no Brasil a propor a idéia da "cultura integral" como base da política educacional.

2277. ――――. Preparação de pessoal docente para escolas primárias rurais (R Br Estud Ped, 20:52, out.-dez. 1953, p. 61-104).
Considerações sobre a formação do pessoal docente para as escolas rurais; mostra os esforços que tem sido realizados no Brasil nesse sentido, de acôrdo com o incremento que vem tendo

êsse tipo de ensino. Analisa duas experiências recentes de preparação especializada de pessoal de ensino para escolas rurais—a de Juazeiro do Norte e a de Fazenda do Rosário—acentuando que ambas mostraram a necessidade de melhoria da formação de pessoal docente e a possibilidade de treinamento de professores do ensino rural. [A. Coutinho]

2278. ――――. Problemas de educação secundária; palestra proferida no curso para inspetores federais do ensino secundário, promovido pela Campanha de Aperfeiçoamento e Difusão do Ensino Secundário. Rio, Campanha de Aperfeiçoamento e Difusão do Ensino Secundário, 1954. 24 p. (Documentário, 4).
Mostrando a disparidade entre o crescimento do ensino secundário e o dos outros graus de ensino, procura explicar as causas prováveis dessa expansão, focalizando ainda os problemas com que se defronta o ensino secundário em decorrência de seu próprio crescimento e da nova realidade social a que deve servir. [E. N. Alves]

2279. ――――. Testes ABC. 4. ed. São Paulo, Melhoramentos, 1952. 122 p.
Em primeiro lugar, o autor passa em revista os critérios adotados para a organização de classes seletivas do primeiro grau das escolas primárias: o da idade cronológica, o da idade escolar, e, por último, o do emprêgo de testes mentais. Observa que a aplicação desses critérios não tem dado resultado satisfatório, e propõe a aplicação dos testes, situando o problema da aprendizagem e da escrita em termos de maturidade. Tendo iniciado suas primeiras pesquisas em 1925, procurou o autor testes de técnica e emprêgo bem conhecidos, os quais, em número de vinte e dois para os primeiros ensaios, foram reduzidos finalmente a oito. Os resultados práticos obtidos por parte de serviços oficiais de psicologia aplicada ou em experiencias menores, tem comprovado o valor da organização de classes seletivas pelos testes ABC. As vantagens de sua aplicação têm sido indiscutíveis na melhoria do rendimento escolar, na definição das responsabilidades dos mestres e no estudo de alunos-problemas. Nesta nova edição, foram acrescentadas indicações sôbre recentes trabalhos de investigadores estrangeiros, a notícia do primeiro ensaio de análise fatorial dos testes, realizado no Rio de Janeiro pelo dr. Otávio Martins e o material completo para exame. [E. N. Alves]

2280. Marcondes Filho, Alexandre. Esbôço de programas básicos; exposição de motivos. Rio, Imp. Nacional, 1955. 14 p.
Traça diretrizes a serem aplicadas pelo Ministério de Educação e Cultura, quanto ao ensino profissional e à formação de elites. [R. Tavares]

2281. Melo, Orlando Ferreira de. Comentários sôbre a monografia *A educação em Santa Catarina.* Rio, Campanha de Inquéritos e Levantamentos de Ensino Médio e Elementar, 1955. 40 p.

2282. Mêrici, Imideo Giuseppe. Os programas e a escola secundária. Rio, Diretoria do Ensino Secundario (Documentário, 8), 1955.

En seu estudo sôbre os programas, examina conceito, tipos, objetivos, características, elaboração e desenvolvimento, bem como a função do professor e do inspetor federal em face do programa. Cita bibliografia. [G. Vieira]

2283. Montenegro, Olívio. O problema da educação (R Ed Cult, 1:1, 1955, p. 56-70).

Considerações sôbre o problema da educação, sua finalidade, seus processos.

2284. Moreira, J. Roberto. O disvirtuamento da escola primária urbana pela multiplicação de turnos e pela desarticulação com o ensino médio (R Br Estud Ped, 22:56, out.-dez. 1954, p. 39-52).

Estuda o problema, analisando a questão das relações entre o ensino elementar e o ensino médio, concluindo por sugerir um mais íntimo entrosamento entre os dois graus de ensino, como se vem fazendo em diversos paises. [A Coutinho]

2285. ————. A educação em Santa Catarina. Rio, Instituto Nacional de Estudos Pedagógicos, Campanha de Inquéritos e Levantamentos do Ensino Médio e Elementar (2), 1954. 103 p.

Sinopse apreciativa sôbre a administração, as origens e a difusão de um sistema estadual de educação. Através de análises e exposições, chega a conclusão de que, apesar do grande esforço desenvolvido pelo governo, desde 1911, para dotar o estado de um sistema de educação popular, amplo e eficiente, o objetivo não foi atingido. Sugere as linhas gerais de um plano capás de proporcionar novos caminhos à educação em Santa Catarina.

2286. ————. O valor da ciência e os estudos educacionais (R Br Estud Ped, 21:53, jan.-março 1954, p. 21-47).

Julga não se justificar no Brasil qualquer tentativa de pesquisa científica pura, têndo em vista uma ciência pura da educação. Indica uma regra de ação científica—a da pesquisa imediatamente comprometida com problemas práticos, específicos, imediatos, de acôrdo com as necessidades prementes do Brasil, onde a educação tem vivido um rosário contínuo de erros, sem o suporte de nenhuma pesquisa objetiva, sistemática. [A. Coutinho]

2287. Mota Filho, Cândido. Servindo à educação. Rio, Ministério da Educação e Cultura, Serviço de Documentação, 1955. 130 p.

Reúne o volume uma série de alocuções proferidas pelo autor, quando Ministro da Educação e Cultura, focalizando problemas de importancia em relação à educação nacional: a educação e a máquina; a teoria e prática da escola primária; a frecuencia na escola primária; problemas da educação de gráu medio; o significado político da escola; o problema do livro, etc. [A. Coutinho]

2288. Neves, Carlos de Sousa. Ensino superior no Brasil: legislação e jurisprudência federais. Rio, Instituto Nacional de Estudos Pedagógicos, 1954-1955. 4 v.

Seleção de toda a matéria que se acha em vigor, constituindo valioso trabalho de referência legislativa, com índices analítico, remissivo e cronológico.

2289. Nóbrega, Vandick Londres da. Enciclopédia da legislação do ensino. V. 2. Rio, Jornal do Comércio, 1954.

Este volume procura completar as lacunas do anterior (1952) e imprime grande desenvolvimento à legislação do ensino superior. Inclúi tambem ensino militar e informações sobre o ensino em alguns paises da Europa, especialmente programas de ensino vigentes na Alemanha. [Regina Tavares]

2290. Observações à margem das conclusões de curso, no ensino superior civil, no ano letivo de 1952 (R Br Estud Ped, 23:58, abril-junho 1955, p. 181-194).

Estudo elaborado pelo Serviço de Estatística e Documentação da Campanha Nacional de Aperfeiçoamento de Pessoal de Nível Superior (CAPES). (Transcrito do Boletim estatístico, editado pelo Conselho Nacional de Estatística do Instituto Brasileiro de Geografia e Estatística, 12:48, out.-dez. 1954).

2291. Pasquale, Carlos. Financiamento da educação secundária. Rio, Ministério da Educação e Cultura (Documentário, 3), 1954. 30 p.

Palestra realizada no curso para aperfeiçoamento de inspetores de ensino secundário, na qual revê o problema grave de financiamento do ensino, mostrando como é pequena a participação da União na educação secundária.

2292. Penteado Júnior, Onofre de Arruda. Introdução ao estudo da orientação educacional. São Paulo, Universidade de São Paulo, Faculdade de Filosofia, Ciências e Letras (Caderno, 3), 1953. 65 p.

2293. ————. O sentido e a ação da Universidade. São Paulo, Universidade de São Paulo, Faculdade de Filosofia, Ciências e Letras (Caderno, 1), 1954. 24 p.

Combate a orientação que reduz as universidades a instrumentos de pura pesquisa científica, pensando que elas são órgãos de ação social e orientação política. [A. Coutinho]

2294. Pereira, Nilo. A universidade democrática e a paz mundial (R Ed Cult, 1:1, 1955, p. 46-55).

Defende, como papel da universidade no mundo atual, a pacificação dos homens pela universalização do espírito universitário. [A. Coutinho]

2295. Piloto, Erasmo. Temas de educação de nosso tempo; teologia pedagógica. Rio,

Oficinas de Aprendizagem do Serviço Nacional de Aprendizagem Industrial, 1954. 224 p.

Exposição crítica das correntes principais da filosofia da educação, a partir do naturalismo pedagógico. En seguida, analisa a reação antinaturalista que caracteriza o momento presente e conclui tentando uma síntese unificadora do pensamento pedagógico.

2296. Querino, Manuel. O Colégio de S. Joaquim (*in* Bahia de outrora. Salvador, Brazil, Liv. Progresso, 1955, p. 107-110, illus.).

Dados sôbre o Colégio de Órfãos de S. Joaquim e sôbre outros colégios existentes na Bahia em 1838, acompanhados de uma nota de rodapé con valiosas informações sôbre o ensino secundário naquela cidade no período de 1810 a 1821. [R. Tavares]

2297. Rafael, Forte. O ensino primário no Brasil (colônia, império e república, fases decisivas). Bahia, Brazil, Era Nova, 1953. 26 p.

Esbôço da evolução da instrução primária no Brasil contendo transcrição e comentários de leis, discursos atos, etc. [A. Coutinho]

2298. Renault, Abgar. Aspectos da crise do ensino no Brasil (Formação, Rio, 16-187, fev. 1954, p. 5-21).

Crítica da situação atual do ensino no Brasil, apontando as raízes do fenómeno da sua decadência, considerando as causas mais sociais que pedagógicas. Assinala a má qualidade do curso primário e em consequência a falha da escola secundária. Julga mister aprofundar a formação do professor secundário e primário e mobilizar tôdas as forças para a regeneração moral dos hábitos no ensino. [A. Coutinho]

2299. Ribeiro, Eloá Brodt, and Gilka Niederauer Fontoura. Sugestões para o desenvolvimento de atividades nos jardins de infância. Rio Grande do Sul, Centro de Pesquisas e Orientação Educacionais, 1954. 47 p.

Atendendo às mais recentes conquistas psicopedagógicas, sintetiza as finalidades da educação pré-primária e apresenta, objetivamente, uma série de sugestões para o desenvolvimento das atividades de jardim de infância. Em diretrizes gerais orienta a jardineira, analisando os fundamentos do curso. Apresenta ainda indicações sôbre mobiliário e material e inclue farta bibliografia. [G. Vieira]

2300. ————, and **Rute Ivotí T. da Silva.** Sugestões para desenvolvimento de atividaes nas escolas primárias rurais (B Cent Pesq Or Ed, 1952-1953, p. 9-26).

Apresentação de um plano de atividades para desenvolvimento dos programas de ensino em escolas primárias rurais.

2301. Ribeiro, José Querino. Racionalização do sistema escolar; contribuição para o estudo das "Diretrizes e bases."

São Paulo, Universidade de São Paulo, Faculdade de Filosofia e Ciências e Letras (Caderno, 7), 1954. 32 p.

Propõe um plano de sistema escolar nacional tomando como ponto de partida os grandes problemas atuais da vida brasileira e baseando-se na reforma francesa projetada por Langevin e Walton e na inglesa, decorrente do "Ato Educacional de 1944."

2302. ————; **José Severo de Camargo Pereira; and Moysés Brejon.** Concurso de ingresso no magistério secundário e normal. São Paulo, Universidade de São Paulo, Faculdade de Filosofia e Letras (Cadeira de administração escolar e educação comparada, Boletim 206; 2).

Resultados das observações procedidas pelos responsáveis pela cadeira de Administração Escolar da Faculdade de Filosofia da Universidade de São Paulo nos concursos para provimento das vagas de magistério oficial do gráu médio em São Paulo, em 1949.

2303. Rios, José Artur. A educação dos grupos. Rio, Serviço Nacional de Educação Sanitária, 1954. 312 p., illus.

Estuda os métodos e princípios que devem orientar a formação dos administradores, assistentes sociais, professores, sanitaristas, agrônomos, etc. Defende a aplicação da educação de grupo, desenvolvendo nos vários capítulos, as normas de educação grupal, a estrutura do grupo, a forma e o conceito da comunidade, os meios de intervenção, a psicologia da liderança, e mostrando como a educação social é uma técnica a serviço do homem. Além da bibliografia dá gráficos e planos de inquéritos aplicaveis ao assunto. [A. Coutinho]

2304. Rodrigues, Chiquinha. Ensaio primário em São Paulo (*in* Instituto Histórico e Geográfico de São Paulo. São Paulo em quatro séculos. . . . V. 1. São Paulo, 1953, p. 343-371).

Estado do ensino primário em São Paulo, onde ainda prevalece o prestígio das escolas públicas: primária, profissional, secundária e superior. No que respeita à escola primária esta importância vem do século XIX, quando os mestres erem habilitados perante juntas selecionadas com apuro. Quanto à escola normal e outros organismos continuaram o esfôrço por engrandecer a escola pública, em detrimento do ensino particular. Apoia em suas observações dados estatísticos. [A. Coutinho]

2305. Rogério, Luis. A missão rural, fator de recuperação do homem do interior (R Camp Nac Ed Rur, 1:1, 1954, p. 42-56).

Observa que a "missão rural," pela sua técnica e objetivos, atende à necessidade de educar não só crianças e adolescentes, mas tambem adultos, podendo, portanto, concorrer para a melhoria dos padrões culturais da comunidade e das condições de vida do camponês, aumentando-lhe a capacidade e fornecendo-lhe níveis mais altos de vida no lar e na sociedade, como já tem demonstrado a experiência brasileira.

2306. Romero, Nelson. Bases para uma política nacional de educação (R Clube Mil, 129, 1954, p. 14-25).

Tece o autor considerações sôbre o aspecto social da educação, afirmando que o ensino, em sua função primordial, se destina a facilitar e aperfeiçoar os indivíduos para plena posse de suas aptidões e integração do homem no meio social. Expõe a iniciativa que, nesse sentido, foi empreendida pelo Ministério de Educação e Cultura que lançou com a de adultos os fundamentos da Campanha de Educação de Base no Brasil.

2307. Silveira, Alfredo Baltazar da. História do Instituto de Educação. Rio, Secretaria de Educàção e Cultura, 1954. 144 p.

Faz o levantamento da legislação que vem regendo o ensino normal no Distrito Federal. a partir da criação da Escola Normal no município da Côrte. Relembra os primeiros mestres e apresenta a seguir um registro biográfico de todos os diretores que o referido educandário tem tido. Relaciona os antigos professores e a atual congregação. Remata a exposição com a menção de cerimônias cívicas, visitas de autoridades e de educadores estrangeiros, festividades escolares, etc. [D. F. Monteiro]

2308. Situação do ensino no Brasil (Anhembi, ano 3, 10:29, abril 1953, p. 209-214; 11:31, junho 1953, p. 1-3; 11:33, agôsto 1953, p. 415-420; 12:36, nov. 1953, p. 411-412; ano 4, 13:37, dez. 1953, p. 1-8; 14:40, março 1954, p. 1-7; 14:42, maio 1954, p. 435-439; 15:43, junho 1954, p. 1-7; 16:46, set. 1954, p. 1-11).

Série de entrevistas realizadas com destacadas personalidades do magistério nacional, escritores, jornalistas, en que são debatidos os problemas do ensino no Brasil. Responderam ao inquérito: Maurício de Medeiros, Mário Casasanta, João Cruz Costa, Dante Moreira Leite, Lourenço Filho, Glaucio Veiga, Querino Ribeiro, Florestan Fernandes, Wilhelm Speyer e o estudante Bento Moulli.

2309. Smith, T. Lynn. Education and the school (*in* Brazil: people and institutions. Baton Rouge, La., State University Press, 1954, p. 545-569).

Analisa o sistema educacional brasileiro, mostrando primeiro os principios que o norteam. Descreve a evolução da educação desde os tempos coloniais. Indica o estado a que chegou a educação, a situação educacional a julgar pelas mais recentes estatísticas a respeito do problema do analfabetismo. Passa então a examinar a educação nos seus diversos graus: elementar, secundário e superior, para afinal apontar as tendências atuais e perspectivas futuras da educação no país. Afirma que a educação primária e secundária continuarão a progredir nas grandes cidades, não sendo tão favoravel a situação para a população do interior. Examina o papel propulsor das missões rurais, de recente organização. E termina afirmando que o grande problema da educação brasileira é o estabelecimento de uma escola

elementar em cada centro rural e de uma escola secundária, ao menos, em cada município. Cita bibliografia. [A. Coutinho]

2310. Teixeira, Anísio. A crise educacional brasileira. Rio, Ministério da Educação e Cultura, Serviço de Documentação (Os cadernos de cultura, 68), 1954. P. 39-76.

Observando que a crise educacional brasileira resulta da aplicação de um sistema educacional aristocrático, intelectualista, visando à formação de um grupo de letrados e políticos ao invés da preparação comum dos homens que compõem uma sociedade de massa, o autor menciona as providências que se impõem para reajustar a educação aos fins da sociedade democrática. Esse processo de readaptação institucional é o que vive o mundo e o Brasil neste momento. E essa readaptação procurará desenvolver a aprendizagem de ordem vocacional ou prática, exigida pela sociedade moderna, sem descurar todavia os aspectos humanos de sua formação. [A. Coutinho]

2311. ————. A educação que nos convém; palestra proferida na Escola Brasileira de Administração Pública, em 8.8.1954. Rio, 1954. 21 p.

Define o panorama escolar do mundo do ponto de vista político, econômico e cívico. Depois de um retrospecto da questão educacional desde o século 19, mostra como as nações mais civilizadas são as mais escolarizadas. Revê o sistema educacional brasileiro, analisando o decréscimo de eficiência de nosso ensino e do professorado, baseado na improvisação e em ilusórias ou falsas condições técnicas, e também num êrro fundamental que é a perda da função da escola primária em benefício da secundária. [A. Coutinho]

2312. ————. A escola secundária em transformação; palestra realizada no Seminário de Inspetoria do Ensino Secundário (R Br Estud Ped, 21:53, jan.-março 1954, p. 3-20).

Assevera que a escola secundária deixou de ser preparatória do ensino superior, para ser uma escola que ensina a viver, a trabalhar, a produzir, e que de educação literária passa a ser educação técnica, isto é, deve habilitar o indivíduo à posse de um instrumental de trabalho, seja no campo técnico seja no científico, seja no literário. Focaliza o outro aspecto da evolução da escola secundária que é o do preparo de todos os homens para a vida. [A. Coutinho]

2313. ————. Padrões brasileiros de educação (escolar) e cultura; conferência. Rio, 1954. 23 p.

Faz um histórico da evolução da educação, como fenômeno social, através dos tempos, observando que no Brasil dominou até bem pouco a escola de preparação do "letrado" e que só na década de 1920 a 1930 procuraram os educadores dar à educação um sentido de educação popular que harmonizasse a inteligência e a ação, num desenvolvimento físico e mental. Analisa a situação da educação nos três graus e defende a descentralização da

educação e sua distribuição nos planos primá-
rios, médio e superior, afin de que possa
exercer-se plenamente em benefício da integração do homem na sociedade. [A. Coutinho]

2314. ————. Sôbre o problema de como
financiar a educação do povo brasileiro;
bases para discussão. Trabalho apresentado ao 11. Congresso Nacional de Educação, realizado em Curitiba, em janeiro
de 1954. Rio, 1954. 17 p.

Focaliza os delineamentos preliminares e mais
gerais do problema, com elementos de análise
demográfica, estatística e comparativa, incluindo os econômicos e sociais. Crítica a delimita-
ção constitucional dos recursos previstos em
percentagens tributárias e defende a transformação de tais recursos em fundos de educação, com administração especial autônoma.
Planeja a administração de tais recursos, sepa-
rando-se as verbas em custeio e investimento,
integrando-se os recursos federais e municipais
numa só obra de educação, ajustando-se o custo
das escolas às condições dos recursos locais.
As escolas seriam municipais, contando com
o auxílio do Estado na formação do professorado, assistência técnica e orientação do ensino.
Esse plano permite não só levar a educação a
tôdas as crianças brasileiras, como tambem uma
unidade orgânica desenvolvida pelo Ministério
da Educação e Cultura, nos estados e nos
municípios.

2315. ————. A universidade e a liberdade humana. Rio de Janeiro, Ministério

da Educação e Cultura, Serviço de Documentação (Os cadernos de cultura, 68),
1954. p. 3-36.

Considerações sobre o papel que compete à
universidade, no regime da plena autonomia
que merece de direito, quanto ao problema da
liberdade humana. Observa que para obtenção
do pleno desenvolvimento desse conceito, é
necessário transforma-la em definitivo na instituição básica do progresso humano, estendendo
os seus efeitos por todos os niveis de cultura,
e tornando-as centros de manutenção e de
criação do saber.

2316. Venâncio Filho, Francisco. Instituto de Educação do Distrito Federal (R
Br Estud Ped, 23:57, jan.-março 1955,
p. 28-41).

A partir de um sumário da história da educação no Brasil, mostra a origem do movimento
renovador que se iniciou pela década de 1920,
e focalisa a atenção sôbre o Instituto de Educação, cuja história, organização, estrutura,
instalação, passa a descrever. [A. Coutinho]

2317. Viveiros, Jerônimo de. Apontamentos para a história da instrução pública
e particular do Maranhão (R Geog Hist,
4:4, 1953, p. 3-43).

Evolução do sistema escolar maranhense, desde
a implantação das primeiras escolas de los
jesuítas até o advento da República. Histórico
minucioso da educação nos períodos colonial
e imperial. [Salvio Oliveira]

Geography

GENERAL

2350. American Geographical Society.
The Americas, 1:12,500,000. N. Y., 1953.
51 x 34 inches. 10 colors. [Map]
An excellent general reference map showing physical features, political boundaries, cities and towns, roads, railroads and airports. Insets show vegetation, agricultural land use, moisture regions, cities, and transportation connections. Being on the bipolar oblique conic projection, the map shows little distortion of land mass shapes, and a straight line between any two points on the map will be very close to a great circle route [A. C. Gerlach]

2351. Carlson, Fred A. Geography of Latin America. 3rd ed. N. Y., Prentice-Hall, Inc., 1952. 569 p., illus., maps.
A textbook that has been standard for many years is brought up to date. [R. E. Crist]

2352. ————. Notes on the Amazon Valley (J Geog, 54:6, Sept. 1955, p. 277-286). [P. E. James]

2353. ————. Views on the Amazon Valley (Sci Month, 79:2, Aug. 1954, p. 90-96).
Is it, or is it not, a region of great natural endowment? [P. E. James]

2354. Chebataroff, Jorge. Las regiones naturales de Río Grande del Sur y de la República Oriental del Uruguay (R Geog Inst Pan Am, 11-12:31-36, 1951-52, i. e. 1953, p. 59-82, maps). [P. E. James]

2355. Federación Interamericana de Automóvil Clubs. Sistema panamericano de carreteras. B. A., 1953. 12½ x 16½ inches. [Map]
This map shows the Pan American Highway and its principal connections throughout the Americas. Symbols designate the highway as paved, all weather surfaced, dry weather only, and not yet open to traffic. Rail and sea connections at breaks in the highway are charted on insets. Text on the verso describes the condition of the highway in each country. [A. C. Gerlach]

2356. Franco, José L. Urbanismo y pro-greso (Cuad Inst Interam Hist Mun Inst, 8, abril 1954, p. 5-41).

2357. García Castellanos, Telasco. Geología de fronteras. Bases geológicas para la determinación de límites internacionales. Córdoba, Argentina, Dirección General de Publicidad de la Universidad Nacional de Córdoba, 1954. 38 p.
An investigation of such factors as geomorphology, sedimentation, ice action, and even biological action (of coral colonies, for example), as regards their influence in the tracing of international boundary lines. [R. E. Crist]

2358. Gheerbrant, Alain. Journey to the far Amazon. An expedition into unknown territory. Translated by Edward Fitzgerald. N. Y., Simon and Schuster, 1954. 353 p., illus.
A popular narrative by an observant traveler through little-known sectors of Colombia, Venezuela, and Brazil. Unfortunately much of the flavor and delicate nuances of the original French have been lost in translation. Although *quién sabe*, for instance, is left in Spanish without translation, the word *machete*, well known in American English, is whittled down to *machet*, and thus looks stark naked, and strange indeed. But the translator has been able to capture much of the naiveté and lyricism that give the book great interest and charm. [R. E. Crist]

2359. Gourou, Pierre. The tropical world. Its social and economic conditions and its future status. N. Y., Longmans, Green (Geographies for advanced study), 1953. 156 p., illus., maps.
A dispassionate, forward-looking discussion of the peoples, soils, diets, agricultural techniques, and their interrelations in the hot, wet tropics, with emphasis on the problems due to European intervention there. The author has had first-hand experience in the tropics and is aware that the physical world does not exert a determinist influence on man, who can be master of his destiny if he is *conscious* of his mastery. "It will not be easy to raise the standard of living of tropical people if Nature's directions are obeyed; but it will be utterly

impossible if her vetoes are disregarded." [R. E. Crist]

2360. Hadlow, Leonard. Climate, vegetation and man. N. Y., Philosophical Library, 1953. 288 p., illus., maps.
A basic discussion of climate and vegetation, and of man's response to them in the various sectors of the globe, including tropical Latin America. [R. E. Crist]

2361. Marrero, Levi. La tierra y sus recursos. Habana, 1955. 392 p.
This is the most significant general geography in Spanish that has come to the attention of the reviewer. The physical world is brilliantly described; numerous pictures and diagrams make it easy for the reader to visualize concepts. Cultural geography is masterfully presented, with well-illustrated chapters on population, foodstuffs, fibers, transportation, minerals, etc. Dr. Marrero is a brilliant geographer, educator, and author, and is able to make his readers keenly aware—to paraphrase the late President Isaiah Bowman—that the earth is not merely something to be described in a textbook; it is something very real, with which every one of us is in daily contact. One wonders why a comparable general geography has not appeared in English. [R. E. Crist]

2362. Murphy, Robert Cushman, and **Dean Amadon** (eds.). Land birds of America. N. Y., McGraw-Hill, 1953. 240 p., illus.
This volume for the bird lover—both of amateur and professional standing—is vivid proof that color photography is a more humane and rewarding form of outdoor activity than gunning. It has an interesting introduction by the genial senior author. 221 photographs. [R. E. Crist]

2363. Pan American Consultation on Geography, III, Washington, July 25-Aug. 4, 1952. Final act. Washington,

Pan American Union (Conferences and organizations series, 28), 1953. v, 29 p.
Resolutions, recommendation and votes of this consultation. [R. E. Crist]

2364. Porto, José Luiz de Almeida Nogueira. Atlas de direito internacional público. Rio, Ministério das Relações Exteriores, 1953. 1 v.
This inexpensive atlas of black and white maps shows very clearly for elementary study the classification of countries: federated vs. unittype states, independent units, protectorates, colonies, and their historical development and areal expansion by dates. [A. C. Gerlach]

2365. Spain. Servicio Geográfico del Ejército. Cartografía de ultramar. Madrid, 1955. 2 v.
For locating historical place names in the U. S., Canada, and Alaska, this work is unique. In v. 1 are listed 138 maps prepared between 1733 and 1803 covering all or parts of those three areas. Following each entry is a list of place names on that map. V. 2 contains facsimiles of the 138 maps on 9½ by 13½ paper. The selection of maps was carefully made to provide the largest possible number of references to historical place locations. [A. C. Gerlach]

2366. Vindel, Francisco. Mapas de América en los libros españoles de los siglos XVI al XVIII (1503-1798). Madrid, Góngora, 1955. 378 p., 241 facsms.
This classic collection of facsimiles of maps from Spanish books which are now scarce, constitutes a valuable aid to the study of American geography and history. The edition is limited to 520 numbered copies on specially made paper. Each book is described in detail and its location given. Following the citation are a few quotations from the text to show the purpose and importance of the work, then a reproduction of the title page and colophon, followed by the facsimile maps. There are both author and area indexes. [A. C. Gerlach]

THE CARIBBEAN AREA

RAYMOND E. CRIST

MIDDLE AMERICA

2400. Andrade Azuara, J. Aníbal. Huaxtecapan, el estado huaxteco. México, 1952? 228 p.
A volume of impassioned special pleading for the creation of a new State.

2401. Blake, Emmett Reid. Birds of Mexico. A guide for field identification. Illustrated by Douglas E. Tibbetts. Chicago, Ill., University of Chicago Press, 1953. 644., illus.
This volume will acquaint the ornithologist with the names of Mexican birds, and make it possible for him to identify them. The au-

thor mentions the landmarks in Middle American ornithology, and hopes that his book will stimulate a wider interest in Mexican birds.

2402. Bonilla, Marcelina. Diccionario histórico-geográfico de las poblaciones de Honduras. 2. ed. Tegucigalpa, Imprenta Calderón, 1952. 310 p.

2403. Carr, Archie. High jungles and low. Gainesville, Fla., University of Florida Press, 1953. 226 p., illus.
A comprehensive picture of Honduras and Nicaragua, from the stately rain forest of the Caribbean seaboard to the high cloud forest of the interior—mute witnesses of "the four-century panorama of cruelty and color and

avarice and courage that has unfolded there. ..."
There is a vivid account of the flora and fauna
and inhabitants of the Mosquito Coast. This
book is highly recommended to the general
reader as well as to the scientist.

2404. Collart Valle, Ángel Antonio
(ed.). Introducción al estudio del desarrollo integral del Valle de Cuyamel.
Tegucigalpa, Banco Nacional de Fomento, 1954. 80 p., illus., tables.
Suggestions as to how to achieve over-all regional development in education, transportation, and agriculture in the Cuyamel valley.
One particularly pertinent recommendation is
for continuity in government-sponsored programs.

2405. Costa Rica. Dirección General
de Estadística y Censos. Sección de
Cartografía y Divulgación. Atlas estadístico de Costa Rica. San José, 1953.
114 p., illus., maps, tables.
Some of the results of the 1950 census are here
presented in graphic form so as to be available
for use in the classroom, and in the library, in
the office and in the home. We are told that
this volume is merely a beginning, but it is an
auspicious beginning, a valuable addition to
the published literature on Central America.

2406. Dondoli B., César. Nota geoagronó-
mica sobre la zona de Cañas Gordas y
Sabalito (R U C R, 7, oct. 1952, p.
27-36).
A reconnaissance soil survey of the Sabalito
area in western Costa Rica, with an eye to the
potentialities of settlement by Italian immigrants. A sketch map would have been most
useful, both for orientation and for pin-point-
ing the data.

2407. Dondoli B., César, and J. Alberto
Torres M. Estudio geoagronómico de
la región oriental de la Meseta Central.
San José, Ministerio de Agricultura e
Industrias, 1954. 180 p.
A detailed soils survey of the eastern sector
of the Meseta Central of Costa Rica, that
should be helpful to those interested in settlement possibilities. The volume is accompanied
by a geological map, with cross-sections, and
by a soils map.

2408. Galerazamba y San Pedrito. Documentos relacionados con los límites entre
los departamentos de Bolívar y Atlántico.
Cartagena, Colombia, Imp. Departamental, 1954. 140 p.

2409. Gavira, Gabriel. Nombres indígenas
de todas las ciudades y municipios de la
República Mexicana, con traducción de
su significado en castellano. México,
1953. 100 p.
A translation into Spanish of the Indian names
of the cities and *municipios* of Mexico. Since
place names are cultural survivals, the correct
translation of which will help make possible

an exact description of a former cultural landscape, this volume is a valuable reference work
for students doing work in the field.

2410. Gutiérrez Braun, Federico. Bibliografía sobre la geografía de Costa
Rica (R Geog Inst Pan Am, 11-12:31-36,
1951-1952, i.e. 1953, p. 97-99).
A usable bibliography.

2411. Hernández Crozo, Gilberto. Fisio-
grafía de la región de Huehuetoca, estado
de México. México, Universidad Nacional Autónoma de México, 1953. 47 p.
The valuable data on physiography, climate,
and soils in this thesis are not easily available
to the uninitiated because of the lack of any
map or sketch.

2412. Kohkemper M., Mainrad. Historia
de las travesías de la cordillera de Talamanca. San José, Museo Nacional, 1955.
97 p., illus.
A brief historical résumé of the many expeditions across the Cordillera de Talamanca between the years 1564 and 1954 is followed by
four chapters on the various facets of Indian
life in the indigenous communities in that sector—from foodstuffs to tribal palavers. Special
credit is given to Mrs. Doris Stone and her
anthropological work in Costa Rica.

2413. México. Dirección General de
Geografía y Meteorología. Bibliografía geográfica de México. Recopilación
y ordenamiento de Ángel Bassols Batalla.
México, 1955. 652 p.
This exhaustive bibliography of works geographic is a valuable reference work.

2414. Rubio, Ángel. Bibliografía básica de
la geografía de Panamá (R Geog Inst
Pan Am, 11-12: 31-36, 1951-1952, i.e.
1953, p. 100-110).
An exhaustive bibliography.

2415. Rubio Melhado, Adolfo. Geografía
general de la república de Honduras.
Tegucigalpa, Ministerio de Educación
Pública, 1953. 267 p., maps, tables.

2416. Sax, Karl. Population problems of
Central America (Ceiba, 4:3, July 31,
1954, p. 153-200).
A timely article on population growth and
available resources in Central America. It is
shown that increases in agricultural production
will result only in large populations living at a
low level unless birth rates can be reduced
rapidly. The percentage of increase of agricultural production is not as great as the percentage increase of population resulting largely
from the public health campaign. Even rich
countries cannot long support a population
resulting from an uncontrolled birth rate and a
controlled death rate.

2417. Termer, Franz. Die halbinsel Yucatan. Hamburg, Germany, Veb Geo-

graphisch-Kartographische Anstalt Gotha, 1954. 72 p., illus.

An excellent regional study of the role of both physical and cultural factors in the development of Yucatan. Present-day economy as seen in historical perspective is admirably analyzed in chapter 4. In spite of his appreciation of the splendid qualities of the happy industrious population, of their progress in education, public health measures, and general standard of living, the author ends on a note of what seems to the reviewer to be unwarranted pessimism. Perhaps he is haunted by the bogeyman of climatic determinism. Indeed, the failure of the scheme to settle in Zoh Laguna some 200 Polish refugees, people neither psychically nor technologically equipped to cope with a tropical environment, gives rise to comments that cause the ghost of Ellsworth Huntington to rise and walk again. This work will receive all too little attention because of the language barrier.

THE WEST INDIES

2418. Crist, Raymond E. Some notes on recent trends in rice production in Cuba (Ec Geog, 32:2, Apr. 1956, p. 126-131).

In several widely separated sectors of Cuba soils that only a few years ago were considered poor to worthless are being used for the production of rice. The rapidly evolving cultural landscape in these sectors is due almost entirely to the favorable economic climate induced by the high price of rice and the favorable economic climate for rice growers is due largely to the liberal credit policy of the Banco de Fomento Agrícola e Industrial de Cuba (Banfaic). Lowland rice is the most effective food crop which can be grown on many very poor tropical soils, because it is adapted to wet soils and because even on extremely poor soils it still produces some foodstuffs. It seems inevitable that more and more people of the world will have rice as their basic food.

2419. Cuba. Dirección General de Estadística. Clave numérica de la división política del territorio nacional. Habana, 1954. 128 p.

2420. Northwestern University. Department of Geography. The rural land classification program of Puerto Rico. Evanston, Ill., 1952. 261 p., illus., maps, tables. (Northwestern University studies in geography, 1).

Some results of the basic research on various aspects of land utilization in Puerto Rico, carried out by Professor C. F. Jones and five graduate students, with the active cooperation of Dr. Rafael Picó, President, Puerto Rican Planning Board. The interrelations between physical land types, economic activities and patterns of settlement are discussed against the background of detailed observations in the field. In a world of rapidly growing population, studies of this kind are extremely valuable and deserve wide dissemination.

2421. Núñez Jiménez, Antonio. Geografía de Cuba. Habana, Lex, 1954. 411 p., illus.

A beautifully-illustrated regional and cultural geography of Cuba, unfortunately marred by many typographical errors. Although not definitive, as is the *Geografía de Cuba* of Professor Levi Marrero, it does show patient research and conscientious organization of material.

2422. Oriol, Raymond B. Aperçu sur la géographie, la cartographie et la géodésie en Haïti. Port-au-Prince, Imprimerie de l'État (Coll. du Cent-cinquantenaire de l'Indépendance d'Haïti), 1953. xiii, 101 p.

Valuable for its bibliography of the geographic and cartographic works compiled in Haiti from its discovery to the present time.

2423. Picó, Rafael; Antonio F. Chaves; and Zayda Buitrago de Santiago. Geografía de Puerto Rico. Parte 1. Geografía física. Río Piedras, Puerto Rico, Editorial Universitaria, 1954. 243 p., illus., maps, tables.

Structural geology and land forms, climatology and mineral deposits, soils and natural vegetation, all are exhaustively treated in this monograph by the outstanding geographer of Puerto Rico and his able collaborators. This is a physical geography, but the emphasis is on the use man has made of the physical resources. In a volume in preparation, economic and demographic factors will be analyzed. The author, one of the most learned and distinguished of the alumni of the University of Puerto Rico, dedicates the volume to his alma mater on the occasion of the 50th anniversary of its founding—a fitting tribute to the role that that institution is playing in the intellectual life of the island.

2424. Roig, Juan T. Plantas medicinales exóticas, plantas aromáticas y plantas medicinales cubanas. Santiago, Cuba, Universidad de Oriente (Departamento de Extensión y Relaciones Culturales, 23), 1953. 18 p.

A description of some of the more common of the medicinal plants of Cuba, used empirically in folk medicine as hemostatics, febrifuges, diuretics, and cold cures.

COLOMBIA

2425. Chaves, Milcíades. La Guajira: una región y una cultura de Colombia (R Colomb Antr, Bogotá, 2. época, 1:1, junio 1953, p. 123-195, illus., maps).

A detailed study of the Colombian Guajira, including observations of the geology, climatology and vegetation. The adjustment of this relatively primitive but resourceful people to the factors of their physical background is carefully studied. The institution of slavery is analyzed. Much space is given to a discussion of the processes of interracial mixing and acculturation. The paper is well illustrated.

2426. Colombia. Instituto Geográfico de Colombia. Plan de diez años para la clasificación de los suelos de Colombia. (Publicación especial, 9). Bogotá, 1952. 35 p., tables.

The preliminary statement regarding the inauguration of the 10-year plan for the classification of soils in Colombia. The advantages of such a survey to the farmer, to the industrialist, and to the political policy maker are outlined. The budget for the 10 years is also drawn up. It is to be hoped that such a soil survey will be made, especially if it is made in conjunction with a land-use survey—actual and potential.

2427. Córdoba, Juan B. Compendio geográfico de la intendencia del Caquetá. Bogotá, Imp. Nacional, 1954. 159 p., illus.

An informative report on an "underdeveloped" area of Colombia which is being opened up by settlers from the Andes. There are some interesting pages on the language and customs of the native Indians. One of the most noteworthy customs is that of drinking an infusion of *yajé* to induce sleep, visions, or even temporary madness.

2428. Crist, Raymond E. Fixed physical boundaries and dynamic cultural frontiers (Am J Ec Sociol, 12:3, Apr. 1953, p. 221-230).

A study of the province of Cauca in southwestern Colombia which has within its boundaries a rapid succession of natural regions: mangrove swamps; tropical rainforest, with minor subdivisions depending on altitude; hot rainshadow deserts, also varying in temperature with elevation; and intermontane, ash-filled depositional peneplain, almost 6000 feet above sea level; mountain terraces at various levels; cold bleak paramos above the tree line. But the patterns of human occupance do not correlate with the changes in the physical environment. The comparable belts, climatically induced, on the opposite sides of the mountain ranges, for instance, have radically different agricultural landscapes, the physiognomies of which are in large part determined not so much by the physical environment as by factors of a cultural, economic, and historical nature.

2429. Gómez, Eugenio J. Diccionario geográfico de Colombia. Bogotá, Banco de la República, 1953. Unpaged, maps.

An authoritative compendium of information, useful to the geographer, historian, and economist.

2430. Guhl, Ernesto. El aspecto económico-social del cultivo del café en Antioquia (R Colomb Antr, Bogotá, 2. época, 1:1, junio 1953, p. 197-257, illus.).

A keen analysis, well-illustrated, of the economic aspect of coffee growing in Antioquia. The summary discussion of the geographic milieu is followed by a detailed examination of the significant factors in the social climate, such as disease, diet, rural hygiene, size of holdings, capital accumulation, the importance

of the family and the trend toward diversification. Higher yields per man and per unit of area should be achieved in order that the coffee industry might hold a labor force and interest investment capital in competition with other areas and other industries.

2431. ————. Aspecto socio-geográfico de la provincia fisiogeográfica formada por el valle del Río San Juan y por el Codo de los Mellizos y sus estribaciones hacia el Río Cauca, departamento de Antioquia (R Colomb Antr, 2:2, 1954, p. 37-87).

A significant contribution, beautifully illustrated, in which is studied population growth in a region which has increased from 38,789 to 193,797 from 1873 to 1951, a five-fold increase in 67 years—phenomenal for a purely rural population. This was due to rapid settlement in its initial phases. Excess population must now emigrate to unsettled areas or to the industrial center of Medellin. There is a good discussion of the cultural influences of roads. Padre Correa established a *despensa del campesino*, where lard, rice, and fish could be purchased at about half what the monopolists had previously charged. Indeed, physical, historical, economic, and social factors are reviewed in this penetrating regional analysis.

2432. ————. Caldas: estudio de su situación geográfica, económica y social como base para el establecimiento de un régimen de seguridad regional. Bogotá, Departamento Técnico de la Seguridad Social Campesina, 1955.

An outstanding contribution to the geography of Colombia. This work was compiled with the collaboration of the distinguished group of social anthropologists, ethnologists and economists: Luis Duque Gómez, Roberto Pineda Giraldo, Milcíades Chaves Ch., and Julio César Cubillos. Of especial interest are the easily readable maps showing the physiographic regions of the country and the distribution of urban and rural population. Transparent maps are effectively used to throw light on what might be termed cultural stratigraphy; for instance, if such a map showing boundaries of economic regions be superimposed on one showing the distribution of population one may see at a glance those areas in which the cultural, social, and economic factors outweigh the edaphic or climatic factors in the evolution of the cultural landscape.

2433. ————. Estudios preliminares de planificación para el seguro social en el Valle del Río Cauca. Bogotá, 1953.

A well-documented analysis of the province of Valle, based on personal observations in the field.

2434. ————. La seguridad social campesina en Colombia. Bogotá, Ministerio de Trabajo, 1954. 68 p., illus., tables.

In this work the distribution and density of population are analyzed in the light of the physical background and the economic regions of Colombia are delimited. The plight of the small farmer is pictured in realistic terms. The acute problem of the *minifundio*, or the division *ad absurdum* of landholdings, is investigated. In Cundinamarca in 1940 there were 2½ times the number of coffee farms there were in 1932, yet the yield was only 370,018 bags of 60 kilograms each, as against 364,379 in 1932. The technological progress of a region depends in large part upon the cultural level attained by its inhabitants.

2435. Pérez Arbeláez, Enrique. Recursos naturales de Colombia. Su génesis . . . . 1. entrega. Bogotá, Instituto Geográfico de Colombia Agustín Codazzi, 1953. xxvi, 128 p., illus.

A kind of potpourri into which the author has brought a number of exceedingly interesting items culled from many sources. Shore line development is taken up in detail, and especial emphasis has been placed on the peripheral sectors of the country and their problems. The monograph is beautifully illustrated, especially with photographs of the Instituto Geográfico.

2436. Philipson, W. R.; C. C. Doncaster; and J. M. Idrobo. An expedition to the Sierra de la Macarena, Colombia (Geog J, 117:2, June 1951, p. 188-199).

A valuable account of botanical and ecological investigations carried out in the vicinity of this inselberg, which "lies in an area of transitional climate between the damper Amazonian region and the drier savannas of the Orinoco . . . very close to the subtropical flora of the middle zones of the Andes."

2437. Rangel Galindo, Aparicio. Forests of Colombia. Bogotá, Universidad Municipal de Bogotá, 1952. 31 p., illus.

A valuable ecological classification of the forests of Colombia, with an eye to the commercial possibilities of the regions in which the various woods are found. In conclusion some of the important roles played by forests in the past are summed up, and it is shown how they will become even more useful in the future as man's technological equipment improves.

VENEZUELA

2438. Crist, Raymond E. Along the llanos-Andes border in Venezuela: then and now (Geog R, 46:2, Apr. 1956, p. 187-208).

A study of the factors of the physical and cultural environments that have caused the transition zone between the llanos and the Andean chain of Venezuela to experience alternate periods of poverty and prosperity. Cultural factors have of recent years become more significant than physical factors. Transportation facilities have been improved, the techniques of production have been bettered, and public-health measures have been introduced, with a general improvement of economic conditions. General economic growth should go a long way toward creating a powerful middle class that would act as a stabilizing influence in society. It is to be hoped that a higher level of living for the entire population will mean a

national upsurge in the development of arts and crafts, of science, and of higher education generally.

2439. González Sirit, Ismael, and Rafael González Sirit. Poliantea del distrito Zamora. Estudio geográfico, político, económico, cultural, folklórico y en especial médico-sanitario y social de la región. Caracas, Tip. Italiana, 1954. 578 p., illus., tables.

An account of human activities, somewhat anecdotal, of the district of Zamora, state of Falcon, from its founding to the present. Since both authors are medical doctors, great emphasis has been placed on the practice of medicine and the development of public health and education.

2440. Perales, Pablo. Manual de geografía económica de Venezuela. Caracas, Ediciones Jaime Villegas, 1955. 503 p., tables, maps.

A textbook of the genre published in the U. S. a generation or so ago under the uninspiring title of "commercial geography."

2441. Sociedad de Ciencias Naturales La Salle. La región de Perijá y sus habitantes. Caracas, Universidad del Zulia, 1953. 556 p., illus.

This little-known region was studied on three successive expeditions made during 1947, 1949, and 1950. Ethnological, ecological and geographic data were gathered. The volume is profusely illustrated with maps, photographs, colored plates, and sketches of plants and animals.

2442. Vila, Marco-Aurelio. Aspectos geográficos del estado Anzoátegui. Caracas, Corporación Venezolana de Fomento, 1953. 267 p., illus., map.

This volume does not devote an undue number of pages to the oil industry. The geology, relief, soils, rainfall regimes and agriculture are adequately treated in separate chapters. The chapter on agriculture is particularly exhaustive and interesting. The author also discusses in detail the ethnological aspects of this area, demography and migration, housing, and endemic diseases. This is an exceedingly well-written and intensive analysis of the state of Anzoategui by a competent geographer. The volume is illustrated with superb photographs, and is printed on excellent paper.

2443. ———. Aspectos geográficos del estado Apure. Caracas, Corporación Venezolana de Fomento, 1955. 234 p., illus., maps, tables.

The state of Apure was once devoted almost entirely to grazing, for the production of beef steers, but the economy has become considerably diversified during the past several decades. This systematic treatment of one of the great llano states is a significant and welcome contribution to geographic literature on South America. Thus the Corporación Venezolana de Fomento continues its series of excellent monographs of the various provinces or states of the country.

2444. ————. Aspectos geográficos del estado Portuguesa. Caracas, Corporación de Fomento (Monografías económicas estadales, 5), 1954. 217 p., illus., tables & folded map.

The state of Portuguesa lies athwart the transition zone between the great chain of the Venezuelan Andes and the vast plains, or llanos. But there were large stocks neither of gold nor of provisions, with the result that the area suffered somewhat from neglect during the colonial epoch, in spite of the fact that as early as 1610 the landholders of the mountains found it advantageous to bring the Indian workers whom they held in encomiendas from the steep mountain slopes to the plains, where the land was more fertile. By the time of the

first agricultural census in 1937, coffee, bananas, cotton, beans, and corn were produced in large quantities. Since that time there has been a veritable revolution in agricultural development. The motto of the government with respect to development is *sembrar el petróleo*, that is, to invest some of the profits from the petroleum industry in industry, agriculture, transportation, and public services.

This keen analysis of an important political division of Venezuela is well written and profusely illustrated, a valuable addition to the geographic literature on that country.

2445. ————. Geografía de Venezuela. Caracas, Fundación Eugenio Mendoza, 1953. 399 p., illus., tables & maps.

A popular, well-illustrated textbook for secondary schools, by the author of a series of excellent regional monographs on Venezuela.

SOUTH AMERICA (EXCEPT BRAZIL, COLOMBIA, AND VENEZUELA)

GEORGE McCUTCHEN McBRIDE
AND
ROBERT C. EIDT

GENERAL

2500. Díaz, Emilio L. El efecto dinámico de la cordillera de los Andes y el aislamiento de la acción perturbadora regional y superior (Meteoros, 3:1, enero-marzo 1953, p. 8-30, maps, tables).

Discussion of the dynamic effects of the Andes on meteorological phenomena east of the Andes. It was found that the mathematical function linking Pacific latitudinal pressure gradients with pressure anomalies on the eastern side of the Andes seems to be exponential. A diminished Pacific gradient results in anticyclogenesis east of the Andes. Comments on the detection of regional and upper-air circulation over Argentina. [R. C. Eidt]

2501. ————. Interrelaciones entre anomalías mensuales de lluvias, temperatura, presión, gradientes y variaciones (Meteoros, 3:4, oct.-dic. 1953, p. 342-382, graphs, maps, tables).

There is a relationship between the rainfall anomalies in the pampas of Argentina and the temperature variations above and below normal conditions in southern Brazil, the Pacific Ocean area, and the Atlantic Ocean area near Santa Cruz. Rainfall excesses in the pampas and intensified temperature gradients are associated with decreased planetary circulation in South America. An increased pressure gradient in the Pacific gives rise to a dynamic pressure trough east of the Andes. [R. C. Eidt]

2502. Heim, Arnold. Naturerlebnisse in fernen Erdteilen. 2. Naturerlebnisse auf Reisen in Chile, Argentinien und Bolivien.

Bern, Switzerland, Huber, 1953. 218 p., illus., maps.

Good travel descriptions of southern South America, including Chilean lake region, glaciated portions of the Andes, northern Argentina, and Bolivia. Detailed ornithological, botanical, and geological observations. Much geographical information throughout. Outstanding color and black-and-white photographs. One color map of southern South America, scale 1:8,000,000. [R. C. Eidt]

2503. Osborn, Fairfield. The limits of the earth. Boston, Mass., Little, Brown, 1953. 238 p.

Plans for improving living standards in the world rest upon development of better agricultural practices, primarily. Europe's agricultural productivity has not greatly changed since 1925 whereas her population since then has increased by almost 50,000,000 people. Criticism of the Intergovernmental Committee for European Migration suggestion of relieving population pressures by sending people to places like Latin America. Pessimistic outlook for increased food production in places like the Amazon basin. Only 3 to 4 percent of the entire inner basin is subject to annual floods, providing an estimated 10,000 square miles for temporary agriculture. Such land exists in only uneven patches, and it would be very expensive to dyke and drain. All such useful parts of the basin are already owned or assigned. There are, thus, no reasonable grounds for believing that the area can produce great surpluses of food although it could absorb some millions more of purely subsistence farmers. In order to improve the situation tax structure needs to be revised. At the present time some 40 percent of the tax goes entirely out of the region, and less than one-fifth of the total collected by the municipalities gets back to those political units. [R. C.. Eidt]

2504. Stackpole, Edouard A. The sea-hunters. The New England whalemen during two centuries, 1635-1835. Philadelphia, Pa., Lippincott, 1953. 510 p., illus.

A history of whaling and sealing, 1635-1835. Description of the beginnings of sperm whaling in the Pacific carried out by rounding Cape Horn after 1789. Early American contacts with South America started when whaling vessels called on ports there from 1792 on. First contacts with the Antarctic by whaling vessels included in a special chapter. Interesting tales of the discovery of many islands in the Pacific and Atlantic oceans. [R. C. Eidt]

ARGENTINA

2505. Anesi, José. Nuevo atlas geográfico metódico universal. 13. ed. B. A., Peuser, 1955. 1 v.

Although the 256 maps cover the physical, political, and economic geography of areas, they are too small for detailed use. They are crowded onto 76 plates, 28 of which are devoted to Latin America, and 18 of them to Argentina. Intended for general reference use as a world atlas, it is especially useful for secondary schools and institutions of higher learning in Argentina. [A. C. Gerlach]

2506. Ardissone, Romualdo, and **Mario F. Grondona.** La instalación aborigen en Valle Fértil. B. A., Universidad de Buenos Aires, Instituto de Geografía (Serie A, 18), 1953. 160 p., illus.

A neat, condensed study of a small valley district in the Argentine province of San Juan, carried out by the two authors, one centering on physiography, the other on anthropogeography. [G. McBride]

2507. Argentina. Instituto Geográfico Militar. Carta aeronáutica de la República Argentina, 1:1,000,000. 4. ed. B. A., 1953-. [Map]

Argentina is covered in 16 sheets compiled on the Gauss Conformal Cylindrical Projection. The base map shows relief by contours and layer colors, drainage, roads and railroads, and the overlay includes the usual aeronautical information. [A. C. Gerlach]

2508. ————. ————. Diccionario geográfico argentino. T. 1. Entre Ríos, Corrientes, Misiones. B. A., 1954. 359 p.

First of eight volumes eventually to be published, giving latitude and longitude and political location of names appearing on *Cartas topográficas de la República Argentina* and on the new maps (1:250,000) edited by the Instituto Geográfico Militar. Populations of political units, cities, and villages, based on 1947 census. Brief descriptions of more important cities and political units. [R. C. Eidt]

2509. ————. ————. Mapa de la República Argentina, 1:2,500,000. B. A., 1954. [Map]

This general reference map in two sheets is too detailed for wall map use at distances beyond ten feet, but it has a background of relief and drainage covered by overlays which show the provinces in colors, four categories of roads, ten railroads according to ownership, and urban centers in seven population categories. [A. C. Gerlach]

2510. ————, Ministerio de Transportes de la Nación; and **Automóvil Club Argentino.** República Argentina, red caminera principal, 1:4,000,000. B. A., 1955. [Map]

Over a relief base, with many place names, is a net of the principal roads in several categories, including paved, surfaced, graded, ungraded, under construction, and projected. The map also shows national and provincial boundaries, with special symbolization for any sections in dispute. Altogether, it is an attractive and useful general reference map about 40 x 22 inches, and is based on an official road map published in 1954 by the Ministerio de Obras Públicas. [A. C. Gerlach]

2511. ————. Servicio Meteorológico Nacional. Atlas agroclimático argentino. B. A., 1953. 1 v. (loose-leaf).

This is a loose-leaf atlas, the 12½ x 9 inch sheets of which are released as they are printed. The first 27 sheets deal with climatic phenomena such as frost free areas, frost free periods, dates of early and late frosts, evapotranspiration zones, precipitation characteristics, etc. The total number of maps to be issued has not been determined in advance. [A. C. Gerlach]

2512. Automóvil Club Argentino. Guía de viaje de la Argentina, zona norte. B. A., Kraft, 1954. 446 p., illus., maps.

Unusually well-written tourist guide to northern Argentina. Includes section on regional geography of the north followed by descriptions of 16 provinces and one territory north of the province of B. A. Descriptions follow an outline of general aspects, climate, flora, fauna, agriculture, mining, industry, commerce, communications, and places of interest. Special section on the city of B. A. [R. C. Eidt]

2513. Azéma, M. A. La conquête du Fitz-Roy. Paris, Flammarion (L'Aventure vécue), 1954. 235 p., illus., maps, ports.

An account of a successful 1952 French climbing expedition in Argentina. Includes a discourse on Alpinism, an historical survey of the region, impressions of Argentina, and the diary of the expedition. Photographs and sketch maps. [R. C. Eidt]

2514. Bassi, Hugo G. L. Estudio geológico-económico de la mina "El Oro," Chilecito (provincia de la Rioja). B. A., Dirección Nacional de Minería (Anales, 4), 1953. 30 p., diagrs., illus., maps. [G. McBride]

2515. Bonfils, Constante G., and Alejandro E. Capello. Levantamiento agrohidrológico de la isla Choele-Choel. Zona económica, no. 63, punto 6, del plan de gobierno. B. A., Instituto de Suelos y Agrotecnia (Publ., 26), 1954. 29 p., illus., maps.
Study of soil conditions and possibility of irrigation in this little island between channels of the Río Negro, a rather typical example of land and water problems in that part of Argentina. [G. McBride]

2516. Ferlet, René, and Guy Poulet. Victoire sur l'Aconcagua. Paris, Flammarion (Coll. L'Aventure vécue), 1955. 247 p., illus.
Ascent of Mt. Aconcagua, 1954, the first (it is claimed) from the south side, with few but excellent photographs. [G. McBride]

2517. Fernández Díaz, Augusto. Cayastá Viejo, Cayastá Chico y Cayastá Nuevo. Rosario, Argentina, Tall. Gráf. Star, 1953. 15 p., maps, plans.
Etymology of the name "Cayastá," found in the vicinity of Santa Fe, from its first documented appearance in 1607. [R. C. Eidt]

2518. Guía Peuser de turismo, 1955. B. A., Peuser, 1955. 447 p., illus., maps.
Usual tourist information for the northern part of Argentina, somewhat briefer descriptions of the south. Separate section on city of B. A. is more detailed. Map of B. A. and surroundings, scale 1:175,000. Photographs. [R. C. Eidt]

2519. Mapa general de la República Argentina, 1:3,750,000. B. A., Ediciones Cartográficas Peuser, 1953. [Map]
A general reference map in colors, containing the province and department boundaries, roads and railroads, and generalized drainage and relief. Folds into 8 x 11½ inch cover for easy use by tourists. [A. C. Gerlach]

2520. Martínez, Mario Hernán. Viento blanco. Episodios vividos en las duras sendas de la alta montaña, en la picada de la selva, en el engañoso desierto y en las rutas de los mares del sur. B. A., Cesarini Hnos., 1954. 208 p., illus.
A series of excursions made in different parts of the Argentine, from the Chaco to Ushuaia. [G. McBride]

2521. Mikenberg, Natalio. Reconocimiento agrohidrológico del Valle Medio del Río Negro entre General Conesa y Segunda Angostura. Plan de gobierno. B. A., Instituto de Suelos y Agrotecnia (Publ., 30), 1954. 36 p., illus., maps.
Classification of soils along the middle Río Negro in the arid border of the Pampa. [G. McBride]

2522. Miranda, Guido. El paisaje chaqueño. Ensayo geográfico regional. Resistencia, Argentina, Editorial Norte Argentino, 1954. 145 p., illus., maps.
Regional description of the Argentine Chaco. Sections on historical development, soils, climate, drainage, vegetation, and fauna. Four "typical subregions" described. [R. C. Eidt]

2523. Newton, Jorge. Misiones; oro verde y tierra colorada. B. A., Gráf. Impresores, 1951. 254 p., illus., maps.
Journalistic presentation of an economic report on the province of Misiones in northeastern Argentina. Contains useful historical data and good generalized maps of hydrography, orography, yerba mate plantations, industries, etc. [R. C. Eidt]

2524. Paul Fantini, Antonio de; Heriberto G. Fisher; and Juan B. Vázquez. Reconocimiento agrohidrológico del área de influencia del dique Río Los Molinos. Plan de gobierno. B. A., Instituto de Suelos y Agrotecnia (Publ., 29), 1954. 31 p., illus., maps.
Relation of geology, climate, and hydrology to the soils along the Río Segundo, south of Cordoba. [G. McBride]

2525. Punzi, Orlando Mario; Valentín Ugarte; and Mario de Biasey. Historia del Aconcagua. Cronología heróica del andinismo. B. A., 1953. 400 p., illus.
A history of attempts to climb Aconcagua; contains good chapter bibliographies, and quotations from classical accounts by men like Güssfeldt, FitzGerald, etc. Photographs. [R. C. Eidt]

2526. Quevedo, Casiano V. (and others). Aptitud de las tierras del partido de San Antonio de Areco. Reconocimiento y clasificación (R Inv Agr, 7:4, oct.-dic. 1953, p. 277-313).
Careful study of erosion as related to soils and vegetation in a northern partido of B. A. province. [G. McBride]

2527. Stäubli, Willy. Argentinien: Führer und Handbuch. Zürich, 1952. 368 p., illus., maps.
Brief descriptions of provinces and territories of Argentina, followed by sections on climates, population, government, business establishments, communications, sports, etc. Good compendium of recent statistical information. [R. C. Eidt]

CHILE

2528. García-Huidobro Guzmán, Andrés Javier. Geografía de Chile. Santiago, La Gratitud Nacional, 1954. 158 p.
A somewhat disorganized description of Chilean geological formations, landforms, and natural resources. Sections on various agricultural products, and appendix with notes on steel industry, communication lines, schools, etc. [R. C. Eidt]

2529. **Housse, P. Rafael.** Animales salvajes de Chile en su clasificación moderna. Su vida y costumbres. Santiago, Universidad de Chile, 1953. 198 p., illus.

Useful descriptions of wild animals of Chile, giving appearance, habits, and geographical distribution. Some photographs. [R. C. Eidt]

2530. **Kaplán C., Óscar.** Geografía de Chile. Aprobada por el Ministerio de Educación. Recomendada por el Ministerio de Defensa Nacional. Santiago, Instituto Geográfico Militar, 1955. 551 p., illus., maps.

A useful volume, with much detailed geographical information on Chile and many phases of human activity, based mainly on official information, with sources cited. [G. McBride]

2531. ————. Nueva geografía de Chile. De acuerdo con los programas aprobados por el Ministerio de Educación. Recomendada por el Ministerio de Defensa Nacional. Santiago, Instituto Geográfico Militar, 1954, i.e. 1953. 552 p., illus., maps.

Usual Latin American compendium of information listing boundaries, rivers, climates, flora, fauna, government offices, transportation facilities, industries, etc. [R. C. Eidt]

ECUADOR

2532. Demostración gráfica de las desmembraciones territoriales del Ecuador en su litigio con el Perú, 1:400,000. Milano, Italy, Officine Litografiche, no date. [Map]

Shows distinctly the boundaries set by the Protocols of 1829 and 1942, and the area still in controversy west of the Rio Santiago and north of the Rio Marañon. [A. C. Gerlach]

2533. **Ecuador. Dirección General de Obras Públicas. Sección Estudios.** República del Ecuador; plan nacional de vialidad, 1:700,000. Quito, 1954. [Map]

Shows roads in six categories, and the international boundary established by the Protocol of Rio de Janeiro, Jan. 29, 1952. [A. C. Gerlach]

2534. **Eichler, Arturo.** Ecuador: snow peaks and jungles. N. Y., Crowell, 1955. 216 p., illus., map.

Accounts of travels in Ecuador and the Galapagos Islands. Particularly interesting descriptions of life on the islands, and good photographs throughout. Translation of *Nieve y selva en Ecuador* (see item below). [R. C. Eidt]

2535. ————. Nieve y selva en Ecuador. Quito, Moritz, 1952. 131 p., illus., map.

See item above. [R. C. Eidt]

PERU

2536. **Bellido B., Eleodoro, and Alberto Manrique P.** Geología de los yacimientos de tungsteno de Mundo Nuevo y la Victoria. Lima, Instituto Nacional de Investigación y Fomento Mineros (Boletín, 12), 1954. 36 p., maps.

Tungsten outcrops at Mundo Nuevo and Mina Victoria, east of Trujillo, Peru. Irregular mineralization varying from 0.8 percent to 2.0 percent WO_3, and highest in ore-shoots along the veins. Economic future depends on high prices for tungsten ore. [R. C. Eidt]

2537. **Cerro de Pasco Corporation. Departamento Geológico.** Mapa del Perú, 1:1,000,000. Cerro de Pasco, Perú, D. G. Baldeon L., 1952. [Map]

Issued as a blue print, 103 x 36 inches, this unusually complete map should eventually be printed. It shows boundaries for departments, provinces, and districts; mines, oil fields, and a detailed transportation pattern including railroads, roads, bridges, tunnels, passes, ports, airfields, power and telecommunication lines; drainage features in detail, mountain areas by hachures, and spot heights at geodetic and astronomical control points. [A. C. Gerlach]

2538. **Clark, Leonard Francis.** The rivers ran east. N. Y., Funk & Wagnalls, 1953. 366 p., illus.

Exploration in Peru's *montaña* from the Gran Pajonal northward into the disputed zone with Ecuador. Deals with Indian trading, jungle healing, etc. Locates petroleum deposits along Perene River in the south and in the disputed border region of the north. Claims much larger extent of Jivaro Indian tribes than generally believed. Interesting description of ephemeral island formations on the Maranon River. Impressive demonstration of how little is really known about interior South America. Appendices on useful plants, edible fish, turtles, etc. [R. C. Eidt]

2539. **Egeler, Cornelis Geoffrey.** Naar onbestegen Andes-toppen. Met medewerking van T. de Booy. Amsterdam, Scheltens & Giltay, 1953. 231 p., illus.

Ascent of the Nevado Huatsan, 21,317 feet, northwest of Chavin, in the Cordillera Blanca of Peru, with imposing photographs. [G. McBride]

2540. **Ghiglione, Piero.** Nelle Ande del sud Perù Milano, Garzanti (Vita vissuta), 1953. 169 p., illus., fold. col. map, ports.

Two expeditions to the southern Peruvian Andes (12° S. to 17° S.) in 1950 and 1952. Descriptions of geology, flora, fauna, and mountain climbing. Separate section on the southeastern Andes bordering the Amazon drainage basin. [R. C. Eidt]

2541. **Kogan, Georges, and Nicole Leininger.** The ascent of Alpamayo. An account of the Franco-Belgian expedition

to the Cordillera Blanca in the high Andes. Foreword by Maurice Herzog. Translated by Peter E. Thompson. London, Harrap, 1954. 134 p., illus.
Graphic account of first ascent (1951) of Mt. Alpamayo, near Huascaran, in the Cordillera Blanca of Peru; good descriptions also of people and villages seen in the Callejon de Huaylas. [G. McBride]

2542. **Perú. Instituto Geográfico Militar.** Mapa del Perú, 1:3,000,000. Lima, 1953. [Map]
A good general reference map, with ribbon boundary lines for departments. It also shows roads and railroads, drainage, and cities and towns. [A. C. Gerlach]

2543. ————. **Ministerio de Relaciones Exteriores.** Mapa del Perú, 1:5,000,000. Lima, 1954. [Map]
Designed for popular distribution, this map shows drainage, main roads, and many place names. On the verso is a description, in English, of geographic features, history, culture, production, transportation facilities, etc., for use by American tourists. [A. C. Gerlach]

2544. **Pierre, Bernard.** La conquête du Salcantay, géant des Andes. Paris, Amiot-Dumont (Bibliothèque de l'alpinisme), 1953. 191 p., illus.
Well-organized report on the climbing of 6300-meter Salcantay, 70 kilometers northwest of Cuzco, by a Franco-American expedition in 1952. The first part is an account of the climbing; the second part contains a general study of Peruvian mountains with bibliographical and cartographical references, and the third part discusses Andean climbing problems along with expeditionary suggestions. A French glossary of the usual mountaineering terms in both Spanish and Quechua is given. [R. C. Eidt]

2545. **Rodríguez, Jesús Jordán.** Pueblos y parroquias de el Perú. T. 2. Lima, Gráf. Saiman, 1953. 508 p., illus.
Monographic description, largely of ecclesiastical organization, but with some general data. [G. McBride]

2546. **Romero, Emilio.** Geografía económica del Perú. 3. ed. Lima, Tip. Salas, 1953. 536 p., illus., maps.
This is something different in geography texts

for Latin American countries. The author is exceptionally well-read and applies modern theories to his homeland. Landforms, soils, and water problems of Peru are discussed by distribution and location. Interesting description of pre-Columbian irrigation works on the coast. Geography of communication, agriculture, sources of power, and mining are all treated. Concluding section discusses regionalism with the division of Peru into Coast, Central Sierra, South, and Amazon. [R. C. Eidt]

2547. **Sack, John.** The ascent of Yerupaja. London, Jenkins, 1954. 191 p., illus.
Well-written journalist's account of the experience of seven college students who climbed Yerupaja, 6632-meter peak in central Peru. First edition published in 1952 under title: The Butcher: the ascent of Yerupaja, N. Y., Rinehart, 213 p. [R. C. Eidt]

OTHER COUNTRIES

2548. **Alborta Velasco, Oscar.** En la ruta de Ñuflo de Chaves (el oriente boliviano). La Paz, Empresa Editora Universo, 1953. 309 p.
Historical, descriptive, and even poetical sketches, but containing much about the Santa Cruz region, about which little has been written by Bolivians or others. [G. McBride]

2549. **United States. Department of the Interior. Office of Geography.** Bolivia. Gazetteer no. 4. Official standard names approved by the U. S. Board on Geographic Names. Washington, U. S. Government Printing Office, 1955. 269 p.
Contains about 18,800 names, with geographical coordinates and indications as to whether they represent human or natural features. There is also a translation of descriptive terms used in place names, such as "abra" (pass), "cachuela" (rapids), etc. [G. McBride]

2550. **Uruguay. Ministerio de Obras Públicas. Dirección de Topografía.** Mapa de la República Oriental de Uruguay, 1:800,000. Montevideo, 1954. [Map]
This is an index of mapping progress in Uruguay. Over a base that shows roads, railroads, administrative boundaries and the principal urban centers, are overlays showing maps published before 1950, since 1950, and those now in process as well as some under study for future production. [A. C. Gerlach]

BRAZIL

PRESTON E. JAMES

This volume of the Handbook covers items published through 1955. Special note should be made of the several articles by geographers in the Conselho Nacional de Geografia, published in volume 15 (1953) of the *Revista brasileira de geografia*, dealing with population and pioneer settlement. Sternberg's paper on Brazilian agriculture, in the *Geographical journal*, 121:4, Dec. 1955, is also noteworthy.

PHYSICAL AND BIO-GEOGRAPHY

2600. **Ab'Sáber, Aziz Nacib.** O planalto dos Parecís, na região de Diamantino, Mato Grosso (B Paulista Geog, 17, julho 1954, p. 63-79, map).

2601. **Almeida, Fernando F. M. de.** Considerações sôbre a geomorfogênese da Serra do Cubatão (B Paulista Geog, 15, out. 1953, p. 3-17, map).
A contribution to the geomorphology of a part of the Serra do Mar.

2602. ————. Geologia do centro-leste mato grossense. Rio, Departamento Nacional da Produção Mineral, Divisão de Geologia e Mineralogia (Boletim, 150), 1954. 97 p., illus., maps.

2603. ————, and **Octavio Barbosa.** Geologia das quadrículas de Piracicaba e Rio Claro, estado de São Paulo. Rio, Departamento Nacional da Produção Mineral, Divisão de Geologia e Mineralogia (Boletim, 143), 1953. 96 p., illus., map, tables.

2604. **Alvim, Paulo de T., and Wilson A. Araújo.** O solo como fator ecológico no desenvolvimento da vegetação no centro-oeste do Brasil (B Geog, Rio, 11:117, nov.-dez. 1953, p. 569-578, map).
Relation of vegetation to soil material.

2605. **Aubreville, A.** A floresta de pinho do Brasil (B Geog, Rio, 12:119, março-abril 1954, p. 164-173).
Reprinted from *Anuário brasileiro de economia florestal,* 2:2, 1949, p. 21-36. The Araucaria forests of the south.

2606. **Bernardes, Lysia Maria Cavalcanti.** Aplicação de classificações climáticas ao Brasil (B Carioca Geog, 6:3-4, 1953, p. 24-33).
A comparative study. Map.

2607. ————. Tipos de clima do estado do Rio de Janeiro (An Geog Estado Rio, 6, 1953, p. 145-159, map).

2608. **Büchele Júnior, Carlos.** A Bacia do Itajaí. Florianópolis, Brazil, Instituto Brasileiro de Geografia e Estatística, Conselho Nacional de Geografia, Diretório Regional do Estado de Santa Catarina (Série 1, Publ. 2), 1952. 75 p. & illus., maps, tables.

2609. **Domingues, Alfredo José Porto.** Conclusões preliminares sôbre a geomorphologia da região dos arredores da cidade de Paraíba do Sul (R Geog Inst Pan Am, 14:40, 1. semestre 1954, p. 13-26).
A detail in the Paraiba Valley.

2610. **Guerra, Antônio Teixeira.** Aspectos geográficos do território federal do Acre (R Br Geog, 16:2, abril-junho 1954, p. 234-251).
This and the following five articles by this author deal with factual details of Brazilian physical geography: "Aspectos geográficos gerais do território federal do Guaporé," B Geog, Rio, 11:112, jan.-fev. 1953, p. 48-62, map; "Aspectos geomorfológicos do Brasil," B Geog, Rio, 11:117, nov.-dez. 1953, p. 603-617, maps; "Geografia do litoral," B Geog, Rio, 11:114, maio-junho 1953, p. 281-292; "Ilha Soares," B Geog, Rio, 12:122, set.-out. 1954, p. 286-290, maps; "Observações geográficas sôbre o território do Guaporé," R Br Geog, 15:2, abril-junho 1953, p. 183-296, maps.

2611. **Guild, Philip W.** Iron deposits of the Congonhas district, Minas Gerais, Brazil (Ec Geol, 48:8, Dec. 1953, p. 639-676, map).

2612. **Kuhlmann, Edgar.** Os grandes traços da fitogeografia do Brasil (B Geog, Rio, 11:117, nov.-dez. 1953, p. 618-628, map).

2613. ————. A vegetação de Mato Grosso—seus reflexos na economia do estado (R Br Geog, 16:1, jan.-março 1954, p. 77-119, maps).

2614. ————. A vegetação original do Rio Grande do Sul (B Geog, Rio, 11:112, jan.-fev. 1953, p. 157-163).
Three important papers on Brazilian plant geography.

2615. **Lamego, Alberto Ribeiro.** Ciclo evolutivo das lagunas fluminensas (An Geog Estado Rio, 7, 1954, i.e. 1955, p. 1-45, maps).
A detail of shore line development near Rio.

2616. **Maack, Reinhard.** O desenvolvimento das camadas gondwânicas do sul do Brasil e suas relações com as formações Karru da África do Sul (Arq Biol Tec, 7:21, julho 1952, p. 201-253, maps).
More data supporting the Wegener hypothesis.

2617. **Mattos, Horácio Peres Sampaio de.** Proteção florestal no Brasil. Rio, Ministerio da Agricultura, Serviço de Informação Agrícola, 1953. 63 p., illus.

2618. **Moreira, Ziede Coelho.** O problema vivo das florestas (An Geog Estado Rio, 6, 1953, p. 117-136).

2619. Robaux, Albert. Recursos de água do Nordeste; estudos e pesquisas necessários ao seu aproveitamento. Rio, Divisão de Fomento da Produção Mineral (Avulso, 78), 1953. 38 p., map.

2620. Romariz, Dora de Amarante. Mapa da vegetação original do estado do Paraná (R Br Geog, 15:4, out.-dez. 1953, p. 597-609, maps).
An important contribution.

2621. Ruellan, Francis. Estudos geomorfológicos na zona urbana do Rio de Janeiro (B Carioca Geog, 6:3-4, 1953, p. 5-13).

2622. ————. O papel das enxurradas no modelado do relêvo brasileiro (B Paulista Geog, 13, março 1953, p. 5-18; 14, julho 1955, p. 3-25).
Man as an agent of geomorphology.

2623. Schröder, Rudolf. Verteilung und jährlicher Gang der Niederschläge im Staat São Paulo (Petermanns Geog Mitteilungen, 99, 3. Quartalsheft 1955, p. 193-209, maps).

2624. Senra, Carlos A. Fragoso. Köppen e Serebrenick—climas da bacia do Rio São Francisco (R Br Geog, 16:3, julho-set. 1954, p. 370-383, maps).
A comparative study.

2625. Setzer, José. Isolinhas de unidade do clima no estado do Rio de Janeiro e no Distrito Federal (R Br Geog, 16:3, julho-set. 1954, p. 315-364, maps).

2626. ————. Os solos do município de São Paulo (B Paulista Geog, 20, julho 1955, p. 3-30).
Soils from a modern point of view.

2627. Simões, Ruth Mattos Almeida. Notas sôbre o clima do estado do Paraná (R Br Geog, 16:1, jan.-março 1954, p. 126-132, maps).

2628. Soares, Lúcio de Castro. Limites meridionais e orientais da área de ocorrência da floresta amazônica em território brasileiro (R Br Geog, 15:1, jan.-março 1953, p. 3-122, maps).
Summaries in French, Spanish, English, German, and Esperanto, p. 120-122. An original contribution which changes the commonly accepted southern boundary of the Amazon forest. Based on air observations.

2629. Souto Maior, Ariadne Soares. Tipos climáticos do Distrito Federal (R Br Geog, 16:2, abril-junho 1954, p. 267-275, maps).

2630. Vageler, Paulo. Contribuição para o problema da sêca (R Br Geog, 15:1, jan.-março 1953, p. 156-161).

ECONOMIC GEOGRAPHY

2631. Abreu, Florencio de. O gado bovino e sua influência sôbre a antropogeografia do Rio Grande do Sul (B Geog, Rio, 11: 116, set.-out. 1953, p. 466-476).

2632. Ackerman, Adolph J. Hydro—the answer to Brazil's power needs (Civ En, 25:5, May 1955, p. 272-277, maps).

2633. Aubert de la Rüe, E. L'essor minier du nord-est du Brésil (Chron Min Colon, 22:217-218, juillet-août 1954, p. 176-184, map).

2634. Avila, Fernando Bastos de. Economic impacts of immigration; the Brazilian immigration problem. With prefaces by A. Camillo de Oliveira and Julius Isaac. The Hague, Research Group for European Migration Problems (Publ. 9), 1954. 102 p., illus.

2635. Botelho, Carlos de Castro. Aspectos geográficos da zona cacaueira da Bahia (R Br Geog, 16:2, abril-junho 1954, p. 161-207, maps).

2636. Brazil. Instituto Brasileiro de Geografia e Estatística. Conselho Nacional de Geografia. Estudos da zona de influência da cachoeira de Paulo Afonso. Rio, 1952. 410 p., illus., tables.
An attempt to survey the market for electric power within range of Paulo Afonso.

2637. ————. ————. ————.
I centenário das ferrovias brasileiras. Rio, 1954. 414 p., illus., maps, tables.

2638. Diégues Júnior, Manuel. Bases econômicas e sociais na formação das Alagoas (B Carioca Geog, 6:1-2, 1953, p. 5-24, maps).

2639. Faissol, Speridião. Alguns aspectos do "Mato Grosso de Goiás" (B Geog, Rio, 11:112, jan.-fev. 1953, p. 63-83; 11:113, março-abril 1953, p. 174-188).

2640. Feio, Mariano. Perspectivas da acudagem no nordeste sêco (R Br Geog, 16:2, abril-junho 1954, p. 213-225).

2641. Geiger, Pedro Pinchas, and Ruth Lyra Santos. Notas sôbre a evolução da ocupação humana na Baixada Fluminense

(R Br Geog, 16:3, julho-set. 1954, p. 291-310, map).

2642. **Gobbato, Celeste.** La coltura della vite e l'industria del vino nel Rio Grande del Sud, Brasile (R Agr Subtrop Trop, 48:1-3, gennaio-marzo 1954, p. 10-20, map).

2643. **Guerra, Antônio Teixeira.** Notas sôbre as zonas econômicas do Território Federal do Acre (B Geog, Rio, 11:115, julho-agôsto 1953, p. 349-366, map).

2644. **Instituto Pan-Americano de Geografia e História.** Estudos sôbre recursos naturais nas Américas. V. 7. Brasil: estudo preliminar sôbre a situação atual dos conhecimentos relativos aos recursos naturais. Rio, 1953. 253 p., maps.
The first part of "Project 29" for the study of natural resources in the Americas. A review of existing sources of information and of technical competence..

2645. **James, Preston E.** Patterns of landuse in northeast Brazil (A Assoc Am Geog, 43:2, June 1953, p. 98-126).
The second part of a report on field studies in northeast Brazil (see *HLAS, no. 18, 1952,* item 1410). Contains maps of land use regions and dot maps of various crops and animals.

2646. ————. Trends in Brazilian agricultural development (Geog R, 43:3, July 1953, p. 301-328).
An analysis of Brazilian agriculture from a geographic viewpoint. Discusses the problem of Brazilian backlands and of the impact of "modern" agricultural methods.

2647. **Joint Brazil-United States Economic Development Commission.** The development of Brazil; report. With appendices. Washington, Institute of Inter-American Affairs, 1954. 324 p., maps, tables.

2648. **Kuder, Manfred.** Entwicklungstendenzen der Wirtschaft Brasiliens (Geog Rundschau, 5:12, Dezember 1953, p. 445-455, maps).

2649. **Lehmann, Edgar.** Zur Wirtschafts- und Sozialstruktur Brasiliens (Petermanns Geog Mitteilungen, 98, 4. Quartalsheft 1954, p. 318-323).

2650. **Le Lannou, Maurice.** Le Brésil. Paris, Colin (Coll. Armand Colin; Section de géographie, 303), 1955. 224 p., maps.

2651. **Long, Robert G.** O vale do médio Paraíba (R Br Geog, 15:3, julho-set. 1953, p. 385-471, maps).

2652. **Maya, William A.** O Brasil e suas florestas; devastação e programa de reflorestamento (R Geog Inst Pan Am, 14: 40, 1. semestre 1954, p. 43-50).

2653. **Mello Pettei, Beatriz Celia Corrêa.** Produçâo de milho e suinos no Brasil meridional (R Br Geog, 16:3, julho-set. 1954, p. 329-364, maps).
A report on a "corn-hog" type of farming.

2654. **Monbeig, Pierre.** Le Brésil. Paris, Presses Universitaires de France, 1954. 126 p., maps.

2655. ————. Fer et métallurgie au Brésil (Inf Géog, 19:2, mars-avril 1955, p. 48-56, maps).

2656. **Paiva, Glycon de.** A existência do petróleo no Brasil e sua influência em nossos destinos políticos e econômicos e na projecão histórica da nacionalidade (B Geog, Rio, 11:114, maio-junho 1953, p. 266-277).
The discovery of oil will be fine for the Brazilian economy.

2657. **Petrone, Pasquale.** Contribuição ao estudo da região do Cariri, no Ceará (B Paulista Geog, 19, março 1955, p. 3-29, map).

2658. ————. Crato, "capital" da região do Cariri (B Paulista Geog, 20, julho 1955, p. 31-55, maps).

2659. ————. As indústrias paulistanas e os factôres de sua expansão (B Paulista Geog, 14, julho 1953, p. 26-37).

2660. **Silva, C. F. dos Santos.** Tipos de propriedades rurais em Santa Cruz do Rio Pardo (Panorama, Santa Cruz do Rio Pardo, 1:5, março 1955, p. 3-19, maps).

2661. **Silva, Moacir Malheiros Fernandes.** Expansões continentais das vias brasileiras de transportes de superficie (R Geog Inst Pan Am, 13-14:37-39, 1953, p. 77-82, maps).
A rather optimistic extension of still projected national lines of transportation.

2662. **Stein, Stanley J.** The Brazilian cotton textile industry, 1850-1950 (Interam Ec Aff, 8:1, summer 1954, p. 69-91).
Also published in *Economic growth: Brazil, India, Japan,* edited by Simon Kuznets, Wilbert E. Moore, and Joseph J. Spengler (Durham,

N. C., Duke University Press, 1955., p. 430-447).

2663. Sternberg, Hilgard O'Reilly. Agriculture and industry in Brazil (Geog J, 121:4, Dec. 1955, p. 488-502).
An excellent review of agricultural and industrial development in Brazil, especially São Paulo and the South. Maps of coffee spread: 1920, 1940, 1950. Frosts in 1948.

2664. ————. Sismicidade e morfologia na Amazônia brasileira (B Geog, Rio, 11:117, nov.-dez. 1953, p. 595-600, maps).
Published in French in A Géog, 64:342, mars-avril 1955, p. 97-105.

2665. United States. Institute of Inter-American Affairs. Brazilian technical studies. Prepared for the Joint Brazil-United States Economic Development Commission. Washington, 1955. 432 p., tables.
Contents: transportation, power, industry, and agriculture.

2666. Urquhart, D. H., and G. A. Ross Wood. The cocoa industry of Bahia in Brazil (World Crops, 7:3, Mar. 1955, p. 97-101, map).

2667. Vieira, Flávio. A ligação ferroviária Pará-Maranhão (B Geog, Rio, 12:119, março-abril 1954, p. 154-163, map).

2668. Wagley, Charles. Brazil. Garden City, N. Y., Doubleday, 1955. 48 p., map.

POPULATION AND SETTLEMENT

2669 Aagesen, Aage. Det japanske folkeelement i Brasilien (Kulturgeografi, 7:37, Feb. 1955, p. 1-8).
The Japanese population of Brazil. Maps.

2670. Ab'Sáber, Aziz Nacib. A cidade de Manaus (B Paulista Geog, 15, out. 1953, p. 18-45, maps).

2671. Alexander, J. L. São Paulo (Geog Mag, 27:7, Nov. 1954, p. 364-374, map).

2672. Azevedo, Aroldo de. Cuiabá, capital de Mato Grosso (B Paulista Geog, 15, out. 1953, p. 69-79).

2673. ————. São Paulo, Stadt des dynamischen Wachstums (Staden-Jahrbuch, 3, 1955, p. 31-42, map).

2674. Barreto, Castro. A população brasileira; formação e evolução (B Geog, Rio, 11:112, jan.-fev. 1953, p. 32-43).

2675. Bernardes, Lysia Maria Cavalcanti. O problema das "frentes pioneiras" no estado do Paraná (R Br Geog, 15:3, julho-set. 1953, p. 335-381, maps).
A good study of the progress of settlement.

2676. Carmin, Robert Leighton. Anápolis, Brazil; regional capital of an agricultural frontier. Chicago, Ill., University of Chicago, Dept. of Geography (Research paper, 35), 1953. 172 p., illus., maps.

2677. Casais, José. Bahía (Brasil); dos ciudades de diferente fisonomía (R Geog Am, 2. época, año 20, 36:216-217, sept.-oct. 1953, p. 109-118).

2678. Castro, Josué de. A cidade do Recife. Ensaio de geografia urbana. Rio, Casa do Estudante do Brasil, 1954. 166 p., illus.

2679. Coelho, Djalma Polli. A localização da nova capital do Brasil (R Geog Inst Pan Am, 15:41, 2. semestre 1954, p. 1-31, maps).
A report on one of the official planning missions.

2680. Egler, Eugênia Gonçalves. Distribuição da população no estado de Minas Gerais em 1940 (R Br Geog, 15:1, jan.-março 1953, p. 123-152, maps).
Summaries in French, Spanish, English, German, and Esperanto, p. 149-152.

2681. Gutersohn, Heinrich. A região central de Minas Gerais; uma contribuição à geografia cultural do Brasil (B Geog, Rio, 12:118, jan.-fev. 1954, p. 5-49, maps).

2682. Keller, Elza Coelho de Sousa. Crescimento da população do estado do Rio de Janeiro. Comparação entre os recenseamentos de 1920 e 1940 (R Br Geog, 15:1, jan.-março 1953, p. 165-169).

2683. ————. Distribuição da população no estado de Mato Grosso em 1940 (R Br Geog, 15:2, abril-junho 1953, p. 303-311, maps).

2684. Korabiewicz, Waclaw. Matto Grosso. Translated from the Polish by M. A. Michael. London, Cape, 1954. 238 p.

2685. Lessa, Maria Luísa de Silva. Crescimento da população do estado do Rio Grande do Norte (R Br Geog, 15:2, abril-junho 1953, p. 312-317, map).

2686. Monbeig, Pierre. Aspectos geográficos do crescimento de São Paulo (B

Geog, Rio, 12:119, março-abril 1954, p. 139-153).

2687. **Mortara, Giorgio.** Caratteristiche demografiche del Brasile (B Inst Intl Stat, 34:3, 1954, p. 175-188).
French and English summaries, p. 187-188.

2688. ————. The development and structure of Brazil's population (Popul Stud, 8:2, Nov. 1954, p. 121-139).

2689. **Pfeifer, Gottfried.** Landwirtschaftliche Betriebssysteme und Kolonisationserfolg in Südbrasilien auf Grund der Forschungen von Leo Waibel (Erdkunde, 7:4, Oktober 1953, p. 241-249).
Leo Waibel's research into farming systems and their bearing on the problem of successful colonization in southern Brazil.

2690. **Platt, Robert S.** Brazilian capitals and frontiers (J Geog, 53:9, Dec. 1954, p. 369-375; 54:1, Jan. 1955, p. 5-17, maps).

2691. **Rios, José Arthur.** Rio de Janeiro (*in* Robson, William Alexander (ed.). Great cities of the world; their government, politics and planning. London, Allen and Unwin, 1954, p. 489-513).

2692. **Roche, Jean.** Les migrations rurales dans le Rio Grande do Sul: un exemple d'instabilité de la population rurale dans un pays neuf (A Éc Soc Civ, 9:4, oct.-dec. 1954, p. 481-504, map).

2693. ————. Pôrto Alegre, metrópole do Brasil meridional (B Paulista Geog, 19, março 1955, p. 30-51, maps).
Abstract in Portuguese of item below.

2694. ————. Porto Alegre, métropole du Brésil méridional (Cahiers d'Outre-Mer, 7:28, oct.-déc. 1954, p. 367-397, maps).

2695. **Schmidt, Carlos Borges.** Habitação rural; alguns de seus aspectos na área do Paraitinga (R Geog Inst Pan Am, 13-14: 37-39, 1953, p. 83-93).

2696. **Silva, C. F. dos Santos.** Rio Turvo. Estudo de geografia urbana (Panorama, Santa Cruz do Rio Pardo, 1:6, abril 1955, p. 3-14, maps).

2697. **Teulieres, Roger.** Bidonvilles du Brésil: les favelles de Belo-Horizonte (Cahiers d'Outre-Mer, 8:29, jan.-mars 1955, p. 30-55, maps).

2698. **Waibel, Leo.** Die europäische Kolo-

nisation Südbrasiliens. Bonn, F. Dümmler's Verlag, 1955. 152 p.
Prepared from the author's notes by Gottfried Pfeifer.

OTHER MATERIALS OF GEOGRAPHIC INTEREST

2699. **Azevedo, Thales de.** Bahia: two-story city (Américas, PAU, 6:11, Nov. 1954, p. 7-11).

2700. **Brazil. Departamento Nacional da Produção Mineral. Divisão de Águas.** Boletim fluviométrico, no. 12. Dados fluviométricos na bacia do Rio Paranaíba (até 1952). Rio, 1953. 228 p., graphs, maps, tables.

2701. ————. Diretoria do Serviço Geográfico. Catálogo das cartes e obras diversas. Rio, 1954. 55 p., maps.

2702. Brazil and her expanding economy (W Today, 10:9, Sept. 1954, p. 397-406).

2703. **Bueno, Jerônimo Coimbra.** Interiorização da capital federal (B Geog, Rio, 12:120, maio-junho 1954, p. 287-297, maps).
He is in favor of it.

2704. **Carvalho, Juvenal de.** Ligeiras notas sôbre o acôrdo de limites com o estado de São Paulo (An Geog Estado Rio, 6, 1953, p. 21-24).

2705. **Castello Branco, José Moreira Brandão.** O Rio Grande do Norte na cartografia dos séculos XVIII a XX (R Inst Hist Geog Br, 226, jan.-março 1955, p. 169-230).

2706. **Coelho, Djalma Polli.** Geógrafos, cartógrafos e demarcadores (*in* Brazil. Diretoria do Serviço Geográfico do Exército. Anuário, 4, 1951-52. Rio, 1954, p. 35-47).

2707. **Deffontaines, Pierre.** Río de Janeiro, ciudad de cabo, dentro de una bahía (Estud Am, 8:38-39, nov.-dic. 1954, p. 439-447).

2708. **Diniz, Almério de Araújo.** Roteiro amazônico (estado do Amazonas e território do Rio Branco); histórico, geográfico, fitológico, zoo-geográfico, etnográfico, e descritivo (R Geog Inst Pan Am, 16:42, 1. semestre 1955, p. 1-87).

2709. **Drumond, Carlos.** Uma "ilha" borôro na toponímia brasileira (B Paulista Geog, 17, julho 1954, p. 22-42, map).

2710. **Duncan, Julian S.** Beef and milk for urban Brazil (Interam Ec Aff, 9:1, summer 1955, p. 3-16).

2711. ————. The improvement of railroad transport in Brazil (Interam Ec Aff, 8:3, winter 1954, p. 83-95).

2712. **Hohenthal, W.** Notes on the Shucurú Indians of Serra de Ararobá, Pernambuco, Brazil (R Mus Paulista, n. s., 8, 1954, p. 93-166).

2713. **Johnston, W. D.** Mineral deposits of Brazil (*in* Conference on Latin American Geology, Austin, 1954. Proceedings. Austin, Tex., University of Texas, Department of Geology, 1955, p. 83-99, maps).

2714. **Maack, Reinhard.** A situação atual das pesquisas geográficas no Paraná e alguns problemas da geografia histórica (Arq Biol Tec, 8, 1953, p. 459-472).

2715. **Mendonça, Valdemar Paranhos de.** A toponímia brasilense (B Geog, Rio, 12:121, julho-agôsto 1954, p. 177-200). Reprinted from *Revista municipal de engenharia,* 19:2, abril-junho 1952.

2716. **Monteiro, Carlos Augusto de Figueiredo.** Guia de excursão a Angra dos Reis (An Geog Estado Rio, 7, 1954, i. e. 1955, p. 121-133, maps).

2717. **Murphy, Charles J. V.,** and **Michael Heilperin.** Brazil: the crisis and the promise (Fortune, 50:5, Nov. 1954, p. 119-125).

2718. **Prewett, Virginia.** Beyond the great forest. N. Y., Dutton, 1953. 302 p. A penetrating view of life in the Brazilian backlands, with special reference to the "American colony" in Goiás.

2719. Quadro sistemático da divisão regional das unidades federadas, Brasil (B Geog, Rio, 11:116, set.-out. 1953, p. 531-536).

2720. **Rodrigues, Lysias A.** Estrutura geopolítica da Amazônia brasileira. Rio, 1953. 39 p. Reprints from *Revista do Instituto de Geografia e História Militar do Brasil,* no. 19-20, 1951, and no. 21-22, 1952.

2721. **São Paulo** (state). **Instituto Geográfico e Geológico.** Coordenadas geográficas dos locais do estado de São Paulo, Brasil. São Paulo, 1953. 21 p. (Boletim, 34).

2722. **Strauch, Ney.** Guia de excursão a Volta Redonda (An Geog Estado Rio, 6, 1953, p. 47-72).

2723. **Texeira, Eurico.** Frutas do Brasil. Rio, Ministério da Educação e Cultura, Instituto Nacional do Livro, 1954. 281 p.

2724. **Valverde, Orlando.** Relatório técnico da excursão ao Rio Grande do Norte (B Carioca Geog, 6:3-4, 1953, p. 34-49, map).

2725. **Weyer, Edward, Jr.** Jungle quest. With photos. by the author. N. Y., Harper, 1955. 198 p., maps.

Government

ASHER N. CHRISTENSEN

The users of earlier volumes of this *Handbook* will recall the comments of the editor of the "Government" section in which he regretted the lack of good monographic studies of those factors which have shaped government and the political process in Latin America. To a certain extent this gap is now being closed.

Several of the books, monographs, and articles listed below refer to the causes of political instability and *caudillismo,* the relationships of political to social and economic institutions, and the societal changes that must come before political democracy can find a firm foot-hold in the area. These fine studies are contributed by both Latin American and U. S. scholars.

Another significant and relatively new development is the increase in the number of items referring to state (in the federal systems) and local government and to the process of administration. The number of administrative studies is the largest in the experience of the current editor.

Although a few of the items among the publications seen this year do refer to the dynamics of the political, as distinct from the governmental, process, and to the ideology, structure, and functioning of Latin American political parties, this remains an area in which further research and writing is urgently needed.

GENERAL

2850. Alba, Víctor. Historia del comunismo en América Latina. México, Ediciones Occidentales, 1954. 150 p.
Despite its brevity this book contains much information on the Communist party in Latin America: its relationships to labor movements, its tactics of infiltration, and its support of dictators who are anti-U. S. There is a short bibliography.

2851. Álvarez, Teodoberto. Ciencia política. Santiago, Editorial Alonso de Ovalle (12), 1953. 355 p.
This book is partly an attempt to establish a "system" for the study of government and partly a text on principles of comparative government. It is general and theoretical in its approach, and there is little reference to Latin American government and how it can fit into the author's outline.

2852. Andréu Iglesias, César. Independencia y socialismo. San Juan, Puerto Rico, Estrella Roja, 1951. 171 p.
This little book has some important material relating to the political role that the Communist party is playing in Latin America generally and more specifically its relationship to Argentine political events.

2853. Arciniegas, Germán. Political instability in Latin America (J Intl Aff, 9:1, 1955, p. 33-36).
It is the thesis of the author that the political instability of Latin America is accounted for, in the main, by the Spanish inheritance of centralism and a feudal society and by the historical process by which the colonies became independent states.

2854. Berraz Montyn, Carlos. Ensayo sobre el justicialismo y la unión americana. 2. ed. Santa Fe, Argentina, Imp. de la Universidad Nacional del Litoral, 1954. 182 p.
It is obvious that the author is an ardent Hispanist and Perón supporter, but the book has some importance as an illustration of the point of view of a typical ultra-nationalist. Although the writer is concerned with an inter-American solidarity, it is interesting to note that there are almost no references to either the Pan American Union or the Organization of American States.

2855. Briceño-Iragorry, Mario. Dimensión y urgencia de la idea nacionalista. Pequeño discurso sobre venezolanidad y americanidad. Madrid, Ediciones Bitácora, 1953. 78 p.

The theme of this interesting essay is that nationalism in Latin America must concern itself with other, and more basic, programs than the politically popular expulsion of foreign economic enterprises.

2856. Castillo Velasco, Jaime. El problema comunista. Santiago, Editorial del Pacífico, 1955. 218 p.
A thoughtful discussion which, although it has little on the Latin American setting of the problem, well sets forth a Latin American view.

2857. Figueres, José. The problems of democracy in Latin America (J Intl Aff, 9:1, 1955, p. 11-23).
The president of Costa Rica holds that the lack of democracy is mainly due to the economic problems, the low standards of living of the region, and the failure to establish an educational system which is really public. He cautions us not to be discouraged; the people of Latin America have never given up in their struggle to establish a true political democracy.

2858. Fitzgibbon, Russell H. Argentina and Uruguay: a tale of two attitudes (Pac Spec, 8:1, winter 1954, p. 6-20).
A fine article addressed to the question: Why are Uruguay and Argentina so different?

2859. García y Mellid, Atilio. La crisis política contemporánea. La sociedad cristiana. La herejía marxista. La democracia funcional. B. A., Emecé, 1953. 132 p.
A discursive pamphlet on the basic ideological conflict between Western Christian civilization and Marxist political thought. The writer is intrigued by what he calls "functional democracy," namely representation on a corporative basis.

2860. Gil, Federico G. Responsible parties in Latin America (J Pol, 15:3, Aug. 1953, p. 333-348).
A brief listing of criteria for the term "party" is followed by an effort to classify the parties, in whatever nations they may be located, as "Aprista," "Peronista," etc. The author seeks also to define the characteristics of these parties which make them indigenously Latin American parties rather than merely European parties imitated in the Americas.

2861. Jorrín, Miguel. Governments of Latin America. N. Y., Van Nostrand, 1953. 385 p., illus.
Professor Jorrín has emphasized *comparative* Latin American government, and does this by discussing broad constitutional and institutional principles. Instead of devoting separate chapters to each of the republics, he approaches the subject under headings such as "The executive power," "The legislature," "Local government," etc. Part 3, "Conflicts of power," and part 4, "The control of power," are very well done.

2862. ————. Political instability in Latin America. Albuquerque, N. Mex.,

University of New Mexico, Division of Research, Department of Government (Publ., 36), 1953. 18 p.
A brief political history of the last five years which notes the number of governments which came to power, or have maintained themselves in power, by the use of force or violence.

2863. MacDonald, Austin F. Latin American politics and government. 2. ed. N. Y., Crowell, 1954. 712 p.
In this second edition of a very useful general text on the governmental organization of the several Latin American states, a new chapter on the relations of the U. S. and Latin America has been added, and the number of charts and graphs has been considerably augmented. The discussion of governmental and political institutions for most of the countries is mainly from a constitutional-legal point of view, although for the major republics this is preceded by a chapter or chapters on political forces and political dynamics.

2864. Matthews, Herbert L., The U. S. and Latin America; and **Holmes, Lula T.,** An atlas of Latin America. N. Y., Foreign Policy Association (Headline series, 100), 1953. 62 p., illus., maps.
The emphasis of this little pamphlet is primarily on economic matters, although the first section discusses with insight the outlook for democracy in Latin America. The atlas includes valuable statistical data on the American republics.

2865. Organization of American States. Chiefs of state and cabinet ministers of the American republics. No. 37. Revised to Jan. 1, 1956. Washington, Pan American Union, 1954. 24 p.
A useful listing of the chiefs of state of the several republics, the persons holding high executive positions, when the president was elected, his predecessor, when the term ends, and the date of the next presidential election. Revised every few months.

2866. Plaza, Galo. Problems of democracy in Latin America. Chapel Hill, N. C., University of North Carolina Press, 1955. 88 p.
In this book of three lectures the author, a former president of Ecuador, expresses optimism over the future of political democracy in Latin America. His case is largely based on the fact that Ecuador, a most typical *caudillo* republic, did make great forward strides in 1948 and succeeding years.

2867. Sampaio, Nelson de Sousa. Ideologia e ciência política. Bahia, Brazil, Livraria Progresso, 1953. 336 p.
An introductory political science textbook with emphasis on the theory of the State. Very little reference to Latin American political thought.

2868. Schurz, William L. This New World: the civilization of Latin America. N. Y., Dutton, 1954. 429 p.

Each of the ten chapters of this fine book is of great importance in the understanding of the factors which have conditioned the nature and role of government in Latin America.

2869. Ugarte, Manuel. El porvenir de América Latina. Estudio preliminar de Jorge Abelardo Ramos. B. A., Editorial Indoamérica, 1953. x1, 160 p.
An enthusiastic "rediscovery" of Ugarte by one who regarded him in 1953 as a precursor of the national revolution of 1945. [B. Wood]

2870. Vilela, Arturo. Interpretación de la historia sud-americana. El fenómeno político-cultural. La Paz, Alcaldía Municipal (Biblioteca paceña), 1953. 220 p.
An excellent discussion of those basic factors which have so profoundly influenced the political evolution of the Spanish-speaking South American republics. The seven essays are: "Land and man"; "Colonial organization"; "Political and social status before Independence"; "Politics and ideology of the revolutionary movements"; "The birth of the independent states"; "The political personality of the republics"; and "Social progress."

ARGENTINA

2871. Alexander, Robert. Peronism and Argentina's quest for leadership in Latin America (J Intl Aff, 9:1, 1955, p. 47-55).
An excellent discussion of how Perón attempted to establish Argentina's leadership by means of economic pressures and programs. Perón's desires were blocked by the weak economic position of his country.

2872. Anzoátegui, Yderla G. La mujer y la política. Historia del feminismo mundial. B. A., Editorial Mendoza, 1953. 289 p., illus.
One gets the impression from this book that Eva Perón was the most important figure in the modern world feminist movement, including the enfranchisement of women in all of the American republics. The chapters on the history of feminism in Latin America, and more particularly the development of the Argentine woman suffrage movement, have some important materials in them.

2873. Bambill, Benjamín A. M. Hacia la realización de una democracia responsable. B. A., Kraft, 1953. 343 p.
The author maintains that the realization of a responsible democracy has come in Argentina owing to the efforts of President and Eva Perón.

2874. Blanksten, George I. Perón's Argentina. Chicago, Ill., University of Chicago Press, 1953. 478 p.
A fully documented and excellently written account of the background, the coming to power, and the development of the Perón administration and its political objectives and strategy.

2875. Damonte Taborda, Raúl. ¿A dónde va Perón? De Berlín a Wall Street.

Montevideo, Ediciones de la Resistencia Revolucionaria Argentina, 1955. 269 p.
It is the writer's view that Perón "sold out" to American capitalists and hence departed from the social justice content of *justicialismo*. The book has some good material on *Peronista* penetration into other Latin American countries.

2876. Erlijman, Jacob. Libertad frente al marxismo y al capitalismo. B. A., 1953. 268 p.
The author finds that *justicialismo* protects the economic and political liberties which are threatened elsewhere by either capitalism or Marxism.

2877. Latella Frías, Donato. Separación de la iglesia del estado y otras intervenciones e iniciativas. B. A., 1955. 37 p.
A collection of the congressional speeches of an Unión Cívica Radical deputy who opposed the suggested changes in Church-State relationships in Argentina. It is of interest as an illustration of the role of an "opposition" deputy during the Perón administration, and his "freedom" to oppose on the floor of the Chamber.

2878. Legón, Faustino J., and Samuel W. Medrano (comps.). Las constituciones de la República Argentina. Madrid, Ediciones Cultura Hispánica (Las constituciones hispanoamericanas, 3), 1953. lxxxiv, 527 p.
This collection of constitutions and organic laws in Argentina, 1811-1949, has a very fine preface which is a brief constitutional history of the nation. It also contains a very complete bibliography on Argentine constitutional history.

2879. Orfila Reynal, Arnaldo. Breve historia y examen del peronismo (Cuad Am, año 14, 84:6, nov.-dic. 1955, p. 7-37).
Mainly an historical account of the rise, the "digging in," and the fall of the Perón administration. The sections that relate to the Church and to the labor unions are the best.

2880. Prewett, Virginia. Beyond the great forest. N. Y., Dutton, 1953. 302 p.
This is mainly an interestingly written account of "pioneering" in Brazil. Chapter 1, however, deals with the Argentine political situation in 1945, and the position of the American correspondents in B. A. with reference to the rapidly expanding press control by the then new Perón administration.

2881. Tristán, Lucía. Yrigoyen y la intransigencia radical. B. A., Indoamérica (Biblioteca de la nueva generación, 6), 1955. 78 p.
Some new light is thrown on Argentine politics of the first two decades of this century, and especially on the internal strains in the Unión Cívica Radical.

BOLIVIA

2882. Fellman Velarde, José. Víctor Paz

Estenssoro; el hombre y la revolución. La Paz, Tejerina, 1954. 284 p.
A political biography by a co-partisan and an obviously great admirer. The book does contain a great deal of material on the origins of the Movimiento Nacionalista Revolucionario and its social and economic program.

2883. Natale E., Remo di. Revolución agraria en Bolivia. Cochabamba, Bolivia, Imprenta Universitaria, 1953. 156 p.
Amplified versions of the author's lectures on this subject at the Universidad Mayor de San Andrés in 1952. The Christian Social point of view is elaborated with respect to the historical perspective, property rights among the indigenes from the earliest times to the present, the nature of the contemporary problem (low economic levels, malnutrition, maldistribution of land ownership and control, and low educational status), the basic elements of a Social Christian agrarian revolution. [T. L. Smith]

2884. Osborne, Harold. Bolivia, a land divided. London and N. Y., Royal Institute of International Affairs, 1954. 144 p.
In each of the three major parts of this little book, "The country," "History and people," and "The economy," one finds constitutional and political information of significance, interestingly written.

2885. Paz Estenssoro, Víctor. Discursos y mensajes. B. A., Ediciones Meridiano, 1953. 184 p.
This collection of speeches and writings, to commemorate the revolution of April 1952, is an important source of information on recent politics and political history of Bolivia. It contains considerable material on the program of the nationalization of the mining enterprises.

2886. Valencia Vega, Alipio. Desarrollo del pensamiento político en Bolivia. (Bosquejo). La Paz, 1953. 122 p.
The four chapters of this short book deal with: "The political organization of pre-Conquest Bolivia"; "The colonial period"; "Revolution and republic"; and "The twentieth century." This last chapter includes several pages on the problem of the nationalization of the mining enterprises. A short bibliography is included.

BRAZIL

2887. Bloem, Ruy. A crise da democracia e a reforma eleitoral. São Paulo, Martins, 1955. 196 p.
An important contribution, which covers material on which we have relatively little information. It is an analysis of Brazil's electoral code and its relation to the political and governmental climate of that country.

2888. Campos, Roberto de Oliveira. Planejamento do desenvolvimento econômico de países subdesenvolvidos. Rio, Fundação Getúlio Vargas, Escola Brasileira de Administração Pública (Cadernos de administração pública, 2), 1954. 53 p.
A training manual for those who are concerned with international economic and technical assistance projects.

2889. Constituição dos Estados Unidos do Brasil promulgada em 18 de setembro de 1946. Com índice alfabético e remissivo. Ed. atualizada. Rio, Gráf. Editôra Aurora, 1953. 102 p.
A very good alphabetical index makes this text of the Brazilian 1946 Constitution an important document.

2890. Escola Brasileira de Administração Pública. The Brazilian School of Public Administration and its activities in 1952 and 1953. Report. Rio, Getulio Vargas Foundation, 1954. 92 p.
This little report offers some insights into the place of public administration in Brazil and the aspects of public administration study and research which are deemed most important. It includes an account of those public agencies and entities in Brazil which have entered in agreements with the School for the training of personnel.

2891. Goiás (state). Governor. Mensagem apresentada à Assembléia Legislativa pelo Governador Dr. Pedro Ludovico Teixeira. Goiânia, Brazil, 1953. 42 p.
A very good report on state activities and state problems in the Brazilian federal system. The report includes several pages of statistical data on the state government of Goias.

2892. Lessa, Gustavo. O distrito na organização municipal. Rio, Fundação Getúlio Vargas, 1952. 64 p.
Although brief, this is a good account of the role of the municipality in Brazil, the development of municipal organization, and the present administrative organization of the city.

2893. Moitinho, Álvaro Pôrto. O ensino da administração no Brasil. Rio, Paulo de Azevedo, 1953. 47 p.
A brief account of the development of the study of public administration in Brazil; there is little attention devoted to public administration itself.

2894. Pimentel, A. Fonseca. Alguns aspectos do treinamento. Rio, Fundação Getúlio Vargas, Escola Brasileira de Administração Pública (Cadernos de administração pública, 5), 1954. 38 p.
A training manual of civil servant "in-service" training.

2895. Pinto, Luiz. Pandiá Calógeras. Rio, Departamento Administrativo do Serviço Público, Serviço de Documentação (Pequenos estudos sôbre grandes administradores do Brasil, 1), 1955. 79 p.
While this is essentially a biography it does contain some information on the administrative history of the federal union and the states in Brazil.

2896. **Silva, Benedicto.** Publicidade administrativa. Rio, Fundação Getúlio Vargas, Escola Brasileira de Administração Pública (Cadernos de administração pública, 3), 1954. 26 p.
A training manual on the public relations of governmental departments and agencies.

2897. ————. Relações públicas, divulgação e propaganda. Rio, Fundação Getúlio Vargas, Escola Brasileira de Administração Pública (Cadernos de administração pública, 1), 1954. 26 p.
A training manual on the public relations of governmental departments.

2898. ————. Teoría dos departamentos de clientela. Rio, Fundação Getúlio Vargas, Escola Brasileira de Administração Pública (Cadernos de administração pública, 4), 1954. 28 p.
A training manual on the theory of departmental organization.

2899. **Smith, T. Lynn.** Brazil: people and institutions. Rev. ed. Baton Rouge, La., Louisiana State University Press, 1954. 704 p., illus., maps, tables.
The second edition of a work originally published in 1947. Although it is not intended to be a political study, the full discussion of social and economic institutions and problems is, of course, directly related to public policy.

2900. **Vargas, Getúlio.** Mensagem ao Congresso Nacional apresentada pelo Presidente da República, Getúlio Vargas, por ocasião da abertura da sessão legislativa de 1953. Rio, 1953. 283 p.
A long and very detailed account of the work of the major governmental departments, well supported by statistical data.

COLOMBIA

2901. **Bushnell, David.** What has happened to democracy in Colombia? (Cur Hist, 24:137, Jan. 1953, p. 38-42).
The author feels that the reputation that Colombia had, of being a democratically organized state, was not fully deserved. He feels that the growing antidemocratic nature of the present regime is partly explained by extremist influences in both Liberal and Conservative parties.

2902. **Colombia. Dirección de Información y Propaganda.** Colombia trabaja. Conferencias radiales de los señores ministros del despacho ejecutivo con motivo del primer año de gobierno. Bogotá, 1954. 422 p., illus.
These radio talks by the several ministers of state are oral reports on the work of their departments. Those relating to the ministries of agriculture, public works, education, and health are well supported with statistical data.

2903. ————. ————. Seis meses de gobierno. Bogotá, 1953. 395 p., illus.
Most of this volume praises the work of the administration. It does contain, however, some important information on the backgrounds of the "movement" of June 13, 1953, and the legalistic attempt to justify the governmental change on constitutional grounds.

2904. **Liévano Aguirre, Nicolás.** Hacia la nueva reforma política. Bogotá, Imp. Municipal (Col. Estado nacional), 1953. 58 p., illus.
The author contends that the most needed reforms in Colombia are programs to reduce the political effects of class conflict and the separatist influence of intense regionalism.

2905. **Molina, Gerardo.** Proceso y destino de la libertad. Bogotá, Biblioteca de la Universidad Libre, 1955. 275 p.
A good treatment of the problem of liberty in general and in its Latin American perspective. Only the last chapter is specifically related to the political tensions and limitations on liberty in Colombia.

CUBA

2906. **Azcuy, Aracelio.** Cuba: campo de concentración. México, Humanismo, 1954. 342 p., illus.
This volume is dedicated to the victims of the tyranny of President Batista. The chapters dealing with the censorship of the media of communication, labor organizations, and the universities contain the most valuable information which this book has to offer.

2907. **Cuba. Ministerio de Información.** The Cuban people tell their true story. What is the matter with Cuba? Habana, 1954. 20 p.
This little pamphlet, issued by the Cuban Ministry of Information, finds that all is well in the Cuba of President Batista.

2908. **Entralgo, Elías.** El resentimiento de un prólogo. Habana, Imp. de la Universidad de la Habana, 1953. 22 p.
A brief essay on the intellectual problem of Cuba at the time of Independence, which, in the view of the author, was essentially this: whether the new republic should continue the Spanish tradition and Spanish institutions or attempt to modify them in an "American" pattern.

2909. **Riera Hernández, Mario.** Cincuenta y dos años de política. Oriente. 1900-1952. Habana, 1953. 584 p.
This is a general account of presidential and congressional elections (the latter broken down into districts) from 1899 to 1952. The data are of considerable importance to those interested in the political party history of Cuba, although there are few references to the parties other than naming them and their candidates. Total votes cast and the number received by each candidate are included.

DOMINICAN REPUBLIC

2910. Constitution of the Dominican Republic, 1947. Washington, Pan American Union, Division of Law and Treaties (Law and treaty series), 1953. 22 p.
An official text in English.

2911. Marrero Aristy, Ramón. Trujillo: síntesis de su vida y de su obra. 2. ed. Ciudad Trujillo, Imp. Dominicana, 1953. 122 p., illus.
An extremely laudatory biography which stresses the social and economic gains made in the Dominican Republic in the Trujillo era.

2912. Trujillo, Rafael L. Discursos, mensajes y proclamas. T. 11. Ciudad Trujillo, Imp. Dominicana, 1953. 336 p.
This collection of speeches made in 1951 and 1952 is very well indexed.

EL SALVADOR

2913. Constitution of the Republic of El Salvador, 1950. Washington, Pan American Union, Division of Law and Treaties (Law and treaty series), 1953. 49 p.
An official text in English.

2914. El Salvador. Ministerio del Interior. Entrevistas con el señor Ministro del Interior, Teniente Coronel José María Lemus. San Salvador, 1953. 32 p.
A transcription of a radio interview relating to the program of the junta which came to power in 1948. A considerable part of the interview revolved about municipal government and municipal functions in El Salvador.

2915. El Salvador. President. Mensaje del Señor Presidente de la República Teniente Coronel Óscar Osorio, dirigido al pueblo salvadoreño el 14 de septiembre de 1953 al cumplir tres años de labores el actual gobierno. San Salvador, 1953. 200 p., graphs, illus., map.
The president summarizes the activities and accomplishments of the past three years. A few tables, graphs, and charts are included.

GUATEMALA

2916. Arévalo, Juan José. Escritos políticos y discursos. Habana, Cultural, 1953. 515 p.
A Cuban reprint of speeches and articles of the former president of Guatemala. Most of the material deals with political events in Guatemala, 1943-1945, but perhaps the better part is found in the first section where ex-President Arévalo writes on a subject that has long held his interest: the unity of the Central American republics.

2917. Geiger, Theodore. Communism versus progress in Guatemala. Washington, National Planning Association (Planning pamphlets, 85), 1953. 90 p.
A good, well-documented, well-balanced, and objective report. The report concludes by emphasizing the great danger of not providing some programs of land redistribution, Indian welfare, and economic reconstruction.

2918. Gutiérrez G., Víctor Manuel, and Gabriel Alvarado. Breves resúmenes de economía política. Guatemala, Ministerio de Educación Pública (Biblioteca de cultura popular, 3), 1950. 107 p.
The first 71 pages of this book are devoted to a consideration of basic economic principles; briefly and sketchily presented. In the last chapter the authors give a brief outline and synopsis of the laws of Guatemala referring to money and banking, labor legislation, and social security. This chapter may serve as a useful guide to more intensive study.

2919. James, Daniel. Red design for the Americas. Guatemalan prelude. N. Y., Day, 1954. 347 p.
Although the author gives way to the temptation to make sweeping generalizations, this volume is primarily a factual account of the expansion of communist influence in Guatemala. Mr. James warns of the danger of replacing a procommunist government with another dictatorship which is not concerned with the basic social and economic problems facing Guatemala.

2920. Silvert, K. H. A study in government: Guatemala. National and local government since 1944. New Orleans, La., Tulane University, Middle American Research Institute (21), 1954. 3 v.
An excellent study of Guatemalan government and politics (before the Castillo Armas administration). Part 1 deals with the backgrounds of the revolution of 1944 and the Constitution of 1945; Part 2 has a fine discussion of the national government under the 1945 Constitution; the final part is concerned with departmental and local government.

2921. Vielman, Julio. Stabilization of the post-revolutionary government in Guatemala (J Intl Aff, 9:1, 1955, p. 73-81).
The author points out that it is essential that the democratic gains in Guatemala, between 1944 and 1954, be maintained and consolidated. He is concerned that this will be extremely difficult owing to the opposition of the landowners who can capitalize on the anticommunist sentiment that exists and who can label the real democratic gains as a communist program.

MEXICO

2922. Chico Alatorre, Carlos. Cauce y horizontes de la Revolución Mexicana. México, Ediciones Alatorre, 1953. 177 p.
Although written by an ardent Partido Revolucionario Institucional supporter, this is an important book on the history and evolution of

that political party. The author denies that the party has a monopoly on political activity in Mexico and that it is not democratically organized and operated.

2923. Guisa y Azevedo, Jesús. La civitas mexicana y nosotros los católicos. México, Polis, 1953. 226 p.

A diffuse tract which presents the views of a Catholic with reference to the policies and programs of the Mexican nation from the Revolution to the present time.

2924. Manzanilla, A. El comunismo en México y el archivo de Carrillo Puerto. 2. ed. corregida y aumentada. México, 1955. 215 p., facsims., illus., ports.

This is the second edition of a book originally published in 1921. The title is somewhat misleading, for most of the work relates to the Communist party activities in Yucatan in 1920 and 1921. The book has some value in its presentation of early Communist activities in Mexico.

2925. México. Dirección General de Estadística. División municipal de las entidades federativas, 30 de junio de 1954. México, 1954. 165 p., tables.

A compilation of important statistical data referring to the municipalities in Mexico. The several categories of local governmental units are classified by states and by date of incorporation or legal establishment.

2926. Puente Arteaga, Martín. Génesis, evolución y desarrollo del municipio en México. México, Universidad Nacional Autónoma de México, 1954. 128 p.

The author discusses, much too briefly, the origins of the municipality in Spain; colonial municipal government and organization; the evolution of the municipality since independence; and the present status, structure, and functions of municipal governments in Mexico. A short bibliography is included.

2927. Rivas Andrade, Aristeo (ed.). Funcionamiento de las juntas de mejoramiento moral, cívico y material en el estado de Veracruz. Xalapa, México, 1953. 73 p., illus.

An interesting account of the plan of the Ruiz Cortines administration to establish local committees whose concern is the betterment of the moral and spiritual life of Mexicans. This pamphlet deals almost exclusively with the junta established at Veracruz.

2928. Sánchez Septién, Salvador (ed.). José María Lozano en la tribuna parlamentaria, 1910-1913. Prólogo de Nemesio García Naranjo. México, Jus, 1953. 204 p.

A collection of the speeches made in the Mexican Congress in the years 1911-1913. A valuable source of information on the politics of the troubled early years of the Mexican Revolution.

2929. Santoyo, Ramón Víctor. Hechos y hombres del Parlamento. México, 1955. 285 p.

The author has served in the Chamber of Deputies of the Mexican Congress. He includes some materials on how that Chamber acts as a legislative body. Another chapter on "The Party" has data on the early development of the present PRI. The long excerpts from speeches made at the time of the oil-well expropriation shed considerable light on the constitutional and institutional backgrounds of the move.

2930. Silva Herzog, Jesús. Nueve estudios mexicanos. México, Imp. Universitaria (Col. Cultura mexicana, 8), 1953. 315 p.

Part 1 contains these five essays: "The problems of Mexico"; "The crisis of the Mexican Revolution"; "Meditations about Mexico," which has a very good section on the relations of geography to the Mexican economy; "The Mexican Revolution"; and "The duties of a Mexican Liberal." The second part, "The era of petroleum in Mexico," has a brief but good account of the development of the petroleum industry, the role of oil in the revolutionary movement, the expropriation, and the recent progress of the industry since nationalization.

2931. Tannenbaum, Frank. Reflections on the Mexican Revolution (J Intl Aff, 9:1, 1955, p. 37-46).

Professor Tannenbaum, in a fine article, argues that basically the changes in Mexico since the Revolution have been in the democratic direction. Despite the continued existence of *personalismo* and corruption, decision-making powers have spread downwards into thousands of small and large groups, and this development has increased the democratic characteristics of Mexican polity.

PERU

2932. Kantor, Harry. The ideology and program of the Peruvian Aprista movement. Berkeley, Calif., University of California Press (University of California publications in political science, 4:1), 1953. 163 p.

An account of the origins and development of APRA, its policies and its programs. It seems evident that the author admires the leader of APRA and that, in general, he is sympathetic to the party's program. He has, however, written a most complete and fully documented account. Spanish translation: *Ideología y programa del movimiento Aprista*, México, Humanismo, 1955, 247 p.

2933. Perú. Presidente. Mensaje presentado al Congreso Nacional por el Sr. Presidente Constitucional de la República General Manuel A. Odría. Lima, 1953. 224 p.

The president summarizes the work and accomplishments of the several ministries. Despite the length of the report, it includes no statistical or tabular materials.

2934. **Sánchez, Luis Alberto.** Haya de la Torre y el Apra. Crónica de un hombre y un partido. Santiago, Editorial del Pacífico, 1955. 475 p.
A political biography by an admirer and party co-worker. It has some good materials on the early years of APRA and the working out of its political program.

2935. **Zárate, Fidel A.** Los derechos políticos de la mujer peruana. Lima, Azángaro, 1954. 47 p.
This little essay discusses in very general terms the development of political rights for the women of Peru.

PUERTO RICO

2936. **Fraga Iribarne, Manuel.** Las constituciones de Puerto Rico. Madrid, Ediciones Cultura Hispánica, 1953. 553 p.
A collection of the constitutions and organic laws governing the period 1812-1952. It includes an extensive bibliography.

2937. **Hansen, Millard, and Henry Wells** (eds.). Puerto Rico: a study in democratic development (A Am Ac Pol Soc Sci, 285, Jan. 1953, 166 p.).
This very fine symposium has articles dealing with "The political development of Puerto Rico"; "Economic development"; "A fusion of cultures"; "Too many people"; and "Future prospects."

2938. **Muñoz Marín, Luis.** La personalidad puertorriqueña en el Estado Libre Asociado. Discurso . . . . San Juan, 1953. 14 p.
Dr. Muñoz Marín has written a thoughtful little essay on what things "American" Puerto Rico should adopt or reject.

2939. ————. Puerto Rico y los Estados Unidos: su futuro en común. San Juan, Departamento de Instrucción Pública, 1954. 16 p.
The governor discusses, in his usual thoughtful manner, the ways in which Puerto Rico is "another American state" and those in which its constitutional status is unique.

2940. **Puerto Rico. Bureau of the Budget. Office of Statistics.** Guía de agencias y funcionarios, agosto 1953. San Juan, 1953. 90 p.
This is a directory of major branches, divisions, agencies, commissions, etc., of the executive, legislative, and judicial departments of the government, including a list of principal officeholders in each.

2941. ————. **Governor.** Discurso de Luis Muñoz Marín, gobernador del Estado Libre Asociado de Puerto Rico, con

motivo de su inauguración el 2 de enero de 1953. San Juan, 1953. 14 p.
The governor examines the juridical status of Puerto Rico under the new constitutional arrangement.

VENEZUELA

2942. **Briceño-Iragorry, Mario.** Problemas de la juventud venezolana. Temas acerca de la presente crisis universitaria. Madrid, Ediciones Bitácora, 1953. 61 p.
A rather rambling essay on the need for the reform of higher education in Venezuela, with few suggestions for specific changes. The author's stress on technical education, in order to prepare for the nationalization of oil resources, has political significance.

2943. **Dávila, Antonio.** La dictadura venezolana. Maracaibo, Venezuela, Tip. Criollo, 1954. 230 p.
A series of brief essays on the major political questions of the period from Oct. 18, 1945, to Nov. 24, 1948, when Acción Democrática was in power.

2944. **Pepper, José Vicente.** Reconstrucción integral de Venezuela. Valencia, Venezuela, Editorial Aborigen, 1953. 544 p., illus., ports.
A laudatory account of the Pérez Jiménez administration, emphasizing its social and economic reforms. One chapter deals with the drafting of the 1953 Constitution.

2945. **Pérez Dupuy, H.** El liberalismo creador frente al socialismo destructor. Caracas, Ragon, 1954. 376 p.
This not-too-well-organized volume has considerable material on the economic development of Venezuela since 1947.

2946. **Rodríguez H., Ivan.** Política contemporánea. Recopilación de artículos publicados. Caracas, Ragon, 1954. 213 p., illus.
The earlier chapters of this book contain some important materials on 20th-century political party evolution.

OTHER AREAS

2947. **Comité de Estudiantes Universitarios Anticomunistas.** Plan de Tegucigalpa. Tegucigalpa, 1954. 65 p.
This is an outline (non-official) to be followed in the drafting of a new constitution. The plan of government which is included is stated in the most general terms.

2948. **Costa Rica. Asamblea Constituyente.** Asamblea Nacional Constituyente de 1949. T. 1. Antecedentes. Proyecto. Reglamento. Actas. San José, 1953. 675 p.
This volume includes a discussion of the back-

grounds of the constitutional reform of 1948, the several plans which were presented to the Constituent Assembly, the organization of the Convention, a report on the principal policy debates, and the text of the constitution which was approved.

2949. Fitzgibbon, Russell H. Uruguay. Portrait of a democracy. New Brunswick, N. J., Rutgers University Press, 1954. 301 p., illus.
This is an excellent study of democratic Uruguay. The author not only clearly portrays the democratic institutions of Uruguay but suggests some valuable explanations of why Uruguay is so different. More books like this on the other American republics would immeasurably advance our knowledge of basic political forces and trends. Includes bibliography and index.

2950. Goytía, Víctor F. (comp.). Las constituciones de Panamá. Prólogo de Manuel Fraga Iribarne. Madrid, Ediciones Cultura Hispánica (Las constituciones hispanoamericanas, 7), 1954. lxvi, 823 p.
A very fine constitutional history of the Republic of Panama, which includes the texts of all organic laws and constitutions from 1841 to 1946.

2951. Hall, John O. La administración pública en el Uruguay. Sugerencias para una reforma de la organización administrativa. Montevideo, Instituto de Asuntos Interamericanos, 1954. 90 p.
An excellent analysis of present administrative organization in Uruguay, and proposals for reform. The chapter on personnel administration and the budget (as a means of administrative control) contains much valuable information.

2952. Honduras. Oficina de Cooperación Intelectual. Acontecimientos en relación al nuevo gobierno de concentración nacional. Tegucigalpa, Ariston, 1954, i.e. 1955. 54 p., illus.
A brief account, based mainly on news items and radio broadcasts, of the succession of Julio Lozano Díaz to the presidency on Nov. 16, 1954.

2953. Jagan, Cheddi. Forbidden freedom. The story of British Guiana. With a foreword by Tom Driberg. N. Y., International Publishers, 1954. 96 p.

The author charges that he and his administration were removed from office because of the pressure which the U. S. exerted on the British government.

2954. Linke, Lilo. Ecuador: country of contrasts. London and N.Y., Royal Institute of International Affairs, 1954. 173 p., maps.
Though this book is not intended to be a political study, the material on the role of the Indian, needed reforms relating to them, and the clerical versus anticlerical feelings extant in Ecuador are of real importance and value.

2955. Pendle, George. Paraguay, a riverside nation. London, N. Y., Royal Institute of International Affairs, 1954. 115 p., maps.
Like the other books in this series of the Royal Institute, this one is very well done and includes much material on constitutions, government, and politics.

2956. The story of British Guiana (New Statesman and Nation, 46:1180, Oct. 17, 1953, p. 449-454).
This article is a criticism of British policy with reference to its colony; its point of view is that the action which was taken was decided too hastily and without a full consideration of the basic colonial problem.

2957. United States. Congress. Senate. Committee on Interior and Insular Affairs. Virgin Islands report by Mr. Butler of Nebraska . . . with reference to proposed revision of the organic act and the governmental, economic, and fiscal structure in the Islands, with recommendations on the federally owned Virgin Islands Corporation. Washington, U. S. Government Printing Office, 1954. 143 p.
A valuable reference book on governmental, economic, and fiscal problems in the Virgin Islands.

2958. Vittini, Manuel Antonio. Cara o cruz del justicialismo. Estudio de exposición y crítica. Santiago, Imp. Universitaria, 1953, i.e. 1954. 150 p.
The author is a Chilean admirer of the program of *justicialismo*. The book has some importance in the discussion that it presents of a closer economic union between Chile and Argentina.

History

GENERAL

3000. Aguirre Beltrán, Gonzalo. Formas de gobierno indígena. México, Imp. Universitaria (Cultura mexicana, 5), 1953. 221 p.

Deals with the subject as a whole, from the 16th century to date, and then discusses the current status separately of the Tarahumares, the Tzotziles, the Tzeltales, and the Tarascans. A little source material is used from the Mexican archives. [R. D. Hussey]

3001. Alumni, José. El Chaco. Figuras y hechos de su pasado. Con motivo del II.° centenario de la fundación de San Fernando del Río Negro, 1750-1950. Resistencia, Argentina, Talleres Gráficos Juan Moro, 1951. 341 p., illus.

A documented survey history of the Chaco from the earliest times with heavy emphasis upon the colonial period. 19th and 20th centuries receive scant attention in the text but provide most of the materials for the large documentary appendix. A chapter is devoted to church history. [C. Gibson]

3002. Antigua Librería Robredo de José Porrúa e hijos. Catálogo 16, agosto 1954. México, 1954.

Item 17,949 deals with "Biblioteca de aportación histórica, publicada por el editor, Vargas Rea, México, 1940-." It is a short-title listing, without much arrangement, of 239 items in the valuable series of *cuadernos* that have now been in publication, in editions of 75 or 100 copies only, for 15 years, to the joy of historians and exasperation of bibliographers. It is probably the nearest to a complete list in existence, although the compiler plaintively comments that "el mismo señor Vargas Rea no pudo informarnos de los títulos faltantes, ya que ni siquiera conserva una lista de lo publicado." By no means all the titles have been entered in the *HLAS*. [R. D. Hussey]

3003. Antilia and America. A description of the 1424 Nautical Chart and the Waldseemüller Globe of 1507 in the James Ford Bell Collection at the University of Minnesota. Minneapolis, Minn., 1955. 10 p., folding colored map.

The 1424 Nautical Chart (formerly Phillipps MS. 25,924) is the one discussed by Armando Cortesão (item 3104) when it was in the hands of a London bookdealer. It was bought for the Bell Collection in 1954. The well-known unique copy of the 1507 printed map was offered in a separate printed catalog by the Parke Bernet Galleries, New York, on May 24, 1950. The upset price of $50,000 was not met and the map was withdrawn. It was bought by the Bell collection in 1954. Both maps are well reproduced in this 1955 item, as well as in the book and the sale catalog mentioned. [R. D. Hussey]

3004. Araneda Bravo, Fidel. Los estudios históricos en Chile (Atenea, año 30, 110: 336, junio 1953, p. 425-441; 111:337-338, julio-agosto 1953, p. 76-93; 113:341-342, nov.-dic. 1953, p. 132-139.

Discussion of some Chilean historians, and some factors conditioning their work, since colonial times. Not a complete review (omits Donoso, Feliú Cruz, and many others), but written with common sense. [C. B. Kroeber]

3005. Armytage, Frances. The free port system in the British West Indies. A study in commercial policy, 1766-1822. London, Longmans, 1953. 176 p., maps, tables.

A careful and detailed account of the drafting of the Free Port Acts and the working of the system. The Acts were a logical extension of the navigation system; they neither conflicted with the Acts of Trade, nor presaged the downfall of protection. Their effectiveness in encouraging trade with Spanish America was limited. Of particular interest is the discussion of the effect of the Acts upon trade with the U. S. after Independence. [J. H. Parry]

3006. Ashby, Charlotte M. (comp.). Cartographic records of the United States Marine Corps. Washington, National Archives (Preliminary inventories, 73), 1954. 17 p.

This catalogue of maps in the National Archives lists many of the Latin American countries or parts thereof. [R. R. Hill]

3007. Bellegarde, Dantès. Haïti et son peuple. Paris, Nouvelles Éditions Latines, 1953. 121 p.

Commemorating 150 years of Haitian independence, the dean of Haitian intellectuals has produced a charming account of Haitian history—written in Gallic style and apparently with French readers principally in mind. One item of especial interest to U. S. readers, however, is the account of 800 Haitians who were sent to aid American independence and most of whom died in the battle of Savannah, Oct. 1779. Possibly a monument there would further U. S.-Haitian friendship. [R. E. McNicoll]

3008. ————. Histoire de peuple haïtien (1492-1952). Port-au-Prince, Held (Coll. du tricinquantenaire de l'Indépendance d' Haïti), 1953. 365 p.

This outgrowth of a series of lectures delivered in 1952 at the Haitian-American Institute is basically a revised edition of M. Bellegarde's superb general study, *La nation haïtienne*, published in Paris 18 years ago. Once again the reader has an opportunity to admire the impeccable style that mirrors the character of a great Haitian. The book ends with a copy of the 1950 Constitution, which was drafted under the direction of Dantès Bellegarde. [M. Cook]

3009. Bierck, Harold A., Jr. Spoils, soils, and Skinner (Md Hist Mag, 49:1, Mar. 1954, p. 21-40; 49:2, June 1954, p. 143-155).

Examines the Latin American interests (privateering, propaganda, exchange of agricultural data) of John Stuart Skinner of Baltimore (1788-1851). [D. Bushnell]

3010. Binayán, Narciso. Zinny en la bibliografía argentina (R Interam Bibl, 3:2, mayo-agosto 1953, p. 121-129).

Account of the works in Argentine, Uruguayan, and Paraguayan historical bibliography of Antonio Zinny (1821-1890), which works have not yet been superseded in value. Mentions also several Argentine bibliographers before Zinny. [C. B. Kroeber]

3011. Black, Clinton V. The archives of Jamaica (Carib Q, 3:3, Dec. 1953, p. 130-135).

An account of the neglect and losses of Jamaican records, together with a brief survey of the documents now in the Archive available for research and a statement of a program for improvements for their care. [R. R. Hill]

3012. Borhegyi, Stephen F. de. The miraculous shrines of Our Lady of Esquipulas in Guatemala and Chimayó, New Mexico (Palacio, 60:3, March 1953, p. 83-111).

Published also in Spanish in *Antropología e historia de Guatemala*, v. 5, no. 1, enero 1953, p. 11-28. Traces something of the early history (from the 16th century) in Guatemala, speculates about the transfer of the cult to New Mexico, and discusses its history there until the 19th century The transfer was probably made by a member of the Abeyta family, and before 1805. There are 16 documents, 1813-1849. [R. D. Hussey]

3013. Burns, Alan C. History of the British West Indies. London, Allen & Unwin, 1954. 821 p., maps.

A compendious history of the British Caribbean colonies, intended for the general reader and making no pretense of original research. Each chapter contains sections on each colony, which makes for easy reference but renders the book difficult to read as a connected story. The last 50 years are not covered, except by a brief list of outstanding events. The bibliography is extensive but unsystematic, with some serious omissions. The book is very well produced, with excellent maps, and contains much out-of-the-way information. It is the only modern work on the subject on so large a scale. [J. H. Parry]

3014. Burrus, Ernest J. An introduction to bibliographical tools in Spanish archives and manuscript collections relating to Hispanic America (HAHR, 35:4, Nov. 1955, p. 443-483).

Valuable and clear information upon guides and printed or manuscript inventories, and to some degree upon the type of materials and their coverage, in a number of the important depositories of Spain. [R. D. Hussey]

3015. Cabrera, Lucio. Suecia ante la independencia de la América Latina. México, Universidad Nacional Autónoma de México, Facultad de Filosofía y Letras, 1951. 66 p.

A brief but capable summary of Swedish intellectual, political, and economic interest in Latin American independence; based only on printed sources (including many in Swedish). [D. Bushnell]

3016. Carreño, Alberto María. La cripta arzobispal en la catedral metropolitana de México. México, Comisión Diocesana de Orden y Decoro, 1954. 23 p. & illus.

Important to historians only for the reproductions of portraits of the Mexican archbishops from Zumárraga to the present incumbent. [R. D. Hussey]

3017. Carrera Stampa, Manuel. Los gremios mexicanos. La organización gremial en Nueva España, 1521-1861. México, EDIAPSA (Colección de estudios histórico-económicos mexicanos de la Cámara Nacional de la Industria de Transformación, 1), 1954. 399 p., illus.

An excellent book, so far as one can be written from the essentially legal and/or official sources. Discusses all the aspects likely to concern the historian of institutions, and gives something upon the life, work and social status of the workers. About 200 guilds are identified, from 1542 on. [R. D. Hussey]

3018. Castillero, Ernesto. Grandeza y decadencia del Castillo de San Lorenzo de Chagres. Panamá, 1954. 24 p.

Reprinted from *Revista de Indias*, Madrid, 14: 57-58, julio-dic. 1954. Except possibly for the notes upon the castle's history after Colombia became independent, the item has no value for specialists. [R. D. Hussey]

3019. Charlier, Étienne D. Aperçu sur la formation historique de la nation haïtienne. Port-au-Prince, Les Presses Libres, 1954. 334 p.
A detailed study of the complex and interrelated factors which caused the people of Haiti to break away from France. French Revolutionary policy and Bonaparte's fatal attitude toward the colony are very carefully analyzed, as are varying reactions which these policies caused among the French colonists and the Negroes, both freedmen and slave, and their leaders. The reader is given a very clear and stirring picture of the process through which the Haitian people moved simultaneously to personal and national freedom. [R. S. Chamberlain]

3020. Cignoli, Francisco. Historia de la farmacia argentina. Rosario, Argentina, Ruiz, 1953. 403 p.
The pharmaceutical history of Argentina is thoroughly chronicled from aboriginal to modern times. Documents and bibliography are appended. [C. Gibson]

3021. Congreso Hispanoamericano de Historia. Causas y caracteres de la independencia hispanoamericana. Madrid, Ediciones Cultura Hispánica, 1953. 519 p.
More on causes than on characteristics. A summary of reports and discussion which took place in 1949 at Madrid and reveal the thinking of an impressive list of Spanish and Spanish American historians who attended the Congress. [D. Bushnell]

3022. Conseil International des Archives. Archivum. Paris. V. 2-4, 1952-1954, i. e. 1953-1955.
Items on Latin American archivology appear in the classified bibliography in each volume. Special articles regarding the Latin American countries may also be included. [R. R. Hill]

2023. Cuba. Archivo Nacional. Catálogo de los mapas, planos, croquis y árboles genealógicos existentes en el Archivo Nacional de Cuba. T. 3. D-H. Prefacio del Capitán Joaquín Llaverías y Martínez. Habana, 1954. 377 p. (Publ. 38).
A listing of maps, plans, and genealogical trees, for names beginning with D to H, which are in the National Archive of Cuba. The entries give the date, a complete identification, the size, and the location in the collections. Indexes of places, persons, engineers and architects, and of the collections are included. See also *HLAS, no. 18, 1952*, item 1642, and *no. 17, 1951*, item 1392. [R. R. Hill]

3024. Cuesta, Luisa, and Modesta Cuesta (comps.). Catálogo de obras iberoamericanas y filipinas en la Biblioteca Nacional. Prólogo del ilustrísimo señor don Fran-

cisco Sintes Obrador. Madrid, Dirección General de Archivos y Bibliotecas (Cátalogos de archivos y bibliotecas, 1) 1953. 322 p.
3364 items, alphabetically arranged, with a subject index. The 18th century is most strongly represented. According to the preface, this is intended as the first volume of a series, and contains only "Obras generales." Volumes on separate countries are planned. [R. D. Hussey]

3025. Cuevas, Mariano. Historia de la Nación Mexicana. 2. ed., anotada por el autor. México, Buena Prensa, 1952-1953. 3 v.
Somewhat revised from the first edition (Mexico, 1940) from notes left by the author at the time of his death in 1949. [R. D. Hussey]

3026. Cuzco. Archivo Histórico. Revista del Archivo Histórico. Cuzco, Perú, Universidad Nacional del Cuzco. Año 1, no. 1, 1950—año 5, no. 5, 1954.
The Archivo Histórico of Cuzco was inaugurated in 1949 in accordance with a presidential decree of 1923. The following year the *Revista* was first published under the direction of the National University of Cuzco and numbers have appeared in each succeeding year. The numbers contain indexes of records, texts of important documents, and articles dealing with the history of Cuzco. [R. R. Hill]

3027. Davis, Edward J. P. Historical San Diego, the birthplace of California. A history of its discovery, settlement, and development. San Diego, Calif., 1953. 120 p., illus.
A hodge podge of "facts" about many aspects of the history of San Diego; gives proportionally adequate attention to the Spanish and Mexican period, but without new value for them. [R. D. Hussey]

3028. Davis, Harold E. The Americas in history. N. Y., Ronald Press, 1953. 878 p., maps.
A college text, with fairly orthodox treatment of the Bolton "History of America" hemispheric approach. [H. F. Cline]

3029. Díaz Soler, Luis M. Historia de la esclavitud negra en Puerto Rico (1493-1890). Madrid, Revista de Occidente (Ediciones de la Universidad de Puerto Rico), 1953. 432 p.
Six chapters on the slave trade, 1508-1866, two on life and work of the slaves, one each on rebellions and on free Negroes, four on abolition (with indemnity), 1864-1890. Extensive printed sources are supplemented by some manuscript for the late 18th and 19th centuries, and appendices offer nine documents, 1735-1855. An invaluable study in an almost unworked field. [R. D. Hussey]

3030. Díaz Vial, Raúl. Una línea Vial en Concepción (1764-1952). Santiago, Imp. Universitaria, 1952. 29 p.

Genealogical and biographical notes on the Vial family in Chile. [C. Gibson]

3031. Encina, Francisco A. Resumen de la historia de Chile. Redacción, iconografía y apéndices de Leopoldo Castedo. Santiago, Ziz-Zag, 1954. T. 1, 1535-1817. T. 2, 1817-1879. 1385 p., illus., maps.

A condensed, rewritten and somewhat re-shaped version of Encina's multi-volume history of Chile since the early 16th century; one volume still to come. Remarkable for the quantity of maps and other graphic material, much of it hard to come by outside Chile. [C. B. Kroeber]

3032. Engenhoff, Elizabeth L. De argento vivo. Historic documents on quicksilver and its recovery in California prior to 1860. A supplement of the *California journal of mines and geology* for October, 1953. Sacramento, Calif., Division of Natural Resources, Division of Mines, 1953. 144 p., illus.

About half the book reprints, or prints in translation, extracts from ancient Greek or Roman, or Muslim, or Renaissance European, works. The rest of the book does the same for California, 1796 and 1846-1860. [R. D. Hussey]

3033. Estudios históricos americanos. Homenaje a Silvio Zavala. Salutación de Alfonso Reyes. México, El Colegio de México, 1953. 786 p., illus.

A large number of essays by different authors, on the occasion of the twentieth anniversary of Zavala's doctorate from the University of Madrid. Mostly on Mexico and the colonial era, but a few of broader interest. The quality varies greatly. Some of the best are entered separately in the proper portion of this handbook. [R. D. Hussey]

3034. Ewing, William S. (comp.). Guide to the manuscript collection in the William L. Clements Library. 2d ed. Ann Arbor, Mich., Michigan University, William L. Clements Library, 1953. 548 p.

Includes all groups, with an index, but refers back to the 1942 *Guide* for details when that is possible. This second edition shows that the collections on Latin American, and especially Mexican, phases are continuing to develop strongly. Nearly a fifth of the listed groups are specifically Latin American, aside from such interest in some other groups. Since 1942 there have been added a few documents on the Jesuits in the Philippines (1615) and on Guatemala (1760-1870) and at least 15 groups on Mexico. The latter include big lots on Mexican Independence, Porfirio Díaz, Zacatecas (1561?-1870), Yucatan 1772-1898, and papers (1785-1789) of the Mexican Botanical Gardens. [R. D. Hussey]

3035. Eyzaguirre, Jaime. The Franciscan teachers of Bernardo O'Higgins (Americas, Franciscan Hist, 12:1, July 1955, p. 43-49).

Brief sketch of the Franciscan college at Chillan (founded 1697), with some data on the attitude of Chilean Franciscans toward the Independence movement. [D. Bushnell]

3036. Faivre, Jean Paul. Expansion française dans le Pacifique de 1800 à 1842. Paris, Nouvelles Éditions Latines, 1953. 550 p., maps.

Excellent historical study, from sources that represent several national viewpoints. The first part of the work deals with the era before 1800, and some of the later portions refer back to it. Although the subject matter primarily concerns the western Pacific, there is much value for French interest in, and trade with, and ship calls at, many parts of the Pacific areas of North and South America, as well as the Philippines. [R. D. Hussey]

3037. Fawcett, Percy H. Exploration Fawcett. Arranged from his manuscripts, letters, log-books, and records by Brian Fawcett. London, Hutchinson, 1953. 312 p., illus.

The explorer's accounts of his Bolivian and Brazilian travels, 1906-1925, as boundary surveyor and searcher for lost cities of the *bandeirantes*. Some useful observations on sordid backland life during the later days of the rubber boom. The American edition (N. Y., Funk & Wagnalls, 1953) has title: *Lost trails, lost cities*. [C. B. Kroeber]

3038. Fernández del Castillo, Francisco. La facultad de medicina, según el Archivo de la Real y Pontificia Universidad de México. México, Editorial Universitaria (Ediciones del IV Centenario de la Universidad de México, 14), 1953. 311 p., facsims.

A large body of documents, with an introduction. Emphasizes the 18th and 19th centuries, but has material also upon the 16th and 17th. [R. D. Hussey]

3039. Finot, Enrique. Nueva historia de Bolivia. Ensayo de interpretación sociológica. 2. ed. La Paz, Gisbert, 1954. 382 p.

Republication of the work first issued in 1946. [C. Gibson]

3040. Fisher, Lillian Estelle. Champion of reform, Manuel Abad y Queipo. N. Y., Library Publishers, 1955. 314 p.

An uncritical, extremely eulogistic, and essentially chronological arrangement of data and extracts from a vast mass of archival sources. Abad y Queipo (1751-1825) was bishop of Michoacan during several troubled years, and a good man and moderate liberal whose advice might have been good for Spain or Mexico had those in authority wished to take it, but there is no evidence whatsoever that he had any such influence as is ascribed to him here. "The Writings" are well discussed, p. 272-277. [R. D. Hussey]

3041. **Fisher, Mary Ann.** Preliminary guide to the microfilm collection in the Bancroft Library. Berkeley, Calif., University of California, 1955. 28 p. (mimeographed).

Describes especially the 2,500,000 frames newly acquired from various foreign archives, for the history of western North America and the Pacific Coast, and to a lesser degree for that of many parts of Latin America. Information is also given on some 2,500 reels of newspaper copies, and more briefly on the older collections of transcripts and photographs from Mexico and Spain. [R. D. Hussey]

3042. **Gabaldón Márquez, Joaquín** (and others). Misiones venezolanas en los archivos europeos. México, Instituto Panamericano de Geografía e Historia (Publ. 181; Comisión de Historia, 73; Misiones, 8), 1954. 230 p.

An account of the labors of Venezuelans in European archives. Part 1 deals with the official missions, giving a description of the documents in 55 volumes of transcripts deposited in the Academy of History. Part 2 treats of the several private missions and includes descriptive lists of the transcripts secured. [R. R. Hill]

3043. **Gianello, Leoncio.** Historia de Entre Ríos (1520-1910). Paraná, Argentina, Ministerio de Educación (Biblioteca enterriana General Perón, Serie: Historia, 3), 1951. 633 p., map, illus.

Useful for orientation purposes, but a quite conventional book based on other books and some published documents. History up to 1860 uses up four-fifths of the space. [C. B. Kroeber]

3044. **Giraldo Jaramillo, Gabriel.** Colombia y Cuba. Bogotá, Minerva, 1953. 185 p. Provocative. [R. E. McNicoll]

3045. **Goveia, Elsa V.** A study on the historiography of the British West Indies to the end of the nineteenth century. México, Instituto Panamericano de Geografía e Historia, 1956. 183 p.

An account of all the more important books within its period which claimed to be histories of the British West Indies or of the individual territories in British possession. Not a historical bibliography, but a study in "a phase of intellectual history." Within the limits of its own definition, this is a full and complete study of a rich and varied field. Describes and criticizes the work of individual historians, and relates changes in the attitudes and methods of historians to corresponding changes in social structure. Well written, penetrating, and scrupulously fair. [J. H. Parry]

3046. **Gurria Lacroix, Jorge.** Monografías históricas sobre Tabasco. Villahermosa, México, Instituto de Historia (Publ., serie 1, 25; Publ. del Gobierno del Estado de Tabasco, Escritores tabasqueños, 72), 1952. 233 p.

Gathers up six essays by the author, one on archaeology, three on the 16th century, and two on the 19th. The first four, though pleasantly written, add nothing for specialists. The others, from good sources, are: "José María Alpuche é Infante, vida y tiempos, 1780-1840," and "La Intervención y el Imperio en el estado de Tabasco." [R. D. Hussey]

3047. **Harrison, John P.** The archives of United States diplomatic and consular posts in Latin America (HAHR, 33:1, Feb. 1953, p. 168-183).

A general discussion of the extent and condition of records transferred from American diplomatic and consular posts to the National Archives, together with a detailed description of the diplomatic records from Argentina and the consular records from Bahia. The conclusion treats of the use of post archives for research. [R. R. Hill]

3048. ————. Opportunities for inter-American studies in the National Archives (*in* Wilgus, A. Curtis (ed.). The Caribbean: peoples, problems, and prospects. Gainesville, Fla., University of Florida Press, 1952, p. 162-174).

A paper read at the Second Annual Conference on the Caribbean, held at the University of Florida in December 1951. It briefly outlines the record group system of the National Archives at Washington and the organization of the documents in the groups. Then descriptive illustrations of a few of the many record groups containing materials for the Caribbean are given. Mention is made of State Department, Naval and other groups, as well as of certain specific items in order to show the vast scope and importance for research in the field of Latin American history. [R. R. Hill]

3049. **Hill, Roscoe R.** Ecclesiastical archives in Latin America (Archivum, 4, 1954, i. e. 1955, p. 135-144).

An outline of the parochial, diocesan, and archdiocesan archives of the Roman Catholic Church in Latin America which contain documents relating to the activities of the bishops and archbishops and the records of births, marriages, and deaths in the parishes. There is a brief description of the ecclesiastical archives of Mexico, giving location, types and groups of records, dates and amounts, including the archbishopric, bishopric, and selected parish archives of Mexico City and selected archives of the states. Also some mention of Brazilian archives. [R. R. Hill]

3050. ————. Latin American archivology, 1951-1953 (HAHR, 34:2, May 1954, p. 256-279).

A general survey of the activities of the Latin American archives for the years 1951-1953, including bibliographic notes. [R. R. Hill]

3051. **Ibáñez Varona, René.** Historia de los hospitales y asilos de Puerto Príncipe

o Camagüey. Período colonial. Habana, Ministerio de Salubridad y Asistencia Social (Cuadernos de historia sanitaria), 1954. 64 p., illus.
A valuable collection of notes from various sources, some of them scarce periodicals. The "colonial period" includes the 19th century. [R. D. Hussey]

3052. **Ibarra, Carlos M.** Hombres e historia en México. Puebla, México, Cajica, 1953. 2 v. 518, 301 p.
Survey history of Mexico. [W. V. Scholes]

3053. The John B. Stetson collection of books in English, Spanish, French and other languages on exploration, history, anthropology, and similar subjects relating to the Western Hemisphere. N. Y., Parke-Bernet Galleries, 1953. 3 parts.
Parts 1 and 3, with over 1400 items (many with more than one title) offer a good working collection for the subjects named, except that not many of the histories written in the last century are represented. The collection has few of the excessively rare items that were offered in the 1935 Stetson sale, but there are many that earn special notes. South America is emphasized more than North America, and, in proportion to what is in print, there is an emphasis on Florida. [R. D. Hussey]

3054. **Lancaster Jones, Ricardo.** La hacienda de Santa Ana Apacuero (B Junta Aux Jalis, 9:4-5, enero-abril 1951, p. 149-178.
Most valuable data upon the history of an enormous estate, slowly accreted from the 16th century on, until "dismembered" in the 19th. The holdings were in present-day Guanajuato and Jalisco. Folding map of 1756. [R. D. Hussey]

3055. **Lansing, Marion F.** Liberators and heroes of the West Indian Islands. Boston, Page, 1953. 294 p., illus.
Juvenile, dealing with Columbus, Diego Columbus, Hatuey, Las Casas, Morgan, George Rodney, Toussaint L'Ouverture, Bolívar, Duarte, Narciso López, and Céspedes. [R. E. McNicoll]

3056. **Llaverías y Martínez, Joaquín.** Biografía del Archivo Nacional de Cuba. Habana, Archivo Nacional de Cuba (Publ., 39), 1954. 59 p.
The text of a conference at the University of Habana, giving briefly the history of the National Archive of Cuba and pointing out the value of its records and the achievements, particularly during the administration of Captain Llaverías, the dean of Latin American archivists. [R. R. Hill]

3057. **Marsland, William D.,** and **Amy L. Marsland.** Venezuela through its history. N. Y., Thomas Y. Crowell, 1954. 277 p., illus., maps.
This work, as its title indicates, traces the history of Venezuela from pre-Columbian times to the present. The content is well balanced between the colonial, independence movement, and national periods. Treatment of the war for independence is kept close to events in Venezuela, but without isolating them from related developments elsewhere. Character sketches of Bolívar and other leaders of the independence period and of principal figures of the national period are particularly good. Economic and other forces at work in Venezuela today which will shape the future receive due and speculative attention. Fast-moving, well-written, and often entertaining, this book can be read with pleasure by both scholars and the general reader. [R. S. Chamberlain]

3058. **Medina, José Toribio.** Tres estudios históricos. Santiago, D. G. de Prisiones, 1952. 32 p., facsim.
Reprint of three short essays by Medina: "El escudo de armas de la ciudad de Santiago"; "El acta del cabildo abierto del 18 de septiembre de 1810"; "¿Quiénes firmaron esa acta?" [C. Gibson]

3059. **Meilink-Roelofsz, M. A. P.** A survey of archives in the Netherlands pertaining to the history of the Netherlands Antilles (West Indische Gids, 35:1-2, april 1954, p. 1-38).
Historical data about records from various archives in the Netherlands West Indies, which are now in the Netherlands archives, with listings of series and groups of the records from each archive. The lists give titles of the series, dates, and number of items. There is an indication of many inventories or descriptions. Also there is brief mention of records created in the Netherlands relating to the West Indies. [R. R. Hill]

3060. **Mendes, Ubirajara Dolácio.** Noções de paleografia. São Paulo, Departamento do Arquivo do Estado de São Paulo, 1953. 123 p.
A brief treatise on paleography. The topics discussed include: definition of paleography; evolution of writing; materials used in writing; conservation and repair of documents; difficulties in reading and interpreting old records; and Brazilian paleography. [R. R. Hill]

3061. **Mörner, Magnus.** Swedish contributions to the historical bibliography of Latin America (HAHR, 34:3, Aug. 1954, p. 393-398).

3062. **Monte y Tejada, Antonio del.** Historia de Santo Domingo. 3. ed. Ciudad Trujillo, Secretaría de Estado de Educación Bellas Artes, Sección de Canje, Difusión Cultural y Publicaciones (Biblioteca dominicana, serie 1, v. 6-8), 1952-1953. 3 v.
A reprint of the first three volumes only of the four-volume edition (1890-1892), with extensive and valuable notes by Gustavo Adolfo Mejía y Ricart. The fourth volume, which was

documentary, 1792-1794, was deliberately omitted. It should be noted that the "first edition" of 1853 was only of the first volume. [R. D. Hussey]

3063. Nakayama, Antonio. Documentos inéditos e interesantes para la historia de Culiacán . . . . Culiacán, Sinaloa, México, 1952. 129 p., 2 maps.
A valuable miscellany of documents from the mid-16th century to 1842. All but one are previously unpublished. [R. D. Hussey]

3064. Navarro y Noriega, Fernando. Memoria sobre la población del Reino de Nueva España, escrita en el año de 1814. . . . Reimpresa ahora por la vez primera con una introducción por Jaime Delgado. Llanes, Spain, José Porrúa Turanzas, 1954. xviii, 30 p., fold. table.
150 numbered copies only. The first edition was published by Arispe in Mexico in 1820. In spite of the title of this 1954 edition, it has been reprinted at least once before (see *HLAS*, no. 9, 1943, item 2729). [R. D. Hussey]

3065. Nieto y Cortadellas, Rafael. Documentos sacramentales de algunos cubanos ilustres (R Bib Nac, Habana, 2. serie, 4:1, enero-marzo 1953—6:3, julio-sept. 1955).
Birth, marriage, and death certificates, from various parish registers of noted Cubans (entries no. 25-84). The source of each document is indicated. To be continued. [R. R. Hill]

3066. Noticias sobre Nueva Galicia. México, Vargas Rea (Biblioteca de historiadores mexicanos), 1953. 42 p.
Data from the 16th century to 1835, in an anonymous document from the archives of the Secretaría de Hacienda. 100 copies only. [R. D. Hussey]

3067. Nueva Vizcaya. Datos. México, Vargas Rea (Biblioteca de historiadores mexicanos), 1954. 42 p.
Data from the 16th century to 1832, from a document in the archives of the Secretaría de Hacienda. 75 copies only. [R. D. Hussey]

3068. Ortega Ricaurte, Enrique. Bibliografía académica. Publicación de la Academia Colombiana de Historia con motivo del cincuentenario de su fundación, 1902-1952. Bogotá, Minerva, 1953. 645 p.

3069. Palacio, Ernesto. Historia de la Argentina, 1515-1938. B. A., Ediciones Alpe (Biblioteca de estudios americanos), 1954. 654 p.
A highly nationalistic, polemical treatment of the course of Argentine history by an author who sees Rosas as the true representative of Argentine nationality and who regrets what he views as the loss of influence by strong provincial leaders who symbolized the true Argen-

tina. He deplores the concentration, despite federal forms, of all power in the hands of politicians in the central government in materialistic Buenos Aires. The overthrow of Rosa, marked the beginning of this process of decay according to the author. [R. S. Chamberlain]

3070. Pares, Richard. Yankees and Creoles. The trade between North America and the West Indies before the American Revolution. London, Longmans, 1956. 168 p.
A fascinating account and description of trade between the North American colonies and the West Indies in the 18th century, based chiefly upon the letters and accounts of North American trading firms and families. Throws new light upon the part played by the West Indies trade in the formation of capital in North America and in the discharge of North American debts to European suppliers. Very well written, in a terse and clear style, and a model of the systematic handling of scattered detail. [J. H. Parry]

3071. Piquion, René. Archives. Port-au-Prince, Deschamps, 1953? 33 p.
By describing research facilities in France, Dr Piquion tactfully reminds his colleagues in Haiti of the importance of primary sources. The preface is by M. R. H. Bautier, French archivist. [M. Cook]

3072. Proctor, Jesse H., Jr. The development of the idea of federation of the British Caribbean territories (R Hist Am, 39, junio 1955, p. 61-105).
An historical sketch of earlier proposals for federation, and the reactions of public opinion towards them. [J. H. Parry]

3073. Puente Arteaga, Martín. El municipio en México. Génesis y evolución. México, Studium, 1954. 128 p.
A thesis, printed in a limited edition of 75 signed copies for sale, plus 50 not put in trade. Concentrates upon the theory, but organized about the history, from the 16th century to the 20th. [R. D. Hussey]

3074. Reyes, Antonio. Caciques aborígenes venezolanos. 3. ed. Caracas, Imp Nacional, 1953. 328 p., illus.
Literary evocations of historical and mythical figures in Venezuelan aboriginal history of pre Conquest and colonial times. [C. Gibson]

3075. Rosenblat, Ángel. La población indígena y el mestizaje en América. I. La población indígena, 1492-1950. II. El mestizaje y las castas coloniales. B. A. Editorial Nova, 1954. 2 v., illus.
Somewhat revised, and the second part appreciably augmented, from the first edition (B. A. 1945). [R. D. Hussey]

3076. Rossel Castro, Alberto. Caciques y templos de Ica. Lima, 1954. 157 p.
Notes on the ecclesiastical history of Ica Valley

rom the 16th to the 20th century, with some 1ew documentation on cacicazgos and religious uildings and organization. [C. Gibson]

3077. Schoen, Wilhelm Albrecht von. Geschichte Mittel- und Südamerikas. Munich, Verlag F. Bruckmann, 1953. 698 p.

λ history by a nonprofessional author who had 3ng experience, as a diplomat or otherwise, in berian countries. It seems to have no unusual characteristics, except a natural tendency to play 1p German activities. [R. D. Hussey]

3078. Siegrist Clamont, Jorge. En defensa de la autonomía universitaria. Trayectoria historico-jurídica de la Universidad Mexicana. Introducción de José Vasconcelos. México, 1955. 2 v.

Primarily a discussion of current aspects, but 1as a few chapters upon the history of the subject from the 16th century. [R. D. Hussey]

3079. Silva Herzog, Jesús. Nueve estudios mexicanos. México, Imp. Universitaria (Col. Cultura mexicana, 8), 1953. 315 p.

Reprints of studies made during the last decade, 1pon four centuries of Mexican history. [R. D. Hussey]

3080. Sociedad Venezolana de Historia de la Medicina. Revista de la. . . . Caracas. V. 1, no. 1, enero-abril 1953.

The first volume of a new periodical on medical history. Contains some notices on Venezuelan medical history, especially of recent imes, but relates also to medical history in more distant times. [C. Gibson]

3081. Soto, Guillermo. Apuntes para la historia médica de los hospitales del Distrito Federal (R Soc Ven Hist Med, 1:1, enero-abril 1953, p. 8-86).

Essay on the hospitals and medical history of the Distrito Federal of Venezuela from the pre-Conquest period to the present. [C. Gibson]

3082. Soto Cárdenas, Alejandro. Misiones chilenas en los archivos europeos. México, Instituto Panamericano de Geografía e Historia (Publ. 149; Comisión de Historia, 47; Misiones americanas en los archivos europeos, 6), 1953. 295 p.

Documentation on 19th- and 20th-century Chilean historians who worked in European archives: Claudio Gay, Diego Barros Arana, Benjamín Vicuña Mackenna, J. T. Medina, and others. The documents copied and works published are enumerated. An important bibliographical source. [C. Gibson]

3083. Spain. Archivo General de Marina Don Álvaro Bazán. Independencia de América. Índice de los papeles de expediciones de Indias. Por Julio F. Guillén. Madrid, Instituto Histórico de Marina, 1953. 3 v. in 1, 384, 280, 133 p.

The first two volumes of this catalog of part of the treasures of this newly available archive present some 4500 items listing the same number of legajos, 1807-1837. V. 3 is an index of proper names and subjects. The papers are organized by the naval stations (apostaderos) with some further subdivisions. The archive is located in Ciudad Real; the papers come from the Navy Ministry. [R. D. Hussey]

3084. ————. ————. Índice de los papeles de la Sección de Corso y Presas. Madrid, 1953-1954. 2 v.

The papers of this Sección, of large value for American affairs, are catalogued here by Julio F. Guillén. They are mostly for the period 1784-1838. An extensive index of persons and places is in the second volume. [R. D. Hussey]

3085. ————. Dirección General de Archivos y Bibliotecas. Guía de las bibliotecas de Madrid. Madrid, Servicio de Publicaciones del Ministerio de Educación Nacional (Catálogos de archivos y bibliotecas), 1953. 556 p.

Basic data upon nearly 300 public or semipublic libraries, the more important described in considerable detail. Many of them would have interest for some students of American affairs. For the corresponding guide to the archives located in Madrid, see HLAS, no. 18, 1952, item 3297. [R. D. Hussey]

3086. Speroni Vener, Julio. La bibliografía en el Uruguay (R Interam Bibl, 4:1-2, enero-junio 1954, p. 35-42).

A good review of publications in Uruguayan historical bibliography, up to and including some current annuals. [C. B. Kroeber]

3087. Tanodi, Aurelio Z. Ediciones de documentos históricos. Córdoba, Argentina, Universidad Nacional de Córdoba, Instituto de Estudios Americanistas (Cuaderno de historia, 29), 1954. xii, 43 p.

Plea for exactness in documentary transcription with remarks on paleography, abbreviations, modernization, and other editorial problems in the publication of texts. [C. Gibson]

3088. Taylor, Virginia H. (comp.). The Spanish archives of the General Land Office of Texas. Austin, Tex., Lone Star Press for the author, 1955. 258 p.

An excellent introduction by the compiler, upon the land grant system and titles, in Spain, Mexico and Texas, and lists of documents. Nearly all of these were in the Mexican period of Texas history. [R. D. Hussey]

3089. Thornton, A. P. West-India policy under the Restoration. Oxford, Clarendon Press, 1956. 280 p., map, illus.

A detailed and painstaking study of the attempts, between 1660 and 1685, to establish a centralized imperial administration to govern the English plantations and enforce the Acts of Trade in the West Indies. Chiefly concerned with developments at the London end, and with the consequent disputes with West Indian Assemblies about finance and governors' powers. Does not differ greatly from accepted views of this period, but adds much new detail on administrative practice and theory. Contains chapter on Anglo-Spanish relations over Jamaica. Closely documented from sources in Public Record Office and British Museum, but makes no use of Spanish sources. [J. H. Parry]

3090. Tudela, José. Los manuscritos de América en las bibliotecas de España. Madrid, Ediciones Cultura Hispánica, 1954. 586 p.

Deals only with public and secular libraries — plus the Escorial as one that belonged to the Royal Patrimony — and omits map collections. If an institution has a satisfactory printed catalog, that is mentioned and additions are noted. If there is none, or even if American items are buried in a general catalog, the editor tries to give full information. His work has been rather severely criticized in Spain and in America, as uneven and incomplete. The criticisms are literally valid. But anyone who has—like the present annotator—tried in past years to use anything except the one or two collections favored by most Americanists, and to use the printed catalogs of provincial libraries, will have little but thanks for Señor Tudela's contribution. [R. D. Hussey]

3091. Universidad de Barcelona. Centro de Estudios Históricos Internacionales. Índice histórico español. Publicación trimestral. Barcelona. 1953-.

V. 1 had eight numbers, for the years 1953 and 1954. No. 9-12 are for 1955. Author index for no. 1-4 in no. 5; for no. 1-8 published separately; future indices to be published annually with the regular issues. The arrangement is by eras first of Spanish and then of Spanish American history, with content indication and critical notes. The work is similar in type to and really a continuation of the well-known bibliography edited by Benito Sánchez Alonso (see *HLAS, no. 12, 1946,* item 1643, and *HLAS, no. 18, 1952,* item 1674). [R. D. Hussey]

3092. Urquiaga y Vento, Juana. Historia de Cuba. Habana, Lux, 1953. 293 p., map.

Simple textbook. [R. McNicoll]

3093. Vidal y Saura, Fulgencio. Haití, primer estado negro. Madrid, Ed. Castilla, 1953. 210 p., pl.

Compares French and English colonization in the West Indies unfavorably with Spanish in a study of Haiti, indicating that "los franceses no han dejado en Haití rastro de su presencia." In regard to the English, he states "no hay en todas las Antillas inglesas un nexo de unión y de compresión entre la masa negra y sus opresores actuales." [R. McNicoll]

3094. Waters, Willard O. Franciscan missions of Upper California as seen by foreign visitors and residents. A chronological list of printed accounts, 1786-1848. Los Angeles, Calif., Glen Dawson (Early California travels, 24), 1954. 53 p.

200 copies, reprinted with revisions from *Bookmen's holiday . . . Tribute to Harry Miller Lydenberg* (N. Y., 1943). [R. D. Hussey]

3095. Wheat, Carl I. Mapping the American west, 1540-1857. A preliminary study. Worcester, Mass., 1954. 194 p.

Chronological and alphabetical indices of the maps, many of which have value for the Spanish and Mexican periods. 300 copies only, reprinted from the *Proceedings* of the American Antiquarian Society, April 1954. [R. D. Hussey]

3096. The world encompassed. A catalogue of an exhibition of the history of maps . . . October-November, 1952. Baltimore, Md., The Trustees of the Walters Art Gallery, 1952. Unnumbered leaves, illus.

This list of 288 items, gathered mostly in the U. S., is one of the finest existing approaches to the history of cartography from ancient days to the end of the 18th century. A large number of items are directly of American interest. The most valuable part of these, because the least known until now, are the maps formerly in the Hauslab-Liechtenstein collection (see the sale catalog in *HLAS, no. 18, 1952,* item 1700a) which had been given to Harvard just as the exhibition was being arranged. [R. D. Hussey]

3097. Zavala, Silvio. Aproximaciones a la historia de México. México, Porrúa y Obregón (México y lo mexicano, 12), 1953. 160 p.

This book is composed of five instructive essays, four on Mexican history and one on the history of the Americas: "Síntesis de la historia del pueblo mexicano" (p. 9-45); "El mexicano en sus contactos con el exterior" (p. 47-66); "El contacto de culturas en la historia de México" (p. 67-101); "Tributo al historiador Justo Sierra" (p. 102-127); and "Formación de la historia americana" (p. 128-160). The first of these essays views the entire course of Mexican history and analyzes the factors which led to the forging of Mexican nationality, the second treats of the outside influences which have played a role in determining the development of Mexico, and the third (originally prepared for UNESCO) focuses upon the cultural and racial fusions witthin Mexico. These three essays form something of an integrated group and provide the Hispanic scholar much food for thought. The fourth essay is an excellent analysis of the place of Sierra as a constructive historian of Mexico. The final essay thoughtfully suggests approaches to the integrated history of the Americas and is essential reading for all Hispanic scholars and students. [R. S. Chamberlain]

SPANISH AMERICA AND HAITI:
THE COLONIAL PERIOD

GENERAL

ROLAND D. HUSSEY
AND OTHERS

3100. Acosta, José de. De procuranda indorum salute. Predicación del Evangelio en las Indias. Introducción, traducción y notas por Francisco Mateos. Madrid, Col. España Misionera, 1952. 621 p.
First translation into Spanish, from the Latin of Salamanca, 1588, but with comparison also with the MS. at the University of Salamanca. It was written in 1576, as a guide for missionaries. The lengthy introduction is an excellent discussion of both the work and the author. [R. D. Hussey]

3101. ————. Obras. Estudio preliminar y edición del P. Francisco Mateos. Madrid, Ediciones Atlas (Biblioteca de autores españoles, 73), 1954. xlix, 633 p.
With a good preface, presents the texts of: *Historia natural y moral de Indias; De procuranda indorum salute;* and a large number of letters, memorials, and *relaciones,* dealing with both Spain and America, 1569-1593. Manuscripts are used in preparing the preface, and for some of the letters and memorials. [R. D. Hussey]

3102. Alba, Duque de. El archivo de la Casa de Alba. Madrid, 1953. 29 p., folding genealogical chart.
A valuable survey of the 41 groups, including those of the 39 houses (or *mayorazgos*), that have been incorporated into that of Alba. There is considerable specific mention of the Indies, and much more is implied for anyone with knowledge of the family names involved. Relatively few of the papers are mentioned as destroyed in the fire of 1936. [R. D. Hussey]

3103. ————. Contribución de España a la defensa de la civilización portuguesa en América durante las guerras holandesas. Campaña de Fadrique de Toledo, marqués de Villanueva y Valdueza, en 1625. Conferencia en Río de Janeiro. 2. ed. Madrid, 1952. 32 p., 7 pls.
A biography of Fadrique de Toledo Osorio, not just or chiefly upon the 1625 episode in Brazil. Mentions also Toledo's voyage of 1630, and expulsion of the English from Nieves and San Cristobal. No scholarly apparatus, but evidently based in part upon the Alba archives. [R. D. Hussey]

3104. Alvarado, Pedro de. Cartas del adelantado (A Soc Geog Hist Guat, año 26, 26:1, marzo 1952, p. 64-68).
Legal documents (not "cartas") dated at Quito on Aug. 26 and 27, 1534, concerning the transfer of his armada to Pizarro and Almagro. [R. D. Hussey]

3105. Anghiera, Pietro Martire d'. Epistolario [de Pedro Mártir de Angleria]. Estudio y traducción de José López de Toro. T. 1, 2. Madrid (Documentos inéditos para la historia de España, 9, 10), 1953. 2 v., illus.
The first complete translation into any language from the Latin, to be completed in three volumes. (The many American letters have long been in French translation, though not widely known, edited by Paul Gaffarel and the Abbé Louvot, Paris, 1885). These first two volumes include Libros 1-24, Epístolas 1-472, years 1488-1511. [R. D. Hussey]

3106. Armytage, Frances. The free port system in the British West Indies. A study in commercial policy, 1766-1822. London, Longmans, Green, 1953. 176 p.
Based upon excellent English sources, but has French and Spanish side only from printed works. The British Free Port system was created in 1766 as an effort to get back into the Spanish American trade in competition with the French and Dutch free ports, and with the recently less restricted Spanish trading system. The effort was not really successful. [R. D. Hussey]

3107. Arocena, Fausto. La introducción del maíz en Guipúzcoa (B Real Ac Hist, 135:2, oct.-dic. 1954, p. 389-393).
A note commenting upon, or correcting, the 1953 item by Bouza Brey (see item 3116) and referring back to articles of 1933 and 1950, by Arocena, in other periodicals. [R. D. Hussey]

3108. Ballesteros Beretta, Antonio. La marina cántabra y Juan de la Cosa. Santander, Spain, Hermanos Bedia, 1954. 429 p., illus., maps.
A well-documented study of Cantabrian maritime affairs from the reign of Alfonso VIII to that of the Catholic Kings, and (p. 129-405) of the life of the famous mariner and map maker named. [R. D. Hussey]

3109. Ballesteros Gaibrois, Manuel. La obra de Isabel la Católica. Con prólogo de Pascual Marín Pérez. Segovia, Spain, Diputación Provincial de Segovia (Publ. históricas, 2), 1953. xx, 468 p., illus.
An excellent study as to the reign and institutions of the Queen, in Castile, but rather trivial as to Indies aspects. [R. D. Hussey]

3110. Bataillon, Marcel. Las Casas et le licencié Cerrato (B Hisp, 55:1, 1953, p. 79-87).
Denunciation in 1552 of the Licenciado Juan López de Cerrato, Presidente of the Audiencia de los Confines, for frauds. [R. D. Hussey]

3111. **Bayle, Constantino.** Colegios de estudios mayores en las Indias españolas (Razón y Fe, año 52, 147:1 (660), enero 1953, p. 24-37).
Primarily but not entirely as to New Spain. Based heavily on the Archivo de Indias. [R. D. Hussey]

3112. ————. Valor histórico de la *Destrucción de las Indias* (Razón y Fe, año 52, 147:4 (663), abril 1953, p. 379-391).
An attack upon the favorable views of Fray Manuel María Martínez (see *HLAS, no. 18, 1952*, item 1717a) and others, including Lewis Hanke and almost anyone else who has defended Las Casas. [R. D. Hussey]

3113. **Benito y Durán, Ángel.** La Universidad de Salamanca y la apología de *La humanidad de los españoles en las Indias* del Padre Juan Nuix y Perpiña (R Indias, Madrid, 14:57-58, julio-dic. 1954, p. 539-547).
Consists chiefly of the texts of the preface which José, brother of Juan the author, added to his edition of the work (Cervera, 1783), and of the official minutes of the *claustro* of the University, showing that body's reaction to the copy sent to the institution by José. [R. D. Hussey]

3114. **Benton, Frederick L.** The last resting place of Christopher Columbus. Edited by George A. Lockward S. Ciudad Trujillo, Impresora Dominicana (Columbus Memorial Lighthouse publications), 1953. 93 p.
Written in 1923 while Benton was in the Dominican Republic with the U. S. occupation; promulgates the Dominican thesis. There is also a Spanish language version, and part of this was also published as "Los verdaderos restos de Cristóbal Colón" in v. 16 (1953) of B Arch Gen, Ciudad Trujillo. [R. D. Hussey]

3115. **Borah, Woodrow.** Early colonial trade and navigation between Mexico and Peru. Berkeley, Calif., University of California Press (Ibero-Americana, 38), 1954. 170 p.
Based upon manuscript materials from Seville and Mexico, with adequate printed materials for Peru. A thorough coverage to 1585, and the last chapter, upon the end of the early trade and start of the era affected by the Philippine trade, carries the story more sketchily to 1631. [R. D. Hussey]

3116. **Bouza Brey, Fermín.** Noticias históricas sobre la introducción del cultivo del maíz en Galicia (B Real Ac Hist, 132:1, enero-marzo 1953, p. 35-72, pl.).
It is obviously of some American interest to know that the introduction referred to was by Gonzalo Méndez de Cancio on his return to Galicia from service as Gobernador y Capitán General de la Florida (1596-1603). But in the bargain, while searching the family papers of the present Casa de Casariego (of the Cancio family) the author discovered a treasure trove of papers on the career of don Gonzalo (1554?-1622) who served as a seaman in American waters from about 17 years of age and who, among other exploits, was Almirante of the 1595 fleet against Drake. [R. D. Hussey]

3117. **Carril, Bonifacio del.** Los Mendoza. Los Mendoza en España y en América en el siglo XV y en la primera mitad del siglo XVI. Comprobaciones sobre la genealogía de don Pedro de Mendoza, fundador de Buenos Aires. B. A., Emecé (Selección Emecé de obras contemporáneas), 1954. 184 p., illus.
A scholarly genealogy of the Mendoza family from the 14th century to its 16th-century representatives in America, including Antonio de Mendoza, viceroy of New Spain, and Pedro de Mendoza, adelantado of the Rio de la Plata. [C. Gibson]

3118. **Carro, Venancio Diego de.** Bartolomé de las Casas y las controversias teológico-jurídicas de Indias. Madrid, Maestre, 1953. 44 p.
Reprint (B Real Ac Hist, 132:2, abril-junio 1953, p. 231-264). Another warm defense of the views of Las Casas, and comparison of them with those of Vitoria and Domingo de Soto. [R. D. Hussey]

3119. **Casas, Bartolomé de las.** The tears of the Indians. Translated by John Phillips. Stanford, Calif., Academic reprints, 1953. 134 p.
A facsimile reproduction of the second English edition (1656) of the famous *Destruction of the Indies*. [R. D. Hussey]

3120. **Castañeda, Carlos.** Spanish medieval institutions in overseas administration: the prevalence of medieval concepts (Americas, Franciscan Hist, 11:2, Oct. 1954, p. 115-130).
An apologetic for Spanish royal policy as humanitarian and just in intention, in spite of the manner of its carrying out. [R. D. Hussey]

3121. **Castro Seoane, José.** La traída de libros y vestuarios en el siglo XVI, de los misioneros desde sus conventos a Sevilla, pagada por el tesoro de la Casa de Contratación (Miss Hisp, 10:30, 1953, p. 495-584; 11:31, 1954, p. 55-133; 11:33, 1954, p. 447-484).
Continuation of the writer's studies in ecclesiastical finance, transport, and commerce. Materials relate to all parts of the 16th-century American colonies. [C. Gibson]

3122. **Cepeda Adán, José.** Una visión de América a fines del siglo XVI (Estud Am, 6:26, nov. 1953, p. 397-421).
A description with commentary on the American portions of the *Historia general de España* (published 1592-1605) of P. Juan de Mariana.

The sense of incipient decline is manifest. [C. Gibson]

3123. Connell-Smith, Gordon. Forerunners of Drake. N. Y., Longmans, Green (Royal Empire Society imperial studies), 1954. 228 p., maps.

A study of Tudor English trade relations primarily with Spain, prior to the reign of Elizabeth, but offers also much upon English ventures in trade or piracy, to America, in the same period. The sources include little used English records, especially from the Admiralty, and some material from Spanish archives. The latter is not voluminous, but is well selected for strategic effect. For an idea of the American content, see the articles by the author which have been entered in previous issues of the *HLAS*. [R. D. Hussey]

3124. Cortesão, Armando. The nautical chart of 1424 and the early discovery and cartographical representation of America. A study on the history of early navigation and cartography. With a foreword by Maximino Correia. Coimbra, Portugal, University of Coimbra, 1954. 123 p., 19 pls.

The essence of this book appeared in an article by the same author: "The North Atlantic nautical chart of 1424," Imago Mundi, London, 10, 1953, p. 1-13, folding map. (For the map, see item 3003). The chart, probably drawn by one Zuane Pizzigano, shows several Atlantic islands, including one called "Antilia." Cortesão believes that these represent the present Antilles, and that they were reached by various ships, perhaps from the Canaries or Madeiras, after resumption of Atlantic voyages in the 13th and 14th centuries. If so, this is the first "American" map. [R. D. Hussey]

3125. Cuesta, Luisa. También los conquistadores se quejaban (R Indias, Madrid, 13:51, enero-marzo 1953, p. 117-118).

Anonymous, undated petition, "Sobre el tratado á los Conquistadores," says that when they come to Spain now from Indies, they fear the *fiscal* of the Consejo, and the bureaucrats of the Casa, who proceed against them for offenses committed before the *Leyes nuevas*. The Crown referred the petition to the Consejo. [R. D. Hussey]

3126. Davies, Arthur. The loss of the *Santa María* Christmas Day, 1492 (Am Hist R, 68:4, July 1953, p. 854-865).

A good article as a criticism of many aspects of the record, by a veteran geographer, but reaches conclusions as to causes and results that are not likely to be received with acclaim by historians with less respect for subconscious guilt feelings as motivations. [R. D. Hussey]

3127. Descola, Jean. Les conquistadors. Paris, Librairie Arthéme Fayard (Les grandes études historiques), 1954. 524 p., maps, tables.

A general history of the discovery of America and of Spanish conquest and colonization to the mid-16th century, based on standard printed sources and secondary works. Treatment of Spanish motives, viewed in time and place, is interesting and sympathetic. Although presenting nothing new, this work is of interest to the general reader and is evidence of continuing French interest in Hispanic history. [R. S. Chamberlain]

3128. Dickson, Sarah Augusta. Panacea or precious bane. Tobacco in sixteenth century literature. N. Y., New York Public Library (Arents tobacco collection, 5), 1954. 227 p., illus.

Reprinted from v. 57 and 58 (1953-1954) of the *Bulletin* of the Library. It deals with European knowledge and interest, as shown in literature chiefly but not entirely English. Some information appears also for the earlier 17th century. Much value for students of American affairs. [R. D. Hussey]

3129. Diggs, Irene. Color in colonial Spanish America (J Negro Hist, 38:4, Oct. 1953, p. 403-427).

A useful summary article on Indians, Negroes, and whites and their ethnic intermixture. Interprets colonial Spanish society as a population of groupings based on color. Considers the nomenclature of mixed groups, their social status, legal position, and similar topics, from secondary sources. [C. Gibson]

3130. Donworth, Albert B. Why Columbus sailed. N. Y., Exposition Press, 1953. 205 p.

The general idea is that Columbus knew about the Viking voyages, and that these had not reached Cathay, so he stayed away from those areas. It seems unlikely that many scholars will be convinced. [R. D. Hussey]

3131. Encinas, Diego. Cedulario indiano, recopilado por . . . . Reproducción facsímil de la edición única de 1596. Estudio e índices por Alfonso García Gallo. Madrid, Ediciones Cultura Hispánica, 1945-1953. 5 v.

For the first four volumes, which completed the textual facsimile, of this invaluable compilation, see HLAS, no. 12, 1946, item 1675. The fifth volume, now finally published, includes the promised study, an excellent statement of what is known about Encinas—who was not mentioned as compiler in the original—and some documents. (Readers should note that although the original is excessively rare, as stated by the editor, copies are not limited to the national libraries of Madrid and Santiago de Chile. There are two, and I think three, in the U. S. alone). [R. D. Hussey]

3132. Enjuto Ferrán, Federico. Régimen comunal de la propiedad rústica en América según las Leyes de Indias (Cuad Inst Interam Hist Mun Inst, 9, junio 1954, p. 23-42).

A handy interpretation, without value for specialists. [R. D. Hussey]

3133. Farley, Rawle. The economic circumstances of the British annexation of British Guiana (R Hist Am, 39, junio 1955, p. 21-59).
An account of British economic interests in Guiana before and during the French wars, and the factors, internal and external, making for annexation. [J. H. Parry]

3134. Fernández de Navarrete, Martín. Obras. Edición y estudio preliminar de C. Seco Serrano. Madrid, Ediciones Atlas (Biblioteca de autores españoles, 75-77), 1954. 3 v.
There is a 60-page introduction upon the life and works of Navarrete, followed by the entire text—but not the maps—of his well-known *Viajes* (5 v., Madrid, 1825-1837). [R. D. Hussey]

3135. Fleuriot de Langle, Paul. La tragique expédition de Lapérouse et Langle. Paris, Hachette, 1954. 249 p.
Popular account, but from good sources, of the voyage of 1785-1788, which touched on the coasts of South America and of California and in the Philippines. [R. D. Hussey]

3136. Foster, G. M. Relationship between Spanish and Spanish American folk medicine (J Am Folk, 66:261, July-Sept. 1953, p. 201-218).
Finds considerable resemblance between 16th-century medical beliefs in Spain and present-day folk medicine in Spain and Spanish America, but more in America than in Spain. [R. D. Hussey]

3137. Fuentes Cervera, Eduardo de. El ejército y las armas en la época de los Reyes Católicos (*in* Curso de conferencias sobre la política africana de los Reyes Católicos. T. 3. Madrid, Consejo Superior de Investigaciones Científicas, Instituto de Estudios Africanos, 1951, p. 67-87).
Intelligent brief review of a subject bearing on Spanish militarism in the New World. Remarks on the Santa Hermandad, the armed forces at Granada, and the creation of a national army. Stresses the personal role of Isabella. [C. Gibson]

3138. Garcés Ferra, Bartolomé. Estudios bibliográficos. Un libro de Nebrija tasado para las Indias (R Hist Am, 37-38, enero-dic. 1954, p. 295-298).
A copy of the *Elegancias romançadas* (Antequera, 1570) in the library of the University of Valencia has a printed cedula of Nov. 26, 1564, on the last page. This orders that the price is to be, per *pliego*: in Spain, 3 *maravedís;* in Santo Domingo and the other islands, and New Spain, 6; in New Granada, 8; in Peru, 10. [R. D. Hussey]

3139. García Gallo, Alfonso. El desarrollo de la historiografía jurídica indiana (R

Estud Pol, año 13, 48:70, julio-agosto 1953, p. 163-185).
A survey of the relevant works from the 16th century to the present, with mention of a good many manuscripts which are still in Spanish libraries. [R. D. Hussey]

3140. Gibson, Charles. The Spanish conquest as reality and symbol. Chicago, The First Newberry Library Conference on Hispanic-American Studies, April 2, 1955. 16 p.
A thoughful and provocative interpretative essay discussing the concept of "conquest" and its implications in writings on Hispanic America since the 16th century. Contains fruitful suggestions for more meaningful syntheses of colonial history. [H. F. Cline]

3141. Giménez Fernández, Manuel. Bartolomé de las Casas. T. 1. Delegado de Cisneros para la reformación de las Indias 1516-1517. Sevilla, Escuela de Estudios Hispano-Americanos de Sevilla (Publ 70), 1953. 776 p., facsms., illus., ports.
Planned as the first of six volumes, which will carry the story to the death in 1556. Based on an enormous documentation, but intensely partisan, seeing everything in black and white. Regards the failure of Cisneros, plans as caused by the attacks of a Fernandino clique of vicious men, chiefly from Aragon, and thinks that the Jeronimite friars whom Cisnero chose as his agents sold out before they left Spain. But no one interested in the period in America or in Spain can afford to neglect this work. The author *is* a first-class scholar, and it seems hopeless to expect anyone to be objective about Las Casas. [R. D. Hussey]

3142. ―――. Dos ensayos polémicos sobre los restos de Cristóbal Colón. Sevilla y los restos de Cristóbal Colón y Los restos de Colón en Sevilla. Sevilla, Escuela de Estudios Hispano-Americanos de Sevilla, 1954. 33, 175 p., illus.
This work brings together two essays which were earlier separately printed. For one, see *HLAS, no. 18, 1952,* item 1706a. The other appeared in *Anuario de estudios americanos,* 10, 1953, p. 1-170. In the two taken together the author says in effect that he does not know where the Discoverer's bones are, but that emphatically they are not in Seville nor Ciudad Trujillo. He says that the 1877 claim of that latter city rests upon an "hallazgo inventado . . . por los señores Billini y Nouel." [R. D. Hussey]

3143. ―――. Más sobre las letras alejandrinas de 1493, referentes a las Indias. V. Réplica a Don Vicente D. Sierra (U Hispalense, 14:2, 1953, p. 241-301).
A warm reply to a hot bombardment, in a battle that has raged since the author's book of 1944. It has been partly reported in various issues of the *HLAS,* including other entries in this one. (On the whole, it has seemed to the compiler of this note that most historians without a strong religious or "Hispanist" bias have

agreed with Giménez Fernández, but probably most users of the HLAS will think that it matters very little either way.) [R. D. Hussey]

3144. ————. Los restos de Cristóbal Colón en Sevilla (An Estud Am, 10, 1953, p. 1-170).
A meticulous post mortem contributing to the debate on the location of Columbus' grave. Argues that the remains were never taken to the New World. [C. Gibson]

3145. González Casanova, Pablo. El auge del comercio francés en las Indias españolas (Com Ext, México, 2:1, enero 1952, p. 24-27; 2:2, feb. 1952, p. 64-67; 2:3, marzo 1952, p. 105-107).
A study based on good French sources, on the trade chiefly through Cadiz, from about 1680 to 1789. [R. D. Hussey]

3146. González Ruiz, Felipe. Evolución de la cultura en América; estudios de iniciación. Madrid, Sapientia, 1953. 592 p., illus.
A lengthy discussion, without much care for chronological sequences, of various aspects of life in the pre-Conquest and the Colonial periods. No authorities are cited, and the bibliography is brief and unannotated. [R. D. Hussey]

3147. Guerra, Francisco. Historiografía de la medicina colonial hispanoamericana. Prólogo de Fidel Carrancedo. México, Abastecedora de Impresos, 1953. 322 p.
500 numbered copies only. The author mentions over 2000 items relevant to his subject, with a valuable general introduction and individual comments. He makes no claim for definitiveness, but has presented a valuable key to the subject. [R. D. Hussey]

3148. Hanke, Lewis. Bartolomé de las Casas, an essay in hagiography and historiography (HAHR, 33:1, Feb. 1953, p. 136-151).
Published also in Spanish: "¿Bartolomé de las Casas, existencialista? Ensayo de hagiografía y de historiografía" (Cuad Am, año 12, 68:2, marzo-abril 1953, p. 176-193). Broadly conceived and independently documented article, but essentially part of a polemic with Edmundo O'Gorman which started with the latter's article in the HAHR, v. 29, 1949. [R. D. Hussey]

3149. ————. Bartolomé de las Casas and the Spanish empire in America: four centuries of misunderstanding (Pro Am Phil Soc, 97:1, Feb. 1953, p. 26-30).
A handy résumé of the work and ideas of half a lifetime by the author, useful to those who have not followed all of his more detailed studies. [R. D. Hussey]

3150. ————, and Manuel Giménez Fernández. Bartolomé de las Casas, 1474-1566. Bibliografía crítica y cuerpo de materiales para el estudio de su vida,

escritos, actuación y polémicas que suscitaron durante cuatro siglos. Santiago, Fondo Histórico y Bibliográfico José Toribio Medina, 1954. xxxvii, 394 p., illus.
Lists 849 items, manuscript and printed, 1492 to 1953, with a dozen more mentioned in the Postscriptum (p. 393-394), and an "Índice analítico." The extensive annotations often include factual data. [R. D. Hussey]

3151. Hernández y Sánchez-Barba, Mario. La población hispanoamericana y su distribución social en el siglo XVIII (R Estud Pol, año 14, 52:78, nov.-dic. 1954, p. 111-142).
A discussion with many statistical tables, and careful indication of what is recorded fact and what is mere surmise. [R. D. Hussey]

3152. Herrera y Tordesillas, Antonio de. Historia general de los hechos de los castellanos en las islas y tierra firme del mar océano. T. 12-14. Madrid, Academia de la Historia, 1953-1954. 3 v., maps, pl.
The three volumes listed include the whole of Década 6, and Década 7 through libro 6. As in earlier volumes of this reprint, which has been under way for many years, the annotations are not extensive, though the scholarly ability of the editors assures their value so far as they go. [R. D. Hussey]

3153. Indexes of volumes I-X (Im Mundi, London, 10, 1953, p. 141-152).
Successively offers a table of contents by volumes since the start in 1935, and then a table by authors, and finally indices by names of cartographers and of publishers, and other indices of books reviewed, maps reproduced, and portraits. Nearly half a hundred of the maps reproduced are "American" in whole or in part, which gives some indication of the wealth of material available to specialists in the series. Only some of the most outstanding of the articles have been entered in the HLAS. [R. D. Hussey]

3154. Konetzke, Richard. Colección de documentos para la historia de la formación social de Hispanoamérica, 1493-1810. V. 1. Madrid, Consejo Superior de Investigaciones Científicas, Instituto Jaime Balmes, 1953. 671 p.
With a short but useful introduction, presents 481 documents, dated from 1493-1592. There are indices of persons, places, and subjects. As several writers have pointed out, the documents are all laws or closely related items, and there are distinct limits to what can be learned from only that sort of record. But more can be learned from them upon the subject than has been learned from anything else so far, at any rate, and students will look forward eagerly to future volumes. [R. D. Hussey]

3155. León Pinelo, Antonio Rodríguez de. El gran canciller de las Indias. Estudio preliminar, edición y notas de Guillermo Lohmann Villena. Sevilla, Escuela de

Estudios Hispano-Americanos (Publ., 76), 1955. clxxxvi, 220 p.
Text of the valuable historical and legal study written in 1625, with an excellent introduction which discusses the author's other writings, presents an extensive biography of him, and carries the story of the office to late in the 19th century. [R. D. Hussey]

3156. Le Riverend Brusone, Julio. Relaciones entre Nueva España y Cuba, 1518-1820 (R Hist Am, 37-38, enero-dic. 1954, p. 45-108).
Concerns especially trade (already strong by 1540), financial relations, and the slave trade. Based on Mexican archival sources, and Cuban sources mostly printed. [R. D. Hussey]

3157. Levene, Ricardo. Nuevas investigaciones históricas sobre el régimen político y jurídico de España en Indias hasta la Recopilación de Leyes de 1680 (Cahiers d'Hist Mond, 1:2, oct. 1953, p. 463-490).
An informative but summary statement on the political and juridical aspects of Spanish imperialism to the late 17th century, by one of the prominent Argentine historians of the subject. Treats the incorporation of the Indies under the crown of Castile, argues that the Indies were not colonies in the strict sense, and traces the antecedents of the *Recopilación* of 1680. [C. Gibson]

3158. Lewin, Boleslao. Mártires y conquistadores judíos en la América Hispana. B. A., Editorial Candelabro, 1954. 274 p., illus.
The author of this unusual book provides biographies of 12 figures of Hebrew descent in colonial Spanish America, most of whom fell into the toils of the Inquisition and a number of whom were condemned. Most prominent of those dealt with are Pedrarias Dávila, Luis de Carvajal, Governor of Nuevo León, and the poet Luis de Carvajal. Many excerpts from trial records are quoted and much valuable information on the Hebrew religious practices which were so anathema to the Inquisition is provided. The author deals most objectively with this story of the intolerance of an earlier period. Unfortunately a bibliography, which would have been of interest and value to Hispanic scholars, is not included in the book. [R. S. Chamberlain]

3159. Leyes nuevas de Indias. Edición facsimilar de la edición de Alcalá de Henares de 1543, con un estudio preliminar de Agustín Millares Carlo. México, Fondo Pagliai (1), 1952. 14 l., 81 p.
100 numbered copies only, plus five not put in trade. Has not been seen, and unfortunately the price required by its sumptuous format makes it unlikely that many historians can see it. But the preliminary study by Millares is said to be all that would be expected of so outstanding a scholar and editor. The text, of course, is widely available even in another modern facsimile. [R. D. Hussey]

3160. Lobo, Eulalia Maria Lahmeyer. Administração colonial luso-espanhola nas Américas. Rio, Editôra Companhia Brasileira de Artes Gráficas, 1952. 444 p., 6 maps.
A scholarly, comprehensive, and well-organized study of the evolution and structure of the colonial administrations of Spain and Portugal in the New World, with due attention to Old World backgrounds. The author has employed a wealth of documentary sources as well as specialized studies, including the most recent. This is an excellent, well-balanced comparative analysis of colonial government which all Hispanic scholars may read with profit. [R. S. Chamberlain]

3162. López de Palacios Rubios, Juan, and Matías de Paz. De las islas del mar océano, por Juan López de Palacios Rubios. Del dominio de los reyes de España sobre los indios, por Matías de Paz. Introducción de Silvio Zavala. Traducción, notas y bibliografía de Agustín Millares Carlo. México, Fondo de Cultura Económica (Biblioteca americana; Serie de cronistas de Indias, 25), 1954. cxxx, 318 p., facsms.
The Paz' *De dominio regum* has been available in Latin, but not previously in Spanish. The author was a Salamancan professor, and a Dominican. Palacios Rubios' *Libellus de insulis oceanis* has not been available in print at all except for a few passages. In addition to those printed by Zavala in 1937, Eloy Bullón presented a number, in Latin, in the notes to his *Problemas jurídicos de la dominación de España en América antes de las "Relecciones" de Francisco de Vitoria*, Madrid, 1933. Palacios Rubios was a lawyer, and a member of the Consejo Real. Both the men were at the Burgos Conference of 1512, and wrote their papers, at the request of Ferdinand, for that meeting. The introduction by Zavala has been printed separately, in 1950-1951 (see *HLAS, no. 18 1952*, item 1733a). The contributions of Millares Carlo, as well as of Zavala, have the high quality that one expects of both men. [R. D. Hussey]

3163. Majo Framis, Ricardo. Vidas de navegantes, conquistadores y colonizadores españoles de los siglos XVI, XVII y XVIII. V. 3. Colonizadores y fundadores de Indias. Madrid, Aguilar, 1954. 1372 p., illus.
As with the earlier volumes (1946-) this is strictly a work of popularization. [R. D. Hussey]

3164. Manzano Manzano, Juan. Historia de las recopilaciones de Indias. I. Siglo XVI. Madrid, Ediciones Cultura Hispánica, 1950. 399 p.
Was not, apparently, published until early 1952 or perhaps late 1951. It is a thoroughly scholarly and well-documented study, in three parts: Before Juan de Ovando; the Project of Ovando, 1569-1575; after Ovando, to 1600. [R. D. Hussey]

3165. Mariluz Urquijo, José María. Ensayo sobre los juicios de residencia indiana. Sevilla, Escuela de Estudios Hispano-Americanos (Publ. 70 (no. general), Ser. 2), 1952. 310 p.
A dissertation presented to the Faculty of Law and Social Sciences, B. A., and the first substantial historical study of the institution of *residencia*. European origins, appointment and character of the judges, legal procedure, and a sober evaluation of the institution's efficacy are presented in detail. The author manages the legal technicalities, particularly of the 18th century, with unusual assurance. Sources include much unpublished archival material. [C. Gibson]

3166. Martínez, Manuel Ma. Las Casas, historiador. II. La *Historia de las Indias* (Ciencia Tomista, año 45, 80:246, enero-marzo 1953, p. 75-103).
For the first part of this apologia, see *HLAS, no. 18, 1952,* item 1717a. [R. D. Hussey]

3167. Mateos, Francisco. Personalidad científica del Padre Constantino Bayle, S. I. (Razón y Fe, año 52, 147:5 (664), mayo 1953, p. 455-468, illus.).
A critical bio-bibliography. The same, or a closely similar item, appears in *Missionalia Hispanica,* 10:28, 1953, p. 5-19, as "El Padre Constantino Bayle, 1882-1953." [R. D. Hussey]

3168. Miranda, María Rosa. El libertador de los indios. Prólogo de Luis Morales Oliver. Madrid, Aguilar (Col. literaria: novelistas, dramaturgos, ensayistas, poetas), 1953. 716 p., illus.
One more highly popularized and uncritical biography of Las Casas. [R. D. Hussey]

3169. Morales Padrón, Francisco. El comercio canario-americano (siglos XVI, XVII y XVIII). Prólogo de Eduardo Arcila Farías. Sevilla, Escuela de Estudios Hispano-Americanos (Publ., Serie 2, 89), 1955. 425 p., facsms., illus., maps.
A soundly documented study, from materials in the Archives of the Indies, of the trade itself and of its legal system and illegal extensions, and of the economic influences of each area upon the other. It is, however, hard to use as a history of its stated topic, since like so many of these institutional studies, it consists essentially of a group of chapters each one of which treats of one aspect for the whole three centuries. [R. D. Hussey]

3170. Morse, Richard M. Language as a key to Latin American historiography (Americas, Franciscan Hist, 11:4, Apr. 1955, p. 517-538).
Stimulating throughout. Essentially, an examination of differences between American and Peninsular language, and what these suggest about underlying cultures and motives. [R. D. Hussey]

3171. Muller, Herman J. British travel writers and the Jesuits (Mid Am, 35:2, Apr. 1953, p. 91-116).
Discusses the extent to which English writers translated, edited, or plagiarized from Jesuit writers on Spanish America. The details concern only Juan de Acosta, Alonso de Ovalle, and Cristóbal de Acuña. [R. D. Hussey]

3172. Muñoz Perez, José. Una descripción comparativa de las ciudades americanas en el siglo XVIII (Estud Geog, 15:54, feb. 1954, p. 89-129).
Calls attention to the document *Consideraciones americanas* (1789) in the Biblioteca de Palacio in Madrid, written by Raimundo Diosdado Caballero. The document contains a comparative description and evaluation of sample English, French, and Spanish cities in the New World, among which Diosdado clearly reveals his partiality for the Spanish. [C. Gibson]

3173. ————. La idea de América en Campomanes (An Estud Am, 10, 1953, p. 209-264).
Discussion of an 18th-century view of Spanish imperialism, the nature of America, and commercial reorganization. The Conde de Campomanes is correctly assigned a position of importance in the intellectual and economic climate of the later Bourbon reforms. [C. Gibson]

3174. Muro Orejón, Antonio. Juan Bautista Muñoz. Las fuentes bibliográficas de la *Historia del Nuevo Mundo* (An Estud Am, 10, 1953, p. 265-337).
Compilation of Muñoz' published sources (mainly 18th-century) and of the manuscripts he accumulated in preparing his *Historia del Nuevo Mundo.* [C. Gibson]

3175. Navarro, José Gabriel. Los franciscanos en la conquista y colonización de América, fuera de las Antillas. Madrid, Ediciones Cultura Hispánica, 1955. 178 p.
One more work of popularization and apologia, for the whole Colonial period. [R. D. Hussey]

3176. Nowell, Charles E. Henry Vignaud (1830-1922), Louisiana historian (La Hist Q, 38:1, Jan. 1955, p. 1-25).
The title refers to Vignaud's place of birth, not his scholarly interests. The latter were in connection with the discovery period of American history, and especially the controversial aspects. It is interesting to note that Vignaud entered into the Toscanelli-Columbus disputes as the result of a meeting with the Peruvian expatriate, Manuel González de la Rosa. [R. D. Hussey]

3177. Ojeda, Gonzalo Miguel. Reivindicación burgalesa de Alonso de Ojeda, famoso conquistador y colonizador del Nuevo Mundo (B Inst Fernán González, 32:122, 1. trimestre 1953, p. 432-449).
An industrious and intelligent, but not very successful, effort to clarify the facts about the

great discoverer's ancestry, by investigation of the locality and the local archives. [R. D. Hussey]

3178. Olmedo, Daniel. La primera evangelización de América, 1492-1504 (Ábside, 17:1, enero-marzo 1953, p. 35-67).
A study, based on newly discovered documentation, of the clerics who accompanied Columbus on his last three voyages. [R. D. Hussey]

3178a. Palacios, Alfredo L. Masas y élites en Iberoamérica. B. A., Columba (Col. Esquemas, 10), 1954. 87 p.
Terse commentary on selected events in the social history of colonial Spanish America, seen in a self--conscious framework of majority-minority relations. Systematic examination of terms (*masa, pueblo, multitud,* etc.), men (Ortega y Gasset, Las Casas, Juan and Ulloa), and insurrections. The *comuneros* of Paraguay are seen as a "conjunction of masses and élites," those of New Granada as "masses without élites." [C. Gibson]

3179. Palmer, Philip Motley. German works on America, 1492-1800. Berkeley, Calif., University of California Press (University of California publications in modern philology, 36:10), 1952. 271-412 p.
About 1900 entries, which, with cross references, variants, etc., list 967 works on all parts of the Americas. There are no indices of any kind. Based upon, but corrects and adds to and locates more copies than, Joseph Sabin's *Dictionary of books relating to America* (26 v., N. Y., 1868-1936). [R. D. Hussey]

3179a. Parks, George B. Columbus and Balboa in the Italian revision of Peter Martyr (Hunt Libr Q, 18:3, May 1955, p. 209-226).
Refers to the composite volume, without a real collective title, published at Venice, 1534, which starts with *Libro primero de la Historia.* This is a translation, but also a revision and often a condensation, of what Peter Martyr wrote. It was done by Andrea Navagero, poet, scholar, and former ambassador to Spain, who was well acquainted with many of the "American" figures at the royal court, even having bought books for Ramusio. [R. D. Hussey]

3180. Parry, J. H. The patent offices in the British West Indies (Eng Hist R, 69:271, Apr. 1954, p. 200-225).
An analysis of the manner of appointment of colonial officials, from the beginnings of the "patent" system under the Commonwealth to its abolition in the 1830's, and a comparison with the analogous system of sale in the Spanish Indies. [J. H. Parry]

3180a. ———. Plantation and provision ground (R Hist Am, 39, junio 1955, p. 1-20).
An historical sketch of the introduction of food crops into Jamaica, and an attempt to show connections between introductions and changes in rural social structure. [J. H. Parry]

3181. ———. The sale of public office in the Spanish Indies under the Hapsburgs. Berkeley, Calif., University of California Press (Ibero-Americana, 37), 1953. 73 p.
A valuable study and analysis of a practice which began under the Catholic Kings, but was systematized and emphasized under Philip II, as the pressure for revenue mounted. Considers the contemporary reaction as well as the long-time results. [R. D. Hussey]

3181a. Peña y de la Cámara, José María de la (comp.). A list of Spanish *resi- dencias* in the Archives of the Indies, 1516-1775. Administrative judicial reviews of colonial officials in the American Indies, Philippine and Canary Islands. Washington, Library of Congress, 1955. 109 p.
A list of the documents in the General Archive of the Indies relating to investigations at the end of the term of service (*residencia*) of officials in the Spanish colonies. The documents are from the sections of Justicia and Escribanía de Cámara. The entries are chronological under the subdivisions of the sections. Each entry gives the date, the name of the official and the place of service, the name of the judge, and the *legajo* designation. [R. R. Hill]

3182. Pérez de Tudela, Juan. La negociación colombina de las Indias (R Indias, Madrid, 14:57-58, julio-dic. 1954, p. 289-357).
Intended as the start of a series of articles analyzing the colonizing effort of Spain in America, 1492-1505, announces the intention of correcting the chronology of documents, using known ones that have been neglected, and using some that are still inedited. The first installment (to 1495) does not advance far enough to make clear if the series will be an apologetic, a polemic, or a distinguished contribution to knowledge. The emphasis on economic aspects is encouraging, but the sources are few and in general only those well known already. [R. D. Hussey]

3182a. ———. Una rectificación y tres documentos: ilustración a dos momentos colombinos (R Indias, Madrid, 13:54, oct.-dic. 1953, p. 609-623).
Provisión real of Granada, Apr. 30, 1492, the text of which has not previously been printed, and two undated documents connected with preparations for the fourth voyage. [R. D. Hussey]

3183. Quirk, Robert E. Some notes on a controversial controversy: Juan Ginés de Sepúlveda and natural servitude (HAHR, 34:3, Aug. 1954, p. 357-364).
An important article examining the meaning of the term *natura servus* as used by Sepúlveda

in reference to the American Indian. Argues that *servus* is to be interpreted in the sense of "serf" rather than in the Aristotelian sense of "slave," and seeks to correct the reputation of Sepúlveda accordingly. [C. Gibson]

3183a. Radaelli, Sigfrido A. La institución virreinal en las Indias. Antecedentes históricos (R Indias, Madrid, 14:55-56, enero-junio 1954, p. 37-56).
A suggestive analysis of the peninsular and early colonial office of viceroy, emphasizing discontinuity rather than progressive development. Dismisses the Castilian viceregal institution, finds no precedent in the Aragonese viceroyalty for Columbus' viceregal status, and concludes that the American viceroyalties of 1535 and after were independent of both European and Columbian "precedents." [C. Gibson]

3184. Ramírez Corría, Filiberto. Reconstrucción crítica del segundo viaje cubano de Colón. La ficción colombina del Cura de Los Palacios. Habana, 1955. 23 p.
This Cuban author, as the result of a cruise along the south coast of his native land, found that it did not fit the account of Columbus' second voyage as given by Andrés Bernáldez, which is a major source for the Cuban part of that voyage. Further study has now made him doubt that Bernáldez even lived, much less wrote a history. The claim can be adequately examined only by experts in the field, but there seems to be something that must be examined. [R. D. Hussey]

3184a. Rodríguez Demorizi, Emilio. Los dominicos en las Antillas y Venezuela en 1632 (Clío, 22:101, oct.-dic. 1954, p. 245-251).
A detailed relation dated Apr. 14, 1632, by Fray Luis de San Moquer, from the Dominican archives in Rome. [R. D. Hussey]

3185. Rodríguez Moñino, Antonio (ed.). Catálogo de memoriales presentados al Real Consejo de Indias, 1626-1630. Descripción bibliográfica de más de 400 rarísimos impresos y manuscritos. Madrid, 1953. 291 p.
200 copies only, reprinted from the periodical version listed in *HLAS, no. 18, 1952,* item 1727a. There are 430 items, often extracted or abstracted in considerable detail, with an extensive index of proper names. The collection is in private hands, bound in three volumes. It was gathered by Luis de Tapia, a member of the Council. [R. D. Hussey]

3185a. Roldán y Guerrero, Rafael. Historia del Cuerpo de Farmacia Militar del ejército español (Arch Iberoam Hist Med, 5:1, enero-junio 1953, p. 3-72; 5:2, julio-dic. 1953, p. 379-431; 6:3, julio-dic. 1954, p. 283-344).
A detailed and competent history of Spanish military pharmacy from the late 15th century to 1800, based largely on the sources in the Simancas archives. There is no portion specifically upon America, and relatively few mentions of America, but the articles deal with service at sea as well as on land, and present information which must apply to American expeditions as well as to European. [R. D. Hussey]

3186. Romoli, Kathleen. Balboa of Darién. Discoverer of the Pacific. Garden City, N. Y., Doubleday, 1953. 431 p.
A meticulously detailed and critical account of the work and times of Balboa, rather than a genuine biography. The scholarly apparatus is cut to a minimum. Appendices discuss weights, measures, currency and prices. [R. D. Hussey]

3186a. Rumeu de Armas, Antonio. Código del trabajo del indígena americano. Madrid, Ediciones Cultura Hispánica (Santo y seña, 14), 1953. 94 p.
Has not been seen. Said to be a good, popularised rearrangement of the *Recopilación.* [R. D. Hussey]

3187. Salas, Alberto. Fernández de Oviedo, crítico de la Conquista y de los conquistadores (Cuad Am, año 13, 74:2, marzo-abril 1954, p. 160-170).
Mostly but not entirely based upon an examination of Oviedo's *Historia general.* [R. D. Hussey]

3187a. Sancho de Sopranis, Hipólito. El maestro Fray Jorge de Sevilla, mercedario. Intento de identificación de un amigo de Colón (Miss Hisp, 10:29, 1953, p. 291-312).
A good discussion, which leaves it as uncertain, but rather probable, that the man studied was the friar of that name who accompanied Columbus on his second voyage. [R. D. Hussey]

3188. ————. Un problema de historia missional hispanoamericana. Los hospicios de Indias en Cádiz (Miss Hisp, 12:36, 1955, p. 515-553).
Concerns residences maintained by the various missionary Orders, from the later 16th century for the earlier cases, because the undeveloped state of the city originally offered no other adequate facilities. [R. D. Hussey]

3188a. Santiago Sanz, Luis. El proyecto de extinción del régimen de las intendencias de América y la ordenanza general de 1803 (R Inst Hist Der, 5, 1953, p. 123-185).
A sound and well-documented examination of the intendancy system and its proposed abolition. The 1803 ordinance, clarifying and modifying the intendancy institution, resulted from the failure of the abolition movement. [C. Gibson]

3189. Sierra, Vicente D. Así se hizo América. La expansión de la hispanidad en el siglo XVI. Madrid, Ediciones Cultura Hispánica (Col. Ambos mundos), 1955. 460 p., illus.

A semi-apologia, and complete popularization. There is more emphasis on cultural aspects than on those of politics or movement-of-population. [R. D. Hussey]

3189a. ————. En torno de las bulas alejandrinas de 1493 (Miss Hisp, 10:28, 1953, p. 73-122).

Continuance of a long polemic, especially with the Sevillian professor, Manuel Giménez Fernández. [R. D. Hussey]

3190. ————. Y nada más sobre las bulas alejandrinas de 1493 (Miss Hisp, 12:36, 1955, p. 401-428).

More of the same. One hopes that the title's "Y nada más" will be taken seriously by all the participants. Many readers of this particular item will perhaps find the note, added by the editors of the periodical, more helpful to comprehension of the underlying reasons for the controversy than the article itself. [R. D. Hussey]

3190a. Skelton, R. A. Explorer's maps (Geog Mag, 26:3, July 1953, p. 119-131 and subsequent issues).

A series of studies, profusely illustrated, with much value for Latin America, or for other parts of the Americas which are likely to interest Latin Americanists. The articles are semi-popular in style, but the author's status as Superintendent of the Map Room in the British Museum guarantees the quality of the scholarship. Among the 11 installments to January 1956, were such subtitles as "Cathay or a New World?" "The Spanish in the Pacific," and (January 1956) "The New World in the 16th century." To be continued. [R. D. Hussey]

3191. Spain. Archivo General de Marina. Índice de los expedientes y papeles de la Sección de Indiferente. . . . 1. 1730-1794. Madrid, Consejo Superior de Investigaciones Científicas, 1951. 291 p.

Since the Secretariat of Marina in the 18th century was often combined with that of Indias or Comercio, its papers have large value for all sorts of happenings and conditions in the Indies. The Sección analysed here is directly upon America, but others have value. The compilation is done by Julio F. Guillén with his usual high competence. Indices to the publication will be furnished in the last volume. [R. D. Hussey]

3191a. ————. Archivo General de Simancas. Títulos de Indias . . . ordenado por Ricardo Magdaleno. Valladolid, Spain, 1954. 980 p. (Catálogos, 20).

Lists, with indices, a vast body of documentation on the appointments of civil, clerical, and military officials for all parts of the Indies, from the Treasury records (mostly from those of Lanzas, Media Annata or Mercedes). Most are for the 18th century, but earlier and later occur. [R. D. Hussey]

3192. ————. Archivo Histórico Nacional. Documentos de Indias, siglos XVI-XIX. Catálogo de la serie existente en la Sección de Diversos. Madrid, 1954. 282 p., facsms.

Compiled by María del Carmen Pescador del Hoyo. Lists 540 documents (including some imprints), 1496-1831 (but only one is of the 15th century and only nine of the 19th) for the history of all parts of the Indies, including the Philippines. About one fifth have been published as Cartas de Indias, Madrid, 1877. [R. D. Hussey]

3192a. Specker, Johann. Die Missionsmethode in Spanisch-Amerika im 16. Jahrhundert, mit besonderer Berücksichtigung der Konzilien und Synoden. Schöneck-Beckenried, Switzerland, Administration der Neuen Zeitschrift für Missionswissenschaft (Neue Zeitschrift für Missionswissenschaft, Supplementa, 4), 1953. 247 p.

A well-documented study of missionary methods, chiefly from printed records, plus new material from the Vatican archives upon the Provincial Councils and Synods. Except for the latter, almost entirely on Mexico. [R. D. Hussey]

3193. Tejera, Emiliano. Los restos de Colón en Santo Domingo, y Los dos restos de Cristóbal Colón. 4. ed. Preparada por fray Cipriano de Utrera por encargo del Comité Ejecutivo Permanente del Faro de Colón. Ciudad Trujillo, Montalvo, 1953. 354 p., illus.

In this one corpus, presents the text of the first editions of two books (1877, 1879), with the appendices from the second and third editions (1926, 1929) and then (p. 283-346) the "Notas" prepared by Tejera (before his death), by his son Emilio, by Cayetano Armando Rodríguez, and by Utrera. [R. D. Hussey]

3193a. Tobar, Baltasar. Compendio de bulario índico. T. 1. Estudio y edición de M. Gutiérrez Arce. Sevilla, Escuela de Estudios Hispano-Americanos de Sevilla, 1954. liii, 558 p.

A compilation of extracts from the bulls, briefs, and similar papal documents that concerned the Indies. Tobar (1669-1707?) was former oidor of the Audiencia of Mexico, was trained at the University of Salamanca and was commissioned for the work by the Consejo de Indias in 1695. There are at least seven manuscripts of the Compendio; the one used is in the Biblioteca del Palacio, Madrid. [R. D. Hussey]

3194. Tudela, José (ed.). Legado de España a América. Madrid, Pegaso, 1954. 2 v.

Essays, of very uneven value, but often by outstanding authorities, on many aspects of the socio-cultural life of the Spanish colonies. There is very little critical apparatus and only brief bibliographies are given. [R. D. Hussey]

194a. Tudisco, Anthony. Hipótesis españolas en el siglo XVIII sobre el origen de los indios (Cien Soc, 5:28, agosto 1954, p. 146-151).
A handy résumé of the ideas of various well-known Spanish writers on America, starting with Acosta, but chiefly on men of the 18th century. [R. D. Hussey]

194b. Verhoog, P. Columbus landed on Caicos (U S Naval Inst Pro, 80:10, Oct. 1954, p. 1101-1111).
An experienced sea captain, with a longtime interest in the Columbus questions, claims that "San Salvador" was present-day Caicos, not Watling Island as usually supposed. [R. D. Hussey]

194c. Verlinden, Charles. Italian influence in Iberian colonization (HAHR, 33: 2, May 1953, p. 199-211).
A detailed study of Hispanic dependence on Genoese and other Italian precedents in colonial economic organizations. The author identifies the beginnings of colonial activity in Spain and Portugal in the early 14th century and connects its techniques with Italian convoy navigation, colonizing companies, Genoese merchants, and other Italian influences. Hispanic American colonization is seen as an outgrowth of Italy's impact on the Iberian peninsula. [C. Gibson]

195. ————. Les origines coloniales de la civilisation atlantique. Antécédents et types de structure (Cahiers d'Hist Mond, 1:2, oct. 1953, p. 378-398).
Another in the author's series of articles calling attention to the similarities between Mediterranean colonization in the Middle Ages and Atlantic colonization in the 16th and later centuries. Slavery, Italian influence, commercial systems, and feudal relationships are cited as critical themes in the continuity of expansion. An antidote to the conventional treatment of Hispanic imperialism, "the historians of which are customarily specialists in the modern period and hence less familiar with medieval European history." [C. Gibson]

195a. ————. Précédents mediévaux de la colonie en Amérique. México, Instituto Panamericano de Geografía e Historia, Comisión de Historia (Programme d'histoire de l'Amérique, 2: Période coloniale, 5), 1954. 61 p.
A call for more research with emphasis on the medieval carry-over and on Italian influences. Names two dozen medieval precedents, with detailed attention to only a few. Concerns Portugal as well as Spain. [R. D. Hussey]

196. Vigneras, L. A. El viaje de Samuel Champlain a las Indias Occidentales (An Estud Am, 10, 1953, p. 457-500, 4 pl.).
A much needed critical examination of the authenticity of the well-known account of Champlain's voyage to the Caribbean from Spain, 1599-1600. The need has long been evident to anyone who read the account with knowledge of conditions in Spanish America at the time. (According to Hubert Deschamps, as editor of Les voyages de Samuel Champlain, Paris, 1951, the Canadian historian Claude de Bonnault had already conducted research upon the subject in Seville. Vigneras mentions no connection with that earlier study, which has never, I think, been printed.) No known manuscript of the narrative is the original. Vigneras regards the Bologna University MS. as textually superior to that of the John Carter Brown Library, which has always been printed, and reproduces four facsimiles from the Bologna item. He mentions the manuscript of the Archivio di Stato, Turin, as inferior. (He does not mention that of the Bibliothèque Nationale, Paris: Nouv. Franç. 9256, which however is a copy made by Pierre Margry of what later became the John Carter Brown copy.)
The bulk of the article searches for traces of Champlain in the voluminous records of the relevant voyages from France to Spain and on to America, as found in Seville and Simancas. Champlain's name does not appear, and if he went to America he must vastly have exaggerated his importance. On the other hand, in spite of some errors, or perhaps careless borrowing from others, he surely was in Spain, and comparison of data makes it probable that he was in the Antilles. He could have got information on that area from Frenchmen who had been there, of course, and in any case seems to discuss Guadeloupe, the Caymans, and some other islands at second hand. His claims to have gone to Veracruz are probably untrue; his information upon the trip from Veracruz to Mexico City and to Puerto Belo is absurdly vague or confused, and the timing is almost impossible.
Vigneras points out that the narrative may not have been written by Champlain—none of the MSS makes any such claim—and that whoever wrote it may have done so some ten years after Champlain's return to Spain. This could account for some of the minor errors and omissions. (From notes made in the 1930's but never used, I may point out for the benefit of some later student that Champlain would have had available, even in 1602, several editions of the works of Acosta and of González de Mendoza, and that perusal of them may adequately explain where he got his "knowledge" of Mexico and Panama.) [R. D. Hussey]

196a. ———— (ed.). Some Spanish documents relating to early French expeditions to Canada (Can Hist R, 35:3, Sept. 1954, p. 217-223).
Translated extracts from seven letters, mostly sent to Spain from Paris, and dated from Feb. 29, 1600, to Nov. 1, 1608. The first deals, among other things, with the Roche-Breton expedition of 1598. [R. D. Hussey]

3197. Villaseñor, Raúl. Luciano, Moro y el utopianismo de Vasco de Quiroga (Cuad Am, año 12, 68:2, marzo-abril 1953, p. 155-175).
With a commentary of his own, the author offers extracts from Lucian's Saturnalia which appear most to have influenced Quiroga. The latter knew them in the Latin text which had been edited by Sir Thomas More. [R. D. Hussey]

3198. **Wright, Louis B.** Elizabethan politics and colonial enterprise (N C Hist R, 32:2, Apr. 1955, p. 254-269).
A valuable essay on the conflict in America with Spain, but solely from English sources. [R. D. Hussey]

3198a. **Ybot León, Antonio.** La Iglesia y los eclesiásticos españoles en la empresa de Indias. Barcelona, Salvat (Historia de América y de los pueblos americanos, 16), 1954. 768 p., illus.
An industrious compilation upon the whole Colonial era, profusely illustrated. The author uses the works of many specialists, but exhibits little care for synthesis or critical accommodation of diverse viewpoints. [R. D. Hussey]

3199. **Zavala, Silvio.** The political philosophy of the conquest of America. Translated by Teener Hall. México, Edit. Cultura, 1953. 140 p.
The original appeared in 1947. See *HLAS, no. 13, 1947,* item 1237. [R. D. Hussey]

3199a. **Zubillaga, Félix.** El procurador de las Indias Occidentales de la Compañía de Jesús, 1574 (Arch Hist Soc Iesu, 22:43, Ian-Iun. 1953, p. 367-417).
A very detailed story, based on the Jesuit archives in Rome, for the period 1568-1576, with a few notes on relevant events to the early 17th century. The Procurador for the Indies, whose office was established only four years after that of the Procurador for the Province of Spain itself, normally resided at Seville. [R. D. Hussey]

MIDDLE AMERICA AND THE WEST INDIES

ROLAND D. HUSSEY

AS I look back on the publications that I have analysed for the *HLAS* since 1940, I am concerned that so little has changed in the historiography of colonial Spanish America. Throughout, one finds about the same dreary polemics, and the same defensive reaction to a *leyenda negra* that has not needed combatting among scholars for a generation. Throughout, there have been additions to factual knowledge of limited aspects of a few favorite old topics such as the history of religious bodies, expansion of settlements, Indian status, the external history of colleges, universities, and printing, and the theory and machinery, though not usually the workings, of governing entities. But such work is more notable for the publishing of documents, criticism of textual accuracies, and interpretation by intuition, than for scholarly synthesis or evaluation of underlying meanings and causes by the only satisfactory method—the stating of hypotheses, the amassing of evidence *pro et con,* and only then the forming of conclusions that will be agreed to by almost anyone else who has seen the same evidence. Under existing conditions, workers in our field are doing little more than make available, by printing them, the materials from which future writers can construct a real history. Is it not time that more, at least of our younger men, turned their attention toward the latter goal?

Without quarrelling further with the type of work that we have, one can say that 1953-1955 has produced the usual accretions of evidence in the older fields, including the usual and welcome reprints or translations, several new collections of documents, contributions to historical cartography, and bibliographies. Among items that are outstanding but essentially "factual" readers should note the newly accessible texts by Acosta, Leon Pinelo, and Peter Martir d'Anghiera, the *Colección Somoza,* the volume upon Haiti from the Cuban archives (item 3384) and the documents edited by Richard Konetzke. A few others join Konetzke in exploring new fields, and/or offer studies notable for synthesis. Their work includes the books on trade by Borah and Morales Padrón, those of Lanning upon the University of Guatemala and that of Chinchilla Aguilar upon the same kingdom's Inquisition, the vast compilations by Calderón Quijano and Incháustegui, the monographs of Parry upon the sale of offices and of Chamberlain upon the early history of Honduras, and finally —but far from least—the pioneering study by Díaz Soler upon slavery in Puerto Rico. Also, though for quite different reasons, readers should note Vindel's controversial claims about the first book published in America and Connell-Smith's valuable clarification of a fringe of Spanish American history.

By an error discovered too late to rectify, I have failed to analyze even the

953 volumes of the valuable Puerto Rican *Historia* and Honduran *Revista del Archivo y Bibliotecas Nacionales.* Interested persons should check these for themselves, since few works upon the countries in question appear outside these reviews. [Roland D. Hussey]

MIDDLE AMERICA

3200. Academia Mexicana de la Historia. Dictamen . . . acerca del primer libro impreso en América según el Señor Francisco Vindel (Mem Ac Mex Hist, 13:1, enero-marzo 1954, p. 5-43; also in Bol Bibl Nac, México, 2. época, 5:2, abril-junio 1954, p. 3-46).
Articles by J. B. Iguíniz, Alberto María Carreño, and Federico Gómez de Orozco, attacking practically every point made by the Spanish book dealer named. The "Dictamen" was approved by the Academy in August 1953, saying in effect that neither the place nor date of printing of the Vindel item can be proved. See item 3375a.

3201. Actas capitulares de Cartago, de 1777 a 1785 (R Arch Nac C R, 18:7-12, julio-dic. 1954, p. 142-249).
A very revealing source for the history of Costa Rica, as well as for that of municipal government. In addition to all the usual subjects of concern to city governments, and to all the sessions in which almost nothing important was dealt with, there is a considerable emphasis on preparations for trouble with foreign interference, or on the interference itself.

3202. Adams, Eleanor B. A bio-bibliography of Franciscan authors in colonial Central America. Washington, Academy of American Franciscan History (Publ., Bibliographical series, 2), 1953. xxi, 97 p.
For the periodical version (Americas, Franciscan Hist, 8:4, Apr. 1952, p. 431-473; 9:1, July 1952, p. 37-86) see *HLAS, no. 18, 1952,* item 1734a.

3203. ————, and John E. Longhurst. New Mexico and the Sack of Rome, one hundred years later (New Mex Hist R, 28:4, Oct. 1953, p. 243-250).
Concerns a bitter Church versus State dispute of 1618-1625 under Governor Eulate. The latter cited the example of the Duke of Bourbon's obedience to Charles V, in 1527, as a precedent for his own unquestioning obedience to the royal orders.

3204. Aguilar, Francisco de. Relación breve de la conquista de la Nueva España. Estudio y notas por Federico Gómez de Orozco. México, Porrúa (Biblioteca José Porrúa Estrada de historia mexicana, 1. serie, 2), 1954. 115 p.

From a manuscript in the Escorial, which has been printed three times already since 1903, the last time as a separate book, Mexico, 1938.

3205. Aguirre, M. C. La acción de los franciscanos en Nuevo México (Miss Hisp, 12:36, 1955, p. 429-452).
A good discussion of the period of the 1590's to 1692, but almost entirely from well-known printed sources.

3206. Aldana, Cristóbal de. Crónica de la Merced de México. Introducción y notas de Jorge Gurría Lacroix. México, 1953. xii, 82 p.
225 copies only. Reprints the edition (also in 225 copies) of the Sociedad de Bibliófilos Mexicanos, Mexico, 1929, which reprinted the rare first edition of about 1770.

3207. Almada, Francisco. La expulsión de los jesuítas de Sonora (B Soc Chihua Estud Hist, 8:2, enero-marzo 1953, p. 631-634).
Detailed as to dates and a list of names, but without documentation.

3208. ————. Gobernadores de la Nueva Vizcaya: Don Francisco Montaño de la Cueva (B Soc Chihua Estud Hist, 8:8, dic. 1954, p. 725-729).
Born in Sevilla; to America very young; active on the northern Indian frontier as a soldier and administrator from early in the 17th century. He was acting governor or lieutenant governor of Nueva Vizcaya for the last 15 years before his death in 1647.

3209. Almoina, José. Las citas clásicas de Zumárraga (Hist Mex, 3:3, enero-marzo 1954, p. 391-419, 2 pl.).
A very careful examination, with quotations, of the Latin citations in the *Regla christiana breve* (1547), that being considered the only one of Zumárraga's works that was essentially original. Unfortunately for many readers, many quotations are left in the Latin.

3210. Altolaguirre y Duvale, Ángel de. Descubrimiento y conquista de México; con una introducción sobre fuentes por Antonio Ballesteros y Beretta. Barcelona, Salvat (Historia de América y de los pueblos americanos, 7), 1954. 448 p., illus., maps.
A standard type narrative, from the discovery of Yucatan to about 1535, with considerable information upon other parts of New Spain than Mexico. As in others of the series, the bibliographical footnotes and the illustrations are interesting and valuable, although the illustrations must be used critically if one is looking for those which are contemporary.

3211. Alvarado, Pedro de. Relación hecha . . . á Hernán Cortés, en que se refieren las guerras y batallas para pacificar las provincias del Antiguo Reino de Goathe-

mala. Estudio y notas por José Valero Silva. México, Porrúa (Biblioteca José Porrúa Estrada de historia mexicana, serie 1, 3), 1954. 120 p.
250 numbered copies. Has been many times printed before.

3212. Alvarado García, Ernesto (ed.). Tratados internacionales. T. 1. Período colonial, República Federal de Centro América y tratados bilaterales con Costa Rica. Tegucigalpa, Secretaría de Relaciones Exteriores, 1954. 515 p.
A collection of treaties and other international documents of Honduras for the Colonial and Central American periods, and similar documents between Honduras and Costa Rica for the National period. Most are from the Honduran archives, and the sources of the others are indicated. [R. R. Hill]

3213. The annals of the Cakchiquels; translated from the Cakchiquel Maya by Adrián Recinos and Delia Goetz. Title of the lords of Totonicapán; translated from the Quiché text into Spanish by Dionisio José Chonay; English version by Delia Goetz. Norman, Okla., University of Oklahoma Press, 1953. 217 p.
A new well-edited English translation of the well-known post-Conquest Mayan documents, both dealing with the pre-Conquest but the first dealing with the era after the Spaniards came. This one is also known as *Memorial de Tecpán Atitlán*.

3214. Arrigunaga y Peón, Joaquín de. Estudio etnográfico-social de la ciudad de Chihuahua durante la colonia (B Soc Chihua Estud Hist, 8:12, junio 1955, p. 791-794; 9:1, julio 1955, p. 804-807).
The second installment has some specific data on marriages, slavery, and other topics, about 1709-1719, as revealed by clerical archives. The author announced hopes of continuing the material, but had not done so in the next two issues.

3215. Ataque y saqueo del puerto de Alvarado, año de 1651 (B Arch Gen, México, 24:3, julio-sept. 1953, p. 501-508).
Testimony of witnesses to the events of the Dutch-French attack.

3216. Babelon, Jean. Un retrato verdadero de Hernán Cortés (Mem Ac Mex Hist, 13:3, julio-sept. 1954, p. 173-178, 3 pl.).
A medal and drawing of 1529, by the German artist Christopher Weiditz, who knew Cortés.

3217. Baratta, María de. Folklore religioso, época de la Conquista. Misa del Ahorcado, primera misa que se cantó en el territorio de Cuzcatlán (A Soc Geog Hist Guat, 27:1-4, marzo 1953-dic. 1954, i.e. 1955, p. 289-297).
With reproduction of two pages (the "Kyrie eleison") discusses a manuscript which is apparently the original of the mass celebrated by Juan Godines on June 19, 1524, in the Cuzcatlan area, and apparently used again in 1538.

3218. Barrera Aceves, Joaquín (ed.). Semblanza de Cuernavaca y México a mediados del siglo XVIII (Mem Ac Nac Hist Geog, 2. época, 9:4, 1953, p. 36-42).
Text of a private letter written, probably, by the Peruvian Antonio Cavedo to someone in Peru, Feb. 28, 1781.

3219. Barrios Berumen, Ernesto. La conquista española. Hernán Cortés y su obra. Prólogo de José Vasconcelos. México, Constancia, 1954. 240 p.
Another item in the apparently never ending polemic between the *indigenistas* and *hispanistas* as to the character of Mexican history. This one is on the *hispanista* side, well documented, and not lacking in value within the possible limits of such items.

3220. Bataillon, Marcel. Zumárraga, reformador del clero seglar. Una carta inédita del primer obispo de México (Hist Mex, 3:1, julio-sept. 1953, p. 1-10).
Copy (signed by Las Casas) of a letter to the Crown, probably written about 1539 or 1540, concerned with "la descompuesta y desordenada vida de los clérigos" in America, and efforts at reform.

3221. Benavides, Alonso de. Benavides memorial of 1630. Translated by Peter P. Forrestal, with an historical introduction and notes by Cyprian J. Lynch. Washington, Academy of American Franciscan History (Publ., Documentary series, 2), 1954. xxv, 96 p.
An effort to present a smoother reading translation than the older one of Chicago 1916, and using information in the notes and introduction which could not be known to the editors of that edition.

3222. Benítez, Fernando. La vida criolla en el siglo XVI. México, Colegio de México, 1953. 322 p., illus.
A readable and interesting discussion, chiefly from published sources, of cultural life; very little upon political, social or economic life.

3223. Berlin, Heinrich. La vida franciscana en la Guatemala de 1700 (Antr Hist Guat, 5:2, junio 1953, p. 9-18).
Text of several chapters of the *Actas capitulares* of the Order in Guatemala.

3224. Bobb, Bernard. Bucareli and the Interior Provinces (HAHR, 34:1, Feb. 1954, p. 20-36).

A careful study, based largely on the Mexican National Archives, of the policy of Viceroy Bucareli (1771-1779). Differs frequently with the major previous writer, Alfred Thomas (now of the University of Alabama), about Bucareli's character.

3225. Borah, Woodrow. Francisco de Urdiñola's census of the Spanish settlements in Nueva Vizcaya, 1604 (HAHR, 35:3, Aug. 1955, p. 398-402).
Lists 472 vecinos (by various definitions of the word) with occupations, marital status, and similar data attached to many names.

3226. Boyd, Mark F. Further consideration of the Apalachee missions (Americas, Franciscan Hist, 9:4, April 1953, p. 459-467).
Translations of documents (1702-1706) which the author listed on pages 18 and 102 of his *Here they once stood*, Gainesville, Fla., 1951 (see HLAS, no. 17, 1951, item 1461) which were received too late for full use in that book.

3227. ———, and José Navarro Latorre. Spanish interest in British Florida, and in the progress of the American Revolution (Fla Hist Q, 32:2, Oct. 1953, p. 92-130).
Documents of 1773-1778, from the Archivo Histórico Nacional, Madrid, with a good introduction.

3228. Buño, Washington. Escorbuto durante la exploración y conquista de América: una epidemia de 1603 descrita por Torquemada (Arch Iberoam Hist Med, 5:2, julio-dic. 1953, p. 576-583, 3 facsms.).
Concerns the Vizcaíno expedition up the western coast of North America, but offers notes upon earlier cases, and points out that the problem of preservable foods was such that almost any 16th-century sea trip that lasted as long as six weeks was sure to have trouble with scurvy.

3229. Burrus, Ernest J. Francesco Maria Piccolo, 1654-1729, pioneer of Lower California, in the light of Roman archives (HAHR, 35:1, Feb. 1955, p. 61-76).
Piccolo had been working among the Tarahumaras for over 13 years when he arrived in Lower California in 1697 to help Salvatierra consolidate the new beach head there. He greatly fostered the growth of the string of missions for the remainder of his life. This article corrects and amplifies what has been known of his life, although data are still inadequate on many aspects.

3230. ———. Francisco Javier Alegre, historian of the Jesuits in New Spain, 1729-1788 (Arch Hist Soc Iesu, 22:43, Ian.-Iun. 1953, p. 439-509, facsms.).
A thorough study of the life and writings, based on Mexican archives as well as Jesuit sources in

Rome. Alegre was born and educated in Mexico, and, except for a few vaguely known years in Havana, was never outside his native land until the exile of 1767. An appendix lists 41 writings, many not now known.

3231. ———. Pedro de Mercado and Mexican Jesuit recruits (Mid Am, 37:3, July 1955, p. 131-139).
Mercado (1546-1619), the first Mexican-born Jesuit, returned to his native land from studies in Spain in 1571. He aided greatly in the work of the new province, especially in work among the Indians and mestizos, in gaining the good will of the Creoles, and in the founding of schools and churches.

3232. Bushnell, David. El Marqués de Branciforte (Hist Mex, 2:3, enero-marzo 1953, p. 390-400).
This article uses practically nothing except Branciforte's letters to his superiors, but finds that they paint him clearly as avid for power and adulation, reactionary toward anything new, and constantly "apologetic" although there is no evidence in them of any specific fault.

3233. Calderón Quijano, José Antonio. Historia de las fortificaciones en Nueva España. Sevilla, Escuela de Estudios Hispano-Americanos, 1953. xxxvi, 334 p., illus.
An extensive and excellently prepared text, accompanied by 183 "figuras." The latter range from reproductions of original 16th-century maps in the Archivo General de Indias, to modern photographs. There are 17 documents in an appendix, and such aids to the user as transcriptions of legends from the maps and plans. The whole Colonial period is covered. The introduction and four plates are also printed in *Estudios americanos*, 6:21-22, junio-julio 1953, p. 37-53.

3234. Carpenter, Edwin H. Copper engraving in Mexico during the late eighteenth century. An inventory of the engravers found in the N. Y. P. L. N. Y., New York Public Library, 1953. 12 p.
A reprint from the *Bulletin* of the Library. Shows that there are no separate 18th-century prints known to exist in N. Y., although the Public Library and others have examples in books, and a few modern copies struck from 18th-century plates are known in other institutions. Discusses the general subject as well as specific examples.

3235. Carreño, Alberto María. Una carta abierta del librero Francisco Vindel (B Bib Nac, México, 2. época, 5:3, julio-agosto 1954, p. 21-37, illus.).
An answer to Vindel's reply to the attack on his thesis by the Academia Mexicana de Historia. See items 3200 and 3375a.

3236. ———. Los primeros años de un municipio del siglo XVI (Mem Ac Nac

Hist Geog, 2. época, 11, primer boletín extraordinario, 1955, p. 16-31). Concerns Coyoacan in the 1520's.

3237. Carrera Stampa, Manuel. Las ferias novohispanas (Hist Mex, 2:3, enero-marzo 1953, p. 319-342, maps).
A scholarly study of the 18th-century *feria* of Jalapa, with some information on those of Acapulco, San Juan de los Lagos, Saltillo, Chihuahua, and Taos.

3238. Cavallini Quiroz, Ligia. Relaciones entre México y Centro América durante el período colonial (Estud Hist Am, 1953, p. 344-405).
Concerns all fields of human activity, with details of considerable minuteness. Especially useful for the area of present-day Guatemala, and for biographical data.

3239. Ceccherelli, Claudio. El bautismo y los franciscanos en México, 1524-1539 (Miss Hisp, 12:35, 1955, p. 209-289).
Primarily from printed materials, but has 15 documentary appendices mostly from the Archivo General de Indias.

3240. Chamberlain, Robert S. The conquest and colonization of Honduras, 1502-1550. Washington, Carnegie Institution of Washington (Publ., 598), 1953. 264 p., map.
A magnificently detailed but also clearly presented study, based upon the archives of Sevilla, Mexico, Guatemala, and Comayagua, Honduras. Clarifies the whole story, and tells it almost for the first time for the period 1539-1544.

3241. ———. Simpson's *The encomienda in New Spain* and recent encomienda studies (HAHR, 34:2, May 1954, p. 238-250).
A valuable article, which should be read both for critique and for substance of the subject.

3242. Chávez Hayhoe, Arturo. Guadalajara en el siglo XVI. Guadalajara, México, Banco Refaccionario de Jalisco, 1953-1954. 2 v.
A collection of abstracts and extracts loosely strung together, rather than synthesized history or description, but a valuable mine of information upon a little treated subject.

3243. Chávez Orozco, Luis (comp.). Índice del Ramo de Indios del Archivo General de la Nación. II. México, Instituto Indigenista Interamericano, 1953. 409 p.
An index of the records regarding Indians found in v. 1-4 of the Ramo de Indios of the Archivo General de la Nación of Mexico. The entries give the year, the volume, the expediente number, the foliation, and the places referred to. There is a brief summary of the content of each document. The entries follow the order

of the documents in the volumes, which are of the last quarter of the 16th century. There are indexes of geographical names and of subjects. [R. R. Hill]

3244. Chinchilla Aguilar, Ernesto. La Inquisición en Guatemala. Guatemala, Instituto de Antropología e Historia de Guatemala, 1953. 335 p.
Based upon the scattered materials of the Ramo de Inquisición of the Mexican National Archives. A very useful work, although such materials are of course spotty, and apparently no effort was made to discover relevant documents which exist in other Ramos.

3245. ———. El Ramo de Aguas de la Ciudad de Guatemala en la época colonial (Antr Hist Guat, 5:2, junio 1953, p. 19-31).
Documents of 1645 and 1782, with a note upon the history of the water supply of the municipality.

3246. ——— (ed.). Ordenanzas de escultura, carpinteros, escultores, entalladores, ensambladores y violeros de la ciudad de México (Antr Hist Guat, 5:1, enero 1953, p. 29-52).
Ordenanzas, mostly of the second half of the 16th century plus one of 1704. The texts are not located, and the introduction is based only on the texts themselves.

3247. Cignoli, Francisco. El *Tractado breve de medicina* por Fray Agustín Farfán, México, 1952. Rosario, México, Talleres Gráficos Emilio Fenner, 1952. 37 p.
"Trabajo publicado en la *Revista de Farmacéuticos Nacionales*, números de agosto y diciembre de 1951 y abril de 1952."

3248. Cline, Howard F. Civil congregation of the Western Chinantec, New Spain, 1599-1603 (Americas, Franciscan Hist, 12:2, Oct. 1955, p. 115-138).
The Chinantla area was around San Pedro Yolox, in the present-day Sierra de Juarez. Work there was part of a major job of investigation and policy-forming under Viceroy Monterrey.

3249. Collis, Maurice. Cortés and Montezuma. N. Y., Harcourt, Brace, 1955. 256 p., illus.
A well-written account, without scholarly apparatus and intended for popular reading, but intended also to be accurate.

3250. Corbitt, D. C., and Roberta Corbitt. Papers from the Spanish archives relating to Tennessee and the Old Southwest (East Tenn Hist Soc Publ, 24, 1952, p. 106-124; 25, 1953, p. 74-88; 26, 1954, p. 60-66).
Installments for the period July 1790 to Decem-

ber 1791 of these valuable transcripts. Earlier installments have occasionally been entered in the *HLAS*. To be continued.

3251. Crespo, Benito. Documents concerning Bishop Crespo's visitation, 1730 (New Mex Hist R, 28:3, July 1953, p. 222-233).
Two letters to Viceroy Casafuerte, Sept. 8 and 25, 1730, with a valuable description of conditions in New Mexico.

3252. Cruz y Moya, Juan José de la. Historia de la santa y apostólica provincia de Santiago de Predicadores de México en la Nueva España. México, Porrúa (Documentos mexicanos, 3, 4) 1954-1955. 2 v.
The Dominican author of this work was born in Spain, 1706, and died in Mexico, 1760. His fine addition to the few chronicles of his Order in New Spain was written in 1756-1757. It was almost unknown until recently, and is now first printed in an edition of 500 copies, with a good introduction, and index, by Gabriel Saldívar.

3253. Dávila Padilla, Agustín. Historia de la fundación y discurso de la provincia de Santiago de México de la Orden de Predicadores. 3. ed. Prólogo de Agustín Millares Carlo. México, Editorial Academia Literaria (Col. de grandes crónicas mexicanas, 1), 1955. 654 p. & illus.
A facsimile of the second edition (Brussels, 1625) with a valuable bio-bibliographical introduction.

3254. Documentos de la gobernación de don Gregorio de Sandoval, 1636-1644 (R Arch Nac C R, 18:1-6, enero-junio 1954, p. 11-16).
Items upon a variety of matters of local governmental concern, especially trade, taxes, and the new port of Matina.

3255. Documentos históricos de Chiapas (B Arch Gen Chiapas, 1:2, abril-junio 1953, p. 7-125).
Text of documents of the 15th to 18th centuries relating to Chiapas, copied from the Archivo General del Gobierno de Guatemala, together with a list of documents microfilmed from that archive. [R. R. Hill]

3256. Documentos para la historia de Nicaragua. Madrid, Imprenta Juan Bravo (Col. Somoza), 1954-1955. 8 v. T. 1, [1503-1529], 536 p.; t. 2, 1529-1530, 579 p.; t. 3, 1531-1536, 535 p.; t. 4, 1536, 788 p.; t. 5, 1536-1538, 563 p.; t. 6, 1539-1540, 561 p.; t. 7, 1541-1543, 563 p., t. 8, 1543-1544, 629 p.
Selected documents from the Archive of the Indies, with a few from other sources, dealing with the Spanish colonial régime in Nicaragua.

In the eight volumes there are 607 documents including royal cedulas, letters of persons in the colony, reports, instructions, memorials, petitions, information on merits and services, powers of attorney, papal bulls, expedientes of residencias of officials, and other types. The records range in date from 1503 to 1544, and present much information on the life and activities in Nicaragua during those years. The documents are in chronological order, and have descriptive headings and an indication of the archival location. Each volume has indexes of names of persons and places. [R. R. Hill]

3257. Documentos relacionados con el Gobernador don Manuel de Bustamante y Vivero, 1693-1696 (R Arch Nac C R, 17:1-6, enero-junio 1953, p. 45-98).
The documents, connected with the governor's retirement in 1696, concern such matters as his powers, infringement on the powers of the alcaldes, and service of Negroes and Indians.

3258. Domínguez, Francisco Atanasio. The missions of New Mexico, 1776. Albuquerque, N. Mex., University of New Mexico Press, 1955. 387 p., illus., maps.
An extremely informative report from the National Library of Mexico, with letters of Domínguez, 1775-1795; translated, edited and annotated by Eleanor B. Adams and Fray Angélico Chávez. The three maps are of 1779 (Miera y Pacheco), of about 1766-1768 (Joseph Urrutia), and one of the Rio del Norte of the 1770's.

3259. Donahue, William H. Mary of Agreda and the southwest United States (Americas, Franciscan Hist, 9:3, Jan. 1953, p. 291-314).
Discusses the miraculous visits of Sor María de Jesús Agreda to the New Mexican area, 1627-1631. A critical article, in technique, even though some readers will have reservations when they realize that Mr. Donahue apparently takes for granted that the visits did occur.

3260. Dunne, Peter Masten. Lower California an island (Mid Am, 35:1, Jan. 1953, p. 37-66).
Detailed study of erroneous geographical ideas from the 16th to the 18th century.

3261. Durand, José. La transformación social del conquistador. México, Porrúa y Obregón (México y lo mexicano, 15, 16), 1953. 2 v.
Interesting essays on various ideas and social trends, chiefly as shown in the writings of 16th-century Mexico. Deals especially with fluidity of social classes; men of low status, upon emigrating to America, "enseñored" themselves, became wealthy, held office, etc.; on the other hand hidalgos might go into trade or even work with their hands. Related articles were published under variant titles in *Historia mexicana*, 3:4, abril-junio 1954, p. 497-515, and *Cuadernos americanos*, 77:1, feb. 1953, p. 175-192.

3262. Fairweather, Gerald Cattouse. The

truth about the so-called Battle of St. George's Caye and conquest of Belice. Guatemala, Imp. El Faro, 1953? 14 p.
The "battle" was on Sept. 10, 1798. It gave the British no sovereignty, and if it did, Spanish rights were restored by the 1802 treaty of Amiens, says the author. In other words, this pamphlet is part of the literature of the Guatemalan-British boundary dispute, without independent historical value, although its statements seem to be accurate enough.

3263. Fernández del Castillo, F. El hospital de San Lázaro, 1571-1862 (G Méd Méx, 82:2, marzo-abril 1952, p. 87-105).

3264. Folmer, Henry. Franco-Spanish rivalry in North America, 1524-1763. Glendale, Calif., Arthur H. Clark (Spain in the West, 7), 1953. 346 p., fold. map.
This work is based upon fairly good sources, and has much useful information in it, but the scholarship is careless and the title claims too much. Of 310 pages of useful text, the chapter upon the period "1727-1763" covers only pages 291-310, and does that poorly.

3265. Fragmentos de un testimonio de causas seguidas contra los Gobernadores don Miguel Gómez de Lara y don Manuel de Bustamante y Vivero, y contra el Capitán Sebastian de Zamora, 1694 (R Arch Nac C R, 18:1-6, enero-junio 1953, p. 67-98).

3266. Fuentes y Guzmán, Francisco. Recordación florida. Discurso historial, demostración material, militar y política del reyno de Goathemala. Libros primero, segundo y tercero de la primera parte de la obra. Guatemala, Ministerio de Educación Pública (Biblioteca de cultura popular, 9), 1951. 127 p.
Has not been seen, but evidently much abridged from the three-volume edition published in Guatemala in 1932-1933.

3267. García Granados, Rafael. Diccionario biográfico de historia antigua de Méjico. México, Instituto de Historia (Publ., 1. série, 23:I-II), 1952-1953. 2 v. 605, 524 p.
Enormously detailed data, with careful citations, upon all the known Indians who were of importance before the Conquest, including the ones who continued to be important during or after it.

3268. García Ruiz, Alfonso. La moneda y otros medios de cambio en la Zacatecas colonial (Hist Mex, 4:1, julio-sept. 1954, p. 20-46).
As Zacatecas became a rich mining and agricultural area in the 16th century, it suffered a shortage of currency which continued to the end of the colonial period, there being no mint outside of Mexico City until 1810. This article

is valuable on the question of mediums of exchange, and has useful information on many related questions.

3269. Gardiner, C. Harvey. The first shipping constructed in New Spain (Americas, Franciscan Hist, 10:4, April 1954, p. 409-419).
Concerns the ships built at Tenochtitlan, by Martín López for Cortés, in 1519-1520.

3270. —————. Tempest in Tehuantepec, 1529. Local events in imperial perspective (HAHR, 35:1, Feb. 1955, p. 1-13).
Concerns the three-month struggle, July to September, between the newly arrived Martín López, as alcalde mayor for the newly established audiencia, and Francisco Maldonado, who had been governing the province for Cortés for several years. Maldonado was defeated.

3271. Garza Treviño, Ciro R. de la. Así nació Tamaulipas. La epopeya escandoniana. Ciudad Victoria, México, 1953. 50 p.
Detailed information, settlement by settlement, mostly of the 18th century. There is no scholarly apparatus.

3272. Geiger, Maynard (ed.). Reply of Mission San Antonio [and San Gabriel] to the questionnaire of the Spanish government in 1812 concerning the native culture of the California mission Indians (Americas, Franciscan Hist, 10:2, Oct. 1953, p. 211-227; 12:1, July 1955, p. 77-84).
The above two installments are part of a series which is appearing irregularly in this periodical. The questionnaire itself, and replies from Mission San Diego and Mission San Carlos de Borromeo, appeared several years ago.

3273. Gerhard, Peter. A Dutch trade mission to New Spain, 1746-1747 (Pac Hist R, 23:3, Aug. 1954, p. 221-226).
Based on ambitious hopes, but after delays that cut these down, two Dutch ships left Manila in July 1746. They were separated by a storm at the Marianas. One reached Lower California and the nearby mainland in December 1746, but was turned away from the mainland and finally sailed back for Batavia. The other reached the mainland coast, apparently was in small harbors there for some two months, and appeared briefly at Acapulco on Mar. 25, 1747, before sailing away. Nothing is known (from the Spanish sources used) about the ultimate fate of either ship.

3274. —————. Misiones de Baja California (Hist Mex, 3:4, abril-junio 1954, p. 600-605).
An examination of the present locations of the libros de misión (records of baptisms, marriages, and deaths) of the missions of Lower California. Most are unknown; others are in Upper California or in other parts of Mexico.

3275. Gibson, Charles. Rotation of alcaldes in the Indian cabildo of Mexico City (HAHR, 33:2, May 1953, p. 212-223). Rotation of officeholding was a well-established principle in Spain and in Spanish America. It also existed in the subordinate Indian cabildo that assisted in the government of the four Indian barrios of Mexico City. Rotation was, apparently, on a basis of choice among the barrios, but the procedure is not certain.

3276. ————. Significación de la historia tlaxcalteca en el siglo XVI (Hist Mex, 3:4, abril-junio 1954, p. 592-599).
A penetrating examination of several old concepts about the favored status of Tlaxcala through privileges that grew from their aid to Cortés in the conquest. Says that the Indians exploited that aid very shrewdly, but that many of the privileges did not last very long, and that by the end of the 16th century, with a considerable number of Spaniards and more mestizos living in the area, the cabildo and Indian *principales* had lost control of their situation.

3277. Giraud, Marcel. Histoire de la Louisiane française. T. 1. Le règne de Louis XIV, 1698-1715. Paris, Presses Universitaires, 1953. 368 p., maps.
A scholarly study which deliberately omits the preliminary explorations and deals with the settlement and related episodes. The latter include relations with other American colonies, and with the Indians.

3278. Gómez de Orozco, Federico. El conquistador anónimo (Hist Mex, 2:3, enero-marzo 1953, p. 401-411).
By internal evidence, pretty well establishes that the author of the well-known chronicle was Alonso de Ulloa.

3279. ————. El libro de rezo del Rosario (B Bibl Nac, México, 2. época, 5:2, abril-junio 1954, p. 35-46).
Attacks the thesis advanced by Francisco Vindel (see item 3375a) as to the first book published in Mexico. Does so less violently than many, but no less emphatically.

3280. Gómez Robledo, Xavier. Humanismo en México en el siglo XVI. El sistema del Colegio de San Pedro y San Pablo. México, Jus, 1954. 182 p., illus.
A series of pleasantly written essays upon various related topics for the last quarter of the century.

3281. González de Cossío, Francisco (ed.). El libro de tasaciones de pueblos de la Nueva España. México, Archivo General de la Nación, 1952, 677 p.
The text of recently discovered documents: the second book—the first being lost—of *Matrícula de tributos*, a register kept by the audiencia. The basic years are for about 1550 to 1570, but much information appears on the earlier period. The entries include laws, administrative decisions, etc., as well as the data upon assessments.

3282. González Navarro, Moisés. Repartimiento de indios en Nueva Galicia. México, Museo Nacional de Historia (Serie científica, 1), 1953. 237 p.
210 documents, 1670-1751, from the audiencia archives of Guadalajara, concerned especially with crops and labor.

3283. Gutiérrez y Ulloa, Antonio. Estado general de la provincia de San Salvador, Reyno de Guatemala (Anaqueles, 5. época, 4, mayo 1953 - abril 1954, p. 101-119).
This item began in issue no. 1, enero-abril 1951, It is a good description, area by area, with the sort of information customary in official documents of the period; drawn up about 1807. To be continued.

3284. Hammond, George P., and Agapito Rey (eds. and trans.). Don Juan de Oñate: colonizer of New Mexico, 1595-1628. Albuquerque, N. Mex., University of New Mexico Press (Coronado Cuarto Centennial publications, 1540-1940, v. 5-6), 1953. 2 v., fold. map.
172 documents, nearly all from the Archive of the Indies, 1584 to 1628 (but mostly 1598-1609), presented in excellent translation and with scholarly commentary. Oñate is merely the central figure in what amounts to a history of the area and period. There is no bibliography, since that is easily available elsewhere.

3285. Harper, Elizabeth Ann. The Taovayas Indians in frontier trade and diplomacy, 1769-1779 (SW Hist Q, 57:2, Oct. 1953, p. 181-201).
Centers around the treaty with the Taovayas Indians made by De Mezières on Oct. 27, 1771. An earlier installment, on the years 1719-1768, appeared in the *Chronicles of Oklahoma*, about the same time, but has not been seen.

3286. Hernández Luna, Juan. El iniciador de la historia de las ideas en México (Fil Let, México, 25:51-52, julio-dic. 1953, p. 65-80).
Concerns the Mexican theologian, orator and bibliographer, Juan José de Eguiara y Eguren, and his *Bibliotheca mexicana* (1755).

3287. Hidalgo, Joseph Domingo. Memoria para hacer una descripción puntual del Reino de Guatemala (A Soc Geog Hist Guat, 26:3-4, sept.-dic. 1952, i.e. 1955, p. 383-413).
Reprinted from the *Gazeta de Guatemala*, 2. época, t. 1-2, 1797-1798. Consists of an introduction by Hidalgo, the editor of the *Gazeta*, and then descriptions of the provinces of Quezaltenango and Totonicapan.

3288. Iriarte Iturri, Romualdo, and Lázaro de Azpurz. Redin, soldado y misionero, 1597-1651. Madrid, Espasa Calpe, 1951. 297 p.

Has not been seen, but is said to be scholarly biography based upon the Vatican and Spanish archives and libraries, including the archive of the present head of Redin's family. Tiburcio de Redin, after a career as an able if truculent and swashbuckling seaman-soldier, became known as a great Capuchin missionary, in the Congo and in Panama, as Francisco de Pamplona.

3289. Ives, Ronald L. "California no es ysla" (Rec Am Cat Hist Soc, 64:4, Dec. 1953, p. 189-198).
A good critical study of the geographical question mentioned, with a reproduction of the Kino map (of 1701, originally) "Passo por tierra á la California." The latter was not much improved upon for 150 years.

3290. Izquierdo, José Joaquín. Montaña y los orígenes del movimiento social y científico de México. Con un prefacio de Henry E. Sigerist. México, Ediciones Ciencia, 1955. 442 p.
Dr. Luis José Montaña (Puebla, 1755-Mexico, 1820) was a pioneer in the effort to start, and on modern lines, the study of botany, chemistry, pharmacy, and related disciplines, in Mexico. He had no great success in his own time. Much information appears for the history of learning, and of politics, in Montaña's day.

3291. ————. A note on the early relations between scientists of Mexico and of the United States: Luis José Montaña and Samuel L. Mitchill (J Hist Med Allied Sci, 10:1, Jan. 1955, p. 45-57).
The famous physician Mitchill (1764-1831) showed an interest in Spanish America as early as 1813. The equally famous Mexican physician Montaña (1755-1820) sent copies of two works by him, published in 1817, to Mitchill, who reviewed them in complimentary manner in the *Medical repository* for 1820. The manner of the first contacts between the two men is not known, but may have involved one Dr. F. Pascalis.

3292. Jacobsen, Jerome V. Pedro Nieto, the ancient porter (Mid Am, 35:1, Jan. 1953, p. 3-17).
Corrects the facts about the Jesuit lay brother, or temporal coadjutor, as given in Andrés Pérez de Ribas' chronicle. Nieto was born about 1545-48, went to America with Menéndez de Ávila in 1568, took his simple vows in 1585, and served until his death in 1637.

3293. Kieman, Mathias C. A document concerning the Franciscan custody of Rio Verde, 1648 (Americas, Franciscan Hist, 11:3, Jan. 1955, p. 295-329).
Primarily a document on the visit of Commissary General Fray Buenaventura de Salinas y Córdoba to the custody (founded in 1607) which lay between present-day San Luis Potosi and Tampico.

3294. Kino, Eusebio Francisco. Kino reports to headquarters. Correspondence

. . . from New Spain with Rome. Edited by Ernest J. Burrus. Roma, Institutum Historicum Societatum Iesu, 1954. 135 p.; maps and facsims. in separately printed supplement.
14 unpublished letters and reports, 1681-1704, in Spanish with English translations. From the Jesuit archives in Rome. Have special value for the Atondo expedition of 1683, about which litte detail has been known.

3295. Kushinsky, Martin. Oviedo on the conquest of New Spain (Rec Am Cat Hist Soc, 64:3, Sept. 1953, p. 155-165).
A critical examination especially of book 33 of the *Historia general*. Decides that this is not particularly important as an independent source of facts about the Conquest, but is important for the remarks and judgments which Oviedo inserts out of his familiarity with the people and the character of the episodes.

3296. Lamadrid, Lázaro. Fray José Antonio Liendo y Goicoechea, O. F. M., y la "Philosophia Recentior" del siglo XVIII (Americas, Franciscan Hist, 11:3, Jan. 1955, p. 363-388).
A survey of various aspects of the Enlightenment in Spanish America, with occasional depth given by the use of new information from Central American archives.

3297. Lanning, John Tate. The legend that Governor Moral Sánchez was hanged (Ga Hist Q, 38:4, Dec. 1954, p. 349-355).
Governor Francisco del Moral Sánchez of Florida made a treaty with James Oglethorpe in 1736 giving England title down to the St. John's River, against the Spanish claim to the Altamaha. The Earl of Egmont reported in 1740 that he had therefore been sent home in chains, and hanged. In fact his residencia, in 1744, caused his punishment for various rather ordinary offenses, and in 1748, upon his appeal, his name was entirely cleared.

3298. ————. The University in the Kingdom of Guatemala. Ithaca, N. Y., Cornell University Press, 1955. 331 p., illus.
This first history in English of any Latin American university is indispensable not only for its own subject, but for the light that it casts upon many aspects of intellectual and social life in all of Spanish America. It is based upon thorough exploitation of the Guatemalan archives and of the Archives of the Indies, in Sevilla. Successive chapters deal with every aspect of its founding, later history to the end of the colonial era, and its academic life and institutions. There is no bibliography, except in footnotes. The "Glossary of academic terms" (p. 309-319) and the related "Foreword" (p. v-ix) can perhaps be appreciated only by those who also have struggled with the questions involved, but should be of value to all.

3299. ———— (ed.). Reales cédulas de la Real y Pontificia Universidad de San

Carlos de Guatemala. . . . Prólogo del Dr. Carlos Martínez Durán. . . . Guatemala, Editorial Universitaria, 1954. xxxvi, 350 p., illus.

134 cedulas, 1620-1819, from the Guatemalan National Archives. The cedulas are indispensable for any future history of the university, and of much value for related aspects of the socio-intellectual history of the colony.

3300. Lardé, Jorge. La población de El Salvador: su origen y distribución geográfica (A Mus Nac, 4:12, marzo 1953, p. 73-92).

3301. Lawson, Edward W. Determination of the first landing place of Juan Ponce de León on the North American Continent in the year 1513. St. Augustine, Fla., Record Press, 1954. 25 p., fold. maps.

Using knowledge of seamanship and an effort at correction for magnetic variation and for errors of the early records, concludes that Ponce de León sailed from Puerto Rico on Mar. 3, 1513 (not 1512); sighted Gran Abaco Island (not Florida) on Easter Sunday; and first sighted Florida, and then landed, at the St. Augustine area, on Apr. 3, 1513.

3302. Leal, Luis. El Códice Ramírez (Hist Mex, 3:1, julio-sept. 1953, p. 11-33).

A critical examination of the 16th-century *Relación del origen de los indios que habitan esta Nueva España*, first completely published (by José M. Vigil) in 1878. Establishes pretty well that it was written about 1588 by P. Juan Tovar, on the basis of an earlier item by him (no longer known) which had meantime been used by Durán. This 1588 item by Tovar was prepared for Acosta, who used it in his *Historia natural y moral*. It is not to be confused with the *Historia de los mexicanos por sus pinturas*, published first by García Icazbalceta, and also called, at times, "Códice Ramírez."

3303. Lewis, Clifford M., and Albert J. Loomie. The Spanish Jesuit mission in Virginia, 1570-1572. Chapel Hill, N. C., Virginia Historical Society, 1953. xviii, 294 p., illus., maps.

A satisfactory account is here given, for the first time, of the Jesuit mission effort at "Ajacan," probably on the York River. The authors relate it as growing from a combination of missionary enterprise, international rivalry, and search for a strait through the continent.

3304. Leza, Jesús de. Fray Juan Ramírez, O. P. Un riojano defensor de los indios (Berceo, 7:22, enero-marzo, p. 41-60; 7:23, abril-junio, p. 309-319; 7:24, juliosept. 1952, p. 457-468).

Fray Juan was a 16th-century humanist of the University of Salamanca, and a missionary in New Spain and Bishop of Guatemala.

3305. Lines, Jorge (ed.). Colección de documentos para la historia de Costa Rica

relativos al cuarto y último viaje de Cristóbal Colón. San José, Academia de Geografía e Historia, 1952. xxxi, 331 p.

A reprinting of documents relating to the fourth voyage of Columbus, with indication of the sources, together with excerpts from early historians and opinions respecting the location of Cariay. [R. R. Hill]

3306. López de Meneses, Amada. El primer regreso de Hernán Cortés a España (R Indias, Madrid, 14:55-56, enerojunio 1954, p. 69-91).

Points out that, contrary to the usual story, Cortés and the King met at Monzon, not Toledo. Uses a document from the Aragonese archives to show who was at the court at the time, and comments about what is known or may be inferred about Cortés' relations with some of those people in later years.

3307. McAlister, Lyle N. The discovery and exploration of the Nicaraguan transisthmian route, 1519-1545 (Americas, Franciscan Hist, 10:3, Jan. 1954, p. 259-276).

A detailed and careful study (from printed documents only) which emphasizes the connection with the early desire for a good route to Asia.

3308. ————. The marine forces of William Augustus Bowles and his "State of Muskogee," 1801-1802 (Fla Hist Q, 32:1, July 1953, p. 3-27).

Bowles' plans for a "State" of the Civilized Indian Tribes of the southeast of the U. S., to be independent of Spanish or U. S. control, as a means to break the trade monopoly of Spain and of Panton-Leslie Co., probably went back to the 1780's.

3309. ————. The reorganization of the Army of New Spain, 1763-1766 (HAHR, 33:1, Feb. 1953, p. 1-32).

Based on the Mexican archives; some information about the subject from the late 17th century.

3310. McCaleb, Walter Flavius. Spanish missions of Texas. San Antonio, Tex., Naylor Co., 1954. 121 p.

A popular account by a veteran amateur historian. Used some materials from the Bejar archives.

3311. McCloskey, Michael B. The formative years of the Missionary College of Santa Cruz de Querétaro, 1683-1733. Washington, Academy of American Franciscan History, 1955. xiv, 128 p.

The College named was established upon a Spanish precedent, to attempt to ensure a steady supply of trained missionaries. It was directly under the *Propaganda Fidei* of Rome, and its graduates worked in Central America and the present U. S., as well as in Mexico. It was the example followed by two other colleges in Mexico and by one in Peru.

3312. McPheeters, D. W. An unknown early seventeenth century codex of the *Crónica mexicana* of Hernando Alvarado Tezozomoc (HAHR, 34:4, Nov. 1954, p. 506-512).
A critical discussion of a manuscript two centuries earlier than those so far used, of the well-known chronicle. It appears to be a copy, and has been in the possession of Boturini and Viceroy Revillagigedo. At the time that Mc-Pheeters used it, it was in the hands of a N. Y. dealer.

3313. Malagón, Javier. Las "ordenanças y copilación de leyes" del Virrey Mendoza para la audiencia de la Nueva España (R Hist Am, 37-38, enero-dic. 1954, p. 109-132, facsms.).
A discussion of the laws printed in Mexico in 1548, to which very little attention has been paid, though they were not incorporated into the Puga *Cedulario* of 1563 (Medina says that they were). They controlled the "buena gobernación y estilo" of officials of the audiencia, such as the *escribanos, relatores, alguaciles,* or *fiscales.*

3314. Mange, Juan Mateo. Unknown Arizona and Sonora, 1693-1701. Translated by Harry J. Karns. Tucson, Ariz., Arizona Silhouettes, 1954. 303 p., illus.
The Spanish, *Luz de tierra incógnita,* was published in Mexico in 1926.

3315. Martínez, Manuel María. El obispo Marroquín y el franciscano Motolinía, enemigos de Las Casas. Examen de los motivos de su enemistad (B Real Ac Hist, 132:2, abril-junio 1953, p. 173-199).
The author (a Dominican) agrees that there were questions involved of differences over methods of evangelization, and influences from Colonial angers against the New Laws. But he finds a strong factor in more petty and personal motives. Marroquín was, he says, jealous of his former subordinate. Motolinía was a friend of Alonso Maldonado, and had been proposed by him, as President of the Audiencia de los Confines, to be Bishop of Yucatan. Maldonado was deposed through the efforts of Las Casas, and with him went Motolinía's hopes of preferment.

3316. Martínez del Río, Pablo. La comarca lagunera a fines del siglo XVI y principios del siglo XVII según las fuentes escritas. México, Instituto de Historia (Publ., 30), 1954. 124 p.
A study, from printed sources, of the Indian culture and of Spanish penetration of the area, chiefly through Jesuit activity. The work centered in the Valle de Parras, in the region of the Nazas and Aguanaval rivers (southern Coahuila, today).

3317. Mata Gavidia, José. Fundación de la Universidad de Guatemala, 1548 a 1688. Guatemala, Editorial Universitaria, 1954. 338 p.

A discussion, documented from the Archivo General de Gobierno of Guatemala, of the long struggle to achieve royal consent for the establishment of the university. It was greatly complicated by rivalry between the Dominicans and the Jesuits.

3318. Maynard, Theodore. The long road of Father Serra. N. Y., Appleton-Century-Crofts, 1954. 297 p., illus.
An honest, but extremely eulogistic, popular biography; incorporates much from modern printed research.

3319. Maza, Francisco de la. El guadalupanismo mexicano. México, Porrúa y Obregón (México y lo mexicano, 17), 1953. 130 p.
A historiographical and bibliographical study, primarily for the Colonial period.

3320. Meade, Joaquín. La evangelización de la Huasteca Tamaulipeca y la historia eclesiástica de la región (Mem Ac Mex Hist, 14:3, julio-sept. 1955, p. 271-296, 16 pl., plan).
Primarily on 16th-century expeditions, and from Mexican archival materials.

3321. ————. Notes on the Franciscans in the Huasteca region of Mexico (Americas, Franciscan Hist, 11:3, Jan. 1955, p. 429-448).
An undocumented summary of basic facts, to 1810, followed by lists of the custodies and parishes and their heads.

3322. Memoria de los servicios que había hecho Nuño de Guzmán, desde que fué nombrado governador de Pánuco en 1525. Estudio y notas por Manuel Carrera Stampa. México, Porrúa (Biblioteca José Porrúa Estrada de historia mexicana, 1. serie; La Conquista, 4), 1955. 209 p., map.
Valuable material, by Nuño de Guzmán or by his companions. Has been printed before, but is here made more available, with a useful introduction.

3323. Meseguer Fernández, Juan. Contenido misionológico de la "Obediencia" e "Instrucción" de Fray Francisco de los Ángeles a los Doce Apóstoles de México (Americas, Franciscan Hist, 11:3, Jan. 1955, p. 473-500).
A scholarly article on the Latin and Spanish texts of the well-known and basic document of 1523.

3324. Millares Carlo, Agustín. Dos nuevos datos para la historia de la imprenta en México en el siglo XVI (Nueva R Filol Hisp, 7:3-4, julio-dic. 1953, p. 702-708, illus.).
A viceregal order of July 10, 1552, for payment to Pedro Ocharte for services as a printer, and

an imprint of the same year, struck off by Pedro Balli, *Iubileo plenissimo, que nuestro muy S. Padre Gregorio 14 ha concedido á la christianidad.* The latter, a broadside, is reproduced.

3325. ————, and Julián Calvo. Juan Pablos, primer impresor que a esta tierra vino. México, Porrúa (Documentos mexicanos, 1), 1953. 220 p., facsims.
A biography, history, and study of Pablos' work (1539-1560) including full details and locations, so far as possible, of 62 items known to have been printed by him. Not all are represented by extant copies. There is an appendix of 26 documents.

3326. ————, and ————. Los protomártires del Japón (Nagasaki, 1557). Ensayo biobibliográfico. México, 1954. Unpaged, 1 pl.
A list, with much detail, of 416 items, mostly printed, from 1592-1953. It is a *tirada aparte* of pages xxvii-ccxl of the *Testimonios auténticos acerca de los protomártires del Japón,* edited by Eduardo Enrique Ríos for the Fondo Pagliai (Mexico, 1954). The martyrs were closely connected with work in New Spain before they went to Japan.

3327. Montero de Miranda, Francisco. Descripción de la provincia de la Verapaz. . . . Relación del siglo XVI (A Soc Geog Hist Guat, 27:1-4, marzo 1953—dic. 1954, i.e. 1955, p. 342-358).
Not dated, but of about the 1570's; from a manuscript in the University of Texas.

3328. Morales Rodríguez, Sergio. Costumbres y creencias en la Nueva España (Estud Hist Am, 1953, p. 425-476).
Presents a variety of data about the daily life, with reference to the Creole, mestizo and Indian groups.

3329. Murdock, Richard M. Report of the forest resources of Spanish East Florida, in 1792 (Agr Hist, 27:4, Oct. 1953, p. 147-151).
A document from the East Florida papers in the Library of Congress. The introductory comment has value for related matters such as the province's food supply.

3330. Navarro, Bernabé. La cultura mexicana frente a Europa (Hist Mex, 3:4, abril-junio 1954, p. 547-561).
Notes on the 18th-century depreciatory attitude in Europe, and reaction in Mexico.

3331. New source material for the history of the North American West including the Spanish possessions in North America. . . . The previously unknown and unpublished papers of Count Revillagigedo, viceroy of Mexico, 1789-1794. . . . N. Y., H. P. Kraus, 1954. 12 p., pls.
A sales catalogue for 37 manuscript volumes, including 25 of correspondence, and 12 of

accounts by explorers and scientists who took part in events during the period. Some of the latter are not, probably, otherwise extant, whatever may be true of the correspondence. The many facsimiles are of some value even in their reduced size. The papers come from the family in Spain.

3332. Ocaranza, Fernando. Algunas noticias acerca de las misiones de California (Mem Ac Mex Hist, 12:4, oct.-dic. 1953, p. 294-298).
A discussion of developments from 1768 to 1780, with data from the Mexican National Archives.

3333. ————. Fundación de nuevas misiones franciscanas en el año 1803 (Americas, Franciscan Hist, 11:3, Jan. 1955, p. 449-472).
A slightly documented article, concerning many areas of northern New Spain.

3334. ————. Las misiones de Sonora en el año de 1658 (Mem Ac Mex Hist, 14:2, abril-junio 1955, p. 119-129).
The history, as well as the status in 1658, mission by mission. Documentation from the Mexican National Archives.

3335. Olmedo, Daniel. ¿Indofilia mitómana o credulidad excesiva? Estudio crítico sobre el catálogo de "Indios célebres" de Antonio Carrión (B Bibl Nac, México, 2. época, 4:1, enero-marzo 1953, p. 9-27).
Documented corrections of biographies of Mexican Jesuits who were listed as Indians in Carrión's "Indios célebres de la República Mexicana," which was published as an *Apéndice* to Anastasio Cerecedo's *Memorias para la historia de las revoluciones en México* (Mexico, 1869).

3336. Omaechevarría, Ignacio. Mártires franciscanos de Georgia (Miss Hisp, 12:34, 1955, p. 5-93; 12:35, 1955, p. 291-370).
A well-documented account of the "Guale" episode of September 1597, and the Spanish reaction to it to the year 1612.

3337. Ortega y Medina, Juan A. México en la conciencia anglosajona. México, Porrúa y Obregón (México y lo mexicano, 13), 1953. 120 p.
Analysis of the ideas shown by well-known English travelers and writers like Hakluyt and Gage.

3338. Palou, Francisco. Life of Fray Junípero Serra. Translated and annotated by Maynard J. Geiger. Washington, Academy of American Franciscan History (Publ., Documentary series, 3), 1955. xxx, 457 p., illus., map.
An effort to provide a better, or at least smoother reading, translation than the only

previous one in English, by George Wharton James (Pasadena, 1913). The editor also provides nearly 200 pages of notes, and a good bibliography and index.

3339. Pazos, Manuel R. Los franciscanos y la educación literaria de los indios mejicanos; Reducciones franciscanas en Méjico; La Asunción de Nuestra Señora en las misiones franciscanas de Méjico; Los misioneros franciscanos de Méjico en el siglo XVI y su sistema penal al respecto de los indios (Arch Ib Am, 2. época, 13: 49, enero-marzo 1953, p. 1-59; 2. época, 13:50, abril-junio 1953, p. 129-164; 2. época, 13:51, julio-sept. 1953, p. 329-352; 2. época, 13:52, oct.-dic. 1953, p. 385-440).

Good compilations on the subjects named, mostly for the 16th century, but entirely from printed and mostly from well-known sources.

3340. Pénicaut, André. Fleur de lys and calumet. Translated and edited by R. G. McWilliams. Baton Rouge, La., State University Press, 1953. xxxiv, 282 p., illus., maps.

A smooth translation, and scholarly annotation, of a chronicle written in 1723 and well known to historians, but never before available, complete, in English. The author accompanied such men as St. Denis, and offers much upon relations with the Spanish and the Indians. The editor points out that until fairly recently the author's name was given as Jean, not André.

3341. Pérez Maldonado, Carlos. El Duque de Alba, Conde de Monterrey (Mem Ac Mex Hist, 13:3, julio-sept. 1954, p. 240-261).

Points out that the late Duque de Alba's titles had included, since 1733, that of Conde de Monterrey, and discusses the work in Mexico, as viceroy (1595-1603), of the fifth Conde, Gaspar de Zúñiga y Acevedo. (The title originated in 1432.)

3342. Peterson, Mendel L. History under the sea. Underwater exploration of shipwrecks. Washington, Smithsonian Institution (Miscellaneous publ., 4174), 1954. 16 p., illus.

Primarily a discussion of methods and problems in the recently instituted Marine Archeology Project of the Department of History of the National Museum. The work has been done off the Florida coast, and the two examples cited in some detail include remains of the Spanish fleet lost in 1733.

3343. Pompa y Pompa, Antonio. Ubicando el lugar de origen de Hidalgo (A Inst Nac Antr Hist, 6, pt. 1 (no. 34), 1952, i.e. 1954, p. 113-124, illus., pl.).

Establishes that Hidalgo was born on the hacienda of San Diego de Corralejo and baptized in the parish church of Penjamo, both near

Guanajuato. The story that he was born at San Vicente de Caño was invented in the mid-19th century by the then proprietors to save their property from expropriation.

3344. Ponce Ramos, Carlos. Una injusticia de la historia. México, 1955. xx, 158 p.

An impassioned labor of love, seeking to redeem the reputation of Moctezuma. The author brings little historical apparatus or critical scholarship to his aid.

3345. Pradeau, Alberto Francisco. Don Antonio de Mendoza y la Casa de Moneda de México en 1543. Documentos inéditos publicados con prólogo y notas; y una introducción por Alberto María Carreño. México, Antigua Librería Robredo (Biblioteca histórica mexicana de obras inéditas, 23), 1953. 150 p., facsims.

With related documents, offers the first full printed text of Licenciado Francisco Tello de Sandoval's *Visitación de la Casa de la Moneda de la Ciudad de México . . . año de 1545,* from the Archivo General de Indias, Justicia 277.

3346. ————. Nentuig's "Description of Sonora" (Mid Am, 35:2, Apr. 1953, p. 81-90).

The *Descripción geográfica natural y curiosa de la provincia de Sonora* has several times been printed, as anonymous. Pradeau convincingly identifies it as written by Padre Juan Nentuig (1713-1768) at Guasavas, Sonora, in 1762.

3347. Prisión de franceses en la Nueva España en 1795 (B Arch Gen, México, 24:1, enero-marzo 1953, p. 91-110).

Documents, contributed by "R. G." Aside from their value for the announced topic, they suggest something of the rather large proportion of foreign population in northern and central Mexico.

3348. Ramírez Flores, José. Sobre la *Nueva Galicia* de Arregui (Hist Mex, 2:3, enero-marzo 1953, p. 421-431).

A critical examination of the history published in Sevilla, in 1946, from a manuscript in the Biblioteca del Palacio, Madrid.

3349. Raup, Halleck F., and William B. Pounds, Jr. Northernmost Spanish frontier in California as shown by the distribution of geographic names (Calif Hist Soc Q, 32:1, Mar. 1953, p. 43-48, map).

Concerns the whole coast of the present state, and the interior to somewhat north of present-day Sacramento. The technique is interesting.

3350. Rebullida, Pablo de. Letter . . . to the Venerable Antonio Margil de Jesús, O. F. M., Urinama, Costa Rica, August 18, 1704 (Americas, Franciscan Hist, 10:1, July 1953, p. 89-92).

'rom the monastery archives in Guatemala and dited by Father Lázaro Lamadrid. Concerns, hiefly, the effort at renewed work among the 'alamancas.

351. **Recinos, Adrián.** Pedro de Alvarado, conquistador de México y Guatemala. México, Fondo de Cultura Económica, 1953. 263 p.

A good narrative biography, based upon study f the considerable amount of relevant documentation which has become available in recent 'ears.

352. Reglamento general de artesanos de la Nueva Guatemala, que la junta comisionada para su formación propone á la general de la Real Sociedad. Por D. Ignacio Beteta en la Nueva Guatemala, Año de 1798 (A Soc Geog Hist Guat, 27:1-4, marzo 1953—dic. 1954, i.e. 1955, p. 264-288).

A reprint, without editorial comment.

353. Relación de los caciques y principales del pueblo de Atitlán, 1° de febrero del año 1571 (A Soc Geog Hist Guat, 26: 3-4, sept.-dic. 1952, i.e. 1955, p. 435-438).

An item from the Muñoz MSS. in the Academy of History, Madrid, vol. 42, fol. 115-118. It has previously been printed in French by Ternaux Compans, Paris, 1838.

354. Relación de los cargos públicos y eclesiásticos desempeñados por individuos de la familia Aycinena y Larrazábal en Guatemala durante la colonia (A Soc Geog Hist Guat, 26:3-4, sept.-dic. 1952, i.e. 1955, p. 445-450).

A document signed by 23 men at Guatemala, Oct. 3, 1820, listing the 62 men of the Aycinena and Larrazábal connection who held offices, from high to low. These had been mostly acquired since an ayuntamiento, dominated by the combine, named don Antonio Larrazábal as Diputado in Madrid, with don José Aycinena there as Consejero de Estado. Variants from another list are indicated.

355. **Rico González, Víctor.** Hacia un concepto de la conquista de México. México, Instituto de Historia (Publ., Serie 1, 29), 1953. 297 p.

An analysis of the work of eight 19th-century historians, including seven Mexicans and Prescott, and an advocacy of a new approach with less bias toward either the Hispanist or Indianist viewpoint.

356. **Robles, Vito Alessio.** La historia de unas fábulas. La fundación y el fundador de Saltillo (Mem Ac Mex Hist, 13:3, julio-sept. 1954, p. 179-196).

The settlement was made about 1578, by Captain Alberto del Canto.

357. **Romero Solano, Luis.** La Nueva

España y las Filipinas (Hist Mex, 3:3, enero-marzo 1954, p. 420-431).

An index of the first four volumes (1718-1768) of the total of 63 bound volumes of the *Ramo de Filipinas* of the Mexican National Archives.

3358. **Ross, Edward Hunter, and Dawson A. Phelps** (eds. and trans.). A journey over the Natchez trace in 1792: a document from the archives of Spain (J Miss Hist, 15:4, Oct. 1953, p. 252-273).

A trip to the Choctaws, March and April, by Stephen Minor of Pennsylvania, a lieutenant in the Spanish army.

3359. **Rowland, Donald W.** (ed.). Spanish information on early English colonization (J South Hist, 20:4, Nov. 1954, p. 530-532).

Translation of a report, undated but undoubtedly the one referred to in a letter of Mar. 28, 1634, on the English in Virginia and *tierra de las Indias mas arriba de la Florida*. It was evidently drawn up in Europe, largely from information sent by the Spanish ambassador in London, and is highly suggestive, for the little information that apparently was available.

3360. **Rubio Mañé, J. Ignacio.** Acusaciones contra el corregidor y teniente general de Veracruz don Diego Ortiz de Larchaga, 1678-1679 (B Arch Gen, México, 24:4, oct.-dic. 1953, p. 701-716).

Four documents on a lawsuit over jurisdiction between the corregidor and Fernando de Solís, who was *castellano* of San Juan de Ulua.

3360a. ————. El Dr. don Diego Vásquez de Mercado, primer obispo de Yucatán del clero secular, 1604-1608 (Mem Ac Mex Hist, 13:4, oct.-dic. 1954, p. 263-270).

Establishes that the bishop was Spanish, not Mexican born, as has been believed, and discusses his career in New Spain and the Philippines until his death in 1616.

3361. ————. Ocupación de la Isla de Términos por los ingleses, 1658-1717 (B Arch Gen, México, 24:2, abril-junio 1953, p. 295-330).

A discussion based on the Spanish and Mexican archives, with much biographical information on officials concerned.

3361a. ————. Política del virrey Flores en la Comandancia General de las Provincias Internas, 1787-1789 (B Arch Gen, México, 24:2, abril-junio 1953, p. 213-257).

Really a history of the Commandancy from origins to Independence, although it centers around the critical problems of Flores.

3362. ————. Proyectos de fundar la Universidad de Guadalajara, 1788 (B

Arch Gen, México, 24:4, oct.-dic. 1953, p. 677-699).
Various documents, with a sketch history of the project from the start of the 18th century.

3362a. ————. La visita del obispo de Yucatán Fray Antonio Alcalde a la provincia de Tabasco, 1764 (B Arch Gen, México, 24:3, julio-sept. 1953, p. 453-470).
Two documents, with a lengthy introductory note.

3363. Rubio Sánchez, Manuel. Apuntes para el estudio del comercio marítimo en la Capitanía General del Reino de Guatemala durante el siglo XVI (Antr Hist Guat, 5:2, junio 1953, p. 63-74).
Bibliographical notes, and documents from the Archivo General del Gobierno of Guatemala.

3363a. Saravia, Atanasio G. El convento de San Juan del Río y Fray Esteban Benítez (Americas, Franciscan Hist, 11:3, Jan. 1955, p. 405-428).
Concerns 17th-century missions in present-day Sonora.

3364. Sedelmayr, Jacobo. Jacobo Sedelmayr, missionary, frontiersman, explorer, in Arizona and Sonora. Four original manuscript narratives, 1744-1751. Translated and annotated by Peter Masten Dunne. Tucson, Ariz. (distributed by Dawson's Book Shop, Los Angeles), 1955. 94 p., maps. (Great Southwest travels series, 1).
Sedelmayr, one of the greatest of the followers of Kino, recounts his several voyages around the head of the Gulf of California.

3364a. Simpson, Lesley Bird. Mexico's forgotten century (Pac Hist R, 22:2, May 1953, p. 113-121).
Points out that the 17th century played a big part in the development of life and institutions, and comments on some of these.

3365. Soler Vidal, José. Pere Fages, descobridor, cronista i governador de la Nova California. México, Ediciones Catalanas de Mexic, 1953. 207 p.
Fages was a prominent figure in the activities on the Sonora and New Mexico border, and in the founding of Upper California.

3365a. Somolinos d'Ardois, Germán. Tras la huella de Francisco Hernández: la ciencia novo-hispana del siglo XVIII (Hist Mex, 4:2, oct.-dic. 1954, 174-197).
Recounts the reaction, in Spain and Mexico in the 18th century, to the rediscovery and printing of Hernández' great Historia natural. A facsimile is included of the 4-page prospectus (Madrid, 1790) which is believed unique.

3366. Spell, Lota M. The first half century of European music in America (Atlante, 1:3, July 1953, p. 158-162).
An undocumented but detailed article, which confuses Mexico with "America."

3366a. Stevenson, Robert. The "Distinguished Maestro" of New Spain: Juan Gutiérrez de Padilla (HAHR, 35:3, Aug. 1955, p. 363-373).
Padilla was director of vocal and instrumental music at the Puebla cathedral from 1629 to his death in 1664. Modern research shows him of a quality to stand with any of the Baroque era in Spain. This article uses the Puebla cathedral archives.

3367. Supresión del oficio de tesorero de la provincia de Costa Rica. Inventario de haberes de la Caja Real de Costa Rica que pasaron a la de Nicaragua, 1635-1637 (R Arch Nac C R, 17:1-6, enero-junio 1953, p. 7-44).

3367a. Susto, Juan Antonio. El precursor de la fundación de la Nueva Ciudad de Panamá fué un portugués (R Hist Am, 39, junio 1955, p. 121-126).
Refers to Gonzalo de Meneses Alencastre e Andrade, called "El Hermano Gonzalo." Gonzalo had been in New Spain for some years before arriving at the old site of Panama in 1669; he promoted the new site after 1670.

3368. Szécsy, Janos de. Santiago de Caballeros de Goathemala, en Almolonga; investigaciones del año 1950. Guatemala, Ministerio de Educación Pública, 1953. 160 p., pl., plans.
Reports upon archaeological investigations of 1950 which seem to establish that the ruins commonly regarded as those of Alvarado's city are not, but more probably are those of the Tlaxcalteca barrio of Santiago.

3368a. Tamaron y Romeral, Pedro. Bishop Tamaron's visitation of New Mexico, 1760. Edited by Eleanor B. Adams. Albuquerque, N. Mex., New Mexican Historical Society (Publ., 15), 1954. 113 p.
Originally published in v. 28 and 29 (1953, 1954) of the New Mexican historical review. The Spanish was edited by Vito Alessio Robles (Mexico, 1937) as Demostración del vastíssimo obispado de la Nueva Vizcaya.

3369. Taracena, Ángel. La obra civilizadora de los frailes dominicanos en el sur de Nueva España (B Soc Mex Geog Est, 76:1-3, julio-dic. 1953, p. 83-131).
Mostly from printed works, but uses valuable scraps from the Archivo del Juzgado de Villa Alta, Oaxaca.

3369a. Tavera Alfaro, Javier. Documentos para la historia del periodismo mexicano, siglo XVIII (Estud Hist Am, 1953, p. 317-344).

3370. Tibesar, Antonine (ed.). A spy's report on the expedition of Jean Ribaut to Florida, 1565 (Americas, Franciscan Hist, 11:4, April 1955, p. 589-592). A detailed report, the result of three days in Dieppe, May 17-19.

3370a. Toscano, Salvador. Cuauhtémoc. México, Fondo de Cultura Económica, 1953. 210 p., illus. Highly popularized account of the life of the son-in-law and successor of Moctezuma, who had become the symbol of Indian resistance to Cortés and of *indianismo* as opposed to *hispanismo*.

3371. Trens, Manuel B. Colegios y universidades. El Colegio de Comendadores Juristas de San Román Nonato (B Arch Gen, México, 25:1, enero-marzo 1954, p. 1-58). Statutes (1691) of the Mercedarian school, and documents on the lawsuit between the school and the Provincial of the Order, from 1686.

3371a. Ulloa Ortiz, Berta (comp.). Catálogo de los fondos del Centro de Documentación del Museo Nacional de Historia. Castillo de Chapultepec. Números 4, 5 (Mem Ac Mex Hist, 12:2, abril-junio 1953, p. 117-144; A Inst Nac Antr Hist, 6, pt. 2 (35), 1952, i.e. 1955, p. 135-171). For the earlier parts of this valuable cataloguing of microfilm records, see *HLAS, no. 18, 1952,* item 3313. Part 4 completes the listing of materials from Monterrey, chiefly for the 17th and 18th century. Part 5 lists materials from the municipal and parish archives of Parral, Chihuahua, from about 1637 to about 1657.

3372. Uribe de Fernández de Córdoba, S. Manuel Orozco y Berra y su *Historia antigua y de la conquista de México* (Estud Hist Am, 1953, p. 517-561). A biography of the author and a critical study of his history with special reference to his sources.

3372a. Valle, Rafael Heliodoro. Bibliografía de Hernán Cortés. México, Jus (Soc. estud. cortesianos, 7), 1953. 269 p. A chronological list, with annotations, of 611 items, probably fairly complete on the writings of Cortés, but far from complete as to writings about him. Part was published, as "Cartas de Cortés" (Hist Mex, 2:4, abril-junio 1953, p. 549-563).

3373. Valle-Arizpe, Artemio de. Juego de cartas. Tradiciones, leyendas y sucedidos del México virreinal. México, Patria, 1953. 222 p.

Popular and semi-factual, like the similar book by the same author, just below.

3373a. ————. Personajes de historia y de leyenda. Tradiciones, leyendas y sucedidos del México virreinal. México, Patria, 1953. 227 p. Popular and semi-factual.

3374. Vásquez de Tapia, Bernardino. Relación de méritos y servicios del conquistador . . . vecino y regidor de esta Gran Ciudad de Tenustitlán, México. Estudio y notas por Jorge Gurría Lacroix. México, Porrúa (Biblioteca José Porrúa Estrada de historia de México, 1), 1953. 147 p.

3374a. Velázquez, María del Carmen. La real fuerza de San Diego de Acapulco (Estud Hist Am, 1953, p. 79-108). A good sketch of the history of the fort, founded in 1615.

3375. Villaseñor Bordes, Rubén. Un obispo y un presidente de audiencia (Hist Mex, 4:1, julio-sept. 1954, p. 99-106). A quarrel over prerogatives, 1678-1693, between Bishop León Garavito of Guadalajara and President Cevallos de Gutiérrez of the Audiencia of Nueva Galicia.

3375a. Vindel, Francisco. El primer libro impreso en América fué para el rezo del Santo Rosario (Méjico, 1532-34). Facsímil, estudios y comentarios. Madrid, Artes Gráf. Faure, 1953. 102 p. In this book, of which 100 numbered copies were printed, this authority upon Spanish incunabula advances the claim that a small primitive prayer book in his possession, without indication of place or printer or date, was in fact printed in Tlaxcala, Mexico, about 1532 to 1534 probably by Pedro Varela, son of a Sevillian printer. Pedro Varela went to New Spain in 1531. The claim is based entirely upon surmise as to what could have happened, plus study of type faces and manner of printing. It has been attacked savagely in Mexico, some only of the resulting articles being entered in this *HLAS*. See item 3200.

3376. ————. Las primeras aeronaves en América fueron de invención española. (México, 1784-1785). Madrid, 1954. 33 p., 11 unnumbered pages of facsimiles. 100 numbered copies, only 50 of which are for sale. Reprinted, with the facsimiles added, from *Revista de aeronáutica,* Madrid, no. 166, October 1954. Using the *Gazeta de México* as sole source, shows that in late 1784 a man was building a small "globo aerostático," and that on Feb. 22, 1785, a man had actually flown one, in Vera Cruz. Others did likewise, later. All such balloons were small and had no passenger. Vindel makes no effort to justify his "primeras" or "incención española." It is in fact evident from his own data that the men active in Spain were at least inspired by events in France and England. As for the question of American priority, men in the vicinity of Philadelphia evidently had information direct from Benjamin Franklin in France and were actively interested by May 1784, and on June 24, 1784, a 13-year-old boy actually ascended some feet from the ground near Baltimore, after the builder of the balloon decided not to risk his own weight.

3376a. Williams, Schafer. The G. R. G. Conway Collection in the Library of Congress: a checklist (HAHR, 35:3, Aug. 1955, p. 386-397).

For some years before his death in 1951 the late Mr. Conway had been distributing his manuscript transcripts and translations among three institutions: the Library of Congress, and the libraries of Aberdeen and Cambridge Universities. Those in the Library of Congress are nearly all upon Englishmen and the Mexican Inquisition in the 16th century.

3377. Wolf, Eric. La formación de la nación: un ensayo de formulación (Cien Soc, 4:21, julio 1953, p. 98-111; 4:22, agosto 1953, p. 146-171).

Concerns the Colonial period of Mexico, especially as to rise of the class structure. The author is much too willing to generalize from works which are themselves generalizations, but he also presents specific data from contemporary sources, including manuscript. The article therefore has real value, though it must be read very critically.

3377a. Wright, Doris Marion. A guide to the Mariano Guadalupe Vallejo Documentos para la Historia de California, 1780-1875. Berkeley, Calif., University of California Press, 1953. 264 p.

A catalogue of the Vallejo papers now in the Bancroft Library. The 36 volumes of the collection comprise: papers addressed to Vallejo and copies of his letters (v. 1-14); military papers, concerning the Presidios of Monterrey, Santa Barbara, San Diego, and San Francisco (v. 15-27); and miscellaneous letters of relatives, friends, and others (v. 28-36). The documents contain interesting data on the military, civil, missionary, economic, and social life of Upper California during the Mexican regime. There is a biography of Vallejo. [R. R. Hill]

3378. Zapatero, Juan Manuel. Del Castillo de San Fernando de Omoa, antigua audiencia de Guatemala (R Indias, Madrid, 13: 52-53, abril-sept. 1953, p. 277-306, illus.).

Based largely upon the resources of the Servicio Histórico Militar, Madrid, and to a lesser degree upon those of the Archivo General Militar, Segovia. Deals with the English attack of 1779 and with that of Aury in 1820, and with conditions around those times. The four plans reproduced are dated from 1769 to 1779.

WEST INDIES

3378a. Barrera y Domingo, Francisco Reflexiones histórico, físico, naturales médico, quirúrgicas. . . . Habana, Ediciones C. R., 1953. 514 p.

Written in 1798. Useful primarily for the historian of medical knowledge, but has value on the status of the Negro in the West Indies.

3379. Beltrán de Heredia, Vicente. La autenticidad de la bula "in apostolatus culmine," base de la Universidad de Santo Domingo, puesta fuera de discusión. Ciudad Trujillo, Universidad de Santo Domingo (Publ., Serie 9, 99:3), 1955. 56 p

One more item in a long series devoted to questions concerned with the papal bull of 1538 which is the key document in the claim of the Dominican Republic to have had the first university of the New World.

3379a. Charlier, Étienne D. Aperçu sur la formation historique de la nation haïtienne. Port-au-Prince, Les Presses Libres 1954. 334 p.

A new and sometimes controversial look at the early history of Haiti. Preface by Thomas H. Lechaud. Reviewed in *Conjonction*, 54, déc. 1954, p. 44-45. [M. Cook]

3380. Debien, Gabriel. Les colons de Saint-Domingue et la Revolution. Essai sur le Club Massiac, août 1789-août 1792. Paris, Colin, (La société coloniale aux XVIIe et XVIIIe siècles, 2), 1953. 411 p.

The Club Massiac, named from its meeting place, was the organization of proprietors of lands in St. Domingue who lived in Paris and carried on propaganda and lobbying in protection of their interests. It was for a time quite influential, the main opposition to the Société des Amis des Noirs.

3380a. ————. Les colons de Saint-Domingue refugiés à Cuba, 1793-1815 (R Indias, Madrid, 13:54, oct.-dic. 1953, p. 559-604; 14:55-56, enero-junio 1954, p. 11-36).

The great exodus from French St. Domingue to Cuba—chiefly to the Santiago area—was from 1803, but there was some before. The immigrants were somewhat persecuted during the years of Napoleonic control of Spain, and thousands moved on to the U. S., or even went to the former Spanish part of the island under Ferrand. Many however, remained in Cuba, where they were influential, especially as to the growth of coffee.

3381. ————. Esprit colonial et esprit d'autonomie à St. Domingue au XVIIIe siècle. 2. ed. Paris, Larose, 1954. 55 p.

Deals with the period from 1690 to about 1793 but as to the earlier half century depends largely on printed studies by others. The later years have independent value, being based on the great variety of manuscripts and contemporary imprints that the author is accustomed to use.

3381a. Dermigny, L., and G. Debien. La révolution aux Antilles: marins et colons; marchands et petits blancs; août 1790-août 1792 (R Hist Am Fr, 8:4, mars 1955, p. 496-517; 9:1, juin 1955, p. 55-73).
Two documents about the revolution in Martinique, one an anonymous letter from Castries, St. Lucie, Dec. 28, 1790, the other a "Journal maritime" of Commandeur de Villevielle, of the frigate *Didon,* September 1790-September 1792. The items come from two provincial archives in France. To be continued.

3382. Dorsinville, Luc. Toussaint Louverture, général haïtien. Port-au-Prince, Imprimerie de l'État, 1953. 63 p., illus. [R. McNicoll]

3282a. Exquemelin, Alexandre Olivier. Historia de los aventureros, filibusteros y bucaneros de América. Traducida de una ed. francesa de La Sirène, París, por C. Armando Rodríguez. Introducción y bosquejo biográfico del traductor por Ramón Lugo Lovatón. Ciudad Trujillo, Montalvo (Archivo General de la Nación, 11), 1953. 157 p.
Reprinted here from v. 15 of the *Boletín del Archivo General de la Nación* (Dominican Republic). It reproduces only the first volume of the original—which has all the material upon Santo Domingo—from the Paris, La Sirène, 1920 edition, which in turn came from the Paris 1744 edition.

3383. Fouchard, Jean. Les joies de la table à St. Domingue (R Soc Haïtienne Hist Geog, 27:97, avril 1955, p. 59-63).
Chiefly upon the 18th century. Rather a slight study, but uses manuscript from several provincial libraries in France.

3383a. ————. Les marrons du syllabaire. Port-au-Prince, Deschamps, 1953. 167 p.
A former editor of *La relève* and *Haïti-journal,* Jean Fouchard moved to Paris shortly after the fall of the Estimé government. He then began his researches, in public libraries and private collections, on the intellectual and cultural history of colonial St. Domingue. This is the first published result of his fruitful labors. In it M. Fouchard studies "various aspects of the problem of instruction and education of slaves and freedmen in Santo Domingo." Advertisements of slave sales and descriptions of fugitives often designated Negroes who, in addition to possessing specialized skills in music, carpentry, tailoring, or even medicine, could read and write. The ABC's, taught by a kindly priest, a sympathetic master, or an educated freedman, courageous enough to defy the unwritten law prohibiting this kind of instruction for slaves, reached a larger number of Negroes than has usually been imagined. M. Fouchard supports

this thesis by photostatic copies of letters and documents, as well as an appendix of 23 pages. The book is appropriately and eloquently prefaced by Dr. Price-Mars. [M. Cook]

3384. Franco, José Luciano (comp.). Documentos para la historia de Haití en el Archivo Nacional. Habana, Archivo Nacional (Publ., 37), 1954. 259 p.
Documents dealing with the relations of Cuba and Haiti during the struggle for and early years of Haitian independence (1790-1844), selected from the National Archive of Cuba and published in connection with the celebration of the sesquicentennial of Haitian independence. They relate to the revolution and its influence on the Caribbean islands. Much is revealed as to the attitude of the Spanish colonial authorities, especially regarding slavery and the slave trade. The introduction gives an interesting account of events and the relations between the Spanish authorities of Cuba and the French of Haiti. [R. R. Hill]

3384a. Incháustegui, J. Marino. La gran expedición inglesa contra las Antillas mayores. T. 1. El plan antillano de Cromwell (1651-1655). México, Gráf. Panamericana, 1953. 655, ccxlviii p.
An enormously detailed compilation, with a documentary appendix of over 200 pages at the back. Many of the documents and such features as the extensive biography of Cromwell lack novelty for persons acquainted with the English studies, but many of the English and most of the Spanish documents are important for everyone. This first volume discusses events only to the arrival of Barbados and the start toward Santo Domingo.

3385. Institut Français d'Haïti. Commemoration du cent-cinquantième anniversaire de l'indépendance d'Haïti (R Hist Colonies, 41:142, 1. trimestre 1954, p. 132-161).
A list of an extensive loan exhibition (1796-1805) of manuscript and printed documents, engravings, maps, and coins and medals, partly from private collectors but also from government depositories in France.

3385a. Jean-Baptiste, St. Victor. Le Fondateur devant l'histoire. Port-au-Prince, Eben-Ezer, 1954. 326 p.
With a preface by Colbert Bonhomme, this is an apologia—at times rhetorical—for Jean-Jacques Dessalines. It begins with 1803 and justifies Dessalines's domestic and foreign policies. No new documents. Reviewed in *Conjonction,* 54, déc. 1954, p. 45-47. [M. Cook]

3386. Karraker, Cyrus H. Piracy was a business. Rindge, N. H., Richard R. Smith, 1953. 244 p.
A cross between a fairly scholarly effort to debunk certain aspects of piracy during its great days in the Caribbean, and an effort to sell a "pirate" book by the usual popularized and overdramatized methods of writing. Has only English language materials, but is not entirely without value.

3386a. Lamb, Ursula. Cristóbal de Tapia versus Nicolás de Ovando. A residencia fragment of 1509 (HAHR, 33:3, Aug. 1953, p. 427-441).

The earliest residencia known to exist, and the first extant record of a case heard in the colonies based on the testimony of eye witnesses, is here discussed. The suit began in Santo Domingo in October 1509, and was sent to the Consejo de Indias for decision on Feb. 23, 1510. It directly concerns a rather trivial question of social standing, governmental practices, and even the postal system and land titles.

3387. Laurent, Gerard M. Toussaint Louverture à travers sa correspondance (1794-1798). Madrid, Industrias Gráf. España, 1953. 480 p.

Very useful. [R. McNicoll]

3387a. Le Riverend Brusone, Julio. Las ideas económicas en el *Papel periódico de la Havana* (1790-1805) (Estud Hist Am, 1953, p. 9-29).

Confined rather closely to the subject matter stated in the title, not to facts of economic history. Shows that the periodical was distinctly an organ of the Enlightenment.

3388. McLarty, Robert Neil. Jamaica prepares for invasion, 1779 (Carib Q, 4:1, Jan. 1955, p. 62-67).

Mainly, a letter from the papers of Lord Shelburne, written by Samuel Jones, Kingston, Jamaica, on Sept. 10, 1779. Danger was seen from Spain as well as from France.

3388a. Massio, Roger. Les Bigordans à St. Domingue au XVIIIᵉ siècle (A Midi, 64:18, avril 1952, p. 151-158; 66:1, jan. 1954, p. 21-46; R Soc Haïtienne Hist Geog, 24:91, oct. 1953, p. 23-39; 27:97, avril 1955, p. 5-21).

From National and local French archives, discusses the colonists of French St. Domingue who were connected with the French province of Bigorre, as to personal and social identity, manner of life, and related aspects. Chiefly for the later 18th century. There is a related item with another title (*R Soc Haïtienne Geog*, 27:98, juillet 1955, p. 65-75).

3389. ⸻. Chronique des sources privées de l'histoire coloniale dans le Pays de Bigorre (R Soc Haïtienne Hist Geog, 24:89, avril 1953, p. 19-36).

Notes on five family archives, with papers on one or another of the French Antilles, 1729-1830, but mostly for the later 18th century to about 1815. Unlike many such lists, has papers with value for the early 19th-century history of Guadeloupe, which are much scarcer than for Saint Domingue.

3389a. ⸻. Un dossier de plantation de St. Domingue, 1745-1823 (R Soc Haïtienne Hist Geog, 27:98, juillet 1955, p. 1-21; 28:99, oct. 1955, p. 55-62; 29: 100, janv. 1956, 1-32).

Data from the letters of the brothers Terrien, agents in Saint Domingue of the absentee owner Navailles-Bonnas, of the Plantation Seguineau-Navailles. They largely concern the history of the period 1790-1798, and the "Question de l'indemnité, 1823-1829."

3390. ⸻. Inventaire de deux habitations à St. Domingue: la habitation de Thèze; la habitation de Lanzac (R Soc Haïtienne Hist Geog, 24:90, juillet 1953, p. 17-29).

Summaries of inventories for the coffee plantation of Thèze, Dec. 8, 1792, and the sugar plantation of Lanzac, probably of Oct. 1788.

3390a. Maza, Diego de la. Memorial . . . sobre el estado del Convento y Universidad de los Dominicos en la Isla Española. . . . Ciudad Trujillo, Universidad de Santo Domingo (Publ., Serie 9, 93:2), 1954. 51 p.

Reproduced from the unique copy in the William L. Clements Library, Ann Arbor, Michigan, and reprinted here from v. 18, 1953, of the *Anales de la Universidad de Santo Domingo.* The Memorial was printed in Madrid, 1693, and concerns religious and intellectual affairs in the colony, with special emphasis upon their low state.

3391. Mejía Ricart, Gustavo Adolfo. Historia de Santo Domingo. V. 6. Ciudad Trujillo, Pol, 1953. 613, li p.

Like earlier volumes of this work, under publication since 1948, this is a massive compilation, mostly from printed sources and with notes often longer than the text. This volume deals with the "era colonial," 1608-1801. It has much strength on foreign aspects, and prints many documents, especially of the 18th century, in their entirety. See HLAS, no. 14, 1948, item 1886, and later issues of the HLAS.

3391a. Nieto y Cortadellas, Rafael. Dignidades nobiliarias en Cuba. Madrid, Ediciones Cultura Hispánica, 1954. 669 p.

Genealogical data regarding persons born in Cuba or residing in the island who held titles of nobility. There is full information on the granting of the title, with dates of the corresponding decrees and a listing of all holders with extensive biographical data respecting each one. The sources of the information are given. The bibliography includes the archives and libraries where searches were made, as well as the published works consulted. [R. R. Hill]

3392. Pietersz, J. L., and H. P. Jacobs (eds.). Two Spanish documents of 1656. Being two letters from the last Spanish Governor of Jamaica, edited and translated by . . ., with a commentary by S. A. G. Taylor (Jam Hist R, 2:2, Oct. 1952, p. 11-35, fold. map).

Concerns Governor Isasi's successful ambush raid of the spring of 1656. The map is modern, and valuable for understanding the events.

3392a. Ratekin, Mervyn. The early sugar

industry in Española (HAHR, 34:1, Feb. 1954, p. 1-19).
A very thorough reconstruction so far as that can be made from printed materials. Quite good for the earliest years; rather spotty for the 16th century as a whole.

3393. Recherches collectives. Chronique documentaire pour une nouvelle histoire coloniale. Les papiers privés et l'Amérique française (R Hist Am Fr, 6:4, mars 1953, p. 536-559; 7:1, juin 1953, p. 88-109; 7:2, sept. 1953, p. 259-286).
A study signed by eight well-known students of French American history, calling for renewed and revisionist study, beginning with the Antilles, and listing bodies of private documentation known to be available.

3393a. Recopilación diplomática relativa a las colonias española y francesa de la isla de Santo Domingo (B Arch Gen, Ciudad Trujillo, año 15, 15:72, enero-marzo 1952, p. 62-78, and issues thereafter to año 18, 18:86, julio-sept. 1955, p. 256-274).
For earlier portions, see HLAS, no. 17, 1951, item 1556. The portions published in the issues named above deal with the years 1685 to 1717. To be continued.

3394. Richard, Robert. À propos de Saint Domingue: la monnaie dans l'économie coloniale, 1674-1803 (R Hist Colonies, 41:142, 1. trim. 1954, p. 22-46).
Until 1803, when Rochambeau imposed use of the French decimal system currency, what money was used was often foreign, and if not was based on the livre, and on the imaginary "écu" worth three livres. But in fact not much money was used. Almost any commodity including indigo or slaves might be quoted in transactions, but most transactions were carried on in terms of tobacco or, from about 1715, in terms of sugar.

3394a. Rodríguez Demorizi, Emilio. Acerca del tratado de Ryswick (Clío, 22:100, julio-sept. 1954, p. 127-132).
Demonstrates by documents of 1700 and 1767 that the Spanish Crown did not regard the treaty of 1697 as having given France title to anything in Hispaniola.

3395. ————. La construcción de barcos en Santo Domingo (Clío, 22:100, julio-sept. 1954, p. 121-123).
Notes upon the 16th and 18th centuries, not enormously important by themselves, but a valuable supplement to those that were furnished by Father Cipriano Utrera in the latter's edition of Sánchez Valverde (Ciudad Trujillo, 1947). For the latter, see HLAS, no. 13, 1947, item 1292.

3395a. ————. El culto de Las Mercedes (Clío, 22:101, oct.-dic. 1954, p. 226-243).

Data largely of the 17th and earlier 18th centuries, about Nuestra Señora de las Mercedes of Santo Domingo, "única Patrona" of the city and the island from 1610, with her fiesta in September.

3396. San Juan Bautista de Puerto Rico (city). Cabildo. Actas. T. 3. 1761-1767. San Juan, 1954. 261 p.
Like the preceding volumes, has extensive indices of names and subjects. For those volumes, see HLAS, no. 15, 1949, item 1455, and HLAS, no. 16, 1950, item 1546.

3396a. Smelser, Marshall. The campaign for the Sugar Islands, 1759. A study of amphibious warfare. Foreword by Samuel Eliot Morison. Chapel Hill, N. C., University of North Carolina Press (Publ. for the Institute of Early American History and Culture at Williamsburg, Virginia), 1955. 212 p., map.
Good monograph upon the British operations against the French West Indies, so far as one can be written depending largely upon British sources. The importance of the French records is minimized for reasons (explained in the preface) which hardly seem satisfactory.

3397. Sobre erección de la Santa Iglesia Catedral del Obispado de Cuba y creación y distribución de diezmos (B Arch Nac, Habana, 51-52, enero 1952-dic. 1953, i.e. 1954, p. 255-261).
Order of Bishop of Santiago de Cuba, Juan de Umite, dated Valladolid, Jan. 8, 1523, and incorporating the Papal Brief of Apr. 28, 1522.

3397a. Thornton, A. P. The Modyfords and Morgan (Jam Hist R, 2:2, Oct. 1952, p. 36-60).
Letters of Sir James Modyford to Sir Andrew King in London, on the affairs of Jamaica and the whole Caribbean, 1667-1672. This is a completely new source for the history of the area, found in a most unexpected depository.

3398. ————. Spanish slave ships in the English West Indies, 1660-1685 (HAHR, 35:3, Aug. 1955, p. 374-385).
Primarily from British sources, but good British sources, and a good discussion of the interplay between the desire to attract Spanish buyers to Jamaica and the struggle over the monopoly of the English African companies.

3398a. Trouillot, Henock. La condition des nègres domestiques à St. Domingue (R Soc Haïtienne Hist Geog, 28:99, oct. 1955, p. 4-34).
From contemporary accounts including the 18th-century Haitian press, shows that domestics had in practice considerable privilege and freedom from ordinary discipline, compared to the field workers.

3399. Utrera, Cipriano de (ed.). La parroquia de Higuey, 1778-1782 (Clío, 21:95, enero-abril 1953, p. 56-65).

Part of an incomplete expediente of 1784, with detailed figures upon the revenues of the parish.

3399a. **Verschueren, R.** Saint-Domingue. La sucrerie Foache à Jean-Rabel (R Soc Haïtienne Hist Geog, 24:91, oct. 1953, p. 1-11; 27:97, avril 1955, p. 22-39; 27: 98, juillet 1955, p. 22-64).
Family activities in Saint-Domingue from about 1763 to 1804, but most of the new detail is upon the *sucrerie* in the 1770's and 1780's.

SOUTH AMERICA
(EXCEPT BRAZIL)

CHARLES GIBSON

The publications in Spanish South American colonial history reviewed below include the regular offerings of 1953 plus a substantial portion of those of 1954. Works of more than regional import occur mainly in European and North American journals, such as *Missionalia hispanica, Estudios americanos, Revista de Indias, The Hispanic American historical review,* and the new UNESCO journal, *Cahiers d'histoire mondiale.* The tendency of South American periodicals to confine attention to matters of limited local history continues—occasionally, as in Peru, with an abundant production of high quality. Monographs and longer writings are less numerous than in the past few years but are exceptionally strong in the ecclesiastical history of Peru, with important work by Rubén Vargas Ugarte, Fernando de Armas Medina, and Antonine Tibesar. The material as a whole reflects emphases upon exploration, mission labors, and prerevolutionary reform as the principal themes of current historical interest.

GENERAL

3410. **Caldas y Tenorio, Francisco José de.** El códice original de los estudios de . . . en fácsimil . . . en la Biblioteca General de la Universidad de Antioquia. Medellín, Colombia, Universidad de Antioquia, 1953. 1 v. (various pagings)
Legible facsimile edition of notes and observations by one of the foremost scientific observers of the Spanish colonies. Astronomical statistics, geometric measurements, and sketches and notes on natural history. *Ca.* 1800.

3411. **Greve, Ernesto.** El conquistador

Francisco de Aguirre. Comentarios y complementos al libro del Pbro. Luis Silva Lezaeta. Santiago, Fondo Histórico y Bibliográfico J. T. Medina, 1953. 204 p.
The author's intention is systematically to correct, amplify, and bring to date the work *El conquistador Francisco de Aguirre* of Luis Silva Lezaeta, published in 1904 and republished by the Fondo Histórico y Bibliográfico J. T. Medina in 1953 (see item 3415). Some fresh light is cast on the activities of Aguirre as a conquistador and administrative officer in Peru, Chile, and La Plata.

3412. **Levillier, Roberto.** Vespucio, descubridor del Plata, en su V centenario (R Indias, Madrid, 13:54, oct.-dic. 1953, p. 515-525).
A re-expression of the writer's well-known thesis on the Vespucci question focussed on the Platine discovery.

3413. **Losada, Ángel.** *Los tesoros del Perú y La apologia contra Sepúlveda,* obras inéditas de Fr. Bartolomé de las Casas (B Real Ac Hist, 133:2, abril-junio 1953, p. 269-333).
Los tesoros del Perú, a rare item in the Las Casas bibliography, is here summarized with partial translations into Spanish. A series of philosophical propositions proves the mortal sin incurred in the looting of Indian graves and the moral obligation of restitution. Las Casas' *La apologia contra Sepúlveda* is briefly commented upon, preparatory to its publication.

3414. **Martínez, Manuel Ma.** Las Casas, historiador. I. Valor histórico de la *Destrucción de las Indias* (Ciencia Tomista, 79:244, julio-sept. 1952, p. 441-468).
A favorable estimate of the *Destrucción de las Indias* as a work of history despite its exaggerations. The evaluation is soberly written but fails to contribute new data or insights.

3415. **Silva Lezaeta, Luis.** El conquistador Francisco de Aguirre. Santiago, Fondo Histórico y Bibliográfico J. T. Medina, 1953, i.e. 1954. 489 p.
Republication of the standard work first issued in 1904. Chapters on Aguirre's exploits in Europe, Peru, Upper Peru, Chile, and Tucuman, with genealogical appendices. Based principally upon Medina documentation.

NEW GRANADA AND VENEZUELA

3416. **Altolaguirre y Duvale, Ángel de** (ed.). Relaciones geográficas de la gobernación de Venezuela, 1767-68. Caracas, Ediciones de la Presidencia de la República de Venezuela, 1954. xli, 332 p.
A collection of interesting descriptive documents of the 18th century, some heretofore unpublished, others extracted from the *Descripción exacta de la provincia de Venezuela* (1765) of José Luis de Cisneros. The documents are principally of the standard *relación geográfica* type with data on a variety of local topics.

3417. **Arcaya, Pedro Manuel.** Historia del estado Falcón, república de Venezuela. 1a. parte. Época colonial. T. 1. Caracas, Tipografía La Nación, 1953. 275 p.
Substantially a re-edition of the work originally published in 1919.

3418. **Arráiz, Antonio.** Historia de Venezuela. T. 1. Antes de la independencia. Texto para la enseñanza secundaria y normal. Caracas, Fundación Eugenio Mendoza, 1954. 306 p., illus.
A school text written with simple clarity and attention to the chronological course of events.

3419. **Ballesteros Gaibrois, Manuel.** "El Antijovio" de Jiménez de Quesada (Bolívar, Bogotá, 22, agosto 1953, p. 169-202; 23, sept. 1953, p. 333-358).
A detailed and scholarly study of a manuscript soon to be published, containing notices of Jiménez de Quesada's opponent, Paulo Jovio, bibliographic commentaries on the manuscript, textual history, sources, and stylistic analysis. The work is a 16th-century defense of Spanish policy, incidentally shedding light on the life of the conquistador of New Granada.

3420. **Carvajal, Alberto.** De la conquista a la liberación. Benalcázar y Cayzedo y Cuero. Cali, Colombia, Carvajal, 1953. 241 p.
Biographical jottings on the conquistador Sebastián de Benalcázar and the revolutionary leader Joaquín de Cayzedo y Cuero.

3421. **Dugand, Armando.** El primer arribo de Humboldt a la Nueva Granada (R Ac Colomb Cien Exact Fís Nat, 9:35, julio 1954, p. 210-213).
Indicates that Baron von Humboldt first landed in New Granada in 1800 rather than, as customarily believed, 1801.

3422. **Friede, Juan.** Breve reseña biográfica del segoviano Don Juan del Valle, primer obispo de Popayán (Bolívar, Bogotá, 19, mayo 1953, p. 707-723).
One of the few accounts of the life of the first bishop of Popayan. It summarizes and anticipates a much fuller study in preparation by the author.

3423. **Giraldo Jaramillo, Gabriel.** Bibliografía selecta de Nariño. Bogotá, Sucre, 1953. 24 p.
Brief statement on the bibliography of Antonio Nariño.

3424. **Groot, José Manuel.** Historia eclesiástica y civil de Nueva Granada. Bogotá, Ministerio de Educación Nacional, Ediciones de la revista Bolívar (Biblioteca de autores colombianos, 57-61), 1953. 5 t. 788, 692, 766, 703, 622 p.
Republication of the celebrated history of José Manuel Groot, from the second edition published in Bogota in 1889.

3425. **Jaramillo Arango, Jaime.** Don José Celestino Mutis y las expediciones botánicas españolas del siglo XVIII al Nuevo Mundo (R Ac Colomb Cien Exact Fís Nat, 9:33-34, mayo 1953, p. 14-31).
A catalogue with commentary of a number of 18th-century scientific expeditions and an evaluation of the role of New Granada in the contributions to scientific knowledge.

3426. **Lacas, M. M.** A sixteenth-century German colonizing venture in Venezuela (Americas, Franciscan Hist, 9:3, Jan. 1953, p. 275-290).
A succinct account of the German period in Venezuela with a qualitative comparison of German and Spanish colonizing practices.

3427. **Lecuna, Vicente.** Los padres de Bolívar (B Ac Nac Hist, Caracas, 36:143, julio-sept. 1953, p. 258-278).
Biographical notes and published documents on Juan Vicente Bolívar and María de la Concepción Palacios y Blanco, parents of Simón Bolívar. The documentation contains material on the Minas de Aroa.

3427a. **Ortega Ricaurte, Enrique,** and **Ana Rueda Briceño.** Historia documental de Choco. Bogotá, Departamento de Biblioteca y Archivos Nacionales, 1954. 293 p., illus.
A collection of documents, mostly from the Archivo Nacional, dealing with the history of the department of Choco. It includes royal orders, commissions, memorials, reports, descriptions, and instructions, all of the Spanish colonial period. [R. R. Hill]

3428. **Ospina Vásquez, L.** Organización colonial del comercio (U Antioquia, 28:111, marzo-mayo 1953, p. 423-445).
An important document summarizing the commercial reform for Venezuela advocated by Álvarez de Abreu in the early 18th century. The author, a member of the Consejo de Indias, served as alcalde visitador in Caracas and the province of Venezuela. The document, from the Archivo Nacional, Colombia, is probably an abstract of the full report, dealing with foreign intrusions, coast guards, goods, prices, and remedial measures.

3429. **Porras Troconis, G.** Cartagena hispánica 1533 a 1810. Bogotá, Ministerio de Educación Nacional, Ediciones de la revista Bolívar (Biblioteca de autores colombianos, 81), 1954. 342 p.
An urban history partly chronological and partly topical. The strategic situation of the city of Cartagena is related to its form and to the dramatic incidents of its military history. A work based in part on unpublished documents, although the apparatus of citation is meager.

3430. **Restrepo Tirado, Ernesto.** Historia

de la provincia de Santa Marta. Bogotá, Ministerio de Educación Nacional, Ediciones de la revista *Bolívar* (Biblioteca de autores colombianos, 63, 64), 1953. 2 t. 438, 408 p.

New edition of a diligently executed history of colonial Santa Marta, largely confined to political-military affairs and organized by successive administrations. Based principally upon materials in the Archivo General de Indias.

3431. Sánchez Pedrote, Enrique. Gil y Lemos y su Memoria sobre el Nuevo Reino de Granada (B Hist Antig, 40:465-467, julio-sept. 1953, p. 424-460).

Publication of the text of the *Memoria* (1789) of Viceroy Francisco Gil Taboada y Lemos to his successor. Though in office only six months the viceroy issued a full report of expenses and income, agriculture, *reducciones,* and related topics. Concludes with a statistical compilation of the troops of New Granada.

3432. Uribe Uribe, Lorenzo. La expedición botánica del Nuevo Reino de Granada: su obra y sus pintores (R Ac Colomb Cien Exact Fís Nat, 9:33-34, mayo 1953, p. 1-13).

Commentary on the 18th-century botanical expedition of José Celestino Mutis to New Granada with an assessment of its achievement and an enumeration of its contributing artists.

3433. Vargas, Marco Tulio. Don Pedro Pinto Vellorino (B Hist Antig, 40:459-461, enero-marzo 1953, p. 41-46).

Summary data on the conquistador and town founder in New Granada. Late 16th and early 17th centuries.

3434. Vargas, Pedro Fermín de. Pensamientos políticos y memorias sobre la población del nuevo reino de Granada. Bogotá, Banco de la República (Archivo de la economía nacional, 10), 1953. 162 p.

Transcription of a lengthy document from the Biblioteca Nacional of Bogota, together with other materials relating to New Granada in the late 18th century. The principal item, the *Pensamientos políticos* of Pedro Fermín de Vargas, provides a survey of agricultural, commercial, and mining economies of the viceroyalty. Other pieces deal with population, building, guaco, and prices in the years 1739 and 1791. First published completely in the *Biblioteca popular de cultura,* no. 53, Bogota, 1944.

3434a. Venezuela. Ministerio de Hacienda. Legislación real sobre hacienda para las provincias coloniales venezolanas. Caracas, 1954. 304 p.

Two long documents, one establishing the intendancy system in Venezuela (1776), the other enumerating the royal instructions for intendants in New Spain (1786). The latter were extended to Venezuela in 1787.

QUITO, PERU, UPPER PERU

3435. Archivo de documentos de la Casa Real de Moneda (B Soc Geog Hist Potosí, 40:12, junio 1953, p. 203-213).

Titles of documents of the mid-18th century relating to the *casa de moneda.*

3436. Armas Medina, Fernando de. Cristianización del Perú (1532-1600). Sevilla, Escuela de Estudios Hispano-Americanos de Sevilla (75), 1953. xxvii, 636 p.

A comprehensive work on the 16th-century conversion of Incaic peoples and the establishment of a Christian society. The mission labors of the pertinent orders receive attention, together with evangelical methods, sacraments, and the social consequences of Christianization, e.g., alcoholism and geographical redistribution. Uniformly adopts a Spanish point of view and uses standard published material with some new documentation from the Archivo General de Indias. Concludes with a thoughtful essay on Christian-pagan *sincretismo religioso,* proposing the essentially Christian character of the Indian of colonial times and assigning a secondary role to pagan survivals.

3437. Basto Girón, Luis J. Las mitas de Huamanga y Huancavelica (Perú Indíg, 5:13, dic. 1954, p. 215-242).

Publication, with editorial commentary, of a documentary historical analysis of Indian labor systems written in the early 19th century by Martín José de Mugica. Contains numerous details of *mita* operation, especially of the late 18th and early 19th centuries.

3438. Billi di Sandorno, Amalia. Los descendientes del conquistador del Perú (R Indias, Madrid, 13:51, enero-marzo 1953, p. 112-116).

A document of 1622 perpetuating the office of regidor in the city of Trujillo within the Pizarro family.

3439. Una botica colonial (R Arch Hist Cuzco, 4:4, 1953, p. 263-282).

An interesting apothecary's inventory from Cuzco, dated 1618. Some 500 drugs are listed.

3439a. Bustamante de la Fuente, Manuel J. Mis ascendientes. Edición privada. Lima, 1955. 717 p. & illus.

An extensive genealogy, partially annotated, with accounts of a number of prominent individuals in colonial Peru. Documentary appendices.

3440. Canedo, Lino G. New data regarding the origins of the Franciscan missions in Peru, 1532-1569 (Americas, Franciscan Hist, 10:4, Jan. 1953, p. 315-358).

An important commentary on Peruvian Franciscan history, with documents from the Archivo General de Indias on the expedition of Fray Francisco de Vitoria and the commissaryships of Fray Hernando de Armellones and Fray Luis Zapata.

3441. **Cardenal de Iracheta, Manuel.** Vida de Gonzalo Pizarro. Madrid, Ediciones Cultura Hispánica (Col. Hombres e ideas), 1953. 127 p.
A perfunctory sketch of the career of Gonzalo Pizarro with adulatory commentary.

3442. Cédulas reales recibidas de 1768 a 1823 (R Arch Hist Cuzco, 4:4, 1953, p. 300-309).
Statement on the royal cedulas received in the Audiencia of Cuzco from 1768 to 1823. The content of each document is cursorily noted.

3443. **Costales Samaniego, Alfredo.** Los jesuítas en la presidencia de Quito (Mus Hist, 6:20, junio 1954, p. 125-135).
Brief exposition of Jesuit history in Quito, to which is appended a list of expelled Jesuits whose deaths occurred prior to 1784.

3444. ————. Riobamba, la ciudad mártir del siglo XVIII (Mus Hist, 6:19, marzo 1954, p. 77-93).
Account of the great earthquake of 1797.

3445. Cuenca: acta de fundación de la ciudad. Introducción y nota de Víctor Manuel Albornoz. Edición conmemorativa del tricentésimo nonagésimo séptimo aniversario. Cuenca, Ecuador, 1954. lx p.
Text of the *Actas de fundación* of Cuenca and related documents referring to the first buildings and land grants and the establishment of the municipal *cabildo* (1556-1557).

3446. **Cuesta, Luisa.** Testamento de D. Pedro Gasca, pacificador del Perú, y la apertura del mismo (R Indias, Madrid, 13:51, enero-marzo 1953, p. 119-122).
First publication of Pedro Gasca's will (1577), from a document in the Archivo Catedral de Palencia.

3447. Diez documentos del siglo XVII (R Arch Hist Cuzco, 4:4, 1953, p. 211-262).
Miscellaneous documents concerning the social and economic history of Peru in the 17th century. All are published in full.

3448. Documentos del siglo XVI (Perú Indíg, 5:12, dic. 1953, p. 143-152).
Miscellaneous 16th-century documents from the Archivo Histórico of Cuzco including regulations of Indian services and the testaments of Fray Domingo de Betanzos and Mancio Sierra de Leguízamo.

3449. Documentos del siglo XVI (R Arch Hist Cuzco, 4:4, 1953, p. 59-102).
Documents on a variety of subjects of the latter half of the 16th century. Indian services, local customs, residencias, taxes, and many other matters are touched upon.

3450. **Escandell Bonet, Bartolomé.** Repercusión de la piratería inglesa en el pensamiento peruano del siglo XVI (R Indias, Madrid, 13:51, enero-marzo 1953, p. 81-88).
An intensely interesting and wholly unexpected reaction to the British acts of piracy is discovered in 16th-century Peru, namely admiration for the British. Anglophilism is explained by the author in terms of a lower-class antipathy to Spanish administration.

3451. **Gangotena y Jijón, C. de.** Documentos históricos (B Ac Nac Hist, Quito, 34:83, enero-junio 1954, p. 131-135).
Publication of an important cedula dated at Aranjuez in 1795 and describing a large number of categories of *gracias al sacar* with the *tarifa* appropriate to each.

3451a. **Hanke, Lewis.** La villa imperial de Potosí. Un capítulo inédito en la historia del Nuevo Mundo. Sucre, Bolivia, Universidad de San Francisco Xavier (Biblioteca Universidad de San Francisco Xavier, Serie historiográfica, 2), 1954. 81 p.
Suggests the problems and outlines the data and bibliography in the light of which a definitive history of Potosi will be written.

3452. Índice de escrituras públicas del Cuzco, año 1560 (R Arch Hist Cuzco, 4:4, 1953, p. 5-58).
The index contains précis of notarial documents in the Archivo Histórico of Cuzco. Sales, receipts, payments, powers, debts, and wills comprise the bulk of the materials. All are dated 1560.

3453. Informe sobre escrituras públicas existentes en el archivo notarial del Cuzco, correspondientes al siglo XVI (R Arch Hist Cuzco, 4:4, 1953, p. 115-168).
Summary enumeration of notarial documents recorded in Cuzco from 1561 to the end of the 16th century. The materials are abundant, important, and in large part unknown.

3454. **Lastres, Juan B.** El pensamiento científico-natural en el Perú a fines del siglo XVIII (R U, Cuzco, 42:105, 2. semestre 1953, p. 89-100).
Discursive commentary on the association between European thought and the appearance of the *Mercurio peruano* in the last decade of the 18th century. The liberating influence of the *Mercurio* is assumed but not analyzed.

3455. **Leonard, Irving A.** On the Lima book trade, 1591 (HAHR, 33:4, Nov. 1953, p. 511-525).
Publication, with an introductory descriptive and analytic commentary, of a document of sale (Lima, 1591) giving 150 book titles. The list "confirms the truth . . . that books of all kinds, excepting only those contrary to the Catholic faith and a few others, enjoyed a relatively free and unhampered circulation in the viceroyalties of the New World."

3456. **Lohmann Villena, Guillermo.** El limeño. Don Juan de Valencia el del

Infante, preceptista taurino y espía mayor de Castilla (Miscel Am, 3, p. 395-464).
Fresh information, carefully documented and recorded, on the life of a 17th-century toreador and dabbler in diplomatic intrigue.

3457. McMahon, Dorothy. Variations in the text of Zárate's *Historia del descubrimiento y conquista del Perú* (HAHR, 33:4, Nov. 1953, p. 572-586).
A revealing textual comparison between the 1555 and the 1577 editions of Zárate's *Historia*. The revised version of 1577 presents a narrative more favorable to Viceroy Blasco Núñez Vela.

3458. Paz y Guiní, Melchor de. Guerra separatista. Rebeliones de indios en Sur América. La sublevación de Túpac Amaru, crónica. Con apostillas a la obra de . . . por Luis Antonio Eguiguren. Lima, 1952. 2 v.
First publication of a manuscript in the New York Public Library with abundant new material on the 18th-century rebellion of Túpac Amaru, written in the 1780's by the viceregal secretary Melchor (de) Paz y Guiní. Important for the historical facts of the uprising and for the Spanish official and unofficial reaction to it. Incorporates many viceregal and other documents. A fundamental source.

3458a. Pérez Ayala, José Manuel. Baltasar Jaime Martínez Compañón y Bujanda. Prelado español de Colombia y el Perú, 1737-1797. Bogotá, Imprenta Nacional (Biblioteca de la Presidencia de Colombia, 13), 1955. 515 p. & illus.
Not an integrated biography but a collection of notes and documents concerning the life of the bishop of Trujillo in the late 18th century. Some new documentation on the *Historia natural, civil y moral de Trujillo* (1780-1785), with indices and illustrations.

3459. Quesada, Vicente G. Crónicas potosinas. T. 2. Potosí, Bolivia, Sociedad Geográfica y de Historia Potosí, 1951. 382 p.
Literary evocations of scenes and persons of colonial Potosi, from secondary sources.

3460. Schadel, Richard P., and José Eulogio Garrido. El obispo D. Baltazar Jaime Martínez Compañón y la etnología del Perú a fines del siglo XVIII (R Mus Nac, 22, 1953, p. 75-103).
An account of the episcopal ethnologist Martínez Compañón with a catalogue of illustrations and an appeal for the publication of his works. Reproductions of sample scenes.

3461. Tauro, Alberto. Los pequeños grandes libros de historia americana (R Interam Bibl, 4:1-2, enero-junio 1954, p. 73-80).
Detailed bibliographical notices of the 16 volumes of *Los pequeños grandes libros de historia americana*, published 1941-1948. The volumes relate wholly to colonial Peru and are here

annotated with brief *précis*, bibliographical commentary, and citations to reviews. The important collection includes much material on Túpac Amaru and other Indian and mestizo figures of the colony as well as writings by Las Casas, Reginaldo de Lizárraga, Blas Valera, Martín de Murúa, and Cristóbal de Molina.

3462. Temple, Ella Dunbar. El testamento inédito de doña Beatriz Clara Coya de Loyola, hija del Inca Sayri Túpac (Fénix, 7, 1950, i.e. 1952, p. 109-122).
First publication of the will of the noble Inca heiress. Her bequests include thousands of pesos in cash as well as numerous lands, a mill, an *obraje*, and a number of encomiendas. The document is dated 1600.

3463. Tibesar, Antonine. Franciscan beginnings in colonial Peru. Washington, Academy of American Franciscan History (Monograph series, 1), 1953. xviii, 162 p., illus.
A superior work of technical historical scholarship on the work of the Franciscans in the conversion of the Indians in Peru. Earliest labors, the foundation of the province of Lima, methods of Christianization, and *doctrinas* of the late 16th century are analyzed in detail. An important contribution.

3464. Valcárcel, Daniel. Libro de oposiciones de la Universidad del Cusco, siglo XVIII (A U San Marcos, 2. época, 9-10, enero-dic. 1953, p. 125-212).
Examination, competition, and qualifying records of the University of Cuzco from 1732 to 1763. Part of a continuing series.

3465. Vargas Ugarte, Rubén. Archivo de la beneficencia del Cuzco (R Arch Hist Cuzco, 4:4, 1953, p. 103-113).
Partial description of a rich and unexploited archive containing much of the material of the lost archive of the *convento* de San Agustin, Cuzco.

3466. ――――. Historia de la iglesia en el Perú (1511-1568). T. 1. Lima, Imprenta Santa María, 1953. 422 p.
A significant work of scholarship, the first volume of a projected series by one of the ablest of Peruvian historians. Examines pre-Conquest Incaic religion, the spiritual conquest, the first ecclesiastical establishments, and the organization and achievement of the Peruvian church to 1568, with a documentary appendix and a full index. Depends in large part upon new archival research. The work is modeled on and takes its inspiration from the *Historia de la iglesia en México* of P. Mariano Cuevas, S.J., with which it may be favorably compared.

3467. Villanueva Urteaga, Horacio. Cajamarca: corregimiento, partido, provincia y departamento (R U, Cuzco, 42: 104, 1. semestre 1953, p. 147-182).
Chronicle of the several political systems established in Cajamarca with lists of its colonial

governors, corregidors, *subdelegados*, and military commanders, and its 19th-century political officers.

CHILE

3467a. **Almeyda, Aniceto** (ed.). Actas del Cabildo de Santiago. T. 28. Santiago, 1953. 351 p. (Col. de historiadores de Chile y documentos relativos a la historia nacional, 51).
The minutes of the sessions of the Cabildo of Santiago for the years 1723 to 1728. [R. R. Hill]

3467b. **Almeyda Arroyo, Elías.** La historia de Chile de don Francisco Antonio Encina. Estudio crítico. Prólogo de Ricardo Donoso. Santiago, Imprenta San Francisco, 1952. 66 p.
Critical essay on Encina as an historian of Chile. Notes defects in style and factual content, invalid historical presuppositions, and a general attitude of prejudice.

3468. **Armond, Luis de.** Frontier warfare in colonial Chile (Pac Hist R, 23:2, May 1954, p. 125-132).
Brief and interesting analysis of Spanish-Araucanian warfare and the reasons for its persistence through colonial times. Comments on strategies, adaptations, and strengths and weaknesses of both sides.

3469. **Cline, Howard F.** The Franciscans in colonial Chile (Americas, Franciscan Hist, 10:4, Apr. 1954, p. 471-480).
Outline history of a virtually unexplored subject, the activity of Franciscans in 16th-century Chile. "Perhaps the most significant legacy . . . was their formulation of problems connected with Indian labor."

3470. **Espejo, Juan Luis.** La provincia de Cuyo del reino de Chile. Santiago, Fondo Histórico y Bibliográfico José Toribio Medina, 1954. 2 v. 740 p.
A wealth of documentation on Cuyo, consisting of extracts of documents from the Archivo Nacional de Chile and other collections. *Encomiendas, mercedes*, contracts, *informaciones* and many other categories of documentation are included. Volume 1 includes material to the late 17th century.

3471. **Gento Sanz, Benjamín** (ed.). The first Franciscans in Chile. Founding of the monasteries of Santiago and Concepción (Americas, Franciscan Hist, 10:4, Apr. 1954, p. 481-489).
Two documents from the Archivo de San Francisco de Lima authorizing the foundation of the monasteries of Concepcion (1553) and Santiago (1556).

3472. **Márquez de la Plata, Fernando.** Arqueología del antiguo reino de Chile.

Santiago, Imprenta Artes y Letras, 1953. 218 p.
An unusual and informative examination of the material culture of colonial Chile. Urban and rural residences, public buildings, fortifications, armaments, tombs, bridges, furniture, and clothing are described and illustrated. Weak in bibliography and in the quality of photographic reproduction, but intelligently presented and informed by frequent comparison with Spain.

3473. **Oñat, Roberto, and Carlos Roa.** Régimen legal del ejército en el reino de Chile. Notas para su estudio. Santiago, Universidad Católica de Chile, Facultad de Ciencias Jurídicas, Políticas y Sociales, 1953. 272 p.
A valuable institutional study of the colonial army in Chile. The examination of the military organization is especially instructive for the 18th century, and such topics as the militia and the military jurisdiction are treated with an unprecedented abundance of detail. Appendix summarizes pertinent documents from the Captaincy General, Contaduría Mayor, Audiencia, Medina, and Fondo Antiguo archives.

3474. **Pérez Bustamante, Ciriaco.** Valdivia, en sus cartas (R Indias, Madrid, 13:51, enero-marzo 1953, p. 9-23).
Reflections on the character and attitudes of Valdivia as they appear in the Conquest letters edited by Medina.

3475. **Ramón Folch, José Armando de.** Descubrimiento de Chile y compañeros de Almagro. Santiago, Universidad Católica de Chile, Facultad de Filosofía y Letras, Instituto de Investigaciones Históricas, 1953, i.e. 1954. 190 p.
A recapitulation of familiar material but with a useful biographical appendix cataloguing 178 of Almagro's companions.

LA PLATA

3476. **Álvarez López, Enrique.** Comentarios y anotaciones acerca de la obra de don Félix de Azara (Miscel Am, 3, 1952, p. 9-61).
Thoughtful essay on the work of Félix de Azara, author of the *Apuntaciones para la historia natural de las aves de la provincia del Paraguay* (1789) and the *Apuntamientos para la historia natural de los cuadrúpedos del Paraguay y Río de la Plata* (written 1783-1796). Analysis of his principal ideas on varieties in artificial selection, the struggle for survival, and natural mutation. Interprets Azara as a neglected precursor of Charles Darwin.

3477. **Brito Stífano, Rogelio.** Dos noticias sobre el estado de los campos de la Banda Oriental al finalizar el siglo XVIII (R Hist, Montevideo, 2. época, año 47, 18:52-54, feb. 1953, p. 301-527).
Two documents from the archive of the Real Academia de la Historia, Madrid. One is an exhaustive and well-informed discussion of

problems of the Banda Oriental (now Uruguay) and, by extension, of the Plata estuary region as of 1793-1794 and earlier; an important source for commercial and agricultural history in particular. The other (p. 517-527) is of the same kind. [C. B. Kroeber]

3477a. Castellanos, Alfredo Raúl. Lectura de historia nacional. Época colonial. Montevideo, Medina, 1954? 204 p.
Précis of about 100 classroom lectures on the colonial history of Uruguay. Sections on discovery, conquest, colonization, institutions, commerce, and society. A useful handbook with scattered bibliographical citations.

3478. Diario del fraile franciscano Antonio Lapa, con referencias a su viaje al Gran Chaco Gualamba ... (R Bibl Nac, B A, 23:56, 4. trimestre 1950, i.e. 1954, p. 477-500).
Description of an *entrada* of 1776 designed to reach peaceful agreements between native caciques and the governor of Tucuman in preparation for Christianization.

3479. Documentos históricos concernientes a Mendoza y el Río Negro (R Bibl Nac, B A, 23:56, 4. trimestre 1950, i.e. 1954, p. 401-422).
Documents of the late 18th century, and continuing to 1804, relating to the disposition of the militia of the city of Mendoza and the extension of the effective frontier to the Rio Negro.

3480. Eguía Ruiz, Constancio. España y sus misioneros en los países del Plata. Madrid, Ediciones Cultura Hispánica, 1953. 634 p.
Historical survey of Jesuit labors in the Platine area to the time of the expulsion. Encomiastic and discursive, but valuable for its comprehension of a large subject.

3481. Expedición al estrecho de Magallanes por Fray García de Loaysa (R Bibl Nac, B A, 23:56, 4. trimestre 1950, i.e. 1954, p. 423-459).
Publication of the *probanza* of Rodrigo de Acuña, captain of a ship in the expedition of Fray García de Loaysa to the Straits of Magellan. The document, dated 1529, provides new and detailed information on the expedition.

3482. Fajardo Terán, Florencia. Historia de la ciudad de San Carlos. Orígenes y primeros tiempos. Montevideo, Oliveras Roses y Villaamil, 1953. 332 p.
A rewarding study of the foundation and early history of the Uruguayan city of San Carlos. The founding families and their earliest political establishments receive primary attention. Confined almost wholly to the late 18th century

3483. Fúrlong, Guillermo. Pedro Juan Andreu y su carta a Mateo Andreu, etc. (1750). B.A., Librería del Plata (Escritores coloniales rioplatenses, 3), 1953. 150 p.

Biography of Pedro Juan Andreu (1697-1777) with special attention to his missionary work in the Chaco and his ecclesiastical career in Paraguay prior to the Jesuit expulsion. The letter to his brother, Mateo Andreu, is a compact description of mission life written from Estancia de la Concepción in 1750. The work is documented and contains a bibliography of Pedro Juan Andreu.

3484. Fúrlong, Guillermo; Raúl A. Molina; and Humberto F. Burzio. Las ruinas de Cayastá son de la vieja ciudad de Santa Fe fundada por Garay. B.A., Ediciones Arayú, 1953. 175 p., illus., maps.
A scholarly and perhaps definitive contribution to the dispute over the location of old Santa Fe. With maps, plans, texts, and archaeological objects the authors identify the traditional Cayasta ruins as occupying the primitive site. The work contains a bibliography of the controversy since 1949.

3485. García, Juan Agustín. La ciudad indiana. Buenos Aires desde 1600 hasta mediados del siglo XVIII. Nueva ed. ... Notas sobre la vida y obra del autor por E. M. S. Danero. Santa Fe, Argentina, Castellví (Clásicos argentinos), 1954. 286 p.
New edition of a classic history of colonial B. A. A biography and bibliography of Juan Agustín García are included.

3485a. Guzmán, Augusto. El kolla mitrado. Biografía de un obispo colonial, Fray Bernardino de Cárdenas. La Paz, Editorial Juventud, 1954. 169 p.
Biography of the bishop of Paraguay (born 1579) with an account of his long struggle with the Jesuits. From published sources.

3485b. Luque Colombres, Carlos A. Antecedentes documentales sobre la topografía del asiento urbano de Córdoba durante los siglos XVI y XVII. Córdoba, Argentina, Universidad Nacional de Córdoba, Instituto de Estudios Americanistas (Cuaderno de historia, 28), 1954. xii, 19 p.
Summary recapitulation of conclusions published by the author in previous studies on the site and urban form of colonial Cordoba.

3486. ————. Un plano de la ciudad de Córdoba del siglo XVIII (R Fac Fil Hum, 5:1-3, 1953, p. 379-383).
Demonstrates that an 18th-century city plan attributed by Félix F. Outes to Tucuman is in reality a plan of the city of Cordoba. The Outes plate is reproduced.

3487. Mariluz Urquijo, José M. La fundación de San Gabriel de Batoví (R Hist, Montevideo, 2. época, año 47, 19: 55-57, sept. 1953, p. 147-179).
Factual account of an Uruguayan settlement ex-

periment in the late 18th century. The short-lived community came to an end in 1801 after Portuguese attack.

3488. ————. Los guaraníes después de la expulsión de los jesuítas (Estud Am, 6:25, oct. 1953, p. 323-330).
The article cites documents to show that the Guarani exodus after the Jesuit expulsion of 1767 was directed in large part toward towns and farms, i.e., that it did not represent a reversion to migrant primitivism. B. A., Montevideo, Asuncion, Santa Fe, and other urban centers are mentioned as having received Guarani exiles.

3489. Mateos, Francisco. Nuevos incidentes en las misiones del Paraguay hasta el final de la demarcación de límites, 1757-1760 (Miss Hisp, 11:31, 1954, p. 135-192).
Diplomacy and local maneuvering over the Spanish-Portuguese colonial boundary of the mid-18th century are recorded in some detail. The dispute centered upon the location of the source of the Ibicuy river.

3490. ————. Pedro de Cevallos, gobernador de Buenos Aires, y las misiones del Paraguay (Miss Hisp, 10:29, 1953, p. 313-375).
Straightforward account of the contribution of Pedro de Ceballos to the maintenance of order in the Paraguayan missions and to the resistance against Brazilian incursion.

3491. Mörner, Magnus. The political and economic activities of the Jesuits in the La Plata region. The Hapsburg era. Stockholm, Sweden, Library and Institute of Ibero-American Studies, 1953. 254 p., maps.
An important scholarly contribution on Jesuit labors among the Guaranis in the 16th and 17th centuries. The local history is understood in its relation to the totality of Jesuit enterprise and is faithfully chronicled to 1700. Many historiographical difficulties of the subject are successfully confronted for the first time.

3492. Molina, Raúl A. La obra franciscana en el Paraguay y Río de la Plata (Miss Hisp, 11:32, 1954, p. 329-400; 11:33, 1954, p. 485-522).
An important study of a subject insufficiently known. The work of Fray Luis de Bolaños receives particular attention and the effectiveness of all Franciscan labor in the Plata area is enthusiastically appraised. Contains a documentary appendix.

3493. Montes, Aníbal. Historia antigua de la ciudad de Río Cuarto. Córdoba, Argentina, Universidad Nacional de Córdoba, Facultad de Filosofía y Humanidades, Instituto de Estudios Americanistas (Cuaderno de historia, 26), 1953. 53 p.
An interesting local history tracing the stages of conquest, encomienda, latifundia, and Indian warfare in and about colonial Rio Cuarto.

3494. Pueyrredón, Alfredo. Algunos aspectos de la enseñanza en la Universidad de Córdoba durante la regencia franciscana. Córdoba, Argentina, Universidad Nacional de Córdoba, Facultad de Filosofía y Humanidades, Instituto de Estudios Americanistas (Cuaderno de historia, 24), 1953. 56 p.
Organization, administration, and teaching methods of the Franciscans in the University of Cordoba after the Jesuit expulsion of 1767. New philosophical doctrines, a decline in scholasticism, the biographies of Franciscan rectors, and the Franciscan library are briefly examined.

3495. Sánchez, Mariquita. Recuerdos del Buenos Aires virreynal. B. A., Ene (Col. Los testimonios, sección historia), 1953. 70 p.
Brief jottings on late colonial scenes and society in B. A.

3496. Tanodi, Aurelio Z. Nomenclatura indígena de un manuscrito del año 1691 (R Fac Fil Hum, 5:1-3, 1953, p. 385-396).
An interesting paleographic study demonstrating standard errors of copyists and methods of correcting such errors in the absence of originals. The manuscript treated relates to the foundation of Tucuman and contains a number of Indian names in variant spellings.

3497. Tepp, Max. Die Indianerreduktion im Jesuitenstaat (Südamerika, 3:6, Mai-Juni 1953, p. 568-573).
Brief and conventional remarks upon Indian life in the Jesuit missions.

3498. Von der Heydte, Fiedrich A. Las reducciones del Paraguay (Estud Am, 6:27, dic. 1953, p. 561-569).
Argues against the concepts of a "Jesuit state" and imposed communistic order in the Paraguayan missions. Asserts that the politico-economic structure consisted of Guarani custom regulated by Spanish law. Lacks documentation.

MEXICO AND CENTRAL AMERICA
WALTER V. SCHOLES

Although the published material on Central America follows in the pattern of the past, authors dealing with Mexico brought out many significant contributions. Certainly Cosío Villegas's political history of Mexico, 1867-1876, the articles in *Historia mexicana* and *Ábside* on Hidalgo's ideas, Potash's economic articles on the 1830's and 1840's, and Cline's survey which calls for more study of the regional aspects of Mexico must be singled out.

MEXICO

3553. Aguayo Spencer, Rafael. Alamán estadista (Hist Mex, 3:2, oct.-dic. 1953, p. 279-290).
A brief study of Lucas Alamán's activities in education, the city council of Mexico City, and international relations.

3554. Álvarez, José Rogelio. Los primeros contactos diplomáticos de México (Hist Mex, 3:1, julio-sept. 1953, p. 87-101).
Description of the first Mexican diplomatic contacts with Spain, Colombia, Peru, and the U. S., after Independence.

3555. Archivo del General Porfirio Díaz. Memorias y documentos. Prólogo y notas de Alberto María Carreño. México, Elede (Col. de obras históricas mexicanas, 3), 1953-1954. V. 16-18. 353, 313, 313 p.
"Esta obra se publica en colaboración con el Instituto de Historia de la Universidad Nacional Autónoma de México." (Publ. no. 7).
Letters to Díaz constitute the bulk of the material. V. 16 covers Jan. 3, 1877—Jan. 21, 1877. V. 17 covers Jan. 22, 1877—Feb. 13, 1877, and v. 18 covers Feb. 13, 1877—Feb. 28, 1877. Material deals primarily with political and military affairs on the state level.

3555a. Arnade, Charles W. The Porfirio Díaz papers of the William Clements library (HAHR, 33:2, May 1953, p. 324-325).
A brief note on the papers of Porfirio Díaz acquired by the William Clements Library. They range from 1856 to 1903, but are mostly for the year 1867. [R. R. Hill]

3556. Arnáiz y Freg, Arturo. Alamán en la historia y en la política (Hist Mex, 3:2, oct.-dic. 1953, p. 241-260).
Brilliant essay on Lucas Alamán: the man, his ideas, and his history.

3557. Bean, Ellis Peter. Les aventures au Mexique et au Texas ..., 1783-1846; ses mémoires. Paris, Honoré Champion, 1952. 220 p.
A translation of Bean's Memoirs covering the period between 1800 and 1816, to which is added the story of his youth and adventures encountered after 1816.

3558. Blaisdell, Lowell L. Was it revolution or filibustering? The mystery of the Flores Magón revolt in Baja California (Pac Hist R, 23:2, May 1954, p. 147-164).
Shows that the Flores Magón revolt had no backing from the government of the U. S. nor from private money in California.

3559. Borah, Woodrow. Race and class in Mexico (Pac Hist R, 23:4, Nov. 1954, p. 331-342).
An essay on "What is an Indian?" Points out how the Mexicans have attempted to define the word.

3560. Brent, Robert A. Nicolas P. Trist and the Treaty of Guadalupe Hidalgo (SW Hist Q, 57:4, Apr. 1954, p. 454-474).
Survey; adds little that is new.

3561. Burleson, Jesse Issac. La vida de Lorenzo de Zavala. México, Universidad Nacional Autónoma de México, 1953. 284 p.
Mimeographed doctoral dissertation. Biography based on personal papers of Zavala and other manuscript.

3562. Burrus, Ernest J. Jesuit exiles, precursors of Mexican independence? (Mid Am, 36:3, July 1954, p. 161-175).
Points out books written by Mexican Jesuit exiles in Europe and indicates that their reports on Mexico were very well done which led Mexicans to be "conscious of their distinct heritage."

3563. Busey, J. L. Don Victoriano y la prensa yanqui (Hist Mex, 4:4, abril-junio 1955, p. 582-594).
In 45 articles studied in various journals the author finds that the press in the U. S. was favorable toward Huerta.

3564. Bustamante, Carlos María de. Continuación del Cuadro histórico de la revolución mexicana. México, Biblioteca Nacional de México (Publ., 2), 1953. 2 v.
Reprint from the 1832 edition.

3565. Call, Tomme Clark. The Mexican venture. From political to industrial revolution in Mexico. N. Y., Oxford University Press, 1953. 273 p., illus.
Author stresses industrialization and nationalism; realizes and deals with the problems created in 1951. Based upon author's residence in Mexico.

3566. Camberos Vizcaíno, Vicente. Más allá del estoicismo. Apuntes biográficos y monográficos. Conclusión de Un hombre y una época. México, Jus, 1953. 325 p.
Another account of religious persecution in Mexico in the 1920's.

3567. Cardoso, Joaquín. Los mártires mexicanos. El martirologio católico de nuestros días. México, Buena Prensa, 1953. 480 p., illus.
Brief biographical sketches of the Catholics killed in Mexico, 1926-1929.

3568. Carrera Stampa, Manuel. Hidalgo y su plan de operaciones (Hist Mex, 3:2, oct.-dic. 1953, p. 192-206).
With some new evidence the author claims, in contradiction to Lucas Alamán and others, that

Hidalgo did have a plan for the Independence movement.

3569. Caruso, John Anthony. The liberators of Mexico. N. Y., Pageant Press, 1954. 342 p.
Biographical studies of Hidalgo, Morelos, and Iturbide. Book is based on the usual secondary sources.

3570. Castillo, Porfirio del. Puebla y Tlaxcala en los días de la Revolución. Apuntes para la historia. México, Zavala, 1953. 321 p.
Autobiography of a political leader who was a Madero supporter and later governor. Gives a good account of the period 1910-1918.

3571. Chamberlin, Eugene Keith. Baja California after Walker: the Zerman enterprise (HAHR, 34:2, May 1954, p. 175-189).
Concludes that the Zerman expedition of 1855 was not a filibustering expedition.

3572. ————. The Japanese scare at Magdalena Bay (Pac Hist R, 24:4, Nov. 1955, p. 345-360).
Gives the historical background of the "scare" by discussing the interests of the American and Japanese promoters in the area.

3573. Cline, Howard F. The United States and Mexico. Cambridge, Mass., Harvard University Press, 1953. 452 p.
An especially important book on Mexico since 1910. The author stresses the need to view Mexico from the point of view of the population, regionalism, and industrialization rather than the traditional national political interpretation. The chapters on the Revolution and the period since 1934 are outstanding.

3574. Cosío Villegas, Daniel. Historia moderna de México. [1]. La República restaurada. La vida política. México, Hermes, 1955. 979 p., maps, pl.
A major contribution to 19th-century Mexican history. This is the first volume of a projected six-volume history of Mexico covering the period 1867-1911; it covers the political history, 1867-1876. The attempt of Díaz to overthrow *juarista* democracy is the key to this volume. Excellent in details on men, congress, revolts, political manipulations, and newspapers. Without question it is the best book on Mexico of 1867-1876.

3575. ————. La historiografía política del México moderno. México, Sobretiro de la Memoria de El Colegio Nacional, 1953. 91 p.
Revised and enlarged. First published in 1949. Short critical statements on the books and documents.

3576. ————. Porfirio Díaz en la revuelta de la Noria. México, Hermes, 1953. 309 p.

Reasons for the failure of the Díaz revolt of 1871-1872. Based on printed and manuscript sources.

3577. Cumberland, Charles C. Border raids in the Lower Rio Grande Valley, 1915 (SW Hist Q, 57:3, Jan. 1954, p. 285-311).
Contant and serious raids from Mexico alarmed Americans; author shows that Carranza could have stopped these raids but used them to force recognition from the U. S.

3578. Dávila Garibi, J. Ignacio. Ascendencia materna de D. Miguel Hidalgo y Costilla a la luz de nuevos documentos. México, Cultura, 1953. 49 p., illus.
Genealogical study.

3579. ————. Genealogía de D. Agustín de Iturbide, emperador de México. México, Cultura, 1952. 68 p., illus.
Genealogical study correcting errors in previous publications on Iturbide.

3580. Delgado, Jaime. España y México en el siglo XIX. V. 2. (1831-1845). Madrid, Consejo Superior de Investigaciones Científicas, Instituto Gonzalo Fernández de Oviedo, 1953, i.e. 1954. 380 p.
V. 1 reviewed in *HLAS, no. 16, 1950,* item 1765. Important study of Mexican-Spanish relations, with stress on the Treaty of 1836.

3581. Diario económico de un convoy de México a Veracruz en 1814 (B Arch Gen, México, 25:3, julio-sept. 1954, p. 357-398).
Diary of a member of a convoy relating the incidents of a round trip, Mexico City-Veracruz.

3582. Dromundo, Baltasar. Tomás Garrido: su vida y su leyenda. México, Guarania (Col. Nezahualcoyotl), 1953. 179 p., illus.
Biographical study that is favorable to Garrido. Author recounts many personal experiences with Garrido.

3583. Ellison, William H., and Francis Price (eds.). The life and adventures in California of Don Agustín Janssens, 1834-1856. San Marino, Calif., Huntington Library, 1953. 165 p.
Good description of Southern California, 1834-1849.

3584. Estep, Raymond. Lorenzo de Zavala and the Texas Revolution (SW Hist Q, 57:3, Jan. 1954, p. 322-335).
Describes Zavala's participation in the Texas independence movement.

3585. Estrada, Francisco J. Recuerdos de mi vida. Introducción, transcripción y notas de Rafael Montejano y Aguiñaga.

San Luis Potosí, México, Universidad Autónoma de San Luis Potosí (Biblioteca de historia potosina, 1), 1954. 319 p.
First published in 1870. Autobiography of a man from San Luis Potosi involved in Mexican politics, 1820-1867.

3586. Fernández MacGregor, Genaro. El istmo de Tehuantepec y los Estados Unidos. México, Elede, 1954. 228 p.
Survey of the diplomacy of the U. S. and Mexico concerning the Isthmus. Stress is placed on the 19th century but the account is carried down to 1937.

3587. Flaccus, Elmer W. Commodore David Porter and the Mexican navy (HAHR, 34:3, Aug. 1954, p. 365-373).
Describes the unsuccessful attempt by Porter to build up the Mexican navy, 1826-1829.

3588. Flores D., Jorge. El primer proyecto de Colegio Militar en México (Hist Mex, 4:1, julio-sept. 1954, p. 68-98).
Contains documents of the first suggested plan for a Mexican military school in 1821, written by Pedro Torréns.

3589. Foland, Frances M. Pugnas políticas en el México de 1808 (Hist Mex, 5:1, julio-sept. 1955, p. 30-41).
Discussion of the political fight in Mexico between the *gachupines* and *criollos* over the question of where sovereignty lies.

3590. Friend, Llerena. Sam Houston, the great designer. Austin, Tex., University of Texas Press, 1954. 394 p.
Good biographical study.

3591. Fuentes Díaz, Vicente. Los partidos políticos en México. T. 1. 1810-1911. México, Talleres Impresiones Perfectas, 1954. 146 p.
Survey.

3592. Fuentes Mares, José. Y México se refugió en el desierto. Luis Terrazas: historia y destino. México, Jus, 1954. 298 p., illus.
Centered around Luis Terrazas, this study is one of the few good biographical studies of a secondary figure in recent Mexican history.

3593. García Ruiz, Alfonso. Ideario de Hidalgo. Prólogo de José Ángel Ceniceros. México, Museo Nacional de Historia, 1955. 132 p.
Excellent summary of the political, social, and economic ideas of Hidalgo.

3594. Geiger, Maynard. Reply of Mission San Antonio to the questionnaire of the Spanish Government in 1812 concerning the native culture of California Mission Indians (Americas, Franciscan Hist, 10:2, Oct. 1953, p. 211-227).

3595. Gilbert, Benjamin F. French warships on the Mexican west coast, 1861-1866 (Pac Hist R, 24:1, Feb. 1955, p. 25-38).
Discusses attempted French blockade of Mexico's west coast.

3596. Gill, Mario. Los Escudero, de Acapulco (Hist Mex, 3:2, oct.-dic. 1953, p. 291-308).
The attempt by Juan Escudero, 1919-1923, to lead the masses in their move against the absolute economic control by the Spanish of the Acapulco-Guerrero region.

3597. ———. Veracruz: revolución y extremismo (Hist Mex, 2:4, abril-junio 1953, p. 618-636).
Points out why Veracruz, since 1920, has been the center of extremes in the revolution. The author feels that the anti-rent strike of 1922 and Herón Proal are the basic causes for this.

3598. Glick, Edward B. The Tehuantepec Railroad: Mexico's white elephant (Pac Hist R, 22:4, Nov. 1953, p. 373-382).
Short history of the building and economic failure of the railroad down to 1921.

3599. Godoy, Bernabé. La batalla de la Mojonera (Hist Mex, 3:4, abril-junio 1954, p. 562-591).
Gives brief background on the life of Lozada and then describes the battle of Mojonera in 1873 where Lozada was defeated.

3600. Gómez, Marte R. Sobre Justo Sierra O'Reilly (Hist Mex, 3:3, enero-marzo 1954, p. 309-327).
Places Sierra O'Reilly and his recently found and published memoirs in their proper historical place by developing the background in Yucatan and the U. S. in the 1840's.

3601. González, Natalicio. Icazbalceta y su obra (Hist Mex, 3:3, enero-marzo 1954, p. 367-390).
Historiographical essay on the published works of Joaquín García Icazbalceta.

3602. González Navarro, Moisés. Alamán e Hidalgo (Hist Mex, 3:2, oct.-dic. 1953, p. 217-240).
Excellent corrective essay on some of Lucas Alamán's errors, especially on Hidalgo, abolition of Indian tribute, abolition of slavery, and land for the Indians.

3603. ———. La política colonizadora del porfiriato (Estud Hist Am, p. 183-239).
Describes the attempt made during the Díaz period to get colonists to come to Mexico.

3604. Goodspeed, Stephen S. The development and use of *facultades extraordinarias* in Mexico (SW Soc Sci Q, 34:3, Dec. 1953, p. 17-33).
Surveys the period down to 1917 and then

stresses period after the constitution in the use of the extraordinary power of the president.

3605. ————. Mexico: president and constitution (Mid Am, 36:2, Apr. 1954, p. 96-115).
Discusses debates in the Constitutional Convention of 1917 on the powers of the president.

3606. Graebner, Norman A. American interest in California, 1845 (Pac Hist R, 22:1, Feb. 1953, p. 13-28).
Little interest expressed in the U. S. on California but interest picked up in 1845 because of possible British interference in the area.

3607. ————. Party politics and the Trist mission (J South Hist, 19:2, May 1953, p. 137-156).
Deals with American politics, 1847-1848, rather than with the diplomacy of the period.

3608. Gringoire, Pedro. El "protestantismo" del Doctor Mora (Hist Mex, 3:3, enero-marzo 1954, p. 328-366).
Article based upon research in the archives of the British and Foreign Bible Society; shows that Mora never became a Protestant. He was interested in spreading knowledge of the Bible in the various languages in Mexico.

3609. Gutiérrez Santos, Daniel. Historia militar de México, 1876-1914. México, Ateneo, 1955. 368 p.
Book is concerned with military history, 1910-1914.

3610. Gutiérrez Zamora, Manuel. El salvamento de don Porfirio Díaz frente a la barra de Tampico (Hist Mex, 5:1, julio-sept. 1955, p. 62-85).
Publication of the manuscript of the author who in 1876 served as the postal agent on the City of Habana and describes how Díaz was saved.

3611. Hafen, LeRoy R., and Ann W. Hafen. Old Spanish trail: Santa Fé to Los Angeles. With extracts from contemporary records and including diaries of Antonio Armijo and Orville Pratt. Glendale, Calif., Arthur H. Clark (The Far West and the Rockies historical series, 1820-1875, v. 1), 1954. 377 p., illus.
First of a projected 15-volume set of documents on the Far West and Rockies. Gives a good general history of the exploration and travel in the west, 1820-1875.

3612. Hammond, George P. (ed.). The Larkin papers. Personal, business, and official correspondence of Thomas Oliver Larkin, merchant and United States consul in California. Berkeley, Calif., University of California Press, 1953-1955. V. 4, 1845-1846. xxxi, 411 p. V. 5, 1846. xxviii, 333 p.

V. 4 covers 1845—May 1846: Tasso affair, letters to Buchanan, descriptions of California, and business affairs. V. 5 contains an excellent introduction by the editor on the Bear Flag revolt, and correspondence with such men as Frémont, Pío Pico, and Buchanan.

3613. Hanna, Kathryn Abbey. The roles of the South in the French intervention in Mexico (J South Hist, 20:1, Feb. 1954, p. 3-21).
Fine article based on extensive research in archives; shows interrelationships of the diplomacy of France, U. S., the Confederacy, and Mexico, 1861-1866.

3614. Hardy, Osgood. Ulysses S. Grant, President of the Mexican Southern Railroad (Pac Hist R, 24:2, May 1955, p. 111-120).
Discusses Grant's interest in the railroad in the 1880's.

3615. Heiliger, Edward M. La revolución mexicana en la prensa de lengua inglesa, 1910-1952 (Hist Mex, 3:3, enero-marzo 1954, p. 451-472).
A list of articles dealing with the Mexican Revolution in American popular journals; excludes most of the scholarly journals.

3616. Hernández Luna, Juan. Hidalgo pintado por los realistas (Hist Mex, 4:1, julio-sept. 1954, p. 1-19).
Descriptions of Hidalgo by those who opposed him.

3617. ————. El mundo intelectual de Hidalgo (Hist Mex, 3:2, oct.-dic. 1953, p. 157-177).
Author shows the depth and learning of Hidalgo. Certainly disproves old thesis that Hidalgo was not learned.

3618. Higuera, Ernesto. Hidalgo. Reseña biográfica con una iconografía del iniciador de nuestra independencia. México, Talleres Gráficos de la Nación (Col. Medallones mexicanos), 1955. 427 p., illus.
Miscellaneous collection of material by and about Hidalgo.

3619. Horgan, Paul. Great river. The Rio Grande in North American history. N. Y., Rinehart, 1954. 2 v. V. 1, Indians and Spain, 447 p.; v. 2, Mexico and the United States, 453-1020 p.
V. 2 deals primarily with Texas.

3620. Iturribarría, Jorge Fernando. El partido "borlado" (Hist Mex, 3:4, abril-junio 1954, p. 473-496).
Deals with the political fight for power in Oaxaca, 1855-Díaz, between the puros and borlados. An important article showing politics on the state level.

3621. Izquierdo, J. Joaquín. Origins and development of the Mexican pharmacopoeiae (B Hist Med, 26:1, Jan.-Feb. 1952, p. 54-70).
A study of the history of the publication of pharmacopoeias, with information on the societies which sponsored them. (Puebla had an Academy before 1824; the first in Mexico City was in 1838.) The article includes facsimiles of six title pages, from that of Puebla, 1832, to that of Mexico, 1896. [R. D. Hussey]

3622. José María Lozano en la tribuna parlamentaria, 1910-1913. Prólogo de Nemesio García Naranjo. Selección y notas de Salvador Sánchez Septién. México, Jus, 1953. xxxii, 204 p.
Speeches given in Mexican parliament by a brilliant Díaz supporter.

3623. Juárez, Benito. Apuntes para mis hijos. Datos autobiográficos del Benemérito de las Américas, tomados de su archivo privado. Prólogo de Vicente Sáenz. México, Cronos, 1955. 174 p.
New edition.

3624. Knapp, Frank A., Jr. A new source on the Confederate exodus to Mexico: The two republics (J South Hist, 19:3, Aug. 1953, p. 364-373).
Discusses the newspaper The two republics founded in Mexico City in 1867 by George W. Clarke. Clarke was a Confederate who went to Mexico. The newspaper contains information about Confederates in Mexico.

3625. ————. Parliamentary government and the Mexican Constitution of 1857 (HAHR, 33:1, Feb. 1953, p. 65-87).
Points out the attempts made to establish a parliamentary government, 1857-1876.

3626. ————. Preludios de la pérdida de California (Hist Mex, 4:2, oct.-dic. 1954, p. 235-249).
Reaction in California and Mexico to Commodore Jones' seizure of Monterrey in 1842.

3627. Lara, J. Andrés. Prisionero de callistas y cristeros. México, Jus, 1954. 117 p.
The Church-State fight in 1929.

3628. Lara y Torres, Leopoldo. Documentos para la historia de la persecución religiosa en México. México, Jus, 1954. 1104 p.
Consists of pastoral letters and private correspondence of the Monsignor, 1926-1929, on Church-State relations.

3629. Mancisidor, José. El huertismo (Hist Mex, 3:1, julio-sept. 1953, p. 34-51).
Brief description of the politics of the Huerta regime.

3630. McCormack, Richard B. Los esta-

dos confederados y México (Hist Mex, 4:3, enero-marzo 1955, p. 337-352).
Based on Pickett's papers in the Library of Congress, the article presents an excellent account of Pickett's activities in Mexico City.

3631. McLean, Malcolm D. Guillermo Prieto (1818-1897), a forgotten historian of Mexico (Americas, Franciscan Hist, 10:1, July 1953, p. 79-88).
Throws some light on Prieto as an historian.

3632. Méndez Plancarte, Gabriel. Hidalgo, reformador intelectual (Ábside, 17:2, abril-junio 1953, p. 135-170).
A study of Hidalgo's dissertation; shows the depth of knowledge of the young Hidalgo. (See also item below).

3633. ———— (ed.). Disertación de Hidalgo (Ábside, 17:2, abril-junio 1953, p. 171-196).
Hidalgo's dissertation: Disertación sobre el verdadero método de estudiar teología escolástica. (See also preceeding item).

3633a. México. Dirección General de Correos. Oficina de Museo y Biblioteca. S.C.O.P. Catálogo de documentos históricos de la Biblioteca Postal. México, 1954. 110 p.
A catalogue, alphabetical by type of document and thereunder chronological, of the historical records in the Postal Library of Mexico. The entries state the content of the document or group of documents, giving dates, places, and names of persons. The Brussels classification number and archival location are indicated. The documents are mostly of the last half of the 19th century. [R. R. Hill]

3634. Mora, J. de la. Apuntes biográficos de Mons. Rafael Guízar Valencia. México, Editorial Josefina, 1955. 221 p., illus.
Brief biography of Guízar Valencia, who became Bishop of Veracruz in 1920.

3635. Nicolau d'Olwer, Luis. Santa-Anna y la invasión vistos por Bermúdez de Castro (Hist Mex, 4:1, julio-sept. 1954, p. 47-65).
Description of Mexico and Santa Anna by the Spanish Minister to Mexico, 1845-1847.

3636. Niemeyer, E. V. Anticlericalism in the Mexican Constitutional Convention of 1916-1917 (Americas, Franciscan Hist, 11:1, July 1954, p. 31-50).
Shows the anticlericalism by discussing the debates on Articles 3, 24, and 130.

3637. Noticia de los conventos del arzobispado de México, 1826 (B Arch Gen, México, 24:3, julio-sept. 1953, p. 471-500).
Document listing the convents of the archbishopric and giving, among other things, the income from their urban holdings.

638. Pani, Arturo. Ayer . . . . México, Stylo, 1954. 387 p.
Autobiography; covers author's activities as a student, engineer, and then as a Mexican diplomat in Europe, in the 1920's.

639. Pelissier, Raymond F. Intensification of competition in Mexico through the entry of American private enterprise (Interam Ec Aff, 7:2, autumn 1953, p. 80-91).
Deals with the present day and suggests the effect on Mexican mass buying of such stores as Sears, Roebuck and Co.

640. Pletcher, David M. México, campo de inversiones norteamericanas, 1867-1880 (Hist Mex, 2:4, abril-junio 1953, p. 564-574).
Although Mexico attempted to obtain American investments, few investments were made because of obstacles in Mexico and because the U. S. itself was a good field for new capital.

641. Potash, Robert A. Alamán y el Banco de Avío (Inv Ec, 13:4, 4. trimestre 1953, p. 499-512).
Excellent article on the bank, covering the 1830's and 1840's. Shows effect of loans and tariff on the establishment of factories.

642. ————. El Comercio esterior de México de Miguel Lerdo de Tejada: un error estadístico (Trim Ec, 20:3, julio-sept. 1953, p. 474-479).
Points out the grave error of Lerdo in calculating the amount of British exports to Mexico. Shows that British exports were much less than Lerdo claimed.

643. ————. La fundación del Banco de Avío (Hist Mex, 3:2, oct.-dic. 1953, p. 261-278).
Important article on the reasons for the establishment of a bank in 1830 to aid Mexican industry. The author shows Lucas Alamán's part in this, and the relationship of the bank to the prohibitive tariff on manufactured goods.

644. Quirk, Robert E. Liberales y radicales en la Revolución mexicana (Hist Mex, 2:4, abril-junio 1953, p. 503-528).
Covers period 1913-1916; shows the difference in ideology of the followers of Carranza as compared with those of Villa and Zapata. Because of Carranza's middle-class beliefs his followers were defeated in the elections for the constitutional convention in 1916.

645. Reyes Heroles, Jesús. Continuidad del liberalismo mexicano (Cuad Am, año 13, 76:4, julio-agosto 1954, p. 167-202).
Suggestive article on what the word "liberal" was meant to Mexicans. Deals especially with the 19th century.

646. Rivera Marín, Guadalupe. Los conflictos de trabajo en México, 1937-1950 (Trim Ec, 22:2, abril-junio 1955, p. 181-208).
Discusses the types of strikes and causes of the strikes in the period given.

3647. Rodríguez Frausto, J. Jesús. Hidalgo no era guanajuatense. Localización histórico-geográfica de la hacienda de San Diego de Corralejo. Ilustraciones del autor. México, Imprenta Manuel León Sánchez, 1953. 170 p.
Claims that Hidalgo was born in Leon and not in Guanajuato.

3648. Romero de Terreros, Manuel. El Condado de Regla en 1810 (Hist Mex, 4:1, julio-sept. 1954, p. 107-114).
Description of the Conde's visit to his vast agricultural holdings in 1810.

3649. Royer, Fanchón. Padre Pro. N. Y., P. J. Kenedy, 1954. 246 p., illus.
Laudatory biography based on secondary works. Padre Pro was shot by the Callistas for his supposed participation in the attempted assassination of Obregón.

3650. Rubio Mañé, J. Ignacio. Movimiento marítimo entre Veracruz y Campeche, 1801-1810 (B Arch Gen, México, 24:4, oct.-dic. 1953, p. 595-676; 25:1, enero-marzo, p. 91-146; 2, abril-junio 1954, p. 237-336).
Author gives background of the importance of the port of Campeche and then publishes documents showing the large number of ships and goods involved in the trade between Campeche and Veracruz.

3651. Sánchez Garza, J. (ed.). La rebelión de Texas. Manuscrito inédito de 1836 por un oficial de Santa Anna. México, A. Frank de Sánchez, 1955. 321 p.
Written in 1836 by Lt. Col. José Enrique de la Peña and now published for the first time. It shows the disastrous results of the Filisola command in the Texas War.

3652. Schmitt, Karl M. The clergy and the independence of New Spain (HAHR, 34:3, Aug. 1954, p. 289-312).
Hierarchy was consistent in its opposition to liberalism. Lower clergy divided sharply in their reactions to the rebellion. Yet the author concludes that "a majority of the lower clergy were probably neutral in the struggle."

3653. Scholes, Walter V. El liberalismo reformista (Hist Mex, 2:3, enero-marzo 1953, p. 343-352).
Shows the influence on mid-19th-century Mexico of the concepts of capitalism, utilitarianism, and equality before the law.

3654. Sierra Casasús, Catalina. El excomulgador de Hidalgo (Hist Mex, 3:2, oct.-dic. 1953, p. 178-191).
Deals with the background, before Hidalgo's

move for independence, of Bishop Abad y Queipo, and then shows how the bishop's views were changed by the revolution.

3655. Sierra O'Reilly, Justo. Segundo libro del diario de mi viaje a los Estados Unidos. La pretendida cesión de la península de Yucatán a un gobierno extranjero. Prólogo y notas de Marte R. Gómez. México, Porrúa, 1953. 159 p.
Publication of the "lost" second volume of the diary. Fills in the gap in the period of early 1848. Contains very little on negotiations with the U. S.

3656. Silva Herzog, Jesús. La epopeya del petróleo en México (Cuad Am, año 12, 67:1, enero-feb. 1953, p. 7-63).
Historical survey of the oil development in Mexico; justifies expropriation in 1938.

3657. Simpson, Lesley Byrd. Unplanned effects of Mexico's planned economy (Vir Q R, 29:4, autumn 1953, p. 514-532).
Critical analysis of the Mexican economy in the period after 1941. Stresses need of change in order to get capital and mechanization.

3658. Sobarzo, Horacio. Crónica de la aventura de Raousset-Boulbon en Sonora. México, Porrúa, 1954. 222 p.
Popular account of the Count's adventures in Sonora in 1854.

3659. Torre Villar, Ernesto de la. Hidalgo y Fleury (Hist Mex, 3:2, oct.-dic. 1953, p. 207-216).
This article is centered around a letter written in 1805 which claimed that Hidalgo upheld the ideas in Fleury's *Historia eclesiástica.*

3661. Valades, José C. Don Melchor Ocampo, reformador de México. México, Patria, 1954. 422 p., illus.
Excellent biography; deals with the man, his ideas, the politician, and the statesman.

3662. Vázquez Alfaro, Guillermo. La reforma agraria de la Revolución mexicana. México, La Artística, 1953. 303 p.
Most of the book deals with the contributions made by the Alemán administration to agrarian reforms.

3663. Vigness, David M. La expedición Urrea-Mejía (Hist Mex, 5:2, oct.-dic. 1955, p. 211-219).
Description of the Federalist attempt to overthrow Bustamante in 1838-1839.

3664. ————. Relations of the Republic of Texas and the Republic of the Rio Grande (SW Hist Q, 57:3, Jan. 1954, p. 312-321).
Although the Texan government was officially neutral it did allow Mexican federalists, in 1840, to recruit volunteers and obtain supplies and arms in Texas.

3665. Villaseñor, Eduardo. La estructura bancaria y el desarrollo económico de México (Trim Ec, 20:2, abril-junio 1953, p. 199-230).
Historical survey.

3666. Villoro, Luis. La revolución de independencia. Ensayo de interpretación histórica. México, Universidad Nacional Autónoma de México, Consejo de Humanidades (Ediciones del Bicentenario del Nacimiento de Hidalgo), 1953. 239 p.
This study, based on primary sources, is centered around an analysis of the human element and the conflict between liberty and order in the Mexican Independence movement.

3667. Young, Otis E. Military protection of the Santa Fé Trail and trade (Mis Hist R, 49:1, Oct. 1954, p. 19-32).
Describes the protection given in the period 1829-1845.

CENTRAL AMERICA

3668. Baylen, Joseph O. American intervention in Nicaragua, 1909-1933. An appraisal of objectives and results (SW Soc Sci Q, 35:2, Sept. 1954, p. 128-154)
Surveys the political and financial intervention by the U. S. The author concludes that though the intervention accomplished certain ends, "the results were not worth the price paid."

3669. ————. Sandino: death and aftermath (Mid Am, 36:2, Apr. 1954, p. 116-139).
Describes political activity in Nicaragua, 1933-1937; stresses the rise to power of Somoza.

3670. Bischoff, Henry C. British investments in Costa Rica (Interam Ec Aff 7:1, summer 1953, p. 37-47).
Brief survey covering especially period after 1870.

3671. Britnell, G. E. Factors in the economic development of Guatemala (Am Ec R, 43:2, May 1953, p. 104-114).
General survey of present-day economic conditions.

3672. Cardoza y Aragón, Luis. Guatemala y el Imperio Bananero (Cuad Am, año 13, 74:2, marzo-abril 1954, p. 19-45).
Shows how the United Fruit Company has controlled the political and economic affairs of Guatemala.

3673. Chapman, Mary Patricia. The mission of Elisha O. Crosby to Guatemala 1861-1864 (Pac Hist R, 24:3, Aug. 1955 p. 275-286).
Describes the activities of one of the few good Ministers of the U. S. to Guatemala.

3673a. **Comisión de Investigación Histórica de la Campaña, 1856-1857.** Proclamas y mensages. San José, 1954. 59 p. ([Publ.], 3).
A collection of proclamations and messages issued by President Juan Rafael Mora and other officials of Costa Rica during the campaign for the expulsion of William Walker from Central America. Many of the documents are inedited and the sources of the others are indicated. [R. R. Hill]

3674. **Gallardo, Miguel Ángel** (comp.). Papeles históricos. San Salvador, 1954. 228 p.
Miscellaneous collection of memoirs and letters of important people in 19th-century San Salvador.

3675. **Greer, Virginia L.** State Department policy in regard to the Nicaraguan election of 1924 (HAHR, 34:4, Nov. 1954, p. 445-467).
From the State Department archives the author shows the unsuccessful attempt of Hughes to obtain a free election in Nicaragua.

3676. **Guardiola Cubas, Esteban.** Vida y hechos del General Santos Guardiola. Tegucigalpa, Talleres Tipográficos Nacionales, 1953. 236 p.
Popular biography of General Guardiola of Honduras.

3677. **Houk, Richard J.** The development of foreign trade and communication in Costa Rica to the construction of the first railway (Americas, Franciscan Hist, 10:2, Oct. 1953, p. 197-209).
Shows the importance of the development of the export of coffee by the port of Puntarenas to 1857.

3678. **Miró, Rodrigo** (ed.). Panamá, 50 años de república. Panamá, Junta Nacional del Cincuentenario, 1953. 626 p.
Comprehensive coverage of social, economic, and political affairs by various authors.

3679. **Moore, J. Preston.** Pierre Soulé, southern expansionist and promoter (J South Hist, 21:2, May 1955, p. 203-223).
Describes Soulé's participation in the Walker filibustering activity in Central America, 1856-1860.

3680. **Panamá. Junta Nacional del Cincuentenario.** Documentos fundamentales para la historia de la nación panameña. Panamá, Imprenta Nacional, 1953. 476 p.
Compilation of various documents from the state papers.

3681. **Parker, Franklin Dallas.** José Cecilio del Valle and the establishment of the Central American Confederation. Tegucigalpa, (Publ. Univ. Honduras, 16), 1954. 85 p.
Brief biographical study. Thesis.

3681a. **Townsend Ezcurra, Andrés.** Misión del Mariscal Santa Cruz en Francia y Bélgica. Contribución a la historia diplomática de Guatemala, 1853-1855 (Antr Hist Guat, 4:2, junio 1952, p. 43-92).
A well-documented account, based on the Guatemalan archives, of the work of Andrés de Santa Cruz, who was made Guatemalan minister to France and then to Belgium while already in Paris as the Bolivian minister. With France, his main business concerned a dispute over treatment of a French consul to Guatemala. With Belgium, his main business was over the failure of a Belgian colonization company to fulfil its contract of 1842-1843. [R. D. Hussey]

3682. **Wright, Almon R.** German interest in Panama's Piñas Bay, 1910-1938 (J Mod Hist, 27:1, Mar. 1955, p. 61-65).
Concentrates on the period 1910-1914, with some material on the 1930's. Attempt of a German company to obtain railroad concession and land in the Piñas Bay region; blocked by the U. S. and Panama.

WEST INDIES

ROBERT E. McNICOLL

The centenary of José Martí's birth directly affected the number of historical writings produced, causing a flood of titles not only in Cuba but in all Latin America. Not all are listed herein. In Cuba, the indefatigable Dr. Fermín Peraza organized the Agrupación Bibliográfica José Toribio Medina, which should supplement the important bibliographical effort he has carried on so long single handed.

CUBA

3700. **Academia de la Historia de Cuba.** Constituciones de la República de Cuba. Habana, 1952, i.e. 1953. Unpaged.
Facsimile reproduction of the signed copies of the nine constitutions of Cuba from 1869 to 1952. [R. R. Hill]

3701. **Álvarez Conde, José.** Homenaje del Archivo Nacional a su primer director, Néstor Ponce de León, el emigrado intransigente. Habana, Archivo Nacional (Publ., 41), 1955. 73 p., illus.
An interesting documented study of the life and activities of Néstor Ponce de León, the first director of the Archive of Cuba under the Republic. The documents include especially correspondence and poetry of Ponce de León, as well as other materials. [R. R. Hill]

3702. **Arce, Luis A. de.** José Antonio Cor-

tina, época y carácter, 1853-1884. Habana, Selecta, 1955. 300 p.
Literary biography of important Cuban.

3703. **Bas Torriente, Eladio.** Siguiendo al sol. Habana, 1953. 131 p.
Description of invasion of Cuba by Gómez' forces from east to west.

3704. **Buttari Gaunaurd, J.** Boceto crítico histórico. Obra escrita en cuatro etapas. Habana, Lex, 1954. 789 p.
Four epochs of Cuban history: the American military government; the administration of Estrada Palma; the American intervention; the period of restoration, from Gómez' to Machado's administration. Personal comment and extensive copies of letters and documents. Agreeable and conversational in style, very critical of men and events.

3705. **Carmona Romay, Adriano G.** Fuentes para el estudio del pensamiento de José Martí en materia municipal. Habana, Editorial Martí, 1953. 15 p.
Study of *krausismo* of Martí as it affected his concept of municipal government.

3706. **Castro de Morales, Lilia** (ed.). Diccionario del pensamiento de José Martí. Ed. del centenario. Habana, Selecta, 1953. 377 p.
An ingenious attempt to create a tabulated *idearium* of Martí's thought—no doubt useful to speakers who desire to quote Martí on their particular subject.

3707. **Chester, Edmund A.** A sergeant named Batista. N. Y., Holt, 1954. 276 p., illus.
Although Mr. Chester is an official public relations man, this fact does not detract from the substantially authentic account he has written. Naturally Batista is the hero of the story, and many will find errors of focus and weighting of concurrent events, but the lively account is of use to the English reader.

3708. **Congreso de Escritores Martianos,** Habana, febrero 20 a 27 de 1953. Memoria. . . . Habana, Comisión Nacional Organizadora de los Actos y Ediciones del Centenario y del Monumento de Martí, 1953. 871 p., illus.
Papers, addresses, and resolutions offered at the Congress.

3709. **Cuba.** Archivo Nacional. El Archivo Nacional en la conmemoración del centenario del natalicio de José Martí y Pérez, 1853-1953. Habana, 1953. 805 p. (Publ., 36).
This commemorative volume comprises everything, both published and inedited, in the National Archive dealing with Martí. Included are: personal documents of Martí, notes, letters, poems, etc.; documents concerning Martí and letters to him; documents relating to the family of Martí; and articles and works treat-ing of Martí which have been published by the Archive. [R. R. Hill]

3710. ————. ————. Inventario general de la Delegación del Partido Revolucionario Cubano en Nueva York (1892-1898). T. 1. Habana, 1955. 322 p. (Publ., 42).
A listing alphabetically under names of writers of correspondence in the Archive of the Delegation of the Cuban Revolutionary Party. The list of Spanish correspondence includes names from A to Z, and that in other languages covers names from A to J. Each of the 8293 entries gives the name of the writer, the addressee, the date and pages. There is no indication of subject matter, but naturally, the documents deal with the purpose and actions of the Revolutionary Party. [R. R. Hill]

3711. ————. ————. Memoria correspondiente a los años de 1951-1953. Habana, 1954. 51 p. (Publ., 40).
A brief survey of the activities of the Archivo for the years indicated. Numerous letters and other documents are included. Also there are notes on searches made and new documents received. [R. R. Hill]

3712. **Esténger, Rafael.** El hombre de las montañas. Habana, Tall. Tip. Alfa, 1954. 107 p.
Speech regarding Antonio Maceo.

3713. **Fernández de la Vega, Óscar** (ed.). Proyección de Martí. Sus mejores textos. Habana, Selecta, 1953. 700 p.
Well-annotated collection of selection of Martí's writings.

3714. **Franco, José L.** La verdad histórica sobre la descendencia de Antonio Maceo. Habana, Municipio de La Habana, Oficina del Historiador de la Ciudad (Cuadernos de historia habanera, 47), 1951. 54 p.
Combats statement that Maceo was out of Cuba during 1870-1871 period.

3715. **Gómez Toro, Bernardo.** La famosa expedición Gómez-Martí (1895). Un eslabón perdido en su cadena de vicisitudes. Habana, Úcar García, 1953. 58 p.
Details on Martí's last trip to Cuba, with facsimiles of two of Martí's letters and a statement of the German captain of the ship on which Martí sailed. It appears that the fact that the captain and Martí were brother Masons helped Martí to gain his aid.

3716. **González, Manuel Pedro.** José Martí. Epic chronicler of the United States in the eighties. With an introduction by Sturgis E. Leavitt. Chapel Hill, N. C., University of North Carolina Press, 1953. 79 p.
This book, a welcome addition to the English titles on Martí, is better on Martí than on the U. S. of that era. The author, an authority on

Spanish literature, has apparently accepted as true many of the myths that still cloud the Latin American view of U. S. civilization.

3717. **Griñán Peralta, Leonardo.** Carlos Manuel de Céspedes. Análisis caracterológico. Santiago, Cuba, Universidad de Oriente, 1954. 284 p.

An excellent work that does a service in preventing the eclipse of interest in Céspedes, the patrician father of his country, by the expansion of works on lesser figures in the 1895-1898 war.

3718. **Habana (city). Oficina del Historiador de la Ciudad.** Homenaje al ilustre habanero Domingo Figarola-Caneda en el centenario de su nacimiento. Habana, Municipio de La Habana (Cuadernos de historia habanera, 52), 1952. 107 p.

First director of the National Library, founded 1901.

3719. **Henríquez Ureña, Max.** La Sociedad de Conferencias de la Habana y su época. Habana, Municipio de La Habana, Oficina del Historiador de la Ciudad (Cuadernos de historia habanera. 58), 1954. 47 p.

The Dominican intellectual, now retired in Cuba, played an important role in the organization described and his comments are important for a period of Cuba's cultural history.

3720. **Horrego Estuch, Leopoldo.** Juan Gualberto Gómez. Un gran inconforme. 2. ed., aumentada y corregida. Habana, La Milagrosa, 1954. 299 p.

A valuable literary biography of Martí's great collaborator.

3721. **Infiesta, Ramón.** El pensamiento político de Martí. Habana, Universidad de La Habana (Cátedra Martiana, III curso, 1952), 1953. 141 p.

3722. **Le-Roy y Gálvez, Luis F.** Breve reseña del origen y desarrollo de la química en Cuba. Habana, Academia de Ciencias Médicas, Físicas y Naturales, 1954. 23 p.

Notes for history of science. "Discurso de contestación" by Horacio Abascal y Vera included.

3723. **Lismore, Thomas.** Las monedas de Cuba (1870-1953). The coinage of Cuba (1870-1953). Habana, Lex, 1955. 84 p., tables, pl.

Text in Spanish and English. Very useful listing and description of Cuban coins.

3724. **Lizaso, Félix.** José Martí. Recuento de centenario. Habana, 1953. 2 v. 330, 452 p.

Two volumes collecting articles published by author between 1930 and 1953 as a result of 25 years of dedication to the study of Martí.

3725. ————. Proyección humana de Martí. B. A., Raigal, 1953. 160 p.

By one of the foremost writers on Martí.

3726. ———— (ed.). José Martí, precursor de la Unesco. Habana, Comisión Nacional Cubana de la UNESCO, 1953. 163 p.

The title would appear flippant to the Anglo-American reader if it were not for the respect due Lizaso's seriousness. As it turns out it is more useful as a sort of *critique* of the UNESCO than for any new light on the Cuban "Apostle."

3727. **Márquez Sterling, Carlos.** Don Tomás. Biografía de una época. Habana, Lex, 1953. 514 p., illus.

Excellent biography that would seem to establish Estrada Palma's place in Cuban history as a man as well as a leader.

3728. **Martí en Moscú.** Homenaje en su centenario. Habana, Páginas, 1953. 86 p., illus.

Addresses given in Moscow commemorating Martí centenary.

3729. **Mesa Rodríguez, Manuel I.** Diez años de guerra. El pacto del Zanjón, la Constitución de Baraguá y el fin de la contienda. Habana, Academia de la Historia de Cuba, 1954. 43 p.

Points out that the "Ten Years War" (1868-1878) lasted only nine years and four months.

3730. ———— (ed.). Centón epistolario de Domingo del Monte. T. 6, 1844-1845. Habana, Academia de la Historia de Cuba, 1953. 297 p.

Excellent source material in the letters of many of the cultural leaders of the Cuban "Golden Century" (19th).

3731. ———— (ed.). Diario de campaña del Comandante Luis Rodolfo Miranda. Habana, Municipio de la Habana, Oficina del Historiador de la Ciudad (Cuadernos de historia habanera, 57), 1954. 121 p.

Valuable war diary of 1896-1898.

3732. **Montiel, Félix.** Reverso del cincuentenario: España. Habana, Academia de la Historia de Cuba, 1953. 41 p.

Valuable for the international aspects of Martí's efforts and the development of the Cuban nation.

3733. **Moral, Luis F. del.** Serafín Sánchez. Un carácter al servicio de Cuba. México, Ediciones Mirador, 1955. 350 p.

Literary biography describing period 1846-1896 and covering life from Sancti-Spiritus to associations with Martí, exile, the war in the *manigua,* up to death in battle of Las Damas.

3734. Morales Patiño, Oswaldo. El capitán chino, Teniente Coronel Quirino Zamora. Historia de un mambí en la provincia de la Habana. Habana, Oficina del Historiador de la Ciudad (Cuadernos de historia habanera, 54), 1953. 135 p., illus.
Interesting but of restricted value.

3735. Moreno Fraginals, Manuel. Nación o plantación. El dilema político cubano a través de José Antonio Saco (Estud Hist Am, p. 241-272).
Study of Saco's attitude towards the Negro and the economic consequences of abolition of the slave trade.

3736. Oficios remitidos del estado Mayor de la columna expedicionaria que salió de la Habana al mando del Exmo. Señor Conde de Mirasol en mayo de 1850, con respecto al desembarco de enemigos en Cárdenas (B Arch Nac, Habana, t. 51-52, 1952-1953, i.e. 1954, p. 261-286). [J. H. Parry]

3737. Ortiz, Fernando. Discurso de. . . . Habana, Comisión Nacional Organizadora de los Actos y Ediciones del Centenario y del Monumento de Martí, 1953. 19 p.
Address in honor of Martí.

3738. ————. Martí y las razas. Habana, Comisión Nacional Organizadora de los Actos y Ediciones del Centenario y del Monumento de Martí, 1953. 33 p.
Useful discussion of Martí's ideas on the Negro.

3739. Palmer, Thomas Waverly, and **Emeterio S. Santovenia.** William Rufus King. Discursos leídos por . . . en la sesión pública celebrada por la misma el día 23 de marzo de 1953, en memoria de William Rufus King. Habana, El Siglo XX, 1953. 38 p.
Commemorating fact that King took oath of office as Vice President of the U. S. on Mar. 24, 1853, in Matanzas, Cuba. He died in Alabama less than a month later.

3740. Peraza Sarausa, Fermín. Carlos M. Trelles. Habana, Municipio de La Habana, Departamento de Educación, 1954. 20 p.
Cuba's leading bibliographer of today talks of his noted predecessor.

3741. Pérez Cabrera, José Manuel. La Academia de la Historia y el centenario de Martí. Discurso . . . . Habana, Academia de la Historia de Cuba, 1954. 23 p.

3742. ————. Martí y el "proyecto Ruz." Habana, Academia de la Historia de Cuba, 1955. 24 p.
Brief account by one of Cuba's major historians

3743. Piedra-Bueno, Andrés de. Lanuza Habana, Juan González, 1953. 39 p.
Short biography of statesman and intellectual José Antonio González Lanuza.

3744. Ponte Domínguez, Francisco. La masonería en la independencia de Cuba Habana, Modas Magazine, 1954. 135 p
This writer, who appears to specialize in the history of Masonry, provides an interesting sidelight on Cuban independence.

3745. Primelles, León. Crónica cubana 1915-1918. La reelección de Menocal y la revolución de 1917. La danza de los millones. La primera guerra mundial. Habana, Lex, 1955. 659 p.
A conscientious effort to list and comment on all important events in Cuban history. Strict chronological order is maintained and the greatest factual detail is given.

3746. Quintana, Jorge. Índice de extranjeros en el ejército libertador de Cuba (1895-1898). Introducción de Joaquín Llaverías. T. 1. Habana, Archivo Nacional de Cuba (Publ., 35), 1953. 388 p
A documented study based on records in the Archive regarding the lives and activities of foreigners who conspired and worked for the independence of Cuba from the time of the Cacique Hatuey down to 1868, including Dominicans, Americans, Mexicans, South Americans, and others. It is an interesting study of a particular phase of Cuban history by the dean of the Provincial College of Journalism. [R. R. Hill]

3747. Remos, Juan J. Deslindes de Martí. Habana, Tip. J. Suárez, 1953. 142 p.
A solid series of essays by a leading literary and historical authority.

3748. Rexach de León, Rosario. El carácter de Martí y otros ensayos. Habana, Comisión Nacional Cubana de la UNESCO, 1954. 108 p.
Attempt to apply character analysis to Martí. Not too successful, though appealing.

3749. Reyna Cossío, René E. Estudios histórico-militares sobre la guerra de independencia de Cuba. Habana, Municipio de la Habana, Oficina del Historiador de la Ciudad (Cuadernos de historia habanera, 59), 1954. 128 p. & maps.
Technical study of several battles.

3750. Rodrigues, Carlos Rafael. José Martí and Cuban liberation. With an introduction by Jesús Colon. N. Y., International Publishers, 1953. 24 p.
Leftist publication depicting Martí as "sure-eyed guide of the Cuban middle class," and indicating that "the social equilibrium Martí sought was unattainable."

3751. Rodríguez Abascal, Pedro. Un español que llegó a coronel por sus hazañas en Cuba. Habana, 1953. 89 p., tables.
Life of José Álvarez Pérez, "el gallego Álvarez" —a Spaniard who fought for Cuba.

3752. ————. El mayor general Pedro E. Betancourt en la guerra y en la paz. Habana, 1954. 113 p.

3753. Rodríguez Altunaga, Rafael. Las Villas. Biografía de una provincia. Habana, Academia de la Historia de Cuba, 1955. 355 p.
A labor of love by a son of Las Villas, but tending more to a chronicle and a listing of events and names than the interpretative social history that could be desired.

3754. Rodríguez Demorizi, Emilio. Martí en Santo Domingo. Habana, Úcar García, 1953. 621 p.
Excellent.

3755. ————. Papeles dominicanos de Máximo Gómez. Ciudad Trujillo, Montalvo, 1954. 447 p.
To celebrate centenary of Martí, the author publishes letters of Gómez sent to relatives and others in Santo Domingo.

3756. Roig de Leuchsenring, Emilio. José Martí: pensamiento político. Martí: síntesis de su vida. Habana, Oficina del Historiador de la Ciudad (Col. del Centenario de Martí, 1), 1953. 236 p.
Another selection of Martí's writings, with a short synopsis of his life.

3757. ————. Martí, antimperialista. Habana, Imp. Modelo, 1953. 106 p.

3758. ————. La república de Martí. Habana, Imp. Modelo, 1953. 124 p.
Emphasis on Martí's ideas that Cuba should avoid monocultivo and a single purchaser.

3759. Rosell Planas, Rebeca. Factores económicos, políticos y sociales de la Guerra Chiquita. Habana, Academia de la Historia de Cuba, 1953. 58 p.
Analysis of the tax burden imposed on Cuba after 1878; for example, flour that cost $5.25 a hundred pounds in the U. S. cost $16.63 in Havana.

3760. Santos Jiménez, Rafael. Ideas de Martí sobre las luchas entre el capital y el trabajo. Habana, Lex, 1953. 30 p.

3761. Torriente, Cosme de la. Juan Gualberto Gómez. Habana, Academia de la Historia de Cuba, 1954. 79 p.
A brief comment as important for its author as for its subject.

3762. Vela, David. Martí en Guatemala. Guatemala, Ministerio de Educación Pública (Col. Contemporáneos, 40), 1954. 366 p.
Guatemala, as well as many other nations omitted in this listing, made a significant contribution to the centenary by this publication.

3763. Vitier, Medardo. Martí. Estudio integral. Habana, Comisión Nacional Organizadora de los Actos y Ediciones del Centenario y del Monumento de Martí, 1954. 334 p.
One of Cuba's profounder thinkers attempts to make a philosophical study of Martí.

3764. Zéndegui, Guillermo de. Ámbito de Martí. Habana, P. Fernández, 1954. 222 p., illus.
Magnificently presented book that retraces in text and pictures the route of Martí, containing some account of every place where Martí lived for any length of time.

OTHER AREAS

3765. Damirón, Rafael. Memorias y comentarios. Ciudad Trujillo, Stella, 1953. 190 p.
Interesting personal reminiscences of period 1894-1930.

3766. Gutiérrez del Arroyo, Isabel. El reformismo ilustrado en Puerto Rico. México, Asomante, 1953. 259 p.
A thorough study of ideas of political and institutional reform dictated by "enlightened despotism" in Puerto Rico, stemming from memoirs of Pedro Tomás de Córdova (1818-1838) directed to the Spanish authorities. A well-documented and footnoted work that is a valuable guide to the Anglo-American scholar, not only to the major theme of the book but also to the state of Puerto Rico in the first half of the 19th century.

3767. Healy, Mary Aquinas. The contributions of Toussaint L'Ouverture to the independence of the American republics, 1776-1826 (Americas, Franciscan Hist, 9:4, April 1953, p. 413-451).
Enthusiastic but not particularly original eulogy. States that "Leclerc's defeat by Toussaint's army was, in its results, one of the most decisive defeats in history." [J. H. Parry]

3768. Jiménez Malaret, René. Epistolario histórico del Dr. Félix Tió y Malaret. Santurce, Puerto Rico, Imp. Soltero, 1953. 189 p.
Illuminating description of independence and autonomist movements during period 1887-1897 documented by letters of the period.

3769. Lhérisson, Lélia J. Les héros de l'Indépendance dans l'histoire d'Haïti. Port-au-Prince, Coll. du Centcinquan-

tenaire de l'Indépendance d'Haïtï, 1953. 68 p.
Thumbnail sketches of some 50 leaders of the Haitian war of independence.

SOUTH AMERICA (EXCEPT BRAZIL)

CLIFTON B. KROEBER AND DAVID BUSHNELL

GENERAL

3800. Bierck, Harold A., Jr. The struggle for abolition in Gran Colombia (HAHR, 33:3, Aug. 1953, p. 365-386).
Describes the beginnings of slave emancipation, offering much new data, especially on practical difficulties faced in administering the manumission law of 1821. [D. Bushnell]

3801. Bolívar, Simón. América y el Libertador. Prólogo del Dr. Cristóbal L. Mendoza. Caracas, Secretaría General de la Décima Conferencia Interamericana (Col. Historia, 3), 1953. xxiii, 55 p.
Selections from the writings of Bolívar dealing with American fraternity, independence, America and the war, America before the World, and political union of the New World. [R. R. Hill]

3802. Brice, Ángel Francisco. Bolívar, libertador y estadista. Caracas, Universidad del Zulia, 1953. 367 p., illus.
Contains the author's essay on Madariaga's Bolívar (HLAS, no. 18, 1952, item 2040), a conventional study on "Bolívar, Libertador del Perú," and a third essay interpreting Bolívar's views on inter-American solidarity in the light of the Panama Congress. [D. Bushnell]

3803. Bushnell, David. The Santander regime in Gran Colombia. Newark, Del., University of Delaware Press (University of Delaware monograph series, no. 5), 1954. 381 p.
A broad-gauge administrative history of Gran Colombia (chiefly of Colombia itself), 1819-1827, clearly treating fields, problems, and policies of the central government's activity. This is a mature and well-written book, important both for its scope and for the depth of its well-digested information. Its obvious fault is lack of a conclusion. [C. B. Kroeber]

3804. Encina, Francisco A. Bolívar y la independencia de la América española. Emancipación de la presidencia de Quito, del virreinato de Lima y del Alto Perú. Santiago, Nascimento, 1954. 666 p.
A detailed and generally readable survey of the final liberation of Ecuador, Peru, and Bolivia. A volume in the author's series Bolívar y la independencia de la América española. [D. Bushnell]

3805. Fragachán, Félix R. (comp.). Simón Bolívar. Síntesis panorámica de la vida del grande hombre. Homenaje a la Semana de la Patria. Caracas, Tip. Americana, 1954. 437 p., illus.
Officially-sponsored anthology of documents, poems, discursos, and articles relating to Bolívar; a useful compendium of bolivarianismo. [D. Bushnell]

3806. Guerra Íñiguez, Daniel. El pensamiento internacional de Bolívar. Caracas, Ragon, 1955. 309 p.
Without pretending to offer new facts or interpretation, discusses backgrounds of the Independence movement, and then in some detail the "Pan Americanist" policies of Bolívar and Gran Colombia. [D. Bushnell]

3807. Lecuna, Vicente. El archivo del Libertador (in La Casa Natal del Libertador. Caracas, 1954, p. 53-77).
A brief description of the papers of Bolívar and related materials assembled by Dr. Lecuna. There is a list of the 206 volumes of the collection, with an indication of the content of each. The collection is deposited in the Casa Natal del Libertador. [R. R. Hill]

3808. ————. Bolívar y el arte militar. Formada sobre documentos, sin utilizar consejas ni versiones impropias. Conclusiones de acuerdo con hechos probados, y la naturaleza de las cosas. N. Y., Colonial Press, 1955. 473 p., facsim., illus., maps.
A further development of themes already handled in Lecuna's Crónica razonada (see HLAS, no. 16, 1950, item 2002). Organized chronologically, with illustrative documents; the latter are mainly from 1813-1816, and many previously unpublished. [D. Bushnell]

3809. ————. Relaciones diplomáticas de Bolívar con Chile y Buenos Aires. Caracas, Sociedad Bolivariana de Venezuela, 1954, i.e. 1955. 2 v. 274, 388 p., illus.
Documents, many published for the first time, fully indexed. [D. Bushnell]

3810. Leturia, Pedro de. Conatos franco-venezolanos para obtener, en 1813, del Papa Pío VII una encíclica a favor de la independencia hispanoamericana (Miscel Am, 3, 1952, p. 355-393).
Brief review of efforts to secure Papal pronouncement on behalf of American independence. [H. Bernstein]

3811. Navarro, Nicolás Eugenio. Un episodio divertido de la primera educación de Bolívar (B Ac Nac Hist, Caracas, 38:149, enero-marzo 1955, p. 3-15).
Describes the escape of young Bolívar, first from the house of his guardian, Carlos Palacios, and then from his teacher, Simón Rodríguez, whose early influence is minimized by Navarro. Based especially on the document that

follows next in the same issue: "Transcripción del expediente original de la Real Audiencia de Caracas, sobre domicilio tutelar del Menor Don Simón de Bolívar ..." (*ibid.*, p. 16-59). [D. Bushnell]

3812. **Palacio Fajardo, Manuel.** Bosquejo de la revolución en la América española. Prólogo de Enrique Bernardo Núñez. Caracas, Secretaría General de la Décima Conferencia Interamericana (Col. Historia, 5), 1953. xxxvi, 221 p., facsim., illus., fold. map.
First Spanish edition of a work, by a Venezuelan patriot leader, which was originally published in London in 1817 as *Outline of the Revolution* ... and also translated into French and German; significant especially for its influence on foreign opinion. Contains a useful bibliographical note as well as the prologue. [D. Bushnell]

3813. **Pérez Vila, Manuel** (ed.). Bolívar y su época. Cartas y testimonios de extranjeros notables. Prólogo del Dr. Vicente Lecuna. Caracas, Secretaría General de la Décima Conferencia Interamericana (Col. Historia, 10, 11), 1953. 2 v. 279, 247 p.
A collection of letters to Bolívar from contemporaries in Europe and America expressing their opinions regarding the labors and position of the Liberator. Most of the items are inedited. Extensive notes are included regarding the activities of Bolívar and respecting the documents. There are also biographical sketches of the correspondents. [R. R. Hill]

3814. **Rivarola, Vicente.** Memorias diplomáticas. El Paraguay en el litigio de límites con Bolivia. La Guerra del Chaco. 2. Misión en la Argentina (1929-1936). B. A., Ayacucho, 1955. 392 p.
Continuing the memoirs of a Paraguayan diplomat, here seen heading the B. A. legation during the preliminaries to and early course of the Chaco War (June 1929-August 1933). A simple account of events, including many documents; a contribution to the history of those difficult dealings in which attempts at mediation, including one by the League of Nations, failed. [C. B. Kroeber]

3815. **Street, John.** La influencia británica en la independencia de las provincias del Río de la Plata, con especial referencia al período comprendido entre 1806 y 1816 (R Hist, Montevideo, 19:55-57, sept. 1953, p. 181-257; 21:61-63, julio 1954, p. 329-391; 22:64-66, agosto 1954, p. 1-83; 24:70-72, agosto 1955, p. 224-317).
A valuable study, based on wide archival research. The first installment reviews at length the British invasions of 1806-1807; the next two, dealing with the period of the Strangford mission in Rio, present conclusions which are also summarized in the following item; the last installment gives epilogue, documentary appendix, and index. [D. Bushnell]

3816. ————. Lord Strangford and Río de la Plata, 1808-1815 (HAHR, 33:4, Nov. 1953, p. 477-510).
Reviews the policy pursued by Britain's minister at Rio toward Spanish American independence; concludes that Strangford sympathized with the patriots but was never actually disloyal to England's Spanish alliance. [D. Bushnell]

3817. **Yrarrázaval Larraín, José Miguel.** San Martín, según documentos del Public Record Office de Londres (B Ac Ch Hist, 21:51, 2. semestre 1954, p. 5-48).
Discusses policy and character of San Martín on the basis of copious citations from reports of British agents, possibly sometimes reading too much into their remarks. The British views of San Martín are very favorable; Yrarrázaval's generally are not, suggesting that San Martín was disloyal toward O'Higgins and too willing to offer concessions to the British. [D. Bushnell]

ARGENTINA

3818. **Alberdi, Juan Bautista.** Cartas inéditas a Juan María Gutiérrez y a Félix Frías. Recopilación e introducción de Jorge M. Mayer y Ernesto A. Martínez. B. A., Luz del Día, 1953. 287 p.
In his direct and honest style. 49 letters to Gutiérrez from Chile, 1845-1852, and Europe, 1856-1876; to Frías, 69 letters, all but 8 from Chile, 1844-1854. The diplomatic missions in Europe and exile in Chile do not seem to yield major new insights, but the letters contain many worthwhile statements and questions as to Alberdi himself, the foreign nations concerned (France, England, Spain, Italy, and Chile), and his own Argentina. [C. B. Kroeber]

3819. **Alem, Leandro N.** Autonomismo y centralismo. Con una introducción sobre "Alem y el federalismo argentino" por Gabriel del Mazo. B. A., Raigal (Biblioteca histórico-política argentina, 2) 1954. xxviii, 207 p.
Speeches as deputy in the legislature of B. A. Province, 1876, 1877, 1879, and 1880, and one as senator (on the uprising of 1890) in 1891, selected to show his resistance to increasing centralization of power in the national government, especially in the executive. These are well worth reading. Alem's complete parliamentary record was published by the provincial Chamber (La Plata, 1949, 6 v.). [C. B. Kroeber]

3820. **Amico, Carlos d'.** Buenos Aires, sus hombres, su política (1860-1890). B. A., Editorial Americana, 1952. 306 p.
Reprint of his *Buenos Aires, su naturaleza, sus costumbres, sus hombres* ..., México, 1890, issued under the nom de plume of Carlos Martínez. D'Amico was once governor of Buenos Aires Province, and his somewhat bitter account of events and personalities was, in part, gained at first hand. [C. B. Kroeber]

3821. **Arana, Enrique** (h.). Juan Manuel

de Rosas en la historia argentina. Creador y sostén de la unidad nacional. B. A., Instituto Panamericano de Cultura, 1954. T. 1, Rosas y la política exterior, con otros estudios, 693 p.; t. 2, Rosas en la evolución política argentina, 781 p.

Synthetic work on the Argentine dictator Rosas; one volume yet to come. Strong, in many tangential passages of value, and in inserting rare old items in entirety. Glaring weaknesses, in the "revisionist" methods of using friendly authors (almost to exclusion of others), and in infrequent resort to new manuscripts. Maintains the complete "revisionist" position, even where recent studies make it untenable—either by printing unmatchable facts and conclusions together (viz. Rosas' role in British invasion of 1807), or merely by overlooking the inconvenient matter (viz. Rosas and Paraguay, Uruguay). Commentary on "revisionism," t. 1, p. 9-123. [C. B. Kroeber]

3822. Archivo del General Juan Andrés Gelly y Obes (R Bib Nac, B A, 21:51, 3. trimestre 1949, i.e. 1951, p. 7-296; 21:52, 4. trimestre 1949, i.e. 1951, p. 309-633; 22:53, 1. trimestre 1950, i.e. 1952, p. 7-237; 22:54, 2. trimestre 1950, i.e. 1953, p. 241-462; 23:55, 3. trimestre 1950, i.e. 1953, p. 7-249; 23:56, 4. trimestre 1950, i.e. 1954, p. 253-373, conclusión).

Documents of General Gelly y Obes (1802-1865) comprising: (1) private correspondence; (2) official correspondence dealing with the defense of the frontiers and the rebellions of Generals Peñazola and López Jordán; and (3) correspondence relative to the war of the Triple Alliance against Paraguay. Each issue of the *Revista* has documents of each of the groups indicated. There is an introduction by Felipe Barreda Laos in no. 51. [R. R. Hill]

3823. **Barreda y Laos, Felipe.** Roque Sáenz Peña. B. A., Lombardi, 1954. 421 p.

An undocumented narrative of the public life of the Argentine diplomat and statesman (1851-1914), national president 1910-1914, and author of the compulsory secret vote law of 1912. This pupil of Leandro Alem was a well-born Conservative helping to break the Conservative monopoly of government. The man does not emerge from this story, but his optimism and individualism become abundantly evident. [C. B. Kroeber]

3824. **Barrionuevo Imposti, V.** El Libertador Don José de San Martín y la provincia de Córdoba (R U Nac, Córdoba, 41:1-2, marzo-junio 1954, p. 191-354).

Describes the role of Cordoba (political, economic, and military) in the Independence movement, 1813-1822, with reference mainly to the campaigns of San Martín. Unpretentious local history, but based on fairly wide research. [D. Bushnell]

3825. **Caballero, Ricardo.** Yrigoyen. La conspiración civil y militar del 4 de febrero de 1905. B. A., Raigal, 1951. 251 p.

Memoirs of the Unión Cívica Radical from before its abortive national uprising of Feb. 4, 1905, until after the national election victory in 1916. These memoirs are very spotty, but contain a whole book of names of participants, and incidents and doctrinal discussion, that will help toward a history of the party, particularly at Rosario and elsewhere in Santa Fe. The author was later a leading Radical senator. [C. B. Kroeber]

3826. **Caillet-Bois, Ricardo.** Noticias acerca de las vinculaciones de Fray Servando Teresa de Mier, Guillermo Walton y Santiago Perry con el gobierno de Buenos Aires, 1812-1818 (R Hist Am, 35-36, junio-dic. 1953, p. 118-132).

Miscellaneous data on the correspondence of the Mexican patriot Fray Servando with the B. A. authorities, and on the propaganda activities of two English sympathizers, Walton and Perry. [D. Bushnell]

3827. **Cánepa, Luis.** Historia de los símbolos nacionales argentinos. B. A., Albatros, 1953. 237 p.

A satisfactory synthesis of history of the Argentine flag, shield, hymn, and other national devices. [C. B. Kroeber]

3828. **Celesia, Ernesto H.** Rosas, aportes para su historia. B. A., Peuser, 1954. 505 p.

Convincing proof, from new documents, on certain disputed points touching the youth and early career of Juan Manuel de Rosas of Argentina, especially 1806-1833. The proof runs against Rosas' reputation. Documents, p. 347 ff. [C. B. Kroeber]

3829. **Colegio Libre de Estudios Superiores.** Veintidos años de labor, 20 de mayo 1930, 16 de julio 1952. B. A., 1953. 117 p.

History and personnel of the free college that so well echoed trends in Argentine scientific, technical, and general scholarly work from 1930 until closed by the government in 1952. Similar information can be had in *Cursos y conferencias*, published by the Colegio from 1931. [C. B. Kroeber]

3830. **Davis, Thomas B., Jr.** Carlos de Alvear, man of revolution. The diplomatic career of Argentina's first minister to the United States. Durham, N. C., Duke University Press, 1955. 305 p.

Careful research on the man known in his time as Carlos María de Alvear (1789-1852); chiefly his lonely and devious missions in the U. S., 1824-1825, 1838-1852, whose reports, says Davis, helped condition the post-1852 official Argentine view of the U. S. This study is done in context, and is informative for Argentine history of the period. [C. B. Kroeber]

3831. **Fernández Zárate, Luis.** Ángel Vicente Peñaloza. El señor de Guaja. El Chacho. La Rioja, Argentina (B. A., Cervantes Tall. Graf.), 1952. 88 p.

A loose account of the wars of one caudillo (1800-1863), evidently an inefficient attempt to give historical backing to Perón's view that past "oligarchic" governments robbed and misled the innocent Argentine poor. [C. B. Kroeber]

3832. Ferns, H. S. Britain's informal empire in Argentina, 1806-1914 (Past Pres, 4, Nov. 1953, p. 60-75).
How Argentina achieved a close and profitable relation with Britain, and thus with the industrial world, without experiencing the tensions characteristic of such relationships. Many insights, and a number of factual errors concerning the revolutionary period. [C. B. Kroeber]

3833. Flores, María [pseud.], i.e. **Mary Foster Main.** The woman with the whip: Eva Perón. Garden City, N. Y., Doubleday, 1952. 286 p.
A biography of María Eva Duarte de Perón, wife and partner-in-government of the former Argentine president, concerning mainly the period from her introduction to Perón until her death in July 1952. The book is undocumented and often heavily anecdotal, but is mature, well written, and very well informed. It is convincing in explaining both Eva Perón's character and her influence in Argentina, and contains much common-sense opinion about present-day Argentina. [C. B. Kroeber]

3834. Fragueiro, Mariano. Organización del crédito. Estudio preliminar de Ricardo M. Ortiz. B. A., Raigal (Biblioteca Manuel Belgrano de estudios económicos), 1954. 253 p.
Originally published in Santiago, Chile, 1850. The Argentine author (1795-1872), active in elective and appointive offices after 1831 and on both sides of the B. A.-provinces struggles of his time, shows how the emerging industrial economy of Argentina should be based on state control, via paper currency, a Bank, and direction of investment. Development by private initiative would yield the greatest good to the greatest number only if overseen by the state. A major work, grouping with Esteban Echeverría's. The essay by Ortiz (p. 7-107) is a worthy history of economic trends and ideas in Argentina after 1810. [C. B. Kroeber]

3835. Funes, Víctor Luis. Caseros. Ensayo histórico. B. A., Tall. Gráf. San Pablo, 1952. 40 p., illus.
A minor example of the revisionism in Argentine history that rehabilitates the name of Juan Manuel de Rosas, dictator 1829-1852. Funes demonstrates that Rosas was popular up to the moment of his defeat; then he gives some examples showing that terrorism did not cease with Rosas' fall in 1852. The work does not focus, and is of value mainly for some inedited documents quoted in the text. [C. B. Kroeber]

3836. Gandía, Enrique de. El 25 de mayo de 1810. La historia tradicional y la historia renovadora (R Cien Jur Soc, 15: 76-77, 1953, p. 223-303).

A long interpretative essay, specifically taking issue with the more traditional views expressed by Pueyrredón (see item 3849, below). Seeks above all to rehabilitate the figure of Martín de Alzaga, leader of the abortive junta attempt of Jan. 1, 1809, who is described as the real precursor of Argentine independence. At the same time, Gandía stresses the limited objectives of the junta finally set up in May 1810; its professions of respect for Ferdinand VII he generally accepts as quite sincere. Similar views are expressed by Gandía in "Antecedentes de los sucesos de mayo de 1810 en B. A." (R Hist Am, 37-38, enero-dic. 1954, p. 277-294), which takes the form of a commentary on a report of the Audiencia dealing with the 1809 junta attempt; and in "El temor a Napoleón en B. A." (B Real Ac Hist, 134:1, enero-marzo 1954, p. 115-135), which deals again with the theme of loyalty to Ferdinand. [D. Bushnell]

3837. Herren, Ricardo A. Azul-celeste y blanca. Génesis de la bandera argentina. Madrid, Ediciones Cultura Hispánica (Santo y seña, 15), 1953. 116 p.
Defends the view that the colors of the Argentine flag are derived, directly or indirectly (e.g., via the flag of B. A. consulado), from the symbolism of the Immaculate Conception; other explanations are discussed and rejected. [D. Bushnell]

3838. Hoffmann, Fritz L. A Franciscan fighter for South American Independence (Americas, Franciscan Hist, 10:3, Jan. 1954, p. 289-300).
Brief sketch of the Argentine friar Luis Beltrán, recording his military and technical services in the armies of San Martín. [D. Bushnell]

3839. Ingenieros, José. La locura en la Argentina. Anotado por Aníbal Ponce. B. A., Meridión, 1954. 158 p.
Reprint of 1st edition, B. A., 1920. Facts on mental disorders, asylums, and studies in psychiatry, legal medicine, neuropathology and related fields, in Argentina between the 1820's and c. 1910. Of interest since some well-known Argentine historians originally took medical degrees and put their special knowledge to (doubtful) historical use. [C. B. Kroeber]

3840. Levene, Ricardo. La anarquía de 1820 y la iniciación de la vida pública de Rosas. B. A., Unión de Editores Latinos (Col. Histórica americana, 1), 1954. 330 p.
Second and slightly altered edition of a work published in B. A., 1932, describing and analyzing the complex politics of B. A. Province in 1820, then following the growing role of Juan Manuel de Rosas (dictator, 1829-1852) into late 1826. Competent. Documents (1820-1825), p. 215-322. [C. B. Kroeber]

3841. Luna, Félix. Yrigoyen. El templario de la libertad. B. A., Raigal (Biblioteca histórico-política argentina; Formato mayor, 1), 1954. 563 p.

Public career of the man (1852-1933) who finally became leader of the Argentine Radical party and first popularly elected president of Argentina (1916-1922; 1928-1930). This is a story rather than an analysis of administration or of the mysterious man himself. Useful for detailed remarks on political shifts and maneuverings within the Radical party, particularly during the twenties, and for occasional comments on previous literature on the man and the period. [C. B. Kroeber]

3842. **Marco, Carlos R.** Don Juan Manuel de Rosas, sus detractores y sus panegiristas. Prólogo del Dr. Luis Alberto de Herrera. T. 1. Mendoza, Argentina, 1953. 283 p.

Discusses four intemperate critics of the Argentine dictator Rosas: Domingo F. Sarmiento and Tomás de Iriarte, at length; José Rivera Indarte and Andrés Lamas, briefly. Some new thoughts appear, but the book is poorly informed and is nearly as partisan (revisionist) as the writers discussed [C. B. Kroeber]

3843. **Mariluz Urquijo, José M.** Antecedentes sobre la política económica de las Provincias Unidas, 1810-1816 (R Fac Der Cien Soc, B A, 3. época, 7:31, nov.-dic. 1952, p. 1313-1328).

A good article, done largely from unpublished papers of the merchant *consulado* of B. A., showing how futile were attempts by the B. A. governments to protect local industries while at the same time encouraging the importation being carried on by aggressive Britons. [C. B. Kroeber]

3844. **Medrano, Samuel W.** Problemas de la organización de la justicia en las primeras soluciones constituyentes (R Fac Der Cien Soc, B A, 9:40, sept.-oct. 1954, p. 1127-1148).

Brief but useful review, covering the period 1810-1817. [D. Bushnell]

3845. **Ortiz, Ricardo M.** El pensamiento económico de Echeverría. Trayectoria y actualidad. B. A., Raigal (Biblioteca Manuel Belgrano de estudios económicos), 1953. 185 p.

Begins with key points of the economic thought of the Argentine poet whose ideas served to found the Argentine historical school and to proclaim a Utopian-socialist program (1837). Ortiz then shows how these economic ideas not only were realistic in their time but are also timely for Argentina today. Those ideas indicated a mixed economy which would aid democracy and militate against class struggle. Ortiz' detailed reading of economic history (1830's nearly to the present) is, as always, lucid and meaningful. [C. B. Kroeber]

3846. **Pavón Pereyra, Enrique.** Perón. Preparación de una vida para el mando, 1895-1942. B. A., Espiño, 1952. 274 p., illus.

A factual if flattering biography of Juan Domingo Perón before he became a government minister and, later, president of Argentina. Emphasizes his interest in sports and the writing he did during his army days, but does not explain his rise to political power. [C. B. Kroeber]

3847. **Peña, Roberto I.** El pensamiento político del deán Funes. Córdoba, Argentina, Universidad Nacional de Córdoba, Instituto de Estudios Americanistas (Serie Histórica, 24), 1953. 258 p.

A useful short study, mainly narrative in approach; discusses Funes' "intellectual formation" and his expressed opinions on political organization (1810-1826) and Church-State relations. (Also in R U Nac, Córdoba, 39:4-5, sept.-dic. 1952, p. 979-1061; 40:1, marzo-abril 1953, p. 49-213). [C. B. Kroeber]

3848. **Perdiguero, César.** Calisto Gauna. Contribución documental para su historia. Salta, Argentina, Ediciones El Estudiante (Col. Salta de antes, historia y tradiciones, 1), 1953. 243 p., illus.

Biography of a "civil hero" of Independence (d. 1833). Based on extensive research in Salta archives; a useful contribution to local history in the revolutionary period. [D. Bushnell]

3849. **Pueyrredón, Carlos A.** 1810. La Revolución de Mayo según amplia documentación de la época. B. A., Peuser, 1953. 670 p., facsims., illus.

A detailed history of the May Revolution and its antecedents from 1806, with numerous basic documents reprinted; treatment is on the whole conventional. See also article by Enrique de Gandía, above. [D. Bushnell]

3850. **Rosa, José María.** Los caudillos populares en la República Argentina (H Id, año 13, 24:104, nov. 1952, p. 233-247).

The author feels that the caudillo (military leader) can only be defined as a truly popular leader, and in Argentina he has been a federalist who has repeatedly saved the people from unitarist traitors. A capsule statement of "revisionism," also of present-day chauvinism. [C. B. Kroeber]

3851. **Ruiz Moreno, Isidoro; José Antonio Ginzo; and Lisandro de la Torre.** En torno a Rosas y el revisionismo. B. A., Bases (1), 1954. 87 p.

Useful reading. The essay by Ginzo included in this volume was noted in *HLAS, no. 18, 1952,* item 2066. Ruiz Moreno carefully uses previous studies to show the weakness of the Argentine revisionists' leading assertion: that Juan Manuel de Rosas (dictator, 1829-1852) was an effective champion of Argentine sovereignty. [C. B. Kroeber]

3852. **Ruiz Moreno, Leandro.** El General Don Francisco Ramírez, fe de bautismo de la democracia y piedra angular del federalismo. Paraná, Argentina, Nueva Impresora. 1955. 466 p.

A diffuse biography of the caudillo of Entre Rios Province, Argentina, Francisco Ramírez (1786-1821), with focus on the anarchy of 1820-1821. Mainly useful for some new documents reproduced in the work. [C. B. Kroeber]

3853. ———— (comp.). César Blas Pérez Colman (B Ac Nac Hist, B A, 28:26, 1952, p. 323-352).
List of the works of the late historian whose subject was the history of Entre Rios Province, Argentina. [C. B. Kroeber]

3854. Smith, O. Edmund, Jr. Yankee diplomacy. U. S. intervention in Argentina. Dallas, Tex., Southern Methodist University Press (Arnold Foundation studies, n. s., 3), 1953. 196 p.
Done mostly from well-known books and articles, this account reaches the usual conclusions in dealing mainly with events of 1942-1946. [C. B. Kroeber]

3855. Tonda, Américo A. Las facultades de los vicarios capitulares porteños, 1812-1853 (Cien Fe, 9:33, enero-marzo 1953, p. 39-72).
Careful exposition of tension between successive *provisores* of the Catholic diocese of B. A. and the ecclesiastical cabildo, as to powers and limitations of the former. Decrees of the Council of Trent on the subject had evidently not been entirely clarified, and the Pope's part in removal of *vicarios capitulares* was not yet what it is today. Valuable research. [C. B. Kroeber]

3856. Vedia y Mitre, Mariano. El deán Funes. Su vida, su obra, su personalidad. B. A., Kraft (Col. Cúpula), 1954. 671 p., illus.
An outstanding historical biography. The author admires Funes for his manifold services to Argentina in the Independence era, and for his general attitude of moderation, but offers no mere eulogy and carefully analyzes all the controversies that have grown up about Funes' career. [D. Bushnell]

3857. Zorraquín Becú, Ricardo. Formación constitucional del federalismo (R Fac Der Cien Soc, B A, 8:33, mayo-junio 1953, p. 459-482).
Authors of the Argentine constitution of 1853 departed from earlier examples to arrive at a "centralized federalism" well calculated to meet local needs, but later changes made at the instance of B. A. Province (due to her dissatisfaction with this "mixed" system) were destructive of the juridical balance of 1853. An intelligent discussion. [C. B. Kroeber]

3858. ————. Marcelino Ugarte, 1822-1872. Un jurista en la época de la organización nacional. B. A., Universidad de Buenos Aires, Instituto de Historia del Derecho (Col. de estudios para la historia del derecho argentino, 5), 1954. 333 p.
Traces the career of a B. A. lawyer who served as provincial legislator, professor of law, Min-

ister of Foreign Relations (1867), and finally, 1870-1872, as justice of the Supreme Court. His contributions were considerable; he was unsuccessful in fighting centralization of government; his project for a civil code (printed here) had much merit. An intelligent book, and a valuable example of the civilians who formed Argentina after 1852. [C. B. Kroeber]

BOLIVIA

3859. Arnade, Charles W. Una figura mediocre en el motín del 18 de abril de 1828 (B Soc Geog Sucre, 45:441, enero-marzo 1954, p. 73-100).
New light on the revolt against Sucre's government; deals with José Antonio Acebey, who was a titular leader of the movement but not one of its dominant figures. [D. Bushnell]

3860. Grisanti, Ángel. El proceso contra los asesinos del gran mariscal de Ayacucho. Caracas, Ediciones Garrido, 1955. 402 p., illus.
Contains the "Causa criminal seguida contra ... Apolinar Morillo" (1. ed., Bogotá 1843), as well as numerous documents relating to Sucre's assassination, some of them published for the first time. There are no startling revelations, but the prologue serves as a convenient if biased recapitulation of the latest exchanges between those affirming and denying the implication of the New Granada liberal José María Obando. The amazing vitality of this debate is attested by the publication of the same "Causa criminal ..." in installments in *Museo histórico* (Quito), starting with 3:10-11, agosto-dic. 1951, and still in progress as of 7:21, mayo 1955. The latter review has included a few related documents and bits of comment, *passim*, and especially "Proceso sobre el asesinato de Sucre que desvirtuaría la culpabilidad del General Juan José Flores," 5:16, marzo 1953, p. 26-49, which is a series of declarations drawn up to clear Flores and implicate Obando. [D. Bushnell]

3861. Pinto, Manuel M. La revolución de la intendencia de La Paz en el virreinato del Río de la Plata con la ocurrencia de Chuquisaca, 1800-1810. La Paz, Biblioteca Paceña (Documentos para la historia de la Revolución de 1809, v. 1), 1953. 207, ccxc p.
Account of the background and progress of the abortive revolution at La Paz in 1809; equally divided between text and documents. The interpretation lays special emphasis on the "democratic" aims (social and economic as well as political) of the revolutionists. [D. Bushnell]

CHILE

3862. Coleman, William J. La restauración del episcopado chileno en 1828, según fuentes vaticanas (R Ch Hist Geog, 121, enero-junio 1953, p. 76-92). [D. Bushnell]

3863. **Domeyko, Ignacio.** Reseña de los trabajos de la Universidad desde 1855 hasta el presente (A U Ch, 112:90-92, 2.-4. trimestre 1953, p. 170-276).

Account of affairs of the University of Chile, 1855-1872 (previously printed, Santiago, Chile, 1872), by the rector, the Polish-born teacher and geologist (1802-1889). Workings of the university in its early years are made clear, with much detail such as names of texts. See also item 3869. A Domeyko bibliography is in this same number. [C. B. Kroeber]

3864. **Donoso, Ricardo.** Alessandri, agitador y demoledor. Cincuenta años de historia política de Chile. V. 2. México, Fondo de Cultura Económica (Col. Tierra firme, 56), 1954. 578 p.

Concluding an ambitious history of Chilean national politics (v. 2 covers 1925-1950), centered on and attacking the late ex-President Arturo Alessandri. A major work, superbly informed, it carries the author's bitter suspicion that events since 1925 leave serious antidemocratic results in government. [C. B. Kroeber]

3865. **Edwards Vives, Alberto.** La organización política de Chile. 2. ed. Santiago, Pacífico, 1955. 137 p.

An able interpretation of the beginnings of national organization; originally published in 1943. [D. Bushnell]

3866. **Encina, Francisco A.** La presidencia de Balmaceda. Santiago, Nascimento, 1952. 2 v. T. 1, El gobierno constitucional, 496 p.; t. 2, La revolución de 1891, 368 p.

Comprises v. 19-20 of the author's *Historia de Chile desde la prehistoria hasta 1891.* [C. B. Kroeber]

3867. **Feliú Cruz, Guillermo.** La imprenta durante el gobierno de O'Higgins. Estudio histórico. Santiago, Imp. Universitaria, 1952. 70 p., illus.

A detailed short study, dealing chiefly with administrative aspects of the Imprenta del Estado, 1817-1923. [D. Bushnell]

3868. **O'Higgins, Bernardo.** Archivo de don Bernardo O'Higgins. T. 12. Santiago, Archivo Nacional, 1953. 336 p.

Reprints the *Gazeta ministerial de Chile*, enero 2 to julio 15, 1819; indexed. [D. Bushnell]

3869. **Poblete Muñoz, Olfa.** Un servidor de la enseñanza: Ignacio Domeyko (A U Ch, 112:90-92, 2.-4. trimestre 1953, p. 277-351).

This chronicle of Domeyko, the teacher, scientist, and administrator of the University of Chile (rector, 1867-1883, and other important posts), covers his entire career, before and after his first connection with the University (1843). [C. B. Kroeber]

3870. **Stuardo Ortiz, Carlos,** and **Juan Eyzaguirre Escobar.** Santiago; contribuyentes, autoridades, funcionarios, agentes diplomáticos y consulares, 1817-1819. Introducción de Raúl Silva Castro. Santiago. Academia Chilena de la Historia, 1952. 111 p., fold. map, plans.

Name lists that should prove a useful research aid. [D. Bushnell]

COLOMBIA

3871. **Cortazar, Roberto** (comp.). Cartas y mensajes del General Francisco de Paula Santander. Bogotá, Librería Voluntad, 1953-1954. V. 1, 1812-1819, 396 p., 1953; v. 2, 1820, 485 p., 1953; v. 3, 1821, 492 p., 1954; v. 4, 1822-1824, 549 p., 1954; v. 5, 1825, 450 p., 1954; v. 6, 1826, 529 p., 1954.

One of the most important publications in Colombia in recent years, bringing together material previously scattered in the *Archivo Santander*, etc., and offering much more for the first time. V. 1 contains mainly familiar items; v. 2 and 3 have more that are new, though often of a routine nature; starting with v. 4 there is much invaluable new material, especially Santander's legislative messages covering every conceivable topic. [D. Bushnell]

A compilation of correspondence, proclamations, and other documents of General Santander, who as general and vice-president of Great Colombia played an important role in the struggle for independence and the early years of the Republic of New Granada. Since many letters are directed to Bolívar, they serve to complement the volumes of the writings of the Liberator. [R. R. Hill]

3872. **Henao Mejía, Gabriel.** Juan de Dios Aranzazu. Bogotá, Ministerio de Educación Nacional, Ediciones de la Revista Bolívar (Biblioteca de autores colombianos, 55), 1953. 401 p.

Competent and readable, though rather general, biography of a noted *antioqueño* (1751-1845) who was active in Colombian politics as a leading moderate and in economic matters as an entrepreneur of land settlement. [D. Bushnell]

3873. **Jacinto María de Quito, Brother.** Historia de la fundación del pueblo de San Francisco en el valle de Sibundoy. Sibundoy, Colombia, Edición del CILEAC, 1952. 70 p., illus.

An interesting account of racial conflict and Capuchin missionaries, loosely organized but adequately documented. San Francisco was founded in 1902 as a means of drawing off intruding *blancos* from the Indian town of Sibundoy. [D. Bushnell]

3874. **Martínez Delgado, Luis.** Noticia biográfica del prócer don Joaquín Camacho. Documentos. Bogotá, Pax (Biblio-

teca de historia nacional, 89), 1954.
368 p.

Biographical sketch of a Tunja patriot (1766-1816), followed by documents and correspondence mostly relating to public and private affairs of Camacho both before and after 1810. Also contains a notebook of pay orders from Nariño's Pasto campaign. [D. Bushnell]

3875. Ortega Ricaurte, Enrique, and Ana Rueda Briceño (eds.). Luis Brión, de la Orden de Libertadores. Primer almirante de la república de Colombia y general en jefe de sus ejércitos, 1782-1821. Bogotá, Departamento de Biblioteca y Archivos Nacionales, 1953. 239 p., illus.

A collection of documents dealing with the life and activities of Admiral Brión, including his reports to Bolívar and Santander. There are also letters of Bolívar and Santander to Brión. The documents are from the Archivo Nacional of Colombia, from the Archivo General de la Nación of Venezuela, and from published works and newspapers, with the sources indicated. They relate to the activities of Admiral Brión and are of the years 1815-1821, but mostly of 1820. [R. R. Hill]

3876. Ospina Vásquez, Luis. Industria y protección en Colombia, 1810-1930. Medellín, Colombia, ESF, 1955. 531 p.

A work notable for both shrewd analysis and quantity of detail. Ospina emphasizes the extent to which protectionism had become firmly entrenched by 1930, while viewing many of its underlying assumptions with skepticism. Despite the title, this book does more than discuss the interrelation of tariff policy and industrial development; by way of background, it offers the best general economic history yet available for Colombia. [D. Bushnell]

3877. Restrepo, José Manuel. Diario político y militar. Bogotá, Biblioteca de la Presidencia de Colombia, 1954. T. 1, 1819-1828, 403 p.; t. 2, 1829-1834, 370 p.; t. 3, 1835-1848, 576 p.; t. 4, 1849-1858, 742 p.

A significant addition to the sources on Colombian history, in which events are set down as they occurred, by an author who was Interior Secretary of Gran Colombia and was closely connected long afterwards with the politics of New Granada. These volumes mirror Restrepo's personal evolution from a decided liberal in the early 1820's to conservative at mid-century; but his work as a chronicler is at all times noteworthy for both honesty and common sense. [D. Bushnell]

3878. Restrepo Sáenz, José María. La provincia del Socorro y sus gobernantes (B Hist Antig, 41:476, junio 1954, p. 321-378).

Brief biographical sketches of provincial rulers from the formation of the province (1795) to its absorption in the department of Santander (1857). Based on meticulous research, as are two rather similar items by the same

author in the same review: "Don Nicolás de Rivas," which brings some new data on a Bogota patriot martyr (1772-1816) (40:459-461, enero-marzo 1953, p. 150-157); and "La familia de Nariño," a genealogical study (41: 473-474, marzo-abril 1954, p. 237-248). [D. Bushnell]

ECUADOR

3880. Carbó, Luis Alberto. Historia monetaria y cambiaria del Ecuador. Desde época colonial. Quito, Imprenta del Banco Central del Ecuador, 1953. 675 p.

A pioneer monetary-financial history of Ecuador from independence to 1953, thinnest for the period 1831-1880. Emphasis is on monetary laws, banks, foreign debts, and financial policy and crises. Appended are a number of reports written in Ecuador since 1940 by the author (late Treasury Minister, now of the Banco Central), and others. An incomplete but most useful work. [C. B. Kroeber]

3881. García Moreno, Gabriel. Cartas. Wilfredo Loor [ed.] T. 1, 1846-1854. Quito, La Prensa Católica, 1953. xxxii, 327 p., illus.

First of a projected series; personal and official correspondence of García Moreno (1821-1875), President of Ecuador 1860-1864, 1869-1875. Almost all these letters are personal, to the Ascásubi family of which Roberto was his brother-in-law; almost all come from the Jesuit archive of Cotocollao, except for a very few documents of official nature. [C. B. Kroeber]

3882. Guarderas, Francisco. El viejo de Montecristi. Biografía de Alfaro. Quito, La Unión, 1953. 453 p.

Eloy Alfaro (1842-1912) turbulent Liberal president of Ecuador, 1897-1901, 1906-1911. Mainly a political history adding something to previous biographies by use of some new manuscripts from family collections. [C. B. Kroeber]

3883. Pérez Concha, Jorge. Vargas Torres. 2. ed. Guayaquil, Ecuador, Casa de la Cultura Ecuatoriana, Núcleo del Guayas, 1953. 287 p., facsims.

A spotty account of small campaigns and maneuvers in which Vargas (1855-1887) helped the later president Eloy Alfaro try to come to power (from 1883 to 1887, when Vargas was executed). Of some small value, chiefly in reprinting a brief journal of Vargas' (1884) and other documents once published at Guayaquil (1885). [C. B. Kroeber]

3884. Salazar y Lozano, Agustín. Recuerdos de los sucesos principales de la Revolución de Quito, desde el año de 1809 hasta el de 1814 (Mus Hist, 5:17, sept. 1953, p. 71-125).

Memoirs, chiefly military, which were written in 1824 and originally published in 1854. The same review has also published a number of documents concerning the first Quito rebellion: "El Ilmo. Cuero y Caicedo, Obispo de Quito en el proceso contra los patriotas del 10 de agosto de 1809," 5:18, dic. 1953, p. 14-65; Tomás de Aréchaga, "Acusación del Fiscal Tomás de Aréchaga, en la causa seguida contra los patriotas del 10 de agosto . . .", 6:19, marzo 1954, p. 37-65; "De los procesos seguidos contra los patriotas del 10 de agosto de 1809," 7:21, mayo 1955, p. 1-49. [D. Bushnell]

3885. Solano, Vicente. Epistolario. Prólogo y notas de Augustín Cueva Tamariz. Cuenca, Ecuador, Casa de la Cultura Ecuatoriana, Núcleo del Azuay (Biblioteca azuaya), 1953. 2 v. liv, 585 p., illus.
Letters of the revered and accomplished Franciscan father, from 1840-1862. Volume 1 contains letters to D. José María Losa (1840-51), first printed at Quito, 1902; volume 2, letters to various churchmen (some printed in 1935), 1842-1862. These reflect his vigorous personality and wide interests, and are a good source for Ecuadorian history. This is one of a number of Solano items issued recently under the same auspices. [C. B. Kroeber]

PERU

3886. Capuñay, Manuel A. Leguía. Vida y obra del constructor del gran Perú. Lima, 1951, i.e. 1952. 279 p.
An impassioned and somewhat incoherent defense of Augusto B. Leguía (1863-1932), president of Peru, 1908-1912 and 1919-1930. Capuñay says that Leguía brought "bourgeois-democratic revolution" to Peru, and that he worked "miracles," as a "divine" personage. The book is a good example of hero worship but does little to demonstrate Leguía's faults, his constructive achievements, or even his road to power. [C. B. Kroeber]

3887. Dulanto Pinillos, Jorge. Castilla. Lima, Compañía de Impresiones y Publicidad, 1952. 405 p.
Third edition of a useful biography that catches the bold spirit of Ramón Castilla (1797-1867), who at 15 was fighting for Spain against revolutionists in Chile, who later became a military caudillo and an able president in Peru (1844-1850, 1855-1862), and who died while raising a personalist revolt against the government there. [C. B. Kroeber]

3888. Fernández Moro, Wenceslao. Cincuenta años en la selva amazónica. Padres domínicos españoles. Vicariato de Puerto Maldonado, Perú. Madrid, 1952. 774 p., illus.
A good, if heavy, book tracing from their beginnings the Dominican missions of the Urubamba River country in Amazonian Peru, north of Cuzco, from 1902. The documentation in the text makes this an especially valuable report. [C. B. Kroeber]

3889. García Rosell, César. Unánue, parlamentario y diplomático (Mer Per, año 30, 36:343, oct. 1955, p. 705-746).

A valuable study of Hipólito Unánue (1755-1833), Peruvian collaborator of both Bolívar and San Martín. This is the most substantial of a number of articles in honor of Unánue's bicentennial, appearing in the same issue and in the preceding one (año 30, 36:342, sept. 1955). [D. Bushnell]

3890. Pavletich, Esteban. Leoncio Prado. Una vida al servicio de la libertad. 2. ed. Lima, Servicio de Prensa, Propaganda y Publicaciones Militares, 1953. 129 p.
Sketch of the violent adventures of a Peruvian who first tasted war at age 13 and who was executed at 30, resisting Chilean forces in Peru (1883). First edition, 1939. [C. B. Kroeber]

3891. Porras Barrenechea, Raúl. José Sánchez Carrión, el tribuno de la República Peruana (Mer Per, año 28, 34: 320, nov. 1953, p. 489-523).
Biographical note on a Peruvian patriot (1787-1825), who defended republicanism against Monteagudo and served later under Bolívar. [D. Bushnell]

URUGUAY

3892. Ardao, María Julia, and Aurora Capillas de Castellanos. Bibliografía de Artigas. T. 1. Montevideo, Comisión Nacional Archivo Artigas, 1953. 935 p.
An invaluable guide to the study not only of Artigas but of the entire River Plate area during his lifetime. This first volume lists books, pamphlets, and a portion of the articles that have appeared on Artigas and his period; for each item there is a full bibliographical citation, and usually an abstract of the contents. [D. Bushnell]

3893. Fitzgibbon, Russell. The political impact on religious development in Uruguay (Church Hist, 22:1, Mar. 1953, p. 21-32).
A balanced and reasonable statement of facts and conclusions, mostly affecting the period since 1919 (separation of Church and State in Uruguay). [C. B. Kroeber]

3894. Informes diplomáticos de los representantes de Francia en el Uruguay, 1855-1859 (R Hist, Montevideo, 2. época, año 47, 18:52-54, feb. 1953, p. 34-300).
Dispatches of the French consul at Montevideo, Nov. 4, 1855—Aug. 30, 1859. Continuation (dispatches for 1851-1855 published in issues for año 45, 17:49-50, dic. 1951, and año 46, 17:51, sept. 1952). As noted in HLAS, no. 18, 1952 (item 2133), these reports are of high quality and are very comprehensive. [C. B. Kroeber]

3895. Instituto Histórico y Geográfico del Uruguay. Artigas. Homenaje en el centenario de su muerte. Curso de conferencias, 1950. Prólogo por Simón S. Lucuix. Montevideo, Imp. Nacional, 1952. xxxix, 466 p., illus. [D. Bushnell]

3896. **Páez Formoso, Miguel A.** Artigas, ciudadano del Plata. Montevideo, Talleres Gráficos Prometeo, 1952. 123 p.
The ideas and achievements of Artigas, viewed and reviewed in connection with the chief events of his life. [H. Bernstein]

3897. **Schiaffino, Rafael.** Historia de la medicina en el Uruguay. T. 3. (1800-1828). Montevideo, Imprenta Rosgal, 1952. 721 p.
Continuation of a minute and documentary work, begun 1927, on Uruguayan medical and public-health history in its politico-social context. Much of the present volume concerns military medicine—such efforts as those to continue hospital service and to revive smallpox vaccination during foreign and civil war. Valuable. [C. B. Kroeber]

3898. **Sosa, Jesualdo.** La escuela lancasteriana. Ensayo histórico-pedagógico de la Escuela Uruguaya durante la dominación luso-brasileña (1817-1825), en especial del método de Lancaster; acompañado de un apéndice documental (R Hist, Montevideo, 2. época, año 47, 20: 58-60, dic. 1953, p. 1-262).
An original and valuable contribution to Latin American intellectual history. [D. Bushnell]

VENEZUELA

3899. **Abello Salcedo, Rafael.** Origen de la prisión de Miranda (Bolívar, Bogotá, 19, mayo 1953, p. 745-767).
Insists that Bolívar had no responsibility for Miranda's arrest, which is ascribed solely to Col. Manuel M. de las Casas and Dr. Miguel Peña. (Also printed in B Ac Nac Hist, Caracas, 36:142, abril-junio 1953, p. 216-233). [D. Bushnell]

3900. **Bierck, Harold A., Jr.** The first instance of U. S. foreign aid: Venezuelan relief in 1812 (Interam Ec Aff, 9:1, summer 1955, p. 47-59).
Discusses the origin and operation of the relief program voted by U. S. Congress after the Venezuelan earthquake of 1812; the desire for commercial advantage is stressed as a motive. [D. Bushnell]

3901. **García Chuecos, Héctor.** Los perdidos archivos de la primera república (R Nac Cult, 12:86, mayo-junio 1951, p. 65-70).
Notes on the loss or partial loss of a number of administrative archives, records of *juntas*, records of the Sociedad Patriótica, and other documents of the early revolutionary period in Venezuela. [C. Gibson]

3902. **Gil, Pío** [pseud.], i.e. **Pedro María Morante.** Amarillo, azul y rojo. Personalismos y verdades. Caracas, Tip. Garrido, 1952. 181 p.
Done in France during 1912-1913, this diffuse series of writings condemns the then dictator of Venezuela, Juan Vicente Gómez. The work may be of use in identifying a few personalities of the time. [C. B. Kroeber]

3903. ————. Los felicitadores. Caracas, Tip. Garrido, 1952. 110 p.
Notes of rejoicing and congratulation sent to Cipriano Castro (1899-1909), or lauding him in various newspapers, on the occasion of one of his successes in 1906. Collected by Morante after these same men had, he says, turned against Castro and joined his successor, Juan Vicente Gómez. Almost 100 items are given here. [C. B. Kroeber]

3904. **González Sabariegos, Rosario.** Un americano al servicio de España: D. Pedro de Urquinaona y Pardo (B Ac Nac Hist, Caracas, 37:148, oct.-dic. 1954, p. 339-351).
Refers chiefly to the feud between Urquinaona (born in Bogota) and the Spanish General Monteverde, arising from differences in policy during the "pacification" of Venezuela; based on research in Spanish archives. [D. Bushnell]

3905. **Grases, Pedro,** and **Alberto Harkness.** Manuel García de Sena y la independencia de Hispanoamérica. Caracas, Secretaría General de la Décima Conferencia Interamericana (Col. Historia, 6), 1953. 63 p., facsims.
A careful monograph, which touches on personal details and political-diplomatic activity but discusses mainly the role of the Venezuelan patriot García de Sena as a publicist in transmitting Anglo-American concepts to Spanish America. [D. Bushnell]

3906. **Grisanti, Ángel.** Miranda. Precursor del Congreso de Panamá y del panamericanismo. El Convenio de París de 1797. Origen del derecho internacional hispanoamericano. Caracas, Grisanti (Documentos inéditos), 1954. 182 p., illus.
The purpose of both text and documents in this volume (whose title is over-ambitious) is to show the wide extent of Miranda's contacts with representatives of other colonies prior to 1810. There is possibly some exaggeration, but also much useful data on the background of Independence. [D. Bushnell]

3907. ————. Miranda juzgado por los funcionarios españoles de su tiempo. Los orígenes de la independencia hispanoamericana según los documentos secretos e inéditos existentes en los archivos españoles. Caracas, Grisanti, 1954. 218 p.
Contains reports, beginning with 1784, from Spanish diplomatic agents in foreign countries through which Miranda passed in the course of his work as "Precursor" of Independence. [D. Bushnell]

3908. ————. Vargas íntimo. Un sabio de carne y hueso. Su niñez, adolescencia y juventud. Caracas, Jesús E. Grisanti, 1954. 378 p.

The early career of the Venezuelan physician, surgeon, and statesman (1786-1854) who became rector of the Universidad Central, Caracas, in 1827, and, briefly, president of the nation, 1835-1836. Copies many documents and gives knowledge of the least-known part of Vargas' life (up to 1813), but does not deal with the later life save in listing his publications and some other facts. [C. B. Kroeber]

3909. Grummond, Jane Lucas de. The Jacob Idler claim against Venezuela, 1817-1870 (HAHR, 34:2, May 1954, p. 131-157).

Follows to the bitter end a dispute over payment for military supplies used in the War of Independence. [D. Bushnell]

3910. King, James F. El Comisionado Regio don Antonio Ignacio de Cortabarría y la Primera República de Venezuela (B Ac Nac Hist, Caracas, 37:146, abril-junio 1954, p. 125-178, with documentary appendix).

Studies the mission of the agent sent out from Cadiz to restore normalcy after the Caracas junta of Apr. 19, 1810, was set up. He never got beyond Puerto Rico, but his activity there throws some light on the evolution of Spanish policy. [D Bushnell]

3911. ————. A royalist view of the colored castes in the Venezuelan War of Independence (HAHR, 33:4, Nov. 1953, p. 526-537).

Report by the acting Captain-General (July, 1815), recommending greater equality of treatment; printed with detailed notes and introduction. [D. Bushnell]

3912. Lavin, John. A halo for Gómez. N. Y., Pageant Press, 1954. 471 p., illus.

Life and times of Juan Vicente Gómez, dictator of Venezuela 1908-1935, and a brief discussion of politics 1935-1950. With few new facts the author gives a reasonable account but also some unreasonable conclusions (p. 465) as to Gómez' achievements. [C. B. Kroeber]

3913. Paredes, Antonio. Cómo llegó Cipriano Castro al poder. Memorias contemporáneas o bosquejo histórico donde se vé cómo llegó Cipriano Castro al poder en Venezuela y cómo se ha sostenido en él. 1906. 2. ed. Caracas, Garrido, 1954. cxxiii, 205 p.

This reprint (1st ed., 1906) is the memoirs of a general who arrayed himself with and against Venezuelan dictators from 1892, when he asked for command of a national revolt at the age of 22, until he was executed in 1907. His prejudiced account is very detailed on the politics of the period after 1892. [C. B. Kroeber]

3914. Parra Márquez, Héctor. Presidentes de Venezuela: el doctor Francisco

Espejo. Ensayo biográfico. 2. ed. corregida y aumentada. Caracas, Imp. López 1954. 293 p., illus.

Biography of a lawyer-statesman and marty of the First Venezuelan Republic, member o the Second Triumvirate (1758-1814). Based on careful research, with documentary appen dices. Former edition appeared in 1944. [D Bushnell]

3915. Pi Sunyer, Carlos. La última fase de la vida del General Miranda (B Ac Nac Hist, Caracas, 36:142, abril-junio 1953, p. 193-215).

Interpretative discussion of Miranda's actions from his final departure from Europe to his capitulation in 1812, based on study of Miranda materials in London. [D. Bushnell]

3916. El publicista de Venezuela (B Ac Nac Hist, Caracas, 37:148, oct-dic. 1954 p. 361-373; 38:149, enero-marzo 1955, p 60-73).

Copy of first two issues (July 4-11, 1811) o official periodical published by the patrio Venezuelan Congress. Series to be continued [D. Bushnell]

3917. Revenga, José Rafael. La hacienda pública de Venezuela en 1828-1830. Misión de José Rafael Revenga como ministro de hacienda. Introducción de Augusto Mijares. Caracas, Banco Central de Venezuela, 1953. 401 p.

Invaluable collection of letters and detailed reports, referring to all phases of governmen finance and economic policy; descriptive o Venezuela, but relevant for any study of Gran Colombia during the Bolivarian dictatorship Fully indexed. [D. Bushnell]

3918. Rodríguez, Simón. Consejos de amigo. Dados al Colejio de Latacunga Introducción y notas de Arturo Guevara Caracas, Imp. Nacional, 1955. 224 p. illus.

Miscellany of pedagogical maxims, social and linguistic commentaries, etc., written by Bolí var's tutor in his declining years. The notes appendices, and the lengthy but rather form less introduction contain general discussion o both Rodríguez and the Liberator. [D. Bushnell]

3919. Roscio, Juan Germán. Obras. Pró logo de Augusto Mijares, compilación de Pedro Grases. Caracas, Secretaría Ge neral de la Décima Conferencia Inter americana (Col. Historia, 7-9), 1953. 3 v T. 1, El triunfo de la libertad sobre e despotismo, xcvii, 496 p.; t. 2, Textos políticos, 276 p.; t. 3, Correspondencia 212 p.

Documents and correspondence of Juan Ger mán Roscio (1763-1821), an active protagonis of the movement for independence in Vene zuela. They throw much light on his role and the events of the era. [R. R. Hill]

3920. **Valdivieso Montaño, A.** José Tomás Boves, caudillo hispano. El más recio batallador realista durante la guerra a muerte: años de 1812 a 1814. Caracas, Línea Aeropostal Venezolana (Ediciones gratuitas, 8), 1953. 178 p., illus.

A readable and generally sound biography, first published in 1931; neither apology nor diatribe (though closer to the former), paying due attention to Boves as a sociological phenomenon of the Venezuelan *llanos*. [D. Bushnell]

3921. **Williamson, John G. A.** Caracas diary, 1835-1840. The journal of John

G. A. Williamson, first diplomatic representative of the United States to Venezuela. Edited by Jane Lucas de Grummond. Baton Rouge, La., Camellia Publishing Co., 1954. xxxiv, 444 p.

He was U. S. consul in Venezuela after 1826, chargé from 1835 until death in 1840. The editor wrote a book on his Venezuelan service (1951), and here annotates the journal and bridges its gap (May 1836—June 1838) with his dispatches to Washington. Has some value for customs and politics of the time, although a product of a conventional mind with the usual prejudices our envoys then had. [C. B. Kroeber]

BRAZIL

MANOEL CARDOZO AND GEORGE BOEHRER

DURING 1953-1955, two centenaries were held, that of the expulsion of the Dutch from Recife (1654) and that of the founding of São Paulo (1554). Historians were active in commemorating both, but the latter, which had the advantage of having the second International Luso-Brazilian Colloquium held in conjunction with the celebrations, attracted more scholarly attention. Publications in honor of São Paulo ranged from the useful *Biblioteca histórica paulista* (items 4000, 4027, 4041, 4049, 4078, and 4079) and excellent monographic items (e.g., item 4037) to ephemera which are not noticed below. If the São Paulo publications were many and the Pernambucan few, the Recife celebration did occasion a number of needed biographies by José Antônio Gonsalves de Mello (items 4050-4053).

Among other monographic works there are two volumes, neither precisely new, which merit special attention. Thales de Azevedo's *Povoamento da cidade do Salvador,* now in a second revised edition, brilliantly brings to bear on Salvador that manifold scholarship of which Gilberto Freyre was the pioneer in Brazil. The second is Luís Martins' *O patriarca e o bacharel* which first appeared as an article and now, in greater depth, interprets the remorse of the revolutionaries of '89 over their part in the overthrow of Dom Pedro II.

Aside from these, the flood of books on Rui Barbosa continues. His complete works are still appearing, as well as other books which might better have been left unpublished. Attention should be called to the comparatively few works devoted exclusively to the imperial period, at one time the focus of interest. Now emphasis is being placed on either the colonial or the republican eras.

Finally, it is regretfully announced that *Atlante,* a quarterly review published by the Hispanic and Luso-Brazilian Councils of Britain, ceased publication with v. 3, no. 4, Oct. 1955. During its three years of existence, 1953-1955, articles of general interest on Brazilian and Hispanic American history and literature were published. [G. Boehrer]

GENERAL

4000. **Alincourt, Luiz d'.** Memória sôbre a viagem do pôrto de Santos à cidade de Cuiabá. Introdução de Afonso de E. Taunay. São Paulo, Martins (Biblioteca histórica paulista, 8), 1953. 207 p., illus.

An engineer's detailed description of a trip made in 1817, first published in 1825. Attached

is an account of the frontier of Mato Grosso, dated 1826. [G. Boehrer]

4001. Aspectos da formação e evolução do Brasil. Estudos publicados em 1952, no *Jornal do commercio,* no seu 125.° aniversario. Rio, 1953. 585 p.

47 largely interpretative and journalistic articles by leading scholars on almost every phase of Brazilian life. [G. Boehrer]

4002. Barbosa, Francisco de Assis. Retratos de família. Rio, Olympio, 1954. 192 p.
Short literary biographies of Rodrigues Alves, Rui Barbosa, Lafayette Rodrigues Pereira, Clovis Bevilacqua, and Sílvio Romero, among others, which were originally published in the *Correio da manhã*. The author secured his information from members of the subjects' families. [G. Boehrer]

4003. Barbosa, Rui. Antologia. Seleção, prefácio e notas de Luís Viana Filho. Rio, Casa de Rui Barbosa, 1953. 225 p.
Rui's opinions on a great variety of subjects. The work is composed of short abstracts from his speeches and essays. [G. Boehrer]

4004. Bittencourt, Adalzira. A mulher paulista na história. Rio, Livros de Portugal, 1954. 359 p. & illus.
This volume contains more than a hundred vignettes of São Paulo women, from the Indian wives of João Ramalho to the present. The presentation is generally enthusiastic, and, for the colonial times, often farfetched. [G. Boehrer]

4005. Boehrer, George C. A. Da monarquia à república. História do Partido Republicano do Brasil (1870-1889). Tradução de Berenice Xavier. Rio, Ministério da Educação e Cultura, Serviço de Documentação, 1954. 300 p.

4006. Brazil. Biblioteca Nacional. Divisão de Obras Raras e Publicações. Catálogo de manuscritos sôbre o Paraná existentes na Biblioteca Nacional. Rio, 1953. 48 p. & facsims.
This volume is a list of 117 items ranging from codices of *cartas régias* to tax protests: with one exception all are official. The years 1642-1902 are covered. There is a thorough index and a fine introduction by José Honório Rodrigues. [G. Boehrer]

4007. ———. ———. ———.
Documentos históricos. Revolução de 1817. Rio, 1953. V. 101, 1953, 302 p.; v. 102, 1953, 295 p.; v. 103, 1954, 294 p.; v. 104, 1954, 288 p.; v. 105, 1954, 268 p.; v. 106, 1954, 256 p.
Six volumes (one more is to follow) on the 1817 Revolution. All aspects are covered, rebel and royal, foreign reaction and intrigue, origins, and repression. Each volume is prefaced by an introduction of José Honório Rodrigues indicating the more significant contents. An excellent continuation of an important series. [G. Boehrer]

4008. ———. ———. ———.
Manuscritos da coleção de Angelis. Rio, 1952. V. 1, Jesuítas e bandeirantes no Guairá (1549-1640), 506 p.; v. 2, Jesuítas e bandeirantes no Itatim (1596-1760), 367 p.
Manuscripts on the Jesuits in the two places noted. The Brazilian government acquired the Pedro de Angelis papers in 1853. Essays on the acquisition, Angelis, his service to Brazil, the collection, and Paraguay precede the main material. [G. Boehrer]

4009. ———. Comissão de Estudo dos Textos da História do Brasil. Bibliografia de história do Brasil. 1. e 2. semestres de 1949. Rio, 1953. 158 p.

4010. Cascudo, Luís da Câmara. História do Rio Grande do Norte. Rio, Ministério da Educação e Cultura, Serviço de Documentação, 1955. 524 p.
A detailed political, cultural, and institutional account which contains information not found elsewhere. There are lists of officeholders, statistical tables, etc. The volume is based on archival research but the references are often vague and haphazard. [G. Boehrer]

4011. Crabtree, Asa Routh. Baptists in Brazil. A history of Southern Baptists' greatest mission field. Rio, Baptist Pub. House of Brazil, 1953. 236 p., illus.
Informative chronicle of the missionary activities of the Baptists during the Empire and the Republic. [G. Boehrer]

4012. Curso Capistrano de Abreu (R Inst Hist Geog Br, 221, out.-dez. 1953, p. 44-245).
Series of lectures on Capistrano and diverse aspects of his writings and influence. Among the authors are Múcio Leão, Artur César Ferreira Reis, José Honório Rodrigues, and A. de E. Taunay. [G. Boehrer]

4013. Docca, E. F. de Souza. História do Rio Grande do Sul. Rio, Organização Simões (Biblioteca Brasil), 1954. 454 p.
A survey from the beginning to our own times. It is a very broad survey indeed: there are sections on geography, anthropology, economics, sociology, politics, religion, education, and intellectual life. The approach is historical, and the results are exceedingly competent. The author does have peeves, i.e., he believes in the *homo americanus*. And the book could have achieved greater unity if the author had had a clearer notion of what history is. [M. Cardozo]

4014. Dunlop, C. J. Apontamentos para a história dos bondes no Rio de Janeiro. Rio, Laemmert, 1953. 333 p., illus.
A popular account of the Jardim Botânico streetcar line from its inception in 1868 by Charles B. Greenough of N. Y. until 1911. There are cartoons and photographs of the epoch. Street names are given in both past and present forms. [G. Boehrer]

4015. Instituto Histórico e Geográfico de São Paulo. São Paulo em quatro séculos. Temas sôbre alguns aspectos da história e da geografia de São Paulo e assuntos correlatos. Obra comemorativa organizada pelo ... e editada sob os auspi-

cios da Comissão do IV Centenário da Cidade de São Paulo. São Paulo, 1953-1954. 2 v. 371, 387 p., maps.
A collection of articles on the city and the province of São Paulo. The essays, which are partially popular, cover a wide variety of subjects: institutions, folklore, religion, history, genealogy, and even mules are treated. [G. Boehrer]

4016. Lacombe, Américo Jacobina. Brazil; a brief history. Translated by W. A. R. Richardson. Rio, Ministry of Foreign Relations, Cultural Division, 1954. 105 p.
This is a translation of the author's *Passeio pela história do Brasil,* a series of four lectures delivered before the Anglo-Brazilian Cultural Society of Rio in 1942. A select bibliography has been added by the translator. [G. Boehrer]

4017. Lafayette, Pedro. Três perfis. Saldanha da Gama. Barão de Penedo. Silveira Martins. Rio, Livraria Clássica Brasileira, 1955? 178 p.
Three laudatory biographies, on the leader of the Naval Revolt and onetime head of the Naval School, on the diplomat who was minster to England during the Christie crisis and pecial envoy to Rome during the bishops' risis, and on the civilian chief of the '93 evolution. [G. Boehrer]

4018. Leão, Múcio. Salvador de Mendonça. Ensaio biobibliográfico. Rio, Publicações da Academia Brasileira, 1952. 133 p., illus.
Life of the journalist, a drafter of the Republican Manifesto of 1870, and a diplomat. His writings and diplomatic career are analyzed. Mendonça was the Brazilian representative at the First Pan American Conference. [G. Boehrer]

4019. Leite, Aureliano; Afonso de E. Taunay (and others). Homens de São Paulo. Antônio Rapôso Tavares, Bartolomeu de Gusmão, José Bonifácio, Diogo Antônio Feijó, Antônio Prado, Prudente de Morais, Júlio Mesquita, Osvaldo Cruz, Monteiro Lobato, Roberto Simonsen. São Paulo, Martins, 1955. 494 p.
Biographical essays of uneven quality on two colonial and eight national figures. The disparity in numbers reflects the state's growing importance. Especially welcome are the articles on Júlio Mesquita, editor of *A província* (now *O estado de São Paulo*) and of Roberto Simonsen, the economic historian. [G. Boehrer]

4020. Matos, Pedro Gomes de. Capistrano de Abreu. Vida e obra do grande historiador. Edição do centenário. Fortaleza, Brazil, A. Batista Fontenele, 1953. 410 p., illus.
A highly eulogistic and semi-scholarly biography of Brazil's great historian. Matos gives a list of Capistrano's works, and reprints the critical judgment of others. [G. Boehrer]

4021. Menezes, Raimundo de. Histórias da história de São Paulo. São Paulo, Melhoramentos, 1954. 275 p., illus.
Tales of São Paulo life. Well written, they illuminate urban and provincial life in areas neglected in more serious works. [G. Boehrer]

4022. Nery, Fernando. Rui Barbosa. Ensaio biográfico. Rio, Casa de Rui Barbosa, 1955. 170 p. & illus.
A new edition of the work first published in 1933 (?) as *Ruy Barbosa (ensaio bio-bibliográfico).* Américo Jacobina Lacombe has omitted the introduction and the bibliography but has corrected and enlarged the notes where needed. [G. Boehrer]

4023. Orico, Osvaldo. Momentos estelares de Rui Barbosa. Rio, Casa de Rui Barbosa, 1954. 89 p., port.
Six highly interesting essays on Rui. Especially to be noted are the author's treatment of Rui's relationship with José do Patrocínio and Joaquim Nabuco. [G. Boehrer]

4024. Palha, Américo. História da vida de Rui Barbosa. 2. ed. Rio, Casa de Rui Barbosa, 1954. 96 p.
A short impressionistic biography of Barbosa in which the high points of his career are recounted. [G. Boehrer]

4025. Reis, José Antônio dos. Relação de livros, verbetes datilográficos de coleções inéditas, fotografias, relações de cartas geográficas e mapas estatísticos, documentos facsimilares em taboletas de decretos, jornais antigos e impressos vários relativos à história de São Paulo do movimento da independência e aos principais acontecimentos da história política do Brasil no século XIX. (Exposição histórica comemorativa do IV centenário da fundação da cidade de São Paulo. . . . Contribuição do Arquivo Nacional). Rio, Companhia Brasileira de Artes Gráficas, 1954. 26 p.
An index of documents in the Arquivo Nacional relating to the history of São Paulo, issued in connection with fourth centenary of the city. [R. R. Hill]

4026. Ricardo, Cassiano. O tratado de Petrópolis. Rio, Ministério das Relações Exteriores, 1954. 2 v. 239, 222 p. & maps.
Not only the treaty itself, but also the background and opposition to it are considered. The author is a devotee of Rio Branco. His exuberance and redundancy detract from an otherwise valuable work. [G. Boehrer]

4027. Saint-Hilaire, Augusto de. Segunda viagem a São Paulo e quadro histórico da província de São Paulo. Tradução e introdução de Afonso de E. Taunay. São Paulo, Martins (Biblioteca histórica paulista, 6), 1953. 223 p., illus.

A new and unedited edition of this famous work about Brazil on the eve of Independence. It presents an adequate picture of São Paulo life in 1822. [G. Boehrer]

4028. São Paulo (state). **Departamento do Arquivo.** Pequeno histórico e prontuário do Departamento do Arquivo do Estado. São Paulo, 1953. 182 p., illus.
A brief history and important information about the State Archive of São Paulo. There are the following sections: reproductions of photographs of the directors with biographies; list of the personnel in 1953; list of former members of the staff; the history of the Archive; and laws and decrees relating to the Archive, 1842-1946. [R. R. Hill]

4029. Soares, José Carlos de Macedo. Fontes da história da igreja católica no Brasil. São Paulo, Tip. Edanee, 1954. 384 p.
A melange of information on sources for Brazilian church history. Pertinent Brazilian and other depositories, research centers, and journals are unevenly treated. There are, however, valuable listings of documents located in several Brazilian archives. [G. Boehrer]

4030. Souza, Affonso Ruy de. Páginas de história do Brasil. Bahia, Brazil, Progresso (Col. de estudios brasileiros), 1955. 139 p.
Essays on various topics including the origins, the Habsburg period, women, the Church, 18th-century nationalism, the revolution, the empire, and the republic. [G. Boehrer]

4031. Viana Filho, Luiz. A vida de Joaquim Nabuco. São Paulo, Companhia Editôra Nacional, 1952. 355 p. & illus.
An extremely competent biography that adds to what we already knew of the man. [M. Cardozo]

COLONIAL PERIOD

4032. Araújo, Antônio d'. Catecismo na língua brasílica. Rio, Pontifícia Universidade Católica, 1952. 179 p.
This facsimile edition of a work first published in 1618 is preceded by an introduction by the Rev. A. Lemos Barbosa. He believes that, although corrected and edited by Padre Antônio d'Araújo, it is a collective work of the Jesuits. [G. Boehrer]

4033. Azevedo, Thales de. Povoamento da cidade do Salvador. 2. ed., revista. São Paulo, Companhia Editôra Nacional (Biblioteca pedagógica brasileira, Brasiliana, 5:281), 1955. 504 p.
Exceptionally penetrating study of colonial Salvador. Every possible aspect of the life of the city is given a careful examination through a synthesis of various disciplines. The author believes that "the cultural and biological mixture had amazingly secured the integration of the Portuguese in the human . . . environment of Brazil, and a great part of that experiment took place in the city of Salvador." [G. Boehrer]

4034. Boiteux, Lucas Alexandre. Figura do passado catarinense. O Capitão-Mo Domingos de Brito Peixoto, Senhor d Laguna: sua prole e seus serviços. Flo rianópolis, Brazil, 1954. 72 p.
A great deal of information on the beginning of Santa Catarina by the dean of Santa Cata rina's historians. [M. Cardozo]

4035. Boxer, C. R. The recovery of Pe nambuco, 1645-1654 (Atlante, 2:1, Jan 1954, p. 1-17).
The expulsion of the Dutch portrayed as a event that was not destined to occur. Th Portuguese position was much worse than th Dutch. [G. Boehrer]

4036. Brazil. Arquivo Nacional. Brev verdadeira e autêntica relação das última tyrannias e crueldades que os pérfidc olandeses usarão com os moradores d Rio Grande. 2. ed. Rio, 1954. 15 p.
Reprint from v. 26 of the *Publicações do A quivo Nacional.* An account of the action the Dutch in Brazil, issued in connection wi the commemoration of the third centenary the restoration of Pernambuco, with an intr duction by Alcides Bezerra. [R. R. Hill]

4037. Cortesão, Jaime. A fundação c São Paulo, capital geográfica do Brasi Rio, Livros de Portugal, 1955. 275 p.
A careful history of 16th-century São Paul The author attempts to put the founding the city in a larger framework of Portugue world policy. 20 documents are reprinted illustrate his thesis. [G. Boehrer]

4038. Costa, Afonso. Baïanos de antanh Série A. Rio, Pongetti, 1955. 104 p.
Brief sketches of well-known Baians of tł past. There is no bibliography. [M. Cardozo]

4039. Costa, F. A. Pereira da. Ana pernambucanos. V. 5. 1701-1739. R cife, Brazil, Arquivo Público Estadua 1953. 497 p. & illus.
A continuation of the careful recording events in Pernambucan history. The episod treated include the Vieira de Melo revolt ar the Guerra dos Mescates. Like previous v umes (see *HLAS, no. 18, 1952,* item 536 this is important for the history of colonial a and architecture. [G. Boehrer]

4040. Delgado, Luiz. A restauração pe nambucana. Recife, Brazil, Editôra No deste, 1954. 59 p.
Contains an interpretative discourse and fo press articles on the restoration. Two are the general problem and three on Maurice Nassau and the Congress of 1640. Delga gives the usual interpretation that the strugg against the Dutch evoked Brazilian nationalisr [G. Boehrer]

4041. Gaspar da Madre de Deus, Fre Memórias para a história da capitania S. Vicente, hoje chamada de S. Paul

Com uma introdução de Afonso de E. Taunay. São Paulo, Martins (Biblioteca histórica paulista, 3), 1953. 250 p., illus. The fourth edition of this work. Sr. Taunay's hort biography is a condensation of his longer one published with the third (1921) edition. Also includes Frei Gaspar's *Notícias*. [G. Boehrer]

4042. **Holanda, Sérgio Buarque de.** As técnicas rurais no Brasil durante o século XVIII (*in* International Colloquium on Luso-Brazilian Studies [see item 6713], p. 260-265).
A discussion of Portuguese borrowing of native techniques in some rural pursuits, the retention and improvement of European techniques in others, and the abandonment of more technically advanced for more suitable native procedures in others. [G. Boehrer]

4043. **Instituto Histórico e Geográfico Brasileiro.** Catálogo dos documentos sôbre São Paulo existentes no arquivo do Instituto Histórico e Geográfico Brasileiro. São Paulo, 1954, i.e. 1953. 354 p.
A printing of the cards in the Institute's catalogue. The documents, which concern only the colonial period, are listed neither in chronological nor in subject order. [G. Boehrer]

4044. **Kiemen, Mathias C.** The Indian policy of Portugal in the Amazon region, 1614-1693. Washington, Catholic University of America Press, 1954. xii, 216 p. Thesis.

4045. **Leite, Serafim.** A cabana de António Rodrigues, primeiro mestre-escola de São Paulo, 1553-1554 (Brotéria, 56:4, abril 1953, p. 433-441).
On the first primary school (Escola de Meninos) as distinguished from the Escola de Latim directed by José de Anchieta. The latter was for pre-seminarians and literate Indians, the former taught the Indians religion and how "to read, write, sing and play instruments." [G. Boehrer]

4046. ————. Artes e ofícios dos Jesuítas no Brasil (1549-1760). Rio, Livros de Portugal, 1953. 324 p.
A description of the various professions exercised by the Jesuits, most of whom were temporal coadjutors of the Society. The usual trades predominated, but there were waxmakers, chemists, geographers, typographers (!), shipwrights, pilots, and even a Director of the Clock. Leite precedes each section with a short essay on the general trades and gives a short biography of the brothers. If nothing else, this work testifies to Jesuit versatility. [G. Boehrer]

4047. ————. Documentos inéditos sobre São Paulo de Piratininga, 1554-1555 (Brotéria, 56:3, março 1953, p. 5-14).
Leite here is concerned with two Cartas Quadrimestres of 1554-1555 and one Carta Trimestral sent by Nóbrega in his capacity as

Provincial of the Jesuits in Brazil. They were edited by José de Anchieta, then master of Latin in Piratininga, and have been hitherto known in truncated Castilian versions. [G. Boehrer]

4048. ————. Fundador e "fundadores" de São Paulo, 1553-1554 (Brotéria, 56:5, maio 1953, p. 541-551).
On Nóbrega and the establishment of the church, school, and house of the Jesuits on Jan. 25, 1554, in the town of Piratininga. Leite again holds that Nóbrega is *the* founder. [G. Boehrer]

4049. **Leme, Pedro Taques de Almeida Paes.** Nobiliarchia paulistana histórica e genealógica. 3 ed.... Com uma biografia do autor e estudo crítico de sua obra por Afonso de E. Taunay. São Paulo, Martins (Biblioteca histórica paulista, 4), 1953. 3 v. 280, 290, 282 p., illus. This third edition includes hitherto unpublished part of the celebrated work by the outstanding historian of colonial São Paulo. [M. Cardozo]

4050. **Mello, José Antônio Gonsalves de.** D. Antônio Filipe Camarão, capitão-mor dos índios da costa do nordeste do Brasil. Recife, Brazil, Universidade do Recife, 1954. 64 p.
One of a series of monographs by one of Brazil's leading historians issued in connection with the third centennial of the expulsion of the Dutch from Pernambuco (1654-1954). The subject of this study was an Indian leader of the movement on the side of the Luso-Brazilians. [M. Cardozo]

4051. ————. Filipe Bandeira de Melo. Tenente de mestre de campo general do estado do Brasil. Recife, Brazil, Universidade do Recife, 1954. 61 p.
Felipe Bandeira de Melo, one of the heroes of the Pernambucan restoration, was a prisoner at Recife, fought in Portugal against the Spaniards, later returned to Brazil and was again a prisoner but participated in the battle of Guarapes. [G. Boehrer]

4052. ————. Francisco de Figueiroa, mestre de campo do têrço das ilhas em Pernambuco. Recife, Brazil, Universidade do Recife, 1954. 51 p.
Figueiroa was active against the Dutch both in Brazil and Angola. As *mestre do campo* of troops he had raised in Madeira, he participated in the final liberation of Pernambuco. Later he was governor of Cape Verde (1656-1662), and seems to have died in Brazil. [G. Boehrer]

4053. ————. Frei Manuel Calado do Salvador, religioso da ordem de São Paulo, pregador apostólico por sua santidade, cronista da restauração. Recife, Brazil, Universidade do Recife, 1954. 119 p.
Frei Manuel was one of the chroniclers of

the movement against the Dutch invaders in Brazil; his book was published in Lisbon in 1648. The author rehabilitates very convincingly the much-maligned figure of Frei Manuel, whose work, he says, must be considered on the whole a primary source for the period and subject treated. [M. Cardozo]

4054. Nemésio, Vitorino. O campo de São Paulo. A Companhia de Jesus e o plano português do Brasil (1528-1563). Lisboa, Comissão do Centenário (IV Centenário da fundação de São Paulo, 2), 1954. 466 p.

This treatment of the Jesuit activity in São Paulo is half devoted to Portuguese and Jesuit backgrounds. It is largely based on secondary sources with the exception of the Jesuit Letters. [G. Boehrer]

4055. Pôrto, J. Costa. História popular da restauração. Recife, Brazil, Prefeitura Municipal do Recife, Departamento de Documentação e Cultura, 1953? 70 p.

An admittedly popular history of the 1645-1654 movement which cast the Dutch out of Brazil. [G. Boehrer]

4056. Portugal. Secretariado Nacional da Informação, Cultura Popular e Turismo. Exposição histórica comemorativa do tricentenário da restauração pernambucana, 1654-1954. Lisboa, 1954. 160 p. & illus.

This Portuguese contribution to the tricentenary of the expulsion of the Dutch from Brazil was arranged by Alberto Iria, director of the Arquivo do Ultramar. It lists documents, maps and plans, paintings, engravings, etc., found in Portuguese depositories. [G. Boehrer]

4057. Reis, Artur Cezar Ferreira. A Amazônia no século XVIII: sugestões para estudos (*in* International Colloquium on Luso-Brazilian Studies [see item 6713], p. 266-271).

An essay calling attention to the need for further research on the state of Maranhão. Missionary activity, the administration, immigration, boundaries, and commerce are among the subjects suggested for further archival study. [G. Boehrer]

4058. Rodrigues, José Honório. O continente do Rio Grande. Rio, Edições S. José, 1954. 81 p., map.

This synthesis of southern Brazil is an enlargement of a chapter of the author's *Programa de história do Brasil colonial*. There is an extensive annotated bibliography. [G. Boehrer]

4059. São Paulo (state). Departamento do Arquivo. Documentos avulsos de interesse para a história e costumes de São Paulo. São Paulo, 1953. V. 2-3. 173, 148 p.

A series designed to contain miscellaneous documents from the archive of São Paulo. Those of

these volumes are from a bundle entitled "Bispo capitular, parocos, conventos, recolhimento, esmolas para a Santa Crusada, 1693-1786." They are of the years 1787-1822, and relate to the bishopric, parishes, convents, hospitals, and charities. Included are letters of the bishop, reports, memorials, inventories, and other papers. Among the papers are orders and proclamations, proposals for official appointments, lists of contributions, letters of agents of the crown, requisitions, papers regarding charities, etc. [R. R. Hill]

4060. ————. ————. Documentos interessantes para a história e costumes de São Paulo. V. 73. Oficios do Capitão General D. Luís Antonio de Souza Botelho Mourão, 1775-1776. São Paulo, 1952. 216 p.

These interesting documents comprise letters of the Captain General for the year 1766. Among the subjects treated are: installation of governors; appointment of officials; limits of São Paulo and Minas; organization of villages; number of inhabitants of São Paulo; land problems; mines and mining; military matters; war materials; Jesuits; discords of the religious orders; and leprosy. [R. R. Hill]

4061. ————. ————. Documentos interessantes para a história e costumes de São Paulo. V. 74-79. Oficios do General Martim Lopes Lobo de Saldanha, 1775-1777. São Paulo, 1954. 6 v. 352, 199, 192, 226, 218, 204 p.

The documents in these volumes comprise letters of the Governor of the Captaincy for the period from June 15, 1775, to Dec. 14, 1777, selected from the Archive of the State of São Paulo. They deal with the activities of the governor and the problems which he handled in the administration of the colony. They reveal much concerning the life and development of the São Paulo region [R. R. Hill]

4062. ————. ————. Inventários e testamentos. São Paulo, 1951-1955. V. 34-40. 260, 164, 259, 182, 192, 225, 175 p.

Wills and inventories of estates of residents of São Paulo for the years 1612-1663. The documents are from the historical section of the archive of the state of São Paulo. They contain important data on genealogy and economic matters. [R. R. Hill]

4063. Sousa, José Antônio Soares de. Açorianos na cidade do Salvador (R Inst Hist Geog Br, 219, abril-junho 1953, p. 3-26).

On the founding of Salvador and Azorean colonization through 1554. [G. Boehrer]

4064. Southey, Robert. História do Brasil. Traduzida do inglés por Luiz Joaquim de Oliveira e Castro e anotada por J. C. Fernandes Pinheiro. Salvador, Brazil, Progresso, 1954. T. 4-6. 276, 320, 314 p.

The continuation of the translation previously noted in *HLAS, no. 14, 1948,* item 2311, and *no. 16, 1950,* item 2218. First published in Paris in 1862. [G. Boehrer]

4064. Southey, Robert. História do Brasil. Sul. Pôrto Alegre, Brazil, Sulina (Col. Meridional, 1), 1953. 132 p., illus.
A short, sound work on the formation and the acquisition of Rio Grande do Sul and Santa Catarina. It is annotated but without page references. Included is a relatively lengthy résumé of the history of the horse in the Americas. [G. Boehrer]

4066. Thevet, André. Le Brésil et les Brésiliens. Paris, Presses Universitaires de France (Col. internationale de documentation, 2. série: Les classiques de la colonisation, 2), 1953. 346 p., illus.
Contains t. 2 of Thevet's *La cosmographie universelle* with the exception of *livre 12.* Also added are the hitherto unpublished *Histoire de deux voyages* (1585?) and *Le grand insulaire et pilotage.* The edition has been made with extreme care and excellence. [G. Boehrer]

4067. Thomaz, Joaquim. Anchieta. Rio, Guanabara, 1954. 334 p.
Although the author gives evidence of wide secondary reading, little light is thrown on Anchieta. There are two appendices of two articles originally published in the *Jornal do commércio* of Rio and in *O estado de São Paulo* against Oscar Pacheco, Tito Lívio Ferreira, and Seraphim Leite, who hold that Nóbrega, not Anchieta, was the founder of São Paulo. [G. Boehrer]

EMPIRE

4068. Barbosa, Rui. Obras completas de .... V. 14, 1887. T. 1. Questão militar, abolicionismo. Trabalhos jurídicos. Swift. Rio, Ministério da Educação e Cultura, 1955. 333 p.
Here are given Rui's activities in the military question and in abolition, his legal practice, and his rare excursion into literary criticism in his preface to the translation of *Gulliver's travels.* [G. Boehrer]

4069. Boiteux, Lucas Alexandre. A marinha imperial e outros ensaios. Rio, Ministério da Marinha, 1954. 443 p.
These uncritical essays designed "para exaltar a nossa marinha," concern heroes, vessels, and battles mainly during the Independence period, the first Argentine and the Paraguayan wars. [G. Boehrer]

4070. Brazil. Ministério da Guerra. Secretaria Geral. Revista militar brasileira. Rio. Ano 41, v. 59, agôsto 25, 1953, edição especial conmemorativa do sesquicentenário do nascimento de Luiz Alves de Lima (Duque de Caxias).
21 uncritical articles on Caxias, on various aspects of his career. Some are by trained historians, the rest by military officers. [G. Boehrer]

4071. Cardozo, Manoel. The Holy See and the question of the bishop-elect of Rio, 1833-1839 (Americas, Franciscan Hist, 10:1, July 1953, p. 3-74).
When Gregory XVI refused to confirm Antônio de Moura, the Regency's nominee, as bishop of Rio, a long Church-State argument resulted. The government lost the contest but not until after the royalists, including Feijó, had aired their views. This article is based on research in the Vatican Archive. [G. Boehrer]

4072. Corrêa, F. de Aquino. Dom José Antônio dos Reis, primeiro bispo diocesano de Cuiabá. Rio, Rodrigues, 1954. 83 p.
A hortatory biography of the man who was bishop of Cuiaba from 1832 to 1876. An *homem de côr,* he was the librarian of the first public library of São Paulo, a lawyer, and a deputy in the national Chamber. He is also reputed to be the author of Dom Manuel do Monte Rodrigues de Araujo's *Compêndio de teologia moral* which was indexed by the Holy Office. [G. Boehrer]

4073. Fouquet, Carlos. Vida e obra do Doutor Blumenau (*in* Centenário de Blumenau. São Paulo, Instituto Hans Staden, 1951, p. 52-113).
A short but penetrating biography of Hermann Blumenau, who arrived in Brazil in 1846 and was principally responsible for the success of the German settlements in Santa Catarina. [G. Boehrer]

4074. Oliveira, José Feliciano de. José Bonifácio e a independência. O homem do fico e o verdadeiro patriarca. São Paulo, Martins, 1955. 362 p.
The author, who promised to write this work in 1909, "wishes only to defend my beloved and great José Bonifácio. . . ." He believes that José Bonifácio had decided upon Brazil's independence when John VI left for Europe. His argument is mostly with those who would give José Clemente Pereira considerable credit and is based on the "demorarei" and the second edital's "Diga ao povo que fico." José Bonifácio's "Memória econômica e metalúrgica" is here reprinted as are other essays of the author. [G. Boehrer]

4075. Quintas, Amaro. Notícias e anúncios de jornal. Recife, Brazil, Departamento de Documentação e Cultura, 1953. 27 p.
This short essay treats of news items, advertisements, and letters published in Pernambucan newspapers during the era 1830-1852. Preceded by an introduction on its sociological significance by Gilberto Freyre. [G. Boehrer]

4076. Sousa, Octavio Tarquinio de. De várias províncias. Rio, Ministério da Educação e Saúde, Serviço de Documentação (Os cadernos de cultura), 1952. 51 p.
Short biographical essays on Teófilo Otoni, Antônio Borges de Fonseca, Cipriano Barata, Caetano Lopes de Moura, Francisco Muniz

Tavares, Antônio Carlos de Andrada e Silva, and Antônio Rodrigues Veloso de Oliveira. [G. Boehrer]

4077. Stein, Stanley J. The passing of the coffee plantation in the Paraiba Valley (HAHR, 33:3, Aug. 1953, p. 331-364).
The coffee planter faced many problems in the second half of the 19th century in Vassomas, in the province of Rio de Janeiro. With widespread misuse of lands, the inefficient application of machinery, financing became more difficult. Emancipation seems to have been the final blow. [G. Boehrer]

4078. Tschudi, J. J. von. Viagem às províncias do Rio de Janeiro e São Paulo. Introdução de Afonso de E. Taunay. Tradução de Eduardo de Lima Castro. São Paulo, Martins (Biblioteca histórica paulista, 5), 1953. 209 p., illus.
A translation of the sections concerning São Paulo of Tschudi's *Reisen durch Süd-Amerika*. Tschudi, who made his trip in 1860, is interesting for his comments on agriculture and on the Swiss and German colonies. While most of the author's notes are retained, some are incorporated within the text. [G. Boehrer]

4079. Zaluar, Augusto-Emílio. Peregrinação pela província de S. Paulo (1860-1861). São Paulo, Martins (Biblioteca histórica paulista, 2), 1952, i.e. 1953. 236 p., illus.
The third edition of this work which religiously retains the typographical errors of the first and adds a few more. José Bonifácio's first *Apontamentos para a civilização dos índios* is again printed without credit despite Inocêncio da Silva's remarks. [G. Boehrer]

REPUBLICAN PERIOD

4080. Barbosa, Rui. D. Pedro II e Francisco de Castro. Rio, Organização Simões (Col. Rui, 17), 1953. 73 p.
Two of these addresses are concerned with the revocation of the banishment of the imperial family. The third is a eulogy of the physician and author. The first two are interesting, for they are Rui's analysis of the Revolution of 1889 and the reasons for the banishment. [G. Boehrer]

4081. ————. Discurso no Colégio Anchieta. Rio, Casa de Rui Barbosa, 1953. xxv, 91 p.
This was one of Barbosa's most famous speeches. Given in 1903, it has become a fount for numerous quotations. It is here preceded by an analysis of Rui's religious position by Américo Jacobina Lacombe who regards this oration as a decisive point in Barbosa's religious evolution. [G. Boehrer]

4082. ————. Obras completas de . . . . V. 24, 1897. T. 1. O partido republicano conservador. Discursos parlamentares. Rio, Ministério da Educação e Saúde, 1952. 322 p.

4083. ————. Obras completas de . . . . V. 25, 1898. T. 6. Discursos parlamentares. Rio, Ministério da Educação e Saúde, 1953. 396 p.

4084. ————. Obras completas de . . . V. 26, 1899. T. 2. Discursos parlamentares. Rio, Ministério da Educação e Cultura, 1955. 230 p.

4085. ————. Obras completas de . . . . V. 29, 1902. Rio, Ministério da Educação e Saúde, 1953. T. 2-3. 440, 445 p.
The defense of Rui's *parecer* on literary criticism of the Civil Law Code project against the attacks of Ernesto Carneiro Ribeiro, Clovis Bevilaqua, and José Verissimo. T. 1, *Parecer sôbre a redação do código civil*, was published in 1949; t. 2 and 3 are entitled *Réplica*. [G. Boehrer]

4086. Castro, Eduardo de Lima. Memórias de um político pernambucano. Revivendo o passado aos 80 anos. Rio, O Cruzeiro, 1955. 222 p.
The autobiography of a prominent Pernambucan businessman and politician. An unsuccessful candidate for governor in 1922, he was a federal deputy in the Chamber disrupted by the Revolution of 1930. Financially ruined in the depression, he turned to translations. [G. Boehrer]

4087. Gabaglia, A. C. Raja. Poder marítimo nas duas guerras mundiais (1914-1918—1939-1945). Rio, Imprensa Naval, 1953. 478 p., tables.
There are two chapters on Brazilian participation in the two World Wars (p. 119-129; p. 404-443). The second section is much more detailed, with charts on convoys, ships lost, rescues, etc. [G. Boehrer]

4088. Konder, Marcos. Lauro Müller. Ensaio biobibliográfico. Rio, Academia Brasileira, 1953. 98 p., illus.
An unannotated life of one of the first eminent German-Brazilians. Son of immigrant parents, Müller was a deputy, a senator, governor of Santa Catarina, minister of transportation, and the successor of Rio Branco in the Foreign Office. He resigned from the last position when Brazil entered World War I. [G. Boehrer]

4089. Lopes, Murilo Ribeiro. Rui Barbosa e a marinha. Rio, Casa de Rui Barbosa, 1953. 393 p., pl.
Rui's relationship with the navy is here portrayed through letters, telegrams, and many parliamentary questions and discourses. Of special interest are the Wandenkolk episode of 1892-1893, the Naval revolt of 1893, the mutiny of 1910, and his defense of Vice-Admiral Silveira da Mota. [G. Boehrer]

4090. Martins, Luís. O patriarca e o bacharel. Prefácio de Gilberto Freyre. São Paulo, Martins, 1953. 228 p.
An enlargement and strengthening of Senhor

Martin's celebrated article in the *Revista do Arquivo Municipal*. The theme is a discussion of the Revolution of November 15 as a revolt against, and a slaying of, a father by his sons. Luís Martins' chapter on the personality and role of Pedro II is, perhaps, the most brilliant analysis of a much misunderstood personality. Among the leading republicans who later re-sented of their activity, or seemed to do so, and who are discussed, are Rui Barbosa, Afonso Celso Júnior, Martim Francisco III, Oliveira Lima, and even the ferocious João Manuel. This work is clearly one of the most significant to appear in Brazilian historiography in many years. [G. Boehrer]

4091. Pessoa, Epitácio. Obras completas de .... V. 1. Discursos parlamentares, 1890-1893. Rio, Instituto Nacional do Livro, 1955. 429 p.

The first volume of the works of Epitácio Pessoa, President of Brazil, 1919-1922. These papers begin with the Constitutional Assembly of 1890 and cover the regimes of Fonseca and Peixoto and the period of the revolts in Rio Grande do Sul and Santa Catarina. [G. Boehrer]

4092. Ponce Filho, Generoso. Generoso Ponce, um chefe. Prefácio de Pedro Calmon. Rio, Pongetti, 1952. 564 p.

A filial biography of Ponce (1852-1911), a politician of Mato Grosso and a major figure during his state's turbulent history in the Republic's first years. Senator, state president, and deputy, at divers times, he was also in exile. [G. Boehrer]

4093. Sousa, José Antônio Soares de. A margem de uma política, 1850-1852 (R Inst Hist Geog Br, 221, oct.-dez. 1953, p. 3-43).

On the diplomatic activity and correspondence of Argentina and Brazil in the years preceding the war against Rosas. Tomás Guido repre-sented Rosas in Brazil, conducting a spy ring and even publishing *O americano*. Rodrigo Silva Pontes represented Brazil in Montevideo and Asunción and had his informants in B. A. There is a long discussion of Pontes' "un-known correspondent." [G. Boehrer]

4094. Villares, Henrique Dumont. Quem deu asas ao homem. Alberto Santos-Du-mont: sua vida e sua glória. São Paulo, Emprêsa Gráf. da Revista dos Tribunais, 1953. 632 p., illus.

A nephew of the aviator, the author hopes that these personal notes will serve to com-plement the extant biographies of his uncle. Santos Dumont's priority over the Wright brothers in heavier-than-air flight is claimed. There are illustrations on every other page, which enhances the volume's value. [G. Boehrer]

International Relations Since 1830

BRYCE WOOD

GENERAL

4200. El asilado "silencioso." Antología del caso Haya de la Torre. Su biografía. México, Fren, 1954. 241 p.
The body of this book consists of texts of articles and editorials about Haya de la Torre during his five years of asylum in the Colombian embassy in Lima.

4201. Cabot, John M. Toward our common American destiny. Speeches and interviews on Latin American problems. Medford, Mass., Fletcher School of Law and Diplomacy, 1955? 214 p., pl.
A career diplomat, Mr. Cabot served as Assistant Secretary of State for Inter-American Affairs from February 1953 to February 1954. These speeches touch on political and economic problems; there is a witty piece on "Why diplomats don't behave like human beings"; his discussion of how the U. S. "learned the unwisdom of interfering in our neighbors' affairs" is of historical as well as topical interest. These speeches are of more than ordinary interest and importance.

4202. Corominas, Enrique V. In the Caribbean political areas. Translated from the Spanish by L. Charles Foresti. Cambridge, Mass., University Press, 1954. 204 p.
Unidiomatic translation of a study of postwar political developments in the Caribbean by a former president of the Council of the OAS. For the original in Spanish, see *HLAS, no. 18, 1952,* item 2177.

4203. Current history. Philadelphia, Pa. V. 28, no. 163, Mar. 1955.
Entire issue devoted to foreign policies in Latin America. Articles by six specialists deal with the interests and influences of Spain, Portugal, France, Germany, Great Britain and the U. S. in Latin America. Synoptic reviews of the Inter-American System by Howard F. Cline, and of aspects of U. S. policy since 1865 by Arthur P. Whitaker, are of special interest to students of international affairs.

4204. Galíndez, Jesús de. Anti-American sentiment in Latin America (J Intl Aff, 9:1, 1955, p. 24-32).
A brief review of the changes in Latin American attitudes toward the U. S.; since 1945 anti-U. S. feeling has increased.

4205. Goodrich, Carter. Bolivia: test of technical assistance (For Aff, 32:3, Apr. 1954, p. 473-481).
A review, by a participant, of the work and plans of a United Nations technical assistance mission in Bolivia.

4206. Haya de la Torre, Víctor Raúl. ¿Adónde va Indoamérica? B. A., Editorial Indoamérica, 1954. 145 p.
A reprint of a work that appeared in its second edition in 1935. The preface gives no explanation of the reasons for republication at this time.

4207. Jobim, Danton. O ciclo da doutrina de Monroe. Rio, Edições Souza, 1955. 107 p.
A Brazilian professor of journalism traces the history of the Monroe Doctrine; once unilateral, the doctrine has become a contribution of the Americas to international law.

4208. Lara, Jesús. El Congreso de los Pueblos por la Paz efectuado en Viena del 12 al 19 de diciembre de 1952. Cochabamba, Bolivia, Imp. Universitaria, 1953. 31 p.
An account of the personalities and resolutions of the Communist-sponsored Congress of Peoples for Peace, in Vienna, by a Bolivian participant.

4209. Morales Yordán, Jorge. La Corte Internacional de Justicia y el caso Haya de la Torre (R Col Abog P R, 16:1, nov. 1955, p. 7-31).
A Puerto Rican lawyer argues that the Court's decisions in the Haya de la Torre case did not lead to a solution of the conflict because the Court did not consider the case in terms of "American international law." He says if the Court persists in the attitude assumed in this case, it will deserve being called weak.

4210. Pani, Alberto J. Las conferencias de Bucareli. México, Jus, 1953. 228 p.
The author was the Secretary of Foreign Relations under Álvaro Obregón. Most of the book

is devoted to the acts of the conference with comments. [W. V. Scholes]

4211. Sánchez Lazo, Carlos Roberto. La ODECA y algunos de sus antecedentes histórico-jurídicos. Guatemala, Universidad de San Carlos de Guatemala, Facultad de Ciencias Jurídicas y Sociales, 1955. 84 p.
A thesis on the origin and legal status of the Organization of Central American States (ODECA).

4212. United Nations. Department of Public Information. World against want. An account of the UN technical assistance programme for economic development. Geneva, 1953. 80 p., illus.
This pamphlet contains brief articles on iron and steel in Latin America and UNESCO's Scientific and Technical Documentation Centre in Mexico, here called "a fortress of knowledge."

ORGANIZATION OF AMERICAN STATES: GENERAL

4213. Canyes, Manuel. La Organización de los Estados Americanos y las Naciones Unidas. 2. ed. Washington, Unión Panamericana, 1953. 36 p.
Official statement of the comparative structure of the OAS and the UN, and description of their relationships. English second edition appeared in 1952.

4214. Fenochio, Andres. Índice por materias de los diversos instrumentos interamericanos, suscritos o aprobados en las conferencias panamericanas principales de 1889 a 1951 inclusive. Washington, Unión Panamericana (Serie sobre conferencias y organismos, 29), 1953. 111 p.
A subject index to conventions and resolutions of American conferences. Issued in Spanish only.

4215. Inter - American Economic and Social Council. Program of Technical Cooperation of the Organization of American States for the calendar year 1954. Approved January 28, 1954. Washington, Pan American Union, 1954. 66 p.
Issued also in Spanish: Programa de Cooperación Técnica . . . , 1954, 67 p. A list and description of technical assistance projects of the Council, in health, education, and other fields.

4216. Organization of American States. Council. Regulations of the Council of the Organization of American States. Washington, Pan American Union, 1954. 21 p.
Published also in Spanish: Reglamento del Consejo de la Organización de los Estados Americanos. Text of the rules of procedure of the Council of the OAS.

4216a. Pan American Union. Manual de la Conferencia Interamericana. Organización y funcionamiento de la Secretaría General. Washington, 1953. 169 p. (Serie sobre conferencias y organismos, 27).
Issued only in Spanish. This is a work on how to hold the inter-American conferences, for the benefit of member states. It seems to be complete. It contains diagrams showing shape and dimensions of cabinets for simultaneous interpreters, sketches of the size and form of boxes used for distributing documents to delegations, tables of office equipment (100 medium size and 5 large wastebaskets), instructions about the designation of documents and about protocol and other matters.

4216b. ————. El sistema interamericano. Washington, 1954? 13 p., illus.
A brief popular description of the structure, principles, and operation of the OAS and inter-Americanism. A more condensed version was issued in English: The inter-American system, 1954, 4 p.

4217. ————. Columbus Memorial Library. Bibliografía de las conferencias interamericanas. Washington, 1954. 277 p. (Bibliographic series, 41).
This work lists, for each inter-American conference from 1889-1951, including meetings of consultation of foreign ministers, and conferences on peace and security (B. A., 1936; Mexico City, 1945; and Rio, 1947) the following: titles of documents prepared for and presented at the conferences; publications relating to the conferences; and reports and articles and books written about the conferences. A useful reference work for students of inter-American organization. Issued in Spanish only.

4218. ————. Department of International Law. Bilateral treaty developments in Latin America, 1942-1952. Washington, 1953. 243 p. (Law and treaty series, 38).
A list of new bilateral treaties, and modifications of old ones.

4219. ————. ————. Manual of inter-American relations. A systematic classification of the treaties, conventions, resolutions, declarations, and recommendations adopted at inter-American conferences and meetings of consultation. Washington, 1953. 296 p.
This work makes it possible "to place in the hands of a delegate to an inter-American conference a complete record of the action taken at previous conferences with respect to the particular subject in which he has a special interest." Issued only in English.

4220. ————. ————. Strengthening of internal security. Report prepared in compliance with resolution VIII, approved by the Fourth Meeting of Consultation of Ministers of Foreign Affairs, Washington, D. C., March 26-April 7, 1951. Washington, 1953. 432 p.

Issued also in Spanish: *Fortalecimiento de la seguridad interna,* 1953, 295 p. This volume is a handbook on methods for the prevention of subversive acts by communists in the Americas. It defines sabotage, espionage, and other activities, and appends the texts of national laws and a large number of resolutions of the Emergency Advisory Committee for the Political Defense of the Americas.

4221. ————. Division of Law and Treaties. Documents and notes on privileges and immunities with special reference to the Organization of American States. Washington, 1953. 146 p. (Law and treaty series).
A collection of provisions of treaties and of the laws of the U. S. concerning privileges and immunities, designed to help members of delegations to the Council of the OAS. English and Spanish texts.

4222. ————. ————. Inter-American peace treaties and conventions. Washington, 1954. 73 p. (Law and treaty series).
Texts of American agreements relating to the pacific settlement of disputes, 1902-1948, and tables showing signatures, ratifications, and deposits with respect to each instrument and each country.

ORGANIZATION OF AMERICAN STATES: NINTH AND TENTH INTER-AMERICAN CONFERENCES

4225. Conferencia Internacional Americana, IX, Bogotá, marzo 30-mayo 2, 1948. Actas y documentos. Bogotá, Ministerio de Relaciones Exteriores, 1953. 7 v. V. 1, Antecedentes; secretaría general; reunión preliminar; sesiones plenarias, 261 p.; v. 2, Comisiones reglamentarias, 592 p.; v. 3, Comisión primera; comisión segunda, 661 p.; v. 4, Comisión tercera; comisión cuarta, 778 p.; v. 5, Comisión quinta; comisión sexta, 653 p.; v. 6, Conclusiones, 414 p.; v. 7, Índice analítico, 33 p.
This beautifully printed record of the Bogotá conference contains verbatim minutes of plenary sessions, and of several of the committees, and all of the resolutions, conventions, and other diplomatic instruments. Summary minutes are provided for subcommittee meetings. Issued in Spanish only.

4226. Inter - American Conference, X, Caracas, Mar. 1-28, 1954. Acta final. Caracas, Secretaría General de la Décima Conferencia Interamericana, 1954. 125 p.
Spanish text issued by the conference secretariat. *Draft final act* issued in English, 1954, 163 p.

4227. ————. Handbook for delegates. Washington, Pan American Union, 1953. 268 p.

Published also in Spanish: *Manual para los delegados,* 1953, 270 p. This publication's purpose "is to make available to the delegates antecedent material on the various topics included in the agenda." The text combines narrative and textual material.

4228. ————. Report on the activities of the Organization of American States, 1948-1953. Washington, Pan American Union, 1953. 209 p.
Issued also in Spanish, *Informe sobre las actividades de la Organización de los Estados Americanos, 1948-1953,* 1953, 215 p., and in French. A five-year review of the activities of the OAS in political, economic, and cultural fields.

4229. ————. Report of the delegation of the United States of America with related documents. Washington, U. S. Government Printing Office (Dept. of State publ., 5692; International organization and conference series, 2; American Republics, 14), 1955. 221 p.
The first 43 pages of this report outline the positions taken by the U. S. delegation on important issues such as communism in the Americas, European colonies in the Western Hemisphere, and the dispute over fishing rights on the west coast of South America. The remainder of the work comprises addresses by the Secretary of State and others, and resolutions and documents of the conference.

ORGANIZATION OF AMERICAN STATES: INTER-AMERICAN COUNCIL OF JURISTS

4230. Herrera Báez, Porfirio. El Consejo Interamericano de Jurisconsultos. Dos reuniones. V. 1. Rio de Janeiro, 1950. Ciudad Trujillo, Editora del Caribe, 1954. 554 p.
Review of discussions and issues at the meeting with special attention to the position of the delegation of the Dominican Republic. See also item below.

4231. ————. El Consejo Interamericano de Jurisconsultos. V. 2 (separata). Los temas sobre el reconocimiento de gobiernos de facto y la protección internacional de los derechos humanos en la II Reunión del Consejo de Jurisconsultos, Buenos Aires, 1953. Ciudad Trujillo, Editora del Caribe, 1954. 154 p.
See also item above.

4232. Inter-American Council of Jurists, 2nd meeting, B. A., Apr. 20-May 9, 1953. Actas y documentos. Washington, Unión Panamericana, 1953. 2 v. V. 1, Actas de las sesiones plenarias; acta final, 192 p.; v. 2, Actas de las sesiones de las comisiones; observaciones y proyectos; índice alfabético, 259 p. (CIJ-19 español).

Minutes, resolutions, and conventions emerging from the second meeting of the Inter-American Council of Jurists. Issued only in Spanish.

4233. ————. Final act. Washington, Pan American Union, Department of International Law, 1953. 70 p. (CIJ-17 Euglish).
Text of resolutions, and, principally, of draft conventions on (1) political exiles, asylees, and refugees, and (2) diplomatic asylum. Issued also in Spanish, *Acta final*, 1953, 72 p., and in Portuguese and French.

4234. ————. Handbook. Washington, Pan American Union, Department of International Law, 1953. 98 p. (CIJ-16 Euglish).
Issued also in Spanish, 1953, 99 p., and in Portuguese. Background documents and other information for delegates to the meeting.

4235. ————. Report of the Executive Secretary of the Inter-American Council of Jurists. Washington, Pan American Union, Department of International Law, 1953. 29 p. (CIJ-18 English).
An interpretation of the work of the meeting, the resolutions and conventions of which are given in item 4232. Issued only in English.

ORGANIZATION OF AMERICAN STATES: INTER-AMERICAN CULTURAL COUNCIL

4236. Inter-American Cultural Council. Carta cultural de América. I. Recopilación de normas culturales. 2. Ciencia. Washington, Unión Panamericana, Departamento de Asuntos Culturales, 1953. 2 v. [Parte] A, Conferencias Internacionales Americanas (1889-1948)—Conferencias panamericanas de uniformidad de especificaciones (1924-1927); [parte] B, Conferencias panamericanas de directores nacionales de sanidad (1926-1948)—Conferencia Interamericana sobre Conservación de los Recursos Naturales Renovables (7-20 de septiembre de 1948).
A collection of resolutions and other texts from inter-American conferences dealing with scientific questions; the range of subjects includes demography, geography, health, botany, oceanography, and others. See also items 2006 and 2007.

4237. ————. Carta cultural de América. I. Recopilación de normas culturales. 3. Cultura. Washington, Unión Panamericana, 1953. 2 v. [Parte] A, Conferencias Internacionales Americanas (1889-1948) —Congresos panamericanos del niño (1916-1948); [parte] B, Congresos americanos de expansión económica y ense-

ñanza comercial (1919-1922)—Conferencias regionales interamericanas de la UNESCO (1948-1950).
See also items 2006 and 1007.

4238. ————. Carta cultural de América. II. Índice analítico de la recopilación de normas culturales. 2. Ciencia. Washington, Unión Panamericana, 1954. 28 p.
See also items above.

4239. ————. Carta cultural de América. II. Índice analítico de la recopilación de normas culturales. 3. Cultura. Washington, Unión Panamericana, 1954. 24 p.
See also items above.

ORGANIZATION OF AMERICAN STATES: INTER-AMERICAN COMMISSION OF WOMEN

4240. Inter-American Commission of Women. Report presented to the 7th session of the United Nations Commission on the Status of Women, New York, N. Y., March-April 1953. Washington, Pan American Union, 1953. 12 p.
Report of the year's activity, and of developments in the Americas concerning political and other rights of women. Also issued in Spanish.

4241. ————, 8th Assembly, Rio, July 23-Aug. 8, 1952. Final act. Washington, Pan American Union (Conferences and organizations series, 22), 1953. 36 p.
Issued also in Spanish and Portuguese. Texts of resolutions of the Assembly; most of them deal with matters involving equal rights for women.

4242. Organization of American States. Agreement between the Council of the OAS and the Inter-American Commission of Women. (English and Spanish texts). Washington, Pan American Union, Division of Conferences and Organizations (Conferences and organizations series, 25), 1953. 9 p.
Published also in Portuguese: *Acôrdo entre o Conselho da OEA e a Comissão Interamericana de Mulheres.*

ORGANIZATION OF AMERICAN STATES: OTHER SPECIALIZED ORGANS

4243. Organization of American States. Agreement between the Council of the OAS and the Inter-American Indian Institute. Washington, Pan American Union, Division of Conferences and Organizations (Conferences and organizations series, 24), 1953. 9 p.
Text, in English and Spanish.

4244. ———. Agreement between the Council of the OAS and the Pan American Railway Congress Association. Washington, Pan American Union, Division of Conferences and Organizations (Conferences and organizations series, 30), 1953. 9 p.
Text, in English and Spanish.

4245. Special Pan American Highway Congress, Mexico City, Oct. 26-Nov. 1, 1952. Final act. Washington, Pan American Union (Conferences and organizations series, 23), 1953. 53 p.
Issued also in Spanish and Portuguese. The main work of this congress was to consider plans for financing the Pan American Highway.

4246. United States. Department of State. Fourth Meeting of Consultation of Ministers of Foreign Affairs of American States, Washington, D. C., March 26-April 7, 1951. Report of the Secretary of State. Washington, 1953. vi, 88 p. (Publ. 4928).
Official report of the U. S. delegation to this mainly economic meeting. 31 appendices give texts of resolutions, declarations, etc.

PAN AMERICANISM

4247. Accioly, Hildebrando. Raízes ou causas históricas do Panamericanismo. Rio, Ministério das Relações Exteriores, Serviço de Publicações, 1953. 77 p.
Brief essays on the growth of Pan Americanism in the 19th century.

4248. Briceño-Iragorry, Mario. El fariseísmo bolivariano y la anti-América. Temas sobre hispanoamericanismo y panamericanismo. Madrid, Ediciones Bitácora, 1953. 59 p.
An attack on the "farce" of Pan Americanism by a Venezuelan in Spain who protests at the holding of the Tenth Inter-American Conference in Caracas.

4249. Burr, Robert N., and Roland D. Hussey. Documents on Inter-American cooperation. Philadelphia, Pa., University of Pennsylvania Press, 1955. V. 1, 1810-1881, 182 p.; v. 2, 1881-1948, 214 p.
Selections from speeches, treaties, articles, editorials and resolutions to illustrate the growth of Pan Americanism. Almost no item is reproduced in full, not even the Rio treaty of 1947. The serious student, dismayed by the great number of indicated omissions, will seek the full flavor and meaning of the sources elsewhere; others may be merely baffled. The authors would have done better to follow the example of *Foreign relations of the United States.*

4250. Franco, Affonso Arinos de Mello. Pela solidariedade continental. Rio,

Ministério das Relações Exteriores, 1953. 74 p.
This small book has a grander title than its substance warrants. It consists of texts of two speeches by the son of Afranio Mello Franco, the peacemaker in the Leticia dispute. The chief value of the speeches is their excellence as models of baroque eloquence in Latin American diplomatic practice.

4251. Padilla, Ezequiel. The meaning of Pan-Americanism (For Aff, 32:2, Jan. 1954, p. 270-281).
The former Mexican foreign minister suggests that the good neighbor policy had, between 1930 and 1940, "cleared the horizon," but that American unity began to break up after 1945 because the American nations "forgot that the essence of Pan-Americanism is economic solidarity."

POLICY OF THE UNITED STATES

4252. Eisenhower, Milton S. United States-Latin American relations. Report to the President (Dept State B, 29:752, Nov. 23, 1953, p. 695-717).
Recommendations for greater respect and understanding, and closer economic cooperation between the U. S. and Latin America. President Eisenhower's brother spent five weeks on a visit to the ten countries of South America. Also issued as Dept. of State Publ., 5240; Inter-American series, 47; Washington, 1953, 23 p.

4253. Fabela, Isidro. La conferencia de Caracas y la actitud anticomunista de México. México, Cultura, 1954. 44 p.
The U. S., it is alleged, is effectively intervening in certain Latin American countries by what the author calls a kind of diplomatic McCarthyism. Writing in a moderate tone, he applauds the efforts of Mexican representatives at the Caracas conference to defend Mexican sovereignty against the proposals of the delegation of the U. S.

4254. Stuart, Graham H. Latin America and the United States. 5th ed. N. Y., Appleton-Century-Crofts, 1955. 493 p. & maps.
This popular textbook first appeared in 1922; the 4th edition was dated 1943. New material on the good neighbor policy has been added, but the original organization is unchanged.

4255. United States. Congress. House. Select Committee on Communist Aggression. 83rd Congress, 2nd session. Report of the Subcommittee to Investigate Communist Aggression in Latin America. Washington, U. S. Government Printing Office, 1954. 18 p.
This report is based on hearings held by the Subcommittee; it provides evidence of what may almost be called a rediscovery of Latin America resulting from the Guatemalan crisis in 1954.

4256. ———. ———. Senate. Committee on Foreign Relations. 83rd Congress, 2nd Session. South America. Report of Senator Theodore Francis Green on a study mission. Jan. 26, 1954. Washington, U. S. Government Printing Office, 1954. 12 p.

Senator Green (Democrat, R. I.) spent five weeks at the end of 1953 on a visit to Latin America. His report is a model of political investigation: cautious, moderate, and specific. He reports low morale in the Foreign Service and makes some recommendations aimed at raising it. [S. Garbuny]

4257. ———. Department of State. Our foreign policy in Latin America. Washington, 1953. 20 p. (Publ. 5285; Inter-American series, 46).

Texts of speeches by President Eisenhower, Assistant Secretary of State John M. Cabot, and Nelson A. Rockefeller, reprinted from the *Department of State bulletin.*

4258. ———. ———. Our southern partners. The story of our Latin American relations. Washington, U. S. Government Printing Office (Dept. of State, Publ. 5604; Inter-American series, 49), 1954. 48 p., illus.

Official interpretation, in broad outlines, of Latin American and inter-American history and current problems.

POLICY OF OTHER COUNTRIES

4259. Alfaro, Ricardo J. Medio siglo de relaciones entre Panamá y los Estados Unidos. Panamá, Imp. Nacional, 1953. 32 p.

A stimulating essay. Diplomatic historians in the U. S. should give serious attention to this eminent Panamanian. He says: "It is foolishness to maintain, as badly documented or ill-intentioned historians and writers have done, that the independence of Panama in 1903 was the result of arbitrary action by Theodore Roosevelt." This is part of a new black legend in Panamanian history; Alfaro claims the Panamanian people gained their own independence.

4260. Bervin, Antoine. Mission à La Havane. Notes et souvenirs, 1942-1945. Port-au-Prince, Coll. du Sesquicentenaire de l'Indépendance d'Haïti, 1952? 136 p. & illus.

These diplomatic memoirs have a 19th-century air, and a sampler-like charm. In these rough-and-ready days it is pleasant to find a book by an envoy containing a picture of "Trois grâces cubaines sur le Malecon"; a vignette of Spruille Braden recalling that he now and then asked the Haitian chargé d'affaires for the etymologies of French words; and a quotable quotation: ". . . In dealing with our Presidents, it is always necessary to guess at what they mean, for they do not clearly expose their thoughts."

4261. Chile. Comisión Chilena de Cooperación Intelectual. 22 años de labor, 1930-1952. Santiago, Editorial Universitaria, 1953. 32 p.

A description of the aims and activities of the Commission, which serves as a Chilean national commission for UNESCO.

4262. Costa Rica. Ministerio de Relaciones Exteriores y Culto. Memoria . . . 1952-1953. San José, 1953. 262 p.

This report demonstrates the scope and complexity of international relations of even one of the smaller states of the modern world. Foreign Minister Fernando Lara Bustamante points out that his ministry constantly needs to increase its personnel because of the growing work of the United Nations, and of technical assistance developments.

4263. Magloire, Paul E. Le Président Magloire parle au Congrès Américain. Port-au-Prince, N. A. Théodore, 1955. 22 p.

The Haitian president's address to the U. S. Congress, Jan. 27, 1955. Text in French and English.

4264. Olea Muñoz, Xavier. La aportación de México al derecho internacional. México, Universidad Nacional Autónoma de México, 1954. 135 p.

Mexican contributions to international law are considered as being three: the Estrada and Carranza doctrines and the Mexican Calvo clause.

4265. Peña Batlle, Manuel A. Política de Trujillo. Ciudad Trujillo, Imp. Dominicana, 1954. 204 p.

Articles and speeches by a Dominican writer and public man, on diverse political matters. In the preface it is stated that: "From the beginning of his remarkable public life, Generalissimo Trujillo showed the ability to avail himself of the fullest cooperation of intellectuals, extracting from each of them the utmost effort for the well-being of the Republic."

4266. Price-Mars, Jean. La République d'Haïti et la République Dominicaine. Les aspects divers d'un problème d'histoire, de géographie et d'ethnologie. Port-au-Prince, Held (Coll. du tricinquantenaire de l'Indépendance d'Haïti), 1953. 2 v. 229, 335 p.

One of the most respected of Haitian intellectuals, Dr. Price-Mars has also served his country as minister of foreign affairs, ambassador to the UN, and as ambassador to Ciudad Trujillo. He is now rector of the University of Haiti. In these two volumes he traces the history of the relations between Haiti and her nearest neighbor, the Dominican Republic. The tensions that divide these two nations stem from historical, geographical, ethnological, and other factors. The author traces these complex problems most skillfully. His excellent analysis of the past and present justifies the apprehension with which he awaits future developments.

Reviewed in HAHR, 35:4, Nov. 1955, p. 538-549. [M. Cook]

4267. Sociedad Mexicana de Geografía y Estadística. La isla de Chipre. La Sociedad Mexicana de Geografía y Estadística contra el sistema colonialista (B Soc Mex Geog Est, 79:1, enero-feb. 1955, 106 p.).

A collection of documents in which the Society places itself on record against "the colonial system" as represented by British policy in Cyprus.

4268. Whitaker, Arthur P. The United States and Argentina. Cambridge, Mass., Harvard University Press, 1954. 272 p.

More than half of this well-informed study deals with the Peronista period.

GUATEMALAN REVOLUTION

4269. Cardoza y Aragón, Luis. La revolución guatemalteca. México, Ediciones Cuadernos Americanos (43), 1955. 215 p.

A bitter accusation against what the author alleges to have been a "Yankee attack" on Guatemala, defended in the United Nations by a representative of "Bostonian imperialism." This book, written by a partisan of ex-president Arbenz, should be read in connection with that by Guillermo Toriello, item 4273.

4270. Grant, Donald. Guatemala and United States foreign policy (J Intl Aff, 9:1, 1955, p. 64-72).

A U. S. journalist says the U. S. "supplied the decisive factors" in the 1954 Guatemalan revolution. Such action, he suggests, might have been unnecessary had the U. S. given economic and other support to the Arévalo government in 1944.

4271. Great Britain. Foreign Office. Report on events leading up to and arising out of the change of régime in Guatemala, 1954. London, H. M. Stationery Office (Cmd. 9277), 1954. 125 p. (Guatemala, 1 (1954)).

Five sixths of this report consists of texts of UN and OAS documents. There is a preface in the form of a dispatch of July 26, 1954, from Guatemala to the Foreign Office and a summary of the proceedings in the Security Council.

4272. Sharpe, Reginald. British Honduras. Report of an inquiry held by Sir Reginald Sharpe into allegations of contacts between the People's United Party and Guatemala. Presented . . . . London, Colonial Office (Cmd. 9139), 1954. 36 p.

Hearings held by a lawyer in Belize. The lawyer, commissioned by the Governor of British Honduras, concluded that there had been efforts made by a leader of the People's United Party in Belize to obtain funds from the government of Guatemala in 1953. Certain funds reached the Party through the Guate-malan consul in Belize, apparently to pay defense costs for individuals charged with sedition.

4273. Toriello, Guillermo. La batalla de Guatemala. México, Ediciones Cuadernos Americanos (39), 1955. 349 p.

The former foreign minister of Guatemala presents a fiery defense of his role in the Guatemalan crisis of 1954, and a bitter attack on the policy of the U. S., which, he writes, "utterly cancelled out what remained of the 'good neighborhood' of Roosevelt, the apostle of democracy." There is a 90-page collection of documents.

4274. United States. Department of State. Intervention of international communism in Guatemala. Washington, U. S. Government Printing Office (Dept. of State publ., 5556; Inter-American series, 48), 1954. 96 p.

The first 35 pages of this "blue book" provide the texts of statements by officials of the Department of State before the Security Council of the UN, the Council of the OAS, and other audiences. The second part of the work presents a study of the Guatemalan Communist Party and a chronology of the growth of communism in Guatemala from 1944-1954.

TERRITORIAL QUESTIONS

4275. Bloomfield, Louis M. The British Honduras-Guatemala dispute. Toronto, Canada, Carswell, 1953. 231 p.

A dispassionate review of the dispute that points out strengths and weaknesses of the case for each side. There is a map and an extensive collection of treaties. The author is a Canadian lawyer.

4276. García Sayán, Enrique. Notas sobre la soberanía marítima del Perú. Defensa de las 200 millas de mar peruano ante las recientes transgresiones. Lima, Villanueva, 1955. 62 p.

A legal statement of the Peruvian case for Peru's sovereignty over waters 200 miles from its coasts. Annexes contain official decrees and other documents.

4277. Hadgialy Divo, Miguel. Así se ha escrito la historia. Los Monjes han sido y son venezolanos. Caracas, Ragon, 1955. 74 p.

Enthusiastic statement of the Venezuelan claim to two groups of islets in the Caribbean, also claimed by Colombia. It is hoped that the problem is less grave than the author claims.

4278. Heron, David Winston. Antarctic claims (For Aff, 32:4, July 1954, p. 661-667, map).

A review of Antarctic claims with special reference to British and Argentine rivalry.

4279. El litigio territorial entre el Ecuador y el Perú. El protocolo de Río de Janeiro, su origen y sus consecuencias. Polémica entre los embajadores del Ecuador y del Perú. Caracas, Áncora, 1953. 47 p., illus., maps.

A spirited debate between Eduardo Garland for Peru and Antonio Parra Velasco for Ecuador. This boundary dispute, thought to have been laid to rest at Rio de Janeiro on Jan. 27, 1942, is very much alive. These letters range in subject from responsibility for the outbreak of fighting in 1941 to details of the unsettled stretch of frontier near the Santiago River. There are excellent maps.

4280. López Contreras, Eleazar. Proceso de límites entre Venezuela y Colombia. N. Y., Las Américas Publ. Co., 1953. 38 p.

The former president of Venezuela describes the background of the boundary settlement with Colombia.

4281. Oxford-López, Eduardo. La Guayana hispano-venezolana. Caracas, Garrido, 1954. 51 p.

The author calls the 1899 arbitral decision on the Venezuela-British Guiana boundary a fraudulent one, basing his allegations on posthumously published papers of S. Mallet-Prevost.

4282. Pedrero, Julián. América, las Malvinas y el derecho internacional. B. A., Argentina Austral, 1954. 11 p., illus.

A cartographical argument for Argentine sovereignty over the Falklands, with reproductions of old maps.

4283. Pinochet de la Barra, Óscar. La Antártica chilena. 3. ed. Santiago, Editorial del Pacífico, 1955. 226 p. & maps.

Substantial statement of Chilean claims to the sector of Antarctica between 53° and 90° W. longitude. First edition, 1944.

4284. ————. Chilean sovereignty in Antarctica. Santiago, Editorial del Pacífico, 1955. 59 p., maps.

Translation of two speeches in Santiago, Oct. 18 and 20, 1954, based on the third edition of the speaker's book. See item above.

4285. Torriente, Cosme de la. Mi misión en Washington. La soberanía de la Isla de Pinos. 1923-1925. Habana, Imp. de la Universidad de la Habana, 1952. 380 p.

The Cuban diplomat's own story of his part in securing Cuban control over the Isle of Pines. The last 300 pages contain official and unofficial texts relating to the subject.

Labor and Social Welfare

LABOR

THOMAS MOSIMANN

4300. Albaa, Víctor. Le mouvement ouvrier en Amérique latine. Paris, Éditions ouvrières (Coll. Masses et militants), 1953. 238 p., illus.

A broad analysis by the well-known Spanish writer of the history of and problems besetting the labor movement in Latin America. Has many penetrating and illuminating observations together with more controversial conclusions which the reader will wish to evaluate for himself. Forcefully and readably written, the work reviews and comments on a surprising number of historical events and problems. A valuable chronology of significant labor events in Latin America is attached.

4301. Argentina. Ministerio de Trabajo y Previsión de la Nación. Revista de trabajo y previsión. B. A. Año 1, no. 1, feb. 1953.

Of broader scope than the earlier (1952) publication of the Ministry, *Revista argentina de previsión social* (listed in *HLAS, no. 18, 1952,* item 2245), this first issue is a valuable review of developments in 1952 in labor and social welfare. A copy of the Second Five-Year Plan of the Perón administration is included.

4302. Colombia. Ministerio del Trabajo. El trabajo de la mujer. Disposiciones legales. Bogotá, Imp. Nacional, 1953. 51 p.

Excerpts from Colombian labor law covering maternity provisions, domestic service, work in the house, and work of minors.

4303. Cueva Tamariz, Carlos. Jurisprudencia ecuatoriana del trabajo. Cuenca, Ecuador, Universidad de Cuenca, 1954. 277 p.

Primarily a jurisprudential study, only those articles of the code being quoted to which the court decisions discussed apply. The author, who is Professor of Labor Law at the University of Cuenca, includes his own valuable independent comments upon the court decisions.

4304. Davis, Horace B. Numerical strength of Mexican unions (SW Soc Sci Q, 35:1, June 1954, p. 48-55).

Estimates number of members for 1953. [W. V. Scholes]

4305. Ferrero Rebagliati, Raúl, and **Carlos Scudellari.** El derecho del trabajo en el Perú. Lima, Centro de Estudios Económicos y Sociales, 1955. 96 p.

Very useful and well-prepared summary of the legal concepts, definitions, and provisions of Peruvian labor law. In addition to chapters on the different provisions relating to labor contracts there are others on work accidents, sicknesses related to work, and social security. Beautifully presented and printed. An indispensable handbook.

4306. García Aybar, José E. El código Trujillo de trabajo y la política social dominicana. Ciudad Trujillo, Editora del Caribe, 1953. 39 p.

This brief address delivered in June 1953 is quite interesting and informative. It summarizes in non-technical form the broader aspects of Dominican labor law.

4307. Garzón Ferreyra, Ignacio. La convención colectiva de trabajo. B. A., Arayú, 1954. 176 p.

An analysis of the provisions and implications of Argentine law regulating collective labor agreements. A summary of 21 conclusions appears as an appendix.

4308. Macin, Francisco J. Salario insuficiente. México, Editorial Veracruz, 1954. 39 p.

A pamphlet of polemical style containing some documented data on wages and the distribution of expenditures but side by side with many figures for which no source or documentation is given. The analysis is superficial, and many of the comparisons cannot be considered reliable.

4309. Maldonado, Abraham (comp.). Legislación boliviana del trabajo. La Paz, Caja Nacional de Seguro Social, 1954. 728 p.

Very valuable compilation of provisions of Bolivian law relating to labor and social legislation in a broad sense. The author has arranged the material alphabetically by subject matter, presenting pertinent provisions of many laws under each heading. Since this necessarily involves some arbitrary grouping, care in using the book for reference must be exercised.

310. **Martínez Fourzan, Óscar.** La habitación de los trabajadores mexicanos. México, 1953. 65 p.
Discusses the problem of housing for Mexican workers and outlines, as conclusions, ten "basic points" for a proposed "law of worker's housing." These points outline proposed standards for housing to be provided by establishments which have the legal obligation to do so. Thesis, University of Mexico.

311. **Muñoz García, Hugo.** Código del trabajo. Leyes, anexas, convenios y recomendaciones internacionales. Concordado y anotado por. . . . Quito, Ministerio de Previsión Social y Trabajo, 1954. 438 p.
The first official edition since 1947. In addition to the complete text of the code, the volume contains summaries of some of the decisions of the Supreme Court of Justice of Ecuador as jurisprudential notes under the various articles. A section of the book also gives the text of various decrees governing the application of the labor code.

312. **Organización Regional Interamericana de Trabajadores.** Serie Libertad. No. 1-. México, 1955?-.
The Inter-American Regional Organization of Workers (ORIT), regional organization of the International Confederation of Free Trade Unions (CIOS), has since its establishment in 1951 published numerous pamphlets and bulletins addressed to the workers of Latin America. The first three publications of the "Serie Libertad" are: 1, "¿Que es la ORIT?," no date, 4 p.; 2, "Cómo llegar a las bases sindicales," no date, 23 p.; and 3, "Los sindicatos y la menaza totalitaria," 1955, 38 p. Among the stated purposes of this series is to make available to the workers materials on "the theoretical bases of free trade unionism."

313. **Pérez Paton, Roberto.** Derecho social y legislación del trabajo. 2. ed. ampliada y actualizada. B. A., Arayú, 1954. 960 p.
This expanded edition contains lectures delivered at the Universidad de La Paz. Discusses (part 1) the origins and concepts of social law, philosophical, historic and economic, and (part 2) the labor contract, and legislation bearing upon it. The treatment is general, but examples are taken primarily from labor law in the Western hemisphere. Scholarly, and complete with interesting comparisons of national laws and jurisprudential details. A discussion of social security and of cooperatives is included.

314. **Perú. Ministerio de Trabajo y Asuntos Indígenas.** Obra del movimiento restaurador en el campo de la justicia social. Lima, 1955. 99 p.
A useful booklet, published on the occasion of the inauguration in 1955 of the new building of the Ministry of Labor and Indigenous Affairs. Groups principal points on: the organization and functions of the Ministry; a directory of officially recognized labor unions; and a chronological index of "the principal decrees promulgated in defense of the worker in the period 1948-54."

4315. **Puerto Rico. Bureau of Labor Statistics.** The labor force of Puerto Rico and its characteristics, Apr. 1950 to July 1952. San Juan, 1953. 32 p. (Special report on the labor force, rev. series, 6).
A statistical publication presenting an analysis of the labor force in Puerto Rico based on a monthly sample survey of households. Estimates are presented of population, labor force, unemployment, and employment, the last also being tabulated by industrial composition and hours worked. An interesting feature is the inclusion of estimates of persons engaged in home needlework.

4316. **Sandoval, José E. de.** Conferencia Internacional del Trabajo, 38 reunión, 1955. Habana, Ministerio de Estado, 1955. 261 p.
Prepared by the delegate of the Cuban government to the 38th meeting, this report summarizes the work of the Cuban delegation both in the plenary sessions and in committees. The reports of the various committees and the resolutions of the meeting relating to them are given in full.

4317. **United States. Bureau of Labor Statistics.** The status of labor in—Puerto Rico, Alaska, Hawaii. Reprint from the *Monthly labor review,* December 1955. Washington, Bureau of Labor Statistics (Bulletin, 1191), 1956. 99 p.
The first section of this booklet, p. 1-26, contains articles on Puerto Rican labor entitled "The labor force and level of living," "Migration to the mainland," "Labor unions and labor relations," "Labor laws and their enforcement," and "Wage structure and minimum wages."

4318.————. **Congress. Senate. Committee on Agriculture and Forestry.** Extension of the Mexican farm labor program. Hearings before the . . . extending for three years the period during which agricultural workers may be made available for employment under such title. March 23 and 24, 1953. Washington, 1953. 106 p.
Hearings on the extension of the Mexican farm labor program. The problems involved in U. S.-Mexican cooperation in the administration of the program are pointed up.

4319. **Vela Monsalve, Carlos.** Derecho ecuatoriano del trabajo. 1. Introducción general. 2. El contrato individual. Quito, La Unión Católica, 1955. 805 p.
A scholarly, if somewhat ponderous, discussion of the principles of Ecuadorian labor law in the general context of the philosophical bases of labor law in general. Hardly useful for quick reference but for interesting study of specific

228   HANDBOOK OF LATIN AMERICAN STUDIES

problems of labor law in Ecuador has much valuable information and criticism.

4320. Vianna, Renato Segadas. O sindi-Brasil. Rio, Serviço de Documentação, 1953. 224 p.

The foreword of this volume, an expansion of an earlier work by the same author, expresses the hope that it will serve to give to the workers of Brazil a better knowledge of unionism and of the advantages of unionization. The author, who served as Minister of Labor under Getúlio Vargas, summarizes and interprets

Brazilian labor legislation as it applies to unio organization and activities. Authoritative.

4321. Vinasco Rengifo, Efraín. Las cor venciones colectivas de trabajo en l legislación colombiana y en la doctrina Bogotá, Pontificia Universidad Católic Javeriana, 1954. 79 p.

Thesis. Discusses different types of collectiv labor agreement and jurisprudence related them, both in general and with particular a plication in Colombian labor law.

SOCIAL WELFARE

CARL H. FARMAN

GENERAL

4400. Crane, Jacob L., Jr. Chozas y casas en los trópicos (Cuad Inst Interam Hist Mun Inst, 5, junio 1953, p. 19-40).

A translation of a brief discussion, by an assistant to the Administrator of the U. S. Housing and Home Finance Agency, of the inadequate housing facilities of the millions of families living in the tropical zones. [T. L. Smith]

4401. Enochs, Elisabeth Shirley. The children of Latin America in an age of anxiety (B Inst Int Am Prot Infan, 29:1, marzo 1955, p. 637-649).

A general review of the countries of Latin America, considered from the child welfare standpoint. The author considers resources, nutrition problems, schools of social work, economic problems, and child welfare work. The international operations organized for welfare are described in some detail in a discussion that includes the OAS and the Pan American Child Congresses.

4402. Escardó y Anaya, Víctor. XI Congreso Panamericano del Niño, Panamá, 6-12 de febrero de 1955 (B Inst Intl Am Prot Infan, 29:2, junio 1955, p. 566-635).

A chronological, official account of this important congress, including a list of delegates and the text of the findings and recommendations issued. These suggestions cover many fields including motion pictures, books and magazines, social services, rural families, and juvenile courts.

4403. Inter-American Conference, X, Caracas, Mar. 1-28, 1954. Social welfare. Washington, Pan American Union, 1953. 34 p. (Doc. 10 (English); SG-10, 10th Dec. 1953; chapter III, topic 17 of the agenda).

A general document, originating in an Argentine resolution that "social welfare conditions throughout the continent" be on the agenda of the conference. The planning of welfare pro-

grams is considered with reference to aid t families, children, the sick and disabled, worke and immigrants, and delinquents and criminal Sections also consider rural problems, welfar administration, and international agencies they relate to new continental trends in welfar The work is one of several prepared by th Pan American Union for the information delegates to the Caracas Conference of 195 Others deal with the cooperative movement America, social aspects of economic develo ment, and causes and effects of the rural e odus.

4404. Inter-American Conference on S cial Security. Resoluciones sobre segur dad social aprobadas por las conferenci regionales de los Estados de Améric miembros de la Organización Intern cional del Trabajo (Chile, 1936; Cub 1939; Uruguay, 1949, y Brasil, 1952 México, 1954. 55 p. (Cuaderno, 13).

The Conference of American States that a members of the International Labour Organiz tion marked the first of the now diverse an widespread regional organizations of that bod and the resolutions adopted on social securi have reflected advanced hemispheric thinkin on many phases of the social insurance que tion. This work is accordingly a useful refe ence tool, increasingly handy with the growin interest in international action.

4405. ————. Sistemas de control d inscripción, cobros, registro de cotiz ciones y vigencia de derechos; sistema d seguro social mexicano. México, 195 144 p. (Cuaderno, 12).

Basic documents include the Mexican social ir surance law as amended, and regulations o employer and worker registration and on pa ment of contributions. There are also instruc tions for the working and control of accountin operations, with reproductions and explana tions of the forms used and other managemen details. Excellent specific administrative guid to this phase of the Mexican program, and possible model for other administrators. Com piled and arranged by Drs. Rafael Morfi Sánchez and Jesús Rodríguez y Rodríguez fficials of the Instituto Mexicano del Seguro ocial.

406. ————, V Session, Mexico, Mar. 1955. Resoluciones adoptadas por la Quinta Conferencia Interamericana de Seguridad Social (Seg Soc, México, 4:15, abril 1955, p. 89-114).
Among the topics studied (on which conclusions were set forth) were the pensionable age in old-age insurance, housing and social security, training and selection of personnel, and mechanization in social insurance institutions.

407. Inter-American Economic and Social Council. Problems of housing of social interest. Washington, Pan American Union, 1954. 232 p.
Through this publication, the Inter-American Economic and Social Council is fulfilling the wishes of the American Republics to have this technical document made known and widely disseminated among the public and private institutions and professional people of Latin America interested in the serious problems of housing of social interest." The main portion is the report of a 1953 Ad Hoc Committee for the Study of Low-Cost Housing Problems. There are several appendixes—with much useful information for the countries concerned—by delegations from Chile, Argentina, Colombia, Cuba, Haiti, Peru, and the U. S.

408. Mijares Ulloa, Luis A. Relaciones entre las instituciones de seguridad social y el cuerpo médico (Seg Soc, México, 3:11, junio 1954, p. 5-42).
Includes an analysis by the author of the results of a questionnaire as answered by Chile, the Dominican Republic, Ecuador, Mexico, Peru, and Venezuela on important aspects of the relationship between social insurance agencies and physicians. Also the text of conclusions and recommendations on the subject adopted by the International Social Security Association, and comments on these conclusions by the author.

409. Morales Beltrami, Guillermo. Cooperación interamericana (B Inst Intl Am Prot Infan, 28:4, dic. 1954, p. 478-487).
The author expresses the thesis that a new era in maternal and child care has arisen in the Americas, namely, "Inter-American cooperation," which is seen as working through five media—financial aid, technical assistance, missions of experts, fellowships, and specialized courses. Suggestions are made for an improved organization to work through the UN Children's Fund.

410. Pan American Child Congress, X, Panamá, 1955. La familia y el servicio social. Washington, Unión Panamericana, División de Trabajo y Asuntos Sociales, 1955. 29 p.
Briefly analyzes some of the problems affecting Latin American families, and the role of social service—actual and potential—in helping to solve them. Emphasis is on the constructive possibilities inherent in family social service.

411. Pan American Union. Division of Housing and City Planning. Directorio de instituciones de vivienda y planeamiento. Washington, 1953. 99 p.
Lists 166 institutions on 20 Latin American countries, giving date of establishment, address, objectives, functions, activities, and publications. Special sections list international agencies and specialized housing and planning institutions in the U. S.

412. Reunión de la Comisión Ejecutiva del Comité Permanente Interamericano de Seguridad Social (Seg Soc, México, 2:7-8, sept.-nov. 1953, p. 60-79).
This meeting was called by invitation of the International Labour Office and met at Geneva in June 1953 to help determine policy respecting both the Inter-American Social Security Conference itself and its relation to the International Labour Organization. Documents making up most of the résumé include the projected new statutes of the Inter-American Social Security Conference, the proposed new regulation to govern the Conference, and the proposed reform of the regulation of the Permanent Inter-American Committee on Social Security, which is the executive organ of the Conference itself.

413. Segundo Congreso Iberoamericano de Seguridad Social (Inf Soc, 9:4, oct.-dic. 1954, p. 69-89).
Reviews the main events of the congress and gives the text of the committee resolutions, which dealt with social security in agriculture, social security finance, conservation of migrants' rights, and related questions. Also has the draft statute of the Organización Ibero-Americana de Seguridad Social.

414. Seminario de trabajo sobre administración de servicios de protección a la infancia, 1953 (B Inst Intl Am Prot Infan, 27:3, sept. 1953, p. 229-363).
Contains 12 essays by holders of UN and OAS scholarships to a child welfare seminar held April to June 1953, in Montevideo. They provide significant and timely data on the programs of Bolivia, Chile, Guatemala, Haiti, Nicaragua, and Uruguay.

415. Seminario de trabajo sobre administración de servicios de protección a la infancia (B Inst Intl Am Prot Infan, 28:2, junio 1954, p. 92-256).
Papers from the third and last of the seminars held in Uruguay on the administration of child protective services. Various phases of this work in Uruguay are considered in several of the 14 papers, and in addition there is information on potentialities of child welfare work in countries having large Indian populations. Data also appear for Bolivia, Chile, Costa Rica, Ecuador, and Paraguay.

416. Los seminarios de Costa Rica, El Salvador, Guatemala, Haití, Honduras, Nicaragua y Panamá (B Inst Intl Am Prot Infan, 27:4, dic. 1953, p. 440-504).

Seven child welfare seminars were held in the above countries, in one of the most significant coordinated inter-American movements in this field of work. Each is described, and information is given on the institutions visited and the recommendations made. Illustrated.

4417. Taylor, Sue H. El centro communal en la vida rural. Washington, Unión Panamericana, División de Trabajo y Asuntos Sociales (Serie sobre organización de la comunidad, 10), 1954. 17 p.

A picture story showing by illustration and carefully written simple text just how a rural community center can be developed into a force helping to stimulate community pride and improvement. The author is a domestic science specialist who has worked with the American International Association for Economic and Social Development in both Venezuela and Brazil. The Association was founded in 1946 by Nelson A. Rockefeller and his brothers.

4418. United States. Public Health Service. Bureau of State Services. 10 years of cooperative health programs in Latin America. An evaluation. Washington, 1953. 175 p.

A comprehensive report on the cooperative health programs in Latin American countries in which the Institute of Inter-American Affairs participated during the years 1942 to 1952. The document contains a considerable amount of information on health, mortality, and sanitation in many parts of Latin America, as well as the description, analysis, and appraisal of the programs that have been undertaken. [T. L. Smith]

4419. Ware, Caroline F. Organización de la comunidad para el bienestar social. Washington, Unión Panamericana, Departamento de Asuntos Económicos y Sociales, 1954. 257 p.

The author, professor of social work at Howard University, Washington, presented this material in Medellin, Colombia, August-September 1953. It is a modern approach to community organization, problems, and resources, and is supplemented by summaries of the classroom discussions prepared by Srta. Marta Ospina Xepes, professor of the School of Social Service, Medellin. A significant social service document looking to research and social betterment in the Latin American community. Bibliography.

4420. Zapata Ballon, Ernesto. El seguro de enfermedad en América Latina. México, Conferencia Interamericana de Seguridad Social, 1956. 47 p. (Asociación Internacional de la Seguridad Social, XII Asamblea General, México, nov.-dic. 1955).

The various aspects of health insurance in Latin America are briefly and competently treated in summaries of the principal legal provisions and in a very useful section on statistics that covers Brazil, Chile, the Dominican Republic, Mexico, Peru, and Venezuela. Special sections deal with the native populations, agri cultural labor, health and medical facilities, an the general health status of the people of Latin America.

ARGENTINA

4421. Goñi Moreno, José M. El nueve ordenamiento administrativo de la previ sión social argentina (Seg Soc, México 3:10, mayo 1954, p. 7-14).

Analysis of reforms effected by law 14,236 o 1953, which had the threefold aim of providing better coordination among the existing socia insurance organizations, expanding the retire ment programs to new sectors of the popula tion, and covering, where possible, additiona risks.

4422. Palacios, Alfredo L. La justicia social. I, Concepto filosófico de la justicia II, Desenvolvimiento histórico de la idea de justicia social; III, La justicia social en el Río de la Plata, desde antes de la emancipación hasta 1943. B. A., Claridad (Biblioteca de ciencias económicas, políticas y sociales, 6), 1954. 527 p.

The final 20 chapters, on social justice in Argentina, deal with many fields and institu tions, including workers in general, Parliament women and children, civil rights of women occupational injuries, dismissal, railway retire ment, and the army. The work of the Nationa Legislature, especially of the Socialist Party tc which the author belongs, receives considerable emphasis. The entire issue of the social develop ment under Perón is by-passed by the self imposed limits of the study, but the larger perspective resulting has much value.

4423. Remorino, Jerónimo. La nueva legislación social argentina. B. A., Ministerio de Relaciones Exteriores y Culto, 1953. 336 p.

The enormous volume of Peronist social legisla tion is here sympathetically reviewed in 25 chap ters dealing with virtually all phases of labor law and related social insurance and social assistance laws. The author's method is to move quickly from one topic to another, giving in each case the essence of relevant laws and decrees, with citations to the source. The method is well suited to the needs of the gen eral reader or the student using it as a reference work.

BOLIVIA

4424. Bolivia: institución en Bolivia de un régimen de subsidios familiares y asigna ción de alquileres; ampliación del régimen de prestaciones de la Caja de Seguro Social de Ferroviarios y anexos (Seg Soc México, 2:7-8, sept.-nov. 1953, p. 159 163).

Summarizes Bolivia's significant 1953 decre introducing nursing and children's allowance for factory, mine, construction, and petroleum workers. Also gives the results of amendment in the country's railway retirement system.

425. Organización de los servicios médicos de la Caja Nacional de Seguro Social (Prot Soc, 16:193-194, marzo-abril 1954, p. 104-114).

A document giving the organizational plan for Bolivia's social insurance medical services, as proposed by Dr. Isidoro Ochoa Pacheco, member of the governing body of the Social Insurance Fund. The plan was officially approved, and took effect Mar. 15, 1954.

426. Soriana Badani, Armando. La protección materno-infantil en el seguro social obligatorio de Bolivia (B Inst Intl Am Prot Infan, 29:1, marzo 1955, p. 515-518).

Briefly summarizes the social insurance cash benefits and medical care offered by the Bolivian social insurance program, with special reference to mothers and children, and notes the provisions of the family allowance system.

427. Valdez, Vicente (comp.). Complemento a la nueva compilación de leyes del trabajo y de previsión social. La Paz, Editorial Nacional, 1953. 280, 22 p.

The compulsory social insurance measures of October 1951 are given, together with various decrees and statutes issued by the government of the Revolutionary Nationalist Movement for the regulation of working conditions in different enterprises. An appendix gives the provisions of 1951 on family allowances and low-cost housing.

COSTA RICA

428. Costa Rica. Caja Costarricense de Seguro Social. Informe a patronos y trabajadores sobre la seguridad social en Costa Rica. San José, Trejos, 1954? 15 p.

With data on the organization and functions of the Caja Costarricense de Seguro Social, the risks covered and classes of persons protected, volume of benefits, and some social aspects of its investment policy. The material is of particular interest in its treatment of health and maternity insurance.

429. ———. ———. Instrucciones sobre el seguro familiar: el trabajador y su familia protegidos por el seguro social. San José, La Española, 1953. 8 p.

Presents details on health and maternity insurance for the dependents of the insured worker as this supplementary program operates in certain parts of Costa Rica. Gives clear directions and spells out the rights of the family to medical care and the conditions for receiving it.

430. ———. ———. Ley constitutiva; reglamento de los riesgos de enfermedad y maternidad; reglamento del seguro de invalidez, vejez y muerte. San José, Trejos, 1954? 117 p.

Contains the laws and regulations governing the two programs that make up the most important sector of social security in Costa Rica.

431. ———. ———. Memoria anual, 1953. San José, 1954. 373 p.

Text and full illustrative data on Costa Rica's health, maternity, and retirement insurance programs and the housing operations of the Fund. An exceptionally comprehensive report, rather informally written, which gives a wealth of information on this well-established Central American institution with over 900 employees (mostly medical) and 75,000 affiliated workers.

432. ———. ———. Departamento Actuarial y Estadístico. Informe estadístico correspondiente al año 1953. San José, 1954. Unpaged.

Arranged in four main parts, this report of about 80 pages covers administration, finance, cash benefits, and benefits in kind. The last section, which is much the largest, provides detailed data on the most important aspect of the Costa Rican social insurance system—the medical, dental, hospital, laboratory, and other services provided the insured worker and (in some zones) his dependents. Earlier sections include statistical analyses of old-age, invalidity, and survivors insurance as well as cash sickness and maternity payments.

433. ———. ———. Oficina de Divulgación. Beneficios del seguro de invalidez, vejez y muerte. San José, Trejos, n.d. 15 p.

An information pamphlet in question-and-answer form which explains the conditions for receiving benefits in the Costa Rican program of old-age, permanent disability, and survivors insurance.

434. Vicenzi, Atilio (ed.). Código de trabajo. Nueva edición con todas las reformas. San José, Librería Las Américas, 1953. 198 p.

Costa Rica's labor code of 1943 included the law of one social security program—insurance against work accidents. The provisions governing that risk are taken almost without change from the work accident law of 1925, making up title 4. Amendments of the entire code are given to October 1953, and other basic documents appear, including relevant portions of the Constitution of 1949 and various statutes and regulations not in the code when first promulgated.

EL SALVADOR

435. Barrett, Maude T. Social welfare programmes in El Salvador. Prepared for the Government of El Salvador. N. Y., United Nations, Technical Assistance Programme, 1954. 18 p. (Doc. ST/TAA/K/El Salvador/1).

Reveals on a broad canvas the entire social welfare picture of the country, including care for children, delinquents, adults, the disabled, and adult offenders. The aim was to present what information could be obtained in two short visits, and, secondly, to make recommendations based on El Salvador's request to the UN for an expert in social welfare administration.

4436. El Salvador. Ministerio de Trabajo y Previsión Social. Esbozo de la situación económico-social en las materias mas estrechamente relacionadas con la seguridad social en la República de El Salvador. San Salvador, 1951. 42 p., tables.

Valuable data are here collected for the first time in a highly informative fact-book that covers such points as population, government, products, and economic activity generally including living standards and per-capita income. Medical and hospital data—highly important in social security planning—are comprehensive on points such as equipment, location, volume of work, number of physicians, and related matters.

4437. ————. ————. Recopilación de leyes y reglamentos sobre trabajo y seguridad social. San Salvador, 1954. 465 p.

Contains the text of 36 laws and decrees, including constitutional law relating to labor and welfare, collective and individual labor law, social insurance, and many related measures. The dedication of the volume by the Ministry of Labor and Social Welfare to the country's workers and employers calls attention to its significance in understanding present legislation and the history of such acts from the work accident law of 1911. A basic document for the study of welfare in El Salvador.

4438. El seguro social en la República de El Salvador (Seg Soc, México, 3:12, 1954, julio 1954, p. 31-42).

Brief summary of the program and its legislative history, followed by the text of decree no. 37, May 10, 1954, which inaugurated this system of health, maternity, and accident insurance in certain regions of El Salvador.

GUATEMALA

4439. Creación del I. G. S. S. y su desarrollo actual (Seg Soc, México, 4:18, dic. 1955, p. 23-29).

A useful historical and statistical review of the programs of the Instituto Guatemalteco de Seguridad Social, which operate with emphasis on high standards of care and broad eligibility for benefit in the comparatively restricted area of maternity protection and benefits in case of both general and work-connected injuries.

4440. Guatemala. Instituto Guatemalteco de Seguridad Social. Informe de la regencia . . . sobre las operaciones del ejercicio comprendido del 1° de julio de 1954 al 30 de junio de 1955. Guatemala, 1955. 65 p., processed.

The many changes in administration and finance that followed the overthrow of the Marxist government in Guatemala are given in valuable detail, along with a substantial amount of statistical and historical information on the development of this program against accident risk and for maternity care.

4441. ————. ————. Reglamento sobre protección materno-infantil. 3. ed. Guatemala, Departamento de Divulgación y Relaciones Públicas, 1955. 107 p.

Contains all official documents for the program of maternity care and cash maternity benefits which the Guatemalan Social Security Institute inaugurated in 1953, in the department of Guatemala. The program covers both insured women workers and the wives or companions of insured male workers.

4442. ————. ————. Reglamento sobre protección relativa a accidentes en general. 4. ed. Guatemala, 1955. 292 p.

In 1949 Guatemala's social security program was extended—in the areas where it operates—from the risk of occupational accidents to all accidents. This pocket-size work is the full legal record of the regulations and orders governing this official program covering 200,000 workers. Includes documents to August 1955.

4443. Reoux, Réné. An approach to minimum wage fixing in Guatemala (Intl Lab R, 71:1, Jan. 1955, p. 1-33).

This account by an International Labour Office technical assistance official contains important material on working-class budgets in Guatemala City, on wages in certain industries, and on related matters, including the national economy in general. Has applicability to other countries at a similar stage of economic evolution.

HAITI

4444. Haïti. Département du Travail. Séminaire de l'enfance en Haïti du 9 au 18 août 1953. Avec la collaboration de l'Institut Interaméricain pour la Protection de l'Enfance. Port-au-Prince, 1954. 162 p., illus.

This national child welfare seminar, which was an outgrowth of the international sessions at Montevideo (see items 4414 and 4415), resulted in more than 20 papers, most of them in the field of education. Included are discussions of the Haitian child in the rural milieu, child health in Haiti, voluntary child welfare in the country, and labor law and children. The sum is an impressive addition to the child welfare literature of Haiti.

4445. ————. Institut d'Assurances Sociales d'Haïti. Rapport annuel, 1er octobre 1954-30 septembre 1955. Port-au-Prince, Imp. de l'État, 1956. 77 p.

Haiti's social insurance act of 1951 created IDASH, the nation's social insurance institution, and set out provisions for work accident insurance and health and maternity insurance. The former program began operating Mar. 1, 1952, and at the time of the present report was operating on an annual budget of one and a quarter million gourdes. The report is a well-presented analysis of administrative and medical information for this program, which covers 34,000 workers in 1141 firms.

4446. El seguro social en Haití (Seg Soc, México, 3:12, julio 1954, p. 17-30).
Systematic and useful review of one of the newer social insurance systems of the hemisphere, which is in practice limited to insurance against work accidents. Includes data on the social and economic background, plus an account of the legislative history and the provisions of the legislation.

MEXICO

4447. Covarrubias Camargo, Manuel. El problema de salubridad y asistencia rurales en relación con el derecho agrario. México, Universidad Nacional Autónoma de México, 1952. 66 p.
The author maintains that legislation for rural health and medical care belongs with agricultural law because of the influence of health on production. Specific shortcomings are noted in connection with Mexican rural conditions, including poor housing, clothing, and nutrition. Includes photographs and some tables, but does not develop its subject in much detail. A final chapter traces the work of the Mexican revolutionary governments in this phase of rural policy. Thesis.

4448. García Cruz, Miguel. La seguridad social: bases, evolución, importancia económica, social y política. México, Instituto Mexicano del Seguro Social, 1955. 231 p.
The author notes the need, in Mexico, for "un manual actualizado, ordenado, sistemático, pedagógico, para fines de enseñanza, que compendie las ideas directrices de la Seguridad Social." His own work, though termed "un modesto compendio antológico del pensamiento de la Seguridad Social en el Mundo y del movimiento mexicano de la seguridad social," is a well-organized comparative study with emphasis on Mexican social security. It includes both principles and facts, describes international organizations in the field, and has a highly informative chapter on the Mexican social security movement from its earliest days.

4449. Herrera Gutiérrez, Alfonso. Problemas técnicos y jurídicos del seguro social. México, Imp. Galeza, 1955. 301 p.
Contains 38 chapters on practical aspects on social insurance in Mexico, particularly problems that have arisen on matters like registration of workers with two or more employers, determination of wage for purposes of benefit payments, how to fix a worker's wage class when his remuneration has varied, and the return to work of a person pensioned for occupational disability. The author is professor of law and social sciences at the University of Mexico and legal adviser to national employer organizations.

4450. Lázaro Salinas, José. La emigración de braceros. Visión objetiva de un problema mexicano. México, Cuauhtemoc, 1955. 204 p.
The author alternates factual but somewhat journalistically colored accounts of the quarter million Mexican migratory workers with attempts to analyze the problem and indicate a solution. Chapters urge international agreement, analyze reasons for the eagerness to go to the U. S., review the system of labor contracting, and show "versiones negras sobre la explotación de braceros." There is no bibliography or index, but appendixes give emigration figures from the Mexican centers for 1953 and 1954.

4451. Moreno Resendiz, Saúl. Nivel de vida del sector agrícola y política de mejoramiento. México, Universidad Nacional Autónoma de México, 1953. 83 p.
Agricultural income in Mexico is low—the 65 percent of the population that is rural receives only 20 percent of the national income. The author notes some of the main facts, devotes attention to estimated cost-of-living requirements, and in particular analyzes causes of the agricultural problem. These include such factors as governmental neglect, rural underemployment, delay in adapting modern techniques to agriculture, inadequate credit, the price system, and others. Suggestions are made on each of these points, but they are somewhat general and academic in tone, and less significant than the statement of the problems. Thesis.

PERU

4452. Ferrero R., Raúl, and **Carlos Scudellari.** Legislación social del Perú y otros países de América Latina. Lima, Tip. Peruana, 1954. 141 p.
A rather ambitiously planned and executed survey that covers, first, Peruvian laws, and, secondly, the social and labor legislation of Argentina, Brazil, Colombia, Chile, Mexico, and Uruguay. The subject matter includes the labor contract, wages, hours, vacations, retirement benefits, workmen's compensation, and other social security programs. The orientation is somewhat conservative—a healthy sign where most discussions of social legislation have the opposite viewpoint—and the facts are stated with admirable accuracy and brevity.

4453. Perú. Caja Nacional de Seguro Social. Décimatercera memoria . . . correspondiente al año 1954. Lima, 1955. 12 p., & tables.
Relatively brief textual comment is followed by extensive statistical tables giving financial and hospital data for this program that has been in operation since 1936. During 1954, 370,868 persons paid contributions to the scheme. Health insurance accounts were approximately balanced at 107 million soles ($5.35 million), but old-age and invalidity pensions paid out much less than the 65 million soles collected. An informative analysis of one of the oldest and best-managed programs in the hemisphere.

4454. ————. ————. Seguro social del empleado; proyecto de estatuto definitivo. Lima, 1955. 38 p.
Peru's long evolution toward a social security program for white-collar workers to match their

wage earners' system reached a further stage with this bill for health, maternity, and pension insurance, the last to include old-age, invalidity, and survivor benefits. Drafted by Antonio Zelenka, International Labour Office actuary, it calls for contributions totaling 7 percent of salaries for health and maternity benefits and 13 percent for pensions. The employee would pay 7.5 percent, the employer 12 percent, and the government 0.5 percent.

OTHER COUNTRIES

4455. Bejarano, Jorge. La protección de la infancia en Colombia (B Inst Int Am Prot Infan, 29:1, marzo 1955, p. 519-525).
The 20th anniversary of the Fundación del Amparo de los Niños, Bogota, is the occasion for this useful review of the institution's activities and of child welfare laws enacted in Colombia.

4456. Brazil (Seg Soc, México, 2:7-8, sept.-nov. 1953, p. 89-127).
Among the documents included in this résumé of Brazilian social insurance developments is a detailed explanation in support of a 1952 bill for an "organic social insurance law." This contains very useful factual information and evaluation of the various social security programs of the country. Another important item is the 1953 decree for the unification of the social insurance "funds" for workers in public utilities and railway enterprises.

4457. Cervera Martínez, Lilia. Organización de la comunidad. Habana, Isidro Hernández, 1953. 137 p.
Sets forth a program for the study of community organization and notes the social worker's role in such activities. The conclusions and some portions of the study pay special attention to Cuban conditions, noting the extent of community resources for social aid and pointing out ways to improve such services. Thesis, University of Habana.

4458. Cordero, Armando. Estudio del seguro social dominicano. Ciudad Trujillo, Imp. Arte y Cine, 1955. 195 p.
Clear factual presentation of all the central points in the law and administrative operation of health, pensions, and accident insurance in the Dominican Republic. This is preceded by an historical and comparative study, and is followed by statistical tables for the years 1948-1954. The program covers approximately 300,000 workers, and operates on a budget of approximately five million dollars a year.

4459. Dominican Republic. Secretaría de Estado de Salud Pública. Legislación sanitaria dominicana y legislación sobre seguridad social. 2. ed. Ciudad Trujillo, 1953. 794 p.
Contains 45 laws, decrees, and regulations on social insurance, rents, child welfare, delinquency, and institutional care. Still more material is given on health matters, this portion re-

placing the out-of-print 1938 edition and including later amendments and regulations in the health field. An official edition, compiled by Dr. Hipólito Sánchez Báez of the Department of Public Health.

4460. Ferrari, Francisco de. Los principios de la seguridad social. Montevideo, Universidad de Montevideo (Biblioteca de publicaciones oficiales, Sec. 3, 74), 1955. 251 p.
Historical, comparative, and theoretical chapters are followed by a section on social security in Uruguay which is in many respects the most useful part of the book since documentation on the interesting and significant developments of Uruguay's programs are all too scarce. However, the largest programs—namely, the retirement systems—are reserved for another volume. The author is professor of labor law and social welfare at the University of Montevideo, and the work is based on a special course given in 1954.

4461. Ley orgánica de seguridad social, administración Somoza. Managua, Tall. Nacionales, 1956. 113 p.
The text of Nicaragua's social security act of December 1955, prefaced by an historical review of its legislative history and by an official explanation of the measure for the members of the National Congress. A basic document in the history of Nicaragua's program.

4462. Mijares Ulloa, Luis. Consideraciones sobre el seguro de enfermedad en América Latina (Seg Soc, México, 4:16, sept.-oct. 1955, p. 7-24).
With data from Venezuelan health and work-accident insurance showing the relation between cash and medical benefits and other aspects of cost and services. The discussion centers on financing and the need for adequate statistics as a basis for providing benefits at the most economical level consistent with efficiency.

4463. Oliveira, Moacir Veloso Cardoso de. Panorama de la previdencia social brasileira (R Iberoam Seg Soc, 4:2, marzo-abril 1955, p. 205-216).
Presents a useful bird's-eye view of coverage, contributions, benefits, and financial operations for Brazil's "funds" and "institutes" for health and pension insurance. Expenditures for benefit in 1953 totaled some 5.7 billion cruzeiros, and coverage, according to the author, was about 14 million, including dependents.

4464. Sección memoria de la Superintendencia de Seguridad Social correspondiente a 1954 (Prev Soc, Santiago, 20:83, 1.-2. semestres 1954, p. 102-128).
A review of legislation, work-accident data, hospital conditions, and social security revenue and expenditure. The statistical section, p. 13-24, has more detailed information on the year 1953 for Chile's long-established system of medical care, family allowances, and related benefits.

4465. La seguridad social en Chile; reforma

del seguro social (Seg Soc, México, 2:6, junio 1953, p. 48-58).

Chile's law of July 27, 1952, completely revamped the hemisphere's oldest social insurance system, setting up modern health and pension insurance, and creating the National Health Service that linked into one organization many institutions of research and applied medicine. The present account is a brief, accurate, and informative review of the changes.

4466. Seguridad social en Cuba (Seg Soc, México, 4:14, enero-marzo 1955, p. 55-59).

Summarizes provisions in two additional Cuban retirement systems—those for construction workers and shorthand reporters. The risks covered are those of old age, permanent disablement, and death (the last giving rise to survivor pensions). Financing of each program includes a substantial government subsidy which is in addition to payroll deductions.

4467. El Seminario de Seguridad Social de Panamá (Seg Soc, México, 3:9, enero-abril 1954, p. 17-42).

The broad subject fields of the seminar, held in January 1954 at Panama City on the initiative of the Inter-American Conference on Social Security, were the creation and development of a social security system, administration, account-ing, statistics, and health insurance. In the present account the delegates are listed and reports of eight addresses given.

4468. Venezuela. Instituto Venezolano de los Seguros Sociales. Anales del . . . . Caracas, 1955. 170 p., tables & graphs, illus.

This fully illustrated publication, which was issued on the occasion of the meeting of the Inter-American Social Security Conference at Caracas, has several parts. It includes annual and ten-year reports on Venezuelan social security, papers given at special social insurance meetings in October 1954, at Caracas, and papers solicited from social security experts of the International Labour Organization, Chile, Brazil, Germany, and Spain. A valuable analysis, both national and international.

4469. Vives Sandoval, Augusto. Las jubilaciones del Estado y el seguro social en Panamá (Seg Soc, México, 4:16, sept.-oct. 1955, p. 29-35).

Text of an address, by the actuary of the Panamanian Social Insurance Fund, which traces the predecessors and history of present public employee pensions, with critical discussion of the many "liberalizing" elements that make the cost actuarially high.

Language and Literature

SPANISH AMERICAN LANGUAGE

DANIEL S. WOGAN

Many significant contributions to the study of American Spanish have appeared since the publication of *HLAS, no. 18, 1952*.[1] The admirable reissues of Lisandro Alvarado's philological writings and the new editions of the Pichardo and Cuervo dictionaries will be welcomed by all scholars in this field. In lexical matters attention should be drawn to the comprehensive vocabulary of Texan Spanish compiled by Cerda, Cabaza, and Farias and also to the exhaustive research on words associated with old technological processes undertaken by Oroz, Dornheim, and Vidal de Battini—all models of scientific investigation, of interest not only to students of American Spanish but to sociologists, folklorists, and cultural historians as well. This observation applies likewise to Gustavo Correa's highly original study of the sources and semantic evolution of the terms designating evil spirits, or devils, in Guatemala. Syntactical studies, which Spanish Americans have tended to neglect, are notably extended by the researches of Lope Blanch in Mexico and Rodríguez Herrera in Cuba, while the authoritative surveys made by Rabanales and Toscano Mateus broaden in many areas our knowledge of the Spanish spoken in Chile and Ecuador.

In magnitude and method, however, all other publications in Hispanic linguistics are overshadowed by the appearance of volumes 1 and 2 of Juan Corominas' monumental *Diccionario crítico etimológico de la lengua castellana*. While final evaluation from the standpoint of American Spanish must await publication of the remaining volumes and the index of Americanisms the author has compiled, the Corominas dictionary takes its place at once as an indispensable reference for the history of a large number of New World terms whose origin and development, in many cases, have been explained differently by Friederici, von Wartburg, Brüch, Sainéan, Malkiel, and other scholars. It is safe to predict that this work will afford a mine of information as well as a source of controversy for years to come.

Finally, it is pertinent to note here the favorable reaction on the part of Spanish American literati to the *Nuevas normas de prosodia y ortografía* issued by the Spanish Royal Academy in 1952. The prosodic and orthographic practices now officially sanctioned are held by Junco and Rosenblat to be sensible, if long overdue, reforms, while the latter sees in them a vindication of the theories of spelling and accentuation advanced by Bello more than a century ago.

[1]The editor has included in this section all books and monographs that have come to his attention before March, 1956, but has omitted studies appearing in journals published after 1953. In the future this bibliography will be brought up-to-date in compliance with the new *HLAS* policy.

4500. Ades, Raphael. My first encounter with the Spanish of Medellín (Hispania, AATSP, 36:3, Aug. 1953, p. 325-327).
Miscellaneous notes on the colloquial speech of Medellin, Colombia.

4501. Alatorre, Margit Frenk. Designación de rasgos físicos personales en el habla de la ciudad de México (Nueva R Filol Hisp, 7:1-2, enero-junio 1953, p. 134-156).
Some 650 expressions, many of Nahuatl derivation, commonly employed in the present-day speech of Mexico City in reference to physical defects, age, health, personal appearance, dress, etc. Very informative study, well indexed.

4502. Alegría, Ricardo E. Origin and diffusion of the term *cacique* (*in* Tax, Sol (ed.). Acculturation in the Americas. Proceedings and selected papers of the XXIXth International Congress of Americanists. Chicago, Ill., University of Chicago Press, 1952, p. 313-315).
The Arawak word *cacique* was heard by Columbus on his first voyage and was soon carried to other parts of the New World. Changing cultural patterns have extended the original meaning, as in Yucatan, where it denotes the master of ceremonies at festivals.

4503. Alonso, Amado. Estudios lingüísticos. Temas hispanoamericanos. Madrid, Gredos (Biblioteca románica hispánica. 2, Estudios y ensayos), 1953. 446 p.
Eight previously published studies, here revised, and one new contribution entitled "La base lingüística del español americano." In this essay Alonso holds that the basic speech type implanted by the *conquistadores* was Castilian rather than Andalusian.

4504. Alvarado, Lisandro. Obras completas. V. 1. Glosario de voces indígenas de Venezuela. Caracas, Ministerio de Educación, Dirección de Cultura y Bellas Artes (Comisión Editora de las Obras Completas de Lisandro Alvarado), 1953. xxvii, 422 p., facsim.
First edition, 1921. The editors have incorporated marginal notes found in Alvarado's personal copy of the *Glosario* and also corrections and additions made by him in a manuscript unearthed in the library of the Ministry of Education. A section entitled *voces geográficas* (p. 369-402), here published for the first time, adds to the value of this edition.

4505. ————. Obras completas. V. 2. Glosarios del bajo español en Venezuela. 1. parte. Acepciones especiales. Caracas, Ministerio de Educación, Dirección de Cultura y Bellas Artes (Comisión Editora de las Obras Completas de Lisandro Alvarado), 1954. 505 p.
A reissue of the first edition (Caracas, 1929) unchanged except for minor revisions by the Comisión Editora under the direction of Santiago Key-Ayala.

4506. ————. Obras completas. V. 3. Glosarios del bajo español en Venezuela. 2. parte. Neologismos y arcaísmos. Otros escritos conexos con ellos. Caracas, Ministerio de Educación, Dirección de Cultura y Bellas Artes (Comisión Editora de las Obras Completas de Lisandro Alvarado), 1955. 397 p.
This volume completes the glossary and reprints four studies Alvarado contributed to various Venezuelan journals.

4507. Amado Alonso (Nueva R Filol Hisp, 7:1-2, enero-junio 1953, p. 3-15).
Useful check list of Alonso's publications, many in the field of American Spanish, from 1922 through 1952, the year he died.

4508. Ángeles Caballero, César A. Peruanismo, lenguaje popular y folklore en un libro de Aurelio Miró Quesada (Letras, 50-53, 1.-2. semestre 1954, p. 105-124).
Classifies and annotates the extensive folk vocabulary used by Miró Quesada in the second edition (Lima, 1947) of *Costa, sierra y montaña*.

4510. Arroyo S., Víctor Manuel. Nauatismos y nahuatlismos en Costa Rica (Tlatoani, 2. época, 7, oct.-dic. 1953, p. 13-17).
Interesting notes on some 48 terms of real or presumed Nahuatl origin widely used in Costa Rica.

4511. Barahona J., Luis. El gran incógnito. Visión interna del campesino costarricense. San José, Editorial Universitaria (Sección Tesis de grado y ensayos, 3), 1953. 164 p.
Contains a glossary of Costa Rican expressions (p. 153-164), some of which are not found in Gagini's *Diccionario de costarriqueñismos*.

4512. Barrenechea, Ana María. Borges y el lenguaje (Nueva R Filol Hisp, 7:3-4, julio-dic. 1953, p. 551-569).
Argues that Jorge Luis Borges' use of regionalisms is conditioned solely by esthetic considerations.

4514. Canfield, Lincoln D. Andalucismos en la pronunciación salvadoreña (Hispania, AATSP, 36:1, Feb. 1953, p. 32-33).
Holds that certain phonetic peculiarities, archaisms, and ultracorrections in the Spanish of El Salvador have parallels in Andalusia.

4515. ————. Two early Quechua-Spanish dictionaries and American Spanish pronunciation (*in* South Atlantic studies for Sturgis E. Leavitt. Edited by Thomas B. Stroup and Sterling Stoudemire. Washington, Scarecrow Press, 1953, p. 63-70).

In the dictionaries of Domingo de Santo Tomás and Diego González Holguín the author finds "further evidence of an early 'southern accent' in American Spanish pronunciation."

4516. Cárdenas, Daniel N. El español en Jalisco. Contribución a la geografía lingüística hispanoamericana (Diss Abs, 14:1, 1954, p. 137-138).
A study of the phonetics, morphology, syntax, linguistic divisions, and historical background of the Spanish spoken in the state of Jalisco, Mexico.

4517. Carrizo, Juan Alfonso. Historia del folklore argentino. B. A., Ministerio de Educación, Instituto Nacional de la Tradición, 1953. 187 p.
Chapter 8, "Folklore lingüístico," offers a valuable review of the bibliography of Argentine folk speech.

4518. Cerda, Gilberto; Berta Cabaza; and Julieta Farias. Vocabulario español de Texas. Austin, Tex., University of Texas Press, 1953. 347 p.
This vocabulary presents material drawn from eight predominantly Spanish-speaking counties of Texas—Cameron, Duval, Edwards, Kinney, Val Verde, Webb, Willacy and Zapata. While open to criticism in certain details (see review by Lawrence Kiddle, *Hispanic review*, 23:2, Apr. 1955, p. 164-169), this compilation remains the most comprehensive survey ever made of the vocabulary of a Spanish-speaking area in the U. S.

4518a. Corominas, Juan. Diccionario crítico etimológico de la lengua castellana. Madrid, Gredos (Biblioteca románica hispánica. 5, Diccionarios etimológicos), 1954—. V. 1, A-C, lxviii, 993 p. V. 2, CH-K, 1080 p.
First two volumes of the etimological dictionary begun by Corominas in 1924. See the introduction to this section for comment and evaluation.

4519. ————. Para la fecha del yeísmo y del lleísmo (Nueva R Filol Hisp, 7:1-2, enero-junio 1953, p. 82-87).
Supports the theory that *yeísmo* was a comparatively late development from several independent foci.

4519a. Correa, Gustavo. El espíritu del mal en Guatemala. Ensayo de semántica cultural. New Orleans, La., Tulane University, Middle American Research Institute, 1955. 103 p.
A fascinating study of semantic fusions and displacements in words denoting or symbolizing concepts of evil (the Devil) in Guatemala. The terms analyzed by the author were obtained from written and oral sources. Among them are: *Cabobil, Cadejo, Juan Nok, Kisin, Patas, Siguanaba, Sisimite* and *Xtabai*.

4520. Cuervo, Rufino José. Diccionario de construcción y régimen de la lengua castellana. T. 1. A-B. Bogotá, Instituto Caro y Cuervo, 1953. lxviii, 922 p.
A facsimile edition of Cuervo's famous unfinished dictionary. The Instituto Caro y Cuervo plans to complete this work in subsequent volumes.

4521. Dabbs, Jack Autrey. Namelore in Latin America (Names, 1:3, Sept. 1953, p. 177-187).
A discussion of the obstacles to onomastic studies in Latin America followed by a tentative working bibliography arranged by countries.

4522. Dávila Garibi, José Ignacio. Algunas analogías fonéticas entre el romanceamiento castellano de voces latinas y la castellanización de vocablos nahuas ... y respuesta ... por Julio Jiménez Rueda. México, Cultura, 1954. 52 p. & illus.
Shows how Latin and Nahuatl words sometimes underwent similar phonetic changes on being incorporated into Spanish.

4523. Dornheim, Alfredo. La alfarería criolla en los Algarrobas, provincia de Córdoba (*in* Homenaje a Fritz Krüger. T. 1. Mendoza, Argentina, Universidad Nacional de Cuyo, Facultad de Filosofía y Letras, 1952, i.e. 1953, p. 335-364).
Detailed investigation of terms used by ceramic workers in an isolated village of the province of Cordoba, Argentina. Photographs and drawings.

4525. Elías Ortiz, Sergio. Estudios sobre lingüística aborigen de Colombia. Bogotá, Kelly (Biblioteca de autores colombianos), 1954. 503 p.
Provides interesting examples of Hispanicisms in the native languages of Colombia.

4526. Erminy Arismendi, Santos. Por entre pueblos de indios. Caracas, Editorial Oceánida, 1953? 61 p., illus.
Notes on the geography and folklore of the state of Sucre, Venezuela. Numerous local terms of indigenous derivation are defined by the author in footnotes.

4527. Flórez, Luis. Lengua española. Bogotá, Instituto Caro y Cuervo (Publ.; Series minor, 3), 1953. 299 p.
21 popular lectures given over radio in 1952 by Colombia's leading dialectologist. Clear, well organized, they have to some extent been reworked for publication. See review by Peter Boyd-Bowman, *Romance philology*, 8:3, Feb. 1955, p. 226-227.

4528. Herrero Mayor, Avelino. Diálogo argentino de la lengua. 50 lecciones para hablar y escribir correctamente. 1. serie. B. A., Hachette, 1954. 122 p.
A professor and his student discuss various linguistic pitfalls peculiar to Argentina. The author began his duties as "catedrático idiomático de LRA Radio del Estado" in 1951.

4529. Junco, Alfonso. ¡Novedad en la Academia! México, Jus, 1953. 59 p.

Jocose remarks by the well-known Mexican publicist on the *Nuevas normas de prosodia y ortografía* issued by the Royal Spanish Academy in 1952. Junco is essentially in agreement with the new regulations.

4530. King, Harold V. Sketch of Guayaquil Spanish phonology (Stud Ling, 11: 1-2, Mar.-June 1953, p. 26-30).
Tentative conclusions based on a phonemic analysis of one speaker from Guayaquil, Ecuador.

4531. Lope Blanch, Juan M. Observaciones sobre la sintaxis del español hablado en México. México, Instituto Hispano Mexicano de Investigaciones Científicas (Publ., 1), 1953. 135 p.
Well-documented observations on departures from normal syntactical usage as revealed in the spoken and written lantuage of the middle class of Mexico City. Leans on previous investigators at times, but offers much new material.

4532. Madueño, Raúl R. Léxico de la borrachera. Palabras y coplas de América y España. B. A., Optimus, 1953. 63 p.
Some 407 terms used in Spain and Spanish America to describe various degrees of alcoholic intoxication. Probably a nearly definitive list of such expressions.

4533. Malaret, Augusto. Correcciones al diccionario de americanismos y al lexicon de fauna y flora (U Pontif Bolivariana, 16:62, agosto-sept. 1951, p. 374-421; 17: 63, oct. 1951-marzo 1952, p. 27-61 (B-C); 17:64, abril-junio 1952, p. 312-352 (Ch-Ll); 17:65, julio-agosto 1952, p. 470-527 (M-Z)).

4534. ————. Esculcando yaguas viejas (U Pontif Bolivariana, 18:67, feb.-abril 1953, p. 228-236).
The Royal Spanish Academy is called to task by Malaret for erroneous definitions in the 1947 edition of its dictionary.

4537. Morínigo, Marcos A. La formación léxica hispanoamericana (Nueva R Filol Hisp, 7:1-2, enero-junio 1953, p. 221-233).
Maintains that the factors responsible for new creations in regional vocabularies are as active now as in the early days of the settlement of America.

4538. Navarro, Tomás. Observaciones sobre el papiamento (Nueva R Filol Hisp, 7:1-2, enero-junio 1953, p. 183-189).
Analysis of Papiamento sounds. Navarro holds that Papiamento did not derive from Spanish but is, rather, an Afro-Portuguese dialect that has gradually become Hispanicized.

4539. Oroz, Rodolfo. La carreta chilena sureña (*in* Homenaje a Fritz Krüger. T. 1. Mendoza, Argentina, Universidad Na-

cional de Cuyo, Facultad de Filosofía y Letras, 1952, i.e. 1953, p. 365-386).
On the evolution of the Chilean *carreta* and the terminology associated with it from colonial times to the present. Illustrations.

4539a. Pichardo, Esteban. Pichardo novísimo; o, diccionario provincial casi razonado de vozes y frases cubanas. Novísima edición, corregida y ampliamente anotada por Esteban Rodríguez Herrera. Habana, Editorial Selecta, 1953. lxiii, 716 p., port., facsms.
First edition (Matanzas, Cuba, 1836) under the title *Diccionario provincial de voces cubanas.* Subsequent editions, 1849, 1861-1862, and 1875.

4539b. Rabanales O., Ambrosio. Introducción al estudio del español de Chile. Santiago, Universidad de Chile, Instituto de Filología (Anexo no. 1 del Boletín de Filología), 1953. 142 p.
Part 2, p. 31-115, "Exposición analítica de nuestra definición de chilenismo."

4540. Ranson, Helen M. "Manitos" and their language (Hispania, AATSP, 36:3, Aug. 1953, p. 310-313).
Random notes on the Spanish of New Mexico.

4541. Robe, Stanley L. Algunos aspectos históricos del habla panameña (Nueva R Filol Hisp, 7:1-2, enero-junio 1953, p. 209-220).
The indigenous languages left little imprint on Spanish in Panama. Words borrowed by early settlers from the Indians, e.g., *cabra,* captive, *ira,* woman, *ochí,* tiger, etc., were forgotten or replaced by Antillianisms.

4542. Rodríguez Herrera, Esteban. La gramática, el lenguaje y los periódicos. Fascículo 1. Habana, P. Fernández, 1953? 222 p.
A member of the Academia Cubana de la Lengua sternly criticizes the grammar and syntax of contemporary journalists, mainly Cuban. To be continued.

4543. Rosaldo, Renato. El léxico como reflejo de la psicología del mexicano (Hispania, AATSP, 36:1, Feb. 1953, p. 67-70).
The author believes that characteristically Mexican attitudes are discoverable in expressions such as *machismo, ningunear, mordelón, pelado,* etc. Highly unflattering to Mexicans.

4543a. Rosenblat, Ángel. Las nuevas normas ortográficas y prosódicas de la Academia Española. Caracas, Universidad Central de Venezuela, Facultad de Filosofía y Letras, Instituto de Filología Andrés Bello, 1953. 31 p.
The famous Argentine philologist holds that the new academic norms are in general liberal, progressive, and in keeping with the spirit of Bello's reforms.

4545. ————. Los venezolanismos de Martí (R Nac Cult, 14:96, enero-feb. 1953, p. 32-53).
Calls attention to a posthumously published article by the Cuban patriot-poet in which he defined and commented on 160 Americanisms, one fourth of which were peculiar to Venezuela.

4546. Schorer, C. E. English loan words in Puerto Rico (Am Sp, 28:1, Feb. 1953, p. 22-25).
On some American English loans to Puerto Rican Spanish and the attitude of Puerto Ricans toward them.

4547. Smither, William J. Dissertations in the Hispanic languages and literatures —1953 (Hispania, AATSP, 37:2, May 1954, p. 171-185).
Lists two doctoral dissertations in the field of American Spanish completed in 1953: Daniel N. Cárdenas, *El español de Jalisco* (Columbia) and Francisco Villegas, *Glosario del argot costarricense* (Michigan). Authors and titles of dissertations begun in U. S. universities during 1953 are: Vito de Vicenzo, *Linguistic study of Spanish in the area of Camagüey* (Middlebury); Charles W. Kreidler, *A study of the influence of English on the speech of Mexican Americans in Detroit* (Michigan); Luis Soto Ruiz, *La lengua dialectal en las novelas de Benito Lynch* (Michigan); Virginia Zúñiga, *Aspectos del habla costarricense* (Tulane).

4548. Tauro, Alberto. Huella de los tamales en el lenguaje y la literatura del Perú (R Nac Cult, 14:96, enero-feb. 1953, p. 81-107).
Extended remarks on various kinds of tamales consumed in Peru, idiomatic expressions derived from the word, together with a short anthology of metrical compositions the tamale has inspired.

4549. Tejera, Emiliano. Palabras indígenas de la isla de Santo Domingo (B Ac Dom Lengua, 13:43, abril 1953, p. 24-34).
Continuation: *maguacochíos* to *mato*. (See HLAS, no. 18, 1952, item 2367). Many of the author's sources have been used by others to better advantage.

4550. Tobón Betancourt, Julio. Colombianismos y otras voces de uso general. 2. ed. Bogotá, Academia Colombiana, 1953. 270 p.
The first edition (Medellín, 1946) here reworked and enlarged.

4550a. Toscano Mateus, Humberto. El español en el Ecuador. Madrid, Consejo Superior de Investigaciones Científicas (Revista de filología española, Anejo 61), 1953. 478 p.
The first systematic, comprehensive study of Ecuadorian Spanish. Conventionally divided into phonetics, morphology, syntax and lexical formations, the author's investigations show that Quechua has affected Ecuadorian Spanish more deeply and in more directions than had

been realized. Invaluable.

4551. Universidad de Puerto Rico. Consejo Superior de Enseñanza. La lengua hablada en la escuela elemental. Temas favoritos y errores comunes de sintaxis y morfología. Río Piedras, Puerto Rico, 1952. 96 p., tables. (Publicaciones pedagógicas, serie 2, no. 14).
Analysis of 3789 syntactical and morphological deviations among rural and urban school children in Puerto Rico. No significant differences were found between the speech of country children and those in cities. Elaborate statistical tables.

4553. Vidal de Battini, Berta Elena. El léxico de los buscadores de oro de La Carolina, San Luis (*in* Homenaje a Fritz Krüger. T. 1. Mendoza, Argentina, Universidad Nacional de Cuyo, Facultad de Filosofía y Letras, 1952, i.e. 1953, p. 303-333).
A study of the terms used by gold miners in the village of La Carolina, an old mining center in the province of San Luis, Argentina. Archaic words and Quechuisms figure prominently in this technical vocabulary. Profusely illustrated.

4554. ————. El léxico de los *yerbateros* (Nueva R Filol Hisp, 7:1-2, enero-junio 1953, p. 190-208).
In vocabulary the pre-Conquest *yerba mate* industry remains basically Guaraní, Spanish, Portuguese, and Quechua have enriched it. Drawings, photographs, and a map add to the usefulness of this excellent study.

4555. Villaverde, Cirilo. Cecilia Valdés o La loma del Ángel. Edición crítica y notas por Esteban Rodríguez Herrera. Habana, Lex, 1953. 753 p.
The abundant notes supplied by Rodríguez Herrera clarify many obscure points of 19th-century Cuban usage in Villaverde's famous *costumbrista* novel. An admirable edition.

4556. Villegas, Francisco. Glosario del argot costarricense (Diss Ab, v. 13, 1953, p. 383-384).
A compilation of current Costa Rican slang words gathered from informants, popular novels, and other sources.

4557. Woodbridge, Hensley C. An annotated bibliography of Mexican Spanish for 1940-1953 (Ky For Lang Q, 1:2, 2nd quarter 1954, p. 80-89).
Continues for the years indicated the Mexican section of *A bibliographical guide to materials for the study of American Spanish* (1941) by Madaline Nichols.

4559. Zárate, Manuel F., and Dora Pérez de Zárate. La décima y la copla en Panamá. Panamá, La Estrella de Panamá, 1953. 548 p.
This extensive collection of folk poetry is a good source for the documentation of Panamanian Spanish.

SPANISH AMERICAN LITERATURE:
THE COLONIAL PERIOD

IRVING A. LEONARD

WHAT immediately strikes the eye in this year's publications, as in preceding years, are the number and variety of items relating to the nun-poetess, Sor Juana Inés de la Cruz (1651-1694). Her magic seems to lure readers of varied types to record in print their tributes. If many of these are more enthusiastic than enlightening, they testify to the continuing popularity of this enigmatic genius. Under examination by distinguished scholars are the metrical form, the language, and the content of her verse, and a new edition of her difficult long poem *Primero Sueño* is issued (item 4604).

The Mexican nun's nearest competitor for attention is the Peruvian mestizo chronicler, Inca Garcilaso de la Vega, about whom appeared in the course of the year some interpretative essays along with a few new documents pertaining to him. But the array of minor or lesser-known figures grows more miscellaneous, and an occasional one is the object of extended scholarly investigation. The most serious study that any received this current year was the Dominican friar, Father Hojeda, author of the notable religious epic poem *La Cristiada,* written in Peru (item 4639).

Invariably of special value in widening the base of available materials are the new editions of rare and inaccessible works and the publication of inedited texts of colonial writings. Of particular interest in this respect are: the collection of 18th-century satirical writings (item 4653) and the 17th-century play by Matías Bocanegra (item 4649).

Other aspects of colonial literary culture such as the history of the printing press, of book circulation, the theater, etc., continue to receive illuminating contributions.

SOR JUANA INÉS DE LA CRUZ

4600. Enríquez Calleja, Isidoro. Las tres celdas de Sor Juana. México, Col. Aquelarre, 1953. 134 p., illus.

The three "cells," inspired by a line of Valle Inclán, are temperament, sentiment, and knowledge, the second "cell" being the stoutest. To the author it was a passionate, frustrated love which dominated her; her scientific interests and intellectual pursuits were mere time-killing hobbies. The "cell" of knowledge was merely acquaintance with poetry and literature. This estimate would seem to do less than justice to the nun-poetess.

4601. Garcés, Jesús Juan. Vida y poesía de Sor Juana Inés de la Cruz. Madrid, Ediciones Cultura Hispánica, 1953. 174 p.

A young Spanish poet expresses his enthusiasm for the Mexican nun-poetess and her verses in a garrulous fashion, and apparently without reading the works cited in his brief bibliography which would clarify the numerous errors in his account of her life and work.

4602. Graves, Robert. Juana Ines de la Cruz (Encounter, 1:3, Dec. 1953, p. 5-13).

With some poetic licence the English poet sketches an interesting "profile" of the nun-poetess, and appends his own translation of her

famous "Hombres necios . . ." and of a *villancico* of 1677.

4603. Juana Inés de la Cruz, Sor. Obras completas. 3. Autos y loas. Edición, prólogo y notas de Alfonso Méndez Plancarte. México, Fondo de Cultura Económica, 1955. xcviii, 739 p., illus.

The third of the projected five-volume collection of Sor Juana's writings, by the late Mexican scholar, is devoted to her *Teatro sacro* (three *autos sacramentales* and their corresponding *loas*, together with 13 other *loas* belonging to her *Teatro profano*). A long introduction traces the history of the *auto* and *loa* as genres. The carefully collated texts have abundant bibliographical, exegetical, and philological notes, totalling 227 pages. Like the preceding volumes of the series it is a masterly edition, and it is important that *Comedias y sainetes* and the prose writings planned for volumes 4 and 5 appear, to complete this monument both to the late editor and the nun-poetess.

4604. ————. Primero sueño. Texto, con introducción y notas por Gerardo Moldenhauer. B. A., Universidad de Buenos Aires, Facultad de Filosofía y Letras, Sección de Literatura Iberoamericana, 1953. 87 p.

A new edition of Sor Juana's most ambitious

poem, based on that of Karl Vossler (Karlsruhe, 1946, 2nd ed.). Two editions of the second volume of the *Obras de Sor Juana Inés de la Cruz* including the *Primer sueño* appeared in Barcelona in 1693, the German scholar using the second and less satisfactory, while the first was used in the present critical edition of the poem. The introduction reproduces the essays of Vossler and Ludwig Pfandl, and Vossler's notes are appended with additional commentary by the present editor.

4605. Leal, Luis. El "Tocotín mestizo" de Sor Juana (Ábside, 18:1, enero-marzo 1954, p. 51-64).
A brief discussion, based largely on notes of Alfonso Méndez Plancarte, of the verses in mixed Spanish and Nahuatl that Sor Juana wrote in her *villancicos* to be sung on March 31, 1677, in honor of San Pedro Nolasco. Linguistic comments are made regarding this festive dance inherited from the Aztecs.

4606. Leonard, Irving A. The *encontradas correspondencias* of Sor Juana Inés. An interpretation (Hisp R, 23:1, Jan. 1955, p. 33-47).
The triangular antitheses occurring in three sonnets, with echoes in her other verses, are interpreted as veiled expressions of a profound intellectual conflict between the methods of seeking truth through the traditional medieval scholasticism and those of the experimentalism of science rapidly developing in the secular world of the 17th century.

4607. Martín, José Luis. El amor en la poesía de Sor Juana (Alma L, 896, enero 31, p. 8, 14; 897, feb. 7, p. 15-16, 27; 898, feb. 14, p. 15, 27; 900, feb. 28, p. 15-16, 32, 34; 901, marzo 7, p. 15-16, 18; 903, marzo 21, 1953, p. 32, 34-35).
A thoughtful essay, inspired by Chávez' *Ensayo de psicología de Sor Juana Inés*, whose author believes "El tema del amor pasional es primero y último en la poesía de Sor Juana." He divides her poetry into: (1) *amor místico*, (2) *amor amistoso*, and (3) *amor pasional*. He asserts that her personality as an intellectual ". . . es artificial y poco íntima. . . . Es un yo más superficial, más retirado del centro psíquico." Comments on poetical names used by Sor Juana.

4608. Navarro, Tomás. Los versos de Sor Juana (Rom Philol, 7:1, Aug. 1953, p. 44-50).
Study of the metrical peculiarities of the nun-poetess. She possessed a perfect command of metrical techniques, using novel and ingenious forms but preferring, on the whole, the simpler and more popular modes.

4609. Newby, Edith O. Sor Juana Inés de la Cruz, científica (R Hisp Mod, 20:3, julio 1954, Sección escolar, p. 17-22).
A perceptive essay emphasizing Sor Juana's intellectual character, with fragments of the famous *Respuesta a Sor Filotea*.

4610. Ricard, Robert. Les vers portugais de Sor Juana Inés de la Cruz. Apropos d'une édition récente (B Hisp, 55:3-4, 1953, p. 243-251).
The incorrectness of language of the six *coplas* in Portuguese included in the nun-poetess's festive *villancico* of 1677 is attributed to her deliberate imitation of the corrupt speech of a Portuguese living in Mexico rather than to an imperfect knowledge of the idiom.

4611. Salceda, Alberto G. Cronología del teatro de Sor Juana (Ábside, 17:3, julio-sept. 1953, p. 333-358).
A valuable article which attempts to establish the dates of the comedies, *loas*, and *autos* of Sor Juana by internal evidence, linking allusions to persons and events with announcements and data recorded in the contemporary *Diario de Robles* and other similar accounts of daily events. In various instances precise dates are established by this method.

4612. Saz, Agustín del. Sor Juana Inés de la Cruz. Barcelona, Industrias Gráficas (Vidas de mujeres ilustres), 1954. 149 p., illus.
A biography based almost entirely on Sor Juana's own writings.

4613. Suárez Galindo, José Guadalupe. La obra literaria de Sor Juana Inés de la Cruz (Armas Let, 10:1, enero 1953, p. 1, 7-8).
Another victim of the spell of the nun-poetess who feels it necessary to externalize his regard in a descriptive essay which makes no new interpretation.

4614. Villegas, Abelardo. El cielo y la tierra en *El sueño* de Sor Juana (Fil Let, México, 27:53-54, enero-junio 1954, p. 241-251).
Author sees the conflict between the "Ciudad de Dios" and the "Ciudad Terrena" as the basic theme of the colonial era of Mexico. This dialectic, he believes, is reflected more clearly in Sor Juana's difficult poem *El sueño* than in any of her other verses. While granting that her preoccupations were intellectual, the author considers her final surrender as evidence that she comtemplated "la Ciudad Divina a través de la Ciudad Terrena."

4615. Yantis, George Davenport. Sor Juana after three hundred years (Poet Lore, 57:1, spring 1953, p. 161-167).
Subtitled "The Mexican phoenix," it is a brief sketch of the life of the nun-poetess, with a bare mention of her work.

INCA GARCILASO DE LA VEGA

4616. Asensio, Eugenio. Dos cartas desconocidas del Inca Garcilaso (Nueva R Filol Hisp, 7:3-4, julio-dic. 1953, p. 583-593).
Reproduces two letters of the Peruvian chronicler, discovered in the archives of a Portuguese family, written from Cordoba in 1592 and 1593

o Juan Fernández Franco, an antiquarian. Among other things they indicate that *La Florida* was completed in 1592 and that a new edition of the Inca's *Diálogos de León Hebreo* was contemplated. The intimacy of the Peruvian mestizo with the Spanish chronicler, Ambrosio de Morales, and the influence of classical antiquarians, particularly Jean Bodin, are tressed by the author of this article.

4617. Cox, Carlos Manuel. Interpretación económica de los "Comentarios" del Inca Garcilaso (Cuad Am, año 12, 70:4, julio-agosto, 1953, p. 205-220).
A somewhat generalized account of the Inca Garcilaso which narrows down in the last page or two to the implications of the title. Garcilaso's references to Jean Bodin's *Traité de la République* and to Giovanni Botero, a contemporary Italian economist, suggest to the author that the Inca opposed current mercantilist theories. The Inca "no fué economista en sí, pero interpretó la historia desde el punto de vista económico. . . ."

4618. Durand, José. El Inca español (Américas, PAU, 5:5, mayo 1953, p. 6-8, 30-31).
A "profile" essay pointing up the contradictions resulting from the dual nature and heritage of the Peruvian mestizo chronicler, Inca Garcilaso de la Vega, "el primer escritor noable en América."

4619. ——————. La redacción de *La Florida del Inca:* cronología (R Hist, Lima, 21, 1954, p. 288-302).
Interesting data concerning the writing and publication of what is, perhaps, Garcilaso's master work. Probably its publication in 1605 was 20 years after he began to write it. The author gives testimony as to the veracity and integrity of the Inca as a writer and historian.

4620. ——————. Un sermón editado por el Inca Garcilaso (Nueva R Filol Hisp, 7: 3-4, julio-dic. 1953, p. 594-599).
A sermon by a Franciscan of Montilla, Spain, Alonso Bernardino, was published by Garcilaso in 1612, dedicated to the Marqués de Priego, who owed a substantial sum of money to the Peruvian mestizo. The author discusses the circumstances associated with this little publication overlooked by scholars.

4621. Miró Quesada, Aurelio. Italia y el Inca Garcilaso (M S, año 5, 10:28, julio-agosto 1953, p. 1-24).
A study of Italian influences on the development of the Peruvian chronicler's style, based on the inventory of books found in his library after his death.

4622. Moreno Báez, Enrique. El providencialismo del Inca Garcilaso (Estud Am, 8:35-36, agosto-sept. 1954, p. 143-154).
A Spaniard looks at the Peruvian mestizo chronicler, and dwells upon the statements in his writings which tend to indicate that he regarded the Spanish conquest and the conversion to Christianity as acts of Providence. The

similar techniques of the Incan emperors in their expansion, it is alleged, prepared this Indian civilization for the acceptance of the new religion "providentially" bestowed.

4623. Porras Barrenechea, Raúl. El Inca Garcilaso en Montilla (1561-1614). Nuevos documentos hallados y publicados por . . . . Lima, Editorial San Marcos, 1955. 300 p., illus.
Over 200 unpublished documents exhumed from notarial records of Montilla, Spain, where the Peruvian chronicler lived mainly from 1561 to 1591 when he moved to nearby Cordoba. A substantial number of these documents are baptismal certificates indicating the Inca as a godfather, but many of his commercial and legal transactions are recorded. These help to establish a more precise chronology of the period least known but most active of the Inca's career. The appendix reproduces several articles written by Porras Barrenechea relating to his researches on the Inca Garcilaso, and includes an extensive bibliography. The whole is obviously a work of fundamental importance.

4624. Sánchez, Luis Alberto. El Inca Garcilaso, escritor (R Nac Cult, 17:109, marzo-abril 1955, p. 36-47).
The Peruvian chronicler reveals the nostalgic romanticism of a *déraciné,* or exile, together with classic diction and lyric, narrative style which partly justifies Menéndez y Pelayo's characterization of the Inca Garcilaso as a novelist.

4625. Williams, Schafer. Hoffman Atkinson, translator of *La Florida del Inca* (R Interam Bibl, 4:1-2, enero-junio 1954, p. 52-62).
A documented sketch of an American (1839-1901) with a varied career in government service abroad and in business, with scholarly interests which led him late in life to make a complete translation of the Inca Garcilaso's account of the De Soto expedition, one that preceded the recently published version of Dr. and Mrs. Varner (University of Texas Press, 1951) by over half a century. The manuscript has remained virtually unnoticed in the Library of Congress since 1903.

OTHER FIGURES

4626. Alayza y Paz Soldán, Luis. Unanue, geógrafo, médico y estadista. Lima, Lumen, 1954. 235 p.
A lengthy study of three aspects of the work of a patriotic Peruvian creole scholar, José Hipólito Unanue (1758-1833), whose life and interests, reflecting 18th-century intellectual influences, vaguely suggest the character and services of Benjamin Franklin. This is the fullest treatment yet of a colonial *sabio* who merits a full-length biography.

4627. Burrus, E. J. Sigüenza y Góngora's efforts for readmission into the Jesuit order (HAHR, 33:3, Aug. 1953, p. 387-391).
Brief documents found in the *Archivum Romanum Societatis Jesu* at the Jesuit headquar-

ters in Rome concerning the refusal to reinstate the Mexican Creole savant (1645-1700) in the Jesuit order from which he had been dismissed for an infraction of their discipline when a novitiate.

4628. Caillet-Bois, Julio. Un olvidado cronista: Fray Reginaldo de Lizárraga, ca. 1539-1609 (Nueva R Filol Hisp, 7:3-4, julio-dic. 1953, p. 600-607).
A succinct account of the *Descripción y población de las Indias* by a 16th-century Dominican, a keen observer and lively describer of types and places in Peru and Chile. Intended as a narrative of travels, it is a handy encyclopedia "de saberes prácticos" and general lore, to which was attached an historical sketch giving it the importance of a chronicle.

4629. Cavazos Garza, Israel. Juan Bautista Chapa, cronista anónimo del *Nuevo Reino de León* (Estud Hist Am, 1953, p. 273-316).
Alonso de León's *Historia de Nuevo León,* written in the late 17th century, was continued by an Italian named J. B. Chapa, whose biography is here sketched, and the text of two documents pertaining to him is reproduced.

4630. Cisneros, Luis Jaime. Estudio y edición de la *Defensa de damas* (Fénix, 9, 1953, i.e. 1955, p. 81-196).
A detailed philological study, with text of a poem in six cantos of octaves, or 3728 verses (Lima, 1603), written by the Seville-born Diego Dávalos y Figueroa as the concluding part of his *Miscelánea austral.* Though a work admittedly lacking in originality and literary merit, it is interesting as a reflection of contemporary influences, classical and Italian.

4631. ————. Sobre la poesía de Dávalos y Figueroa. Un descuidado poema colonial (M S, año 5, 9:26, marzo-abril 1953, p. 38-49).
In the *Miscelánea austral* by Diego Dávalos Figueroa published in Lima in 1602, the author finds clear indications of Italian influences through Garcilaso de la Vega, Camoens, Petrarch, and Cervantes' *Galatea,* mainly in verses quoted.

4632. Dinamarca, Salvador. Los estudios de Medina sobre Ercilla. N. Y., Hispanic Institute in the United States, 1953. 86 p.
A reprinting in booklet form (250 numbered copies) of a bibliographical essay published in *Atenea,* año 29, 107:327-328, sept.-oct. 1952, p. 341-374 (cf. *HLAS, no. 18, 1952,* no. 2411) as part of commemoration of the centennial of the birth of the great Chilean bibliographer and historian, José T. Medina.

4633. Forero, Manuel José. Un capítulo de la historia de la literatura colombiana: Fray Pedro Simón (Bolívar, Bogotá, 28, abril 1954, p. 473-488).
Commentary on the content, style, and sources of the *Noticias historiales* by the Franciscan chronicler (1572-?), recently published by the author of this article. Reproduced from this

work are two short chapters reciting the mis adventures of some Spanish conquistadors.

4634. ————. Un poeta cortesano de Santafé (Bolívar, Bogotá, 21, julio 1953 p. 145-152).
Francisco Antonio Vélez Ladrón de Guevara

4635. Garrido, José Eulogio. Un obispe humanista en Trujillo a fines del sigl(XVIII (R U, Trujillo, 3. época, 2:3-4 1.-2. semestres 1954, p. 1-30).
Biographical sketch of a colonial Enlighten ment figure, Bishop Baltasar J. Martínez Com pañón of the Trujillo (Peru) diocese from 177 to 1790. Includes a discussion of his writing as a geographer, naturalist, and ethnologist.

4636. Lefebvre, Alfredo. La poesía de Capitán (1537-1578). Concepción, Chile 1953. 234 p.
Francisco de Aldana. Cf. Elias L. Rivers, "A example of Hispanic originality" (Hispania AATSP, 37:3, Sept. 1954, p. 310-312).

4637. Lohmann Villena, Guillermo. L *Historia de Lima* de Antonio de Leó Pinelo (M S, año 5, 9:25, enero-feb. 1953 p. 1-20).
See *HLAS, no. 18, 1952,* item 2418.

4638. Lucero Ontiveros, Dolly María El Renacimiento y América en *La Argen tina,* de Martín del Barco Centener (Cuad Hispanoam, 59, nov. 1954, p. 179 189).
A superficial, tabular listing of the "aspecto renacentistas" and "aspectos americanos" c one of the many pedantic and prosaic epic inspired by the success of Ercilla's *La Arau cana.*

4639. Meyer, Mary Edgar. The source of Hojeda's *La Cristiada.* Ann Arboi Mich., University of Michigan Pres (University of Michigan publ. in languag and literature, 26), 1953. 233 p.
A very erudite and distinguished study of th classical, medieval, Renaissance, and contem porary literature, sacred history, and mytholog mystical, and patristic writings which influ enced the Dominican friar, Diego de Hojed (1571?-1615), in composing, in Peru, a reli gious epic considered the best in the Spanis language and frequently likened to Milton *Paradise lost.*

4640. Moreno, Rafael. Alzate, educado ilustrado (Hist Mex, 2:3, enero-marz 1953, p. 371-389).
A discussion of the activities of Juan Antoni Alzate (1729-1799), editor of periodica (*Diario literario,* 1768; *Asuntos varios,* 177 *Observaciones varias,* 1778, and *Gaceta d México,* 1788-1795), stressing his work as a educator.

4641. Moreyra y Paz Soldán, Manuel Una carta del virrey Conde de la Mon

clova sobre Pedro Peralta Barnuevo (M
S, año 5, 10:28, julio-agosto 1953, p.
36-39).
Data on the eminent Peruvian savant and
iterato (1664-1743), together with the text of
a letter of the viceroy, dated August 28, 1696,
to the king regarding the purchase of the office
of accountant by Peralta.

4642. Oroz, Rodolfo. Reminiscencias vir-
gilianas en Pedro de Oña (Atenea, año
31, 115:348, junio 1954, p. 278-286).
Slight similarities of brief phrases noted in the
long poems of the Chilean bard (*Arauco do-
nado, Ignacio de Cantabria*, and *El Vasauro*)
to those in the *Aeneid* and the *Eclogues*.

4643. Pardo, Isaac J. Juan de Castellanos
(R Nac Cult, 17:109, marzo-abril 1955,
p. 58-78).
A chapter of a forthcoming book entitled *Esta
Tierra de Gracia, imagen de Venezuela en el
siglo XVI*, which comments on the long poem
Elegías de varones ilustres de Indias by the
conquistador and *cura* of Tunja (1522-1607),
with numerous quotations from this work, indicating the sources and broad culture of this
16th-century Spaniard whose life was spent
mostly in Venezuela.

4644. Riva Agüero, José de la. Diego
Mexía de Fernangil y la segunda parte
de su *Parnaso antártico* (R Hist, Lima,
21, 1954, p. 37-75).
A reprinting of an excellent critical article by
the late Peruvian historian (1885-1944), first
published in 1914 in the *Actas del Congreso de
Historia y Geografía Hispano-Americanas* at
Seville. It sketches the life and work of a late
16th- and early 17th-century *sevillano* mer-
chant-poet who spent many years in Peru. He
was distinguished for his translations of Ovid's
Heroidas and the first part of his *Parnaso
antártico*, a collection of his poems published
at Seville in 1608. The unpublished second
part is described by Riva Agüero.

4645. Rodríguez Mendoza, Emilio. Francisco de Pineda y Bascuñán. Santiago,
Imp. Universitaria, 1953?
A lively lecture on the 17th-century author of
El cautiverio feliz. This curious prose narrative is described as a mixture of history, fiction,
and personal recollection. "En realidad, tiene
de todo como la vida misma."

4646. Toussaint, Manuel. Nuevos datos
sobre Arias de Villalobos (A Inst Inv
Estét, 6:21, 1953, p. 92-94).
From the *Actas del Cabildo* of Mexico City
the author extracts two petitions of the early-
17th-century poet. The first, dated June 10,
1613, requests an increased water supply for his
school, and the second, dated Sept. 20, 1622,
asks aid for the publication of a *relación* that
he had written.

4647. Valton, E. Fray Alonso de la Vera
Cruz (B Bib Nac, México, 2. época,
5:4, oct.-dic. 1954, p. 3-8).

Gives a brief biography of this 16th-century
humanist and an analysis of his *Recognitio
sumularum dialectica resolutio* . . . with geographical data on Mexico, transcribed from the
fourth edition of the *Phisica speculatio* (Salamanca, 1573).

TEXTS

4648. Arriola, Juan José de. Décimas de
Santa Rosalía. Selección y nota de Alfonso Méndez Plancarte. México, Los
Presentes, 1955. 110 p.
A selection of 23 hitherto unpublished poems
in *décimas* by a Mexican Jesuit (1698-1768)
in homage to the 12th-century saint.

4649. Arrom, José Juan. Una desconocida
comedia mexicana del siglo XVII (R
Iberoam, 19:37, oct. 1953, p. 79-103).
An unrecorded edition of a 1641 *relación* describing the ceremonious reception of the viceroy, Marqués de Villena, written by the gifted
Jesuit poet of colonial Mexico, Matías de
Bocanegra (1612-1668). It includes the text
of a well-written play, *Comedia de San Francisco de Borja*, revealing the influence of Lope
de Vega and particularly of the then recent
La vida es sueño of Calderón. The theme is
a dramatization of Bocanegra's *Canción a la
vista de un desengaño*, the text of which is
reproduced as an appendix of this study.

4650. Díaz del Castillo, Bernal. Historia
verdadera de la conquista de la Nueva
España. Introducción y notas de Joaquín
Ramírez Cabañas. México, Porrúa, 1955.
2 v. 514, 518 p.
This classic work belongs in colonial literature
as well as history, if not for its contents nor its
esthetic qualities, for its sheer readability and
interest.

4651. Espinosa, Aurelio Macedonio.
Romancero de Nuevo Méjico (R Filol
Esp, anejo 58, 1953, 302 p.).
A six-part collection of "Romances novelescos
tradicionales, Romances novelescos varios, Romances religiosos tradicionales, Romances religiosos varios, Corridos, Cuandos, Inditas,"
etc., and "Fragmentos de romances sobre la
historia de España y . . . de Nuevo Méjico,"
with an historical introduction, by the veteran
folklorist of Stanford University, California.

4652. Fiestas celebradas en Quito cuando
la Católica Majestad de Carlos III pasó
del trono de Nápoles al de España, celebradas el año de 1760 (Mus Hist 5:17,
sept. 1953, p. 126-148).
This *descripción* includes the text of an anonymous allegorical *loa* in verse.

**4653. Miranda, José, and Pablo González
Casanova.** Sátira anónima del siglo
XVIII. México, Fondo de Cultura Económica (Letras mexicanas, 9), 1953.
234 p.

A series of 21 unpublished satirical writings in prose and verse drawn from records of the Inquisition and others in the General Archive of the Nation and similar repositories. They are interesting examples of the anonymous, popular literature circulating in manuscript which reflect the growing tensions of social and political life in 18th-century Mexico. Archbishops and lesser clergy as well as viceroys and royal officials are the objects of satire often expressed in crude language, and the hostility of Creole and Peninsular elements is thus indicated. These examples are preceded by two essays by the editors entitled "Carácter y temática" and "Sentido y figura."

4654. Murcia de la Llana, Francisco. Canciones lúgubres y tristes, a la muerte de don Christoval de Oñate, teniente de governador y capitán general de las conquistas del Nuevo México. Valencia, Spain (Duque y Marqués, Opúsculos literarios rarísimos, 3), 1953. 154 p.
Reproduction of a "homage volume" of more historical than literary value, from a unique copy in the John Carter Brown Library.

4655. Vargas Ugarte, Rubén. Rosas de Oquendo y otros. Introducción y notas de. . . . Lima, 1955. 167 p.
This is the fifth in the series of *Clásicos peruanos* which the indefatigable Father Vargas Ugarte has produced on the colonial literature of Peru. It includes selections relating to Peru from Spanish-born poets who, like Caviedes and Terralla y Landa, possessed "facilidad para la versificación, espíritu satírico, erudición propia de la época, desenfado picaresco y mucha sal." Also included are poems by Pedro de Torre, Enrique Garcés, Diego Dávalos y Figueroa, Diego Mexía de Fernangil, Príncipe de Esquilache, Marqués de Montesclaros, Francisco Bejarano de Loaiza, Juan J. de Zaballos y Dávalos, and religious verses by nuns of the period.

ESSAYS, TRANSLATIONS, AND MISCELLANY

4656. Adams, Eleanor B. An English library at Trinidad, 1633 (Americas, Franciscan Hist, 12:1, July 1955, p. 25-41).
A collection of 35 volumes seized by Spaniards from an English group on Trinidad and delivered to the Holy Office on the island of Margarita. Mostly secular in character, they are an interesting sidelight on the larger subject of book circulation in the Spanish Indies.

4657. Alegría, Fernando. La poesía chilena. Orígenes y desarrollo del siglo XVI al XIX. Berkeley, Calif., University of California Press, 1954. 311 p.
Four of the six chapters of this valuable critical study are devoted to the colonial period and the versifiers of the War for Independence. The first two are extended studies of Ercilla's *La Araucana* and Oña's *Arauco domado*, while the third treats of the *repentistas* or improvis-

ors of occasional verse. The approach to the early epic poems is original and untraditional.

4658. Alone (i.e., Díaz Arrieta, Hernán) La literatura chilena durante el siglo XVIII (Atenea, año 30, 113:341-342 nov.-dic. 1953, p. 15-43).
A discussion of causes of the decadence of Chilean letters in the last colonial century which is centered about three Jesuit writers: Miguel de Olivares, a moralist; Juan Ignacio Molina, a naturalist; and Manuel de Lacunza a theologian.

4659. Anderson-Imbert, Enrique. Estudios sobre escritores de América. B. A. Raigal (Biblioteca Juan María Gutiérrez) 1954. 222 p.
The first two of these 11 essays are "Un episodio quijotesco en el Padre Las Casas" and "Fernando Oviedo y Bernal Díaz del Castillo." These are of interest to literature because of their comments on the style and subjective qualities of these early chroniclers.

4660. Asencio, José. Cronistas franciscanos (Mem Ac Mex Hist, 13:3, julio-sept 1954, p. 220-248).
An account of some 140 chronicles written by Franciscans from 1525 to the present.

4661. Barker, George C. (ed.). The shepherd's play of the prodigal son (Coloquio de pastores del hijo pródigo). A folk drama of old Mexico . . . . Berkeley, Calif. University of California Press (Folklore studies, 2), 1953. 167 p.
The text and English translation of the manuscript play discovered in Jalisco, Mexico, at a Christmas performance in 1948. Combining the nativity and prodigal son themes, it harks back to the 16th- and 17th-century *autos*. "It is perhaps not too much to say that this Mexi can play constitutes a major link in the chain of evidence connecting the religious folk dramas of Mexico . . . with the autos del nacimiento of Spain."

4662. Barrera, Isaac J. Historia de la literatura ecuatoriana. V. 1. Siglos XVI y XVII. Quito, Casa de la Cultura Ecuatoriana, 1953. 301 p.
New edition of a useful work.

4663. Boggs, R. S. Caribbean ballads of the Spanish conquest (Carib Cont Trends p. 91-99).
Comments on the lack of ballads in the Caribbean area inspired by the conquerors' exploits and possible explanation. "We may have to recognize it as a fact that the conquerors who won the Caribbean for Spain . . . by an unfortunate combination of circumstances of geography, history, and the nature of the folk groups on which Spanish balladry has depended for its existence, simply did not interest the folklore form and its propagators."

4664. Bopp, Marianne O. de. Autos mexicanos del siglo XVI (Hist Mex, 3:1 julio-agosto 1953, p. 113-123).

A succinct summary of the author's recent book on the subject, showing that the early Mexican *autos*, because of their didactic purpose, resembled those of the early Middle Ages more than the contemporary Spanish *autos sacramentales*. Primitive, hybrid compositions, they were somewhat like a religious opera combining Indian music, song, dance, and acting with simple Biblical themes.

4665. Capote, Higinio. Las Indias en la poesía española del Siglo de Oro (Estud Am, 6:21-22, junio-julio 1953, p. 5-36).
Fragments of verses relating to the New World by Spanish poets (various of whom, including Ercilla, Juan de la Cueva, Bernardo Balbuena, Ruiz de Alarcón, Luis de Belmonte, had lived or traveled in parts of these overseas dominions) together with brief commentary.

4666. Castanien, Donald G. The Mexican Inquisition censors a private library (HAHR, 34:3, Aug. 1954, p. 374-392).
An analysis of one of the richest private book collections of the colonial period, the property of Melchor Pérez de Soto, a Mexico City architect, who incurred the displeasure of the Holy Office by his fondness for "judicial astrology." After his tragic death in prison, his library, seized by the Inquisition, was returned to his widow, with a few exceptions. The inventory lists many secular and fictional works, including novels of chivalry, whose importation was allegedly banned.

4667. Castro Seoane, José. La traída de libros y vestuarios en el siglo XVI de los misioneros desde sus conventos a Sevilla, pagada por el tesorero de la Casa de la Contratación (Miss Hisp, 10:30, 1953, p. 495-584; 11:31, 1954, p. 55-133; 11:33, 1954, p. 417-484).
Curious data on the freighting and handling of a part of the book trade with America from 1539 to 1595.

4668. Cervantes de Salazar, Francisco. Life in the imperial and loyal city of Mexico in New Spain, and the Royal and Pontifical University of Mexico. As described in the dialogues for the study of the Latin language prepared by ... for use in his classes and printed in 1554 by Juan Pablos. Now published in facsimile with a translation by Minnie Lee Barrett Shepard and an introduction and notes by Carlos Eduardo Castañeda. Austin, Tex., University of Texas Press, 1953 [i.e., 1954]. 113 p. & 71 p. of facsim.
The first English translation of this well-known and useful description of university life and customs in mid-16th-century Mexico by the Spanish humanist and disciple of Vives and Erasmus.

4669. Cossío, José María de. Romances sobre *La Araucana* (*in* Estudios dedicados a Menéndez Pidal. Madrid, Patronato

Marcelino Menéndez y Pelayo, 1954, p. 201-229).
Comments on 15 ballads of the late 16th century deriving from episodes in Alonso de Ercilla's celebrated historical poem.

4670. Echaiz, René León. Romancero en la zona central (B Ac Ch Hist, 21:50, 1. semestre 1954, p. 107-121).
A study which assembles various Spanish ballads, dealing with American themes, preserved in the central region of Chile.

4671. Fúrlong, Guillermo. Escritores coloniales rioplatenses. B. A., Librería del Plata, 1953. T. 2, José Cardiel, S. J., y su carta-relación (1747); t. 3, Pedro Juan Andreu y su carta a Mateo Andreu (1750).

4672. ———. Historia y bibliografía de las primeras imprentas rioplatenses, 1700-1850. T. 1. La imprenta en las reducciones del Paraguay, 1700-1727; la imprenta en Córdoba, 1765-1767; la imprenta en Buenos Aires, 1780-1784. B. A., Guaranía, 1953. 596 p., illus.
First volume of a cooperative work to carry the record of the River Plate region printing presses from the colonial period through the 19th century, supplementing rather than supplanting Medina's earlier (1892) work on the colonial press.

4673. Gómez Robleda, José. Humanismo en México en el siglo XVI. El sistema del Colegio de San Pedro y San Pablo. México, Jus, 1954. 182 p., illus.
Traces humanistic studies in the Jesuit institutions of Mexico City from 1574 to 1600, describing methods of instruction, obstacles to humanistic training, and "un día de clases en S. Pedro y S. Pablo (1591-1600)."

4674. Hesse, Everett W. Calderon's popularity in the Spanish Indies (Hisp R, 23:1, Jan. 1955, p. 12-27).
The *comedias* and *autos* of the great peninsular dramatist were widely and repeatedly performed throughout colonial Spanish America in the 17th century and increasingly in the 18th. A compilation of recorded performances, particularly in Mexico City and Lima, is appended to this valuable study, which affirms once again the wide diffusion of Castilian literary culture in the American realms.

4675. Johnson, Harvey L. Compañías teatrales en Arequipa en 1621 y 1636 (Nueva R Filol Hisp, 7:3-4, julio-dic. 1953, p. 449-460).
Text of two contracts of stock companies performing in the inland Peruvian city, with a brief introduction and notes giving data on individual actors. These documents are interesting for the light that they throw upon the kinds of agreements entered into by strolling players in the viceroyalty during the Golden Age of Spanish drama.

4676. Leonard, Irving A. Los libros del conquistador. México, Fondo de Cultura Económica (Lengua y estudios literarios), 1953. 399 p., 8 pl.
A translation of *Books of the brave* (Harvard University Press, 1949), by the same author (see *HLAS, no. 15, 1949*, item 2203). With slight revision of text and notes it also includes a documentary appendix of nine selected book lists of the late 16th and early 17th centuries, a feature lacking in the original edition in English.

4677. ————. On the Lima book trade, 1591 (HAHR, 33:4, Nov. 1953, p. 511-525).
A bill of sale, found in the National Archive of Peru, covering some 1186 volumes which are listed by abbreviated titles. Among them are numerous historical works, novels of chivalry, epic poems, and secular nonfiction. This document is reproduced, preceded by an historical impression of Lima in 1591, and an analysis of the titles appearing in the list.

4678. Lohmann Villena, Guillermo. Los libros españoles en Indias (*in* Historia de España, estudios publicados en la revista *Arbor*, Madrid, 1953, p. 422-444).
Reprinting of an article published in *Arbor*, 2:6, nov.-dic. 1944, describing the free circulation of books in colonial Spanish America, with an analysis of the types of literature then in vogue.

4679. Manchester, P. T. Criticism of *La Araucana* by Ercilla's contemporaries (*in* Stroup, Thomas B., and Sterling A. Stoudemire (eds.). South Atlantic studies for Sturgis E. Leavitt. Washington, Scarecrow Press, 1953, 39-54).
The "contemporaries" are mainly those who contributed prefaces to the early editions, references to *La Araucana* found in literary and historical writings of the 16th and 17th centuries, and comments from unpublished manuscripts, practically all laudable rather than penetrating.

4680. Maria y Campos, Armando de. Las comedias en el Corpus mexicano colonial (Humanismo, 2:11-12, mayo-junio 1953, p. 111-114).
Curious details extracted from the *Actas del Cabildo* concerning arrangements in Mexico City at the close of the 16th century for the annual performances of the religious plays on Corpus Christi day.

4681. Millares Carlo, Agustín. Dos datos nuevos para la historia de la imprenta en México en el siglo XVI (Nueva R Filol Hisp, 7:3-4, julio-dic. 1953, p. 702-708).
Two newly discovered incunabula of the 16th century: "Para el rezo del Santo Rosario," allegedly printed about 1534, and "Nuevo vergel de olorosas flores sembradas por la muerte dolorida y cogidas por la trabajada vida," a work of Bernal de las Indias, previously published in Seville. Author gives text of letter,

dated at Mexico City, July 10, 1592, and addressed to Pedro Ocharte, "ympresor," and reproduces a page of "IUBILEO Plenissimo . . ." printed by Pedro Balli in Mexico City in 1592, here described for the first time.

4682. Miramón, Alberto. Un aspecto interpretativo de *El Carnero* (Bolívar, Bogotá, 17, marzo 1953, p. 313-320).
On the 17th-century gossipy chronicle of New Granada or Colombia by Juan Rodríguez Fresle.

4683. Monterde, Francisco. La literatura mexicana en los siglos XVI y XVII (*in* Historia general de las literaturas hispánicas. V. 3. Renacimiento y barroco. Barcelona, Editorial Barna, 1953, p. 997-1019).
Brief survey of literary activities in New Spain of native Mexicans and transient Spaniards.

4684. Sánchez, Luis Alberto. La novela en los cronistas (Atenea, año 31, 114: 343-344, enero-feb. 1954, p. 109-130).
Excerpt from the author's recently published *Proceso y contenido de la novela hispanoamericana* which surveys the 16th and 17th centuries.

4685. Stols, Alexander A. M. Historia de la imprenta en el Ecuador de 1755 a 1830. Quito, Casa de la Cultura Ecuatoriana, 1953. 261 p., 51 facsim.
An account of the colonial press and the influence of the Jesuits on its diffusion. Much new documentation on the first press of Ambato and its first printer, the Jesuit Adam Schwartz. Indicates 274 publications on colonial press in 74 years.

4686. Tavera Alfaro, Xavier. Una reseña histórica del periodismo (Cuad Am, año 13, 74:2, marzo-abril 1954, p. 171-190).
Chiefly an analysis of the short-lived *gacetas, diarios, compendios de noticias,* etc., of 18th-century Mexico, indicating that they reflect a dawning sense of national consciousness and a preoccupation with "useful" knowledge so characteristic of the Enlightenment.

4687. Torres Ríoseco, Arturo. Ensayos sobre literatura latinoamericana. Berkeley, Calif., University of California Press, 1953. 207 p.
The first three of the 16 essays of this miscellany deal with the "Teatro indígena de México" (p. 7-25), "Tres dramaturgos mexicanos del período colonial (Eslava, Alarcón, Sor Juana)," p. 26-56, and "El *Apologético* en favor de don Luis de Góngora," p. 57-64.

4688. Vega, Miguel Ángel. Literatura chilena de la conquista y de la colonia. Santiago, Nascimento, 1954. 163 p.
A welcome synthesis which begins with a brief discussion of geographical, social, and psychological factors conditioning literary expression in Chile. Chroniclers, particularly Góngora Marmolejo, Mariño de Lobera, and

SPANISH AMERICAN LITERATURE 249

Valdivia, and figures of the "Literatura de la colonia" such as Ercilla, Oña, Ovalle, Rosales, Núñez de Pineda y Bascuñán, Gómez de Vidaurre, and Lacunza receive succinct comments with lengthy illustrative passages from their works. Mainly *prosistas*, a relatively short chapter is devoted to poetry, mostly ballads and satirical verses. Though repeating disproved clichés such as the alleged noncirculation of fiction in the colonial centuries, and adding little to previous investigations and criticism, this survey is both interesting and useful.

4689. Vindel, Francisco (ed.). El primer libro impreso en América fué para el rezo del Santo Rosario (Méjico, 1532-34). Facsímil, estudios y comentarios. Madrid, Artes Gráficas Faure, 1953. 102 p.

Facsimile edition of a work allegedly printed in Tlaxcala about 1534 by a manufacturer of playing cards.

BIBLIOGRAPHICAL WORKS

4690. Araujo Espinoza, Graciela. Adiciones a *La imprenta en Lima, 1584-1824* (Fénix, 8, 1952, i.e. 1954, p. 467-704).

Includes items assembled by José Toribio Medina for a new edition, together with others gathered by Rubén Vargas Ugarte in his *Impresos peruanos (1584-1650)*, arranged by years and in alphabetical order.

4691. Beltrán Martínez, Román. Bibliografía de Joaquín Fernández de Lizardi, el Pensador Mexicano (B Bibl S Hac Cr Púb, 26, dic. 15, 1954, supl., 4 p.; 27, enero 15, 1955, supl., 4 p.; 29, feb. 15, 1955, supl., 2 p.; 30, marzo 1, 1955, supl., 2 p.; 32, abril 1, 1955, supl., 2 p.; 33, abril 15, 1955, supl., 2 p.; 36, junio 1, 1955, supl., 2 p.).

A new bibliography of the writings of the Mexican pamphleteer and novelist, supplementing the earlier efforts of Luis González Obregón and J. R. Spell, with illustrations from the early editions of Lizardi's works.

4692. Cody, W. F. An index to the periodicals published by José Antonio Alzate y Ramírez (HAHR, 33:3, Aug. 1953, p. 442-475).

A complete index of literary and scientific writings published in the late-18th-century periodical *Gaceta de México*, with biobibliographical data on its editor (1729-1799).

4693. García Icazbalceta, Joaquín. Bibliografía mexicana del siglo XVI. Catálogo razonado de libros impresos en México de 1539 a 1600. Con biografías de autores y otras ilustraciones. Precedido de

una noticia acerca de la introducción de la imprenta en México. Nueva ed., por Agustín Millares Carlo. México, Fondo de Cultura Económica, 1954. 581 p., facsms.

By incorporating items from bibliographies of Medina, León, Wagner, Valton, González de Cossío, etc., some 80 documentary references to 16th-century printers appear in place of the nine, and data on 180 imprints in place of the 118 of the original edition are given, along with a new index. Reviewed by Antonio Alatorre in an article entitled "Los libros de México en el siglo XVI" (Cuad Am, año 14, 79:1, enero-feb. 1955, p. 219-226).

4694. Lohmann Villena, Guillermo. La literatura peruana de los siglos XVI y XVII (*in* Historia general de las literaturas hispánicas. V. 3. Renacimiento y barroco. Barcelona, Editorial Barna, 1953, p. 975-995).

A rapid summary of poetic, dramatic, and prose literature written in viceregal Peru, with bibliographical commentary.

4695. Medina, José Toribio. Adiciones inéditas a *La imprenta en Lima* (Fénix, 8, 1952, p. 434-461).

Items assembled during the last years of Medina's life and transferred to Feliú Cruz; arranged in chronological order from 1623 to 1824, with three undated items of the 18th century.

4696. Valle, Rafael Heliodoro. Bibliografía de Rafael de Landívar. Bogotá, Instituto Caro y Cuervo, 1953. 48 p.

A two-part work with the first, "Bibliografía de Landívar," in chronological order, and the second, "Bibliografía sobre Landívar," in alphabetical order. Many items have brief critical commentary and quotations.

4697. Vargas Ugarte, Rubén. Impresos peruanos (1584-1650). Lima, Editorial San Marcos (Biblioteca peruana, 7), 1953. liv, 272 p.

First volume of a new listing of printed works appearing in Peru from the beginnings to 1829. While supplementing J. T. Medina's earlier work on the press in Lima, it does not follow that model in inserting the text of pertinent documents or in giving a minute description of the various items. See also item below.

4698. ————. Impresos peruanos (1651-1699). Lima, Editorial San Marcos (Biblioteca peruana, 8), 1954. 331 p.

Second volume of a listing of works published in Lima and Peru to extend to 1829. The two volumes now available list 1107 items or about 400 more than J. T. Medina offered in his earlier work covering the same period. See also item above.

SPANISH AMERICAN LITERATURE:
NINETEENTH AND TWENTIETH CENTURIES

GENERAL

ÁNGEL FLORES

4700. Academia Mexicana. Memorias de la . . . Correspondiente de la Española. Discursos académicos. T. 9. México, Jus, 1954. 377 p.
Speeches on Mexican and foreign literatures, delivered during 1925-1950; none of permanent value.

4701. Almafuerte [pseud.], i.e., **Pedro Bonifacio Palacios.** Obras de . . . . Poesías y prosas. Ordenadas y anotadas por Romualdo Brughetti. B. A., Ediciones Peuser, 1954. 629 p. & illus.
Brughetti's introduction is a fine initiation to the significant work of the much neglected Argentine poet Pedro B. Palacios, better known as Almafuerte (1854-1917); the anthology is arranged according to themes.

4702. Alone [pseud.], i.e., **Hernán Díaz Arrieta.** Estado actual de la literatura chilena (Panorama, 2:8, 1953, p. 89-99).
Excellent over-all picture of contemporary Chilean letters, reprinted from the *Revista nacional de cultura,* of Caracas.

4703. Anaya Juárez, Elsa. Escritores mexicanos de leyendas. México, 1953. 119 p.
Doctoral thesis covering the Mexican 19th-century writers, mostly second-raters, who created a huge body of "legends" drawn from criminal annals, oral tradition, history and fantasy: among others, Luis González Obregón (1865-1938), Juan de Dios Peza (1852-1910), Vicente Riva Palacio (1832-1896).

4704. Anderson Imbert, Enrique. Estudios sobre escritores de América. B. A., Raigal (Biblioteca Juan María Gutiérrez), 1954. 222 p.
11 articles on sundry topics: the early historians of America, the Latin American novel, Sarmiento, Echeverría, etc.

4705. —————. Spanish-American literature in the last twenty-five years (Panorama, 3:10, 1954, p. 25-50).
An introductory essay on recent Spanish American writing.

4706. Andrade y Cordero, César. Hombre, destino y paisaje. Registro vario. Cuenca, Ecuador, Casa de la Cultura Ecuatoriana (Núcleo del Azuay), 1954. 429 p. & illus.
A young poet raves in prose about his native land and its aesthetic expression. The book includes four of his own short stories.

4707. Arrieta, Rafael Alberto. La ciudad y los libros. B. A., Editorial Sudamericana (Ediciones Librería del Colegio), 1955. 207 p.
Rambling considerations of Argentine book production and book trade, highlighting the role of the Librería del Colegio in the cultural life of B. A.

4708. Aubrun, Charles Vincent. Histoire des lettres hispano-américaines. Paris, Armand Colin (Section de langues et littératures, 291), 1954. 223 p.
Concise and stimulating manual dealing with the cultural development of Spanish America.

4709. Balaguer, Joaquín. Literatura dominicana. B. A., Américalee, 1950. 365 p.
Conventional panorama of Dominican literature focussed on the 19th and 20th centuries.

4710. Barnola, Pedro Pablo. Estudios crítico-literarios. 2. serie. Caracas, La Torre, 1953. 243 p.
A Jesuit critic's view of Venezuelan literature; especially interested in Pedro Emilio Coll, Teresa de la Parra, Mario Briceño, and Arvelo Torrealba.

4711. Bazin, Robert. Histoire de la littérature américaine de langue espagnole. Paris, Librairie Hachette, 1953. 354 p.
Bird's-eye view of Spanish American literature by a French professor gifted with the art of synthesis and condensation.

4712. Beltrán Guerrero, Luis. Razón y sinrazón. Temas de cultura venezolana. Caracas, Ariel, 1954. 249 p.
A Venezuelan journalist appraises the new poets and critics of his native country.

4713. Berenguer Carisomo, Arturo. Historia de la literatura. Para cuarto año de bachillerato, magisterio y comercial. B. A., FIDES, 1955. 650 p.
A textbook embracing Spanish literature (first 300 pages) and the literatures of Latin America; sketchy, superficial.

4714. Briceño-Iragorry, Mario. Pasión venezolana. El caballo de Ledesma. Mensaje sin destino. Tratado de la presunción. Caracas, Edime, 1954. 179 p.
A reprint of four of his shorter works.

4715. Bueno, Salvador. Las ideas literarias de Domingo Delmonte. Habana, Comisión Nacional Cubana de la UNESCO (Cuadernos de divulgación cultural, 10), 1954. 22 p.
Concise but searching study of the critic Domingo Delmonte y Aponte (1804-1853).

4716. Cardona Peña, Alfredo. Semblanzas mexicanas. Artistas y escritores del México actual. México, B. Costa-Amic (Biblioteca mínima mexicana, 10), 1955. 150 p., illus.
Eulogistic sketches of Mexican painters (Frida Kahlo, Toscano, etc.) and writers (Henestrosa, Pellicer, Villaurrutia).

4717. Caro, José Eusebio. Epistolario. Prólogo de Lucio Pabón Núñez. Edición dirigida por Simón Aljure Chalela. Bogotá, Ministerio de Educación Nacional, Ediciones de la revista Bolívar (Biblioteca de autores colombianos, 62), 1953. 454 p.
Letters which reveal the multiple interests of the Colombian poet and philosopher (1817-1853).

4718. Carrasquilla, Rafael María. Sermones y discursos. Bogotá, Ministerio de Educación Nacional, Ediciones de la revista Bolívar (Biblioteca de autores colombianos, 65), 1953. 428 p.
Sermons, funeral orations, and academic speeches by the Colombian priest (1884-1910).

4719. Castilla Barrios, Olga. Breve bosquejo de la literatura infantil colombiana. Tesis para optar el título de doctor en filosofía, letras y pedagogía. Bogotá, Pontificia Universidad Católica Javeriana, 1954. 371 p.
A doctoral dissertation on a little-known field: the juvenile literature of Colombia—fiction, history, poetry, drama, and fable-writing.

4720. Díaz Mirón, Salvador. Prosa. Compilación, prólogo y comentarios de Leonardo Pasquel. México, Biblioteca de autores veracruzanos, 1954. 328 p.
Newspaper articles, parliamentary speeches, and letters by the 19th-century Mexican poet.

4721. Díaz Ruanova, Oswaldo. Bajo el signo de Tláloc. Dibujos de Fernando Castro Pacheco. México, Porrúa y Obregón, 1953. 384 p., illus.
Evocation of Mexico's mythological Indian past, with some references to present-day conditions.

4722. Díaz Seijas, Pedro. Espejos del tiempo . . . Ensayos. Caracas, Jaime Villegas, 1953. 165 p.
On the intellectual crisis of Venezuela and some present-day writers: Lucila Palacios, Ramón Díaz Sánchez, Guillermo Meneses.

4723. ————. Historia y antología de la literatura venezolana. Caracas, Editorial Villegas Venezolana, 1953. 2 t. 843 p.
Well-organized annotated anthology of Venezuelan literature from the Colonial period to date.

4724. Diez de Medina, Fernando. Literatura boliviana. Introducción al estudio de las letras nacionales. Del tiempo mítico a la producción contemporánea. La Paz, Alfonso Tejerina, 1953. 379 p.
Impressionistic and often erratic over-all picture of Bolivian literature.

4725. Esténger, Rafael. Caracteres constantes en las letras cubanas. Habana, Alfa, 1954. 66 p.
Speech before the Cuban National Academy demonstrating the social awareness of Cuban writers throughout the last century.

4726. Estrella Gutiérrez, Fermín. Nociones de historia de la literatura española, hispanoamericana y argentina. Con antología. Para cuarto año de las escuelas de comercio. B. A., Kapelusz, 1954. 454 p., illus.
Textbook. The first 225 pages devoted to the literature of Spain, the balance to Argentina and Spanish America—rather choppy and trite.

4727. Flores, Ángel. Índices de *Cuadernos americanos* 1942-1952. México, Ediciones de Cuadernos Americanos, 1953. 172 p.
Subject and author index of the Mexican literary journal for 1942-1952.

4728. ————. Latin American literature (*in* The Americana annual, 1955. N. Y., Americana Corp., 1955, p. 415-416).
Survey of literary activity in Latin America during 1954.

4729. ————. Latin American literature (*in* Britannica book of the year, 1953. Chicago, Ill., Encyclopaedia Britannica, 1953, p. 408-409).
Survey of literary activity in Latin America during 1952.

4730. Fombona-Pachano, Jacinto. Obras completas. T. 1. Poesía. Caracas, Edime, 1953. 358 p.
V. 1 contains the most memorable verse of the Venezuelan poet (1901-1951), and v. 2 his prose writings: travel impressions, literary sketches, political speeches, lectures.

4731. Garrido, Luis. Alfonso Reyes. México, Imp. Universitaria (Cultura mexicana, 12), 1954. 117 p.
Brief considerations on Alfonso Reyes' poetry, short-story writing, humanism, and scholarship. Bibliography.

4732. Ghiano, Juan Carlos. De la literatura argentina, siglo XX (Panorama, 2:7, 1953, p. 53-67).
Reprint of a résumé of contemporary Argentine literature, originally published in *Revista de Guatemala* in 1952.

4733. Girondo, Oliverio. En la masmédula. B. A., Losada, 1954. 45 p.
Sophisticated game of creating new words and

new phonetic combinations, ostensibly by an imitator of Ramón Gómez de la Serna and Jean Cocteau.

4734. Giusti, Roberto F. Momentos y aspectos de la cultura argentina. B. A., Raigal (Problemas de la cultura en América, 2), 1954. 126 p.
Endeavors to show the highlights in the cultural development of Argentina. Rather superficial.

4735. Gómez Carrillo, Enrique. Páginas escogidas. T. 1. Evocación de Guatemala. Crítica. T. 2. Impresiones de viaje. T. 3. Cuentos, crónicas, poemas en prosa. Selección y prólogo por Edelberto Torres. Guatemala, Ministerio de Educación Pública (Biblioteca de cultura popular, 46-48), 1954. xxx, 372 p.
Selected critiques and short stories culled from the 27-volume legacy of Guatemala's great writer (1873-1927).

4736. Henríquez Ureña, Max. Breve historia del modernismo. México, Fondo de Cultura Económica, 1954. 544 p. & pls.
Although called "breve" this is a sprawling history of the *modernista* movement with very little that is new or stimulating. "El modernismo en España," p. 501-522.

4737. Jaimes Freyre, Raúl. Anecdotario de Ricardo Jaimes Freyre. Potosí, Bolivia, Ed. Potosí (Col. de la cultura boliviana, Colección tercera, Los escritores modernos, no. 1, v. 2), 1953. 168 p., pl.
Sidelights on the life of Bolivia's greatest poet, Ricardo Jaimes Freyre (1868-1933), by his brother, also a poet.

4738. José Gil Fortoul y Pedro-Emilio Coll. Caracas, Academia Nacional de la Historia, 1953. 24 p.
Two speeches, one by Jesús Antonio Cova on Gil Fortoul and the other by Santiago Key-Ayala on Coll, on the occasion of the unveiling of their pictures at the National Academy of History.

4739. Lazo, Raimundo. La personalidad, la creación y el mensaje de Alfonso Reyes. Habana, 1955. 24 p.
Eulogy of Alfonso Reyes before the Academia Cubana de la Lengua.

4740. Lillo, Samuel A. Literatura chilena. 7. ed. Santiago, Nascimento, 1952. 304 p.
Originally published in 1918, this is a classic survey of Chilean literature from Ercilla to Huidobro.

4741. Liscano, Juan. Caminos de la prosa. Comentarios. Caracas, Ediciones El pensamiento vivo, 1953. 126 p., illus.
Notes on the development of Venezuelan prose writing from Pocaterra to Arráiz.

4742. López Velarde, Ramón. Prosa política. Prólogo y recopilación de Elena Molina Ortega. México, Imp. Universitaria, 1953. 335 p.
Trivia by a much admired Mexican poet.

4743. Loprete, Carlos Alberto. La literatura modernista en la Argentina. B. A., Poseidón (Biblioteca de estudios breves), 1955. 126 p.
Brief survey of the *modernista* movement in Argentina: its journals, its polemics, its precursors (especially Carlos Guido y Spano), its cultivators and its lyrical fruition in the work of Larreta and Lugones.

4744. Mallea, Eduardo. Notas de un novelista. B. A., Emecé (Cuadernos de ensayos), 1954. 141 p.
In addition to the sundry essays on some of his favorite writers, his "Introducción al mundo de la novela" and his diary while writing *Los enemigos del alma* are revealing and of considerable interest.

4745. Marechal, Leopoldo, and Elbia R. de Marechal. Antología didáctica de la prosa argentina. B. A., Kapelusz, 1954. 656 p.
Excerpts showing the development of Argentine prose from the Colonial period to the work of Ricardo Güiraldes.

4746. Maria y Campos, Armando. Imagen del mexicano en los toros. México, Editorial Al Sonar el Clarín, 1953. 268 p.
A Mexican "Death in the afternoon" detailing the art of bullfighting from 1796 to the death of Camelio Pérez in 1931.

4747. Mariátegui, José Carlos. La novela y la vida. Siegfried y el Profesor Canella. Nota preliminar de Alberto Tauro. Portada de José Sabogal. Lima, Biblioteca Amauta, 1955.
On the occasion of the 25th anniversary of Mariátegui's death, his admirers publish this variation on the Siegfried theme, as sophisticated as Giraudoux's *Siegfried et le limousin*.

4748. Martí, José. Sección constante. Historia, letras, biografía, curiosidades y ciencia. Artículos aparecidos en *La opinión nacional* de Caracas, desde el 4 de noviembre de 1881 al 15 de junio de 1882. Compilación y prólogo de Pedro Grases. Caracas, 1955. 451 p.
"Sección constante" was the title of a column contributed by Martí in 1881-1882 to a Caracas newspaper; the articles deal with the most varied topics of interest, especially oddities and strange happenings.

4749. Martínez, José Luis. Problemas literarios. México, Panamericana (Colección literaria Obregón, 3), 1955. 228 p.
Compilation of book reviews and articles on Mexico's cultural problems.

4750. Martínez Cuitiño, Vicente. El café de los inmortales. B. A., Kraft (Col. Vértice), 1954. 401 p.
Reminiscences about the artistic life in the B. A. cafe "Los Inmortales" which was patronized by Darío, Quiroga, Viana, Florencio Sánchez, Gerchunoff, Ingenieros, and a host of other writers, playwrights, actors, painters, and musicians.

4751. Masferrer, Alberto. Páginas escogidas. Selección de José Luis Martínez. San Salvador, Ministerio de Cultura, Dirección General de Bellas Artes, 1953. 309 p.
The Mexican critic José Luis Martínez has chosen some of Masferrer's finest pages which reflect his struggles in uplifting the cultural level of his native El Salvador.

4752. Maya, Rafael. Estampas de ayer y retratos de hoy. Bogotá, Ministerio de Educación Nacional (Biblioteca de autores colombianos, 80), 1954. 450 p.
Lyrical rather than critical essays on Spanish American writers, past and present, with special emphasis on Colombian literary figures.

4753. Miranda Ruano, Francisco. Las voces del terruño. San Salvador, Ministerio de Cultura, Departamento Editorial (Biblioteca popular, 2), 1955. 155 p.
Posthumous work of a Salvadorean writer who deeply loved his native country and evokes in this volume its countryside, its people and customs, its fauna and flora.

4754. Miró, César. Don Ricardo Palma. El patriarca de las tradiciones. B. A., Losada, 1953. 206 p.
Eminently readable biography of Peru's greatest writer.

4755. Montello, Josué. Ricardo Palma, clássico da América. Rio, Gráfica Olímpica, 1954. 120 p.
A Brazilian teacher compares his fellow countryman Machado de Assis with Peru's Don Ricardo.

4756. Montes, Hugo, and Julio Orlandi. Historia de la literatura chilena. Santiago, Editorial del Pacífico, 1955. 338 p.
A textbook of uneven merit; repertorial, anecdotical.

4757. Nervo, Amado. Semblanzas y crítica literaria. México, Imp. Universitaria, 1952. 195 p.
Reminiscences of Mexico's literary life in the 1890's. The critical aspect of this volume is the least important.

4758. Núñez, Estuardo. Autores germanos en el Perú. Florilegio de la poesía alemana en versiones peruanas. Lima, Ministerio de Educación Pública, 1953. 192 p.

The impact of the *Sturm und Drang* and German romanticism on Peruvian writing; the translations of Palma, Prado, and More.

4759. Owen, Gilberto. Poesía y prosa. México, Imp. Universitaria, 1953. 259 p.
Exciting compilation of prose and verse by the prematurely dead Gilberto Owen (1905-1952).

4760. Piedra-Bueno, Andrés de. La Virgen María en la literatura cubana. Edición del *Boletín de las provincias eclesiásticas de Cuba*. Habana, Albino Rodríguez, 1955. 58 p.
The recurrence of the Immaculate Conception in Cuban literature; this brochure was awarded a prize in the Concurso Mariano held in 1955.

4761. Portuondo, José Antonio. José Martí, crítico literario. Washington, Unión Panamericana (Pensamiento de América), 1953. 112 p.
A perceptive study of the backgrounds and trends of Martí's literary criticism.

4762. Prisco C., R. Di. (comp.). Autores barquisimetanos. T. 1. Acosta Ortiz— Garmendia. Caracas, Vargas (Biblioteca de cultura larense, 11), 1953. 536 p.
Anthology containing verse and prose by writers born in Barquisimeto. Of the 26 included in this first volume, Antonio Arráiz and Julio Garmendia are perhaps the ones best known.

4763. Rabasa, Emilio. La guerra de tres años. Seguido de poemas inéditos y desconocidos. Edición y prólogo de Emmanuel Carballo. México, Ediciones Libro-Max (Biblioteca mínima mexicana, 12), 1955. 103 p.
Reprint of a little classic originally published in 1891, with 30 poems hitherto unpublished combining a light vein with a Becquerian tragic sense; excellent introduction.

4764. Ramos, Jorge Abelardo. Crisis y resurrección de la literatura argentina. B. A., Editorial Indoamérica, 1954. 82 p.
A proletarian attack on Borges and Martínez Estrada.

4765. Reyes, Alfonso. Memorias de cocina y bodega. México, Tezontle, 1953. 174 p.
Reyes, the literary virtuoso, meets Reyes, the gourmet.

4766. ———. Quince presencias, 1915-1954. México, Panamericana (Colección literaria Obregón, 2), 1955. 190 p.
15 articles on travel and myth making.

4767. Ríos Patrón, José Luis. Jorge Luis Borges. B.A., La Mandrágora, 1955. 179 p.
Brilliant study of Argentina's greatest contemporary writer; chapters devoted to his style, his thought, his verse, fiction, and critical work, followed by extensive bibliography.

HANDBOOK OF LATIN AMERICAN STUDIES

4768. Rodríguez Demorizi, Emilio. Martí y la patria de Darío. Apuntes. Managua, Editorial San José, 1953. 34 p.

Martí's rapprochement with Darío and Nicaragua.

4769. Rojas Paz, Pablo. El canto de la llanura. Meditaciones pampeanas. B. A., Nova, 1955. 185 p.

The pampas as mirrored in Argentine literature, especially in the work of Echeverría, Sarmiento, Hudson, Hernández, and Güiraldes.

4770. Sánchez, Luis Alberto (comp.). Repertorio bibliográfico de la literatura latino-americana. Fasciculo 1 del tomo 1. Santiago, Universidad de Chile, 1955. 124 p.

Brochure no. 1 in a bibliographical series which eventually will cover all of Latin America's literature; however, the beginning is dreadful —it is incomplete and includes irrelevant materials, such as textbooks used in the U. S. for the study of the Spanish language. Misspellings galore.

4771. Sanín Cano, Baldomero. El humanismo y el progreso del hombre. B. A., Losada, 1955. 260 p.

The 96-year-old Colombian humanist casts his expert eye over wide areas, showing the vicissitudes of our age and lingering over some of its important writers, from Chesterton to Isherwood.

4772. Sarmiento, Domingo Faustino. Recuerdos de provincia. Selección, prólogo y notas de Fermín Estrella Gutiérrez. B. A., Kapelusz, 1953. xvi, 110 p.

Nothing unique in this new edition of an old classic.

4773. Stolk, Gloria. Apuntes de crítica literaria. Caracas, Edime (Autores venezolanos, 37), 1955? 259 p.

Although circumstantial, these jottings frequently shed light on Venezuelan contemporary literature.

4774. Stroup, Thomas B., and Sterling A. Stoudemire (eds.). South Atlantic studies for Sturgis E. Leavitt. Washington, Scarecrow Press, 1953. 215 p.

Of the 17 contributions in this homage to Professor Leavitt upon his retirement from the editorship of the *South Atlantic bulletin,* five have to do with Latin America: P. T. Manchester on *La Araucana* (see item 4679); L. D. Canfield on the pronunciation of Spanish in America (see item 4515); Lawrence S. Thompson on resources for research in Latin American literature in U. S. Southern libraries (p. 97-108); John A. Crow on some aspects of Spanish American fiction (p. 109-125); and John E. Englekirk on Mariano Azuela (p. 127-135). Crow especially says some very new things about Spanish American fiction.

4775. Suárez, Marco Fidel. Escritos escogidos. Medellín, Colombia, Imp. Departamental de Antioquia, 1954. 321 p.

To commemorate the 100th anniversary of his birth.

4776. Subercaseaux, Benjamín. Santa materia. Ensayos y lecciones de visión y tacto. Santiago, Zig-Zag (Col. Ensayos), 1954. 420 p.

Poematic approaches to sex, the black arts, and death.

4777. Tamayo, Marcial, and Adolfo Ruiz-Díaz. Borges, enigma y clave. B. A., Editorial Nuestro Tiempo, 1955. 170 p.

Biographical study with careful consideration of Borges' handling of time and memory, and his stylistic peculiarities.

4778. Tiempo, César. Protagonistas. B. A., Kraft (Col. Cúpula), 1954. 304 p.

35 sketches and critiques of outstanding personalities in the arts and letters; among the Spanish Americans treated: Isaacs, Martí, Quiroga, Gerchunoff, and Gabriela Mistral.

4779. Tinker, Edward Larocque. The horsemen of the Americas and the literature they inspired. N. Y., Hastings House (Book of the Americas, 1), 1953. 149 p., illus.

Life and saga of Gauchos, *charros,* and cowboys, and the literature reflecting their epos and ethos.

4780. Torrealba Lossi, Mario. Anotaciones literarias venezolanas. Misceláneas. Caracas, Tip. Garrido, 1954. 78 p.

Jottings on Bello, Teresa de la Parra, Gallegos, and other Venezuelan writers.

4781. Torres Bodet, Jaime. Tiempo de arena. México, Fondo de Cultura Económica (Letras mexicanas, 18), 1955. 349 p.

Autobiographical notes by Mexico's most distinguished poet: his literary beginnings and influences, travels, friendships, and all the stimulating factors responsible for his literary production.

4782. Torres Ríoseco, Arturo. Ensayos sobre literatura latinoamericana. Berkeley, Calif., University of California Press, 1953. 207 p.

16 essays on diverse aspects of Latin American literature: the indigenous theatre, humor, *Don Segundo Sombra,* the poetry of Chocano and Villaurrutia.

4783. Uslar Pietri, Arturo. Las nubes. Prólogo de Mariano Picón Salas. Caracas, Ministerio de Educación, Dirección de Cultura y Bellas Artes (Biblioteca popular venezolana, 43), 1951. 239 p.

Fugitive essays on Venezuelan culture and world writers; interesting but often banal and conceited.

254

4784. Valencia, Guillermo. Oraciones panegíricas. Bogotá, Editorial ABC (Biblioteca de autores colombianos), 1952. 284 p.
20 eulogies of Bolívar, Julio Arboleda, Isaacs, and other leading figures.

4785. Vargas, Moisés. La diversión de las familias. Lances de noche buena. Prólogo y notas de Juan Uribe-Echeverría. Santiago, Universidad de Chile, Instituto de Investigaciones Histórico-Culturales (Col. de libros raros o curiosos de la literatura chilena, 1), 1954. 306 p., illus.
Originally published in 1865, it depicts Chilean life and manners during the middle of the 19th century.

4786. Vela, Arqueles. Fundamentos de la literatura mexicana. México, Editorial Patria (Col. Cultura para todos, 26), 1953. 120 p.
Synoptical analysis of Mexican literature, teeming with erratic generalizations and conclusions.

4787. Zum Felde, Alberto. Índice crítico de la literatura hispanoamericana. Los ensayistas. México, Guarania, 1954. 606 p.
Ambitious attempt at a critical index of Latin American literature; in this volume the author is focused on the essay.

PROSE FICTION

E. NEALE-SILVA

EN la novela y el cuento de años recientes se observa gran interés por el análisis psicológico, especialmente en la Argentina, en donde sigue marcando una ruta Eduardo Mallea, con dos libros recientes: *Chaves* y *La sala de espera*. En el mismo campo se destacan también cuatro novelistas, dos hombres y dos mujeres: Manuel Mujica Laínez, que nos ha dado *Los ídolos* y *Los viajeros;* Max Dickman, cuya novela *Los habitantes de la noche* está entre lo mejor de su producción; Estela Canto, autora de un excelente estudio de la demencia *(El hombre del crepúsculo)* y Silvina Bullrich, a quien se recordará por el bello volumen *Bodas de cristal,* publicado por primera vez en 1951 y reeditado en 1953. Entre los cuentistas merecen especial mención: Nicolás Olivari *(La noche es nuestra)* y Velmiro Ayala Gauna, autor de dos colecciones de cuentos correntinos.

Fuera de la Argentina, el cuento sobre la intimidad humana ha sido cultivado extensamente, interesados como están los hombres de letras por comprender el alma del hombre y de los pueblos. Son especialmente significativas cinco colecciones: *Luto eterno y otros relatos* del ecuatoriano Pedro Jorge Vera; *El polvo y el tiempo* de Víctor Molina Neira, autor justamente premiado en Chile; *Los demás,* de Luis A. Heiremans; *El girasol enfermo,* de Surama Ferrer, cuyas magníficas narraciones la ponen entre las maestras del género, y *El reino azul,* del escritor mexicano José Martínez Sotomayor.

El tema existencialista, que ha interesado a tantos intelectuales, aparece en la novela ya como asunto mismo de la obra o como parte de una discusión filosófica; hasta ahora, sin embargo, no ha aparecido una novela existencialista definitiva, con excepción de aquellas en que el caudal ideológico es sólo intención y no tema propiamente tal.

Entre los autores interesados en recrear una época o en comparar el pasado con el presente, hay dos que sobresalen: Mariano Picón Salas, autor de la finísima y sugerente novela *Los tratos de la noche,* y Ernesto L. Castro, quien nos dió en 1953 la excelente novela *Campo arado.* Como novelización de hechos históricos se singulariza también el volumen *Cuando los guayacanes florecían* de Nelson Estupiñán Bass.

Es también abundante la producción realista, especialmente la dedicada a pintar los barrios bajos, ya sea como simple visión pormenorizada *(Con el pan bajo el brazo,* de Orlando D'Aniello y *La cruz nuestra de cada día,* de Roberto Mariani) o como "aguafuerte" de tipo angurrientista. En esta última categoría está *El mundo herido,* de Armando Méndez Carrasco, la novela más fuerte y conmovedora de 1955, aunque no la más agradable.

En el polo opuesto están dos tipos de novela contemporánea que se acusan cada vez con más fuerte relieve: la novela de realismo onírico en que se superponen esotéricas concepciones y se hace gala de audacia verbal *(El derrumbamiento,* de Armonía Somers) y la novela de la vida subconsciente, en la cual se ve la realidad a través de ensueños, visiones y recuerdos o dentro de atmósferas imprecisas cargadas de subjetivismo. De este tipo son *El falso cuaderno de Narciso Espejo,* del venezolano Guillermo Meneses, *Juan Páramo*, del mexicano Juan Rulfo y *Ausencias*, de Carlos Valdés.

El tema indio, que tanto ha obsesionado a algunos novelistas en época reciente, empieza a decaer, excepto en Bolivia, nación que entra en la vida moderna con gran empuje desde los días de la revolución minera. De hondo patetismo son la minuciosa novela *Yanakuna*, de Jesús Lara, en la cual se estudia la vida serrana, y dos novelas sobre el indio minero: *Socavones de angustia*, de Fernando Ramírez Velarde y *Mina*, novela póstuma, de Alfredo Guillén Pinto y Natty Peñaranda de Guillén Pinto.

Hay, por último, una que otra novela de intriga que podría compararse con las mejores *mystery stories* de la literatura norteamericana. En este grupo está *Los tallos amargos*, de Adolfo Jasca.

En el campo de la crítica, la obra de mayor amplitud es el extenso y prolijo *Proceso y contenido de la novela hispanoamericana*, de Luis Alberto Sánchez, que es sin duda un esfuerzo totalizador digno de encomio.

NOVELS AND SHORT STORIES

4850. Alayza y Paz Soldán, Luis. La capa roja. Novela peruana de los tiempos del General Salaverry. Lima, Imp. Santa María, 1953. 235 p.

Mezcla de historia y ficción en que se reconstruyen los años que siguieron a la independencia. Pasan ante los ojos del lector, con mayor o menor nitidez, las figuras de Gamarra, su mujer, Orbegoso, Santa Cruz y Salaverry. Termina la obra con el fusilamiento de este último. La trama amorosa es sólo una excusa para reconstruir la historia.

4851. ————. La higuera de Pizarro. Novela peruana de los últimos días del guano y del salitre. Lima, Imp. Santa María, 1953. 259 p.

Otra novela de la pluma de un historiador en que se da vida al pasado peruano. En esta edición reformada se cambiaron las primeras 80 páginas del original y se acortó el epílogo. Véase el párrafo anterior.

4852. Alvarado, José. El personaje. México, Los Presentes (16), 1955. 76 p.

Un hombre cualquiera—"el personaje" de esta novela corta—deambula por una pequeña ciudad muerta rodeado de visiones y recuerdos. Con este maridaje de vida real y fantasía crea el autor un ambiente de alucinación y subjetividad.

4853. Ambrogi, Arturo. El libro del trópico. San Salvador, Ministerio de Cultura, Departamento Editorial, 1955. 369 p.

Contiene este libro (publicado por primera vez en 1910) 44 cuadros de la vida campesina y pueblerina de El Salvador: detallismo, incursión en el alma de las cosas, vibración lírica. Algunos cuadros son magníficos porque en ellos se encierra una profunda emoción terrígena mezclada con rasgos a veces irónicos, humorísticos o dramáticos.

4854. Argentino Golz, Adolfo. El hombre incompleto y otros cuentos. Prólogo de Rafael Rovira Vilella. Paraná, Argentina, Prensa (Col. Letras, 2), 1954. 104 p.

Narraciones varias acerca de la vida en sociedad. En casi todas ellas predomina el interés por la aventura y el desenlace inesperado, llegándose a veces a la peripecia "hollywoodesca," como, por ejemplo, en el penúltimo cuento, "Princesa azul." El autor tiene verdaderas aptitudes narrativas, pero no maneja siempre la lengua con soltura y propiedad.

4855. Asla Moreno, Raquel de. El alféizar. B. A., Tall. Gráf. Optimus, 1953. 126 p.

Estudio psicológico de un hombre "raro," intelectualista y abúlico, que se deja llevar del remolino de la vida sin alcanzar lo que desea —el amor de la mujer admirada. Escenas inconexas, motivaciones poco plausibles.

4856. Ayala Gauna, Velmiro. Otros cuentos correntinos. Santa Fe, Argentina, Castellví, 1953. 178 p.

Segunda serie de cuentos (véase *HLAS, no. 18, 1952*, item 2510) sobre el hombre de Corrientes "con su mansedumbre estoica, con el peso de las supersticiones, con su ignorancia, con su resignado patetismo, con sus lacras y sus virtudes." Narraciones de gran dramatismo algunas, y de honda emoción otras. El autor es digno discípulo de Horacio Quiroga y conoce muy bien los recursos del género.

4857. Ayora, Augusto Mario. Escamas de culebra y otros cuentos. Guayaquil, Ecuador, Concejo Cantonal, 1953. 154 p., illus.

Diez narraciones de un joven escritor ecuatoriano. En todas ellas prima el interés por el hombre y la tierra, pero sin insistir especialmente en las influencias de ésta sobre aquél. El autor sabe crear interés fijando la atención en los hechos extraordinarios, misteriosos o macabros. Lengua natural y de gran fuerza, pero algo descuidada. Algunas narraciones no están bien rematadas.

4858. Azuela, Mariano. La maldición. México, Fondo de Cultura Económica (Letras mexicanas, 21), 1955. 227 p.

Novela en cuatro partes, de las cuales la tercera bien pudo fundirse con la última. Más que el estudio de personajes al autor le interesa destacar el ambiente de corrupción que hace posible el ascenso de ignaros y arribistas. Se sirve para ello de la familia de Rodulfo, vilmente sacrificada a las ambiciones de éste. Por fortuna, los fines didácticos del novelista son menos obvios aquí que en otros libros suyos posteriores a 1940.

859. **Baliñas, Ricardo.** El perro desollado y otros relatos. Montevideo, Salamanca, 1955. 108 p.
●cho cuentos sobre temas variadísimos, pero nificados por su realismo. Interesado en egar a la brevedad máxima, recurre el autor a ● superposición de diferentes planos de acción, estruyendo algunas veces la efectividad dramá-ca del relato. Véanse, como ejemplos, los ●entos *El maneador* y *Los zapatos lustrados*. .l mejor de todos es el titulado *Los cuervos,* ● que se describe la tortura de seis prisioneros ● guerra.

860. **Beltrán, Germán.** El diablo sube el telón. Bogotá, Espiral, 1955. 213 p.
●fancia, adolescencia y juventud de un mu-●acho, hijo de familia bogotana venida a ●enos. En su primera parte, este libro pro-●ete ser una excelente novela porque presenta ● cuadro convincente de la vida y de la ●aturaleza humana. Se transforma después en ●ovela picaresca y el personaje central, Ernesto ●añola, pasa de un ambiente a otro, sin trayec-●ria fija, impelido por su espíritu aventurero, ●sconformidad e imperativo sexual. Las escenas ● personajes se repiten, la acción pierde en ●erisimilitud y por fin decae el interés de la ●ama. Todo esto es lamentable por ser evi-●entes, en otros respectos, las dotes literarias ● el autor.

861. **Berti, José.** Oro y orquídeas. Caracas, Fragua, 1955. 306 p.
●ida de un buscador de oro en el corazón de ● selva venezolana; a través de sus aventuras ● intenta captar el alma de la tierra y el ●spíritu apasionado y tumultuoso del hombre ●el interior. Hay en este libro vigorosos cuadros ●letóricos de sol y de verdor y también escenas ● violencia y primitivismo. Algunos pasajes ●ecan por falta de intensidad y otros por ●xceso de adjetivación.

862. **Booz, Mateo.** Tres lagunas. Santa Fe, Argentina, Castellví, 1953. 194 p.
●dición póstuma de 16 relatos; prólogo enco-●iástico de Horacio Caillet-Bois. Cada relato ● compone de varias escenas costumbristas. ●ás importante que la trama misma es la ●inucia de la vida provinciana, observada con ●jos comprensivos y con espíritu regocijado.

863. **Borges, Jorge Luis.** Historia universal de la infamia. B. A., Emecé (Obras completas de Jorge Luis Borges, 3), 1954. 137 p.
●ueva edición de un libro publicado por ●rimera vez en 1935. Contiene tres piezas ●uevas al final.

864. **Borges, Jorge Luis, and Levinson, Luisa Mercedes.** La hermana de Eloísa. B. A., Ene, 1955. 71 p.
●inco cuentos: dos escritos por Borges, otros ●os por Luisa Mercedes Levinson y uno escrito ●n colaboración. El mejor de todos es "El ●bra," de Levinson, intensísimo relato de amor ● odio. El último cuento, que da título a la ●olección, aun siendo obra de ambos autores, ●eja la impresión de haber quedado inconcluso.

4865. **Boschetti, Luis R.** El amor oculta el corazón. Santa Fe, Argentina, Castellví, 1953. 228 p.
Mediocre relato con injertos de historia local del Entre Ríos de 1850 y una trama amorosa de poco interés.

4866. **Bosco, María Angélica.** La muerte baja en el ascensor. B. A., Emecé (El séptimo círculo, 123), 1955. 155 p.
Novela policíaca con todas las características del Entre Ríos de 1850 y una trama amorosa máticos, coincidencias, interrogatorios, recapitulaciones, etc. Obvia imitación de modelos norteamericanos.

4867. **Bullrich, Silvina.** Bodas de cristal. B. A., Editorial Sudamericana, 1953. 183 p.
Finísimo estudio psicológico de un hombre perseguido por la pasión y el vértigo de la vida moderna. Enlázanse en la vida de éste los dilemas de cuatro mujeres—tres admiradoras y la esposa. Esta última es quien hace el balance de 15 años de vida matrimonial. Libro cargado de adivinaciones y sutilezas, extremadamente interesante por presentar una visión femenina del hombre contemporáneo.

4868. **Canto, Estela.** El hombre del crepúsculo. B. A., Editorial Sudamericana, 1953. 141 p.
Historia de amor, odio, locura y muerte. El atormentado Evaristo Lérida intenta guiar los pasos de una joven enamorada sin distinguir entre la verdad y el error, el bien y el mal, llevándola por fin a la desesperación y a la muerte. Magnífico estudio psicológico. En él contrastan las rarezas de Lérida con el prosaico "equilibrio" de los que le rodean.

4869. **Canto, Rosa.** Renunciación. B. A., Editoriales Reunidas, 1954. 164 p.
Novela amorosa de poco interés por la trivialidad del tema—"amor de angustia, de dolor y de celos desesperados"—y por el ambiente de romanticismo pueril en que se agitan los protagonistas.

4870. **Carleton de Millán, Verna.** La mujer que quiso ser infiel. José Nicolás. Evocación a Felisa. Cuentos. México, Porrúa, 1955? 69 p.
Tres cuentos de una escritora norteamericana que conoce el alma y manera de ser de México y que escribe en español y en inglés. En el primero hay un estudio de la vida matrimonial moderna y sus problemas; el segundo se destaca por su brevedad y finura; el tercero, que es el mejor de todos, es notable por su delicadeza, penetración psicológica y honda vibración dramática. Estos relatos merecían una edición más esmerada.

4871. **Carpena, Elías.** Enrique Dávinson. El inglés del bañado. B. A., Guatraché (Col. Novelistas argentinos actuales), 1953. 279 p.
Novela de aventuras y espeluznantes acontecimientos entre criminales y ladrones de los barrios bajos. Lo único que le interesa al autor

es la aventura por la aventura, aunque sea a expensas de la verisimilitud y los requisitos formales del relato.

4872. Castro, Ernesto L. Campo arado. B. A., Losada, 1953. 246 p.
Magnífico estudio de la transformación de la pampa argentina en el curso de tres generaciones. Se contrasta aquí el espíritu libérrimo del gaucho de antaño (personificado en Ceferino) con el amor a la gleba, al "campo arado" (personificado en Pancho, el personaje principal). Méritos especiales de este libro son su proyección en el tiempo, la variedad de personajes secundarios (algunos de los cuales son excelentes), la honda comprensión del espíritu terrígena y el interés dramático de la acción. Culmina el relato en una escena inolvidable en que se enfrentan la terquedad del campesino y el espíritu libertario de la nueva generación. Es éste un libro de primer orden.

4873. Cerretani, Arturo. Confesión apócrifa. B. A., Kraft (Col. Cúpula), 1955. 249 p.
Incidentes de la infancia y la niñez vistos a través del recuerdo e integrados en un relato carente de relieve y de poco interés.

4874. Chamico [i.e., Conrado Nalé Roxlo]. Libro de quejas. B. A., Orientación Cultural, 1953. 123 p.
Nueva serie de relatos humorísticos por el conocido poeta y comediógrafo argentino.

4875. Chaves, Fernando. Plata y bronce. La embrujada. Quito, Casa de la Cultura Ecuatoriana, 1954. 351 p.
Nueva edición de una novela premiada en 1927 por la revista *América*. En realidad no es ésta una obra notable, por su falsa retórica y manifiesta intención didáctica. Lo mejor en ella son los cuadros de costumbres y el estudio de la vida india. Los pasajes ensayísticos en que vierte el autor sus teorías sociales son particularmente chocantes, aun cuando encierran verdades innegables. Este libro fué más una promesa que una realización. En esta edición se ha añadido "La embrujada," novela corta sobre la venganza de un indio supersticioso y sádico.

4876. Chávez Guerrero, Herminio. Surianos. Grabados de Leopoldo Méndez. México, 1953. 192 p., illus.
Novela folklórica y de aventuras compuesta de numerosos incidentes en ventas, ferias y polvorientos caminos. Organización muy floja, estilo inseguro. Lo mejor del libro son las descripciones de algunos paisajes. Más que novela es éste un extenso relato costumbrista.

4877. D'Aniello, Orlando. Con el pan bajo el brazo. B. A., Unión de Editores Latinos, 1955. 242 p.
Visión caleidoscópica de los barrios bajos: diversiones, trabajo diario, alegrías, obscuras tragedias. Algunas escenas son conmovedoras en su sencillez y hondura; otras, en cambio, adolecen de excesivo verismo.

4878. Delgado, Rafael. Cuentos y notas.

Prólogo de Francisco Sosa. Notas de Pedro Caffarel Peralta. México, Porrúa 1953. xliii, 360 p.
Nueva edición del texto de Agüeros, al cual se han añadido tres relatos publicados en 1942 por Francisco Monterde.

4879. Diego, Celia. Bosquejo bárbaro. B A., Ene, 1955. 150 p.
Encierra este libro dos tipos de narraciones: unas en que predomina el sondeo anímico y el prurito intelectualista, y otras más humanas y sencillas en que la vida se impone por sobre el elemento discursivo. Sólo estas últimas tienen verdadero calor humano. En casi todo el volumen hay, además, un intento, a veces artificial o innecesario, de relacionar la vida de los insectos con las acciones humanas.

4880. 16 cuentos argentinos. Selección, prólogo y notas por Mignon Domínguez. B. A., Lajouane (Col. de folklore argentino, 6), 1955. 194 p.
Esta colección fué preparada teniendo presentes los méritos de los cuentos mismos y su valor como exponentes del folklore de distintas regiones argentinas. Trabajo serio, hecho con tino y buen gusto. Cada selección va acompañada de un comentario explicativo y de un breve ensayo bío-bibliográfico. A algunos de los cuentos se les ha añadido, además, un glosario.

4881. Dobles, Fabián. Historias de Tata Mundo. San José, Trejos, 1955. 110 p.
Narraciones costumbristas escritas sin otro fin que comunicar al lector algo de la gracia y sabiduría populares de Costa Rica.

4882. Domínguez, María Alicia. Vida de una calle. B. A., Acanto, 1954. 282 p.
Historia de un muchacho sentimental que se sobrepone a sus dificultades de familia y triunfa al fin con la ayuda de un bondadoso protector. Son notables las páginas en que se relata la infancia de Alfonso Miranda y la vida interior de éste. Hacen desmerecer al relato el empleo de lo fortuito y la falta de tonalidades en el diseño de algunos caracteres.

4883. Espinosa, Miguel A. Bastardo. Habana, Selecta, 1955. 208 p.
Novela archirromántica sobre unos amores imposibles que a la postre terminan bien, a pesar de las dificultades que acumula el autor para hacerlos más interesantes. Técnica elemental; tema de escasa novedad.

4884. Estupiñán Bass, Nelson. Cuando los guayacanes florecían. Quito, Casa de la Cultura Ecuatoriana, 1954. 307 p.
La rebelión de los montuvios en los días que siguieron a la muerte de Alfaro. La trama la componen los incidentes de la rebelión misma y las miserias de los "conciertos." Historia intensa y dolorosa, cuyos personajes son víctimas del terrateniente poderoso y también de su propia naturaleza selvática. En medio de la bestialidad y violencia del conjunto humano aquí estudiado, logra el autor destacar algunas virtudes del pueblo bajo—sentido de justicia, distinción entre el bien y el mal, compasión etc. Al final del relato se incluye un mensaje

umanitario en pro de los oprimidos. Este ibro debe colocarse entre las mejores obras del grupo de Guayaquil.

4885. Feldman, Jacobo. Relato de una fuga. B. A., América-Sapucai (Novelas americanas), 1955. 151 p.

Homicidio, fuga y encarcelamiento de un hombre. He aquí los tres hechos primordiales que le sirven al autor para hacer un sondeo de una alma agitada por el remordimiento y as pasiones. Libro sugerente, rico en meditaciones y hallazgos psicológicos.

4886. Ferrer, Surama. El girasol enfermo. Cuentos. Habana, Impresora Mundial, 1953. 147 p.

Magníficas narraciones sobre muy variados temas: amores encontrados, odios, violencias, celos, afectos entrañables, supremos sacrificios, etc., todo visto dentro de ambientes de alta tensión, algunos de los cuales llegan a los bordes de lo macabro. Extraordinaria penetración en los móviles humanos y mano segura para captar las notas fundamentales del escenario. Imágenes certeras, economía de medios, diálogo rápido y natural.

4887. Francheri López, Eduardo. Nueve extraños relatos. Santa Fe, Argentina, Castellví, 1953. 202 p.

Tres tipos de narraciones: cuentos de agonía y muerte, con voces de ultratumba y aparecidos, relatos sobre fenómenos naturales extraordinarios y cuentos sobre hombres y cosas de la tierra. Los mejores son los del último tipo; los demás son de valor muy relativo.

4888. Fuentes, Carlos. Los días enmascarados. México, Los Presentes, 1954. 97 p.

Seis fantasías que recuerdan el realismo mágico de Jorge Luis Borges y los malabarismos intelectuales de la literatura vanguardista, todo aplicado a las más peregrinas concepciones —el retorno de un dios prehispánico, visiones de ultratumba y mil aventuras en mundos imaginarios.

4889. Gálvez, Manuel. Las dos vidas del pobre Napoleón. B. A., Losada, 1954. 147 p.

Un hombre real en busca de un personaje. . . . Napoleón Machuca, al verse retratado en la figura de Alejandro Magno Pacheco delineada por un novelista, amigo suyo, siente la imperiosa necesidad de ser como su "otro yo" y, después de no pocas peripecias, va a parar en un sanatorio. Novela de asunto ligero que trae a la memoria la figura de Davis en *El socio,* de Jenaro Prieto.

4890. ————. Miércoles santo. B. A., Emecé (Novelistas argentinos contemporáneos), 1953. 147 p.

Nueva edición de la discutida novela sobre la vida pecaminosa del hombre, publicada por primera vez en 1930 y traducida al inglés en 1934.

4891. ————. El uno y la multitud. B. A., Alpe (Poema y prosa de América), 1955. 316 p.

La realidad político-social de la Argentina entre los años 1942 y 1947: efectos de la guerra europea, conflictos ideológicos, reajustes sociales, vuelcos políticos, etc. Dentro de este ambiente coloca el autor a varios grupos humanos de diferentes procedencias y variada categoría social, los cuales le sirven para exponer ideas, dejando especialmente en claro el conflicto entre el individuo y las masas. A pesar de que predomina el material ideológico, las mejores páginas están entre las que Gálvez dedica a la peripecia humana.

4892. ————. Y así cayó don Juan Manuel . . . (1850-1852). B. A., Espasa-Calpe (Col. Austral, 1205), 1954. 289 p.

Novela sobre los últimos años del período rosista; mezcla de historia y ficción, tal como en la trilogía sobre la guerra del Paraguay.

4893. Gambaro, Griselda. Cuentos. B. A., Américalee, 1953. Unpaged, illus.

Sencillos cuentos sobre la vida de todos los días en que se presentan las ironías del destino humano. Algunos apenas son breves escenas sobre acontecimientos minúsculos.

4894. González Martínez, Enrique. Cuentos y otras páginas. Prólogo y selección de Ana María Sánchez. México, Libro-Mex (Biblioteca mínima mexicana, 19), 1955. 126 p.

Contiene dos bellos cuentos ("Una hembra" y "La chiquilla"), varios pasajes tomados de *El hombre del buho* y una conferencia, "Problemas mexicanos," dictada por el poeta ante la Sociedad Económica Matritense de Amigos del País.

4895. Gramonte, Marcos. Cuando al demonio le toca perder. Santa Fe, Argentina, Dina, 1955. 227 p.

Tema: la fidelidad conyugal ante los mandatos de la moral y las leyes de la sociedad. Personajes de poco interés, exceso de detallismo sobre la vida de todos los días, problema central mal planteado.

4896. Guillén Pinto, Alfredo, and Natty Peñaranda de Guillén Pinto. Mina. Novela póstuma. La Paz, Tall. Gráf. Bolivianos, 1953. 383 p.

Los horrores de la vida minera en Bolivia: trabajo brutal, miseria fisiológica, embrutecimiento, escenas de sangre y muerte, masacres. Novela episódica y de intención social; personajes casi siempre unilaterales. Hay en ella algunas partes bien logradas, especialmente las que describen el interior de las minas y la impasividad de la naturaleza.

4897. Helguera, Ignacio. El hallazgo engañoso y otros cuentos. México, Muñoz, 1955. 221 p.

Relatos de desigual valor sobre acontecimientos cuotidianos. Algunos son flojos de estructura ("Pipo el cruzado"), otros apenas tienen trama, sin que por ello dejen de ser interesantes ("Guerra con México") y otros, en fin, insisten en sucesos de poca significación ("Marion La Rochelle"). En todos hay, sin embargo, una nota de espontaneidad y buen diálogo.

4898. House, Guillermo. Anselmo Coronel. B. A., Ediciones La Posta, 1955. 235 p.

Sencillo relato de amores y aventuras en la pampa de antaño, cuando aún había malones de indios y empezaban a llegar contingentes de inmigrantes europeos. Narración algo morosa, pero no desprovista de interés.

4899. ————. El fortín de los hombres sin miedo. B. A., Raigal (La aventura creadora), 1953. 224 p.

18 narraciones sobre la vida en la pampa argentina entre peones, mayordomos y ganaderos. En algunas se apunta una nota humorística y en otras el interés en la descripción de la agonía y de la muerte. Interés dramático, naturalidad del diálogo.

4900. Jasca, Adolfo. Los tallos amargos. B. A., Emecé (Novelistas argentinos contemporáneos), 1955. 173 p.

Historia de un crimen "perfecto," escrita en estilo sencillo y ameno y desarrollada dentro de los límites de lo plausible. Excelente relato en su género.

4901. Kirschbaum, Manuel. Las diversiones exasperadas. B. A., Dilema, 1953. 190 p.

Novelística "pura"—empleando palabras de uno de los personajes—compuesta de fragmentos entrecruzados de vida humana. El prurito de novelería lleva al retorcimiento lingüístico y a la indefinición conceptual, con la consiguiente perdida de eficacia expresiva.

4902. Labarca, Guillermo. Mirando al océano. Santiago, Editorial del Pacífico (Col. El umbral), 1953. 123 p.

Nueva edición de una novela corta que es ya obra "clásica" en la literatura chilena por su finura, dramaticidad, poesía y estilo. Excelente prólogo de Alone.

4903. Labrador Ruiz, Enrique. El gallo en el espejo. Habana, Lex, 1953. 163 p.

Hay en esta colección gran abundancia de elementos utilizables en una buena narración —sentido humorístico, variedad de personajes, dimensión humana—pero faltan la coordinación y unidad temática necesarias a todo buen cuento. El autor a menudo olvida el hilo central del relato y cae en la escena costumbrista o el incidente chistoso. Reseña de E. Padilla (Nueva Dem, 35:4, oct. 1953, p. 93-94).

4904. Lamas Carísimo de Rodríguez Alcalá, Teresa. La casa y su sombra. B. A., América-Sapucai (Novelas americanas), 1955. 125 p.

Contiene este volumen tres tipos de narraciones: rememoraciones del pasado paraguayo, escenas sentimentales y cuentos sobre las tremendas conmociones producidas por la guerra del Chaco. Estos últimos son los mejores, especialmente "Oyere-bo Chaco-güi" (Al volver del Chaco) y "Drama de una soledad." Dan carácter al volumen la delicada emotividad, buen gusto y sentido dramático de la autora.

4905. Lancelotti, Mario A. El traficante. B. A., Ed. Sudamericana, 1954. 142 p.

Intrigas y aventuras policiales; trama dispersa sin interés.

4906. Larreta, Enrique. Gerardo o la torre de las damas. Madrid, Aguilar, 1953. 196 p.

En la introducción se llama a este libro "un testimonio de las encrucijadas vitales de nuestro tiempo." Dentro de una trama bastante pobre, hecha a base de incidentes muchas veces antojadizos y de forzado dramatismo, se presentan las aventuras de Gerardo, las cuales sirven de apoyo a las disquisiciones sobre el pasado español, grandezas granadinas y singularidad del paisaje.

4907. Lombardo de Caso, María. Muñecos de niebla. México, Imp. Nuevo Mundo, 1955. 99 p.

Anécdotas, recuerdos, incidentes de la vida diaria narrados con espíritu comprensivo y suma sencillez.

4908. López Negrete, Ladislao. Fuego en las cumbres. México, Botas, 1953. 199 p.

Mediocre relato de las aventuras amorosas de un donjuanesco charro y de dos parejas jóvenes. Personajes estereotipados, demasiado ocurrentes y parlanchines. Trabajo tipográfico pobre, papel malo.

4909. Luna, Félix. La última montonera. Cuentos bárbaros. B. A., Ediciones Doble P (Grandes escritores argentinos, Cuentos 2), 1955. 100 p.

Vida de los montoneros riojanos en los días de transformación social que siguieron a la batalla de Monte Caseros. Algunos de estos cuentos apenas tienen trama y son más bien bocetos psicológicos. Otros nos dan el aliento épico y honda humanidad del hombre del interior. Entre los mejores están "Se moría el Chacho" y "Muerte en el Paraguay."

4911. Mallea, Eduardo. Chaves. Novela. B. A., Losada, 1953. 101 p.

Historia de un solitario cuya hipocondría se convierte en huraña ofensiva ante los ojos de los que no comprenden su angustia y su silencio. Estudio interesante del ensimismamiento en el dolor.

4912. ————. La sala de espera. B. A., Editorial Sudamericana (Col. Horizonte), 1953. 224 p.

Excelente novela poemática sobre siete motivos de angustia: la ambición arribista, la erotomanía, la bancarrota espiritual, la envidia, el apocamiento, el orgullo y la discordia conyugal. La sala de espera es el lugar a donde convergen con su carga de tristezas los siete personajes principales del libro—cuatro hombres, dos mujeres y un niño.

4913. Mariani, Roberto. La cruz nuestra de cada día. B. A., Ariadna (Col. Flor de leer), 1955. 319 p.

Pormenorizada visión de una casa de vecindad en que aparece toda una galería de personajes, cada cual con "la cruz de cada día," esto es, en lucha cuotidiana con la pobreza, el dolor y el hambre. Tiene esta novela el mérito muy especial de presentar un conjunto social (el sector de la Boca) como simple humanidad y no como vehículo para probar la superioridad de tal o cual teoría socio-económica. Es éste un libro hondamente humano sobre la clase baja, con todas sus sencillas virtudes, afectos y alegrías y también con sus enredos, bajezas y crímenes.

4914. Márquez, Edmundo. Guerrilleros. Novela histórica. Santiago, Alonso de Ovalle, 1953. 175 p.
La primera mitad del libro la ocupa la novela corta que da título al volumen. En ella se narran los esfuerzos de los patriotas chilenos por obtener la independencia en los días de San Martín y O'Higgins. La segunda mitad está integrada por diez leyendas de la región de Curicó. Es éste el primer esfuerzo novelístico del autor.

4915. Mazzanti, Carlos. El sustituto. B. A., Botella al Mar, 1954. 136 p.
Teoría existencialista en una novela sobre la vida psicológica subconsciente. Enlázanse aquí el pasado de un hombre abatido por la pérdida de su mujer e hijo y la realidad de un crimen perpetrado por persona desconocida. El cuerpo de la novela lo constituyen los recuerdos de la infancia y las angustias de la edad madura; culminan éstas en la auto-demolición al confesar el héroe un crimen que no ha cometido. Libro poético, sugerente y dramático, que debe ponerse entre las buenas realizaciones de 1954.

4916. Méndez Carrasco, Armando. El mundo herido. Santiago, Editorial Cultura, 1955. 303 p.
Pavorosa y conmovedora visión de las clases bajas de Valparaíso: hambre, brutalidad, prostitución, crimen. Este libro no busca probar nada; el autor sólo se propuso dar forma novelística a una atroz realidad. Obra intensa, de un realismo áspero y punzante, que no desdeña ni lo procaz, ni lo mefítico para representar la vida de los desesperados de toda ilusión. En algunos momentos el relato cae en el más franco mal gusto.

4917. Meneses, Guillermo. El falso cuaderno de Narciso Espejo. Novela. Caracas, Ediciones Nueva Cádiz (Biblioteca de escritores venezolanos), 1955? 209 p.
Libro concebido en dos partes: una contiene el supuesto relato de Narciso Espejo y la otra, la historia de varios amigos del biografiado vistos fuera del ámbito del relato anterior. Son notables por su penetración y calidad artística las páginas de la primera parte en que se narra la evolución espiritual de Narciso al enfrentarse éste con la noción de Dios y con los problemas de la vida: el pecado, la fe, el deber cívico, la presencia de la muerte y el amor. Sobre el significado del título y la calidad poética de esta obra véase la reseña de Pedro Pablo Paredes (R Nac Cult, 16:103, marzo-abril 1954, p. 154-156).

4918. Molina Neira, Víctor. El polvo y el tiempo. Santiago, Nascimento (Col. Araucaria, 6), 1953. 172 p.

Extraordinaria colección de cuentos, premiada por la Sociedad de Escritores de Chile: finura poética, excelente técnica narrativa, estilo cargado de sugerencias. Una de las mejores obras de 1953.

4919. Mujica Laínez, Manuel. Los ídolos. B. A., Editorial Sudamericana, 1953. 255 p.
Novela psicológica en tres partes; la primera —titulada "Lucio Sansilvestre"—es una obra completa en sí, en la cual se hace un magnífico estudio de una alma sensitiva, apasionada por el arte de un poeta, cuya misteriosa vida encierra un apasionante enigma. Las partes restantes son elaboraciones de temas ancilares y no tienen ni la estructuración ni el interés del comienzo.

4920. Murena, H. A. La fatalidad de los cuerpos. B. A., Sur, 1955. 249 p.
Es ésta una novela mal organizada en que no concuerda el espíritu moroso y funerario de la primera parte con el dinamismo de la segunda. Quedan en el aire varias acciones secundarias y algunos hechos, que parecen apuntar hacia un desenlace lógico, llevan a soluciones fortuitas. Al novelizar la tiranía de la carne, el autor se dejó arrastrar, en más de una ocasión, por un prurito ensayístico. Este libro revela indiscutibles aptitudes narrativas, pero, considerado en su totalidad como obra literaria, deja defraudado al lector.

4921. Nuestros cuentos. Por Juan de la Cabada, Eglantina Ochoa Sandoval, Julia Hernández, Alberto Quiroz, Máximo Magdaleno, Celedonio Martínez, Patricia Cox, Héctor Morales Saviñón y Ramiro Aguirre. México, Unidad Mexicana de Escritores (Col. Tehutli, 2), 1955. 106 p., illus.
Nueve relatos por nueve autores distintos. Entre éstos se destaca Juan de la Cabada por su excelente cuento "La llovizna." En los demás se nota o bien superficialidad temática, pobreza narrativa o falta de verisimilitud.

4922. Palomino, Pablo. Autopsia. México, Obregón, 1955. 164 p.
Autopsia de un mundo de crápulas, *demimondaines*, prostitutas y gente del hampa. Mézclanse en este relato la corrupción moral de hombres y mujeres con discusiones sobre política, arte, moral y existencialismo. Más que novela es éste un muestrario de envilecimientos y aberraciones.

4923. Pareja, Carlos H. El monstruo. B. A., Editorial Nuestra América (Col. Novelistas de nuestra América), 1955. 218 p.
Novela política basada en los sucesos del 9 de abril de 1948 promovidos por el asesinato de Jorge Eliécer Gaitán. La trama amorosa es lo de menos. Este libro es fundamentalmente expresión de una ideología política.

4924. Peraza, Celestino. Los piratas de la sabana. Cuarta edición. Caracas, Editorial Nueva, 1953? 237 p.
Novela romántica publicada por primera vez en

folletín. Cuenta la historia de un crimen y el
destino de los culpables y sus perseguidores.
Hay en ella un robo, varias muertes, amores
contrariados, un incendio, dos suicidios y, de
"yapa," en las páginas finales, una escena de
antropofagia. Aunque basada en algunos hechos
reales, esta novela tiene muy escaso mérito
literario. Con razón la ha llamado un crítico
"casi-novela."

4925. Pérez Zelaschi, Adolfo. El terra-
plén. B. A., Emecé, 1955. 222 p.
Vida, amores y desilusión de un joven estan-
ciero. La trama de la novela rota alrededor de
un solo asunto que queda planteado en la
segunda mitad del libro: el problema de
acomodación de dos temperamentos distintos
—Alberto Lagos y su esposa Estela. Al autor
le interesa la intriga amorosa más que la
creación de fuertes personalidades o la interpretación a fondo de los ambientes en que
actúan sus personajes.

4926. Picón-Salas, Mariano. Los tratos
de la noche. Barquisimeto, Venezuela,
Editorial Nueva Segovia, 1955. 206 p.
Se presenta en esta excelente novela el resurgi-
miento de Venezuela tras los días aciagos de
la tiranía asociándolo al advenimiento de inmigrantes europeos, víctimas también de la barbarie. En esta urdimbre se enlazan el pasado
romántico de doña Doloritas y su hermano, el
indómito general Segovia (padre del héroe),
la infamia del gomezolato, el mundo eufórico
de las grandes empresas, honestas y deshonestas,
y una visión esperanzada de un futuro de paz
y de trabajo. Este hermoso libro se destaca
entre las obras de 1955 por su estilo, armonía
interna y hábil manejo de un material humano
interesante y variado.

4927. Prato, Luis F. Mi coronel . . . Madrid, Caracas, Edime, 1953. 246 p.
La barbarie venezolana en los días de Juan
Vicente Gómez, personificada en la figura de
Secundino Fanundes, en el cual ha puesto el
autor los rasgos esenciales de un personaje
real, un indio analfabeto y sombrío que llena
no pocas páginas de la historia del gomezolato.
Sin duda el autor fué testigo presencial de gran
parte de lo que relata. Como novela este libro
carece de suficiente organización interna. Hay
en ella, además, exceso de anécdota y de dialec-
talismo lingüístico.

4928. ———. Ventisca. Madrid-Caracas,
Edime, 1953. 238 p.
Dice el autor en la introducción que el objeto
de esta novela es dar a conocer al andino de
Venezuela, especialmente su sencillez, bravura
y amor a la tierra, pero no logra del todo su
propósito porque sus personajes no actúan de
acuerdo con las características que a ellos se
les atribuye o resultan un tanto desleídos.
Buenas descripciones del paisaje; mensaje
optimista.

4929. Quiroga, Carlos B. Lázaro resuci-
tado. Prólogo por Roberto F. Giusti.
B. A., Raigal (La aventura creadora),
1955. 273 p.
La vida de Lázaro enfrentada con la de Judas
y Barrabás. Novelización dramática en que se

hace uso del diálogo tal como en una pieza
teatral. El prólogo de Roberto F. Giusti es
excelente.

4930. Ramírez Velarde, Fernando. Socavones de angustia. La Paz, Biblioteca
Paceña, 1953. 250 p.
Dramática visión de la vida minera en Bolivia
sin los ex-abruptos de la vehemencia política.
Al autor parece interesarle más la dolorosa y
elemental realidad de una multitud humana que
la creación de personajes singulares. Son de
especial interés los detalles que se dan sobre la
vida del minero indio.

4931. Ramos, Bautista Juan. Mala calle
de brujos. B. A., Gleizer, 1954. 230 p.
Romántico relato en que se contrastan los
amores inefables de Victorio y Zelmira con
el odio de Agú, la hija del brujo Dimas.
Personajes borrosos o improbables, trama melo-
dramática, mal encadenamiento de causas y
efectos. El autor tiene innegables dotes narrativas, que resaltarían aún más si no insistiese
tanto en lo espectacular y misterioso.

4932. Ramos Mejía, María Elena. Un
hombre y su destino. B. A., Kraft (Col.
Vértice), 1953. 250 p.
Niñez y juventud de Eduardo Quesada, hijo de
terratenientes, en quien se da el consorcio de
amor elemental a la tierra y el gusto por los
refinamientos parisinos. Al tomar contacto una
vez más con su tierra natal, llega a un remanso
pasional y al descubrimiento de su verdadero
yo. Libro interesante por presentar el problema
espiritual de no pocos argentinos, rico en meditaciones y atisbos psicológicos.

4933. Reyes Nevares, Salvador. Frontera
indecisa. México, Los Presentes (23),
1955. 78 p.
Cinco narraciones escritas en estilo sencillo y
ameno. Las tres primeras—que son las mejores
—apuntan hacia un suceso inesperado que se
presenta cerca del final.

4934. Ripoll del Río, Eloy. Tranvía,
primavera y otros cuentos. México, Jus,
1953. 151 p.
Cinco relatos sobre los enigmas y contrasentidos
del diario vivir. El destino humano está pasado
por un alambique intelectual que destila dudas,
desesperanzas y derrotas.

4935. Rodríguez-Acosta, Ofelia. Hágase
la luz. La novela de un filósofo existencialista. México, Impresora Galve, 1953.
322 p.
Intento de verter lo filosófico en lo novelístico
haciendo que los incidentes de la trama sirvan
de sostén a la disquisición conceptual sobre
los temas del existencialismo. La insistencia
en el comentario abstracto debilita la realidad
vital de los personajes.

4936. Rosenthal, Mauricio. Las cenizas
de Dios. B. A., Kraft (Col. Cúpula),
1955. 391 p.
Romántica historia de un abnegado médico
de su esposa, quienes se entregan a laborear

humanitarias en Mendoza durante los años que precedieron a la catástrofe sísmica de 1861. Acción lenta; trama sentimental.

4937. Rulfo, Juan. El llano en llamas y otros cuentos. México, Fondo de Cultura Económica (Letras mexicanas, 11), 1953. 170 p.

15 cuentos sobre la vida del pueblo bajo mexicano: miserias, hambres, chismes, pequeñas ilusiones, etc., reflejados todos a través del yo subjetivo de los personajes, en el cual se advierte siempre una fuerte nota existencialista. Entre los mejores está el primer cuento ("Macario"); en él se da, con hondo patetismo, una visión del mundo estrafalario en que vive un niño idiota. Véase el extenso estudio de Carlos Blanco A., "Realidad y estilo de Juan Rulfo," *Revista mexicana de literatura,* no. 1, sept.-oct. 1955, p. 59-86.

4938. ————. Pedro Páramo. México, Fondo de Cultura Económica (Letras mexicanas, 19), 1955. 155 p.

Vida de un terrateniente, Pedro Páramo, vista a través de un prisma que descompone la acción en múltiples planos y que los reorganiza, superponiéndolos o imbricándolos, sin relación con una idea de espacio o tiempo. Novela altamente poética, rica en símbolos, imágenes auditivas y detalles ambientales. Esta obra hay que ponerla en la corriente novelística última.

4939. Salado Álvarez, Victoriano. Cuentos y narraciones. Prólogo de Ana Salado Álvarez. México, Porrúa (Col. de escritores mexicanos, 71), 1953. xxix, 318 p.

Mezcla del "tradicionismo" picaresco de don Ricardo Palma con el costumbrismo del siglo XIX. Edición ampliada del libro *De autos* (1901), con un estudio preliminar, un resumen biográfico y un juicio crítico de José López Portillo y Rojas.

4940. Salvador Porta, Eliseo. Con la raíz al sol. Montevideo, Asir, 1953. 277 p.

Vida agraria del Uruguay. Se entrelazan aquí las miserias de los colonos y las de un viejo agricultor con las marrullerías del terrateniente. Esta novela se parece a muchas otras sobre el mismo tema.

4941. Sánchez G., Ángel Porfirio. Senderos. Relatos regionales hondureños. Comayaguela, Honduras, Imp. Libertad, 1952. 85 p.

11 relatos sobre incidentes de la vida diaria en que se acusa un marcado interés por lo costumbrista y sobrenatural. Expectación, detallismo, lengua de las clases bajas. En general, el asunto de las narraciones es de importancia secundaria.

4943. Sierra, Dante. A la izquierda de la luna. B. A., Ediciones Siglo Veinte (Col. La rosa de los vientos), 1955. 189 p.

Una teoría de la vida llevada a la novela. Están a la izquierda de la luna los que "viven un remedo de la vida, aun cuando sus voces y ademanes crean la casi perfecta visión de la realidad." Este libro tiene un defecto básico:

la novelización no está a la altura de la teoría en que se sustenta. Los personajes son meros símbolos y se desenvuelven en un ambiente desarticulado, dentro de una cuadrícula intelectual.

4944. Somers, Armonía. El derrumbamiento. Montevideo, Ediciones Salamanca, 1953. 138 p.

Cinco relatos fantasmales, transidos de pesadilla y de pasión, en que afloran los instintos primarios dentro de la absurda lógica de los más enrevesados sueños, todo ello expresado en un lenguaje selecto, con abundantes metáforas inesperadas. Libro para reducidos cenáculos.

4945. Stolk, Gloria. Los miedos. 10 cuentos literarios. Caracas, EDIME, 1955, 122 p.

Diez narraciones sobre las ironías de la vida. Tienen en común la sencillez de la exposición y del estilo. Entre las mejores está el cuento "¡Dinero!" que relata la vacuidad de una vida sacrificada a la ambición del dinero. Véase la reseña de Juan Ramón Medina (R Nac Cult, 17:111, julio-agosto 1955, p. 180-181).

4946. Stoll, Antonio. El desierto poblado. B. A., Raigal (Biblioteca de novelistas argentinos), 1953. 237 p.

Transformación de un olvidado rincón de la Patagonia bajo la influencia bienhechora de una maestra. La mayor parte del libro describe las labores educacionales de ésta y su vida doméstica como mujer soltera y, mas tarde, como esposa. El tema no es nuevo, pero está aquí tratado con gran delicadeza. El desenlace optimista no es del todo convincente.

4947. Tamayo Vargas, Augusto. Búsqueda. Lima, D. Miranda, 1953. 193 p.

Primera novela del conocido intelectual peruano. En ella se esboza la figura de un hombre inteligente con alma de poeta que se busca a sí mismo en la soledad selvática de la montaña peruana. Desfilan por estas páginas infinidad de personas, dentro de un ambiente que recuerda muchas veces *La serpiente de oro* de Ciro Alegría. Estructuralmente la novela es un poco floja por acusarse en ella demasiado interés en lo anecdótico.

4948. Tiempo, César. Así quería Gardel. B. A., Bell, 1955. 159 p.

Los amores de Carlos Gardel y una bella joven de provincia, rematados por la trágica muerte del famoso cantor argentino en el aeródromo de Medellín, Colombia. Biografía novelada con todas las trazas de una novela sentimental. Ocupan el primer plano las relaciones amorosas de los protagonistas.

4949. Tinoco, Manuel Vicente. Rastro en el alba. Caracas-Madrid, Gabriel Jordán, 1953. 206 p.

Primera parte de una trilogía en que se da la historia de la infancia, adolescencia y juventud de un muchacho venezolano que vive las inquietudes y oprobios de los días gomecistas. La novela no ahonda en la psicología de los personajes ni entra a fondo en el significado de la tiranía.

4950. Valdés, Carlos. Ausencias. México, Los Presentes (10), 1955. 73 p.
Aventura espiritual en mundos de la imaginación, ya pasando del ámbito de la vida al de la muerte, infundiendo vida en la materia inerte o contrastando la vida común con la heterodoxia de un personaje. Minúsculo libro que llama la atención por sus agudezas y rebeldías intelectuales.

4951. Valdés, Ignacio de J., Jr. Cuentos panameños de la ciudad y del campo. 2. ed., corregida y aumentada. Panamá, Imprenta Nacional, 1955. 172 p.
Nueva edición de un libro publicado por primera vez en 1928. Dice el autor en la introducción que fué su intención "retratar lo más fielmente el alma de nuestros campesinos, con sus grandes pasiones y sus odios, sus creencias y costumbres patriarcales." Colección de sencillos cuentos, que han gozado de gran popularidad en Panamá; trágicos algunos, cómicos y zumbones otros. En estos últimos se advierten a veces reminiscencias del estilo y técnica de don Ricardo Palma.

4952. Velázquez, Luis Horacio. El juramento. B. A., Emecé, 1954. 201 p.
Aventuras de un grupo expedicionario interesado en rescatar a Alberto Suárez, a quien se supone en manos de una tribu salvaje. Dos tercios del libro los dedica el autor a intercalar escenas de la niñez y juventud del amigo perdido, revelando con ello la poca importancia de la aventura selvática. Hay algunas escenas interesantes; lo demás es más que mediocre.

4953. Vera, Humberto B. Aroma de tilos. Estudiantina. B. A., Signo, 1953. 163 p.
Vida estudiantil en La Plata: estudios, aventuras, política universitaria, amoríos y franca-chelas, todo contado con sencillez y espíritu jubiloso. Libro hecho de anécdotas y recuerdos, sin grandes pretensiones.

4954. Vera, Pedro Jorge. Luto eterno y otros relatos. Guayaquil, Ecuador, Casa de la Cultura Ecuatoriana, Núcleo del Guayas, 1953. 211 p.
Notable colección de cuentos en que el autor se separa de la corriente nativista—paisaje, folklorismo, fuerzas telúricas—para introducirse en el alma del hombre actual y revelar sus veleidades, anhelos y pasiones. En todos sus personajes encuentra el autor una veta dramática que presenta escuetamente y con gran interés. Véase la reseña de G. Rabassa (R Hisp Mod, 21:2, abril 1955, p. 151-152).

4955. Vieyra, Jaime Julio. Un rostro agrio. B. A., Botella al Mar, 1954. 121 p.
Tres novelas cortas. "Un rostro agrio": estudio de la timidez y soledad de un adolescente; "La dicha": cómo se forjan un momento de felicidad dos almas desesperanzadas; "La cosecha": análisis de la incomprensión entre dos seres disímiles. Elementos comunes: patetismo, emoción del paisaje, reiteración poética.

4956. Villaverde, Cirilo. Cecilia Valdés o la loma del ángel. Novela de costumbres cubanas. Edición crítica y notas por

Esteban Rodríguez Herrera. Habana, Lex, 1953. lxviii, 753 p.
Nueva y esmerada edición de la conocida novela cubana. Extensa introducción, glosario y abundantes notas críticas.

4957. Zúñiga, Olivia. Entre el infierno y la luz. Introducción de Arturo Rivas Sáinz. Guadalajara, México, Instituto Tecnológico de Guadalajara (Col. Nueva), 1953. 102 p.
Desorganizado relato sobre las tribulaciones de Francisca, esposa, madre y mujer de mundo, quien relata su vida destacando las angustias del pasado y la quiebra espiritual del presente. Ambiente de falso dramatismo. Algunos incidentes están a los bordes de lo absurdo.

4958. Zuno, José G. La muerte de un lago. Los cuentos de Chapala. Guadalajara, México, Fénix, 1955. 190 p.
Mediocre colección de ensayos periodísticos que casi nada tienen de cuento. En ellos se repite siempre el mismo asunto, la "muerte" gradual del lago de Chapala. Intención satírica, alusivismo político, burla, chiste barato.

STUDIES

4959. Azuela Arriaga, María. Mariano Azuela, novelista de la Revolución Mexicana. México, Universidad Nacional Autónoma de México, Facultad de Filosofía y Letras, 1955. lxxix p.
Trabajo superficial en que se recogen datos aclaratorios ya discutidos por otros críticos o presentados por el propio Azuela. En la segunda mitad de este opúsculo se da una bibliografía.

4960. Caldiz, Juan Francisco. Lo que no se ha dicho de Don Segundo Sombra. La Plata, Argentina, A. Domínguez, 1952. 67 p.
Ensayo crítico en que se parte de un supuesto muy discutible ("hay y hubo exceso de elogio para Don Segundo Sombra") y se llega, tras un brevísimo estudio de detalles menores y de poca significación estética, a esta audaz conclusión: "Don Segundo Sombra no es ni puede considerarse una obra literaria de excepción." Es obvio que el autor ha pasado por alto los méritos artísticos de la novela.

4961. Cobo, Armando J. ¿A dónde va la literatura argentina? La novela. Redescubrimiento de Max Dickmann. B. A., Losange (Col. Ensayos de ayer y de hoy, 1), 1954. 49 p.
Apreciación encomiástica de la obra de Dickmann. Se estudian personajes y temas y su valor representativo, pero sin entrar en mayores detalles.

4962. Cruz, Salvador de la. Nuevos novelistas iberoamericanos. México, 1955. 64 p.
Colección de brevísimas notas impresionistas

destinadas a servir de introducción a las distintas partes de una antología. Entre los veinte autores "iberoamericanos" se incluye a José Antonio Zunzunegui.

4963. Fabbiani Ruiz, José. El cuento en Venezuela. Caracas, Pensamiento Vivo, 1953. 24 p.

Presentación sumaria de los más destacados cuentistas de tres generaciones: la de *El Cojo ilustrado* y *Cosmópolis;* la de *Alborada,* y la generación de 1928. Los cuentistas posteriores a 1940 apenas están mencionados. Bibliografía al final.

4964. Guzmán, Augusto. La novela en Bolivia. Proceso 1847-1954. La Paz, Juventud, 1955. 180 p.

Revisión y ampliación del libro sobre el mismo tema publicado por el autor en 1938: los románticos (1847-1905); los realistas (1905-1932); los naturalistas (1932-1954). Con este plan—por cierto demasiado estrecho para organizar bien el libro—examina el autor la producción literaria boliviana dentro de tres corrientes, viéndose obligado a veces a presentar a un autor en dos secciones distintas. Manual de positiva utilidad porque presenta un campo hasta ahora no bien estudiado. Es muy discutible, sin embargo, la conveniencia de sistematizar y aislar dentro de cada corriente en vez de captar el proceso novelístico en sus aspectos generales más significativos.

4964a. Luque Valderrama, Lucía. La novela femenina en Colombia. Bogotá, Pontificia Universidad Católica Javeriana, 1954. 248 p.

Extenso estudio de la producción novelística femenina en Colombia durante los siglos XIX y XX. Tras los pequeños ensayos bio-bibliográficos de las primeras 70 páginas, se abre la parte verdaderamente significativa de este libro. En ésta se estudian las obras de un considerable número de escritoras colombianas clasificándolas por géneros y corrientes literarias. Quizás sobran a veces los detalles de la trama de algunos libros. Hay en este trabajo un honrado propósito de comprender y valorar y un espíritu reverente, a veces demasiado unilateral. Sin duda, algunas de las escritoras discutidas son de escasa estatura literaria. Tesis, Facultad de Filosofía, Letras y Pedagogía.

4965. Navarro, Joaquina. La novela realista mexicana. México, Compañía General de Ediciones, 1955. 33 p.

Concienzudo trabajo sobre el género realista en que se destacan las figuras de Emilio Rabasa, Rafael Delgado, José López Portillo y Rojas y Federico Gamboa. Véase la reseña de Ermilo Abreu Gómez (R Interam Bibl, 5:4, oct.-dic. 1955, p. 336-337).

4966. Sánchez, Luis Alberto. Proceso y contenido de la novela hispanoamericana. Madrid, Biblioteca Románica Hispánica (Estudios y ensayos, 2), 1953. 664 p.

Minuciosa exposición del campo novelístico hispanoamericano en que se amplía considerablemente el tema (tratado ya por el autor en *América, novela sin novelistas,* Lima, 1933). Libro aluviónico, arsenal de datos, impresiones y juicios personales.

4966a. Santana, Francisco. La biografía novelada en Chile. Santiago, Flor Nacional, 1953. 31 p.

Breve estudio de carácter informativo más que crítico en que se presentan las obras del género en orden cronológico. Al final dice el autor: "Al hacer este panorama no hemos tenido el propósito agobiante de buscar defectos . . . sino de exponer e interpretar a los autores. . . ."

4967. Silva Castro, Raúl. Alberto Blest Gana. Santiago, Zig-Zag, 1955. 352 p.

Muy nutrida biografía del gran novelador chileno y estudio cronológico de su producción literaria. Obra de erudición y honradez crítica.

4968. ————. Panorama de la novela chilena (1843-1953). México, Fondo de Cultura Económica (Col. Tierra firme, 59), 1955. 224 p.

Valioso manual hecho por un experto en la materia. Abarca desde los precursores hasta el presente. Cada capítulo va acompañado de una nota bibliográfica. Es de lamentar que la falta de espacio no le haya permitido al autor explayarse sobre algunos de los temas que aborda. Esto se nota en particular en el último capítulo, "Novelistas de la nueva generación."

4969. Warner, Ralph E. Historia de la novela mexicana en el siglo XIX. México, Antigua Librería Robredo (Clásicos y modernos, Creación y crítica literaria, 9), 1953. xvii, 124 p.

Manual útil por los datos y referencias que en él se recogen. Véase la reseña de Luis Monguió (Hisp R, 23:2, April 1955, p. 149-151).

POETRY
FRANCISCO AGUILERA

The period 1953-1955 produced a considerable quantity of material eligible for this section. Among anthologies, Borges and Bioy Casares' *Poesía gauchesca,* Fernández Spencer's *Nueva poesía dominicana,* Saz' *Nueva poesía panameña,* and Mendoza's *El corrido mexicano* are outstanding contributions. The same praise is deserved by the collected poems of four Spanish American masters— Darío, Gutiérrez Nájera, Almafuerte, and López Velarde.

For Fombona-Pachano and Ballagas, who died prematurely in 1951 and 1956 respectively, we have now complete editions of their verse, as well as for the venerable Dublé Urrutia (who began to publish in 1895) and poets in full production such as César Tiempo, Carranza, and Vitier. A word of commendation should be given to the anthologies of Ibero-American poetry that Ediciones

Cultura Hispánica of Madrid has been issuing since 1949 (two of which were mentioned above under the compilers' names, Fernández Spencer and Saz). Translation into English did not fare so well, as witness the poems of love and the Andrés Bello ode listed below.

Among the contemporaries, importance must be attached to the new works of Mistral, Neruda, Claudia Lars, and Andrés Eloy Blanco (who died in 1955).

Scholarly criticism was brilliantly represented by Alegría's *La poesía chilena* and Monguió's *La poesía postmodernista peruana*. Biography of enduring value was produced by Brughetti in his *Vida de Almafuerte*. Toussaint's *Bibliografía mexicana de Heredia* and Mapes' key to the score of pseudonyms and hundreds of inedited pieces in prose or verse of Gutiérrez Nájera are welcome tools which augur well for the future of research in this field.

VERSE

5000. Alberti, Altana. Poemas de . . . (escritos de los 12 a los 13 años). Retrato de Raúl Soldi. B. A., Imp. López, 1955. 45 p.
Really extraordinary for one so young. Who is she?

5001. Almafuerte [pseud.], i.e., **Pedro Bonifacio Palacios.** Obras de Almafuerte. Ordenadas y anotadas por Romualdo Brughetti. B. A., Peuser, 1954. 629 p., pl.
Divided into "Libro I, Poesías," and "Libro II, Prosas." Most adequate memorial to Almafuerte on the centenary of his birth.

5002. Antología de poemas de la Revolución. La Paz, Tall. Gráf. Bolivianos (Publ. SPIC), 1954. 103 p., illus.
13 poets, some of distinct talent, inspired by the proletarian and nationalistic aspects of the Paz Estenssoro program. Published by the Subsecretaría de Prensa, Informaciones y Cultura (SPIC).

5003. Ballagas, Emilio. Obra poética de . . . . Edición póstuma. Con un ensayo preliminar de Cintio Vitier. Habana, Úcar García, 1955. xli, 313 p.
The Cuban Emilio Ballagas (1908-1954), noted both for his *poesía negra* of the early 1930's and his *poesía pura* before and after those years, looms as one of Spanish America's principal poets of the last quarter century. Exhaustive compilation, intelligently organized.

5004. Becco, Horacio Jorge, and Osvaldo Svanascini (eds.). Poesía argentina moderna. B. A., Pedestal, 1953. 96 p.
19 poets who have been active in the last ten years, represented by poems selected in accordance with intricate canons explained in the introduction (13 pages including 37 footnotes).

5005. Bello, Andrés. A georgic of the tropics. Charlottesville, Va., King Lindsay Printing Corp., 1954. 39 p.
English translation by John Cook Wyllie of "A la agricultura de la zona tórrida" (1826). Spanish and English texts on opposite pages. Limited edition.

5006. Blanco, Andrés Eloy. Giraluna. México, Yocoima, 1955. 245 p.
Last volume of verse published while alive by the beloved Venezuelan poet, then a political exile in Mexico. A few months after publication the author died in an automobile accident (May 1955). Introductory statements by Rómulo Gallegos, Alfonso Reyes, Manuel Altolaguirre, and Pedro Sotillo. Announced as "en prensa," a book of poems, La juambimbada. See review by Luis Alberto Sánchez (Atenea, año 32, 121:359, mayo 1955, p. 265-270); review-obituary by Ricardo A. Latcham (Atenea, año 32, 121:360, junio 1955, p. 474-482); and moving tribute by the Spanish poet León Felipe, "Andrés Eloy Blanco, muerto en la Giranoche de su Giraluna" (Cuad Am, año 14, 82:4, julio-agosto 1955, p. 221-231).

5007. Borges, Jorge Luis. Poemas. 1923-1953. B. A., Emecé (Obras completas de Jorge Luis Borges, 2), 1954. 174 p.
The last four poems in this volume are the only ones not included in his *Poemas, 1922-1943* (B. A., Losada, 1943).

5008. ————, and Adolfo Bioy Casares (eds.). Poesía gauchesca. México, Fondo de Cultura Económica (Biblioteca americana, 29, 30), 1955. 2 v. xxvii, 633; 798 p.
Here are gathered for the first time, and in a format that leaves nothing to be desired, the complete texts of the works of the Argentine and Uruguayan genuine *gauchesco* poets: Bartolomé Hidalgo, Hilario Ascasubi, Estanislao del Campo, Antonio D. Lussich, and José Hernández. Notes and glossary are reduced to an acceptable minimum.

5009. Bustamante, José Ignacio. La poesía en Popayán, 1536-1954. 2. ed. Popayán, Colombia, Editorial Universidad del Cauca, 1954. 495 p.
Enlarged edition of *Historia de la poesía en Popayán, 1536-1939* (Popayán, Tall. Editoriales del Departamento, 1939, 431 p.).

5010. Carranza, Eduardo. Canciones para iniciar una fiesta. Poesía en verso, 1935-1950. Ilustraciones de José Caballero. Madrid, Ediciones Cultura Hispánica (Col. La encina y el mar, 12), 1953. 173 p.

Selections from the books *Canciones para iniciar una fiesta, Seis elegías y un himno, Azul de ti, La sombra de las muchachas, Este era un rey . . . , Canto en voz alta, Los días que ahora son sueños,* and *El olvidado,* published by the distinguished Colombian poet between 1936 and 1950.

5011. Cruchaga Santa María, Ángel. Pequeña antología. Selección del autor. Santiago, Escuela Nacional de Artes Gráficas (Col. Premios nacionales de literatura), 1953. 182 p.

The poet's own selection—from three to six poems from each of his books, beginning with *Las manos juntas* (1915). For earlier anthology, edited by Pablo Neruda, see *HLAS, 1946, no. 12,* item 2630.

5012. Cuadernos trimestrales de poesía. Trujillo, Perú. No. 1, dic. 1951—no. 11, sept. 1955.

About 15 local poets have been represented so far in this interesting poetry magazine.

5013. Danero, E. M. S. (comp.). Antología gaucha. Santa Fé, Argentina, Castellví, 1953. 363 p.

An excellent all-inclusive compilation, not for scholars but for the edification of and enjoyment by the general public. Subdivisions: Los precursores; Los tres grandes; Los últimos gauchos; Los ecos gauchescos; Menores y payadores; Cancionero popular.

5014. Darío, Rubén. Poesías completas. Edición, introducción y notas de Alfonso Méndez Plancarte. Madrid, Aguilar, 1954. lxxii, 1487 p.

This "segunda impresión" adds 21 poems and many notes to the original edition of 1952. Unquestionably the most adequate Darío compilation. See item 5081.

5015. Dublé Urrutia, Diego. Fontana cándida. Poemas, 1895-1952. Prólogo de Francisco García Krautz. Santiago, Nascimento, 1953. 341 p.

Most of the verse of a major Chilean poet known only by an international elite. This book is named after a 1916 composition, written in Rome, which gave notice that Dublé Urrutia was still living.

5016. Durand, René L. F. (ed., trans.). Algunos poetas venezolanos contemporáneos. Quelques poètes vénézuéliens contemporains. Textos escogidos y traducción al francés con una presentación de los autores. Prólogo de Mariano Picón-Salas. Caracas, Universidad Central de Venezuela, Instituto de Lenguas Modernas (Lenguas modernas, 1), 1954. 243 p.

Siv poets identified with the "1918" and "Viernes" groups (Fernando Paz Castillo, Enrique Planchart, Andrés Eloy Blanco, José Ramón Heredia, Luis Fernando Álvarez, Vicente Garbasi), and two others thus far unlabeled (Antonio Arráiz, Juan Liscano) are here presented in French translation, with Spanish original on opposite page. M. Durand is professor of French literature at the Central University of Venezuela. Each group of poems is preceded by a cogent introduction.

5017. Fernández Spencer, Antonio (ed.). Nueva poesía dominicana. Antología. Madrid, Ediciones Cultura Hispánica, 1953. 341 p.

A large number of compositions (some not as yet published in book form) by nine poets rigorously selected: Domingo Moreno Jimenes, Rafael Américo Henríquez, Tomás Hernández Franco, Manuel del Cabral, Franklin Mieses Burgos, Héctor Incháustegui Cabral, Pedro Mir, Freddy Gatón Arce, and Antonio Fernández Spencer. They represent the period 1916-1947, from the emergence of *postumismo* to the discontinuance of *La poesía sorprendida.* The compiler, a poet in his own right, does not claim distinction for the poets who flourished before World War I in the Dominican Republic (possible exception, Fabio Fiallo). Thoughtful, informative introduction (p. 11-70). A valuable addition to the Ibero-American anthologies issued in Madrid by Cultura Hispánica (Nicaragua, 1949; Brazil, 1952; Puerto Rico, 1952; Panama, 1954).

5018. Fombona-Pachano, Jacinto. Obras completas. Caracas, Edime, 1953. 2 v. T. 1: Poesía, 356 p.; t. 2, Prosa, 709 p.

Volume 1 is a welcome publication containing most distinguished verse by the late poet (1901-1951).

5019. Gutiérrez Nájera, Manuel. Poesías completas. Edición y prólogo de Francisco González Guerrero. México, Porrúa (Col. de escritores mexicanos, 66, 67), 1953. 2 v. xxv, 372; 409 p.

Don Justo Sierra's 1896 compilation of all the available verse of Gutiérrez Nájera (1859-1895) —a labor of love—included 158 compositions. In 1943, E. K. Mapes issued as addenda 27 unknown poems. The present edition adds 20 more, making a total of 205.

5020. Johnson, Mildred Edith. Spanish poems of love. N. Y., Exposition Press, 1955. 64 p.

20 poets from Spanish America and four from Spain represented. About half of the poems feature love between man and woman; the rest, love for God, country, children, etc.

5021. Lars, Claudia [pseud.], i.e., Carmen Brannon de Samayoa. Donde llegan los pasos. San Salvador, Ministerio de Cultura, Dirección General de Bellas Artes, 1953. 82 p., illus.

Under the title, "El horizonte mágico de Claudia Lars," Fernando Alegría wrote a fervidly enthusiastic article on this book (Atenea, año 30, 111:337-338, julio-agosto 1953, p. 64-75).

5022. ————. Escuela de pájaros. San

Salvador, Ministerio de Cultura, Departamento Editorial, 1955. 127 p., illus.

5023. López Velarde, Ramón. Poesías completas y El minutero. Edición y prólogo de Antonio Castro Leal. México, Porrúa (Col. de escritores mexicanos, 68), 1953. xxii, 374 p.
One of Sr. Castro Leal's exemplary editions, worthy of the subject. *El minutero* is a collection of sketches in prose.

5024. Martínez M., Guillermo E. (comp.). La poesía en el Valle del Cauca. Cali, Colombia, Imp. Departamental, 1954. 500 p.
A comprehensive anthology of poets born in Valle del Cauca, one of Colombia's 16 "departamentos." Useful notes, scrupulous selection.

5025. Maya, Rafael (ed.). La musa romántica en Colombia. Antología poética. Bogotá, Ministerio de Educación Nacional (Biblioteca de autores colombianos, 79), 1954. 538 p.
Selections from nine Romantic poets who flourished in Colombia during the second half of the 19th century. Authoritative evaluation with a minimum of information is supplied by the editor.

5026. Mendoza, Vicente T. (ed.). El corrido mexicano. México, Fondo de Cultura Económica (Letras mexicanas, 15), 1954. xliv, 467 p.
A fascinating anthology preceded by an authoritative introduction. 172 compositions with 120 musical notations. "El corrido es un género épico-lírico-narrativo, en cuartetas de rima variable, ya asonante o consonante en los versos pares, forma literaria sobre la que se apoya una frase musical compuesta generalmente de cuatro miembros, que relata aquellos sucesos que hieren poderosamente la sensibilidad de las multitudes. . . ." "El corrido . . . uno de los más firmes soportes de la literatura genuinamente mexicana. . . ."

5027. Mistral, Gabriela. Desolación. Santiago, Editorial del Pacífico (Obras selectas, 2), 1954. 259 p.
Publisher plans a six-volume series. First two volumes issued (no. 2 and 6, respectively) are *Desolación* (first edition, 1922) and *Lagar* (see below).

5028. ————. Lagar. Santiago, Editorial del Pacífico (Obras selectas, 6), 1954. 188 p.
First new book of Mistral since *Tala* (1938). Initial poem, "La otra," may well be interpreted as a clue to a new phase in the most prodigious career since the time of Darío.

5029. Moreno Jimenes, Domingo. Antología. Selección y prólogo de Flérida de Nolasco. 2. ed. Ciudad Trujillo, Librería

Dominicana (Col. Pensamiento dominicano, 3), 1953. 187 p.
This second edition includes two additional poems under the subtitle "América." See *HLAS, no. 15, 1949,* item 2370.

5030. Neruda, Pablo. Alturas de Macchu Picchu. Santiago, Nascimento, 1954. 77 p. & photos.
"Edición definitiva . . . impresa con ocasión del cincuentenario de Pablo Neruda el 12 de julio de 1954. . . ."

5031. ————. Poesía política. Discursos políticos. Santiago, Editora Austral, 1953. 2 v. 244, 242 p.
Most of his political poems since 1936. In v. 2, p. 95-239, are included some of his speeches as a Communist leader. Introduction by Ilya Ehrenburg.

5032. ————. Todo el amor. Santiago, Nascimento, 1953. 255 p., illus.
70 love poems selected from his various books. An enterprising publisher thus responds to those who are weary of the political content in Neruda's verse and pine for the good old "Farewell."

5033. ————. Las uvas y el viento. Santiago, Nascimento, 1954. 422 p.
Verse written in 1952-1953, mostly while travelling in Europe and Asia.

5034. Nieto, Ricardo. Obra poética de . . . . Prólogo de Armando Romero Lozano. Cali, Colombia, 1955. 344 p.
Useful introduction (p. 11-47) by Armando Romero Lozano. Nieto (1878-1952) was active as a poet between 1914 and 1935. Born in the Cauca Valley like Guillermo Valencia, he was, unlike the latter, a hard-to-explain Romantic who commingled Hugo and Musset, Núñez de Arce and Gutiérrez Nájera. Memorial edition sponsored by the government of the Cauca Valley Department.

5035. Novo, Salvador. Las aves en la poesía castellana. México, Fondo de Cultura Económica (Letras mexicanas, 10), 1953. 139 p.
One brief chapter (p. 117-139) touches on birds in Mexican poetry.

5036. Rincón y Serna, Jesús. La Bolivaríada. Bogotá, Ministerio de Educación Nacional (Biblioteca de autores colombianos, 37), 1953. 263 p.
Rafael Maya, in a brief introduction, commends this contemporary Colombian poet for his relatively successful attempt to compose an epic poem.

5037. Rugeles, Manuel F. Cantos de sur y norte. B. A., Losada (Poetas de España y América), 1954. 139 p.
Poems written in different countries by the poet-diplomat. The poem "Evocación geográfica de la isla de Margarita" was issued in

1953 as the first of the series of brochures sponsored by the Dirección de Cultura y Bellas Artes, Ministerio de Educación, Caracas. See review of Rugeles' *Antología poética* (1952) by Félix Armando Núñez (Atenea, año 30, 111: 337-338, julio-agosto 1953, p. 25-37), in which the Venezuela poet is called "uno de los más altos valores de nuestra América."

5038. Saz, Agustín del (ed.). Nueva poesía panameña. Madrid, Ediciones Cultura Hispánica, 1954. 430 p.

Another excellent number in the series variously called "Poesía de España y América," "La encina y el mar," "Antologías hispanoamericanas," "Colección de veintiuna antologías de poesía nueva." In "Estudio preliminar" (p. 11-34), the editor intelligently reviews 50 years of verse writing, through *modernismo, nativismo, vanguardismo,* and *los novísimos.* Among the 35 poets represented, well-deserved emphasis is given—both in the introduction and in the anthology proper—to Ricardo Miró, Demetrio Korsi (spelled "Corsi" in the running headline), Rogelio Sinán, and Demetrio Herrera. Bibliography includes a useful list of "periódicos y revistas."

5039. Tiempo, César [pseud.], i.e., Israel Zeitlin. Sábado pleno. B. A., Gleizer, 1955. 238 p.

The Argentine poet who, since 1930, has distinguished himself for his Jewish fervor and themes offers here a "cumulative" edition of the poems included in *Libro para la pausa del sábado* (1930), *Sabatión argentino* (1933, actually an enlargement of the first book), and *Sábadomingo* (1938), plus a number of poems published in periodicals.

5040. Vitier, Cintio. Vísperas, 1938-1953. Habana, Orígenes, 1953. 313 p.

A compilation of published and inedited verse by one of Cuba's most distinguished poets.

STUDIES

5041. Alegría, Fernando. La poesía chilena. Orígenes y desarrollo del siglo XVI al XIX. México, Fondo de Cultura Económica (Col. Tierra firme, 55), 1954. 311 p.

Scholarly study of Chilean poetry from Ercilla to about 1900—first of its kind ever attempted. With the exception of Ercilla (a Spaniard) and Oña ("un español nacido en Chile"), the poets studied seem to justify Menéndez y Pelayo's low opinion of Chilean poetry. Dr. Alegría, however, thinks it is possible to find in the products of those centuries elements which may reasonably be considered legitimate antecedents of the great heights reached by Chilean poets in the 20th century. The author does not neglect the consideration of political and social events; on the contrary, he boldly fills in the gaps which he detects in the voluminous works of the professional historians. See thoughtful review of Dr. Alegría's work by Ricardo A. Latcham (Atenea, año 31, 118:353-354, nov.-dic. 1954, p. 130-140). Part of this first edition was published with the imprint of the University of California Press, Berkeley and Los Angeles.

5042. ————. Walt Whitman en Hispanoamérica. México, Ediciones Studium (Col. Studium, 5), 1954. 419 p.

Chapters 5 and 6, on Whitman's influence in Spanish America and on Whitman's translators (both Spaniards and Spanish Americans) are of special interest to this section. To the excellent bibliography (p. 411-419) now can be added a book which came out in Ecuador too late for Alegría to include it in his discerning examination of texts—Walt Whitman, *Hojas de hierba,* Versión directa e íntegra conforme al texto de la edición definitiva de 1891-1892 por Francisco Alexander, Quito, Casa de la Cultura Ecuatoriana, 1953, lxxiii, 603 p. Alegría was ideally equipped to undertake this important work of research, evaluation—and revaluation. See review by the Nicaraguan Whitmanist Juan Felipe Toruño (Atenea, año 31, 118:353-354, nov.-dic. 1954, p. 120-130).

5043. Alfau Durán, Vetilio (ed.). Historia de la poesía en Santo Domingo. Documentos para su estudio (A U Sto Domingo, 18:67-68, julio-dic. 1953, p. 301-345).

Documents relating to the Royal Spanish Academy's inquiry of 1891 which led to the preparation, by Menéndez Pelayo, of an epoch-making anthology of Spanish-American poetry. Included (p. 303-330) is the virtually unknown "Reseña histórico-crítica de la poesía en Santo Domingo," an important report submitted in 1892 by a committee composed of Salomé Ureña de Henríquez, Federico Henríquez y Carvajal, César Nicolás Penson, José Pantaleón Castillo, and Francisco Gregorio Billini. Issued as a separate under the title *Apuntes para la historia de la poesia en Santo Domingo.*

5044. Arias, Juan de Dios. El romance en la tradición santandereana (Bolívar, Bogotá, 16, enero-feb. 1953, p. 137-165).

Spanish survivals in the department of Santander, Colombia, and original local *romances* as well.

5045. Aub, Max. Alfonso Reyes, según su poesía (Cuad Am, año 12, 68:2, marzo-abril 1953, p. 241-274).

Notes on Reyes' *Obra poética* (see *HLAS, no. 18, 1952,* item 2602).

5046. Borges, Jorge Luis. Evaristo Carriego. B. A., Emecé (Obras completas de Jorge Luis Borges, 4), 1955. 175 p.

Includes the *Evaristo Carriego* published in 1930 and, in pages 121-174, various papers on related topics. Argentina's leading man of letters—erudite and sophisticated—vindicates the validity of Carriego's fame as the poet of the B. A. slums.

5047. ————, and Margarita Guerrero. El *Martín Fierro.* B. A., Editorial Columba (Col. Esquemas, 2), 1953. 79 p.

"He sido muchas veces interrogado sobre literatura argentina e invariablemente he respondido que esa literatura (tan desdeñada por quienes la ignoran) existe y que comprende, por lo menos, un libro, que es el *Martín Fierro.*" The present essay—the distillation of much knowledge and wisdom—lucidly explains Borges' conviction. An important pronouncement.

5048. Brughetti, Romualdo. Vida de Almafuerte. El combatiente perpetuo. B. A., Peuser, 1954. 255 p., illus.
Authoritative and eminently readable biography of Pedro Bonifacio Palacios (1854-1917), whom author places together with Darío and Neruda as "los más intensos del continente."

5049. Cabrera de Tablada, Nina. José Juan Tablada en la intimidad. Con cartas y poemas inéditos. México, Imp. Universitaria, 1954. 216 p.
Pious reminiscences of the Mexican poet-theosophist Tablada by his wife; the letters and poems appended add very little to our knowledge of the writer. [A. Flores]

5050. Cañizales-Márquez, José. Dos poetas contemporáneos venezolanos (Atenea, año 30, 110:335, mayo 1953, p. 246-264).
On Luis Pastori, Ana Enriqueta Terán, and recent Venezuelan poetry in general. With respect to Pastori we should like to call attention to *Palabras de otros años,* a selection of poems issued in 1954 as number 7 of the attractive series of poetry brochures issued since 1953 by the Dirección de Cultura y Bellas Artes, Ministerio de Educación, Caracas.

5051. Chapman, Arnold. Heredia's Ossian translation (Hisp R, 23:3, July 1955, p. 231-236).
José María Heredia translated Ossian into Spanish verse while he was in the U. S. as an exile, from Dec. 1823 to May 1824. Only six of his Ossian pieces are known today.

5052. Dromundo, Baltasar. Vida y pasión de Ramón López Velarde. México, Guarania, 1954. 88 p.
A prize-winning literary biography with penetrating comment on the poet's work.

5053. Duffau, Eduardo Héctor (comp.). Nuevos encuentros con Rubén Darío (Ábside, 17:2, abril-junio 1953, p. 211-238).
Ten poems and six prose items by Darío exhumed from Buenos Aires periodicals (all but one dated 1894-1898).

5054. Elliott, Jorge. La nueva poesía chilena (Atenea, año 30, 111:337-338, julio-agosto 1953, p. 94-108; 112:339-340, sept.-oct. 1953, p. 122-130; año 31, 116: 349-350, julio-agosto 1954, p. 121-139; 117:351-352, sept.-oct. 1954, p. 160-175).
A thoughtful study of major value for evaluating Chilean poetry since 1919. It concentrates on the most significant figures.

5055. Fein, John M. La correspondencia de Rafael Pombo y Henry W. Longfellow (Bolívar, Bogotá, 31, julio 1954, p. 25-47).
Originals and translations of a number of letters exchanged between the two poets. Pombo was one of the most devoted Colombian translators of Longfellow.

5056. García, Pablo. Contrafigura de Nicanor Parra (Atenea, año 32, 119:355-356, enero-feb. 1955, p. 150-163).
On the author of *Cancionero sin nombre* and *Poemas y antipoemas,* a poet whose contribution will tend to emancipate the younger Chilean generation from the all-pervading influence of Huidobro and Neruda.

5057. ————. Juvencio Valle o relación del guardabosque maravillado (Atenea, año 30, 110:335, mayo 1953, p. 280-292).
A beautiful tribute to the poet of Imperial, Chile, a unique personality among the Chilean poets of the 1920's.

5058. ————. La poética de Pablo Neruda (Atenea, año 30, 112:339-340, sept.-oct. 1953, p. 76-90).
On the latest phase of Neruda's poetic art—simplicity, clarity, to make his social message accessible to the masses.

5059. García-Girón, Edmundo. "La azul sonrisa." Disquisición sobre la adjetivación modernista (R Iberoam, 20:39, oct. 1954-marzo 1955, p. 95-116).
Emphasizes the need for a general study of the vocabulary of Modernist poetry.

5060. Gatica de Montiveros, María Delia. Examen de la poesía puntana actual. San Luis, Argentina, Universidad Nacional de Cuyo, Facultad de Ciencias de la Educación (Publ. de la Cátedra de estudios sanluiseños, 2. serie, 6), 1951. 36 p.
An informative study on regional poetry—inspired by the province of San Luis, Argentina.

5061. González, Ariosto D. Las evocaciones históricas en la poesía uruguaya. Montevideo, 1953. 76 p., facsms.
An historian of ideas, upon being inducted into the Academia Nacional de Letras, summarizes the historical content in the compositions of Uruguayan poets, from José Prego de Oliver to the present.

5062. González, Manuel Pedro. Una influencia inexplorada en Ignacio Rodríguez Galván (Cuad Am, año 14, 84:6, nov.-dic. 1955, p. 256-278).
Echoes of Heredia in the poetry of Mexico's first (chronologically) Romantic (1816-1842). Valuable contribution to the history of Romanticism in Spanish America.

5063. ————. Un notable estudio argentino sobre Julián del Casal (R Iberoam, 19:38, abril-sept. 1954, p. 253-260).

A significant review article on José María Monner Sans' *Julián del Casal y el modernismo hispanoamericano*, reviewed in *HLAS, no. 18, 1952,* item 2633.

5064. ————. Una notable revaloración del modernismo (Cuad Am, año 14, 80:2, marzo-abril 1955, p. 283-292).
In praise of Max Henríquez Ureña's *Breve historia del modernismo* (México, Fondo de Cultura Económica, 1954).

5065. González Guerrero, Francisco. Revisión de Gutiérrez Nájera. México, Imp. Universitaria, 1955. 105 p.
An address (p. 9-56) read on the occasion of joining the Academia Mexicana Correspondiente de la Española. It discloses the antecedents of Gutiérrez Nájera's epoch-making poem "Pax animae." There follows Alfonso Méndez Plancarte's welcoming speech (which was read by Alfonso Junco owing to Father Méndez Plancarte's death on Feb. 8, 1955, eight days before the Academy's meeting). Published also in *Ábside,* 19:2, abril-junio 1955, p. 221-267.

5066. González Lanuza, Eduardo. Alfonso Reyes o la conciencia del oficio (Cuad Am, año 14, 80:2, marzo-abril 1955, p. 267-282).
A sound appreciation of Alfonso Reyes' stature as a poet by one of Argentina's most distinguished poets.

5067. ————. Almafuerte, existencialista "avant la lettre" (Sur, 229, julio-agosto 1954, p. 65-80).
One of three fine articles honoring the hundredth anniversary of the birth of Pedro Bonifacio Palacios ("Almafuerte"). The other two articles in this issue of *Sur* are: Carlos Mastronardi, "El pobre Almafuerte" (p. 60-65), and Aldo Prior, "Almafuerte en la conciencia de todos" (p. 80-89).

5068. González Martínez, Enrique. Para el epistolario de . . . (Ábside, 17:2, abril-junio 1953, p. 203-210; 18:3, julio-sept. 1954, p. 351-365; 18:4, oct.-dic. 1954, p. 496-519).
Continuation. Letters from the poet to friends (see *HLAS, no. 18, 1952,* item 2622). See also item below.

5069. ————, and **Alfonso Reyes.** Correspondencia de . . . (Ábside, 17:3, julio-sept. 1953, p. 283-308; 17:4, oct.-dic. 1953, p. 439-462; 18:1, enero-marzo 1954, p. 89-105).
An unusual unit in the *epistolario* in progress. See item above.

5070. Illanes A., Graciela. La tierra de Gabriela Mistral (Atenea, año 30, 109:331-332, enero-feb. 1953, p. 115-121).
On the Elqui Valley, famous in poetical geography. Worthy addition to item mentioned in *HLAS, no. 18, 1952,* item 2640.

5071. Jimenes Grullón, J. I. Seis poetas cubanos. Ensayos apologéticos. Regino E. Boti. María Luisa Milanés. Manuel Navarro Luna. Nicolás Guillén. Dulce María Loynaz. Eugenio Florit. Habana, Cromos, 1954. 169 p.
Notwithstanding its diffuseness and verbiage, this little book succeeds in communicating a warm appreciation for Cuban poetry.

5072. Kosice, Gyula. Peso y medida de Alberto Hidalgo. B. A., Ediciones SIGLA, 1953. 60 p.
Extravagant praise, in tortuous discourse, of a cryptic poet of undeniable talent and distinction, the Peruvian Hidalgo.

5073. Lefebvre, Alfredo. Descripción de la poesía de Gonzalo Rojas (Atenea, año 30, 109:331-332, enero-feb. 1953, p. 122-137).
On the author of *La miseria del hombre* (Valparaiso, Chile, 1948).

5074. Lerín, Manuel. Apuntes sobre la poesía de Alfonso Reyes (Cuad Am, año 14, 81:3, mayo-junio 1955, p. 212-226).

5075. Lindo, Hugo. Presentación de poetas salvadoreños (Atenea, año 32, 119:355-356, enero-feb. 1955, p. 78-116).
Selections from contemporary Salvadorean poets, with some biographical comments. Authoritative, informative.

5076. Louvel Bert, René. Homenaje de la Universidad de Concepción al poeta Ignacio Verdugo Cavada (Atenea, año 32, 121:358, abril 1955, p. 87-99).
Verdugo Cavada, born in 1887, is the author of a poem, "Los copihues," which every other Chilean knows by heart.

5077. Mapes, E. K. Manuel Gutiérrez Nájera: seudónimos y bibliografía (R Hisp Mod, 19:1-4, enero-dic. 1953, p. 132-204).
As a result of many years of search in Mexican repositories, Professor Mapes presents this invaluable tool to students of "el primer precursor del movimiento modernista." Only ten percent of Gutiérrez Nájera's production is available in book form; the rest (some verse and much prose) is in newspapers and magazines.

5078. Marasso, Arturo. Rubén Darío y su creación poética. B. A., Kapelusz, 1954. 428 p., illus.
"Definitive edition" of a most important book published in 1934 by the University of La Plata. Enlarged edition, 1941 (B. A., Biblioteca Nueva). The present edition adds quantitatively little: "Filosofía y hermetismo," p. 27-32, and comments on three or four poems not featured before. As in earlier editions, the author offers the following apology: "El desorden que se advierte en este libro se debe a que está hecho, casi siempre, por agregación de partes. . . . La

imposibilidad de reunir en capítulos la materia que quedó dispersa en el volumen, se remedia con el índice analítico." It is our considered judgment that Professor Marasso has committed no wrong. We would even favor further enlargements of his work without changing his method of exposition. This is a work of scholarship and of art as well.

5079. Marrero, Carmen. Luis Lloréns Torres: vida y obra (R Hisp Mod, 19:1-4, enero-dic. 1953, p. 3-84, photos.).
Life and works of Puerto Rico's most beloved poet (1876-1944), conscientiously studied and methodically presented. Bibliography, compiled by Félix L. Alegría, on p. 85-87, and selection of poems on p. 119-131.

5080. Méndez Plancarte, Alfonso. Díaz Mirón, poeta y artífice. México, Antigua Librería Robredo (Clásicos y modernos, Creación y crítica literaria, 10), 1954. 392 p., illus.
A rambling study of influences, meters, and rhymes, with valuable bibliographical information, and some portraits and facsimiles. Last major work of Father Méndez Plancarte (Sept. 2, 1909—Feb. 8, 1955). Two issues of *Ábside*, the literary review which he edited for five years, were dedicated to him (19:2 and 19:3, abril-junio and julio-sept. 1955).

5081. ————. Rubén: la primavera innumerable (Ábside, 17:1, enero-marzo 1953, p. 109-123).
The editor of the *Poesías completas* of Darío (Madrid, Aguilar, 1952) shows that the publisher was wrong in labelling it "Séptima edición, corregida y aumentada," since it is not based on the Alberto Ghiraldo edition (printed six times by Aguilar between 1932 and 1949). An interesting item for Darío's bibliography.

5082. Monguió, Luis. El origen de unos versos de "A Roosevelt" (Hispania, AATSP, 38:4, Dec. 1955, p. 424-426).
Did Darío "adapt" a phrase of Alberdi?

5083. ————. La poesía postmodernista peruana. México, Fondo de Cultura Económica (Col. Tierra firme, 57), 1954. 251 p.
Following a 50-page introductory chapter on *modernismo* in Peruvian poetry, Professor Monguió discusses the *postmodernista* period 1916-1950: *vanguardismo* in general, p. 60-86; *nativismo* (*indigenismo, cholismo*, etc.), p. 87-131; socio-political verse, p. 132-149; and "pure" verse, p. 150-183. Bibliography, p. 207-239. A thoroughly documented study that presents a dramatic chapter in the intellectual history of Peru. The author's discernment and insight, his method, and the lucidity of his style would be difficult to match nowadays.

5084. Nervo, Amado. Prosas y versos para Margarita. Nuevos inéditos de . . . (Ábside, 18:2, abril-junio 1954, p. 157-193).
Documents (mostly letters) of biographical sig-

nificance. Introductory note by Alfonso Méndez Plancarte.

5085. Nolasco, Flérida de. Rutas de nuestra poesía. Ciudad Trujillo, Impresora Dominicana, 1953. 155, vi p.
Journalistic papers of varying length on a dozen Dominican poets.

5086. Núñez, Estuardo. El poeta Chocano en Nueva York (Cuad Am, año 13, 75:3, mayo-junio 1954, p. 292-298).
Brief stop in 1909 and longer visit in 1914 to 1915 or 1916.

5087. Percas, Helena. La original expresión poética de Silvina Ocampo (R Iberoam, 19:38, abril-sept. 1954, p. 283-298).
Her first book, *Enumeración de la patria y otros poemas* (1942) was an event in Argentine literary circles because of the contrasting reactions of critics.

5088. ————. La poesía de María Alicia Domínguez (R Hisp Mod, 21:2, abril 1955, p. 127-140).
Descriptive account of the 11 books of verse published between 1925 and 1949 by a distinguished Argentine writer born in 1908.

5089. Phillips, Allen W. Nuevos estudios sobre López Velarde (R Hisp Mod, 19: 1-4, enero-dic. 1953, p. 94-99).

5090. Ponce, Manuel. Dios y el poeta (Ábside, 19:3, julio-sept. 1955, p. 324-340).
On Gorostiza, Villaurrutia and other modern Mexican poets vis-à-vis *arte cristiano*.

5091. Quintero, J. Humberto. El Padre Borges. Caracas, Imp. Nacional, 1953. 15 p.
Additional information on Carlos Borges, 1867-1932 (see *HLAS, no. 16, 1950*, item 2759).

5092. Rivera, Héctor M. Fernández Moreno: sus años de médico y poeta de Chascomús. Chascomús, Argentina, Editorial del Lago (Biblioteca de Chascomús, 3), 1953. 62 p.
Baldomero Fernández Moreno (1886-1950) moved from B. A. to Chascomús in 1912. In this provincial town he initiated his medical practice (for which he admittedly had no vocation), published his first poems, and married Dalmira López Osornio. No mention is made of the length of his residence in Chascomús.

5093. Rokha, Pablo de. Neruda y yo. Santiago, Multitud, 1955. 129 p. & illus.
Uncompromising attack on Neruda as poet and political leader. The critic "Alone" (i.e., Hernán Díaz Arrieta) gets a share of the blame.

5094. Russell, Dora Isella. Autobiografía poética (Bolívar, Bogotá, 38, abril 1955, p. 597-618).

The distinguished Uruguayan poetess quotes from her five books (1943 to 1954) in an attempt to explain some inexplicable processes. See also Agustín Rodríguez Garavito's warm appreciation of Dora Isella's accomplishments in pages 564-573 of the same issue, and Manuel Scorza's note (Cuad Am, año 12, 67:1, enero-feb. 1953, p. 293-295).

5095. ————. Carlos Sabat Ercasty, el poeta (Bolívar, Bogotá, 41, julio 1955, p. 19-36).
A Uruguayan woman poet's engaging exegesis of some texts by a master poet and compatriot.

5096. ————. Juana de Ibarbourou (Bolívar, Bogotá, 36, enero-feb. 1955, p. 55-81).
Brings nearly up to date a fine article published in *Revista nacional*, Montevideo, February 1951.

5097. Sánchez, Juan Francisco. De la métrica en Rubén Darío. Ciudad Trujillo, Pol Hermanos, 1955. 64 p., folding chart.
Excellent unpretentious study. Includes a folding chart with a detailed numerical analysis of metrical lines in Darío's complete verse production (32,408 lines). The three highest frequencies are: octosyllables, 9861; hendecasyllables, 8446; Alexandrines, 4213.

5098. Sánchez, Luis Alberto. Amanecer, ocaso y mediodía de José Santos Chocano (Cuad Am, año 13, 78:6, nov.-dic. 1954, p. 241-249).
Suggests that a revaluation of Chocano's poetry —nowadays underestimated—is now due.

5099. ————. González-Prada, olvidado precursor del modernismo (Cuad Am, año 12, 72:6, nov.-dic. 1953, p. 225-234).
A persuasive statement.

5100. ————. Presencia de la muerte en la poesía de Eguren (Bolívar, Bogotá, 37, marzo 1955, p. 353-360).
Brief article notable for the author's insight.

5101. Sánchez Quell, Hipólito. Tríangulo de la poesía rioplatense. B. A., Américalee, 1953. 126 p.
Includes: "Itinerario de la actual poesía argentina" (p. 9-35), "La poesía paraguaya, incógnita evelada," (p. 39-72), "Mapa de la poesía uruguaya contemporánea" (p. 75-99), and a selection of Sánchez Quell's own poems. The three studies mentioned contain, in an unassuming manner, data on poets and some samples of their best work. The paper on Paraguay justifies the book—the author, a Paraguayan and a poet in his own right, supplies information generally unavailable.

5102. Santana, Francisco. Poesía romántica chilena. Santiago, Flor Nacional, 1953. 31 p.
Mere generalities.

5103. Sarmiento, Ángel Martín. Sentido religioso de la poesía de Rafael Maya (Bolívar, Bogotá, 37, marzo 1955, p. 255-288; 38, abril 1955, p. 517-532).
A new approach to Maya's poetry.

5104. Silva Castro, Raúl. Efigie de Carlos Pezoa Velis (Atenea, año 32, 121:360, junio 1955, p. 370-385).
Life and vicissitudes of Pezoa Velis (1879-1908), with new significant information. His maternal surname is more often spelled "Véliz."

5105. Stelingis, Pablo. Carlos Pezoa Véliz, poeta modernista innovador (Atenea, año 30, 113:341-342, nov.-dic. 1953, p. 99-112; año 31, 114:345, marzo 1954, p. 274-295; 115:348, junio 1954, p. 287-312; 116:349-350, julio-agosto 1954, p. 106-115; 117: 351-352, sept.-oct. 1954, p. 120-159).
Overly long study, too prodigal of references to innumerable poets, which fails to prove the commendable thesis that Pezoa Véliz was not a lesser poet and a mere "criollista."

5106. Torres Rioseco, Arturo. Génesis de la formación literaria de Rubén Darío. Los raros (Atlante, 1:3, July 1953, p. 149-157).
On the importance of *Los raros* (B. A., 1896) for understanding the springs of Darío's later major works.

5107. Toussaint, Manuel. Bibliografía mexicana de Heredia. México, Secretaría de Relaciones Exteriores, Departamento de Información para el Extranjero (Monografías bibliográficas mexicanas, 2. serie, 5), 1953. 146 p.
Exhaustive bibliography of the Cuban poet José María Heredia (1803-1839) in Mexico. [A. Flores]

5108. Ugarte, Manuel. Cabral. Un poeta de América. Su poesía, la tierra, el hombre, el drama. 2. ed. B. A., Américalee (Biblioteca de cultura social, 15), 1955. 184 p.
An exegesis, often exasperatingly detailed and farfetched, of the poems in some of Manuel del Cabral's books. This distinguished son of the Dominican Republic is noted for the noble ideals contained in his verse as well as for his poetic gift. Ugarte ranks him among the great —with Neruda, Vallejo, and others.

5109. Undurraga, Antonio de. ¿Fueron doce los sonetos de la muerte de Gabriela Mistral? (Atenea, año 30, 110:336, junio 1953, p. 379-385).
Reveals the existence of another sonnet, dated 1909. The famous three compositions grouped under the title "Los sonetos de la muerte" won a poetry prize in 1914 and appeared in a book for the first time in 1922.

5110. Uribe Muñoz, Bernardo. Biografía de Aurelio Martínez Mutis. Sus mejores poesías. Medellín, Colombia, Editorial Granamérica, 1955. 232 p.

Informal account of key events in the literary life of a Colombian poet who became widely known in 1913 upon winning the coveted award offered by *Mundial,* the magazine edited by Darío in Paris. Martínez Mutis (1884-1954) was to some a veritable oracle and a major poet, and to others no more than a gifted versifier.

5111. Warner, Ralph E. Los *Poemas rústicos* de Manuel José Othón. Estudio bibliográfico analítico (Ábside, 19:4, oct.-dic. 1955, p. 438-447).

Interesting details about Othón as a book designer, the book being his famous *Poemas rústicos* (1902).

5112. Zardoya, Concha. La muerte en la poesía femenina latinoamericana (Cuad Am, año 12, 71:5, sept.-oct. 1953, p. 233-270).

Agustini, Mistral, Storni, and Ibarbourou are lineal descendants of the Spanish Santa Teresa de Jesús, when it comes to the sense of death in their poetry, according to the Spanish critic.

DRAMA

FRANK DAUSTER

THE note of hope expressed in the last number of the *Handbook* seems justified by the dramatic production of the last three years. The Latin American theater must now be regarded as a fact; the period of experimentation has been left behind. In addition to the established figures, a group of highly promising young authors has appeared. There is still a depressing quantity of inferior theater acted and published each year, but the quantity of good and even excellent plays is on the increase.

Among the most important events was the publication of four volumes of theater of the Guatemalan satirist, Manuel Galich. 1953 saw the publication of the complete works of Xavier Villaurrutia, one of the leaders in Mexico's attempt to develop a vital theater. Evidence of the effectiveness of the effort is the appearance of two new playwrights of exceeding promise, Héctor Mendoza and Carlos Solórzano. Mendoza's *Las cosas simples* and the two tragedies of Solórzano, *Doña Beatriz* and *El hechicero,* rank as the best new plays published in the period covered, along with Antonio Pagés Larraya's *Santos Vega, el payador.*

Criticism has not been so fortunate.

The only full-length studies of importance to come to our attention were Raúl Castagnino's *El circo criollo* and Julio Imbert's biography of Florencio Sánchez.

In sum, if it has not yet achieved recognition as a major genre in Latin America, the theater is developing. If it has not quite arrived, at least no longer need we adduce proof that it exists. The titles which follow are ample proof indeed.

PLAYS

5150. Angulo Guridi, Javier. Iguaniona. Drama histórico en verso y en tres actos (1867). Ciudad Trujillo, Montalvo (Col. conmemorativa del primer centenario de la Logia Cuna de América, 1), 1953. xxxiii, 112 p.

Second edition of the *indigenista* drama published in 1881. The play suffers from a dialogue unduly influenced by Zorrilla, and a dramatic conception whereby the Indians act according to the Spanish code of honor.

5151. Arriví, Francisco. Una sombra menos. Club de solteros. Madrid, Talls Gráfs. Méndez (Teatro puertorriqueño) 1953. 159 p.

Una sombra menos is a poetic-psychological drama which wavers between real meaning and the vapidity of a self-conscious, turgid and overly sensual dialogue. At its best, it is charged with dramatic power, and certain scenes are models of true clarity and compression. *Club de solteros* is a sparkling and thoroughly amusing grotesque of the war between the sexes.

5152. Blanco-Amor, Eduardo. Farsas B. A., López Negri, 1953. 102 p.

Three delightfully witty farces originally written for puppets, ranging from sheer humor through grotesque. The author is a master of the double-edged word and uses it to excellent advantage.

5153. Cervantes, Dagoberto de. Lorenzo Corrido del vengador. México, Helio México (Col. Teatro mexicano), 1954 86 p.

Uneven retelling of the *Agamemnon* in terms of the Revolution of 1910. There are moments of sober dramatic power, which often decay into melodrama.

5154. Cuzzani, Agustín. El centro-forward murió al amanecer. B. A., Ariadna, 1955 61 p.

A fantasy of man's isolation in society, better executed than conceived. The author demonstrates a real feeling for the theater and a solid command of its resources.

5155. Eichelbaum, Samuel. Un tal Ser

vando Gómez. B. A., Losange (Publ. teatral periódica, 4), 1954. 84 p.
Unnecessary lapses of time during the action vitiate an otherwise effective drama of a man's love for a woman and her son. The mastery of dialogue does not compensate for the disruption of dramatic unity and the consequent clouding of motivation.

5156. Ferretti, Aurelio. Farsas. Segunda edición. B. A., Tinglado, 1952, i.e. 1953. 172 p.
Two new and three previously published works. Their humor, ranging from mordant satire to broad farce, and a liberal use of music, make them somewhat qualified successes in a minor genre.

5157. Fuente, Sindulfo de la. El ruedo de Calatrava. Comedia en tres actos. México, Tezontle, 1954. 167 p.
A sentimental *costumbrista* comedy about a traditionalist *tabernero* who is converted to the acceptance of modernity. The moral is unimportant; the play's chief virtue is a vivid dialogue.

5158. Galich, Manuel. De lo vivo a lo pintado. Comedia en tres actos. Guatemala, Ministerio de Educación Pública (Col. Contemporáneos, 37; M. Galich, Obras de teatro, 3), 1953. 103 p.
An attack on hypocrisy and unfair legal practices, more theatrical than dramatic. The continuity is frequently destroyed by the author's intrusion.

5159. ————. M'hijo el bachiller. Comedia en tres actos. Guatemala, Editorial del Ministerio de Educación Pública (Col. Contemporáneos, 35; M. Galich, Obras de teatro, 1), 1953. 142 p.
A comedy of thesis, attacking the custom of wealthy families of attempting to force their children into professions, regardless of abilities. Through an agile and amusing dialogue, making effective use of puns and verbal games, the play amuses without losing the point of its satire.

5160. ————. La mugre. Comedia en tres actos. Guatemala, Editorial del Ministerio de Educación Pública (Col. Contemporáneos, 38; M. Galich, Obras de teatro, 4), 1953. 143 p.
This sequel to *Papá-Natas* is a bitter attack on cynicism, reaction, and intrigue in politics. The dramatic value of the play suffers from the vitriolic nature of its content, and dialogue is sometimes replaced by propaganda. This is, nevertheless, satire of a particularly dynamic sort.

5161. ————. Papá-Natas. Comedia en tres actos. Guatemala, Editorial del Ministerio de Educación Pública (Col. Contemporáneos, 36; M. Galich, Obras de teatro, 2), 1953. 128 p.
This "comedia trágica" is a searing attack on modern society's willingness to sacrifice the ideal in return for material well-being. Suffers the defect common to Galich's plays; the satire is so acid that it occasionally burns the life from the characters, converting the play into a tract. Fortunately, this is not usual, and *Papá-Natas* remains a dramatic indictment of individuals as well as a sociological indictment of a society.

5162. Hernández, Fausto. El inventor del saludo. Drama en tres actos. Rosario, Ruiz, 1955. 58 p.
On the framework of his fable of a famous clown who wishes to abandon the personality and relationships forced on him by his role, the author has constructed an amusing and thoughtful dramatic comedy. The agile dialogue and broad humor do not detract from the fundamentally serious nature of the play.

5163. Imbert, Julio. El diente. B. A., Losange (Publ. teatral periódica, 15), 1954. 63 p.
A one-act fable of man's inability to understand man. A very well executed play marred badly by the use of coincidence as motivation.

5164. Jiménez, Wilfredo. Pasión de Florencio Sánchez. Biografía dramatizada en tres actos. B. A., Losange, 1955. 79 p.
The author has yet to learn the differences between his profession of writing film scripts and writing for the stage, with its peculiar advantages and limitations. The complexities of staging, with rapid shifts of scene and an enormous cast, render this dramatically infeasible, despite its virtues: excellent individual scenes and fine understanding of character.

5165. Magaña, Sergio. Los signos del zodíaco. México, Editorial Intercontinental (Col. Teatro mexicano), 1953. 171 p.
A pessimistic drama of man's defeat in society, ending in an overly violent apocalyptic fury of blood, atonement, and frustration. The play makes excellent use of staging to integrate the large number of characters.

5166. Mendoza, Héctor. Las cosas simples. Comedia en tres actos y un entremés. México, Librería Studium (Col. Studium, 6), 1954. 82 p.
A comedy of Mexican student life distinguished by its delicate treatment of adolescence and the soundness of its conception. The dream sequence of the *entremés* is excellently integrated, and shows another aspect of the author's brilliant promise. Without falling into mawkishness or crudity, he has created a sympathetic and vivid picture of the problems and joys of the very young.

5167. Mora, Juan Miguel de. Primero es la luz. México, Helio-México (Col. Teatro mexicano), 1955. 45 p.
A promising symbolic drama of man's refusal to betray his moral heritage. The excellent first act is betrayed for the sake of shock power, and the last act is slipshod and rhetorical.

5168. Olivari, Nicolás. La seca. B. A., Ene, 1955? 83 p.
Unnecessary Lorquian reminiscences hinder this drama of a man's love for his brother's wife. The tragic undertones are never quite clarified in the protagonist's inability to break the spiritual drought which oppresses him, although the climactic moment of release demonstrates the author's understanding of its implications.

5169. Ordóñez, Eduardo. Por encima de todo. Comedia dramática en cuatro actos. Habana, Lex, 1953. 106 p.
A slick and talkative melodrama of World War III, well developed and professional.

5170. Pagés Larraya, Antonio. Santos Vega, el payador. Leyenda trágica en un preludio y tres actos. B. A., Ediciones "Doble P," 1953. 94 p.
In this poetic recreation of the myth of the legendary *payador*, the author has successfully avoided what is dead in the Gaucho dramatic tradition—external realism, superficial "gauchismo"—and created the mythic atmosphere required. Through an effective use of light and other scenic devices, the dramatic moments take on an air of illusion. The interest grows constantly until the climax, the duel between Santos Vega and the Devil. An excellent play.

5171. Plaza Noblia, Héctor. Teatro de cámara. La cajita de música. Tarde. Montevideo, Gaceta Comercial, 1954. 55 p.
Two one-act plays written as dramatic exercises. The author demonstrates an understanding of the importance of staging and the effectiveness of properties in the dramatic movement. *Tarde* provides an interesting new answer to the special problems of the monodrama.

5172. Rial, José Antonio. Nuramí. Drama en tres actos. Caracas, Tip. La nación (Cuadernos literarios de la Asociación de escritores venezolanos, 85), 1954. 130 p., illus.
This drama of a triangle between a newlywed couple and the husband's best friend suffers from a deliberate attempt at poetic dialogue and an overdose of Freudianism. It has the virtues of excellent theatrical sense and a gift for the creation of mood.

5173. Sepúlveda Iriondo, Ariel. Fernando Morales; comedia breve en un acto dividido en tres cuadros. Rosario, Imprenta de Revista Moderna, 1953. 42 p.
A promising first play which studies the idle dilettantism of a wealthy, handsome group of young people. Their tragedy is not overly convincing, but the author demonstrates an ability with dialogue and the development of character.

5174. Solana, Rafael. Estrella que se apaga. México, Editorial Intercontinental (Col. Teatro mexicano), 1953. 102 p.
This incisive satire of the world of movie-mak-ing skirts the edge of caricature, without losing the undertone of humanity. Several characters are brilliantly drawn; the excellent dialogue helps the development from pure comedy through satire to the almost tragic overtones of the climax.

5175. Solórzano, Carlos. Doña Beatriz. Auto histórico en tres actos. México, 1954. 84 p.
This tragedy of Beatriz de Alvarado, destroyed by her hatred of the alien world into which her conquistador husband brought her, is one of the best plays of the year. Her fanatical struggle and final self-destruction are heightened by an unusual economy of dialogue and the author's thorough understanding of dramatic unity and structure. See *HLAS, no. 17, 1951,* item 2563.

5176. ————. El hechicero. Tragedia en tres actos. México, Cultura (Cuadernos americanos, 40), 1955. 70 p.
In this, one of the year's best plays, the author has expressed man's struggle to harmonize the material and the spiritual in terms of the medieval search for the philosophers' stone. The tragedy of Merlin and the salvation of his people through his death are developed in a series of scenes which culminate in a third act worthy of the term "tragedy." *El hechicero* and *Doña Beatriz* (see above) demonstrate that Solórzano must be considered among Spanish America's most promising dramatists.

5177. Villaurrutia, Xavier. Poesía y teatro completos. México, Fondo de Cultura Económica (Letras mexicanas, 13), 1953. xxxiv, 539 p.
This edition of the works of the outstanding Mexican poet and playwright (1903-1950) includes the previously unpublished *Juego peligroso,* a typically Villaurrutian comedy of manners, although, paradoxically, it is more human and less a game than much of his other work. The introduction of Alí Chumacero provides a good preparation for reading Villaurrutia's cerebral dramas. Lacking El solterón, a one-act adaptation of a short story by Schnitzler, and the book of the opera, La mulata de Córdoba.

5178. ————. El solterón. México, Helio-México (Col. Teatro mexicano), 1954. 51 p.
A cynically witty adaptation for the stage of Schnitzler's short story, Der Tod des Jung-gesellen. Previously published in *Revista de Guatemala* (1:1, julio-sept. 1945, p. 114-129) and omitted in the collected works, it is accompanied here by 18 critical comments which stress the author's central position in the development of the Mexican theater.

STUDIES

5179. Arrom, José Juan. Perfil del teatro contemporáneo en Hispanoamérica (Hispania, AATSP, 36:1, Feb. 1953, p. 26-31; Bolívar, Bogotá, 21, julio 1953, p. 69-78).
A brief but lucid and informative sketch of the

levelopments during the last few years. In-
:ludes an extremely valuable list of outstanding
authors.

5180. Beck, Vera F. La fuerza motriz en
la obra dramática de Rodolfo Usigli (R
Iberoam, 18:36, sept. 1953, p. 369-383).
This analysis of Usigli's work classifies the
plays as politico-social and studies of psycho-
pathology. The author confesses *Corona de
ombra* to belong to both categories. The play-
y-play analysis is interesting and carefully
done, although it places such heavy emphasis on
these categories that other aspects are lost.
Vithal, an important contribution to the grow-
ig list of studies of Mexico's finest playwright.

5181. Castagnino, Raúl H. El circo
criollo. Datos y documentos para su historia, 1757-1924. B. A., Lajouane, 1953.
143 p., illus.
Devotes a considerable space to the origins in
he "circo" of the *teatro gauchesco*. Aside
rom its historical value, this study is interesting
nd well written. Includes a copious quantity of
eproductions of playbills and photographs.

182. Englekirk, John E. "Y el Padre
Eterno se ardía . . ." En torno al teatro
popular mexicano (Hispania, AATSP,
36:4, Nov. 1953, p. 405-411).
argely a classification of the themes of the
opular theater of northern Mexico, this work
the forerunner of a series of others, a result
uch to be desired.

183. Imbert, Julio. Florencio Sánchez.
Vida y creación. B. A., Schapire, 1954.
320 p., illus.
 rather subjective but thoroughly interesting
iography of the fine Uruguayan dramatist.
he section devoted to the plays is, unfortu-
ately, only a rapid discussion of a few points.
ánchez' work remains in need of a solid
:itical analysis.

184. Lamb, Ruth S. Xavier Villaurrutia

and the modern Mexican theatre (Mod
Lang For, 29:2, Dec. 1954, p. 108-114).
In this résumé of Villaurrutia's work as director
and playwright, the author stresses his experimentalism and the importance of his role in the
development of the theater. She feels, quite
correctly, that he died as he was attaining
mastery of his dramatic idiom.

5185. Lizarralde, Fernando. El Ollántay
argentino. Ensayo sobre la tragedia andina
de Ricardo Rojas. B. A., Término, 1953.
118 p.
An evaluation of a distinguished play in which
literary criticism is subordinated to an attempt
to treat it as an expression of the Argentine
national consciousness. The author recognizes
the 18th-century origin of the Quechua
Ollántay, and stresses the importance of Rojas'
work in uncovering the real legend.

5186. Maria y Campos, Armando de.
El teatro está siempre en crisis. Crónicas
de 1947 a 1950. México, Ediciones Arriba
el Telón, 1954. 240 p.
Another in the series of volumes of drama
criticism published by the Mexican critic. Although the articles are largely personal
impressions or reviews, they will be extremely
helpful to the scholar interested in the panorama of the modern theater in Mexico.

5187. Speratti Piñero, Emma Susana.
Dos aspectos de la literatura mexicana
del siglo XIX. I. Lo histórico y lo an-
tihistórico en *Muñoz, visitador de México*,
de Ignacio Rodríguez Galván. II. El teatro neoclásico en la literatura mexicana.
Indulgencia para todos, de Manuel Eduardo de Gorostiza (R Iberoam, 19:38, sept.
1954, p. 321-332).
The author emphasizes the individuality of
these two playwrights, stressing the romantic
disregard of historical fact in *Muñoz*, and the
eclecticism of Gorostiza within his neoclassical
framework.

BRAZILIAN LANGUAGE AND
LITERATURE

RALPH EDWARD DIMMICK

THE years 1953-1955 were marked by a pre-eminence of non-fiction in Brazilian
etters. Of outstanding importance was a group of works autobiographical in nature.
These included the stark *Memórias do cárcere* of Graciliano Ramos, whose death in
he year of their publication (1953) doubtless contributed to the widespread public
nterest which they aroused; Manuel Bandeira's literary memoirs, *Itinerário de Pasár-
ada;* the first volume of Oswald de Andrade's autobiography, *Um homem sem
rofissão;* the charming boyhood recollections of Thiers Martins Moreira, *O menino
o palacete;* the equally delightful volumes of Gilberto Amado dedicated to his
hildhood and student days, *História da minha infância* and *Minha formação no*

Recife; and two works by authors long dead, the *Diário íntimo* of Lima Barreto and the semiscandalous *Diário secreto* of Humberto de Campos. In the field of literary scholarship the most notable contribution was doubtless made by J. Galante de Sousa, with his monumental *Bibliografia de Machado de Assis*. Two new histories of Brazilian literature appeared: Antônio Soares Amora's *História da literatura brasileira* and the first volume (actually number 2) of *A literatura no Brasil*, a collaborative work under the general editorship of Afrânio Coutinho. Of a more restricted nature are Fred P. Ellison's *Brazil's new novel*, a study of the *romance nordestino*, and Jamil Almansur Haddad's lengthy *Revisão de Castro Alves*. A reference work of unusual value is Luís da Câmara Cascudo's *Dicionário do folclore brasileiro*.

In the field of fiction, the more important novels were produced by writers of long standing: Cornélio Penna (*A menina morta*), Jorge Amado (*Os subterrâneos da liberdade*), Lúcia Miguel Pereira (*Cabra-cega*), José Lins do Rêgo (*Cangaceiros*), Dinah Silveira de Queiroz (*A muralha*), and Érico Veríssimo (*Noite*). Of these works it can generally be said that they neither added to, nor detracted from, the authors' reputations. The most promising new figure to appear was Antônio Callado, with *Assunção de Salviano*. Better-than-average collections of short stories are *O pátio*, of Saldanha Coelho, and *Quatro histórias*, of Maurício Caminha de Lacerda.

The situation with regard to poetry was for the most part disappointing. Manuel Bandeira, Carlos Drummond de Andrade, Cassiano Ricardo and Vinícius de Moraes published collected editions, or selections from their previous production. Among the younger poets Antônio Rangel Bandeira (*O retrato-fantasma*) and José Escobar Faria (*Rosa dos ritos*) are perhaps most worthy of mention.

The extraordinary renaissance which the Brazilian theater has been experiencing in the last decade—chiefly on the basis of translations from English and French—is beginning to attract the attention of major figures in Brazilian letters. While Raquel de Queiroz's *Lampião*, Josué Montello's *Verdugo*, and Antônio Callado's *Cidade assassinada* are not truly successful as dramas, they are possessed of far greater distinction than the melodramas or farces which had previously constituted the bulk of Brazilian writing for the stage. One may hope that the long neglect of this genre is coming to an end.

Figures besides Graciliano Ramos to disappear from the scene in 1953 were Américo Facó, Jorge de Lima, Lindolfo Gomes, Said Ali, and Miguel Osório de Almeida. Oswald de Andrade died in 1954.

Tavares Bustos' *Anthologie de poètes brésiliens contemporains* won the Capdeville Prize in 1954 from the Académie Française, the first occasion on which a work of Brazilian literature had been so honored by that august body. Its counterpart in Rio, the Academia Brasileira de Letras, decided in the same year to raise the amount of its awards, but to make them biennial. The chief among them, the Machado de Assis Prize for *conjunto de obra*, was given to Dinah Silveira de Queiroz and to Onestaldo de Pennafort. The period moreover was characterized by a rash of literary contests sponsored by reviews, political figures, and private individuals. It is interesting to note that in the competition commemorating the Fourth Centenary of São Paulo, awards were made only in the fields of poetry (to João Cabral de Melo Neto) and the novel (to Gastão de Holanda), it being felt that the entries in the fields of the essay and the short story were not of a quality deserving recognition.

The editor would call attention to the fact that omissions from this statement or from the bibliography which follows do not all result from the *Handbook*'s principle of selectivity. The difficulties of obtaining books from Brazil are such that probably half of the works earning high critical praise there never become available for consultation. Thus not one of the eight short-story collections which *Jornal de letras* declared outstanding in 1954 has ever reached the editor's hands. It is hoped that such works as Cecília Meireles' *Cancioneiro da Inconfidência*, João Cabral de Melo Neto's *O rio*, Gastão de Holanda's *Os escorpiões*, Carlos Drummond de

Andrade's *O fazendeiro do ar*, Eneida's *Cão de madrugada*, and Edgard Cavalheiro's life of Monteiro Lobato—all presumably of major importance—may at least be included in future issues of the *Handbook*.

BIBLIOGRAPHY AND LANGUAGE

5200. Albuquerque, A. Tenório d'. Cubanismos e brasileirismos (Kriterion, 7: 29-30, julho-dez. 1954, p. 320-340).
Words, chiefly of African origin, which have had similar evolutions in the Spanish of Cuba and the Portuguese of Brazil.

5201. ————. Gauchismos. A linguagem do Rio Grande do Sul. Pôrto Alegre, Brazil, Livraria Sulina (Col. Meridional, 4), 1954? 101 p.
Notes on words which the author considers peculiar to the state of Rio Grande do Sul, with discussion of their origin (Spanish, African, Amerindian).

5202. Brazil. Biblioteca Nacional. Boletim bibliográfico. Rio. V. 1, no. 1, 1-2. trimestre 1951, i.e. 1952, and subsequent numbers.
Section on Brazilian literature valuable for current bibliography.

5203. Carpeaux [i.e., Karpfeu], Otto Maria. Pequena bibliografia crítica da literatura brasileira. 2. ed. revista e aumentada. Rio, Ministério da Educação e Cultura, Serviço de Documentação, 1955. 297 p.
Revised edition of a work of greatest bibliographical and critical value. See also *HLAS, no. 18, 1952,* item 2718.

5204. Cascudo, Luís da Câmara. Dicionário do folclore brasileiro. Rio, Instituto Nacional do Livro, 1954. 660 p.
Monumental work, covering all aspects of Brazilian folklore, by the recognized authority in the field. Valuable reference work for students of literature.

5205. Griffin, William J. Brazilian literature in English translation (R Interam Bibl, 5:1-2, enero-junio 1955, p. 21-37).
Highly complete bibliography of Brazilian works in English, including even brief excerpts. The period covered extends to about mid-1954.

5206. Jorge, J. David. O Tupi em São Paulo (R Arq Mun, 19:156, abril-junho 1953, p. 19-89).
Information concerning Tupi place names in the state of São Paulo.

5207. Jornal de filologia. São Paulo, Saraiva. Ano 1, v. 1, julho-set. 1953.

5208. Montenegro, Tulo Hostílio. O cumprimento do período como característica de estilo. Aplicação do processo de

Yule a amostras extraídas dos romances de Graciliano Ramos, Jorge Amado e José Geraldo Vieira (R Br Est, 16:63, junho-set. 1955, p. 1-82).
This elaborate statistical study shows an appreciable increase in sentence length in the later works of Amado and Ramos, with greater homogeneity in the case of Vieira.

5209. Moser, Gerald. "A gíria acadêmica": Portuguese student slang (Hispania, AATSP, 38:2, May 1955, p. 159-168).
Expressions used at the Universities of Coimbra and São Paulo form the basis of this entertaining study.

5210. Nascentes, Antenor. A gíria brasileira. Rio, Livraria Acadêmica (Biblioteca brasileira de filologia, 3), 1953. 181 p.
No dictionary of slang can hope to be complete or entirely up to date, but, with this reservation, the present work is in every respect the best for Brazil which has yet appeared.

5211. Nogueira, Júlio. Vocabulário ortográfico da língua portuguêsa. São Paulo, Companhia Editôra Nacional, 1953. 175 p.
Practical spelling book covering only the more common difficulties, following the principles of the *Pequeno vocabulário ortográfico da língua portuguêsa* of 1943, but noting the variants of the 1945 system.

5212. Nunes, José de Sá. Como vai o caso ortográfico? (Ocidente, ano 17, 47: 197, set. 1954, p. 96-105).
Those who are confused by the wavering state of spelling in Brazil will here find an account of the official actions taken in regard to the matter since 1943.

5213. Pereira, Manuel da Cunha (ed.). Vocabulário ortográfico brasileiro da língua portuguêsa. Organizado por . . . com a colaboração de Luiz Peixoto Gomes Filho. Supervisão e prefácio do Prof. Aurélio Buarque de Hollanda Ferreira. 2. ed. revista e aumentada. Rio, Livro Vermelho dos Telefones, 1954. 702 p.
Reproduces the material of the long-out-of-print *Pequeno vocabulário ortográfico da língua portuguêsa*, with corrections, about 15,000 additions, indications of plurals of compound nouns and the conjugation of irregular verbs, etc. Authoritative and highly useful.

5214. Revista brasileira de filologia. Rio, Livraria Acadêmica. V. 1, no. 1, junho 1955.

5215. Sampaio, Mário Arnaud. Dicionário guarani-português (R Mus Castilhos, 2:3, jan. 1953, p. 365-390).
Vocabulary of Guarani terms, E through Y.

5216. Schnerr, Walter J. The three verbs of location in Brazilian Portuguese (Hispania, AATSP, 38:4, Dec. 1954, p. 417-424).
Excellent study of contemporary usage of *ser*, *estar*, and *ficar*.

5217. Silveira, Valdemar César. A língua do Brasil e os italianismos de São Paulo (Diário de São Paulo, 6. caderno, jan. 25, 1954, p. 10-13).
Information on Brazilianisms in general, on localisms of the state of São Paulo, and especially Italianisms.

5218. Sousa, J. Galante de. Bibliografia de Machado de Assis. Rio, Instituto Nacional do Livro (Col. B I; Bibliografia, 10), 1955. 772 p., facsims.
Catalog of editions of Machado's work, periodicals and other publications in which he collaborated or in which transcriptions of his work appear, manuscripts, pieces set to music and adaptations; account of pseudonyms used by Machado; chronological list of his writings, in which the history of each item is set forth in detail; alphabetical index; facsimiles of title pages of first editions. Not entirely complete, but done with great care and honesty. A major contribution to literary scholarship, which must form the basis of all future research on Machado.

5219. Vallandro, Leonel, and Lino Vallandro. Dicionário inglês-português. Riqueza de explanação e exemplificação, têrmos técnicos e científicos, vocabulário de nomes próprios, abreviaturas, estudo da pronúncia e da gramática inglêsa. Pôrto Alegre, Brazil, Globo, 1954. 1135 p.
Contains a few errors, chiefly in usage ("a boy of eight years old"), but the large number of entries, the wealth of examples, and the up-to-date character of the information make this unquestionably the best English-Portuguese dictionary which has yet appeared.

CRITICISM, BIOGRAPHY, ESSAYS

5220. Aita, Giovanna. Due poeti brasiliani contemporanei. M. Bandeira, Ribeiro Couto. Napoli, Italy, Libreria Scientifica Editrice, 1953. 96 p.
Brief presentation of two contemporary poets, with selections and Italian translations. Sympathetic treatment, but shows only the more conventional side of their work.

5221. Amado, Gilberto. História da minha infância. Rio, Olympio, 1954. 287 p.
Sr. Amado grew up in small back-country towns of the Brazilian "bulge," and here brings vividly to life the people and happenings of 60 years ago: shopkeepers, schoolchildren, and politicians; holidays, missions, and amateur theatricals. The social historian should consider this a gold mine, and so will the general reader. The freshness of the observations and the roguish spirit of the telling make this a completely delightful book.

5222. ————. Minha formação no Recife. Rio, Olympio, 1955. 373 p.
Continuation of Amado's memoirs, covering the period of his legal studies. Highly interesting account of his intellectual awakening —the impressions made upon him by contact with great thinkers and writers.

5223. Amora, Antônio Soares. História da literatura brasileira (séculos XVI-XX). São Paulo, Saraiva, 1955. 169 p.
The critic Wilson Martins wrote of this book: ". . . é a nossa primeira história literária a se fundar exclusivamente em critérios estéticos. . . . Aos esforços descritivos dos seus antecessores, opõe o sr. Soares Amora os mais inteligentes esforços interpretativos; à mania acumulativa . . . responde com rigorosa prática selecionadora." Much more than a mere school text, this attempt at interpreting the leading figures and movements in Brazilian literature is worthy of the attention of all students thereof. One regrets, however, that there is no index or bibliography.

5224. ————. Perspective of contemporary Brazilian literature (Books Abroad, 27:4, autumn 1953, p. 359-367).
Sr. Amóra discusses trends since 1920 (anarchy, modernism, nationalism, regionalism), and declares: ". . . all sectors of Brazilian life have shown a determined effort to penetrate our national reality, to arrive at a comprehension of it, to interpret it, to solve its problems, especially its social problems. This determination is evident in our literary movements. . . ."

5225. Andrade, Oswald de. Um homem sem profissão. Memórias e confissões. V. 1. 1890-1919. Sob as ordens de mamãe. Prefácio de Antônio Cândido. Rio, Olympio, 1954. 220 p.
Oswald de Andrade was the *enfant terrible* of modernism, and this first volume of his memoirs, with its disorderliness, irreverence, lack of reticence, and colloquial style, would seem to opponents of the movement ample justification for all their outraged protests of 30 years ago. It is unfortunate that the book gives no clear picture of Andrade's early years: it is often obscure and much that one would like to know goes unmentioned. It gives interesting glimpses of a provincial São Paulo of the turn of the century and a fascinating gallery of portraits, notably that of the author. This is unquestionably artificial, but important as offering the view he wished others to entertain in his regard.

5226. ————. O modernismo (Anhembi, ano 5, 17:49, dez. 1954, p. 26-32).

Highly diverting account of Andrade's part in the initiation of the modernist movement and the Semana de Arte Moderna.

5227. Ballstaedt, Élio. A "idéia nova," de Cruz e Sousa e Virgílio Vársea (Sul, 7:23, dez. 1954, p. 1-10).
The reaction against romanticism in Santa Catarina in the 1880's, with emphasis on the rôle played by Cruz e Sousa.

5228. Bandeira, Manuel. Apresentação da poesia brasileira seguida de uma antologia de versos. 2. ed. aumentada. Rio, Casa do Estudante do Brasil, 1954. 443 p.
Revised and enlarged edition of what is unquestionably the best introduction to poetry in Brazil extant. Should be in every library of Brazilian literature.

5229. ————. O *humour* na poesia brasileira (Américas, PAU, 6:10, out. 1954, p. 16-19, 39).
Dealing chiefly with contemporary poets, this interesting article treats an aspect of Brazilian literature which had previously been almost completely ignored. Appears in the September issue of the English edition of the magazine.

5230. ————. Itinerário de Pasárgada. Rio, Jornal de Letras, 1954. 131 p.
Not so much a literary autobiography as a series of informal conversations, in which Bandeira comments upon aspects of his art and poetic experience—influences, inspiration, views on versification, the problem of translation, the relation of poetry to music. The frankness of the book makes it a valuable document to students of modern Brazilian literature.

5231. Barbosa, Rui. Antologia. Seleção, prefácio e notas de Luís Viana Filho. Rio, Casa de Rui Barbosa, 1953. 225 p.
The editor declares that Rui's enduring fame must rest, not upon his action as a statesman, but upon his literary production. This is a mistake. Few knew the Portuguese language so well, but Rui's florid style is wearisome today: he is a model to be avoided rather than followed. Sr. Viana has nevertheless rendered real service by culling from the vast body of Rui's writing passages representative of the best in his work, possessing for posterity some of the interest they afforded his contemporaries.

5232. Barreto, Lima. Diário íntimo. São Paulo, Mérito, 1953. 330 p.
Contains the "diário extravagante" kept from 1903 to 1921, the "Diário do hospício" (notes on the period spent in a mental institution), fragments of "Cemitério dos vivos" (an unfinished novel based on the author's experiences in that institution), and the inventory of Barreto's library. Interest chiefly biographical, especially for the light thrown on Barreto's alcoholism and the unhappiness and inferiority he felt at being a mulatto.

5233. ————. Feiras e mafuás. São Paulo, Mérito, 1953. 312 p.

Collection of newspaper articles on a variety of subjects, only a few of which (e.g. "A estação") have so much as a picturesque value today.

5234. ————. Marginália. São Paulo, Mérito, 1953. 320 p.
Previously scattered newspaper and magazine articles, including "impressões de leituras" and some ventures into folklore. Unimportant, but often amusing.

5235. Batchelor, Malcolm. Stories and storytellers of Brazil. V. 1. Folklore. Habana, Ucar García, 1953. 226 p.
Introduction to folk tales which circulate in Brazil. Aimed at the general public, highly readable. At the same time, evidences sound scholarship.

5236. Braga, Rubem. A borboleta amarela. Crônicas. Rio, Olympio, 1955. 333 p.
Poignancy is the term which best describes the works in this excellent collection. Usually inspired by a fleeting impression or recollection, all reflect Braga's highly sensitive nature, his melancholy at the transitoriness of human existence, and his talent for truly poetic expression.

5237. Brito, Mário da Silva. Notas para a história do modernismo brasileiro (Anhembi, ano 4, 14:40, março 1954, p. 73-89, and each succeeding issue through ano 5, 18:52, março 1955, p. 74-82 (conclusão)).
Covers all aspects of the movement. Poorly organized, but valuable for the bibliographical indications given.

5238. Campos, Humberto de. Diário secreto. Rio, O Cruzeiro, 1954. 2 v. 384, 479 p.
This diary of the semi-public life of one of the most popular writers of the 20's contains enough of the *chronique scandaleuse* (intrigues in the Academy, the amorous misbehavior of prominent public figures) to justify the stipulation that it appear only 20 years after his death, and the appeal which it has had for a certain segment of the public today. Though covering chiefly the period of Campos' maturity (1928-1934), it reveals an essentially shallow mind; nor does the tragedy of his disease-ridden last years make up for his lack of a sense of human dignity with regard to others.

5239. Cannabrava, Euryalo. Crítica e julgamento estético (R Br Poe, ano 5, 2:6, junho 1953, p. 28-46).
The author finds that the essence of the work of art consists in its ability to suggest a variety of meanings. Highly thoughtful essay.

5240. Carneiro, José Fernando. Apresentação de Jorge de Lima. Rio, Ministério da Educação e Cultura, Serviço de Documentação (Os cadernos de cultura, 66), 1954. 94 p.
Brief anthology of poems from the principal periods of Lima's production, preceded by an

appreciation. The editor's comparison of Lima and Castro Alves as poets of the Negro is well taken, but his remarks concerning Lima's philosophy and obscurities in his style are not illuminating.

5241. ————. Aspectos da poesia de Jorge de Lima (Ordem, 50:5, nov. 1953, p. 27-54).

The author studies "sua poesia negra, o problema do hermetismo em muitos dos seus poemas, a presença da Esperança em tôda sua obra." He finds Lima's attitude toward the Brazilian Negro less artificial than that of Castro Alves; his style at one and the same time that of "um clássico e um primitivo." The obscurity of some poems derives from the fact that they are faithful transcriptions of dreams. Lima did not, strictly speaking, write religious verse; faith underlies his work. An excellent appreciation.

5242. ————. Obscuridade na poesia de Jorge de Lima (Anhembi, ano 4, 13:38, jan. 1954, p. 233-244).

The obscurity of Jorge de Lima's later poems results from the fact that he was "o nosso melhor exemplo de autêntica poesia noturna, na qual o autor se limitou . . . a escrever aquilo que sua memória ainda guardava dos sonhos da véspera, coibindo-se de qualquer colaboração posterior."

5243. Cascudo, Luís da Câmara. Cinco livros do povo. Introdução ao estudo da novelística no Brasil. Pesquisas e notas. Textos das cinco tradicionais novelas populares: *Donzela Teodora, Roberto o Diabo, Princesa Magalona, Imperatriz Porcina, João de Calais.* Informação sobre a *História do Imperador Carlos Magno e dos Doze Pares de França.* Rio, Olympio (Documentos brasileiros, 72), 1953. 449 p.

Extensive consideration of survivals of romances of chivalry.

5244. Castello, José Aderaldo. Aspectos da poesia de Manuel Bandeira (Anhembi, ano 5, 20:59, out. 1955, p. 353-366).

Careful analysis of Bandeira's poetic development, especially with regard to content and emotions expressed.

5245. ————. Aspectos do realismo-naturalismo no Brasil (R Hist, São Paulo, 4:14, abril-junho 1953, p. 437-456).

The author studies Machado de Assis, Aluísio de Azevedo, Rodolfo Teófilo, Domingo Olímpio, and Inglês de Sousa, and concludes that the last-mentioned's *O missionário* is the sole truly naturalistic novel produced in Brazil.

5246. ————. Poesia de Carlos Drummond de Andrade (Anhembi, ano 4, 16:46, set. 1954, p. 110-119; 47, out., p. 353-362; 48, nov. 1954, p. 580-587).

Extended analysis of Carlos Drummond's poetic development.

5247. ————. Raul Pompéia: *O Ateneu* e o romance modernista (Anhembi, ano 4, 15:45, agôsto 1954, p. 472-482).

Castello finds the true position of *O Ateneu* to be that of " 'um esbôço de romance' precursor do romance modernista."

5248. ————. Tendências do romance modernista brasileiro (Anhembi, ano 5, 18:54, maio 1955, p. 549-555).

Excellent analysis of the general characteristics of the Brazilian novel of the modernist period. ". . . O nosso modernismo não é, senão, em última análise, um esfôrço de revisão total da temática da literatura brasileira e a preocupação de lhe oferecer novas contribuições, procurando, voluntária ou involuntáriamente, o seu traço de unidade, do século XVI até os nossos dias."

5249. ———— (ed.). A polêmica sôbre *A confederação dos Tamoios.* Críticas de José de Alencar, Manuel de Araújo Pôrto-Alegre, D. Pedro II e outros, coleidas e precedidas de uma introdução por José Aderaldo Castello. São Paulo, Universidade de São Paulo, Faculdade de Filosofia, Ciências e Letras (Col. Textos e documentos, 2), 1953. xlvii, 139 p.

The publication of Gonçalves de Magalhães' attempt at epic poetry, *A confederação dos Tamoios,* provoked a literary discussion of more interest for the light it throws on aspects of romanticism as it was conceived in Brazil in the 19th century than as criticism of Magalhães' work. Sr. Castello republishes the principal documents, accompanied by an excellent study of all sides of the question.

5250. Cavalheiro, Edgard. A correspondência entre Monteiro Lobato e Lima Barreto. Rio, Ministério da Educação e Cultura, Serviço de Documentação (Os cadernos de cultura, 76), 1955. 71 p.

Interesting for the light it throws on relations between two important forerunners of the generation of 1930.

5251. ————. Evolução do conto brasileiro. Rio, Ministério da Educação e Cultura (Os cadernos de cultura, 74), 1954. 47 p.

The title essay is essentially an aesthetic appreciation, eminently readable and showing excellent critical judgment, rather than a work of literary history. Also included is an essay on "Valdomiro Silveira, pai do conto regional brasileiro."

5252. Cegalla, Domingos Paschoal. Paulo Setubal e o sentido de sua obra (Ordem, 50:6, dez. 1953, p. 476-487).

Concerned chiefly with *Confiteor,* the apology of Setubal's reconversion to Catholicism.

5253. Coutinho, Afrânio (ed.). A literatura no Brasil. V. 2. Direção de Afrânio Coutinho com a assistência de Eugênio

Gomes e Barreto Filho. Rio, Editorial Sul Americana, 1955. 394 p.

Covering realism, naturalism, and Parnassianism in Brazilian literature, this volume includes essays by Josué Montelo (M. A. de Almeida, Naturalist fiction); Barreto Filho (Machado de Assis); Eugênio Gomes (Raul Pompéia, Lima Barreto); Otávio de Faria (Coelho Neto); Peregrino Júnior, Aderbal Jurema, Adonias Filho, Wilson Lousada, Edgard Cavalheiro, and Augusto Meier (regionalism); Herman Lima (short story); Décio de Almeida Prado (drama); Péricles Eugênio da Silva Ramos (Parnassian poetry). The last of these is probably the best; some of the others are little more than catalogs. Coutinho's introductory essay is rewarding, and the biobibliography organized by Xavier Placer is helpful. Useful for reference, but not a work of profound scholarship.

5254. ————. Poética: conceito e evolução (R Br Poe, ano 5, 2:6, junho 1953, p. 9-19).

The author urges a return to the classic distinction between poetry and rhetoric.

5255. Cruz-Coronado, Guillermo de la. Graciliano Ramos: trayectoria y personalidad (Estud Am, 8:37, oct. 1954, p. 283-301).

Acute observations upon Graciliano's temperament and upon the character of his work.

5256. Diegues Júnior, Manuel. As sêcas no folclore regional (Obs Ec Fin, 18:207, maio 1953, p. 55-60).

Reflections of the droughts of northeastern Brazil in popular literature.

5257. Ellison, Fred P. Brazil's new novel. Berkeley, University of California Press, 1954. 191 p.

One of the most original features of modern Brazilian literature is the *romance nordestino*. Passing beyond the superficial regionalism of the past century, it effectively relates characters to the local background and gives a voice to the masses of plantation workers, city proletarians, and dwellers in the backlands. Mr. Ellison analyzes the art and social views of José Lins do Rego, Jorge Amado, Graciliano Ramos, and Rachel de Queiroz. He shows the documentary value of José Lins' picture of decadent sugar-cane society; he recognizes the talent for creating fiction possessed by Amado, but notes his artistic deficiencies, especially the tendency to sink into propaganda. Ramos is presented as the greatest master of the novel since Machado de Assis, combining sociological interest with psychological revelation. Rachel de Queiroz contributes an understanding of feminine nature and emphasizes the social inequality of woman. Well written, admirably documented, indicative of wide knowledge and an excellent understanding of the subject, this book is a notable contribution to the study of Brazilian letters.

5258. Ennes, Ernesto. Uma poetisa brasileira, 1711 ou 1712-1793 (R Hist, São Paulo, 4:14, abril-junho 1953, p. 421-436).

Information concerning the family troubles of Teresa Margarida da Silva e Orta, best known as the authoress of the first Brazilian novel.

5259. Fragoso, Augusto. Seis pseudônimos de Patrocínio (Rio, 45:225, jan.-fev. 1954, p. 8-10, 50).

Notes on an important literary figure of the latter part of the last century.

5260. Freyre, Gilberto. Reinterpretando José de Alencar. Rio, Ministério da Educação e Cultura, Serviço de Documentação (Os cadernos de cultura, 79), 1955. 39 p.

"Seu paisagismo, seu naturismo, seu indianismo parecem representar todo êsse esfôrço socialmente crítico e românticamente reformador da sociedade e não apenas literáriamente romântico. . . . O que êle desejava era uma literatura, e mais do que isso, uma cultura brasileira, que resultasse de um maior contacto do brasileiro civilizado com a natureza, as gentes e os valores rùsticamente tropicais." Highly suggestive essay.

5261. Frieiro, Eduardo. Do Lazarilho de Tormes ao filho do Leonardo Pataca (Kriterion, 7:27-28, jan.-junho 1954, p. 65-82).

Manuel Antônio de Almeida's *Memórias de um sargento de milícias* viewed as a continuation of the picaresque tradition.

5262. Gomes, Eugênio. Prata de casa. Ensaios de literatura brasileira. Rio, A Noite, 1954? 181 p.

Sr. Gomes is a critic of the back-to-the-text school, and while his observations seldom go beyond the purely descriptive, they are singularly acute and thought provoking. Of special interest are the essays on Alvares de Azevedo, Castro Alves, Machado de Assis, and Adelino Magalhães.

5263. Haddad, Jamil Almansur. Castro Alves e a Revolução Praieira (R Hist, São Paulo, 4:13, jan.-março 1953, p. 211-221).

Discussion of the principles of the Pernambuco revolution of 1848-1849, and of Castro Alves' agreement therewith.

5264. ————. Revisão de Castro Alves. São Paulo, Saraiva (Col. Cruzeiro do Sul, 1, 2, 3), 1953. 3 v. 268, 235, 281 p., illus.

The author's admirable intent was to view his subject from all angles, in as much detail as possible, but his ambition o'erleapt itself. Ideas not without a kernel of truth are developed to the point of exaggeration; detail often becomes digression. While not without value, the work leaves the reader with the confused sense of not being able to see the forest for the trees.

5265. Hilton, Ronald. Brazilian literature (*in* Brazil and Portugal; an introduction.

Made by friends of Edgar Prestage and Aubrey Fitz Gerald Bell. Edited by H. V. Livermore, with the assistance of W. J. Entwistle. Oxford, Clarendon Press, 1953, p. 334-348).
Considerations upon the cultural background of Brazilian literature rather than a historical account thereof. Refreshing for the frankness and independence of the views expressed.

5266. Ivo, Lêdo. O preto no branco. Exegese de um poema de Manuel Bandeira. Rio, Livraria São José, 1955. 94 p.
Thought-provoking analysis of Bandeira's "Água-forte" by a leading poet of the younger generation.

5267. Jorge de Lima (J Let, 5:54, dez. 1953, p. 1, 14).
Biographical sketch of the late poet, plus an extensive bibliography of his works.

5268. Lessa, Orígenes. Literatura popular em versos (Anhembi, ano 6, 21:61, dez. 1955, p. 60-87).
Considerations on popular verse.

5269. Lima, Alceu Amoroso. Sílvio Romero and the evolution of literary criticism in Brazil (Americas, Franciscan Hist, 10:3, Jan. 1954, p. 277-288).
Good short account of literary criticism in Brazil, with emphasis on the figure of Sílvio Romero, whose case, Lima finds, is that of a personality greater than his written work.

5270. Lima, Medeiros. José Lins do Rêgo não foi menino prodígio (J Let, 6:56, fev. 1954, p. 2, 10, 15).
Interesting information concerning the writer and his art.

5271. Lisboa, Henriqueta. Convívio poético. Belo Horizonte, Brazil, Secretaria da Educação do Estado de Minas Gerais (Col. Cultural, 4), 1955. 202 p.
Reflections on the poetic art and a few of its practitioners, among others Cruz e Sousa, Varela, Alvares de Azevedo, João Alphonsus, Mário de Andrade, Carlos Drummond de Andrade, and Cecília Meireles.

5272. Lopes, Albert R., and Willis D. Jacobs. Ronald de Carvalho (R Iberoam, 19:36, sept. 1953, p. 391-399).
Brief but useful account of the work of a leading poet of the first third of this century.

5273. Lousada, Wilson. O caçador e as raposas. Rio, Ministério da Educação e Saúde, Serviço de Documentação (Os cadernos de cultura), 1953. 90 p.
Contains an essay on "Alencar e o romance de aventura." "Sua imaginação . . . sua riqueza de estilo, seu lirismo, seus dotes de grande paisagista . . . são virtudes de um legítimo narrador de histórias que em poucos outros românticos ou naturalistas serão encontradas."

5274. Machado, José Bettencourt. Machado of Brazil. The life and times of Machado de Assis. N. Y., Bramerica, 1953. 246 p.
Essentially the work of an amateur, this book adds nothing new concerning Machado (and perpetuates a number of errors), but serves to present him to the English-reading public.

5275. Magalhães Júnior, R. Arthur Azevedo e sua época. 2. ed. ilustrada, refundida e aumentada. São Paulo, Martins, 1955. 326 p.
Though it won an Academy prize in 1952, this is not a work of serious scholarship, nor does it contain much real information about Azevedo. It is a highly readable collection of literary gossip, however.

5276. ———. Machado de Assis desconhecido. Rio, Civilização Brasileira, 1955. 381 p.
As a journalist, Magalhães is chiefly interested in Machado's work for newspapers and magazines, attempting to show he was more interested in the surrounding world than some have said. Interesting ideas, but form of presentation is not helpful to scholars.

5277. Martins, Wilson. Poesia e prosa. Distinção. Histórico dessa distinção (R Br Poe, ano 5, 2:6, junho 1953, p. 47-62).
The author finds the history of the distinction between prose and poetry a highly confused one, and that only in France has there been a clear consciousness of the problem involved.

5278. Milliet, Sérgio. Panorama da moderna poesia brasileira. Rio, Ministério da Educação e Saúde, Serviço de Documentação, 1952. 133 p.
Brazilian poetry has known no more penetrating—and at the same time sympathetic —critic than Sérgio Milliet. Here he gathers together his views on all poets of significance to appear between 1920 and 1950. One regrets only that the series of individual studies is not accompanied by general observations and conclusions. A work of great critical value.

5279. Moreira, Thiers Martins. O menino e o palacete. Rio, Organização Simões, 1954. 136 p.
This highly sensitive and evocative work is unusual in the field of childhood reminiscences for confining itself to impressions made upon a boy by the house in which he spent his formative years. For the author, the old mansion which his immigrant parents had transformed into a provincial hotel was the world: all the perceptions to which he gradually awakened either originated within its walls or penetrated through its windows and doors. So personal was the relation between the two that Moreira speaks of it as a "dialog." This is a book of remarkable interest and merit.

5280. Nery, J. de Castro. O catolicismo de Joaquim Nabuco (Verbum, 10:2, junho 1953, p. 129-141).

Study of three phases of Nabuco's religious belief: "catolicismo incipiente e hereditário," "catolicismo partidarista e rebelde," "catolicismo voluntário e integral."

5281. Nunes, Cassiano. Vicente de Carvalho vivo. São Paulo, 1953. 15 p.
The author emphasizes Carvalho's constant self-criticism, his search for truth, and the continuation in him of the old Lusitanian lyric tradition.

5282. Pacheco, Armando Correia. La novela brasileña: una visión panorámica (Cursos Conf, año 24, 46:269, junio 1955, p. 97-109).
Good short account of the development of the Brazilian novel, with emphasis on the 19th century.

5283. Pereira, Lúcia Miguel. As mulheres na literatura brasileira (Anhembi, ano 5, 17:49, dez. 1954, p. 17-25).
The social status of Brazilian women of the past as reflected in literature.

5284. Proença, M. Cavalcanti. Ritmo e poesia. Rio, Organização Simões, 1955. 116 p.
Highly detailed and perceptive analysis of rhythmic patterns in Portuguese and Brazilian verse, of considerable interest to critics and interpreters.

5285. Ramos, Graciliano. Graciliano Ramos através de sua correspondência íntima (J Let, 5:54, dez. 1953, p. 3).
Letters of the late novelist, of interest to future biographers.

5286. ————. Memórias do cárcere. 3. ed. Rio, Olympio, 1954. 4 v. 232, 243, 234, 164 p.
First edition appeared in 1953. Published posthumously, with a concluding chapter by the author's son Ricardo, this memoir covers the period of Ramos' imprisonment for political reasons in 1936. Vividly realistic, the book recreates the nightmare of a shy, sensitive, semi-infirm genius, suddenly thrust into forcible and constant contact with everything most repugnant to him, deprived of all opportunity for solitude. While Ramos was revolted by much of that to which he was exposed, and while he underwent considerable suffering (the period in the penal colony was responsible for the definite ruin of his health), there is no self-commiseration and, more surprisingly, no expression of regret for lost liberty. Ramos was interested by the opportunity to study human types, and at times even displays a certain sense of humor. Highly significant as a social document, the *Memórias* are an invaluable contribution to knowledge of one of the most important figures in the history of Brazilian letters.

5287. Ricardo, Cassiano. A poesia na técnica do romance. Rio, Ministério da Educação e Cultura, Serviço de Docu-mentação (Os cadernos de cultura, 59), 1953. 52 p.
The author has some interesting observations on novelists, Brazilian and foreign, but arrives at the not very surprising conclusion that "a poesia na técnica do romance quer dizer um recurso a mais entre os muitos de que o romancista lança mão em seu ofício maravilhoso."

5288. Sánchez-Sáez, Braulio. La crítica literaria en el Brasil (Bolívar, Bogotá, 40, junio 1955, p. 1007-1015).
Brief history of literary criticism in Brazil, from Sílvio Romero to Antônio Cândido.

5289. ————. Monteiro Lobato, propulsor de una generación (Bolívar, Bogotá, 27, marzo 1954, p. 219-228).
The author discusses Lobato's publishing activities and other claims to leadership of the literary generation of the 1920's.

5290. Silva, J. Romão da. Luís Gama e suas poesias satíricas. Rio, Casa do Estudante do Brasil, 1954. 221 p.
The essay on Gama and his work is not particularly enlightening, but the volume includes the text of the *Primeiras trovas burlescas de Getulino.* It is curious that Gama, a prominent abolitionist, makes no reference to the slavery question in his attacks on the society of his day.

5291. Silveira, Edmund A. da. Literary aspects of José Lins do Rêgo's *Sugar cane cycle* (Hispania, AATSP, 38:4, Dec. 1955, p. 404-413).
Excellent discussion of the art of Lins do Rêgo as a novelist of the Brazilian Northeast. Silveira finds him to be "a descriptive rather than analytical writer" and his language "that of the spoken word." The novelist's chief defect lies in his "inability to assimilate a situation that lies outside the orbit of his experience."

5292. Souza, Antônio Cândido de Mello e. A literatura brasileira no século XX (*in* Proceedings of the International Colloquium on Luso-Brazilian Studies. Nashville, Tenn., Vanderbilt University Press, 1953, p. 149-153).
Interesting views on recent literary developments in Brazil by one of the country's most penetrating critics.

5293. Thiollier, René. Depoimento inédito sôbre a "Semana de Arte Moderna" (Habitat, 3:12, set. 1953, p. 44-49).
According to Thiollier, he was the person chiefly responsible for the organization of the Semana de Arte Moderna.

5294. Thomas, Earl W. Folklore in Brazilian literature (*in* Brazil. Papers presented in the Institute for Brazilian Studies, Vanderbilt University. Nashville, Tenn., Vanderbilt University Press, 1953, p. 91-135).

The author discusses the basic elements of folk literature in Brazil, the gradual appearance of folklore in literature in the colonial and romantic periods, the development of folklore studies, the appearance of urbanized folk poets such as Catulo da Paixão Cearense, and the increasing use of folk elements in poetry and the novel since 1920. An excellent synthesis.

5295. Torres Ríoseco, Arturo. Graciliano Ramos (Cuad Am, año 12, 71:5, sept.-oct. 1953, p. 281-288).
Brief but interesting analysis of the novelist's work.

5296. Valbuena Prat, Ángel. Panorama de poesía en un paisaje. Temas del Brasil (Cor Lit, 4:68, marzo 15, 1953, p. 1, 10).
Enthusiastic account of Brazilian poetry, as seen in Manuel Bandeira's Panorama de la poesía brasileña (HLAS, no. 17, 1951, item 2627), by a leading Spanish critic.

5297. Veríssimo, Érico. Reflexiones sobre un enigma literario: Machado de Assis (R Iberoam, 19:37, oct. 1953, p. 13-26).
Discussion chiefly of the influence which Machado's epilepsy may have had upon his work.

5298. ————. ¿Torre de marfil? ¿Torre de hierro? (Cuadernos, 4, enero-feb. 1954, p. 7-13).
A leading novelist discusses the problem of art for art's sake versus art with a social purpose in Brazil. He strikes a compromise, finding that: (1) "el novelista puede y debe participar íntegramente en la vida, con todas sus pasiones y luchas"; but that (2) "se salvarán tan sólo los escritores que hayan mantenido una fe profunda, apasionada y activa en su arte."

5299. Veríssimo, José. História da literatura brasileira. 3. ed. Rio, Olympio (Col. Documentos brasileiros, 74), 1954. 359 p.
Despite its age (first edition 1916), Veríssimo's history is, like Sílvio Romero's, still basic. The approach is that of a book reviewer rather than a literary critic: Veríssimo gives brief sketches of leading authors and evaluations of their work, with little attempt at synthesis or the development of principles of judgment. He has been criticized for a lack of appreciation of poetry, but, in general, time has confirmed his opinions. It is regrettable that there is no index and that there are a truly impardonable number of misprints in this edition, some so serious as to alter the meaning of the text.

5300. Woodbridge, Benjamin Mather, Jr. Machado de Assis—o encontro do artista com o homem (Prov São Pedro, 18, 1953, p. 18-25).
Only in 1879 did Machado's "artistic" writing begin to evidence that pessimism (not skepticism) to which the author had long given vent in his more personal crônicas. An article of unusual interest.

PROSE FICTION

5301. Amado, Jorge. Os subterrâneos da liberdade. São Paulo, Martins (Obras de Jorge Amado, 13), 1954. 3 v. 323, 240, 396 p.
Part 1 of a trilogy having the general title O muro de pedras, in which "o autor pensa apresentar um quadro da luta do povo brasileiro, dirigido pela classe operária, nos anos que vêm do golpe de Estado de 1937 até os dias atuais." Quite aside from any consideration of Amado's politics or the slant given to his narrative, from the point of view of probability his explanation of events is so elementary and his Communist heroes are so wooden in their perfection as to be entirely unconvincing. Amado tells a lively story however, and the villains keep the reader's interest, if not his sympathy.

5302. Anjos, Cyro dos. El amanuense Belmiro. México, Tezontle, 1954. 267 p.
Spanish translation, by Daniel Tapia Bolívar, of an important psychological novel of the 30's.

5303. Assis, Machado de. Dom Casmurro. Translated by Helen Caldwell. With an introduction by Waldo Frank. N. Y., Noonday Press, 1953. 283 p.
The elegance and distinction of Machado's style are unfortunately lacking in this translation of one of his major works.

5304. ————. Philosopher or dog? N. Y., Noonday Press, 1954. 271 p.
Translation, by Clotilde Wilson, of Quincas Borba.

5305. ————. Quincas Borba. Traduction de Alain de Acevedo. Introduction de Roger Bastide. Paris, Éditions Nagel (Coll. UNESCO d'œuvres représentatives, Série Ibéro-américaine, 8), 1955. 270 p.
French translation of a Brazilian classic. Good introduction.

5306. Branco, Carlos Castello. Continhos brasileiros. Rio, A Noite, 1952. 70 p.
Shrewd observation, humor, and better-than-average writing characterize these brief stories, each of which captures a particular psychological moment in the life of the protagonist.

5307. Callado, Antônio. Assunção de Salviano. Rio, Olympio, 1954. 219 p.
This story of a pair of Communist agitators in the back country who induce one of their adepts to pose as a mystic, hoping to turn the festivities of the Assumption into a popular revolt, only to have the "saint" fall victim to his own harangues, is one of the most original to appear in Brazil in many years. The irony of the situations is handled in delightfully humorous fashion, and, while the author has perhaps attempted to combine too many elements in one short book, he displays considerable mastery of the narrative art.

5308. Coelho, Saldanha. O pátio. Contos. Rio, Revista Branca, 1953? 126 p.

These stories are less a slice of life than a slice of soul. Evidence strong social consciousness on the part of the author. Well done.

5309. Damião, Antônio [pseud.]. Apenas o verde silêncio. Pôrto Alegre, Brazil, Globo, 1954. 78 p.

Composed in one week by Sílvio Duncan, Jorge Cezar Moreira, Heitor Saldanha and Joaquim Azevedo, as a last-minute entry in the ill-publicized competition for the "Prêmio da Cidade de Pôrto Alegre," this tale of marital infidelity on a ranch in Rio Grande do Sul is interesting chiefly as a *tour de force*.

5310. Donato, Mário. Madrugada sem Deus. Rio, Olympio, 1954. 475 p.

Telling the story of a descendant of an old Paulista family, this novel of urban life re-creates rather well the atmosphere of the 30's and 40's, although it does not delve very profoundly into the sociological bases of the changes effected. Save for a weak and unconvincing ending, the book is well constructed and interestingly written, and marks a distinct advance over Donato's previous preoccupations with sexual abnormalities.

5311. Dupré, Sra. Leandro [i.e. Maria José Dupré]. Vila Soledade. São Paulo, Saraiva, 1953. 311 p.

Sra. Dupré's sources of narrative inspiration seem to have dried up. This novel of an unloved wife who seeks solace in the arms of an egotistical lover may present an accurate picture of high society in São Paulo, but is totally lacking in interest.

5312. Ferreira, Ondina. Mêdo. São Paulo, Saraiva (Col. Romances do Brasil, 5), 1953. 233 p.

Story of a woman painter and sculptor and her fear of facing up to life and death. Not particularly convincing as a study of an artist, but better than average from the point of view of writing and psychology.

5313. Figueiredo, Guilherme. Viagem. São Paulo, Martins, 1955. 286 p.

A Utopian tale is a novelty in Brazilian letters; the author claims that his compatriots reserve their flights of fancy for politics! Though marred structurally by the inclusion of large sections of extraneous material, the book is not without interest for its implied criticism of contemporary society, often manifested in humorous style.

5314. Fonseca, Emi Bulhões Carvalho da. Lua cinzenta. Rio, O Cruzeiro (Col. Aurora, 5), 1953. 202 p.

As a study of jealousy, this novel had possibilities; unfortunately the heroine is too much of a pathological case to be truly interesting to the reader.

5315. ————. Siá Menina. Rio, O Cruzeiro (Col. Aurora, 6), 1953. 335 p.

Family chronicle, presented through the eyes of a portrait. Sentimental, and lacking in literary distinction, but not uninteresting.

5316. Fontana, Maria Elena. Biografia de uma rua. Rio, O Cruzeiro (Col. Aurora, 7), 1954. 223 p.

Family chronicle, presumably of Curitiba. Not uninteresting, but undistinguished.

5317. Lacerda, Maurício Caminha de. Quatro histórias. Rio, Revista Branca, 1954. 100 p.

Lacerda has a brilliant gift of caricature and a delightful style; unfortunately he does not yet know how to bring off a dénouement.

5318. Melo, Osvaldo Ferreira de, and Salim Miguel (comps.). Contistas novos de Santa Catarina. Introdução de Nereu Correa. Florianópolis, Brazil, Edições Sul (5), 1954. 100 p.

This collection testifies more to the desire of the Brazilian intellectual to call himself an *escritor* than to any sudden literary flowering in Santa Catarina. Of the 13 authors represented, only A. Boos Jr., Marcos de Farias, and Salim Miguel show any narrative talent.

5319. Menezes, Maria Wanderley. Os pecados de Maria Quitéria. Rio, O Cruzeiro, 1955. 150 p.

Although not exceptionally original, these tales of the backlands of Pernambuco (which received an Academy prize) evidence a narrative talent of genuine promise.

5320. Mucinic, José. Serpentinas. Recife, Brazil, Oficinas Gráficas da Fôlha da Manhã, 1954. 105 p.

Short stories, chiefly of unfortunate members of the lower classes. The author possesses a certain talent, but does not yet seem to have achieved a definite personality.

5321. Penna, Cornélio. A menina morta. Rio, Olympio, 1954. 458 p.

Penna writes very well, and no one in Brazil is more adept at creating an air of mystery. The reader would like at least some of the mystery dispelled by the end of the book, however. It is never made clear just what evil force causes the disintegration of this plantation family in the days of the Empire.

5322. Pereira, Armindo. Flagelo. Rio, Organização Simões, 1954. 157 p.

Attempt at renovation of the *romance nordestino*, dealing with a flood rather than a drought, and taking subjective lyricism rather than external realism as the approach. Shows promise.

5323. Pereira, Lúcia Miguel. Cabra-cega. Rio, Olympio, 1954. 202 p.

Novel of an adolescent girl of an upper-middle-class family of Rio, who gradually discovers the skeletons in the family closet. These are so numerous as to render the novel unbelievably melodramatic in the last analysis; nevertheless, the author tells her story with an unusual degree of art.

5324. Queiroz, Dinah Silveira de. A muralha. Romance comemorativo do IV centenário da fundação de São Paulo, Rio, Olympio, 1954. 459 p.

A somewhat strange tribute to São Paulo in view of the unfavorable light thrown upon the character of the Paulistas, this historical novel tells the tale of a haughty girl from Portugal and her inability to adapt herself to Brazil, with some account of the gold wars in Minas during the early part of the 18th century. An interesting story, well written for the most part. The men are somewhat shadowy figures—and the Indians straight out of Alencar—but the women are well drawn.

5325. Rêgo, José Lins do. Cangaceiros. Rio, Olympio, 1953. 315 p.

José Lins returns to his native Nordeste, dealing this time with the harsh existence of the *sertão*, whose inhabitants are victims, in turn, of bandit bands and the punitive forces supposedly sent in pursuit thereof. The grimness of this life is vividly set forth, but as a narrative *Cangaceiros* leaves much to be desired: the episodes, none of significant importance, are connected with a variety of characters and follow no apparent line of development. Bento, the central figure, can hardly be called a protagonist: he is at most an exasperating do-nothing. This is material for a novel rather than a finished product.

5326. Santos, Ruy. Agua barrenta. Rio, Olympio, 1953. 318 p.

Though called a novel, this book is essentially a series of sketches of life along the Rio São Francisco, connected by the thinnest of narrative threads. Interesting for its picture of aspects of Brazil little touched upon in literature up to now.

5327. Schmidt, Afonso. Obras. São Paulo, Editôra Brasiliense, 1954? 10 v. 1, Menino Felipe; Primeira viagem, 378 p.; 2, Saltimbancos; Adventuras de Indalécio, 294 p.; 3, O assalto; No tempo do protocolo, 293 p.; 4, A marcha; Lua nova, 348 p.; 5, A sombra de Júlio Frank; A vida de Paulo Eiro, 316 p.; 6, Colônia Cecília; Zanzalá; Reino do Céu, 260 p.; 7, Os impunes e outros contos, 325 p.; 8, Tesouro de Cananéia; Brutalidade, 212 p.; 9, Pirapora; O desconhecido, 316 p.; 10, São Paulo de meus amôres; Lembrança, 340 p.

Collected works of a minor novelist.

5328. Veríssimo, Érico. Noite. Pôrto Alegre, Brazil, Globo, 1954. 210 p.

Sr. Veríssimo's nameless protagonist is a victim of temporary amnesia, resulting from emotional shock, who falls into vaguely sinister company with whom he goes the rounds of the city by night. Told entirely from his point of view, the story has the air of a bad dream, from which, with the dawn, there comes a Freudian awakening. Absorbingly told, this represents a new departure by Sr. Veríssimo in the narrative art. The Portuguese edition (Lisboa, Livros do

Brasil, 1954, 243 p.) also contains a short story, "Sonata."

VERSE

5329. Abreu, Casimiro de. Obras de . . . Apuração e revisão do texto, escôrço biográfico, notas e índices por Sousa da Silveira. 2. ed. melhorada. Rio, Ministério da Educação e Cultura (Col. de textos da língua portuguêsa moderna, 1), 1955. xxxvi, 471 p.

Revised and augmented edition of a work which first appeared in 1940, and in which the editor not only restored Casimiro's text but rehabilitated his reputation in matters of usage and versification. A model of scholarship in every respect.

5330. Álvarez Alonso, Isidro. Poetas del Brasil en lengua española (R U Cat São Paulo, ano 2, 4:7, set. 1953, p. 62-90).

Translations of 19 poets, from Gonçalves Dias to Maria Eugênia Celso, with brief commentaries.

5331. Andrade, Carlos Drummond de. Viola de bôlso. Novamente encordoada. Rio, Olympio, 1955. 125 p.

New, enlarged edition of work published in 1952 (see HLAS, no. 18, 1952, item 2785). The section "Prima & contra-prima" contains verse of very high quaity, the tone of which runs from quiet resignation to sly humor. Interesting to compare the *vers de circonstance* composing the rest of the volume with Manuel Bandeira's *Mafuá do malungo.*

5332. Araujo, Murillo. O candelabro eterno. Rio, Pongetti, 1955. 105 p.

Critics have called attention to the "sentido da infância" shown in Araujo's work, and it is possible that children will enjoy these pedestrian tributes to the great men and events of Brazil's past.

5333. Bandeira, Antônio Rangel. O retrato-fantasma. Composições líricas. Jôgo partido. São Paulo, Clube de Poesia de São Paulo (Col. Centenário), 1953. 60 p.

Discretion and sobriety are the hallmarks of Sr. Bandeira's poetry, as is a strong sense of reality. "Poeta, teu reino é dêste mundo," he declares in "Poética," and he goes on to counsel faithfulness to self and the search for preciseness of expression. The result is verse of admirable sincerity, depth of emotion, and power of suggestion.

5334. Bandeira, Manuel. Mafuá do malungo. Versos de circunstância. Nova ed. aumentada. Rio, Livraria São José, 1955. 120 p.

Written exclusively for the amusement of the poet's friends, these verses were never meant to be taken seriously. Nevertheless, a few ("Autorretrato," "Casa grande & senzala") are outstanding examples of Bandeira's humorous manner. First edition privately printed in a limited edition (see *HLAS, no. 14, 1948,* item 3057).

5335. ————. Poesias. A cinza das horas. Carnaval. Ritmo dissoluto. Libertinagem. Estrêla da manhã. Lira dos cinqüent'-anos. Belo belo. Opus 10. 6 ed. aumentada. Rio, Olympio, 1955. 401 p.

The "Saint John the Baptist of the modernist movement" continues to add to his distinguished poetic production. Wrote José Aderaldo Castello of this most recent edition: "Poesia carregadamente individualista, pelo seu sentido autobiográfico na dependência da memória, do temperamento, do sofrimento físico, da emoção mais íntima, mesmo quando aborda temas sociais ou retrata amigos, ela é uma constante auto-definição essencialmente subjetiva, às vêzes espontâneamente confidencial, às vêzes exaltada, quase virtuosa, quando não ostenta a intenção anti-lírica dos modernistas."

5336. Brandão, Théo. Trovas populares de Alagoas. Maceió, Brazil, Edições Caeté, 1951. 122 p.

1143 quatrains (with Portuguese and Spanish variants) from the Northeast, arranged alphabetically by first lines.

5337. Couto, Ribeiro. Entre mar e rio. Lisboa, Livros do Brasil, 1952. 140 p.

A nostalgic tribute to the Portugal of Couto's forebears. Many of these short poems have the simplicity and charm of verse of popular origin.

5338. ————. Rive étrangère. Paris, Presses du Livre Français (Coll. Le soleil bleu), 1951.

A distinguished Brazilian poet tries his hand at French verse.

5339. Faria, José Escobar. Poemas e elegias. São Paulo, Martins, 1953? 74 p.

The poet seems to be striving throughout this collection to give expression to the ineffable. It may well be, as Sérgio Milliet declares, that this is the *raison d'être* of poetry, but the result in the present case is undeniably obscurity. Conciseness of expression and musicality are among Faria's more positive qualities.

5340. ————. Rosa dos ritos. São Paulo, Edições Leia, 1954. Approx. 44 unnumbered pages.

The solitude of man before the universe is the theme of Sr. Faria's latest collection. Greater simplicity and musicality of expression, and deeper, more sincere feeling make it also the best. Outstanding.

5341. Guimaraens, Alphonsus de [i.e., **Alfonso Henriques da Costa Guimarães**]. Poesias. 2. ed. aumentada e revista. Rio, Organização Simões, 1955. 2 v. 701 p., illus.

The reputation of Alphonsus de Guimaraens, as one of the two great Brazilian symbolists, seems to be constantly on the rise. The 1938 edition of his collected poems, long out of print, is here reprinted with 19 additions, a chronology and a biographical sketch, abundant notes, an extensive bibliography, and numerous illustrations. Highly valuable work for all students of Brazilian literature.

5342. Lopes Neto, J. Simões (comp.). Cancioneiro guasca. Antigas danças, poemetos, quadras, trovas, dizeres, poesias históricas, desafios. Pôrto Alegre, Brazil, Globo (Col. Província, 6), 1954. 260 p.

First published in 1910, this is still one of the best and most extensive collections of popular poetry of Rio Grande do Sul.

5343. Medauar, Jorge. Prelúdios, noturnos e tema de amor. 1949-1954. Rio, Olympio, 1954. 90 p.

Lyric expansion, in a sort of communion with the entire circumambient world. Unusually felicitous choice of words and figures of speech produces at times verse of strikingly beautiful effect.

5344. Mendes, Murilo. Contemplação de Ouro-Prêto. Rio, Ministério da Educação e Cultura, Serviço de Documentação, 1954. 171 p., illus.

Handsome volume of somewhat uneven content. Some parts are little more than a rhymed guidebook; other sections (e. g., "A lua de Ouro Prêto") show genuine poetic inspiration.

5345. Moraes, Vinicius de. Antologia poética. Rio, A Noite, 1955? 271 p.

This collection gives an excellent view of the evolution of one of the most important poets writing in Brazil today. In subject matter he has progressed from a semireligious mysticism through open carnality to verse of social inspiration; in style he has tended toward greater conciseness and clarity, away from long, meandering lines and vague terminology.

5346. Oliveira, Manuel Botelho de. Música do Parnasso. Prefácio e organização do texto por Antenor Nascentes. Rio, Instituto Nacional do Livro (Biblioteca popular brasileira, 2), 1953. 2 v. 252, 238 p.

Scholarly edition of the works of the first Brazilian-born poet. Interest purely historic; over half of the material in Spanish.

5347. Ramos, Saulo. Café. A poesia da terra e das enxadas. São Paulo, Martins, 1953. 177 p.

In these poems, Sr. Ramos treats a wide variety of aspects of the social impact of the coffee cycle upon the growers and the region in which they dwell. He is best when, instead of waxing consciously "poetic," he gives a simpler, and more truly expressive, turn to his verse.

5348. Ricardo, Cassiano. Martim Cererê. Traductor, Emilia Bernal. Madrid, Ediciones Cultura Hispánica, 1953. 241 p.

Spanish translation of one of the notable poetic works of Brazilian modernism. Prefaces by the translator and Menotti del Picchia.

5349. ————. Meu caminho até ontem. Poemas escolhidos. Introdução de Mário da Silva Brito. São Paulo, Saraiva, 1955. 254 p.

"Sabendo cultivar a forma sem ser formalista; escrevendo uma poesia de pensamento sem ser 'pensador'; conseguindo valer-se dos recursos da prosa e das expressões e palavras mais chãs, sem jamais ser prosaico ou vulgar, Cassiano Ricardo se firma cada vez mais entre os primeiros nomes da moderna poesia em língua portuguêsa" writes Domingos Carvalho da Silva. Of all contemporary Brazilian poets, Cassiano Ricardo has had perhaps the most notable evolution, from Parnassianism, through the "verde-amarelo" excesses of modernism, to an expression which is best described as purely personal. While this is supposedly an anthology of his work to date, it is to be noted that the poems from earlier collections frequently appear in greatly altered form.

5350. Tavares, Adelmar. Um ramo de cantigas. Rio, Gráfica Editôra Aurora, 1955. 139 p.

Selection of quatrains in the popular manner taken from the author's previously published work.

5351. Vargas Netto, Manoel. Tropilha crioula e gado xucro. Versos gauchescos. Pôrto Alegre, Brazil, Globo (Col. Província, 8), 1955. 146 p.

Though the work of a minor poet, much of the verse in the folk vein possesses distinct charm.

DRAMA

5352. Callado, Antônio. A cidade assassinada. Peça em 3 atos e 7 quadros. Rio, Olympio, 1954. 109 p.

Historical drama of the forcible abandonment of Santo André to the benefit of São Paulo. The dénouement is not entirely convincing, but the work does possess dramatic power and the style is far above the usual level of playwriting in Brazil.

5353. Montello, Josué. O verdugo. Teatro. Rio, Gráfica Olímpica Editôra, 1954. 107 p.

Symbolistic drama of the pass to which misfortune can bring "good" people.

5354. Nascimento, Abdias. Sortilégio. Mistério negro (Anhembi, ano 3, 12:36, nov. 1953, p. 544-565).

One-act play with candomblé setting. An educated Negro relates, as if in hallucination, his unhappy relations with white society, and his murder of his mistress. Performance by the Teatro Experimental do Negro forbidden in São Paulo as tending to create racial tension.

5355. Oliveira, D. Martins de. Baile pastoril. Rio, Editôra Borsoi, 1954. 142 p.

Observations on traditional religious playlets of the São Francisco valley. Includes texts.

5356. Queiroz, Rachel de. Lampião. Drama em cinco quadros. Rio, Olympio, 1953. 142 p.

Srta. Queiroz has attained great distinction as a novelist, but her first attempt at dramatic writing is a distinct disappointment. There is no real plot; the dialog frequently seems improbable; and no clear impression is given of the character of the celebrated bandit and his followers.

5357. Teatro brasileiro. São Paulo. No. 1, nov. 1955.

New magazine, dedicated to the theater. Edited by Alfredo Mesquita, who, more than any other, is responsible for the extraordinary renaissance of the drama in Brazil in the last decade.

HAITIAN LANGUAGE AND LITERATURE

MERCER COOK

THE emphasis was on history as Haiti celebrated the 150th anniversary of her Independence, in 1953. Intensifying the Haitian's traditional and understandable pride in the achievements of Toussaint, Dessalines, Christophe, and Pétion, the sesquicentennial inspired several historical works of special significance. One such volume, Jean Fouchard's Les marrons du syllabaire (item 3383a), was particularly refreshing because the author, following the lead of an indefatigable French scholar, Gabriel Debien, consulted sources not utilized by other Haitian historians. Two volumes by Dantès Bellegarde (items 3007, 3008, and 6603) and one by Dr. J. Price-Mars (item 4266) brought new laurels to long-established reputations. In addition, as a member of the UN Commission on Race Relations in South Africa, M. Bellegarde collaborated on the three reports published to date.

The harvest in belles lettres was somewhat more meager than that in the social sciences. To stimulate literary production, various prizes were offered in connection with the celebration. Jean F. Brierre and Clovis N. Bonhomme won the President's Prize for the best drama; Régnor C. Bernard received the poetry award (item 5391). Moreover, many of the works published during the period were grouped in the Collection de Cent Cinquantenaire de l'Indépendance d'Haïti. On the whole, however, the increased output proved more impressive from a quantitative than from a qualitative standpoint.

Several authors discussed this relative decline in literary merit. Frenchman Auguste Viatte attributed it to preoccupation with racial, nationalistic themes, "la littérature engagée." A Haitian critic, Pradel Pompilus, disagreed in a review of Viatte's *Histoire littéraire de l'Amérique française.* In a stimulating volume of essays, Joseph D. Baguidy blamed economic causes. Another essayist, Régnor C. Bernard, also cited economics, along with a milieu "almost hostile to culture·" Significantly, perhaps the finest poetry published by a Haitian in 1955 was written by Jean F. Brierre in 1932 and 1934 (cf. *Pétion y Bolívar,* and *El adiós a la Marsellesa*).

Why, one wonders, do poets like Émile Roumer and Carl Brouard remain silent? Has Roussan Camille abandoned poetry for journalism? What has become of J. B. Cinéas, who pioneered in the peasant novel? When may we expect the next novel by the Marcelin brothers, the second volume of Pradel Pompilus's literary history, or René Piquion's long-awaited *Colosses de bronze?* These are some of the questions that come to mind as one surveys the contemporary Haitian scene.

Paradoxically, the insistence on financial difficulties of publishing—to which we alluded in no. 13 of the *Handbook*—occurs at a time when Haitian revenue is at a record high. In unprecedented numbers, tourists are flocking to the island, but their interests, alas, rarely include Haitian books. Especially designed for tourists are two volumes lately published in this country: Cave's *Haiti, highroad to adventure,* and Rodman's *Haiti, the black republic.* In linguistics, a significant recent volume is *Haitian Creole,* by Robert A. Hall, Jr. Still unpublished, unfortunately, is the excellent dissertation on Haitian poetry that Naomi M. Garrett prepared at Columbia University. The closest approach to it in French, though the authors differ somewhat in point of view, is Viatte's aforementioned detailed study of Haitian letters.

Conjonction, the magazine published by the Institut Français d'Haïti, continued its interesting career, and a most promising monthly, *Optique,* entered the field in February 1954.

No analysis, however brief, of contemporary Haitian letters should fail to mention two grievous losses sustained in 1954. Dr. Catts Pressoir, historian, scientist, and educator, died on September 8, and Luc Grimard, poet, novelist, and journalist, passed away on October 25 of that year. In February 1955 *Conjonction* carried a bibliography of Dr. Pressoir's works; M. Grimard's writings were listed in the December 1954 issue of the same periodical.

5375. Alexis, Jacques Stephen. Compère général soleil. Paris, Gallimard, 1955. 350 p.

This violently communistic novel tells of a Haitian peasant who struggles against poverty, injustice, illness, imprisonment, and massacre. In these pages, Haiti under Sténio Vincent is depicted as a chamber of horrors, and conditions in the neighboring Dominican Republic, where the hero seeks asylum, are even worse. Perhaps the most sympathetic characters are a handful of Stalinists on either side of the border. In fact, the author's tribute to Stalin (p. 224) must doubtless prove embarrassing in the light of the official Soviet reappraisal of the former dictator. Neither the love story nor occasional bits of local color render the propaganda palatable. Nevertheless, as a Gallimard publication, the book will probably reach large numbers of French readers.

5376. Baguidy, Joseph D. Incidences. Essais et témoignages. Port-au-Prince, 1955. 105 p.

Eight short essays on such subjects as Africa, Haitian folklore, Haitian problems, foreign policy, and the future of Haitian letters.

5377. Bellegarde, Dantès. Le créole haï-

tien, patois français (Panorama, 3:11, 1954, p. 56-63).
An excerpt from M. Bellegarde's *Haïti et son peuple*. Here he stresses the relationship of Creole to French and suggests a method for facilitating the study of the latter for the Haitian child.

5378. Bernard, Régnor C. Sur les routes qui montent. Port-au-Prince, Les Presses Libres (Coll. du cent cinquantenaire), 1954. 67 p.
The first and third of these four essays are largely historical. The second is a splendid tribute to Robert Lataillade, a Haitian poet who died prematurely in 1931. The final essay reveals the responsibilities and the plight of the Haitian author. A remarkable preface by F. Morisseau-Leroy and the title of the book indicate, along with the text proper, that M. Bernard is no defeatist.

5379. Brierre, Jean F. Dessalines nous parle. Port-au-Prince, Deschamps (Coll. du sesquicentenaire de l'Indépendance d'Haïti), 1953. 8 p.
A poetic tribute to the founder of Haitian independence by one of Haiti's most talented poets.

5380. ————. Pétion y Bolívar. El adiós a la marsellesa. B. A., Ediciones Troquel, 1955. 200 p.
Two poetic dramas written in 1932 and 1934 by the poet-diplomat who is Haitian Ambasador in B. A. The text is in the original French and in Spanish translation by Hugo E. Lezama. The subjects, taken from Haitian history, are treated with the fervor and eloquence that have always characterized the vibrant voice of Jean F. Brierre. His sparkling Alexandrines provide an appropriate background for the greatness of Pétion, Bolívar, and Toussaint Louverture.

5381. Charles, Paul-Émile. Caraïbes en fleurs. Port-au-Prince, Imp. de l'État (Coll. du cent cinquantenaire de l'Indépendance nationale), 1954. 102 p.
Poems of local inspiration in free verse. In his preface, M. Maurice Laraque notes that the verses reflect "our rich natural setting and the torments of our Afro-Latin soul."

5382. Chauvet, Marie. Fille d'Haïti. Paris, Fasquelle, 1954. 297 p.
In *HLAS, no. 13, 1947* (item 2363), we called attention to Mme. Pierre Chauvet's poetic *La légende des fleurs*. The present work, a novel, tells the story of an illegitimate Haitian girl, Lotus, whose mother becomes a prostitute in order to support her. After the mother's death, Lotus falls in love with a young Haitian journalist; both risk their lives preparing for the revolution (that of 1946?), which finally disavows them because they are mulattoes. A new régime brings promise of justice, but by now the hero is dead and Lotus's house has become a day-nursery. The author's talent is undeniable, though she has not yet realized the promise of her earlier work. *Fille d'Haïti* is something of a mélange—psychological, mystic, political—with strong doses of naturalism and a bit of *vodun* thrown in for good measure.

5383. Dartiguenave, Edith. Héroisme d'une haïtienne. Port-au-Prince, 1955? 46 p.
A short story of peasant life, the struggle between *vodun* and Christianity. As Jean Brierre tactfully suggests in his preface, the character delineation leaves much to be desired. But this is the author's first attempt at fiction; we shall await her next.

5384. Dauphin, Marcel. Boisrond-Tonnerre. Port-au-Prince, Dorsinville, 1954. 101 p.
Historical play in three acts. The action takes place in 1806.

5385. Figaro, George J. Le papillon noir. Port-au-Prince, Imp. de l'État, 1953. 23 p.
A simple tale of a peasant mother's vain attempt to save her consumptive son's life by resorting to *houngan* rather than physician. Unfortunately, much of the dialogue is in Creole without explanatory footnotes.

5386. Fouchard, Jean. Plaisirs de Saint-Domingue. Port-au-Prince, Imp. de l'État, 1955. 181 p.
Continuing his study of newspapers, memoirs, and manuscripts in French libraries, M. Fouchard paints a well-documented picture of social life in Santo Domingo. His chapter on the "Artistic and literary life of the Colony," (p. 51-127), is especially noteworthy.

5387. Garrett, Naomi M. The renaissance of Haitian poetry. Unpublished Ph.D. thesis, Columbia University, 1954.
During World War II the author spent two years in Haiti as a teacher of English. Her interest in Haitian poetry continued after her return to the States to study at Columbia University and later to teach at West Virginia State College. The result of her literary labors is a brilliant analysis of Haitian verse from its origins to the present, with major emphasis upon the contemporary poets, such as Laleau, Brierre, Roumer, Camille. She traces the influence of French and American Negro poetry, notes the dominant themes, and evinces sound critical judgment. Here is a manuscript richly deserving of publication. In the meantime, *Dissertation Abstracts* (14:9, 1954), notes that a "microfilm copy of complete manuscript of 311 pages [is] available from University Microfilms, Ann Arbor, Michigan, $3.89."

5388. Haïti (Formes Coul, 12. série, 1, 1954, unpaged).
Entire issue devoted to Haiti. Many of Haiti's finest writers have contributed to this de luxe edition: poets Jean Brierre, Damoclès Vieux, Luc Grimard, Christian Werleigh, Tertulien Guilbaud, Émile Roumer, Ida Faubert, Charles Moravia, Léon Laleau, Dominique Hippolyte, Oswald Durand, Arsène Chevry, and Virginia Sampeur. In addition, there are two articles by Dantès Bellegarde, two by Louis Maximilien,

one each by Roussan Camille, Dr. Camille Lhérisson, Morisseau-Leroy, Mme. H. Magloire Prophète, Antoine Bervin, and a summary of 150 years of Haitian literature by Pradel Pompilus. There is also an article on Haitian painting by André Held.

5389. Hall, Robert A., Jr. Haitian Creole. Grammar, texts, vocabulary by . . . with the collaboration of Suzanne Comhaire-Sylvain, H. Ormonde McConnell and Alfred Métraux. Philadelphia, American Folklore Society (Memoirs, 43), 1953. 309 p.

This scholarly work is "a scientific description of modern Haitian Creole, as spoken especially in Port-au-Prince and in the Valley of the Gosseline." After a grammatical analysis, (p. 17-72), there are texts of various kinds—an autobiography, folk tales, proverbs, riddles, etc. —in Creole and in English translation (p. 72-221). The third section of the book provides useful glossaries (Creole-English and English-Creole). Most of these texts are presented according to the McConnel-Laubach method, which the author justifies on the bases of "typographical ease and economy and to emphasize the value, both practical and scientific of this orthography." This is still a moot question among Haitians, some of whom would prefer a method that might lead the peasant more readily to regular French orthography. The book is partly the result of a study undertaken in 1949 for UNESCO's Fundamental Education Project. It is a significant addition to the literature on the subject of Haitian Creole, which, as the author points out, "is the native speech of almost all the inhabitants of the Republic."

5390. Lubin, J. Dieudonné. Héros et héroines de la liberté d'Haïti et du monde. Port-au-Prince, Imp. de l'État (Coll. du tri-cinquantenaire), 1953? 89 p.

Sonnets on Haitian heroes and heroines and on such foreign celebrities as George Washington, Martí, Maceo, John Brown, Lincoln, Bolívar, Joan of Arc, Hugo, Gandhi, etc. The poems are dated 1952.

5391. 1803, Liberté ou la mort — 1953, l'Union fait la force. Port-au-Prince, 1953. 20 p. (Coll. du cent-cinquantenaire).

In this pamphlet, one finds *Au milieu des*

flammes, a play in two acts in verse by Jean F. Brierre and Clovis Bonhomme. This historic drama was awarded the Prize of the President of the Republic. Also included in the pamphlet is *C'était à l'Arcahaie*, the prize-winning poem by Régnor C. Bernard.

5392. Morpeau, Hélène M. Pages de Marie et d'Hélène. Port-au-Prince, Les Presses Libres (Coll. du tricinquantenaire de l'Indépendance d'Haïti), 1954.

This book is a curious mixture of biographical and autobiographical material. There are brief sketches on varied subjects—Catholicism, education, Haitian women—pages the author had published in various periodicals, as well as family photographs.

5393. Phareaux, Lallier C. La vie contemporaine. Port-au-Prince, Imp. de l'État, 1953. 630 p.

A collection of short articles on varied subjects, with a preface by Félix Courtois. Of particular interest to the student of Haitian literature are reviews of three plays presented in 1940: Jean Brierre's *Adieu à la marseillaise; Le faisceau*, by Stephen Alexis; and *Le torrent*, by Dominique Hippolyte and Placide David.

5394. Trouillot, Ernst. Hommage à Luc Grimard. Port-au-Prince, Imp. de l'État, 1955. 61 p.

The death of Luc Grimard, poet, editor of *La phalange*, and rector of the University of Haiti, was a severe blow for Haitian letters. In 1950 he collaborated with André Chevallier on a novel, *Bakoulou*, (see *HLAS, no. 16, 1950*, item 2938). M. Trouillot briefly traces the career of his distinguished compatriot and reproduces the funeral orations pronounced over the man who will long live in Haitian hearts for his magnificent poem on Henry Christophe.

5395. Viatte, Auguste. Histoire littéraire de l'Amérique française. Quebec, Canada, Presses Universitaires, 1954. 545 p.

A study of French literature in the old French colonies of the New World. The discussion of Haitian literature is found on pages 329-479. In the author's opinion, the literary efforts of Haitians and French Canadians are most notable. He feels, however, that the former, in recent years, have been too slanted toward racial and social considerations. Reviewed in *Conjonction*, 55, fevr. 1955, p. 34-36.

Law

HELEN L. CLAGETT

COLLECTIONS OF LAWS, COMPILED WORKS AND BIBLIOGRAPHIES

5400. Albi, Fernando. Derecho municipal comparado del mundo hispánico. Madrid, Aguilar, 1955. 678 p.
Using a general approach from a comparative viewpoint, the author covers many aspects of municipal law, including the financial and tax powers, public services, zoning and construction, and many other activities and duties. U. S. practice is referred to in comparison with that of French and Hispanic countries.

5401. Benson, Jesse Guy. Report on Venezuelan tax, labor, corporation law. Albany, N. Y., Fallon Law Book Co., 1953. 1 v. (loose-leaf), 1955 supplement inserted.
Tabs are used to separate the work into divisions relating to introductory materials, taxes, labor law, corporation law, tax forms, and index. Very useful reference tool in English.

5402. Carteira do advogado (permanente). V. 1. São Paulo, Limonad, 1954. Various paginations.
Appearing first in temporary form, the editor periodically will collect and publish the compiled legislations in permanent volumes. The present tome contains sections on constitutional law by Carlos Eduardo Barreto, labor law by Hélio de Miranda Guimarães and Ylves de Miranda Guimarães, criminal code by Darcy Arruda de Miranda, and penal procedure by the latter also.

5403. Dias, José Aguiar de, and **Floriano Aguiar Dias.** Carteira da *Revista forense.* Rio, Revista Forense, 1955. 2744 p.
Very comprehensive handbook, comprising the texts of the constitution, all basic codes, and organic laws, followed in each case by amendatory, implementary or regulatory measures.

5404. Directorio de abogados de Cuba. Habana, La Milagrosa, 1953. 1 v., ports.

5405. Guía jurídica del Uruguay. Monte-

video, Agencia Londres. Año 1, no. 1, 1955-.
Annual directory of lawyers, judges, courts, notaries and public accountants in Montevideo, with an appendix containing names of persons living in the interior of the country. In all cases, no biographical material is given but merely addresses and telephone numbers, with the exception of judges, whose courts are indicated.

5406. Parra, Francisco J. Estudios de derecho venezolano. N. Y., Las Américas Publishing Co., 1955. 214 p.
The author has collected in this work a number of his unpublished studies together with others which have appeared in newspapers and periodicals in past years. There is no pattern followed, but the studies are grouped under civil law, political studies, administrative, penal, and mercantile law. The author was for many years Minister of Finance of his country.

5407. Vade-mecum forense; coletânea de leis do Brasil. Constituição de 1946, códigos, leis, decretos-leis, decretos, portarias e regulamentos em vigor. 4. ed. atualizada. Distribuidos em ordem alfabética por asunto e seguidos de minuciosos índices organizados pelo Dr. Osny Duarte Pereira. Rio, Konfino, 1955. 1732 p.

PHILOSOPHY OF LAW, HISTORY OF LAW, JURISPRUDENCE

5408. Alecrim, Octacilio. Idéias e instituições no império; influências francêsas. Rio, Instituto de Estudos Políticos (Publ., 1), 1953. 240 p.
History of law showing specifically the French influence in the days of the Brazilian Empire.

5409. Bascuñán Valdés, Aníbal. Pedagogía jurídica. Santiago, Editorial Jurídica de Chile (Col. de estudios jurídicos y sociales, 37), 1954. 216 p.
There has been very little literature, outside of periodical articles, dealing with legal education as such. The author includes five studies on

basic matters, including the relation of the State to the university, the law faculties, use of seminars, and proposals for teaching law, The author is professor of a course on introduction to the study of law, and will use this work as a supplementary textbook.

5410. Canal Ramírez, Gonzalo. Función social de la propiedad; prospecto histórico, filosófico y jurídico. Bogotá, Antares, 1953. 270 p.

5411. Carranza, Enrique F. Introducción al derecho. Córdoba, Argentina, Imp. de la Universidad, 1954. 421 p.
General textbook on principles of law, specializing on their development in Argentina.

5412. Cossio, Carlos. La valoración jurídica y la ciencia del derecho. B. A., Ediciones Arayú (Col. de la teoría general del derecho; Col. menor), 1954. 155 p.
Philosophic and theoretical discussion of law as a science.

5413. Dantas, Francisco Clementino San Tiago. Problemas de direito positivo. Rio, Revista Forense, 1953. 428 p.
Compilation of studies and opinions of the author covering a number of unrelated subjects, including modern developments in contract law, due process of law, administrative acts, public lands, war damages, protection of purchasers in sales, corporation law, incapacity of mentally deranged persons to make wills, clandestine publication of a literary work over the radio, and others.

5414. Goytía, Víctor Florencio. 1903: biografía de una república. Panamá, Ediciones del Cincuentenario, 1953. 408 p.
Dr. Goytía divides this constitutional and political history of Panama into three periods of its 50 years of existence as a republic, namely, the period of development, the period of realization as a legal republic, and a third period of frustration. Much of the latter is attributed to U. S. activities in the Canal Zone.

5415. Jacobini, H. B. A study of the philosophy of international law as seen in works of Latin American writers. The Hague, Nijhoff, 1954. 158 p.
The preliminary chapters are devoted to general philosophical background, and to the various schools of legal philosophy established between the 15th and 20th centuries. The writers of the 19th and 20th centuries in Latin America, beginning with Andrés Bello and Juan Bautista Alberdi, are discussed fully, divided into various classifications. One chapter is devoted to American international law, which has assumed characteristics of its own as contrasted with the classical and other international law.

5416. Jorquera F., Francisco. Derecho romano. Santiago, Editorial Jurídica de Chile (Colección de estudios jurídicos y sociales, 31-32), 1953. 2 v.

5417. Laplaza, Francisco P. Las ideas penales de Alberdi en el *Fragmento preliminar al estudio del derecho*. B. A., Ediciones Arayú (Col. blanca), 1954. 84 p.
The author first comments on the great value to history of law of "ideas" contributed by eminent lawyers and statesmen in many countries. Among these he evaluates the contribution of Alberdi's ideas on criminal law, from which subsequent legislation was developed. The philosophical and theoretical tract written by Alberdi is commented on in the second half of the small monograph.

5418. Legislación real sobre hacienda para las provincias coloniales venezolanas. (Antecedentes de la legislación fiscal de la República de Venezuela). Caracas, Tip. de la Nación, 1954. 307 p.
Officially authorized by President Pérez Jiménez, this work is an excellent contribution to history of law, giving a background to the present tax laws and internal revenue organization.

5419. Morineau, Óscar. El estudio del derecho. México, Porrúa, 1953. 521 p.
Intended for use as a textbook in the author's law course. It deals generally with the theoretical, logical, and philosophical bases of law as a field of knowledge, and discusses the various schools of thought and doctrines developed by well-known authorities in other countries.

5420. Mouchet, Carlos, and **Miguel Sussini.** Derecho hispánico y "common law" en Puerto Rico. B. A., Perrot, 1953. 134 p.
The interlacing of two great legal systems has apparently been successful in Puerto Rico, as described by Argentine lawyers.

5421. Peláez, Carlos. Estado de derecho y estado de sitio; la crisis de la constitución en Colombia. Bogotá, Temis, 1955. 211 p.
Study of article 121 of the constitution compared with measures on state of siege and emergency provisions taken in European and other American nations. The subject is also approached from an historical angle.

5422. Pérez Gorrín, José Antonio, and **Eloy G. Merino Brito.** Martí y el derecho. Habana, J. Montero (Biblioteca jurídica de autores cubanos y extranjeros, 163; Publ. de la A.N.F.P.J., 7), 1953. 132 p.
Devoted to the legal aspects of José Martí's tremendous contributions to literature and culture in general.

5423. Rojas R., Abelardo. El derecho subjetivo y el deber jurídico. México, Tip. Mercantil (Seminario de filosofía del derecho), 1954. 136 p.
Study of concepts of law from the viewpoint of legal philosophy and technical jurisprudence.

COURTS AND JUDICIAL PROCEDURE (CIVIL AND CRIMINAL)

ARGENTINA

5424. Allende Iriarte, Jorge. Evolución del proceso escriturario. . . . Allende, Ignacio M. Apreciaciones jurídicas notariales. B. A., 1953. 123 p.

The first work deals with modern trends in the notarial and scrivener's duties insofar as concerns the documents which formerly were all in handwriting. The typewritten master copy, photo duplications in issuing certified copies, and similar matters are discussed. The second work, paged continuously with the first, treats of the scientific aspects of notarial law, the faith and credit given notarial documents, and notarial functions.

5425. Coronas, Juan Enrique; Hugo A. Oderigo; and Fernando Horacio Payá. La reforma procesal civil. Ley 14.237. B. A., Ediciones Arayú, 1954. 414 p.

A new law in 1954 created substantial changes in the civil and commercial procedure used in the courts of the capital city, B. A., and applicable also to the entire nation in certain fields. The development of similar procedures in the provinces and comparison with former legislation is brought out in various chapters.

5426. Ibáñez de Aldecoa, Alfonso. Meditaciones sobre la cientificidad dogmática del derecho procesal. B. A., Ediciones Arayú (Col. menor de la teoría general del derecho), 1954. 148 p.

The "meditations" pursue the philosophical and theoretical aspects of procedural law, dealing in generalities for the most part.

5427. Levene, Ricardo, Jr. Manual de derecho procesal penal. B. A., Perrot, 1953. 462 p.

The discussion of penal procedure is divided into a description of sources and background, and then the actual procedures at the pre-trial and trial stages. Special procedures and types of defendants are covered, including habeas corpus, juvenile delinquents, courts martial, police trials and others.

5428. Sánchez de Bustamante, Miguel. Acción revocatoria; caracteres y naturaleza. B. A., Perrot, 1954. 96 p.

The rights of the creditor under varying circumstances to revoke acts of the debtor are discussed from the viewpoints of theory and practice. The remedy may be invoked in relation to property rights, personal rights, and may be for specific performance, rescission, compensation or other objectives.

5429. Ymaz, Esteban. La esencia de la cosa juzgada y otros ensayos. B. A., Ediciones Arayú (Col. de la teoría general del derecho; colección menor), 1954. 282 p.

A fine exhaustive treatment of *res adjudicata* from numerous aspects, and including the more recent developments under administrative and constitutional law concepts.

BRAZIL

5430. Bastos Tornaghi, Hélio. Processo penal. Rio, Coelho Branco, 1953. 367 p.

A generalized text on penal procedure, with numerous citations to foreign authorities. Brazilian law, naturally, is highlighted.

5431. Castro Nunes, José de. Soluções de direito aplicado; julgados e votos vencidos. Rio, Freitas Bastos, 1953. 535 p.

A Supreme Court justice writes about his own decisions and dissenting opinions during his terms on the bench. These cover a variety of subjects showing application of law in the fields of constitutional, electoral, and procedural law, and other subjects. The growing importance of judicial precedent is acknowledged by the author.

5432. Muller, Yara. Da propositura e do processamento de ações. Rio, Pongetti, 1954. 669 p.

A practical work on trial of cases, giving advice on the steps to be taken in order to bring the action, and the subsequent procedures in the court. Special actions are covered, and forms are included by the author, who is a noted woman lawyer. She has produced many other works in this field.

5433. Santos, Moacyr Amaral. Introdução ao estudo do processo cominatório. São Paulo, Limonad, 1953. 186 p.

Special action and procedure seeking a judicial threat or warning.

OTHER COUNTRIES

5434. Abeliuk Manasevich, René; Olga Rojas Bescaín; and Kireya Tasso Fuentes. Estudio crítico de la jurisprudencia del código civil: la sucesión legal, la sucesión intestada. . . . Santiago, Editorial Jurídica de Chile (Col. de seminarios e institutos, 1; Derecho civil), 1955. 419 p.

The seminar students undertaking a criticism of the interpretation by the courts of the book of the civil code dealing with testate and intestate succession have taken a stand against the classic and traditional criteria and classification of succession followed by the courts. This analytical and well-documented treatise is worthy because of the novelty of its approach to the subject.

5435. Alzamora Valdez, Mario. Derecho procesal civil; teoría general del proceso. Lima, Lumen, 1953. 340 p.

Comparative theoretical treatise on civil procedure, with frequent citations and references to Peruvian practice.

LAW 297

5436. Castro, Juventino V. La suplencia de la queja deficiente en el juicio de amparo. México, Asociación Nacional de Funcionarios Judiciales, Instituto Nacional del Amparo (Publ., 4; Col. de estudios jurídicos), 1953. 148 p.
A fine monograph, on one specific procedural point, which exhausts the substantive and adjective law available in Mexico.

5437. Manrique Pacanins, Gustavo. Jurisprudencia y crítica de la doctrina de la casación venezolana, 1924-1950. Con un índice sintético de todos los fallos dictados por la Corte desde 1876 a 1950. Caracas, Tip. Americana, 1953. 2 v. (A-L; M-V).

5438. Rodríguez Garcés, Sergio. Tercerías. Intervención de terceros en los diversos procedimientos. Santiago, 1953. 606 p.
Procedural aspects of rights of third parties in court actions. The author covers special types of suits, as well as labor law and criminal law actions.

ADMINISTRATIVE LAW (INCLUDING TAXATION)

ARGENTINA

5439. Quirós, César. Organización administrativa. La tercera posición en organización administrativa. B. A., 1955. 197 p.
Dedicated specifically to the administration set-up under President Perón. The coverage takes in government centralization, personnel, financial and economical measures, and other administrative provisions. The author eulogizes Perón for the solution of many administrative problems.

5440. Wallace, Donald O. (ed.). Argentina income tax service. Hempstead, N. Y., Foreign Tax Law Association, 1953. 2 v. (loose-leaf).

BRAZIL

5441. Brazil. Ministério da Fazenda. Trabalhos da Comissão Especial do Código Tributário Nacional. Rio, 1954. 547 p.
Useful for the researcher, since it contains the actual debates and decisions of the commission entrusted with the codification of a federal tax code.

5442. British Chamber of Commerce for Brazil. Brazilian income tax regulations. Rio, 1955. 71 p.
English translation of the 1954 regulation to the income tax law.

5443. Fernandes, Celso Frois, and Jayme Geraque Murta. A função do agente fiscal na administração pública federal. Rio, Coelho Branco, 1953. 675 p.

A handbook for use of the internal revenue collector or agent, containing the texts of excerpts from pertinent laws on internal revenue taxes and fees, and the procedure for collection, together with forms of various kinds.

5444. Loureiro, Raul R. Questões fiscais. São Paulo, Saraiva, 1953. 324 p.
Opinions and decisions of the attorney general for tax matters in São Paulo, interpreting provisions of decree-law 960.

5445. Novo regulamento do imposto de renda: decreto no. 36.773 de 13/1/955. Rio, Aurora, 1955. 150 p.

5446. Rezende, Tito, and J. O. Castro Viana Júnior (eds.). Imposto de renda; anotações. 2. ed. muito aumentada. Rio, 1953. 2 v. 933 p. (Biblioteca da Revista fiscal e de legislação de fazenda, 22).
The work relates to the 1942 income tax law, which has been repealed in 1954. This exhaustive work is very useful because of the careful annotations of the editors and the forms and indexes contributed by them.

5447. ———, and ———. Novo regulamento do impôsto de renda. Rio, 1955. 240 p. (Biblioteca da Revista fiscal e de legislação de fazenda, 28).
The 1954 regulation is annotated by the joint editors, who have searched out case law of the past which is still pertinent to the present law, and have enhanced the value of the work by incorporation of numerous forms and samples of returns, and a fine index.

CUBA

5448. Hernández Corujo, Enrique. Procedimientos administrativos internos. Habana, Lex, 1955. 303 p.
Administrative procedures as employed within the government departmental organization, as differentiated from those used for conflicts between the government and individuals or entities outside the departments or agencies. Some of the matters treated refer to registration, dispatches, reports, inter-governmental relations, administrative resolutions and decisions, personnel conflicts, and internal affairs.

5449. Menocal y Barreras, Juan Manuel. Derecho fiscal; constitución, legislación y jurisprudencia cubanas. Habana, Minerva, 1953. 302 p.
Each chapter contains a "lesson" devoted to some aspect of tax law, commencing with constitutional provisions in point, and then dealing individually with each type of tax or impost. This orderly work has been much needed for some time, in view of the confused legislative picture of taxation in general in Cuba.

5450. Montiel, F. Félix. Administración y "self government"; una experiencia cubana. Santiago, Cuba, Universidad de Oriente, Facultad de Derecho y Ciencias Comerciales, 1954. 162 p.

Decentralization of services and public works is discussed, with examples of early Spanish attempts in irrigation communities. The author believes self government can be used in professions or "guilds," and other special fields.

5451. Wallace, Donald O. (ed.). Cuban income tax service. Hempstead, N. Y., Foreign Tax Law Association, 1953. 2 v. (loose-leaf).

MEXICO

5452. Albareda, José Daniel. Conozca sus nuevas obligaciones fiscales. Impuesto sobre la renta; impuesto sobre ingresos mercantiles; impuesto del timbre. México, Revista Fiscal y Financiera, 1955. 613 p.

The 1954 edition of this very useful work covered only 161 practical cases and presented 137 tax accounting problems, while the 1955 edition has collected 200 practical cases and 400 problems on the three types of important taxes. To the editor's knowledge, this is the first attempt in Mexico to produce a practical handbook in this style.

5453. Ley del impuesto sobre la renta y su reglamento. Puebla, México, J. M. Cajica (Colección de leyes mexicanas; Serie Leyes federales), 1954. 317 p.

5454. Martínez López, Luis. Ensayo de derecho fiscal mexicano. Comentarios al código fiscal federal. . . . México, 1953. 343 p.

Both substantive and procedural law are covered in this work on the State's right to tax and collect taxes administratively and judicially. The decisions of the tax court form the basis of the study.

5455. México. Dirección General del Impuesto sobre la Renta. Ley del impuesto sobre la renta. México, Tall. de Impresión de Estampillas y Valores, 1954. 190 p.

5456. ————. ————. Ley del impuesto sobre la renta y su reglamento. México, 1954. 1007 p.

The use of colored pages indicates the various parts of the work, which covers not only the texts of the income tax law, its regulation, and subject indexes to both, but also forms for taxpayers' returns, administrative organization of the tax department, statistics, and other useful information.

URUGUAY

5457. Peirano Facio, Juan Carlos. El impuesto a las ventas. Montevideo, Universidad de Montevideo, Facultad de Derecho y Ciencias Sociales (Biblioteca de publicaciones oficiales, Sec. III, 80), 1955. 469 p.

Practical treatise on the sales tax, dealing first with a comparison of this tax in other lands, and then a discussion of development, legislation, administration and procedure as related to this type of tax.

5458. El presupuesto de 1953 y sus normas complementarias. Montevideo, Servicio de Información de Derecho Positivo Uruguayo, 1954. 687 p.

The budget for 1953, with all related legislative and administrative measures, is incorporated in this volume. A digest of legislation, covering 400 pages, is arranged under subject matter, and is a very useful adjunct.

5459. Sayagués Laso, Enrique. Tratado de derecho administrativo. V. 1. Montevideo, Bianchi Altuna, 1953. 687 p.

The author is a recognized authority on administrative law, as well as professor of same subject, and has contributed with his prolific pen to the literature of his country in this specific field. The present work promises completely to exhaust the subject, approached from all aspects.

5460. Valdés Costa, Ramón, and Herbert Porro. Régimen tributario del gobierno departamental de Montevideo. Montevideo, Bianchi Altuna, 1955. 486 p.

The joint authors are representatives of the pedagogical and governmental professions, respectively, and the seminar work produced correspondingly represents the theory and practice.

VENEZUELA

5461. Aragon, Víctor. Vocabulario aduanero de Venezuela. Elaborado sobre los textos oficiales. Caracas, Imp. Nacional, 1953. 2 v. 776, 591 p.

In addition to the actual customs tariff, the editor has supplied in digest form, under an alphabetical subject arrangement, all laws, decrees, regulations, and administrative decisions that might have some relation to customs law. This includes entire texts or provisions from laws on merchant marine, postal regulations, airports and aviation, stamp laws, codes, exchange and monetary regulations.

5462. Cover, Gilbert Grace. Venezuelan income tax law of 1955: with its original Spanish text and its English translation; also a carefully revised index in both languages. Caracas, Ragon, 1955. 78 p.

5463. Venezuela. Ministerio de Hacienda. Jurisprudencia de impuesto sobre la renta. Caracas, 1955. 474 p.

Compilation of decisions of the Appellate and Federal Court (Supreme Court), as well as of the highest Tax Court, chronologically arranged, but with a good subject index for cross reference. An introductory portion gives a good picture of organization of tax courts, of jurisdiction in this field by other courts, and other matters of related significance.

LAW 299

5464. Venezuelan customs law, as published in the *Official gazette*, extraordinary issue, no. 208, August 28, 1948. Caracas, Translation Service, 1953. 103 p.

OTHER COUNTRIES

5465. Aramayo, Óscar. Legislación económica. Santiago, Editorial Jurídica de Chile, 1953. 516 p.
The author is legal adviser to the Ministry of Economy, and has had access to materials and experience in their use. Part of this extensive work is analytical and part devoted to the texts of the legal and administrative measures. The Ministry of Economy is playing a very vital role in the development of economy and industry of Chile.

5466. Caro, Néstor. Trujillo y el derecho agrario. Ciudad Trujillo, Imp. Dominicana, 1954. 131 p.
Monograph devoted to legislation promoting and developing agriculture under the aegis of the Generalissimo.

5467. Code fiscal haïtien: recettes internes et communales. Port-au-Prince, Imp. de l'État, 1953. 1182 p.; Supplément, 1954, 254 p.
Texts of the principal laws and decrees on taxes, customs, budget, and other measures of financial and economic nature, with an occasional note in boldface type.

5468. Mersán, Carlos A. Legislación fiscal del Paraguay. Con la legislación bancaria y las normas del Convenio de Unión Económica Paraguayo-Argentina. 2. ed. Asunción, Cía. Imp. Argentina, 1954. 804 p.
Exhaustive compilation of all measures falling in the categories of finance or economics. These embrace laws on banking, public services, public lands, administration of financial or economic programs, taxes, imposts, and other sources of revenue. International agreements between Argentina and Paraguay are also included.

5469. Raisbeck, James W. Codificación del impuesto sobre la renta, patrimonio y exceso de utilidades. Bogotá, Iqueima, 1954-1955. 2 v. 577, 631 p.
The first volume is devoted to the legislation and administrative regulations, while in the second we find tables of depreciation, forms, case law, and some legislation enacted since the appearance of the first volume. This is a valuable reference tool.

5470. Sandoval Cerna, Ernesto. Compilación de disposiciones legales y reglamentarias sobre urbanizaciones, 1900-1953. Con inclusión de construcciones para Lima y Balnearios. Autori-

zada oficialmente por R. M. 57 de 21 de febrero de 1953. Lima, Rimac, 1953. 434 p.

5471. Wallace, Donald O. (ed.). El Salvador income tax law service. Centerport, N. Y., Foreign Tax Law Association, 1955. 1 v. (loose-leaf).

5472. ———— (ed.). Haitian income tax service. Centerport, N. Y., Foreign Tax Law Association, 1955. 1 v. (loose-leaf).

5473. ———— (ed.). Honduras income tax service. Centerport, N. Y., Foreign Tax Law Association, 1955. 1 v. (loose-leaf).

5474. ———— (ed.). Paraguay income tax service. Centerport, N. Y., Foreign Tax Law Association, 1955. 1 v. (loose-leaf).

CONSTITUTIONAL LAW

ARGENTINA

5475. Casiello, Juan. Derecho constitucional argentino. B. A., Perrot, 1955. 619 p.
A professor of constitutional law in Rosario writes his own textbook, making it current with a discussion of the 1949 amendments to the charter, and the consequent implementary and regulatory legislation. Both Argentine and U. S. case law are cited.

5476. Heredia Moyano, Hugo A. Historia constitucional. B. A., Perrot, 1955. 519 p.
General theoretical treatise on constitutional history and law, dealing with its development from the first social and political manifestations to date. Argentine history from 1810 through the 1949 constitutional reforms is traced in more detail.

5477. Linares Quintana, Segundo V. Tratado de la ciencia del derecho constitucional argentino y comparado. B. A., Alfa, 1953. T. 1, Constitucionalismo y derecho constitucional; t. 2, Teoría de la constitución.
A fine contribution to literature of the world on constitutionalism and constitutional law. The author speaks of political science in general, developments in various nations leading up to adoption of fundamental charters, the constitutions of today, and similar matters. The Argentine history is specifically examined, with references to judicial interpretation in Argentina and in the U. S., which helped to shape the practice in constitutional law.

MEXICO

5478. Basulto Jaramillo, Enrique. Libertad de prensa en México. México, 1954. 172 p.
Freedom of press in its constitutional and criminal law concepts forms the basis of the author's contribution. A chapter each is devoted to this freedom in relation to international organizations and to the nation's economy.

5479. Burgoa, Ignacio. Dos estudios jurídicos. Algunas consideraciones sobre el artículo 28 constitucional. Las normas de orden público y el interés social. México, Porrúa, 1953. 115 p.
Delivered originally as addresses of major importance, the two studies concern article 28 of the constitution on monopolies, and the conflict of public order regulations and social interest.

5480. ———. Las garantías individuales. 2. ed. México, Porrúa, 1954. 529 p.
A professor of constitutional law brings out a much enlarged and modernized edition of an earlier work dealing with the personal rights guaranteed constitutionally in Mexico.

5481. Ponce Lagos, Antonio. Historia de las reformas a los artículos 34 y 115 constitucionales, que conceden la ciudadanía a la mujer mexicana. México, Taranzas del Valle, 1954. 350 p.
Collection of addresses, debates, and legislative history leading to amendment of the constitution giving civic rights to women. The author was a member of the congress at the time the amendment was debated and adopted.

OTHER COUNTRIES

5483. Amiama, Manuel A. Notas sobre derecho constitucional. Ciudad Trujillo, Montalvo, 1954. 190 p.
General constitutional law textbook, with specific references in each chapter to the law and practice in the Dominican Republic on each topic discussed.

5484. Amunátegui, Gabriel. Principios generales del derecho constitucional. Santiago, Editorial Jurídica de Chile (Colección de estudios jurídicos y sociales, 35), 1953. 335 p.
Discusses in general terms constitutional law of other nations, and treats domestic concepts and practice more specifically.

5485. Colombia. Comisión de Estudios Constitucionales. Estudios constitucionales. Bogotá, Imp. Nacional, 1953. 2 v. 500, 433 p.
Preparatory work in drafting of a new constitution.

5486. Demicheli, Alberto. Formación constitucional rioplatense. Montevideo, Barreiro y Ramos, 1955. 3 v.
Extremely readable historical and constitutional treatment on the territory which later formed Argentina and Uruguay. The exhaustive work is well documented, covering all aspects in vast detail. The author has been characterized as a perfectionist, and has received much encomium from jurists at home and abroad for this particular contribution.

5487. Goytía, Victor F. Las constituciones de Panamá. Madrid, Ediciones Cultura Hispánica, 1954. 823 p.
One of a series of works being issued in Madrid, each work edited and preceded by introductory material contributed by a well-known author in the individual country. The present work contains a historical portion by Dr. Manuel Fraga Iribarne, and a constitutional history by Dr. Goytía. The various charters are illustrated with excerpts from debates and other notes.

5488. Valencia Vega, Alipio. Fundamentos de derecho político. La Paz, Juventud, 1954. 784 p.
Beginning with Plato, the author traces the history and theory of State and political law to the present time. The textbook for the Law School of San Andrés University contains chapters on the various kinds of government, political parties, public opinion, the relations of Church and State, and theory of revolution and de facto government, among other matters.

CIVIL LAW

ARGENTINA

5489. Borda, Guillermo A. Derecho civil; parte general. B. A., Perrot, 1953. 2 v.
A narrative treatment of the civil code, as contrasted with the usual exegetic style which is more popular. The author is apparently following Dr. Raymundo Salvat's methods, but is bringing the contents up to date with the very substantial legislative changes which have occurred in the past 25 years. He thus emulates and complements the "old master."

5490. Cejas, Horacio E., and Horacio W. Bliss. Nociones de derecho civil. B. A., Ciencias Económicas, 1953. 556 p.
Textbook for first-year law students, covering superficially the entire scope of the civil code.

5491. Gásperi, Luis de. Tratado de derecho hereditario. B. A., Tip. Editorial Argentina, 1953. 4 v. 565, 471, 544, 372 p.
Exhaustive treatise on inheritance law, of which two volumes are labelled "general part" and two "special part." The treatment does not differ in the entire treatise, which is written from a comparative and very generalized viewpoint, with occasional references to Paraguay and Argentina specifically. The distinction may lie in

he topics which in the first two volumes refer to the general and common elements in succession and inheritance, while the last two deal with such topics as types of heirs, kinds of wills, legatees, procedure, etc. Dr. Gásperi is also author of a work of the same exhaustive nature dealing with contracts and obligations. His works show careful and comprehensive research and reading, are well documented, and contain copious footnotes and explanations.

5492. **Goldstein, Mateo,** and **Fernando M. Morduchowicz.** El divorcio en el derecho argentino, legislación de amparo de la familia. B. A., Editorial Logos, 1955. 413 p.
A recent attempt to incorporate within the text of a law on minors a provision admitting absolute divorce in Argentina raised a furore among the lawyers, church, and legal writers. Since Perón's overthrow, this law has already been repealed, but the present book was written before that time. The author covers history and opinions of authorities on absolute and relative divorces, dissolution of marriage by other means, and legal death declarations based on absence. Numerous cases are cited, and of interest are those which were filed immediately following the December 1954 law, but were still pending at the time of the writing of the above work.

5493. **González, Carlos Emérito.** Teoría general del instrumento público. B. A., Ediar, 1953. 475 p.
Historical and legal treatment on notarial law, both domestic and comparative. The law and practice of Spain, France, Italy, Mexico, Cuba, and Uruguay are commented upon briefly.

5494. **Lapa, Eduardo L.** La venta de ganado por el martillero. B. A., Ediciones Arayú, 1953. 123 p.
A monograph on forced sales and judicial attachment with relation to the cattle industry, one of the most important in Argentina.

5495. **Llambías, Jorge Joaquín.** Efectos de la nulidad y de la anulación de los actos jurídicos. B. A., Ediciones Arayú, 1953. 206 p.
Full discussion of void and voidable acts under law. The effects of absolute or relative nullity which require or do not require judicial determination are of great interest in contract law and domestic relations. The rights of third parties are also described in this connection.

5496. **Martínez Paz, Enrique.** Introducción al derecho de la sucesión hereditaria. B. A., Editora Argentina, 1953. 599 p.
A condensed version of the theory and practice in the field of inheritance and succession, which the author intends to develop later into a larger three-volume work. Argentine law and practice are highlighted.

5497. **Quinteros, Federico D.** La trasmisión mortis causa y la responsabilidad del heredero. B. A., Librería Jurídica (Col.

de monografías de derecho, 19), 1954. 93 p.
A general discussion of the historical background and status of gifts *inter vivos* under various regimes, including the Napoleonic Code, canon law, customary law. Special attention is given to the effect of such gifts on the liability of the heir.

5498. **Racciatti, Hernán.** Propiedad por pisos o por departamentos. B. A., Depalma, 1954. 224 p.
Since 1948, when a law was adopted in this field, cooperative ownership of apartment houses and business buildings has been made possible. Because of the classic theory in civil law that title and ownership must be in the same person, this legal fiction about owning a "horizontal" portion of a building in mid-air was evolved to permit modern practice to become legal realities.

BRAZIL

5499. **Batalha, Wilson de Souza Campos.** Loteamentos e condomínios, sistema jurídico da propriedade fracionada. São Paulo, Limonad, 1953. 2 v. 461, 535 p.
Commences with the history of ownership of property in general, tracing it from primitive times to the present, dealing particularly with the Roman and Germanic influences. Joint ownership and condominium, and community ownership of lands are the subject of the latter part of the work.

5500. **Costa Filho, João Mendes da.** Propriedade, desapropriação, inquilinato. O "bem estar social" da Constituicão de 1946. Rio, Freitas Bastos, 1953. 478 p.
In the light of constitutional provisions for the common welfare, the author discusses property rights including expropriation and landlord-tenant relations.

5501. **Medeiros, João.** Erro essencial de pessoa. (Moléstia grave e transmissível, causa de anulação de casamento). Teoria e prática. Rio, Konfino, 1954. 226 p.
Treatment of a single ground for annulment of marriage, where there is error as to person.

5502. **Monteiro, Washington de Barros.** Cursos de direito civil. Direito das coisas. São Paulo, Saraiva, 1953. 394 p.
See also item below.

5503. ————. Curso de direito civil. Direito das sucessões. Rio, Saraiva, 1954. 283 p.
Although not labelled as volumes in a collection or series, these published volumes follow directly the contents of the civil code. In 1952 the volume on family law appeared (see *HLAS, no. 18, 1952,* item 2916), in 1953 and 1954 the two above.

5504. **Oliveira, Arthur Vasco Itabaiana**

de. Curso de direito das sucessões. Com a colaboração de Aires Itabaiana de Oliveira. Rio, Andes (Estante jurídica, 2), 1954. 360 p.
From his long career as a judge, the author has produced a substantial and practical treatise on his favorite subject of inheritance and succession.

5505. Pontes de Miranda, Francisco Cavalcante. Tratado de direito privado. Rio, Borsoi, 1954-1955. 13 v.
The plan of this exhaustive commentary on private law has in 13 volumes so far covered only part of the civil code. Six volumes have been devoted to the "general part" of the code, two to family law and persons, and four to "things" or property rights. If it is intended to cover the entire field, there are still several "books" of the civil code as well as other laws and codes on "private" law to be embraced herein.

URUGUAY

5506. Arias Barbé, Óscar. Arrendamientos rurales y desalojo. Montevideo, Imp. El Siglo Ilustrado, 1954. 435 p.
Leases, transfers, and other negotiations involving agricultural lands have received high attention from the legislature because of the importance of the industry to the nation. The specific legislation on which this monograph is based are two laws enacted in 1954 on leases and eviction. Comparative references to other countries and to case law are included from time to time.

5507. Barbagelata, Héctor Hugo. El derecho común sobre el despido y su interpretación jurisprudencial. Montevideo, Universidad de Montevideo, Facultad de Derecho y Ciencias Sociales (Biblioteca de publicaciones oficiales, Sec. III, 70), 1953. 164 p.
The subject of dismissal of employees is not limited herein to the labor law aspects, but covers private and government employees, and other categories not included elsewhere.

5508. Luna, Isabel M. P. de. Capacidad para contratar. Montevideo, Universidad de Montevideo, Facultad de Derecho y Ciencias Sociales (Biblioteca de publicaciones oficiales, Sec. III, 67), 1953. 232 p.
Not only is the topic of legal capacity to enter contracts discussed, but incidentally also the importance of the work of mental and welfare institutions in their role of guardians to incapacitated persons. Women and corporate bodies in relation to capacity are covered in special chapters.

5509. Peirano Facio, Jorge. Responsabilidad extracontractual. Montevideo, Barreiro y Ramos, 1954. 699 p.
Dividing this excellent work on torts into three parts, the author discusses general elements, the elements of extra-contractual liability, and the sources for this liability. This work shows intensive research, and is well documented.

5510. Quagliata, Pascual. La propiedad horizontal en los registros públicos. Montevideo, Bianchi Altuna, 1953. 227 p.
The author, as a notary, is interested in the aspects of property registration as affected by cooperative or joint ownership of buildings and real property, a fairly recent innovation in the civil law countries. Comparison is made with Chilean practice in this field, and proposed amendments of the Uruguayan law are offered.

5511. Sánchez Fontáns, José. Capacidad y legitimación en derecho contractual. Montevideo, Bianchi Altuna, 1953. 69 p.
Monograph on the right and capacity to enter contracts of all categories, the effect of incapacity thereon, void and voidable contracts, and specific types or categories, such as agency, labor, bailment, and gifts.

5512. ————. El contrato de construcción. V. 1. Montevideo, Universidad de Montevideo, Facultad de Derecho y Ciencias Sociales (Biblioteca de publicaciones oficiales, Sec. III, 66), 1953. 478 p.
All legal aspects of the construction business are to be discussed in this treatise. This first volume covers general elements, the civil and commercial aspects, public works contracts, prices, legal guarantees and a few other details.

OTHER COUNTRIES

5513. Argüello Hurtado, Roberto. La propiedad horizontal. León, Nicaragua, Universidad Nacional, 1955. 65 p.
Joint or cooperative ownership in real property is admitted only indirectly under the provisions of the Civil Code of Nicaragua. The author discusses the practice in his country, and offers proposed amendments on the subject matter.

5514. Batiza, Rodolfo. Tres estudios sobre el fideicomiso. México, Imp. Universitaria, 1954. 194 p.
Some aspects of the common law trust have been incorporated in Mexican legislation, although alien to classic civil law concepts. The subject is dealt with principally in connection with contracts, the rule against perpetuities, and insurance law.

5515. Contreras A., Cesáreo A. Los principios fundamentales de la ley de registros de tierras. Ciudad Trujillo, Universidad de Santo Domingo (Publ., 90; Serie 3, Derecho y ciencias sociales, 4), 1953. 153 p.
The Dominican Republic has used the Torrens system of land registration for many years. The author discusses this Australian system, together with the French, German, and Spanish system of land registration.

5516. **Gómez Gil, Orlando.** La propiedad horizontal en Cuba. Habana, Lex, 1954. 220 p.
The work on cooperative ownership of real property, treated from the viewpoint of comparative law, was awarded a prize in 1953 by the Havana Bar Association.

5517. **Hernández-Bretón, Armando.** Código civil venezolano. Caracas, La Torre (Col. Arandina), 1955. 295 p.
Annotated article by article, with references to other codes, conflict of laws measures, and specialized legislation.

5518. **Muñoz, Luis.** Comentarios a los códigos civiles de España e Hispanoamérica. V. 1. España. México, Ediciones Jurídicas Herrero, 1953. 1008 p.
The great detail with which the commentaries are to be made has limited the first volume to a single country, and it is over 1000 pages in length.

5519. **Pérez Vives, Álvaro.** Compraventa y permuta en derecho colombiano. 2. ed. Bogotá, Temis, 1953. 602 p.
Sales and transfers of property as applied and interpreted judicially under Colombian law.

5520. **Ruiz Tejada, Manuel Ramón.** Estudio sobre la propiedad inmobiliaria en la República Dominicana. Ciudad Trujillo, Universidad de Santo Domingo (Publ., 85; Serie 3, Derecho y ciencias sociales, 2), 1952. 446 p.

5521. **Sandoval Saavedra, Hugo.** Código civil boliviano, con secciones de legislación, doctrina y jurisprudencia. Recopilado, concordado y ordenado por . . . . V. 1. La Paz, 1955.
Written in an exegetic style, this is the first volume of a badly needed reference tool for Bolivian law. The code provisions are given, and each is followed by excerpts from laws, learned opinion, and case law. Other volumes will cover other basic codes and laws.

5522. **San Martín y Torres, Xavier.** Nacionalidad y extranjería. México, Editorial Mar, 1954. 347 p.
Important contribution on aliens in Mexico. The texts of basic laws on nationality, population, and other legislation in point are given at the back of this excellent source book.

5523. **Soler, Juan José.** Introducción al derecho paraguayo. Madrid, Ediciones Cultura Hispánica, 1954. 577 p.
Exhaustive work on inheritance law, with few additional topics, in spite of the title of the work.

5524. **Somarriva Undurraga, Manuel.** Derecho sucesorio; explicaciones de clases revisadas. Santiago, Nascimento, 1954. 2 v. 312, 368 p.
Notes taken from the professor's lecture course by René Abeliuk, and published following the former's revision of the text. Prof. Somarriva has written and taught for many years in the field of civil law and specifically on inheritance and succession, and is considered an outstanding authority by his compatriots as well as foreigners.

5525. **Trujillo Gómez, Rafael.** Compilación sobre notariado, registro y estado civil. Bogotá, Minerva, 1953. 380 p.

5526. **Yaquián Otero, Carlos Rafael.** El delito de abandono de familia o incumplimiento de los deberes de asistencia familiar. Guatemala, Imp. Universitaria, 1954.
Law school thesis.

CRIMINAL LAW

ARGENTINA

5527. **Laplaza, Francisco P.** El delito de genocidio o genticidio. B. A., Ediciones Arayú (Col. blanca), 1953. 100 p.
Genocide has attained international importance since World War II, especially in view of the UN efforts to have a universal treaty with regard to it.

5528. **Levene, Ricardo, Jr.** El delito de homicidio. B. A., Perrot, 1955. 297 p.
All aspects of homicide are discussed from viewpoints of both law and criminology. Justifiable homicide, suicide, deaths occurring during sports events, and euthanasia are covered in addition to the more usual forms of this crime.

5529. **Pessagno, Rodolfo G.** Temas de historia penal. B. A., Perrot, 1953. 254 p.

BRAZIL

5530. **Gomes, Amynthas Vidal.** Novo manual do delegado. Rio, Revista Forense, 1955. 709 p.
Handbook for the criminal investigator on the local level. Includes all measures concerning police, crime, procedure, criminology, forensic medicine, finger-printing and other matters.

5531. **Lyra, Roberto.** Expressão mais simples do direito penal. (Introdução e parte general). Rio, Konfino, 1953. 259 p.
Philosophical and theoretical approach to criminal law as a science. Covers only the general subjects found in the first book of the Criminal Code.

5532. **Silveira, Valdemar César da.** Tratado da responsabilidade criminal. São Paulo, Saraiva, 1955. 3 v. 1656 p.
Exhaustive treatise covering Brazilian law and practice on criminal liability, with copious footnotes on documentation and comparative

law comments. Legal aspects are highlighted, although the author also approaches the subject with respect to anthropology, psychology, pathology, biology, and criminology. Case law is liberally referred to in the text.

5533. Teixeira, Napoleão Lyrio. Psicologia forense e psiquiatria médico-legal. Curitiba, Brazil, 1954. 299 p.

A professor on forensic medicine gives an analysis of authorities and actual cases in his field.

5534. Vergara, Pedro. Fanatismo e homicídio. Rio, 1953. 177 p.

A criminological monograph on homicide committed by fanatics, who may be impelled by religion, superstition, mob violence, political aspirations, war measures, and others. The crime of genocide is discussed in this connection.

COLOMBIA

5535. Barrientos Restrepo, Samuel. Elementos de derecho penal. Medellín, Colombia, Universidad Pontificia Boliviariana, 1953. 306 p.

Theory and history of criminal law, with specific application to Colombia.

5536. Rendón G., Gustavo. Derecho penal colombiano. Medellín, Colombia, 1953. 280 p.

Covers various general categories of crimes and delicts, including those against persons, property, family relations, life and body, administration of justice, and others.

5537. Serpa Flores, Roberto. Manual de psiquiatría forense. Bogotá, Cooperativa Artes Gráficas, 1953. 279 p.

The use of psychiatry in court to prove capacity or lack of capacity to contract, make wills, to be responsible for one's acts, and similar matters, is discussed from various viewpoints, as legislated in the various codes and laws of the country. This includes, among others, civil and criminal codes, labor and canonical law.

MEXICO

5538. Ceniceros, José Ángel. Derecho penal y criminología. México, Ediciones Botas (Publ. Criminalia), 1954. 391 p.

Dr. Ceniceros' prolific pen adds another contribution to the literature on criminal law, a field in which he has long been an outstanding authority at home and abroad.

5539. Jiménez Huerta, Mariano. La tipicidad. México, Porrúa, 1955. 325 p.

Contribution to criminal law literature dealing with characteristics customary to specific crimes in order to determine into which category they would fall as judged by standards, and also to determine the proper penalty. To judge by simple analogy in this field is prohibited by the Mexican Constitution. The rule is to judge

rather by "precise and unequivocal" lines which must be technically drawn in determining what is an unlawful act.

5540. Martínez Licona, R. Aristeo. Dogmática del delito en la legislación veracruzana y en la del Distrito y territorios federales. México, 1953. 152 p.

Philosophical and jurisprudential treatment of the subject of crime, with particular reference to the advanced measures on criminal law adopted by the state of Veracruz.

5541. Molina Pasquel, Roberto. Contempt of court; correcciones disciplinarias y medios de apremio. México, Fondo de Cultura Económica, 1954. 430 p.

An eminent proceduralist in spite of being still a young man, the author gives us a comparison of "contempt" and "desacato" under common and civil law. He refers to contempt of legislature as well as contempt of court, and devotes several chapters to European practice as differentiated from Mexican and other Latin American countries, and the U. S. and Great Britain.

OTHER COUNTRIES

5542. Palomino Arana, Helí. Jurisprudencia penal comentada. Lima, Cultura Hispana (Col. Francisco García Calderón), 1953. 657 p.

Digest of case law in the criminal field, with correlation to provisions of law in other fields. The Supreme Court decisions are given in full, followed by the editor's comments thereon.

5543. Torre Reyes, Carlos de la. El delito político: su contenido jurídico y proyecciones sociales. Quito, La Unión, 1954. 739 p.

Doctoral dissertation worthy of special mention. The subject matter deals with the legal and social aspects of the so-called political crime and related matters of political and diplomatic asylum. It is well planned and contains copious references to practices in European and Asiatic countries, including those behind the Iron Curtain, but devotes itself chiefly to the crime as dealt with in the Americas.

5544. Vides Menéndez, Bernardo. Introducción al estudio del derecho penal guatemalteco: parte especial. Guatemala, Tip. Nacional, 1953. 311 p.

Doctoral dissertation of unusual depth and coverage. Each chapter is followed by a brief bibliography of sources consulted. The various classifications of crimes are discussed separately in chapters, following a dissertation of general elements and matters related to the criminal law field.

COMMERCIAL LAW

ARGENTINA

5545. Baker, Wallace R. The Argentine foreign investment law of 1953. N. Y., Thomas Ashwell, 1955. 13 p.

An analysis by an American attorney, with English translations of the laws and decrees. This is a partial reprint of articles appearing previously in *Export trade and shipper.*

5546. **Becú, Carlos Teodoro.** El control del dinero en la Argentina. B. A., Librería Jurídica, 1953. 156 p.
Legal and economic aspects of money, including exchange control.

5546a. **Beveraggi Allende, Walter M.** El servicio del capital extranjero y el control de cambios. México, Fondo de Cultura Económica, 1954, 238 p.
Although published in Mexico, the work relates to Argentine law and practice in exchange control covering the period of 1900 to 1943.

5547. **Cámara, Héctor.** Sociedades de economía mixta. B. A., Ediciones Arayú, 1954. 156 p.
Domestic law and practice in the field of public and so-called "mixed" public and private corporations and agencies is compared with those of European, Asiatic, and American nations. In detail, Argentine provincial and national entities are discussed in two chapters while four chapters are needed to describe the historical and legal antecedents to the national law finally adopted as Law 12.962 in 1946.

5548. **Cavagna Martínez, Ildefonso F.** Sistema bancario argentino. B. A., Ediciones Arayú, 1954. 493 p.
The legal history of the banking system deals principally with the effects on it of President Perón's economic and social programs. Two useful chapters deal with international agreements with other countries on commerce and payments, covering about 50 pages, and one on foreign capital and investment.

5549. **Cholvis, Francisco.** La revaluación de los bienes activos. B. A., Prometeo (Biblioteca de ciencias comerciales, económicas y sociales), 1954. 174 p.
The effect of currency devaluation and depreciation on assets of persons and corporations is treated from a comparative point of view. The bulk of the work, however, relates to domestic legislation and practice in revaluating the assets, indicating the legal and financial aspects.

5550. **Garo, Francisco J.** Derecho comercial. B. A., Depalma, 1955. 528 p.
The first volume of what appears to promise an exhaustive treatment of the commercial code contents. The present volume deals only with the "general part," on rights of merchants in general, books to be kept, and types of persons in commerce, such as brokers, agents, salesmen, etc.

5551. ————. Sociedades anónimas. B. A., Ediar, 1954. 2 v.
An expert on commercial and business law, the author makes a fine contribution in this exhaustive work on the organizations which are most similar to the common law corporation.

5552. **Segura, Luis G.** Breves nociones sobre reaseguro. B. A., Librería Jurídica (Colección de monografías de derecho, 20), 1954. 61 p.
A brief commentary on reinsurance from the historical and legal points of view.

5553. **Varangot, Carlos Jorge.** Derecho comercial; parte general. B. A., Perrot, 1953. 3 v.
The three volumes which have already appeared cover the "general part" of the commercial code, and the "books" on contracts and corporations, or business associations. Apparently other parts of the commercial code will be covered by subsequent volumes. There have been numerous legislative changes in recent years affecting the code provisions.

5554. **Wallich, Henry C., and Robert Triffin.** Monetary and banking legislation of the Dominican Republic. N. Y., Federal Reserve Bank of New York, 1953. 98 p.
Consists of reports by the authors on proposed legislation on money, a central bank and general banking measures, giving texts in English. A fine introductory chapter on the economic background to 1950 supplies a great deal of useful information.

BRAZIL

5555. **Lacerda, Jozé Cândido Sampaio da.** Curso de direito comercial marítimo e aeronáutico. 2. ed. melhorada e atualizada. Rio, Freitas Bastos, 1954. 496 p.
Covers, in textbook style, all aspects of maritime and navigation law as found in the commercial code and special legislation. As applicable to aeronautical trade the commercial code provisions are interpreted by analogy, and there are also special measures affecting this type of transportation of goods.

5556. Legislação bancária. Rio, Coelho Branco (Coleção de códigos e leis vigentes, 9), 1954.
The compilation of all laws and other legislative and administrative measures, including those emanating from the bank itself, is unannotated.

5557. **Luz, Fábio.** Teoria e prâtica das sociedades cooperativas. 4. ed. refundida e atualizada. Rio, Pongetti, 1953. 748 p.
The growing importance and use of cooperatives in Brazil have prompted the author to enlarge and bring up to date his treatise on theory and practice.

5558. **Nabuco, José Thomaz.** A statement of the laws of Brazil in matters affecting business. 2d. ed., revised and enlarged. Washington, Pan American Union, Division of Law and Treaties, 1955. 158 p.

5559. **Pontes de Miranda, Francisco**

Cavalcante. Tratado de direito cambiário. 2. ed. São Paulo, Limonad, 1954-1955. 4 v.

The first edition of 1937 was out of print as well as out of date. There have been many important and substantial changes in Brazilian exchange law in recent years.

5560. Rudge, Raul Telles. Seguro contra incêndio no direito brasileiro. Rio, Freitas Bastos, 1954. 365 p.

There has been little or nothing written on the legal aspects of insurance law in Brazil. The present work is limited to fire insurance, and is very complete.

COLOMBIA

5561. Cavelier, Germán. A statement of the laws of Colombia in matters affecting business. 2d. ed., revised and enlarged. Washington, Pan American Union, Division of Laws and Treaties, 1953. 186 p.

5562. Código de sociedades. Bogotá, Librería Voluntad (Colección Codex brevis), 1953. 286 p.

5563. Vanegas Lasprilla, Santiago. Sociedades (constitución, prueba y control). Bogotá, Imp. Departamental, 1953. 85 p. Law school thesis.

MEXICO

5565. Cervantes Ahumada, Raúl. Títulos y operaciones de crédito. México, Porrúa, 1954. 449 p.

Negotiable instruments are taking on an added importance as the trade relations of Mexico with other countries keeps growing. The present work approaches the subject of credit instruments theoretically and practically. One chapter is devoted to the Anglo-American trust, as used in Mexico.

5566. Hernández Zanabria, Gonzalo. La sociedad de responsabilidad limitada. Ensayo hermenéutico. México, 1954. 208 p.

Dissertation on the general elements and development of the so-called limited liability company, a hybrid organization between a partnership and a corporation. This is a well-documented monograph.

5567. Mantilla Molina, Roberto L. Derecho mercantil. 2. ed. México, Porrúa, 1953. 429 p.

Revised and enlarged edition made necessary by the many recent changes taking place in the substantive commercial law. This volume covers the general concepts of mercantile law and corporation law.

5568. Salinas Puente, Antonio. Derecho

cooperativo. México, Editorial Cooperativismo, 1954. 416 p.

Excerpts and citations from national and foreign authorities together with legal and judicial interpretation are included in this monograph on corporation law. The general historical development, the various methods of establishing and making use of cooperatives, registration, labor problems related thereto, taxation, and other aspects are touched upon..

5569. Siqueiros P., José Luis. Las sociedades extranjeras en México. México, Imp. Universitaria, 1953. 199 p.

International problems related to corporations and business associations have formed the bases for a number of works by the author. One of his earlier works was awarded honors by Harvard University.

5570. Translation of the commercial code of Mexico, as enacted in 1889, with all amendments up to 1953. México, Traducciones, S. A., 1954. 141 leaves.

The title is misleading, since the basic commercial code of 1889 has been amended in practically two thirds of its contents. The amendments are merely cited in this translation, and not included, as might be gathered from the words "with all amendments."

PERU

5571. Boesen, Richard M. Rights and duties of foreign businesses under Peruvian law. Lima, Andean Air Mail & Peruvian Times, 1953. 227 p.

The Peruvian and U. S. provisions of law are analyzed in this English-language contribution. The law forming the basis of the analysis concerns business principally, including contracts, sales, labor, and other provisions.

5572. Lavalle Vargas, Hernando de. La emisión de obligaciones por las sociedades anónimas. Lima, T. Scheuch, 1953. 138 p.

This fills a gap in the legal literature of Peru, which has little on this particular subject. As a matter of fact, it is a subject that has been neglected even in the legislation itself, according to the author.

5573. Ulloa y Sotomayor, Alberto. A statement of the laws of Peru in matters affecting business. 2d. ed., revised and enlarged. Washington, Pan American Union, Division of Law and Treaties, 1955. 133 p.

OTHER COUNTRIES

5574. Código de comercio, sancionado por el Congreso Nacional en 1955. Caracas, A. Almeda Cedillo, 1955. 350 p.

5575. Couture, Eduardo J., and H. Bar-

bagelata. A statement of the laws of Uruguay in matters affecting business. 2d. ed., revised and enlarged. Washington, Pan American Union, Division of Law and Treaties, 1953. 122 p.
Supplement no. 1, March 31, 1954, has appeared.

5576. Gurdián, Raúl, and Harry Zurcher. A statement of the laws of Costa Rica in matters affecting business. 2d. ed., revised and enlarged. Washington, Pan American Union, Division of Law and Treaties, 1954. 118 p.

5577. Iriarte Paz, Augusto. Compendio y compilación general de legislación económica para el comercio y la industria. Defensa de la economía privada y pública frente al agio y la especulación. La Paz, 1953. 503 p.
In recent years, extortion and speculation in connection with essential foods and other products has produced a situation requiring restrictive and control legislation. Matters covered include price control, exchange control, export-import controls, government monopolies, and others.

5578. Morales, Carlos. Comentarios al código de comercio venezolano. V. 1. Caracas, Ediciones Garrido, 1954. 316 p.
Each article of the code is treated in a narrative explanatory form, some provisions being covered very briefiy and others at great length. Only the first 205 articles of code are included in this first volume.

5579. Pressoir, Charles Fernand; Georges Baussan, fils; and Pierre Chauvet. A statement of the laws of Haiti in matters affecting business. 2d. ed., revised and enlarged. Washington, Pan American Union, Division of Law and Treaties, 1955. 77 p.

5580. Ricci, Denis de. Investissements en Amérique latine. Paris, A. Peone, 1955. 104 p.
Demonstrating that the growing interest in trade and investment in Latin America is not imited to the U. S., the author describes for European investors the legal and tax aspects of trading or investing in Brazil, Colombia, Ecuador, Peru, and Venezuela.

5581. Sapena Pastor, Raúl. A statement of the laws of Paraguay in matters affecting business. Washington, Pan American Union, Division of Law and Treaties, 1953. 138 p.

5582. Serrano Moscoso, Eduardo. A statement of the laws of Ecuador in matters affecting business. 2d. ed., revised and enlarged. Washington, Pan American Union, Division of Law and Treaties, 1955. 190 p.

5583. Supervielle, Bernardo. El establecimiento comercial: noción, disciplina, naturaleza. Montevideo, Imp. Uruguaya, 1953. 586 p.
Comparative study of concepts of business organizations in the economic field, including new forms developed more or less recently, caused by changes in the business world. Various measures on acquisition of business and trade, unfair competition, duties, obligations and legal aspects of regulation of business, are all discussed in this work.

5584. Tellado (hijo), Antonio. A statement of the laws of the Dominican Republic in matters affecting business. 2d. ed., revised and enlarged. Washington, Pan American Union, Division of Law and Treaties, 1953. 209 p.

5585. Urquidi, Carlos Walter. A statement of the laws of Bolivia in matters affecting business. 2d. ed., revised and enlarged. Translated and edited by Taylor W. Gannett and Paul A. Colborn. Washington, Pan American Union, Division of Law and Treaties, 1955. 158 p.

PRIVATE INTERNATIONAL LAW

5585a. Alfonsín, Quintín. Curso de derecho privado internacional con especial referencia al derecho uruguayo y a los tratados de Montevideo de 1889. V. 1. Montevideo, Bianchi Altuna, 1955. 690 p.
An authority on conflicts of law discusses this subject in a general introductory method in this first volume, to be followed by more specific application of the rules under the laws of his own country and under treaties of private international law.

5586. ————. Régimen internacional del divorcio. Montevideo, Universidad de Montevideo, Facultad de Derecho y Ciencias Sociales (Biblioteca de publicaciones oficiales, Sec. III, 72), 1953. 166 p.
Problems of private international law related to divorce and recognition of its validity in other countries.

5586a. Muñoz Meany, Enrique. Derecho internacional privado. Guatemala, Ministerio de Educación Pública (Colección científico-pedagógica, 8), 1953. 250 p.
The author having died before completion of his work, the task was carried through in his memory by Drs. Julio Camey Herrera and Carlos Hall Lloreda. The treatise discusses generally the conflicts of laws field, the various doctrines and schools of thought developed in different countries. As practiced in Guatemala,

the topics cover nationality, contracts, labor, criminal law, civil law, and procedure.

5587. Salazar Flor, Carlos. Generalización del derecho penal internacional. Quito, Casa de la Cultura Ecuatoriana, 1955. 189 p.
Conflict of laws in the field of criminal law is the basis of discussion, including such topics as extradition, asylum, and treaties for prevention of smuggling and other crimes practiced across borders.

PUBLIC INTERNATIONAL LAW

5587a. Altamira y Crevea, Rafael. El derecho al servicio de la paz; cuestiones internacionales. México, Imp. Universitaria, 1954. 528 p.
A posthumous publication of the author's views on pacifism and the use of the rule of law to promote universal peace.

5588. Moreno Quintana, Lucio Manuel. Preliminares del derecho internacional. B. A., Perrot, 1954. 124 p.
A generalized text for use in the first-year courses of international law.

OTHER TOPICS

5588a. Aguerrevere, Ángel Demetrio. Elementos de derecho minero. Caracas, Ragon, 1954. 270 p.
Relates specifically to Venezuelan legislation and practice.

5589. Bonifaz, Miguel. Legislación agrario-indigenal. Cochabamba, Bolivia, Universidad Mayor de San Simón, Facultad de Derecho, 1953. 595 p.
Systematic, orderly compilation of all enactments affecting the Bolivian Indian, insofar as agricultural, land, and labor rights are concerned. The period covered commences with independence from Spain and goes to the present.

5589a. Chiossone Lares, Germán. Principios generales de derecho aeronáutico venezolano. Caracas, Ragon, 1954. 231 p.
Many aspects of aeronautical law are discussed, including dominion of airspace, mortgage and liens on aircraft, insurance, and others.

5590. Código de minería. San José, Imp. Nacional, 1953. 24 p.
Official text, unannotated.

5590a. Código del petróleo. Bogotá, Ediciones Revista del Petróleo, 1953. 40 p.

5591. Corrêa, Eduardo. Moratórias e reajustamentos (pecuaristas e agricultores). Rio, Freitas Bastos, 1954. 524 p.
The laws on agricultural and cattle-industry financing are annotated with excerpts from

learned opinion, legislation, legislative history, case law, and statistics.

5591a. Cuban traffic code, effective August 6, 1955. English translation by J. de D. Tejada, revised by Hardy L. Spatz. Habana, Cárdenas, 1955. 84 p.
Enacted by Law-decree 2037 of Jan. 27, 1955, and published in the official gazette of Feb. 5, 1955.

5592. Enciclopédia da legislação do ensino. Rio, Lex, 1952-1954. 2 v. 712 p.
Under a subject classification, the entire texts of national and provincial laws and regulations on education are copied.

5592a. Ledesma, Julio O. Función social de las marcas de fábrica y de comercio. B. A., Librería Jurídica (Col. de monografías de derecho, 16), 1955. 111 p.
Property rights, public interest, and protection against unfair competition are the highlights discussed in connection with trade-marks and commercial names. Argentine legislation and case law attempting to balance private and public interests are discussed in this work.

5593. Legislación boliviana del indio; recopilación de resoluciones, órdenes, decretos, leyes, decretos supremos y otras disposiciones legales, 1825-1953. La Paz, Fénix, 1953. 518 p.
Measures of all categories taken to meet and solve problems connected with the large Indian population in Bolivia.

5593a. López González, Norma. Problemas sanitarios y soluciones legislativas. Santiago, 1953. 116 p.
A law school thesis dealing with a subject not commonly selected, and one on which very little literature has been contributed in Chile, insofar as concerns the legal aspects.

5594. Noguera Laborde, Rodrigo. Código de petróleos. Bogotá, Imp. Nacional, 1953. 2 v. 145 p.; Apéndice, 125 p.

5594a. The oil code of Colombia, decree 1056 of 1953 (April 20). English translation by James W. Raisbeck. Bogotá, Ospina-Racines, 1954. 70 p.

5595. Pasini Costadoat, Carlos Alberto. El espacio aéreo (dominium coeli). B. A., Depalma, 1955. 151 p.

5595a. Plazas, Arcadio. Los derechos de autor en las obras musicales. Bogotá, Saycco, 1953. 28 p.
Reprint of a radio address concerning musical copyright.

5596. Reglamento del código de petróleo; decreto número 445. Guatemala, Ministerio de Economía y Trabajo, 1955. 140 p.

5596a. Sánchez Espejo, Carlos. El patronato en Venezuela. Caracas, Tall. Civa (Pontificium Institutum Internationale Angelicum), 1953. 198 p.

A thesis which was awarded a prize by the School of Ecclesiastical Law. The author is a member of the priesthood.

5597. Santos, Moacyr Amaral. Direito usual para engenheiros. São Paulo, Limonad, 1953. 391 p.

The author is professor of law and legislation in the School of Engineering of Mackenzie University in São Paulo. This work is intended for his students and for other engineers who may be required to know legal aspects of their profession and of law touching on any undertakings they might have to work with. Among the topics discussed are laws on public works, construction, mining, labor, land and water, in addition to laws governing the profession of engineering itself.

5597a. Siegrist Clamont, Jorge. En defensa de la autonomía universitaria. México, Jus, 1955. 2 v. 571, 190 p.

The development of the University of Mexico is discussed from historical and legal viewpoints, from its creation, when Mexico was part of the Viceroyalty of New Spain, up to the present time. The second volume deals principally with its role as a government institution.

5598. Sociedade Brasileira de Compositores e Editôres de Música. Direito autoral de execução pública e radiodifusão. São Paulo, 1954. 154 p.

Contains a collection of national laws in force, the text of the Washington and Berne Conventions, as well as excerpts from case law and opinions dealing with this particular phase of copyright law.

5598a. Valdés Otero, Estanislao. Derechos de autor; régimen jurídico uruguayo. Montevideo, Universidad de Montevideo, Facultad de Derecho y Ciencias Sociales (Biblioteca de publ. oficiales, Sec. III, 68), 1953. 414 p.

Historical and legislative background of domestic copyright law is followed by a full discussion of practice and judicial interpretation of same.

5599. Velloso, Lycurgo. Legislação açucareira e alcooleira. Rio, Instituto do Açúcar e do Alcool, 1955. 2 v.

Annotated compilation of legislative and administrative acts on sugar and alcohol enacted between 1931 and 1952. The annotations consist principally of the excerpts from related legislation and some case law.

5599a. Viteri Echeverría, Ernesto R. La protección marcaria y la legislación guatemalteca. Guatemala, 1953. 134 p.

Includes discussion of U. S. laws and authorities in a comparative analysis of trade-mark protection. The author also touches on problems of trade-marks belonging to enemy aliens.

Music

RICHARD A. WATERMAN

DURING the years 1953-1955 there appears to have been a slump in significant musical publications, possibly because the backlog of articles not published during the war had been used up. The number of musical works of Latin American composers coyprighted in the U. S. also showed a decline during the period. Musical performances and musical groups, however, increased in number in most countries.

Argentina's distinguished record in the field of concert life was maintained, and many musical organizations functioned during the years in question. Among the symphonic groups may be listed the Orquesta Sinfónica de la Ciudad de Buenos Aires, the Orquesta Sinfónica de la Radio del Estado, the Orquesta Sinfónica del Estado, the Orquesta Filarmónica de Buenos Aires, the Orquesta Sinfónica Universitaria, and the Orquesta Juvenil de la Radio del Estado. Opera was best represented by the Teatro Colón de Buenos Aires. Chamber music groups include the Agrupación Nueva Música, the Conjunto Instrumental de la Asociación Sinfónica de Buenos Aires, the Conjunto Instrumental de la Asociación del Profesorado Orquestal, the Conjunto de Instrumentos de Viento de Buenos Aires, the Cuarteto Argentino, the Cuarteto Pro-Arte, the Cuarteto Renacimiento, the Cuarteto Acedo, and the Cuarteto de la Asociación Wagneriana.

Choral music was performed in Argentina by many groups, including the Asociación Coral de Cámara de Pamplona and the Agrupación Coral de Buenos Aires. The list of Argentine associations for the promotion of musical culture is a long one, including such varied groups as the Mozarteum Argentino, the Buenos Aires Sociedad de Conciertos de Cámara, the Sociedad Musical Daniel, the Asociación Wagneriana, the Asociación Sinfónica Femenina, the Círculo Juan Sebastián Bach, the Asociación Amigos de la Música, the Asociación Tárrega de Buenos Aires, and the Asociación Pro Cultura Musical de Rosario.

Argentine musical nationalism was undoubtedly spurred considerably by the presidential decree of Dec. 29, 1952, requiring that at least one work by an Argentine composer be included in each concert of any kind, on pain of suspension from musical activities for 30 days for the first offense, 90 days for the second, and permanently for the third.

There was much activity in many fields of music in Mexico. Symphonic groups included the Orquesta Sinfónica Nacional, the Orquesta Filarmónica Ciudad de México, and the Orquesta Sinfónica de la Universidad de México, as well as the Orquesta Sinfónica de Guanajuato, the Orquesta Sinfónica de Xalapa, and the Orquesta Sinfónica de Guadalajara. Chamber music was played by the Orquesta de Cámara de México, the Cuarteto Breda, the Quinteto de Instrumentos de Aliento del Instituto Nacional de Bellas Artes, the Cuarteto Haydn, and the Dúo de Cámara of Mexico City. The Conjunto Vocal de Cámara was organized in Mexico City in 1953. Choral groups giving concerts included the Coro del Conservatorio Nacional de Música and the Coro de Varones of the same institution, and Los Niños Cantores de Morelia.

Operas were produced by the Academia de Ópera del Instituto Nacional de Bellas Artes, the Teatro de Bellas Artes, and the Ópera Nacional. The Juventudes Musicales de México presented many concerts, including both opera and ballet. Promotional associations included the Asociación Musical del Instituto Francés de la América Latina and the Sociedad Leonense de Conciertos, of León, Guanajuato, both organized in 1953, as well as the Asociación Música de Cámara de México, the Asociación Veracruzana de Conciertos, the Asociación Musical Manuel M. Ponce, and the Sociedad Musical Daniel.

In Cuba, the Orquesta Filarmónica de La Habana, sorely beset by problems both of management and of finance, was revived a few times during the period but was moribund at its close, leaving the Western Hemisphere to feel the loss of one of its outstanding orchestras. Chamber music was provided by many groups, including the Sociedad de Música de Cámara de Cuba and the Cuarteto de la Sociedad de Conciertos; many chamber music events were scheduled and arranged by the consistently active Sociedad Pro-Arte Musical de La Habana. The Grupo Coral Madrigalista de la Universidad de Oriente, La Coral de Cienfuegos, and La Coral del Conservatorio Municipal de La Habana were among the organizations providing concerts of choral music during the 1953-1955 period. Ballet was presented by El Ballet Alicia Alonso and El Ballet de Cienfuegos. Musical societies included the Sociedad Pro-Arte Musical de La Habana, the Sociedad de Conciertos de La Habana, the Sociedad Lyceum de La Habana, the Sociedad Filarmónica, Juventudes Musicales de Cuba, la Sociedad Pro-Artes y Ciencias de Cienfuegos, the Sociedad de Arte Musical de Santa Clara, and the Sociedad Amigos de la Cultura Cubana, in Matanzas.

Symphony orchestras functioned in several Brazilian centers, with São Paulo, in this as in other musical respects, seeming to threaten to supplant Rio as the focus of Brazilian concert life. Among the active symphonic groups of the period may be mentioned the Orquestra Filarmônica de São Paulo, the Orquestra Sinfônica Municipal de São Paulo, the Orquestra do Teatro Municipal de São Paulo, the Orquestra Sinfônica Brasileira, the Orquestra Sinfônica de Recife, and the Orquestra Sinfônica de Pôrto Alegre. Among the chamber music concerts of the period were those given by the Quarteto de São Paulo, the Orquestra de Cordas do Angelicum do Brasil, of São Paulo, and the Conjunto Mineiro de Música de Câmara of Belo Horizonte. Notable among Brazilian choral groups was the Côro Evangélico, of São Paulo. Many orchestral concerts, as well as opera and ballet, were offered by the Teatro Nacional de Rio de Janeiro.

Of the remaining Latin American countries, Chile and Uruguay were outstanding in terms of the numbers of musical organizations and concerts, the latter perhaps because of the extremely active leadership of SODRE *(Servicio Oficial de Difusión Radio Eléctrica)*, in Montevideo. During the period Colombia saw the formation of the Orquesta Sinfónica de Colombia, which gave its first concert in July 1953, as well as the organization of the Orquesta Sinfónica del Conservatorio de Caldas, Manizales, in June 1955. In Peru the Orquesta Sinfónica de Chiclayo, and in Chile the Orquesta Filarmónica de Chile were also formed in 1955.

Easily the most important event of the 1953-1955 period, in terms of American music as a whole, was the First Festival of Latin American Music, held in Caracas from Nov. 22 to Dec. 10, 1954. Organized by the José Ángel Lamas Institution, the festival was presided over by Inocente Palacios, Enrique de los Ríos, Pedro Antonio Ríos Reyna, and Alejo Carpentier. Guests of honor, who represented their respective countries, were Juan José Castro, Jacobo Ficher, and Enzo Valenti Ferro, of Argentina; Heitor Villa-Lobos, of Brazil; Domingo Santa Cruz, of Chile; Guillermo Uribe Holguín, Guillermo Espinosa, and Pedro Biava, of Colombia; Harold Gramatges, Edgardo Martín, Julián Orbon, and Hilario González, of Cuba; Carlos Chávez, Blas

Galindo, and Rodolfo Halffter, of Mexico; Jesús María Sanromá, Héctor Campos Parsi, and Alfredo Matilla, of Puerto Rico; Aaron Copland and Virgil Thompson, of the U. S.; and Héctor Tosar Erecart and Alberto Soriano, of Uruguay. Jack Bornoff of UNESCO, Guillermo Espinosa of the Pan American Union, and James Fasset of the Columbia Broadcasting Company were also in attendance as representatives of their organizations.

In connection with the Festival, a contest for Latin American composers had been announced some time previous to the event. The panel of judges included Carlos Chávez, Heitor Villa-Lobos, Erich Kleiber, Edgard Varese, and Vicente Emilio Sojo. Juan José Castro, of Argentina, was awarded the José Ángel Lamas prize of $10,000 for his "Corales criollos"; Carlos Chávez, of Mexico, was given the Caro de Boesi prize of $5,000 for his "Symphony No. 3"; and Julián Orbon, of Cuba, received the Juan Landaeta prize of $5,000 for his "Tres versiones sinfónicas."

Ten concerts were given during the festival, for the most part featuring contemporary music of the various countries represented, and several round table discussions dealt with the problem of Latin American musical nationalism and with an exploration of possible ways and means to promote international musical interchange and mutual understanding in the Western Hemisphere. As one of the results of these discussions, AIM (Asociación Interamericana de Música) was founded, with Dr. Inocente Palacios as its first president.

Some three months later, and in line with the purpose of AIM, SODRE organized and held in Montevideo the first Congreso Pro Intercambio Musical Americano. Argentina, Brazil, Chile, and Uruguay were represented. The executive committee of the congress, after much discussion, adopted a series of 23 resolutions designed to implement the program of Latin American musical cooperation.

The spread of musical information was facilitated during 1953-1955 by numerous Latin American periodicals and serials dealing wholly or in part with music. Among those whose publication commenced during the period are the following: *Boletín del Instituto de Folklore,* Dirección de Cultura, Ministerio de Educación, Edificio Fermín Toro, Caracas, September 1953.

Comissão Nacional de Música, Instituto Brasileiro de Educação, Ciência e Cultura, Rio, March 1955.

Cristalomandia, San Martín y Eva Perón, piso 1°, B. A., November 1953.

Folclore, orgão da Comissão Paulista de Folclore e do Centro de Pesquisas Folclóricas Mário de Andrade, Caixa Postal 309, São Paulo, December (?) 1952.

Inter música, Álvarez Fonte 4278, B. A., August 1955.

Medellín musical, Apartado 21-22, Medellín, Colombia, September-October 1953.

Música, Escuela Vocacional de Música, Tegucigalpa, January 1955.

Plática, Donato Álvarez 1588, B. A., August 1953.

Pro-Arte, Casilla 2446, La Paz, March 1953.

Revista de la Comisión de Cultura, French 70, Avellaneda, Provincia de Buenos Aires, March 1953.

GENERAL

5600. Boggs, Ralph Steele. Folklore bibliography for 1955 (South Folk Q, 20:1, Mar. 1956).

Ballad, song, dance, game, music, verse, as related to Latin America, p. 48-53. The March issues of this periodical for 1953-1955 contained several pages each of Latin American folklore items, by the same compiler, for 1952-1954.

5601. Cotton, Marion, and Adelaide Bradburn. Music throughout the world. Boston, C. C. Birchard, 1953. 293 p., illus.

Chapter 6, p. 36-42, "Central and South America," deals in an extremely superficial and curtailed manner with Latin American folk and art music.

5602. Fracassi del Carrill, Salvador. Manual de cultura musical. B. A., Julio

Korn (Selecciones de cultura popular), 1954. 215 p.

A musical primer in four chapters dealing respectively with the history and aesthetics of music, brief (3-20 lines) biographies of composers, slightly less brief biographies of Argentine composers, and finally a series of paragraphs on the folklore and the famous musicians of each of the Latin American countries. Bibliography.

5603. Franco Lao, Meri. Ensayo introductivo al atonalismo (SODRE, 2, 1955, p. 21-33).

In discussion of Schoenberg's 12-tone technique, the author tries to strike a happy medium between the attitudes of those who praise it and those who scorn it, and actually succeeds in explaining some aspects of it.

5604. Martí, Samuel. Música aborigen americana (SODRE, 2, 1955, p. 15-20).

Brief summary of structure and functions of Central and South American Indian music.

5605. Pan American Union. Division of Music and Visual Arts. Music of Latin America. 3rd ed. Washington, 1953. 49 p.

Third edition of publication originally issued in 1942. Contains annotated bibliography, p. 43-49.

5606. Peña, Israel. Música sin pentagrama. Caracas, Sucre, 1955. 330 p.

60 short essays, some delightful, reflecting Peña's impressions of various musical subjects, objects, and events.

ARGENTINA

5607. Berruti, P. Manual de danzas nativas. Coreografías, historia y texto poético de las danzas. 1. ed. B. A., Escolar, 1954. 265 p., illus.

A textbook in the field of Argentine native dances, this presentation is remarkably complete and understandable. Many photographic plates, diagrams, and choreographic charts add to its clarity. Bibliography.

5608. Catálogo cronológico de las obras del compositor argentino Alberto Williams (B Música y Artes Visuales, 45-46, nov.-dic. 1953, p. 36-49).

List of the works of Williams, with a sample page from his work.

5609. Catálogo cronológico de las obras del compositor argentino Carlos Gustavino (B Música y Artes Visuales, 44, oct. 1953, p. 14-19).

List of the works of Gustavino, with a sample page of his work.

5610. Catálogo cronológico de las obras del compositor argentino Floro M. Ugarte (B Música y Artes Visuales, 42-43, agosto-sept. 1953, p. 20-24).

List of the works of Ugarte, with reproduction of a page from "Lamento campero."

5611. Catálogo cronológico de las obras del compositor argentino Juan Carlos Paz (B Música y Artes Visuales, 48, feb. 1954, p. 16-22).

List of the works of Paz, with a sample page of his work.

5612. Chronological catalog of the works of the Argentine composer Honorio Siccardi (B Música y Artes Visuales, 63-64, mayo-junio 1955, p. 40-48).

In English and Spanish. Includes facsimile page of his manuscript.

5613. Chronological catalog of the works of the Argentine composer Jacobo Ficher (B Música y Artes Visuales, 69-70, nov.-dec. 1955, p. 44-54).

In English and Spanish. Includes a facsimile page of his manuscript.

5614. Lamuraglia, Nicolás J. Athos Palma: vida, arte, educación. B. A., Ricordi Americana, 1954. 109 p.

Biographic eulogy of Palma as composer, educator, and administrator. Many facsmile plates of Palma's manuscript.

5615. López Flores, Joaquín. Danzas tradicionales argentinas. 2. ed. B. A., Ateneo (Col. Cultura universal), 1954. 386 p., illus.

Extended treatise on the choreography of Argentine folk dance. More than 50 dances are explained, and full directions for dancing are given by means of a special choreographic notation. A few musical examples.

5616. ————. Señuelo. Indicaciones esenciales para guía del cultor de las danzas tradicionales argentinas. B. A., Tall. Beca, 1953. 26 p.

Directions for performing Argentine folk dances, with charts indicating the choreography of eight dances.

5617. Vega, Carlos. Bailes tradicionales argentinos: el cielito. B. A., Julio Korn, 1952, i.e. 1953. 70 p.

History, origin, music, words, and choreography of this traditional Argentine group dance. One plate, several musical examples, and line drawings. Bibliography.

5618. ————. Bailes tradicionales argentinos: el malambo. B. A., Julio Korn, i.e. 1953. 42 p.

History, origin, music, words, and choreography of this traditional Argentine foot-stamping solo dance. One plate, one musical example, line drawings and charts. Bibliography. Includes brief essays on "el solo inglés," "la campana," and related dances.

5619. ————. Bailes tradicionales argen-

tinos: el montonero. El minué federal. B. A., Julio Korn, 1952, i.e. 1953. 36 p.
History, origin, music, words, and choreography of this Argentine traditional minuet. Two pages of music, one plate, many diagrams and line drawings, bibliography of Vega.

5620. ————. Bailes tradicionales argentinos: el pericón. B. A., Julio Korn, 1952, i.e. 1953, 52 p.
History, origins, music, words, and choreography of this Argentine country square dance. Line drawings illustrate some of the figures. Bibliography, and classification chart of dances.

5621. ————. Bailes tradicionales argentinos: el pericón. B. A., Julio Korn, 1952, 1952, i.e. 1953. 21 p.
History, origins, music, words, and choreography of this dance which is unique among traditional Argentine dances in that the movements of the independently dancing couples follow the directions given by the words of the song, as in the U. S. square dance. Two pages of music, one plate, and numerous diagrams and line drawings illustrating the movements of "la firmeza." Bibliography. Classification scheme for dances, in chart form.

5622. ————. Bailes tradicionales argentinos: la media caña. B. A., Julio Korn, 1952, i.e. 1953. 38 p.
History, origin, music, words, and choreography of this traditional Argentine circle dance dating from the first decade of the Revolution of 1810. One plate, and a few illustrative line drawings. Bibliographies of the "media caña" dance, and of Carlos Vega.

5623. ————. Bailes tradicionales argentinos: la resbalosa. B. A., Julio Korn, 1952, i.e. 1953. 38 p.
History, origin, music, words, and choreography of this couple dance of central and western Argentina. One plate, two pages of music, several line drawings to illustrate the steps of the dance. Bibliography.

5624. ————. Bailes tradicionales argentinos: la zamacueca (cueca, zamba, chilena, marinera); la zamba antigua. B. A., Julio Korn, 1952, i.e. 1953. 156 p.
A fairly lengthy discussion of the history of the zamacueca and its relation to the zamba, followed by brief essays on the origin, music, words, and choreography of this Peruvian-derived dance. The second paper contains a brief amplification of what has previously been said concerning connections between zamacueca and zamba. Many plates, two pages of music, line drawings and diagrams, bibliography.

5625. ————. Bailes tradicionales argentinos: los aires. B. A., Julio Korn, 1952, i.e. 1953. 23 p.
History, origins, music, words, and choreography of this traditional lively couple-dance. Has two pages of music, one plate, and numerous diagrams and line drawings illustrating the "los aires" dance. Bibliography.

BRAZIL

5626. Cascudo, Luís de Câmara. Dicionário do folclore brasileiro. Rio, Instituto Nacional do Livro, 1954. 660 p., illus.
Deals with folklore terms derived from both Portugal and Africa. In the proper alphabetical places are a good many articles on dances, musical instruments, and song types, and a remarkably concise treatment of the subject of Brazilian popular and folk music.

5627. Chronological catalog of the works of the Brazilian composer Luiz Cosme (B Música y Artes Visuales, 61-62, marzo-abril 1955, p. 20-26).
In English and Spanish. Includes a sample page of his work.

5628. Guinle, Jorge. Jazz panorama. Rio, Agir, 1953. 184 p.
For its size, this is the most comprehensive, most nearly accurate, best balanced (least polemic) book on jazz yet to come out of the Western Hemisphere. Its most obvious lack is that of musical examples and some consideration of the musical structure of the various jazz styles.

5629. Martins, Saul. A danca de São Gonçalo. Folclore. 2. ed. Belo Horizonte, Brazil, Mantiqueira, 1954. 79 p., illus.
An account of the rural cult of São Gonçalo, with songs, music, and dance. The dance for the saint is usually held to redeem a promessa, i. e., to repay the saint for supernatural and favorable intervention in one's affairs. An occasional part of the ceremony is the round dance, orgiastic in type, that may follow the very sedate dance in honor of the saint. Line drawings, musical examples, glossary, bibliography.

5630. Melo, Veríssimo de. Rondas infantis brasileiras. São Paulo, Departamento de Cultura, 1953. 356 p., illus.
A scholarly and very worthwhile work on Brazilian children's game-songs, considered in terms of the following categories: amorous, satirical, imitative, religious, and dramatic. Each song is presented in musical notation. Bibliography.

5631. Muricy, Andrade. Contribuição do Brasil à música universal (Panorama, 2:5, 1953, p. 42-56).
Discussion of the contributions to Western music made by three Brazilians: Joaquim Manuel, Carlos Gomes, and Heitor Villa-Lobos.

5632. Rezende, Carlos Penteado de. Cronologia musical de São Paulo (1800-1870) (in São Paulo em quatro séculos. V. 2. São Paulo, Instituto Histórico e Geográfico de São Paulo, 1954, p. 233-268).
This essay is a completely chronological listing

of musical events during the 70-year period treated. Several plates, bibliography.

5633. ————. Tradições musicais da Faculdade de Direito de São Paulo. São Paulo, Saraiva, 1954. 270 p., illus.
An elaborate and fully documented treatment of the musical aspects of the history of the Faculdade de Direito from its beginning, in 1828, until 1873. The approach is, in the main, biographical, and deals with important personalities both on the faculty and among the students. Several portraits, reconstructed views of São Paulo, and facsimile reproductions of newspaper clippings.

CHILE

5634. Acevedo Hernández, Antonio. La cueca. Orígenes, historia y antología. Santiago, Nascimento, 1953. 434 p.
Deals only with the words—not the music—of the cueca. The author equates this dance with the zamacueca.

5635. Aguilar, Miguel. La evolución estilística en la obra de René Amengual (R Music Ch, 9:47, oct. 1954, p. 9-17).
The author sees four distinct evolutionary stages in the development of the work of the late director of the National Conservatory of Music.

5636. Becerra, Gustavo. Próspero Bisquertt, premio nacional de arte 1954 (R Music Ch, 9:47, oct. 1954, p. 18-29).
Short biography of Bisquertt and an assessment of his personality, works, and influence.

5637. Chronological catalog of the works of the Chilean composer Alfonso Letelier-Llona (B Música y Artes Visuales, 65-66, julio-agosto 1955, p. 30-34).
In English and Spanish. Includes facsimile page of his manuscript.

5638. Chronological catalog of the works of the Chilean composer Humberto Allende (B Música y Artes Visuales, 67-68, sept.-oct. 1955, p. 44-55).
In English and Spanish. Includes facsimile page of his manuscript.

5639. Lavín, Carlos. El rabel y los instrumentos chilenos (R Music Ch, 10:48, enero 1955, p. 15-28).
The author traces the line of descent from the three-stringed medieval "viol," similar to the Arabic rebab, to the *guitarrón* of Chile (quite different from the *guitarrón* of Mexico) and indicates that the original instrument was brought to the Western Hemisphere by the colonizers of New Spain. Musical examples, six photographs.

5640. Salas Viú, Vicente. Ramón Carnicer, músico y liberal (R Music Ch, 10:48, enero 1955, p.. 8-14).
Biography and appreciation of don Ramón

Carnicer (1789-1855), Spanish composer of the Chilean national hymn.

CUBA

5641. Catálogo cronológico de las obras más importantes del compositor cubano Amadeo Roldán (B Música y Artes Visuales, 38, abril 1953, p. 18-21).
List of the works of Roldán, with a facsimile manuscript page and the first page of one of his published songs.

5642. Ortiz, Fernando. Los instrumentos de la música afrocubana. Habana, Cárdenas, 1954-1955. V. 4, Los membranófonos abiertos, Ñ a Z; los bimembranófonos y otros tambores especiales, 452 p.; v. 5, Los pulsativos, los fricativos, los insuflativos y los aeritivos; índices generales, 529 p.
These two volumes complete the monumental and scholarly 2103-page work, publication of which started in 1952 (see *HLAS, no. 18, 1952,* item 3014) and brings to a close the series started by *La africanía de la música folklórica de Cuba* (see *HLAS, no. 16, 1950,* item 3183) and *Los bailes y el teatro de los negros en el folklore de Cuba* (see *HLAS, no. 17, 1951,* item 2861). Profusely illustrated.

MEXICO

5643. Acevedo López, Santos (comp.). Macehualcuicatl. Cantos populares. México, Vargas Rea (Biblioteca de historiadores mexicanos), 1954. 42 p.
Limited edition of 75 copies only. The songs were collected in the Xochimilco region from old residents, apparently in recent years. They are given in Nahuatl, with Spanish translation. [R. D. Hussey]

5644. Catálogo cronológico de las obras del compositor mexicano Rodolfo Halffter (B Música y Artes Visuales, 55-56, sept.-oct. 1954, p. 30-35).
List of the works of Halffter, with a sample page of his work.

5645. Catálogo cronológico de las obras del compositor mexicano Silvestre Revueltas (B Música y Artes Visuales, 40, junio 1953, p. 22-24).
List of the works of Revueltas, with a sample page from his "Cuauhnahuac."

URUGUAY

5646. Ayestarán, Lauro. La música en el Uruguay. V. 1. Prólogo de Juan E. Pivel Devoto. Montevideo, Servicio Oficial de Difusión Radio Eléctrica, 1953. 818 p.
First two parts of a larger projected work on primitive music and art music up to 1860. Yet

to come are the part on folk music and an anthology and critical essay on Uruguayan music. Several plates, and many musical examples. Includes, p. 303-435, a complete chronology of Uruguayan theatre music from 1829 to 1860. This is an extremely valuable reference work.

5647. Chronological catalog of the works of the Uruguayan composer Eduardo Fabini (B Música y Artes Visuales, 67-68, sept.-oct. 1955, p. 56-61).
In English and Spanish. Includes facsimile page of his manuscript.

OTHER COUNTRIES

5648. Catálogo cronológico de las obras del compositor costarricense Julio Fonseca (B Música y Artes Visuales, 60, feb. 1955, p. 22-26).
List of the works of Fonseca, with a facsimile page of his manuscript.

5649. Catálogo cronológico de las obras del compositor nicaragüense Luis A. Delgadillo (B Música y Artes Visuales, 49-50, marzo-abril 1954, p. 24-30).
List of the works of Delgadillo, with a sample page of his work.

5650. Catálogo cronológico de las obras del compositor peruano Andrés Sas Orchassal (B Música y Artes Visuales, 59, enero 1955, p. 22-29).

List of the compositions of Orchassal, with a facsimile page of his manuscript.

5651. Chronological catalog of the works of the Dominican composer Juan Francisco García (B Música y Artes Visuales, 63-64, mayo-junio 1955, p. 34-38).
In English and Spanish. Includes facsimile page of his manuscript.

5652. Honorat, Michel L. Les danses folkloriques haïtiennes. Port-au-Prince, Imp. de l'État, 1955. 155 p.
A Haitian ethnologist studies the dances of his country, with special emphasis on those connected with vodun, though other types are also analyzed. The monograph is illustrated by photographs of musical instruments utilized in Haiti and pictures of various dancers in costume. Several Haitian songs are also included. M. Honorat's treatment of this difficult subject is rendered even more interesting by an approach that is at once historical, sociological, and psychological. [M. Cook]

5653. Ramón y Rivera, Luis Felipe. El joropo, baile nacional de Venezuela. Caracas, Ministerio de Educación, Biblioteca Venezolana de Cultura (Col. Folklore y etnología), 1953. 92 p., illus.
An excellent musicological treatise on the polyrhythmic national dance of Venezuela, dealing with its history, its social aspects, its melodic, rhythmic, and harmonic structure, the instruments, the verses, and the choreography. 12 plates, 42 musical examples, 16 complete transcriptions, bibliography.

Philosophy

ANÍBAL SÁNCHEZ REULET

POCOS cambios de orientación pueden anotarse en la producción filosófica del año 1953. Desde un punto de vista estrictamente bibliográfico, es importante destacar el hecho de que comenzaron a publicarse otras dos nuevas revistas de carácter especializado. En primer término, la *Revista pernambucana de filosofía,* que edita la Universidad de Recife bajo la dirección de los profesores Pinto Ferreira y Glaucio Veiga. Esta revista es órgano oficial de la Sección Pernambucana del Instituto Brasileño de Filosofía. Por su parte, la Sección de Ciencias Filosóficas de la Casa de la Cultura Ecuatoriana ha iniciado la publicación de una revista semestral titulada *Filosofía* que dirige el Dr. Emilio Uzcátegui.

Dos reuniones de carácter internacional tuvieron lugar en 1953. En el mes de enero, organizadas por la Sociedad Cubana de Filosofía, y como parte del homenaje a Martí en su centenario, se realizaron en La Habana las "Conversaciones Filosóficas Interamericanas," a las que asistieron, además de un grupo numeroso de filósofos cubanos, representantes de la Argentina, Bolivia, el Brasil, Chile, Colombia, Costa Rica, España, los Estados Unidos, la India, Panamá, el Perú y Venezuela. Los debates fueron dirigidos por el presidente de la Sociedad, Profesor Humberto Piñera Llera, y versaron sobre dos temas principales: "La esencia del hombre y de lo humano" y "¿Es posible una filosofía americana?" En la última sesión se decidió crear una Sociedad Interamericana de Filosofía, cuya acta constitutiva fue firmada por todos los participantes, en carácter de socios fundadores (véase párrafo 5723).

En el mes de abril, en Quito, se efectuó el Primer Congreso de Filosofía y Filosofía de la Educación convocado por la Facultad de Filosofía, Letras y Ciencias de la Educación de la Universidad Central del Ecuador, con motivo de cumplir los veinticinco años de su fundación. Concurrieron delegaciones del Brasil, Colombia, Chile, España, Francia, Honduras, Panamá, República Dominicana, Suiza, el Uruguay y Venezuela y representantes de las tres universidades nacionales, de la Casa de la Cultura y de otras instituciones del Ecuador. El presidente titular del Congreso fue el Dr. Emilio Uzcátegui, decano de la mencionada facultad.

De acuerdo con el criterio que se ha adoptado para la preparación de esta bibliografía, figuran en ella obras y artículos escogidos de autores latinoamericanos, cualquiera que sea el asunto de que se ocupen, y de autores no latinoamericanos, siempre que traten temas relacionados con el pensamiento y la filosofía de América Latina. Todos los trabajos referentes a la filosofía latinoamericana se agrupan en un apartado especial de la subsección de "Estudios críticos." Las reediciones de obras clásicas del pensamiento latinoamericano figuran en la subsección de "Obras generales." Los estudios que se refieran a aspectos no estrictamente filosóficos del pensamiento latinoamericano, aparecen bajo el título "Historia de las ideas." Con el propósito de dar una visión más completa de lo que se está publicando en América Latina se incluye, en un apéndice, una lista mínima de nuevas traducciones de obras clásicas y contemporáneas importantes.

317

OBRAS GENERALES Y MISCELÁNEA

5700. Álvarez González, Francisco. Historia de la filosofía. Con una selección de textos originales de los principales filósofos. Cuenca, Ecuador, Publicaciones de la Universidad, 1953-1954. 2 v. 1254 p.

Texto para la enseñanza elemental de la filosofía en cursos secundarios y universitarios. Abarca desde Grecia hasta la filosofía actual. El último autor tratado es Ortega y Gasset. Incluye, al final, una pequeña bibliografía. La selección de los textos de los filósofos es excelente y se han utilizado, en general, las mejores versiones castellanas existentes.

5701. Astrada, Carlos. Mito, tiempo e historicidad (Cuad Fil, año 5-6, fasc. 7, no. 10-12, marzo 1952-oct. 1953, p. 27-33).

Notas sobre el sentido del tiempo y la vivencia de la temporalidad histórica, en la mentalidad primitiva. La conciencia mítica, al parecer, tiende a una concepción circular y cíclica del tiempo.

5702. Bello, Andrés. Obras completas. V. 3. Filosofía. Caracas, Ministerio de Educación, 1951. lxxx, 710 p., facsms.

Contiene *La filosofía del entendimiento,* publicada originalmente en Santiago de Chile, en 1881, y de la que no se había hecho ninguna edición posterior. Incluye además, algunos otros trabajos menores de carácter filosófico. El volumen lleva un prólogo y un estudio sobre el pensamiento filosófico de Bello por Juan David García Bacca.

5703. Berndtson, Arthur. Teaching Latin American philosophy (Americas, Franciscan Hist, 9:3, Jan. 1953, p. 263-271).

Comenta las ventajas y problemas que presenta la enseñanza de la filosofía latinoamericana en los Estados Unidos, en relación con el curso que el autor dicta desde hace años en la Universidad de Missouri. Contiene referencias a autores y bibliografía utilizada.

5703a. Brito, R. de Farias. A base física do espírito. 2. ed. Rio, Ministério da Educação e Saúde (Obras de Farias Brito, 2), 1953. 304 p.

Segundo volumen de la reedición de las obras de Farias Brito (1862-1917) emprendida por el Instituto Nacional do Livro, Brasil. Esta obra se publicó por primera vez en Rio de Janeiro, en 1912.

5703b. ————. A verdade como regra das ações. 2. ed. Rio, Ministério da Educação e Saúde (Obras de Farias Brito, 3), 1953. 141 p.

Primera edición, Pará, 1905.

5704. Casanovas, Domingo. La duda peregrina. Una breve historia de la filosofía. Filosofía contemporánea. Prólogo por Luis Beltrán Guerrero. Caracas, Ediciones Ariel, 1953. 325 p.

Reúne una serie de artículos publicados en diferentes periódicos y revistas. Da una rápida visión del desarrollo de la filosofía, desde Grecia hasta nuestros días. Entre los autores tratados, figura el mexicano Antonio Caso. Contiene retratos de algunos filósofos importantes.

5705. Derisi, Octavio Nicolás. La existencia en el tomismo y en el existencialismo (Sapientia, Eva Perón, 8:29 julio-sept. 1953, p. 193-198).

5708. Frankl, Víctor. Espíritu y camino de Hispanoamérica. T. 1. La cultura hispanoamericana y la filosofía europea. Bogotá, Ministerio de Educación Nacional, Ediciones de la Revista Bolívar (Biblioteca de autores colombianos, 42), 1953. 582 p.

Serie de artículos, ensayos y conferencias publicados ya con anterioridad en revistas y periódicos. El autor se propone la ambiciosa tarea de descubrir, no sólo las profundas raíces de la espiritualidad hispanoamericana, para lo cual empieza por remontarse a la filosofía de San Agustín, sino también la dirección y destino futuros de la vida y la cultura de la América Hispánica. Cree que en los países hispanoamericanos existe, en gestación, una nueva Edad Media que no haría sino prolongar la tradición escolástica de España por debajo de las transitorias influencias de la Ilustración, el nacionalismo y el liberalismo modernos. De los trabajos incluidos en este volumen, quizás el más interesante sea el dedicado a examinar el pensamiento político, histórico y económico del Virrey de Nueva Granada, Caballero y Góngora. La tesis más discutible del libro se encuentra en el ensayo titulado "Arte y filosofía en Hispanoamérica," en el cual se afirma que el arte hispanoamericano carece de "estilo verdadero" porque, con la sola excepción del mexicano Orozco, los artistas están desvinculados de la tradición cristiana.

5709. Gaos, José. Sobre los estudios filosóficos en nuestra Facultad (Fil Let, México, 25:51-52, julio-dic. 1953, p. 41-63). Informe sobre el plan de estudios.

5710. García de Onrubia, Luis F. Psicología intencional. B. A., Universidad de Buenos Aires, Facultad de Filosofía y Letras, Sección de Psicología (Monografías psicológicas, 8), 1953. 73 p.

Después de indicar la transformación que las concepciones de la psicología han experimentado desde la época de Wundt por obra de Brentano, Stumpf y la Escuela de Wurzburgo, estudia, en los capítulos siguientes, las contribuciones de Husserl y de Sartre al desarrollo de la psicología intencional.

5711. Lalande, A. Vocabulario técnico y crítico de la filosofía. Traducción española de la quinta edición. 2 v. B. A., El Ateneo, 1953. 1502 p.

La traducción, del francés, fué hecha por un conjunto de colaboradores bajo la dirección de Luis Alfonso, y ha sido revisada por Vicente Quintero. Tomo 1, letras A-L; tomo 2, letras LL-Z, y apéndice.

5712. Moraes Filho, Evaristo de. Francisco Sanches e a dúvida metódica na renascença portuguesa (R Br Fil, v. 3, fasc. 1, no. 9, jan.-março 1953, p. 68-96; fasc. 2, no. 10, abril-junho 1953, p. 260-297).

5713. Piñera Llera, Humberto. The teaching of philosophy in Cuba (*in* The teaching of philosophy; international enquiry. Paris, UNESCO, 1953, p. 27-38).
Breve informe sobre la enseñanza de la filosofía en Cuba. Después de una rápida introducción histórica, el autor examina el carácter, programas, métodos, tendencias, etc. que dicha enseñanza tiene en los colegios secundarios y universidades. Hace, también, algunas consideraciones sobre el papel de la filosofía en la vida cultural de Cuba y acerca del valor educacional de la filosofía.

5714.————. El Undécimo Congreso Internacional de Filosofía (B Comis Nac Cub UNESCO, 2:10, oct. 1953, p. 1-4).
Breve informe sobre el Congreso realizado en Bruselas, desde 20 al 28 de agosto de 1953.

5715. Pita, Enrique B. Problemas fundamentales de filosofía. B. A., Peuser, 1952. 345 p.
Texto de introducción a la filosofía. Comprende cuatro partes dedicadas, respectivamente, a considerar los problemas del conocimiento, de las condiciones de la filosofía, de la búsqueda de Dios y de la valoración moral.

5716. Quiles, Ismael. Manuscritos filosóficos de la época colonial en Chile (Cien Fe, 9:34, abril-junio 1953, p. 39-61).
Catálogo crítico de manuscritos existentes en archivos y bibliotecas de Chile. No incluye ningún manuscrito nuevo que no figurara ya en repertorios anteriores, pero rectifica datos y permite situarlos con mayor rigor histórico, como así también, establecer la filiación filosófica de sus autores.

5717. Reale, Miguel. Filosofia do direito. V. 1 [en dos tomos]. São Paulo, Saraiva, 1953. 647 p.
Texto de enseñanza universitaria. Comprende sólo la parte general. El autor, que enseña la materia en la Facultad de Derecho de la Universidad de San Pablo, se propone publicar más adelante dos volúmenes destinados al estudio especial de la epistemologia, la ontología y la culturología. Incluye extensa bibliografía.

5718. Romero, Francisco. Estudios de historia de las ideas. B. A., Losada (Biblioteca filosófica), 1953. 207 p.

Ensayos sobre diversos autores, períodos y problemas vinculados con la historia de la filosofía y de las ideas. Entre ellos, se destacan: "Descartes en la filosofía y en la historia de las ideas," "Sobre la oportunidad histórica del cartesianismo," "Antecedentes e incitaciones para la *Enciclopedia,*" "El tiempo y la cultura" y "Confesiones filosóficas."

5719.————. Qué es la filosofía. B. A., Editorial Columba (Col. Esquemas, 1), 1953. 71 p.
Breve tratado de introducción a la filosofía. Incluye, al final, una bibliografía selecta.

5720. Sánchez Reulet, Aníbal. Crisis de la idea del hombre en la filosofía contemporánea (Torre, 1:4, oct.-dic. 1953, p. 119-130).
Analiza las diversas concepciones del hombre en la filosofía contemporánea. A pesar de los rasgos comunes que pueden destacarse en ellas, se carece de una idea unitaria del hombre. Existe una oposición radical, inconciliable, entre los filósofos que reconocen la posibilidad de una trascendencia absoluta y los que la niegan. Esa antinomia no es sino la expresión teórica de la crisis del hombre moderno.

5721. Schwartzmann, Félix. El sentimiento de lo humano en América. Antropología de la convivencia. T. 2. Santiago, Universidad de Chile, 1953. 219 p.
La primera parte de esta obra fué publicada en 1950 (véase *HLAS, no. 16, 1950,* párrafo 3236). Este segundo volumen completa el análisis de las características que el sentimiento de lo humano ha adquirido, o va adquiriendo, en América. Una de las notas típicas del hombre americano, indicadas por el autor en la primera parte de la obra, es su tendencia al aislamiento. En el presente volumen se estudia la dinámica peculiar que lleva del aislamiento subjetivo a la acción y a la participación social, en el sentido de lo que el autor llama una "antropología de la convivencia." Para su análisis, Schwartzmann utiliza ejemplos tomados de la literatura, el arte y el pensamiento social y político de América Latina. En tres breves apéndices explica y justifica los cambios que se ha visto obligado a introducir en el plan original de la obra.

5722. Silva, Vicente Ferreira da. Sôbre a teoria dos modelos (R Br Fil, v. 3, fasc. 1, no. 9, jan.-março 1953, p. 39-43).
Sobre el papel que corresponde a las figuras ejemplares o heroicas en la historia, y su reflejo en la conciencia colectiva.

5723. Sociedad Cubana de Filosofía. Instituto de Filosofía. Conversaciones filosóficas interamericanas. Habana, 1953. 214 p., illus.
Actas de la reunión que, con el nombre de "Conversaciones Filosóficas Interamericanas," se efectuó en La Habana del 26 de enero al 1. de febrero de 1953, como parte del homenaje rendido a José Martí al cumplirse el centenario de su nacimiento. Además de los discursos, y de un resumen de las discusiones, el volumen

contiene las ponencias presentadas por los distintos participantes. En la primera parte figuran los trabajos que, sobre el tema "La esencia del hombre y de lo humano," presentaron Alejandro Aguilar Machado (Costa Rica), Pedro V. Aja (Cuba), Julio César Arroyave (Colombia), Diego Domínguez Caballero (Panamá), Guillermo Francovich (Bolivia), Eduardo García Maynez (México), Mercedes García Tudurí y Rosaura García Tudurí (Cuba), Manuel Granell (Venezuela), Edgar Henderson (Estados Unidos), Dionisio de Lara (Cuba), N. A. Nikam (India), Humberto Piñera Llera (Cuba), Luis Recaséns Siches (Guatemala) y Raimundo Suárez (España). La segunda parte agrupa los trabajos de Máximo Castro Turbiano (Cuba), Diego Domínguez Caballero (Panamá), Francisco Miró Quesada (Perú), Marcelo Pogolotti (Cuba), Miguel Reale (Brasil), Aníbal Sánchez Reulet (Argentina), Emilio Uranga, Luis Villoro y Leopoldo Zea (México), sobre el tema "¿ Es posible una filosofía americana?" Se incluyen, también, los debates y el acta constitutiva de la Sociedad Interamericana de Filosofía.

5724. Vaz Ferreira, Carlos. Fermentario. Montevideo, Ministerio de Instrucción Pública y Previsión Social, Biblioteca Artigas (Col. de clásicos uruguayos, 5), 1953. 203 p.
Esta obra, una de las más significativas del autor, fué editada por primera vez en Montevideo, en 1938. Hay una edición de B. A., de 1940.

5725. ————. Sobre la propiedad de la tierra. Montevideo, Ministerio de Instrucción Pública y Previsión Social, Biblioteca Artigas (Col. de clásicos uruguayos, 6), 1953. 375 p.
Primera edición, 1918.

5726. ————. Sobre los problemas sociales. Montevideo, Ministerio de Instrucción Pública y Previsión Social, Biblioteca Artigas (Col. de clásicos uruguayos, 5), 1953. 143 p.
Primera edición, 1922.

5727. Viteri, Atanasio. Primer Congreso Latinoamericano de Filosofía General y Filosofía de la Educación (Let Ecuad, 8:83, marzo-abril 1953, p. 10-11).
Informe detallado acerca de la organización y desarrollo del Congreso que, a iniciativa de la Facultad de Filosofía, Letras y Ciencias de la Educación de la Universidad Central del Ecuador, se realizó entre el 10 y el 15 de abril de 1953 en la ciudad de Quito.

5728. Washington, Luiz. Estética fenomenológica (R Br Fil, v. 3, fasc. 4, no. 12, out.-dez. 1953, p. 635-647).
Sobre la aplicación del método fenomenológico al estudio de los problemas estéticos.

5729. Zea, Leopoldo. América como conciencia. México, Editorial Cultura (Cuadernos americanos, 30), 1953. 184 p.

Plantea el problema de la cultura y la filosofía americanas. Independientemente de la originalidad con que los filósofos americanos traten los temas universales y permanentes de la filosofía, existe una problemática propia de la cultura y la filosofía en América como consecuencia de las peculiares circunstancias históricas y sociales del Nuevo Mundo. El pensamiento filosófico americano debe tratar de entender sus propias experiencias y vincular la teoría metafísica con las exigencias prácticas concretas de su existencia. De ese modo podrá contribuir a resolver la crisis por la que atraviesa la cultura occidental. El libro, rico en incitaciones, ofrece perspectivas originales para entender la posición y el futuro de la cultura americana. De gran interés es el capítulo titulado "Las dos Américas," en el cual el autor juzga y enfrenta la cultura y la filosofía anglosajonas con las de Hispanoamérica. La obra resume las ideas y opiniones expresadas anteriormente por el autor en innumerables ensayos y trabajos menores.

5730. ————. La conciencia del hombre en la filosofía. Introducción a la filosofía. México, Imp. Universitaria (Cultura mexicana, 4), 1953. 384 p.
Reúne las lecciones dictadas por el autor en El Colegio de México durante el primer semestre de 1944. Es un curso de introducción a la filosofía encarado históricamente. Expone el desarrollo de las ideas filosóficas desde Grecia hasta el siglo XVII.

ESTUDIOS CRÍTICOS
FILOSOFÍA ANTIGUA Y MEDIEVAL

5731. Almeida, Enrique P. Los comienzos del idealismo en los filósofos griegos (Fil, Quito, 1:1, enero-junio 1953, p. 33-72).

5732. Álvarez González, Francisco. La evolución del concepto de substancia en la filosofía griega (Fil, Quito, 1:1, enero-junio 1953, p. 6-32).

5733. Diez Aguado, Antonio. Teoría del conocimiento de Santo Tomás de Aquino (A U Sto Domingo, 18:67-68, julio-dic. 1953, p. 347-365).

5734. Frankl, Víctor. El agustinismo franciscano del siglo XIII como raíz de la física matemática moderna (Bolívar, Bogotá, 16, enero-feb. 1953, p. 25-68).
Se refiere a los aportes de Roger Bacon, y de algunos de sus discípulos, y a los de los occamistas del siglo XIV.

5735. ————. La posición de Santo Tomás en la evolución de la filosofía matemática (Bolívar, Bogotá, 25, nov.-dic. 1953, p. 729-750).

5736. Muñoz Sanz, Juan Pablo. Los sofistas presocráticos y la teoría del conocimiento (Fil, Quito, 1:1, enero-junio 1953, p. 101-122).

5737. **Van Acker, Leonardo.** O espírito da filosofía medieval (R Br Fil, v. 3, fasc. 3, no. 11, julho-set. 1953, p. 367-383).
Resume las posiciones principales de la filosofía medieval, representadas por el ajustinismo, el tomismo y el averroísmo latino, respecto de las relaciones entre la fe y la razón. Cree que la filosofía de la Edad Media puede constituir una fuente eficaz de inspiración para el hombre contemporáneo.

FILOSOFÍA CONTEMPORÁNEA

5738. **Armstrong, A. MacC.** Contemporary Latin-American philosophy (Philos Q, 3:11, Apr. 1953, p. 167-174).
Comentario a las Actas del Primer Congreso Nacional de Filosofía celebrado en Mendoza (Argentina) en 1949 (véase *HLAS, no. 16, 1950,* párrafo 3222). La filosofía latinoamericana, a diferencia de la europea, le parece tener un mayor contacto con los problemas de la calle y las preocupaciones del momento: es "an outdoor philosophy." Aunque América Latina no ha producido, todavía, filósofos excepcionales ha dado, al menos, algunos profesores notables, como en el caso del argentino Luis Juan Guerrero. Este breve estudio, a pesar de sus naturales limitaciones, constituye una interesante contribución a la escasa bibliografía que sobre el tema existe en inglés.

5739. **Babini, José.** La filosofía científica de los "científicos" (Cursos Conf, año 12, 43:256-258, julio-sept. 1953, p. 165-180).
Expone las ideas epistemológicas del círculo de Viena, y de Russell, Jeans y Eddington.

5740. **Fatone, Vicente.** La existencia humana y sus filósofos. B. A., Raigal, 1953. 193 p.
Dedica sendos capítulos a exponer las ideas fundamentales de Heidegger, Jaspers, Barth, Chestov, Berdiaeff, Zubiri, Marcel, Lavelle, Sartre y Abbagnano. La obra se cierra con un epílogo en que se resumen los temas capitales de la filosofía existencialista. Bien escrito, y con un tono muy personal, este libro contiene la mejor presentación de conjunto que se haya hecho hasta ahora en América Latina del existencialismo contemporáneo.

5741. **Ferrater Mora, José.** Dos obras maestras de historia de la lógica (Notas Estud Fil, 4:14, abril-junio 1953, p. 145-158).
Sobre dos obras recientes de los filósofos polacos J. Lukasiewicz y I. M. Bochenski.

5742. **Mañach, Jorge.** El pensamiento de Dewey y su sentido americano. Habana, Comisión Nacional Cubana de la UNESCO (Cuadernos de divulgación cultural, 9), 1953. 31 p.
Breve exposición de las ideas de Dewey, especialmente las que se relacionan con su teoría del conocimiento, su psicología, su pedagogía y su concepción política democrática. El autor cree que la filosofía de Dewey es la mejor expresión de la cultura y de las modalidades propias del pueblo norteamericano, pero que es representativa, también, de lo americano en general.

5743. **Olguín, Manuel.** El fenomenalismo de Alfred Ayer (Fil Let, México, 25:49-50, enero-junio 1953, p. 23-25).

5744. **Romano Muñoz, José.** Hacia una filosofía existencial. Al margen de la nada, de la muerte y de la náusea metafísica. México, Imp. Universitaria (Cultura mexicana, 3), 1953. 172 p.
Obra de carácter polémico en la que el autor, colocándose en una posición que él mismo califica de existencialista, combate los aspectos negativos de la filosofía de Heidegger y Sartre. Considera que es un deber denunciar las consecuencias nihilistas a que conduce la metafísica de Heidegger y muy especialmente la de Sartre. La crítica del autor se concentra, sobre todo, en el análisis de los conceptos de la nada y de la libertad tal como los entiende el existencialismo francés. En oposición al existencialismo nihilista propugna una concepción de la existencia humana en que subsistan, con sentido nuevo, los valores tradicionales.

5745. **Soler Grimma, Francisco.** El origen de la obra de arte y la verdad en Heidegger. Bogotá, Universidad Nacional de Colombia, Facultad de Filosofía y Letras, 1953. 133 p.
Contiene una exposición del autor y la traducción de "Der Ursprung der Kunstwerkes," primera parte de la obra de Heidegger titulada *Holzwege* (Frankfurt, 1950). Al final, incluye un glosario de términos heideggerianos.

5746. **Uzcátegui, Emilio.** Jorge Santayana, un filósofo incomprendido (Fil, Quito, 1:1, enero-junio 1953, p. 123-127).

5747. **Wagner de Reyna, Alberto.** Presente y futuro de la filosofía en Hispanoamérica (Bolívar, Bogotá, 21, julio 1953, p. 5-23).
Analiza las características y posibilidades de la filosofía hispanoamericana. Cree que el futuro del pensamiento filosófico hispanoamericano ha de consistir en prolongar, conservándola y acrecentándola, la tradición de la filosofía occidental.

FILOSOFÍA LATINOAMERICANA

5748. **Alberini, Coriolano.** Génesis y evolución del pensamiento filosófico argentino (Cuad Fil, año 5-6, fasc. 7, no. 10-12, marzo 1952-oct. 1953, p. 7-18).
Breves notas sobre el desarrollo de la filosofía en la Argentina, destinadas a servir de prólogo al libro de Luis Farré, *Cincuenta años de filosofía en Argentina.*

5749. Apéndice: El tomismo en Córdoba (Arqué, 2:1-3, 1953, p. 251-294).

Reseña las contribuciones de los neotomistas cordobeses, o formados en la Universidad de Córdoba, desde fines del siglo XVIII hasta el momento actual.

5750. Brüning, Walther. La antropología filosófica actual en Iberoamérica (R U Nac Córdoba, 40:3-5, julio-dic. 1953, p. 935-965).

Dedica atención preferente a los autores neotomistas, pero considera, también, otras direcciones filosóficas contemporáneas recientes en Hispanoamérica y en el Brasil. Incluye, al final, una breve bibliografía.

5751. Cavalcanti Filho, Teófilo. A filosofia jurídica de Farias Brito (R Br Fil, v. 3, fasc. 2, no. 10, abril-junho 1953, p. 225-241).

5752. Elboux, Luiz Gonzaga da Silveira d'. O Padre Leonel Franca, S. J. Rio, Livraria Agir, 1953. 537 p.

Estudio sobre el religioso y filósofo brasileño fallecido en 1948.

5753. Elías de Tejada, Francisco. Las doctrinas políticas de Raimundo de Farias Brito. Sevilla, Escuela de Estudios Hispano-Americanos de Sevilla (Publ., 79; Seminario de historia del pensamiento; Col. Mar adentro, 2), 1953. 195 p.

5754. Farré, Luis. Introducción a "Cincuenta años de filosofía en Argentina" (Cuad Fil, año 5-6, fasc. 7, no. 10-12, marzo 1952-oct. 1953, p. 19-26).

Introducción a una obra de próxima aparición.

5755. Gaos, José. En torno a la filosofía mexicana. México, Porrúa y Obregón (México y lo mexicano, 11), 1953. 83 p.

Contra la opinión de que no puede haber historia de la filosofía en México, porque no existen filósofos originales de importancia, señala el autor que la historia de la filosofía se da como un elemento integrante de la historia general de las ideas. Después de reseñar los esfuerzos que se han hecho en México, para elaborar esa historia de las ideas, destaca el carácter imperativo de la tarea, como un modo de contribuir, en la parte que a ella le toca, al desarrollo de la filosofía mexicana.

5756. Gutiérrez Girardot, Rafael. Sobre la filosofía en Hispanoamérica (Correo literario, Madrid, 4:71, mayo 1, 1953, p. 10).

Rápido panorama de las tendencias dominantes en la filosofía hispanoamericana contemporánea.

5757. Harris, Marjorie S. Romero on Cartesian reason (J Philos, 50:8, Apr. 9, 1953, p. 242-249).

Ponencia presentada a la reunión anual de la Southern Society for Philosophy and Psychology realizada en 1951. Estudia la tesis de Romero según la cual la razón cartesiana tiene un carácter inmanente.

5758. Miró Quesada, Francisco. Outline of my philosophic position (S Philos, 2:4, Sept. 1953, p. 1-5).

En este breve trabajo, el joven profesor de la Universidad de San Marcos hace una sucinta presentación de los problemas que en el orden de la lógica, de la epistemología, de la antropología y de la metafísica le han preocupado más intensamente en los últimos tiempos y expone, a la vez, la posición personal que ha asumido frente a ellos en procura de su solución. Con relación al problema antropológico y metafísico, define su actitud como un "ateísmo nostálgico" que afirma el supremo valor ético de la solidaridad humana.

5759. Molina, Enrique. La filosofía en Chile en la primera mitad del siglo XX. Notas y recuerdos. 2. ed. aumentada. Santiago, Nascimento, 1953. 164 p.

La primera edición se publicó, en 1951, por la misma editorial. La presente edición no agrega nada substancial a la anterior.

5760. Perdomo García, José. La filosofía hispanoamericana y su ritmo asincrónico (Cuad Hispanoam, 16:45, sept. 1953, p. 331-345).

Según el autor, tanto en Hispanoamérica como en España, se ha filosofado "a destiempo," en relación con el movimiento general de ideas de Europa. La tesis es particularmente válida respecto de los siglos XVIII y XIX. En cambio, a medida que avanza el siglo XX la sincronía es cada vez más notable.

5761. ———. En torno a la filosofía hispanoamericana (Estud Am, 6:23-24, agosto-sept. 1953, p. 141-163).

Discute la posibilidad de una filosofía que pueda llamarse propiamente hispanoamericana. El problema es común a toda la filosofía de lengua española y es en estos términos que él debe plantearse.

5762. Romero, Francisco. Notice on my philosophy (S Philos, 2:3, May 1953, p. 1-5).

Expone las ideas fundamentales contenidas en su obra *Teoría del hombre* (véase *HLAS, no. 18, 1952,* párrafo 3129) y en algunos de sus trabajos menores, como "Programa de una filosofía." Importante como presentación resumida de su concepción filosófica.

5763. Rubio y Rubio, Alfonso. La filosofía mexicana actual. Los antecedentes: El positivismo y la generación del centenario (R Indias, Madrid, 13:52-53, abril-sept. 1953, p. 307-324).

Después de referirse al influjo del positivismo, analiza la posición asumida por la llamada generación del Ateneo.

5764. Sciacca, Michele Federico. Observaciones sobre la filosofía en América

Latina (R Fil, Eva Perón, 6, 1953, p. 47-54).
Reproduce un fragmento del segundo volumen de la obra *La filosofía, oggi*, del mismo autor.

5765. Zea, Leopoldo. El positivismo en México. México, Ediciones Studium (Col. Studium, 3), 1953. 254 p.
Reproduce, sin modificaciones, el texto de la primera edición (México, 1943).

HISTORIA DE LAS IDEAS

5766. Alarco, Luis Felipe. Pensadores peruanos. Lima, Tip. Santa Rosa, 1952. 119 p.
Estudia las figuras de Hipólito Unánue, Bartolomé Herrera, Manuel González Prada, José de la Riva Agüero, José Carlos Mariátegui y César Vallejo.

5767. Batllori, Miguel. El abate Viscardo. Historia y mito de la intervención de los jesuítas en la independencia de América. Caracas, Instituto Panamericano de Geografía e Historia, Comisión de Historia, Comité de Orígenes de la Emancipación (Publ., 10), 1953. 334 p.
La primera parte comprende un estudio biográfico de Juan Pablo Viscardo, el autor de la famosa *Carta a los españoles americanos*. En capítulo especial, se analiza las circunstancias históricas en que fue escrito este importante documento, como asimismo el contenido doctrinario y el influjo que tuvo en América y en Europa. El epílogo está dedicado a discutir el papel de los jesuítas en la emancipación de las colonias españolas de América. En el volumen se transcriben, además, importantes documentos relacionados con la vida de Viscardo. Al final, se incluye la reproducción facsímil de la primera edición de la *Carta*.

5768. Bustamante, Pedro. Páginas desconocidas: la doctrina de Bentham. Su influencia en el Uruguay (R Nac, año 16, 60:179, nov. 1953, p. 303-315).
Estudio escrito en 1876, que había permanecido inédito. Señala la influencia de la filosofía de Bentham en los primeros años de la República, particularmente a través de la acción ejercida por Lucas José Obes durante la presidencia de Rivera.

5769. Caturelli, Alberto. El pensamiento de Mamerto Esquiú (Arqué, 2:1-3, 1953, p. 53-250).
Largo y documentado estudio sobre las ideas religiosas, sociales y políticas del notable pensador y orador sagrado argentino. Extensa bibliografía.

5770. Costa, J. Cruz. O positivismo na república. Notas para a história das idéias no Brasil (Kriterion, 6:25-26, julho-dez. 1953, p. 304-314).
Estudia, especialmente, la actitud asumida por Teixeira Mendes, con relación al militarismo,

en una serie de artículos publicados en el *Jornal do commercio*, en 1908.

5771. Hernández Luna, Juan. El iniciador de la historia de las ideas en México (Fil Let, México, 25:51-52, julio-dic. 1953, p. 65-80).
Estudia la obra de Eguiara y Eguren, el gran historiador y bibliógrafo mexicano del siglo XVIII.

5772. Labrousse, Roger. Echeverría y la filosofía política de la Ilustración (Sur, 219-220, enero-feb. 1953, p. 79-92).
Junto a las influencias de Mazzini, Leroux y Saint-Simon, se puede rastrear, en la obra de Echeverría, el influjo de autores del siglo XVIII, especialmente de Rousseau y Condorcet. Echeverría tomó de sus contemporáneos no tanto las ideas novedosas y originales, como aquellas otras que coincidían con la tradición dieciochesca.

5773. Machado, Lourival Gomes. O tratado de direito natural de Tomás Antônio Gonzaga. Rio, Ministério da Educação e Saúde, Serviço de Documentação, 1953. 144 p.
Estudio sobre el conocido tratado del escritor y poeta lusobrasileño, una de las figuras características de la Ilustración portuguesa.

5774. Mejía Valera, Manuel. El pensamiento filosófico de Manuel González Prada (Cuad Am, año 12, 71:5, sept.-oct. 1953, p. 122-135).

5775. Mijares, Augusto. Rousseau y el Libertador (R Nac Cult, 14:100, sept.-oct. 1953, p. 103-111).
Documenta la influencia de Rousseau sobre Bolívar y señala ciertas aproximaciones psicológicas entre los dos.

5776. Peña, Roberto I. El pensamiento político del Deán Funes. Córdoba, Argentina, Ministerio de Educación, Universidad Nacional de Córdoba, Facultad de Filosofía y Humanidades, Instituto de Estudios Americanistas (Serie histórica, 24), 1953. 258 p.
Estudio documentado de la formación intelectual de Gregorio Funes, del desarrollo de su pensamiento político y de la acción que ejerció en el proceso de la independencia y en el primer período de la organización nacional argentina. Influído por las ideas de la Ilustración francesa, Funes supo mantener una actitud realista y conciliadora en materia política. El volumen reproduce, en un apéndice, documentos vinculados con la vida de Funes.

5777. Romero Flores, Jesús. Don Melchor Ocampo; el filósofo de la Reforma. Morelia, México, Ediciones de la Universidad Michoacana de San Nicolás de Hidalgo, 1953. 292 p.

5778. **Zea, Leopoldo.** El Occidente y la conciencia de México. México, Porrúa y Obregón (México y lo mexicano, 14), 1953. 87 p.
Inspirándose en las ideas de Toynbee acerca de la posición de la civilización occidental en relación con las otras culturas del mundo, Zea nos da una interpretación filosófico-sociológica de la evolución histórica de México desde la Conquista hasta el momento actual en que se manifiestan los efectos integradores de la Revolución de 1910.

GNOSEOLOGíA Y METAFíSICA

5779. **Cannabrava, Euryalo.** On truth, knowledge and valuation (Phil Phen Re, 13:4, June 1953, p. 525-530).
Defiende la autonomía del valor, especialmente en la esfera de la estética, frente a las doctrinas epistemológicas que niegan importancia a la actividad ética y estética y que desconocen los rasgos peculiares que el conocimiento adquiere cuando se aplica a los productos del arte o a la conducta moral.

5780. **Lima, Carlos Cirne.** O indeterminismo na mecânica quântica (R Br Fil, v. 3, fasc. 3, no. 11, julho-set. 1953, p. 400-421).
Expone el principio de indeterminación de Heisenberg y las interpretaciones de von Neumann y Henry-Hermann. El principio de indeterminación, bien interpretado, no afecta el valor del principio de causalidad física.

5781. **Fragueiro Lascano, José M.** Prioridad de la aprehensión del ente (Arqué, 2:1-3, 1953, p. 313-315).
Afirma la primacía del problema ontológico.

5782. **Frondizi, Risieri.** Empiricism and humanism (S Philos, 2:5, Nov. 1953, p. 1-10).
El objeto de la filosofía es el estudio de la realidad en su conjunto. Al conjunto de la realidad llama el autor "experiencia humana." Los tres componentes de la realidad son: el *yo*, lo que el *yo* hace, y el objeto al cual se aplica su actividad. De los tres aspectos que constituyen la "experiencia humana," el autor analiza con algún detalle en este trabajo sólo el primero, resumiendo las ideas ya expuestas en su obra *The nature of the self* (véase párrafo 5783).

5783. ———. The nature of the self. A functional interpretation. New Haven, Conn., Yale University Press, 1953. 210 p.
Versión inglesa de la obra original publicada en 1952 en B. A. y que fué comentada en *HLAS, no. 16, 1950,* párrafo 3302 y *no. 18, 1952,* párrafo 3122.

5784. **García Bacca, Juan David.** Sobre la analogía del ser (Fil Let, Quito, 6: 18, abril-junio 1953, p. 7-26).
Fragmento de una obra en preparación que se titulará *Metafísica.*

5785. **Haas, João Nepomuceno.** Filosofia do organismo (R Br Fil, v. 3, fasc. 3, no. 11, julho-set. 1953, p. 437-455; fasc. 4, no. 12, out.-dez. 1953, p. 648-662).
Ensayo de filosofía biológica. Después de referirse a algunas concepciones contemporáneas de la vida, expone una teoría de los organismos vivos directamente inspirada en la doctrina aristotélico-tomista de la unidad substancial.

5786. **Larroyo, Francisco.** El valor lógico de los métodos estadísticos (Fil Let, México, 25:49-50, enero-junio 1953, p. 63-71).

5787. **Lins, Mario.** A lógica aristotélica como um caso limite de uma lógica mais geral (R Br Fil, v. 3, fasc. 2, no. 10, abril-junho 1953, p. 221-224).

5788. **Nicol, Eduardo.** La vocación humana. México, El Colegio de México, 1953. 352 p.
Colección de ensayos, artículos y conferencias, escritos o pronunciadas en diferentes ocasiones. El libro tiene, sin embargo, cierta unidad temática. En la primera parte, se destaca el ensayo que da título a la obra y en el cual el autor expone una concepción personal, aunque muy teñida de existencialismo, de la vida humana y del papel que la filosofía juega en ella. De gran interés es, también, el estudio "La marcha hacia lo concreto," en que discute la crisis actual de la razón o, mejor dicho, del racionalismo, y la posibilidad de una experiencia que, rebasando el marco del conocimiento empírico, nos permita aprehender y entender "la variedad y riqueza de cualidades del mundo concreto en que el hombre vive su vida." El volumen contiene, además de los ensayos de carácter estrictamente filosófico, varios trabajos de psicología y de teoría política. Entre estos últimos, los más significativos son, sin duda, los dos que dedica a estudiar las ideas jurídico-políticas de Francisco Suárez, comparándolas y enfrentándolas con las de Locke y Marx.

5789. **Reale, Miguel.** Para um criticismo ontognoseológico (R Br Fil, v. 3, fasc. 1, no. 9, jan.-março 1953, p. 32-38).
Discute la posibilidad de desarrollar un nuevo tipo de criticismo que tenga en cuenta, a un mismo tiempo, los factores ontológicos y gnoseológicos del conocimiento.

5790. **Roig, Arturo Andrés.** Fundamento y "aformé" de la metafísica (Philosophia, 10:18, enero-dic. 1953, p. 5-31).
Discute el problema del fundamento y de los supuestos del conocimiento metafísico, con especial referencia a textos de Platón, Aristóteles, San Agustín, Descartes, Malebranche, Leibniz y Kant.

5791. **Wagner de Reyna, Alberto.** El desengaño: experiencia metafísica (Cien Fe, 9:34, abril-junio 1953, p. 23-27).
Análisis del desengaño, como momento existencial en la búsqueda de la verdad. "El desengaño es el impacto por el cual la verdad afecta a la existencia."

5792. Xirau, Ramón. Sentido de la presencia. Ensayos. México, Tezontle, 1953. 134 p.

Colección de ensayos breves en los que el autor expresa de un modo personal y libre, y en prosa clara y concisa, sus puntos de vista sobre el sentido de la vida humana, de su aparente fugacidad y de su esencial permanencia. En última instancia, no hay cambio sin presencia: "Cambiando, el hombre, reposa, porque el sujeto, la ley misma del cambio, es estancia, es perennidad."

ÉTICA Y FILOSOFÍA JURÍDICA Y POLÍTICA

5793. Arocha Morton, Carlos A. Crítica al jusnaturalismo tomista. México, 1953. 199 p.

Tesis universitaria. Critica la concepción tomista del derecho natural desde su punto de vista marxista.

5794. Betancur, Cayetano. Introducción a la ciencia del derecho. Bogotá, Ministerio de Educación Nacional (Biblioteca de autores colombianos, 39; Crítica y ensayo), 1953. 366 p.

5795. Bruera, José Juan. Filosofía de la paz. B. A., Losada (Biblioteca filosófica), 1953. 213 p.

En una serie de ensayos entrelazados, el autor discute el problema de la paz en su relación con la dialéctica, la oposición, la acción, el mito, el lenguaje, el derecho, la religión y el valor. En el capítulo final resume sus ideas acerca de la paz, tanto en el orden colectivo como en el individual. Frente a los que proclaman la paz en la guerra, en la oposición, o en la muerte, afirma la paz en la satisfacción del deber propuesto, en el cumplimiento de la norma.

5796. Cabrera Macia, Manuel. Bases para una fundamentación de la sociología. Prólogo de José Gaos. México, Imp. Universitaria (Col. de cultura mexicana), 1953. 96 p.

La investigación del fundamento de la sociología debe comenzar por el problema del conocimiento del yo ajeno. El autor rechaza las teorías corrientes acerca del conocimiento del prójimo y propone una nueva, según la cual el conocimiento de los otros yos es un dato primario: existe una solidaridad ontológica entre el yo y el tú. Este principio se puede expresar, según el autor, en la fórmula: "Pienso, luego soy en sociedad."

5797. Filosofía y sociedad. Ciclo de conferencias a cargo de la Sociedad Cubana de Filosofía (Instituto de Filosofía). Habana, Comisión Nacional de la UNESCO, 1953. 248 p.

Contiene los textos de las conferencias pronunciadas por Mercedes García Tudurí, sobre "Lo humano como fundamento y objeto de la democracia" y sobre "Medios y fines de la estructura democrática"; de Humberto Piñera Llera, sobre "El papel de la filosofía en la enseñanza del presente" y "La filosofía y la cultura"; de Rosaura García Tudurí, sobre "Los valores y progresos humanos" y "Actualidad de la educación en la cultura occidental"; de Dionisio de Lara Mínguez, sobre "John Locke, filósofo de la democracia" y "Mazzini, profeta de la democracia"; de Máximo Castro Turbiano, sobre "La idea kantiana de la paz perpetua y los derechos del hombre" y "El *debe ser* en la convivencia humana"; y dos conferencias de Pedro V. Aja Jorge sobre "El cristianismo: significado de su valor en el presente." Como lo declara en el prólogo, el presidente de la Sociedad Cubana de Filosofía, profesor Humberto Piñera Llera, el propósito de este ciclo de conferencias, que contó con los auspicios de la Comisión Nacional Cubana de la UNESCO, fué el de ofrecer "un aporte de sus mejores esfuerzos en el orden teórico a las nobles y oportunas finalidades prácticas que justifican la existencia de la UNESCO."

5798. García Maynez, Eduardo. Los principios de la ontología formal del derecho y su expresión simbólica. México, Imp. Universitaria (Cultura mexicana, 1), 1953. 173 p.

Completa las investigaciones que en el campo de la lógica jurídica ha venido efectuando el autor desde hace años y cuyos principios formuló sistemáticamente por primera vez en su obra *Introducción a la lógica jurídica*, publicada en 1951 (véase *HLAS, no. 17, 1951*, párrafo 2957). En este libro, intenta dar formulación simbólica a los axiomas jurídicos, cuyo conjunto constituye, para García Maynez, una verdadera "ontología formal" del derecho. El volumen incluye, además, en apéndice, otros estudios y trabajos de fecha anterior.

5799. Labrousse, Roger. Introducción a la filosofía política. B. A., Editorial Sudamericana (Biblioteca de filosofía), 1953. 332 p.

Expone las ideas políticas de Platón, Aristóteles, Cicerón, San Agustín, Santo Tomás, Ockham, Hobbes, Locke, Rousseau, Fichte, Marx y Sorel. En el último capítulo, estudia las relaciones entre el "totalitarismo" y el "pluralismo" desde una posición próxima a la del personalismo francés. Incluye bibliografía.

5800. Quintanilla, Luis. Bergsonismo y política. México, Fondo de Cultura Económica, 1953. 205 p.

En los dos primeros capítulos se expone la filosofía de Bergson destacando aquellas ideas que pueden servir para establecer las consecuencias prácticas del bergsonismo. La filosofía de Bergson, interpretada por el autor como una forma extrema de anti-intelectualismo, lleva igualmente, en el orden práctico y político, a actitudes de tipo irracionalista. No es extraño, por lo tanto, que Sorel, el autor de la *Apologie sur la violence*, se haya inspirado fuertemente en la filosofía bergsoniana. Esta filosofía constituye la base teórica del anarcosindicalismo revolucionario de Sorel y, en una dirección diferente, ha influído en ciertos aspectos del "nacionalismo integral" francés. Es conocida, además, la influencia que Sorel ejerció sobre el fascismo italiano y la de éste sobre el nazismo alemán. El irracionalismo bergsoniano, llevado a sus últimas consecuencias prácticas, conduce a posiciones políticas antidemocráticas y totalitarias, haya sido ésa o no la intención original del filósofo. El núcleo esencial de esta obra constituyó el tema de la tesis doctoral presentada por el autor a la Universidad Johns Hopkins.

5801. Russo Delgado, José. Sentido ontológico de la paz. Guatemala, Imp. Universitaria, 1953. 24 p.

Conferencia dictada en la Facultad de Humanidades de la Universidad de San Carlos de Guatemala. Plantea el problema moral de la guerra y la posibilidad de una paz efectiva fundada en la verdad, la buena voluntad y el amor universal.

TRADUCCIONES

5802. Alembert, Jean-Baptiste Le Rond d'. Discurso preliminar de la enciclopedia. Trad. de Consuelo Bergés. B. A., Aguilar, 1953. 190 p.

5803. Anselmus Cantuarienses, Sanctus. Proslogion. En favor del insensato. Respuesta a Gaunilo. Trad. de Manuel Fuentes Benot. B. A., Aguilar, 1953. 101 p.

5804. Augustine, Saint. La inmortalidad del alma. Texto y traducción de José Bezie. Nota preliminar de Octavio Nicolás Derisi. Ciudad Eva Perón, Argentina, Universidad Nacional, Instituto de Filosofía, 1953. 87 p.

5805. Berkeley, George. Tres diálogos entre Hilas y Filonus. Trad. de A. P. Masegora. B. A., Aguilar, 1953. 162 p.

5806. Bréhier, Emile. La filosofía de Plotino. Trad. de Lucía Piosseck Prebisch. B. A., Editorial Sudamericana, 1953. 254 p.

5807. Cassirer, Ernst. El problema del conocimiento en la filosofía y en la ciencia modernas. I. El renacer del problema del conocimiento. El descubrimiento del concepto de la naturaleza. Los fundamentos del idealismo. Trad. de Wenceslao Roces. México, Fondo de Cultura Económica, 1953. 619 p.

5808. Cohen, Morris R. Introducción a la lógica. Trad. de E. de Gortari. México, Fondo de Cultura Económica, 1952. 254 p.

5809. Comte, Auguste. Discurso sobre el espíritu positivo. Trad. de Consuelo Bergés. B. A., Aguilar, 1953. 170 p.

5810. Croce, Benedetto. Ética y política, seguidas de la contribución a la crítica de mí mismo. Trad. de la 3. edición italiana por Enrique Pezzoni. B. A., Imán (Panorama de la filosofía y de la cultura), 1952. 351 p.

5811. ———. Teoría e historia de la historiografía. Trad. de Eduardo J. Prieto. B. A., Imán, 1953. 300 p.

5812. Dilthey, Wilhelm. Vida y poesía. Prólogo y notas de Eugenio Ímaz. Trad. de Wenceslao Roces. 2. ed. México, Fondo de Cultura Económica, 1953. 520 p.

5813. Erasmus, Desiderius. Elogio da loucura. Trad. de Aldo Della Nina. São Paulo, Ed. do Brasil, 1953. 160 p.

5814. Faggin, Giuseppe. Meister Eckhart. Trad. de Elena Sella. B. A., Editorial Sudamericana, 1953. 402 p.

5815. Heidegger, Martin. Comentarios a la poesía de Hölderlin. Trad. de Rafael Gutiérrez Girardot (Bolívar, Bogotá, 18, abril 1953, p. 577-595).

5816. ———. La doctrina de Platón acerca de la verdad. Trad. de Norberto V. Silvetti (Cuad Fil, año 5-6, fasc. 7, no. 10-12, marzo 1952-oct. 1953, p. 35-57).

5817. Jaeger, Werner. La teología de los primeros filósofos griegos. Trad. de José Gaos. México, Fondo de Cultura Económica, 1952. 262 p.

5818. Jaspers, Karl. La filosofía desde el punto de vista de la existencia. Trad. de José Gaos. México, Fondo de Cultura Económica, 1953. 151 p.

5819. ———. La razón y sus enemigos en nuestro tiempo. Trad. de Lucía Piosseck Prebisch. B. A., Editorial Sudamericana, 1953. 100 p.

5820. Jolivet, Régis. Curso de filosofia. Trad. de Eduardo Prado de Mendonça. Rio, Agir, 1953. 474 p.

5821. ———. Curso de filosofía. Trad. de Leandro de Sesma. B. A., Desclée de Brouwer, 1953. 426 p.

5822. Jouffroy, Théodore. Sobre la organización de las ciencias filosóficas. Trad.

de Miguel Ángel Virasoro. B. A., Losada, 1953. 261 p.

5823. **Kuhn, Helmut.** Encuentro con la nada. Trad. de Raúl Alberto Piérola. B. A., Editorial Sudamericana, 1953. 255 p.

5824. **Marcel, Gabriel.** El misterio del ser. Trad. de María Eugenia Valentié. B. A., Editorial Sudamericana, 1953. 358 p.

5825. **Mirandola, Pico della.** De la dignidad del hombre. Traducción de Elizabeth Goguel de Labrousse (Notas Estud Fil, 4:16, oct.-dic. 1953, p. 353-370).

5826. **Plato.** Fedro, o de la belleza. Trad. de María Araujo. B. A., Aguilar, 1953. 140 p.

5827. **Reichenbach, Hans.** La filosofía científica. Trad. de Horacio Flores Sán-

chez. México, Fondo de Cultura Económica, 1953. 299 p.

5828. **Santayana, George.** Dominaciones y potestades. Trad. del inglés por J. A. Fontanilla. Madrid, Aguilar, 1953. 550 p.

5829. **Schopenhauer, Arthur.** Aforismos para a sabedoria na vida. Trad. de Genésio de Almeida Moura. São Paulo, Melhoramentos, 1953. 232 p.

5830. **Schweitzer, Albert.** El pensamiento de la India. Trad. de Antonio Ramos-Oliveira. México, Fondo de Cultura Económica, 1952. 231 p.

5831. **Seneca, Lucius Annaeus.** Cartas morales. T. 2. Trad. de M. Gallegos Rocafull. Méxxico, Universidad Nacional Autónoma de México, 1953. 553 p.

5832. **Uexküll, Thure von.** Vida, ciencia y realidad: esbozo de una filosofía de la naturaleza. Trad. de Ricardo Krebs. Santiago, 1953. 384 p.

Sociology

T. LYNN SMITH

THE years 1953-1955 were ones of general and rapid progress in the sociological study of Latin American peoples and institutions. A Latin American sociological association was organized at a meeting in B. A., with annual meetings planned for the future. In Mexico the fourth, fifth, and sixth annual meetings of the Asociación Mexicana de Sociología met under the presidency of Dr. Lucio Mendieta y Núñez. The last of these, devoted exclusively to the sociology of rural life, was held November-December 1955, with more than 80 scholars participating, including representatives from Colombia, Cuba, Ecuador, France, Uruguay, and the U. S. Publication annually of the proceedings of these meetings is adding a highly significant series to Mexican sociological literature.

Noteworthy books are appearing in increasing numbers, with special consideration being due Solari's treatise of rural sociology published in Uruguay (item 6021), and Rios' brilliant study of group education in Brazil (item 6074). In the U. S. many contributions of major proportions are appearing, particularly the following: *Turrialba*, by Charles P. Loomis and associates; *Man and land in Peru*, by Thomas R. Ford; and *Peasant Society in the Colombian Andes*, by Orlando Fals-Borda. The last of these is especially significant. It is probably the first book-length study of a single community in Latin America by one who has combined intimate knowledge and insight of the native, thorough training in the North American sociological frame of reference and methodology, and a lengthy period of observation and interviewing in the community itself. It should be particularly helpful in its contribution to understanding of the more elusive aspects of Latin American society, especially the religious and domestic institutions and social processes in general.

The increasing numbers of those receiving Ph.D. degrees in sociology who are writing their dissertations on Latin American subjects also bodes well for the future of studies of Latin American society. Among those completing such dissertations between 1953 and 1955 are the following: at Columbia University, Jerry W. Combs, Rivera G. Jiménez, and Clarence O. Senior; at the University of Florida, Orlando Fals-Borda, John Van Dyke Saunders, and Sam Schulman; and at Michigan State University, Manuel Alers-Montalvo.

GENERAL

6000. **American Academy of Political and Social Science.** Puerto Rico, a study in democratic development (A Am Ac Pol Soc Sci, 285, Jan. 1953, 246 p.).
Among the many excellent articles in this symposium, the following should be of basic interest to the sociologist: "Culture patterns of Puerto Rico," by Julian H. Steward; "The transformation of the Spanish heritage," by Francisco Ayala; "Puerto Rico, a crowded island," by Kingsley Davis; "Social structure as affecting fertility in Puerto Rico," by Arnold S. Feldman and Paul K. Hatt; "Migration and Puerto Rico's population problem," by Clarence Senior; and "The prospects of birth control in Puerto Rico," by J. Mayone Stycos and Reuben Hill.

6001. **Arze, José Antonio.** Hacia la crea-

ción de un Instituto Sociográfico de América Latina (ISAL). Proyecto de estatuto
. . . . Prólogo de Alfredo Poviña . . . .
La Paz, Fénix, 1952, i.e. 1953. 151 p.
An ambitious proposal for the establishment of a Latin American Sociographic Institute. In addition to the draft of the proposed constitution, some documentary supplements present valuable directories of social science organizations and useful lists of Latin American social science periodicals and other important bibliographical information.

6002. Caldera Rodríguez, Rafael. Idea de una sociología venezolana; discurso . . . Contestación del académico doctor Edgard Sanabria. Caracas, El Cojo, 1953. 101 p.
In this discourse, delivered during the ceremonies in which the author was inducted into the Academia de Ciencias Políticas y Sociales, an outline for the development of a sociology of Venezuela is presented. Much emphasis is also placed upon the developments of social and sociological thinking and writing in Venezuela.

6003. Caldeira, Clovis. Fazendas de cacau na Bahia. Rio, Ministério da Agricultura, Serviço de Informação Agrícola (Documentário da vida rural, 7), 1954. 58 p. & illus.
A comprehensive description of life and labor in the cacao-producing area near Ilheus in Bahia.

6004. Doherty, Donald K. (c o m p .). Bibliografia preliminar de colonização e povoamento nas Américas Latina e Anglo-Saxônica (R Geog Inst Pan Am, 11-12:31-36, 1951-1952, i.e. 1953, p. 111-153).
An extensive listing of titles relating to colonization and settlement throughout the Americas, arranged by countries. Maps are given in separate lists.

6005. Echanove Trujillo, Carlos A. La sociología en Hispanoamérica. Habana, Imp. Universitaria, 1953. 175 p., illus.
The published versions of a short series of lectures given by the author at the Centre d'Études Sociologiques, Paris, May 1949, and at the Universidad Nacional Autónoma de México, February 1950. The summaries of sociological personnel and writings are given on a regional basis with the following divisions: Mexico, Central America, the Antilles, and South America.

6006. Fals-Borda, Orlando. Peasant society in the Colombian Andes. A sociological study of Saucío. Gainesville, Fla., University of Florida Press, 1955. 277 p., illus., figs., tables.
Probably the most intensive sociological study of a rural community in Latin America that has ever been done. The volume developed, with much additional study and restudy, out of

the author's M. A. thesis at the University of Minnesota. After tracing the history of the settlement from pre-Columbian days, Fals-Borda centers attention upon social organization and culture and personality. In the former, with skill and insight, he analyzes, describes, and interprets masses of data relating to the morphology of the neighborhood, the population, the relations of man to the land, the settlement process, the economic institutions, the level of living, social stratification, and the basic social institutions. In the latter, with the penetration, deftness in handling nuances, and sympathetic understanding that only a gifted native of a country can command, the author presents the all-important materials, probably unequalled in the literature, relative to the development of the *campesino's* personality, the role of religion in the community's life, and the ethos of Saucio.

6007. Fitzgibbon, Russell H. Uruguayan regional problems (Social Science, 29:2, Apr. 1954, p. 75-85).
A penetrating analysis of Uruguayan social problems, with particular emphasis upon the capital-*campo* or rural-urban basis of many of the differentials and conflicts.

6008. Fretz, Joseph Winfield. Pilgrims in Paraguay. The story of Mennonite colonization in South America. Scottdale, Pa., Herald Press, 1953. 247 p.
A sympathetic but on the whole objective account and analysis of the Mennonite colonies in Paraguay, along with briefer statements relating to the work of the Mennonites in Brazil, Uruguay, Argentina, and Colombia. Major attention is given to the family and the home, education and the school, religion and the church, government and social welfare, manners and customs, health and medical facilities. The book constitutes a significant addition to the literature on colonization and settlement.

6009. Lambert, Jacques. Le Brésil: structure sociale et institutions politiques. Paris, Armand Colin (Cahiers de la Fondation Nationale des Sciences Politiques), 1953. 165 p.
An ably prepared summary by a scholar who knows Brazil well. The major topics treated are as follows: Brazil's place in South America; the Brazilian population, natural increase and immigration, racial structure and social structure; the bases of the Brazilian economy; political institutions and life; and foreign policy and cultural relations with France.

6010. Leonard, Olen E., and Charles P. Loomis (eds.). Readings in Latin American social organization and institutions. Lansing, Mich., Michigan State College, Department of Sociology and Anthropology, 1953. 320 p.
A useful collection of recent periodical literature in English dealing with the basic social institutions, social ecology, social stratification, race relations, locality groupings, and social change in Latin America.

6011. Loomis, Charles P.; Julio O.

Morales; Roy A. Clifford; and Olen E. Leonard (eds.). Turrialba: social systems and the introduction of social change. Glencoe, Ill., Free Press, 1953. 288 p.
This volume "reports the results of an inter-disciplinary research program on the introduction of change and the nature of the social systems in the . . . community of Turrialba, Costa Rica. . . ." In addition to the four directors and editors, Paul C. Morrison, Sakari Sariola, Juvenal Valerio, Thomas L. Norris, Charles Proctor, Norman W. Painter, Nevin Scrimshaw, Antonio Arce, Eduardo Arze Louriera, Fernando del Río, and Ralph Allee all contributed to the analysis and interpretation. The following subjects receive detailed consideration: social status and communication; informal social systems; large and small land holdings; the ecological basis of social systems; demographic characteristics of the population; health systems; religious systems; educational systems; agricultural extension systems; political systems; levels of living; and the strategy of change. Throughout the volume the situation on the large estates, or haciendas, is compared and contrasted with that on the small farms in the area. An important report on the most thoroughly studied community in Latin America.

6012. López Núñez, Carlos. La sociología general de Azevedo (Estud Am, 4:13, abril 1952, p. 229-240).
A critical analysis of the sociological system of Fernando de Azevedo as it is set forth in the latter's Princípios de sociologia. López Núñez ranks Azevedo alongside Mariano H. Cornejo as a social theorist.

6013. Mendieta y Núñez, Lucio. La orientación sociológica de la economía (Cong Nac Soc, V, 1954, Estud Soc, p. 35-41).
A general statement distinguishing between economics, sociology, and economic sociology, prepared as an orientation for those participating in Mexico's Fourth National Sociological Congress which was devoted to economic sociology.

6014. Morse, Richard M. São Paulo in the twentieth century: social and economic aspects (Interam Ec Aff, 8:1, summer 1954, p. 3-60).
An examination and description of the "new patterns of urban society," industrialization, changing political functions and activities, and ecological arrangements in Brazil's great industrial and commercial center.

6015. Reinaga, Fausto. Tierra y libertad. La revolución nacional y el indio. La Paz, Ediciones Rumbo Sindical, 1953. 88 p.
A vigorous call for bettering the lot of the Bolivian Indian and for agrarian reform.

6016. Rios, José Arthur. O conceito de rural e urbano (R Geog Inst Pan Am, 11-12:31-36, 1951-1952, i.e. 1953, p. 11-17).
A penetrating analysis of the difficulties of determining adequate criteria for a rural-urban classification of the population.

6017. Rodríguez Vega, Eugenio. Apuntes para una sociología costarricense. San José, Universidad de Costa Rica (Sección Tesis de grado y ensayos, 4), 1953. 130 p.
A study of the individualism of the Costa Rican, its origins and psychological components, accompanied by a brief analysis of the class structure of Costa Rican society. Thesis, Facultad de Derecho.

6018. Senior, Clarence. Strangers and neighbors: the story of our Puerto Rican citizens. N. Y., Anti-Defamation League of B'nai B'rith, 1952. 53 p., illus.
A summary, intended for the general reader, of Senior's studies of the Puerto Rican migration to N. Y. and the process of assimilation and acculturation in the metropolis.

6019. Shatzky, Jacob. Comunidades judías en Latinoamérica. B. A., American Jewish Committee, 1952. 179 p.
Based on questionnaire. Material on religion, education, community life. No historical data and generally thin, but of some value to the sociologist. [C. C. Griffin]

6020. Smith, T. Lynn. Brazil: people and institutions. Rev. ed. Baton Rouge, La., Louisiana State University Press, 1954. 704 p., illus., figs, tables.
A revised edition of a book that appeared in 1946. The organization is the same, with major parts devoted to cultural diversity, demography, levels and standards of living, the relations of people to the land, and the major social institutions. The abundant statistical data in the text, tables, and charts is much more recent and current, thanks to the completion in the interim of the 1950 censuses of population and agriculture and the publication of the definitive results of the 1940 enumerations. Results of studies by Brazilian and other scholars since 1945, and additional field work by the author, enabled the documentation to be considerably improved.

6021. Solari, Aldo E. Sociología rural nacional. Montevideo, Universidad de Montevideo, Facultad de Derecho y Ciencias Sociales (Biblioteca de publicaciones oficiales, Sección 3, 69), 1953. 572 p.
A noteworthy attempt at producing a sociology of rural life in Uruguay. The author presents a fairly comprehensive frame of reference for the study of rural society (borrowed largely from Sorokin and Zimmerman's Principles of rural-urban sociology and Smith's Sociology of rural life) and fits into it appropriate descriptions and analyses of rural social phenomena as observed in Uruguay. The author's procedure deserves serious consideration by those who are concerned with the production of "national sociologies" for the other Latin American countries.

6022. **Universidad de Buenos Aires.** Instituto de Sociología. Boletín del Instituto de Sociología. B. A. Año 10, no. 6, 1952. 334 p.
A special issue containing papers presented to the Primer Congreso Latinoamericano de Sociología held in B. A. Sept. 20-25, 1951. The work at the conference was divided between two commissions, the first of which considered the necessity for and existence of a Latin American sociology and national sociologies, common and specific problems, and the university chairs and sociological works in Latin America. The second included the papers classified as having to do with sociological questions as they are related to the physical and geographical environment or demographic factors, including ethnic types, immigration, and rural-urban contrasts. The list of contributors is as follows: Argentina, Alicia G. Eguren de Catella, Gino Germani, Ricardo Levene, Alfredo Poviña, Julio E. Soler Miralles, Juan Antonio Villoldo, Carlos Alberto Alumi, Juan Dalma, and Plácido Alberto Horas; Bolivia, José Antonio Arze; Brazil, Pinto Ferreira, Mário Lins, Djacir Menezes, Pessoa de Morais, Miguel Diégues Júnior, Anobio Graça, and Laudelino Teixeira de Medeiros; Chile, Óscar Álvarez Andrews and Julio Vega; Italy, Corrado Gini; Nicaragua, Julio Ycaza Tigerino; and Venezuela, Miguel Acosta Saignes and Marco-Aurelio Vila.

6023. **Universidad Nacional Autónoma de México.** Instituto de Investigaciones Sociales. Memoria. México, Imprenta Universitaria, 1952. 177 p., illus.
A description of the organization of Mexico's major institution for social research and a summary statement of its accomplishments during the period 1939-1951. The contents of the *Revista mexicana de sociología* are listed year by year. The bulk of the report is devoted to photographs and lists of publications of the numerous sociologists from other countries who have contributed to the *Revista*.

6024. **Urquidi, Arturo.** Aspectos sociológicos de Bolivia (R Mex Soc, año 15, 15:1, enero-abril 1953, p. 67-82).
A brief summary of sociological realities in Bolivia with emphasis upon population changes, immigration, the mixture of races, and levels of living.

6025. **Vidart, Daniel D.** La vida rural uruguaya. Montevideo, Ministerio de Ganadería y Agricultura, Departamento de Sociología Rural (Publ., 1), 1955. 212 p.
A general study, largely literary and lyrical, of rural life in Uruguay. Stress is placed upon rural and urban contrasts and the competition between agriculture and stockraising as ways of life. Special consideration is given to human types and particularly the Gaucho and the caudillo.

COMMUNITY

6026. **Barney Almeida, Carlos.** La colonización menonita en Chihuahua (Estud Am, 5:20, mayo 1953, p. 581-588).
A short history and description of the successful Mennonite colonies in Chihuahua, Mexico.

6027. **Cámara Barbachano, Fernando.** Chacaltianguis, comunidad rural en la ribera del Papaloapan. V. 1. México, Gobierno del Estado de Veracruz (Serie Configuración cultural de la cuenca del Papaloapan, 1), 1952. 170 p., illus., maps.
A summary of materials assembled in a sociological study of the *municipio* of Chacaltianguis, Veracruz, Mexico, made between September 1947 and June 1948. Part 3, "Vida social," p. 123-151, which analyzes and describes the socio-cultural configurations, the population, marital condition, and family organization in the small seat of the *municipio* are of great interest to the sociologist. Further sociological material is promised in a second volume.

6028. **Jones, Robert Cuba.** Investigación de los programas de ayuda propia en la zona del Caribe y México, organizada por las Naciones Unidas (R Mex Soc, año 16, 16:1, enero-abril 1954, p. 77-81).
A brief report on self-help in various communities throughout the Caribbean area and in Mexico, observed by a group of experts from the United Nations during a ten-week period in 1952.

6029. **Vásquez-Calcerrada, P. B.** A research project on rural communities in Puerto Rico (Rural Soc, 18:3, Sept. 1953, p. 221-226).
Case studies of the most successful and the least successful of the new planned communities in the coffee area, the suger-cane area, and the tobacco-and-minor-crops area of Puerto Rico.

6030. **Wagley, Charles.** Amazon town. A study of man in the tropics. N. Y., Macmillan, 1953. 305 p., illus.
Intimate, detailed facts about life in a small Amazon community gathered by the author, his Brazilian wife, and two Brazilian companions in 1948. This study rivals that by Pierson of a community in São Paulo (fictitiously called *Cruz das Almas*) as the most exhaustive investigation that has been made of a specific Brazilian community. Attention is concentrated upon the economic institutions, social relations, family affairs, recreation, and dealings with the supernatural. The volume is a fundamental contribution to the understanding of life and work in the great Amazon basin.

LEVELS OF LIVING

6031. **Buitrón, Aníbal.** Éxodo rural en Venezuela. Washington, Pan American Union, 1955. 272 p., illus., figs., tables.
A careful study of 199 rural families in the states of Táchira, Mérida, and Trujillo, and of

232 families who had migrated from these Andean sections and currently were living in a workers' district in the city of Caracas. This research is equally important for those interested in levels and standards of living and those interested in the movements of population from the rural to the urban districts. The detailed analysis is relative to housing, clothing, food and diet, occupations, family organization, religious practices, and educational status.

6032. Germani, Gino. Sociología del consumo (Cong Nac Soc, V, 1954, Estud Soc, p. 145-153).

A theoretical treatment of consumption patterns, including an examination of the influence of socio-cultural differences upon income.

6033. Ortega Mata, Rolfo. La industrialización y el nivel de vida de la población del país (Cong Nac Soc, V, 1954, Estud Soc, p. 341-356).

A study establishing a correlation between industrialization and level of living in Mexico.

6034. Poblete Troncoso, Moisés. El standard de vida y sus repercusiones económicas y sociales (Cong Nac Soc, V, 1954, Estud Soc, p. 213-231).

An important attempt to describe and measure differences in the levels of living which prevail throughout the Americas. Factors influencing the level of living are classified as social (demographic and sanitary condtions, food and nutrition, housing and conveniences, clothing, conditions of work and employment, and social security), economic (labor market and occupation, earnings and expenses, economic development, communications, and energy), and educational and cultural (illiteracy; professional, technical, and university training; development of the press and publications; cultural centers; and others). Available statistics for recent years are presented on mortality, infant mortality, birth rates, intake of calories, percentages of income going for food, housing, clothing, etc., economically active population, gross income per capita, proportions of illiteracy, consumption of newsprint, and newspapers per 1000 inhabitants. All of these are accompanied by appropriate comment designed to stimulate and facilitate the comparisons.

MAN-LAND RELATIONS

6035. Diégues Júnior, Manuel. População e açúcar no nordeste do Brasil. Rio, Comissão Nacional de Alimentação, 1954. 236 p.

This volume contains one of the most basic sociological studies of rural life so far completed for any region of Brazil or any other portion of Latin America. Particular attention is focused upon the formation of an agrarian society in a sugar plantation area, slavery, miscegenation, *latifundismo*, the relations of people to the land, the development of modern plantations and sugar factories, and the demographic and social effects of the latifundium and monoculture.

6036. Ferreira, Pinto. El problema de la reforma agraria (Cong Nac Soc, V, 1954, Estud Soc, p. 181-190).

A brief description of the problem of the concentration of ownership and control of the land in Brazil, preceded by fragmentary comments upon the nature of the problem in general, attempts at agrarian reform in socialistic programs in Spain and China, programs of land reform in Russia and its satellites, and the size of farms and increase of agricultural production in the U. S.

6037. Ford, Thomas R. Man and land in Peru. Gainesville, Fla., University of Florida Press, 1955. 176 p.

A basic study of the highly important institutionalized relationships of man to the land in one of the principal Latin American countries. Land tenure, the concentration of land ownership and control, proposals for agrarian reform, and the relation of these to the Aprista movement, the so-called "Indian problem," and the work of the communists, are handled with the insight and objectivity of one thoroughly oriented in his subject who has done much work in the field. The book ranks among the more important contributions sociologists have made in the area of Latin American studies.

6038. Leal, Héctor Alfonso. Tierra de liberación para el campesino. Colonias agrícolas auténticamente nacionales. Guatemala, Tip. Nacional, 1955. 190 p., illus.

Basic documents and statistical data pertaining to the program of land reform in Guatemala in the first six months of the government of President Castillo Armas. The preliminary chapters discuss the communist-dominated activities in the same field under his predecessor.

6039. Schulman, Sam. The *colono* system in Latin America (Rural Soc, 20:1, Mar. 1955, p. 34-40).

A penetrating analysis and discussion of a large, much neglected, and highly significant tenure category in Latin America.

6040. Taylor, Carl C. Some land situations and problems in Caribbean countries (Carib Cont Trends, series 1, 3, 1952, i.e. 1953, p. 59-73).

A brief but competently done survey of the problem aspects of man-land relationships, and a description of some of the activities designed to ameliorate the condition.

6041. United Nations. Department of Economic Affairs. Progress in land reform. Analysis of replies by governments to a United Nations questionnaire. N. Y., 1954. 322 p. (Doc. E/2526; ST/ECA/21; sales no. 1954.II.B.3).

Published also in Spanish: *Progresos en materia de reforma agraria.* An analysis and summary of the materials submitted by the governments of the various countries to a United Nations questionnaire. Data included are those relating to general policy with respect to agrarian reform, measures undertaken (land redistribution, colonization projects, quality and location of the land, conditions of agricultural labor, the reduction of minifundia, fragmentation of holdings, etc.), and recommendations. Even though far from complete, this is a valuable source for those interested in man-land relations.

6042. Villalobos-Domínguez, C., a n d Julio Villalobos. Colonización integral en tierra de propiedad común y concesión vitalicia individual y la enfiteusis rivadaviana. B. A., El Ateneo, 1953. 150 p.
Elaboration of the authors' plans for an ideal "rurban" community and for a thoroughgoing change in the nature of property rights in the land.

6043. Vivanco, Antonino Carlos. Contribución al estudio de la sociología rural (R Fac Der Cien Soc, B A, 3. época, 7:28, enero-abril 1952, p. 235-253).
A short essay designed to introduce students of law to the nature of the rural environment, the rural family, and the rural community.

POPULATION

6044. Achille, Aristide. Quelques aspects du problème de la population en Haïti. Port-au-Prince, Imp. de l'État, 1955. 61 p.
The first part of this pamphlet is a paper presented at the Planned Parenthood Conference held at San Juan, Puerto Rico, in 1955. The second part is a lecture delivered in June 1955, giving the author's impressions of the conference. [M. Cook]

6045. Brazil. Instituto Brasileiro de Geografia e Estatística. Conselho Nacional de Estatística. Pesquisas sôbre a natalidade no Brasil. 2. série. Rio, 1953. 97 p. (Estatística demográfica, 16).
A study of the ratio of young children to women of childbearing ages as a measure of the rate of reproduction of a population, followed by analyses of the fertility of the population in the rural and urban portions of Brazil, and of differential fertility and infant mortality in the states of Rio Grande do Sul and Bahia and the *municípios* containing the state capitals in Ceara and Pernambuco.

6046. ——————. ——————. ——————.
Pesquisas sôbre as populações urbanas e rurais do Brasil. Rio, 1954. 89 p. (Estatística demográfica, 17).
A comparison of the demographic characteristics of Brazil's rural and urban populations, followed by a study of the growth of towns and cities and the changes in the numbers and proportions of rural and urban populations in the decade 1940 to 1950.

6047. Germani, Gino. Nuevas tendencias en la natalidad de los países de cultura occidental: el caso argentino (R Mex Soc, año 17, 17:1, enero-abril 1955, p. 65-83).

A study of the trends in Argentina's birth rate, with some analysis of the factors responsible for the changes. Since 1942, definitely, and probably since the middle of the 1930-1940 decade, there has been a slight increase in the birth rate in Argentina. The increase appears to have been more rapid in the capital, B. A., than in other parts of the republic; and the changes have been more pronounced among members of the upper and middle social classes than among the lower social strata.

6048. Kuczynski, R. R. Demographic survey of the British colonial empire. V. 3. West Indian and American territories. London, Royal Institute of International Affairs, 1953. 497 p.
A compilation and analysis, by one of the world's foremost demographers, of the population materials for the Bahamas, Barbados, Bermuda, British Guiana, British Honduras, Jamaica and dependencies, Windward Islands, Falkland Islands and dependencies, and St. Helena and dependencies. This should be a basic reference on the British possessions in and about the Caribbean for many years to come.

6049. Martí Bufill, Carlos. Nuevas soluciones al problema migratorio. Madrid, Ediciones Cultura Hispánica (Instituto Iberoamericano de Cooperación Económica, 2), 1955. 547 p.
A comprehensive analysis of facts, politics, and policies relative to international migrations. Special consideration is given to problems and policies in the Latin American countries and the movement of persons from Spain to the Americas.

6050. Mortara, Giorgio. Les erreurs dans les déclarations de l'âge dans les recensements brésiliens de 1940 et 1950. Rio, Serviço Gráf. do Instituto Brasileiro de Geografia e Estatística, 1953. 27 p.
An investigation of the extent of error in age declarations and of the extent to which these have been reduced by an improvement of the questions on the census schedules.

6051. Stycos, J. Mayone. La dinámica del control de la natalidad en la clase baja de Puerto Rico (R Mex Soc, año 15, 15:1, enero-abril 1953, p. 27-65).
A summary report of the findings in a study of attitudes towards birth control and birth-control practices among 48 couples of lower-class status in Puerto Rico. One half of the cases studied were from the villages and the others from the open country.

RACE

6052. Comas, Juan. Un ensayo sobre "raza" y economía (Cong Nac Soc, V, 1954, Estud Soc, p. 127-144).
A significant study of the relationship, principally in the Americas, between racial characteristics, such as color, and economic status.

6053. **Entralgo, Elías.** La liberación étnica cubana. Habana, Imprenta de la Universidad de La Habana, 1953. 272 p.

The texts of three lectures presented at the Club Atenas de la Habana and the Centro de Estudios Superiores de Oriente in 1942 and 1944. These were entitled "Los hechos negros," "Las ideas blancas," and "El fenómeno mulato." Together they represent a fundamental contribution to the study of race and race relations in Cuba.

6054. **Morse, Richard M.** The Negro in São Paulo, Brazil (J Negro Hist, 38:3, July 1953, p. 290-306).

A study of racial contact and assimilation in the city of São Paulo, with emphasis on the degree to which the patterns differ from those observed and described in Bahia and other parts of Brazil.

6055. **Pinto, L. A. Costa.** O negro no Rio de Janeiro. Relações de raças numa sociedade em mudança. São Paulo, Companhia Editôra Nacional (Biblioteca pedagógica brasileira, Série 5, Brasiliana, 276), 1953. 355 p.

A comprehensive study of the Negro in Rio de Janeiro with emphasis upon his position in the social pyramid, the natural areas in which he resides, his educational and cultural opportunities and accomplishments, the stereotypes which govern race relations in the city, and the tensions and movements which indicate his changing position in a changing society.

6056. **Ramos, Guerreiro.** Patologia social do "branco" brasileiro. Rio, Jornal do Commercio, 1955. 28 p.

The author posits a sharp contradiction between the facts and the ideas relating to race relationships in Brazil. He attributes this largely to the writings of whites, such as Arthur Ramos and Gilberto Freyre, who suffer serious personality conflicts; he maintains that in Brazil whiteness as a value is very precarious.

6057. **Ribero, René.** Preconceito racial entre os universitários nordestinos (Neurobiologia, 16:4, dez. 1953, p. 348-364).

A modified version of Bogardus' social-distance test was administered to 249 students at the University of Recife in 1952, and the results are compared with those of similar tests made in São Paulo and the U. S. Only 13.6 percent expressed willingness to intermarry with Negroes, 24.1 percent with mulattoes; and 8.8 percent would exclude Negroes from the country, and 7.2 percent would exclude mulattoes. Foreign nationalities receiving the highest degree of acceptation on the tests are the French, Italian, Spanish, Canadian, Uruguayan, Mexican, and Portuguese. Those towards whom the attitudes were most ambivalent are the Germans, North Americans, Argentines, and English. And those to whom the attitudes were most hostile are the Russians, Syrians, Jews, Hindus, Chinese, and Japanese.

6058. **Souza, Yvonildo de.** Posição do negro no direito brasileiro. Contribuição

ao estudo sociológico do negro nas Américas. Recife, Brazil, Editôra Nordeste, 1954. 62 p.

Brief comments upon the extent to which Portuguese and Brazilian law have dealt specifically with the Negro and race relations.

SOCIAL CHANGE

6059. **Blanchet, Jules.** Idéologies et transformation sociales. Port-au-Prince, Imp. de l'État, 1955. iii, 18 p.

An impressive essay prefaced by Professor Karl Lowenstein. The preface first appeared in Bulletin international des sciences sociales, 5:1, 1953. [M. Cook]

6060. **Lewis, Oscar.** Tepoztlán restudied. A critique of the folk-urban conceptualization of social change (Rural Soc, 18:2, June 1953, p. 121-137).

Selected materials from a restudy of the Mexican village on which Robert Redfield worked 17 years earlier, with special reference to methodological and theoretical aspects of the study of social change.

6061. **Marroquín, Alejandro D.** Factor económico y cambio social (Cong Nac Soc, V, 1954, Estud Soc, p. 329-339).

A study of the variations in the roles of economic factors in the social changes that have been taking place in three Mexican communities, Tepoztlan, Tlaxiaco, and Ojitlan.

6062. **Smith, T. Lynn.** Algumas tendéncias sociais correntes na América Latina (Sociologia, 16:3, agôsto 1954, p. 236-247).

Brief discussion of several major social trends throughout Latin America, including the rapid growth of population, the mushrooming of towns and cities, the changing functions of urban centers in Latin America, the great increase in social differentiation, the emergence of a middle class, and the improvement in the educational status of the population.

SOCIAL INSTITUTIONS

6063. **Araújo, Heitor.** Vinte anos de sertão. Bahia, Brazil, Empresa Gráfica Limitada, 1953. 154 p.

Intimate description of the ways of life and social problems of the people in the interior of Bahia by a priest who spent 20 years in the area. Particularly valuable for one interested in the religious institutions, including the schismatic movements and the activities of the Protestant denominations.

6064. **Azevedo, Thales de.** As famílias dos alunos de uma escola primária (R Br Estud Ped, 22:56, out.-dez. 1954, p. 116-143).

This article gives the results of a detailed social survey made of 150 families, of a total of about 600, whose children were enrolled in one of the schools in the city of Bahia. The interviewing was done by university and college students with the assistance of specified schedules of questions. The analysis presents basic data about the section of the city in which the families live, and then presents the detailed data about family organization and relationships in the area. It is a study that deserves to be imitated widely throughout Latin America.

6065. Barahona J., Luis. El gran incógnito. Visión interna del campesino costarricense. San José, Editorial Universitaria (Sección Tesis de grado y ensayos, 3), 1953. 164 p.

A collection of essays on the Costa Rican *campesino*, his characteristics, recreations, religious beliefs and practices, households, etc.

6066. Bastide, Roger. Estudos afro-brasileiros. São Paulo, Universidade de São Paulo, Faculdade de Filosofia, Ciencias e Letras (Boletim, 154; Sociologia, 1:3), 1953. 104 p.

Four fundamental studies of various aspects of the Afro-Brazilian religious cults in Brazil. The first essay deals with the stereotypes of the Negro as exhibited in Brazilian literature. The second is a thoroughgoing examination of the mystic trance into which the "daughter of the saint" falls when she becomes the "horse of the saint." The third study is of the much neglected baptism of the necklace, or "lavagem das contas"; and the fourth and final is an analysis and description of the Angolian ritual of Axexe.

6067. Bermúdez, María Elvira. La vida familiar del mexicano. México, Antigua Librería Robredo (México y lo mexicano, 20), 1955. 142 p.

An essay based upon personal observation and materials gathered from folklore and literature and dealing with family life in Mexico. The author attempts to portray class differences and stresses many of the maladjustments in the relations between the sexes.

6068. Burma, John H. Spanish-speaking groups in the United States. Durham, N. C., Duke University Press (Sociological series, 9), 1954. 214 p., maps.

This excellent study is the most comprehensive to date of the various Spanish-speaking groups in the U. S., their numbers and distribution, their social institutions and social problems. The case study of the Penitentes of northern New Mexico and southern Colorado deserves special mention.

6069. Galvão, Eduardo. Vida religiosa do caboclo da Amazônia (B Mus Nac, Rio, Antropologia, no. 15, 29 de abril de 1953, p. 1-18).

A valuable description of the fundamental religious beliefs and practices of the rural inhabitants of the great Amazon Valley.

6070. Hamburger, Adelaide. A família numa pequena comunidade paulista (Sociologia, 16:3, agôsto 1954, p. 284-292).

An objective study of some of the characteristics of the family in a small rural community in the state of São Paulo.

6071. Lago, Tomás. El huaso. Ensayo de antropología social. Santiago, Ediciones de la Universidad de Chile, 1953. 325 p., illus.

Huaso signifies two things in Chile: first, the *campesino*, or rural inhabitant, as distinct from the urbanite; and, second, one lacking in the social graces, or the "hombre incultivado." This comprehensive study traces the Chilean "horse complex" from its origins in Spain to the present, and describes in detail modern horsemanship, the equipment used, and especially the dress of the *huaso*.

6072. Pierson, Donald. Santos em Cruz das Almas (Sociologia, 15:1, março 1953, p. 31-43).

The Portuguese translation of a portion of the analysis and description of religious institutions in the monographic study of a rural community in the state of São Paulo.

6073. Ribeiro, René. Cultos afrobrasileiros do Recife. Um estudo de ajustamento social. Recife, Gráf. Editôra do Recife (Boletim do Instituto Joaquim Nabuco), 1952. 150 p., illus.

An important monograph presenting the results of intensive studies in the years 1947-1948 and 1951-1952. Part of the material was used in the author's M. A. thesis at Northwestern University. The major divisions of the work are: (1) the Negro in Pernambuco; (2) group structure of the Afro-Brazilian cults; (3) the functioning of cult groups; and (4) the behavior and role of the individual.

6074. Rios, José Arthur. A educação dos grupos. Rio, Serviço Nacional de Educação Sanitária e Serviço Especial de Saúde Pública do Ministério da Saúde, 1954. 312 p.

This is a work of great merit. In a brilliant manner the author has brought together the tested knowledge and theory of the nature and processes of social groups, community organization, social diagnosis, leadership, and the ways of inducing social change; and he has applied these to the special problem of group or mass education. No comparable work in any other language is known to the editor.

6075. Willems, Emílio. The structure of the Brazilian family (Soc Forces, 31:4, May 1953, p. 339-345).

On the basis of 19 years of residence in Brazil, during which he was actively engaged in sociological research in various parts of the country, the author attempts to correct many widely held ideas about the Brazilian family. The antithetic roles of males and females of the upper and middle classes is stressed, and the fact that the pattern prevailing among the members of the very large lower class differs sharply from that of the other classes is emphasized.

SOCIAL PROBLEMS

6076. Guhl, Ernesto. La seguridad social campesina en Colombia. Bogotá, Ministerio del Trabajo, 1954. 68 p., illus., tables.

A general sketch describing the system and setting of rural social security in Colombia, with special reference to the following: the economic regions of Colombia; density and distribution of the population; labor and wages; the situation of the *campesino;* the national income and its distribution; the habitat and social security; compulsory social security; the budget for social welfare; *minifundismo* and social security; and the raising of the standard of living.

6077. Hopper, Rex D. Aumento de la criminalidad de la América Latina pre-revolucionaria (R Mex Soc, año 17, 17:1, enero-abril 1955, p. 95-111).

A preliminary report on the author's extensive study of criminality in Latin America during the colonial epoch.

6078. Lins, Mario. Los factores de la delincuencia (R Mex Soc, año 16, 16:3, sept.-dic. 1954, p. 365-373).

A short, theoretical study of the nature of delinquency, the physical, biological, psychological, and socio-cultural factors involved, and the problems involved in its control and reduction.

6079. Mendoza, José Rafael. Estudio de sociología criminal venezolana. (Trabajo presentado al II Congreso Internacional de Criminología reunido en París en septiembre de 1950). Caracas, 1952. 58 p.

An important study of crime and juvenile delinquency in Venezuela. Types of criminal behavior are identified, their incidence studied, and their relationships to various factors such as age, sex, residence, etc., investigated.

6080. Ruiz Funes, Mariano. La defensa social, el delito y el peligro (R Mex Soc, año 15, 15:2, mayo-agosto 1953, p. 197-209).

A brief analysis of the fundamental problems involved in the control of crime and delinquency.

6081. Viqueira, Carmen, and Ángel Palerm. Alcoholismo, brujería y homicidio en dos comunidades rurales de México (Am Indíg, 14:1, enero 1954, p. 7-36).

A study of three of the problems the authors consider as typical of those found in many rural communities throughout Mexico. The authors contend that childhood experiences and education are not the determining factors in drunkenness, but that it arises from the socio-cultural influences. In one of the communities studied alcoholism helps maintain psycho-cultural stability, in the other it unleashes aggressive impulses. In one community magic

and political organization provide channels for aggressiveness and its control, and in the other the lack of such leads to homicide.

SOCIAL PROCESSES

6082. Aguirre Beltrán, Gonzalo. Teoría de los centros coordinadores (Cong Nac Soc, V, 1954, Estud Soc, p. 315-328).

A significant attempt to analyze the role of Mexican cities as agencies of regional integration and of acculturation in general.

6083. Cañón, José J. Organización y funciones de las cooperativas agropecuarias. Bogotá, Ministerio de Agricultura, Sección de Economía Agrícola, 1953. 90 p., illus.

A significant report on the attempts to apply Rochdale principles in the development of contractual cooperative activities among Colombia's farmers and cattlemen.

6084. Fals-Borda, Orlando. Notas sobre la evolución del vestido campesino en la Colombia central (R Colomb Folk, 2. época, 2, junio 1953, p. 139-147).

A study of Chibcha-Spanish acculturation as exemplified in the origin and evolution of the costumes of the rural folk in central Colombia.

6085. Saito, Hiroshi. O cooperativismo na região de Cotia. Estudo de transplantação cultural, I (Sociologia, 16:3, agôsto 1954, p. 248-283).

An excellent and highly significant study of the cooperative movement introduced by Japanese settlers in the Cotia area near the city of São Paulo.

6086. Suárez, Luis A. Cooperatives in Puerto Rico: history, problems, and research (Rural Soc, 18:3, Sept. 1953, p. 226-233).

A survey of the development of the cooperative movement in Puerto Rico, the problems encountered, and the need for additional study of cooperative undertakings.

6087. Yescas Peralta, Pedro. Teotitlán del Valle, muestra del proceso de transculturación (R Mex Soc, año 16, 16:3, sept.-dic. 1954, p. 397-408).

An analysis of the problems of acculturation as exemplified by the contacts between the rural and largely indigenous society in the small community of Teotitlan del Valle and the more urban forms of society in Oaxaca and Tlacolula.

SOCIAL STRATIFICATION

6088. Adams, Richard N. A change from caste to class in a Peruvian sierra town (Soc Forces, 31:3, Mar. 1953, p. 238-244).

In 1880 the town of Muquiyauyo, Peru, was sharply divided into an "Indian community" and a mestizo remainder, with basic differences in clothing, land ownership, language, family names, political and governmental functions and privileges, physical features, and religious activities separating the two. Intermarriage was strictly forbidden. Since that time the differences have been largely obliterated, a fusion of the two has occurred, and a grouping into upper, middle, and lower social strata, with each class containing elements from both the former Indian and mestizo communities, has emerged.

6089. Beals, Ralph. A estratificação social na América Latina (Sociologia, 16:3, agôsto 1954, p. 219-235).
The Portuguese translation of the study by Beals published in the *American journal of sociology*, January 1953 (see following item).

6090. ————. Social stratification in Latin America (Am J Sociol, 58:4, Jan. 1953, p. 327-339).
A critical analysis and appraisal of recent literature dealing with the class systems in the Latin American countries, along with promising suggestions for the further study of social stratification in those countries.

6091. Fals Borda, Orlando. Estratos sociales entre los campesinos colombianos (Ec Colomb, año 2, 5:14, junio 1955, p. 593-604).
The application of a scale, based on those of Chapin, Sewell, and Guttman, in the study of social stratification in the neighborhood of Saucio, Cundinamarca, Colombia. Only the owner of one large hacienda could be placed in the upper class, and there were none of the inhabitants rating middle-class status. However, those in the lower class ranged on the scale from 45 to 87, with 15 of the 69 families scoring 50 or above. Those rating 59 or above, the author believes, have possibilities of becoming members of a genuine middle class if sufficient educational opportunities are provided.

6092. Germani, Gino. Estructura social de la Argentina. Análisis estadístico. B. A., Raigal, 1955. 273 p.
A statistical study of the composition of population, growth and redistribution of population, socio-economic classes, educational status, and the relationship between class structure and political attitudes in Argentina.

6093. Sariola, Sakari. Social class and social mobility in a Costa Rican town. Turrialba, Costa Rica, Inter-American Institute of Agricultural Sciences, 1954. 136 p.
An intensive study of class components, the obstacles to vertical social mobility, and the amount of shifting from one class to another in the town of Turrialba, Costa Rica.

OTHER

6094. Agramonte, Roberto. La ecología humana y su importancia sociológica (Cong Nac Soc, V, 1954, Estud Soc, p. 111-126).

An able synthesis of the development, scope, and principal features of the field of human ecology.

6095. Cárdenas Ojeda, Mauro, and Camilo Valiente. Las relaciones laborales, la opinión dentro de la fábrica y la calificación de méritos de los trabajadores (Cong Nac Soc, V, 1954, Estud Soc, p. 155-168).
An interesting attempt to measure the quality of the worker through opinions secured from 88 supervisors in Mexican factories.

6096. Chacón, Vamireh. O antisemitismo no Brasil. Tentativa de interpretação sociológica. Recife, Brazil, Clube Hebraico, 1955. 34 p.
Anti-Semitism in Brazil is said, on the basis of a rather general study of the pertinent literature, to lack the degree of virulency necessary to justify the designation. Anti-Judaism is suggested as a more appropriate term. Theological and religious bases are said to be the primary factors producing the prejudice, although accusations of clannishness or unassimilability, sharp practices in business, and aims at world domination are also made.

6097. Dotson, Floyd. A note on participation in voluntary associations in a Mexican city (Am Sociol R, 18:4, Aug. 1953, p. 380-386).
A survey of 415 adult residents of Guadalajara to determine the organizations with which they were affiliated and the extent of their participation in the activities of the same.

6098. Dotson, Floyd, and Lillian Ota Dotson. Ecological trends in the city of Guadalajara, Mexico (Soc Forces, 32:4, May 1954, p. 367-374).
A significant study of the changing ecological arrangements in a large and rapidly growing Mexican city.

6099. Fernandes, Florestán. Apontamentos sôbre os problemas da indução na sociologia. São Paulo, Universidade de São Paulo, Secção de Publicações (Col. Cursos e conferências, 3), 1954. 123 p.
A collection of essays on the problems of induction in sociological study, with special attention given the work of Émile Durkheim, Max Weber, and Karl Marx.

6100. Garcés Pachano, Wilson. Estudio sobre la vivienda en El Salvador. Preparado para el Gobierno de El Salvador. N. Y., Naciones Unidas, Programa de Asistencia Técnica, 1954. 86 p. (UN Doc. ST/TAA/K/El Salvador/9).
A significant analysis of housing problems in El Salvador, rural and urban, and of the factors which make them acute, accompanied by recommendations for improving the situation.

6101. Humphrey, N. D. Ethnic images

and stereotypes of Mexicans and Americans (Am J Ec Sociol, 13:2, Jan. 1954, p. 305-313).

A report of the author's study of the Mexican town of Tecolotlan, Jalisco, Mexico (population about 4500). He contrasts the personality traits of the Mexican with the stereotypes of the same commonly possessed by middle class citizens of the U. S., and he also describes the stereotypes of U. S. society prevailing in the minds of the Mexicans.

6102. Lenoir, Raymond. La sociología en México (R Mex Soc, año 16, 16:1, enero-abril 1954, p. 93-101).

A few observations on sociology in Mexico, its origin and development, with special emphasis upon the work of Lucio Mendieta y Núñez.

6103. Mendieta y Núñez, Lucio. Juan Bautista Vico, precursor de la sociología (R Mex Soc, año 15, 15:1, enero-abril 1953, p. 33-35).

An able review of the life and social theories of Vico (1668-1743).

6104. Molina Enríquez, Luis. Sociedad, derecho y estado (R Mex Soc, año 16, 16:3, sept.-dic. 1954, p. 409-426).

Society, law, and the State, and the interrelations between the three as a field of sociological study. Examples are drawn for the most part from Mexican society, codes, and constitutions.

6105. Treviño, Víctor L., and Rafael González Montemayor. La educación del obrero manual en México (R Mex Soc, año 16, 16:1, enero-abril 1954, p. 83-91).

An exposition of what must be done by the Mexican government, industrialists, the workers, and Mexican leaders if the members of the nation's labor force are to receive the training they need.

6106. Uribe Villegas, Óscar. La asistencia técnica. Relación socio-económica contemporánea (R Mex Soc, año 17, 17:1, enero-abril 1955, p. 113-121).

A clear and concise exposition of the legal and logical bases and forms for a technical assistance program conducted by the United Nations.

6107. ————. La libertad como problema psico-sociológico (R Mex Soc, año 15, 15:2, mayo-agosto 1953, p. 229-249).

A study, largely philosophical, of the nature of liberty and of its various types.

6108. Violich, Francis. Urbanization in Venezuela—an object lesson for the Caribbean area (Carib Cont Trends, series 1, 3, 1952, i. e. 1953, p. 74-87).

An important study of urbanization, its causes, the social problems it produces, and what may be done to guide its development.

General

STATISTICS

PHYLLIS G. CARTER

In view of the fact that most of the results of the 1950 census of the Americas have become available, this section now presents a roundup of the latest population census volumes available for Latin America, as well as recent housing census results. (For censuses of agriculture, commerce, and industry, see Economics.)

MOST RECENT CENSUSES

6250. **Inter American Statistical Institute.** The story of the 1950 census of the Americas. An account prepared by . . . in cooperation with the General Bureaus of Statistics and the National Census Offices of the American Nations. Washington, 1953. 89 p.
". . . Prepared for the general public, to tell how the 1950 Census of the Americas came about, how the effort was organized, and what the program undertook to do, and why." History of the effort by the Inter American Statistical Institute and other bodies to get all the American nations to take censuses during 1950, and to use the same definitions, minimum set of questions, tabulations, etc.

6251. **Argentina. Dirección Nacional del Servicio Estadístico.** IV censo general de la nación. T. 1. Censo de población. B. A., 1956? xci, 727 p.
1947 census. Analysis includes information on mortality and expectation of life, origins of the population, and some history; organization of the census is explained; data on age by sex, citizenship, civil status; number of families, of other households, and of persons living alone; religion; physical handicaps; literacy; employment and unemployment, branch of economic activity; urban centers.

6252. **Bahama Islands.** Report on the census of the Bahama Islands taken on the 6th December 1953. Nassau, 1953. 10, 18 p.

6253. **Bermuda.** Census of Bermuda, 9th October, 1950. Report of Census Committee and statistical tables compiled in accordance with the Census Act, 1950. 118 p.

6254. **Bolivia. Dirección General de Estadística y Censo.** Resultados generales del censo de población de la República de Bolivia levantado el día 5 de septiembre de 1950. La Paz, 1951. 139 p.
Urban and rural population by departments, provinces, and cantons; an estimate of tribal Indians in each department and province; and area and density of each department and province.

6255. **Brazil. Instituto Brasileiro de Geografia e Estatística. Conselho Nacional de Estatística. Serviço Nacional de Recenseamento.** VI recenseamento geral do Brasil - 1950. Série regional. Rio, 1954-.
Being issued as a separate volume for each state, some in more than one tome (in which case t. 1 always contains the "Censo demográfico"). The demographic census includes data on population (urban, rural, and suburban residence; age; sex; color; marital status; religion; citizenship; birthplace; language spoken; literacy; educational level; highest course of schooling completed; occupation; branch of economic activity; occupational status; economically active population; population dependent on agriculture; fertility), households, and housing. The volume for the Federal District includes four pages of definitions and explanations in English. The household schedule is inserted at the end of all the volumes.

6256. ————. ————. ————.
————. VI recenseamento geral do Brasil. Censo demográfico (1.o de julho de 1950). . . . Seleção dos principais dados. Rio, 1951-1953. 23 v. (a volume for each state, one for the Federal District, one for the territories, and one for Brazil).
De jure population, and de facto population by age and sex, urban-suburban-rural distribution, color, marital status, religion, nationality, liiteracy, branch of economic activity, and place of birth, for the states and for those *municípios* containing the state capitals.

6257. ————. ————. ————. VI recenseamento geral do Brasil (1.o-VII-1950). Selected tables of the population census. Tableaux choisis du recensement de la population. Rio, 1953. vii, 15 p.

De facto population, age by sex, urban-rural distribution, citizenship, literacy, branch of economic activity; urban centers having more than 25,000 inhabitants.

6258. Chile. Dirección General de Estadística. XII censo general de población y lo. de vivienda, levantado el 24 de abril del año 1952. Escrutinio oficial. Santiago, 1953. 14 p.

First final results to appear.

6259. Colombia. Departamento Administrativo Nacional de Estadística. Censo de edificios y viviendas de 1951. Bogotá, 1953-1955. (A separate volume for each department.)

6260. ————. ————. Censo de población de 1951. Bogotá, 1954-.

Being issued as a separate volume for each department. Urban and rural population, age, sex, civil status, nationality, literacy, school years completed, occupation, economic activity, occupational status, households.

6261. Costa Rica. Dirección General de Estadística y Censos. Censo de población de Costa Rica, 22 de mayo de 1950. San José, 1953. 237 p., tables, charts, maps.

There is a brief analysis of the census results, and data on population density, urban-rural distribution, age by sex, place of birth, color or race, native language, civil status, households, education, and occupation. An appendix includes definitions, laws, and the census questionnaire.

6262. ————. ————. Censo urbano de edificios y viviendas, noviembre y diciembre de 1949. San José, 1954. 70 p.

6263. Cuba. Oficina Nacional de los Censos Demográfico y Electoral. Censos de población, viviendas y electoral, enero 28 de 1953. Informe general. Habana, 1955. xlviii, 325 p.

Urban-rural population, age, sex, race, women by number of children ever born, place of birth, citizenship, civil status, relation to head of family, households, school attendance, educational level, literacy, branch of economic activity, labor force, hours of work in week preceding census, weeks worked in year preceding census, occupation; housing characteristics; electoral population. Appendixes include data on intercensal births and deaths.

6264. Dominican Republic. Dirección General de Estadística. Oficina Nacional del Censo. Población de la República Dominicana censada en 1950. Distribución según la división territorial al lo. de julio de 1954. Ciudad Trujillo, 1954. 126 p.

1950 census results, total population only, for administrative divisions according to their territorial boundaries as of July 1, 1954.

6265. ————. ————. ————. Tercer censo nacional de población, 1950. V. 1. Común de San Cristóbal. Ciudad Trujillo, 1952. xxxv, 170 p.

Detailed data on age, sex, urban-rural distribution, color, civil status, religion, place of birth, citizenship, nationality, literacy, school years completed, attendance at schools, physical and mental defects, women by number of children ever born, economically active and inactive population, occupation, branch of economic activity, and occupational status, households, relations to heads of households, housing.

6266. ————. ————. ————. Tercer censo nacional de población, 1950. Resumen general. Ciudad Trujillo, Sección de Publicaciones, 1953. xvii, 75 p., tables.

Includes brief notes on history and geography of the country, history of national censuses, and explanation of census methods, as well as data on households, housing (including number of persons per dwelling by number of bedrooms), and on age, sex, color, civil status, relation to head of family, religion, place of birth, nationality, language, education (literacy, completed years of schooling, attendance at schools), physical defects, number of children ever born, economic characteristics (occupation, branch of economic activity, occupational status, wages and salaries, income).

6267. Ecuador. Dirección General de Estadística y Censos. Boletín de información censal. Resultados definitivos del censo nacional de población de 1950 sobre: edad y sexo, estado civil, alfabetismo, población económicamente activa e inactiva. No. 1-17, 17A. Quito, 1951-1952. 18 v.

A bulletin for each province and for the Archipelago of Columbus (Galapagos).

6268. ————. ————. Información censal. Resumen de los resultados definitivos del censo nacional de población de 1950 sobre sexo, edad, estado civil, alfabetismo y población económicamente activa e inactiva. Quito, 1952. 61 p.

6269. ————. ————. Población de acuerdo con la actual división político-territorial del Ecuador al 29 de noviembre de 1950. Quito, 1954. 41 p.

Final census figures for slightly different administrative divisions from those by which the enumeration was done.

6270. ————. ————. Primer censo de población del Ecuador, 1950. Quito, 1954. T. 1, Población por edad y sexo, 320 p.; t. 2, Población urbana, suburbana y rural, 133 p.; t. 3, Población por estado civil, 137 p.

Results of the first population census of Ecuador. The first volume contains data by age and sex for each province, *cantón* (civil division), and *parroquia* (minor civil division), as well as for the country as a whole; the preface includes provisional data on area and density by provinces, and brief explanatory notes and analyses.

6271. El Salvador. Dirección General de Estadística y Censos. Primer censo de la vivienda urbana, febrero 1950. San Salvador, 1953. 965 p.

6272. ————. ————. Segundo censo de población, junio 13 de 1950. San Salvador, 1954. xxxi, 622 p.

Urban-rural distribution, age, sex, civil status, population born in the country by age and sex and urban-rural distribution (but not by place of birth), foreign-born by age and sex and urban-rural distribution and country of birth and nationality, school-age population attending school, literacy, school years completed, unemployment, economically active population by occupation and occupational status and branch of economic activity, households (*familias censales*).

6273. Falkland Islands. Report of census taken on the night of the 28th March, 1953. Stanley, 1954. 9 p.

Vital and migration statistics as well as census data on age by sex, civil status, nationality and place of birth, and religion.

6274. France. Service Colonial des Statistiques. Résultats du recensement de 1946. Territoires d'outre-mer (Français d'origine métropolitaine et étrangers): Guyane et Inini. Paris, 1948. 43p. (Bulletin mensuel de statistique d'outre-mer, Supplément série "Statistique," 7).

6275. ————. ————. Résultats du recensement de 1946 dans les territoires d'outre-mer (Français d'origine métropolitaine et étrangers): Martinique. Paris, 1948? 34 p. (Bulletin mensuel de statistique d'outre-mer, Supplément série "Statistique," 5).

6276. Guatemala. Dirección General de Estadística. Oficina Permanente del Censo. Censo de la vivienda urbana, 1949. T. 1. Guatemala, 1954. 390 p.

The first volume of a projected two-volume summary in a series of eight volumes giving the definitive results of the 1949 census of housing. This volume contains the simple tabulations of results by departments and *municipios*. [T. L. Smith]

6277. ————. ————. ————. Sexto censo general de población, abril 18 de 1950. Guatemala, 1953. 244 p.

Data on number of families (households), age, sex, ethnic group, literacy, school attendance, use of shoes or sandals, and population in municipal capitals and outside them.

6278. Haïti. Bureau de Recensement de la République d'Haïti. Premier dénombrement de la population. Port-au-Prince, 1951. 47 p.

Population by department, arrondissement, commune, and town and section, from the census of August 1950.

6279. ————. Institut Haïtien de Statistique. Recensement de 1950. Département du Nord-Ouest. Personnes en chômage (B Trim Stat, 18, sept. 1955, p. 165-169).

6280. ————. ————. Recensement général, août 1950. Démographie, économie, famille et habitation, agriculture et élevage. V. 1. Département du Nord-Ouest. Port-au-Prince, 1955? 318 p.

Urban-rural distribution of population, age and sex, civil status, place of birth, literacy and level of education; economically active and inactive, occupation, branch of industry; families (households) and housing; and agriculture and livestock. Definitions are given in the preface.

6281. Honduras. Dirección General de Censos y Estadísticas. Detalle del censo de población por departamentos, levantado el 8 de junio de 1950. T. 1. Tegucigalpa, 1955. 69 p.

The first volume contains data on the provinces of Atlantida, Colon, Comayagua, Copan, Cortes, Choluteca, El Paraiso, and Francisco Morazan, on urban-rural population, age by sex, civil status, place of birth, citizenship; literacy and educational level; households; population using or not using shoes, eating or not eating wheat bread, and by type of bed used (with mattress, with *petate*, hammock, etc.).

6282. ————. ————. Resultados generales del censo general de la República levantado el 18 de junio de 1950. Tegucigalpa, 1952. 373 p.

Cover title: *Resumen general del censo de población levantado el 18 de junio de 1950.* Data on age, sex, civil status, urban-rural distribution, place of birth, nationality, citizenship, literacy, school years completed, households, relation to head of family, economically inactive population, economically active by branch of economic activity, occupation, occupational status, use or not of shoes, use or not of wheat bread, and type of bed used. An introduction gives brief notes on methodology, and reproduces the questionnaire.

6283. ————. Dirección General de Estadística. Resumen general del censo de vivienda levantado el 10 de julio de 1949. Tegucigalpa, 1950? 245 p.

6284. Jamaica. Central Bureau of Statistics. West Indian census 1946. Kingston, 1950. 8 parts in 2 v.

Issued originally as eight separate parts. V. 1 contains part A, General report on the census of population, and part B, Census of agriculture in Barbados, the Leeward Islands, the Windward Islands and Trinidad and Tobago. V. 2 contains part C, Census of the colony of Barbados; part D, Census of population of the colony of British Guiana; part E, Census of population of British Honduras; part F, Census of population of the Leeward Islands; part G, Census of population of the colony of Trinidad and Tobago; part H, Census of population of the Windward Islands (Dominica, Grenada, St. Lucia, St. Vincent).

6285. ———. ———. West Indian census 1946. Bulletin 1-13. Kingston, 1946-1950. 13 parts.

No. 1, Population and dwellings in the Leeward Islands; no. 2, Agriculture and fishing in the British Virgin Islands; no. 3, Trinidad employment and unemployment; no. 4, Trinidad birthplaces; no. 5, Conjugal condition and fertility in the Leeward Islands; no. 6, Summary census tables for the colony of British Honduras, 17 p.; no. 7, Summary census tables for the presidency of St. Kitts-Nevis-Anguilla, 12 p.; no. 8, Summary statistics of the labour force (British West Indies), 11 p.; no. 9, Life tables for Jamaica 1879-82 to 1945-47, 10 p.; no. 10, Life tables for Trinidad and Tobago and for Barbados, 22 p.; no. 11, Special population bulletin, 1 p.; no. 12, Life tables for British Guiana and British Honduras, 14 p.; no. 13, Vital statistics of the British Caribbean, 1921-1948, 14 p.

6286. México. Dirección General de Estadística. Integración territorial de los Estados Unidos Mexicanos. Séptimo censo general de población, 1950. México, 1952. 734 p.

Number of inhabitants in every minor and major civil division, with indication of the census district in which small localities were enumerated. Data are not final; according to the preface they are still subject to minor modification.

6287. ———. ———. Séptimo censo general de población, 6 de junio de 1950. México, 1952-.

Detailed data on each state and territory, being published in a separate volume for each.

6288. ———. ———. Séptimo censo general de población, 6 de junio de 1950. Parte especial. México, 1955. 303 p.

Special tabulations of the data pertaining to the labor force and to the incomes of employed persons, classified according to the industry in which they were engaged. [T. L. Smith]

6289. ———. ———. Séptimo censo general de población, 6 de junio de 1950.

Resumen general. México, 1953. 264 p., map.

Data on households, age, sex, education, civil status, number of children ever born, education (literacy, attendance at school, number of school years completed), relation to head of family, occupation, branch of economic activity, occupational status, days worked in week preceding census, wages and salaries and other income, place of birth, nationality, language, food costs, rent, religion, use of wheat bread, use of shoes or sandals or no footwear; housing characteristics.

6290. Nicaragua. Dirección General de Estadística y Censos. Censo general de población de la República de Nicaragua, mayo 1950. Managua, 1951-.

Being issued as a separate volume for each department, with results for the country as a whole in v. 17 (1954, 472 p.). Data on urban-rural distribution, households, relation to head of family, age, place of birth, nationality, language or dialect spoken, civil status, fertility (child-woman ratios), literacy, school attendance and educational level, religion, economically active and inactive, occupation, branch of economic activity, occupational status. V. 17 includes an explanation of definitions and concepts, a reproduction of the schedule, and authorizing laws.

6291. Panamá. Dirección de Estadística y Censo. Censos nacionales de 1950. Quinto censo de población. Panamá, 1954. V. 1, Características generales, 331 p.; v. 2, Características educativas, 299 p.

V. 1 includes increase and density, urban and rural population, Indian population by province and sex, age by sex, place of birth, foreign-born by sex and nationality, language, civil status, women by number of children ever born, and electoral population.

6292. ———. ———. Censos nacionales de 1950. Quinto censo de población. Primer censo de vivienda. Lugares poblados. Panamá, 1954. 168 p. (Boletín informativo, 5).

Population by sex, and number of occupied dwellings, for each populated place in 1950, as well as total population of each place of 100 or more at the 1920 and 1930 censuses, and population of towns of 1500 and more and of district seats at the 1930, 1940, and 1950 censuses. Supersedes *Boletín informativo*, no. 3, which is out of print.

6293. Paraguay. Dirección General de Estadística y Censos. Censo nacional de población y viviendas, 28 de octubre de 1950. Boletín informativo. No. 1-11. Asunción, 1953-1954.

No. 1, Departamento de Concepcion; no. 2, Departamento de San Pedro; no. 3, Departamento de Las Cordilleras; no. 4, Departamento de Guaira; no. 5, Departamento de Caaguazu; no. 6, Departamento de Caazapa; no. 7, Departamento VII, Itapua; no. 8, Departamento VIII, Misiones; no. 9, Departamento IX, Paraguari; no. 10, Departamentos XIV, Pte. Hayes; XV,

Boqueron, y XVI, Olimpo; no. 11, Ciudad de Asuncion. Data on urban-rural distribution, place of birth, citizenship, civil status, language; literacy, educational level, school attendance; economically active and inactive population, occupation and industry group, population dependent on agriculture; households; housing.

6294. Perú. Dirección Nacional de Estadística. Censo nacional de población y ocupación, 1940. Lima, 1944-1949. 9 v.: V. 1, Resúmenes generales, 1944, cc, 673 p.; v. 2-9, Provincia de . . . .

6295. Surinam. Welvaartsfonds Suriname. Tweede algemeene volkstelling Suriname 1950. De eigenlijke volkstelling. Serie A. Aantal, landaard en geslacht, geographische spreiding, leeftijdsopbouw en herkomst der getelde woonbevolking. 1954-
Being issued in parts. The second general census of Surinam, 1950; series A, on number, origin, sex, geographical distribution, and age composition of the resident population.

6296. Trinidad. Census Office. Census, colony of Trinidad and Tobago, 1946. Port-of-Spain, 1948. 616 p.

6297. ─────. Colony of Trinidad and Tobago census album containing a brief geographical, historical and economic review of the Colony of Trinidad and Tobago with meteorological observations, vital, trade and other statistics and 75 maps based on the 1946 census. Port-of-Spain, 1948. 114 p.

6298. United States. Bureau of the Census. Census of housing: 1950. (Taken as part of the seventeenth decennial census of the United States). V. 1. General characteristics. Part 7. Alaska, Hawaii, Puerto Rico, Virgin Islands of U. S. Washington, 1953. Various pagings.

6299. ─────. ─────. Census of population: 1950. V. 2. Characteristics of the population, number of inhabitants, general and detailed characteristics of the population. Parts 51-54. Territories and possessions. Washington, 1953. 591 p.
Part 53 is on Puerto Rico. Part 54 includes data on the Canal Zone and on the Virgin Islands of the U. S.

6300. Uruguay. Dirección General de Estadística. Censo general de la República en 1908 (An Est Ur, 1908, t. 2, v. 3, p. 755-1260).
No later census has been taken.

6301. Venezuela. Dirección General de Estadística. Oficina Central del Censo

Nacional. Octavo censo general de población, 26 de noviembre de 1950. Caracas, 1953-
A separate volume is being issued for each state and one for the Federal District.

6302. ─────. ─────. ─────. Octavo censo general de población (26 de noviembre de 1950). Edad y estado civil por entidades y distritos, y resumen nacional. Caracas, 1954. 138 p., tables. Age and civil status by sex.

6303. ─────. ─────. ─────. Octavo censo general de población, 26 de noviembre de 1950. Alfabetismo, asistencia escolar y nivel educacional. Caracas, 1955. 121 p.

6304. ─────. ─────. ─────. Octavo censo general de población, 26 de noviembre de 1950. Población urbana y rural y lugar de nacimiento. Caracas, 1955. 148 p.

6305. ─────. ─────. ─────. Octavo censo general de población (26 de noviembre de 1950). Resultados generales por entidades, distritos y municipios. Caracas, 1954. 66 p., tables.
Population by sex for states, state capitals, districts, and *municipios*, as well as urban and rural population of states, and some summary comparative data from earlier censuses.

BIBLIOGRAPHIES

6306. United Nations. Statistical Office. Bibliography of recent official demographic statistics. N. Y., 1954. 80 p. (Statistical papers, series M, 18; ST/-STAT/SER.M/18).
Reprint from the *Demographic yearbook, 1953.* Citations to available official publications containing census and other demographic statistics for each area of the world. References are given to (a) the most recent published census returns, final or preliminary, and in selected instances to earlier censuses which represent more comprehensive coverage in the field of demography including population, occupation, and housing; (b) sources of periodic and other demographic statistics since 1920; and (c) life tables since 1900. Supplemented by bibliographies in the 1954 and 1955 editions of the *Demographic yearbook.*

6307. United States. Library of Congress. Census Library Project. Statistical bulletins; an annotated bibliography of the general statistical bulletins of major political subdivisions of the world. Prepared by Phyllis G. Carter. Washington, 1954. 93 p.
A companion to the item listed below. These bibliographies are limited to the general statis-

tical yearbooks and bulletins, usually issued by the national statistical offices, which have the function of providing a summary of all the important available recent statistics in their countries; i.e., statistical bulletins and yearbooks on specialized subjects are not included.

6308. ————. ————. ————.
Statistical yearbooks; an annotated bibliography of the general statistical yearbooks of major political subdivisions of the world. Prepared by Phyllis G. Carter. Washington, 1953. 123 p.
See also item above.

BIBLIOGRAPHIES, LISTS, AND INDEXES*

6400. Albanell MacColl, Norah (comp.). Bibliografía selecta sobre inmigración en la República Argentina. Washington, Pan American Union, Columbus Memorial Library (Bibliographic series, 40), 1953. 27 p.

6401. Anuario bibliográfico salvadoreño, 1951 (Anaqueles, 5. época, 3, mayo 1952-abril 1953, p. 89-106).

6402. Archila, Ricardo. Bibliografía médica venezolana. Contribución. 2. ed. Colaboradora especial: Sra. María T. de Guerra. Caracas, Editorial Bellas Artes, 1955. 1041 p.

6403. Argentina. Dirección General de Cultura. Boletín bibliográfico nacional, años 1952 y 1953. No. 31. B. A., 1954. xxviii, 216 p.

6404. ————. Ministerio de Agricultura y Ganadería. Secretaría General. Departamento de Bibliotecas. Catálogo centralizado de la Biblioteca Justicialista. B. A., 1955. 186 p. (Circular bibliográfica interna, 5).

6405. Biblioteca Almeida Cunha. Índice da *Revista do patrimônio histórico e artístico nacional* (números 1 a 10, 1937-1946). Recife, Brazil, 1954. 18 p. (Boletim, 1).

6406. Bio-bibliografía del R. P. Rubén Vargas Ugarte, S. J. (B Bibl, Lima, 24:1-4, 1955, 27 p.).

6407. Brazil. Biblioteca Nacional. Divisão de Obras Raras e Publicações. Boletim bibliográfico. V. 2, no. 2, 2. semestre 1952. Rio, 1953. 320 p.

6408. ————. Instituto Nacional do Livro. Bibliografia brasileira, 1942-1945. V. 1. A-I. Rio, 1953. 444 p.

6409. ————. ————. Bibliografia brasileira, 1953. Rio, 1954. 240 p.

6410. Castro de Morales, Lilia (comp.). Bibliografía de José Antonio Fernández de Castro. José Antonio Fernández de Castro por Salvador Bueno. Habana, Biblioteca Nacional, 1955. 48 p.

6411. ————. El libro en Cienfuegos. Catálogo de las obras relacionadas con Cienfuegos que se exhiben en la Biblioteca Nacional como homenaje al libro cubano. Con la colaboración del Ateneo de Cienfuegos. Habana, Biblioteca Nacional, 1954. 80 p.

6412. Chile. Biblioteca Nacional. Anuario de publicaciones periódicas chilenas. Santiago, 1953. 79 p.

6413. Colombia. Biblioteca Nacional. Primera exposición bibliográfica bolivariana con ocasión de cumplirse el 143° aniversario de la independencia de Venezuela. Preparada con la colaboración de la Embajada de Venezuela en Colombia. Bogotá, 1954. 240 p.

6414. ————. Contraloría General de la República. Consejo Técnico. Biblioteca. Catálogo de la sección Colombia. Bogotá, 1955. 26 p.

6415. Conover, Helen F. (comp.). Current national bibliographies. Washington, Library of Congress, General Reference and Bibliography Division, 1955. 132 p. "Latin America," p. 17-27.

6416. Costa Rica. Biblioteca Nacional. Boletín bibliográfico. Algunas de las publicaciones nacionales correspondientes al año 1952. San José, 1954. 28 p.

6417. Cuesta, Luisa (ed.). Catálogo de obras iberoamericanas y filipinas de la Biblioteca Nacional de Madrid. Madrid, Dirección General de Archivos y Bibliotecas, Servicio de Publicaciones, 1953. 322 p.

6418. Dardón Córdova, Gonzalo. Índice bibliográfico guatemalteco, 1952. Guatemala, Biblioteca Nacional, 1953? 50 p.

* Specialized bibliographies are listed in the appropriate sections.

An effort at a national annual bibliography, and as such, highly to be encouraged. Leaves a good deal to be desired in completeness of entries. Topically arranged entries without author index. [C. C. Griffin]

6419. ————— (comp.). Monografía bibliográfica de libros escritos por los catedráticos de la Facultad de Humanidades. Guatemala, 1953. 7 p.

6420. Díaz C., Miguel (comp.). Bibliografía de Honorato Vásquez. Cuenca, Ecuador, Casa de la Cultura Ecuatoriana, Núcleo del Azuay (Biblioteca ecuatoriana, 1), 1955. 187 p.

6421. Díaz Thomé, Hugo. Bibliografía ibérica y latinoamericana en las Islas Británicas de 1808 a 1833 (Estud Hist Am, p. 719-786).
Publications in England, 1808-1833, by Spanish and Latin Americans living there. [W. V. Scholes]

6422. El Salvador. Biblioteca Nacional. Anuario bibliográfico salvadoreño, 1952. San Salvador, 1954. 39 p.

6423. —————. —————. Bibliografía salvadoreña. Lista preliminar por autores. San Salvador, 1953? 430 p.
A pioneering effort, a copy of which has been made available to the Library of Congress by the Director of the National Library, San Salvador.

6424. Fúrlong, Guillermo. Historia y bibliografía de las primeras imprentas rioplatenses, 1700-1850. B. A., 1953-1955. T. 1, La imprenta en las reducciones del Paraguay, 1700-1727; la imprenta en Córdoba, 1765-1767; la imprenta en Buenos Aires, 1780-1784 (1953, Editorial Guarania, 596 p.); t. 2, La imprenta en Buenos Aires, 1785-1807 (1955, Librería del Plata, 596 p.).

6425. Giraldo Jaramillo, Gabriel. Apuntes para una bibliografía colombo-cubana (R Bib Nac, Habana, 2. serie, 4:1, enero-marzo 1953, p. 109-152).

6426. ————— (comp.). Bibliografía de bibliografías colombianas. Bogotá, Biblioteca Nacional, 1954. 192 p.

6427. Gropp, Arthur E. (comp.). Union list of Latin American newspapers in libraries in the United States. Washington, Pan American Union, Department of Cultural Affairs (Bibliographic series, 39), 1953. 235 p.

6428. Guatemala. Tipografía Nacional. Tipografía Nacional. Guatemala, enero de 1954. 71 p.
Quarterly.

6429. Iguíniz, Juan B. El éxodo de documentos y libros mexicanos al extranjero (B Bib Nac, México, 4:3, julio-sept. 1953, p. 3-27).

6430. Instituto Brasileiro de Bibliografia e Documentação. Bibliografia brasileira de ciências sociais (continuação da Bibliografia econômico-social). Rio. V. 1, no. 1, 1954.

6431. Jaramillo, Miguel Ángel (comp.). Índice bibliográfico de las revistas de la Biblioteca Jaramillo de Escritos Nacionales. Cuenca, Ecuador, Casa de la Cultura Ecuatoriana, Núcleo del Azuay, 1953. 180 p.

6432. Lugo Lovatón, Ramón. Periódicos dominicanos en el Archivo General de la Nación. Ciudad Trujillo, Montalvo, 1953. 49 p.

6433. Manrique de Lara, Juana, and Guadalupe Monroy Baigén (comps.). Seudónimos, anagramas e iniciales de escritores mexicanos, antiguos y modernos. 2 ed. México, Secretaría de Educación, Departamento de Divulgación, 1954. 115 p.

6434. Metford, J. C. J. British contributions to Spanish and Spanish-American studies. London, Longmans, Green, 1950. 86 p.
A competent bibliographical survey. [C. C. Griffin]

6435. Moliner, Israel M. (comp.). Índice cronológico de la prensa en Matanzas. Matanzas, Cuba, 1955. 18 p.

6436. Moncayo de Monge Germania (Comp.). Índice general de la revista sur, Argentina, 1931-1954. Washington, Unión Panamericana, Biblioteca Conmemorativa de Colón (Bibliographic series, 46), 1955. 259 p.
"La recopilación de este índice originalmente fué iniciada por Geraldine McCrum y Pauline Leiner bajo la dirección del Profesor Ángel Flores en Queens College, en Flushing, estado de Nueva York."

6437. Morales Padrón, Francisco (ed.). Historiografía y bibliografía americanista, 1954. Sevilla, Escuela de Estudios Hispano-Americanos, 1956. 258 p. (Tirada

aparte del *Anuario de estudios americanos*, 11).
First of a proposed separate series, placing in one volume the bibliographical portions of the *Anuario*. This contains two articles, a series of bibliographies on the 1954 production on Latin America in the Antilles, Argentina, Bolivia, Colombia, Mexico, Peru, Sweden, Venezuela, and Spain, as well as reviews. An important and useful tool for all fields. [H. F. Cline]

6438. Núñez González, Ana Rosa. La vida bibliográfica de Don Antonio Bachiller y Morales. Habana, Librería Martí, 1955. 20 p.

6439. Pan American Union. Columbus Memorial Library. Índice de la *Revista iberoamericana* (mayo 1939 a enero 1950). Memorias del Congreso Internacional de Catedráticos de Literatura Iberoamericana (primera 1938 al cuarto 1949). Washington, 1954. 51 p. (Bibliographic series, 42).

6440. ―――. ―――. Índice general de *Atenea*, revista mensual de ciencias, letras y artes publicada por la Universidad de Concepción (Chile), 1924-1950. Washington, 1955. 205 p. (Bibliographic series, 44).

6441. Peraza Sarausa, Fermín (comp.). Bibliografía martiana, 1853-1953. Edición del centenario. Habana, Comisión Nacional Organizadora de los Actos y Ediciones del Centenario y del Monumento de Martí, 1954. 692 p.

6442. ―――. Bibliografía martiana, 1953. Habana, Biblioteca Municipal de la Habana (Serie C: Guías bibliográficas, 22), 1955. 35 p.

6443. Perú. Biblioteca Nacional. Anuario bibliográfico peruano de 1949-1950. Preparado bajo la dirección de Alberto Tauro. Lima, 1954. 427 p. (Ediciones, 9).
Books and pamphlets on or about Peru, published in or out of the country. [Ed.]

6444. Sánchez, Manuel Segundo. Bibliografía de índices bibliográficos relativos a Venezuela (Viejo y Raro, 1, marzo 1955, p. 19-23; 2, mayo, p. 21-28; 3, julio 1955, p. 37-46).
133 entries, arranged alphabetically by compiler, with a subject index at the end. [Ed.]

6445. Sindicato Nacional das Emprêsas Editôras de Livros e Publicações Culturais. Boletim bibliográfico brasileiro. V. 1, no. 1-2, nov. 1952-fev. 1953.
Bimonthly classified list of current Brazilian publications.

6446. Spell, Lota M. Research materials for the study of Latin America at the University of Texas. Austin, University of Texas Press (Latin American studies, 14), 1954. 107 p., facsms.

6447. Suárez, Víctor M. Bibliografía yucateca de 1951 (Cuad Estud Yucatecos, 1, primavera 1953, p. 85-101).

6448. Torre Revello, José. Bibliografía de las Islas Malvinas. Obras, mapas y documentos. B. A., Universidad de Buenos Aires, Instituto de Investigaciones Históricas (Publ., 99), 1953. 260 p., plans.
This massive bibliography contains 1702 entries of materials on the Falklands from discovery to 1950. All items have been seen by Professor Torre Revello, who comments on the significance of many items, such as Julius Goebel's work. There are indexes of names of authors, names of ships, and geographical place names. [B. Wood]

6449. Trotier, Arnold H., and Marian Harman (comps.). Doctoral dissertations accepted by American universities, 1952-1953. No. 20. Compiled for Association of Research Libraries. N. Y., H. W. Wilson Co., 1953. 305 p.

6450. United Nations Educational, Scientific and Cultural Organization. UNESCO bulletin for libraries. Paris. V. 7, no. 11-12, Nov.-Dec. 1953. 68 p.
Special issue devoted to a "Guide to national bibliographical centers." Entries for all the American republics except Bolivia, Honduras, Panama, and Paraguay. [Ed.]

6451. ―――. Misión de Asistencia Técnica. Centro de Documentación Científica, Técnica y Económica. Catálogo de las revistas científicas, técnicas y económicas publicadas en Uruguay desde 1850. Montevideo, Biblioteca Nacional, 1954. 29 p.

6452. Universidad de Chile. Biblioteca Central. Centro de Información Bibliográfica. Anales de la Universidad de Chile. Índice general, 1843-1950. Índice por autores. Santiago, 1954. 283 p.

6453. Universidade de São Paulo. Índice bibliográfico das publicações da Universidade de São Paulo. São Paulo, 1953. V. 1, fasc. 2, 156 p.; v. 1, fasc. 4, 73 p.; v. 1, fasc. 8, 41 p.
Fascsicules 1 and 9 of v. 1 appeared in 1952.

6454. Velázquez, Gonzalo (comp.). Anuario bibliográfico puertorriqueño. Índice alfabético de libros, folletos, revistas y periódicos publicados en Puerto Rico durante 1952. Río Piedras, Puerto Rico, Editorial Universitaria, 1954. 199 p.

6455. Wilgus, A. Curtis (comp.). Doors to Latin America. Gainesville, Fla., Inter-American Bibliographical and Library Association (University of Florida Library). V. 1, no. 1, January 1954.

BIOGRAPHY

6500. Anzola, David. Barquisimetanos ilustres. Edición conmemorativa del IV centenario de la ciudad de Barquisimeto. Caracas, Ávila Gráfica (Biblioteca de cultura larense, 9), 1952. 121 p.
Short eulogies of six prominent figures in the history of Barquisimeto in the 19th and 20th centuries. Scientific, clerical, and military professions are represented. [C. Gibson]

6501. Briceño-Iragorry, Mario. Obras selectas. Caracas, Edime, 1954. 1103 p.
The best works of Briceño-Iragorry, a frequent prize-winner in the field of Venezuelan biography. [A. Flores]

6502. Cardoso, Leontina Licinio. Licinio Cardoso. Seu pensamento, sua obra, sua vida. 2. ed. revista e aumentada. Rio, Souza, 1952.
The life of the remarkable philosopher, sociologist, and mathematician, by his daughter. Originally written to commemorate the first centenary of his birth (Rio Grande do Sul, 1852). [M. Cardozo]

6503. Femmes haïtiennes. Port-au-Prince, Ligue Feminine d'Action Sociale (Coll. du tricinquantenaire de l'Indépendance d'Haïti), 1953. 263 p.
Short biographical sketches of distinguished Haitian women and a concluding chapter by Jeanne G. Sylvain on "Les œuvres sociales." There is a brilliant preface by Dantès Bellegarde and an introduction by Marie Thérèse Colimon, Secretary General of the Feminine League for Social Action. [M. Cook]

6504. Goff, Frederick R. Henry Harrisse: Americanist (R Interam Bibl, 3:1, enero-abril 1953, p. 3-10).
Contains quotations from one of Harrisse's letters. [C. C. Griffin]

6505. Luzian, Juan. Richard Black Newton, un caballero de Chascomús. Chascomús, Argentina, Editorial del Lago, 1953. 51 p.
Slight sketch of the life of an Englishman who pioneered in the introduction of purebred sheep in Argentina. [C. C. Griffin]

6506. Moreno, Daniel. Colima y sus gobernadores. Un siglo de historia política. México, Ediciones Studium, 1953. 108 p.
Very brief biographical studies of every governor of Colima. [W. V. Scholes]

6507. Moreno, Pablo C. Galería heroica de México. Torreón, Coahuila, México, Editorial Guerrero, 1954. 466 p., illus.
Very brief sketch of famous Mexicans. [W. V. Scholes]

6508. Parr, Charles McKew. So noble a captain. The life and times of Ferdinand Magellan. N. Y., Crowell, 1953. 253 p.
A literary biography of Magellan "written in compliance to do justice to the memory of . . . Magellan." The book is not documented but is based on extensive reading in both primary and secondary sources. [G. Boehrer]

DESCRIPTION AND TRAVEL

6600. American Automobile Association. International Travel Department. Touring Central and South America. N. Y., 1953. 173 p., illus.
A guide for the ingenuous tourist. [R. E. Crist]

6601. Barranquilla, José Agustín de. Así es la Guajira. Itinerario de un misionero capuchino. 2. ed. Bogotá, Imprenta Nacional, 1953. 237 p., illus.
A well-illustrated travel book in which many significant facts about this little-known region are brought to light. The laws and customs of the people are treated at length, and the present and future work of the Church is dealt with. Unfortunately, this ethnic and cultural unit is cut by the international frontier between Venezuela and Colombia. [R. E. Crist]

6602. Bedford, Sybille. The sudden view. A Mexican journey. London, Victor Gollancz, 1953. 288 p.
A funny book of erroneous impressions. [A. Flores]

6603. Bellegarde, Dantès. Haïti et son peuple. Paris, Nouvelles Éditions Latines, 1953. 121 p.
This is a magnificent brief introduction to Haiti, designed to attract and to inform European tourists. In seven delightful chapters, M. Bellegarde discusses the island, its population, economic activity, religion, literature, language, folklore, education, Franco-Haitian relations, and Haiti's long record of international cooperation dating back to Miranda and Bolívar. Once again the distinguished statesman, educator, and author—now in his 79th year—has rendered an invaluable service to his beloved *patrie*. [M. Cook]

6604. Brivio, Ernesto T. Cuba, isla de las maravillas. 2. ed. Habana, Pedro Fernández, 1953. 329 p., illus.
A picture book primarily. Text in Spanish, English, and French. [R. McNicoll]

6605. **Bruce, James.** Those perplexing Argentines. N. Y., Longmans, Green, 1953. 362 p.
Interesting discussion of national prejudices and attitudes as seen by an American ambassador who is generally sympathetic. [C. C. Griffin]

6606. **Cajigas Langner, Alberto.** Monografía de Tehuantepec. 1. ed. Con cuatro tricromías y 26 grabados originales. México, Imp. M. L. Sánchez, 1954. 164 p., illus.
Generally thin. Contains one interesting document on Tehuantepec in 1580. [C. C. Griffin]

6607. **Cave, Hugh Barnett.** Haiti, highroad to adventure. With photographs by the author. N. Y., Holt, 1952. 306 p., illus.
An interesting account of experiences of an American family in Haiti. Excellent for prospective tourists. [M. Cook]

6608. **Clissold, Stephen.** Chilean scrapbook. N. Y., Frederick A. Praeger, 1952. 315 p., illus.
A first-rate general descriptive work which includes a certain amount of historical information along with geographical and cultural data. [C. C. Griffin]

6609. **De Gamez, Tana,** and **Arthur R. Pastore.** Mexico and Cuba on your own. N. Y., Cortina, 1954. 390 p.
A guidebook which can be recommended because it contains a good deal of background on the history and culture of the area covered. [C. C. Griffin]

6610. **Del Villar, Mary,** and **Fred Del Villar.** Where the strange roads go down. N. Y., Macmillan, 1953. 244 p., illus.
A rather unusual travel book. An American couple walked from Patzcuaro to the Pacific. Vivid description of area off the beaten track. [C. C. Griffin]

6611. **Ford, Norman D.** The fiesta lands. Through Cuba, Mexico, Guatemala, and other lands along the Pan-American Highway on a shoestring. What to see. Where to stay, eat and shop. How to say it in Spanish. Greenlawn, N. Y., Harian Publications, 1953. 164 p., illus.
The title is self-explanatory. [R. E. Crist]

6612. **Haïti.** Sur la route du progrès. Port-au-Prince, Deschamps, 1954. Unpaged, illus.
Magnificent photographs and occasional texts showing progress realized by present régime. [M. Cook]

6613. **Hancock, Ralph; Ray Haller; Mike McMahan;** and **Frank Alvarado.** Baja California. Hunting, fishing and travel in Lower California, Mexico. Los Angeles, Calif., Academy Publishers, 1953. 179 p., illus.
The narration of a leisurely motor trip the length of the Peninsula of Lower California, written with zest and much *joie de vivre*. Illustrations are excellent. [R. E. Crist]

6614. **Helfritz, Hans.** Mexiko und Mittelamerika. Berlin, Safari-Verlag, 1954. 737 p., illus. & map.
Enjoyable survey of Mexico and Central America. [W. V. Scholes]

6615. **Linke, Lilo.** Ecuador, country of contrasts. London, Royal Institute of International Affairs, 1954. 173 p.
An excellent brief handbook. [C. C. Griffin]

6616. **Moreno, Daniel A.** (and others). Collimán. T. 2. Literatura y biografía de Colima. México, Studium, 1953. 132 p., illus.
A combined Who's Who, statistical summary, and album, of a remote and little-known Mexican state, Colima. The second of three projected volumes; the first appeared in 1952 (see *HLAS, no. 18, 1952,* item 3360). [A. Flores]

6617. **Ortiz, Alicia.** Amanecer en Bolivia. B. A., Hemisferio, 1953. 198 p.
Quite a good series of journalistic and impressionistic sketches of Bolivia since the recent nationalist revolution. By a sensitive and sympathetic Argentine woman. [C. C. Griffin]

6618. **Osborne, Harold.** Bolivia. A land divided. London, Royal Institute of International Affairs, 1954. 144 p.
The author has had long experience in Bolivia and knows the country well. A sound general survey with especially good material on the Beni region. Includes bibliography and index. [C. C. Griffin]

6619. **Osorio Gómez, Juan A.** Salcedo; o, Una provincia en la historia. Ciudad Trujillo, Imprenta San Francisco de Papelera Industrial Dominicana, 1952. 188 p.
Data, rather than a history, on the Dominican province of Salcedo. [R. McNicoll]

6620. **Regler, Gustav.** Verwunschenes Land Mexiko. München, Paul List Verlag (List-Bücher, 37), 1954. 210 p.
Observant, impressionistic, and literary description of Mexico and of the writer's experiences during his recent 12 years of residence there. Anecdotes revelatory of Mexican popular and official attitudes, effectively told by a modern German novelist who came to know his subject well. [C. Gibson]

6621. **Roberts, W. Adolphe.** Havana. The portrait of a city. N. Y., Coward-McCann, 1953. 282 p., illus.
An excellent work, like most from the same pen. Intelligent interpretation leagues beyond

the usual run of travel books, without attempting to attain the formal field of history or sociology. [R. McNicoll]

6622. Rodman, Selden. Haiti: the black republic. The complete story and guide. N. Y., Devin-Adair, 1954. 168 p.
A rewarding book for tourists who do not take its ambitious subtitle too seriously. Beautifully illustrated. [M. Cook]

6623. Salmon, Ross. Jungle cowboy. London, Hodder and Stoughton, 1953. 191 p., illus.
A straightforward and honest account of life on British-owned cattle ranches near Valencia, Venezuela, and Barranquilla, Colombia, by a young Englishman. [C. C. Griffin]

6624. Schenck, Fr. von. Viajes por Antioquia en el año de 1880. Bogotá, Banco de la República (Archivo de la economía nacional, 9), 1953. 76 p., maps.
A translation from the German of this travel classic by a keen observer. During the past 75 years material progress in Antioquia has been great indeed. Travellers were so few that Cartago, a rural village of 3000 inhabitants, could boast of neither hotel nor boarding house. [R. E. Crist]

6625. Snow, Sebastian. My Amazon adventure. London, Odhams Press, 1953. 224 p.
The author, a young Englishman, walked, rode, and rafted from the headwaters of the Marañon to Iquitos. Very interesting and valuable down-to-earth record of people and places in the Peruvian *montaña*. [C. C. Griffin]

6626. Tariffi, Terzo, and Natalia Rosi de Tariffi. Caracas. Guía histórico-artística e indicador general. Caracas, Editorial Nueva Venezuela, 1953? 366 p., illus.
A guide for the discerning tourist. [R. E. Crist]

6627. Zavala Paz, José. Bocetos michoacanos. México, Tall. Gráf. de la Nación, 1953. 157 p., illus.
Excellent photographs: architecture and landscape. [C. C. Griffin]

OTHER TOPICS

6700. Amado, Gilberto. Sabor do Brasil. Rio, Edições O Cruzeiro, 1953. 138 p.
A collection of charming essays on contemporary Brazil, with some treatment of the early 19th century. These are followed by interviews with Amado. [G. Boehrer]

6701. Babini, José. La evolución del pensamiento científico en la Argentina. B. A., La Fragua, 1954. 249 p., illus.
Brings together a good deal of data which is generally known but fails to make any new contribution to the subject. [C. C. Griffin]

6702. Diffusion haïtienne, 1804-1954. T. 1. Port-au-Prince, Held, 1954. 325 p., illus.
Various aspects of Haitian life are treated in this item: geography, history, education, folklore, sports, religion, etc. Another de luxe edition, lavishly illustrated. [M. Cook]

6703. Encinas, Luis. Progreso y problemas de México. México, Stylo, 1954. 284 p.
A survey of contemporary Mexican problems from the point of view of the official revolutionary party line. [C. C. Griffin]

6704. Fraser, Ronald. Latin America: a personal survey. London, Hutchinson, 1953. 239 p.
A book that shows real insight into many important problems and aspects of Latin America. [C. C. Griffin]

6705. Galbraith, W. O. Colombia, a general survey. London, N. Y., Royal Institute of International Affairs, 1953. 140 p., maps.
A survey of the historical, institutional, and economic factors operative in the modern Colombian scene. [R. E. Crist]

6706. Gallegos, Rómulo. Una posición en la vida. México, Ediciones Humanismo, 1954. 560 p.
A collection of essays and speeches of the celebrated Venezuelan author and politician. [C. C. Griffin]

6707. Gheerbrant, Alain. Journey to the Far Amazon. An expedition into unknown territory. Trans. by Edward Fitzgerald. N. Y., Simon and Schuster, 1954. 353 p., illus.
This volume on explorations has an authentic feel. Descriptions of tropical rain forests are unsurpassed. The volume teems with ethnological data. The reviewer withdrew the book intending to read only the section dealing with Colombia, but his interest was held to the very last page. [R. E. Crist]

6708. González Ruiz, Felipe. Evolución de la cultura en América. Estudios de iniciación. Madrid, Sapientia, 1953. 592 p., illus.
An ambitious elaborate attempt to describe the evolution of culture in America from the Spanish Catholic point of view. Badly organized, based on haphazardly chosen miscellaneous sources, unreliable and confused. [C. C. Griffin]

6709. Haïti. Institut Haïtien de Statistique. Bulletin trimestriel de statistique. No. 10, sept. 1953 (Coll. du cent-cinquantenaire). 231 p.
One of the mosts useful publications of recent years is the quarterly issued by the Institut Haïtien de Statistique (26, rue des Casernes, Port-au-Prince). This special number is in three parts: a statistical panorama, statistical tables, and results of the 1950 census (Department of the West). [M. Cook]

6710. Hilton, Ronald (ed.). Handbook of Hispanic source materials and research organizations in the United States. 2d. ed. Stanford, Calif., Stanford University Press, 1956. 448 p.

First published in 1942, the *Handbook* is a standard reference work long difficult to obtain. This second edition in near-print form brings the material to about Dec. 31, 1955. Extensive revisions appear. The revised version is an essential item for individual investigators and libraries. Its arrangement is the same as described for the first edition, in *HLAS, no 8, 1942,* item 41. [H. F. Cline]

6711. Hyppolite, Michelson Paul. Une étude sur le folklore haïtien. Port-au-Prince, Imp. de l'État, 1954. 53 p.

A lecture delivered on Nov. 14, 1952, for the Alliance Française of Kingston, Jamaica. An introduction to *vodun* and to its manifestations in Haitian history, folklore, and life. A glossary of Creole terms and a brief bibliography are included. [M. Cook]

6712. Instituto Hans Staden. Staden-Jahrbuch. Beiträge zur Brasilkunde. Band 1. São Paulo, 1953. 160 p.

A new publication designed to portray Brazilian life to the German-speaking public. This issue includes 11 articles in the fields of anthropology, biography, literature, economics, history, and on São Paulo. Some were translated from the Portuguese. [G. Boehrer]

6713. International Colloquium on Luso-Brazilian Studies, Washington, Oct. 15-20, 1950. Proceedings of the . . . under the auspices of the Library of Congress and Vanderbilt University. Nashville, Tenn., Vanderbilt University Press, 1953. 335 p.

Contributions in English or Portuguese to sessions on cultural anthropology, linguistics, fine arts, literature, instruments of scholarship, history, and the development of Brazilian and Portuguese studies in the U. S. in 1920-1950. [Ed.]

6714. Livermore, H. V., and W. J. Entwistle (eds.). Portugal and Brazil. An introduction. Oxford, Clarendon Press, 1953. 418 p.

A collection of essays in honor of Edgar Prestage and Aubrey F. G. Bell, which cover Portugal, her empire, and Brazil. The Brazilian section, smaller than the Portuguese, is nonetheless a fine synthesis of Brazilian life. The contributors are mostly British. The topics covered are land and people, history, religion, institutions, literature, and art. [G. Boehrer]

6715. Lobato Filho, João Bernardo. Fronteiras sudoeste. Rio, Pongetti, 1953. 241 p.

A potpourri of essays and speeches on the geography, history, etc. of Paraguay; on contemporary Brazilian politics; and on rubber and

the exploitation of the Amazon region. [G. Boehrer]

6716. Martí, José. La clara voz de México. Prólogo de Raúl Carrancá y Trujillo. Compilación y notas de Camilo Carrancá y Trujillo. México, Imprenta Universitaria, 1953. 397 p., illus.

Articles, on various subjects, published by Martí, 1875-1876, in Mexican papers and journals. [W. V. Scholes]

6717. Newbery, George Harkness. Pampa grass. The Argentine story as told by an American pioneer to his son, Diego Newbery . . . . B. A., Guarania, 1953. 244 p., illus.

Adventures in Argentina in the 1880's. Interesting data on life in the western pampa shortly after Roca's famous campaign. [C. C. Griffin]

6718. Ortega Ricaurte, Enrique. Heráldica nacional. Estudio documental. Bogotá, Banco de la República, 1954. 178 p.

Reproductions of flags and coats of arms of Colombia in color or black and white, with documentary studies of each one. [R. R. Hill]

6719. Otero, Gustavo Adolfo. La cultura y el periodismo en América. 2. ed., aumentada y rev. Quito, Liebmann, 1953. 545 p.

Essays on urban culture in Hispanic America followed by summaries of the history of journalism in each nation. [C. Gibson]

6720. Pan American Union. Américas. Washington. V. 5, no. 11, nov. 1953.

This issue honors the 150th anniversary of Haitian independence. It contains articles by Haitians Jules Blanchet and Léon Laleau, along with a piece by Jason Seley entitled "A sculptor in Haiti," and a remarkable analysis of Haitian verse by William Jay Smith. In the same issue, Charles Nutter writes of "America's biggest bargain," noting the role played by Haiti in the Louisiana Purchase. [M. Cook]

6721. Perspective of Brazil. An *Atlantic monthly* supplement. N. Y., Intercultural Publications, Inc., 1956. 73 p., illus., map.

Also included in *The Atlantic monthly,* 197:2, Feb. 1956. Fifth in a series of anthologies prepared by Intercultural Publications (established by the Ford Foundation in 1952) and published in cooperation with *The Atlantic monthly.* A sampling of the work of contemporary Brazilian writers, artists, and architects in English translation. [Ed.]

6722. Revert, Eugène. Les Antilles. Paris, Armand Colin (Coll. Armand Colin, 288), 1954. 220 p.

A brief, well-organized survey from a French viewpoint. The area as a whole and prospects for international organization. [C. C. Griffin]

6723. Schurz, William Lytle. This New World. The civilization of Latin America. N. Y., 1954. 429 p.

This is the work of a mature scholar who has lived many years in Latin America, who is a keen observer of physical and cultural features, and who is capable of writing his material in a fascinating style. There is a summary chapter on the physical background and then the author turns the spotlight on the characters who have acted out the Latin American drama. The chapters on the role of the Negro and of the more modern foreigner in Latin America are especially penetrating. Both these elements have made substantial contributions to their countries, and few Latin American leaders question the net worth as ingredients in the national societies of the African and recent European contingents. It is a tribute to the erudition and competence of the author that he has been able to treat in such a few pages a subject so extensive spatially and chronologically. [R. E. Crist]

6724. Skeaping, John. The big tree of Mexico. Bloomington, Ind., Indiana University Press, 1953. 234 p., illus.

A British sculptor's account of how he worked with his fellow craftsmen, the Indian potters of Oaxaca, and came to see their point of view,

while recuperating from a serious operation. This is a vivid picture of some of the fascinating facets of the Indian world—habits of daily life, fiestas, inter-village trips in beat-up buses, drinking bouts, and so on—even though one may disagree with some of the author's sociological judgments. [R. E. Crist]

6725. Solari, Manuel Horacio. Historia de la cultura argentina. 2. ed. B. A., Ateneo, 1954. 345 p.

A general survey which gives very little attention to the 20th century and is of little value except as a general introduction to the subject. [C. C. Griffin]

6726. Universidade da Bahia. Faculdade de Filosofia. Arquivos da Universidade da Bahia. Salvador, Brasil. V. 1, 1942-1952; v. 2, 1953; v. 3, 1954.

In its first issue this new review contained articles in various fields. While still true in subsequent numbers, heavy emphasis has been placed on psychology and philosophy. [G. Boehrer]

Key to Periodical and
Other Title Abbreviations

A Am Ac Pol Soc Sci...The Annals of the American Academy of Political and Social Science. Philadelphia, Pa.

A Assoc Am Geog.....Annals of the Association of American Geographers. Lancaster, Pa.

A Éc Soc Civ..........Annales, Économies, Sociétés, Civilisations. Paris, France.

A Inst Arte Am........Anales del Instituto de Arte Americano e Investigaciones Estéticas. Universidad de Buenos Aires. Buenos Aires, Argentina.

A Inst Étn Nac........Anales del Instituto Étnico Nacional. Ministerio de Asuntos Técnicos. Dirección Nacional de Migraciones. Buenos Aires, Argentina.

A Inst Inv Estét.......Anales del Instituto de Investigaciones Estéticas. Universidad Nacional Autónoma de México. México, D. F., México.

A Inst Nac Antr Hist...Anales del Instituto Nacional de Antropología e Historia. México, D. F., México.

A Midi...............Annales du Midi. Universités de Toulouse et de Bordeaux. Fédération Historique du Sud-Ouest. Fédération des Sociétés Academiques e Savants Languedoc-Pyrénées-Gascogne. Toulouse, France.

A Mus Hist Nat.......Anales del Museo de Historia Natural. Montevideo, Uruguay.

A Mus Nac...........Anales del Museo Nacional David J. Guzmán. San Salvador, El Salvador.

A Soc Geog Hist Guat..Anales de la Sociedad de Geografía e Historia de Guatemala. Guatemala, Guatemala.

A U Cent Ven........Anales de la Universidad Central de Venezuela. Caracas, Venezuela.

A U Ch..............Anales de la Universidad de Chile. Santiago, Chile.

A U Hispalense........Anales de la Universidad Hispalense. Sevilla, Spain.

A U San Marcos......Anales de la Universidad Nacional Mayor de San Marcos. Lima, Perú.

A U Sto Domingo......Anales de la Universidad de Santo Domingo. Ciudad Trujillo, Dominican Republic.

Ábside ....Ábside. México, D. F., México.

Acta Cien Ven........Acta Científica Venezolana. Asociación Venezolana para el Avance de la Ciencia. Caracas, Venezuela.

Acta Méd Ven........Acta Médica Venezolana. Colegio de Médicos del Distrito Federal y Seccional de Medicina de la Asociación Venezolana para el Avance de la Ciencia. Caracas, Venezuela.

Acta Trop...........Acta Tropica. Zeitschrift für Tropenwissenschaften und Tropenmedezin. Review of Tropical Science and Tropical Medicine. Basel, Switzerland.

Afr Aff..............African Affairs. Royal African Society. London, England.

Agr Hist.............Agricultural History. Agricultural History Society. Washington, D. C.

Alma L..............Alma Latina. San Juan, Puerto Rico.

Am Anthr............American Anthropologist. Organ of the Central States Branch of the American Anthropological Association and other societies. New York, N. Y.

Am Antiq............American Antiquity. The Society for American Archaeology. Menasha, Wisconsin.

Am Ec R............American Economic Review. Evanston, Ill.
Am Hist R............The American Historical Review. New York, N. Y.
Am Indíg............América Indígena. Instituto Indigenista Interamericano. México, D. F., México.
Am J Ec Sociol........American Journal of Economics and Sociology. Robert Scholkenvach Foundation. New York, N. Y.
Am J Phys Anthr......American Journal of Physical Anthropology. American Association of Physical Anthropologists. Philadelphia, Pa.
Am J Sociol...........The American Journal of Sociology. The University of Chicago Press. Chicago, Ill.
Am Sociol R..........American Sociological Review. American Sociological Society. Pittsburg, Pa.
Am Sp...............American Speech. Columbia University Press. New York, N. Y.
Americas, Franciscan Hist   The Americas. Academy of American Franciscan History. Washington, D. C.
Américas, PAU........Américas. Pan American Union. Washington, D. C.
An Estud Am.........Anuario de Estudios Americanos. Escuela de Estudios Hispano-Americanos de la Universidad de Sevilla. Sevilla, Spain.
An Geog Estado Rio...Anuário Geográfico do Estado do Rio de Janeiro. Conselho Nacional de Geografia. Instituto Brasileiro de Geografia e Estatística. Niteroi, Brazil.
An Mus Incon.........Anuário do Museu da Inconfidência. Ouro Preto, Brazil.
Anaqueles ....Anaqueles. Biblioteca Nacional. San Salvador, El Salvador.
Anhembi ....Anhembi. São Paulo, Brazil.
Anthr Q..............Anthropological Quarterly. Publication of the Catholic Anthropological Conference. Catholic University of America. Washington, D. C.
Anthropologie ....L'Anthropologie. Editée avec le concours du Centre National de la Recherche Scientifique. Paris, France.
Anthropos ....Anthropos. Fribourg, Switzerland.
Antiquity ....Antiquity. Gloucester, England.
Antr Hist Guat........Antropología e Historia de Guatemala. Instituto de Antropología e Historia de Guatemala. Guatemala, Guatemala.
Arch Antr Etn.........Archivio per l'Antropologia e la Etnologia. Societa Italiana de Antropologia. Firenze, Italy.
Arch Ethnos..........Archivos Ethnos. Buenos Aires, Argentina.
Arch Hist Soc Iesu.....Archivum Historicum Societatis Iesu. Roma, Italy.
Arch Ib Am...........Archivo Ibero-Americano. Madrid, Spain.
Arch Iberoam Hist Med.Archivos Iberoamericanos de Historia de la Medicina. Instituto Arnaldo de Vilanova. Consejo Superior de Investigaciones Científicas. Madrid, Spain.
Arch Ven Folk........Archivos Venezolanos de Folklore. Universidad Central de Venezuela. Facultad de Filosofía y Letras. Caracas, Venezuela.
Archaeology ....Archaeology. Archaeological Institute of America. Cambridge, Mass.
Archiv für Völkerkunde.Museum für Völkerkunde. Wien, Austria.
Archivum ....Archivum. Conseil International des Archives. Paris, France.
Armas Let............Armas y Letras. Universidad de Nuevo León. Monterrey, México.
Arq Biol Tec.........Arquivos de Biologia e Tecnologia. Instituto de Biologia e Pesquisas Tecnológicas. Curitiba, Brazil.
Arq Br Psico.........Arquivos Brasileiros de Psicotécnica. Rio de Janeiro, Brazil.
Arqué ....Arqué. Córdoba, Argentina.
Arquivos, Recife.......Arquivos. Prefeitura Municipal do Recife. Diretoria de Documentação e Cultura. Recife, Brazil.
Art B...............Art Bulletin. The College of Art Association of America. New York, N. Y.
Atenea ....Atenea. Universidad de Concepción. Concepción, Chile.
Atlante ....Atlante. Hispanic and Luso-Brazilian Councils. London, England.

B Ac Ch Hist..........Boletín de la Academia Chilena de la Historia. Santiago, Chile.
B Ac Dom Lengua.....Boletín de la Academia Dominicana de la Lengua. Ciudad Trujillo, Dominican Republic.
B Ac Hist Valle Cauca..Boletín de la Academia de Historia del Valle de Cauca. Cali, Colombia.

B Ac Nac Hist, B A....Boletín de la Academia Nacional de la Historia. Buenos Aires, Argentina.
B Ac Nac Hist, Quito...Boletín de la Academia Nacional de Historia. Quito, Ecuador.
B Arch Gen Chiapas...Boletín. Archivo General de Chiapas. Tuxtla Gutiérrez, México.
B Arch Gen, Ciudad Trujillo   Boletín del Archivo General de la Nación. Ciudad Trujillo, Dominican Republic.
B Arch Gen, México....Boletín del Archivo General de la Nación. México, D. F., México.
B Arch Nac, Habana...Boletín del Archivo Nacional. Habana, Cuba.
B Ac Nac Hist, Caracas   Boletín de la Academia Nacional de la Historia. Caracas, Venezuela.
B Azuc Mex..........Boletín Azucarero Mexicano. Unión Nacional de Productores de Azúcar. México, D. F., México.
BBAA ....Boletín Bibliográfico de Antropología Americana. Instituto Panamericano de Geografía e Historia. México, D. F., México.
B Bib Nac, México....Boletín de la Biblioteca Nacional. Universidad Nacional Autónoma de México. México, D. F., México.
B Bibl, Lima..........Boletín Bibliográfico. Biblioteca Central. Universidad Mayor de San Marcos. Lima, Perú.
B Bibl S Hac Cr Púb..Boletín Bibliográfico de la Secretaría de Hacienda y Crédito Público. México, D. F., México.
B Carioca Geog.......Boletim Carioca de Geografia. Associação dos Geógrafos Brasileiros. Secção Regional do Rio de Janeiro. Rio de Janeiro, Brazil.
B CBAI..............Boletim da C. B. A. I. Comissão Brasileiro-Americana de Educação Industrial. Rio de Janeiro, Brazil.
B Cent Pesq Or Ed.....Boletim do Centro de Pesquisas e Orientação Educacionais. Rio de Janeiro (?), Brazil.
B Comis Nac Cub UNESCO   Boletín de la Comisión Nacional Cubana de la UNESCO. Habana, Cuba.
B Dept Est............Boletim do Departamento de Estatística. São Paulo, Brazil.
B Direc Gen Est.......Boletim de la Dirección General de Estadística. Guatemala, Guatemala.
B Est, Rio............Boletim Estatístico. Instituto Brasileiro de Geografia e Estatística. Conselho Nacional de Estatística. Rio de Janeiro, Brazil.
B Estud Espec.........Boletín de Estudios Especiales. Banco Nacional de Crédito Ejidal, S. A. México, D. F., México.
B Geog, Rio..........Boletim Geográfico. Instituto Brasileiro de Geografia e Estatística. Conselho Nacional de Geografia. Rio de Janeiro, Brazil.
B Hisp...............Bulletin Hispanique. Annales de la Faculté des Lettres de Bordeaux. Bordeaux, France.
B Hist Antig..........Boletín de Historia y Antigüedades. Academia Colombiana de Historia. Bogotá, Colombia.
B Hist Med...........Bulletin of the History of Medicine. Organ of the American Association of the History of Medicine and the Johns Hopkins Institute of the History of Medicine. The Johns Hopkins Press. Baltimore, Md.
B Indig..............Boletín Indigenista. Instituto Indigenista Interamericano. México, D. F., México.
B Indig Ven..........Boletín Indigenista Venezolano. Ministerio de Justicia. Comisión Indigenista. Caracas, Venezuela.
B Inf CAPES.........Boletim Informativo CAPES. Campanha Nacional de Aperfeiçoamento do Pessoal de Nivel Superior. Rio de Janeiro, Brazil.
B Inf Cient Nac.......Boletín de Informaciones Científicas Nacionales. Casa de la Cultura Ecuatoriana. Quito, Ecuador.
B Inst Antr..........Boletín del Instituto de Antropología. Universidad de Antioquia. Medellín, Colombia.
B Inst Fernán González. Boletín de la Institución Fernán González. Burgos, Spain.
B Inst Int Am Prot Infan   Boletín del Instituto Internacional Americano de Protección a la Infancia. Montevideo, Uruguay.
B Inst Intl Stat ....Bulletin de l'Institut International de Statistique. Roma, Italy.
B Inst Pesq Educacionais   Boletim do Instituto de Pesquisas Educacionais. Secretaria General de Educação e Cultura. Rio de Janeiro, Brazil.
B Inst Psicol..........Boletim do Instituto de Psicologia. Rio de Janeiro (?), Brazil.
B Junta Aux Jalis......Boletín de la Junta Auxiliar Jalisciense de la Sociedad Mexicana de Geografía y Estadística. Guadalajara, México.

B Mém Soc Anthr.....Bulletins et Mémoires de la Société d'Anthropologie de Paris. Paris, France.
B Mus Nac, Rio......Boletim do Museu Nacional. Ministério da Educação e Saúde. Rio de Janeiro, Brazil.
B Música y Artes Visuales   Boletín de Música y Artes Visuales. Unión Panamericana. Washington, D. C.
B Paulista Geog.......Boletim Paulista de Geografia. Associação dos Geógrafos Brasileiros. São Paulo, Brazil.
B Real Ac Hist........Boletín de la Real Academia de la Historia. Madrid, Spain.
B Soc Antr Per........Boletín de la Sociedad para la Antropología Peruana. Lima, Perú.
B Soc Chihua Estud Hist....Boletín de la Sociedad Chihuahuense de Estudios Históricos. Chihuahua, México.
B Soc Geog Hist Potosí   Boletín de la Sociedad Geográfica y de Historia "Potosí." Potosí, Bolivia.
B Soc Geog Sucre......Boletín de la Sociedad Geográfica Sucre. Revista de Geografía, Historia y Estadística. Sucre, Bolivia.
B Soc Mex Geog Est...Boletín de la Sociedad Mexicana de Geografía y Estadística. México, D. F., México.
B Soc Suisse Am......Société Suisse des Américanistes. Bulletin. Genève, Switzerland.
B Tex Archaeol Soc....Bulletin of the Texas Archaeological Society. Lubbock, Tex.
B Trim...............Boletín Trimestral. Banco de México, S. A. Departamento de Estudios Económicos. México, D. F., México.
B U Archaeol Soc......Bulletin of the University Archaeological Society. Brigham Young University. Provo, Utah.
B U Mus.............Bulletin of the University Museum. University of Pennsylvania. Philadelphia, Pa.
Bancos ....Bancos. México, D. F., México.
Belas Artes...........Belas Artes. Academia Nacional de Belas Artes. Lisboa, Portugal.
Berceo ....Berceo. Instituto de Estudios Riojanos. Consejo Superior de Investigaciones Científicas. Logroño, Spain.
Bolívar, Bogotá.......Bolívar. Ministerio de Educación Nacional de Colombia. Bogotá, Colombia.
Books Abroad.........Books Abroad. University of Oklahoma. Norman, Okla.
Br Arquit Cont.......Brasil: Arquitetura Contemporânea. Rio de Janeiro, Brazil.
Brotéria ....Brotéria. Lisboa, Portugal.

Cahiers d'Hist Mond....Cahiers d'Histoire Mondiale. Journal of World History. Cuadernos de Historia Mundial. Paris, France.
Cahiers d'Outre-Mer....Les Cahiers d'Outre-Mer. Institut de la France d'Outre-Mer. Bordeaux, France.
Calif Hist Soc Q......California Historical Society Quarterly. San Francisco, Calif.
Can Hist R...........The Canadian Historical Review. Canadian Historical Association. Toronto, Canada.
Carib Cont Trends.....The Caribbean: contemporary trends. A. Curtis Wilgus, editor. (See item 6455).
Carib Q..............Caribbean Quarterly. Port-of-Spain, Trinidad.
Carnegie Mag.........Carnegie Magazine. Carnegie Institute; Carnegie Library of Pittsburg; and Carnegie Institute of Technology. Pittsburg, Pa.
Ceiba ....Ceiba. Escuela Agrícola Panamericana. Tegucigalpa, Honduras.
Chron Min Colon......La Chronique des Mines Coloniales. Groupement des Productions Minières Coloniales. Paris, France.
Church Hist..........Church History. The American Society of Church History. Chicago, Ill.
Cien Fe..............Ciencia y Fe. Colegio Máximo de San José. Buenos Aires, Argentina.
Cien Soc.............Ciencias Sociales. Pan American Union. Washington, D. C.
Ciencia Tomista.......Ciencia Tomista. Salamanca, Spain.
Civ En..............Civil Engineering. American Society of Civil Engineers. New York, N. Y.
Clío ....Clío. Academia Dominicana de la Historia. Ciudad Trujillo, Dominican Republic.
Com Ext, México......Comercio Exterior. Banco Nacional de Comercio Exterior. México, D. F., México.

Cong Nac Soc, V, 1954, Estud Soc — Congreso Nacional de Sociología, V, 1954. Estudios sociológicos. México, Universidad Nacional Autónoma de México, Instituto de Investigaciones Sociales, 1955.

Conjonction . . . . Bulletin de l'Institut Français d'Haïti. Port-au-Prince, Haïti.

Contrib Am Anthr Hist. Contributions to American Anthropology and History. Carnegie Institution of Washington. Washington, D. C.

Cor Lit. . . . . Correo Literario. Barcelona, Spain.

Cuad Am. . . . . Cuadernos Americanos. México, D. F., México.

Cuad Estud Yucatecos. . Cuadernos de Estudios Yucatecos. Mérida, México.

Cuad Fil. . . . . Cuadernos de Filosofía. Universidad de Buenos Aires. Instituto de Filosofía. Buenos Aires, Argentina.

Cuad Hispanoam. . . . . . Cuadernos Hispanoamericanos. Seminario de Problemas Hispanoamericanos. Madrid, Spain.

Cuad Hist Arqueol. . . . . Cuadernos de Historia y Arqueología. Casa de la Cultura Ecuatoriana. Guayaquil, Ecuador.

Cuad Inst Interam Hist Mun Inst — Cuadernos del Instituto Interamericano de Historia Municipal e Institucional. Habana, Cuba.

Cuadernos . . . . Cuadernos. Congreso por la Libertad de la Cultura. Paris, France.

Cur Hist. . . . . Current History. New York, N. Y.

Cur Rept. . . . . Current Reports. Carnegie Institution of Washington. Department of Archaeology. Washington, D. C.

Cursos Conf. . . . . Cursos y Conferencias. Colegio Libre de Estudios Superiores. Buenos Aires, Argentina.

Dept State B. . . . . Department of State Bulletin. U. S. Department of State. Washington, D. C.

Diário de Pernambuco. . Diário de Pernambuco. Recife, Brazil.

Diário de São Paulo. . . . Diário de São Paulo. São Paulo, Brazil.

Diss Abs. . . . . Dissertation abstracts. University Microfilms. Ann Arbor, Mich.

Domus . . . . Domus. Arte nella casa. Milano, Italy.

Dyestuffs . . . . Dyestuffs. Allied Chemical and Dye Corporation. National Aniline Division. New York, N. Y.

East Tenn Hist Soc Publ — East Tennessee Historical Society's Publications. East Tennessee Historical Society. Knoxville, Tenn.

Ec Colomb. . . . . Economía Colombiana. Contraloría General de la República. Bogotá, Colombia.

Ec Geog. . . . . Economic Geography. Clark University. Worcester, Mass.

Ec Geol. . . . . Economic Geology and the Bulletin of the Society of Economic Geologists. Lancaster, Penn.

Ed Ad . . . . Educação de Adultos. Rio de Janeiro (?), Brazil.

Encounter . . . . Encounter. The Congress of Cultural Freedom. London, England.

Eng Hist R. . . . . English Historical Review. London, England.

Erdkunde . . . . Erdkunde; Archiv für wissenschaftliche Geographie. Bonn, Germany.

Estud Am. . . . . Estudios Americanos. Escuela de Estudios Hispano-Americanos. Sevilla, Spain.

Estud Hist Am. . . . . Estudios Históricos Americanos. Homenaje a Silvio Zavala. Salutación de Alfonso Reyes. México, El Colegio de México, 1953. 786 p., illus. (See item 3033)

Estud Geog. . . . . Estudios Geográficos. Instituto Juan Sebastian Elcano. Consejo Superior de Investigaciones Científicas. Madrid, Spain.

Ethnos . . . . Ethnos; Statens Etnografiska Museet. Stockholm, Sweden.

Fénix . . . . Fénix. Biblioteca Nacional. Lima, Perú.

Fil, Quito. . . . . Filosofía. Sección de Ciencias Filosóficas y de la Educación de la Casa de la Cultura Ecuatoriana. Quito, Ecuador.

Fil Let, México. . . . . Filosofía y Letras. Facultad de Filosofía y Letras. Universidad Nacional Autónoma de México. México, D. F., México.

Fil Let, Quito. . . . . Filosofía y Letras. Facultad de Filosofía, Letras y Ciencias de la Educación. Universidad Central del Ecuador. Quito, Ecuador.

Fla Anthr. . . . . The Florida Anthropologist. Florida Anthropological Society. University of Florida. Gainesville, Fla.

Fla Hist Q . . . . The Florida Historical Quarterly. The Florida Historical Society. Jacksonville, Fla.
Folk Am . . . . Folklore Americano. Comité Interamericano de Folklore. Lima, Perú.
Folk-Lore . . . . Folk-Lore. Transactions of the Folk-Lore Society. London, England.
For Aff . . . . Foreign Affairs. Council on Foreign Relations, Inc. New York, N. Y.
Formação . . . . Formação. Rio de Janeiro, Brazil.
Formes Coul . . . . Formes et Couleurs. Lausanne, France.
Fortune . . . . Fortune. New York, N. Y.

G Campesina . . . . Gaceta Campesina. Instituto Indigenista Boliviano. Ministerio de Asuntos Campesinos. La Paz, Bolivia.
G Méd, Guayaquil . . . . . Gaceta Médica. Servicio San Gabriel, Hospital Luis Vernaza, Guayaquil, Ecuador.
G Méd Méx . . . . Gaceta Médica de México.. Academia Nacional de Medicina. México, D. F., México.
Ga Hist Q . . . . Georgia Historical Quarterly. Georgia Historical Society. Savannah, Ga.
Genetica . . . . Genetica. Martin Nijhoff. 's-Gravenhage, Netherlands.
Geog J . . . . Geographical Journal. London, England.
Geog Mag . . . . The Geographical Magazine. London, England.
Geog R . . . . The Geographical Review. American Geographical Society of New York. New York, N. Y.
Geog Rundschau . . . . Geographische Rundschau. Zeitschrift für Schulgeographie. Georg Westermann Verlag. Braunschweig, Germany.
Gleanings Bee Cult . . . . . Gleanings in Bee Culture. The A. I. Root Company. Medina, Ohio.

HAHR . . . . Hispanic American Historical Review. Duke University Press. Durham, N. C.
H Id . . . . Hechos e Ideas. Buenos Aires, Argentina.
Habitat . . . . Habitat. São Paulo, Brazil.
Hisp R . . . . Hispanic Review. University of Pennsylvania Press. Philadelphia, Pa.
Hispania, AATSP . . . . . . Hispania. American Association of Teachers of Spanish and Portuguese. Wallingford, Conn.
Hist Mex . . . . Historia Mexicana. El Colegio de México. México, D. F., México.
Hum Biol . . . . Human Biology. Johns Hopkins Press. Baltimore, Md.
Hum Org . . . . Human Organization. Society for Applied Anthropology. New York, N. Y.
Humanidades . . . . Humanidades. Facultad de Humanidades. Universidad de San Carlos. Guatemala, Guatemala.
Humanismo . . . . Humanismo. México, D. F., México.
Hunt Libr Q . . . . Huntington Library Quarterly. Henry E. Huntington Library and Art Gallery. San Marino, Calif.

Ilus Br . . . . Ilustração Brasileira. Rio de Janeiro, Brazil.
Illus London News . . . . . Illustrated London News. London, England.
Im Mundi, London . . . . . Imago Mundi. London, England.
Inf Géog . . . . L'Information Géographique. J.-B. Baillière et Fils. Paris, France.
Inf Soc . . . . Informaciones Sociales. Caja Nacional de Seguro Social. Lima, Perú.
Interam Ec Aff . . . . Inter-American Economic Affairs. Institute of Inter-American Studies. Washington, D. C.
Intl Colloq . . . . International Colloquium on Luso-Brazilian Studies, Washington, Oct. 15-20, 1950. Proceedings of the . . . under the auspices of the Library of Congress and Vanderbilt University. Nashville, Tenn., Vanderbilt University Press, 1953. 335 p. (See also item 6713)
Intl J Am Ling . . . . International Journal of American Linguistics. Indiana University. Bloomington, Indiana.

Intl Lab R...........International Labour Review. International Labour Office. Geneva, Switzerland.
Inv Ec..............Investigación Económica. Universidad Nacional Autónoma de México. Escuela Nacional de Economía. México, D. F., México.
Isis ....Isis. History of Science Society. Cambridge, Mass.

J Am Folk...........Journal of American Folklore. Philadelphia, Pa.
J Dent Re...........Journal of Dental Research. International Association for Dental Research. St. Louis, Mo.
J Geog..............The Journal of Geography. National Council of Geography Teachers. Menasha, Wis.
J Her...............Journal of Heredity. American Genetic Association. Baltimore, Md.
J Hist Med Allied Sci..Journal of the History of Medicine and Allied Sciences. Department of the History of Medicine. Yale University. New Haven, Conn.
J Intl Aff...........Journal of International Affairs. New York, N. Y.
J Let................Jornal de Letras. Rio de Janeiro, Brazil.
J Miss Hist...........Journal of Mississippi History. Mississippi Historical Society in co-operation with the Mississippi Department of Archives and History. Jackson, Miss.
J Mod Hist..........The Journal of Modern History. Published in cooperation with the Modern European History Section of the American Historical Association. Chicago, Ill.
J Negro Hist.........The Journal of Negro History. The Association for the Study of Negro Life and History. Washington, D. C.
J Philos.............Journal of Philosophy. New York, N. Y.
J Pol................The Journal of Politics. The Southern Political Science Association in cooperation with The University of Florida. Gainesville, Florida.
J Royal Anthr Inst.....Journal of the Royal Anthropological Institute of Great Britain and Ireland. London, England.
J Soc Am.............Journal de la Société des Américanistes, publié avec le concours du Centre National de la Recherche Scientifique et du Viking Fund. Paris, France.
J Soc Archit Hist......Journal of the Society of Architectural Historians. Louisville, Ky.
J South Hist..........The Journal of Southern History. Southern Historical Association. Nashville, Tenn.
Jam Hist R..........Jamaican Historical Review. Kingston, Jamaica.

Kriterion ....Kriterion. Faculdade de Filosofia da Universidade de Minas Gerais. Belo Horizonte, Brazil.
Kroeber Anthr Soc Pap. Kroeber Anthropological Society Papers. Berkeley, Calif.
Kulturgeografi ....Kulturgeografi, Tidsskrift for Befolkningsgeographi. Bebyggelsesgeografi Erhvervsgeographi. Politish Geografi. Historisk Geografi. Kommission Hos Gyldendalske Boghandel. Köbenhavn, Denmark.
Ky For Lang Q.......Kentucky Foreign Language Quarterly. University of Kentucky. Lexington, Ky.

La Hist Q............Louisiana Historical Quarterly. Louisiana Historical Society. New Orleans, La.
Language ....Language. Linguistic Society of America. Baltimore, Md.
Let Ecuad...........Letras del Ecuador. Casa de la Cultura Ecuatoriana. Quito, Ecuador.
Letras ....Letras. Faculdad de Letras. Universidad Nacional Mayor de San Marcos. Lima, Perú.
Libr J..............Library Journal. R. R. Bowker Co. New York, N. Y.
Life ....Life. Chicago, Ill.

M S.................Mar del Sur. Lima, Perú.
Man ....Man. The Royal Anthropological Institute. London, England.

Manchete .... Manchete. Rio de Janeiro, Brazil.
Masterkey .... The Masterkey. Southwest Museum. Los Angeles, Calif.
Md Hist Mag......... Maryland Historical Magazine. Maryland Historical Society. Baltimore, Md.
Mem Ac Mex Hist..... Memorias de la Academia Mexicana de la Historia. México, D. F., México.
Mem Ac Nac Hist Geog. Memorias de la Academia Nacional de Historia y Geografía. México, D. F., México.
Mém IFAN........... Mémoire de l'Institut Français de l'Afrique Noire. Dakar, French West Africa.
Mem Soc Cien Nat   Memoria de la Sociedad de Ciencias Naturales La Salle. Caracas,
La Salle   Venezuela.
Mem Soc Cub Hist   Memorias de la Sociedad Cubana de Historia Natural Felipe Poey.
Nat "Felipe Poey"   Museo Poey. Universidad de La Habana. Habana, Cuba.
Mens Est, DF......... Mensário Estatístico. Secretaria Geral do Interior e Segurança. Departamento de Geografia e Estatística. Rio de Janeiro, Brazil.
Mer Per.............. Mercurio Peruano. Lima, Perú.
Merc Val............. El Mercado de Valores. Nacional Financiera, S. A. México, D. F., México.
Mesoam Notes........ Mesoamerican Notes. Department of Anthropology. Mexico City College. México, D. F., México.
Meteor Mono......... Meteorological Monographs. American Meteorological Society. Boston, Mass.
Meteoros .... Meteoros. Servicio Meteorológico Nacional. Buenos Aires, Argentina.
Mex This Month....... Mexico This Month. México, D. F., México.
Mid Am.............. Mid America. Loyola University. Institute of Jesuit History. Chicago, Ill.
Mid Am Research Rec.. Middle American Research Records. Tulane University of Louisiana, Middle American Research Institute. New Orleans, La.
Mis Hist R........... Missouri Historical Review. State Historical Society of Missouri. Columbia, Mo.
Miscel Am............ Miscelánea Americanista. Instituto Gonzalo Fernández de Oviedo. Madrid, Spain.
Miss Hist............ Missionalia Hispanica. Consejo Superior de Investigaciones Científicas. Instituto Santo Toribio de Mogrovejo. Madrid, Spain.
Mod Lang For........ Modern Language Forum. Los Angeles, Calif.
Mundo Hisp........... Mundo Hispánico. Ediciones Iberoamericanas. Madrid, Spain.
Mus Genève.......... Les Musées de Genève. Genève, Switzerland.
Mus Hist............. Museo Histórico. Museo de Historia de la Ciudad de Quito. Quito, Ecuador.
Museum .... Museum. United Nations Educational, Scientific and Cultural Organization. Paris, France.

N C Hist R.......... North Carolina Historical Review. Raleigh, N. C.
N Y Times............ The New York Times. New York, N. Y.
Names .... Names. American Name Society. University of California Press. Berkeley, Calif.
Nat Hist. .... Natural History. American Museum of Natural History. New York, N. Y.
Natura .... Natura. Administración General de Parques Nacionales. Buenos Aires, Argentina.
Neurobiologia .... Neurobiologia. Sociedade de Psiquiatria, Neurologia e Higiene Mental do Nordeste Brasileiro. Recife, Brazil.
New Mex Hist R....... New Mexico Historical Review. Historical Society of New Mexico and University of New Mexico. Albuquerque, N. Mex.
New Statesman and   The New Statesman and Nation. London, England.
Nation
New W Antiq......... New World Antiquity. London, England.
Notas Estud Fil........ Notas y Estudios de Filosofía. Tucumán, Argentina.
Notas Mus Eva   Notas del Museo Eva Perón, Antropología. Universidad Nacional
Perón,Antropología   de Eva Perón. La Plata, Argentina.
Notes Mid Am   Notes on Middle American Archaeology and Ethnology. Carnegie
Archaeol Ethn   Institution of Washington. Washington, D. C.

Nueva R Filo Hisp..... Nueva Revista de Filología Hispánica. El Colegio de México.
México, D. F., México.

Obs Ec Fin........... O Observador Econômico e Financeiro. Rio de Janeiro, Brazil.
Ocidente .... Ocidente. Lisboa, Portugal.
Ohio J Sci........... Ohio Journal of Science. Ohio State University and Ohio Academy
of Science. Columbus, Ohio.
Ordem .... A Ordem. Rio de Janeiro, Brazil.

Pac Discov........... Pacific Discovery. California Academy of Sciences. Berkeley,
Calif.
Pac Hist R........... The Pacific Historical Review. University of California Press.
Los Angeles and Berkeley, Calif.
Pac Spec............. The Pacific Spectator. American Council of Learned Societies.
Pacific Coast Committee for the Humanities. Stanford University Press. Stanford, Calif.
Palacio .... El Palacio. School of American Research, Museum of New
Mexico, and Archaeological Society of New Mexico. Santa
Fe, N. Mex.
Panorama .... Panorama. Pan American Union. Washington, D. C.
Panorama, Santa Cruz Panorama. Instituto de Educação Leônidas do Amaral Vieira.
do Rio Pardo   Centro de Estudos Geográficos Moraes Rego. Santa Cruz do
Rio Pardo, Brazil.
Past Pres............. Past and Present. London, England.
Pediatrics .... Pediatrics. American Academy of Pediatrics. Springfield, Ill.
Perú Indig........... Perú Indígena. Instituto Indigenista Peruano. Lima, Perú.
Petermanns Geog   Petermanns Geographische Mitteilungen. Veb Geographisch-
Mitteilungen   Kartographische Anstalt. Gotha, Germany.
Phil Phen Re......... Philosophy and Phenomenological Research. Buffalo, N. Y.
Philos Q............. The Philosophical Quarterly. St. Andrews, Scotland.
Philosophia .... Philosophia. Universidad Nacional de Cuyo. Facultad de Filosofía y Letras. Mendoza, Argentina.
Photographie und   Photographie und Forschung; the Contax in the Service of Science.
Forschung   Zeiss Ikon. Stuttgart, Germany.
Phylon .... Phylon. Atlanta University. Atlanta, Ga.
Poet Lore .... Poet Lore. Boston, Mass.
Popul B............. Population Bulletin. Population Reference Bureau. Washington,
D. C.
Popul Stud........... Population Studies. London School of Economics and Political
Science. Population Investigation Committee. London, England.
Prev Soc, Santiago..... Previsión Social. Departamento de Previsión Social. Ministerio
de Salubridad, Previsión y Asistencia Social. Santiago, Chile.
Pro Am Phil Soc....... Proceedings, American Philosophical Society. Philadelphia, Pa.
Prob Agr Ind Méx..... Problemas Agrícolas e Industriales de México. México, D. F.,
México.
Prot Soc............. Protección Social. Caja Nacional de Seguro Social. La Paz,
Bolivia.
Prov São Pedro........ Provincia de São Pedro. Pôrto Alegre, Brazil.
Pub Fin............. Public Finance/Finance Publique. Amsterdam, Netherlands.
Publ Mus Soc Arqueol Publicaciones del Museo y de la Sociedad Arqueológica de la
La Serena B   Serena—Boletín. La Serena, Chile.

R Ac Colomb Cien   Revista de la Academia Colombiana de Ciencias Exactas, Físicas
Exact Fís Nat   y Naturales. Bogotá, Colombia.
R Agr Subtrop Trop.... Rivista di Agricoltura Subtropicale e Tropicale. Instituto Agronomico per l'Africa Italiana. Firenze, Italy.
R Antr.............. Revista de Antropologia. Universidade de São Paulo. Faculdade
de Filosofia, Ciências e Letras. São Paulo, Brazil.
R Antr, Roma......... Rivista di Antropologia. Societa Romana di Antropologia. Roma,
Italy.
R Arch Hist Cuzco..... Revista del Archivo Histórico del Cuzco. Universidad Nacional
del Cuzco. Cuzco, Perú.

R Arch Nac C R....... Revista de los Archivos Nacionales de Costa Rica. San José, Costa Rica.
R Arq Mun........... Revista do Arquivo Municipal. Secretaria de Educação e Cultura. São Paulo, Brazil.
R Arqueol Etn........ Revista de Arqueología y Etnología. Junta Nacional de Arqueología y Etnología. Habana, Cuba.
R Banc.............. Revista Bancaria. Asociación de Banqueros de México. México, D. F., México.
R Banco Cen C R..... Revista del Banco Central de Costa Rica. San José, Costa Rica.
R Bib Nac, B A....... Revista de la Biblioteca Nacional. Buenos Aires, Argentina.
R Bib Nac, Habana.... Revista de la Biblioteca Nacional. Habana, Cuba.
R Br Est............. Revista Brasileira de Estatística. Instituto Brasileiro de Geografia e Estatística. Rio de Janeiro, Brazil.
R Br Fil............. Revista Brasileira de Filosofia. Instituto Brasileiro de Filosofia. São Paulo, Brazil.
R Br Estud Ped....... Revista Brasileira de Estudos Pedagógicos. Instituto Nacional de Estudos Pedagógicos. Rio de Janeiro, Brazil.
R Br Geog........... Revista Brasileira de Geografia. Instituto Brasileiro de Geografia e Estatística. Conselho Nacional de Geografia. Rio de Janeiro, Brazil.
R Br Poe............. Revista Brasileira de Poesia. São Paulo, Brazil.
R Camp Nac Ed Rur... Revista da Campanha Nacional de Educação Rural. Rio de Janeiro (?), Brazil.
R Ch Hist Geog....... Revista Chilena de Historia y Geografía. Santiago, Chile.
R Cien.............. Revista de Ciencias. Facultad de Ciencias de la Universidad Nacional Mayor de San Marcos. Lima, Perú.
R Cien Jur Soc........ Revista de Ciencias Jurídicas y Sociales. Facultad de Ciencias Jurídicas y Sociales de la Universidad Nacional del Litoral. Santa Fe, Argentina.
R Clube Mil........... Revista do Clube Militar. Rio de Janeiro (?), Brazil.
R Col Abog P R....... Revista del Colegio de Abogados de Puerto Rico. San Juan, Puerto Rico.
R Colomb Antr....... Revista Colombiana de Antropología. Instituto Colombiano de Antropología. Bogotá, Colombia.
R Colomb Folk........ Revista Colombiana de Folklore. Instituto Colombiano de Antropología. Bogotá, Colombia.
R Ec, México.......... Revista de Economía. México, D. F., México.
R Ed Cult............ Revista de Educação e Cultura. Rio de Janeiro (?), Brazil.
R Estud Pol........... Revista de Estudios Políticos. Instituto de Estudios Políticos. Madrid, Spain.
R Fac Der Cien Soc, B A ... Revista de la Facultad de Derecho y Ciencias Sociales. Universidad de Buenos Aires. Buenos Aires, Argentina.
R Fac Dir, Paraná..... Revista da Faculdade de Direito. Universidade do Paraná. Curitiba, Brazil.
R Fac Fil Hum........ Revista de la Facultad de Filosofía y Humanidades. Universidad Nacional de Córdoba. Córdoba, Argentina.
R Fac Let............ Revista da Faculdade de Letras. Universidade de Lisboa. Lisboa, Portugal.
R Filol Esp........... Revista de Filología Española. Consejo Superior de Investigaciones Científicas. Instituto Miguel de Cervantes. Madrid, Spain.
R Fisc Fin............ Revista Fiscal y Financiera. Instituto Mexicano de Técnicos Fiscales. México, D. F., México.
R Fr................. La Revue Française de l'Élite Européene. Paris, France.
R Geog Am........... Revista Geográfica Americana. Sociedad Geográfica Americana. Buenos Aires, Argentina.
R Geog Hist.......... Revista de Geografia e História. Rio de Janeiro (?), Brazil.
R Geog Inst Pan Am... Revista Geográfica do Instituto Pan-Americano de Geografia e História. Rio de Janeiro, Brazil.
R Hist, Lima.......... Revista Histórica. Instituto Histórico del Perú. Lima, Perú.
R Hist Am........... Revista de Historia de América. Instituto Panamericano de Geografía e Historia. México, D. F., México.
R Hist Am Fr......... Revue d'Histoire de l'Amérique Française. Institut d'Histoire de l'Amérique Française. Montreal, Canada.
R Hist Colonies........ Revue d'Histoire des Colonies. Paris, France.

R Hisp Mod..........Revista Hispánica Moderna. Hispánic Institute in the United States, Columbia University, New York, N. Y., and Departamento de Estudios Hispánicos, Universidad de Puerto Rico, Río Piedras, Puerto Rico.

R Hist, Montevideo....Revista Histórica. Museo Histórico Nacional. Montevideo, Uruguay.

R Hist, São Paulo......Revista de História. São Paulo, Brazil.

R Hist Relig...........Revue de l'Histoire des Religions. Presses Universitaires de France. Paris, France.

R Hitos..............La Revista Hitos. Guayaquil, Ecuador.

R Iberoam...........Revista Iberoamericana. Instituto Internacional de Literatura Iberoamericana. México, D. F., México.

R Iberoam Seg Soc.....Revista Iberoamericana de Seguridad Social. Instituto Nacional de Previsión, Ministerio de Trabajo. Madrid, Spain.

R Indias, Madrid.......Revista de Indias. Instituto Gonzalo Fernández de Oviedo. Consejo Superior de Investigaciones Científicas. Madrid, Spain.

R Inst Antr...........Revista del Instituto de Antropología. Universidad Nacional de Tucumán. Tucumán, Argentina.

R Inst Hist Der........Revista del Instituto de Historia del Derecho. Universidad de Buenos Aires. Buenos Aires, Argentina.

R Inst Hist Geog Br....Revista do Instituto Histórico e Geográfico Brasileiro. Rio de Janeiro, Brazil.

R Interam Bibl........Revista Interamericana de Bibliografía (Inter-American Review of Bibliography). Unión Panamericana. Washington, D. C.

R Intl Soc............Revista Internacional de Sociología. Instituto Balmes de Sociología. Consejo Superior de Investigaciones Científicas. Madrid, Spain.

R Inv Agr............Revista de Investigaciones Agrícolas. Dirección General de Investigaciones Agrícolas. Buenos Aires, Argentina.

R Mex Estud Antr.....Revista Mexicana de Estudios Antropológicos. Sociedad Mexicana de Antropología. México, D. F., México.

R Mex Soc...........Revista Mexicana de Sociología. Universidad Nacional Autónoma. Instituto de Investigaciones Sociales. México, D. F., México.

R Mex Trab..........Revista Mexicana del Trabajo. Secretaría del Trabajo y Previsión. México, D. F., México.

R Mus Castilhos.......Revista do Museu Júlio de Castilhos e Arquivo Histórico do Rio Grande do Sul. Pôrto Alegre, Brazil.

R Mus Inst Arqueol....Revista del Museo e Instituto Arqueológico. Universidad Nacional del Cuzco. Cuzco, Perú.

R Mus Nac...........Revista del Museo Nacional. Lima, Perú.

R Mus Nac Antr   Revista del Museo Nacional de Antropología y Arqueología.
Arqueol   Lima, Perú.

R Mus Paulista........Revista do Museu Paulista. São Paulo, Brazil.

R Mus U Eva Perón....Revista del Museo de la Universidad Eva Perón. La Plata, Argentina.

R Music Ch...........Revista Musical Chilena. Universidad de Chile. Instituto de Extensión Musical. Santiago, Chile.

R Nac...............Revista Nacional. Ministerio de Instrucción Pública. Montevideo, Uruguay.

R Nac Cult..........Revista Nacional de Cultura. Ministerio de Educación Nacional. Dirección de Cultura. Caracas, Venezuela.

R Pat Hist Art Nac.....Revista do Patrimônio Histórico e Artístico Nacional. Ministério de Educação e Saúde, Diretoria do Patrimônio Histórico e Artístico Nacional. Rio de Janeiro, Brazil.

R Ped...............Revista de Pedagogia. Rio de Janeiro (?), Brazil.

R Sci Leg Fin.........Revue de Science et de Législation Financières. Librairie Générale de Droit et de Jurisprudence. Paris, France.

R SENAC...........Revista SENAC. Serviço Nacional de Aprendizagem Comercial. Rio de Janeiro, Brazil.

R Serv Espec Saú Púb..Revista do Serviço Especial de Saúde Pública. Rio de Janeiro, Brazil.

R Soc Ami Arqueol.....Revista de la Sociedad Amigos de Arqueología. Montevideo, Uruguay.

R Soc Haïtienne   Revue de la Société Haïtienne d'Histoire et de Géographie. Port-
Hist Geog   au-Prince, Haïti.
R Soc Ven Hist Med....Revista de la Sociedad Venezolana de Historia de la Medicina.
                        Caracas, Venezuela.
R U, Cuzco...........Revista Universitaria. Universidad Nacional del Cuzco. Cuzco,
                        Perú.
R U, Trujillo..........Revista Universitaria. Universidad Nacional de Trujillo. Trujillo,
                        Perú.
R U C R.............Revista de la Universidad de Costa Rica. San José, Costa Rica.
R U Cat São Paulo....Revista da Universidade Católica de São Paulo. São Paulo, Brazil.
R U Nac, Córdoba....Revista de la Universidad Nacional de Córdoba. Córdoba,
                        Argentina.
R U Nac Litoral.......Revista de la Universidad Nacional del Litoral. Santa Fe,
                        Argentina.
Razón y Fe ....Razón y Fe. Madrid, Spain.
Rec Am Cat Hist Soc...Records of the American Catholic Historical Society. Philadelphia,
                        Pa.
Rio ....Rio. Rio de Janeiro, Brazil.
Rom Philol...........Romance Philology. University of California Press. Berkeley and
                        Los Angeles, Calif.
Runa ....Runa. Universidad de Buenos Aires. Instituto de Antropología.
                        Buenos Aires, Argentina.
Rural Soc.............Rural Sociology. Rural Sociological Society. North Carolina State
                        College of Agriculture and Engineering. Raleigh, N. C.

Sapientia ....Sapientia. La Plata, Argentina.
Sci Am...............Scientific American. New York, N. Y.
Sci Month............The Scientific Monthly. American Association for the Advance-
                        ment of Science. Washington, D. C.
Science ....Science. American Association for the Advancement of Science.
                        Washington, D. C.
Seg Soc, México.......Seguro Social. Asociación Internacional de la Seguridad Social
                        de la Conferencia Interamericana de Seguridad Social. Oficina
                        Internacional del Trabajo. México, D. F., México.
Soc Ec Stud..........Social and Economic Studies. Institute of Social and Economic
                        Research. University College of the West Indies. Mona, St.
                        Andrew, Jamaica.
Soc Forces...........Social Forces. University of North Carolina Press. Chapel Hill,
                        N. C.
Soc Méx..............La Sociología en México. México, D. F., México.
Social Science ....Social Science. National Social Science Honor Society Pi Gamma
                        Mu. The Social Science Publishing Co. Winfield, Kan.
Sociol Soc Re........Sociology and Social Research. University of Southern California
                        Press. Los Angeles, Calif.
Sociologia ....Sociologia. Revista Didática e Científica. Publicação da Escola
                        de Sociologia e Política de São Paulo. São Paulo, Brazil.
SODRE ....SODRE. Servicio Oficial de Difusión Radio Eléctrica. Monte-
                        video, Uruguay.
South Folk Q.........Southern Folklore Quarterly. The University of Florida in co-
                        operation with the Southeastern Folklore Society. Gainesville,
                        Fla.
Staden-Jahrbuch ....Staden-Jahrbuch, Beiträge zur Brasilkunde. Instituto Hans Staden.
                        São Paulo, Brazil.
Stud Ling............Studies in Linguistics. University of Oklahoma. Norman, Okla.
Südamerika ....Südamerika. Buenos Aires, Argentina.
Sul ....Sul. Florianopolis, Brazil.
Sur ....Sur. Buenos Aires, Argentina.
SW Hist Q............Southwestern Historical Quarterly. Austin, Tex.
SW J Anthr..........Southwestern Journal of Anthropology. University of New Mexico
                        and Laboratory of Anthropology, Santa Fe. Albuquerque,
                        N. Mex.
SW Soc Sci Q........Southwestern Social Science Quarterly. Southwestern Social
                        Science Association. University of Oklahoma. Norman, Okla.

Tierra Firme ....Tierra Firme. Caracas, Venezuela.

Timehri. . . . . Royal Agricultural and Commercial Society of British Guiana. Demerara, British Guiana.
Tlalocan . . . . Tlalocan. La Casa de Tlaloc. México, D. F., México.
Tlatoani . . . . Tlatoani. Sociedad de Alumnos de la Escuela Nacional de Antropología e Historia. México, D. F., México.
Tomorrow . . . . Tomorrow. New York, N. Y.
Torre . . . . La Torre. Universidad de Puerto Rico. Río Piedras, Puerto Rico.
Trans Am Philos Soc. . . Transactions of the American Philosophical Society. Philadelphia, Pa.
Trans NY Ac Sci. . . . . . Transactions of the New York Academy of Sciences. New York, N. Y.
Trim Ec. . . . . El Trimestre Económico. Fondo de Cultura Económica. México, D. F., México.
Trop Agr. . . . . Tropical Agriculture. Imperial College of Tropical Agriculture. Trinidad, B. W. I.

U Antioquia. . . . . Universidad de Antioquia. Medellín, Colombia.
U Calif Publ Am   University of California Publications in American Archaeology
   Archaeol Ethn   and Ethnology. Berkeley, Calif.
U Pontif Bolivariana. . . Universidad Pontificia Bolivariana. Medellín, Colombia.
Universitas, Stuttgart. . . Universitas. Zeitschrift für Wissenschaft, Kunst und Literatur. Wissenschaftliche Verlagsgesellschaft M. B. H. Stuttgart, Germany.
U S Naval Inst Pro. . . . . United States Naval Institute Proceedings. United States Naval Institute. Annapolis, Md.
Umschau in Wissen-   Die Umschau in Wissenschaft und Technik. Frankfurt-am-Main,
   schaft und Technik   Germany.

Verbum . . . . Verbum. Universidade Católica. Rio de Janeiro, Brazil.
Viejo y Raro . . . . Viejo y Raro. Librería Viejo y Raro. Caracas, Venezuela.
Vir Q R. . . . . Virginia Quarterly Review. University of Virginia. Charlottesville, Va.
Virchows Archiv . . . . . . Virchows Archiv. Springer-Verlag. Berlin, Germany.

W Today. . . . . World Today. Royal Institute of International Affairs. London, England.
Water Power . . . . Water Power. London, England.
West In Med J. . . . . West Indian Medical Journal. University College of the West Indies. Mona, St. Andrew, Jamaica.
West Indische Gids. . . . . De West-Indische Gids. 's-Gravenhage, Netherlands.
World Crops . . . . World Crops. London, England.

Y Am Philos Soc. . . . . . Year Book, American Philosophical Society. Philadelphia, Pa.
Yan. . . . . Centro de Investigaciones Antropológicas de México. México, D. F., México.

Zeit Ethn. . . . . Zeitschrift für Ethnologie. Berlin, Germany.
Zeit Morph Anthr. . . . . . Zeitschrift für Morphologie und Anthropologie. E. Schweizerhart'sche Verlagsbuchhandlung. Stuttgart, Germany.

Index I: Author

Aagesen, Aage, 2669
Abeliuk Manasevich, René, 5434, 5524
Abello Salcedo, Rafael, 3899
Abramo, Lívio, 1284
Abreu, Casimiro, 5329
Abreu, Florencio de, 2631
Abreu, Jaime, 2200, 2201
Abreu Gómez, Ermilo, 4965
Ab'Sáber, Aziz Nacib, 2600, 2670
Abu-Merhy, Nair Fortes, 2202
Academia de la Historia de Cuba, 3700
Academia Mexicana, 4700
Academia Mexicana de la Historia, 3200
Accioly, Hildebrando, 4247
Acevedo, Alain de, 5305
Acevedo Hernández, Antonio, 5634
Acevedo López, Santos, 5643
Achille, Aristide, 6044
Ackerman, Adolph J., 2632
Acosta, Jorge R., 95
Acosta, José de, 3100, 3101
Acosta Saignes, Miguel, 250, 292, 821, 822, 6022
Adams, Eleanor B., 3202, 3203, 3368a, 4656
Adams, Richard N., 6088
Adams, Robert M., Jr., 96
Ades, Raphael, 4500
Adonias Filho, 5253
Agramonte, Roberto, 6094
Aguayo Spencer, Rafael, 3553
Aguerrevere, Ángel Demetrio, 5588a
Aguilar, Francisco de, 3204
Aguilar, Miguel, 5635
Aguilar M., Alonso, 1985
Aguilar Machado, Alejandro, 5723
Aguilar P., Carlos H., 97
Aguirre, M. C., 3205
Aguirre, Ramiro, 4921
Aquirre Beltrán, Gonzalo, 1, 624, 625, 634, 3000, 6082
Ahumada, Jorge, 1850
Aita, Giovanna, 5220
Aja Jorge, Pedro V., 5723, 5797
Alanís Patiño, Emilio, 1851, 1930, 1931
Alarco, Luis Felipe, 2000, 5766
Alatorre, Antonio, 4693
Alatorre, Margit Frank, 4501
Alayza y Paz Soldán, Luis, 4626, 4850, 4851
Alba, Duque de, 3102, 3103
Alba, Víctor, 2850, 4300
Albanell MacColl, Norah, 6400
Albareda, José Daniel, 1985a, 5452

Alberdi, Juan Bautista, 3818
Alberini, Coriolano, 5748
Alberti, Altana, 5000
Albi, Fernando, 5400
Albornoz, Víctor Manuel, 3445
Alborta Velasco, Óscar, 2548
Albuquerque, A. P. de, 1215
Albuquerque, A. Tenório d', 5200, 5201
Alcocer, Mariano, 1965a
Aldana, Cristóbal de, 3206
Alecrim, Octacilio, 5408
Alegría, Fernando, 4657, 5041, 5042
Alegría, Ricardo E., 280, 695, 4502
Alem, Leandro N., 3819
Alembert, Jean-Baptiste Le Rond d', 5802
Alencar, José de, 5249
Alencastre G., Andrés, 811
Alexander, Francisco, 5042
Alexander, J. L., 2671
Alexander, Robert, 2871
Alexis, Jacques Stephen, 5375
Alfaro, Ricardo J., 4259
Alfau Durán, Vetilio, 5043
Alfonsín, Quintín, 5585a, 5586
Alfonso, Luis, 5711
Alicina Franch, José, 440
Alincourt, Luiz d', 4000
Aljure Chalola, Simón, 4717
Allee, Ralph, 6011
Allende Iriarte, Jorge, 5424
Almacenes Nacionales de Depósito, 1852, 1853, 1854, 1855
Almada, Francisco, 3207, 3208
Almafuerte. See Palacios, Pedro Bonifacio.
Almeida, Enrique P., 5731
Almeida, Fernando F. M. de, 2601, 2602, 2603
Almeida, João Carlos de, 2203, 2204
Almeida, M. A. de, 5253
Almeida Júnior, A., 2205, 2206, 2207
Almeyda, Aniceto, 3467a
Almeyda Arroyo, Elías, 3467b
Almoina, José, 3209
Alone. See Díaz Arrieta, Hernán.
Alonso, Amado, 4503
Altamira y Crevea, Rafael, 5587a
Altolaguirre y Duvale, Ángel de, 3210, 3416
Alumi, Carlos Alberto, 6022
Alumni, José, 3001
Alvarado, Frank, 6613
Alvarado, Gabriel, 2918
Alvarado, José, 1900, 4852

Anonymous (continued)

Legislación real sobre hacienda para las provincias coloniales venezolanas, 5418

Ley del impuesto sobre la renta y su reglamento, 5453

Ley orgánica de seguridad social, administración Somoza, 4461

Leyes nuevas de Indias, 3159

El litigio territorial entre el Ecuador y el Perú, 4279

Mapa general de la República Argentina, 1:3,750,000, 2519

Martí en Moscú, 3728

Mauritz de braziliaan; tentconstelling, 1235

Memoria de los servicios que había hecho Nuño de Guzmán, desde que fué nombrado governador de Pánuco en 1525, 3322

New source material for the history of the North American West including the Spanish possessions in North America . . . ., 3331

Nossa Senhora nas artes, 1236

Noticia de los conventos del arzobispado de México, 1826, 3637

Noticias sobre Nueva Galicia, 3066

Novo regulamento do imposto de renda; decreto no. 36.773 de 13/1/955, 5445

Nuestros cuentos, 4921

Nueva Vizcaya, 3067

Observações à margem das conclusões de curso, no ensino superior civil, no ano letivo de 1952, 2290

Oficios remitidos del estado Mayor de la columna expedicionaria que salió de la Habana al mando del Exmo. Señor Conde de Mirasol en mayo de 1850, con respecto al desembarco de enemigos en Cárdenas, 3736

The oil code of Colombia, decree 1056 of 1953 (April 20), 5594a

Outras peças do Museu Pigorini de Roma, 1210

Paliteiros nuna coleção, 1262

Perspective of Brazil, 6721

El petróleo y la economía mexicana, 1962

Prisión de franceses en la Nueva España en 1795, 3347

El publicista de Venezuela, 3916

Quadro sistemático do divisão regional das unidades federadas, Brasil, 2718

Recherches collectives, 3393

Recopilación diplomática a las colonias española y francesa de la isla de Santo Domingo, 3393a

Recuperação do solo e do homem brasileiros, 1730

Reglamento del código de petróleo; decreto número 445, 5596

Reglamento general de artesanos de la Nueva Guatemala . . . ., 3352

Reitoria da Universidade da Bahia, 1240

Relación de los caciques y principales del pueblo de Atitlán, 1° de febrero del año 1571, 3353

Relación de los cargos públicos y eclesiásticos desempeñados por individuos de la familia Aycinena y Larrazábal en Guatemala durante la colonia, 3354

Relíquias de Nicolau Taunay, 1241

Revista brasileira de filologia, 5214

Revista de historia da economia brasileira, 1731

Reunión de la Comisión Ejecutiva del Comité Permanente Interamericano de Seguridad Social, 4412

São Paulo e o "art nouveau," 1264

Sección memoria de la Superintendencia de Seguridad social correspondiente a 1954, 4464

II Bienal do Museu de Arte Moderna de São Paulo, 1283

La seguridad social en Chile; reforma del seguro social, 4465

Seguridad social en Cuba, 4466

El seguro social en Haití, 4446

El seguro social en la república de El Salvador, 4438

El Seminario de Seguridad Social de Panamá, 4467

Seminario de trabajo sobre administración de servicios de protección a la infancia, 1953, 4414, 4415

Seminario Interamericano de Educación Secundaria, 2016

Los seminarios de Costa Rica, El Salvador, Guatemala, Haití, Honduras, Nicaragua y Panamá, 4416

Situação do ensino no Brasil, 2308

Sobre erección de la Santa Iglesia Catedral del Obispado de Cuba y creación y distribución de diezmos, 3397

As soluções indicadas pela Comissão Mista Brasil—EE. UU., 1700

The story of British Guiana, 2956

Supresión del oficio de tesorero de la provincia de Costa Rica, 3367

Teatro brasileiro, 5357

Terceiro Bienal de Arte de São Paulo, 1284

III Bienal do Museu de Arte Moderna de São Paulo, 1285

El tomismo en Córdoba, 5749

32 masterworks of Andean art, 371

Tomorrow, quarterly review of psychical research, 610

Translation of the commercial code of Mexico, as enacted in 1889, with all amendments up to 1953, 5570

Una botica colonial, 3439

Bervin, Antoine, 4260, 5388
Betancur, Cayetano, 5794
Beteta, Ignacio, 3352
Beveraggi Allende, Walter M., 5564a
Bezie, José, 5804
Biasey, Mario de, 2525
Biblioteca Almeida Cunha, 6405
Bidney, David, 6
Bierck, Harold A., Jr., 3009, 3800, 3900
Billi di Sandorno, Amalia, 3438
Binayán, Narciso, 3010
Biocca, E., 767
Bioy Casares, Adolfo, 5008
Bird, Junius, 352, 443, 812
Bischoff, Henry C., 3670
Bittencourt, Adalzira, 4004
Bittencourt, Raul, 2216
Black, Clinton V., 3011
Blaisdell, Lowell L., 3558
Blake, Emmett Reid, 2401
Blanchet, Jules, 6059, 6720
Blanco, Andrés Eloy, 5006, 5016
Blanco A., Carlos, 4937
Blanco-Amor, Eduardo, 5152
Blanksten, George I., 2874
Bliss, Horacio W., 5490
Bloem, Ruy, 2887
Blom, Frans, 104, 857
Bloomfield, Louis M., 4275
Blough, Glenn O., 2011
Bobb, Bernard, 3224
Bocanegro, Matías de, 4649
Boehrer, George C. A., 4005
Boesen, Richard M., 5571
Boggs, Ralph Steele, 4663, 5600
Boiteux, Lucas Alexandre, 4034, 4069
Bolívar, Simón, 3801
Bolivia. Dirección General de Economía Rural. Departamento de Muestreos y Padrones, 1408
Bolivia. Dirección General de Estadística y Censo, 6254
Bolivia. Subsecretaría de Prensa, Informaciones y Cultura, 1409
Bonfils, Constante G., 2515
Bonhomme, Clovis, 5391
Bonifaz, Miguel, 5589
Bonilla, Marcelina, 2402
Bonilla Domínguez, Celia, 629
Booz, Mateo, 4862
Bopp, Marianne O. de, 4664
Borah, Woodrow, 3115, 3225, 3559
Borba, Rosy Frontini de, 1271
Borda, Guillermo A., 5489
Borges, Jorge Luis, 4863, 4864, 5007, 5008, 5046, 5047
Borhegyi, Stephen F. de, 7, 51, 52, 53, 54, 55, 56, 105, 3012
Bórmida, Marcelo, 876
Boschetti, Luis R., 4865
Bosco, María Angélica, 4866
Botelho, Carlos de Castro, 2635
Bourguignon, Erika E., 589, 590
Bouza Brey, Fermín, 3116
Boxer, C. R., 4035
Boyd, Mark F., 3226, 3227

Boyd-Bowman, Peter, 4527
Boyrie Moya, Emile de, 281, 282
Bradburn, Adelaide, 5601
Braga, Rubem, 1272, 5236
Brainerd, George W., 57, 58, 72, 424
Braithwaite, Lloyd, 700, 701
Brambila, David, 630
Brancante, E. F., 1220, 1284
Branco, Carlos Castello, 5306
Brandão, Théo, 5336
Brandão Filho, A., 2217
Brannon de Samayoa, Carmen, 5021, 5022
Bravo, Manuel, 1860, 1942
Brazil. Arquivo Nacional, 4036
Brazil. Biblioteca Nacional, 5202
Brazil. Biblioteca Nacional. Divisão de Obras Raras e Publicações, 4006, 4007, 4008, 6407
Brazil. Campanha de Aperfeiçoamento e Difusão do Ensino Secundário, 2218
Brazil. Campanha Nacional de Aperfeiçoamento de Pessoal de Nível Superior, 2219
Brazil. Campanha Nacional de Educação Rural, 2220
Brazil. Comissão de Abastecimento do Nordeste, 1705
Brazil. Comissão de Estudo dos Textos da História do Brasil, 4009
Brazil. Conselho Nacional do Petróleo, 1706
Brazil. Departamento Nacional da Produção Mineral. Divisão de Águas, 2700
Brazil. Departamento Nacional de Educação, 2221
Brazil. Diretoria de Aeronáutica Civil. Divisão do Tráfego. Secção de Estatística, 1707
Brazil. Diretoria do Ensino Secundário, 2222, 2223, 2224, 2225, 2226, 2227, 2228, 2229
Brazil. Diretoria do Serviço Geográfico, 2701
Brazil. Distrito Federal. Prefeitura. Departamento de Geografia e Estatística, 2230
Brazil. Distrito Federal. Prefeitura. Secretaria Geral de Educação e Cultura, 2231
Brazil. Instituto Brasileiro de Geografia e Estatística. Conselho Nacional de Estatística, 2232, 2233, 2234, 2235, 2236, 6045, 6046
Brazil. Instituto Brasileiro de Geografia e Estatística. Conselho Nacional de Estatística. Serviço Nacional de Recenseamento, 6255, 6256, 6257
Brazil. Instituto Brasileiro de Geografia e Estatística. Conselho Nacional de Geografia, 2636, 2637
Brazil. Instituto de Pesquisas Tecnológicas, 1708
Brazil. Instituto de Resseguros do Brasil, 1709
Brazil. Instituto Nacional do Livro, 6408, 6409
Brazil. Instituto Nacional do Mate, 1710
Brazil. Ministério da Educação e Cultura, 2237, 2238, 2239

Capuñay, Manuel A., 3886
Carballo, Emmanuel, 4763
Carbano de Kretschmer, Elba, 1713
Carbó, Luis Alberto, 3880
Cardenal de Iracheta, Manuel, 3441
Cárdenas, Daniel N., 4516, 4547
Cárdenas Ojeda, Mauro, 6095
Cardona Peña, Alfredo, 4716
Cardoso, Alfonso, 1863
Cardoso, Joaquín, 3567
Cardoso, Leontina Licinio, 6502
Cardoso, Luis, 1406
Cardoza y Aragón, Luis, 585, 3672, 4269
Cardozo, Manoel, 4071
Carey Jones, N. S., 1468
Carleton de Millán, Verna, 4870
Carlson, Fred A., 2351, 2352, 2353
Carluci, María Angélica, 753
Carmin, Robert Leighton, 2676
Carmona Romay, Adriano G., 3705
Carnegie Institution of Washington. Department of Archaeology, 80
Carneiro, José Fernando, 5240, 5241, 5242
Carnicelli, Mick, 1208
Caro, José Eusebio, 4717
Caro, Néstor, 5466
Carpeaux [i. e., Karpfeu], Otto Maria, 5203
Carpena, Elías, 4871
Carpenter, Edwin H., 3234
Carr, Andrew, 702
Carr, Archie, 2403
Carrancá y Trujillo, Camilo, 6716
Carrancá y Trujillo, Raúl, 6716
Carrancedo, Fidel, 3147
Carranza, Eduardo, 5010
Carranza, Enrique F., 5411
Carrasco, Pedro, 632, 633
Carrasquilla, Rafael María, 4718
Carreño, Alberto María, 3016, 3200, 3235, 3236, 3345, 3555
Carrera Stampa, Manuel, 3017, 3237, 3322, 3568
Carril, Bonifacio del, 3117
Carrillo, Alejandro, 1964
Carrillo, Carlos A., 2078
Carrillo Flores, Antonio, 1351, 1864, 1865, 1866, 1923, 1945, 1969, 1969a
Carrión Cachot, Rebeca, 444
Carrizo, Juan Alfonso, 4517
Carro, Venancio Diego de, 3118
Caruso, John Anthony, 3569
Carvajal, Alberto, 3420
Carvalho, Irene Mello, 2249
Carvalho, Joaquim Bertino de Moraes, 1714
Carvalho, Juvenal de, 2704
Casais, José, 2677
Casanovas, Domingo, 5704
Casas, Bartolomé de las, 3119
Casas Fernández, Baldomero, 1427
Casasanta, Mário, 2308
Cascudo, Luís da Câmara, 4010, 5204, 5243, 5626
Casiello, Juan, 5475
Caso, Alfonso, 79, 108, 203, 204, 551, 552, 634
Caspar, Frank, 769
Cassaigne, Héctor, 1946

Cassidy, Frederic G., 613
Cassinelli, Carlos Monge, 910
Cassirer, Ernst, 5807
Castagnino, Raúl H., 5181
Castañeda, Carlos, 3120
Castañeda, Carlos Eduardo, 4668
Castanien, Donald G., 4666
Castedo, Leopoldo, 3031
Castellanos, Alfredo Raúl, 3477a
Castello, José Aderaldo, 5244, 5245, 5246, 5247, 5248, 5249
Castello Branco, José Moreira Brandão, 2705
Castilla Barrios, Olga, 4719
Castillero, Ernesto, 3018
Castillo, Porfirio del, 3570
Castillo Velasco, Jaime, 2856
Castro, Carlo Antonio, 227, 635, 691
Castro, Eduardo de Lima, 4078, 4086
Castro, Ernesto L., 4872
Castro Turbiano, Máximo, 5723, 5797
Castro, Josué de, 2678
Castro, Juventino V., 5436
Castro de Morales, Lilia, 3706, 6410, 6411
Castro Leal, Antonio, 5023
Castro Nunes, José de, 5431
Castro Pacheco, Fernando, 4721
Castro Seoane, José, 3121, 4667
Caturelli, Alberto, 5769
Cavagna Martínez, Ildefonso F., 5548
Cavalcanti, Araujo, 2244
Cavalcanti Filho, Teófilo, 5751
Cavalheiro, Edgard, 5250, 5251, 5253
Cavallini Quiroz, Ligia, 3238
Cavazos Garza, Israel, 4629
Cave, Hugh Barnett, 6607
Cavelier, Germán, 1418, 5561
Cebollero, Pedro Ángel, 2011
Ceccherelli, Claudio, 3239
Ceceña, José Luis, 1988
Cegalla, Domingos Paschoal, 5252
Cejas, Horacio E., 5490
Celesia, Ernesto H., 3828
Ceniceros, José Ángel, 2075, 2076, 3593, 5538
Cepeda Adán, José, 3122
Cepero, Rafael, 272
Cerda, Gilberto, 4518
Cerda, R. de la, 667
Cerezo, Hugo, 120, 160
Cerretani, Arturo, 4873
Cerro de Pasco Corporation. Departamento Geológico, 2537
Cervantes, Dagoberto de, 5153
Cervantes Ahumada, Raúl, 1970, 5565
Cervantes de Salazar, Francisco, 4668
Cervantes Mejía, Rodolfo, 1867
Cervera Martínez, Lilia, 4457
Chacón, Vamireh, 6096
Chacón y Calvo, José María, 2065
Chamberlain, Robert S., 708, 3240, 3241
Chamberlin, Eugene Keith, 3571, 3572
Chamico. *See* Nalé Roxlo, Conrado.
Chapman, Arnold, 5051
Chapman, Mary Patricia, 3673
Charles, Paul-Émile, 5381
Charlier, Étienne D., 3019, 3379a

Costa, Afonso, 4038
Costa, F. A. Pereira da, 4039
Costa, João Cruz, 2308, 5770
Costa, Lúcio, 1275
Costa Filho, João Mendes da, 5500
Costa Rica. Asamblea Constituyente, 2948
Costa Rica. Biblioteca Nacional, 6416
Costa Rica. Caja Costarricense de Seguro Social, 4428, 4429, 4430, 4431, 4432, 4433
Costa Rica. Dirección General de Estadística y Censos, 6261, 6262
Costa Rica. Dirección General de Estadística y Censos. Sección de Cartografía y Divulgación, 2405
Costa Rica. Ministerio de Relaciones Exteriores y Culto, 4262
Costales Samaniego, Alfredo, 3443, 3444
Cotter, C. S., 284
Cotton, Marion, 5601
Courlander, Harold, 610
Coutinho, Afrânio, 5253, 5254
Couto, Ribeiro, 5220, 5337, 5338
Couture, Eduardo J., 1469, 5575
Cova, Jesús Antonio, 4738
Covarrubias, José F., 1948
Covarrubias, Miguel, 62, 108
Covarrubias Camargo, Manuel, 4447
Cover, Gilbert Grace, 5462
Cowan, George M., 640, 641
Cox, Carlos Manuel, 4617
Cox, Patricia, 4921
Crabtree, Asa Routh, 4011
Crane, Jacob L., Jr., 4400
Crane, Jane Watson, 403
Créqui-Montfort, Georges de, 819
Crespo, Benito, 3251
Crist, Raymond E., 2418, 2428, 2438
Croce, Benedetto, 5810, 5811
Crow, John A., 4774
Crowley, Daniel J., 553, 706
Crowley, José, 1948a
Cruchaga Santa María, Ángel, 5011
Cruxent, J. M., 293, 294, 295, 296
Cruz, Ernesto, 1224
Cruz, Salvador de la, 4962
Cruz-Coronado, Guillermo de la, 5255
Cruz Santos, Abel, 1423
Cruz y Moya, Juan José de la, 3252
Cuba. Archivo Nacional, 3023, 3709, 3710, 3711
Cuba. Comisión Nacional de Propaganda y Defensa del Tabaco Habano, 1428, 1429
Cuba. Dirección General de Estadística, 2419
Cuba. Ministerio de Información, 2907
Cuba. Oficina Nacional de los Censos Demográfico y Electoral, 6263
Cubillos Ch., Julio César, 404, 409
Cuervo, Rufino José, 4520
Cuesta, Luisa, 3024, 3125, 3446, 6417
Cuesta, Modesta, 3024
Cueva Tamariz, Agustín, 3885
Cueva Tamariz, Carlos, 4303
Cuevas, Mariano, 3025
Cumberland, Charles C., 3577

Cumper, George E., 616
Cunha, Armando, 1225
Cuoco, Francisco C. P., 1284
Cuspinera, Juan L., 1971
Cuzco. Archivo Histórico, 3026
Cuzzani, Agustín, 5154

Dabbs, Jack Autrey, 807, 4521
Dahlgren de Jordan, Barbro, 3, 63, 554
Delma, Juan, 6022
Damião, Antônio, 5309
Damirón, Rafael, 3765
Damonte Taborda, Raúl, 2875
Danero, E. M. S., 3485, 5013
D'Aniello, Orlando, 4877
Dantas, Francisco Clementino San Tiago, 5413
Darbois, Dominique, 803
Dardón Córdova, Gonzalo, 6418, 6419
Darío, Rubén, 5014
Dark, Philip J. C., 804
Dartiguenave, Edith, 5383
Dauphin, Marcel, 5384
Dávalos Hurtado, Eusebio, 550, 875a
Dávalos y Figueroa, Diego, 4655
Davies, Arthur, 3126
Dávila, Antonio, 2943
Dávila Garibi, José Ignacio, 3578, 3579, 4522
Dávila Gómez Palacios, Roberto, 1971a
Dávila Padilla, Agustín, 3253
Davis, Edward J. P., 3027
Davis, Harold E., 3028
Davis, Horace B., 4304
Davis, Kingsley, 6000
Davis, Thomas B., Jr., 3830
DeBeers, John S., 1972
Debenedetti, Emma, 1256
Debien, Gabriel, 3380, 3380a, 3381, 3381a
Deevey, E. S., 253
Deffontaines, Pierre, 2707
De Gamez, Tana, 6609
Deinhard, Hanna, 1205
Dekoster Fuentes, Pedro, 1872
Delgado, Jaime, 3064, 3580
Delgado, Luiz, 4040
Delgado, Rafael, 4878
Del Villar, Fred, 6610
Del Villar, Mary, 6610
Demicheli, Alberto, 5486
Denis, Lorimer, 592
Deren, Maya, 593, 610
Derisi, Octavio Nicolás, 5705, 5804
Dermigny, L., 3381a
Descola, Jean, 3127
Devereux, George, 10
De Wolf, Marian, 285
Dias, Floriano Aguiar, 5403
Dias, João Pereira, 1226
Dias, José Aguiar de, 5403
Díaz, Emilio L., 2500, 2501
Díaz Arrieta, Hernán, 4658, 4702
Díaz C., Miguel, 6420
Díaz del Castillo, Bernal, 4650
Díaz Mirón, Salvador, 4720
Díaz Ruanova, Oswaldo, 4721

Flores de la Peña, Horacio, 1879, 1880
Flores Sánchez, Horacio, 5827
Flórez, Luis, 4527
Flornoy, Bertrand, 803, 831, 906
Foland, Frances M., 3589
Folmer, Henry, 3264
Fombona-Pachano, Jacinto, 4730, 5018
Fonseca, Emi Bulhões Carvalho da, 5314, 5315
Fontana, Maria Elena, 5316
Fontanilla, J. A., 5828
Fontoura, Amaral, 2255
Fontoura, Gilka Niederauer, 2299
Ford, James A., 455
Ford, Norman D., 6611
Ford, Thomas R., 6037
Forero, Manuel José, 4633, 4634
Foresti, L. Charles, 4202
Forrestal, Peter P., 3221
Foshag, William F., 117
Foster, George M., 13, 3136
Fouchard, Jean, 3383, 3383a, 5386
Fouquet, Carlos, 4073
Fracassi del Carril, Salvador, 5602
Fraga Iribarne, Manuel, 2936, 2950, 5487
Fragachán, Félix R., 3805
Fragoso, Augusto, 5259
Fragueiro, Mariano, 3834
Fragueiro Lascano, José M., 5781
Franca, Leonel, 2256
France. Service Colonial des Statistiques, 6274, 6275
Francheri López, Eduardo, 4887
Franco, Affonso Arinos de Mello, 4250
Franco, José L., 2356, 3384, 3714
Franco, Maria E., 1284
Franco Lao, Meri, 5603
Francovich, Guillermo, 5723
Frank, Waldo, 5303
Frankl, Víctor, 5708, 5734, 5735
Fraser, Ronald, 6704
Freier, Koka, 652
Freitas, Carlos A. de, 490, 491, 492, 493
Freitas, Zoraide Rocha de, 2257
Fretz, Joseph Winfield, 6008
Freyre, Gilberto, 2258, 4075, 4090, 5260
Friede, Juan, 754, 3422
Frieiro, Eduardo, 5261
Friend, Llerena, 3590
Frikel, G. P., 772
Frondizi, Risieri, 5782, 5783
Fuente, Julio de la, 644
Fuente, Sindulfo de la, 5157
Fuentes, Carlos, 4888
Fuentes Benot, Manuel, 5803
Fuentes Cervera, Eduardo de, 3137
Fuentes Díaz, Vicente, 3591
Fuentes Irurozqui, Manuel, 1355
Fuentes Mares, José, 3592
Fuentes y Guzmán, Francisco, 3266
Funes, Víctor Luis, 3835
Fúrlong, Guillermo, 3483, 3484, 4671, 4672, 6424
Furtado, Celso, 1718

Gabaglia, A. C. Raja, 4087
Gabaldón Márquez, Joaquín, 3042
Gaffarel Peralta, Pedro, 4878
Gaines, Thomas A., 1356
Gajardo Tobar, R., 399
Galbraith, W. O., 6705
Galich, Manuel, 5158, 5159, 5160, 5161
Galimberti Miranda, Carlos A., 354
Galindez, Jesús de, 4204
Gallardo, Miguel Ángel, 3674
Gallegos, Rómulo, 6706
Gallegos Rocafull, M., 5831
Galvão, Alfredo, 1207
Galvão, Eduardo, 773, 6069
Gálvez, Manuel, 4889, 4890, 4891, 4892
Gambaro, Griselda, 4893
Gandía, Enrique de, 3836
Gangotena y Jijón, C. de, 3451
Gannett, Taylor W., 5585
Gaos, José, 5709, 5755, 5796, 5817, 5818
Garcés, Enrique, 4655
Garcés, Jesús Juan, 4601
Garcés Ferra, Bartolomé, 3138
Garcés Pachano, Wilson, 6100
García, Juan Agustín, 3485
García, Pablo, 5056, 5057, 5058
García Aybar, José E., 4306
García Bacca, Juan David, 5702, 5784
García Castellanos, Telasco, 2357
García Chuecos, Héctor, 3901
García Cruz, Miguel, 4448
García de Onrubia, Luis F., 5710
García Gallo, Alfonso, 3131, 3139
García-Girón, Edmundo, 5059
García Granados, Rafael, 3267
García-Huidobro Guzmán, Andrés Javier, 2528
García Icazbalceta, Joaquín, 4693
García Krautz, Francisco, 5015
García Maynez, Eduardo, 5723, 5798
García Moreno, Gabriel, 3881
García Naranjo, Nemesio, 2928, 3622
García Rosell, César, 3889
García Ruiz, Alfonso, 68, 3268, 3593
García Sáinz, Ricardo, 1953
García Sayán, Enrique, 4276
García Treviño, Rodrigo, 1881, 1900
García Tudurí, Mercedes, 5723, 5797
García Tudurí, Rosaura, 5723, 5797
García y Grave de Peralta, Fernando, 263, 264
García y Mellid, Atilio, 2859
Gardiner, C. Harvey, 3269, 3270
Garibay K., Ángel María, 208, 645, 680
Garland, Eduardo, 4279
Garo, Francisco J., 5550, 5551
Garrett, Naomi M., 5387
Garrido, José Eulogio, 3460, 4635
Garrido, Luis, 2077, 4731
Garza Treviño, Ciro R. de la, 3271
Garzón Ferreyra, Ignacio, 4307
Gaspar de Madre de Deus, Frei, 4041
Gásperi, Luis de, 5491
Gates, R. Ruggles, 861
Gatica de Montiveros, María Delia, 5060
Gatón Arce, Freddy, 5017

Mariátegui, José Carlos, 4747
Mariluz Urquijo, José María, 3165, 3487, 3488, 3843
Marín Pérez, Pascual, 3109
Márquez, Edmundo, 4914
Márquez, Javier, 1976a
Márquez de la Plata, Fernando, 3472
Márquez Miranda, Fernando, 361, 377, 391
Márquez Sterling, Carlos, 3727
Marrero, Carmen, 5079
Marrero, Levi, 2361
Marrero Aristy, Ramón, 2911
Marroquín, Alejandro D., 661, 1898, 6061
Mars, Louis, 598, 610
Marshall, Enrique L., 2059
Marsland, Amy L., 3057
Marsland, William D., 3057
Martí, José, 4748, 6716
Martí, Samuel, 75, 133, 561, 5604
Martí Bufill, Carlos, 6049
Martín, José Luis, 4607
Martín Echeverría, Leonardo, 1895, 1958
Martínez, Celedonio, 4921
Martínez, Ernesto A., 3818
Martínez, José Luis, 4749, 4751
Martínez, Manuel Ma., 3166, 3315, 3414
Martínez, Mario Hernán, 2520
Martínez Cuitiño, Vicente, 4750
Martínez de Paulotti, T., 883
Martínez del Rio, Pablo, 76, 134, 870, 3316
Martínez Delgado, Luis, 3874
Martínez Domínguez, Guillermo, 1896
Martínez Durán, Carlos, 3299
Martínez Fourzan, Óscar, 4310
Martínez Licona, R. Aristeo, 5540
Martínez López, Luis, 5454
Martínez M., Guillermo E., 5024
Martínez Paz, Enrique, 5496
Martins, Luís, 1282, 4090
Martins, Saul, 5629
Martins, Wilson, 5277
Marx, W. G., 708
Marx, Jr., Daniel, 1470
Maryssael, Gustavo, 1946
Masegora, A. P., 5805
Masferrer, Alberto, 4751
Masnata de Quesada, David, 1431
Massey, William C., 649
Massio, Roger, 3388a, 3389, 3389a, 3390
Mastronardi, Carlos, 5067
Mata Gavidia, José, 3317
Mateos, Francisco, 3100, 3101, 3167, 3489, 3490
Matos, Pedro Gomes de, 4020
Matteson, Esther, 815
Matthews, Dom Basil, 703
Matthews, Herbert L., 2864
Mattos, Horacio Peres Sampaio de, 2617
Maximilien, Louis, 610, 5388
Maya, Rafael, 4752, 5025, 5036
Maya, William A., 2652
Mayer, Jorge M., 3818
Mayer-Oakes, Nita, 135
Mayhew, Frank, 704
Maynard, Theodore, 3318
Maza, Antonio de la, 662

Maza, Diego de la, 3390a
Maza, Francisco de la, 3319
Mazière, Francis, 803
Mazo, Gabriel del, 3819
Mazzanti, Carlos, 4915
Mead, Margaret, 27
Meade, Joaquín, 665, 3320, 3321
Medauar, Jorge, 5343
Medeiros, João, 5501
Medeiros, Laudelino Teixeira de, 6022
Medeiros, Maurício de, 2308
Medellín Zenil, Alfonso, 136
Medem, Federico, 411
Medina, José Toribio, 3058, 4690, 4695
Medina, Juan Ramón, 4945
Medrano, Samuel W., 2878, 3844
Meggers, Betty J., 252, 289, 304, 428
Mehren, George L., 1460
Meier, Augusto, 5253
Meilink-Roelofsz, M. A. P., 3059
Meillet, A., 28
Mejía Ricart, Gustavo Adolfo, 3391
Mejía Sánchez, Ernesto, 680
Mejía Valera, Manuel, 5774
Melgarejo Vivanco, José Luis, 666, 875a
Mello, José Antonio Gonsalves de, 4050, 4051, 4052, 4053
Mello Pettei, Beatriz Celia Corrêa, 2653
Melo, Orlando Ferreira de, 2281
Melo, Osvaldo Ferreira de, 5318
Melo, Veríssimo de, 5630
Mendes, Antônio Lopes, 1201
Mendes, Murilo, 5344
Mendes, Ubirajara Dolácio, 3060
Méndez, Leopoldo, 4876
Méndez Carrasco, Armando, 4916
Méndez Plancarte, Alfonso, 4603, 4648, 5014, 5080, 5081, 5084
Méndez Plancarte, Gabriel, 3632, 3633
Mendieta y Núñez, Lucio, 667, 6013, 6103
Mendonça, Eduardo Prado de, 5820
Mendonça, Valdemar Paranhos de, 2715
Mendoza, Angélica, 362
Mendoza, Cristóbal L., 3801
Mendoza, Héctor, 5166
Mendoza, José Rafael, 6079
Mendoza, Vicente T., 680, 5026
Mendoza, Virginia de, 680
Meneses, Guillermo, 4917
Menezes, Djacir, 6022
Menezes, Maria Wanderley, 5319
Menezes, Raimundo de, 4021
Menghin, Osvaldo F. A., 378, 379, 390
Mennesson-Rigaud, Odette, 599, 606
Menocal y Barreras, Juan Manuel, 5449
Mêrici, Imideo Giuseppe, 2282
Merino Brito, Elroy G., 5422
Mersán, Carlos A., 5468
Mesa Andraca, Manuel, 1931, 1958a
Mesa Rodríguez, Manuel I., 3729, 3730, 3731
Meseguer Fernández, Juan, 3323
Metford, J. C. J., 6434
Métraux, Alfred, 600, 601, 602, 603, 5389
Mexía de Fernangil, Diego, 4655
México. Comisión Nacional Bancaria, 1977

Rubin de la Borbolla, Daniel F., 84, 120, 159, 160
Rubio, Ángel, 120, 2414
Rubio Mañé, J. Ignacio, 3360, 3360a, 3361 3361a, 3362, 3362a, 3650
Rubio Melhado, Adolfo, 2415
Rubio Orbe, Gonzalo, 758
Rubio Sánchez, Manuel, 3363
Rubio y Rubio, Alfonso, 5763
Rudge, Raul Telles, 5560
Rübbo Müller, Antonio, 759
Rueda Briceño, Ana, 3407, 3875
Ruellan, Francis, 2621, 2622
Rugeles, Manuel F., 5037
Ruiz-Díaz, Adolfo, 4777
Ruiz Funes, Mariano, 6080
Ruiz Moreno, Isidoro, 3851
Ruiz Moreno, Leandro, 3852, 3853
Ruiz Tejada, Manuel Ramón, 5520
Rulfo, Juan, 4937, 4938
Rumeu de Armas, Antonio, 3186a
Ruppert, Karl, 161, 162, 163, 180
Russell, Dora Isella, 5094, 5095, 5096
Russo Delgado, José, 5801
Ruz Lhuillier, Alberto, 164, 165, 166, 167, 168, 169
Rydén, Stig, 363, 475

Sabogal, José, 4747
Sacchetti, Alfredo, 892
Sack, John, 2547
Sáenz, Vicente, 3623
Sahagún, Bernardino de, 220, 222
Saint-Hilaire, Augusto de, 4027
Saito, Hiroshi, 6085
Salado Álvarez, Ana, 4939
Salado Álvarez, Victoriano, 4939
Salas, Alberto, 3187
Salas Viú, Vicente, 5640
Salazar Flor, Carlos, 5587
Salazar Páez, Antonio, 2078
Salazar y Lozano, Agustín, 3884
Salceda, Alberto G., 4611
Saldanha, Heitor, 5309
Salinas Puente, Antonio, 5568
Salmon, Ross, 6623
Salmoni, Anita, 1256
Salvador Porta, Eliseo, 4940
Sampaio, Mário Arnaud, 785, 5215
Sampaio, Nelson de Sousa, 2867
Samper, Baltasar, 680
Sampeur, Virginia, 5388
San Juan Bautista de Puerto Rico (city), 3396
San Martín y Torres, Xavier, 5522
Sanabria, Edgard, 6002
Sánchez, Ana María, 4894
Sánchez, Juan Francisco, 5097
Sánchez, Luis Alberto, 2934, 4624, 4684, 4770, 4966, 5006, 5098, 5099, 5100
Sánchez, Manuel Segundo, 6444
Sánchez, Mariquita, 3495
Sánchez, Roberto M., 2073
Sánchez Agramonte, Aurelio, 272
Sánchez Báez, Hipólito, 4459
Sánchez de Bustamante, Miguel, 5428

Sánchez Espejo, Carlos, 5596a
Sánchez Fontáns, José, 5511, 5512
Sánchez G., Ángel Porfirio, 4941
Sánchez Garza, J., 3651
Sánchez Lazo, Carlos Roberto, 4211
Sánchez Pedrote, Enrique, 3431
Sánchez Quell, Hipólito, 5101
Sánchez Reulet, Aníbal, 5720, 5723
Sánchez-Sáez, Braulio, 5288, 5289
Sánchez Septién, Salvador, 2928, 3622
Sánchez Urteaga de Peña, Isabel, 2090
Sancho Castro, Álvaro, 1473
Sancho de Soranis, Hipólito, 3187a, 3188
Sanders, William T., 170, 675, 676, 677
Sandoval, Fernando B., 1983a
Sandoval, José E. de, 4316
Sandoval, Luis, 897
Sandoval Cerna, Ernesto, 5470
Sandoval Saavedra, Hugo, 5521
Sanín Cano, Baldomero, 4771
Santana, Francisco, 4966a, 5102
Santander, Francisco de Paula, 3871
Santayana, George, 5828
Santiago Sanz, Luis, 3188a
Santiana, Antonio, 898, 899, 900
Santos, Moacyr Amaral, 5433, 5597
Santos, Noronha, 1211, 1242
Santos, Ruy, 5326
Santos Jiménez, Rafael, 3760
Santovenia, Emeterio S., 3739
Santoyo, Ramón Víctor, 2929
Sanz, Víctor, 494
São Paulo (state). Departamento do Arquivo, 4028, 4059, 4060, 4061, 4062
São Paulo (state). Instituto Geográfico e Geológico, 2721
Sapena Pastor, Raúl, 1474, 5581
Sapper, Herbert D., 586
Saravia, Atanasio G., 3363a
Sariola, Sakari, 6011, 6093
Sarmiento, Ángel Martín, 5103
Sarmiento, Domingo Faustino, 4772
Satterthwaite, Linton, Jr., 171, 221
Sauer, Carl O., 567
Sawyer, Alan R., 476
Sax, Karl, 2416
Sayagués Laso, Enrique, 5459
Saz, Agustín del, 4612, 5038
Schadel, Richard P., 3460
Schaden, Egon, 760, 780, 786
Schaedel, Richard, 368
Schaeffer, Wendell Karl Gordon, 1911
Schenck, Fr. von, 6624
Schenone, Héctor, 1243
Schiaffino, Rafael, 3897
Schmidt, Afonso, 5327
Schmidt, Carlos Borges, 2695
Schmitt, Karl M., 3652
Schnerr, Walter J., 5216
Schoen, Wilhelm Albrecht von, 3077
Scholes, Walter V., 3653
Schopenhauer, Arthur, 5829
Schorer, C. E., 4546
Schreider, Eugène, 873
Schröder, Rudolf, 2623
Schulman, Sam, 6039

Thompson, Peter E., 2541
Thornton, A. P., 3089, 3397a, 3398
Thornton, Phyllis, 611
Tibbetts, Douglas E., 2401
Tibesar, Antonine, 3370, 3463
Tiempo, César, 4778, 4948, 5039
Tinker, Edward Larocque, 4779
Tinoco, Manuel Vicente, 4949
Tirado Benedí, Domingo, 2080, 2081
Tobar, Baltasar, 3193a
Tobón Betancourt, Julio, 4550
Törnberg, Gerda, 581
Tofini, Paolo, 884
Toledo Morán, Salvador, 1446
Tonda, Américo A., 3855
Toriello, Guillermo, 4273
Torrealba Lossi, Mario, 4780
Torriente, Cosme de la, 3761, 4285
Torre, Benjamín de la, 1454
Torre, Lisandro de la, 3851
Torre, Pedro de, 4655
Torre Revello, José, 6448
Torre Reyes, Carlos de la, 5543
Torre Villar, Ernesto de la, 3659
Torrente, Vicente, 1366
Torres, Edelberto, 4735
Torres, Heloisa Alberto, 1213
Torres Bodet, Jaime, 4781
Torres Gaitán, Ricardo, 1914, 1929
Torres M., J. Alberto, 2407
Torres Martínez, Manuel de, 1367
Torres Ríoseco, Arturo, 4687, 4782, 5106, 5295
Torrico Prado, Benjamín, 2057
Toruño, Juan Felipe, 5042
Toscano, Salvador, 3370a
Toscano Mateus, Humberto, 4550a
Tosco, M., 1449
Tosta, Virgilio, 2091
Tourinho, Borba, 1736
Toussaint, Manuel, 4646, 5107
Towle, Margaret Ashley, 489
Townsend, William Cameron, 1915
Townsend Ezcurra, Andrés, 3681a
Travis, Martin, 573
Trens, Manuel B., 3371
Treviño, Víctor L., 6105
Triffin, Robert, 5554
Trik, Aubrey S., 196
Trimborn, Hermann, 783
Trinidad. Census Office, 6296, 6297
Tristán, Lucía, 2881
Trotier, Arnold H., 6449
Trouillot, Ernst, 5394
Trouillot, Henock, 3398a
Trujillo, Rafael L., 2912
Trujillo Gómez, Rafael, 5525
Tschudi, J. J. von, 4078
Tucumán (prov.). Estación Experimental Agrícola, 1403
Tudela, José, 3090, 3194
Tudela de la Orden, José, 686
Tudisco, Anthony, 3194a
Turner, John Kenneth, 1916

Uexküll, Thure von, 5832
Ugarte, Manuel, 2869, 5108
Ugarte, Salvador, 205
Ugarte, Valentín, 2525
Ugarteche, Pedro, 2017
Ulloa Ortiz, Berta, 3371a
Ulloa y Sotomayor, Alberto, 5573
Ulving, Tor, 226
Undurraga, Antonio de, 5109
United Nations. Department of Economic Affairs, 1368, 1369, 1370, 6041
United Nations. Department of Public Information, 4212
United Nations. Economic Commission for Latin America, 1371, 1372, 1373, 1374
United Nations. Population Division, 1917
United Nations. Statistical Office, 6306
United Nations Educational, Scientific and Cultural Organization, 2019, 2058, 2082, 6450, 6451
United States. Bureau of Labor Statistics, 4317
United States. Bureau of the Census, 6298, 6299
United States. Congress. House, 4255
United States. Congress. Senate, 4256
United States. Congress. Senate. Committee on Agriculture and Forestry, 4318
United States. Congress. Senate. Committee on Interior and Insular Affairs, 2957
United States. Department of State, 1461, 4246, 4257, 4258, 4274
United States. Department of the Interior. Office of Geography, 2549
United States. Institute of Inter-American Affairs, 2665
United States. Library of Congress. Census Library Project, 6307, 6308
United States. Public Health Service. Bureau of State Services, 4418
United States. Senate, 1375
United States-Brazil Development Commission, 1700
Universidad de Barcelona. Centro de Estudios Históricos Internacionales, 3091
Universidad de Buenos Aires. Instituto de Sociología, 6922
Universidad de Chile, 2059
Universidad de Chile. Biblioteca Central. Centro de Información Bibliográfica, 6452
Universidad de Costa Rica, 2092
Universidad de Puerto Rico, 2086, 2087
Universidad de Puerto Rico. Consejo Superior de Enseñanza, 4551
Universidad de San Carlos de Guatemala, 2093, 2094
Universidad Nacional Autónoma de México, 1918, 2083
Universidad Nacional Autónoma de México. Instituto de Investigaciones Sociales, 2084, 6023
Universidad Nacional de Buenos Aires. Facultad de Ciencias Económicas, 1404
Universidad Nacional de Colombia, 2063
Universidad Nacional de Córdoba. Facultad

Index II: Subject

ture, 4694, 4787, 5203, 5205. Medicine, 6402. Population statistics, 6303. Social sciences, 6430. Sociology, 6001, 6004. Spanish language, 4557. Statistics, 6307, 6308.
See also Printing presses
Bill, Max, 1268, 1275
BIOGRAPHY
Brazil, 1208, 1233, 4002, 4038. Chile, 3475. Guatemala, 3354. Haiti, 6503. Mexico, 3566, 3567, 6506, 6507. Spain, 3163. Venezuela, 6500, 6501.
BIRDS, 2362, 2401.
Bisquertt, Próspero, 5636
Blumenau, Hermann, 4073
Bochenski, J. M., 5741
Bolívar, Simón, 2091, 3055, 3427, 3802, 3804-3809, 3811, 3813, 5036, 5775
BOLIVIA
General, 2884, 6254, 6618. Anthropology, 363, 388-394, 828, 830, 834, 891, 892. Description and travel, 2548, 3037, 6617, 6618. Economics, 1408-1411, 1863, 4205. Education, 2055-2057. Geography, 2548, 2549. Government, 2882-2886. History, 2886, 3039, 3435, 3451a, 3459. International relations, 4205. Labor, 4309. Law, 4309, 4427, 5488, 5521, 5577, 5585, 5589, 5593. Literature, 4724, 4737, 4896, 4930, 4964, 5002. Social welfare, 4424-4427. Sociology, 3039, 6015, 6024.
BOOK TRADE
General, 4667. Argentina, 4707. Mexico, 4666. Peru, 4677. Spanish America, 4678. Trinidad, 4656.
Borges, Carlos, 5091
Borges, Jorge Luis, 4512, 4764, 4767, 4777
Boti, Regino E., 5071
Boves, José Tomás, 3920
Bowles, William Augustus, 3308
Braden, Spruille, 4260
Branciforte, Marqués de, 3232
BRAZIL
General 2676, 2708, 2718, 2880, 2899, 6009, 6020, 6255-6257, 6405, 6407-6409, 6430, 6445, 6700, 6712-6714, 6721, 6726. Anthropology, 251, 298-307, 750-751, 764-795, 803, 886-890, 2631, 2712, 5206, 5215. Art and architecture, 298, 1200-1286. Description and travel, 794, 1201, 2358, 2684, 2691, 2693, 2694, 2697, 2699, 2707, 2718, 2722, 2725, 2880, 3037. Economics, 1700-1737, 2631-2668, 2702, 2710, 2711, 2717. Education, 1736, 2017, 2200-2317, 5592. Geography, 791, 2600-2725, 6035, 6036. Government, 1737, 2244, 2691, 2887-2900. History, 298, 1731, 1734, 2215, 2216, 2256, 2257, 2296, 2317, 2705. Labor, 1715, 1716, 4320. Language, 5200, 5201, 5206-5217, 5219. Law, 2231, 2240, 2288, 2289, 4320, 5402, 5403, 5407, 5408, 5413, 5441-5447, 5499-

5505, 5530-5534, 5555-5560, 5591, 5592, 5597, 5598, 5599. Literature, 5202-5205, 5218, 5220-5357. Music and dance, 5626, 5633. Philosophy, 5751-5753, 5770, 5773, 5779, 5780, 5785, 5787, 5789, 6726. Social welfare, 4456, 4463. Sociology, 1721, 1724, 2248, 2634, 2641, 2669-2698, 4075, 6003, 6009, 6014, 6020, 6035, 6036, 6045, 6046, 6050, 6054-6058, 6063, 6064, 6066, 6069, 6070, 6072-6075, 6085, 6096, 6099, 6430.
Briceño, Mario, 4710
Brión, Luis, 3875
BRITISH COLONIES
Aruba, Anthropology, 707; History, 707. Bahamas, General, 6252; Anthropology, 553, 706. Bermuda, General, 6253; British Guiana, Anthropology, 289; Government, 2953, 2956; International relations, 4281; Sociology, 6048. British Honduras, Anthropology, 195, 221; Economics, 1468; International relations, 4272, 4275; Sociology, 6048. British West Indies, General, 6284, 6285; Anthropology, 569; Government, 3072; History, 3005, 3011, 3013, 3045, 3072, 3089, 3106, 3180, 3180a, 3388, 3392, 3397a, 3398; Sociology, 569, 6048. Dominica, Anthropology, 715; Geography, 715. Falkland Islands, General, 6273; Sociology, 6048. Grenadines, Anthropology, 709, 714; Music and dance, 714. Jamaica, Anthropology, 284, 285, 569, 611-623; Economics, 617; History, 618, 620; Language, 613; Music, 622; Sociology, 569, 612, 614-616, 618, 619, 621, 623. St. Lucia, Anthropology, 286. Trinidad, General, 6296, 6297; Anthropology, 253, 283, 700-704; Literature, 4656; Sociology, 701, 703.
British Guiana. See Guianas; British Colonies.
British Honduras. See British Colonies.
British West Indies. See British Colonies.
Brito, Raimundo de Farias, 5751, 5753
Bucareli, Virrey, 3224
BUCCANEERS, FILIBUSTERS, AND PIRATES, 3123, 3382a, 3386, 3450, 3571, 3673a, 3679.
BULLFIGHTS, 4746.
Bustamante, Anastasio, 3663
Bustamante y Vivero, Manuel de, 3257, 3265

Caballero, Raimundo Diosdado, 3172
Cabral, Manuel del, 5108
Calderón, Fernando, 4674
Camacho, Joaquín, 3874
Camarão, Antônio Filipe, 4050
Campomanes, Conde de, 3173
Canto, Alberto del, 3356
Cárdenas, Lázaro, 1900, 1906, 1915
Cárdenas, Bernardino de, 3485a
Cardiel, José, 4671
Cardoso, Licinio, 6502
Cardoso Jr., José Bernardo, 1272